Blackie's Compact Etymological Dictionary

Prepared by

RICHARD JOHN CUNLIFFE

M.A. LL.B.

Editor of "A New Shakespearean Dictionary"

BLACKIE & SON LIMITED

LONDON AND GLASGOW

BLACKIE & SON LIMITED
50 *Old Bailey, London*
17 *Stanhope Street, Glasgow*

BLACKIE & SON (INDIA) LIMITED
Warwick House, Fort Street, Bombay

BLACKIE & SON (CANADA) LIMITED
Toronto

Printed in Great Britain by Blackie & Son, Ltd., Glasgow

PREFACE

The compiler of this work wishes to state at the outset that the pains bestowed upon it have not been proportioned to its size. Indeed a larger work could have been produced with much less labour.

For the etymologies, which are the special feature of the book, recourse has been had to the latest and best authorities. In particular, the highest authority, the *New English Dictionary* of the late Sir James Murray and his co-editors, has been consulted throughout; and its guidance has been accepted on all doubtful questions. For the small portion of the alphabet (about a tenth) not yet covered by the *N. E. D.* use has been made of the *Imperial Dictionary*, of the *Century Dictionary*, and of Skeat's Dictionaries.

Every endeavour has been made to state without qualification nothing but what may reasonably be regarded as being as certain as anything in the somewhat uncertain science of etymology can well be. It will be noticed that in a large number of cases—some may think in a disappointingly large number—the origin of the word is simply stated to be "unknown", "obscure", &c. In many of these cases etymologies have been current which have been shown by recent research, and in particular by the labours of Sir James Murray and his fellows, either to be positively wrong or to be mere conjectures, not supported by any evidence, and quite as likely to be wrong as to be right. It seemed to be better to omit such conjectures rather than to run the risk of perpetuating error in however humble a way.

To exhibit the interconnection of words—many of them dissimilar in appearance—extensive use has been made of cross-references by means of SMALL CAPITALS in the manner explained at the foot of the Table of Abbreviations. This has been carried out on a scale not hitherto attempted, at any rate in a dictionary of this size; and it is hoped that it will add to the interest of the work.

Greek words have been transliterated letter for letter into the conventional English equivalents, the rough breathing being represented by *h*, and the smooth being neglected. In the Latin words all the long vowels have been marked.

It has, of course, been impossible to include within the assigned limits of space anything like the whole of the current English vocabulary. The compiler's aim has been to include all words likely to be met with in reading modern works with claims to be regarded as literature.

CONTENTS

ABBREVIATIONS

a., adjective.
abb., abbreviation, abbreviated.
absol., absolute, absolutely.
acc., accusative.
act., active.
adj., adjectival.
adv., adverb.
advbl., adverbial.
A.F., Anglo-French.
aft., after.
Anglo-L., Anglo-Latin.
app., apparently.
Arab., Arabic.
arch., architecture.
arith., arithmetic.
attrib., attributive, attributively.
aug., augmentative.
aux., auxiliary.

cf., compare.
chem., chemistry, chemical.
cogn., cognate.
collect., collectively.
comb., combination.
comp., comparative.
Com. Teut., Common Teutonic (indicating that similar forms occur in the various Teutonic languages).
conj., conjunction.
conn., connected.
contr., contracted.
corr., corruption.
corresp., corresponds, corresponding.

Da., Danish.
dat., dative.
dem., demonstrative.
deriv., derivative.
dial., dialectal.
dim., diminutive.
Du., Dutch.

Eccles.L., Ecclesiastical Latin.
ellipt., elliptical, elliptically.
Eng., English.
esp., especially.

f., from.
F., (Modern) French.
fem., feminine.
fig., figurative, figuratively.
freq., frequentative.
Fris., Frisian.
fut., future.

G., Greek.
Gael., Gaelic.
gen., general, generally.
genit., genitive.
ger., gerundive.
Ger., (Modern) German.
Goth., Gothic.

Heb., Hebrew.
H.G., High German.

Icel., Icelandic.
imp., imperative.
impers., impersonal.
impf., imperfect.
indic., indicative.
inf., infinitive.
int., interjection.
intrans., intransitive.
Ir., Irish.
It., Italian.

L., Latin.
L.G., Low German.
lit., literally.
L.L., Late Latin.

masc., masculine.
math., mathematics.
M.Du., Middle Dutch.
M.E., Middle English.
Med.L., Mediæval Latin.
M.H.G., Middle High German.
M.L.G., Middle Low German.
Mod.L., Modern Latin.
M.Sw., Middle Swedish.
mus., music.

n., noun.
neut., neuter.
nom., nominative.
Norw., Norwegian.

obs., obsolete.
O.Da., Old Danish.
O.Du., Old Dutch.
O.E., Old English (Anglo-Saxon).
O.F., Old French.
O.H.G., Old High German.
O.It., Old Italian.
O.L.G., Old Low German.
O.N., Old Norse (Old Icelandic).
O.N.F., Old Norman French.
orig., origin, original, originally.
O.S., Old Saxon.
O.Teut., Original Teutonic.

pa., past.
pass., passive.
Per., Persian.
perf., perfect.
perh., perhaps.
Pg., Portuguese.
pl., plural.
Pop.L., Popular Latin.
pos., positive.
poss., possibly.
poss., possessive.
ppl., participial.
pple., participle.
Pr., Provençal.
prec., the preceding word or article.
pred., predicative.
pref., prefix.
prep., preposition.
pres., present.
priv., privative.
pron., pronoun.

refl., reflexive, reflexively.
rel., relative.
repg., representing.

sc., *scilicet*, understand, supply.
Scand., Scandinavian.
sim., similar, similarly
sing., singular.
Skr., Sanskrit.
Sp., Spanish.
spec., specifically.
subj., subjunctive.
suff., suffix.
superl., superlative.
Sw., Swedish.

t., tense.
Teut., Teutonic.
trans., transitive.

us., usual, usually.

v., verb.
var., variant.
vbl., verbal.
vi., intransitive verb.
vt., transitive verb.

W.S., West Saxon.

= equivalent to.
+ with the addition of.

Note.—When a word, a prefix, or a suffix is printed in SMALL CAPITALS the reader is referred for further information to the word in its alphabetical place in the body of the work or to the prefix or suffix in the List of Prefixes and Suffixes.

In the etymologies a prefixed asterisk (*) indicates that a form is not actually recorded, but is assumed to have existed. A line (—) indicates 'derived from'.

BLACKIE'S COMPACT DICTIONARY

A, An. O.E. *án*, ONE. The indefinite article.

Aback', *adv.* A-[1] + BACK, to or in the rear. Backwards; behind.

Abaft', *adv.* and *prep.* A-[1] + *baft*, O.E. *beæftan*, f. *be*, about + *æftan*, behind. AFT. Behind.

Aban'don, *vt.* O.F. *abandoner*, f. *à bandon*, *à*, at + *bandon*, Med.L. *bannum*, proscription, order (BAN), *mettre à bandon*, tc leave one to oneself. To give up absolutely.—**Aban'doned**, *ppl.a.* Depraved.—**Aban'don**MENT, *n.*

Abase', *vt.* O.F. *abaissier*, f. *à*, to + *baissier*, to lower—L.L. *bassus*, low. BASE, *a.* To lower, humiliate.—**Abase'**MENT, *n.*

Abash', *vt.* O.F. *esbaïr*=F. *ébahir* (*es*=L. *ex*, out), f. *bah!* of astonishment. To put to confusion.

Abate', *vt.* O.F. *abatre*, f. *à*, to + *batre*, L.L. *battuĕre*, to beat. BATTLE. COMBAT. To lessen; to deduct, strike off.—*vi.* To become less.—**Abate'**MENT, *n.*

Ab'bey, *n.* O.F. *abaïe*, f. L.L. *abbas*, ABBOT. A monastery of religious persons, men or women.

Ab'bot, *n.* L.L. *abbas*, *abbātis*, through G. f. Syriac *abbā*, father. The head of an abbey.—*fem.* **Ab'**BESS.

Abbre'viate, *vt.* L. AB*breviāre*, *abbreviātum*, to shorten, f. *brevis*, short. ABRIDGE. BRIEF. To shorten.—**Abbrevi**A'TION, *n.*

Ab'dicate, *vt.* L. *abdicāre*, *abdicātum*, to renounce, f. AB- + *dicāre*, to proclaim. DEDICATE. To resign formally.—*vi.* To resign power.—**Abdic**A'TION, *n.*

Abdo'men, *n.* L., of unknown orig. The belly.—**Abdom'in**AL, *a.*

Abduct', *vt.* L. AB*dūcĕre*, *abductum*, to lead away. ADDUCE. DUKE. To carry off, kidnap.—**Abduc'**TION, *n.*

Abed', *adv.* A-[1] + BED. Confined to bed.

Aber'rant, *a.* L. *aberrans*, *aberrantis*, pres. pple. of AB*errāre*, to wander away. ERR. Deviating from a standard.—**Aberr**A'TION, *n.*

Abet', *vt.* O.F. *abeter*, f. *à*, to + *beter*, to hound on, prob. f. O.N. *beita*. BAIT. In bad sense, to instigate.—**Abet't**ER, *n.*—Legal and also gen., **Abet't**OR.

Abey'ance, *n.* O.F. *abeance*, f. *abeer*, to gape after, f. *à*, to + *beer*, *baer*, *bader*, L.L. *badāre*, to gape, of unknown orig. A state of suspension.

Abhor', *vt.* L. *abhorrēre*, to shrink back, f. AB- + *horrēre*, to stand aghast. HORROR. To loathe.—**Abhor'**RENCE, *n.*—**Abhor'**RENT, *a.* Hating; repugnant; inconsistent.

Abide', *vi.* O.E. *abīdan*, f. A-[3], intensive + *bīdan*. BIDE. To remain, continue, reside.—*vt.* To await, withstand, endure.

Abil'ity, *n.* O.F. *ableté*—L. *habilis*. ABLE. Capacity; mental capacity; a faculty of the mind (gen. *pl.*).

Ab'ject, *a.* L. *abjicĕre*, *abjectum*, to throw away, f. AB-+*jacĕre*, to throw. JET, *v.* Brought low; despicable.—**Abjec'**TION, *n.*

Abjure', *vt.* L. AB*jūrāre*, to swear away. JURY. To renounce on oath; to disclaim.—**Abjur**A'TION, *n.*

Ab'lative, *a.* and *n.* AB*lātīvus*, f. *auferre*, *ablātum*, to carry away. CONFER. A noun case properly giving notion 'away from'.

A'ble, *a.* O.F. *able*—L. *habilis*, handy, fit, f. *habēre*, to hold. HABIT. Qualified, capable; clever.—**A'b**LY,[2] *adv.*

Ablu'tion, *n.* L. AB*luĕre*, *ablūtum*, to wash off. A washing.

Ab'negate, *vt.* L. AB*negāre*, *abnegātum*, to deny. NEGATIVE. To renounce.—**Abnega**'TION, *n.*

Abnor'mal, *a.* F. *anormal*—Med. L. *anormalus*—G. *anōmalos*, ANOMALOUS. Irregular; unusual.—**Abnor'mal**LY,[2] *adv.*—**Abnormal'**ITY, *n.*

Aboard', *adv.* A-[1] + BOARD. On board.—*prep.* On board of.

Abode', *n.* *Vbl.n.* of ABIDE. Dwelling; a home.

Abol'ish, *vt.* F. *abolir*—L. AB*olēre*, *abolitum*. ADULT. To do away with, destroy.—**Aboli'**TION, *n.*

Abom'inable, *a.* L. AB*ōminārī*, *abōminātus*, to deprecate as a bad OMEN. Offensive, odious.—**Abom'inab**LY,[2] *adv.*—**Abom'in**ATE,[3] *vt.*—**Abomin**A'TION, *n.*

Aborig'inal, *a.* L. *ab origine*, from the beginning (ORIGIN) + -AL. Earliest, strictly native.—**Aborig'ines**, *n.pl.* The original inhabitants of a country.

Abort', *vi.* L. *aborīrī*, *abortus*, f. AB- + *orīrī*, to arise. ORIENT. To miscarry.—**Abor't**ION, *n.* Untimely birth; something misshapen or nugatory.—**Abor't**IVE, *a.*

Abound', *vi.* L. *abundāre*, to overflow, f. AB- + *unda*, a wave. UNDULATE. To be plentiful; to teem or swarm.

About', *adv.* O.E. *abútan*, f. A-[1]+*bútan*, without, outside of. *Bútan* = *be*, by, near + *útan*, locative of *út*, CUT. BUT. On every side; in all directions; near, nearly; to and fro; on foot, astir; on the point of.—*prep.* All round; near, close to; appertaining to; dealing with; round.

Above', *adv.* O.E. *abufan*, f. A-[1] + *bufan*, above. *Bufan*=*be*, by + *ufan*, upward. Cf. O.H.G. *uf*, UP. On high; in a higher place; before in order.—*prep.* On the top of; higher than; in excess of; surpassing.

Abrade', *vt.* L. AB*rādĕre*, *abrāsum*, to scrape off. RASE. RAZOR. To rub off; to wear down. —**Abra'**SION, *n.*

Abreast', *adv.* A-[1], in + BREAST. Side by [side.

Abridge', *vt.* O.F. *abreger*—L. *abbreviāre*, to ABBREVIATE. To shorten, curtail.—**Abridg'**MENT, *n.*

Abroach', *adv.* A-[1] + BROACH. Broached, pierced; afloat, astir.

Abroad', *adv.* A-[1], at + BROAD. Broadly; widely asunder; at large; out of home or country; astray.

Ab'rogate, *vt.* L. *abrogāre*, *abrogātum*, to repeal, f. AB- + *rogāre*, to propose. ROGATION. To repeal, cancel.—**Abroga'**TION, *n.*

Abrupt', *a.* L. *abruptus*, pa.pple. of AB*rumpĕre*, to break off. RUPTURE. Hasty; steep. —**Abrupt'**LY,[2] *adv.*—**Abrupt'**NESS, *n.*

Ab'scess, *n.* L. *abscessus*, a going away, an abscess, f. AB*scēdĕre*, *abscessum*, to go away. CEASE. A collection of pus.

Abscind', *vt.* L. AB*scindĕre*, *abscissum*, to tear off. To cut off or away.—**Abscis'**SION, *n.*

Abscond', *vi.* L. AB*scondĕre*, to stow away. RECONDITE. To withdraw oneself, decamp.

Ab'sent, *a.* L. *absens*, *absentis*, pres.pple. of AB*esse*, to be away. Not present; not existing; wanting in attention.—**Absent'**, *v.refl.* To keep oneself away.—**Ab'sent**LY,[2] *adv.* Without attention.—**Ab'**SENCE, *n.*—**Absent**EE', *n.* One away; one who systematically stays away.

Ab'solute, *a.* L. *absolūtus*, loosened, free, pa.pple. of *absolvĕre*, to ABSOLVE. Free from limitation; perfect; independent.—**Ab'solute**LY,[2] *adv.*—**Ab'solute**NESS, *n.*

Absolve', *vt.* L. AB*solvĕre*, *absolūtum*, to set free. SOLVE. To set free from sin, &c.; to remit; to discharge.—**Absolu'**TION, *n.*

Absorb', *vt.* L. AB*sorbēre*, *absorptum*, to swallow up. To swallow up, incorporate; to engross; to suck in.—**Absorp'**TION, *n.*—**Absorb'**ENT, **Absorp'**TIVE, *aa.*

Abstain', *vi.* L. *abstinēre*, *abstentum*, to withhold, f. ABS- + *tenēre*, to hold. TENABLE. TENANT. To withhold oneself, refrain.—**Absten'**TION, *n.*—**Ab'stin**ENCE, *n.*—**Ab'stin**ENT, *a.*—**Ab'stinent**LY,[2] *adv.*

Abste'mious, *a.* L. *abstēmius*, f. ABS- + *tēmētum*, strong drink. Temperate, sparing.—**Abste'mious**NESS, *n.*

Ab'stract, *ppl.a.* L. *abstractus*, pa.pple. of ABS*trahĕre*, to draw away. TREAT. Withdrawn from matter, practice, &c., not concrete; ideal; abstruse.—*n.* A compendium or summary.—**Ab'stract**LY,[2] *adv.*

Abstract', *v.* Formed f. the prec. To purloin; to separate and consider by itself; to summarize.—**Abstrac'**TION, *n.*—**Abstract'ed**, *ppl.a.* Absent in mind.

Abstruse', *a.* L. *abstrūsus*, pa.pple. of ABS*trūdĕre*, to thrust away. INTRUDE. OBTRUDE. Obscure, difficult.—**Abstruse'**LY,[2] *adv.*

Absurd', *a.* L. *absurdus*, foolish, f. AB- (here intensive) + *surdus*, deaf. SURD. Contrary to reason; ridiculous, silly.—**Absurd'**LY,[2] *adv.*—**Absurd'**ITY, *n.*

Abun'dance, *n.* O.F. *abundance*, *abondance*—L. *abundantia*, f. *abundāre*. ABOUND. Overflowing state, plentifulness; plenty; affluence.—**Abun'd**ANT, *a.*—**Abun'dant**LY, *adv.*

Abuse', *vt.* F. *abuser*—L. *abūti*, *abūsus*, to misuse, f. AB- + *ūti*, to USE. To misuse; to ill-use; to revile.—**Abuse'**, *n.*—**Abus'**IVE, *a.* —**Abus'ive**LY,[2] *adv.*—**Abus'ive**NESS, *n.*

Abut', *vi.* O.F. *abouter*, to thrust towards, f. *à*, to + *bouter*, to thrust. BUTT.[3] To border or end *on*, lean *upon*.—**Abut'**MENT, *n.* A support, esp. for the end of a bridge.

Abyss', *n.* G. *abussos*, f. A[4] + *bussos*, bottom. The great deep; a bottomless or deep gulf.—**Abys'm**AL, *a.*

Acad'emy, *n.* G. *Akadēmeia*, the garden at Athens where Plato taught. The system of Plato; a higher school; a place of training; a literary, scientific, &c., society.—**Academ'**IC, **Academ'**ICAL, *aa.*—**Academi'**CIAN, *n.*

Acan'thus, *n.* G. *akanthos*, f. *akantha*, thorn, f. *akē*, point. ACID. The brank-ursine; in *arch.*, an imitation of the leaves.

Accede', *vi.* L. *ac*(=AD-)*cēdĕre*, *accessum*, to go to, approach. ACCESS. CEASE. To enter upon an office; to assent. agree.—**Acces'**SION, *n.* Entrance upon an office; a joining oneself to; assent; an addition.

Accel'erate, *vt.* L. *accelerāre*, *accelerātum*, to quicken, f. *ac*-(=AD-) + *celer*, swift. CELERITY. To quicken; to hasten.—*vi.* To become swifter. —**Acceler**A'TION, *n.*

Ac'cent, *n.* L. *accentus*, f. *ac*- (=AD-) + *cantus*, singing. CANT.[2] Stress of the voice; a mark indicating quality of sound; one's mode of speech; modulation of the voice.—**Accent'**, *vt.* To utter with stress; to heighten, intensify; to mark with accents.—**Accent'u**ATE,[3] *vt.* In same senses.—**Accentu**A'TION, *n.*

Accept', *vt.* L. *acceptāre*, freq. of *ac*(=AD-)*cipĕre*, *acceptum*, f. and = *capĕre*, to receive. CAPABLE. To receive; to admit, believe; to undertake; to sign (a bill) as engaging to pay.—**Accept'**ER, **Accept'**OR, *nn.* (The latter of a bill).—**Accept'**ABLE, *a.* Pleasing, agreeable. —**Accept'ab**LY,[2] *adv.*—**Accepta**BIL'ITY, *n.* —**Accept'**ANCE, *n.* An accepting; favourable reception; belief; agreeableness; an accepted bill.—**Accepta**'TION, *n.* Belief; meaning.

Ac'cess, *n.* L. *accessus*, f. *accēdĕre*. ACCEDE. Admittance; accessibility; an entrance; an attack; an outburst.—**Acces'**SIBLE, *a.* Affording entrance; easy of access.—**Acces**SIBIL'ITY, *n.*—**Ac'cess**ARY, *n.* An aider, esp. in a crime; an adjunct, accompaniment.—*a.* Aiding, esp. in a crime.—**Ac'cess**ORY, *a.* Additional; adventitious; aiding, esp. in a crime.—*n.* An aider, esp. in a crime; an adjunct, accompaniment.

Ac'cidence, *n.* App. a corr. of *Accidents*, L. *accidentia*, *neut. pl.* of *accidens* (ACCIDENT) in sense 'inflections'. The part of grammar treating of inflections; rudiments.

Ac'cident, *n.* L. *accidens*, *accidentis*, pres. pple. of *accidĕre*, to happen, f. *ac*-(=AD-) + *cadĕre*, to fall. A casualty, contingency; a mishap; a property or quality not essential, an accompaniment.—**Accident'**AL, *a.* In senses f. the *n.*—*n.* In *music*, a sharp, &c., specially introduced.—**Accident'al**LY,[2] *adv.*

Acclaim', *vt.* L. *ac*(=AD-)*clāmāre*, to shout at. CLAIM. CLAMOUR. To applaud; to proclaim with applause.—*n.* Applause; a shout of applause.—**Acclama**'TION, *n.*

Accli'matize, *vt.* F. *acclimater*, f. *à*, to + *climat*, CLIMATE. To habituate to a new climate or environment.

Accliv'ity, *n.* L. *acclīvis*, steep, f. *ac-* (=AD-) + *clīvus*, slope. An ascending slope.

Accolade', *n.* F.—L. *ad*, to + *collum*, the neck. COLLAR. Strictly, an embrace about the neck; the salutation on the bestowal of knighthood.

Accom'modate, *vt.* L. *ac*(=AD-)*COMmodāre*, *accommodātum*, to suit, f. *modus*, measure, MODE. To adapt, fit; to harmonize; to bring to agreement; to supply; to oblige.—**Accom'modating**, *ppl.a.* Obliging, pliant. —**Accommod**A'TION, *n.* Adaptation; a settlement; a convenience, an appliance; lodgings; a loan.

Accom'pany, *vt.* O.F. *accompagner*, f. *à*, to + *compaing*, COMPANION.[1] To go along with, attend; to characterize; to join (another) in singing or playing; with *with*, to supplement (a thing) by.—**Accom'pani**MENT, *n.* That which accompanies; *mus.*, a subsidiary part.—**Accom'pan**IST, **Accom'pany**IST, *nn.*

Accom'plice, *n.* From the earlier *Complice*, L. *complex*, *complicis*, participant, f. COM- + stem *plic-* of *plicāre*, to fold. The *ac-* not accounted for. COMPLICITY. An associate in guilt.

Accom'plish, *vt.* O.F. *acomplir*—L.L. *ac*(=AD-)*complēre*, to fill up. COMPLETE. To perform, carry out; to complete; to equip; to finish off.—**Accom'plished**, *ppl.a.* Fulfilled; complete, perfect.—**Accom'plish**MENT, *n.* Fulfilment; a personal attainment.

Accord', *vt.* O.F. *acorder*—L.L. *accordāre*, f. *ac-* (=AD-)+*cor*, *cordis*, HEART. (Lit., to bring heart to heart.) CORDIAL. To compose, settle; to grant, award.—*vi.* To agree; to be consistent.—*n.* Agreement, harmony; assent; a treaty.—**Accord'**ANT, *a.*—**Accord'**ANCE, *n.* —**Accord'ing**, *a.* Harmonious; with *as*, just as; with *to*, consistent with, agreeably to.—**Accord'ing**LY,[2] *adv.* Correspondingly; in due course.

Accord'ion, *n.* It. *accordare*, to attune, cogn. with ACCORD. A portable musical hand-instrument.

Accost', *vt.* F. *accoster*—L.L. *accostāre*, to be side by side, f. *ac-* (=AD-) + *costa*, rib. COAST. To approach, make up to; to address.

Accouche'ment, *n.* F., n. of action f. *accoucher*, f. *à*, to + *coucher*, to put to bed. COUCH. Delivery in child-bed.

Account', *vi.* O.F. *acunter*—L.L. *accomptāre*, for *ac*(=AD-)*computāre*, to calculate. COMPUTE. COUNT, *v.* To reckon for moneys; to give a reason *for*.—*vt.* To reckon, estimate.—*n.* A reckoning for moneys, a statement; profit; an answering for conduct; estimation, worth; a relation, report.—**Account'**ABLE, *a.* Responsible; explicable.—**Account'**ANT, *n.* One skilled in accounts.

Accou'tre, *vt.* O.F. *accoustrer* of uncertain orig. To equip.—**Accou'tre**MENT, *n.* In *pl.*, equipments.

Accred'it, *vt.* F. *accréditer*, f. *à*, to + *crédit*, CREDIT. To vouch for; to recommend; *to accredit* one *with*, to ascribe or attribute to him.

Accresce', *vi.* L. *ac*(=AD-)*crescĕre*, *accrētum*, to grow to. CRESCENT. DECREASE. To accrue. —**Accre'**TION, *n.* Growth; coherence; an extraneous addition; an accession.

Accrue', *vi.* O.F. *acrewe*, growth—L. *accressĕre*. (See prec.) To come by way of addition; to result.

Accum'ulate, *vt.* L. *accumulāre*, *accumulātum*, to heap up, f. *ac-* (=AD-) + *cumulāre*, to heap. CUMULATE. To amass.—*vi.* To grow into a mass, increase.—**Accumul**A'TION, *n.*

Ac'curate, *a.* L. *accūrātus*, pa.pple. of *accūrāre*, to apply care to, f. *ac-* (=AD-) + *cūrāre*, to care for, f. *cūra*, care. CURE. Exact; correct.—**Ac'curate**LY,[2] *adv.*—**Ac'cur**ACY, *n.*

Accurs'ed, *ppl.a.* A-[3], intensive + O.E. *cursian*, to CURSE. Under a curse; hateful.—Also **Accurst'**.

Accuse', *vt.* O.F. *acuser*—L. *accūsāre*, for *ac*(=AD-)*causāre*, to call to account, f. *causa*, CAUSE, process. To blame, censure, charge.—**Accus**A'TION, *n.*—**Accus'**ER, *n.*—**Accus'**ATIVE, *a.* and *n.* A noun case indicating an object.

Accus'tom, *vt.* O.F. *acostumer*, f. *à*, to + *costume*, CUSTOM. To habituate, familiarize. —**Accus'tomed**, *ppl.a.* Habitual, usual.

Ace, *n.* L. *as*, a unit, perh. f. G. *heis*, one. The one at dice or cards; a jot, atom.

Acerb'ity, *n.* L. *acerbitas*, f. *acerbus*, harsh to the taste, cogn. with ACID. Sourness with bitterness; keen harshness.

Acet'ic, *a.* L. *acētum*, vinegar, cogn. with ACID. Of the nature of or pertaining to vinegar.—So **Ac'et**OUS, *a.*

Ache, *n.* O.E. *æce*, f. *acan*, the *v.* Cogn. with L. *agĕre*, to drive. ACT. A continuous pain.—*vi.* To be in pain; to throb with pain.

Achieve', *vt.* A.F. *achever*, f. O.F. *à chef* (*venir*), L.L. *ad caput venīre*, to come to a head (with). CHIEF. To finish, complete; to attain.—**Achieve'**MENT, *n.* In *heraldry*, an escutcheon granted in memory of some notable feat. HATCHMENT.

Achromat'ic, *a.* G. *achrōmatos*, f. A[4] + *chrōma*, colour. Free from or not showing colour.

Ac'id, *a.* L. *acidus*, f. *acēre*, to be sour, root *ac-* as in G. *akē*, *akmē*, point, L. *acuĕre*, to sharpen. EAGER. EDGE. VINEGAR. Sour, sharp to the taste.—*n.* A sour substance: *chem.*, a compound of hydrogen.—**Acid'**IFY, *vt.*—**Acid'**ITY, *n.*

Acid'ulous, *a.* L. *acidulus*, sourish. (See prec.) Sourish.

Acknowl'edge, *vt.* A[1], changed to *ac* as if f. AD- + KNOWLEDGE. To admit; to recognize; to own as genuine or valid; to own with gratitude.—**Acknowl'edg**MENT, *n.*

Ac'me, *n.* G. *akmē*, point. ACID. The highest point.

Ac'olyte, *n.* F.—G. *akolouthos*, following. An attendant on a priest or deacon; a novice.

A'corn, *n.* O.E. *æcern*. Cogn. with Goth. *akran*, prob. 'fruit of the unenclosed land, the forest', f. *akrs*, plain. ACRE. The fruit of the oak.

Acous'tic, *a.* G. *akoustikos*, f. *akouein*, to hear. Pertaining to hearing.—In *pl.* as *n.*, the science of sound.

Acquaint', *vt.* O.F. *acointer*—L.L. *accognitāre*—L. *ac*(=AD-)*cognoscĕre*, *accognitum*, to KNOW well. COGNITION. To make to know; to inform.—**Acquaint'**ANCE, *n.* Personal knowledge; mutual knowledge between persons (in this sense also **Acquaint'ance**SHIP); a person known.

Acquiesce', *vi.* F. *acquiescer*—L. *ac*(=AD-)*quiescĕre*, to rest, f. *quies*, QUIET. To agree tacitly, concur.—**Acquies'**CENCE, *n.*—**Acquies'**CENT, *a.*

Acquire', *vt.* L. *acquīrĕre*, *acquīsitum*, to get besides, f. *ac-* (=AD-) + *quaerĕre*, to seek. QUEST. To gain, receive.—**Acquire'**MENT, *n.* An acquiring; a personal attainment.—**Acquisi'**TION, *n.* An acquiring; a material gain.—**Acquis'**ITIVE, *a.* Given to make acquisitions.

Acquit′, *vt.* O.F. *aquiter*—L. *ad*, to + *quiētus*, at rest, QUIET. To settle, discharge; to exculpate, exonerate; *refl.*, to perform one's part.—**Acquit′t**AL, *n.* Exoneration.—**Acquit′t**ANCE, *n.* Discharge or release from a debt; a receipt.

A′cre, *n.* O.E. *æcer*. Cogn. with Goth. *akrs*, L. *ager*, G. *agros*, Skr. *ajras*, field. ACORN. A measure of land.

Ac′rid, *a.* A recent formation on L. *ācer*, *acris*, sharp, from root *ac-*, as in ACID. Bitter and hot to the taste; bitterly irritating.—**Acrid′**ITY, *n.*

Ac′rimony, *n.* L. *acrimōnia*, f. *ācer*, sharp, cogn. with ACID. Irritating bitterness, asperity.—**Acrimo′ni**OUS, *a.*

Ac′robat, *n.* G. *akros*, highest + *-batos*, f. stem *ba-* of *bainein*, to go. BASE, *n.* A rope-dancer, tumbler.—**Acrobat′**IC, *a.*

Acrop′olis, *n.* G., f. *akros*, topmost + *polis*, city. A citadel dominating a city, esp. that of Athens.

Across′, *adv.* A-[1], in + CROSS. In the form of a cross; from side to side; on the other side.—*prep.* From side to side of; at right angles or an angle with; *to come across*, to meet with.

Acros′tic, *n.* G. *akros*, extreme + *stichos*, row or verse. A poem in which the first letters of the lines form a word or words.

Act, *n.* F. *acte*—L. *actus*, a doing, f. *agĕre*, *actum*, to drive, do. ACHE. A thing done, a deed; the process of doing; *in the act*, in the process, on the point; a decree of a legislative body; a written instrument; a division of a play.—*vt.* To perform (a play), to personate.—*vi.* To produce effects, fulfil a function; to behave or comport oneself; *to act as*, to serve as.—**Ac′t**ION, *n.* Working, operation, influence; a deed; gesture; legal process, a suit; fighting, a fight.—**Ac′tion**ABLE, *a.* Giving ground for an action at law.—**Ac′t**IVE, *a.* Exhibiting action; working, effective; energetic, diligent; in *grammar*, denoting action.—**Ac′tive**LY,[2] *adv.* — **Activ′**ITY, *n.* — **Ac′t**OR, *fem.* **Ac′tr**ESS, *nn.* A stage-player.—**Ac′tu**ATE,[3] *vt.* To act upon, move, impel.

Ac′tual, *a.* F. *actuel*—L. *actuālis*, f. *actus*, ACT. Real; present, current.—**Ac′tual**LY,[2] *adv.*—**Actual′**ITY, *n.*

Ac′tuary, *n.* L. *actuārius*, a keeper of accounts, f. *actus*, ACT. A skilled accountant.—**Actua′ri**AL, *a.*

Acu′men, *n.* L. *acūmen*, sharpness, cogn. with ACID. Sharpness of wit; quick perception.

Acute′, *a.* L. *acūtus*, pa.pple. of *acuĕre*, to sharpen. ACID. Sharp, pointed; poignant, keen; sensitive; sharp-witted, shrewd; of diseases, coming sharply to a crisis; shrill in tone; *acute accent*, a mark (′) placed on vowels to give various indications.—**Acute′**LY,[2] *adv.*—**Acute′**NESS, *n.* [verb.

Ad′age, *n.* F. *adage*—L. *adagium*. A proverb.

Ada′gio, *a.* and *adv.* It. *ad agio*, at leisure. *Mus.*, slowly, leisurely, with grace.

Ad′amant, *n.* G. *adamas*, *adamantos*, f. A-[4] + *dama-ein*, to TAME. DIAMOND. Something of great hardness.—**Adamant′**INE, *a.*

Adapt′, *vt.* F. *adapter*—L. AD*aptāre*, to fit to. APT. To fit, make suitable; to alter for a new use.—**Adapt**A′TION, *n.*—**Adapt′**ABLE, *a.*—**Adapta**BIL′ITY, *n.*

Add, *vt.* L. *addĕre*, *additum*, f. AD- + *dăre*, to give. DATE.[2] To join (one thing to another). —*vi.* To make an addition *to*; to say further; *math.*, to unite sums into one.—**Addi′t**ION, *n.*—**Adden′dum**, *pl.* **-a.** *Ger.* of *addĕre*. Something to be added; an appendix.

Ad′der, *n.* O.E. *nædre*, with *n* lost in M.E. Cf. APRON, AUGER. A small venomous serpent.

Addict′, *vt.* L. *addictus*, made over, pa.pple. of *addicĕre*, f. AD- + *dicĕre*, to pronounce. DICTION. To devote, give up habitually *to*. —So *refl.* and *pass.*—**Addic′t**ION, *n.*

Ad′dle, *a.* O.E. *adela*, mire. Putrid, rotten. —*vt.* To make addle; to muddle, spoil.—*vi.* To grow addle.

Address′, *vt.* F. *adresser*—L. type *AD*drictiāre*, to make straight, f. *dīrectus*, DIRECT. To direct, dispatch; to direct words *to*; to speak to.—*v.refl.* To turn oneself *to* in speech; to apply oneself *to*.—*n.* Dexterity; the direction on a letter; manner in speech; a discourse; in *pl.*, courteous approach.—**Address**EE′, *n.*

Adduce′, *vt.* L. *addūcĕre*, *adductum*, to bring forward, f. AD- + *dūcĕre*, to lead. ABDUCT. DUKE. To cite, allege.—**Adduc′t**ION, *n.*

Ad′enoid, *a.* G. *adēn*, gland + -OID. Glandlike.—In *pl.* as *n.*, small growths at the back of the throat.

Adept′, *a.* L. *adeptus*, having attained, pa.pple. of AD*ipisci*, *adeptus*, f. *apisci*, to attain. Skilled.—*n.* One skilled.

Ad′equate, *a.* L. *adaequātus*, pa.pple. of AD*aequāre*, *adaequātum*, to make equal, f. *aequus*, EQUAL. Fully sufficient, suitable.—**Ad′equate**LY,[2] *adv.*—**Ad′equ**ACY, *n.*

Adhere′, *vi.* F. *adhérer*—L. AD*haerēre*, *adhaesum*, to stick to. HESITATE. To stick *to*; to cleave *to* a person, opinion, &c.—**Adher′**ENCE, *n.*—**Adher′**ENT, *a.* and *n.*—**Adhe′**SION, *n.*—**Adhe′**SIVE, *a.*

Adhib′it, *vt.* L. AD*hibēre*, f. *habēre*, to hold. HABIT. To affix.

Adieu′, *int.* F. *à dieu*, to God. Farewell.—*n.* A farewell.—*pl.* **Adieux** or **Adieus**.

Ad′ipose, *a.* L. *adipōsus*, fatty, f. *adeps*, *adipis*, fat. Fatty.

Adja′cent, *a.* L. *adjacens*, pres.pple. of AD*jacēre*, to lie near. GIST. JOIST. Lying near.—**Adja′c**ENCY, *n.*

Ad′jective, *n.* L. *adjectīvus*, f. *adjectus*, pa.pple. of AD*jicĕre*, to lay to, f. *jacĕre*, to throw, lay. ABJECT. A word added to a noun to express quality or circumstance.—**Adjecti′v**AL, *a.*

Adjoin′, *vt.* F. *adjoindre*—L. AD*jungĕre*, to JOIN to. To add, annex; to be contiguous to.

Adjourn′, *vt.* O.F. *ajorner*—L.L. *adjurnāre*, f. AD- + *jurnus* (F. *jour*), a day. Cf. L. *diurnus*. DIURNAL. JOURNAL. To defer to another day, postpone.—*vi.* To suspend proceedings; to proceed (to another place).—**Adjourn′**MENT, *n.*

Adjudge′, *vt.* O.F. *ajuger*—L. *adjūdicāre*, to ADJUDICATE. To decide; to sentence; to award.

Adju′dicate, *vt.* L. AD*jūdicāre*, *adjūdicātum*, to award, to give sentence, f. *jūdicāre*, to JUDGE. To try; to pronounce judicially.—*vi.* To sit in judgment.—**Adjudic**A′TION, *n.*

Ad′junct, *a.* L. *adjunctus*, pa.pple. of AD*jungĕre*, to JOIN to. Joined or added.—*n.* Something or a person joined or added; a qualifying addition.

Adjure′, *vt.* L. AD*jūrāre*, to swear to, in L.L., to put on oath. JURY. To entreat.—**Adjur**A′TION, *n.*

Adjust′, *vt.* F. *adjuster*, f. Med.L. *adjustāre* (as if f. AD- + L. *justus*, exact, JUST), formed f. O.F. *ajuster*, to put side by side, arrange, f.

a-(=AD-) + L. *juxta*, near. To settle, harmonize; to arrange, dispose.—**Adjust'**MENT, *n.*
Ad'jutant, *n.* L. *adjūtans*, pres.pple. of *adjūtāre*, freq. of ADjuvāre, to assist. AID. An officer in the army assisting superiors.—**Ad'jutan**CY, *n.*
Admin'ister, *vt.* O.F. *aministrer*—L. AD*ministrāre*, to minister to, manage. MINISTER. To manage; to dispose of as executor; to dispense (justice, a sacrament, &c.); to tender (an oath); to furnish, supply.—**Administr**A'TION, *n.* — **Admin'istr**ATIVE, *a.*—**Admin'istrat**OR, *n.*
Ad'miral, *n.* O.F. *amiral*, f. Arab. *amīr*, commander, with the addition of the Arab. article *al*, (of) the (*sc.* ships). A naval officer of the highest rank.—**Ad'miral**SHIP, *n.*—**Ad'miral**TY, *n.* Cf. SHRIEVALTY. His jurisdiction; maritime affairs; the board managing the navy; the building in which it sits.
Admire', *vt.* O.F. *amirer*—L. AD*mīrāri*, to wonder at. MIRACLE. To regard with surprise and approbation; to delight in.—**Ad'mir**ABLE, *a.*— **Ad'mirab**LY,[2] *adv.*—**Admir**A'TION, *n.*—**Admir'**ER, *n.*
Admit', *vt.* O.F. *amettre*—L. AD*mittĕre*, to let into. MISSION. To let in, receive; to permit; to acknowledge; to concede; to have room for.—*vi.* To grant: with *of*, to lie open to, be compatible with.—**Admis's**IBLE, *a.* —**Admis's**ION, *n.*—**Admit't**ANCE, *n.*
Admix'ture, *n.* AD- + MIXTURE. A mixing; an alloy.
Admon'ish, *vt.* O.F. *amonester*—L.L. *admonestāre*, f. L. AD*monēre*, to warn. MONITION. To exhort, warn, caution; to inform. —**Admoni't**ION, *n.*—**Admon'it**ORY, *a.*
Ado', *n.* Properly an *inf.*=*at do*, a N. English idiom, *at* being used as the sign of the infinitive as in Norse. Business, fuss, trouble, esp. with *much*, *little*, &c.
Adoles'cent, *n.* L. *adolescens*, *adolescentis*, pres.pple. of *adolescĕre*, to grow up. ADULT. A youth.—*a.* Growing to maturity.—**Adoles'c**ENCE, *n.*
Adopt', *vt.* F. *adopter*—L. AD*optāre*, to choose for oneself. OPTION. To take into a relationship, esp. as one's child; to take up (principles, &c.) as one's own.—**Adop't**ION, *n.* —**Adop't**IVE, *a.* Due to adoption; fitted or inclined to adopt.
Adore', *vt.* F. *adorer*—L. AD*ōrāre*, to speak to, salute. To worship; to reverence and love. —*vi.* To offer worship.—**Ador'**ABLE, *a.*—**Ador**A'TION, *n.*—**Ador'**ER, *n.*
Adorn', *vt.* O.F. *aörner*—L. AD*ornāre*, to fit out, to adorn. ORNAMENT. To beautify, add lustre to; to deck, embellish.
Adrift', *adv.* A[1] + DRIFT. Floating free.
Adroit', *a.* F. *adroit*, f. *à droit*, according to right—L. *directus*, right. DIRECT. Dexterous, clever, ready.—**Adroit'**LY,[2] *adv.*—**Adroit'**NESS, *n.*
Ad'ulate, *vt.* L. *adūlāri*, to fawn upon. To flatter servilely.—**Adul**A'TION, *n.*—**Ad'ulat**ORY, *a.*
Adult', *a.* L. *adultus*, pa.pple. of AD*olescĕre*, to grow up, f. obs. *olēre*, to grow. ABOLISH. Grown up, full-grown.—*n.* One grown up.
Adul'terate, *vt.* L. *adulterāre*, *adulterātum*, to corrupt, f. *adulter*. ADULTERY. To debase, esp. by admixture.—**Adulter**A'TION, *n.*
Adul'tery, *n.* O.F. *avouterie*—L. *adulterium*, f. *adulter*, adulterer, f. *ad*, to + *alter*, another. ALTER. Violation of the marriage bed.—**Adul'ter**ER, *fem.* **Adul'ter**ESS, *nn.*—**Adul'ter**OUS, *a.*
Adum'brate, *vt.* L. AD*umbrāre*, *adumbrātum*, to shadow out, f. *umbra*, shadow. UMBRAGE. UMBRELLA. To outline, give an indication of; to typify; to overshadow.—**Adumbr**A'TION, *n.*
Advance', *vt.* O.F. *avancer*—Pop.L. *abanteāre*, f. L.L. *abante* (F. *avant*), away before, f. *ab*, away + *ante*, before. AVAUNT. VAN.[1] To move forward; to help on, aid; to put forward, propose; to hasten, accelerate; to lend; to promote, prefer.—*vi.* To go forward, proceed. —*n.* Forward motion, progress; a forward step; an overture; a rise in amount, &c.; a loan; *in advance*, in front, beforehand, before the due date.—**Advance'**MENT, *n.* Promotion, preferment; furtherance.
Advan'tage, *n.* F. *avantage*, f. *avant*, forward, + -AGE. ADVANCE. Superiority; a favouring circumstance; profit.—*vt.* To favour, profit; to further.—**Advanta'ge**OUS, *a.*—**Advanta'geous**LY,[2] *adv.*
Ad'vent, *n.* L. *adventus*, arrival, f. AD*venīre*, *adventum*, to come to. EVENT. The coming of Christ; the four weeks before Christmas; any important arrival.
Adventi'tious, *a.* L. *adventicius*, coming from abroad. ADVENT. Accidental, casual.
Adven'ture, *n.* O.F. *aventure*—L. *adventūra* (sc. *res*), (a thing) about to happen, fut. pple. of *advenīre*. ADVENT. Risk; a daring feat; daring; a striking event; a speculation. —*vt.* To risk.—*vi.* To run a risk.—**Advent'ur**ER, *fem.* **Advent'ur**ESS, *nn.* Esp., one who lives by his wits.—**Advent'ur**OUS, *a.*
Ad'verb, *n.* L. *adverbium*, f. AD- + *verbum*, word. VERB. A word modifying a verb, adjective, or other adverb.—**Adver'b**IAL, *a.* —**Adver'bial**LY,[2] *adv.*
Ad'verse, *a.* O.F. *avers*—L. *adversus*, turned to or against, pa.pple. of AD*vertĕre*, *adversum*, to turn to. VERSE. Hostile; hurtful, injurious. —**Ad'verse**LY,[2] *adv.*—**Ad'vers**ARY, *n.* An enemy.—**Adver's**ATIVE, *a.* Expressing opposition or contrariety.—**Adver's**ITY, *n.* Distress, affliction; a misfortune.
Advert', *vi.* F. *avertir*—L. *advertĕre* (sc. *animum*, the mind). ADVERSE. To turn one's mind or attention; to refer.—**Adver't**ENCE, **Adver't**ENCY, *nn.*
Advertise', *vt.* F. *avertir*. ADVERT. To notify, inform; to make known, indicate; to give in print public notice of.—*vi.* To give public notice in print.—**Advertis'**ER, *n.*—**Adver'tise**MENT, *n.*
Advice', *n.* O.F. *avis*—Pop.L. *advīsum*, opinion, f. AD- + *visum*, seen, pa.pple. of *vidēre*, to see. VISION. Opinion given, counsel; intelligence, news.
Advise', *vi.* F. *aviser*, f. Pop.L. *advīsum*. (See prec.) To take or give counsel.—*vt.* To counsel; to inform; to announce.—**Advis'**ABLE, *a.*—**Advised'**, *ppl.a.* Considered; judicious.—**Advis'ed**LY,[2] *adv.* Intentionally, deliberately.—**Advis'**ER, *n.*
Ad'vocate, *n.* O.F. *avocat*—L. *advocātus*, pa.pple. of AD*vocāre*, to call in aid to. AVOUCH. A barrister, counsel; an upholder. —*vt.* To uphold.—**Ad'voc**ACY, *n.*
Advow'son, *n.* A.F. *advoeson*, patronage—L.L. *advocātus*, patron, f. L. *advocāre*. (See prec.) The right to confer an ecclesiastical benefice.
Adze, *n.* O.E. *adesa*, orig. unknown. An axe with the edge at right angles to the handle.

A'erate, *vt.* L. *āër*, AIR. To expose to air; to charge with carbonic acid.—**Aera**'TION, *n.*
Aer'ial, *a.* L. *āerius*, f. *āër*, AIR. Connected with or like the air; unsubstantial.
A'erie, **A'ery**, *n.* Med.L. *aeria*—F. *aire*. Orig. doubtful. The nest of a bird of prey; the brood. [A meteoric stone.
A'erolite, *n.* G. *aēr*, AIR + *lithos*, stone.
A'eronaut, *n.* G. *aēr*, AIR + *nautēs*, sailor, f. *naus*, ship. NAVY. One who sails in the air.—**Aeronaut**'IC, *a.* In *pl.* as *n.*, aerial navigation.
Æsthet'ic, **Esthet'ic**, *a.* G. *aisthētikos*, perceptive, perceptible, f. *aisthanesthai*, to perceive. Relating to criticism of the beautiful; of or in good taste.—In *pl.* as *n.*, the philosophy of taste.—**Æsthet'ic**AL, *a.*
Ætiol'ogy, *n.* G. *aitia*, cause + -LOGY. The assignment of a cause; the science of causation.
Afar', *adv.* A-[2] + FAR. From far; far away.
Af'fable, *a.* L. *af*(=AD-)*fāri*, to speak to + -ABLE. FAME. Easy of conversation, courteous.—**Af'fab**LY,[2] *adv.*—**Affab**IL'ITY, *n.*
Affair', *n.* O.F. *afaire*, f. phrase *à faire* (L. *facĕre*), to do. FACT. A business, operation; a matter, concern.
Affect', *v.*[1]*t.* L. *affectāre*, to aim at, freq. of *afficĕre*, *affectum*, to act on, f. *af-* (= AD-) + *facĕre*, to do. FACT. To have a liking for, like, fancy; to make a display of, assume; to pretend.—**Affect**A'TION, *n.* Always with sense of ostentation or pretence. —**Affect'ed**, *ppl.a.* Artificial, pretended; assuming airs.—**Affect'ed**LY,[2] *adv.*
Affect', *v.*[2]*t.* L. *afficĕre*, *affectum*. (See prec.) To attack, as a disease; to influence, move.—**Affec'**TION, *n.* A being affected; goodwill, fondness. — **Affec'tion**ATE,[2] *a.* — **Affec'tionate**LY,[2] *adv.*
Affi'ance, *n.* O.F. *afiance*, f. *afier*—L.L. *af*(=AD-)*fīdāre*, to trust, f. L. *fidus*, trusty. FAITH. The plighting of marriage troth.—*vt.* To betroth.
Affida'vit, *n.* L.L., 3rd sing. perf. of *affīdāre*, in sense 'has sworn'. (See prec.) A written statement on oath.
Affil'iate, *vt.* L. *affiliāre*, *affiliātum*, to adopt, f. *af-* (=AD-) + *filius*, son. FILIAL. To adopt; to attach (*to* a larger institution); to father *on*. —**Affili**A'TION, *n.*
Affin'ity, *n.* F. *afinité*—L. *affinis*, related, f. *af-* (=AD-) + *finis*, end, border. FINAL. Relationship by marriage or in general; resemblance; liking, attractiveness.
Affirm', *vt.* O.F. *afermer*—L. *af*(=AD-)*firmāre*, to make firm, f. *firmus*, FIRM. To confirm, ratify; to assert.—*vi.* To declare, aver; to make a formal declaration.—**Affirm**A'TION, *n.*—**Affirm'**ATIVE, *a.* Affirming.—*n.* A word or phrase expressing assent.—**Affirm'ative**LY,[2] *adv.*
Affix', *vt.* L. *af*(=AD-)*fīgĕre*, *affixum*, to FIX to. To fix to; to subjoin.—**Af'fix**, *n.* Something added, esp. at the end of a word.
Afflict', *vt.* L. *af*(= AD-)*flīgĕre*, *afflictum*, to dash against, f. *flīgĕre*, to strike. To distress, vex.—**Afflic'**TION, *n.*—**Afflic'**TIVE, *a.*
Af'fluent, *a.* L. *affluens*, *affluentis*, pres.pple. of *af*(=AD-)*fluĕre*, to flow to. FLUENT. Flowing freely; wealthy.—*n.* A tributary stream.—**Af'flu**ENCE, *n.* Profusion; wealth.
Afford', *vt.* M.E. *aforthen*, to provide—O.E. *geforthian*, to further, f. *ge-*, pref. + *forth*, FORTH. To be able to give, buy, &c.; to yield. —*vi.* To have the means.
Affor'est, *vt.* Med.L. *afforestāre*, f. *af-* (=AD-) + *foresta*, FOREST. To make forest of.—**Afforest**A'TION, *n.*
Affray', *vt.* O.F. *esfreer*—L.L. *exfridāre*, f. EX- + *fridus*, O.H.G. *fridu*, peace. DEFRAY. To terrify.—*n.* A brawl.
Affright', *vt.* Formed on FRIGHT, *v.*, with A-[3], intensive. To terrify.—*n.* A cause of terror; terror.
Affront', *vt.* O.F. *afronter*, to encounter, f. L. *ad frontem*, to the face. FRONT. To insult; to put to shame; to confront; to face.—*n.* An insult; an offence to one's dignity.
Afield', *adv.* A-[1] + FIELD. To or in the field.
Afloat', *adv.* A-[1] + FLOAT. Floating; current.
Afoot', *adv.* A-[1] + FOOT. On foot; in action.
Afraid', *ppl.a.* Orig. pa.pple. of AFFRAY. In fear.
Afresh', *adv.* A-[2] + FRESH. Anew, again.
Aft, *adv.* O.E. *æftan*, cogn. with Goth. *afta*, behind. At or near a ship's stern; towards the stern.
Af'ter, *adv.* O.E. *æfter*, orig. compar. of *af* (L. *ab*, G. *apo*) with sense 'farther off'. OF. Behind; subsequently.—*prep.* Behind; in pursuit of; succeeding; subsequent to; in accordance with, like.—*a.* Next; later, hinder.
Af'terbirth, *n.* The membrane extruded after a birth.
Af'termath, *n.* AFTER, *a* + obs. *Math*, mowing, O.E. *mǽth*, f. O.Teut. root *mæ-*, to MOW. A second crop. [ing noon.
Af'ternoon, *n.* The part of the day following noon.
Af'terward, **Af'terwards**, *adv.* O.E. *æftanweard*, f. *æftan*, AFT + -WARD(S). Subsequently.
Again', *adv.* M.E. *ayein*—O.E. *ongegn*, f. *on* (A-[1]) + *gegn*, app. orig. meaning direct, straight. GAINSAY. Back; in reply; anew, once more; moreover; besides.
Against', *prep.* Formed on *ayein*, AGAIN, by genitive ending *-(e)s*, with parasitic *-t*. Facing; with respect to, in regard to; into or in contact with; contrary to; in opposition to; instead of; in anticipation of.
Ag'ate, *n.* F. *agathe*—L. *achātes*, f. the river Achates in Sicily, as found there. A semi-pellucid mineral with blended bands of colour.
Age, *n.* O.F. *aäge*—L. *aetas*, f. *aevum*, age. AY, ever. Length of existence; the duration of life; years of discretion; a stage of life; old age; a generation; an indefinitely long time; an epoch.—*vt.* To make old.—*vi.* To grow old. —**A'ged**, *ppl.a.* Old; having reached the age of.
Agen'da, *n.pl.* *Pl.neut.* of L. *agendus*, gerundive of *agĕre*, to do, ACT. A note of business to be done.
A'gent, *n.* L. *agens*, *agentis*, pres.pple. of *agĕre*, to ACT. One who or that which acts or produces an effect; a cause; a natural force; one who acts as representative of another.—**A'g**ENCY, *n.* Action; instrumentality; the business or place of business of a representative.
Agglom'erate, *vt.* and *i.* L. *ag*(=AD-)*glomerāre*, *agglomerātum*, to wind into a ball, f. *glomus*, a clew. To gather or collect into a mass.—**Agglomer**A'TION, *n.*
Ag'grandize, *vt.* F. *agrandir*—L. *ag*(=AD-)*grandīre*, to make great, f. *grandis*, large. GRAND. To enlarge; to add to the power of; to exaggerate.—**Aggrand'ize**MENT, *n.*
Ag'gravate, *vt.* L. *ag*(=AD-)*gravāre*, *aggravātum*, to make heavy, f. *gravis*, heavy. GRAVE, *a.* To make worse, intensify; to exasperate, provoke.—**Aggrav**A'TION, *n.*

Ag'gregate, *ppl.a.* L. *ag*(=AD-)*gregāre*, *aggregātum*, to collect, f. *grex*, *gregis*, flock. GREGARIOUS. Collected together; collective.—*n.* A sum total; an assemblage.—*vt.* To collect together.—*Elliptically*, to amount to.—**Aggrega'**TION, *n.*

Aggres'sion, *n.* F. *agression*, f. *agresser*—L. *aggredi*, *aggressus*, to march to, attack, f. *ag*-(=AD-) + *gradi*, to go, f. *gradus*, step. GRADE. An unprovoked attack; attack, assault.—**Aggres'**SIVE, *a.*—**Aggres'**SOR, *n.*

Aggrieve', *vt.* F. *agrever*—L. *aggravāre*, to AGGRAVATE. To afflict.

Aghast', *ppl.a.* Pa.pple. of *agast*, f. A-3, intensive + O.E. *gǽstan*, to alarm. GHASTLY. Horror-struck.

Ag'ile, *a.* F. *agile*—L. *agilis*, f. *agĕre*, to do, ACT. Nimble, active.—**Ag'ile**LY,2 *adv.*—**Agil'**ITY, *n.*

Ag'itate, *vt.* L. *agitāre*, *agitātum*, freq. of *agĕre*, to drive, ACT. To shake; to perturb, excite; to discuss, push forward.—**Agita'**TION, *n.*—**Ag'itat**OR, *n.* An exciter of discord.

Ag'nate, *n.* L. *agnātus* (AD*gnātus*), born to, f. *gnasci*, *nasci*, to be born. COGNATE. NATAL. A kinsman by the father's side.—*a.* Related by the father's side.

Agnos'tic, *n.* G. *agnōstos*, unknown, unknowing, f. A-4 + *gno*-, root of *gignōskein*, to learn to KNOW. One disclaiming knowledge of existence beyond material phenomena.—*a.* Pertaining to such a one or his views.—**Agnos'tic**ISM, *n.* [by, past.

Ago', *ppl.a.* and *adv.* A-3, away + GO. Gone

Ag'onize, *vi.* G. *agōnizesthai*, to contend, f. *agōn*, contest. To suffer anguish.—*vt.* To torture.

Ag'ony, *n.* G. *agōnia*, f. *agōn*, contest. Anguish, mental or bodily; the pains of death.

Agra'rian, *a.* L. *agrārius*, f. *ager*, field. ACRE. Relating to the land or to landed property.

Agree', *vi.* O.F. *agréer*—L.L. *ag*(=AD-) *grātāre*, to make pleasing, f. *grātus*, pleasing. GRACE. To consent, accede; to come to or be in harmony.—**Agree'**ABLE, *a.*—**Agree'ab**LY,2 *adv.*—**Agree'**MENT, *n.*

Ag'riculture, *n.* L. *agri cultūra*, land culture. ACRE. CULT. The art or science of cultivating the soil; farming.—**Agricul'tur**AL, *a.*—**Agricul'tur**IST, *n.*

Aground', *adv.* A-1 + GROUND. Stranded.

A'gue, *n.* O.F. *ague*—Med.L. *acūta*, sharp, as *n.*, an 'acute fever'. ACUTE. A malarial fever; a quaking. [ward.

Ahead', *adv.* A-1, at + HEAD. In front, onward.

Aid, *vt.* O.F. *aider*—L. *adjūtāre*, freq. of AD*juvāre*, to give help to. To help.—*n.* Help.

Aide-(*pl.* **Aides-**)**de-camp'**, *n.* F. Lit., camp assistant. An officer attending a general.

Aig'rette, *n.* F., the egret or Lesser White HERON. A tuft of feathers like the egret's; a spray of gems.

Ail, *v.impers.* O.E. *eglan*, to pain. Cf. O.E. *ege*. AWE. To trouble, physically or mentally.—*vi.* To be ill.—**Ail'**MENT, *n.*

Aim, *vi.* M.E. *eimen*. Prob. two words blended—A.F. *esmer*, L. *aestimāre*, to estimate, aim, and O.F. *aësmer*—L.L. AD*aestimāre*. ESTEEM. To direct one's course or efforts; to strike or throw (*at* something).—*vt.* To direct (a blow or missile).—*n.* An aiming; intention, purpose; an object.

Air, *n.* O.F. *air*—L. *āĕr*—G. *aēr*, f. *aein*, to blow. The fluid which we breathe; the atmosphere; a breeze, a vapour.—Through F. *air*, look, tune (which, however, may be in this sense another word), manner; affected manner; a tune.—*vt.* To expose to air or view; to dry or warm.—**Air'**Y,2 *a.*—**Air'**ILY,2 *adv.*

Aisle, *n.* F. *aile*—L. *āla*, wing. The wing or lateral division of a church. [open.

Ajar', *adv.* A-1 + CHAR(E), a turn. Partly

Akin', *adv.* A-2 + KIN. Of kin; near in nature.—*a.* Of the same kin; of the same kind.

Al'abaster, *n.* L. *alabaster*—G. *alabastros*, of doubtful orig. A soft marble-like mineral.

Alac'rity, *n.* L. *alacritas*, f. *alacer*, brisk. Briskness, liveliness, sprightliness.

Alarm', *n.* O.F. *alarme*—It. *allarme*, *all' arme*, to the arms, f. L. *arma*. ARM.2 A call to arms; a warning; consternation.—*vt.* To put on the alert; to terrify.—**Alarm'**IST, *n.* A panic-monger.

Albi'no, *n.* Sp., f. L. *albus*, white. (See next.) A person or animal lacking colouring pigment in the skin, hair, and eyes.

Al'bum, *n.* L. *album*, a blank tablet, f. *albus*, white. AUBURN. A blank book for receiving verses, drawings, &c.

Albu'men, *n.* L., the white of an egg. The white of an egg; a constituent thereof and of animals and plants.—**Albu'min**OUS, *a.*

Al'chemy, *n.* Arab. *al*, the + *kimia*, chemistry. CHEMIST. The old chemistry, which aimed at getting gold from base metals, sought the elixir of life, &c.—**Al'chem**IST, *n.*

Al'cohol, *n.* Arab. *al*, the + *kohl*, fine powdered antimony, hence, anything of great tenuity, spirits of wine. The intoxicating element of wine, &c.—**Alcohol'**IC, *a.*—**Al'cohol**ISM, *n.*

Al'cove, *n.* Arab. *al*, the + *qobbah*, vault. A recess. [A tree related to the birch.

Al'der, *n.* O.E. *alor*. Cogn. with L. *alnus*.

Al'derman, *n.* O.E. *aldor* (*ald*, OLD + *or*, n. suffix) + MAN. A magistrate in towns.

Ale, *n.* O.E. *alu*, cogn. with O.S. *alo*, O.N *öl*. Beer or a kind of beer.

Alert', *a.* F. *alerte*—It. *all'*, at the + *erta*, look-out place—L. *ērigĕre*, to ERECT. Vigilant; brisk.

Alexan'drine, *n.* F. *alexandrin*, of doubtful orig. A line of six feet or twelve syllables.

Al'gebra, *n.* Arab. *al*, the + *jabr*, a repairing, a reducing fractions to integers. The science of computing by symbols.—**Algebra'**IC, **Algebra'**ICAL, *aa.* [name.

A'lias, *adv.* L. Otherwise.—*n.* An assumed

Al'ibi, *n.* L., elsewhere. The plea of having been elsewhere at the time of a crime.

Al'ien, *a.* L. *aliēnus*, f. *alius*, other. ELSE. Foreign; not of one's own; inconsistent, repugnant.—*n.* A foreigner.—**Al'ien**ATE,3 *vt.* To estrange; to transfer.—**Aliena'**TION, *n.*

Alight', *vi.* O.E. *alihtan*, f. A-3 + *lihtan*. LIGHT, *v.*1 To get down; to settle or lodge.

Alight', *a.* A-1 + LIGHT, *n.* On fire.

Alike', *a.* M.E. *alike*—O.E. *onlic*, f. *-líc*, LIKE, with *on*- = A-1. Like, similar.—*adv.* Similarly.

Al'iment, *n.* L. *alimentum*, f. *alĕre*, to nourish. COALESCE. Food, support.—*vt.* To support.—**Alimen'**TARY, *a.*

Al'imony, *n.* L. *alimōnia*, f. *alĕre*. ALIMENT. Maintenance, esp. of a wife on separation.

Al'iquot, *a.* L., some, so many. Said of a number which divides another without remainder.

Alive', *a.* A-1, in + LIFE. In life, living.

Al'kali, *n.* Arab. *al*, the + *qalī*, ashes of saltwort, which abound in soda. A substance, such as soda, &c., which neutralizes acids and forms soap with oil.—**Al'kaline**, *a.*—**Al'kaloid**, *a.* and *n.*

All, *a.* O.E. *eal, al.* Common Teut. Every one of, the whole of.—*adv.* Wholly.—*n.* The whole.

Allay', *vt.* A-3 + LAY. To assuage, abate.

Allege', *vt.* and *i.* L. *al*(=AD-)*lēgāre*, to send to, to adduce. f. *lēgāre*, to depute. LEGATE. To plead; to assert, affirm.—**Allega'tion**, *n.*

Alle'giance, *n* M.E. *alegeaunce*, f. F. *à*, to + O.F. *ligance, ligeance*, homage, f. *lige, liege.* LIEGE. Loyalty.

Al'legory, *n.* G. *allēgoria*, lit., speaking otherwise than one seems to speak, f. *allos*, other + *agoreuein*, to speak. A discourse with a meaning different from the literal one; an emblem.—**Allegor'ic**, -ICAL, *aa.*—**-ically**,[2] *adv.*—**Al'legorize**, *vt.* and *i.* [*Mus.*, lively.

Alleg'ro, *a.* and *adv.* It., f. L. *alacer*, brisk.

Allev'iate, *vt.* L. *alleviāre, alleviātum*, to lighten, f. *al*-(=AD-) + *levis*, light. LEVITY. To mitigate.—**Allevia'tion**, *n.* [or passage.

Al'ley, *n.* O.F. *alee*, f. *aler*, to go. A walk

Al'ligator, *n.* Sp. *al lagarto*, the lizard. An American genus of Saurians of the crocodile family.

Allitera'tion, *n.* L. *al*- (=AD-) + *littera*, LETTER. The beginning of two or more words in close succession with the same sound.—**Allit'erative**, *a.*

Al'locate, *vt.* L. *al*(=AD-)*locāre, allocātum*, to place, f. *locus*, place. LOCAL. To set apart; to fix the locality of, localize.—**Alloca'tion**, *n.*

Al'locute, *vi.* L. *al*(=AD-)*loqui, allocūtus*, to speak to. LOQUACIOUS. To give a formal address.—**Allocu'tion**, *n.*

Allo'pathy, *n.* G. *allos*, other + *pathos*, suffering. The curing of a diseased action by inducing an action of a different kind.—**Allopath'ic**, *a.*—**Allopath'ically**,[2] *adv.*

Allot', *vt.* O.F. *aloter*, f. *à*, to + *loter*, to divide by lot, f. *lot*, LOT. To assign, apportion; to appoint.—**Allot'ment**, *n.*

Allow', *vt.* and *i.* O.F. *alouer*, blending L. *al*(=AD-)*laudāre*, to praise (LAUD), and *al*-(=AD-)*locāre*, to place, stow. ALLOCATE. To acknowledge, concede; to permit; to give; to take into a reckoning.—**Allow'able**, *a.* Permissible.—**Allow'ably**,[2] *adv.*—**Allow'ance**, *n.* The act of allowing; a sum given or credited; a portion or sum allotted.

Alloy', *vt.* F. *aloyer*—O.F. *aleier*—L. *alligāre.* ALLY. (North. F. *alayer*, whence *Allay*, the earlier Eng. form). To mix with a baser metal; to debase.—*n.* A baser metal mixed with a finer; a metallic compound.

Allude', *vi.* L. *al*(=AD-)*lūdĕre, allūsum*, to jest at, touch lightly on. LUDICROUS. To have or make a covert reference *to.*—**Allu'sion**, *n.*—**Allus'ive**, *a.*—**Allus'ively**,[2] *adv.*

Allure', *vt.* O.F. *aleurrer*, f. *à*, to + *leurrer*, to LURE. To entice, win over; to charm.—**Allure'ment**, *n.*

Allu'vium, *n.* L. *neut. a.*, f. *al*(=AD-)*luĕre*, to wash against. DELUGE. DILUTE. A deposit left by water.—**Allu'vial**, *a.*

Ally', *vt.* O.F. *alier*—L. *al*(=AD-)*ligāre*, to bind to. ALLOY. LEAGUE.[1] LIGAMENT. To join in friendship or marriage, by treaty, &c.—**Ally'**, *n.* One joined with another by treaty, generally of states.—**Alli'ance**, *n.*

Al'manac, *n.* F. *almanach*—Sp. *almanaque*, app. Sp. Arabic. A table of months, days, &c.

Almight'y, *a.* ALL + MIGHTY. All-powerful.

Al'mond, *n.* O.F. *almande*, corr. of L. *amygdala*, G. *amugdalē.* The kernel of a fruit allied to the peach; the tree bearing the fruit; in *pl.*, the tonsils of the throat. [all but.

Al'most, *adv.* ALL + MOST, *adv.* Nearly,

Alms, *n.* (treated as *pl.*). O.E. *ælmysse*—L.L. *eleēmosyna*, f. G. *eleēmosunē*, pity. A charitable gift.—**Al'moner**, *n.* O.F. *aumoner*, f. *eleēmosyna.* A distributer of alms.—**Al'monry**, *n.* A place where alms are distributed.—**Alms'-house**, *n.* A house for lodging poor persons.

A'loe, *n.* L. *aloē*—G. *aloē.* A genus of bitter plants; in *pl.*, a medicine made therefrom.

Aloft', *adv.* O.N. *á lopt*, in the air. LOFT. On high. [rately.

Alone', *a.* ALL + ONE. Solitary.—*adv.* Sepa-

Along', *prep.* O.E. *andlang*, f. *and*-, over against + *lang*, long. LONG, *a.* From end to end of, by the side of.—*adv.* Lengthwise; forward; side by side *with*; together *with.*

Aloof', *adv.* *On* (A[1].) *loof*=Du. *te loef*, to windward. LUFF. At or from a distance, apart.

Aloud', *adv.* A-1 + LOUD. Loudly.

Alp, *n.* L. *Alpēs, pl.*, a Swiss mountain range. *Pl.* The Alps.—*Sing.* A high hill.—**Al'pine**, *a.*

Alpac'a, *n.* Sp. A Peruvian quadruped with long wool; cloth made from the wool.

Al'phabet, *n.* G. *alpha, bēta*, the first two letters. The set of letters representing the sounds of a language.—**Alphabet'ic, Alphabet'ical**, *aa.*

Alread'y, *adv.* ALL + READY. Before, even now. [too.

Al'so, *adv.* ALL + SO (O.E. *al* + *swā*). Further,

Al'tar, *n.* L. *altāre*, f. *altus*, high. ALTITUDE. A raised structure for sacrifice or the celebration of the Eucharist.

Al'ter, *vt.* F. *altérer*—Med.L. *alterāre*, f. *alter*, other. To change, vary.—*vi.* To change—**Altera'tion**, *n.*—**Al'terative**, *a.* As *n.*, a medicine or treatment inducing a salutary change.

Al'tercate, *vi.* L. *altercāri, altercātus*, to wrangle, f. *alter*, another. To dispute, wrangle.—**Alterca'tion**, *n.*

Alter'nate, *a.* L. *alternātus*, pa.pple. of *alternāre*, to do by turns, f. *alternus*, alternate. Done or changed by turns.—**Al'ternate**, *vt.* To arrange or do by turns.—*vi.* To occur by turns, vary.—**Alter'nately**,[2] *adv.*—**Alterna'tion**, *n.*—**Alter'native**, *a.* As *n.*, an alternative statement, course, &c.—**Alter'natively**,[2] *adv.* [Granting that.

Although', *conj.* ALL, even if + THOUGH.

Al'titude, *n.* L. *altitūdo*, f. *altus*, high. ALTAR. Height.

Al'to, *n.* It. *alto*, L. *altus*, high. ALTAR. The highest male voice; the part for this voice; a singer with a voice of this pitch.

Altogeth'er, *adv.* ALL + TOGETHER. Entirely, wholly.

Alto-relie'vo, *n.* It. *alto-rilievo.* High relief; sculpture with figures projecting more than half.

Al'truism, *n.* F. *altruisme*—It. *altrui*, of or to others—L. *alteri huic*, to this other. Unselfishness.—**Al'truist**, *n.*—**Altruist'ic**, *a.*

Al'um, *n.* L. *alūmen.* A white astringent salt.

Alumin'ium, *n.* Orig. *Aluminum.* From *Alumina*, the oxide, f. L. *alūmen*, ALUM. A white ductile metal, very light. [At all times,

Al'ways, *adv.* ALL + WAY, with genit. *-s*.

Amal'gam, *n.* F. *amalgame*—G. *malagma*, a soft mass, f. *malassein*, to soften. A compound of mercury and another metal; a compound of different things.—**Amal'gam**ATE,[3] *vt.* and *i.* To make or become such a compound.—**Amalgam**A'TION, *n.*

Amanuen'sis, *n.*; *pl.* **-es.** L., f. phrase (*servus*) *a manu*, (servant) by or from the hand, secretary. MANAGE. One who writes from dictation.

Amass', *vt.* F. *amasser*, f. *à*, to + *masser*, f. *masse*, MASS.[2] To pile up, collect.

Amateur', *n.* F.—L. *amātor*, f. *amāre*, *amātum*, to love. One who is fond *of* a thing or cultivates it as a pastime.

Am'atory, *a.* L. *amātōrius*, f. *amāre*, to love. Relating to a lover or to love-making.

Amaze', *vt.* A-[3], intensive + MAZE. To astound, astonish.—**Amaze'**MENT, *n.*

Am'azon, *n.* G. *amazōn*, explained as if f. A-[4] + *mazos*, breast, from the fable that the Scythian Amazons destroyed the right breast, as impeding the use of the bow. Real orig. of the name unknown. A female warrior; a masculine woman.—**Amazon'**IAN, *a.*

Ambas'sador, *n.* F. *ambassadeur*, f. L.L. **ambactiāre*, to go on a mission, f. L. *ambactus*, servant. A representative of a sovereign or state at a foreign court.—*Fem.*, **Ambas'sadr**ESS, *n.*

Am'ber, *n.* F. *ambre*—Arab. *'anbar*, AMBERGRIS, to which the name originally belonged. A yellowish pellucid fossil resin.

Am'bergris, *n.* F. *ambre* (AMBER) *gris*, gray amber. A fragrant waxy ash-coloured substance.

Ambidex'ter, **-trous**, *aa.* Med.L. *ambidexter*, f. *amb(i)-*, both + *dexter*, right-handed. Able to use both hands alike.

Ambig'uous, *a.* L. *ambiguus*, f. *ambigĕre*, to be undecided, f. *amb-*, both ways + *agĕre*, to drive. Doubtful; of double meaning.—**Ambig'uous**LY,[2] *adv.*—**Ambigu'**ITY, *n.*

Am'bit, *n.* L. *ambitus*, a going round, f. *ambīre*, to go round, f. *amb-*, about + *īre*, to go. Compass, scope.

Ambi'tion, *n.* L. *ambitio*, *ambitiōnis*, f. *ambīre*. (See prec.) Desire of distinction or power; the object of the desire.—**Ambi'**TIOUS, *a.*—**Ambi'tious**LY,[2] *adv.*

Am'ble, *vi.* F. *ambler*—L. *ambulāre*, to walk. Of a horse, to move by lifting the feet on each side alternately; hence, to ride or move with an easy motion.—**Am'ble**, *n.* The pace or movement.

Ambro'sia, *n.* G., f. A-[4]+(*m*)*brotos*. MORTAL. The food of the gods.—**Ambro'si**AL, *a.*

Am'bulance, *n.* F.—L. *ambulāre*, to walk. A moving hospital; a conveyance for the sick or injured.

Ambuscade', *n.* F. *embuscade*, f. *imboscāre*. (See next.) An ambush; a force in ambush.

Am'bush, *vi.* O.F. *embuscher*—Late Latin **im*(=IN-[1])*boscāre*, to place in a wood, f. *boscus*, wood. BUSH. To lie in wait.—*vt.* To waylay.—*n.* A lying in wait.

Amel'iorate, *vt.* and *i.* Formed on MELIORATE after F. *améliorer*. To improve.—**Amelior**A'TION, *n.*

Amen', *int.* Heb. *āmēn*, certainty. Verily, [surely.

Amen'able, *a.* F. *amener*, to lead to, f. *à*, to + *mener*, to lead—L. *mināri*, to MENACE. DEMEAN. Liable to answer; tractable.

Amend', *vt.* O.F. *amender*—L. *ēmendāre*, to correct, f. E- + *mendum*, fault. To free from faults or errors; to improve.—*vi.* To reform oneself. — **Amend'**MENT, *n.* — **Amends'**, *n.pl.* Reparation.

Amen'ity, *n.* L. *amoenitas*, f. *amoenus*, pleasant. Pleasantness. In *pl.*, pleasant ways, civilities.

Amerce', *vt.* A.F. *amercier*, f. *à*, at + *merci*, MERCY. To punish by an arbitrary fine; to fine.

Am'ethyst, *n.* G. *amethustos*, not drunken, f. A[4] + *methu*, wine. A violet precious stone, formerly said to prevent intoxication.

A'miable, *a.* O.F. *amiable*—L. *amīcābilis*. AMICABLE. Afterwards confused with O.F. *amable*, L. *amābilis*, lovable, f. *amāre*, to love. Of temper, mood, &c., friendly, kindly; of a disposition awakening liking.—**A'miab**LY,[2] *adv.*—**Amiab**IL'ITY, *n.*

Am'icable, *a.* L. *amīcābilis*, f. *amīcus*, friend, f. *amāre*, to love. Friendly.—**Am'icab**LY,[2] *adv.*

Amid', *prep.* O.E. *on* (A-[1]) *middan* (dat. of *midde*, the middle, f. *midd*, middle), in the middle. MID. With genit. *-s* and addition of *t*, **Amidst'**. In the middle of, among.

Amid'ships, *adv.* 'In the ship's middle', with genit. *-s* after prep. AMID. In the middle of a ship.

Amiss', *adv.* A-[1] + MISS, *n.*, failure, deficiency. Faultily.—*a.* Faulty, deficient.

Am'ity, *n.* F. *amitié*, as if f. Pop. L. **amīcitas*, f. L. *amīcus*. AMICABLE. Friendship, friendliness.

Ammo'nia, *n.* The name given to the gas obtained from *sal-ammoniac*, SALT of Ammon, a hard white salt said to have been first made near the temple of Jupiter Ammon in Libya. A colourless pungent alkaline gas.

Ammuni'tion, *n.* F. *amunition*, corr. of *munition*, MUNITION. Supplies for firearms.

Am'nesty, *n.* F. *amnestie*—G. *amnēstia*, oblivion, f. A-[4] + *mna-esthai*, to remember. MNEMONIC. A general pardon.—*vt.* To give amnesty to.

Among', *prep.* O.E. *onmang*, f. *on*, in + *mang*, mixture. MINGLE. Like AMIDST, **Amongst'**. Mixed or conjoined with, amidst, throughout.

Am'orous, *a.* L. *amorōsus*, f. *amor*, love. Inclined to love; in love; loving.—**Am'orous**LY,[2] *adv.*

Amor'phous, *a.* G. *amorphos*, f. A-[4] + *morphē*, form. Shapeless.

Amount', *vi.* O.F. *amonter*—L. *ad montem*, to the MOUNT. To come *to*, be equivalent *to*.—*n.* Sum total; full effect or significance.

Amphib'ious, *a.* G. *amphibios*, f. *amphi-*, on both sides + *bios*, life. Living both on land and in water.

Amphithe'atre, *n.* G. *amphitheatron*, f. *amphi-*, on both sides + *theatron*, THEATRE. An oval or circular seated building surrounding an open space.

Am'ple, *a.* F.—L. *amplus*, large. Broad, capacious, extensive, abundant, full, copious.—**Am'p**LY,[2] *adv.*—**Am'ple**NESS, *n.*—**Am'pli**FY, *vt.* — **Ampli**FICA'TION, *n.* — **Am'pli**TUDE, *n.*

Am'putate, *vt.* L. *amputāre*, *amputātum*, to cut off, f. *am-*, *amb-*, about + *putāre*, to prune. To cut off (a limb or other part of the body).—**Amput**A'TION, *n.*

Amuck', *adv.* Malay *amoq*, fighting furiously.—*To run amuck*, to run in frenzy for blood.

Am'ulet, *n.* L. *amulētum*, of unknown orig. Something worn as a charm against evil.

Amuse', *vt.* O.F. *amuser*, to cause to stare

about, f. *à*, to, with causal force + *muser*. MUSE, *v.* To divert; to while away (time).—**Amuse'**MENT, *n.*

Anabap'tist, *n.* G. *ana-*, over again + *baptizein*, to BAPTIZE. A baptist who believes in adult baptism only, and holds that baptized children should be baptized again when adult.

Anach'ronism, *n.* G. *ana-*, backwards + *chronos*, time. CHRONIC. The reference of an event. &c., to a wrong date; something occurring out of date.

Anæ'mia, *n.* G. *anaimia*, f. AN- + *haima*, blood. Lack of blood.—**Anæ'mic**, *a.*

Anæsthet'ic, *a.* AN- + G. *aisthētikos*. ÆSTHETIC. Producing insensibility. —*n.* An agent doing this.

An'agram, *n.* G. *ana-*, backwards + *gramma*, a letter. A transposition of the letters of a word or sentence forming a new word or sentence.

Anal'ogy, *n.* G. *analogia*, proportion, f. *analogos*, proportionate, f. *ana-*, up to + *logos*, account, ratio. Equivalence or likeness of relations; similarity. — **Analog'**ICAL, *a.*— **Anal'ogous**, *a.*—**Anal'ogous**LY,[2] *adv.*

Anal'ysis, *n.* G. *analusis*, f. *analuein*, to unloose, f. *ana-*, up, back + *luein*, to loose. The resolution of a compound into its elements; the consideration of a thing in its separate parts.—**An'alyse**, *vt.* To subject to analysis. —**An'alyst**, *n.* One who analyses.—**Analyt'**IC, -ICAL, *aa.*—**-ical**LY,[2] *adv.*

An'apæst, *n.* G. *anapaistos*, struck back, f. *ana-*, back + *paiein*, to strike. A reversed dactyl, a foot of two shorts followed by a long. —**Anapæst'**IC, *a.*

An'archy, *n.* G. *anarchia*, f. AN- + *archos*, leader. A state of lawlessness.—**Anarch'**IC, -ICAL, *aa.* — **-ical**LY,[2] *adv.* — **An'arch**ISM, *n.*—**An'arch**IST, *n.*

Anath'ema, *n.* G. *anathema*, a thing devoted to evil, f. *anatithenai*, to set up, f. *ana-*, up + *the-*, to place. ANTITHESIS. THEME. THESIS. Anything accursed; a formal curse; a curse in general.—**Anath'ema**TIZE, *vt.*

Anat'omy, *n.* G. *anatomē*, a cutting up, f. *ana-*, up + *tem-*, *tom-*, to cut. The dissection of the body; a very thin person; the science of the structure of the body; detailed examination. — **Anatom'**ICAL, *a.* — **-ical**LY,[2] *adv.*—**Anat'om**IST, *n.*—**Anat'om**IZE, *vt.*

An'cestor, *n.* O.F. *ancestre*—L. *antecessor*, a foregoer, f. ANTE- + *cēdĕre*, *cessum*, to go. CEASE. A progenitor, forefather.—**Ances'tr**AL, *a.*—**An'cestr**Y,[1] *n.*

An'chor, *n.* O.E. *ancor*—L. *ancora*—G. *agkura*, f. *agkos*, bend. ANGLE [1] and [2]. An appliance for mooring a ship to the bottom.—*vt.* To moor thus.—*vi.* To cast anchor.—**An'chor**AGE, *n.*—A place suitable or the dues payable for anchoring.

An'choret, -ite, *n.* G. *anachōrētēs*, one who retires, f. *ana-*, back + *chōre-ein*, to go. A hermit.

Ancho'vy, *n.* Sp. *anchova*, of doubtful orig. A small fish of the herring kind.

An'cient, *a.* F. *ancien*—L.L. *antiānus*, f. L. *ante*, before. ANTIQUE. Old; of long standing; time-worn.—*n.* One who lived in ancient times; an old man.—**An'cient**LY,[2] *adv.*

An'cillary, *a.* L. *ancilla*, servant. Subservient, subordinate, ministering *to.*

And, *conj.* O.E. *and*, *end*. A connecting particle.

Andan'te, *a.* and *adv.* It., pres.pple. of *andare*, to go. *Mus.*, moderately slow and distinct.

An'diron, *n.* O.F. *andier*, of unknown orig. A utensil for supporting burning logs.

An'ecdote, *n.* G. *anekdotos*, unpublished, f. AN- + *ek-*, out + *didonai*, to give. A story of a detached incident or a single event.—**An'ecdot**AL, -ICAL, *aa.*—**An'ecdot**IST, *n.*

Anemom'eter, *n.* G. *anemos*, wind + *metrein*, to measure. An instrument for measuring the force and velocity of the wind.

Anem'one, *n.* G. *anemōnē*, lit., daughter of the wind, f. *anemos*, wind. The wind-flower.

An'eroid, *a.* A-[4] + G. *nēros*, moist + -OID. Of a barometer, made without liquid.

An'eurism, *n.* G. *aneurusma*, dilatation, f. *ana-*, up + *eurunein*, to widen, f. *eurus*, wide. Dilatation of an artery.

Anew', *adv.* A-[2] + NEW. Of new, afresh.

An'gel, *n.* L. *angelus*—G. *aggelos*, a messenger. A ministering or guardian spirit; a divine messenger.—**Angel'**IC, -ICAL, *aa.*

An'ger, *n.* O.N. *angr*, affliction, f. root *ang-*, to squeeze. ANGUISH. Wrath, ire.—*vt.* To make angry.—**An'gr**Y,[2] *a.*—**An'gri**LY,[2] *adv.*

An'gle, *n.*[1] O.E. *angul*, fish-hook, cogn. with O.N. *öngull*, and L. *angulus*. (See next.) A fish-hook; fishing tackle. —*vi.* To fish.—**An'gl**ER, *n.*

An'gle, *n.*[2] F. *angle*—L. *angulus*, angle, corner, cogn. with G. *agkos*, bend, f. Aryan root *ank-*, to bend. (See prec.) ANCHOR. ANKLE. The inclination of two meeting lines or planes; a corner; a sharp projection.—**An'gul**AR, *a.*

An'glican, *a.* Med.L. *Anglicānus*, f. *Angli*, the Angles or English. Of or relating to England or the English Church.

An'glicize, *vt.* L. *Anglicus*, English, f. *Angli* + -IZE. (See prec.) To make English.—**An'glic**ISM. An English idiom.

An'guish, *n.* O.F. *anguisse*—L. *angustia*, straitness, f. root *ang-*. ANGER. Extreme suffering, bodily or mental.

An'iline, *n.* Formed f. *Anil*, indigo, f. Arab. *an-nil*, *al*, the + *nil*, indigo. A chemical base furnishing brilliant dyes first got from indigo.

Animadvert', *vi.* L. *animadvertĕre*, *animadversum*, to turn the mind to, f. *animum* AD*vertĕre*. To take note; to pass censure or criticism.—**Animadver'**SION, *n.*

An'imal, *n.* L. *animal*, f. *anima*, breath, life. A living being; a beast as distinguished from man.—*a.* Pertaining to animals or the part of man shared with them; carnal, fleshly.—**An'imal**ISM, *n.*

Animal'cule, *n.* L. *animalculum*, dim. of *animal*, ANIMAL. A microscopic animal.

An'imate, *ppl.a.* L. *animātus*, pa.pple. of *animāre*, to give *anima* or breath to. Living; lively.—*vt.* To give life or liveliness to; to inspirit; to actuate.—**Anima'**TION, *n.*

An'imism, *n.* L. *anima*, life + -ISM. The doctrine that natural phenomena are due to spirits; the attribution of spirits to inanimate objects.

An'imus, *n.* L. *animus*, mind, spirit, passion. Actuating feeling; active enmity. So, f. *animōsus*, spirited + -ITY, **Animos'ity**, *n.* Active enmity.

An'ise, *n.* L. *anisum*—G. *anison*. A plant prized for its aromatic seeds.—**An'iseed**, *n.* The seed.

Ank'er, *n.* Du. Orig. doubtful. A liquid measure, 8½ gallons; a keg holding this quantity.

Ank'le, *n.* M.E. *ancle*, prob. f. Norse. Cf. O.E. *ancleow*, O.N. *ökkla* for *ankula*. All f. root *ank-*, to bend. ANGLE[1] and [2]. The joint between the foot and the leg.

An'nals, *n.pl.* L. *annāles* (*libri*), year (-books), f. *annus*, year. A chronicle of events set down year by year.—**An'nal**IST, *n.*

Anneal', *vt.* O.E. *onǽlan*, to burn, f. *on* (A-[1]) + *ǽlan*, to burn. To toughen by slowly diminished heat.

Annex', *vt.* F. *annexer*—L. AD*nectĕre*, *adnexum*, to tie to. To add, attach; to appropriate, seize upon.—**Annex**A'TION, *n.*

Anni'hilate, *vt.* L. *annihilāre*, *annihilātum*, f. *an-* (=AD-) + *nihil*, nothing. To reduce to nothing, destroy; to make null and void.—**Annihil**A'TION, *n.*

Anniver'sary, *a.* L. *anniversārius*, f. *annus*, year + *vertĕre*, *versum*, to turn. Annual, yearly.—*n.* The day of an annual celebration.

An'notate, *vt.* L. AD*notāre*, *adnotātum*, to put a note to, f. *nota*, a mark. NOTE. To comment on by notes.—**Annot**A'TION, *n.*—**An'notat**OR, *n.*

Announce', *vt.* L. AD*nuntiāre*, to make known, f. *nuntius*, messenger. NUNCIO. To make known, proclaim, declare. — **Announce'**MENT, *n.*

Annoy', *vt.* O.F. *anoier*—L. *in odio*, in hatred, common in L.L. phrase *in odio* (*habēre*), (to have) in hatred. To vex, molest; to hurt, harm.—**Annoy'**ANCE, *n.*

An'nual, *a.* L.L. *annuālis*, yearly, f. *annus*, year. Yearly; lasting a year.—*n.* A plant that lives for a year; a book published yearly.—**An'nual**LY,[2] *adv.*

Annu'ity, *n.* F. *annuité*—Med.L. *annuitas*, f. *annus*, year. A sum paid yearly.—**Annu'it**ANT, *n.* One who receives such a sum.

Annul', *vt.* O.F. *anuller*—L.L. *an*(=AD-) *nullāre*, to make NULL, f. *nullus*, none. To extinguish, cancel, make void. — **Annul'**MENT, *n.*

An'nular, *a.* L. *annulāris*, f. *annulus*, ring. Pertaining to a ring; ring-formed.

Annuncia'tion, *n.* L. *adnuntiātio*, *adnuntiātiōnis*, f. *adnuntiāre*. ANNOUNCE. An announcing; the angel's intimation to the Virgin Mary, and its day (25th March).

An'odyne, *a.* G. *anōdunos*, free from pain, f. AN- + *odunē*, pain. Assuaging pain.—*n.* A medicine with this power.

Anoint', *vt.* O.F. *enoindre*—L. IN*ungĕre*, to put OINTMENT upon. To smear with an UNGUENT; to consecrate by the use of oil.

Anom'alous, *a.* G. *anōmalos*, uneven, f. AN- + *homalos*, even, f. *homos*, SAME. Irregular.—**Anom'al**Y,[1] *n.* Irregularity; something exhibiting irregularity.

Anon', *adv.* O.E. *on án*, into ONE (state, course, &c.). In a short time; now and again; every now and then.

Anon'ymous, *a.* G. *anōnumos*, nameless, f. AN- + *onoma*, NAME.—Nameless; without the author's name. — **Anonym'**ITY, *n.*—**Anon'ymous**LY,[2] *adv.*

Anoth'er, *pron.* Orig. two words. One more; a different.

An'swer, *n.* O.E. *andswaru*, f. *and-*, against, in reply + *swerian*, to speak, to SWEAR. A reply; a solution.—*vt.* To justify; to reply to; to pay, meet; to satisfy, fulfil, suit.—*vi.* To reply; to succeed.—**An'swer**ABLE, *a.* Accountable; fitting; commensurate.

Ant, *n.* O.E. *ǽmette*. Cf. O.H.G. *āmeiza*, Ger. *ameise*. EMMET. A small social insect.

Antag'onist, *n.* G. *antagōnistēs*, opponent, f. *ant-* (=ANTI-) + *agōnizesthai*, to contend. AGONIZE. An opponent.—**Antag'on**ISM, *n.*—**Antagonis'**TIC, *a.*

Antarc'tic, *a.* G. *antarktikos*, opposite the north. f. *ant-* (=ANTI-) + *arktos*, the Great Bear. Of the south polar regions.—*n.* These regions.

Antece'dent, *a.* L. *antecēdens*, *antecēdentis*, pres.pple. of ANTE*cēdĕre* to go before. CEASE. Going before, preceding; previous to investigation, presumptive.—*n.* That which goes before; the noun to which a pronoun refers; in *pl.*, the events of one's history.—**Ante-ce'dent**LY,[2] *adv.*

An'techamber, *n.* F. *antichambre* f. *anti* for ANTE- + *chambre*, room. A room leading to a larger room.

An'tedate, *n.* ANTE- + DATE.[2] An assigned date earlier than the actual date.—*vt.* To assign such a date to; to precede; to anticipate.

Antedilu'vian, *a.* ANTE + L. *diluvium*, DELUGE. Before the Flood; antiquated, primitive.

An'telope *n.* O.F. *antelop*—G. *antholops*. Orig. language and meaning unknown. A swift and graceful deer-like ruminant.

Antemerid'ian, *a.* L. *antemeridiānus*, f. ANTE- + *meridies*, noon. Pertaining to the forenoon.

Anten'na, *n.*; *pl.* **-æ**. L., a sail-yard, perh. f. G. *anateinein*, to stretch out. An insect's feeler.

Antenup'tial, *a.* ANTE- + NUPTIAL. Before marriage.

Antepenult'imate, *a.* ANTE- + PENULTIMATE. The last but two.—*n.* The last syllable but two.

Ante'rior, *a.* L., comp. of *ante*, before. More to the front, fore; earlier, preceding.

An'teroom, *n.* ANTE- + ROOM. Similar in sense to ANTECHAMBER.

An'them, *n.* O.E. *antefne*—L.L. *antiphōna*—G. *ta antiphōna*, things sounding in response, f. ANTI-, in return + *phōnē*, sound. PHONETIC. A prose composition sung in churches (orig. responsively by two choirs).

Anthol'ogy, *n.* G. *anthologia*, f. *anthos*, flower + *legein*, to gather. A collection of choice poems.

An'thracite, *n.* G. *anthrakitēs*, coal-like, f. *anthrax*, coal. A hard coal burning almost without flame.

An'thropoid, *a.* G. *anthrōpos*, man + -OID. Resembling man, man-like.

Anthropol'ogy, *n.* G. *anthrōpos*, man + -LOGY. The science of man and his nature.

Anthropomor'phism, *n.* G. *anthrōpos*, man + *morphē*, form. The ascription of human form and attributes to a deity.

An'tic, *a.* From It. *antico* (lit. old, L. *antiquus*, old, ANTIQUE), in sense 'grotesque'. Grotesque, odd.—*n.* A grotesque figure, gesture, or trick; a clown.

Antic'ipate, *vt.* L. *anticipāre*, *anticipātum*, f. ANTE + *capĕre*, to take. CAPABLE. To use in advance; to forestall; to cause to happen earlier, accelerate; to enjoy or suffer prospectively; to expect.—**Anticip**A'TION, *n.*

Anticli'max, *n.* ANTI- + CLIMAX. The opposite of climax; a descent towards the ridiculous.

Anticy'clone, *n.* ANTI- + CYCLONE. The rotatory outward flow of air from an area of high pressure; the system of such flow and pressure.

An'tidote, *n.* G. *antidoton*, a remedy, f. ANTI- + *dotos*, given, f. *didonai*, to give. DATE.[2] A remedy against a poison.
An'timony, *n.* Med.L. *antimōnium*, prob. of Arab. orig. A whitish brittle metal.
Antip'athy, *n.* G. *antipatheia*, f. ANTI- + *pathos*, feeling. Dislike, aversion.—**Antipath**ET'IC, *a.*
An'tiphon, *n.* F. *antiphone*—L.L. *antiphōna.* A versicle sung responsively; an ANTHEM.
Antip'odes, *n.pl.* G. ANTI-, opposite + *pous, podos*, FOOT. A region directly opposite to ours.
Antique', *a.* L. *antiquus*, f. *ante*, before. ANCIENT. Ancient; old-fashioned; archaic. —*n.* A relic of ancient times.—**Antiq'u**ITY, *n.* Great age; ancient times; a relic of ancient times.—**An'tiqu**ARY, **Antiqua'ri**AN, *nn.* A student or collector of antiquities. The latter also as *a.*, connected with the study of antiquities.—**An'tiqu**ATE,[3] *vt.* To make obsolete or antique.
Antisep'tic, *a.* ANTI- + G. *sēptikos*, putrefying, f. *sēpein*, to rot. Counteracting putrefaction.—*n.* A substance of this nature.
Antith'esis, *n.*; pl. **-eses.** G. *antithesis*, opposition, f. ANTI + *the-*, stem of *tithenai*, to place. An opposition of ideas; contrast; the direct opposite.—**Antithet'**IC, **Antithet'**ICAL, *aa.*—**Antithet'ical**LY,[2] *adv.*
An'titype, *n.* G. *antitupos*, f. ANTI- + *tupos*, stamp, TYPE. That which is shadowed forth by a symbol.—**Antityp'**ICAL, *a.*
Ant'ler, *n.* O.F. *antoillier*, perh. f. L. ANTE- + *oculus*, eye. A branch (orig. the lowest) of the horn of a stag or deer.
A'nus, *n.* L. The lower orifice of the bowels.
An'vil, *n.* O.E. *anfilte, onfilti*, f. *an, on*, on + **filtan*, to weld. A smith's block.
Anx'ious, *a.* L. *anxius*, troubled, f. root *ang-* (as in ANGER, ANGUISH). Troubled, uneasy; solicitous, desirous.—**Anx'ious**LY,[2] *adv.*—**Anxi'**ETY, *n.*
An'y, *a.* and *pron.* O.E. *ǽnig*, f. *án*, ONE + suff. *-ig.* One indefinitely; whatever; one; some.—*adv.* At all, in any degree.
A'orist, *n.* G. *aoristos*, indefinite, f. A-[4] + *horizein*, to limit. HORIZON. A Greek tense denoting simple occurrence.
Aor'ta, *n.* G. *aortē*, lit. that which is hung, f. *airein*, to raise. ARTERY. The great artery which rises from the left ventricle of the heart.—**Aor'**TAL, **Aort'**IC, *aa.*
Apace', *adv.* A-[1], of manner + PACE. With speed.
Ap'anage, Ap'panage, *n.* F. *apanage*, f. *apaner*, Med.L. AD*panāre*, to furnish with bread, f. L. *pānis*, bread. COMPANION. A provision for the younger sons of kings, &c.; a perquisite; a dependency; an attribute.
Apart', *adv.* F. *à part*, *à*, to, *part*, side, place. Separately; aside; away from others; at a distance.
Apart'ment, *n.* F. *appartement*—Med.L. *appartimentum*, f. L. *ap*(=AD-)*partīre*, to apportion. A room.
Ap'athy, *n.* G. *apatheia*, f. A-[4] + *pathos*, feeling. Insensibility; indifference.—**Apath**ET'IC, *a.*
Ape, *n.* O.E. *apa.* Cf. O.N. *api*, Sw. *apa.* A monkey; an imitator.—*vt.* To imitate, mimic.—**Ap'**ISH, *a.*
Ape'rient, *a.* and *n.* L. *aperīre, apertum*, to uncover, open. Opening, something opening, the bowels.—**Ap'erture**, *n.* L. *apertūra*, f. *aperīre.* An opening.

A'pex, *n.*; *pl.* **A'pices, A'pexes.** L. *apex, apicis*, peak, tip. The tip, top or peak of anything.
Aphæ'resis, Aphe'resis, *n.* G. *aph*(=APO-) *aire-ein*, to take away. The suppression of a letter or syllable at the beginning of a word.
Aphe'lion, *n.* *Aph-* (=APO-) + G. *helios*, sun. The point of a planet's orbit farthest from the sun.
Aph'esis, *n.* G. *aphesis*, a letting go, f. *aph*(=APO-)*ienai*, to send away. The gradual aphæresis of a short unaccented vowel.—**Aphet'**IC, *a.*
Aph'orism, *n.* G. *aphorismos*, definition, f. *aph-* (=APO-) + *horizein*, to bound. HORIZON. A maxim.
A'piary, *n.* L. *apis*, bee. A bee-house.
Apiece', *adv.* Orig. two words. Each, for each, to each.
Apoc'alypse, *n.* G. *apokalupsis*, f. APO-*kaluptein*, to uncover, f. *kaluptein*, to cover. The Revelation of St. John, the last book of the New Testament; any revelation or disclosure.—**Apocalyp'**TIC, *a.*
Apoc'ope, *n.* G. APO*koptein*, to cut off. The omission of the last letter or syllable of a word.
Apoc'rypha, *n.* G. *apokruphos*, hidden, hence spurious, f. APO*kruptein*, to hide away. CRYPT. A writing of doubtful authenticity, esp. the books excluded from the Sacred Canon.—**Apoc'ryph**AL, *a.* Spurious, fictitious, sham.
Ap'ogee, *n.* APO- + G. *gē*, the earth. The point of the moon's or a planet's orbit farthest from the earth.
Ap'ologue, *n.* G. *apologos*, fable, f. APO- + *logos*, speech. A moral fable.
Apol'ogy, *n.* G. *apologia*, speech in defence, f. APO- + *logos*, speech. Defence, justification; acknowledgment of offence and expression of regret.—**Apolog**ET'IC, *a.*—**Apol'og**IST, *n.*—**Apol'og**IZE, *vi.*
Ap'ophthegm, Ap'othegm (ap'o-them), *n.* G. *apophthegma*, a terse saying, f. APO*phtheggesthai*, to speak forth. A terse saying.
Ap'oplexy, *n.* G. *apoplēxia*, f. APO*plēssein*, to strike so as to disable, f. *plēssein*, to strike. A sudden arrest of sense and motion.—**Apoplec'**TIC, *a.*
Apos'tasy, *n.* G. *apostasis*, a standing off, f. APO- + *sta-*, to STAND. Renunciation of faith or allegiance.—**Apos'tate**, *n.* and *a.*—**Apos'tat**IZE, *vi.*
Apos'tle, *n.* O.E. *apostol*—G. *apostolos*, one sent off, f. APO*stellein*, to send off. One of Christ's chief disciples sent forth to preach his gospel.—**Apos'tle**SHIP, *n.*—**Apostol'**IC, **Apostol'**ICAL, *aa.*
Apos'trophe, *n.* G. *apostrophē*, a turning away, f. APO*strephein*, to turn away. A stopping in discourse and turning to address a person or thing, present or absent; a sign (') indicating the omission of a letter or letters.—**Apos'troph**IZE, *vt.*
Apoth'ecary, *n.* O.F. *apotecaire*—L. *apothēca*, G. *apothēkē*, a store-house, f. APO*tithenai*, to lay away. One who prepares and sells drugs.
Apothe'osis, *n.* G. *apotheōsis*, f. APO*theo-ein*, to deify, f. *theos*, god. A ranking or being ranked among the gods; deification.
Appal', Appall', *vt.* O.F. *apalir*, to make pale—L. *pallidus*, PALLID, PALE. To dismay, terrify.—**Appall'ing**, *ppl.a.* Dismaying, shocking.
Appara'tus, *n.*; *pl.* **-a'tus, -a'tuses.** L.

f. *ap*(=AD-)*parāre, apparātum*, to make ready for. PARE. The equipment for performing any operation or experiment.

Appar'el, *vt.* O.F. *apareiller*, to dress, f. *à*, to + *pareiller*, to assort, arrange, f. *pariculus*, assumed dim. of L. *par*, equal. To clothe, deck.—*n.* Clothing.

Appar'ent, *a.* O.F. *aparant*—L. *apparēre*, to APPEAR. Plainly seen; obvious; seeming. —**Appar'ent**LY,[2] *adv.*

Appari'tion, *n.* F. *apparition*—L. *appārēre*, to APPEAR. Appearance; an appearance, esp. of a remarkable kind; a spectre, a ghost.

Appeal', *vi.* O.F. *apeler*—L. *appellāre, appellātum*, to accost, to appeal to, a secondary form of *ap*(=AD-)*pellĕre*, to drive towards. COMPEL. PULSATE. To refer a cause to a higher court; to refer to another or to something for justice or corroboration; to address oneself; to make entreaty.—*vt.* To refer to a higher court.—*n.* In senses from the *v.*—**Appeal'**ABLE, *a.*—**Appel'l**ANT, *n.* One who appeals a cause.—**Appel'l**ATE,[2] *a.* Dealing with appeals.

Appear', *vi.* O.F. *apereir*—L. *ap*(=AD-) *parēre, apparitum*, to come in sight. To come into view, be visible; to come before; to be plain; to seem.—**Appear'**ANCE, *n.*

Appease', *vt.* O.F. *apaisier*, f. *à*, to + *pais*, L. *pax, pācis*, PEACE. To pacify, quiet, allay. —**Appeas'**ABLE, *a.*

Appella'tion, *n.* F. *appellation*—L. *appellāre*. APPEAL. A calling by a name; a name or title given.—**Appel'lat**IVE, *a.* Denoting a class.—*n.* A noun or name applicable to a class; a name, title.

Append', *vt.* L. *ap*(=AD-)*pendĕre*, to hang to. PENDANT. To join on or add as an accessory or supplement.—**Appen'd**AGE, *n.*, **Appen'dix**, *n.*; *pl.* **-ices, -ixes**. Something so joined on; the latter also, a small prolongation from the surface of an organ.—**Appendici**'TIS, *n.* Inflammation of such a prolongation in a particular part of the intestines.

Appertain', *vi.* L.L. AD*pertinēre*, to belong to, f. *per*, thoroughly + L. *tenēre*, to hold. ABSTAIN. To belong; to pertain, relate.

Ap'petite, *n.* L. *appetītus*, f. *ap*(=AD-)*petĕre, appetītum*, to strive after, seek. PETITION. Desire, inclination; hunger, capacity for food. —**Ap'pet**IZE, *vt.*—**Ap'petiz**ER, *n.*

Applaud', *vi.* L. *ap*(=AD-)*plaudĕre, applausum*, to clap, esp. the hands. PLAUDIT. To clap the hands or otherwise express approval loudly.—*vt.* To express approval of, esp. loudly.—**Applause'**, *n.*

Ap'ple, *n.* O.E. *æppel*. Common Teut. The fruit of a well-known tree; the pupil of the eye.

Apply', *vt.* O.F. *aplier*—L. *ap*(=AD-)*plicāre, applicātum*, to fold. COMPLEX. PLAIT. PLIGHT.[2] To place in contact; to administer, bring to bear, put into operation; to devote, employ; to make use of (a word).—*vi.* To have a bearing on; to attend assiduously.—*v. refl.* To employ one's energies.—**Appli'**ANCE, *n.* An applying; something applied, apparatus.— **Ap'plic**ABLE, *a.*—**Applic**ABIL'ITY, *n.*— **Ap'plic**ANT, *n.*—**Applic**A'TION, *n.*

Appoint', *vt.* O.F. *apointer*, f. *à point*, to the POINT, into condition. To prescribe, fix; to nominate, set up; to equip.—**Appoint'**MENT, *n.* An engagement; nomination; an office; equipment (gen. in *pl.*).

Appor'tion, *vt.* O.F. *apportionner*, f. *à*, to + *portion*, PORTION. To assign, portion out. —**Appor'tion**MENT, *n.*

Ap'posite, *a.* L. *appositus*, pa.pple. of *ap*(=AD-)*pōnĕre*, to place near. POSITION. Well put, apt.—**Ap'posite**LY,[2] *adv.*—**Ap'posite**NESS, *n.*—**Apposi'**TION, *n.* Application; proximity; the placing of a word beside another by way of explanation.

Appraise', *vt.* O.F. *apreisier*—L. *ad*, at + *pretium*, PRICE. PRAISE. PRECIOUS. To estimate, value.—**Appraise'**MENT, *n.*—**Apprais'**ER, *n.*

Appre'ciate, *vt.* L. *appretiāre, appretiātum*, to appraise, f. *ap-* (= AD-) + *pretium*, price. APPRAISE. To estimate; to estimate aright or highly, be sensitive to.—*vi.* To rise in value.—**Appre'ci**ABLE, *a.*—**Apprecia'**TION, *n.*—**Appre'ci**ATIVE, *a.*

Apprehend', *vt.* F. *appréhender*—L. *ap*(=AD-)*prehendĕre, apprehensum*, orig. to lay hold of. PRISON. PRIZE, *n.*[1] To arrest; to be conscious of, recognize, understand; to consider, view; to anticipate; to fear.—*vi.* To understand; to fear.—**Apprehen'**SIBLE, *a.*—**Apprehen'**SION, *n.*—**Apprehen'**SIVE, *a.*

Appren'tice, *n.* O.F. *aprentis*, representing L.L. **apprenditivus* as if f. **apprenditus* as pa.pple. of L. *apprendĕre*, to learn, short for *apprehendĕre*. (See prec.) One bound to a master to learn a craft; a novice.—*vt.* To bind as an apprentice.—**Appren'tice**SHIP, *n.*

Apprise', *vt.* F. *apprendre* (pa.pple. *appris*), O.F. *aprendre*, in sense to teach, inform, f. L. *apprendĕre*. (See prec.) To inform, acquaint.

Approach', *vi.* O.F. *aprochier*—L.L. AD*propiāre*, to draw near to, f. L. *prope*, near. APPROXIMATE. PROPINQUITY. To draw near; to be nearly equal.—*vt.* To come near to, physically or figuratively; to bring near.—*n.* A coming near; a means of access; an approximation.—**Approach'**ABLE, *a.*

Approba'tion, *n.* L. *approbātio, approbātiōnis*, f. *approbāre, approbātum*, to APPROVE. Sanction; approval.

Appro'priate, *ppl.a.* L. *appropriātus*, pa.pple. of *appropriāre*, to make one's own, f. *ap*(=AD-), with idea of rendering + *proprius*, own. PROPER. Peculiar to, own; fitting, proper.—*vt.* To take to oneself; to set apart, assign.— **Appro'priate**LY,[2] *adv.*—**Appro'priate**NESS, *n.*—**Appropri**A'TION, *n.*

Approve', *vt.* O.F. *aprover*—L. *approbāre*, to assent to, f. *ap-* (=AD-) + *probāre*, to try the goodness of, PROVE, f. *probus*, good. PROBABLE. PROBITY. To confirm; to make proof of; to prove, show; to sanction, commend.—*vi.* To judge well *of*.—**Approv'**AL, *n.*

Approx'imate, *ppl.a.* L. *approximātus*, pa.pple. of *ap*(=AD-)*proximāre*, to draw near to, f. *proximus*, next, superl. of *prope*, near. APPROACH. Nearly resembling; fairly correct. —*vt.* To bring close *to*.—*vi.* To come close *to*. —**Approx'imate**LY,[2] *adv.*—**Approxima**'TION, *n.*

Appur'tenance, *n.* A.F. *apurtenance*—L.L. *adpertinēre*. APPERTAIN. An appendage, accessory.

A'pricot, *n.* Pg. *albricoque*, assimilated to cogn. F. *abricot*—Late G. *praikokion*, f. L. *praecoquus, praecox*, early ripe, PRECOCIOUS. A stone-fruit of the plum kind.

A'pril, *n.* O.F. *avrill*—L. *aprīlis* (*mensis*, month), perh. f. *aperīre* (APERIENT), from the opening and softening of the earth. The fourth month.

A'pron, *n.* With loss of *n* (ADDER, AUGER), f. O.F. *naperon*, dim. of *nappe*, table-cloth—

L. *mappa*, NAPKIN. A cloth, &c., worn in front to protect the clothes, or as a covering.

Apse, *n.* G. (*h*)*apsis*, a loop, wheel, arch, f. *haptein*, to join. APT. A semicircular or polygonal recess with an arched or domed roof, esp. at the east end of a church.

Apt, *a.* L. *aptus*, fitted, *ppl.a.* f. *apĕre*, to fasten, cogn. with G. *haptein*. (See prec.) Suitable, apposite; calculated, likely; inclined, prone; quick-witted.—**Apt**'LY,[2] *adv.*—**Ap'ti**TUDE, *n.*—**Apt**'NESS, *n.*

Aqua'rium, *n.*; *pl.* **-iums**, **-ia**. L., neut. sing. of *aquārius*, a. f. *aqua*, water. A pond or tank for aquatic plants and animals.

Aquat'ic, *a.* L. *aquāticus*, a. f. *aqua*, water. Living in water; relating to water-sports.—*n.pl.* Water-sports.

Aq'ueduct, *n.* L. *aquaeductus*, conveyance of water, f. *aqua*, water + *dūcĕre, ductum*, to lead. DUCT. An artificial water-channel.

A'queous, *a.* L. *aqua*, water + -OUS. Watery.

Aq'uiline, *a.* L. *aquilīnus*, f. *aquila*, eagle. Belonging to the eagle; curved like an eagle's beak.

Ar'abesque, *a.* F. *arabesque*, Arabian. Of Arabian design; fantastic.—*n.* A kind of decoration in flowing lines fancifully intertwined.

Ar'able, *a.* L. *arābilis*, f. *arāre*, to plough. EAR, *v.* Fit for tillage.

Ar'biter, *n.* L. *arbiter*, a judge. One whose opinion is authoritative: an arbitrator, umpire; a despot.—*Fem.*, **Ar'bitr**ESS.—**Ar'bitrate**, *vi.* L. *arbitrāri*, to give judgement, f. *arbiter*. To act as umpire.—*vt.* To submit to decision by an umpire.—**Arbit'ra**MENT, *n.* Decision.—**Ar'bitr**ARY, *a.* Discretionary; capricious; despotic.—**Ar'bitrari**LY,[2] *adv.*—**Arbitra'**TION, *n.*—**Arbitra'tor**, *n.*

Arbo'real, *a.* L. *arboreus*, f. *arbor*, tree + -AL. Pertaining to or inhabiting trees.

Arbore'tum, *n.* L., a plantation, f. *arbor*, tree. A place for the cultivation of rare trees.

Ar'boriculture, *n.* L. *arbor*, tree + *cultūra*, tending, rearing, f. *colĕre*. CULT. The cultivation of trees.

Ar'bour, -or, *n.* M.E. *herbere*—O.F. *herbier*, L. *herbārium*, a herb-garden, an orchard, f. *herba*, grass, HERB. App. there has been confusion with L. *arbor*, tree. Formerly a lawn, a garden, an orchard, trained trees. A bower of trees or shrubs.

Arc, *n.* O.F. *arc*—L. *arcus*, a bow. ARROW. Part of a circle or curve.

Arcade', *n.* F. *arcade*—It. *arcata*, an arched place—L. *arcus*, a bow. (See prec.) A walk under arches or trees; a covered avenue.

Arca'num, *n.*; *pl.* **-ana**. L., f. *arcēre*, to shut up A mystery.

Arch, *n.* O.F. *arche*, a box (L. *arca*, f. *arcēre*, to shut up. ARK. COERCE), by confusion used also for *arc*, ARC, in sense 'arch'. A curved structure supported by the mutual pressure of its parts; a vault.—*vt.* To furnish with or form into an arch.

Arch, *a.* ARCH-, pref., as a separate word. Chief, principal; also, from such expressions as *arch-rogue*, &c., clever, roguish, slily saucy.—**Arch**'LY,[2] *adv.*—**Arch**'NESS, *n.*

Archæol'ogy, *n.* G. *archaios*, old + -LOGY. The study of antiquities.—**Archæolog'**ICAL, *a.*—**Archæol'og**IST, *n.*

Archa'ic, *a.* G. *archaikos*, f. *archaios*, old. Old-fashioned, primitive, esp. of language.—**Ar'cha**ISM, *n.*

Archan'gel, *n.* ARCH- + ANGEL. A chief [angel.

Archbish'op, *n.* ARCH- + BISHOP. A chief bishop, superintending the bishops of his province.—**Archbish'opric**, *n.* -*Ric*=O.E. *rīce*, realm, province.

Archdea'con, *n.* ARCH- + DEACON. A chief deacon; now a dignitary next in rank to a bishop.—**Archdea'con**RY, *n.* His jurisdiction; his office; his residence.—ARCHI**diac'on**AL, *a.* L. *archidiāconus*, archdeacon + -AL.

Arch'er, *n.* A.F. *archer*—L. *arcus*, bow. ARC. A bowman.—**Arch'**ERY, *n.* The archer's art; his weapons.

Ar'chetype, *n.* G. *archetupon*, f. *archē*, beginning + *tupos*, stamp, TYPE. An original from which copies are made.

Archiepis'copal, *a.* ARCHI-+G. *episcopos*, BISHOP + -AL. Pertaining to an archbishop.

Archipel'ago, *n.* It. *arcipelago*, f. *arci-*, chief (=ARCH-) + *pelago*, deep, gulf—L. *pelagus*, G. *pelagos*, sea. The Ægean Sea; a sheet of water with many islands; a group of islands.

Ar'chitect, *n.* G. *architektōn*, f. ARCHI- + *tektōn*, builder, craftsman. One skilled in the art of building; gen., a contriver, builder-up.—**Architecton'**IC, *a.*—**Ar'chitect**URE, *n.*—**Architec'tur**AL, *a.*

Ar'chitrave, *n.* F. *architrave*, f. ARCHI- + *trave*, L. *trabs*, a beam. *Arch.*, the main beam forming the lowest division of the entablature.

Ar'chive, *n.* F. *archif*—L.L. *archīvum*, G. *archeion*, public office, f. *archē*, rule. ARCH-. A place where public records are kept (always in *pl.*); such a record (gen. in *pl.*).

Arch'way, *n.* ARCH + WAY. An arched passage.

Arc'tic, *a.* G. *arktikos*, northern, f. *arktos*, the Great Bear. Of north polar regions.—*n.* These regions.

Ar'dour, Ar'dor, *n.* A.F. *ardour*—L. *ardor*, heat, f. *ardēre, arsum*, to burn. ARID. ARSON. Fierce heat; vehemence; eagerness.—**Ar'd**ENT, *a.*—**Ar'dent**LY,[2] *adv.*—**Ar'd**ENCY, *n.*

Ar'duous, *a.* L. *arduus*, steep. Steep; difficult, laborious; strenuous.—**Ar'duous**LY,[2] *adv.*

A'rea, *n.* L., a vacant piece of ground. An open space; a sunken court before a house; superficial contents; scope, extent.

Are'na, *n.* L. *arēna*, sand. The centre of an amphitheatre (originally strewn with sand); sphere or scene.

Ar'gent, *n.* F. *argent*—L. *argentum*, silver, cogn. with G. *arguros*, silver, f. *argos*, bright. (See next.) Silver.—*a.* Silvery white, esp. in *Heraldry*.

Ar'gue, *vt.* O.F. *arguer*—L. *argūtāre*, freq. of *arguĕre, argūtum*, to make clear, cogn. with G. *argos*. (See prec.) To prove, betoken; to treat by reasoning.—*vi.* To prove, betoken; to reason, dispute.—**Ar'gu**MENT, *n.*—**Argument**A'TION, *n.*—**Argument'**ATIVE, *a.*

Ar'id, *a.* L. *āridus*, f. *ārēre*, to be dry, cogn. with *ardēre*. ARDOUR. Dry, barren, bare; uninteresting.—**Arid'**ITY, *n.*

Aright', *adv.* A-[1] + RIGHT, *n.* Rightly, correctly.

Arise', *vi.* A-,[3] up, away + RISE. To come into existence, spring up; to originate or result *from*.

Aristoc'racy, *n.* L. *aristocratia*—G. *aristokratia*, f. *aristos*, best + *kratia*, rule, f. *kratos*, power. Government by the best; government by the highest by birth or fortune; a state so governed; this ruling class.—**Aris'tocrat**, *n.* F. *aristocrate*. One of the class.—**Aristo-**

crat'IC, **Aristocrat'**ICAL, *aa.*—**Aristocrat'ical**LY,[2] *adv.*

Arith'metic, *n.* G. *arithmētikē* (*technē*), (art) of counting, f. *arithmos*, number. The science of numbers; computation, reckoning. —**Arithmet'ic**AL, *a.*—**Arithmet'ical**LY,[2] *adv.*—**Arithmeti'**CIAN, *n.*

Ark, *n.* O.E. *arc.* Common Teut.—L. *arca*, box. ARCH, *n.* A box, coffer; Noah's vessel; a place of refuge; a ship, boat.

Arm, *n.*[1] O.E. *earm.* Common Teut., f. Aryan root *ar-*, to fit, join. ART. Cf. L. *armus*, shoulder, *artus*, joint; G. *harmos*, joint; and see next. The upper limb; the fore limb of an animal; anything like an arm, as an inlet of the sea, a branch of a river, &c.—*v.*[1]*t.* To give one's arm to.

Arm, *n.*[2] Gen. in *pl.* F. *armes*—L. *arma*, pl., arms, gear, f. root *ar-*. (See prec.) *Pl.* Weapons; war; the military profession; heraldic devices. *Sing.* A particular weapon. *Pl.* and *sing.* Each of the components of an army.—*v.*[2]*t.* To furnish with arms, a protective covering, requisites, &c.—*vi.* To take up arms. —**Ar'ma**MENT, *n.* A warlike force; munitions of war, esp. a ship's guns.

Ar'mistice, *n.* Mod.L. *armistitium*, f. L. *arma* (ARM[2]) + *sistĕre*, to check, stop, f. root *sta-* of *stāre*, to STAND, with reduplication. INSIST. A cessation from arms, truce.

Ar'mory, *n.* O.F. *armoierie*, f. *armoier*, to blazon, f. *arma.* ARM.[2] The science of heraldry.—**Armo'ri**AL, *a.* Pertaining to heraldic arms.

Ar'mour, *n.* O.F. *armeüre*—L. *armātūra*, f. *armāre, armātum*, to arm. ARM.[2] Defensive covering for fighting.—*vt.* To put armour on. —**Ar'mour**ER, *n.* A maker, or one in charge, of arms.—**Ar'moury**,[1] *n.* An arsenal.

Arm'pit, *n.* ARM, *n.*[1] + PIT, *n.* The hollow [under the arm.

Ar'my, *n.* F. *armée*—L. *armāre.* ARMOUR. An armed force, a host; a vast multitude.

Aro'ma, *n.* F. *aromat*—G. *arōma, arōmatos.* A distinctive fragrance, a sweet smell; a subtle charm.—**Aromat'**IC, *a.*

Around', *adv.* A-[3] + ROUND. In a circle; on every side.—*prep.* About, encircling; on all sides of.

Arouse', *vt.* A-[3] + ROUSE. To awaken; to stir up.—*vi.* To wake up; to bestir oneself.

Arraign', *vt.* A.F. *arainer*—L. *adratiōnāre*, f. AD- + *ratiōnāre*, to reason, f. *ratio, ratiōnis*, REASON. To indict, accuse, censure.—**Arraign'**MENT, *n.*

Arrange', *vt.* O.F. *arangier, arengier*, f. *à*, to + *rangier, rengier*, to range, f. *rang, reng*, RANK. To set in order, adapt; to settle, adjust; to plan.—*vi.* To come to an understanding; to make an agreement.—**Arrange'**MENT, *n.*

Ar'rant, *a.* A variant of ERRANT, roving, whence worthless. Notorious, downright, 'regular'.

Array', *vt.* O.F. *arraier*, f. *arrai, arroi*, preparation, f. *ar-* (=AD-) + *rai, roi*, order. CURRY, *v.*[1] To set in order; to attire, equip, deck.—*n.* Order, esp. martial order; a host; a collection or assemblage; attire, dress.

Arrear', *n.* Absolute use of obs. adv. *arrear*, O.F. *arere*—Merovingian L. *ad retro*, to backward—L. *retro*, backward. REAR, *n.* The state of being behindhand; a duty or liability overdue and undischarged (gen. in *pl.*).

Arrest', *vt.* O.F. *arester*, f. *a*, AD- + L. *restāre*, to remain, f. RE- + *stāre*, to STAND. REST.[2] To stop; to capture, apprehend; to catch (attention, &c.); to catch the attention of.—*n.* Stoppage; apprehension; imprisonment.

Arrive', *vi.* O.F. *ariver*—L.L. *adrīpāre*, f. AD- + *ripa*, shore. RIVER. To reach a destination, come upon the scene; with *at*, to attain to a certain result or state.—**Arri'v**AL, *n.*

Ar'rogate, *vt.* L. *ar*(=AD-)*rogāre, arrogātum*, to claim for oneself. ROGATION. To claim unduly or insolently.—**Ar'rog**ANCE, *n.* Aggressive conceit, presumption.—**Ar'rog**ANT, *a.* Presumptuous.—**Ar'rogant**LY,[2] *adv.*

Ar'row, *n.* M.E. *arewe*—O.E. *arwe, earh*, f. Teut. stem *arhw-*, cogn. with L. *arcus*, bow. ARC. A pointed weapon to be shot from a bow.—**Ar'row**Y,[2] *a.*

Ar'rowroot, *n.* A West Indian plant whose tubers were used to cure wounds made by poisoned *arrows*; a nutritious starch prepared from the tubers.

Ar'senal, *n.* Sp. *arsenal*—Arab. *dār aç-çinā'ah*, workshop, *dār*, house + *al*, the + *çinā'ah*, art, trade. A magazine of warlike stores.

Ar'senic, *n.* G. *arsenikon*, 'male', yellow orpiment, a compound of arsenic, so called from its powerful qualities. A brittle, steel-grey, semi-metallic substance; in pop. use, an oxide of this, a virulent poison.—**Arsen'i**CAL, *a.*

Ar'son, *n.* O.F. *arson*—L. *ardēre*, to burn. ARDOUR. The malicious or fraudulent setting on fire of a house, &c.

Art, *n.* O.F. *art*—L. *ars, artis*, prob. f. root *ar-*. ARM[1] and [2]. Skill; skill applied to music, poetry, painting, &c.; any of the subjects to which skill is thus applied; a branch of learning; a system of rules; a craft, business; a knack; cunning; a wile, trick.—**Art'**FUL, *a.*—**Art'ful**LY,[2] *adv.*—**Art'ful**NESS, *n.*—**Art'**LESS, *a.*—**Art'less**LY,[2] *adv.*—**Art'less**NESS, *n.*—**Ar'**TIST, *n.*—**Artis'tic**, **Artis'**TICAL, *aa.*—**Artis'tical**LY,[2] *adv.*

Ar'tery, *n.* G. *artēria*, perh. f. *airein*, to raise. AORTA. A vessel carrying blood from the heart.—**Arte'ri**AL, *a.*

Arte'sian, *a.* F. *artésien*, f. *Artois.* Applied to a kind of well in early use at Artois, made by boring down to water, which rises spontaneously.

Arthri'tis, *n.* G. *arthron*, joint + -ITIS. Gout.

Ar'tichoke, *n.* It. *articiocco*, prob. of Arab. orig. A plant allied to the thistle, having flowers parts of which are edible.—**Jerusalem artichoke**, said to be so named by corruption of It. *girasóle*, sunflower. A species of sunflower having edible tuberous roots.

Ar'ticle, *n.* F. *article*—L. *articulus*, dim. of *artus*, joint, f. root *ar-*. ARM[1] and [2]. ART. The point, the very moment; a clause, statement, head; a paragraph, section; a literary composition in a journal, &c.; a commodity; an adjectival part of speech used before nouns. —*vt.* To set forth (offences); to indict; to bind as apprentice.—**Artic'ul**ATE,[2] *a.* Jointed; of speech, distinct, clear.—*vt.* To joint; to utter distinctly.—*vi.* To speak; to speak distinctly.—**Artic'ulate**LY,[2] *adv.*—**Articul**A'TION, *n.*

Ar'tifice, *n.* F. *artifice*—L. *artificium*, f. *ars*, ART + *-ficium*, making, f. *facĕre*, to make. FACT. Address, cunning; a device, trick.—**Artif'ic**ER, *n.* A craftsman; a deviser.—**Artifi'ci**AL, *a.* Produced by art, not natural; fictitious; affected.—**Artifi'cial**LY,[2] *adv.*

Artil'lery, *n.* O.F. *artillerie*, f. *artiller*, to equip—L.L. **artillāre*, to make machines, f. *ars*, ART. Cannon; the troops using them.

Ar'tisan, *n.* F. *artisan*—L. *artīre*, to endue with art, f. *ars*, ART. A mechanic, handicraftsman,

A'ryan, *a.* Skr. *ārya*, noble, but app. in earlier use a national name for the worshippers of the Brahman gods. Indo-European; applied to the family of languages which includes Sanskrit, Persian, Greek, Latin, Teutonic, &c.

As, *adv.* and *conj.* Worn down f. *all-so*, O.E. *al-swa*, wholly so. ALSO. Expressing equality, similarity of manner or character, likeness, proportion, accordance; while; when; because.

Asbes'tos, *n.* G. *asbestos*, unquenchable, f. A-⁴ + *sbennunai*, to quench. An incombustible (and so unquenchable) mineral.

Ascend', *vi.* L. *a*(=AD-)*scendĕre*, *ascensum*, f. *scandĕre*, to climb. SCAN. To go or come up, soar, rise; to go back in time.—*vt.* To walk up, climb, mount.—**Ascen'**SION, *n.*—**Ascent'**, *n.* Upward movement, rise; a method or means of ascending; an acclivity.—**Ascen'd**ANCY, -ENCY, *nn.* Domination; control.—**Ascen'd**ANT, -ENT, *aa.* Rising; predominant.—*nn.* Superiority, predominance.

Ascertain', *vt.* and *i.* O.F. *acertener*, f. *à*, to + *certain*, CERTAIN. To find out, get to know.—**Ascertain'**ABLE, *a.*

Ascet'ic, *a.* G. *askētikos*, f. *askētēs*, a hermit, f. *aske-ein*, to exercise. Severely abstinent, austere.—*n.* One rigorous in self-denial.—**Ascet'i**CISM, *n.*

Ascribe', *vt.* L. *a*(=AD-)*scrībĕre*, *ascriptum*, f. *scrībĕre*, to write. SCRIBE. To assign, attribute.—**Ascrib'**ABLE, *a.*—**Ascrip'**TION, *n.*

Asep'tic, *a.* A-⁴ + G. *sēptikos*, putrefying, f. *sēpein*. ANTISEPTIC. Not liable to putrefy.—*n.* A substance of this nature.

Ash, *n.*¹ O.E. *æsc*. Common Teut. A well-known forest tree; its wood.—**Ash'**EN,¹ *a.*

Ash, *n.*² O.E. *asce*, *axe*. Common Teut. *Pl.* and *sing.* What is left after combustion. *Pl.* Mortal remains.—**Ash'**Y,² *a.*—**Ash Wednesday**. So called from the custom in the R. C. Ch. of sprinkling ashes on the heads of penitents. The first day of Lent.

Ashame', *vt.* A-³ + O.E. *sceamian*, to SHAME. To put to shame.—**Ashamed'**, *pred.a.* Affected by shame.

Ashore', *adv.* A-¹ + SHORE. To or on shore.

Aside', *adv.* A-¹ + SIDE. To or on one side; apart; at a small distance.—*n.* Words spoken aside.

As'inine, *a.* L. *asinīnus*, f. *asinus*, ASS. Belonging to or resembling the ass.

Ask, *vt.* O.E. *ácsian*. Common Teut. To request: to question: to invite.—*vi.* To request or petition; to make inquiry.

Askance', **Askant'**, *adv.* Orig. unknown. Awry; obliquely; with a side or indirect meaning.

Askew', *adv.* and *a.* Perh. f. A-¹ + SKEW. Awry.

Aslant', *adv.* A-¹ + SLANT. On the slant, obliquely.—*prep.* Athwart.

Asleep', *adv.* and *pred.a.* A-¹ + SLEEP. Sleeping; at rest.

Aslope', *a.* A-¹ + SLOPE. Sloping.—*adv.* Aslant, obliquely.

Asp, *n.* L. *aspis*—G. *aspis*. A small venomous serpent of Egypt.

Aspar'agus, *n.* G. *asparagos*, of doubtful orig. A well-known esculent plant.

As'pect, *n.* L. *aspectus*, f. *a*(=AD-)*spicĕre*, *aspectum*, to look at, f. *specĕre*, to look. SPECIES. Position; point of view; appearance.

As'pen, *n.* O.E. *æspe*, *æps*, the aspen. Common Teut. *Aspen* is, like *golden*, an adjective (*sc.* tree). A species of the poplar.

Asper'ity, *n.* L. *asperitas*, f. *asper*, rough. Roughness, rigour, acrimony.

Asperse', *vt.* L. *a*(=AD-)*spergĕre*, *aspersum*, f. *spargĕre*, to sprinkle. SPARSE. To besprinkle; to calumniate, slander.—**Asper'**SION, *n.*

As'phalt, *n.* G. *asphaltos*, of foreign orig. A bituminous substance, mineral pitch; a composition of this and sand, &c., used for paving.—**Asphal'**TIC, *a.*

Asphyx'ia, *n.* G. *asphuxia*, f. A-⁴ + *sphuxis*, pulse. Stoppage of the pulse; suffocation.—**Asphyx'i**ATE,³ *vt.* To affect with asphyxia; to suffocate.

Aspire', *vi.* L. *a*(=AD-)*spīrāre*, to breathe upon, hence to seek to reach. SPIRIT. To long, seek to attain; to mount up, tower.—**Aspir'**ANT, *a.* and *n.*—**As'pir**ATE,³ *vt.* To pronounce with a full breathing or with the sound of *h*; to add an *h* sound to.—*n.* A sound aspirated; the letter *h*, or an equivalent mark.—**Aspir**A'TION, *n.* Desire or longing; aspirating, an aspirated sound.—**Aspir'**ER, *n.*

Ass, *n.* O.E. *assa*, prob. cogn. with L. *asinus*. A well-known quadruped akin to the horse; a dolt.

Assail', *vt.* O.F. *asalir*—L. *as*(=AD-)*silīre*, *assultum*, to leap on, f. *salīre*, to leap. DESULTORY. INSULT. SALIENT. To attack, ASSAULT.—**Assail'**ANT, *n.*

Assas'sin, *n.* F. *assassin*—Arab. *hashāshīn*, pl., eaters of *hashīsh*, an intoxicant. One maddened to murder by intoxication; hence, one who undertakes to kill by treacherous violence.—**Assas'sin**ATE,³ *vt.* To kill thus.—**Assassin**A'TION, *n.*

Assault', *vt.* O.F. *asauter*, f. AD- + L. *saltāre*, freq. of *salīre*. ASSAIL. To attack, assail.—*n.* An attack.

Assay', *n.* O.F. *assai*—L. *exagium*, weighing, f. EX*igĕre*, to EXAMINE, weigh out, f. *agĕre*, to bring. ESSAY. A trial, esp. of the fineness of metals; standard of fineness.—*vt.* To test; to attempt.—*vi.* To make the attempt.

Assem'ble, *vt.* O.F. *asembler*—L. *assimulāre*, f. AD- + *simul*, together. SIMILAR. To bring together, collect.—*vi.* To come together, meet.—**Assem'bl**AGE, *n.* A collection of persons or things.—**Assem'bl**Y,¹ *n.* A gathering together; a concourse; a deliberative body.

Assent', *vi.* O.F. *asenter*—L. *as*(=AD-)*sentīri*, to join one in opinion, f. *sentīre*, to think. SENSE. To concur, comply, agree.—*n.* Concurrence, agreement.

Assert', *vt.* L. *as*(=AD-)*serĕre*, *assertum*, to join to, claim. SERIES. To insist upon, vindicate; to declare, aver.—**Asser'**TION, *n.*

Assess', *vt.* O.F. *assesser*—L.L. *assessāre*, freq. of *as*(=AD-)*sidēre*, *assessum*, to sit by (as assistant-judge), f. *sedēre*, to sit. ASSIDUOUS. RESIDE. SEDENTARY. To fix the amount of (a fine or tax); to impose (a fine or tax); to value for taxation.—**Assess'**ABLE, *a*.—**Assess'**MENT, *n.*—**Asses'**SOR, *n.* One who assesses; an adviser to a judge.

As'sets, *n.pl.* O.F. *asez*, enough—Pop.L. *ad satis*, to sufficiency—L. *satis*, enough. Effects available to SATISFY debts. *Sing.* An item of one's assets.

Assev'erate, *vt.* and *i.* L. *asseverāre*, to assert seriously, f. AD- + *sevērus*, serious.

SEVERE. To assert positively, affirm solemnly. —**Assevera**'TION, *n.*

Assid'uous, *a.* L. *assiduus*, f. *assidēre*, to sit down to. ASSESS. Persevering.—**Assiduous**LY,[2] *adv.*—**Assidu'**ITY, *n.*

Assign', *vt.* O.F. *asigner*—L. *as*(=AD)*signāre* to mark out to, f. *signum*, SIGN. To allot, apportion, fix; to transfer; to ascribe, refer —**Assign'**ABLE, *a.*—**Assigna'**TION, *n.* Apportionment; transference; an appointment, tryst.—**Assign**EE' and **Assign'**, *nn.*—**Assign'**ER, *n.*—**Assign'**MENT, *n.*

Assim'ilate, *vt.* L. *assimilāre*, *assimilātum*, to liken, f. AD- + *similis*, like, f. *simul*, together. SIMILAR. To cause to resemble; to liken, compare; to absorb into the system.—*vi.* To be or become like *to*; to be absorbed into the system.—**Assimila'**TION, *n.*

Assist', *vt.* L. *as*(=AD-)*sistĕre*, to stand near, f. root *sta-* of *stāre*, to STAND, with reduplication. To be present; to help, further.—**Assist'**ANCE, *n.*—**Assist'**ANT, *n.*

Assize', *n.* O.F. *asise*, act of sitting—L. *assidēre*, to sit down to. ASSESS. ASSIDUOUS. Regulation of price; customary standard; in *pl.*, judicial sessions held periodically in counties for civil and criminal cases.

Asso'ciate, *ppl.a.* L. *associātus*, pa.pple. of *as*(=AD-)*sociāre*, to join to, f. *socius*, allied. SOCIAL. Joined, allied, confederate.—*n.* A comrade, colleague, confederate.—*vt.* To unite, ally; to combine in action; to connect in idea.—*vi.* To combine; to keep company, have intercourse.—**Associa'**TION, *n.*

As'sonance, *n.* F. *assonance*—L. *as*(=AD-) *sonāre*, to sound to, f. *sonus*, SOUND.[1] Likeness in sound.—**As'son**ANT, *a.*

Assort', *vt.* O.F. *asorter*, f. *à*, to + *sorte*, SORT. To classify.—*vi.* To match; to consort. —**Assort'**MENT, *n.*

Assuage', *vt.* O.F. *asouager*, f. AD- + L. *suāvis*, sweet. SUAVE. To mitigate, pacify, appease.—**Assuage'**MENT, *n.*

Assume', *vt.* L. *as*(=AD-)*sūmĕre*, *assumptum*, to take to oneself. CONSUME. To take to oneself or into partnership, use, &c.; to put on (a garb, form, &c.); to lay claim to; to pretend; to take for granted, suppose.—**Assump'**TION, *n.*

Assure', *vt.* O.F. *aseürer*, f. AD- + L. *sēcūrus*, SECURE. To make safe or stable; to insure; to confirm, encourage; to make one certain, to tell him confidently.—**Assured'**, ppl.a. Certain; verified; confident, convinced; bold, self-satisfied.—**Assur'ed**LY,[2] *adv.* Certainly; confidently.—**Assur'**ANCE, *n.* Presumption, impudence; and in senses from the *v.*

As'ter, *n.* G. *astēr*, STAR. A plant with star-like flowers.

As'terisk, *n.* G. *asteriskos*, dim. of *astēr*, STAR. The figure of a star (*) used in printing.

Astern', *adv.* A-[1] + STERN. At the stern; behind; stern foremost.

As'teroid, *n.* G. *astēr*, STAR + -OID. A small planet.

Asth'ma, *n.* G. *asthma*, breath, f. *aein*, to blow. Difficulty of breathing.—**Asthmat'**IC, **Asthmat'**ICAL, *aa.*

Astig'matism, *n.* A[4] + G. *stigma*, point. A state of the eye in which rays are not brought to a common focus on the retina.

Astir', *adv.* A-[1] + STIR, *n.* Out of bed; in motion.

Aston'ish, **Astound'**, *vv.t.* O.F. *estoner*—L.L. EX*tonāre*, to THUNDER out. To amaze, surprise greatly.—**Aston'ish**MENT, *n.*

As'tral, *a.* L. *astrālis*, f. *astrum*, STAR. Of the stars, starry.

Astray', *adv.* or *a.* A-[1] + STRAY. Out of the right way.

Astride', *adv.* A-[1] + STRIDE. With the legs wide apart.

Astrin'gent, *a.* L. *astringens*, *astringentis*, pres.pple. of *a*(=AD-)*stringĕre*, to bind close. DISTRESS. DISTRICT. STRAIN.[1] STRICT. Binding, constrictive.—**Astrin'**GENCY, *n.*

Astrol'ogy, *n.* G. *astrologia*, account of the stars, f. *astron*, STAR + *logos*, discourse. The pretended art of divination by the heavenly bodies.—**Astrol'og**ER, *n.*—**Astrolog'**ICAL, *a.*

Astron'omy, *n.* G. *astronomia*, f. *astronomos*, star-arranger, f. *astron*, STAR + *-nomos*, f. *nemein*, to arrange. The study of the heavenly bodies.—**Astron'om**ER, *n.*—**Astronom'**ICAL, *a.*

Astute', *a.* L. *astūtus*, f. *astus*, craft. Shrewd, wily, crafty.—**Astute'**LY,[2] *adv.*—**Astute'**NESS, *n.*

Asun'der, *adv.* A-[1] + SUNDER. Apart; in two, in pieces.

Asy'lum, *n.* G. *asulos*, inviolate, f. A-[4] + *sulē*, right of seizure. A refuge, sanctuary; an institution for the care of the unfortunate, esp. of lunatics.

Asyn'deton, *n.* G. *asundetos*, unconnected, f. A-[4] + *sun*, with + *de-ein*, to bind. The omission of connecting words.

At, *prep.* O.E. *æt*. Common Teut. Cogn. with L. *ad*. Expressing nearness or presence; near to, by, in; in a state of; engaged or employed in, on, or with; in the direction of.

At'avism, *n.* F. *atavisme*—L. *atavus*, ancestor. Resemblance to ancestors rather than to parents.

A'theism, *n.* F. *athéisme*—G. *atheos*, without a god, f. A-[4] + *theos*, god. Disbelief in, or denial of, the existence of a god.—**A'the**IST, *n.*—**Atheist'**IC, **Atheist'**ICAL, *aa.*

Ath'lete, *n.* G. *athlētēs*, f. *athlos*, contest. One trained to physical exercises.—**Athlet'**IC, *a.* In *pl.* as *n.* The practice of physical exercises.—**Athlet'ic**ISM, *n.*

Athwart', *adv.* A-[1] + THWART. Across, transversely; perversely.—*prep.* Across; across the course of.

At'las, *n.* G. *Atlas*, who was said to bear up the earth on his shoulders. His figure was often put on the title-page of atlases. A volume of maps.

At'mosphere, *n.* G. *atmos*, vapour + *sphaira*, SPHERE. The mass of gas surrounding a heavenly body, esp. that surrounding the earth; environment.—**Atmospher'**IC, *a.*

Atoll', *n.* Native word, Maldive Islands, which are typical examples. A ring-shaped coral island.

At'om, *n.* G. *atomos*, indivisible, f. A-[4] + *-tomos*, cut, f. *temnein*, to cut. A hypothetical ultimate particle of matter; a particle, jot.—**Atom'**IC, *a.*

Atone', *vi.* Short for (*Set*) *at one*. To make satisfaction *for*.—*vt.* To expiate.—**Atone'**MENT, *n.*

Atrabil'ious, *a.* L. *atra bilis*, G. *melagcholia*, black bile, MELANCHOLY. Melancholy; splenetic.

Atro'cious, *a.* L. *atrox*, *atrōcis*, cruel, f. *āter*, black. Excessively cruel or wicked.—**Atro'cious**LY,[2] *adv.*—**Atroc'**ITY, *n.*

At'rophy, *n.* G. *atrophia*, f. A-[4] + *trophē*, nourishment. A wasting away through want of nourishment.—*vt.* To affect with atrophy —*vi.* To waste away.

Attach′ *vt.* O.F. *atachier, attacher*, f. *à*, to + *tache*, nail. TACK. ATTACK. DETACH. To arrest, seize, to tack on, join on, connect; to join in affection *to*; to win over, attract.—*vi.* To adhere, cling *to*; to be incident *to*.—**Attach′**MENT, *n.*

Attache, *n.* Pa.pple. of F. *attacher*, to ATTACH. One attached to another, esp. to the suite of an ambassador.

Attack′, *vt.* F. *attaquer*, cogn. with *attacher*. ATTACH. To assail, fall upon; of disease, to seize upon.—*n.* An onset, seizure.

Attain′, *vt.* O.F. *ateindre*—L. *at*(=AD-) *tingĕre*, to reach, f. *tangĕre*, to touch. ATTAINT. TANGENT. To arrive at, reach; to gain, accomplish.—*vi.* To reach a state, condition, &c.—**Attain′**MENT, *n.* Esp., a personal acquirement or accomplishment.

Attaint′, *vt.* O.F. *ateindre*, to ATTAIN, associated with TAINT, *v.* To condemn to **Attain′der**, *i.e.* to death and extinction of rights; to infect, sully.—*n.* Stain.

Attempt′, *vt.* O.F. *attempter*—L. *at*(=AD-) *temptāre*, to strive after, f. *temptāre*, to test. TEMPT. To try, endeavour; to attack, assail.—*n.* An endeavour, effort; an assault.

Attend′, *vt.* O.F. *atendre*—L. *at*(=AD-) *tendĕre*, to stretch toward. TEND.[1] To wait upon, accompany, tend, be present at; to await.—*vi.* To direct the ears, mind, energies (*to* anything).—**Atten′d**ANCE, *n.*—**Atten′d**ANT, *a.* and *n.*—**Atten′t**ION, *n.*—**Atten′t**IVE, *a.*—**Atten′tive**LY,[2] *adv.*

Atten′uate, *vt.* L. *at*(=AD-)*tenuāre*, *attenuātum*, f. *tenuis*, THIN. TENDER, *a.* To make thin or slender; to rarefy; to weaken, reduce.—*vi.* To become slender or weak.—**Attenu**A′TION, *n.*

Attest′, *vt.* L. *at*(=AD-)*testāri*, f. *testis*, witness. TESTAMENT. To bear witness to, certify.—**Attest**A′TION, *n.*

At′tic, *a.* G. *attikos*. Of Attica or Athens; pure, elegant.—*n.* From the *Attic* order of architecture, a parapet wall terminating an upper façade; hence, a room in the highest storey of a house.

Attire′, *vt.* O.F. *atirer*, f. *à tire*, into row or order. TIER. To dress, array.—*n.* Dress, apparel.

At′titude, *n.* Orig. a painter's term—It. *attitudine*, aptness, attitude—L. *aptitūdo*, *aptitūdinis*, f. *aptus*, APT. A posture of the body; behaviour or manner of acting.—**Attitu′dini**ZE, *vi.* To assume affected attitudes.

Attor′ney, *n.* O.F. *atorné*, one appointed, f. *atorner*, to direct, prepare, constitute, f. *à*, to + *torner*, L. *tornāre*, to TURN. One appointed to act for another; a solicitor.

Attract′, *vt.* L. *at*(=AD-)*trahĕre*, *attractum*, to draw to. ABSTRACT. TREAT. To draw to or towards, literally or figuratively; to entice, allure.—**Attrac′t**ION, *n.*—**Attrac′t**IVE, *a.*—**Attrac′tive**LY,[2] *adv.*—**Attrac′tive**NESS, *n.*

Attrib′ute, *vt.* L. *at*(=AD-)*tribuĕre*, *attribūtum*, to assign, bestow. TRIBUTE. To ascribe, impute, refer *to*.—**At′tribute**, *n.* A quality or character; a characteristic; a symbol; a word expressing an attribute.—**Attrib′ut**ABLE, *a.*—**Attribu′t**ION, *n.*—**Attrib′ut**IVE, *a.* and *n.*—**Attrib′utive**LY,[2] *adv.*

Attri′tion, *n.* L. *attritio*, *attrītiōnis*, f. *at*(=AD-)*terĕre*, *attritum*, to rub upon TRITE. A rubbing away, wearing down.

Attune′, *vt.* *At-* (=AD-) + TUNE, *v.* To harmonize; to tune.

Au′burn, *a.* O.F. *auborne*—L. *alburnus*, whitish, f. *albus*, white ALBUM. Formerly flaxen; now golden brown.

Auc′tion, *n.* L. *auctio*, *auctiōnis*, f. *augēre*, *auctum*, to increase (*sc.* bids). AUGMENT. A sale to the highest bidder.—**Auction**EER′, *n.*

Auda′cious, *a.* L. *audax*, *audācis*, bold, f. *audēre*, to dare. Daring; in bad sense, impudent, shameless.—**Audac′**ITY, *n.*

Au′dible, *a.* Med.L. *audibilis*, f. *audire*, *audītum*, to hear, cogn. with *auris*, EAR. AURAL. Able to be heard.—**Au′dib**LY,[2] *adv.*

Au′dience, *n.* L. *audientia*, f. *audīre*, to hear. (See prec.) The action of hearing; hearing; formal hearing; a formal interview; an assembly of hearers.

Au′dit, *n.* L. *auditus*, a hearing, f. *audire*, to hear. AUDIBLE. A formal examination of accounts; a periodical settlement.—*vt.* To examine (accounts) formally.—**Au′dit**OR, *n.*

Au′ditory, *a.* L. *auditōrius*, f. *audīre*, to hear. AUDIBLE. Relating to hearing.—*n.* An assembly of hearers; the place where they sit, also called **Audito′rium**.

Au′ger, *n.* With loss of *n* (ADDER, APRON) O.E. *nafu-gár*, nave-borer, f. *nafu*, nave (of a wheel) + *gár*, piercer. NAVE, *n.*[1] GORE, *v.*[1] A tool for boring.

Aught, *n.* O.E. *áht*, f. *á*, ever + *wiht*, a creature, WHIT, WIGHT. Anything.—*adv.* To any extent.

Augment′, *vt.* L. *augmentāre*, f. *augēre*, to increase. AUCTION. AUTHOR. AUXILIARY. EKE, *v.* To increase, enlarge.—*vi.* To increase, grow.—**Aug′ment**, *n.* A prefixed vowel indicating a past tense.—**Augment**A′TION, *n.*—**Augment′**ATIVE, *a.* Augmenting; of a word, denoting greatness.—*n.* A derivative denoting something great.

Au′gur, *n.* L. *augur*, perh. f. *avis*, bird + *-gur*, allied to *garrire*, to chatter. GARRULOUS. A Roman official who made predictions chiefly from observation of birds; a soothsayer.—*vt.* and *i.* To divine.—**Au′gur**Y,[1] *n.*

August′, *a.* L. *augustus*, venerable, perh. f. *augur* (see prec.) as if 'consecrated by augury'. Majestic, dignified, worshipful.—**Au′gust**, *n.* From *Augustus* Cæsar, the first Roman Emperor. The eighth month.—**August′**AN, *a.* Of the emperor's reign, the palmy period of Latin literature; hence, classical.

Auk, *n.* Cogn. with Sw. *alka*, O.N. *álka*. A northern sea-bird with short wings used as paddles.

Aunt, *n.* O.F. *aunte*—L. *amita*. The sister of one's father or mother; also, an uncle's wife.

Aural, *a.* L. *auris*, EAR. Pertaining to the ear.

Aure′ola, **Au′reole**, *n.* L. *aureola* (*corōna*), golden (crown), f. *aurum*, gold. An illumination painted round the head or figure of a holy person; a halo.

Aur′icle, *n.* L. *auricula*, dim. of *auris*, EAR. The external ear; the name of the two upper cavities of the heart.—**Auric′ul**AR,[1] *a.* Told in the ear, esp. of confession.

Aurif′erous, *a.* L. *aurifer*, f. *aurum*, gold + *ferre*, to produce. Yielding or containing gold.

Aur′ist, *n.* L. *auris*, EAR + -IST. An ear-doctor.

Auro′ra, *n.* L., the dawn. EAST. A luminous atmospheric phenomenon radiating from the poles, that from the north distinguished as *aurōra boreālis* (BOREAL), and that from the south as *aurōra austrālis* (AUSTRAL).

Auscultа'tion, *n.* L. *auscultātio, auscultātiōnis*, f. *auscultāre*, to listen to. (*Aus-* = *aur-* in *auris*, EAR. The rest is doubtful.) Diagnosis by listening to the sound of the movement of the heart, lungs, &c.

Aus'pice, *n.* Gen. in *pl.* L. *auspicium*, f. *auspex, auspicis*, in same sense as AUGUR, f. *avis*, bird + *specĕre*, to observe. A token given by birds; a prognostication; propitious influence, patronage.—**Auspic'ious**, *a.* Of good omen; favourable; propitious; prosperous.—**Auspic'ious**LY,² *adv.*

Austere', *a.* L. *austērus*—G. *austēros*, drying the tongue, harsh, f. *auein*, to dry. SERE. Rough to the taste; harsh, strict, severe.—**Austere'**LY,² *adv*.—**Auster'**ITY, *n.*

Aus'tral, *a.* L. *austrālis*, f. *auster*, south wind. Southern.

Authen'tic, *a.* O.F. *autentique*—L. *authenticus*—G. *authentikos*, of first-hand authority, f. *authentēs*, one who does a thing himself, a master. Reliable, trustworthy; of undisputed origin, genuine.—Sim., **Authen'tic**AL, *a.*—**Authen'tical**LY,² *adv.*—**Authen'ticate**, *vt.* Med.L. *authenticāre, authenticātum*. To make or prove authentic.—**Authentic**A'-TION, *n.*—**Authentic**'ITY, *n.*

Au'thor, *n.* *Fem.* **Au'thor**ESS A.F. *autour*—L. *auctor*, f. *augēre, auctum*, to make to grow. AUGMENT. A constructor, originator; the writer of a book.—**Au'thor**SHIP, *n.*

Author'ity, *n.* F. *autorité*—L. *auctoritas*, f. *auctor* (see prec.). Power to command; derived or delegated power, authorization; those in authority (often in *pl.*); influence, personal or intellectual title to be believed; a book, person, &c., settling a question.—**Author'i**TATIVE, *a.* Imperative; having or proceeding from authority.—**Author'itative**LY,² *adv.*—**Au'thor**IZE, *vt.* To sanction; to empower; to warrant, justify.—**Authoriz**A'TION, *n.*

Autobiog'raphy, *n* AUTO- + BIOGRAPHY. One's history writter by himself.—**Autobiog'rapher**, *n.* **Autobiograph'**IC, -ICAL, *aa.*—**Autobiograph'ical**LY,² *adv.*

Au'tocrat, *n.* G. *autokratēs*, f. AUTO- + *kratos*, power. An absolute sovereign.—**Autoc'**RACY, *n.*—**Autocrat'**IC, **Autocrat'**ICAL, *aa.*—**Autocrat'ical**LY,² *adv.*

Au'tograph, *n.* G. *autographos*, written by oneself, f. AUTO- + *graphē*, writing, f. *graphein*, to write. GRAPHIC. Something written by oneself; one's handwriting or signature.

Autom'aton, *n.* G. *automatos*, acting of itself. A self-acting machine, esp. one simulating the actions of living beings.—**Automat'**IC, -ICAL, *aa.* Self-acting mechanical, instinctive.—**Automat'ical**LY,² *adv.*

Auton'omy, *n.* G. *autonomia*, f. *autonomos*, independent, free, f. AUTO- + *nomos*, law. Self-government.—**Auton'om**OUS, *a.*

Au'topsy, *n.* G. *autopsia*, f. AUTO- + *opsis*, sight, f. *ops.* OPTIC. Personal observation; a post-mortem examination.

Au'tumn, *n.* O.F. *autompne*—L. *autumnus*, of doubtful orig. The third season.—**Autum'n**AL, *a.*

Auxil'iary, *a.* L. *auxiliāris*, f. *auxilium*, help, f. *augēre*, to increase. AUGMENT. Aiding; subsidiary, additional; of a verb, such as is described below.—*n.* A helper; a verb used to form the tenses, &c., of other verbs; foreign troops in a nation's service (gen. in *pl.*).

Avail', *vi.* O.F. *à*, to + *vail-*, stem of *valoir*, to be of use, f. L. *valēre*, to be strong. VALIANT. To be of use, afford help; to be of profit.—*vt.* To benefit, help; *to avail oneself of*, to profit by, turn to account, make use of. —*n.* Benefit, service, in phrases such as *to little avail*, &c.—**Avail'**ABLE, *a.* At one's disposal.

Av'alanche, *n.* F., f. O.F. *avaler*, to let fall down, f. *à val*, L. *ad vallem*, to the VALLEY. A mass of snow or ice descending swiftly from a mountain.

Av'arice, *n.* L. *avāritia*, f. *avārus*, greedy, cogn. with *avidus*. AVID. Greediness of gain. —**Avari'cious**, *a.*—**Avari'cious**LY,² *adv.*

Avatar', *n.* Skr. *avatāra*, descent. The descent of a Hindoo deity in an incarnate form; manifestation, incarnation.

Avaunt', *int.* F. *avant*, to the front, forward —L.L. *abante*, away before. ADVANCE. VAN.¹ Be off! away!

Avenge', *vt.* O.F. *avengier*—L. *vindicāre*, to lay claim to, to avenge. VINDICATE. To take vengeance on behalf of (a person) or on account of (a wrong).—*v.refl.* To take vengeance for oneself.—**Aveng'**ER, *n.*

Av'enue, *n.* F., *n.* f. fem. pa.pple. of *avenir*, L. ADvenire, to come to. ADVENT. An access or approach; a roadway bordered by trees.

Aver', *vt.* and *i.* F. *avérer*—L.L. AD*vērāre*, to affirm to be true, f. *vērus*, true. VERY. To assert, affirm.—**Aver'**MENT, *n.*

Av'erage, *n.* With -AGE, f. F. *avarie*, now damage, formerly (like Sp. *averia*, Pg. and It. *avaria*) a maritime term, duty charged on goods. Orig. unknown. A charge on goods over and above the freight; loss from damage at sea; the incidence of this; the determination of an arithmetical mean; the generally prevailing quantity, rate, &c.—*a.* Estimated by average; medium, ordinary.—*vt.* To take the average of; to amount to, to do, gain, &c., on an average.

Avert', *vt.* O.F. *avertir*—L. *ā*(=AB-)*vertĕre*, to turn away. VERSE. To turn away; to ward off.—**Averse'**, *a.* From *āversus*, pa.pple. of *āvertĕre*. Disinclined, unwilling.—**Aver'**SION, *n.* Dislike, antipathy; something disliked.

A'viary, *n.* L. *aviārium*, f. *avis*, bird. A place for keeping birds.

Av'id, *a.* L. *avidus*, cogn. with *avārus*. AVARICE. Very eager, greedy.—**Avid'**ITY, *n.*

Avoca'tion, *n.* L. *āvocātio, āvocātiōnis*, f. *ā*(=AB-)*vocāre*, to call off. VOICE. Distraction; a by-work; usual occupation.

Avoid', *vt.* O.F. *esvuidier*, to clear out, get quit of, f. *es* (=L. *ex*), out + *vuit, vuide*, empty. VOID. To invalidate; to keep clear of; to escape.—**Avoid'**ABLE, *a.*—**Avoid'**ANCE, *n.*

Avoirdupois', *a.* and *n.* Formerly *avoir-de-pois*—O.F. and A.F. *aveir de peis*, goods of weight, *aveir* (L. *habēre*, to have), goods + *de*, of + *peis*, L.L. *pensum*, a portion, weight, f. pa.pple. of L. *pendēre*, to weigh. PENSION. (More fully *avoirdupois weight*.) The British standard system of weights.

Avouch', *vt.* O.F. *avochier*—L. *advocāre*, to call to, summon as a witness. ADVOCATE. To guarantee; to affirm, assert; to acknowledge.

Avow', *vt.* O.F. *avouer*—L. *advocāre* (see prec.). To affirm; to own, acknowledge.—**Avow'**ABLE, *a.*—**Avow'**AL *n.*—**Avowed'**, *ppl.a.* — **Avow'ed**LY,² *adv.* Confessedly, openly.

Await', *vt.* O.F. *awaitier*, to wait for, f. *à*, to + *waitier*, to watch, f. O.H.G. *wahtên*, to watch, f. *wahta*, a watching. WAIT. To wait for; to be in store for.

Awake', **Awa'ken**, *vv.* Two O.E. verbs confused, both intrans.—*awacian*, weak verb, whence *awake*, and *awæcnan*, with strong pa.t. *awóc*, whence *awaken*. The strong pa.t. *awoke* (*awóc*) was, after *awakened* came into common use, referred to the former verb, and a trans. sense was developed in both. Pref. prob. A-1. WAKE, WAKEN. *Intrans.* To cease from sleep; to bestir oneself. *Trans.* To rouse from sleep; to stir up, make active.—**Awake'**, *ppl.a.* Not asleep; in activity, on the alert.

Award', *vt.* A.F. *awarder*—O.F. *eswarder*, *esgarder*, to examine, adjudge, f. *es* (=L. *ex*), out + *warder*, *garder*, to GUARD. To appoint by judicial sentence; to adjudge.—*n.* A judicial decision; something awarded.

Aware', *pred.a.* M.E. *iwar*, *ywar*, f. O.E. *gewær*, *wær*, WARE, WARY, the pref. *ge-* not altering the sense. Informed, conscious.

Away', *adv.* A-1 + WAY. Absent, apart, at or to a distance. Often intensive, or giving notion of consuming or destroying.

Awe, *n.* M.E. *aghe*, O.N. *agi*; also M.E. *eghe*, O.E. *ege*; all cogn. with G. *achos*, pain. Dread mingled with veneration or reverential wonder.—*vt.* To terrify; to strike with awe.—**Aw'**FUL, *a.*—**Aw'ful**LY,2 *adv.*

Awhile', *adv.* Strictly two words. WHILE. (For) a short time, (for) a little.

Awk'ward, *a.* With -WARD f. M.E. *awk*, contrary, perverse, f. O.N. *afug*, turned the wrong way, a derivative of *af*, away (cogn. with Eng. *of*, *off*, G. *apo*). Ill-adapted, inconvenient, difficult to deal with; bungling, clumsy, ungainly, embarrassed. — **Awk'ward**LY,2 *adv.*—**Awk'ward**NESS, *n.*

Awl, *n.* O.E. *æl*. Cf. O.H.G. *ala*, O.N. *alr*. A tool for piercing holes, esp. in leather.

Awn, *n.* O.N. *ōgn*. Cogn. with G. *achnē*, chaff. The beard of corn or grass.

Awn'ing, *n.* Of obscure orig. Perh. f. F. *auvent*, penthouse. A canvas covering to shelter from the sun, &c.

Awry', *adv.* A-1 + WRY. Crookedly, askew; improperly, amiss.—*a.* Crooked, distorted; turned from the right course, perverted, wrong.

Axe, **Ax**, *n.* O.E. *æx*. Common Teut. Cogn. with G. *axinē*. An implement with a cutting edge in line with the handle.

Ax'iom, *n.* G. *axiōma*, that which is thought right, f. *axio-ein*, to hold worthy, f. *axios*, worthy. A self-evident proposition.—**Axiomat'**IC, *a.*

Ax'is, *n.* L. *axis*, axle-tree, axis, f. *agĕre*, to drive. Cogn. with G. *axōn* and AXLE. A straight line round which a body revolves; a line or column about which parts are arranged.

Ax'le, **Ax'le-tree**, *nn.* O.N. *ōxull*, axis, whence *ōxul-tré*, *axle*-TREE (*tree* here=block of wood). AXIS. The pole or bar on which a wheel turns.

Ay, **Aye**, *adv.* M.E. *ay*—O.N. *ei*. Cogn. with O.E. *á*, G. *aei*; also G. *aiōn*, L. *aevum*, AGE. Ever.

Aye, **Ay**. *int.* Orig. unknown. Yes.—*n.* An affirmative answer or vote; in *pl.*, those voting affirmatively.

Az'ure, *n.* O.F. *azur*, corr. of *lazur*, Arab. *lazward*, blue. A bright blue pigment or dye; the clear blue of the sky.—*a.* Sky-coloured; clear, cloudless; in *heraldry*, blue.

B

Bab'ble, *vi.* Prob. from *ba*, *ba*, a child's cry. To talk idly, prate.—*vt.* To utter idly.—*n.* Idle talk; murmur.—**Bab'ble**MENT, *n.*

Babe, *n.* Prob. formed like BABBLE. An infant.

Baboon', *n.* O.F. *babuin*, of unknown orig. [A kind of large monkey.

Ba'by, *n.* Pet-form of BABE. An infant.

Bac'carat, **Bac'cara**, *n.* F. *baccara*. A game of cards.

Bac'chanal, *n.* G. *Bakchos*, god of wine. A votary of Bacchus; a reveller; a revel.—*a.* Riotously drunken.—**Bacchana'l**IAN, *a.*

Bach'elor, *n.* O.F. *bacheler*, of doubtful orig. An unmarried man; name of the lowest university degree.—**Bach'elor**SHIP.

Bacil'lus, *n.*; *pl.* **-il'li** L.L., little rod. A microscopic organism causing disease.

Back, *n.* O.E. *bæc*. Common Teut. The hinder part.—*a.* Situated behind.—*vt.* To support; to cause to recede.—*vi.* To move backwards.—*adv.* To the rear; to a former state; in return.—**Back'**ER, *n.* One who supports.

Back'bite, *vt.* BACK + BITE, *v.* To slander (an absent person).—**Back'bit**ER, *n.*

Backgam'mon, *n.* App.=*back-game*, pieces taken being put back. A game played by two on a board with draught-men and dice.

Back'ground, *n.* BACK, *a.* The part of a picture represented as farthest away; a position not prominent.

Back'ward, **Back'wards**, *adv.* BACK, *n.* + -WARD(s). Back forwards, back. — **Back'ward**, *a.* Directed to the back; lagging, reluctant, late; dull.

Ba'con, *n.* O.F. *bacon*—O.H.G. *bacho*, buttock, ham. Cogn. with BACK. Cured pig's flesh.

Bacte'rium, *n.*; *pl.* **-ia**. G. *baktērion*, dim. of *baktron*, stick. A microscopic organism causing disease. — **Bacteriol'**OGY, *n.* The study of bacteria.

Bad, *a.* M.E. *badde*, of doubtful orig. Not good; wicked; immoral; injurious.

Badge, *n.* Orig. unknown. A device or mark.

Badg'er, *n.* Orig. doubtful. A burrowing night animal.—*vt.* To worry, pester.

Bad'inage, *n.* F. Raillery, banter.

Baf'fle, *vt.* Orig. doubtful. To elude, frustrate.

Bag, *n.* Orig. doubtful. A sack; a bagful; a measure of goods.—*vt.* To put into a bag; to distend.—*vi.* To swell like a bag.

Bagatelle', *n.* F.—It. *bagatella*. A trifle; a game somewhat like billiards.

Bag'gage, *n.* O.F. *bagage*, a collection of bundles. Luggage; a worthless woman.

Bail, *v.*1*t.* O.F. *baillier*, to keep in custody —L. *bājulāre*, to carry, hence to carry on, manage, be guardian. BAILIFF. To liberate on security for reappearance.—*n.* The security given; the person giving it.

Bail, *v.*2*t.* **Bale**. F. *baille*, bucket. To free (a boat) from water; to throw out (the water).

Bai'liff, *n.* O.F. *baillif*—L.L. *bājulīvus*, manager—L. *bājulāre*. BAIL.1 A subordinate civil officer; a steward. — **Bai'liwick**, *n.* O.E. *wic*, district—L. *vicus*. His jurisdiction.

Bait, *n.* M.E. *beyten*—O.N. *beita*, causal of *bíta*, to BITE. ABET. A lure, enticement; a halt for refreshment.—*vt.* To furnish with a lure; to feed and water (transport animals); to harass, annoy.—*vi.* To take refreshment on a journey.

Baize, *n.* F. *baies* (*pl.* of *bai*), orig. BAY cloth. A coarse woollen stuff.
Bake, *vt.* O.E. *bacan.* Common Teut. Cogn. with G. *phōgein*, to roast. BATCH. To cook or harden by dry heat.—*vi.* To make bread; to be scorched.—**Ba'k**ER, *n.*
Bak'sheesh, Bakh'shish, *n.* Per. A tip.
Bal'ance, *n.* F. *balance*—L. *bilanx*, two-scaled, BI- + *lanx*, scale. A pair of scales; equilibrium; surplus; difference of two sums; the sum due on an account.—*vt.* To bring to an equilibrium; to weigh; to adjust, as an account.—*vi.* To be in equilibrium; to be exactly adjusted.
Bal'cony, *n.* It. *balcone*, f. *balco*, scaffold —O.H.G. *balcho* = BALK. A platform projecting from a window.
Bald, *a.* M.E. *balled*, of uncertain orig. Hairless; meagre, unadorned.—**Bald'**LY,[2] *adv.* Meagrely.
Bal'dachin, *n.* It. *baldacchino.* A canopy.
Bal'dric, *n.* O.F. *baldrei*, perh. f. L. *balteus*, BELT. A belt worn diagonally.
Bale, *n.*[1] O.F. *bale, balle.* A bundle.
Bale, *n.*[2] O.E. *balu.* Evil, woe.—**Bale'**FUL, *a.*
Bale, *vt.* See BAIL.[2]
Balk, Baulk, *n.* O.E. *balca*, ridge = O.H.G. *balcho*, beam. Common Teut. A strip of land left unploughed; a beam; a hindrance.—*vt.* To shirk; to thwart.—*vi.* To swerve, shy.
Ball, *n.*[1] M.E. *bal*—O.N. *böllr.* A globe; a globular body or mass.
Ball, *n.*[2] F. *bal*, f. *baler*, L.L. *ballāre*, to dance. An assembly for dancing.
Bal'lad, *n.* O.F. *balade*, dancing-song—L.L. *ballāre.* (See prec.) A simple song or poem.—Technically **Ballade'**, a special form of poem.
Bal'last, *n.* In most European languages. Orig. doubtful. Heavy matter carried in a ship to keep her steady.—*vt.* To load with ballast; to steady.
Bal'let, *n.* F. A theatrical dance.
Balloon', *n.* It. *ballone*, aug. of *balla*, ball, cogn. with BALL.[1] A large bag filled with a light gas which makes it rise in the air.
Bal'lot, *n.* It. *ballotta*, ball for voting, dim. of *balla.* (See prec.) Secret voting; lot-drawing.—*vi.* To vote secretly.
Balm, *n.* O.F. *basme.* BALSAM. An aromatic substance; a soothing influence.
Bal'sam, *n.* L. *balsamum.* An aromatic juice or preparation.
Bal'uster, *n.* F. *balustre*—G. *balaustion*, the wild pomegranate flower, the calyx of which has a double curve. A short curved pillar.—*pl.* The posts and handrail of a staircase.—**Balustrade'**, *n.* A row of balusters.
Bamboo', *n.* Malay. A large reed-like plant.
Ban, *n.* O.F. *ban*—Med.L. *bannum*, proclamation with penalty, f. *bannīre*, to proscribe, of Teut. orig. ABANDON. BANISH. BANDIT. An ecclesiastical denunciation; a curse; an interdict.—*pl.* **Banns**, proclamation of marriage.—*vt.* To curse.
Ban'al, *a.* F. Commonplace, trite.
Bana'na, *n.* Sp. A tropical or subtropical tree; its luscious fruit.
Band, *n.*[1] M.E. *band, bond*—O.N. *band*—O.Teut. *bindan*, to BIND. That which binds; a bond.
Band, *n.*[2] M.E. *bande*—F. *bande*—O.Teut. *bindan*, to BIND. A strip; a stripe.—**Band'**AGE, *n.* A strip for binding or covering up.—*vt.* To apply a bandage to.
Band, *n.*[3] F. *bande*—L.L. *banda*, a gang, prob. allied to *bandum*, BANNER. An organized company; a company of musicians.—*vt.* and *i.* To join into a band.
Band'box, *n.* BAND[2] + BOX, orig. made for *bands*, broad collars formerly worn. A thin box for caps or millinery.
Ban'dit, *n.*; *pl.* **-it'ti, -its.** It. *bandito*, proscribed—Med.L. *bannīre.* BAN. An outlaw, a brigand.
Bandoleer', Bandolier', *n.* F. *bandoulière*—It. *bandoliera*, f. *bandola*, dim. of *banda*, band. A shoulder-belt for cartridges.
Ban'dy, *n.* Orig. obscure. A game = HOCKEY; the bent club used therein.—*vt.* To strike to and fro; to exchange (compliments, &c.).—*a.* Of legs, bent inwards.—Hence **Ban'dy-legged.**
Bane, *n.* O.E. *bana*, murderer. Common Teut. Cogn. with G. *phonos*, slaughter. That which causes ruin; ruin; poison.—**Bane'**FUL, *a.*
Bang, *vt.* Cf. O.N. *banga*, to beat. To thump.—*vi.* To strike noisily.—*n.* A heavy blow; an explosion.
Ban'gle, *n.* From a Hindoo word. An ornamental ring for the arms or ankles.
Ban'ish, *vt.* O.F. *banir*—Med.L. *bannire.* BAN. To exile; to drive away.—**Ban'ish**MENT, *n.*
Ban'isters. Corr. of BALUSTERS.
Ban'jo, *n.* Negro corr. of Eng. *bandore*—It. *pandora*—G. *pandoura*, a musical instrument. A stringed instrument played with the fingers.
Bank, *n.*[1] M.E. *banke*, prob. f. O.N. and cognate with Teut. type *bankiz*, BENCH. A shelving elevation in water: the side of a river, &c.—*v.*[1]*t.* To confine within a bank; to hem in.
Bank, *n.*[2] F. *banque*—It. *banca*, money-changer's BENCH, f. Teut. An establishment for the custody of money.—*v.*[2]*t.* To put in a bank.—*vi.* To keep or deal with a bank.—**Bank'**ER, *n.*
Bank'rupt, *n.* From F. *banqueroute*, bankruptcy—It. *banca* (BANK[2]), *rota*, broken (L. *ruptus*). One who cannot pay his debts.—*a.* Unable to pay debts.—**Bank'rupt**CY, *n.*
Ban'ner, *n.* O.F. *banere*—L.L. *bandum*, standard. BAND.[3] A flag bearing a device.
Banns. See BAN.
Ban'quet, *n.* F. *banquet*, dim. of *banc*, bench, cogn. with BANK. A feast, sumptuous entertainment.—*vt.* To treat with a feast.—*vi.* To feast.
Ban'tam, *n.* Prob. f. *Bantam* in Java. A small domestic fowl with feathered shanks.
Ban'ter, *vt.* Orig. unknown. To make fun of, rally.—*n.* Raillery, pleasantry.
Bant'ling, *n.* Prob. Ger. *bänkling*, a child begotten on a bench (BANK[1]), not in the marriage-bed. A brat.
Baptize', *vt.* G. *baptizein*, to immerse. To immerse in or sprinkle with water ceremoniously.—**Bap'**TISM, *n.*—**Bap'**TIST, *n.* A believer in baptism by immersion only.
Bar, *n.* O.F. *barre*—L.L. *barra*, of unknown orig. A long piece of wood or metal; a bolt; an obstacle; an obstruction at the mouth of a river; an inclosure in a law-court; a body of barristers; a counter for serving liquors.—*vt.* To make fast; to obstruct, hinder; to except.
Barb, *n.* F. *barbe*—L. *barba*, BEARD. The recurved points of an arrow or hook.—*vt.* To furnish with barbs.
Bar'barous, *a.* G. *barbaros*, foreign, outlandish. Uncultured, savage. rude.—**Bar'barous**LY,[2] *adv.*—**Barba'r**IAN, *a.* and *n.*—**Barbar'**ITY, *n.*—**Bar'bar**ISM, *n.*

Bar'bel, *n.* O.F. *barbel*—L.L. *barbellus*, f. *barba*, BEARD. A fish with beard-like appendages on its upper jaw.
Bar'ber, *n.* C.F. *barbeor*—L. *barba*, BEARD. A shaver of beards and hair-dresser.
Bard, *n.* Ir. and Gael. A minstrel; a poet.
Bare, *a.* O.E. *bær*. Common Teut. Uncovered; unfurnished; napless; bald.—*vt.* To make bare.—**Bare'**LY,[2]*adv.* Hardly, scarcely. —**Bare'faced**, *a.* Audacious, shameless.
Bar'gain, *n.* O.F. *bargaine*, of obscure orig. A contract, purchase; a gainful transaction. —*vi.* To make a bargain.
Barge, *n.* O.F. *barge* = *barca*. BARK, *n.*[2] A boat of state; a flat-bottomed freight-boat. **Barg**EE', *n.* A bargeman.
Bark, *n.*[1] M.E. *bark*. Scand. The rind of a tree.—*vt.* To strip the bark from.
Bark, *n.*[2], **Barque**, *n.* F. *barque*—It. and L.L. *barca*. BARGE. A small ship; a rowing-boat; a three-masted ship of a particular rig.
Bark, *vi.* O.E. *beorcan*. To utter a sharp cry, esp. of dogs.—**Bark**, *n.*[3] The sound.
Bar'ley, *n.* O.E. *bere*, *bærlic*. BARN. A kind of grain used mainly for malt.
Barm, *n.* O.E. *beorma*. Yeast.
Barn, *n.* O.E. *bere-ern* = *bere*+*ern*, BARLEY-place. A store-house for grain, hay, &c.
Bar'nacle, *n.* M.E. *bernekke*, of unknown orig. A shellfish, often found on ships' bottoms; a species of wild goose.
Barom'eter, *n.* G. *baros*, weight+*metre-ein*, to measure. An instrument measuring atmospheric pressures.—**Bar'ograph**, *n.* *Baros* +*graphein*, to write. A recording barometer.
Bar'on, *n.* O.F. *barun*—L.L. *baro*, *barōnis*, (king's) man. A peer ranking lowest.—*fem.* **Bar'on**ESS.—**Bar'on**AGE, *n.*
Bar'onet, *n.* Dim. of BARON. One of an hereditary order ranking next below a baron.
Barouche', *n.* Ger. *barutsche*—It. *biroccio*—L. *bis*, double+*rota*, wheel. ROTARY. A four-wheeled carriage with a collapsible top.
Barque. See BARK, *n.*[2]
Bar'rack, *n.* Gen. in *pl.* F. *baraque*—It. *baracca*. A building for soldiers.
Bar'rel, *n.* F. *baril*, Med. L. *barile*, *barillus*, of unknown orig. A round wooden vessel; a barrelful; a hollow cylinder.—*vt.* To put in a barrel.
Bar'ren, *a.* O.F. *brehaing*, of unknown orig. Sterile, unfruitful; unsuggestive.—**Bar'ren**NESS, *n.*
Barricade', *n.* F. Prob. conn. with BARREL, from the use of barrels as gabions. An improvised barrier against an enemy.—*vt.* To obstruct, bar.
Bar'rier, *n.* O.F. *barrière*—L.L. *barra*, BAR. A fence, obstruction.
Bar'rister, *n.* A strange formation f. BAR. An advocate in the superior courts.
Bar'row, *n.*[1] M.E. *barewe*—O.E. *beran*, to BEAR. A small wheeled carriage propelled by hand.
Bar'row, *n.*[2] O.E. *beorg*, hill. A sepulchral [mound.
Bar'ter, *vi.* O.F. *barater*, to cheat, of doubtful orig. To traffic by exchange.—*vt.* To exchange in commerce.—*n.* Traffic by exchange.
Bar'ytone, *a.* G. *barus*, heavy+*tonos*, pitch. Having a voice between tenor and bass.—*n.* Such a voice; one having such a voice.
Basalt', *n.* L. *basaltes*. A dark volcanic rock often found in columnar form.
Base, *a.* F. *bas*—L.L. *bassus*, low. ABASE. BASS. Low in value or station; despicable.—**Base'**LY,[2] *adv.*

Base, *n.* F.—G. *basis*, a going, a base, f. *bainein*, to go. ACROBAT. COME. A bottom, foundation, pedestal, starting-point.—*vt.* To found, establish.
Base'ment, *n.* BASE, *n.* + -MENT. The lowest storey of a building.
Bash'ful, *a.* For ABASH-FUL. Modest, wanting confidence.
Ba'sin, *n.* M.E. and O.F. *bacin*—L.L. *bachinus*, of doubtful orig. A broad circular dish; a dock; the tract of country drained by a river.
Ba'sis, *n.*; *pl.* **-ses**. BASE, *n.* A base, foundation, groundwork.
Bask, *vi.* O.N. *bathask*, to bathe oneself. To lie in genial warmth.
Bas'ket, *n.* Orig. unknown. A vessel of wickerwork; a basketful.
Bas-relief', *n.* F.—It. *basso-rilievo*, low (BASE, *a.*) RELIEF. Sculpture in which the figures do not stand out prominently.
Bass, *n.* BASE, *a.* The lowest part in musical harmony; the lowest male voice; one having such a voice.—*a.* Low in the scale; deep.
Bassinet', *n.* F., dim. of *bassin*, BASIN. A wicker cradle; a perambulator.
Bassoon', *n.* BASS. A wooden wind-instrument used as a bass.
Bast, *n.* O.E. *bæst*—O.N., Sw., Da. *bast*. The inner bark of the lime tree; rope or matting made of this.
Bas'tard, *n.* O.F. *bast*, pack-saddle. 'Pack-saddle child.' Cf. BANTLING. An illegitimate child.—*a.* Illegitimate; not genuine.—**Bas'tard**Y,[1] *n.*
Baste, *v.*[1]*t.* Orig. uncertain. To beat soundly.
Baste, *v.*[2]*t.* O.F. *bastir*. Perh. conn. with BAST. To sew together loosely.
Baste, *v.*[3]*t.* Orig. unknown. To moisten with melted fat.
Bastina'do, *n.* Sp. *bastonada*, f. *baston*, stick. A cudgelling.—*vt.* To cudgel.
Bas'tion, *n.* F.—It. *bastione*, f. *bastire*, to build. A projecting part of a fortification.
Bat, *n.*[1] M.E. *bakke*, app. f. Scand. A flying mouse-like mammal.
Bat, *n.*[2] M.E. *bat* or *batte*, of uncertain orig. A stick; a club for striking a ball; a lump: a piece of a brick with one end entire.—*vi.* To use a bat.
Batch, *n.* M.E. *bache*, f. O.E. *bacan*, to BAKE. Quantity of bread baked at one time; a quantity or number.
Bate, *v.* Aphetic form of ABATE.
Bath, *n.* O.E. *bæth*. Common Teut. The action of bathing; a vessel for bathing.—*vt.* To wash.
Bathe, *vt.* and *i.* O.E. *bathian*. To wash.
Ba'thos, *n.* G. *bathos*, depth. A ludicrous descent to the commonplace.
Battal'ion, *n.* F. *bataillon*—It. *battaglione*, f. *battaglia*, BATTLE. Troops in battle array; a division of a regiment.
Bat'ter, *vt.* F. *battre*, to beat—L.L. *battuĕre*. BATTLE. To strike continuously.—*n.* Ingredients beaten up with a liquid.
Bat'tery, *n.* F. *batterie*, f. *battre*, to beat. BATTER. A beating; a number of cannon; the place where they are mounted; an apparatus for producing electricity.
Bat'tle, *n.* O.F. *bataille*—L.L. *battuĕre*, to beat. ABATE. A fight.—*vi.* To fight.
Bat'tledore, *n.* Perh. f. Pr. *batedor*, beater. An instrument for striking a shuttlecock.
Bat'tlement, *n.* O.F. *bateillier*, to fortify. An indented parapet on a wall.
Bau'ble, *n.* Prob. two words blended—O.F.

babel, baubel, a toy, and M.E. *babyll*, f. *bablyn*, to waver. A pretty trifle; a jester's stick.
Baulk. See BALK.
Bawl, *vi*. Med.L. *baulāre*, to bark. To shout.
Bay, *a*. F. *bai*—L. *badius*. Reddish-brown.
Bay, *n*.[1] O.F. *baie*—L. *băca*, berry. The laurel tree. In *pl*., leaves or sprigs of the tree woven into a wreath. [sea.
Bay, *n*.[2] F. *baie*—L.L. *baia*. An arm of the
Bay, *n*.[3] O.F. *baer*, to gape. An opening in a wall; a recess.—**Bay-win'dow**, *n*. A recessed window.
Bay, *vi*. O.F. *abayer*, *bayer*. To bark.—*vt*. To pursue with barking.—*n*.[4] Barking.—**At bay**. Unable to flee farther and compelled to turn and face the hounds.
Bay'onet, *n*. Perh. f. *Bayonne*, as first made there. A stabbing weapon fixed to a rifle.—*vt*. To stab with a bayonet.
Bazaar', *n*. Per., market. A fancy fair.
Be, *v*. Conjugation effected by inflexions of three orig. distinct *vv*.—(1) the orig. Aryan substantive *v*., stem *es*-; whence *is*; (2) the *v*. with stem *wes*-, to remain; Skr. *vas*-, Teut. *wes*-; whence *was*; (3) the stem *beu*-, to become; Skr. *bhū*-, Teut. *beo*-; whence *be*. To exist; stating where or how; as copula.
Beach, *n*. Orig. unknown. The shore of the sea, &c.—*vt*. To run (a vessel) up on the beach.
Bea'con, *n*. O.E. *béacn*. BECK. BECKON. A signal-fire; a founded, artificial sea-mark, not lighted.—*vt*. To give light to, lead.
Bead, *n*. M.E. *bede*—O.E. *gebed*, *bed*, prayer, f. *biddan*, to pray. BID. A small perforated ball threaded with others and used to count prayers; such a ball in gen.; a narrow moulding.
Bea'dle, *n*. M.E. *bedel*—O.E. *bydel*, f. *béodan*, to BID. A mace-bearer; an inferior parish officer. [dog.
Bea'gle, *n*. Orig. unknown. A small hunting
Beak, *n*. F. *bec*—L.L. *beccus*. The bill of a bird; anything like a beak.
Beak'er, *n*. M.E. *biker*—O.N. *bikarr*. A large drinking-cup.
Beam, *n*. O.E. *béam*, tree. Common Teut. BOOM.[2] A long piece of squared timber; the bar of a balance; a ray of light.—*vt*. To emit in rays.—*vi*. To shine.
Bean, *n*. O.E. *béan*. Common Teut. The name of various vegetables; the kidney-shaped seed.
Bear, *vt*. O.E. *beran*, cogn. with L. *ferre*, G. *pherein*. FERTILE. To carry; to support; to produce; to press *upon*.—*Refl*. To conduct oneself.—*vi*. To suffer, be patient; with *upon*, to relate to.
Bear, *n*. O.E. *bera*. A heavily-built partly carnivorous quadruped; the constellations the 'Great' and 'Lesser Bear'; a speculator for a fall in stocks.
Beard, *n*. O.E. *beard*, cogn. with L. *barba*. BARB. BARBEL. The hair on the chin; a similar growth on plants.—*vt*. To defy.
Beast, *n*. O.F. *beste*—L. *bestia*. BESTIAL. A four-footed animal; a brutal man.—**Beast'**LY,[1] *a*. Bestial, vile.
Beat, *vt*. O.E. *béatan*. Common Teut. To strike repeatedly; to overcome.—*vi*. To throb; to sail against the wind.—*n*. A stroke; a pulsation; a course regularly trodden.
Beat'ify, *vt*. F. *béatifier*—L. *beātificāre*, f. *beātus*, blessed+*facĕre*, to make. To make happy; *R. C. Ch*., to pronounce to be in enjoyment of heavenly bliss (the first step towards canonization).—**Beati**F'IC, *a*.—**Beati**FICA'TION, *n*.—**Beat'i**TUDE, *n*. Blessedness; one of the ascriptions of blessedness in the Sermon on the Mount.
Beau'ty, *n*. O.F. *beaute*—L. *bellus*, lovely. Loveliness, grace; a beautiful person or thing.—**Beau'te**OUS, *a*.—**Beau'ti**FUL, *a*.—**Beau'tiful**LY,[2] *adv*.—**Beau'ti**FY, *vt*.
Bea'ver, *n*. O.E. *beofor*. Common Aryan. Cogn. with Aryan type *bhru*-, BROWN, and L. *fiber*, beaver. A rodent quadruped; beaver-fur or a hat made of it.
Becalm', *vt*. BE- (2) + CALM, *v*. To calm; to deprive of wind.
Because', *adv*. BY + CAUSE, *n*. For the reason that.—*adv*. By reason *of*.
Beck, *vi*. Shortened f. BECKON. To make a mute signal.—*n*. Such a signal.
Beck'on, *vi*. O.E. *bíecnan*, f. *béacn*, sign, BEACON. To make a mute signal.—*vt*. To make such a signal to.
Become', *vi*. O.E. *becuman*, to arrive, happen, f. BE- (2) + *cuman*, to COME. To come to be; to come into being.—*vt*. To suit, grace.—**Becom'ing**, *a*. Befitting, suitable.
Bed, *n*. O.E. *bed*, *bedd*. Common Teut. Something to sleep or rest on; the bottom of a river, &c.; a garden plot; a layer, stratum.—*vt*. To lay in a bed; to plant out.—*vi*. To go to bed. [gaudily.
Bediz'en, *vt*. BE- (2) + DIZEN. To adorn
Bed'lam, *n*. A corruption. The Hospital of St. Mary of *Bethlehem* in London, used as a mad-house; a lunatic asylum in general.
Bed'rid, **Bed'ridden**, *a*. O.E. *bedrida*, bedrider, f. *bed*, BED + *rídan*, to RIDE. Confined to bed through infirmity.
Bed'stead, *n*. O.E. *bed*, BED + *stede*, station, place. STEAD. The framework of a bed.
Bee, *n*. O.E. *béo*. Common Teut. A honey-making insect.
Beech, *n*. O.E. *bóece*. BOOK. A large smooth-barked tree bearing nuts.—**Beech'**EN,[1] *a*.
Beef, *n*. O.F. *boef*—L. *bōs*, *bovis*, ox. COW, *n* The flesh of an ox, bull, or cow.
Beer, *n*. O.E. *béor*. Common W.Ger. Orig. uncertain. A fermented alcoholic liquor made from malt and hops.
Beet, *n*. O.E. *béte*—L. *bēta*. A vegetable with a succulent root yielding sugar.
Bee'tle, *n*.[1] O.E. *bitela*, f. *bítan*, to BITE. A coleopterous insect.
Bee'tle, *n*.[2] O.E. *bíetel*, f. *béatan*, to BEAT. A heavy wooden mallet.
Bee'tle, ? *a*. Orig. uncertain. In **Bee'tle-browed**, having prominent brows. Hence **Bee'tle**, *vi*. (first in Shakespeare) to project, overhang.
Befall', *vi*. O.E. *befallan*, f. BE- (2) + *fallan*, to FALL. To happen. [for.
Befit', *vt*. BE- (2) + FIT, *v*. To be fit or right
Before', *prep*. O.E. *beforan*, f. BE-, by, about + *foran*, FORE. In front of; in presence of; ahead of; superior to; in preference to; earlier than.—*adv*. In front; ahead; earlier.—*conj*. Previous to the time when, sooner than.—**Before'hand**, *adv*. In advance.
Befoul', *vt*. BE- (4) + FOUL, *a*. To make foul.
Befriend', *vt*. BE- (5) + FRIEND. To help, assist.
Beg, *vt*. Orig. uncertain. To ask in charity; to ask earnestly; to take for granted.—*vi*. To ask or live on alms.—**Beg'gar**, *n*. One who begs.—*vt*. To reduce to beggary; to exhaust the resources of.—**Beg'gar**LY,[1] *a*. Befitting a beggar; mean, sordid.—**Beg'gar**Y,[1] *n*. Extreme poverty.

Beget', *vt.* O.E. *begitan* = Goth. *bigitan*, f. *bi*, BE- (2) + *-gitan*, to GET. To procreate; to produce.

Begin', *vi.* O.E. *biginnan*, f. *bi-*, BE-, about + *ginnan*, to begin. To take rise; to do the first act; to commence.—*vt.* To enter on, originate.

Begrudge', *vt.* BE- (2) + GRUDGE, *v.* To grumble at; to give reluctantly.

Beguile', *vt.* BE- (2) + obs. *Guile*, *v.* To delude, cheat; to wile on; to charm away.

Behalf', *n.* O.E. BE-, by + *healf*, side. Interest, side. Only in phrases *on, in behalf (of), on, in (his, &c.) behalf.*

Behave', *v.refl.* BE- (2) + HAVE. To conduct or bear oneself; to conduct oneself well.—*vi.* In same senses.—**Beha'viour**, *n.*

Behead', *vt.* O.E. *behéafdian*, f. BE- (with privative force) + *héafod*, HEAD. To deprive of the head. [A command.

Behest', *n.* M.E. *biheste*—O.E. *hǽs*, HEST.

Behind', *prep.* O.E. *bihindan*, f. *bi-*, BE-, by, about + *hindan*, HIND, *a.* In the rear of; remaining after; inferior to.—*adv.* In the rear; remaining; backwards.—**Behind'hand**, *adv.* and *a.* In arrear; late; ill provided.

Behold', *vt.* O.E. *bihaldan*, f. *bi*, BE- (2) + *haldan*, to HOLD. To hold in view, watch; to see.

Behoof', *n.* O.E. *bihof.* Use, benefit.—**Behove'**, *vi.* To be incumbent on; to be due to.

Bela'bour, *vt.* BE- (3) + LABOUR, *v.* To beat hard.

Belate', *vt.* BE- (4) + LATE, *a.* To make late.—**Bela'ted**, *ppl.a.* Overtaken by night.

Belch, *vi.* O.E. *bealcian.* To void wind through the mouth.—*vt.* To give vent to; to emit (wind) by belching.—*n.* The action of the *v.*

Bel'dam, *n.* *Bel-* (L. *bellus* (BEAUTY), expressing relationship) + DAM[1], mother. Orig. a grandmother; now an old woman, a hag.

Belea'guer, *vt.* Du. *belegeren*, f. *leger*, camp. To blockade, besiege.

Bel'fry, *n.* M.E. *berfrey*—O.F. *berfrei*—Teut. **bergfrid*, wooden tower. A bell-tower.

Belie', *vt.* BE- (3) + LIE, *v.* To tell lies about; to misrepresent; to be false to; to falsify.

Believe', *vt.* Early M.E. *bi*(BE- (2))*leven*—O.E. (Anglian) *léfan*, shortened f. *geléfan*, lit., to hold dear, f. Teut. root *leub-*. LIEF. LOVE. To give credence to.—*vi.* To have credence or faith.—**Belief'**, *n.*

Belit'tle, *vt.* BE- (4) + LITTLE, *a.* To make small; to dwarf; to depreciate.

Bell, *n.* O.E. *belle*, perh., from its sound, f. O.E. *bellan*, to roar. A hollow metallic body formed to emit a musical sound when struck; various bell-shaped objects. [Warlike.

Bel'licose, *a.* L. *bellicōsus*, f. *bellum*, war.

Bellig'erent, *a.* L. *belligerāre*, f. *bellum*, war + *gerĕre*, to carry on. Waging regular war.—*n.* A nation or person doing so.

Bel'low, *vi.* Of uncertain orig. BULL.[1] To roar as a bull; to shout.—*n.* The roar of a bull; a deep cry or roar.

Bel'lows, *n.*, now always in *pl.* M.E. *bely*, *below*, bag, also in sense 'bellows'—O.E. *blǽst-belg*, 'blast-bag'. BLAST. BELLY. An instrument constructed to furnish a strong blast of air.

Bel'ly, *n.* M.E. *bely*, O.E. *belg*, bag, hence belly. BELLOWS. The part of the body which contains the bowels; anything like this.—*vi.* and *t.* To swell out.

Belong', *vi.* M.E. *belongen*, intensive of *longen*, in same sense, f. O.E. *gelang*, at hand, dependent on. To be appropriate *to*; to be the property or an attribute of; to be connected with.

Belove', *vt.* M.E. *beluven*, f. *bi*, BE- (2) + *luven*, to LOVE. Only in passive. To be loved.—**Belov'ed**, *ppl.a.*

Below', *adv.* BE-, by + LOW, *a.* In or to a lower position; lower down.—*prep.* Lower than; underneath; lower in amount, degree, &c., than; unworthy of.

Belt, *n.* O.E. *belt*—L. *balteus*, girdle. BALDRIC. A girdle; a band.—*vt.* To furnish with a belt; to surround; to mark with a band.

Bemoan', *vt.* BE- (3) + MOAN, *v.* To lament, weep for.

Bench, *n.* O.E. *benc*—Teut. type *bankiz.* BANK,[1] and [2]. A long seat; a seat or a body of judges or other dignitaries.—**Bench'**ER, *n.* One of the senior members of the Inns of Court.

Bend, *vt.* O.E. *bendan*, orig. to string a bow. To bring (a bow, &c.) into tension; to curve, crook; to subdue; to deflect; to direct, bring to bear; *to be bent*, to be determined.—*vi.* To take a curved form, to incline from the straight line; to submit.—*n.* Bent condition; a curve.

Beneath', *adv.* O.E. *beneothan*, f. BE-, by + *neothan*, below, f. *neothera*, NETHER. In or to a lower position.—*prep.* Under, underneath; lower in degree, &c., than; unworthy of.

Ben'edict, Ben'edick, *n.* From the character in Shakespeare's *Much Ado.* A newly married man, esp. of a confirmed bachelor who marries.

Benedic'tion, *n.* L. *benedictio*, *benedictiōnis*, f. *bene*, well + *dīcere*, to speak. The utterance of a blessing; blessedness.

Ben'efit, *n.* M.E. and A.F. *benfet*—L. *benefactum*, f. *bene*, well + *facĕre*, *factum*, to do. Advantage, profit, good.—*vt.* To do good to, improve, help forward.—*vi.* To receive benefit.—**Benefac'**TION, *n.* A doing good; a benefit.—**Benefac'**TOR, *n.*; *fem.* **Benefac'tr**ESS.—**Benef'ic**ENT, *a.* Doing good.—**Benef'icent**LY,[2] *adv.*—**Benef'ic**ENCE, *n.*—**Benefi'ci**AL, *a.* Advantageous; profitable.—**Benefi'cial**LY,[2] *adv.*—**Ben'efice**, *n.* An ecclesiastical living.

Benev'olent, *a.* O.F. *benivolent*—L. *benevolens*, *benevolentis*, f. *bene*, well + *velle*, to wish. Kindly, charitable.—**Benev'olent**LY,[2] *adv.*—**Benev'ol**ENCE, *n.*

Benight', *vt.* BE- (5) + NIGHT. To involve in darkness.—**Benight'ed**, *ppl.a.* In intellectual or moral darkness.

Benign', *a.* O.F. *benigne*—L. *benignus*, kindly. Kindly, gentle, mild, propitious.—**Benign'**LY,[2] *adv.*—**Benig'n**ITY, *n.* Kindness; a kind deed. Similarly **Benig'n**ANT, *a.*—**Benig'nant**LY,[2] *adv.*—**Benig'n**ANCY, *n.*

Bent, *n.*[1] O.E. *beonet* (in place-names). A wiry grass. [turn of mind.

Bent, *n.*[2] From BEND. A turn, inclination;

Benumb', *vt.* Use as *v.* of obs. *benumb*, orig. *benomen*, O.E. *benumen*, pa. pple. of *beniman*, to deprive. To deprive of sensation; to stupefy, deaden.

Bequeath', *vt.* O.E. *becwethan*, f. BE- (3) + *cwethan*, to say, assert. QUOTH. To leave by will; to hand down.—**Bequest'**, *n.* The act of bequeathing; a legacy.

Bereave', *vt.* O.E. *beréafian.* BE- (2) + REAVE. To deprive, rob of.—**Bereave'**MENT, *n.* [small stoneless fruit.

Ber'ry, *n.* O.E. *berie.* Common Teut. A

Berth, *n.* Of uncertain orig. Convenient

sea-room; a mooring-place; a sleeping-place in a ship; a situation, appointment.—*vt.* To moor; to allot a berth to.

Ber'yl, *n.* O.F. *beril*—L. *beryllus*—G. *bērullos*, prob. of Eastern orig. BRILLIANT. A pale-green precious stone.

Beseech', *vt.* BE- (2) + M.E. *sechen*, *seken*, to SEEK. To supplicate, entreat, implore.

Beseem', *vi.* BE- (2) + SEEM. To befit (with dative object).

Beset', *vt.* O.E. *besettan*, f. BE- (1) + *settan*, to SET. To surround *with*; to assail, invest, occupy.

Beside', *adv.* O.E. *be sídan*, f. BE-, by + *sídan* (dat. sing.), SIDE. In addition; moreover; otherwise, else.—*prep.* By the side of; in addition to; other than; out of (a mental state); wide of (a mark, &c.).

Besides', *adv.* BESIDE + *-s* of the adverbial genitive. In same senses as BESIDE, and more usual.—*prep.* In addition to; other than.

Besiege', *vt.* M.E. *besegen*, f. BE- (1) + *segen*, *asegen*, O.F. *asegier*, L.L. *assediāre*—L. *sedēre*, to SIT. To beleaguer, invest.

Besmear', *vt.* BE- (1) + SMEAR, *v.* To smear over, sully.

Be'som, *n.* O.E. *besema*, *besma*. A broom, us. of twigs.

Besot', *vt.* BE- (4) + SOT. To infatuate; to make stupid.

Bespeak', *vt.* O.E. *besprecan*, f. BE- (3) + *sprecan*, *specan*, to SPEAK. To engage beforehand; to ask for; to speak to; to indicate.

Best, *a*, *superl.* of GOOD. O.E. *betst*. Of the highest excellence; largest, most.—*adv.*, *superl.* of WELL. In the most excellent way; to the fullest extent, most.—*vt.* To get the better of, outwit.

Bestead', *pa.pple.* M.E. BE- (2) + *stad*, later *sted*, placed. Situated, circumstanced, gen. with *ill* or the like.

Bes'tial, *a.* O.F. *bestial*—L. *bestiālis*, f. *bestia*, BEAST. Of the lower animals; like a beast.—**Bestial'**ITY, *n.*

Bestir', *vt.* O.E. *bestyrian*, f. BE- (2) + *styrian*, to STIR. To rouse into activity.—*v.refl.* To show activity.

Bestow', *vt.* M.E. *bistowen*, f. *bi-*, BE- (2) + *stowen*, to STOW. To place; to stow away; to lodge, quarter; to employ *in*, devote *to*; to give.—**Bestow'**AL, *n.*

Bestrew', *vt.* O.E. *bestréowian*, f. BE- (1) + *stréowian*, to STREW. To strew; to lie scattered over.

Bestride', *vt.* O.E. *bestrídan*, f. BE- (3) + *strídan*, to STRIDE. To ride, sit across; to stand over with legs astride.

Bet, *n.* Possibly aphetic from ABET in sense 'to maintain, back'. A wager; the sum staked.—*vt.* and *i.* To wager.

Betake', *v.refl.* M.E. *bitaken*, f. *bi-*, BE- (2) + *taken*, to TAKE. To have recourse or resort; to resort, make one's way.

Bethink', *v.refl.* O.E. *bithencan*, f. *bi*, BE- (3) + *thencan*, to THINK. To reflect, consider; to propose to oneself.

Betide', *vi.* M.E. *bitiden*, f. *bi*, BE- (2) + *tiden*, to happen. To happen, befall.

Betimes', *adv.* M.E. *bi-*, *by-time*, by time, with *-s* of the adverbial genitive. Early.

Beto'ken, *vt.* M.E. *bitacnien*, f. *bi-*, BE- (2) + O.E. *tácnian*, to signify—O.E. *tácn*, TOKEN. To give promise of; to indicate, show.

Betray', *vt.* M.E. *betraien*, f. BE- (2) + O.F. *traïr*, L. *trādĕre*, to hand over. TRADITION. TRAITOR. To give up by treachery; to be disloyal to; to mislead; to disclose with treachery or against one's will; to reveal, show signs of, generally.—**Betray'**AL, *n.*

Betroth', *vt.* M.E. *bitreuthien*, f. *bi-*, BE- (5) + *treuthe*, TRUTH. To bind to marry.—**Betroth'**AL, **Betroth'**MENT, *nn.*

Bet'ter, *a.*, *comp.* of GOOD. O.E. *betera*. Of greater excellence; larger, more.—*adv.*, *comp.* of WELL. In a more excellent way; in a superior degree; *to be better*, to be improved in health.—*vt.* To improve; to surpass.—*vi.* To improve.

Between', *prep.* O.E. *betwéonan*, *betwéonum*, f. *be*, by + *twéonum*, dat. pl. of *twéone*, double, cogn. with *twegen*, TWO. Expressing position in or motion into, across, or along an interval; intermediate position or state; connection; joint action, ownership, &c.; separation; reciprocal relation; motion to and from; indicating alternatives of judgment, choice, &c.—*adv.* Midway, in the midst; in the interval, at intervals.

Betwixt', *prep.* and *adv.* M.E. and O.E. *betwix*, extended f. *betwih*, between. In same senses as BETWEEN.

Bev'el, *a.* App. f. O.F. **buvel*, implied in F. *buveau*, a kind of carpenter's rule. Oblique, slant.—*n.* A tool for setting off angles; a slope.—*vt.* To cut away to a slope.—*vi.* To slant.

Bev'erage, *n.* O.F. *bevrage*, drink, f. *bevre*, L. *bibĕre*, to drink. IMBIBE. Drink, liquor for drinking.

Bev'y, *n.* M.E. *bevey*, of doubtful orig. A company of maidens, birds, &c.; a company generally.

Bewail', *vt.* and *i.* BE- (3) + WAIL. To lament.

Beware', *vi.* BE + WARE, *a.* To be on one's guard.—*vt.* To be on one's guard against.

Bewil'der, *vt.* App. f. O.N. *villr*, WILD, also astray. To perplex, confound.—**Bewil'der**MENT, *n.*

Bewitch', *vt.* M.E. *biwicchen*, f. *bi-*, BE- (2) + *wicchen*, O.E. *wiccian*, to WITCH. To enchant; to fascinate.

Bewray', *vt.* M.E. *bewraien*—O.E. BE- (2) + *wrégan*, to accuse. To reveal, us. unintentionally.

Beyond', *adv.* O.E. *begeondan*, f. BE-, by + *geond*, across, f. *geon*, YON. Farther away; besides.—*prep.* On or to the farther side of; later than; out of the reach of; surpassing; in addition to.

Bez'el, *n.* O.F. **besel*, implied in F. *biseau*, bevel. The part of a ring which holds the stone.

Bi'as, *n.* F. *biais*, of unknown orig. An oblique line; a term at bowls; a leaning, bent; a swaying impulse.—*vt.* To influence, affect.—**Bi'ased**, *ppl. a.* Prejudiced.

Bib, *n.* Perh. conn. with L. *bibĕre*, to drink. IMBIBE. A cloth under a child's chin to keep the dress clean.

Bi'ble, *n.* F. *bible*—G. *ta biblia*, the books. The Scriptures.—**Bib'**LICAL, *a.*

Bibliog'raphy, *n.* G. *biblion*, book + *graphein*, to write. A history and description of books.—**Bibliograph'**ICAL, *a.*

Bib'liophile, *n.* G. *biblion*, book + *phile-ein*, to love. A lover of books.—**Bib'liopole**, *n.* The same + *pōle-ein*, to sell. A bookseller.

Bib'ulous, *a.* L. *bibulus*, drinking freely, f. *bibĕre*, to drink. IMBIBE. Absorbent; given to drinking.

Bi'ceps, *n.* L. *bi-*, two + *-ceps* = *caput*, head. A two-headed muscle, esp. that of the arm; so *biceps muscle*.

Bick'er, *vi.* M.E. *bickeren*, of uncertain orig. To skirmish, fight; to patter; to brawl; to flash.—*n.* A quarrel.
Bi'cycle, *n.* BI- + G. *kuklos*, wheel. CYCLE. A two-wheeled vehicle propelled by the rider. —**Bi'cycl**IST, *n.*
Bid, *vt.* Two O.E. *vv.* blended—*béodan*, to offer, hence to announce, command, and *biddan*, to pray, to ask pressingly, require, command. BEAD. To offer (a price); to command. —*n.* The offer of a price; the price offered.
Bide, *vi.* O.E. *bídan*. Common Teut. ABIDE. To remain.—*vt.* To await.
Bien'nial, *a.* L. *biennis*, f. *bi-*, two + *annus*, year. Lasting two years; happening every two years.—*n.* A plant which lives two years.— **Bien'nial**LY,[2] *adv.*
Bier, *n.* O.E. *bær*, f. *beran*, to BEAR. A stand for a corpse; that on which a corpse is carried to the grave.
Bi'furcate, *vt.* and *i.* BI-+L. *furca*, fork. To divide into two forks, branches, or peaks.
Big, *a.* M.E., of unknown orig., prob. Scandinavian. Large; pregnant; haughty.
Big'amy, *n.* BI- + G. *gamos*, marriage. The having two wives or husbands at once.— **Big'am**IST, *n.*
Bight, *n.* O.E. *byht*—O.Teut. *būgan*, to BOW. The loop of a rope; a bend or curve; a bay.
Big'ot, *n.* F. *bigot*, of unknown orig. One obstinately and unreasonably wedded to an opinion or creed.—**Big'oted**, *a.*—**Big'ot**RY, *n.*
Bilat'eral, *a.* BI-+L. *latus*, side. Two-sided.
Bil'berry, *n.* App. of Norse orig. The whortleberry.
Bile, *n.* F. *bile*—L. *bilis*. The bitter fluid secreted by the liver; anger, ill-temper.— **Bil'**IOUS, *a.*
Bilge, *n.* Prob. a corr. of BULGE. The bottom of a ship's hull; foulness collecting there. —*vt.* To stave in (a ship).—*vi.* To be stove in.— **Bilge'-water**, *n.*
Bilin'gual, *a.* L. BI*linguis* (f. *lingua*, tongue) + -AL. Having or written in two languages.
Bilk, *vt.* Of uncertain orig. To balk; to cheat; to elude.
Bill, *n.*[1] O.E. and O.S. *bil*. An obsolete weapon, a halberd; an implement for pruning, &c.
Bill, *n.*[2] O.E. *bile*, poss. cogn. with BILL.[1] A bird's beak; a beaklike projection.—*v.*[1]*i.* To stroke bill with bill (as doves).
Bill, *n.*[3] M.E. *bille*—Med.L. *bulla*, a seal, hence a document. BULL.[2] The draft of an Act of Parliament; a note of charges; an advertisement; a negotiable commercial document.—*v.*[2]*t.* To announce by bill.
Bil'let, *n.*[1] M.E. and A.F. *billette*—Anglo-L. *billetta*, dim. of *billa*, BILL.[3] A note; an order for a soldier's accommodation.—*vt.* To quarter (troops).
Bil'let, *n.*[2] O.F. *billete*, dim. of *bille*, trunk of tree, of unknown orig. A short, thick piece of wood for burning.
Bil'liards, *n.pl.* F. *billard*—O.F. *billard*, a cue, dim. of *bille*. BILLET.[2] A game played on a table with balls and cues.
Bil'lion, *n.* BI- substituted for initial letter of MILLION. A million millions.
Bil'low, *n.* App. f. O.N. *bylgja*, billow. A great swelling wave.—*vi.* To rise in billows.
Bimet'allism, *n.* BI- + METAL + -ISM. A system recognizing two metals as legal currency.—**Bimetal'l**IC, *a.*—**Bimet'all**IST, *n.*
Bimonth'ly, *a.* BI- + MONTHLY. Occurring or appearing every two months.
Bin, *n.* O.E. *binn*, manger. A receptacle, esp. for corn, &c.; a division in a wine-cellar.
Bind, *vt.* O.E. *bindan*. Com. Teut. To tie fast; to tie about, bandage, gird; to tie together; to restrain, constrain, unite; to put (a book) into a cover.—*vi.* for *refl.* To cohere.
Bin'nacle, *n.* Corr. of *bittacle*.—Sp. *bitácula* —L. *habitāculum*, little dwelling, f. *habitāre*. HABITATION. A ship's compass-box.
Binoc'ular, *a.* L. *bīni*, two + *oculi*, eyes + -AR.[1] By or adapted to both eyes.—*n.* A telescope so adapted.
Biog'raphy, *n.* G. *bios*, life + *graphein*, to write. The history of the lives of men; a record of a man's life.—**Biog'rapher**, *n.*— **Biograph'**ICAL, *a.*
Biol'ogy, *n.* G. *bios*, life + -LOGY. The science of life.—**Biol'og**IST, *n.*
Bipar'tite, *a.* L. *bipartītus*, pa.pple. of *bipartīre*, *bipartītum*, to divide into two, f. *bi-*, two + *partīre*, to divide. Having two parts.
Bi'ped, *n.* L. *bipēs*, *bipedis*, f. *bi-*, two + *pēs*, FOOT. A two-footed animal.
Birch, *n.* O.E. *berc*, *bierce*. A tree with smooth tough bark and slender branches.
Bird, *n.* O.E. *brid*, of unknown orig. A feathered animal.
Biret'ta, **Beret'ta**, *n.* It. *berretta*—L.L. *birretum*, cap. A square cap worn by R.C. clerics.
Birth, *n.* M.E. *burthe*. Cf. Icel. *byrthr*. Cogn. with BEAR, *v.* The bearing or the being born of offspring; parentage.—**Birth'day Birth'place**, *nn.*
Bis'cuit, *n.* L. *bis*, twice + *coctus*, cooked. COOK. A kind of crisp dry bread, generally in thin flat cakes.
Bisect', *vt.* BI- + L. *secāre*, *sectum*, to cut. SECTION. To divide into two parts, generally equal.—**Bisec'**TION, *n.*
Bish'op, *n.* O.E. *biscop*—G. *episcopos*, f. *epi*, on + *scopos*, watcher. SCOPE. A spiritual overseer.—**Bish'opric**, *n.* His province; his office.
Bis'muth, *n.* Ger. Orig. unknown. A red-dish-white metal.
Bi'son, *n.* L. *bison*, f. Teut. A species of wild ox.
Bissex'tile, *a.* L. *bissextus* (f. *bis*, twice + *sextus*, sixth), the name of the day intercalated in the Julian calendar every fourth year after the *sixth* day before the first of March. Containing the day.—*n.* Leap-year.
Bis'tre, *n.* F. A brown pigment.
Bit, *n.*[1] O.E. *bita*, morsel, f. *bītan*, to BITE. A morsel, fragment.
Bit, *n.*[2] O.E. *bite*, a biting, f. *bītan*, to BITE. The biting part of a tool; the mouthpiece of a horse's bridle.—*vt.* To put the bit in the mouth of.
Bitch, *n.* O.E. *bicce*. The female of the dog.
Bite, *vt.* O.E. *bītan* = O.N. *bíta*. BAIT. BEETLE.[1] BIT[1] and [2]. BITTER. To cut into with the teeth; to cut into generally; to corrode.—*n.* The act of biting; a wound made by biting; a mouthful.
Bit'ter, *a.* O.E. *biter*, prob. f. *bītan*, to BITE. Sharp tasting; virulent; stinging.—**Bit'ter**LY,[2] *adv.*—**Bit'ter**NESS, *n.*—**Bit'ters**, *n.pl.* Bitter medicines.
Bit'tern, *n.* O.F. *butor*, of obscure orig. A bird like a heron.
Bitu'men, *n.* L. A kind of mineral pitch; a mineral inflammable substance.
Bi'valve, *a.* BI- + L. *valvae*, folds of a door

Having a double shell.—*n.* A molluscous animal with such a shell.—So **Bival'vul**AR,[1]*a.*

Biv'ouac, *n.* F. *bivouac, bivac*, of uncertain orig. A temporary encampment without tents. —*vi.* To remain, esp. at night, in such an encampment.

Blab, *n.* M.E. *blabbe*, chatterer. Perh. imitative. An indiscreet talker; loose talk.—*vi.* and *t.* To talk or to reveal indiscreetly.

Black, *a.* O.E. *blac, blæk.* Cf. O.N. *blakkr*, dark. Destitute of light; dark; baneful.—*n.* Black colour; a black paint or fabric; a negro.—*vt.* To make black.—Also **Black'**EN,[2] *vi.* and *t.*—**Black'ing**, *vbl.n.* A making black; a preparation for blacking boots.—**Black'berry**, **Black'bird**, *nn.*

Black'guard, *n.* Lit. *Black Guard.* Possibly applied to kitchen menials from their dirty work. A scoundrel.—*a.* Scoundrelly.—*vt.* To revile.—**Black'guard**LY,[1]*a.*—-ISM,*n.*

Black'-lead, *n.* Graphite or plumbago.

Black'-letter, *n.* The form of type of the early printers.

Black'-mail, *n.* From *mail*, Late O.E. *mál*, rent, tribute, f. O.N. *mál*, speech, agreement, but in sense seeming rather to represent the O.N. derivative *mále*, contract, stipulated pay. Money extorted by threats.—*vt.* To extort from thus.

Black'smith, *n.* A smith who works in iron or *black* metal.

Blad'der, *n.* O.E. *blǽdre, blédre.* Common Teut. A membranous bag in the body, esp. that containing the urine; a prepared bladder used for various purposes.

Blade, *n.* O.E. *blæd.* Common Teut. Cogn. with BLOW, *v.*[2] A leaf; a leaf-like part of anything; the cutting edge of a tool.

Blain, *n.* O.E. *blegen.* Cf. Du. *blein.* A pustule.

Blame, *vt.* O.F. *blasmer*—G. *blasphēme-ein*, to BLASPHEME. To censure; to make answerable.—*n.* Censure; culpability.—**Blame'**ABLE, **Blam'**ABLE, *a.*—**Blame'**LESS, *a.*

Blanch, *vt.* F. *blanchir*, f. *blanc*, white. BLANK. To make white or pale.—*vi.* To become white; to pale.

Blancmange', *n.* O.F. *blanc-manger*, white food, f. *blanc*, white + *manger*, to eat. An opaque white jelly.

Bland, *a.* L. *blandus*, soft. Smooth in manner; pleasing to the senses, mild.—**Blan'dish**, *vt.* F. *blandir*—L. *blandīri*, to flatter. To coax, cajole.—**Blan'dish**MENT, *n.*

Blank, *a.* F. *blanc*—O.H.G. *blanch*, white. White; not written upon; void; fruitless; of the look, vacant or discomfited; unmixed, sheer.—*Blank verse*, verse without rhyme.—*n.* A space not written upon; a lottery ticket carrying no prize; a void.—**Blank'**LY,[2] *adv.*

Blank'et, *n.* O.F. *blankete, blanquette*, f. *blanc*, white (see prec.) + dim. suff. *-ette.* A woollen covering for a bed, &c.

Blare, *vi.* Perh. an imitative word. Cf. L.G. *blaren*, M.H.G. *blēren.* To roar, bellow; to sound a trumpet, to trumpet.—*n.* A roaring, bellowing, trumpeting.

Blaspheme', *vi.* O.F. *blasfemer*—L. *blasphēmāre*—G. *blasphēme-ein*, f. *blasphēmos*, evil speaking, f. *blas-*, perh. conn. with *blaptein*, to hurt + *-phēmos*, speaking, f. *phēmi*, I say. BLAME. To talk profanely.—*vt.* To speak irreverently of; to revile.—**Blas'phemy**, *n.* G. *blasphēmia.* Profane speaking.—**Blasphem'**ER, *n.*—**Blas'phemo**US, *a.*—**Blas'phemous**LY,[2] *adv.*

Blast, *n.* O.E. *blǽst*, f. O.Teut. *blǣsan*, to blow. BLAZE, *v.*[2] BELLOWS. A gust of wind; a current of air; a sound made by blowing; blight, a curse; an explosion.—*vt.* To blow up; to blight; to discredit, ruin.

Bla'tant, *a.* Of unknown orig. App. invented by Spenser ('the Blatant beast', F. Q., VI, 12 (Heading)). Noisy, clamorous.

Blaze, *n.* O.E. *blase, blæse*, chiefly in sense 'torch', cogn. with M.H.G. *blas*, a torch, Mod.G. *blass*, pale, orig., shining. A bright flame or fire; brightness, brilliancy, splendour; a violent outburst.—*v.*[1]*i.* To burn brightly; to burn with passion, excitement, &c.; to shine, glitter, be conspicuous.

Blaze, *v.*[2]*t.* O.N. *blása*, O.Teut. *blǣsan*, to blow. Cogn. with L. *flāre*, to blow. BLOW, *v.*[1] BLAST. BLISTER. To proclaim (as with a trumpet), divulge, publish.

Bla'zon, *n.* F. *blason*, of doubtful orig. Earliest meaning 'shield'. A coat of arms; a description of arms; a description in general. —*vt.* To describe or depict (arms); to illuminate, adorn; to describe; to make public.

Bleach, *vt.* O.E. *blǽcan.* (See next). Common Teut. To whiten (linen, &c.); to blanch. —*vi.* To become white, pale, pure.

Bleak, *a.* M.E. *bleik*—O.N. *bleikr*, pale, cogn. with O.E. *blícan*, to shine, and *blǽcan* (see prec.). Exposed, chilly, dreary.

Blear, *a.* M.E. *blere*, of uncertain orig. Of the eyes, dim; dim, misty.—*vt.* To dim, blur, blind.

Bleat, *v.* O.E. *blǽtan.* Common W.Ger.; of imitative orig. To cry, as a sheep, goat, &c.—*n.* The cry.

Bleed, *vi.* O.E. *blédan*, f. O.Teut. type *blôdo-m*, BLOOD. To emit or lose blood; to pay dearly.—*vt.* To draw blood from; to extort money from.

Blem'ish, *vt.* O.F. *blemir*, to make pale, f. *bleme*, pale, of uncertain orig. To mar, spoil; to impair, damage, sully.—*n.* A disfigurement; defect, stain.

Blench, *vi.* Of uncertain orig. BLINK. To flinch, quail.

Blend, *vt.* and *i.* M.E. *blenden*, prob. f. O.N. *blanda*, to blend. To mix, mingle.—*n.* A blending, mixture.

Bless, *vt.* O.E. *blétsian*, app. formed on O.Teut. type *blôdo-m*, BLOOD; hence, to consecrate with blood. To consecrate, hallow; to extol, give thanks to; to invoke happiness upon, wish well to; to make happy.—*v.refl.* To account oneself happy.—**Bless'ed**NESS, *n.*—**Bless'ing**, *vbl.n.* The act of blessing; a benediction; a boon.

Blight, *n.* Of unknown orig. A baleful influence; mildew.—*vt.* To affect with blight, mar, frustrate.

Blind, *a.* O.E. *blind.* Common Teut. Destitute of sight; lacking intellectual or moral light, heedless, random; dim, indistinct, obscure; closed at one end.—*vt.* To make blind; to conceal; to darken.—*n.* Something intercepting light; a screen for a window; a pretext.—**Blind'**LY,[2] *adv.*—**Blind'**NESS, *n.*—**Blind'fold**, *vt.* M.E. *blind-fellen*, to strike blind. FELL. To cover the eyes.—*a.* Having the eyes covered.—**Blind'-worm**, *n.* A reptile, the slow-worm, with very small eyes.

Blink, *vi.* Of uncertain orig. App. cogn. with BLENCH. Cf. Ger. and Du. *blinken* in same sense. To look with half-closed eyes; to wink; to twinkle.—*vt.* To shut the eyes to, shirk.—*n.* A momentary gleam; a glimmer. —**Blink'**ER, *n.* A screen to prevent a horse from seeing sideways.

Bliss, *n.* O.E. *bliths*, f. *blithe*, BLITHE. Perfect happiness.—**Bliss'**FUL, *a.*—**Bliss'ful**LY,[2] *adv.*—**Blissful'**NESS, *n.*

Blis'ter, *n.* M.E. *blester*, perh. f. O.F. *blestre*, swelling, of Teut. orig. Cf. O.N. *blástr*, a blowing, a swelling, f. *blása*, to blow. BLAZE, *v.*[2] A vesicle containing fluid; an application to produce one.—*vt.* To raise blisters on. —*vi.* To become covered with blisters.

Blithe, *a.* O.E. *blíthe*. Common Teut. BLISS. Gay, merry. — **Blithe'**LY,[2] *adv.*— **Blithe'**NESS, *n.*—**Blithe'**SOME, *a.*

Bliz'zard, *n.* A modern word from U.S., prob. onomatopœic. A furious blast of wind and snow.

Bloat, *a.* M.E. *blout*—O.N. *blautr*, soft. Puffed, swollen.—*vt.* To inflate, swell.—*vi.* To become swollen.

Block, *n.* O.F. *bloc*, said to be of Teut. orig. A solid piece of wood, a log, a stump; a pulley; any compact mass; an impediment; a stoppage; a stupid or hard-hearted person.—*vt.* To obstruct, to shut *up*; to shape on a block; to sketch out; to make into blocks.—**Blockade'**, *n.* The blocking up of a place.—*vt.* To block up.—**Block'head**, *n.* A stupid fellow.

Blond, Blonde, *a.* F. *blond*, fem. *blonde*, yellow-haired—Med.L. *blondus*, *blundus*, yellow, of uncertain orig. Of a light golden brown, fair.

Blood, *n.* O.E. *blód*. Common Teut. O.Teut. type *blôdo-m.* BLEED. BLESS. The vital fluid; something resembling or suggesting this; shedding of blood, death; passion, mettle, anger; race or kindred; good parentage; offspring.—*vt.* To draw blood from; to inure to blood.—**Blood'**Y,[2] *a.*—**Blood'**ILY,[2] *adv.* — **Blood'**LESS, *a.* — **Blood'-heat, Blood'hound, Blood'money, Blood'-shed, Blood'-vessel**, *nn.*—**Blood'shot, Blood'thirsty**, *aa.*

Bloom, *n.* M.E. *blome*—O.N. *blóm*, a flower. Cogn. with BLOW, *v.*[2] The blossom or flower of a plant; blossoming, flowers; prime, perfection; flush, glow; the delicate powdery deposit on a fruit.—*vi.* To be in flower; to flourish; to glow.—*vt.* To give a glow to.— **Bloom'**Y,[2] *a.*

Blos'som, *n.* O.E. *blóstm*. Perh. f. the same root as BLOOM. A flower; a mass of flowers.—*vi.* To flower.

Blot, *n.* Of obscure orig. App. Teutonic. A spot or stain; a blemish, a disgrace.—*vt.* To spot or stain; to obliterate; to dry with **Blot'ting-paper**.

Blotch, *n.* App. formed on BLOT. A boil; a large spot or blot.—*vt.* To make blotchy.— **Blotch'**Y,[2] *a.*

Blouse, *n.* F., of obscure orig. A light, loose, upper garment.

Blow, *v.*[1]*i.* O.E. *bláwan* = O.H.G. *blâhan*. Cogn. with L. *flāre*, to blow. BLAZE, *v.*[2] FLATULENT. INFLATE. To make a current of air; to pant; to sound a blast, to give forth a sound; with *up*, to undergo explosion.—*vt.* To breathe out; to drive or carry by air; to direct air against; to make (an instrument) sound, to sound (a note); to inflate, swell *out* or *up*; with *up*, to shatter by explosion.—*n.*[1] A blowing, a blast.—**Blow'**ER, *n.* One who blows; a contrivance for producing a draught. —**Blow'pipe**. A pipe through which air is blown into a flame.

Blow, *v.*[2]*i.* O.E. *blówan* = O.H.G. *bluojan*. Cogn. with L. *flōs*, FLOWER. BLOOM. BLOSSOM. FLOURISH. To blossom; to flourish.— *n.*[2] A blossoming, bloom; a display.

Blow, *n.*[3] Orig. doubtful. A stroke, literally or figuratively.

Blub'ber, *n.* M.E. *blober*, *bluber*, prob. imitative, from the action of the lips in making a bubble. Formerly a bubble. A jelly-fish; the fat of whales.—*vi.* To weep effusively.

Blud'geon, *n.* Orig. unknown. A short club with a thick end.—*vt.* To strike with a bludgeon.

Blue, *a.* M.E. *blew*, *bleu*—O.F. *bleu*—O.Teut. type *blǣwo-z.* Of the colour of the sky; livid; low-spirited; of women, learned, pedantic.— *n.* The colour; a blue pigment; blue clothing. —*vt.* To make blue.—**Blu'**ISH, *a.*—**Blue bell**, *n.* The wild hyacinth.—**Blue'bottle**, *n.* The blue corn-flower; a large fly.

Bluff, *a.* Of uncertain orig. Steep; abrupt, blunt; rough and hearty.—*n.* A cliff with a broad steep face.

Bluff, *vt.* Of uncertain orig. To impose on by a show of strength.—*vi.* To practise imposition thus.

Blun'der, *vi.* Of uncertain orig. To flounder, stumble; to err stupidly.—*vt.* To mismanage. —*n.* A gross mistake.

Blun'derbuss, *n.* App. corr. f. Du. *donderbus*, f. *donder*, thunder + *bus*, gun. A short gun with a wide bore.

Blunt, *a.* Orig. unknown. Dull, insensitive; not sharp, without edge or point; abrupt of speech, curt.—*vt.* To dull.—**Blunt'**LY,[2] *adv.* —**Blunt'**NESS, *n.*

Blur, *n.* Orig. unknown. A smear, a stain; indistinctness.—*vt.* To stain, sully; to make indistinct; to dim (the sight, &c.).

Blurt, *vt.* App. expressive of a discharge of breath after retention. With *out*, to ejaculate impulsively.

Blush, *vi.* M.E. *bluschen*, of uncertain orig., app. related to sim. words in O.N. and L.G. pointing to a root *blus-*, to glow. To become red in the face; to be ashamed; to be or become red.—*n.* A glance, glimpse; a reddening of the face; a rosy glow, a flush of colour.

Blus'ter, *vi.* Of uncertain orig. Of wind, to blow boisterously; to swagger, hector.—*n.* A stormy blast; swaggering.

Bo'a, *n.* L. *boa*, of unknown orig. A genus of large serpents without poison fangs; a snake-like coil of fur worn by ladies round the neck.

Boar, *n.* O.E. *bár*—O.Teut. type *bairo-z.* The male of the swine.

Board, *n.* O.E. *bord*, representing two distinct words, both Common Teut., meaning (1) board, plank, (2) BORDER, ship's side. A plank, slab, or tablet of wood used for various purposes; *the boards*, the stage; thick, stiff paper; a table, daily meals; a council or administrative body; a ship's side; *on board*, in or into a ship.—*vt.* To approach or enter (a ship); to furnish with planks; to provide with daily meals.—*vi.* To be so provided.—**Board'**ER, *n.* One so provided; one who boards a ship.—**Board'ing-house, -school**, *nn.*

Boast, *n.* M.E. *bōst*, with *bōsten*, *v.* Orig. unknown. A vaunt, brag; a cause of boasting. —*vi.* and *refl.* To vaunt.—*vt.* To brag of; to have to show.—**Boast'**ER, *n.*—**Boast'**FUL, *a.*

Boat, *n.* O.E. *bát*, of doubtful orig. A small open vessel; a ship or steamer.—*vi.* To go in a boat, row.—**Boat'swain**, *n.* Lit. 'boat-lad'. A ship's officer in charge of the boats, sails, &c., and who summons the men to duty.

Bob, *n.*[1] Orig. unknown. The weight of a pendulum, plumb-line, &c.; a knot or bunch of hair yarn, ribbons, &c.

Bob, *v.*[1]*t.* M.E. *boben*, of uncertain orig., perh. imitative. To rap with a light blow; to cause to rap against.—*n.*[2] A light blow, a tap.
Bob, *v.*[2]*t.* App. imitative of short jerking motion. To cause to move with such a motion.—*vi.* To move with such a motion; to curtsy.—*n.*[3] A curtsy.
Bob'bin, *n.* F. *bobine*. Orig. unknown. An article round which thread or yarn is wound.
Bode, *vt.* O.E. *bodian*, f. *boda*, messenger, *bod*, message. Cogn. with *béodan*, to BID. To betoken, portend; to have a presentiment of.
Bod'ice, *n.* Shortened from 'a pair of bodies' in old sense 'stays'. Now, the upper part of a woman's dress.
Bod'kin, *n.* Of unknown orig. A small instrument for perforating cloth, &c.; a pin for the hair.
Bod'y, *n.* O.E. *bodig*. Cf. O.H.G. *potach*. The frame of a living being; a corpse; the trunk; a bodice; the main, principal, or larger part; an individual; a number of persons associated or organized; a collective mass; a collection of details; a material thing; bulk, amount; of colours, &c., substantial quality.—*vt.* To embody; to put into tangible form; to symbolize.—**Bod'i**LESS, *a.*—**Bod'i**LY,[1] *a.*—**Bod'i**LY,[2] *adv.*—**Bod'y-guard**, *n.*
Bog, *n.* Ir. or Gael. *bogach*, f. *bog*, soft. A piece of wet spongy ground.—*vt.* To entangle in a bog.
Bog'gle, *vi.* App. f. BOGLE. To take alarm, shy; to hesitate, demur; to palter; to bungle, fumble. [BUG. A spectre.
Bo'gle, *n.* Perh. conn. with Welsh *bwg*, ghost.
Bo'gus, *a.* From U.S. Orig. unknown. Sham.
Boil, *n.*[1] O.E. *býl*. Common Teut., f. O.Teut. root *bul-*, to swell. BOLSTER. BOWL.[1] A suppurating tumour.
Boil, *vi.* O.F. *boillir*—L. *bullire*, to bubble up, boil, f. *bulla*, a globular object, a bubble. BILL.[3] BUDGE. BULL.[2] BULLET. BULLETIN. BULLION. To bubble up from the action of heat; to be agitated, seethe; to be cooked by boiling.—*vt.* To cause to bubble up; to subject (food, clothes, &c.) to the action of boiling water.—*n.*[2] The act or state of boiling.—**Boil'**ER, *n.* A vessel in which water is boiled.
Bois'terous, *a.* Orig. unknown. Stormy; clamorous, noisy; exuberant in spirits.—**Bois'terous**LY,[2] *adv.*
Bold, *a.* O.E. *beald*, *bald*. Common Teut. Daring, fearless; presumptuous; prominent.—**Bold'**LY,[2] *adv.*—**Bold'**NESS, *n.*
Bole, *n.* O.N. *bolr*. The trunk of a tree.
Bol'ster, *n.* O.E. *bolster*. Common Teut., f. O. Teut. root *bul-*, to swell. BOIL, *n.*[1] A long pillow; various things like this.—*vt.* To support, uphold; to pad.
Bolt, *n.* O.E. *bolt*. Cf. O.H.G. *bolz*. Root unknown. A short arrow; a discharge of lightning; a stout pin for fastening a door or holding things together; a dart, rush.—*v.*[1]*i.* To enter suddenly *into*; to dart *out*, rush *off*; to break from control.—*vt.* To blurt *out*; to swallow hastily; to secure with a bolt; to fasten together with bolts.—*adv.* As straight as a bolt; suddenly, with one bolt, straight.
Bolt, *v.*[2]*t.*, **Boult**. O.F. *bulter*, a corruption of **bureter*, to sift through *bure*, coarse cloth. BUREAU. To sift.—**Bolt'**ER, *n.* A piece of cloth or a machine for sifting.
Bomb, *n.* Imitative. F. *bombe*—Sp. *bomba*—L. *bombus*, a humming noise. BOOM, *v.*[1] BOUND, *v.*[2] An explosive projectile, a shell.
Bombard', *vt.* F. *bombarder*, f. *bombarde*, a cannon, prob. f. L. *bombus*. BOMB. To batter with cannon.—**Bombard'**MENT, *n.*—**Bombardi**ER', *n.* A non-commissioned artillery officer.
Bombasine', **Bombazine'**, *n.* F. *bombasin*—L. *bombycinus*, silken, f. G. *bombux*. (See next.) A fabric of silk and worsted.
Bom'bast, *n.* O.F. *bombace*—L.L. *bombax*, cotton, padding—G. *bombux*, silk. (See prec.) High-sounding words, fustian.—**Bombas'**TIC, -ICAL, *a.*—**Bombas'tical**LY,[2] *adv.*
Bond, *n.*[1] M.E. *bond*, a variant of BAND.[1] A shackle; in *pl.* confinement; something used for tying up; a constraining or uniting force; a covenant, an obligation to pay money; of goods, *in bond*, stored till duty is paid.—*vt.* To bind together; to burden with debt; of goods, to put in bond.
Bond, *a.* Adj. use of obs. *Bond*, a vassal or serf—O.E. *bonda*—O.N. *bónde(-i)*, *bóande*, *búande*, husbandman, f. *búa*, to dwell, till. BOOR. BOOTH. BOUND, *ppl.a.*[1] BOWER, *n.*[1] BUILD. BYRE. Enslaved.—**Bond'**AGE, *n.*
Bone, *n.* O.E. *bán*. Common Teut. Any of the parts of the hard framework of the body; various things made of bone.—*vt.* To take the bones out of.—**Bon'**Y,[2] *a.*
Bon'fire, *n.* BONE + FIRE, fire of bones. A fire to burn up rubbish or to express rejoicing.
Bon'net, *n.* O.F. *bonet*, short for *chapel de bonet*, hat of *bonet*, a material not identified. A head-dress.
Bo'nus, *n.* An application of L *bonus*, good, perh. for neut. *bonum*, a boon. An extra payment or dividend.
Boob'y, *n.* Prob. f. Sp. *bobo* in sim. sense, of doubtful orig. A dunce.
Book, *n.* O.E. *bóc*, book, also, a beech-tree (the original 'books' having been writings scratched on beechen boards). Common Teut. Cogn. with L. *fāgus*. BEECH. A printed or written literary work; a volume for records; a main division of a work.—*vt.* To record; to enrol; to engage; to undertake or arrange for the conveyance of.—**Book'**ISH, *a.*—**Book'-worm**, *n.* A maggot which preys on books; a close student.
Boom, *v.*[1]*i.* Imitative. Allied to BOMB. To hum; to make a loud deep sound.—*n.*[1] Such a sound.
Boom, *n.*[2] Du. *boom*, tree, pole, cogn. with BEAM. A long spar; a barrier of connected spars.—*v.*[2]*t.* To extend with a boom; to push off with a pole.
Boom, *n*[3]. From U.S. Of uncertain orig. Sudden commercial activity; a vigorous impetus or writing-up.—*v.*[3]*i.* To go off with a boom.—*vt.* To give a boom to.
Boon, *n.* M.E. *bone*—O.N. *bón*, a petition. A thing asked for; a favour bestowed; a benefit, advantage. [convivial.
Boon, *a.* O.F. *bon*, L. *bonus*, good. Benign;
Boor, *n.* Prob. f. Du. *boer*, peasant. Cogn. with *búa*. BOND, *a.* A rustic; a rude, ill-bred fellow.—**Boor'**ISH, *a.*
Boot, *n.*[1] O.E. *bót*. Common Teut. Cogn. with BETTER. Profit, use; *to boot*, into the bargain.—*v.*[1]*impers.* To profit, avail.—**Boot'**LESS, *a.*
Boot, *n.*[2] O.F. *bote*—Med.L. *botta*, of uncertain orig. A covering for the foot and lower leg.—*v.*[2]*t.* To put boots on.—*vi.* To put on one's boots.
Booth, *n.* M.E. *bōthe*, prob. f. O.Da. *bóth*, O.N. *búth*, dwelling, f. *búa*. BOND, *a.* A temporary shed or stall.

Boot'y, *n.* Prob. f. F. *butin.* Cf. Ger. *beute*; also O.N. *býti*, barter, also spoil. Plunder, spoil, gain.

Bor'der, *n.* O.F. *bordure*—L.L. *bordātūra*, edging—Teut. *bord*, side. BOARD. A side, margin, edging; a frontier; a frontier line; a strip of garden ground; a limit, boundary.—*vt.* To put a border on; to bound; to adjoin. *vi.* To be contiguous *upon*; to verge *on*, resemble.—**Bor'der**ER, *n.*

Bore, *v.*[1]*t.* O.E. *borian.* Common Teut., f. same root as L. *forāre*, to PERFORATE; G. *pharos*, plough. To pierce, perforate; to make (a hole).—*vi.* To make a hole, esp., in mining, to sink one in the earth.—*n.*[1] The cavity of a tube, gun, &c.; the calibre of a gun; in mining, a bore-hole.

Bore, *n.*[2] Orig. unknown. An annoyance, nuisance; a tiresome person.—*v.*[2]*t.* To weary.

Bore, *n.*[3] Perh. f. O.N. *bára*, wave. A tidal surge in a river.

Bo'real, *a.* L. *boreālis*, f. G. *boreas*, north wind. Northern.

Bor'ough, *n.* O.E. *burg, burh*, a fort. O.Teut. stem *burg-*, f. *bergan*, to keep, protect, hide. BURGESS. BURGLAR. BURY. SCABBARD. A town with a municipal corporation.

Bor'row, *vt.* O.E. *borgian*, f. *borg, borh*, pledge, f. root *burg-*. BOROUGH. To take on credit; to adopt, appropriate.—**Bor'row**ER, *n.*

Bo'som, *n.* O.E. *bósm.* Cf. Du. *boezem*, Ger. *busen.* The breast; the enclosure formed by the breast and the arms; the part of the dress covering the breast; the space between this and the breast; the breast as the seat of thought and feelings.—*attrib.* Cherished; intimate.—*vt.* To put in the bosom; to embrace, conceal, cherish.

Boss, *n.* O.F. *boce*, O.N.F. *boche*, a swelling, perh. f. O.H.G. *bōzan*, to beat, a bump being the result of a blow. BOTCH, *n.*[1] A knob; a round ornamental prominence.—**Boss'**Y,[2] *a.*

Bot'any, *n.* G. *botanikos*, relating to plants (*botanic*, see below, is historically the parent word), f. *botanē*, plant. The science of plants.—**Botan'**IC, **Botan'**ICAL, *aa.*—**Bot'an**IST, *n.*—**Bot'an**IZE, *vi.*

Botch, *n.*[1] O.N.F. *boche.* BOSS. A boil, pimple; an eruptive disease.

Botch, *vt.* M.E. *bocchen*, of uncertain orig. To patch or put together clumsily; to bungle.—*n.*[2] A clumsy patch; a bungled piece of work.—**Botch'**ER, *n.*

Both, *a.* M.E. *bāthe*, app. f. O.N. *báthar.* Cf. O.E. *bá*, G. *am-phō*, L. *am-bo.* The one and the other.—*adv.* and *conj.* As well.

Both'er, *vt.* Orig. unknown. Perh. Mod. Irish. To pester, worry.—*vi.* To fuss, take trouble; to be troublesome.—*n.* Worry, fuss.—**Bother**A'TION, *n.*—**Both'er**SOME, *a.*

Bot'tle, *n.* O.F. *bouteille*—L.L. *buticula*, dim. of *butis, buttis*, vessel. BUTT.[1] A vessel with a narrow neck for holding liquids; the contents of a bottle.—*vt.* To put into a bottle; to shut *up, in*, &c.

Bot'tom, *n.* O.E. *botm.* Cogn. with Ger. *boden*, L. *fundus* (*fud-nus*), G. *puthmēn.* FOUND, *v.*[1] The lowest part; the bed of a sea, &c.; the inmost part; a ship; staying power.—*vt.* To put a bottom to; to base *upon*; to get to the bottom of.—**Bot'tom**LESS, *a.*—**Bot'tom**RY, *n.* After Du. *bodmerij.* A loan on the security of a ship.

Bou'doir, *n.* F., lit. 'a place to sulk in', f. *bouder*, to sulk. A lady's private sitting-room.

Bough, *n.* O.E. *bóg, bóh*, orig., an arm=O.N. *bōgr*, shoulder, hence, the bow or shoulder of a ship. Cogn. with G. *pēchus*, fore-arm. BOW, *n.*[3] A branch of a tree.

Boul'der, *n.* Shortened f. **Boulder-stone**, M.E. *bulderston*, of doubtful orig. A large water-worn stone.

Bounce, *vt.* M.E. *bunsen*, to beat. Prob. imitative. To bully; to scold roundly.—*vi.* To bluster, swagger; to bound, throw oneself about; to burst *into, out of.*—*n.* A thump; a leap; a boast, a boastful falsehood.—*adv.* Abruptly.—**Bounc'**ER, *n.* A blusterer, boaster, bully; a 'thumping' lie; a fine specimen.—**Bounc'ing**, *ppl.a.* Big, strapping, vigorous.

Bound, *n.*[1] A.F. *bounde*—Med.L. *bodina*, a limit, perh. of Celtic orig. A limit; in *pl.*, a district, tract.—*v.*[1]*t.* To limit, restrain; to form the limit of.—**Bound'**ARY, *n.*—**Bound'**LESS, *a.*

Bound, *v.*[2]*i.* F. *bondir*, orig. to resound, f. L. *bombitāre*, to hum, f. *bombus*, a humming noise. BOMB. To leap, spring upwards; to move by leaps.—*n.*[2] A leap.

Bound, *ppl.a.*[1] M.E. *boun* + excrescent *d*—O.N. *búinn*, prepared, f. *búa*, to dwell, till, prepare. BOND, *a.* Ready or purposing to go, starting, destined.

Bound, *ppl.a.*[2] Pa.pple. of BIND. Made fast; under obligation; obliged; fated, certain.

Boun'ty, *n.* O.F. *bontet*—L. *bonitas*, f. *bonus*, good. BOON, *a.* Gracious liberality, munificence; a boon, gift, premium.—**Boun'te**OUS, **Boun'ti**FUL, *aa.*

Bou'quet, *n.* F.—O.F. *bosquet*, orig. 'a little wood', dim. of *bos*, f. L.L. *boscus*, wood. BUSH. A bunch of flowers; the perfume of wine.

Bout, *n.* = obs. *Bought*, bend, turn, cogn. with BIGHT. A turn, spell; occasion, time; a combat, match.

Bo'vine, *a.* L. *bovīnus*, f. *bōs, bovis*, ox. BUGLE.[1] COW, *n.* Of the ox tribe.

Bow, *n.*[1] O.E. *boga.* Common Teut. f. O.Teut. *beugan-, būgan-*, to bend. ELBOW. A bend, a bent line; a rainbow; a weapon for shooting arrows; an ornamental knot of ribbons, a necktie; an instrument for playing a violin, &c.—Hence *v.*[1]*t.* and *i.* To use the bow (on a violin, &c.)—**Bow-win'dow**, *n.*

Bow, *v.*[2]*i.* O.E. *būgan*, f. *beugan.* (See prec.) To bend the neck, submit; to bend the body in respect, salutation, submission, assent.—*vt.* To incline, lower; to cause to stoop, crush.—*n.*[2] An inclination in respect, &c.

Bow, *n.*[3] The same in origin as BOUGH; adopted f. L.G., Du., or Da. The fore-end of a ship.

Bow'el, *n.* O.F. *boel, bouel*—L.L. *botellus*, dim. of *botulus*, sausage. An intestine, gen. in *pl.*; in *pl.*, pity, feeling.

Bow'er, *n.*[1] O.E. *búr*, dwelling, f. root of O.N. *búa.* BOND, *a.* BYRE. A lady's room; a shady retreat, an arbour.

Bow'er, *n.*[2] BOW, *n.*[3] + -ER. An anchor at a ship's bow.

Bowl, *n.*[1] O.E. *bolla*, f. its round form. Common Teut., f. O.Teut. root *bul-*, to swell. BOIL, *n.*[1] A large cup-like vessel; the contents.

Bowl, *n.*[2] F. *boule*—L. *bulla*, bubble, ball. BOIL, *v.* A round solid body used in certain games; in *pl.*, a game played with bowls.—*vi.* To play at bowls; to move like a bowl; to launch the ball at cricket.—*vt.* To cause to roll; at cricket, to put (a player) out by bowling.—**Bowl'**ER, *n.*

Bow'sprit, *n.* In all mod. Teut. langs. (Du. *boegspriet*); conn. with BOW, *n.*[3] and a word sim. to O.E. *spréot*, pole, Du. *spriet*, spear. A large spar running out from a ship's bow.

Box, *n.*[1] O.E. *box*—L. *buxus*—G. *puxos*. A small evergreen tree; a dwarf variety used for edgings; the wood of the tree.

Box, *n.*[2] O.E. *box*, prob. an altered form of Med.L. *buxis*, L. *pyxis*, a box, f. G. *puxos*. (See prec.) BUSHEL. PYX. A case, gen. with a lid; the contents; the driver's seat on a carriage; a compartment partitioned off; a shelter, hut, small house; a case for the needle of a compass.—*v.*[1]*t.* To put into a box; to confine; *to box the compass*, to repeat the names of the thirty-two points in order, to go round to the direct opposite, make a complete turn.

Box, *n.*[3] M.E. *box*, of unknown orig. Perh. imitative. A blow, cuff.—*v.*[2]*t.* To cuff.—*vi.* To fight with the fists.

Boy, *n.* M.E. *boi*, *boy*, of obscure orig. A male child.

Boy'cott, *vt.* From Capt. *Boycott*, the original victim. To unite in refusing to deal with.—*n.* Such a union.

Brace, *n.* O.F. *brace*, the two arms, f. *pl.* of L. *bracchium*, the arm. EMBRACE. A clasp, clamp; a strap with a buckle, a trousers-suspender; a pair, couple; a support.—*vt.* To surround; to clasp; to stretch, strain, string up; to make firm, fix.

Brace'let, *n.* O.F. *bracelet*, dim. of *bracel*—L. *bracchiāle*, bracelet, f. *bracchium*. (See prec.) An ornamental ring or band worn on the wrist.

Brack'en, *n.* M.E. *braken*. Cf. Icelandic *burkni*, Sw. *bräken*, fern. A kind of large fern.

Brack'et, *n.* Formerly *bragget*; said to be f. Sp. *bragueta*, bracket, corbel, dim. of *bragas*, breeches, f. L. *brācae*, breeches. The name seems to have come from some resemblance to the front part of a pair of breeches as formerly made. A small shelf; a support; a pipe supplying gas to a gas burner; a mark to enclose words.—*vt.* To enclose (words) within brackets; to couple, connect.

Brack'ish, *a.* Prob. Du. *brak*, brackish + -ISH. Saltish.

Brag, *n.* Orig. uncertain. Boastful language. —*vi.* To vaunt, boast.—**Braggado'cio**, *n.* Formed by Spenser on *brag* with an Italian termination. A boaster; vaunting.—**Brag'gart**, *n.* A boaster.—*a.* Boastful.

Braid, *vt.* O.E. *bregdan*, *brédan*, to pull, brandish, weave. Cf. O.N. *bregtha*, to brandish, change, braid, &c. BRIDLE. To interweave, plait; to bind (the hair); to trim with braid. —*n.* A plait; a woven band or fabric.

Brain, *n.* O.E. *brægn*, perh. cogn. with G. *brechmos*, forehead. The nervous matter in the skull; the understanding.—*vt.* To dash out the brains of.—**Brain'**LESS, *a.*

Braise, **Braize**, *vt.* F. *braiser*, f. *braise*, hot coals, of Teut. orig. BRAZIER. To stew in a close pan with herbs, &c.

Brake, *n.*[1] Cf. M.L.G. *brake*, brake, cogn. with BREAK, originally meaning tree-stumps or broken branches. A clump of bushes; a thicket.

Brake, *n.*[2] M.L.G. *brake*, Du. *braak*, flax-brake, f. *breken*, to BREAK. An implement for beating and crushing flax; a harrow for crushing clods.—*v.*[1]*t.* To beat and crush (flax); to crush (clods).

Brake, *n.*[3] Orig. doubtful. A contrivance for retarding the motion of a wheel.—*v.*[2]*t.* To apply a brake to.

Brake, *n.*[4] See BREAK, *n.*[2]

Bram'ble, *n.* O.E. *brémel* (dim. of *bróm*, BROOM), *brembel*. A prickly shrub; specifically, the blackberry.

Bran, *n.* O.F. *bren*, *bran*. The ground husk of corn.

Branch, *n.* F. *branche*—L.L. *branca*, paw. A limb of a tree or plant; anything like this; a division or subdivision; a component part. —*vi.* To bear branches: to ramify; to diverge.

Brand, *n.* O.E. *brand*, a burning, a (gleaming) sword, f. Teut. type *brennan-*, to BURN. A burning piece of wood, a torch; a mark made by a hot iron, a mark, trade-mark; a class of goods; the blade of a sword, a sword. —*vt.* To burn with an iron; to mark; to stigmatize.—**Brand'-**, **Bran'-new'**, *a.* Quite new, as if fresh from the furnace.

Bran'dish, *vt.* F. *brandir*, f. Teut. BRAND, sword. To flourish, wave about. — *n.* A flourish or wave.

Bran'dy, *n.* Orig. *brandwine*, f. Du. *brandewijn*, burnt (i.e. distilled) wine—Du. *branden*, cogn. with BURN. A spirit distilled from wine.

Brass, *n.* O.E. *bræs*, of unknown orig. An alloy of copper and zinc; effrontery.—**Braze**, *vt.* To make hard like brass, harden to impudence; to solder with an alloy of brass and zinc. (In the latter sense perh. f. F. *braser*, to solder, in O.F. to burn.)—**Brass'**Y,[2] *a.*—**Bra'**ZEN,[1] *a.*—**Bra'**ZIER, *n.* One who works in brass.

Brat, *n.* Of uncertain orig. A child, in [contempt.

Brava'do, *n.* F *bravade*—It. *bravata*, f. *bravo*, BRAVE. An ostentatious display of boldness.

Brave, *a.* F. *brave*, f. It. *bravo*, brave, gallant, fine. Courageous, daring; finely dressed; splendid, showy.—*n.* A warrior.—*vt.* To challenge; to encounter, defy.—**Brave'**LY,[2] *adv.* —**Bra'**VERY, *n.*—**Bra'vo**, *n.* A hired assassin, a daring villain.—*int.* Capital! well done!

Brawl, *v.* M.E. *brawlen*. Orig. uncertain. To wrangle, make a disturbance; to flow noisily.—*n.* A squabble.

Brawn, *n.* O.F. *braon*, flesh for roasting. —O.H.G. *brâtan*, to roast. Fleshy part, muscle; boar's flesh.

Bray, *v.*[1]*i.* F. *braire*—Med.L. *bragire*, to cry, perh. of Celtic orig. To cry out, of the ass.—*n.* The ass's cry.

Bray, *v.*[2]*t.* O.F. *breier*, perh. f. O.Teut. *brek-*, BREAK. To beat small, pound, generally in a mortar.

Bra'zier, *n.* F. *brasier*, f. *braise*, hot coals. BRAISE. A pan for holding burning charcoal.

Breach, *n.* M.E. *breche*, partly f. O.E. *bryce*, O.Teut. *bruki-z*, f. *brek-*, BREAK, partly f. F. *brèche*, a fracture. Cf. Ger. *brechen*, to break. The breaking of waves; the breaking of a rule, duty, &c.; a breaking of relations; a broken place, a gap.—*vt.* To make a breach in.

Bread, *n.* O.E. *bréad*, orig., piece, bit. Cf. O.N. *brauth*, Du. *brood*, Ger. *brot*. Food of meal or flour kneaded and baked; livelihood.

Breadth, *n.* Formed after *length*, &c., on obs. *Brede*, breadth—O.E. *brǽdu*, f. *brád*, BROAD. Extent across, width; largeness (of mind, &c.).

Break, *vt.* O.E. *brecan*, f. O.Teut. stem *brek-*, cogn. with L. *frangĕre* (*frag-*). FRACTION. Orig. sense, to crack with noise. To sever into parts by force; to divide, part; to burst, crack, bruise; to crush, shatter; to destroy, foil. frustrate; to make bankrupt; to discard, cashier; to weary, impair; to tame, train; to trangress; to dissolve, loosen; to sever by breaking; to tell with discretion.—*vi.* To become broken; of waves, to dash against an obstacle and become surf; to burst; to crack; to become bankrupt; to fail in health, decay; to fall into disorder; to disperse; to deviate; to sever a connexion; to escape forcibly, come out, emerge; to dawn.—*n.*[1] Fracture; the dawn; a gap; an interruption of continuity.—**Break'**AGE, *n.*—**Break'**ER. *n.* In senses from the verb; an ocean wave breaking into foam.—**Break'fast**, *n.* The first meal of the day.—**Break'water**, *n.* A structure protecting a harbour.

Break,[2] **Brake,**[4] *n.* App. f. BREAK, in sense 'to break a horse'. A carriage-frame for breaking in horses; a large wagonette.

Breast, *n.* O.E. *bréost*—Teut. stem *brust-*. Perh. conn. with O.S. *brustian*, to bud. Each of the protuberances on the female chest; the front of the chest; the part of a garment covering this; the affections, private thoughts; various things like the breast.—*vt.* To face, oppose.—**Breast'-plate**, *n.* PLATE. A piece of armour for the breast.

Breath, *n.* M.E. *breth*—O.E. *brǽth*, exhalation, odour, f. Teut. root *brǽ-*, *bro-*, to heat. BREED. BROOD. The air from the lungs; existence, life; a respiration; power of breathing; utterance, speech.—**Breathe**, *vi.* M.E. *brethen*, f. *breth*. Not in O.E. To exhale, or to inhale and exhale, air from the lungs; to live; to pause; to speak, sing.—*vt.* To exhale; to inhale and exhale; to whisper, make known; to express, manifest, evince; to let breathe, recreate.—**Breath'**LESS, *a.*

Breech, *n.* O.E. *bréc*, breeches, *pl.* of *bróc*, in same sense. Common Teut. Trousers (in this sense always in *pl.* **Breeches**); the hinder parts.—*vt.* To put into breeches.

Breed, *vt.* O.E. *brédan*—O.Teut. *brôdâ-*, warmth, hatching, BROOD, f. *bro-*, to heat. BREATH. BROOD. (*Brood, breed*, as *food, feed.*) To produce (offspring); to give rise to, engender; to rear (cattle, &c.); to train, bring up.—*vi.* To be produced.—*n.* The offspring produced, a race, kind.—**Breed'**ER, *n.*—**Breed'ing**, *vbl.n.* Training; good manners.

Breeze, *n.* App. f. O.F. *brise* = F. *bise*, north wind, of unknown orig. Formerly, a north wind. A gentle wind; *fig.*, a quarrel, a whisper, rumour.—**Breez'**Y,[2] *a.*

Breve, *n.* Variant of *bref*, BRIEF. A letter of authority; a summary; *mus.*, a note equal to four minims.

Brevet', *n.* F. *brevet*, dim. of *bref*, BRIEF. A document conferring nominal rank on an officer.

Brev'iary, *n.* L. *breviārium*, a summary, f. *brevis*, short. BRIEF. In the *R. C. Ch.*, a book of the daily prayers.

Brev'ity, *n.* L. *brevitas*, f. *brevis*, short. BRIEF. Shortness, esp. of time; conciseness, terseness.

Brew, *vt.* O.E. *bréowan*. Common Teut. App. f. an O.Teut. root *bru-*, to boil, make a decoction. BROTH. To make (beer, &c.) by boiling and fermentation; applied to other liquids; to contrive, bring about.—*vi.* To be in preparation.—**Brew'**AGE, *n.*—**Brew'**ER, *n.*—**Brew'**ERY, *n.*

Bribe, *n.* App. f. O.F. *bribe*, a piece of bread given to a beggar, of unknown orig. A gift to corrupt the judgement or conduct.—*vt.* To influence by such a gift.—**Brib'**ER, *n.*—**Brib'**ERY, *n.*

Bric'-à-brac, *n.* F., said to be formed after *de bric et de broc*, by hook or by crook. Old curiosities.

Brick, *n.* Prob. f. F. *brique*, quoted in O.F. in sense 'broken piece, bit', app. f. Teut. *brek-*, to BREAK. A rectangular mass of hardened clay; a brick-shaped block; a good fellow.—*vt.* To lay or surround with bricks.—**Brick'bat**, *n.* BAT, *n.*[2] A piece of a brick.

Brid'al, *n.* O.E. *brýd-ealo*, BRIDE-ale, bride-feast. A wedding.

Bride, *n.* O.E. *brýd*. Common Teut. A woman about to be married or just married.—**Bride'groom**, *n.* *Brýd* + *guma*, man, cogn. with L. *homo*. A man about to be married or just married.

Bridge, *n.* O.E. *brycg*. Common Teut. A structure for crossing a river, &c.; a raised narrow structure across a ship; the upper part of the nose; the part of a violin, &c., supporting the strings.—*vt.* To make a bridge over.

Bri'dle, *n.* O.E. *brídel*, for *brigdel*, f. *bregdan*, to pull, twitch. BRAID. The head-gear of a horse's harness.—*vt.* To put a bridle on.—*vi.* To throw up the head like a horse when reined in, expressing resentment, &c.

Brief, *n.* M.E. and O.F. *bref*—L. *breve*, letter, summary, neut. of *brevis*, short. ABBREVIATION. BREVE. BREVET. BREVIARY. BREVITY. A papal letter; a summary for the use of counsel.—*a.* Short in duration; concise, succinct.—**Brief'**LY,[2] *adv.*

Bri'er, Bri'ar, *n.* O.E. *brǽr*, *brér*, of unknown origin. A prickly shrub or bush, esp. the wild rose.

Brig, *n.* Abb. f. BRIGANTINE. Differs from a brigantine in carrying also square sails on the main mast.

Brigade', *n.* F., f. It. *brigata*, troop, f. *brigare*, to brawl, strive after—L.L. *briga*, strife. (See next.) A body of troops; a subdivision of an army; an organized band.—**Brigad**IER', *n.* An officer commanding a brigade.

Brig'and, *n.* O.F., f. It. *brigante*, orig. pres.pple. of *brigare*. (See prec.) A robber, bandit.—**Brig'and**AGE, *n.*

Brig'antine, *n.* F. *brigandin*, f. It. *brigantino*, pirate-ship, f. *brigante*. (See prec.) A two-masted vessel carrying square sails on the fore mast and fore-and-aft sails on the main.

Bright, *a.* O.E. *beorht*. Common Teut. O.Teut. stem *berh-*. Cogn. with L. *flagrāre*, to blaze. Shining, clear; cheerful; of conversation, &c., clever, sparkling; quick-witted, keen.—**Bright'**EN,[2] *vt.*—**Bright'**LY,[2] *adv.*

Brill'iant, *a.* F. *brillant*, pres.pple. of *briller*, to glitter, prob. f. L. *beryllus*, BERYL. Glittering, shining; splendid, distinguished.—*n.* A fine diamond.—**Brill'**IANCE, **Brill'i**ANCY, *nn.*—**Brill'iant**LY,[2] *adv.*

Brim, *n.* M.E. *brimme* of uncertain orig. Cf. O.N. *barmr*, brim; Sw. *bräm*, border. The edge, margin, esp. of a cup, &c.—*vt.* and *i.* To fill, or to be filled, to the brim.

Brim'stone, *n.* M.E. *brimston*, *bremstoon*, f. Teut. *brennan-*, to BURN + *stoon*, STONE. Sulphur.

Brin'dled, *a.* A var. of **Brin'ded**, *a.*, which = *branded*. BRAND. Tawny and streaked.

Brine, *n.* O.E. *brýne*, of unknown orig. Cf. Du. *brijn*, pickle. Salt water; the sea.—**Brin'**Y,[2] *a.*

Bring, *vt.* O.E. *bringan.* Common Teut. To make to come with oneself; to fetch; to procure; to set on foot; to adduce; to cause to come *into, from,* &c. a certain state.

Brink, *n.* M.E. Not in O.E. Prob. f. Scand. Cf. O.N. *brekka* (for *brinka*), a slope. The edge of a steep place.

Brisk, *a.* Orig. uncertain. Active, lively; effervescent.—*vt.* and *i.* To make or to be brisk.—**Brisk'**LY,[2] *adv.*

Bris'tle, *n.* M.E. *bristle, birstle,* dim. of O.E. *byrst,* a bristle. Cf. O.N. *burst.* A stiff hair of the hog, &c.—*vi.* To become stiff like bristles; to raise the bristles, show temper.—*vt.* To erect like bristles.—**Bris't**LY,[1] *a.*

Brit'tle, *a.* M.E. *britul, britil*—O.E. *bréotan,* to break. Easily broken, fragile; frail, unstable.

Broach, *n.* O.F. *broche*—L.L. *brocca,* spike. BROCADE. The same as BROOCH. A spit; a perforation.—*vt.* To pierce (a cask); to tap; to make public, introduce, moot.

Broad, *a.* O.E. *brád.* Common Teut. Wide; extensive, ample; of day, &c., fully come; clear, plain; outstanding; unreserved; indecent; unrestrained; of pronunciation, strongly dialectal; inclusive, general; tolerant.—**Broad'**EN,[2] *vt.* and *i.*—**Broad'**LY,[2] *adv.*—**Broad'side**, *n.* A ship's side; a discharge of all the guns on one side; a single sheet printed on one side.—**Broad'sword**, *n.*

Brocade', *n.* Sp. *brocado,* corresp. to It. *broccato,* bossed stuff, f. *brocca*=O.F. *broche.* BROACH. A fabric richly wrought with a raised pattern.

Broc'ard, *n.* From a Bishop *Brocard's* 'Sentences'. A maxim.

Brochure', *n.* F., f. *brocher,* to stitch. A [pamphlet.

Brogue, *n.*[1] Ir. and Gael. *brōg,* shoe, app. cogn. with O.E. *bróc.* BREECH. A rude shoe.

Brogue, *n.*[2] Orig. unknown. Perh. the same as the prec. from some vague reference to Irish brogues. A strong dialectal pronunciation, esp. of English by Irishmen.

Broil, *v.*[1]*i.* F. *brouiller,* to disorder, corresp. to It. *brogliare,* f. *broglio,* confusion. Orig. unknown. IMBROGLIO. To engage in a brawl.—*n.* A brawl.

Broil, *v.*[2]*t.* Of uncertain origin. App. conn. with O.F. *bruiller,* to boil, roast. To cook on a gridiron; to scorch.—*vi.* To be very hot.

Brok'er, *n.* A.F. *brocour,* agent, orig. 'broacher' or seller of wine, f. L.L. *broccātor,* agent-n. f. *brocca.* BROACH. An agent who buys and sells for others; an intermediary; a dealer in second-hand goods; an appraiser of goods distrained for rent.—**Brok'er**AGE, *n.* The action or remuneration of a broker.

Bron'chial, *a.* G. *brogchia,* the ramifications of the *brogchos,* or windpipe. Pertaining to the windpipe or its ramifications.—**Bronchi**'TIS, *n.*

Bronze, *n.* F. *bronze*—It. *bronzo,* of uncertain orig. An alloy of copper and tin; a work of art in bronze.—*vt.* To make like bronze; to harden. — **Bronzed**, *ppl.a.* Coated with bronze; sunburnt; grown shameless, hardened.

Brooch, *n.* The same as BROACH. An ornamental fastening.

Brood, *n.* O.E. *bród,* f. Teut. root *bro-,* to heat. BREATH. BREED. A family of young, esp. from eggs; a race, species.—*vt.* To cherish.—*vi.* To sit, as a hen on eggs; to meditate moodily *on* or *over.*

Brook, *n.* O.E. *bróc.* Cf. Ger. *bruch,* marsh. A small stream.

Brook, *vt.* O.E. *brúcan,* to use, enjoy (the original sense), cogn. with L. *frui.* FRUIT. To put up with, endure.

Broom, *n.* O.E. *bróm,* cogn. with Du. *brem,* L.G. *braam,* broom. BRAMBLE. A shrub bearing yellow flowers; a brush for sweeping (originally one of twigs).

Broth, *n.* O.E. *broth.* Common Teut. Root *bru-.* BREW. A decoction of meat, often with vegetables.

Broth'el, *n.* M.E. *brothel,* degenerate, a lewd person, f. O.E. *bréothan,* to go to ruin. There was confusion (through the use of *brothel-house,* a resort for the lewdly given) with *bordel*—M.E. and O.F. *bordel,* hut, brothel, f. Teut. *bord,* BOARD, plank. *Brothel* finally replaced *bordel* as the name of the place. A house of ill fame.

Broth'er, *n.*; *pl.* **Broth'ers, Breth'ren**. O.E. *bróthor.* Common Teut. and Aryan. Cogn. with G. *phratēr,* clan-brother; L. *frāter,* brother. A son of the same parents, or having a common parent; one closely united with another.—**Broth'er**HOOD, *n.* The relation of a brother; fellowship; a fraternity.—**Broth'er-in-law**, *n.* The brother of one's husband or wife; the husband of one's sister.—**Broth'er**LY,[1] *a.*

Brougham, *n.* From the name of the first Lord *Brougham.* A one-horse closed carriage.

Brow, *n.* O.E. *brú,* eye-lash, cogn. with G. *ophrus,* eye-brow. The forehead; in *pl.,* its prominences; a projecting edge.—**Brow'-beat**, *vt.* To bear down with looks or words, bully.

Brown, *a.* O.E. *brún.* Common Teut. Aryan type *bhru-.* Cogn. with Med.L. *brūnus,* F. *brun.* BEAVER. BURNISH. Of a colour compounded of red, yellow, and black.—*n.* The colour.—*vt.* and *i.* To make or to become brown.

Browse, *vi.* F. *brouster* (now *brouter*), to nibble off sprigs, f. *broust,* sprig, bud, cogn. (with idea of breaking into bud) with O.E. *bréotan.* BRITTLE. To feed *on* leaves and shoots, often *fig.*—*vt.* To crop and eat these.

Bruise, *vt.* O.E. *brýsan,* to bruise. Influenced by F. *bruisier,* to break, perh. of Celtic orig. DEBRIS. To injure by a heavy blow; to bray, pound.—*n.* A contusion.

Bruit, *n.* F. *bruit,* noise, poss. f. L. *rugīre,* to roar. Rumour.—*vt.* To rumour; to celebrate.

Brunette', *n.* F., fem. of *brunet,* brownish, f. *brun,* BROWN. A woman of a dark complexion.

Brunt, *n.* Orig. unknown. Perh. imitative. The shock (of an attack); the chief stress, crisis.

Brush, *n.* Prob. f. O.F. *broce* (F. *brosse*), brushwood, a brush—L.L. *bruscia,* a thicket, perh. Celtic. Small shrubs in a wood (also **Brush'wood**); a utensil for sweeping (orig. one of twigs); a utensil for painting, colouring, &c.; a bushy tail; a short sharp fight.—*vt.* To clean or to remove with a brush; to graze lightly.—*vi.* Perh. f. F. *brosser,* to dash through brushwood. To be off; to move briskly *by, against, &c.,* anything.

Brusque, *a.* F.—It. *brusco,* tart, sour, of unknown orig. Rough in manner, blunt.

Brute, *a.* F. *brut*—L. *brūtus,* stupid. Lacking reason, stupid; sensual; merely material.—*n.* One of the lower animals; a man like a brute.—**Bru't**AL, *a.*—**Bru'tal**LY,[2] *adv.*—**Brutal**'ITY, *n.*—**Bru'tal**IZE, *vt.*—**Bru't**ISH, *a.*

Bub'ble, *n.* Prob. imitative. Cf. Da. *boble*, Du. *bobbel*. A vesicle of a fluid filled with air; anything unsubstantial, a swindle.—*vi.* To form bubbles; to rise like bubbles.—*vt.* To swindle, cheat.

Buccaneer', -ier', *n.* F. *boucanier*, orig. a hunter, f. *boucaner*, to dry meat, f. *boucan*, a frame for drying flesh, said to be f. Brazilian. A sea-rover, pirate.

Buck, *n.*[1] O.E. *buc* and *bucca*, blended, said to have meant male deer and he-goat respectively. Cogn. with O.F. *boc*, he-goat. BUTCHER. The male of the fallow-deer and other animals; a dandy.—*v.*[1]*i.* Of a horse, to leap up like a deer.—*vt. To buck off.*

Buck, *v.*[2]*t.* M.E. *bouken* as if f. an O.E. *búcian*. Cf. Sw. *byka*, F. *buer*. To steep in lye.—*n.*[2] Lye for steeping clothes, &c.; the quantity of clothes, &c., bucked at once.

Buck'et, *n.* Orig. uncertain. App. f. O.F. *buket*, washing tub. Cf. O.E. *búc*, pitcher. A vessel for water.

Buck'le, *n.* F. *boucle*—L. *buccula* (dim. of *bucca*, cheek), cheek-strap of a helmet, boss of a shield. An instrument to fasten straps, &c. —*vt.* To fasten with a buckle; to warp, bend. —*v.refl.* and *i.* To apply oneself *to*.—*vi.* To warp, bend.—**Buck'ler**, *n.* O.F. *boucler*, f. *buccula*. A small round shield.

Buck'ram, *n.* Orig. unknown. Cf. O.F. *boquerant*, It. *bucherame*. A coarse cloth stiffened with paste.

Bucol'ic, *a.* G. *boukolikos*, f. *boukolos*, herdsman. Pastoral, rustic.—*n.pl.* Pastoral poems.

Bud, *n.* Late M.E. *budde*, *bodde*, of uncertain orig. The first shoot of a leaf, &c.; various things like this.—*vi.* To put forth buds; to develop.—*vt.* To graft by inserting a bud.

Budge, *vi.* F. *bouger*, prob. = It. *bulicare*, to bubble up, f. L. *bullīre*. BOIL, *v.* To stir, move.

Budg'et, *n.* F. *bougette*, dim. of *bouge*, f. Gaulish L. *bulga*, bag. BULGE. A bag; its contents, a collection; a yearly statement of national ways and means.

Buff, *n.* App. f. F. *buffle*, buffalo, f. *būfalus*. (See next.) Leather made from buffalo-, or more usually from ox-hide; buff colour, a dull light yellow.—*a.* Of buff colour.

Buf'falo, *n.* Pg. *búfalo* or It. *buffalo*—Pop. L. *būfalus* (in Literary Latin *būbalus*) —G. *boubalos*, an antelope, a wild ox. The name of several species of large oxen.

Buf'fer, *n.* M.E. *buffen*, to strike, f. *buffe* (see next). Lit., 'a striker'. An apparatus for deadening concussion.

Buf'fet, *n.*[1] O.F. *buffet*, dim. of *buffe*, a blow. Prob. imitative. A blow, usually with the hand.—*vt.* To beat, esp. with the hand; to contend against.

Buf'fet, *n.*[2] F., of unknown orig. A sideboard or cupboard for china, &c.; a refreshment bar.

Buffoon', *n.* F. *buffon*—It. *buffone*, f. *buffare*, to puff. A jester, a maker of grimaces.—**Buffoon'**ERY, *n.*

Bug, *n.* Said to be a transferred sense of obs. *Bug*, a bugbear, hobgoblin, poss. f. Welsh *bwg*, ghost. BOGLE. A small blood-sucking insect.—**Bug'bear**, *n.* App. *Bug* + BEAR, *n.* An object of dread, gen. of needless dread.

Bu'gle, *n.*[1] O.F. *bugle*, wild ox—L. *būculus*, dim. of *bōs*, ox. BOVINE. A hunting-horn (orig. of ox-horn; shortened f. *bugle-horn*); a military brass instrument.—**Bu'gl**ER, *n.*

Bu'gle, *n.*[2] Orig. unknown. A glass bead, usually black.

Build, *vt.* M.E. *bulden*—Late O.E. *byldan*, f. O.E. *bold*, house, conn. with O.N. *búa*. BOND, *a.* To construct (a house, ship, &c.); to construct, frame, in gen.; to found (hope, &c.) *on* a basis.—*n.* Make, form.

Bulb, *n.* G. *bolbos*, onion, bulbous root. The roundish head of an onion, &c.; various things like this.—*vi.* To form a bulb.—**Bul'b**OUS, *a.*

Bulge, *n.* O.F. *boulge*, or Gaulish L. *bulga*, bag. BILGE. BUDGET. An irregular protuberance.—*vi.* To swell out.

Bulk, *n.* M.E. *bolke*, heap, app. conn. with O.N. *búlki*, heap, cargo. A cargo, the whole lot; volume, esp. considerable; a mass; greater part.—*vi.* To appear of weight or importance. —**Bulk'**Y,[2] *a.*

Bull, *n.*[1] M.E. *bole*. Not in O.E.; but the dim. *bulluc*, BULLOCK, occurs. Perh. conn. with BELLOW. The male of cattle; a speculator for a rise in stocks.—**Bull's'-eye**, *n.* Cf. F. *œil de bœuf*. A boss of glass; a lantern glass of this shape, a lantern; the centre of a target.

Bull, *n.*[2] L. *bulla*, in Med.L. sense 'seal'. BILL.[3] BOIL, *v.* Formerly, the Pope's leaden seal; hence, a papal edict.

Bull, *n.*[3] Orig. unknown. A ludicrous inconsistency.

Bul'let, *n.* F. *boulette*, dim. of *boule*, ball, f. L. *bulla*. BOIL, *v.* A ball for loading firearms.

Bul'letin, *n.* F.—It. *bullettino*, dim. of *bulletta*, passport, f. L. *bulla*. BULL, *n.*[2] An official report.

Bul'lion, *n.* Perh. f. F. *bouillon*, a boiling, f. L. *bullīre*, to BOIL, with sense changed into 'melting'. Uncoined gold or silver; solid gold or silver.

Bul'lock, *n.* O.E. *bulluc*. BULL.[1] Formerly, a young bull. A castrated bull.

Bul'ly, *n.* Orig. unknown. An overbearing fellow.—*vt.* To intimidate, overawe.—*vi.* To play the bully.

Bul'rush, *n.* Orig. uncertain. Poss. an attrib. use of BULL[1] + RUSH, *n.*[1] A tall rush.

Bul'wark, *n.* Cf. Du. and M.H.G. *bolwerk*. Poss. Scand., f. the words represented by BOLE + WORK, a work of tree-trunks. A rampart; a breakwater; the raised side of a ship.—*vt.* To protect.

Bum'ble-bee, *n.* Obs. *Bumble*, *v.* (f. BOOM, *v.*[1]) + BEE. A large bee; a humble-bee.

Bump, *n.* Imitative. A heavy blow, dull in sound; a swelling caused by a blow; a prominence.—*vt.* To strike against.—*vi.* To come with a bump *against*.

Bum'per, *n.* Perh. f. prec. with notion of a 'bumping', *i.e.* 'thumping' glass. A glass filled to the brim.

Bump'kin, *n.* Orig. uncertain. A rustic, lout.

Bump'tious, *a.* App. a humorous formation, perh. f. BUMP. Self-assertive, self-conceited.

Bun, *n.* Orig. uncertain. A small sweet cake.

Bunch, *n.* Orig. uncertain. A collection, cluster, 'lot'; part of a dress in folds.—*vt.* To make into a bunch.

Bun'combe, **Bun'kum**, *n.* From *Buncombe* in N. Carolina. Its member insisted, in spite of cries for the 'Question', on making *a speech for Buncombe*, as his people, he said, expected it. Speaking for effect, humbug.

Bun'dle, *n.* Ultimately f. Teut. *bindan*, to BIND. History obscure. A package, parcel. —*vt.* To tie in a bundle; to send *off*, *away*, &c., unceremoniously.—*vi.* To go *off*, *in*, &c., precipitately.

Bung, *n.* Cf. Mod.Du. *bonghe.* Poss. f. L. *puncta*, in sense 'hole'. A stopper for a cask. —*vt.* To stop close.

Bun'galow, *n.* From Hindustani. Said to mean 'belonging to Bengal'. A one-storied house or temporary building, lightly built.

Bun'gle, *vt.* App. imitative. To spoil through want of skill.—*vi.* To work or act unskilfully.—*n.* A blunder, muddle.—**Bun'gLER**, *n.*

Bun'ion, *n.* Orig. obscure. An inflamed swelling on the foot.

Bunk, *n.* Orig. unknown. A box or recess used as bed, esp. on board ship.

Bun'ker, *n.* Orig. unknown. A receptacle for coal, esp. on a ship; a sandy hollow on a golf course.

Bunt'ing, *n.*[1] Orig. unknown. A bird allied to the larks.

Bunt'ing, *n.*[2] Orig. unknown. Stuff for flags; flags.

Buoy, *n.* Corresponds to O.F. *boye*, Du. *boei*, buoy, the same word as O.F. *boie*, chain, L. *boia*, a collar for the neck. A floating mark fixed, us. by a chain, to the bottom; something to keep a person afloat.—*vt.* To keep from sinking, support, raise (us. with *up*); to furnish with a buoy.—**Buoy'ANCY**, *n.*—**Buoy'ANT**, *a.*

Bur, Burr, *n.* Orig. uncertain. App. identical or cogn. with Da. *borre*, bur. A prickly head of a plant (us. spelt *bur*); a rough ridge or edge (us. spelt *burr*).

Bur'den, Bur'then. O.E. *byrthen*, f. stem *bur-* of *beran*, to BEAR. A load; a ship's carrying capacity. Showing confusion with *Bourdon* (F., the continuous bass of the bagpipe=Med.L. *burdo*, *burdōnis*, drone, prob. imitative): the chorus of a song; the chief theme.—*vt.* To load, encumber.—**Bur'densome, Bur'thensome**, *a.*

Bureau', *n.* F., a desk, because covered with *bureau*, O.F. *burel*, a kind of cloth, dim. of *bure*, coarse cloth, baize, of uncertain orig. BOLT, *v.*[2] A writing-desk with drawers for papers, &c.; an office.—**Bureau'cracy**, *n.* G. *-kratia*, rule, f. *kratos*, power. Government by officials; officials collectively.

Bur'gess, *n.* O.F. *burgeis*—L.L. *burgensis*, f. *burgus*, town, cogn. with O.E. *burg*. BOROUGH. An inhabitant of a borough, esp. an inhabitant with full municipal rights.

Bur'glar, *n.* A.F. *burgler*—Law L. *burgulātor*, f. *burgulāre*, to break into a house. Cf. O.E. *burg*. BOROUGH. One who breaks into a house by night.—**Burg'lary**,[1] *n.*

Burlesque', *a.* F.—It. *burlesco*, f. *burla*, ridicule, dim. f. L. *burrae*, trifles. Derisively imitative.—*n.* Grotesque imitation, a mockery; a travesty.—*vt.* To travesty, caricature.

Bur'ly, *a.* M.E. *burli*, of doubtful orig. Stout, sturdy.

Burn, *n.*[1] O.E. *burna*. Common Teut. Primitive sense 'spring, fountain'. A small stream.

Burn, *v.* Two words blended: (1) *intrans.*, O.E. *beornan*, f. Teut. type *brennan-*. BRAND. BRIMSTONE; (2) *trans.*, O.E. *bærnan*, f. Teut. type *brannjan-*, causal of the former. *Intrans.*, To be on fire, glow, literally and figuratively; to shine; to be consumed by fire.—*Trans.* To destroy, consume, mar, harden, by fire.—*n.*[2] An injury or mark caused by fire.—**Burn'ER**, *n.* In an apparatus for lighting, the part from which the flame comes.

Bur'nish, *vt.* O.F. *burniss-*, stem of *burnir*, ger. of *brunir*, to brown, polish, f. *brun*, BROWN. To polish, make to shine.

Burr, *n.* App. imitative. A rough sounding of *r*; a rough pronunciation.—*vi.* To speak with a burr.

Bur'row, *n.* Prob. a var. of BOROUGH in sense 'shelter'. The hole of a rabbit, fox, &c. —*vi.* To make a burrow, hide oneself; to bore, penetrate.

Bur'sar, *n.* Med.L. *bursārius*, f. *bursa*, bag, purse—G. *bursa*, hide, wine-skin. PURSE. A treasurer, esp. of a college.

Burst, *vi.* O.E. *berstan*. Common Teut. To fly asunder or in pieces; to break forth into activity; to issue forth suddenly; to find utterance; to come suddenly *into*.—*vt.* To shatter, rend.—*n.* A bursting; a sudden issuing forth; an explosion; an outbreak, spurt.

Bur'y, *vt.* O.E. *byrgan*, app. f. stem *burg-*. BOROUGH. To put underground, hide away, overwhelm.—**Bur'iAL**, *n.*

Bush, *n.* M.E. *busch*, *busk*—O.N. *buskr*—L.L. *boscus*, wood, of unknown orig. AMBUSH. BOUQUET. A close-growing shrub; woodland. —*vi.* To grow bushy.—**Bush'Y**,[2] *a.*

Bush'el, *n.* O.F. *boissiel*, dim. of *boiste*, Med.L. *buxis*, box. BOX, *n.* A dry measure, 8 gallons.

Busk'in, *n.* Cf. F. *brousequin*, Sp. *borcegui*, It. *borzacchino*, of unknown orig. A half-boot, esp. that of the Attic tragic actors.

Bust, *n.* F. *buste*—It. *busto*, upper part of the body, of unknown orig. A sculptured figure representing the head, shoulders, and breast; the front upper part of the body.

Bus'tle, *vi.* and *t.* Orig. uncertain. To bestir oneself or to hurry (a person or thing) fussily. —*n.* Stir, fuss.

Bus'y, *a.* O.E. *bisig*, active. Cf. Du. *bezig*, busy. Actively engaged; officious, meddlesome; carried on with vigour.—*vt.* and *refl.* To employ, keep busy.—**Bus'iLY**,[2] *adv.*—**Bus'iNESS**, *n.* A task, duty, occupation; work; a piece of work.—**Bus'yNESS**, *n.*

But, *prep.* O.E. *be-útan*, *bútan*, *búta*, lit., without, *be*, by, *útan*, without, f. *út*, OUT. Except.—*conj.* Except; yet, still, nevertheless.

Butch'er, *n.* O.F. *bochier*, orig. goat-killer, f. *boc*, he-goat. BUCK, *n.*[1] One who kills animals for food or sells meat; a bloody or brutal man.—*vt.* To slaughter, murder.—**Butch'ERY**,[1] *n.*

But'ler, *n.* O.F. *bouteillier*—Med. L. *buticulārius*, f. L.L. *buticula*. BOTTLE. BUTT.[1] A servant in charge of the wine-cellar.

Butt, *n.*[1] F. *botte*—L.L. *butis*, *buttis*. BOTTLE. BUTLER. A large cask for wine or ale.

Butt, *n.*[2] Of obscure orig. Cf. Da., Du. *bot*, blunt, short. BUTTOCK. The thicker end of anything.

Butt, *n.*[3] F. *but*, a mark, f. O.F. *bouter*, *buter*, *boter*, to thrust, hit—L.L. *buttāre*, *bottāre*, to thrust, put forth. ABUT. BUTTON. A target; an object of ridicule.—*vi.* and *t.* From *buter*. To strike, shove, esp. with the head or horns.

But'ter, *n.* O.E. *butere*—L. *būtyrum*—G. *bouturon*, prob. Scythian. The fatty substance got by churning cream.—*vt.* To spread with butter; to flatter grossly.—**But'tercup**, *n.* (From the yellow cup-like flowers.)—**But'terfly**, *n.* (The reason of the name unknown.)

But'tock, *n.* BUTT,[2] + dim. *-ock*, O.E. *-uc*. Gen. in *pl.* The rump, posteriors.

But'ton, *n.* O.F. *boton*, bud, knob—L.L. *botto*, *bottōnis*, app. conn. with *bottāre*. BUTT.[3] A knob or stud, esp. one for fastening parts of dress; a bud.—*vt.* To fasten with buttons.

But'tress, *n.* Perh. f. O.F. *bouterez*, *pl.* of *bouteret*, a prop, app. conn. with *bouter*, to push. BUTT.[3]. A structure to support a wall: a prop.—*vt.* To support with a buttress.

Bux'om, *a.* M.E. *buxom, buhsum*, f. stem of O.E. *búgan*, to bow + -SOME. BOW, *v.*[2] Formerly, pliant, tractable. Full of health and good temper; plump, comely.

Buy, *vt.* O.E. *bycgan*, corresp. to Goth. *bugjan*, of unknown orig. To get by payment or for some equivalent.

Buzz, *vi.* Imitative. To make a humming sound.—*vt.* To whisper, rumour.—*n.* A humming noise.

Buz'zard, *n.* O.F. *busart*, said to be f. L. *būteo* in same sense. A genus of birds of the falcon family.

By, *prep.* O.E. *bí* (*big*), *bi, be*, prob. cogn. with L. prefix *am-bi-*, G. *am-phi*, about. Denoting agent, instrument, manner, succession of groups or quantities; at; near; beside; with, through; in; for; according to; at the rate of; not later than.—*adv.* Near, close at hand; aside, out of the way; past, beyond.—**By, bye**, *a.* Out of the way, situated to one side; secondary, incidental, secret.—**By and by**, *advbl.phrase.* App. from the use of the *prep.* to denote succession. Soon, shortly.

By'gone, By'-gone, *ppl.a.* BY, *adv.*, past + *gone.* Elapsed, past.—*n.pl.* Past offences, troubles, &c.

By'-law, Bye'-law, *n.* BY, BYE, *a.*, secondary + LAW. A local law made by a subordinate authority.

By'path, By'-path, *n.* BY, *a.*, out of the way + PATH. A side path.

By'-play, *n.* BY, *a.*, incidental + PLAY. Action carried on aside, esp. on the stage.

Byre, *n.* O.E. *býre*, shed, perh. f. O.E. *búr*, dwelling. BOWER.[1] A cow-house.

By'stander, *n.* BY, *adv.*, near + STANDER. One who stands by, a passive spectator.

By'word, *n.* BY, *a.*, incidental + WORD. A proverb; a person or thing become proverbial.

C

Cab, *n.* Shortened from *cabriolet*—F. *cabriolet*, a light carriage, f. *cabriole*, bound. CAPER.[2] A public one-horse carriage.

Cabal', *n.* F. *cabale*—Med.L. *cabbala.* CABBALA. A secret intrigue; a small body of persons engaged therein.—*vi.* To combine in plotting; to intrigue.

Cab'bage, *n.* M.E. and F. *caboche*—L. *caput*, head. CAPITAL. A well-known vegetable.

Cab'bala, *n.* Med.L. f. Heb. A mysterious Jewish tradition; mystery; secret doctrine.

Cab'in, *n.* M.E. and F. *cabane*—L.L. *capanna*, hut. A hovel; a room in a ship.—*vi.* To live in a cabin.—*vt.* To shut up in narrow bounds.

Cab'inet, *n.* Dim. of CABIN. A repository for valuables; a council-chamber; a body of statesmen.

Ca'ble, *n.* M.E. *cable, cabel* = Du., Ger. *kabel.* Cf. F. *câble*—L.L. *capulum*, halter, perh. f. L. *capĕre*, to take. CAPABLE. A strong rope; a submarine telegraph line; a message sent by such a line (also **Ca'blegram**).—*vt.* To furnish with a cable; to transmit by cable.

Cach'innate, *vi.* L. *cachinnāre, cacchinātum*, to laugh. To laugh loudly or immoderately.—**Cachinna'tion**, *n.*

Cack'le, *vi.* M.E. *cakelen.* Imitative. Cf. Ger. *gackeln.* To make a noise as a hen; applied also to other birds and to persons.—*n.* Cackling; silly chatter.

Caco'phony, *n.* G. *kakos*, bad + *phōnē*, voice, sound. PHONETIC. The quality of having an ill sound; dissonance.

Cac'tus, *n.* L. f. G. *kaktos.* A prickly plant.

Cadav'erous, *a.* F. *cadavéreux*—L. *cadāver*, corpse. Corpse-like.

Cad'die, Cad'dy, *n.* F. *cadet.* CADET. A golf-player's attendant.

Cad'dy, *n.* App. f. *kati*, a Malay weight. A small box for tea.

Ca'dence, *n.* M.E. and F. *cadence*—L. *cadĕre*, to fall. CHANCE. DECAY. The flow of verses; the beat of music; the fall or modulation of the voice; the close of a musical movement.

Cadet', *n.* F. *cadet*, younger brother—L.L. *capitellum*, dim. of L. *caput, capitis*, head. CAPITAL. A younger son or brother; a student in a naval or military college.

Cæsu'ra, *n.* L. *caedĕre, caesum*, to cut. CHISEL. CONCISE. In classical prosody, the division of a foot between two words; in English, a pause about the middle of a line.

Caf'feine, *n.* F. *caféine*, f. *café*, COFFEE. A vegetable alkaloid found in the coffee and tea plants.

Cage, *n.* F. *cage*—L. *cavea*, CAVE, coop, cage, f. *cavus*, hollow. DECOY. JAIL. A box fitted with wires or bars.—*vt.* To put in a cage.

Cais'son, *n.* F. *caisson*, large chest, f. *caisse*, L. *capsa*, a chest. CASE.[2] An ammunition chest; a water-tight case for operations in water; an apparatus for raising sunken ships.

Cai'tiff, *n.* O.N.F. *caitif*—L. *captivus*, CAPTIVE. A despicable wretch.

Cajole', *vt.* F. *cajoler*, of uncertain orig. To prevail upon by flattery or specious promises.

Cake, *n.* M.E. *kake*, prob. f. O.N. *kaka.* Cf. Ger. *kuchen.* A composition of bread with sugar, spices, &c.; fancy bread; a solidified mass.—*vt.* and *i.* To form into a cake.

Calam'ity, *n.* F. *calamité*—L. *calamitas.* Deep distress, misery; a disaster.—**Calam'itous**, *a.*

Calca'reous, *a.* L. *calcāreus* (f. *calx, calcis*, a stone, lime) + -OUS. CHALK. Of the nature of lime; containing lime.

Cal'cine, *vt.* Med.L. *calcināre*, to reduce to *calx*, lime. (See prec.) To reduce to quick-lime by heat; to burn to ashes.—*vi.* To suffer calcination.—**Calcina'tion**, *n.*

Cal'culate, *vt.* L. *calculāre, calculātum*, to count, f. *calculus*, dim. of *calx*, a stone (used in counting). CALCAREOUS. To compute, reckon; to adjust, adapt.—*vi.* To perform calculations; to reckon *upon.*—**Calcula'tion**, *n.*—**Cal'culable**, *a.*

Cal'culus, *n.* L., a stone. (See prec.) A concretion occurring accidentally in the body; a method of calculation.

Cal'endar, *n.* L. *calendārium*, an account-book, f. *calendae*, the first of the month, on which day accounts were due. A table of months and days; a list or register.

Cal'ender, *n.* F. *calandre*—L. *cylindrus*, roller, CYLINDER. A machine with rollers for smoothing or glazing cloth, &c.—*vt.* To pass through a calender.

Calf, *n.*[1]; *pl.* **Calves**. O.E. *cealf.* Common Teut. The young of the cow, also of deer, &c.; leather made from a calf's skin.—**Calve**, *vi.* O.E. *cealfian.* To give birth to a calf.—*vt.* To bring forth (a calf).

Calf, *n.*[2]; *pl.* **Calves**. App. f. O.N. *kalfi*, of

unknown orig. The fleshy hinder part of the shank of the leg.
Cal'ibre, *n.* F. *calibre*, of uncertain orig. The internal diameter of a gun or of any tube; personal capacity.
Cal'ico, *n.* From *Calicut* in India, as first imported thence. Cotton cloth.
Call, *vi.* M.E. *callen*—O.N. *kalla*, to shout, name. Common Teut. To shout, cry; to pay a visit; to stop in passing, as a carrier or ship. —*vt.* To utter, announce; to summon; to convoke; to name, designate; to awaken.—*n.* A shout; the characteristic sound made by an animal; a visit; a passing stop; a summons; a demand, claim; a duty, need.—**Cal'ling**, *vbl.n.* The action of the *v.*; one's occupation.
Callig'raphy, *n.* G. *kallos*, beauty+*graphein*, to write. GRAPHIC. Fine writing or penmanship; handwriting generally.
Cal'liper, *n.* Us. in *pl.* The same as CALIBRE. Compasses for measuring internal diameters.
Callisthen'ic, *a.* G. *kallos*, beauty+*sthenos*, strength. Developing strength with beauty.—In *pl.* as *n.*, callisthenic exercises.
Cal'lous, *a.* L. *callōsus*, f. *callum*, hard skin. Hardened, indurated; unfeeling, insensible.—**Callos**'ITY, *n.* Hardness; a hard lump.
Cal'low, *a.* O.E. *calu*, bald, perh. f. L. *calvus*, bald. Not fledged; inexperienced, raw.
Calm, *n.* M.E. and F. *calme*, of doubtful orig. Stillness, quiet; want of wind.—*a.* Still; windless.—*vi.* and *t.* To become, to make, calm.—**Calm**'NESS, *n.*—**Calm'**LY,[2] *adv.*
Cal'omel, *n.* F., of doubtful orig. A preparation of mercury.
Cal'umny, *n.* F. *calomnie*—L. *calumnia*. CHALLENGE. Slander; a slanderous report. —**Calum'ni**ATE,[3] *vt.* To slander.—**Calumni**A'TION, *n.*—**Calum'ni**OUS, *a.*—**Calum'nious**LY,[2], *adv.*
Ca'lyx, *n.* G. *kalux*, shell, husk, f. *kaluptein*, to cover. The covering of a bud.
Cam'bric, *n.* From *Cambray* in Flanders, as first made there. A fine white linen.
Cam'el, *n.* L. *camēlus*—G. *kamēlos*, f. Semitic. A large ruminant quadruped of W. Asia and N. Africa.
Camel'lia, *n.* After *Kamel*, the botanist. A genus of evergreen shrubs of the tea family.
Camel'opard, *n.* L. *camēlopardus*—G. *kamēlopardalis*, f. *kamēlos*, CAMEL+*pardalis*, PARD. The giraffe.
Cam'eo, *n.* It. *cammeo*, of unknown orig. A stone of two layers of different colours cut in relief.
Cam'era, *n.* L. *camera*, vaulted CHAMBER. Short for *camera obscura*, applied esp. to the form used in photography.—**Cam'era obscu'ra**. L. *obscūrus*, dark. OBSCURE. A darkened box in which an image of external objects is formed.
Cam'omile, *n.* L.L. *camomilla*, G. *chamaimēlon*, earth-apple, f. *chamai*, on the ground +*mēlon*, apple. An aromatic creeping herb.
Camp, *n.* F. *camp*—L. *campus*, field of military exercise. CHAMPION. DECAMP. The place where an army or other body of men is lodged in tents, &c.; an army on a campaign. —*vi.* To form or lodge in a camp.
Campaign', *n.* F. *campagne*—L. *campus*. (See prec.) The continuance of an army in the field; its operations.—*vi.* To serve in a campaign.—**Campaign'**ER, *n.*
Campanol'ogy, *n.* L.L. *campāna*, bell+-LOGY. The art or principles of bell-founding, bell-ringing, &c.

Cam'phor, *n.* F. *camfre*—Med.L. *camphora*, f. Arabic. A whitish aromatic crystalline substance used in medicine.—**Cam'phor**ATE,[3] *vt.* To impregnate with camphor.
Can, *n.* O.E. *canne*. App. Common Teut. A vessel for liquids.
Can, *vi.* O.E. *can*, 1st sing. pres. (orig. preterite) of *cunnan*, to KNOW. CUNNING. KEN. UNCOUTH. To be able; to have the power; to be permitted.
Canal', *n.* F. *canal*, O.F. *chanel*—L. *canālis*. CHANNEL. An artificial watercourse; a duct of the body.
Cana'ry, *n.* From the *Canary* Islands, as first brought thence. A yellow domestic singing-bird.
Can'cel, *vt.* L. *cancellāre*, to cross out (writing), f. *cancelli*, lattice. CHANCEL. To cross out (writing); to annul; to abolish; to make up for.—*n.* The act of cancelling.—**Cancel**la'TION, *n.*
Can'cer, *n.* L. *cancer*, crab, malignant tumour. A malignant growth or tumour.—**Can'cer**OUS, *a.*
Can'did, *a.* L. *candidus*, white, pure, f. *candēre*, to shine. INCENDIARY. Impartial; open, sincere.—**Can'did**LY,[2] *adv.*—**Can'dour**, *n.* L. *candor*, f. *candēre*.—**Can'didate**, *n.* L. *candidātus*, clothed in white (as were candidates for office), f. *candidus*. One who seeks an office, privilege, &c.
Can'dle, *n.* O.E. *candel*—L. *candēla*, f. *candēre*. (See prec.) CHANDLER. A cylindrical body of wax, &c., with a wick.—**Can'dlestick**, *n.*—**Can'dlemas**, *n.* MASS.[1] The feast of the Purification of the Virgin, celebrated with candles; the day, 2nd February.
Can'dy (Su'gar Can'dy), *n.* F. (*sucre*) *candi*—Arab. *qand*, sugar, *qandah*, candy, of Indian orig. Crystallized sugar.—*vt.* To preserve with sugar; to form into or cover with crystals.—*vi.* To become incrusted with sugar.
Cane, *n.* O.F. *cane*—L. *canna*, G. *kanna*, reed, perh. Semitic. CANISTER. CANNON. CANON. The hollow jointed stem of various reeds and grasses; a walking-stick, a rod.—*vt.* To beat with a cane.
Canine', *a.* L. *canīnus*, f. *canis*, dog. HOUND. Belonging to or characteristic of a dog.
Can'ister, *n.* L. *canistrum*, G. *kanastron*, basket, app. f. *kanna*. CANE. A small case.
Can'ker, *n.* O.N.F. *cancre*—L. *cancer*. CANCER. An eating sore; a disease of plants; a destructive insect, a **Can'ker-worm**.—*vt.* To infect, corrupt.—*vi.* To become cankered.
Can'nibal, *n.* Sp. *Canibales*, the man-eating Caribes of the West Indies. A man-eater.
Can'non, *n.* F. *canon*—It. *cannone*, great tube, gun-barrel, f. *canna*, L. *canna*. CANE. A great gun; at billiards, a striking of two balls successively with the player's ball (in this sense app., a perversion (with notion 'heavy shot') of *carambole*, *carrom*—F. *carambole*—Sp. *carambola*, of unknown orig.).—*vi.* To make this stroke.—*t.* and *i.* To strike with rebounding collision.—**Cannonade'**, *n.* An attack with cannon.—*vt.* To attack thus. —*vi.* To discharge cannon continuously.
Canoe', *n.* Sp. *canoa*, the native Haytian name. A rude boat used by savages; a light boat propelled by paddles.—**Canoe'**IST, *n.*
Can'on, *n.* O.E. *canon*—L. *canon*, rule—G. *kanōn*, rod, rule, f. *kanna*. CANE. A rule of the Church; a law, principle, axiom; a standard of judgement; a body of books, &c., accepted

as genuine; the list of acknowledged saints. —From O.E. *canonic*—L.L. *canonicus*. A member of a cathedral chapter.—**Canon'**ICAL, *a.*—*n.pl.* A priest's full robes.—**Can'on**IZE, *vt.* To put in the canon of saints.—**Canoniz**A'TION, *n.*—**Can'on**RY, *n.*

Can'opy, *n.* F. *canapé*—L. *cōnōpēum*, mosquito curtains—G. *kōnōpeion*, a bed with these, f. *kōnōps*, gnat, mosquito. A covering over a throne, bed, &c.—*vt.* To cover with a canopy.

Cant, *n.*[1] Cf. M.L.G. *kant*, border, point, Du. *kant*, Ger. *kante*, border, edge, prob. all f. Romanic; It. *canto*, corner, edge. A slanting face of a bank, &c.; a toss, pitch; a tilting up; a slope, inclination.—*v*[1]*.t.* To bevel; to turn over, tilt up; to pitch.—*vi.* To tilt, to lie aslant.

Cant, *n.*[2] Presumably represents in some way L. *cantus*, singing, f. *canĕre*, *cantum*, to sing. ACCENT. CANTICLE. CANTO. CHANT. INCENTIVE. A whine; the secret jargon of beggars, &c.; professional or technical jargon; a pet phrase; insincere or hypocritical language.—*v*[2]*.i.* To use the language of cant.

Canteen', *n.* F. *cantine*—It. *cantina*, cellar, of doubtful orig. A shop in a camp, &c.; a case with an outfit for cooking, &c.; a small tin vessel.

Can'ter, *n.* Shortened f. *Canterbury* (*gallop*). An easy galloping pace (supposed to designate the pace of mounted pilgrims).—*vi.* To run in a canter.

Can'ticle, *n.* L. *canticulum*, dim., f. *cantus*. CANT.[2] A hymn; applied to parts of the Church Service.

Can'to, *n.* It., f. *cantus*. CANT.[2] One of the divisions of a long poem.

Can'ton, *n.* O.F. *canton* = It. *cantone*, augmentative of *canto*. CANT.[1] A small district. —*vt.* To quarter (soldiers).—**Canton'**MENT, *n.*

Can'vas, *n.* O.N.F. *canevas*—L. *cannabis*, G. *kannabis*, HEMP. A coarse cloth of hemp or flax; used for painting on, hence, a picture.—

Can'vass, *vt.* Formerly, to toss in a sheet. To discuss, scrutinize; to solicit the support of.—*vi.* To solicit support.—*n.* Such solicitation.

Caou'tchouc, *n.* Carib, through F. The juice of certain trees which coagulates on exposure to air, and becomes highly elastic, india-rubber.

Cap, *n.* O.E. *cæppe*—L.L. *cappa*, cloak, cap. CAPARISON. CHAPEL. CHAPERON. A covering for the head, of varying shape and material; various cap-shaped things.—*vt.* To cover with a cap; to outdo, surpass, follow up with something better.

Ca'pable, *a.* L.L. *capābilis*, able to hold, f. *capĕre*, *captum*, to hold, take. ACCEPT. CAPTIVE. Susceptible *of*; having the needful ability or fitness; able, gifted.—**Capa**BIL'ITY, *n.*

Capac'ity, *n.* F. *capacité*—L. *capācitas*, f. *capax*, *capācis*, able to hold, f. *capĕre*. (See prec.) Ability to receive or contain; mental receiving power or ability, talent; possibility; position, character.—**Capac'it**ATE,[3] *vt.* To endow with capacity.—**Capa**'CIOUS, *a.* Roomy, wide.

Capar'ison, *n.* O.F. *caparasson*—Sp. *caparazon*, saddle-cover, f. *capa*, L.L. *cappa*, cloak, cape. CAP. (See next.) A covering for the saddle and harness of a horse; equipment, outfit.—*vt.* To put trappings on, deck.

Cape, *n.*[1] F. *cape*—L.L. *cappa*. (See prec.) CAPE. ESCAPE. A covering for the shoulders.

Cape, *n.*[2] F. *cap*—It. *capo*—L. *caput*, head. CAPITAL. A piece of land jutting into the sea, a headland.

Ca'per, *n.*[1] M.E. *caperis*—L. *capparis*—G. *kapparis*. A prickly shrub; its flower-buds, used for pickling.

Ca'per, *n.*[2] App. abb. f. *Capriole* in same sense—F. *capriole* (now *cabriole*), caper; It. *capriola*, kid, caper—L. *capra*, she-goat. CAB. CAPRICE. A frolicsome leap; a freak.—*vi.* To leap in a frolicsome way.

Cap'illary, *a.* L. *capillāris*, f. *capillus*, hair. Pertaining to hair; hair-like; having a very small bore; pertaining to capillaries.—*n.* A vessel with a very small bore, esp. a minute blood-vessel.

Cap'ital, *a.* L. *capitālis*, f. *caput*, *capitis*, head. CADET. CAPTAIN. CATTLE. CHIEF. Affecting the life; serious, vitally injurious; of letters, of the size used in a leading position; chief, head; main, leading; excellent.—*n.* A capital letter; a chief town; a stock or fund.—From L. *capitellum*, dim. f. *caput*. The head of a pillar.—**Cap'ital**IST, *n.* One who owns accumulated capital.—**Cap'ital**IZE, *vt.* To convert into capital.

Capita'tion, *n.* L. *capitātio*, *capitātiōnis*, poll-tax, f. *caput*, head. (See prec.) The levying of a tax, &c., by the head; the tax, &c.

Capit'ulate, *vi.* L.L. *capitulāre*, *capitulātum*, to draw up under heads, f. *capitulum*, CHAPTER, head, dim. of L. *caput*, head. CAPITAL. To surrender on terms.—**Capitula**'TION, *n.*

Ca'pon, *n.* O.E. *capun*—L. *cāpo*, *cāpōnis*. [A castrated cock.

Caprice', *n.* F.—It. *capriccio*, sudden start, freak, app. f. *capro*, L. *caper*, goat. CAPER.[2] A freak, whim; capriciousness.—**Capri'**CIOUS, *a.*—**Capri'cious**LY,[2] *adv.*

Capsize', *vt.* and *i.* Orig. unknown. To upset, overturn.—**Capsiz'**AL, *n.*

Cap'stan, *n.* Pr. *cabestan*, Sp. *cabestrante*—L. *capistrāre*, to fasten, f. *capĕre*, to take hold of. CAPABLE. An apparatus for raising weights, esp. on board ship.

Cap'sule, *n.* L. *capsula*, dim. of *capsa*. CASE.[2] A dry seed-vessel; a gelatine envelope for a drug.

Cap'tain, *n.* O.F. *capitaine*—L.L. *capitāneus*, f. L. *caput*, head. CHIEF. A chief, leader; the commander of a ship, of a troop of horse, &c.

Cap'tious, *a.* L. *captiōsus*, sophistical, f. *capĕre*, to take. CAPABLE. Apt to catch one, sophistical; apt to catch at faults, cavilling.—**Cap'tious**LY,[2] *adv.*

Cap'tive, *a.* L. *captīvus*, f. *capĕre*, to take. CAITIFF. CAPABLE. Taken prisoner.—*n.* A prisoner.—**Captiv'**ITY, *n.*—**Cap'tiv**ATE,[3] *vt.* To fascinate.

Cap'ture, *n.* L. *captūra*, f. *capĕre*, to take. CAPABLE. Seizure, catching.—*vt.* To seize, catch.—**Capt'**OR, *n.*

Car, *n.* O.N.F. *carre*—L.L. *carra*, L. *carrus*, waggon. CAREER. CARGO. CARICATURE. CARRY. CHARGE. CHARIOT. A wheeled vehicle (chiefly poetic); a tramway carriage.

Car'at, *n.* F. *carat*—It. *carato*. Cf. Sp. *quirate*, f. Arab. *qīrāt*, a weight. A measure of weight used for diamonds, &c.; a proportional measure of one twenty-fourth used in stating the fineness of gold.

Car'avan, *n.* Per. *kārwān*. VAN.[2] A company of merchants, &c., travelling together, esp. in the East; a covered carriage or cart.—

Caravan'serai, -era, -ary, *n.* *Kārwān* + *serai*, inn. A kind of inn in the East where caravans put up.

Car'bine, Car'abine, *n.* F. *carabine*, the weapon of the *carabin* (a word of doubtful orig.), a mounted musketeer. A firearm shorter than a rifle.

Carbol'ic, *a.* *Carb-* (= CARBON) + *-ol* (as in alcohol, &c.) + -IC. In *carbolic acid*, a powerful antiseptic.

Car'bon, *n.* F. *carbone*, coined by Lavoisier f. L. *carbo*, *carbōnis*, charcoal. A non-metallic element found in most organic compounds. —**Car'bon**IZE, *vt.* To convert into carbon.

Car'buncle, *n.* L. *carbunculus*, in both senses below, dim. of *carbo.* (See prec.) A fiery red gem; a malignant inflammatory tumour.

Car'cass, Car'case, *n.* F. *carcasse*—It. *carcassa*, of doubtful orig. A dead body.

Card, *n.*[1] F. *carde*—It. *carda*, thistle, card—L. *carduus*, thistle. An instrument for combing wool, &c.—*vt.* To comb (wool, &c.).

Card, *n.*[2] F. *carte*—It. *carta*, paper, letter, playing-card—L. *charta*, G. *chartēs*, papyrus leaf, perh. Egyptian. CARTEL. CARTOON. CARTRIDGE. CHART. One of a set of small pieces of pasteboard used in various games; a flat piece of pasteboard used for various purposes; the dial of a compass.—**Card'board**, *n.* Pasteboard for making cards, &c.

Car'diac, *a.* L. *cardiacus*—G. *kardiakos*, f. *kardia*, HEART. Pertaining to the heart.

Car'dinal, *a.* L. *cardinālis*, pertaining to a hinge, chief, f. *cardo*, *cardinis*, hinge. Chief, principal; of numbers, 'natural', as distinguished from the ordinal; *cardinal points*, the four chief points of the compass.—*n.* One of the seventy dignitaries composing the pope's council.—**Car'dinal**ATE,[1] *n.*

Care, *n.* O.E. *caru*, *cearu*. Common Teut. (Not allied to L. *cūra*.) CHARY. Anxiety, solicitude; pains, heed; charge, oversight; an object of care.—*vi.* To feel concern; to be disposed *to do*; to have regard or liking *for*.—**Care'**FUL, **Care'**LESS, *aa.*—**Care'ful**NESS, **Care'less**NESS, *nn.*

Careen', *n.* F. *carène*, L. *carīna*, keel. The position of a ship laid on its side.—*vt.* To lay (a ship) over for cleaning, &c.—*vi.* To lie over.

Career', *n.* F. *carrière*, race-course, career—L. *carrāria* (*via*), carriage-road, f. *carrus*, waggon, CAR. A running, course; course of action, height of activity; course through life. —*vi.* To run or move at full speed.

Caress', *n.* F. *caresse*—It. *carezza*—L. *cārus*, dear. CHARITY. CHERISH. A fondling touch or action.—*vt.* To fondle, to pet.

Car'go, *n.* Sp. *cargo*, load—L.L. *carricāre*, to load, cart, f. *carrus*, CAR. A ship-load.

Caricature', *n.* It. *caricatura*, an 'overloaded' representation, f. *caricare*, to load—L.L. *carricāre*. (See prec.) A ludicrous representation by exaggeration of characteristics.—*vt.* To represent thus.

Ca'rious, *a.* L. *cariōsus*, f. *caries*, decay. Decayed.

Car'mine, *n.* Sp. *carmin*, a. f. *carmesí*, Arab. *qirmazī*, CRIMSON. A bright-red pigment got from cochineal; the colour.—*a.* Of the colour.

Car'nage, *n.* F. *carnage*—L.L. *carnāticum*, flesh-meat, f. L. *caro*, *carnis*, flesh. CARRION. CHARNEL. Slaughter, butchery.

Car'nal, *a.* L. *carnālis*, f. *caro*, flesh. (See prec.) Fleshly, sensual; worldly.—**Carnal'**ITY, *n.*—**Car'nal**LY,[2] *adv.*

Carna'tion, *n.*[1] L. *carnātio*, *carnātiōnis*, fleshiness, f. *caro*, flesh. CARNAGE. A rosy pink colour.—*a.* Rose pink.

Carna'tion, *n.*[2] Of uncertain orig. The cultivated pink.

Car'nival, *n.* It. *carnevale*—Med.L. *carnilevāmen*, removal of flesh, f. L. *caro*, flesh + *levāre*, to remove. CARNAGE. The season, devoted to revelry, immediately preceding the abstinence of Lent.

Carniv'orous, *a.* L. *carnivorus*, f. *caro*, flesh + *vorāre*, to devour. CARNAGE. VORACITY. Eating or feeding on flesh.

Car'ol, *n.* O.F. *carole*, a dance with song, of uncertain orig. Formerly, a dance. A joyous song, esp. a song sung at Christmas.—*vi.* To sing joyously.

Carouse', *n.* The obs. *Carouse*, adv. (Ger. *garaus* (*trinken*), (to drink) right out) taken as *n.* in phrase *to drink carouse*. A drinking bout.—*vi.* To drink freely.—**Carou's**AL, *n.*

Carp, *n.* O.F. *carpe*—L.L. *carpa*, of unknown orig. A freshwater fish, gen. bred in ponds.

Carp, *v.* Prob. f. O.N. *karpa*, to brag. Formerly, to speak, to recite. Now (influenced by L. *carpĕre*, to pluck, to slander (CARPET)), to find fault, cavil.

Car'penter, *n.* A.F. *carpenter*—L.L. *carpentārius*, carriage-maker, f. *carpentum*, waggon, app. of Celtic orig. An artificer in wood.

Car'pet, *n.* O.F. *carpite*—Med.L. *carpīta*, thick cloth, poss. f. L. *carpĕre*, to pluck, the fabric being made of shreds. EXCERPT. A floor-covering.—*vt.* To cover with a carpet.

Car'rion, *n.* O.N.F. *caroigne*, app. f. a Romanic type **carōnia*, perh. f. L. *caro*, flesh. CARNAGE. CRONE. Dead rotting flesh.

Car'rot, *n.* F. *carotte*—L. *carōta*—G. *karōton*, poss. f. *kara*, head, top. A vegetable the root of which is edible.

Car'ry, *vt.* O.N.F. *carier*—L.L. *carricāre*. CARGO. To transport, convey; to gain, capture; to extend, continue; to support, sustain; to bring as a result; to import, comprise.—*v.refl.* To behave or conduct oneself.—*vi.* Of a weapon, to be effective to a specified distance.—**Car'ri**AGE, *n.* Carrying, conveyance; a vehicle; cost of transport; behaviour, conduct.—**Car'ri**ER, *n.* One who transports for hire.

Cart, *n.* M.E. *carte*, *cart*, prob. f. O.N. *kartr*, of uncertain orig. A two-wheeled vehicle, properly one without springs.—*vt.* To carry in a cart.—**Cart'**AGE, *n.*—**Cart'**ER, *n.*—**Cart'wright**, *n.* A maker of carts.

Car'tel, *n.* F.—It. *cartello*, dim. of *carta*. CARD.[2] A challenge to a duel; an agreement for exchanging prisoners.

Car'tilage, *n.* F.—L. *cartilāgo*, *cartilāginis*, gristle. A firm elastic tissue, gristle.—**Cartilag'in**OUS, *a.*

Cartoon', *n.* It. *cartone*, aug. f. *carta*. CARD.[2] A drawing as a design for a painting, &c.; an illustration in a journal, esp. one relating to current events.

Car'tridge, *n.* A corr. of *Cartouche*. F. *cartouche*—It. *cartoccio*, a roll of paper, aug. f. *carta*. CARD.[2] A case containing a charge for a firearm.

Carve, *vt.* O.E. *ceorfan*. Common Teut. Prob. cogn. with G. *graphein*, to scratch, write. To cut (a way); to hew, sculpture; to cut, engrave; to cut up (meat, &c.).

Cascade', *n.* F.—It. *cascata*, fall, f. *cascare*, L. *cadĕre*. (See next.) A small waterfall.

Case, *n.*[1] O.F. *cas*—L. *cāsus*, fall, occurrence, f. *cadĕre*, *cāsum*, to fall. CASUAL. CASUIST. An instance; state of matters; condition, plight; a suit, cause; a decided cause; a suitor's grounds of claim; a form in the inflection of nouns, &c.

Case, *n.*[2] O.F. *casse*—L. *capsa*, f. *capĕre*, to hold. CAPABLE. CAPSULE. CASH. ENCHASE. SASH.[1] A receptacle; a box, sheath, covering; a box with its contents.—*vt.* To put into a case; to cover, surround *with*.

Case'mate, *n.* F. *casemate*. Cf. Sp. *casamata*, It. *casamatta*, app. f. Sp. and It. *casa*, house: the second element uncertain. A bomb-proof vault.

Case'ment, *n.* CASE, *v.* + -MENT. A frame forming a window.

Cash, *n.* F. *casse*, box, case—L. *capsa*, CASE.[2] Money; ready money; coin, bank-notes.—*vt.* To give or obtain cash for.—**Cash'-book**, *n.* A book recording cash paid and received.—**Cashier'**, *n.* One in charge of cash.

Cashier', *vt.* Du. *casseren*—F. *casser*, to break, cashier—L. *quassāre*, to break, shatter, freq. of *quatĕre*, to shake, which took the senses of *cassāre*, to annul, f. *cassus*, void, null. QUASH. To dismiss; to discard, cast off.

Cash'mere, *n.* A shawl of wool from *Cashmere* in India; the material.

Cask, *n.* F. *casque*—Sp. *casco*, orig. sense 'husk', conn. with L. *quassāre*. QUASH. A barrel.

Cask'et, *n.* Of uncertain orig. A small case [for jewels, &c.

Cas'sock, *n.* F. *casaque*=It. *casacca*, a horseman's coat, of uncertain orig. A long tunic worn by clergymen.

Cast, *vt.* O.N. *kasta*. Cf. Sw. *kasta*, Da. *kaste*. Not in O.E. To throw; to throw down, defeat at law; to throw off, shed, vomit, discard; to put, place, with haste, decisiveness, force; to put *into prison*; to reckon, calculate, add up; to allot (parts in a play), appoint (actors); to found (metal).—*vi.* *To cast about one*, to look about.—*n.* A throw; a throw of dice; distance covered by a missile; a sample; motion or turn of the eye; a slight squint; form, mould; a tinge, hue, slight degree; sort, kind; something formed in a mould; the actors to whom parts in a play are assigned.

Cas'tanet, *n.* Sp. *castañeta*, dim. of *castaña*, L. *castanea*, CHESTNUT. (From the crackling of roasted chestnuts.) An instrument to produce a rattling sound.

Caste, *n.* Sp. and Pg. *casta*, race, orig. a pure breed—L. *castus*, pure, CHASTE. A hereditary class of society.

Cas'tigate, *vt.* L. *castigāre*, *castigātum*, lit. to keep pure, f. *castus*, pure, CHASTE. To chastise; to punish or rebuke severely.—**Castiga'tion**, *n.*—**Cas'tigator**, *n.*

Cast'le, *n.* O.E. *castel*—O.N.F. *castel*—L. *castellum*, dim. of *castrum*, fortified place. A fortified building; a stronghold.

Cas'tor, *n.*[1] F. and L. *castor*—G. *kastōr*. The beaver; a drug got therefrom; a hat, orig. of beaver's fur.

Cas'tor, *n.*[2] A var. of *Caster*, f. CAST, in sense 'to veer, turn' + -ER. A small vessel with a perforated top for pepper, &c.; a small wheel below a leg of a chair, &c.

Cas'tor oil, *n.* Of doubtful orig. Perh. so named by confusion with the drug CASTOR.[1] A vegetable medicinal oil.

Cas'trate, *vt.* L. *castrāre*, *castrātum*. To deprive of generative power, emasculate.

Cas'ual, *a.* F. *casuel*—L. *cāsuālis*, f. *cāsus*, CASE.[1] Subject to chance, accidental; uncertain; unmethodical.—**Cas'ually**,[2] *adv.*—**Cas'ualty**, *n.* An accident; a loss in war.

Cas'uist, *n.* F. *casuiste*—L. *cāsus*. CASE.[1] One skilled in cases of conscience.—**Casuis'tic**, **Casuis'tical**, *aa.*—**Cas'uistry**, *n.*

Cat, *n.* O.E. *cat*. Common European of unknown orig. O.N. *köttr*; L. *cātus*; Byzantine G. *katta*, *kattos*. CATERPILLAR. CATKIN. KITTEN. A well-known domestic animal; extended to the lion, tiger, &c.; an instrument for flogging.—**Cat'gut**, *n.* Dried intestines (never, however, of cats) used for strings for musical instruments, &c.

Cat'aclysm, *n.* G. *kataklusmos*, f. CATA*kluzein*, to dash down on. A deluge; an upheaval.

Cat'acomb, *n.* F. *catacombe*—It. *catacomba*—L.L. *catacumbas*, of unknown sense and orig. An underground place of burial with excavated galleries.

Cat'alepsy, *n.* G. *katalēpsis*, f. CATA*lambanein*, to seize upon. EPILEPSY. A seizure or trance.—**Catalep'tic**, *a.*

Cat'alogue, *n.* G. *katalogos*, f. CATA*legein*, to pick out, enroll. A systematic descriptive list.—*vt.* To make a catalogue of; to enter in a catalogue.

Cat'aract, *n.* G. *katarrhaktēs*, perh. f. CATA(*r*)*rhēgnunai*, to break down. A large waterfall; a violent downpour; an opacity of the lens of the eye.

Catarrh', *n.* G. *katarrhoos*, f. CATA(*r*)*rhe-ein*, to flow down. An inflammatory discharge from the nose, &c.

Catas'trophe, *n.* G. *katastrophē*, an overturning, f. CATA*strephein*, to turn down, overturn. The final turn of events in a tragedy; ruin; a signal disaster.

Catch, *vt.* O.N.F. *cachier*, O.F. *chacier* (F. *chasser*), to hunt—L.L. **captiāre*, extended f. L. *captāre*, to catch, f. *capĕre*, to seize. CAPABLE. CATER. CHASE. To capture, lay hold of; to ensnare, deceive; to overtake (gen. with *up*); to reach, get to, in time; to surprise, detect; to hit; to seize, grasp; to snatch; to intercept; to incur, take, contract; to apprehend, hear, see; to captivate, charm.—*vi.* To become entangled or fixed; to be communicated, spread.—*n.* A catching; anything that takes hold, stops motion, &c.; a stopping of the breath; an advantage taken or to be gained; a song taken up in parts.

Cat'echize, *vt.* L.L. *catēchizāre*—G. *katēchizein*, f. CAT*ēche-ein*, to din down, din into one's ears, f. *ēchē*, sound. ECHO. To instruct by question and answer; to interrogate.—**Cat'echism**, *n.* A manual of such instruction.—**Cat'echist**, *n.*—**Catechu'men**, *n.* From *katēchoumenos*, pres.pple. pass. of *katēche-ein*. One under such instruction.

Cat'egory, *n.* G. *katēgoria*, accusation, assertion, f. CAT*ēgoros*, accuser, &c., f. *agora*, place of assembly. A general class of terms, &c.; a class or division in gen.—**Categor'ical**, *a.* Belonging to categories; unqualified, unconditional.—**Categor'ically**,[2] *adv.*

Ca'ter, *vi.* From obs. *Cater*, caterer—M.E. *catour*, aphetic form of Anglo-Norm. *acatour*, buyer—L.L. *ac*(=AD-)*captāre*, to CATCH at, acquire. To provide food (also things desired, &c.) *for*.—**Ca'terer**, *n.*

Cat'erpillar, *n.* Poss. f. O.F. *chatepelose*, caterpillar, lit. 'hairy she-cat', f. *chate*, fem. of *chat*, L. *catus*, CAT + *pelose*, L. *pilōsus*, hairy, f. L. *pilus*, hair. DEPILATORY. The hairy grub of a butterfly or moth.

Cathe'dral, *a.* Med.L. *cathedrālis*—L. *cathedra*, G. *kathedra*, seat, f. *kata*, down + *hed-*, to sit. CHAIR. Pertaining to a bishop's throne or see.—*n.* (Orig. *cathedral church*). The principal church of a diocese.

Cath'olic, *a.* G. *katholikos*, universal, f. CATH*olon*, according to the whole, universally, f. *holos*, whole. Universal; affecting all men; having sympathies with all men; of the universal church; applied esp. to that part of the Western Church which is under the Roman obedience; of this church.—*n.* A member of this church or of the universal church.—**Cathol'ic**ISM, **Catholic'**ITY, *nn.*

Cat'kin, *n.* Du. *katteken*, kitten, catkin, dim. of *katta*, CAT. The downy-looking flower of the willow, &c.

Cat'tle, *n.pl.* O.N.F. *catel*—L.L. *captāle*, *capitāle* (in sense 'principal property'), neut. of *capitālis*, principal, CAPITAL. CHATTEL. CHIEF. Live stock (us. of bovine animals).

Cau'dal, *a.* Med.L. *caudālis*, f. L. *cauda*, tail. Of the tail.

Caul, *n.* F. *cale*, small cap, of unknown orig. Formerly, a woman's head-dress. The membrane enclosing the fœtus.

Caul'dron, **Cal'dron**, *n.* A.F. and O.N.F. *caud(e)ron*—L. *caldārium*, hot bath, f. *caldus*, *calidus*, hot, f. *calēre*, to be hot. CHAFE. SCALD. A large kettle or boiler.

Cau'liflower, *n.* Formerly *colyflory*—M.E. and O.F. *col*, L. *caulis*, cabbage + O.F. *flori*, *fleuri*, pa.pple. of *fleurir*, L. *flōrēre*, to flower. FLOURISH. COLE. A cabbage the flower of which forms a white edible head.

Caulk, *vt.* O.F. *cauquer*, L, *calcāre*, to tread, press in, f. *calx*, heel. CAUSEY. To stop up (a ship's seams) with oakum or the like.

Cause, *n.* F. *cause*—L. *causa*, in sim. senses. ACCUSE. BECAUSE. A thing or person producing an effect; reason, origin; reason for action, motive; end, purpose; a suit at law; a movement, claim, &c., which one supports.—*vt.* To effect, bring about.—**Cau'**SAL, *a.* Of, acting as, expressing a cause.—**Causal'**ITY, *n.*—**Causa'**TION, *n.*—**Cause'**LESS, *a.*

Cau'sey, *n.* O.N.F. *caucie*—L.L. *calciāta* (*via*), paved (way), prob. f. *calciāre* (interchanging with L. *calcāre*. CAULK), to tread. Also **Cause'way**, *n.* CAUSEY + WAY. A raised way.

Caus'tic, *a.* G. *kaustikos*, f. *kaiein* (fut. *kausein*), to burn. Burning, corrosive; sarcastic, bitter.—**Caus'tically**, *adv.* -AL. -LY.[2]

Cau'terize, *vt.* L.L. *cautērizāre*—G. *kautērion*, branding-iron, f. *kaiein*. (See prec.) To burn with a hot iron or a caustic substance.—**Cau'ter**Y,[1] *n.*

Cau'tion, *n.* L. *cautio*, *cautiōnis*, heedfulness, f. *cavēre*, *cautum*, to take heed. A warning, hint; heedfulness, care.—*vt.* To warn.—**Cau'**TIOUS, *a.*—**Cau'tious**LY,[2] *adv.*

Cavalcade', *n.* F. *cavalcade*—It. *cavalcata*, f. *cavalcare*, L.L. *caballicāre*, to ride, f. *caballus*, horse. A procession on horseback; a company of riders; a procession.

Cavalier', *n.* F. *cavalier*, It. *cavaliere*, L.L. *caballārius*, horseman, f. *caballus*. (See prec.) CHIVALRY. A horseman; a courtly gentleman, a gallant; an adherent of the king in the Civil War.—*a.* Careless, disdainful.—**Cavalier'**LY,[2] *adv.*

Cav'alry, *n.* F. *cavallerie*, It. *cavalleria*, cavalry, f, *caballārius*. (See prec.) Mounted troops.

Cave, *n.* O.F. *cave*—Pop.L. *cava*, f. L. *cavus*, hollow. Also **Cav'ern**, *n.* F. *caverne*—L. *caverna*, f. *cavus*. CAGE. A hollow under ground.—**Cav'ity**, *n.* F. *cavité*, f. *cavus*. A hollow place, an empty space.

Cave, *vi.* Said to have been introduced by Dutch navvies, and to be properly *calve in*, changed through confusion with prec. Cf. E. Fris. *kalfen*, to calve (as a cow), whence *kalfen in*, to cave in, falling earth being likened to a dropped calf. Of earth, &c., to fall *in* over a hollow; to give *in*, submit.

Caviar', **Caviare'**, *n.* F. *caviar*—It. *caviaro*. The roe of the sturgeon pressed and salted.

Cav'il, *vi.* O.F. *caviller*—L. *cavillāri*, to jeer, criticize, f. *cavilla*, a jeering. To find fault without good reason.—*n.* A frivolous objection; cavilling.—**Cav'ill**ER, *n.*

Caw, *n.* Imitative. The cry of a crow, &c.—*vi.* To utter the cry.

Cayenne', *n.* Brazilian *kyýnha*, *quiýnha*. A pungent red pepper.

Cease, *vi.* F. *cesser*, L. *cessāre*, freq. of *cēdĕre*, *cessum*, to go, give way, give up, CEDE. ABSCESS. ANCESTOR. DECEASE. To give over, desist; to come to an end.—*vt.* To discontinue.—**Cease'**LESS, *a.*—**Cease'less**LY,[2] *adv.*

Ce'dar, *n.* O.F. *cedre*—L. *cedrus*—G. *kedros*. A well-known evergreen conifer; the wood.

Cede, *vt.* F. *céder*—L. *cēdĕre*. CEASE. To give up, surrender, said esp. of a portion of territory.

Ceil, *vt.* Perh. f. F. *ciel*, heaven (L. *caelum*), in sense 'canopy, roof'. CELESTIAL. To construct an inner roof for (a building).—**Ceil'ing**, *n.* An inner roof.

Cel'andine, *n.* With intrusive *n* f. O.F. *celidoine*—L. *chelīdonia*—G. *chelidonion*, f. *chelidōn*, a swallow. (The juice was said to be applied by swallows to the eyes of their young.) The name of two plants with yellow flowers, the Greater and Lesser Celandine.

Cel'ebrate, *vt.* L. *celebrāre*, *celebrātum*, f *celeber*, frequented, honoured by an assembly, famous. To perform duly (a ceremony); to observe solemnly (a festival, &c.); to publish abroad; to praise, extol.—**Cel'ebr**ANT, *n.*—**Celebra'**TION, *n.*—**Celeb'r**ITY, *n.* Fame; a famous or well-known person.

Celer'ity, *n.* F. *célérité*, f. L. *celer*, swift. ACCELERATE. Swiftness.

Cel'ery, *n.* F. *céleri*, perh. f. dial. It. *sellari*, pl. of *sellaro*, repg. G. *selinon*, parsley. A plant the stalks of which are used as a salad and vegetable.

Celest'ial, *a.* O.F. *celestial*—L. *caelestis*, f. *caelum*, sky, heaven. CEIL. Pertaining to the sky or to heaven; divine.

Cel'ibacY, *n.* L. *caelibātus*, f. *caelebs*, unmarried. The state of living unmarried.—**Cel'ib**ATE,[2] *a.* and *n.*

Cell, *n.* O.F. *celle*—L. *cella*, small room. Cf. L. *cēlāre*, to CONCEAL. CELLAR. A small dwelling or room; a minute cavity; a minute portion of protoplasm, the ultimate unit in organic structures.—**Cell'ule**, *n.* L. *cellula*, dim. of *cella*. A minute cell.—**Cell'ul**AR,[1] *a.*—**Cell'ulose**, *n.* Mod.L. *cellulōsus*, full of cellules. A substance forming the solid framework of plants.—**Cell'ul**OID, *n.* Formed loosely f. *cellulose*. A substance like ivory consisting chiefly of cellulose.

Cel'lar, *n.* A.F. *celer*—L. *cellārium*, set of cells, receptacle for food, f. *cella*, CELL. An underground room for storage.—**Cel'lar**AGE, *n.*—**Cel'laret**, *n.* Dim. suff. *-et*. A case with compartments for bottles, &c.

Cement', *n.* O.F. *ciment*—L. *caementum*, unhewn stone, chip, f. *caedĕre*, to cut. CONCISE.

(App. chips mixed with lime; the mortar so formed; mortar generally; and hence): A substance used to bind stones, &c., and setting hard; any substance applied to cause cohesion. —*vt.* To unite with or as with cement.

Cem'etery, *n.* L. *coemētērium*—G. *koimētērion*, dormitory, f. *koima-ein*, to put to sleep. A burial-ground.

Cen'otaph, *n.* F. *cenotaphe*—G. *kenotaphion*, f. *kenos*, empty + *taphos*, tomb. EPITAPH. A sepulchral monument in honour of one whose body is elsewhere.

Cen'ser, *n.* O.F. *censier*, abb. f. *encensier*—L. type **incensārium*, f. *incensum*, INCENSE. A vessel in which incense is burnt.

Cen'sor, *n.* L. *censor*, f. *censēre*, to give an opinion, estimate. A supervisor of morals; an official who examines books or plays before publication or production.—**Censo'r**IOUS, *a.* —**Censo'rious**LY,[2] *adv.*—**Cen'sor**SHIP, *n.* —**Cen'sure**, *n.* L. *censūra*, f. *censēre*. Hostile criticism, blame.—*vt.* To blame.—**Cen'sur**ABLE, *a.*—**Cen'surab**LY,[2] *adv.*

Cen'sus, *n.* L. *census*, a registering, f. *censēre*. CENSOR. EXCISE, *n.* An official enumeration of population.

Cent, *n.* L. *centum*, a HUNDRED, *Per cent*, for, in, to, every hundred; a hundredth part of an American dollar.—**Cen'tenary**, *a.* L. *centēnārius*, consisting of a hundred, f. *centum*. Of or relating to a hundred or a hundred years.—*n.* A hundred years; the celebration of a hundredth anniversary. —**Centena'ri**AN. *n.* One a hundred years old.—**Centen'nial**, *a.* *Centum* + L. *annus*, year. Cf. BIENNIAL. Consisting of or lasting a hundred years; happening every hundred years.—*n.* A centenary celebration. —**Cen'tury**, *n.* L. *centuria*, a hundred things, f. *centum*. A hundred; a period of a hundred years.

Cen'tigrade, *a.* L. *centum* + *gradus*. GRADE. Divided into a hundred degrees.

Cen'tipede, *n.* L. *centipeda*, f. *centum*, a hundred + *pēs*, *pedis*, FOOT. A worm-like animal with many feet.

Cen'to, *n.* L. *cento*, patchwork, cento. A composition made up of scraps by various hands; a rigmarole.

Cen'tre, *n.* F. *centre*—L. *centrum*. ECCENTRIC. The middle point of a circle, sphere, line, &c.; middle point or part in general; an axis, pivot; a nucleus; a point to which things tend, or from which things, influences, &c., proceed. —**Cen'tr**AL, **Cen'tr**IC, **Cen'tri**CAL, *aa.*—**Cen'tral**IZE, *vi.* and *t.* To come or bring to a centre, concentrate.—**Centraliza'**TION, *n.*—**Centrif'ug**AL, *a.* *Centrum* + L. *fugĕre*, to flee. Tending from a centre.—**Centrip'et**AL, *a.* *Centrum* + L. *petĕre*, to seek. Tending to a centre.

Centu'rion, *n.* L. *centurio*, *centuriōnis*, f. *centuria*. CENTURY. A commander of a hundred men.

Ceram'ic, *a.* G. *keramikos*, f. *keramos*, pottery. Pertaining to pottery.—In *pl.* as *n.*, the ceramic art.

Ce'real, *a.* L. *cereālis*, f. *Ceres*, goddess of corn. Pertaining to corn.—*n.* The plants yielding corn or grain (us. in *pl.*).

Cer'ebral, *a.* F. *cérébral*—L. *cerebrum*, brain. Pertaining to the brain.—**Cerebr**A'TION, *n.* Brain-action.

Cer'emony, *n.* O.F. *cerymonie*—L. *caerimōnia*. A sacred rite; a merely formal observance; a usage of courtesy or politeness; formal observances collectively; formality.—**Ceremo'ni**AL, *a.* As *n.*, a series of formalities, a ritual.—**Ceremo'ni**OUS, *a.*

Cer'tain, *a.* O.F. *certain*—L. *certus*, sure, orig. pa.pple. of *cernĕre*, to decide. CRIME. Fixed, sure, settled, trustworthy, inevitable, unfailing; indubitable; having no doubt; a particular, some particular; of some (even if not great) quantity, degree, &c.—**Cer'tain**LY,[2] *adv.* —**Cer'tain**TY, *n.* —**Cer'ti**TUDE, *n.*—**Cer'tify**, *vt.* F. *certifier*—Med.L. *certificāre*, f. *certus* + *-fic-*, for L. *facĕre*, to make. To attest as certain; to declare or attest formally; to inform (a person) certainly.—**Certif'icate**, *n.* F. *certificat*. A document certifying a fact or something relating to the bearer.

Ceru'lean, *a.* L. *caeruleus*, dark blue or green. Pure deep blue, azure.

Cessa'tion, *n.* L. *cessātio*, *cessātiōnis*, f. *cessāre*, to CEASE. Ceasing, discontinuance, stoppage.

Ces'sion, *n.* L. *cessio*, *cessiōnis*, f. *cēdĕre*, to yield. CEDE. A surrender, esp. of territory.

Cess'pool, *n.* Orig. uncertain. A receptacle for sewage.

Chafe, *vt.* O.F. *chaufer*—L. *calefacĕre*, to make warm, f. *calēre*, to be warm + *facĕre*, to make. CAULDRON. To rub to restore warmth; to gall; to vex, irritate.—*vi.* To press with friction *on*, *against*, &c.; to be angry, rage.

Chaff, *n.*[1] O.E. *ceaf.* Cf. Du. *kaf*, L.G. *kaff.* The husks of corn; refuse, worthless matter.

Chaff, *vt.* Perh. a playful use of CHAFE, to irritate. To banter playfully.—*n.*[2] Light banter.

Chaf'fer, *vi.* M.E. *chapfare*, a bargaining—O.E. *cēap*, bargain, price + *faru*, a journey, also business, conn. with *faran*, to FARE. CHEAP. To bargain, higgle.—*n.* Bargaining.

Chagrin', *n.* F. *chagrin*, (1) rough skin; such a skin used for rubbing, &c.; hence (2) 'gnawing trouble', displeasure, ill-humour, &c.—Turkish *saghrī*, rump of a horse, skin prepared from it. SHAGREEN. Vexation from disappointment, mortification.—*vt.* To vex by disappointing, mortify.

Chain, *n.* O.F. *chaeine*—L. *catēna*. CONCATENATE. A series of links forming a ligament; a fetter, bond (gen. in *pl.*); a personal ornament; a sequence; a measuring line; the length of the line, 66 feet.—*vt.* To secure with a chain; to confine, restrain.

Chair, *n.* O.F. *chaëre*—L. *catedra*, *cathedra*. CATHEDRAL. A movable seat; a seat of authority, &c.; a professor's seat, hence, his office; a socket supporting a rail on a railway. —*vt.* To place or carry in a chair.—**Chair'man**, *n.* The president of a meeting; the head of a company or corporate body.

Chaise, *n.* F. *chaise* (= the O.F. form in prec.), a chair, also a chaise. A light carriage.

Chal'dron, *n.* = CAULDRON. A measure used for coals.

Chal'ice, *n.* A.F. *chalice*—L. *calix*. A drinking-cup, esp. that used for the eucharist.

Chalk, *n.* O.E. *cealc*—L. *calx*, lime. CALCAREOUS. A soft white limestone.—*vt.* To mark with chalk; to write with chalk; to sketch or trace *out*.—**Chalk'**Y,[2] *a.*

Chal'lenge, *vt.* O.F. *chalonger*—L.L. *calumniāre*, f. L. *calumnia*, false accusation. CALUMNY. Of a sentinel, to call to account; to object to; to dispute; to claim; to defy, summon to fight.—*n.* The action of the *v.*; a letter containing a challenge.—**Chal'lenge**ABLE, *a.*—**Chal'leng**ER, *n.*

Chalyb'eate, *a.* L. *chalybs*, G. *chalups*, steel. Containing iron.—*n.* A chalybeate spring.

Cham'ber, *n.* F. *chambre*—L. *camera*, G. *kamara*, vault, vaulted room. CAMERA. COMRADE. A room; the meeting-place of a legislative, &c., body; such a body; an artificial cavity for various purposes.—**Cham'berlain**, *n.* O.F. *chamberlain*, *-lenc.* An officer in charge of the apartments of a sovereign or nobleman; a steward.

Chamel'eon, *n.* G. *chamaileōn*, f. *chamai*, on the ground, dwarf + *leōn*, lion. A small lizard-like reptile which can change the colour of its skin.

Cham'ois, *n.* F., prob. f. Swiss Romanic. A goat-like mountain animal; soft leather, orig. made from its skin.

Champ, *vt.* Perh. imitative and conn. with JAM, *v.* To crush and chew with the jaws, munch; to bite upon.—*vi.* To keep biting.

Champagne', *n.* From *Champagne* in Eastern France. A sparkling wine made there.

Cham'pion, *n.* O.F. *champiun*—L.L. *campio*, *campiōnis*, professional fighter, f. L. *campus*. CAMP. A fighting man; one who fights for another or maintains a cause; one holding a first place by contest.—*vt.* To fight for, maintain.—**Cham'pion**SHIP, *n.*

Chance, *n.* O.F. *cheance*—L.L. *cadentia*, a falling, f. L. *cadĕre*. CADENCE. Fortune; a casual circumstance; an opportunity; a possibility or probability; absence of assignable cause.—*a.* Casual.—*vi.* To happen.

Chan'cel, *n.* O.F.—L.L. *cancellus*, f. L. *cancelli*, bars of lattice-work (the sense extended to a place enclosed). CANCEL. The eastern part of a church screened off from the rest.

Chan'cellor, *n.* O.F. *chancelier*—L. *cancellārius*, an usher stationed at the *cancelli* or bar of a court. (See prec.) Formerly, an official secretary; now applied to high officers of state, esp. the Lord Chancellor and the Chancellor of the Exchequer.—**Chan'cellor**SHIP, *n.*—**Chan'cery**, *n.* A worn-down form of *Chancell*ERY, f. *chancelier*. The court of the Lord Chancellor.

Chand'ler, *n.* O.F. *chandelier*—L.L. *candēlārius*, candle-seller, f. L. *candēla*, CANDLE. A retail dealer in provisions, groceries, &c.

Change, *vt.* O.F. *changer*—L.L. *cambiāre*—L. *cambīre*, to exchange, barter. To substitute something else for; to quit for another state or thing; to give or receive another kind of money for; to exchange, interchange; to alter, vary.—*vi.* To be altered.—*n.* Variation, alteration; conversion of money; small money; balance of money received on a payment.—**Change'**ABLE, *a.*—**Change'**FUL, *a.*—**Change'ling**, *n.* -LING (1). A child secretly substituted for another.

Chan'nel, *n.* M.E. *chanel*, *canel*—O.F. *chanel*. CANAL. KENNEL.[2] The bed of running waters; a water-course; a narrow piece of water connecting two larger pieces; line of action, thought, &c.; means, agency.—*vt.* To form channels in; to cut into a channel; to convey as a channel does.

Chant, *vi.* and *t.* F. *chanter*—L. *cantāre*, freq. of *canĕre*, to sing. CANT.[2] SHANTY.[2] To sing, warble.—*n.* A song; a short melody used in churches for canticles, &c.; a canticle, &c.

Chan'ticleer, *n.* O.F. *chantecler*, name of the Cock in *Reynard the Fox*, f. *chanter*, to sing, crow + *cler* (F. *clair*), clear. A cock.

Cha'os, *n.* G. *chaos*, empty space. CHASM. The primordial abyss; utter confusion; a confused mass.—**Chaot'**IC, *a.*

Chap, *vt.* Of unknown orig. CHOP, *v.*[1] Of the skin, to cause (it) to crack.—*vi.* To burst into cracks.—*n.*[1] A crack in the skin.

Chap, *n.*[2] See CHOP, *n.*[2]

Chap'el, *n.* O.F. *chapele*—L.L. *cappella*, orig. dim. of *cappa*, cloak, cape. CAP. (The *cappella* or cloak of St. Martin was kept as a relic by the Frankish kings. Hence the name was applied to its sanctuary, and then to a sanctuary in general.) A place of worship not a parish or cathedral church; a private place of worship.—**Chap'lain**, *n.* O.F. *chapelain*, f. *cappella*. The clergyman of a chapel; a clergyman attached to a ship, garrison, prison, &c.—**Chap'lain**CY, *n.*

Chap'eron, *n.* F. *chaperon*, hood—O.F. *chape*, cape, head-dress—L.L. *cappa*. CAP. A married lady accompanying a young unmarried lady in public as protector.—*vt.* To act as chaperon to.

Chap'let, *n.* O.F. *chapelet*, dim. of *chape*. (See prec.) A wreath; a rosary.

Chap'ter, *n.* O.F. *chapitre*—L. *capitulum*, dim. of *caput*, *capitis*, head. CAPITULATE. A section of a book; a meeting of the canons of a cathedral or of the members of an order; the body of canons collectively.

Char, *vt.* App. taken from the first element of CHARCOAL. To make charcoal of, to burn partially.

Char'acter, *n.* L. *charactēr*—G. *charaktēr*, marking tool, mark, f. *charassein*, to cut into, engrave. A mark; a symbol for a sound; a set of letters; handwriting; a feature, trait; nature, kind; mental or moral constitution; good character; estimate, repute; a testimonial; status, position; a personage, a personality.—**Characteris'tic**, *a.* -IST. -IC. Displaying character.—*n.* A distinctive trait.—**Characteris'tical**LY,[2] *adv.*—**Char'acter**IZE, *vt.* To describe the character of; to be a characteristic of.

Charade', *n.* F., of doubtful orig. A riddle upon the syllables of a word.

Char'coal, *n.* *Char*, of uncertain orig. + COAL. The black substance obtained by the imperfect combustion of wood, bones, &c.

Chare, *n.* O.E. *cerr*, a turn. AJAR. A turn of work, odd job.—*vi.* To do odd jobs.—**Char'woman**, *n.*

Charge, *vt.* O.F. *charger*—L.L. *carricāre*, to load, f. L. *carrus*, waggon. CAR. To fill (a vessel, &c.) *with*; to fill, furnish fully; to load (a firearm); to burden, commission *with*; to order, enjoin; to deliver official instruction to (a jury, &c.); to blame, accuse; to impute (as a fault); to subject to liability; to ask as a price *for*; to put as a charge *to* or *against*; to put (a weapon) in position; to attack impetuously.—*n.* The load of a firearm; the quantity which a receptacle, machine, &c., can take in, bear, &c.; a burden, weight; a price asked; an expense; a liability; a task, duty, responsibility; something entrusted; an order; official instruction; accusation; an impetuous attack.—**Charge'**ABLE, *a.*—**Charg'**ER, *n.* An officer's horse; a large flat dish (in this sense poss. f. O.F. *chargeoir, utensil for loading).

Char'iot, *n.* O.F., aug. of *char*, car, f. L. *carrus*. CAR. A car of state; a war-car.—**Chariot**EER', *n.*

Char'ity, *n.* O.F. *charité*—L. *cāritas*, love, f. *cārus*, dear. CARESS. CHERISH. Love, kindness, natural affection; leniency, fair-mindedness; practical beneficence, alms-giving; alms; a bequest, foundation.—**Char'it**ABLE, *a.*—**Char'itab**LY,[2] *adv.*

Char'latan, *n.* F.—It. *ciarlatano*, babbler, mountebank, f. *ciarlare* (prob. imitative), to babble. An impostor in medicine; in general, a pretentious impostor.

Charm, *n.* F. *charme*—L. *carmen*, song, incantation. A magic spell; something worn to avert evil; a fascinating attribute; attractiveness.—*vt.* To bewitch; to fortify against evil; to soothe; to fascinate.—**Charm'**ER, *n.*

Char'nel, *n.* O.F., in same sense—L.L. *carnāle*, app., 'larder', f. L. *caro*, flesh. CARNAGE. A place for the dead or their bones.—So **Char'nel-house**, *n.*

Chart, *n.* O.F. *charte*, card, map, &c.—L. *charta*. CARD.[2] A sea-map; a graphical representation.—*vt.* To make a chart of, to lay down in a chart.

Char'ter, *n.* O.F. *chartre*—L. *cartula*, charter, dim. of *charta*. (See prec.) A document granting privileges or incorporating a borough, &c.; a written evidence or contract.—*vt.* To grant a charter to; to privilege, license.

Cha'ry, *a.* O.E. *cearig*, full of care, f. *cearu*, CARE. Formerly, sorrowful. Careful, wary; careful, sparing *of*; fastidious.—**Cha'ri**LY,[2] *adv.*—**Cha'ri**NESS, *n.*

Chase, *v.*[1]*t.* O.F. *chacier*. CATCH. To pursue; to hunt; to drive forcibly *from*, *into*, &c.—*n.* Pursuit, hunting; a hunting-ground; the thing chased.

Chase, *v.*[2]*t.* Short for ENCHASE. To adorn with embossed work; to engrave.

Chasm, *n.* L. *chasma*, G. *chasma*, yawning hollow, f. *chaskein*, to gape, cogn. with *chaos*, and with L. *hiāre*. CHAOS. HIATUS. A deep rent or cleft; a gap, break.

Chaste, *a.* O.F. *chaste*—L. *castus*, pure. CASTE. CASTIGATE. Continent; stainless; modest; pure in style.—**Chaste'**LY,[2] *adv.*—**Chas'ti**TY, *n.*—**Chas't**EN,[2] *vt.* To punish; to make chaste; to moderate.—**Chastise'**, *vt.* O.F. *chastier*, f. *castus*. In same senses. —**Chas'tise**MENT, *n.*

Chat, *vi.* App. shortened f. CHATTER. To talk lightly and familiarly.—*n.* Such talk.—**Chat't**Y,[2] *a.*

Chat'tel, *n.* O.F. *chatel*—L.L. *captāle*, in sense 'goods'. CATTLE. A movable possession (gen. in *pl.*).

Chat'ter, *vi.* Imitative. To utter short sounds rapidly; to talk rapidly and idly; of the teeth, to shiver, shake.—*n.* Idle talk.

Cheap, *a.* Shortened f. adj. phrase *good cheap*, low-priced—M.E. *chep*, *cheep*, O.E. *céap*, bargain, price. Common Teut. CHAFFER. Costing little; supplying commodities at small cost; well worth the price; easily got; paltry, little esteemed.—**Cheap'**LY,[2]*adv.*—**Cheap'**EN,[2] *vt.* To bargain for; to make cheap.

Cheat, *vt.* Short for ESCHEAT. Formerly, to confiscate. To deprive *of* by deceit, defraud; to impose upon, trick.—*vi.* To practise deceit.—*n.* A fraud, trick; a swindler.

Check, *int.* O.F. *eschec*, a check at chess—Per. (through Arab.) *shāh*, SHAH, king, king at chess. CHESS. CHEQUE. CHEQUER. A call at chess intimating that the adversary's king is in danger—'King!', 'Mind your king!'—*n.* A threatening the king at chess; a rebuff, repulse; a sudden stoppage; restraint; a stop or restraint; a token, a ticket; a mark showing that an item in an account has been found correct.—*vt.* To stop; to repress, restrain; to curb, control; to examine to ensure accuracy. —**Check'mate**, *int.* O.F. *eschec mat*—Arab. *shāh-māt*, the king is dead. An intimation that the king is in inextricable check.—*n.* The move effecting this (often *fig.*).—*vt.* To defeat, frustrate.

Ched'dar, *n.* From *Cheddar* in Somersetshire. A rich cheese.

Cheek, *n.* O.E. (Anglian) *céce*. Cf. M.L.G. *kāke*, Du. *kaak*. The side of the face below the eye; insolence, effrontery.

Cheer, *n.* O.F. *chiere*, L.L. *cara*, face, of uncertain orig. Formerly, the face. Mood, frame of mind; mirth, joy; viands, fare; comfort; a shout of welcome, approval, &c.—*vt.* To comfort, solace; to gladden; to encourage, esp. by shouts, applaud.—*vi.* To shout applause.—**Cheer'**FUL, **Cheer'**Y,[2]*aa.*—**Cheer'ful**LY,[2] **Cheer'**ILY,[2] *advv.*—**Cheer'**LESS, *a.*

Cheese, *n.* O.E. (Anglian) *cése*—L. *cāseus*. The curd of milk coagulated and pressed into a mass.—**Cheese'monger**, *n.* MONGER. One who deals in cheese, butter, &c.

Chemise', *n.* O.F.—L.L. *camisia*, *camisa*, shirt, of uncertain orig. An undergarment worn by women.

Chem'ist, *n.* F. *chimiste*—Mod.L. *chimista*, shortened f. Med.L. *alchimista*, f. Arab. *al-kimia*, ALCHEMY. One versed in chemistry; a seller of drugs.—**Chem'ist**RY, *n.* The science which deals with the elementary substances composing matter.—**Chem'**ICAL, *a.*

Cheque, *n.* An altered spelling of CHECK, *n.*, in sense 'something indicating verification'. Formerly, a counterfoil. A written order to a banker.

Cheq'uer, Check'er, *n.* M.E. *cheker*, aphetic f. *escheker*—O.F. *eschekier*—L.L. *scaccārium* chess-board, f. *scacci*, CHESS. EXCHEQUER Marking like that of a chess-board; in *pl.* squares like those of a chess-board.—*vt.* To mark like a chess-board; to variegate.

Cher'ish, *vt.* F. *chérir*, f. *cher*, L. *cārus*, dear. CARESS. To treat tenderly; to encourage (a hope, &c.).

Cher'ry, *n.* O.North.F. *cherise* (taken for a *pl.*)—L. *cerasus*, G. *kerasos*, cherry-tree, said to have been brought from *Cerasos* in Pontus. A well-known stone-fruit.

Cher'ub, *n.*; *pl.* **Cher'ubs, Cher'ubim**. O.E. *cherubin*, through F., L., and G. f. Heb. *k'rūb*, pl. *k'rūbim*, of unknown derivation. In extant use, an angel of the second order.—**Cherub'**IC, *a.*

Chess, *n.* O.F. *eschès*, pl. of *eschec*, CHECK. Cf. L.L. *scacci*, It. *scacchi*, both *pl.* A game for two played with 32 pieces on a board with 64 squares.—**Chess'-board**, *n.*

Chest, *n.* O.E. *cest*—L. *cista*, G. *kistē*. CIST. CISTERN. A box; a coffer; a treasury, the money therein; the upper part of the trunk of the body.—*vt.* To put in a chest.

Chest'nut, *n.* From obs. *Chesteine*, *Chesten*, the tree (O.F. *chastaigne*—L. *castanea*, the tree, the nut, f. G. *kastanon*, the nut, prob. f. Armenian) + NUT. CASTANET. A large nut of a deep reddish-brown; the tree bearing it.

Chew, *vt.* O.E. *céowan*. Cf. O.H.G. *chiuwan*. To grind with the teeth, masticate.

Chicane', Chica'nery, *nn.* F. *chicane*, *chicanerie*, of doubtful orig. Legal trickery, quibbling.—**Chicane'**, *vi.* To quibble.—*vt.* To quibble over; to overreach by chicanery.

Chick, *n.* Shortened f. **Chick'en**, *n.* O.E. *cicen*. Cf. Du. *kicken*. The young of the hen.

Chic'ory, *n.* F. *cichorée*—L. *cichorium*—G. *kichora*, pl. A plant the root of which is ground and roasted as an addition to coffee.

Chide, *vt.* O.E. *cidan*. Not elsewhere in

Teut. To scold, rebuke; applied to various sounds.

Chief, *n.* O.F. *chef*, L. *caput*, head. ACHIEVE. CATTLE. KERCHIEF. A leader, ruler.—*a.* Taking the first place; principal, foremost, leading.—**Chief**LY,[2] *adv.*—**Chief'tain**, *n.* O.F. *chevetaine*—L.L. *capitāneus*, f. *caput.* CAPTAIN. The chief of a clan or tribe.

Chil'blain, *n.* A BLAIN caused by a CHILL.

Child, *n.*; *pl.* **Chil'dren**. O.E. *cild.* Cf. Goth. *kilthei*, womb. An infant; a boy or girl; a son or daughter.—**Child'**ISH, **Child'**LESS, *aa.*—**Child'bed**, *n.* The state of a woman in labour.

Chill, *n.* O.E. *cele, ciele.* O.Teut. stem *kal-*, to be COLD. Coldness seizing upon the body; coldness of the air, &c.; something dispiriting. —*a.* Unpleasantly cold; shivering; dispiriting. —*vi.* To become cold.—*vt.* To make cold; to dispirit.—**Chil'l**Y,[2] *a.*—**Chil'l**INESS, *n.*

Chime, *n.* App. derived in some way f. L. *cymbalum*, CYMBAL. A set of church-bells; the sound of bells in harmony.—*vt.* To strike (a bell).—*vi.* To ring harmoniously; to agree, harmonize; *to chime in*, to strike into a conversation as expressing agreement.

Chime'ra, *n.* F. *chimère*—G. *chimaira*, she-goat. A fabled monster, part lion, part goat, part serpent; a horrible phantasm; a wild fancy.—**Chimer'**ICAL, *a.* Fanciful, visionary.

Chim'ney, *n.* O.F. *cheminée*—L.L. *camīnāta*, f. L. *caminus*, G. *kaminos*, furnace. A passage for smoke; a glass funnel for a lamp.

Chin, *n.* O.E. *cin.* Cogn. with L. *gena*, cheek, G. *genus*, jaw. The point of the lower jaw.

Chi'na, *n.* Fine earthenware, orig. from *China.*

Chink, *n.*[1] Orig. unknown. A cleft, crack.

Chink, *n.*[2] Imitative. The sound of pieces of metal, &c., striking each other; coin.—*vi.* To emit a chink.—*vt.* To cause to do so.

Chintz, *n.* Orig. *chints*, pl. of *chint*, Hindī *chīnt*, f. Skr. *chitra*, variegated. Cotton cloth printed with designs in a number of colours.

Chip, *v.* App. related (with a lighter vowel as expressing a less degree of action) to CHOP, *v.*[1] To break off fragments from; to shape thus; to break off (fragments).—*n.* A fragment broken off.

Chirop'odist, *n.* App. f. G. *cheir*, hand + *pous, podos*, foot. One who treats the hands and feet.

Chirp, *vi.* Imitative. To utter a short sharp thin sound, as a bird.—*n.* The sound.

Chis'el, *n.* O.N.F. *chisel*, Cent. O.F. *cisel*—L.L. **cīsellum*—L. *caedĕre*, to cut. CÆSURA. SCISSORS. A cutting tool with the edge across the axis.—*vt.* To cut with a chisel; to cheat. (The history of the last sense is obscure.)

Chiv'alry, *n.* O.F. *chevalerie*—L.L. *caballārius.* CAVALIER. Horsemen; gallant gentlemen; the feudal knightly system; brave, honourable, and courteous character.—**Chiv'al**RIC, **Chiv'al**ROUS, *aa.*

Chlo'rine, *n.* With chemical suff. *-ine*, f. G. *chlōros*, yellowish green. A yellowish-green gas, one of the elements.

Chlo'roform, *n.* From prec. and *formic* acid, formerly obtained from red ants—L. *formica*, ant. A liquid used as an anæsthetic.

Choc'olate, *n.* Sp. *chocolate*—Mexican *chocolatl.* Not allied to *cacao.* (See COCOA.[2]) A paste of the seeds of the cacao-tree; a beverage made from the paste.—*a.* Of the colour of chocolate, dark brown.

Choice, *n.* O.F. *chois*, f. *choisir*, to choose. Teut. Cf. Goth. *kiusan*, to CHOOSE. A choosing; the power of choosing, option; something specially chosen; scope for choice; an alternative.—*a.* Exquisite; well-chosen, fit.

Choir, Quire, *n.* O.F. *cuer*—L. *chorus*, company of dancers (in Med.L., body of singers in a church, their place)—G. *choros*, company of dancers. CHORUS. A body of singers in a church; the part appropriated to them; a body of singers in general.

Choke, *vt.* M.E. *choke, cheke*, of doubtful orig. Not elsewhere in Teut. To throttle; of anything which blocks up the windpipe; to smother, stifle; to close (a tube, &c.); to congest.—*vi.* To suffer choking.—*n.* The action and noise of choking.

Chol'er, *n.* O.F. *colre, colère*—L. *cholera*, G. *cholera*, CHOLERA, of doubtful orig. App. f. *cholē*, bile. The L. term was used also in sense 'bile', 'bitter anger'. Bile, biliousness; anger, wrath.—**Chol'er**IC, *a.*

Chol'era, *n.* L. (See prec.) A disorder characterized by vomiting, purging, and cramps.

Choose, *vt.* O.E. *céosan.* Cf. Du. *kiesen*, Goth. *kiusan.* Cogn. with. G. *geuesthai*, L. *gustāre*, to taste, L. *gustus*, taste. CHOICE. GUST.[2] To take by preference, select; to think fit *to do.*—*vi.* To exercise choice.

Chop, *v.*[1]*t.* Another form of CHAP, *v.* App. related to CHIP. To cut with a hewing instrument; to cut into pieces.—*n.*[1] A hewing blow; a slice of meat.

Chop, *v.*[2]*i.* Of doubtful orig. Formerly, to barter. In phrase *to chop and change* (the meaning of *chop* having passed to 'to change, alter'), to change about, be inconstant. Sim. *chop* alone, esp. of the wind.—*vt.* To exchange or bandy (words), esp. in *to chop logic*, to bandy logic, argue.—**Chop'p**Y,[2] *a.* Of the sea, breaking in short waves.

Chop, *n.*[2] Also **Chap.** Orig. unknown. In [*pl.*, the jaws.

Chord, *n.*[1] A 16th cent. refashioning of CORD. A string of a musical instrument; a straight line joining the ends of an arc.

Chord, *n.*[2] Orig. *Cord*, aphetic f. ACCORD, *n.* A combination of musical notes.

Cho'rus, *n.* L. *chorus.* CHOIR. A band of singers; something sung or uttered by many at once; the refrain of a song.—**Cho'r**IC, *a.*—

Chor'ister, *n.* A.F. *cueristre* — Med.L. *chorista*, f. *chorus.* A member of a choir.

Chrism, *n.* O.E. *crisma*—L. *chrisma*, G. *chrisma*, an anointing, f. *chriein*, to anoint. CREAM. Consecrated oil mingled with balm.

Chris'ten, *vt.* O.E. *cristnian*, lit., 'to make Christian', f. *cristen*, Christian. To baptize; to name.—**Chris'tendom**, *n.* O.E. *cristendóm*, f. *cristen* + *-dóm*, -DOM. The Church; the countries professing Christianity collectively.

Christ'ian, *a.* L. *Christiānus*, f. *Christus*, G. *Christos*, Christ, the anointed, f. *chriein.* CHRISM. Following Christ; pertaining to Christ or his religion; *Christian name*, that given at baptism.—*n.* A follower of Christ.—**Christian'**ITY, *n.* The religion of Christ; Christian condition or spirit.—**Christ'ian**IZE, *vt.*—**Christ'mas**, *n.* O.E. *cristes mæsse*, Christ's festival, f. *Crist*, Christ + *mæsse.* MASS.[1] The festival of Christ's nativity.

Chromat'ic, *a.* G. *chrōmatikos*, f. *chrōma*, colour. Relating to colour; *chromatic scale*, a scale proceeding by semitones.

Chron'ic, *a.* F. *chronique*—G. *chronikos*, relating to time, f. *chronos*, time. Of diseases, long-continued; gen., continuous, constant.—

Chron'icle, *n.* A.F. *cronicle*—G. *chronika* (neut. pl. of *chronikos*), annals. An historical record.—*vt.* To record.—**Chron'icl**ER, *n.*—**Chrono**L'OGY, *n.* The science of dates.—**Chronolog'**ICAL, *a.*—**Chronol'og**IST, *n.*—**Chronom'eter**, *n. Chronos* + G. *metre-ein*, to measure. An instrument for measuring time very accurately.

Chrys'alis, *n.* G. *chrusallis*, the gold-coloured sheath of butterflies, f. *chrusos*, gold. The form of an immature insect in its sheath; the sheath.

Chub, *n.* M.E. *chubbe*, of unknown orig. A thick fat river fish.—**Chub'b**Y,[2] *a.* Round-faced, plump.

Chuck, *n.*[1] Imitative. Cf. CLUCK. The noise of a hen calling her chickens.—*v.*[1]*i.* To make the noise.

Chuck, *v.*[2]*t.* Of uncertain orig. Cf. F. *choquer*, to shock, knock. To tap under the chin; to toss, throw.—*n.*[2] A tap under the chin; a toss, a throw.

Chuck'le, *vi.* CHUCK, *v.*[1] + freq. suff. *-le.* To laugh in a suppressed manner.—*n.* Such a laugh.

Church, *n.* M.E. *chirche*—O.E. *circe*, perh. f. G. *kuriakon*, Lord's house, neut. of *kuriakos*, a. f. *kurios*, lord. A building for Christian worship; the Christian community; an organized Christian society; the body of clergy; the clerical profession.—*vt.* To give in church thanks on behalf of (a woman) after childbirth.—**Churchwar'den**, *n.* A lay officer managing various church affairs.—**Church'yard**, *n.* A burial ground by a church.

Churl, *n.* O.E. *ceorl*, one of the lowest rank of freemen. Cf. Sw. and Da. *karl*, man, freeman. A rustic; a low-bred fellow; a niggard.—**Churl'**ISH, *a.*

Churn, *n.* O.E. *cyrin.* Common Teut. A vessel for making butter.—*vt.* To agitate (cream) in a churn to make butter.

Cic'atrice, *n.* F., f. L. **Cica'trix**. A scar.—**Cic'atr**IZE, *vt.* To induce a scar upon (a wound); to mark with a scar.—*vi.* To become cicatrized.

Cicero'ne, *n.* It., f. *Cicero*, app. referring to his learning. A guide who explains antiquities.

Ci'der, *n.* O.F. *sidre*, repg. L.L. *sicera*, G. *sikera*, translating Heb. *shēkār*, strong drink. A fermented beverage made from apples.

Cigar', *n.* Sp. *cigarro*, of doubtful orig. A roll of tobacco-leaves for smoking.—**Cigarette'**, *n.* Dim. suff. *-ette.* Cut tobacco rolled in paper for smoking.

Cinc'ture, *a.* L. *cinctūra*, f. *cingĕre*, *cinctum*, to gird. PRECINCT. SHINGLES. A girding or encompassing; a girdle or belt.

Cin'der, *n.* Misspelt for *sinder* (by confusion with F. *cendre*, L. *cinis* (see next), with which it has no connexion). O.E. *sinder*, slag. Cf. O.N. *sindr.* A piece of glowing coal; a piece of coal not wholly burnt; in *pl.*, ashes.

Cin'erary, *a.* L. *cinerārius*, f. *cinis*, *cineris*, ashes. Cogn. with G. *konis*, dust. Of or pertaining to ashes, esp. of the dead.

Cin'namon, *n.* L. *cinnamōmum*—G. *kinnamōmon*, of Semitic orig. The inner bark of an East Indian tree, used as a spice.

Ci'pher, Cy'pher, *n.* O.F. *cyfre*—Sp. *cifra*—Arab. *sifr*, empty (translating Skr. *cūnya*, empty), used as *n.* ZERO. An arithmetical symbol (0) taking value only by position; a person of no importance; a numeral or figure; a secret writing; a monogram.—*vi.* To use figures.—*vt.* To write in secret characters.

Cir'cle, *n.* M.E. and F. *cercle*—L. *circulus*, dim. of *circus*, G. *kirkos*, a round, circle, ring. Cogn. with O.E. *hring*, RING.[1] SEARCH. A perfectly round plane figure; anything similar; a cycle, period; persons gathered round another or some object of interest; a class or division of society; a sphere of influence.—*vt.* To surround; to move round.—*vi.* To move in a circle; to form a circle.—**Cir'cular**, *a.* A.F. *circuler*—L. *circulāris*, f. *circulus.* In the form of, or moving in, a circle; *circular letter* or *circular*, a letter in identical terms sent to several persons.—**Cir'cul**ATE,[3] *vi.* To move round a circuit, through a system of pipes, &c.; to pass freely from place to place; to pass into readers' hands.—*vt.* To cause to circulate.—**Circul**A'TION, *n.*

Cir'cuit, *n.* F. *circuit*—L. *circuitus*, a going round, f. CIRCUM*īre*, to go round. A line passing round an area; the distance round; area, extent; a roundabout course; a visitation of judges; their district; the path of an electric current.—**Circu'it**OUS, *a.* Roundabout, indirect.—**Circu'itous**LY,[2] *adv.*

Cir'cumcise, *vt.* O.F. *circonciser*—L. *circumcīdĕre*, *circumcīsum*, to cut round, f. CIRCUM- + *caedĕre*, to cut. CONCISE. To cut off the foreskin of.—**Circumci'**SION, *n.*

Circum'ference, *n.* L. *circumferentia*, f. CIRCUM- + *ferre*, to BEAR. The bounding line of anything round.

Cir'cumflex, *n.* L. *circumflexus*, pa.pple. of CIRCUM*flectĕre*, to bend round. FLEXIBLE. An accent mark (ˆ or ˜) placed on a long vowel.

Circumlocu'tion, *n.* L. *circumlocūtio*, *circumlocūtiōnis*, f. CIRCUM- + *loqui*, *locūtus*, to speak. ALLOCUTE. Roundabout speaking.

Circumnav'igate, *vt.* L. CIRCUM*nāvigāre*, *circumnāvigātum*, to sail round. NAVIGATE. To sail round.—**Circumnaviga**'TION, *n.*

Circumscribe', *vt.* L. CIRCUM*scrībĕre*, to write, draw a line, round. SCRIBE. To bound; to limit, confine.

Cir'cumspect, *a.* L. *circumspectus*, well-considered, hence, of persons, cautious, pa. pple. of *circumspicĕre*, to look around, f. CIRCUM- + *specĕre*, to look. Well-considered; watchful, heedful.—**Circumspect'**LY,[2] *adv.*—**Circumspec'**TION, *n.*

Cir'cumstance, *n.* L. *circumstantia*, surrounding condition, f. CIRCUM*stāre*, to stand round. STATE. In *pl.*, the surroundings or adjuncts of an action; the state of affairs; condition in life. In *sing.*, a detail; an event, a matter of fact.—**Cir'cumstanced**, *ppl.a.* Situated.—**Cir'cumstan'**TIAL, *a.* Dependent on circumstances, indirect; incidental; minutely detailed; particular as to details.—**Circumstantial'**ITY, *n.*—**Circumstan'ti**ATE,[3] *vt.* To set forth with details.

Circumvent', *vt.* L. CIRCUM*venīre*, *circumventum*, to come round, hence, to beset, deceive. ADVENT. To entrap; to outwit, overreach.—**Circumven'**TION, *n.*

Cir'cus, *n.* L *circus*, CIRCLE. Among the Romans, a building for public spectacles; now a place for equestrian and other performances.

Cir'rus, *n.*; *pl.* **Cir'ri**. L. *cirrus*, curl, fringe. A tendril; a high fleecy cloud.

Cist, *n.* L. *cista*, G. *kistē*, box. CHEST. A place of interment formed of slabs of stone.

Cis'tern, *n.* O.F. *cisterne*—L. *cisterna*, f. *cista.* (See prec.) A tank for storing water.

Cit'adel, *n.* F. *citadelle*—It. *cittadella*, dim. of *città*, L. *cīvitas*, CITY. An inner (and usually upper) fortified city; hence, a fort commanding a city.

Cite, *vt.* F. *citer*—L. *citāre*, freq. of *ciēre*, to set in motion, call. EXCITE. SOLICIT. To summon officially; to quote; to adduce, allege; to refer to *as*.—**Cit**A'TION, *n.*

Cit'izen, *n.* A.F. *citeseyn* (the *s* unexplained) —O.F. *citeain* (F. *citoyen*)—L. *cīvitas*, CITY. A burgess of a city or town; a townsman; a member of a state.—**Cit'izen**SHIP, *n.*

Cit'ron, *n.* F. *citron*—L. *citrus*, citron-tree. A fruit like a lemon; the tree bearing it.

Cit'y, *n.* O.F. *cité*—L. *cīvitas*, state, city, f. *cīvis*, citizen. A large town.

Civ'ic, *a.* L. *cīvicus*, f. *cīvis*. (See prec.) Pertaining to citizens, a city, or citizenship.

Civ'il, *a.* F. *civil*—L. *cīvilis*, f. *cīvis*. CITY. Of or pertaining to citizens, to the individual citizen, or to the state; not barbarous, refined; polite, courteous; not military or naval; in law, distinguished from criminal; *civil war*, war between fellow-citizens; *the Civil Law*, the Roman Law.—**Civ'il**LY,[2] *adv.* Politely, courteously.—**Civil'ian**, *n.* O.F. *civilien*, f. *civilis*. One skilled in the Civil Law; a non-military person.—**Civil'**ITY, *n.* Politeness, courtesy; an act or expression of politeness.—**Civ'il**IZE, *vt.* To bring out of barbarism, refine.—**Civiliz**A'TION, *n.*

Clack, *n.* Imitative. CLICK. CLUCK. Cf. Du. *klak*. A sharp sound like that of one hard substance, such as a piece of wood, striking another; chatter.—*vi.* To make such a sound; to chatter, prate.

Claim, *vt.* O.F. *clamer*—L. *clāmāre*, to call out, declare aloud. DECLAIM. To demand, require; to demand recognition of, assert one's right to possession of; to call for, deserve. —*n.* A demand, assertion of right; right or title.—**Claim'**ANT, *n.*

Clam'ant, *a.* L. *clāmans*, *clāmantis*, pres.pple. of *clāmāre*. (See prec.) 'Crying', urgent.

Clam'ber, *vi.* App. a deriv. of CLIMB (the pa. tense of which in M.E. is *clamb*, *clam*). To climb with hands and feet, or with effort.

Clam'my, *a.* App. f. obs. *Clam*, moist, sticky (cf. Du. and L.G. *klam*) + -Y.[2] Soft, moist, and sticky; suffused with damp.

Clam'our, *n.* O.F. *clamor*—L. *clāmor*, f. *clāmāre*. CLAIM. Loud shouting, outcry; popular outcry; loud noise.—*vi.* To shout; to call importunately *for* or *to do*.—**Clam'or**OUS, *a.*—**Clam'orous**LY,[2] *adv.*

Clamp, *n.* Orig. doubtful. Cf. Du. *klamp*, Ger. *klampe*. A brace, clasp; a tool for holding or compressing.—*vt.* To fix with a clamp.

Clan, *n.* Gael. *clann*, family, race, app. not orig. Celtic, but f. L. *planta*, sprout, shoot. A tribal group claiming a common descent; a fraternity, party.—**Clan'n**ISH, *a.*

Clandes'tine, *a.* L. *clandestinus*, f. *clam*, secretly. Secret, underhand. —**Clandes'tine**LY,[2] *adv.*

Clang, *n.* App. f. L. *clangĕre*, to ring (as a trumpet), to scream (as a bird). Cf. G. *klazein*, in sim. senses. A loud ringing sound; a harsh cry.—*vi.* To make such a sound.—*vt.* To strike together with a ringing sound.—**Clan'gor**, **Clan'gour**, *n.* L. *clangor*, f. *clangĕre*. A loud ringing sound.

Clank, *n.* Perh. f. Du. *klank* in sim. sense. Cf. CLINK. A short abrupt sound as of pieces of metal struck together.—*vi.* and *t.* To make, move with, cause to make such a sound.

Clap, *vi.* M.E. *clappen*, not represented in O.E. Cf. O.N. *klappa*, M.L.G., L.G., Du. *klappen*. To make a hard explosive noise; to applaud with the hands.—*vt.* To strike (the hands) together; to clap the hands at; to slap with the hand in approval or encouragement; to put, set, place; to put *in* or *into* prison; to impose (a liability, &c.).—*n.* A hard, explosive noise; a plaudit, applause; a slap.—**Clap'per**, *n.* An apparatus for clapping, esp. the tongue of a bell.

Clar'et, *n.* O.F. *claret*, dim. f. *clair*, L. *clārus*, CLEAR. Formerly, like the O.F. word, a yellowish or light red wine; now a red wine imported from Bordeaux.

Clar'ify, *vt.* O.F. *clarifier*—L.L. *clārificāre*, f. *clārus*, CLEAR + *-fic-* for *facĕre*, to make. To make (a subject) clear; to clean, make pure. —*vi.* To become clear.—**Clari**FICA'TION, *n.*

Clar'ion, *n.* O.F. *claron*—Med.L. *clārio*, *clāriōnis*, f. *clārus*, CLEAR. A shrill-sounding trumpet.

Clar'ionet, *n.* Prec. + dim. *-et*. Also **Clar'inet**. A wooden single-reed instrument.

Clash, *n.* App. imitative. A loud broken sound as of weapons meeting, &c.; conflict, collision.—*vi.* To make a clash; to come into collision; to conflict, disagree *with*.—*vt.* To strike (things) together so as to produce a clash

Clasp, *n.* Orig. unknown. A means of fastening; an embracing or grasping; a military decoration.—*vt.* To fasten; to surround, enfold; to embrace, to grasp.

Class, *n.* F. *classe*—L. *classis*. A rank of society; rank, caste; a division of pupils; a division according to quality or merit; a kind, sort, division generally.—*vt.* To assign to the proper class. —**Clas'si**FY, *vt.* To arrange methodically in classes.—**Classi**FICA'TION, *n.*—**Clas'sic**, *a.* L. *classicus*, of the highest class, f. *classis*. Standard, leading; of or belonging to, or in the style of, Greek or Roman literature or art; historically famous; recognized, approved.—*n.* A writer, esp. in Greek or Latin, of recognized excellence; in *pl.*, the body of Greek and Roman literature.—**Clas'sic**AL, *a.*—**Clas'sic**ISM, *n.*—**Clas'sic**IST, *n.*

Clat'ter, *n.* O.E. *clatrung*, a clattering. Imitative. Cf. Du. *klateren*, to clatter. A rattling noise made by the collision of hard bodies; noisy talk.—*vi.* To make a clatter, to rattle; to chatter.—*vt.* To cause to rattle.

Clause, *n.* O.F. *clause*—L.L. *clausa*, conclusion, clause, f. L. *claudĕre*, *clausum*, to CLOSE. A part of a sentence; an article in a formal document.

Claw, *n.* O.E. *clawu*. Cf. Du. *klaauw*, Ger. *klaue*. The sharp nail of a bird or beast; a foot armed with a claw.—*vt.* To tear with the claws; to grip.—*vi.* To grasp or clutch.

Clay, *n.* O.E. *clǽg*. Common Teut. Cogn. with G. *gloios*, sticky matter, L. *glūten*, GLUE. A stiff viscous earth; earth, the earthly part of man.—**Clay'**EY,[2] *a.*

Clean, *a.* O.E. *clǽne*, clear, pure. Common Teut. Pure, not adulterated; free from dirt, not soiled; undefiled, chaste; trim, shapely; clear of obstructions or unevenness; entire, sheer.—*adv.* So as to leave no dirt; entirely, quite.—*vt.* To free from dirt.—**Clean'**NESS, *n.*—**Clean'**LY,[1] *a.* Clean in habits; conducing to cleanness.—**Clean'li**NESS, *n.*—**Clean'**LY,[2] *adv.*—**Cleanse**, *vt.* O.E. *clǽnsian*. To make clean; to clear, rid *of*, *from*.

Clear, *a.* O.F. *cler*—L. *clārus*, bright, clear, manifest. DECLARE. Free from cloud or mist; transparent, pellucid; bright, lustrous; of pure colour; well-marked; easily understood; distinct, free from confusion; evident, plain; seeing distinctly, discerning without confusion; convinced, determined; distinctly heard, ringing; unsullied, innocent; net, unencumbered; free from obstacles, open.—*adv.* Brightly; entirely, quite.—*vt.* To make clear; to explain; to acquit; to remove; to get through or away from; to leap or pass over; to free (a ship) by payment of dues; to make as clear profit.—*vi.* To become clear, bright, transparent; of a ship, to sail on payment of dues. —**Clear'**LY,[2] *adv.*—**Clear'**ANCE, *n.*

Cleave, *v.*[1]*t.* O.E. *clēofan.* Common Teut. Cogn. with G. *gluphein*, to cut, carve. To hew asunder, split.—*vi.* To split, fall asunder. —**Cleav'**AGE, *n.*—**Cleft**, *n.* Not represented in O.E. Cf. O.N. *kluft.* A split, fissure.

Cleave, *v.*[2]*i.* O.E. *clifan, clifian.* Common Teut. To stick fast, adhere; to cling, be devoted *to*.

Clef, *n.* F. *clef*—L. *clāvis*, key. One of the symbols indicating pitch in music.

Clem'atis, *n.* G. *klēmatis*, some kind of creeping plant, f. *klēma*, twig, shoot, f. *klaein*, to break off. The generic name of woody climbing plants.

Clem'ent, *a.* L. *clēmens, clēmentis.* Lenient, merciful; of weather, &c., mild.—**Clem'**ENCY, *n.*—**Clem'ent**LY,[2] *adv.*

Clench, *vt.* O.E. *clenc(e)an.* Cf. O.H.G. *klenkan.* Cogn. with CLING with causal sense. To make fast; to set (the teeth, &c.) firmly together; to grasp firmly; to confirm, drive home (an argument, &c.).

Clere'story, *n.* App. CLEAR, in sense 'light, lighted' + STOREY. An upper part of a church set with windows.

Cler'gy, *n.* O.F. *clergie*, lit. clerkship, f. *clerc*, CLERK. The body of men ordained for service in the Church.—**Clerg'yman**, *n.*

Cler'ic, *a.* L.L. *clēricus.* CLERK. Of or pertaining to the clergy.—*n.* A clergyman.—**Cler'ic**AL, *a.*—**Cler'ical**ISM, *n.*

Clerk, *n.* O.E. and O.F. *clerc*—L.L. *clēricus*, G. *klērikos* (properly *aa.*, of or pertaining to the *klēros*, lit. 'lot', and hence, the clergy, app. because the Lord was their portion). A clergyman; a layman who leads in the responses; an officer in charge of the records, correspondence, &c., of a department, corporation, &c.; a subordinate in an office.—**Clerk'**LY,[1] *a.*—**Clerk'**SHIP, *n.*

Clev'er, *a.* App. for M.E. *cliver*, ready to seize, allied to M.E. *cliver*, claw, and perh. to CLEAVE.[2] Deft, nimble; skilful, adroit.—**Clev'er**LY,[2] *adv.*—**Clev'er**NESS, *n.*

Clew, **Clue**, *n.* O.E. *cliwen, cleowen.* Cf. M.L.G. and Du. *kluwen.* A ball of thread; such a ball as a means of guidance; an indication; a lower corner of a sail.—*vt.* *To clew up*, to draw up the lower ends of (sails) for furling.

Click, *n.* Imitative. A weakened form of CLACK. Cf. Du. and Ger. *klick*, O.F. *clique.* A sound like a clack, but thinner; a catch which falls into a notched wheel.—*vi.* To make a click.

Cli'ent, *n.* L. *cliens, clientis* = *cluens*, f. *cluēre*, to hear, perh. one who is at the call of a patron. A dependant, a 'hanger-on'; one who employs a professional man, esp. in legal matters.

Cliff, *n.* O.E. *clif.* Cf. O.N. and Du. *klif.* A steep face of rock.—**Cliff'**Y,[2] *a.*

Climacter'ic, *a.* G. *klimaktērikos*, f. *klimaktēr*, a round of a ladder, critical period, f. *klimax*, ladder. CLIMAX. Pertaining to a critical period of life; critical, fatal.—*n.* A critical period of life.

Cli'mate, *n.* F. *climat*—L.L. *clima, climatis*—G. *klima, klimatos*, slope, region at a particular elevation, climate, f. *klinein.* CLIMAX. Condition (of a country) in relation to the prevailing atmospheric phenomena.—**Climat'**IC, *a.*

Cli'max, *n.* G. *klimax*, a LADDER, f. *klinein*, to make to slope or lean. LEAN, *v.* A rhetorical figure in which the expressions used rise gradually in dignity and force; the highest term of a climax; culmination, height.

Climb, *vi.* O.E. *climban.* Cf. Du., Ger. *klimmen.* CLAMBER. To raise oneself by grasping or clinging; to creep up, rise, ascend.—*vt.* To creep up, scale, mount.

Clime, *n.* L. *clima*, CLIMATE. Climate; a tract or region of the earth.

Clinch, *vt.* Variant of CLENCH. To make fast; to confirm, drive home (an argument, &c.).

Cling, *vi.* O.E. *clingan*, to shrivel up. Cf. E.Fris. *klingen* in same sense. Of skin, &c., to stick *to* bone, &c., as the result of shrivelling; to stick fast, attach oneself *to*; to cleave, be devoted *to*.

Clin'ic, *n.* L. *clīnicus*—G. *klinikos*, pertaining to a bed, f. *klinē*, bed, f. *klinein.* CLIMAX. One confined to bed.—*a.* Pertaining to a sick-bed.—**Clin'**ICAL, *a.* In same sense, used esp. of medical instruction given at a sick-bed.

Clink, *n.* Perh. f. Du. *klink* in sim. sense. Cf. CLANK. A sharp ringing sound, thinner than a clank, as of small pieces of metal or glasses struck together.—*vi.* and *t.* To make move with, or cause to make such a sound.-

Clink'er, *n.* Du. *klinker.* A very hard kind of brick; a mass of slag.

Clip, *v.*[1]*t.* O.E. *clyppan.* Cf. O.Fris. *kleppa.* To embrace, hug; to encircle; to grip, clutch.—*n.*[1] A device for clipping objects.

Clip, *v.*[2]*t.* M.E. *clippen*, prob. f. O.N. *klippa.* To cut with scissors or shears; to shear (sheep); to cut short, curtail.—*vi.* To run quickly.—*n.*[2] The wool shorn at a place or in a season; an act of clipping.—**Clip'**PER, *n.* One who or that which clips; a fast-sailing vessel.

Clique, *n.* F. *clique*, a noisy gang—O.F. *cliquer*, Du. *klikken*, to CLICK. A small exclusive set.

Cloak, *n.* O.F. *cloke*—Med.L. *cloca*, bell, also horseman's cape, so called from the shape. CLOCK. A loose outer garment; a pretext, pretence.—*vt.* To cover with a cloak; to conceal, disguise.

Clock, *n.* M.Du. *clocke* or O.N.F. *cloke*, *cloque* = Cent. F. *cloche*, Med. L. *cloca*, of Celtic orig., all meaning 'bell'. CLOAK. An instrument for measuring time, properly one which strikes.

Clod, *n.* A var. of, and formerly synonymous with CLOT. A lump of earth; a blockhead.

Clog, *n.* Orig. unknown. A block of wood, &c., impeding motion; an impediment; a wooden-soled overshoe.—*vt.* To put a clog on; to hinder; to choke *up*.

Clois'ter, *n.* O.F. *cloistre*—L. *claustrum*, bolt, hence, shut up place, f. *claudĕre*, to CLOSE. A convent; a covered walk or arcade. —*vt.* To place in a cloister; to confine.

Close, *a.* F. *clos*—L. *clausus*, pa.pple. of *claudĕre.* (See prec.) Closed, shut; confined, narrow; hidden, secret; stifling; reticent; niggardly; dense, compact; near; intimate, confidential; strict, searching.—*adv.* Near; tightly, fast.—*n.*[1] The precinct of a cathedral. —**Close'**LY,[2] *adv.*—**Close'**NESS, *n.*

Close, *vt.* O.E. *clos-*, stem of *clore*, f. L. *claudĕre, clausum*, to close. CLAUSE. CLOISTER. CONCLUDE. FORECLOSE. To shut, to stop up; to conclude, finish.—*vi.* To become shut; to come to an end; to join, combine; to grapple *with*; to come to terms *with*.—*n.*[2] End.

Clos'et, *n.* O.F. *closet*, dim. of *clos*, an enclosed space—L. *clausum*, neut. of *clausus*. CLOSE, *a.* A small private room.—*vt.* To shut up in a closet.

Clos'ure, *n.* O.F. *closure*, barrier—L. *clausūra*, f. *claudĕre*, to CLOSE. A closing; the closing of a debate by vote or other authority.

Clot, *n.* O.E. *clott, clot.* Cf. M.H.G. *kloz* (Ger. *klotz*), lump, block. CLOUD. CLUSTER. A mass, lump; a semi-solid lump, esp. of blood.—*vi.* To form into clots.

Cloth, *n.* O.E. *cláth.* Cf. Du. *kleed*, Ger. *kleid*, a dress. A piece of woven or felted stuff; a woven or felted fabric; one's profession (as marked by garb), esp. the clerical profession.—**Clothe**, *vt.* M.E. *clothen, clathen*, formed f. *cláth.* To put clothes on; to cover.—**Clothes**, *n.pl.* O.E. *cláthas*, pl. of *cláth.* Dress, raiment; bed-coverings.—**Clo'thIER**, *n.* Orig. *clothER.* A seller of clothes.

Cloud, *n.* O.E. *clúd*, mass of rock, hill. Cogn. with CLOD, CLOT. A mass of condensed vapour floating in the air; a cloud-like mass; a dimness or obscurity; a multitude; a state of gloom, &c.—*vt.* To cover with clouds, overshadow; to dim, obscure, darken.—*vi.* To become cloudy.—**Cloud'LESS**, *a.*—**Cloud'Y**,[2] *a.*

Clout, *n.* O.E. *clút.* Cf. Sw. *klut*, Norw. and Da. *klud*, rag, shred. A piece of cloth, a patch.—*vt.* To patch.

Clove, *n.*[1] O.E. *clufu.* Cogn. with CLEAVE.[1] One of the small bulbs constituting a compound bulb, as of garlic.

Clove, *n.*[2] Formerly *clowe de gilofre, clowe-gilofre*—F. *clou de girofle*, lit., 'nail of clove', f. *clou* (L. *clāvus*), nail, and *girofle* (through L.L. f. G. *karuophullon*, lit., 'nut-leaf', f. *karuon*, nut + *phullon*, leaf), clove, referring to a resemblance of the bud with its stalk to a nail. GILLYFLOWER. The dried flower bud of an East Indian tree used as a spice; the tree.

Clo'ver, *n.* M.E. *claver*—O.E. *clāfre.* Cf. Du. *klaver*, Sw. *klöfver.* The common name of species of trefoil.

Clown, *n.* Prob. f. some L.G. source and cogn. with CLOT in sense 'lump'. Cf. Mod. Icelandic *klunni*, a clumsy fellow. A rustic; a rude ill-bred fellow; a jester.—**Clown'ISH**, *a.*

Cloy, *vt.* O.F. *cloyer*, to cloy, stop up = *cloer*, to nail, f. *clo*, F. *clou*, a nail. CLOVE.[2] To surfeit; to weary by sweetness, sameness, &c.

Club, *n.* O.N. *klubba, klumba*, thick stick. Cogn. with CLUMP. (The development into sense 'association' is obscure.) A stick thickening towards the end; a stick or bat used in various games; in *pl.*, one of the suits at cards, marked with a trefoil (F. *trèfle*, which gives the suit its name in that language), in *sing.*, a card of this suit (the word being in the card sense a translation of Sp. *basto* (cf. *baston* under BASTINADO), the 'club' figured on Sp. cards); an association for a common object, social, political, &c.—*vt.* To strike with a club; to gather together, put into a common stock; to make *up*, put *together* (a sum) jointly.—*vi.* To join and contribute for a common end.

Cluck, *n.* Imitative. A var. of CLACK. Cf. CHUCK.[1] The noise of a hen calling her chickens.—*vi.* To make the noise.

Clue. See CLEW.

Clump, *n.* Cf. L.G. *klump*, Du. *klomp*, lump, mass. With *p* for *b* cogn. with O.N. *klumba.* CLUB. A compact mass; a cluster of trees or growing plants.

Clum'sy, *a.* Of doubtful orig. Cf. Sw. dial., *klummsen*, benumbed. Formerly, benumbed. Ungainly, awkward; ill-contrived; unwieldy, inelegant.—**Clum'sILY**, *adv.*—**Clum'siNESS**, *n.*

Clus'ter, *n.* O.E. *cluster, clyster.* Cf. L.G. *kluster.* App. cogn. with CLOT. A collection of things growing together, a bunch; an assemblage, group.—*vt.* To gather in a cluster.—*vi.* To gather or grow in a cluster.

Clutch, *vt.* M.E. *clucchen, clicchen*—O.E. *clyccean.* Cf. M.E. *cloke*, a claw. To seize eagerly, snatch; to grip.—*vi.* To make a clutch *at.*—*n.* Tight grip or grasp; *in one's clutches*, in one's grip or power; a grasping *at*; something that grips.

Coach, *n.* F. *coche.* Said to be from Magyar *kocsi* (in form an *a.*, app. = of *Kocs* in Hungary), coach, as first made at Kocs. A large four-wheeled carriage; a railway carriage; a tutor.—*vi.* To ride in a coach.—*vt.* To tutor.

Coadju'tor, *n.* L. *coadjūtor*, f. *adjuvāre, adjūtum*, to assist. ADJUTANT. An assistant.

Coag'ulate, *vt.* L. *coāgulāre, coāgulātum*, to curdle, f. *coāgulum*, rennet, f. *cōgĕre* (CO- + *agĕre*), to drive together, constrain. COGENT. ACT. SQUASH. To curdle; to form into a mass.—*vi.* To curdle.—**CoagulA'TION**, *n.*

Coal, *n.* M.E. and O.E. *col.* Cf. O.N., Sw. *kol*, Du. *kool.* A glowing ember; a mineral, consisting of carbonized vegetable matter used as fuel.—*vt.* To supply with coal.—*vi.* To take in coal.

Coalesce', *vi.* L. *coalescĕre*, to grow together, f. *alĕre*, to nourish. ALIMENT. To unite.—**Coales'CENCE**, *n.*—**Coali'tion**, *n.* L. *coalitio, coalitiōnis*, f. *coalescĕre.* Combination, fusion; an alliance.

Coarse, *a.* Formerly also *course.* Of uncertain orig. Conjectured to be an adj. use of COURSE, with sense 'ordinary', as in *of course*, 'of the usual order'. Wanting in fineness or delicacy; rough or harsh to the taste, perception, &c.; stormy; unrefined, uncivil; indecent.—**Coarse'LY**,[2] *adv.*—**Coarse'NESS**, *n.*

Coast, *n.* O.F. *coste*—L. *costa*, rib, side. COSTAL. CUTLET. The sea-shore, the margin of the land.—*vi.* To sail along the coast.—**Coast'ER**, *n.* A vessel trading from port to port of the same country.

Coat, *n.* O.F. *cote*—Med.L. *cotta*, of doubtful orig. COTILLION. An outer garment worn by men; a petticoat, skirt; an animal's fur or feathers; a covering; a layer, as of paint, &c.; *coat of arms*, distinctive heraldic devices.—*vt.* To clothe; to cover with a layer of paint, &c.

Coax, *vt.* From obs. *Cokes*, of obscure orig., a fool, simpleton; *to make a cokes of*, to fool, to gull, to pet. To wheedle, flatter, cajole.

Cob, *n.* Of unknown orig. A short-legged stout horse; a lump; a knot of hair.

Cob'ble, *vt.* Of unknown orig. To repair roughly, esp. of shoes; to put together roughly.—**Cob'blER**, *n.*

Cob'ble, *n.* Of unknown orig. App. cogn. with COB. A water-worn rounded stone.

Cob'le, *n.* Cf. Welsh *ceubal*, ferry-boat, skiff. A flat-bottomed sea fishing-boat.

Cob'web, *n.* M.E. *coppeweb*, f. *coppe*, spider + WEB—O.E. *coppa*, as in *āttorcoppa*, spider, f. *āttor*, poison + *cop*, head. A spider's web.

Coca'ine, *n.* Chemical suff. *-ine.* An alkaloid got from the S. American shrub *coca*, used as a local anæsthetic.

Coch'ineal, *n.* F. *cochenille*—Sp. *cochinilla* —L. *coccineus*, scarlet-coloured, f. *coccum*, G. *kokkos*, grain, seed, also the kermes berry (or rather insect). A scarlet dye-stuff got from the dried bodies of an insect found in Mexico and elsewhere.

Cock, *n.*[1] M.E. *cok*—O.E. *cocc*, *coc*, *kok*, prob. f. the bird's cry. Cf. O.N. *kokkr*, and F. *coq*. The male of the domestic fowl and of various other birds; a tap for liquids; the hammer of a gun; the position of the hammer when drawn back; a pronounced upward turn, a significant turn (of the eye).—*v.*[1]*t.* To set or turn up assertively or jauntily; to draw back the cock of (a gun).—**Cockade'**, *n.* F. *cocarde*, f. *coq*, perh. as resembling the cock's comb. A knot of ribbons on a hat.—**Cock's'-comb**, **Cocks'comb**, *n.* A cock's comb; a jester's cap. Spelt **Cox'comb**, a conceited, showy person, a fop.—**Cox'comb**RY, *n.*

Cock, *n.*[2] Cf. dial. Ger. *kocke*, dial. Da. *kok*, hay-cock. A conical heap, generally of hay.—*v.*[2]*t.* To put up (hay, &c.) in cocks.

Cock, *n.*[3] (Now always **Cock'-boat**.) O.F. *coque*, a kind of boat, orig. a shell, prob. f. L. *concha*, shell-fish, shell, f. G. *kogchē*. COCKLE.[2] A small ship's-boat.

Cockatoo', *n.* Malay *kakatúa*, perh. f. the bird's cry. A crested bird of the parrot kind.

Cock'atrice, *n.* O.F. *cocatris*—L.L. *cōcātrix*, answering to L. type **calcātrix*, the tracker (f. *calcāre*, to tread, in L.L. to track, f. *calx*, heel), used to render G. *ichneumōn*, ICHNEUMON. By some confusion *cockatrice* came to be used to denote the *basilisk* (G. *basiliskos*, some kind of serpent, dim. of *basileus*, king, said to be so called from a spot on the head like a crown), a fabulous deadly serpent said to kill by its mere glance.

Cock'er, *vt.* Prob. a derivative of COCK,[1] with the notion 'to make a nestling-cock or darling of'. To indulge, pamper; to foster (an appetite, idea, &c.).

Cock'le, *n.*[1] O.E. *coccel*, of unknown orig. A weed with purple flowers growing in corn.

Cock'le, *n.*[2] M.E. *cokille*—F. *coquille*, shell, through L. f. G. *kogchulion*, dim. f. *kogchē*, mussel, cockle. COCK.[3] CONCH. A small shell-fish.—*vi.* and *t.* Cf. F. *coquiller*, of bread, to have (shell-shaped) blisters on the crust, f. *coquille*. To contract into wrinkles.

Cock'ney, *n.* M.E. *cokeney*, *-ay*, app. = *coken*, of cocks + *ey*, *ay* (O.E. *ǽg*), EGG, lit. 'cocks' egg'. Prob. from 'cocks' eggs' being applied to small or mis-shapen eggs came the obs. senses 'a child that sucks long', 'a cockered child', 'a milksop', 'a townsman' (as the type of effeminacy); hence applied contemptuously to one born in the City of London.—*a.* Pertaining to or characteristic of the cockney.

Cock'roach, *n.* Sp. *cucaracha*. The black-beetle.

Co'co, **Co'coa**,[1] *n.* Pg. and Sp. *coco*, gen. identified with *coco* in the same langs., grinning face, grimace, the name thus referring to the face-like appearance of the base of the shell. The tropical palm-tree bearing the **Co'co-** (or **Co'coa-**) **nut**.

Co'coa, *n.*[2] A corr. of *Cacao*. CHOCOLATE. A powder made from the seeds of the *cacao*, a tropical American tree; a beverage made from the powder.

Cocoon', *n.* F. *cocon*, app. f. *coque*, shell. COCK.[3] The sheath of an insect in the chrysalis state.

Cod, *n.*[1] Orig. unknown. A large sea fish.

Cod, *n.*[2] O.E. *codd*. Cf. early Mod. Du. *kodde*, testicle. The pod or husk of a plant.

Cod'dle, *vt.* Orig. uncertain. To nurse overmuch, to treat as an invalid, to feed *up*.

Code, *n.* F.—L. *cōdex*, earlier *caudex*, a tree-trunk, wooden tablet, book, code. Cf. BOOK. A collection of laws or regulations; a system of signals or abbreviations.—**Cod'**IFY, *vt.*—**Cod**IFICA'TION, *n.*

Cod'icil, *n.* L. *cōdicillus*, dim. of *cōdex*. (See prec.) A supplement to a will.

Cod'ling, **Cod'lin**, *n.* Poss., with -LING (3), f. Ir. *cueirt*, apple-tree. A variety of apple.

Coeffi'cient, *a.* CO- + EFFICIENT. Co-operating.—*n.* A joint agent or factor; a number or quantity multiplying another.

Coerce', *vt.* L. *coercēre*, to compel, f. CO- + *arcēre*, to shut up, restrain. ARCH, *n.* To constrain or restrain by forcible means.—**Coer'**CION, *n.*—**Coer'**CIVE, *a.*

Coe'val, *a.* With -AL f. L. *coaevus*, f. CO- + *aevum*, AGE. Equally old; contemporary; lasting to the same time.

Coexist', *vi.* CO- + EXIST. To exist together or in conjunction.—**Coexist'**ENCE, *n.*—**Coexist'**ENT, *a.*

Cof'fee, *n.* Arab. *qahwah*, the beverage, through the Turkish form *kahveh*. A beverage made from the seeds of a shrub orig. a native of Arabia and Abyssinia; the seeds collectively; the shrub.

Cof'fer, *n.* O.F. *cofre*—L. *cophinus*, G. *kophinos*, basket. A chest for valuables.—**Cof'fer-dam**, *n.* A water-tight case used in building bridges, &c.

Cof'fin, *n.* O.F. *cofin*, a chest = *cofre*. (See prec.) A case for a dead body.—*vt.* To put in a coffin.

Cog, *n.* Cf. Sw. *kugge*, Norw. *kug*, in same sense. One of a series of teeth on a wheel.

Cog, *vi.* Orig. unknown. To cheat.—*vt.* *To cog a die* or *the dice*, to play at dice fraudulently.

Co'gent, *a.* L. *cōgens*, *cōgentis*, pres.pple. of *cōgĕre*. COAGULATE. Forcible; convincing.—**Co'gent**LY,[2] *adv.*—**Co'**GENCY, *n.*

Cog'itate, *vi.* L. *cōgitāre*, *cōgitātum*, to think. To think, reflect.—*vt.* To devise, plan.—**Cogit**A'TION, *n.*

Cognac', *n.* From *Cognac* in France. Brandy distilled from Cognac wine.

Cog'nate, *a.* L. *cognātus*, allied by birth, f. CO- + *gnātus*, old form of *nātus*, pa.pple. of *nasci*, to be born. AGNATE. NATAL. Of the same stock or origin, akin.

Cogni'tion, *n.* L. *cognitio*, *cognitiōnis*, f. *cognoscĕre*, *cognitum*, to get to know well, f. CO- + *gnoscĕre*, old form of *noscĕre*, to get to KNOW. The action or faculty of knowing; a perception, sensation, notion.

Cog'nizance, **-sance**, *n.* O.F. *conisance*, *conoisance*, f. *conoistre*, to know—L. *cognoscĕre*. (See prec.) CONNOISSEUR. Knowledge, state of being aware, perception, observation; a device, badge, emblem. — **Cog'niz**ABLE, **-**SABLE, **Cog'niz**ANT, **-**SANT, *aa.*

Cohab'it, *vi.* L. *cohabitāre*, to dwell together. HABITATION. To live together as husband and wife.

Cohere', *vi.* L. *cohaerēre*, *cohaesum*, to cleave or stick together. ADHERE. HESITATE. To cleave or stick together; to be consistent.—**Cohe'r**ENCE, -ENCY, *nn.*—**Cohe'r**ENT, *a.*—**Cohe'rent**LY,[2] *adv.*—**Cohe'**SION, *n.*

Co'hort, *n.* F. *cohorte*—L. *cohors*, *cohortis*, COURT, company of soldiers, f. CO- + *hort-*, found also in *hortus*, GARDEN. In the Roman army, a tenth of a legion; a body of warriors.

Coif, *n.* O.F. *coife, coiffe*—L.L. *cofea*, supposed to represent O.H.G. *chuppha*, cap. A close-fitting cap.—*vt.* To cover with a coif.

Coil, *vt.* Supposed to be identical with F. *cueillir*, L. *colligĕre*, to gather. COLLECT. To lay up (a rope, &c.) in rings; to twist into a winding shape.—*vi.* To assume a winding form, twist *round*.—*n.* A series of rings into which a rope, &c., is wound; a convolution.

Coin, *n.* F. *coin*, wedge, die for stamping (the die being like a wedge), stamp on money—L. *cuneus*, wedge. CONE. CUNEATE. A piece of money; money.—*vt.* To make (money), to make (metal) into money, by stamping; to fabricate; to invent.—**Coin'**AGE, *n.* The action or right of coining; coins collectively; fabrication, invention; an invention.

Coincide', *vi.* F. *coïncider*—Med.L. *coincidĕre*, f. CO- + IN-[1] + L. *cadĕre*, to fall. CADENCE. To agree in position; to happen together; to agree exactly; to concur.—**Coin'cid**ENCE, *n.*—**Coin'cid**ENT, *a.*

Coke, *n.* Orig. uncertain. The residue left on distillation of coal.—*vt.* To make into coke.

Col'ander, Cul'lender, *n.* Med.L. *cōlātōrium*, f. L. *cōlāre*, to strain. A vessel used as a sieve.

Cold, *a.* O.E. (Anglian) *cald*, f. O.Teut. stem *kal-*, to be cold, cogn. with L. *gel-* in *gelu*, frost, *gelidus*, cold. CHILL. CONGEAL. COOL. JELLY. Lacking heat; not heated; indifferent; apathetic; not cordial; dispiriting.—*n.* The absence of heat; lack of zeal; depression; an inflammatory ailment caused by cold.—**Cold'**LY,[2] *adv.*—**Cold'**NESS, *n.*

Cole, *n.* M.E. *col, cole*—O.E. *cál, cáwel*, or O.N. *kál*—L. *caulis*, stem, cabbage. CAULIFLOWER. KALE. The general name for various kinds of cabbage, esp. rape.

Coleop'terous, *a.* G. *koleopteros*, f. *koleon*, sheath + *pteron*, wing. Having wing-covers.

Col'ic, *n.* F. *colique*—L. *cōlicus*, G. *kōlikos* (incorrectly for *kolikos*), pertaining to the *kolon* or lower bowel. Severe griping pains in the intestines.

Collab'orate, *vi.* L. COL*laborāre, collaborātum*, to work together, f. *labor*, toil. LABOUR. To work with another, esp. in literature and art.—**Collabor**A'TION, *n.*

Collapse', *vi.* L. COL*lābi, collapsus*, to fall together. LAPSE. To fall together, give way; to fail, to lose force or health.—*n.* The action of collapsing.—**Collap'**SIBLE, **Collap'**SABLE, *a.*

Col'lar, *n.* A.F. *coler* = O.F. *colier*—L. *collāre*, f. *collum*, neck. A part of a garment worn round the neck; a band, &c., round the neck.—*vt.* To seize by the collar, capture; to appropriate, master.

Collate', *vt.* L. CON*ferre, collātum*, to bring together, to compare, consult together, bestow. BEAR, *v.* CONFER. To compare carefully or critically; to appoint *to* a benefice.—*vi.* To make, or be entitled to make, such an appointment.—**Colla'**TION, *n.* In senses f. the *v.*; also, a light meal.

Collat'eral, *a.* Med.L. *collaterālis*, f. COL- + L. *latus*, side. LATERAL. Placed side by side; accompanying; corresponding; subordinate; of the same stock but descended in a different line.—*n.* A collateral kinsman.

Col'league, *n.* F. *collègue*—L. *collēga*, f. COL- + *legĕre*, to choose. COLLEGE. An associate in office.

Collect', *vt.* O.F. *collecter*, to collect money—L. *colligĕre, collectum*, to gather together, f. COL- + *legĕre*, to gather, to choose. COIL. CULL. LEGEND. To gather together; to gather (taxes, &c.); to make a collection of (books, &c.); to recall (one's faculties, &c.) to order; to deduce, infer.—*vi.* for *refl.* To assemble.—**Collect'ed**, *ppl.a.* Composed, self-possessed.—**Collec'**TIVE, *a.*—**Collec'tive**LY,[2] *adv.*—**Collec'tiv**ISM, *n.* The theory that the State ought to own all the means of production.—**Collec'**TION, *n.*—**Collec'**TOR, *n.*

Col'lect, *n.* F. *collecte*—L. *collecta*, a gathering together (f. *colligĕre* (see prec.)), in Med.L. used in sense 'a collect'. A short prayer.

Col'lege, *n.* O.F. *collége*—L. *collēgium*, a fraternity, f. *collēga*, COLLEAGUE. A body of colleagues, an association; a society of scholars; an institution for higher education; the building occupied by a college.—**Colle'gi**AN, *a.* and *n.*—**Colle'gi**ATE,[2] *a.*

Collide', *vi.* L. *collīdĕre, collīsum*, to strike together, f. COL- + *laedĕre*, to injure. LESION. To strike or dash together; to clash, conflict.—**Colli'**SION, *n.*

Col'lier. *n.* M.E. *colier*, f. *col*, COAL. A coal-miner; a coal-ship.—**Col'lier**Y,[1] *n.* A coal-mine.

Col'locate, *vt.* L. COL*locāre, collocātum*, to place together, arrange, f. *locus*, place. COUCH. LOCAL. To place side by side, arrange; to set in a position.—**Colloc**A'TION, *n.*

Col'loquy, *n.* L. *colloquium*, a speaking together, f. COL*loqui*, to speak together. LOQUACIOUS. A conversation; converse.—**Collo'qui**AL, *a.* Conversational; informal, familiar.

Collude', *vi.* L. COL*lūdĕre, collūsum*, to play, to act secretly, together. LUDICROUS. To connive, play false.—**Collu'**SION, *n.*—**Collu'**SIVE, *a.*

Co'lon, *n.* G. *kōlon*, limb, clause. A mark (:) indicating a break in construction.

Colonel (cur'nel), *n.* F. *colonel*—It. *colonello* (dim. of *colonna*, L. *columna*, COLUMN), 'the upholder of the regiment', as leading it. The highest regimental officer.—**Colonel**CY, *n.*

Colonnade', *n.* F. *colonnade*—It. *colonnata*, f. *colonna*. (See prec.) A regular range of columns.

Col'ony, *n.* O.F. *colonie*—L. *colōnia*, f. *colōnus*, husbandman, f. *colĕre*, to till. CULT. A body of people settling in a new country; the community so formed; its territory.—**Colo'ni**AL, *a.*—**Col'on**IST, *n.*—**Col'on**IZE, *vt.*—**Coloniz**A'TION, *n.*

Colos'sus, *n.*; *pl.* **-i**, **-uses**. G. *kolossos*. A very large statue.—**Colos'**SAL, *a.* Huge.

Col'our, *n.* O.F. *color*—L. *color*. That which gives bodies different appearances independently of form; a hue or tint; complexion, freshness of hue; a coloured device or dress; a flag (gen. in *pl.*); a colouring matter, paint; outward appearance, show *of*; a pretext.—*vt.* To give colour to, paint, stain, dye; to disguise, excuse; to misrepresent.—*vi.* To become coloured; to blush.—**Col'our**ABLE, *a.* Specious, plausible; pretended, feigned.

Colt, *n.* O.E. *colt*, young camel, young ass, &c. Orig. obscure. The young of the horse.

Col'umn, *n.* O.F. *colompne*—L. *columna*, a collateral form of *columen*, summit. Cf. *collis*, HILL. COLONEL. CULMINATE. A long cylindrical body erected vertically as a support, a pillar; various things resembling this; a division of a page or sheet; a body of troops of great depth.—**Colum'n**AR,[1] *a.*

Co'ma, *n.* G. *kōma, kōmatos.* Unnaturally deep sleep, stupor, lethargy.—**Co'mat**OSE, *a.*
Comb, *n.* O.E. *comb, camb.* Common Teut. Cogn. with G. *gomphos*, peg, pin. A toothed instrument for cleaning and arranging the hair, or for ornament; the crest of a cock; a honeycomb.—*vt.* To apply a comb to.
Com'bat, *vi.* F. *combattre*, f. COM- + *battre*, L.L.**battĕre, battuĕre*, to beat. ABATE. BATTLE. DEBATE. To fight.—*vt.* To fight with; to oppose.—*n.* A fight, encounter, struggle.—**Com'bat**ANT, *n.*—**Com'bat**IVE, *a.*
Combine', *vt.* L.L. *combīnāre*, to join two by two, f. COM- + *bīni*, two together. To join together; to ally; to possess in union (qualities, &c., *vs.* separate).—*vi.* To come together, coalesce; to confederate.—**Combin**A'TION, *n.*
Combus'tion, *n.* L.L. *combustio, combustiōnis*, L. *combūrĕre, combustum*, to burn up. Destruction by fire; the development of light and heat accompanying chemical combination.—**Combus'ti**BLE, *a.*—**Combusti**BIL'ITY, *n.*
Come, *vi.* M.E. *comen*—O.E. *cuman.* Common Teut. Cogn. with G. *bainein*, L. *venīre.* To move (towards something), to approach; to arrive; to be brought *to* a position; to extend, reach; to fall, happen *to*; to emanate, be descended *from*; to proceed, attain *to*; to become, get to be; to turn out to be.
Com'edy, *n.* F. *comédie*—L. *cōmoedia*—G. *kōmōidia*, prob. f. *kōmos*, revel+*aoidos*, singer, f. *aeidein*, to sing. COMIC. ENCOMIUM. ODE. The branch of the drama which deals in a mirthful way with the lighter passions and actions of man; a drama of this kind.—**Come'di**AN, *n.* A player in, or a writer of, comedies.
Come'ly, *a.* M.E. *comli*;—O.E. *cýmlic*, f. *cýme*, exquisite (allied to O.H.G. *chûmo*, with difficulty, *chûmig*, weak, delicate) + *-lic*, like = -LY.[1] M.E. *comli*, being associated with *comen*, to COME, gained the sense 'becoming, pleasing'. BECOME. Fair, pretty, pleasing; becoming, seemly.—**Come'li**NESS, *n.*
Comes'tible, *n.* F. *comestible*—L. COM*edĕre, comēsum*, to EAT up. An article of food.
Com'et, *n.* O.E. *cometa*—L. *comēta*—G. *komētēs* (*astēr*), long-haired (star), f. *komē*, hair. STAR. A celestial body with a luminous train.—**Com'et**ARY, *a.*
Com'fit, *n.* O.F. *confit*—L. *confectum*, use as *n.* of neut. of *confectus*, pa.pple. of *conficĕre*, to put together, prepare, f. CON- + *facĕre*, to make. CONFECTION. A sweetmeat.
Com'fort, *vt.* O.F. *conforter*—L. *confortāre*, to strengthen, f. CON- + *fortis*, strong. FORCE. To console, solace; to gladden, cheer.—*n.* Consolation, solace; well-being; a source of comfort, well-being, or satisfaction.—**Com'fort**ABLE, *a.* Comforting; at ease.—**Com'fort**ABLY,[2] *adv.*—**Com'fort**ER, *n.*
Com'ic, *a.* L. *cōmicus*—G. *kōmikos*, pertaining to COMEDY, prob. f. *kōmos.* Of, proper to, belonging to comedy; funny, causing mirth.—**Com'ic**AL, *a.*
Com'ity, *n.* L. *cōmitas*, f. *cōmis*, courteous. Courtesy; friendly understanding.
Com'ma, *n.* L. *comma*—G. *komma*, piece cut off, short clause, f. *koptein*, to strike, cut. Formerly, a short clause. A mark (,) separating the smallest members of a sentence.
Command', *vt.* O.F. *comander*—L.L. *commandāre*, f. COM- + L. *mandāre*, to commit, enjoin. MANDATE. To order, enjoin; to sway, rule; to be commander of; to have within one's power or disposal; to exact, compel; to dominate, overlook.—*vi.* To exercise command.—*n.* Ordering; an order; sway, rule; power of control or disposal; power of dominating or overlooking; the post of a commander, those under him, his district.—**Command**ANT', **Command'**ER, *nn.*—**Command'**MENT, *n.*—**Commandeer'**, *vt.* S. African Du. *kommanderen*, f. F. *commander.* To force into, seize for, military service.
Commem'orate, *vt.* L. *commemorāre, commemorātum*, to bring to remembrance, f. COM- + *memorāre*, to mention, f. *memor*, mindful. MEMORY. To celebrate, eulogize; to keep in memory by some solemnity.—**Commemo**RA'TION, *n.*—**Commem'or**ATIVE, *a.*
Commence', *vt.* O.F. *comencer*—L.L. type *COM*initiāre*, f. L. *initiāre*, to begin, f. *initium*, beginning. INITIAL. To begin, enter upon.—*vi.* To begin *to*; to make a start.—**Commence'**MENT, *n.*
Commend', *vt.* L. COM*mendāre*, intensive f. *mandāre*, to commit, entrust. MANDATE. To commit, entrust; to recommend; to praise.—**Commend'**ABLE, *a.*—**Commend**A'TION, *n.*—**Commend'at**ORY, *a.*—**Commen'dam**. *Acc. sing.* of Med.L. *commenda*, charge, trust, f. *commendāre.* In phrase *in commendam*, in trust, said of the tenure of a benefice given in charge to be held until the appointment of an incumbent.
Commen'surable, *a.* L. COM*mensūrābilis*, having a common measure, f. *mensūra*, MEASURE. Having a common measure.—**Commen'sur**ATE,[2] *a.* Of equal magnitude or duration *with*; proportionate, adequate *to*.
Com'ment, *vi.* F. *commenter*—L. *commentāri*, to consider, make a note on, f. COM*minisci*, to devise, f. *min-* for *men-* in *meminisse*, to remember, *mens*, MIND. MENTAL. To write notes or make remarks (gen. unfavourable) *on* or *upon*.—*n.* A note; a body of notes; criticism.—**Com'ment**ARY, *n.* An expository treatise; a remark.—**Com'mentat**OR, *n.*
Com'merce, *n.* F. *commerce*—L. *commercium*, f. COM- + *merx, mercis*, merchandise, wares. MERCHANT. Buying and selling, trading; intercourse, dealings.—**Commer'c**IAL, *a.*
Com'minate, *vt.* L. COM*mināri*, to menace. MENACE. To threaten (with divine vengeance).—**Commin**A'TION, *n.* Such a threatening; in the Liturgy, a recital of divine threatenings. [To mix together.
Commin'gle, *vi.* and *t.* COM- + MINGLE.
Com'minute, *vt.* L. COM*minuĕre, comminūtum*, to reduce to fragments, f. *min-*, base of *minor*, less. MINOR. To reduce to small fragments.—**Comminu't**ION, *n.*
Commis'erate, *vt.* L. COM*miserāri, commiserātus*, to pity, f. *miser*, wretched. MISER. To pity, bewail, condole with.—**Commise**RA'TION, *n.*
Com'missary, *n.* Med.L. *commissārius*, L. *committĕre*, to COMMIT. A deputy, delegate; an officer representing a bishop; a military officer in charge of supplies and transport.—**Commissa'riat**, *n.* -AT(E).[1] The military department in charge of these.
Commis'sion, *n.* L. *commissio, commissiōnis*, f. *committĕre*, to COMMIT. Order, command; delegated authority; a warrant, esp. one from the sovereign, conferring such authority; a body charged with a specified function; something entrusted for performance; remuneration by a percentage; the committing (of a crime, &c.).—*vt.* To empower, authorize; to give an order for.—**Commis'sioner**, *n.*

A.F. and F. *commission(n)aire.* A delegate; a member of a commission.—In F. form **Commis'sionaire**, *n.* A messenger.

Commit', *vt.* L. COM*mittĕre, commissum,* to put together, also, to put for safety, entrust, f. *mittĕre,* to put forth, send. MISSION. To give in charge, entrust, consign; to perpetrate, be guilty of; to involve, compromise; to engage, pledge.—**Commit'**MENT, *n.* Esp., commitment to prison. — **Commit't**AL, *n.* — **Commit't**EE, *n.* A body elected for some special business.

Commode', *n.* F. *commode*—L. *commodus,* fit, suitable, f. COM-+*modus,* measure, MODE. A piece of furniture with drawers and shelves; a night-stool.—**Commo'dious**, *a.* Med.L. *commodiōsus,* useful, f. *commodus.* Convenient; roomy, spacious.—**Commo'dious**LY,[2] *adv.* —**Commod'ity**, *n.* L. *commoditas,* fitness, f. *commodus.* Convenience; a convenience; an article of commerce; in *pl.*, goods, wares.

Com'modore, *n.* Formerly also *commandore.* Poss. f. Du. *kommandeur* = COMMANDER. A naval officer ranking next above a captain; the president of a yacht-club.

Com'mon, *a.* O.F. *comun*—L. *commūnis,* cogn. with MEAN, *a.*[1] Belonging to more than one or to all; joint, united; general, public; ordinary, usual, prevalent; mere, bare; mean, of little worth; vulgar.—*n.* A tract of ground open to all; that which is common or ordinary. —*Pl.*, the common people; the Lower House of Parliament; food provided for a community; rations, daily fare.—**Com'mon**LY,[2] *adv.*—**Com'monalty**, *n.* O.F. *comunalté.* A corporation; the common people; the general body.—**Com'mon**ER, *n.* One of the common people.—**Com'monplace**, *n.* = L. *locus commūnis,* a passage of general application. A striking passage noted in a **Commonplace'-book**; a truism; anything ordinary or every-day; triviality. — *a.* Trite, trivial, ordinary.—**Com'monwealth**, *n.* (*Wealth* here in old sense 'well-being'.) Also **Com'monweal**. WEAL.[1] The body of the people, a state; a democratic state.

Commo'tion, *n.* L. *commōtio, commōtiōnis,* f. *commovēre, commōtum,* to move violently, disturb. MOVE. Violent agitation; stir; tumult; a tumult, insurrection.

Commune', *vi.* O.F. *comuner,* to make common, share, f. *comun,* COMMON. To hold intimate intercourse *with.* — **Commu'nicate**, *vt.* L. *commūnicāre, commūnicātum,* f. *commūnis,* COMMON. To give a share of, impart; to impart (information); to impart by way of information.—*vi.* To receive the Communion; to impart or exchange information, &c.—**Commu'nic**ANT, *n.* One who or that which communicates; one who receives the Communion, esp. habitually. — **Commu'nic**ABLE, *a.*—**Communic**A'TION, *n.* The action of communicating; that which is communicated, a paper containing information, a letter; access or means of access between places or persons; a line of connexion, channel.—**Commu'nic**ATIVE, *a.* Free in conversation, open.—**Commun'ion**, *n.* L. *commūnio, commūniōnis,* f. *commūnis.* Sharing, participation; fellowship, mutual intercourse; a body professing a particular faith; communication, intercourse; participation in the sacrament of the Lord's Supper, the sacrament.—**Commu'nity**, *n.* L. *commūnitas,* f. *commūnis.* Joint ownership, tenure, &c.; agreement, identity; a state; a body of men inhabiting a district; a body of men having nativity, a religion, &c., in common.—**Com'mun**ISM, *n.* The doctrine of a common ownership of property.—**Com'mun**IST, *n.*

Commute', *vt.* L. COM*mūtāre,* to alter wholly, to exchange. MUTABLE. To exchange; to change a liability, punishment, &c., into something less burdensome, often into a money payment.—**Commut**A'TION, *n.*

Com'pact, *n.* O.F. *compact*—L. *compactum,* use as *n.* of neut. pa.pple. of COM*pacisci,* to covenant together. PACT. A covenant.

Compact', *ppl.a.* L. *compactus,* pa.pple. of *compingĕre,* to put together or fasten closely, f. COM-+*pangĕre,* to fasten. Framed, composed *of.*—*a.* Solid, firm; neatly packed or arranged; terse, pithy.—*vt.* To join firmly together; to condense; to make up or compose.— **Compact'**LY,[2] *adv.*—**Compact'**NESS, *n.*

Compan'ion, *n.*[1] O.F. *compaing, compaignon*—L.L. *compānio,* f. COM- + *pānis,* bread. PANNIER. PANTRY. A mate, fellow, associate. — **Compan'ion**ABLE, *a.* Sociable.— **Compan'ion**SHIP, *n.*

Compan'ion, *n.*[2] O.F. *compagne,* It. *compagna,* a store-room on the deck of a galley, f. L.L. *compānāticum,* things eaten with bread, provisions, f. COM- + *pānis.* (See prec.) A raised cover over the staircase of a cabin; deck sash-lights lighting a cabin.

Com'pany, *n.* O.F. *compaignie* — Med.L. *compānies,* a taking of meals together, f. COM- + *pānis.* COMPANION. Companionship; a party, band; companions collectively; a social party; guests collectively; an association formed to carry on an undertaking; a subdivision of an infantry regiment.

Compare', *vt.* O.F. *comperer*—L. *comparāre,* lit., to pair together, f. COM- + *pār,* equal. PAR. PAIR. PEER, *n.* To liken *to*; to mark or point out difference or likeness of (things); to form the comparative and superlative degrees of an *a.* or *adv.*—*vi.* To be compared; to vie *with.* — **Com'par**ABLE, *a.* — **Compar'**ATIVE, *a.* Involving comparison; estimated by comparison; not positive or absolute, relative; applied to a form of an *a.* or *adv.* expressing a higher degree of quality or attribute than the simple word.—*n.* The comparative degree of an *a.* or *adv.*—**Compar'ative**LY,[2] *adv.*—**Compar'ison**, *n.* O.F. *comparaison,* f. *comparāre.* Comparing, likening; an act of comparing or likening; comparable condition or character; a simile; the action of comparing an *a.* or *adv.*

Compart'ment, *n.* F. *compartiment*—L.L. *compartīre,* to share, f. COM- + L. *partīre,* to share, f. *pars, partis,* a PART. A division or section; a space partitioned off.

Com'pass, *n.* F. *compas,* measure, pair of compasses—L.L. *compassus,* a circuit, f. COM- + L. *passus,* a PACE. An instrument for measuring and for describing circles, gen. in *pl.*, also *pair of compasses*; a circumference, boundary; measurement round; space, area; reach, scope; an instrument for indicating the north.—*vt.* To contrive, devise; to make the circuit of; to surround, hem in; to encircle; to achieve, accomplish, attain.

Compas'sion, *n.* F. *compassion*—L.L. *compassio, compassiōnis*—L. COM*pati, compassus,* to suffer or endure with, pity. PASSION. Pity, sympathy.—**Compas'sion**ATE,[2] *a.* Pitiful, sympathetic. — *vt.* To pity, commiserate.— **Compas'sionate**LY,[2] *adv.*

Compat'ible, *a.* F. *compatible* — Med.L.

compatibilis (of a benefice which could be held along with another)—L. *compati.* (See prec.) Accordant, consistent. — **Compat'ib**LY,[2] *adv.*—**Compati**BIL'ITY, *n.*

Compat'riot, *n.* L. *compatriōta*, f. COM- + *patriōta*, countryman. PATRIOT. A fellow-countryman.

Compeer', *n.* O.F. *comper*, f. COM- + *per*, an equal, f. L. *pār*, equal. COMPARE. An equal; a comrade.

Compel', *vt.* O.F. *compeller*—L. COM*pellĕre*, *compulsum*, to drive together, constrain. APPEAL. PULSATE. To constrain, oblige; to bring about by force.—**Compul'**SION, *n.* Constraint, obligation.—**Compul'**SIVE, *a.* Exercising compulsion.—**Compul'**SORY, *a.* Exercising compulsion; compelled, forced.

Compend', **Compen'dium**, *n.* L. *compendium*, that which is weighed together, a sparing, shortening, f. COM*pendĕre*, to weigh together. EXPEND. An abridgment, summary.—**Compen'di**OUS, *a.* Brief but comprehensive.—**Compen'dious**LY,[2] *adv.*

Com'pensate, *vt.* L. COM*pensāre*, *compensātum*, to weigh one thing against another, f. *pensāre*, freq. of *pendĕre.* (See prec.) To make up for, make amends for; to remunerate *for*.—*vi.* To make up *for*.—**Compens**A'TION, *n.*

Compete', *vi.* L. *competĕre* in post-class. sense 'to strive after together', f. COM- + *petĕre*, to seek. PETITION. To contend, strive, vie *with*.—**Competi'**TION, *n.*—**Compet'it**IVE, *a.*—**Compet'it**OR, *n.*

Com'petent, *a.* F. *compétent*—L. *competens, competentis*, pres.pple. of *competĕre* (see prec.) in class. sense 'to come together, to be suitable'. Suitable, sufficient; properly qualified; legally qualified or sufficient; proper, due; permissible, legitimate.—**Com'petent**LY,[2] *adv.* —**Com'pet**ENCE, **Com'pet**ENCY, *nn.*

Compile', *vt.* F. *compiler*, to put together, collect, commonly taken as f. L. COM*pilāre*, to plunder. (But perh. the idea is rather that of mixing in a mortar, L. *pila.*) To put (materials) together to form a treatise; to make up (a book) from materials from various sources. —**Compil'**ER, *n.*—**Compil**A'TION, *n.*

Compla'cent, *a.* L. *complacens, complacentis*, pres.pple. of COM*placēre*, to PLEASE. Self-satisfied. — **Compla'cent**LY,[2] *adv.*— **Compla'**CENCE, -ENCY, *nn.*—**Com'plaisant**, *a.* F. *complaisant*, obsequious, pres.pple. of *complaire*, f. *complacēre.* Disposed to please, obliging, compliant.—**Com'plais**ANCE, *n.*

Complain', *vi.* F. *complaindre*—L.L. *complangĕre*, to bewail, f. COM- + *plangĕre*, to beat (the breast), hence, to lament, bewail. PLAINT. With *of*, to let it be known that one is suffering from (a pain, a malady, &c.); to murmur, grumble; to lodge a complaint, bring a charge.—**Complaint'**, *n.* F. *complainte.* Utterance of grievance; a subject of complaint; a formal statement of wrong; an illness.—**Complain'**ANT, *n.*

Complete', *a.* L. *complētus*, pa.pple. of COM*plēre*, to fill up, cogn. with *plēnus*, FULL. PLENARY. Entire, full; ended, finished; entire, thorough; perfect, without defect.—*vt.* To bring to an end, finish; to make whole, entire, perfect, of full number or amount.— **Complete'**LY,[2] *adv.*—**Complete'**NESS, *n.* —**Comple'**TION, *n.*—**Com'plement**, *n.* L. *complēmentum.* COMPLIMENT. Complete quantity, &c., full allowance; something making up a whole.—*vt.* To make complete. —**Complemen'**TARY, *a.*

Com'plex, *a.* L. *complexus*, entwined, hence, intricate, pa.pple. of *complecti*, to entwine, surround, f. COM- + *plectĕre*, to plait, allied to *plicāre*, to fold. ACCOMPLICE. APPLY. COMPLICATE. DISPLAY. PLY. Composite, compound; complicated, involved.—**Complex'**ITY, *n.*

Complex'ion, *n.* L. *complexio, complexiōnis*, combination, association, later, physical constitution, f. *complecti.* (See prec.) The natural appearance of the skin, esp. of the face; colour, look; quality, character.

Com'plicate, *vt.* L. COM*plicāre*, *complicātum*, to fold together. COMPLEX. To mix up *with* in an intricate way; to make intricate or involved.—*ppl.a.* Compound, mixed; intricate, involved.—**Complic**A'TION, *n.*

Complic'ity, *n.* F. *complicité*, f. *complice*, a confederate—L. *complex, complicis*, participant, f. *complicāre.* (See prec.) ACCOMPLICE. Partnership in evil.

Com'pliment, *n.* F. *compliment*—It. *complimento*, f. L. *complēmentum* (COMPLEMENT under COMPLETE) with sense 'fulfilment of the forms of courtesy'. COMPLY. An act or expression of courtesy; a neatly-turned remark involving praise; in *pl.*, formal respects, greetings.—**Compliment'**, *vt.* To pay a compliment to; to congratulate *on* or *upon*; to present *with*, to bestow, in compliment.— **Compliment'**ARY, *a.*

Comply', *vi.* It. *complire*, f. L. *complēre* (COMPLETE) with sense 'to fulfil the forms of courtesy'. COMPLIMENT. Formerly, to use compliments, be complaisant. With *with* or absol., to yield, accede, consent.—**Compli'**ANCE, *n.*—**Compli'**ANT, *a.*

Compo'nent, *a.* L. *compōnens, compōnentis*, pres.pple. of *compōnĕre*, to COMPOUND. Composing, constituting.—*n.* A constituent part or element.

Comport', *vi.* F. *comporter*, to endure, to behave—L. COM*portāre*, to bring together. PORT, *v.*[2] With *with*, to agree with, to suit.— *v.refl.* To behave oneself.

Compose', *vt.* F. *composer*, f. COM- + *poser*, to place. POSE.[1] To constitute, make up; of literary work, to write; of music, to invent and put into form; to set up (types); to arrange artistically; to settle, arrange (disputes, &c.); to adjust or address (the body or mind) to some attitude, esp. to that of repose; to arrange, adjust; to calm (emotions, &c.).— **Composed'**, *ppl.a.* Free from agitation, tranquil.—**Compos'**ER, *n.*—**Com'posite**, *a.* L. *compositus*, pa.pple. of *compōnĕre*, to COMPOUND. Not simple, compound.—**Composi'tion**, *n.* F. *composition*, L. *compositio, compositiōnis*, f. *compositus.* In senses from the *v.*—**Compos'it**OR, *n.* A type-setter.— **Compo'sure**, *n.* App. of Eng. formation on analogy of *enclosure*, &c. Tranquillity, calmness.

Compound', *vt.* M.E. *compounen*—O.F. *componre*—L. COM*pōnĕre*, to put together. POSITION. (The *d* is excrescent.) To put together, combine; to make up (a composite product); to construct, form; to compromise; to discharge (a liability) by a money payment, a partial payment, or payment of a lump sum; to condone.—*vi.* To come to terms, make a pecuniary arrangement; to settle *with* (one's creditors).—**Com'pound**, *a.* Not simple; complex, composite; collective.—*n.*[1] A union, combination; a compound substance or word.

Com'pound, *n.*[2] Of disputed orig. Perh.

f. Malay *kampong*, enclosure. In the East, an enclosure in which houses stand.

Comprehend′, *vt.* L. COM*prehendĕre, comprehensum*, to grasp. APPREHEND. PREHENSILE. To understand; to apprehend, take in; to include, comprise, contain.—**Comprehen′**SIBLE, *a.*—**Comprehen′**SION, *n.*—**Comprehen′**SIVE, *a.*—**Comprehen′sive**LY,[2] *adv.*—**Comprehen′sive**NESS, *n.*

Compress′, *vt.* O.F. *compresser*—L. *compressāre*, freq. of *comprimĕre, compressum*, to press together, f. COM-+*premĕre*, to PRESS.[1] To press or squeeze together; to reduce in volume, condense.—**Com′press**, *n.* A soft mass of lint, &c., for compressing an artery, &c.—**Compres′**SIBLE, *a.*—**Compres′**SION, *n.*

Comprise′, *vt.* F. *compris*, pa.pple. of *comprendre*, L. *comprehendĕre*, to COMPREHEND. To include, contain, extend to, embrace.

Com′promise, *n.* F. *compromis*, orig. pa. pple. of *compromettre*, to compromise—L. COM*prōmittĕre, comprōmissum*, to promise mutually to abide by a decision, f. *prōmittĕre*, to PROMISE. A coming to terms, terms offered; adjustment of rival claims, &c., by partial surrender; exposure to risk or suspicion.—*vt.* To come to terms about; to expose to risk or suspicion.—*vi.* To come to terms.

Comptrol′ler, *n.* An erroneous spelling of CONTROLLER.

Compunc′tion, *n.* L. *compunctio, compunctiōnis*, prick of conscience, f. COM*pungĕre, compunctum*, to prick. PUNGENT. Remorse; passing regret for wrong-doing, regret for a slight offence.—**Compunc′tious**, *a.*

Compute′, *vt.* L. *computāre*, to sum up, reckon, f. COM-+*putāre*, to reckon, COUNT. To reckon, estimate.—**Comput**A′TION, *n.*

Com′rade, *n.* F. *camarade*—Sp. *camarada*, chamberful, hence, chamber-mate, f. *camara*, chamber—L. *camera*. CHAMBER. A mate, fellow.

Con, *v.*[1]*t.* A var. of CAN, *v.*, with sense 'to learn'. To learn; to pore over, scan, examine.

Con, *v.*[2]*t.* App. f. obs. *Cond* in same sense, shortened f. obs. *condue*, to conduct, guide—O.F. *conduire*—L. *condūcĕre*. CONDUCT. To direct the steering of (a ship).

Concat′enate, *vt.* L. CON*catēnāre, concatēnātum*, to link together, f. *catēna*, CHAIN. To connect as with a chain, link together.—**Concaten**A′TION, *n.*

Con′cave, *a.* F. *concave*—L. CON*cavus*, hollow. CAVE. Curved so as to present a hollow to the point of observation, the reverse of CONVEX.—**Concav′**ITY, *n.*

Conceal′, *vt.* O.F. *conceler*—L. CON*cēlāre*, to hide. CELL. HALL. To keep secret; to put or keep out of sight.—**Conceal′**MENT, *n.*

Concede′, *vt.* L. CON*cēdĕre, concessum*, to give way. CEDE. To admit, grant, acknowledge; to yield, surrender.—**Conces′**SION, *n.*—**Conces′**SIVE, *a.*

Conceit′, *n.* App. formed f. CONCEIVE on the analogy of *deceive, deceit*. Favourable opinion, esp. in phrase *out of conceit with*, dissatisfied with; an overweening opinion of oneself; a fancy, whim; fancy, imagination; an affectation in thought or style, the use of conceits.—**Conceit′ed**, *ppl.a.* Having an overweening opinion of oneself.

Conceive′, *vt.* O.F. *conceveir*—L. *concipĕre, conceptum*, f. CON-, altogether+*capĕre*, to take. CAPABLE. To become pregnant with; to take or admit into the mind; to devise, evolve the idea of; to imagine, think of; to understand; to formulate, couch.—*vi.* To become pregnant; to fancy, imagine, think.—**Conceiv′**ABLE, *a.*—**Conceiv′**ABLY,[2] *adv.*—**Con′cept**, *n.* From neut. of *conceptus*, pa.pple. of *concipĕre*. A general notion or idea.—**Concep′tion**, *n.*

Concen′tre, Con′centrate, *vv.t.* F. *concentrer*, f. CON-+L. *centrum*, CENTRE. To draw to a common centre; to bring into small space, to increase the vigour or intensity of.—*vv.i.* To come to a common centre or into closer union.—**Concentr**A′TION, *n.*—**Concen′tric**, *a.* Having a common centre.

Concern′, *vt.* F. *concerner*—Med.L. *concernĕre*, to refer to, regard, in L., to mix together for sifting, f. CON-+*cernĕre*, to separate, perceive, decide, cogn. with G. *krinein*, to separate, decide. CRIME. DECREE. SECRET. To relate or refer to; to be of importance to, be the business of.—*v.refl.* To interest oneself *with, in*, &c.—In *pass.*, to feel interested; to be troubled; to be engaged *with, in*; to be involved *in*; to be affected.—*n.* An affair; importance, moment; care, anxiety; a commercial, &c., establishment.—**Concern′ing**, *prep.* Regarding, respecting.

Concern′MENT, *n.*

Concert′, *vt.* F. *concerter*—It. *concertare*, to agree, to sing or play in concert, poss. f. L. *concertāre*, to contend zealously (hence perh. to argue out, come to terms), f. CON-+*certāre*, to decide by contest, contend, freq. of *cernĕre*. (See prec.) To contrive mutually; of one person, to contrive, plan.—**Con′cert**, *n.* Agreement, harmony; agreement in a course of action; a combination of voices; a public musical entertainment.—**Concert′ed**, *ppl.a.* Mutually contrived; arranged for performance by a company of musicians.—**Concerti′na**, *n.* Fem. ending *-ina*. A portable musical instrument with a bellows and keys.—**Concert′o**, *n.* It., f. *concertare*. A composition for a solo instrument and orchestra.

Conch, *n.* L. *concha*—G. *kogchē*. COCKLE.[2] A shell-fish; the shell of such a fish; such a shell used as an instrument of call.—**Conchol′**OGY, *n.* The science of shells and shell-fish.—**Concholog′**ICAL, *a.*—**Conchol′o**GIST, *n.*

Concil′iate, *vt.* L. *conciliāre, conciliātum*, to bring together, make friendly, to bring about, procure, f. *concilium*, COUNCIL. RECONCILE.—To gain (goodwill, esteem, &c.); to reconcile; to soothe, pacify; to get over (objections), make (things) amicable.—**Concili**A′TION, *n.*—**Concil′iat**ORY, *a.*

Concise′, *a.* L. *concisus*, pa.pple. of *concīdĕre*, to cut up, f. CON-+*caedĕre*, to cut. CEMENT. CHISEL. DECIDE. Brief and comprehensive.—**Concise′**LY,[2] *adv.*—**Concise′**NESS, *n.*—**Concis′**ION, *n.* Mutilation; conciseness.

Con′clave, *n.* F. *conclave*—L. *conclāve*, a place that may be locked up, f. CON-+*clāvis*, key. The place of meeting, the assembly, for the election of a Pope; a private assembly.

Conclude′, *vt.* L. *conclūdĕre, conclūsum*, to shut up closely, end, f. CON-+*claudĕre*, to shut, CLOSE. CLOISTER. To end, finish; to settle, arrange.—*vi.* To come to an end; to infer, deduce; to decide, resolve.—**Conclu′**SION, *n.*—**Conclu′**SIVE, *a.* Final; decisive, convincing.—**Conclu′sive**LY,[2] *adv.*

Concoct′, *vt.* L. CON*coquĕre, concoctum*, to COOK together. To prepare from a variety of ingredients; to devise in concert, make up, fabricate.—**Concoc'tion**, *n.*

Concom'itant, *a.* L. *concomitans, concomitantis*, pres.pple. of CON*comitāri*, to accompany, f. *comes, comitis*, companion. COUNT, *n.*[2] Going together, accompanying.—*n.* An attendant circumstance, &c.; an accompaniment.—**Concom'itance, -ancy**, *nn.*

Con'cord, *n.* F. *concorde*—L. *concordia*, f. *concors, concordis*, agreeing, f. CON- + *cor*, HEART. CORDIAL. Agreement, harmony; a state of amity; harmony of sounds; agreement of words in construction.—**Concor'dance**, *n.* Agreement, harmony; an index of the principal words of a book.—**Concor'dant**, *a.* —**Concor'dat**, *n.* From pa.pple. of L. *concordāre*, to be *concors*. A compact between Church and State.

Con'course, *n.* O.F. *concours*—L. *concursus*, f. *concurrĕre*. CONCUR. A flocking together; a crowd; a flowing or meeting together.

Con'crete. *a.* L. *concrētus*, pa.pple. of CON*crescĕre*, to grow together. ACCRESCE. Solidified; embodied in matter, actual practice, &c. —*n.* A concrete mass; a mixture of stone chippings, sand, &c., with cement used in building.—**Concrete'**, *vt.* To render solid.—*vi.* To run into a mass.—**Con'cretely**,[2] *adv.* —**Concre'tion**, *n.* The action or process of being concreted; a concreted mass.

Con'cubine, *n.* F. *concubin*—L. *concubīna*, f. CON- + *cubāre*, to lie. CUBICLE. A woman not his wife who cohabits with a man.—**Concub'inage**, *n.*

Concu'piscence, *n.* L. *concupiscentia*, f. *concupiscĕre*, inceptive of CON*cupĕre*, to long much for. CUPIDITY. Eager desire; lust.—**Concu'piscent**, *a.*

Concur', *vi.* L. CON*currĕre, concursum*, to run together. CONCOURSE. COURSE. CURRENT. INTERCOURSE. To happen together, coincide; to combine in action, co-operate; to agree in opinion.—**Concur'rence**, *n.*—**Concur'rent**, *a.*—**Concur'rently**,[2] *adv.*

Concuss', *vt.* L. *concutĕre, concussum*, to shake violently, f. CON- + *quatĕre*, to shake. QUASH. To intimidate by threats.—**Concus'sion**, *n.* Violent shaking, a shock; injury, esp. to the brain, by a blow, fall, &c.

Condemn', *vt.* O.F. *condemner*—L. *condemnāre, condemnātum*, to condemn wholly, f. CON- + *damnāre*, to condemn. DAMN. To censure, blame; to convict, find guilty; to devote, doom; to pronounce forfeited, unfit for use, &c.—**Condemna'tion**, *n.*—**Condem'natory**, *a.*

Condense', *vt.* L. *condensāre, condensātum*, f. CON*densus*, very thick, DENSE. To concentrate, compress; to reduce from the gaseous to the liquid form; to compress into few words.—*vi.* To become dense; to be reduced to the liquid state.—**Condensa'tion**, *n.*

Condescend', *vi.* F. *condescendre*—L. CON*dēscendĕre, condēscensum*, to stoop, condescend, f. *dēscendĕre*, to DESCEND. To stoop, deign; to be gracious or complaisant.—**Condescen'sion**, *n.*

Condign', *a.* F. *condigne*—L. CON*dignus*, wholly worthy. DIGNIFY. Well merited.—**Condign'ly**,[2] *adv.*

Con'diment, *n.* L. *condīmentum*, f. *condīre*, to preserve, pickle. Seasoning, a relish.

Condi'tion, *n.* O.F. *condition*—L. *conditio, conditiōnis*, for *condicio, condiciōnis*, a compact, stipulation, f. *condīcĕre*, to talk over together, f. CON- + *dīcĕre*, to speak. DICTION. A provision, stipulation; something on which existing or happening depends; state of being; social position, rank.—*vt.* To govern, limit, qualify; to determine the existence or happening of; to make dependent on; to stipulate for, make it a condition.—**Condi'tional**, *a.*

Condole', *vi.* L. CON*dolēre*, to grieve with. DOLE.[2] To grieve or sympathize *with*.—**Condole'ment, Condol'ence**, *nn.*

Condone', *vt.* L. *condōnāre, condōnātum*, to give up, forgive, f. CON- + *dōnāre*, to give. DONATE. To forgive, overlook (an offence), esp. tacitly.—**Condona'tion**, *n.*

Conduce', *vi.* L. CON*dūcĕre, conductum*, to lead together, also, to be serviceable. DUKE. With *to*, to aid in bringing about, promote.—**Condu'cive**, *a.*

Con'duct, *n.* L.L. *conductus*, defence, escort, also, a canal, tube, f. L. *condūcĕre*. (See prec. and next.) CON.[2] Guidance, leading; leadership; direction, management; behaviour.—**Conduct'**, *vt.* To guide, lead, direct; to manage, carry on; to direct (an orchestra, &c.) —*v.refl.* To behave oneself.—**Conduc'tor Conduc'tress**, *nn.*

Con'duit, *n.* O.F. *conduit*—L.L. *conductus*. (See prec.) A channel or pipe for water.

Cone, *n.* L. *cōnus*, cone—G. *kōnos*, pine-cone, cone, cogn. with L. *cuneus*, wedge (COIN). Cf. Skr. *çi*, to sharpen. A solid figure with a circular base and tapering regularly to a point; the fruit of pines, firs, &c.—**Con'ic, Con'ical**, *aa.*—**Con'ifer**, *n.* L. *cōnifer*, cone-bearing, f. *cōnus* + *-fer*, bearing, f. *ferre*, to BEAR. A tree bearing cones.—**Conif'erous**, *a.*

Confab'ulate, *vi.* L. CON*fābulāri, confābulātus*, to talk together, f. *fābula*, a tale, discourse. FABLE. To talk together familiarly, chat.—**Confabula'tion**, *n.*

Confec'tion, *n.* O.F. *confeccion*—L. *confectio, confectiōnis*, a preparing, f. *conficĕre*. COMFIT. Preparation, making up; a sweetmeat, comfit.—*vt.* To prepare as a condiment or delicacy.—**Confec'tionary**, *a.* Of the nature of a confection.—*n.* A place where sweetmeats are made; a sweetmeat.—**Confec'tioner**, *n.*—**Confec'tionery**, *n.* Things sold by a confectioner, his art and business, his shop.

Confed'erate, *a.* L. *confoederātus*, pa.pple. of CON*foederāre*, to unite by a treaty, f. *foedus*. FEDERAL. Allied, leagued.—*n.* An ally; an accomplice.—*vt.* and *i.* To unite in alliance or as accomplices.—**Confed'eracy**, *n.*—**Confedera'tion**, *n.*

Confer', *vt.* L. *conferre*. COLLATE. To bestow, grant.—*vi.* To converse, take counsel.—**Con'ference**, *n.*

Confess', *vt.* O.F. *confesser*—L.L. *confessāre*, freq. f. L. *confitēri, confessus*, to confess, f. CON- + *fatēri* in same sense, cogn. with *fāri*, G. *phanai*, to speak. FATE. To acknowledge, own (a crime, &c.); to grant, admit (an assertion, &c.); to declare belief in; of a priest, to hear the sins of, shrive.—*vi.* To acknowledge; to acknowledge sins orally as a religious duty (so also *refl.*).—**Confes'sedly**,[2] *adv.* By general admission.—**Confes'sion**, *n.*—**Confes'sional**, *n.* The box in which a priest hears confessions.—**Confes'sor**, *n.* One who confesses; one who adheres to his faith under persecution, but is not a martyr; a priest who hears confessions, a spiritual director.

Confide', *vi.* L. CON*fīdĕre*, to have full trust. FAITH. To trust, have faith *in*.—*vt.* To impart as a secret; to entrust.—**Confidant'**, *n.*

Formation obscure. One entrusted with secrets.—**Con'fid**ENCE, *n.* Trust; assurance, certitude; boldness; hardihood, presumption; trustful intimacy.—**Con'fid**ENT, *a.* Fully assured; bold; presumptuous; dogmatical.—*n.* A trusted friend; one entrusted with secrets.—**Con'fident**LY,[2] *adv.*—**Confiden'**TIAL, *a.* Communicated in confidence; betokening private intimacy; entrusted with secrets.—**Confiden'tial**LY,[2] *adv.*

Config'ure, *vt.* L. *configūrāre*, to fashion after something, f. CON- + *figūrāre*, to fashion, f. *figūra*, FIGURE. To fashion after a model, put together in a certain form.—**Configura**A'TION, *n.* Form, shape.

Confine', *vt.* F. *confiner* in same senses—L. CON*finis*, bordering, f. *finis*, boundary. AFFINITY. To imprison, shut up; to keep within bounds; to keep indoors or in bed; to limit, restrict; to restrain (the bowels) from acting; *pass.*, to be in childbed.—**Con'fines**, *n.pl.* F. *confins*—L. *confīnia*, pl. of *confīnium*, a boundary, f. *confīnis*. Bounds, borders, border-lands.—**Confine'**MENT, *n.*

Confirm', *vt.* O.F. *confermer*—L. CON*firmāre*, *confirmātum*, to make firm, strengthen, f. *firmus*, FIRM. To make firm, settle, establish; to make valid, ratify; to fortify, encourage; to make certain, verify; to administer the rite of confirmation to.—**Confirma**A'TION, *n.* In senses from the *v.*; a rite administered by a bishop to baptized persons admitting to the privileges of the Church.—**Confirm'**ATIVE, **Confirm'at**ORY, *aa.*

Con'fiscate, *vt.* L. CON*fiscāre*, *confiscātum*, to lay up for safety, confiscate, f. *fiscus*, purse, treasury. FISC. To appropriate to the public treasury; to seize.—**Confisca**A'TION, *n.*—**Confiscat'**ORY, *a.*

Con'flagrate, *vi.* L. CON*flagrāre*, to burn. FLAGRANT. To burst into flame.—*vt.* To set ablaze.—**Conflagr**A'TION, *n.*

Conflict', *vi.* L. CON*fligĕre*, *conflictum*, to clash, contend, f. *flīgĕre*, to strike. To contend *with*; to clash, be at variance.—**Con'flict**, *n.* A struggle; clashing or variance.

Con'fluence, *n.* L. *confluentia*, f. CON*fluĕre*, *confluxum*, to flow together. Also **Con'flux**, f. the ppl. stem. AFFLUENT. A flowing together, a union of streams; the place of union; concourse; a multitude, assemblage, collection.—**Con'flu**ENT, *a.*

Conform', *vt.* F. *conformer*—L. CON*formāre*, to fashion, shape, f. *forma*, FORM. To make like; to adapt.—*vi.* To comply, be conformable.—**Conform'**ABLE, *a.* Like; adapted; compliant *to*; tractable.—**Conform'ab**LY,[2] *adv.*—**Conforma**A'TION, *n.* Adaptation; putting into form; structure.—**Conform'**ITY, *n.* Likeness; compliance.

Confound', *vt*, O.F. *confondre*—L. CON*fundĕre*, *confūsum*, to pour together, mix up. FUSE, *v.* To defeat, bring to nought; to discomfit; to disconcert, bewilder; to bring into confusion or disorder; to mix up in idea.

Confront', *vt.* F. *confronter*—Med.L. CON*frontāri*, to be near to, f. *frons*, *frontis*, forehead. FRONT. To face; to stand against, oppose; to bring face to face *with*.

Confuse', *vt.* Occurs first in the pple., adapted f. F. *confus* or L. *confūsus*, f. *confundĕre*. CONFOUND. To disconnect, bewilder; to disorder; to mix up in idea.—**Confu'**SION, *n.*

Confute', *vt.* L. CON*fūtāre*, to repress, confute, of disputed orig. REFUTE. To convict of error; to refute, disprove; to render futile.—**Confut**A'TION, *n.*

Congeal', *vt.* O.F. *congeler*—L. CON*gelāre*, to cause to freeze up, f. *gelu*, frost. COLD. To freeze; to stiffen, curdle.—*vi.* To become congealed.—**Congel**A'TION, *n.*

Con'gee, **Congé**, *n.* F. *congé*, O.F. *congie*, *cunge*—L. *commeātus*, leave of absence, f. COM*meāre*, *commeātum*, to pass to and fro, f. *meāre*, to go. A bow, orig. on taking leave; dismissal.

Conge'ner, *n.* L. CON*gener*, of the same kind, f. *genus*, *generis*, kind. GENUS. One of the same kind or class.

Conge'nial, *a.* CON- + GENIAL. Of the same genius or temperament, sympathetic; to one's liking; suited.—**Conge'nial**LY,[2] *adv.*—**Congenial'**ITY, *n.*

Congen'ital, *a.* With -AL f. L. CON*genitus*, born with, f. *genitus*, pa. pple. of *gignĕre*, to beget. GENITAL. Dating from birth, born with one.

Congest', *vi.* L. CON*gerĕre*, *congestum*, to gather together, heap up. GESTATION. To accumulate to excess.—*vt.* To accumulate to excess; to affect with congestion.—**Conges'**TION, *n.* Abnormal accumulation of blood, population, &c.—**Conge'ries**, *n.* L., f. *congerĕre*. A collection of things heaped together, a mass.

Conglom'erate, *vt.* and *i.* L. CON*glomerāre*, *conglomerātum*, to heap together. AGGLOMERATE. To collect into a coherent mass.—*a.* Gathered into a mass, clustered.—*n.* A rock composed of pebbles cemented into a compact mass.—**Conglomer**A'TION, *n.*

Congrat'ulate, *vt.* L. *congrātulāri*, *congrātulātus*, to congratulate, f. CON- + *grātulāri* in same sense, f. *grātus*, pleasing. GRACE. To compliment *on* or *upon* any happy event, felicitate.—*v.refl.* To account oneself happy.—**Congratul**A'TION, *n.*—**Congrat'ula**TORY, *a.*

Con'gregate, *vt.* L. *congregāre*, *congregātum*, to bring together into a flock, f. CON- + *gregāre* in same sense, f. *grex*, flock. AGGREGATE. To gather together into a mass or assembly.—*vi.* and *refl.* To flock or assemble together.—**Congreg**A'TION, *n.* A congregating or assembling; a gathering, assemblage, esp. for religious worship; a local assembly meeting regularly for worship.—**Congrega'tion**AL, *a.* Relating to a congregation or to the Congregationalists.—**Congrega'tional**IST, *n.* One who holds that each local religious congregation forms an independent body.—**Congrega'tional**ISM, *n.*

Con'gress, *n.* L. *congressus*, a coming together, f. *congredi*, *congressus*, to meet with one, f. CON- + *gradi*, to go, f. *gradus*, step. AGGRESSION. A meeting; a formal assembly for discussion or for the settlement of a question; a national legislative body, esp. that of the United States.—**Congres'sion**AL, *a.*

Con'gruous, *a.* With -OUS f. L. *congruus*, agreeing, f. CON*gruĕre*, to meet together, coincide, of doubtful orig. Accordant, suitable; fitting, appropriate; self-accordant, coherent.—**Con'gruous**LY,[2] *adv.*—**Con'gruent**, *a.* L. *congruens*, *congruentis*, pres.pple. of *congruĕre*. Accordant, suitable.—**Congru'**ITY, *n.*

Conjec'ture, *n.* L. *conjectūra*, a throwing together, an inference, f. *conjicĕre*, *conjectum*, to throw together, infer, f. CON- + *jacĕre*, to throw. ABJECT. A guessing or surmising; an opinion founded on surmise.—*vt.* To guess; to propose (a conjectural reading).—*vi.* To make a guess.—**Conjec'tur**AL, *a.*

Conjoin′, *vt.* F. *conjoindre*—L. *conjungĕre.* (See next.) To join together; to unite, ally.—*vi.* To unite.—**Conjoint′**, *a.* F. *conjoint*, pa.pple. of *conjoindre.* United, associated; belonging to or constituted by two or more in combination.—**Conjoint′**LY,[2] *adv.*

Con′jugal, *a.* L. *conjugālis*, f. *conjunx, conjugis*, a spouse, f. CON*jungĕre, conjunctum*, to join together, cogn. with *jugum*, YOKE. SUBJUGATE. JOIN. Of or relating to marriage, matrimonial.—**Con′jugate**, *vt.* L. CON*jugāre, conjugātum*, to join together, f. *jugum.* To inflect (a verb) in its various forms.—*a.* Coupled; kindred in origin and meaning.—**Conjug**A′TION, *n.*

Conjunct′, *a.* L. *conjunctus*, pa.pple. of *conjungĕre.* (See prec.) In same senses as CONJOINT.—**Conjunct′**LY,[2] *adv.*—**Conjunc′**TION, *n.* Union; a combination of events or circumstances; a combination, association; of heavenly bodies, apparent proximity; a part of speech connecting sentences, clauses, or words.—**Conjunc′**TIVE, *a.*—**Conjunc′**TURE, *n.* A combination of events or circumstances; a crisis.

Conjure′, *vt.* O.F. *conjurer*—L. CON*jūrāre*, to swear together, combine. JURY. To appeal to solemnly, implore.—**Con′jure**, *vt.* To summon (a devil, &c.) by invocations; to effect, bring *out*, convey *away* by magic arts; to bring, get, convey as by magic.—**Conjur**A′TION, *n.* A solemn appeal; an incantation.—**Con′jur**ER, **Con′jur**OR, *n.* A magician; a juggler.

Connect′, *vt.* L. CON*nectĕre, connexum*, to bind together. ANNEX. To join together; to join in sequence or order; to associate in occurrence, action, idea; to unite *with* by ties of relationship, &c.—*vi.* To become joined or united.—**Connex′ion**, **Connec′**TION, *n.*—**Connec′**TIVE, *a.*

Connive′, *vi.* L. CON*nivēre*, to close the eyes, app. cogn. with *nicĕre*, to beckon, *nictāre*, to wink. To pretend ignorance; to wink *at*, be secretly privy.—**Conniv′**ENCE, **Conniv′**ANCE, *nn.*

Connoisseur′, *n.* F. (now *connaisseur*)—O.F. *conoistre*, to know. COGNIZANCE. A critical judge of art or matters of taste.

Connote′, *vt.* Med.L. CON*notāre*, to mark along with, f. *nota*, a mark. NOTE. To signify in addition to the primary meaning; to involve or imply as a consequence or accompaniment.—**Connot**A′TION, *n.*

Connu′bial, *a.* L. *connūbiālis*, f. *connūbium*, marriage, f. CON + *nūbĕre*, to marry. NUPTIAL. Pertaining to marriage or a spouse.

Con′quer, *vt.* O.F. *conquerre*—L. CON*quaerĕre*, to seek for earnestly, hence, in L.L., to gain, conquer. QUEST. To win by war; to win, gain; to overcome, vanquish.—*vi.* To be victorious.—**Con′quer**ABLE, *a.*—**Con′quer**OR, *n.*—**Con′quest**, *n.* L.L. *conquesta*—L. *conquīsīta*, fem. pa.pple. of *conquaerĕre.* Subjugation; gaining of victory; what is acquired by conquest.

Consanguin′eous, *a.* L. *consanguineus* (f. CON- + *sanguis, sanguinis*, blood) + OUS. SANGUINE. Related by blood, akin.—**Consanguin′**ITY, *n.*

Con′science, *n.* F. *conscience*—L. *conscientia*, f. CON*scīre* (*sibi*), to know with oneself, in one's own mind. SCIENCE. The inward sense of right and wrong.—**Conscien′**TIOUS, *a.*—**Conscien′tious**LY,[2] *adv.*—**Con′scion**ABLE, *a.* App. formed f. *conscion*, assumed as sing. of *conscience.* Conformable to conscience, scrupulous, reasonable.—**Con′scious**, *a.* L. *conscius*, aware (f. *conscīre*) + -OUS. Having internal perception; having the faculty of such perception; having one's mental faculties awake; aware of what one is doing; preoccupied with one's own personality; known to oneself, felt; aware of itself.—**Con′scious**LY,[2] *adv.*—**Con′scious**NESS, *n.*

Conscribe′, *vt.* L. CON*scrībĕre*, to write together (in a list), enroll. SCRIBE. To enlist for the army or navy compulsorily.—**Con′script**, *a.* L. *conscriptus*, pa.pple. of *conscrībere.* So enlisted.—*n.* One so enlisted.—**Conscrip′**TION, *n.*

Con′secrate, *vt.* L. *consecrāre, consecrātum*, f. CON- + *sacrāre*, to set apart as SACRED. DESECRATE. To set apart as sacred; to dedicate or devote *to*; to hallow, sanctify.—**Consecr**A′TION, *n.*

Consecu′tion, *n.* L. *consecūtio, consecūtiōnis*, f. CON*sequi, consecūtus*, to follow closely. CONSEQUENT. SEQUEL. Logical sequence, inference; sequence (of events).—**Consec′u**TIVE, *a.* Expressing consequence; following continuously.—**Consec′utive**LY,[2] *adv.*

Consent′, *vi.* O.F. *consentir*—L. CON*sentīre*, to feel together, agree. SENSE. To acquiesce, comply.—*n.* Acquiescence, compliance; agreement in a course of action, concert.

Con′sequent, *a.* L. *consequens, consequentis*, pres.pple. of *consequi.* CONSECUTION. Following as an effect, resulting; logically consistent.—**Con′sequent**LY,[2] *adv.*—**Con′sequ**ENCE, *n.* A result, effect; a logical result; importance, weight.—**Consequen′**TIAL, *a.* Following as a result or effect; not direct or immediate; having a high opinion of one's own importance.—**Consequen′tial**LY,[2] *adv.*

Conserve′, *vt.* F. *conserver*—L. CON*servāre, conservātum*, to keep safe, PRESERVE. To keep from harm or decay.—*n.* A medicinal or confectionary preparation preserved with sugar.—**Conserv**A′TION, *n.* A keeping from harm or decay, esp. *of* existing conditions or institutions.—**Conser′v**ATIVE, *a.* Tending to conserve; adhering to existing institutions.—*n.* One of such a party.—**Conser′vat**ISM, *n.*—**Conser′vat**ORY, *n.* A place for keeping tender plants.

Consid′er, *vt.* F. *considérer*—L. CON*siderāre, considerātum*, to look at closely, orig. (it is said) to observe the stars, f. *sīdus, sīderis*, star. (The simple *siderāre* does not occur.) DESIDERATE. SIDEREAL. To survey, examine; to think over, give heed to; to regard, make allowance for; to respect, esteem; to look upon *as*, think *to be.*—*vi.* To bethink one self, reflect.—**Consid′er**ABLE, *a.* Important of consequence; somewhat large, a good deal of.—**Consid′erab**LY,[2] *adv.*—**Consid′er**ATE,[2] *a.* Careful, deliberate; thoughtful for others.—**Consid′erate**LY,[2] *adv.*—**Consider**A′TION, *n.* Reflection; the taking of something into account, something taken into account; a reward, equivalent; thoughtfulness for others; importance, consequence.

Consign′, *vt.* L. CON*signāre*, to seal, f. *signum*, mark, seal, SIGN. To deliver formally, commit *to* (a fate, &c.); to commit for custody; to deliver (goods) for transit and sale or custody.—**Consign**EE′, *n.*—**Consign′**ER, **Consign′**OR, *nn.*—**Consign′**MENT, *n.*

Consist′, *vi.* L. CON*sistĕre*, to stand still, remain, consist. ASSIST. To agree, harmonize *with*; to be comprised or contained *in*; to be made up or composed *of*.—**Consis'tent**, *a.* Agreeing, according; having its parts in agreement; constant in adherence to principles, &c.—**Consis'tence, Consis'tency**, *nn.* Coherence, permanence of form; degree of density; agreement, harmony; constant adherence to principles, &c.—**Consis'tently**,[2] *adv.*—**Con'sistory**, *n.* L. *consistōrium*, waiting-place, hence, meeting-place, f. *consistĕre.* The senate of the Pope; a bishop's court.

Con'sole, *n.* F. *console*, of uncertain orig. A bracket supporting a cornice, &c.

Console', *vt.* F. *consoler*—L. CON*sōlāri*, *consōlātus*, to comfort. SOLACE. To comfort in distress.—**Consol'able**, *a.*—**Consola'tion**, *n.*—**Consol'atory**, *a.*

Consol'idate, *vt.* L. CON*solidāre*, *consolidātum*, to make firm, f. *solidus*, SOLID. To make into a compact mass; to make firm, strengthen; to combine into a connected whole; to unite into one fund or stock.—**Consolida'tion**, *n.*—**Con'sols**, *n.pl.* Abb. of *Consolidated Annuities*, i.e. the British Government securities.

Con'sonant, *a.* F. *consonant*—L. *consonans*, *consonantis*, pres.pple. of CON*sonāre*, to sound together. ASSONANCE. In agreement or harmony, consistent.—*n.* An alphabetic or phonetic element always combined with a vowel; a letter representing this.—**Con'sonance**, *n.*

Con'sort, *n.* F. *consort*—L. CON*sors*, *consortis*, a partner, f. *sors*, lot. SORT. A ship sailing with another; a spouse.—**Consort'**, *vt.* To associate together.—*vi.* To associate; to accord.

Conspic'uous, *a.* With -OUS f. L. *conspicuus*, f. *conspicĕre*, to look at attentively, f. CON- + *specĕre*, to look at. SPECIES. Clearly visible; striking, noteworthy.—**Conspic'uously**,[2] *adv.*

Conspire', *vi.* F. *conspirer*—L. CON*spīrāre*, *conspīrātum*, to breathe together, hence, to combine, to plot. ASPIRE. To combine for an evil purpose, plot; to combine or concur towards some end.—*vt.* To plot, devise.—**Conspir'acy**, *n.*—**Conspir'ator**, *n.*

Con'stable, *n.* O.F. *cunestable*—L.L. *comes stabuli*, COUNT or officer of the STABLE, who became the chief household officer of the Frankish kings, and ultimately commander of the army in the king's absence and supreme judge of military offences and questions of chivalry: hence *Constable of France*, *Constable of England*. The governor of a royal fortress; an officer of the peace; a police officer.—**Constab'ulary**, *a.* Pertaining to peace or police officers.—*n.* The body of peace or police officers of a district.

Con'stant, *a.* F. *constant*—L. *constans*, *constantis*, standing firm, stable, pres.pple. of CON*stāre*, to stand together, stand firm. COST. STATE. Steadfast, resolute; faithful, true *to*; fixed, unchanging; invariably present or occurring; incessant, unremitting (*in* something).—*n.* A quantity which does not vary.—**Con'stantly**,[2] *adv.*—**Con'stancy**, *n.*

Constella'tion, *n.* L. *constellātio*, *constellātiōnis*, a cluster of stars, f. CON- + *stellātus*, pa.pple. of *stellāre*, to set with stars, f. *stella*, a STAR. A group of stars.

Con'sternate, *vt.* L. *consternāre*, *consternātum*, said to be a collateral form of *consternĕre*, to overthrow, f. CON- + *sternĕre*, to spread out, overthrow. STRATUM. To fill with terror, dismay.—**Consterna'tion**, *n.*

Con'stipate, *vt.* L. CON*stipāre*, *constipātum*, to press closely together. COSTIVE. STEVEDORE. To make costive.—**Constipa'tion**, *n.*

Con'stitute, *vt.* L. *constituĕre*, *constitūtum*, to set up, establish, f. CON- + *statuĕre*, in same sense. STATUTE. To appoint to the office of, to establish or set up as; to set up, found; to give legal form to (an assembly, &c.); to frame, form, determine; to be the elements of, make up, compose.—**Constitu'tion**, *n.* The action of constituting; make, composition; character of the body in regard to health; disposition, temperament; the mode in which a state is organized, the body of principles regulating its government.—**Constitu'tional**, *a.* Belonging to, affecting, beneficial to one's constitution; essential; belonging to, dealing with, in harmony with, ruling according to a political constitution.—**Constitu'tionally**,[2] *adv.*—**Constit'uent**, *a.* L. *constituens*, *constituentis*, pres.pple. of *constituĕre*. Component; electing a representative; having authority to frame or alter a constitution.—*n.* A component part; an elector.—**Constit'uency**, *n.* A body of electors.

Constrain', *vt.* O.F. *constreindre*—L. CON*stringĕre*, *constrictum*, to bind tightly together, restrain. ASTRINGENT. To force, oblige, compel; to confine, imprison; to limit.—**Constraint'**, *n.* O.F. *constreinte*, fem. n. f. *constreint*, pa.pple. of *constreindre*. Compulsion; confinement; restraint.

Constrict', *vt.* L. *constringĕre*. (See prec.) To contract, compress; to cause to contract.—**Constric'tion**, *n.*—**Constric'tive**, *a.*

Construct', *vt.* L. CON*struĕre*, *constructum*, to heap together, to make, form. STRUCTURE. To make, frame, build; to combine (words) grammatically; to draw or form geometrically.—**Con'strue**, *vt.* From pres. stem of *construĕre*. To combine (words) grammatically; to analyse grammatically, translate; to expound, interpret.—*vi.* To admit of grammatical analysis.—**Construc'tion**, *n.*—**Construc'tive**, *a.* Tending to construct; pertaining to construction; structural; inferential.—**Construc'tively**,[2] *adv.*

Con'sul, *n.* L. Cogn. with next. One of the annually elected chief magistrates of Rome; applied to the chief magistrates of the French Republic, 1799 to 1804; an agent appointed by a state to protect its subjects and commerce in a foreign town.—**Con'sular**,[1] *a.*—**Con'sulate**,[1] *n.* Government by consuls, their office or dignity; the office or establishment of a commercial consul.—**Con'sulship**, *n.*

Consult', *vi.* L. *consultāre*, freq. of CON*sulĕre*, *consultum*, to deliberate, ask COUNSEL of. (The simple *sulĕre* does not occur.) To take counsel together, confer.—*vt.* To keep in view, be mindful of; to ask advice of; to refer to (a book, &c.).—**Consulta'tion**, *n.*

Consume', *vt.* L. CON*sūmĕre*, *consumptum*, to take wholly, hence, to destroy. ASSUME. To destroy, esp. of fire; to use up; to swallow, eat up (food); to take up, spend (time).—*vi.* To waste away; to burn away.—**Consump'tion**, *n.* Destruction; using up; amount consumed; decay; wasting of the body, esp. by phthisis.—**Consump'tive**, *a.* Wasteful, destructive; wasted, sickly; having a tendency to or affected with phthisis.

Con'summate, *vt.* L. *consummāre*, *consummātum*, to sum up, complete, f. CON- + *summa*, SUM. To complete, finish.—**Consum'mate**,[2] *a.* Supremely qualified, accomplished; perfect.—**Consum'mately**,[2] *adv.*—**Consumma'tion**, *n.*

Con'tact, *n.* L. *contactus*, f. *contingĕre*, *contactum*, to touch on all sides, f. CON- + *tangerĕ*, to touch. CONTAMINATE. CONTIGUOUS. CONTINGENT. TACT. A touching, the mutual relation of touching bodies.—**Conta'gion**, *n.* F. *contagion*—L. CON*tāgio*, *contāgiōnis*, f. *tangĕre*. The communication of disease by contact; a pestilence; moral corruption; the influence of example, &c.—**Conta'gi**OUS, *a.*

Contain', *vt.* O.F. *contenir*—L. *continēre*, *contentum*, to hold together, contain, f. CON- + *tenēre*, to hold. CONTENT. CONTINENT. CONTINUE. COUNTENANCE. TENANT. To hold; to have capacity for; to comprise, include; to have (as a constituent element); to restrain (oneself).

Contam'inate, *vt.* L. *contāmināre*, *contāminātum*, f. *contāmen* for **contagmen*, contact, infection, f. CON- + *tag-*, stem of *tangĕre*, to touch. CONTACT. To sully, taint.—**Contamin**A'TION, *n.*

Contemn', *vt*, O.F. *contemner*—L. CON*temnĕre*, *contemptum*, to despise. To despise, scorn; to treat with disregard.—**Contempt'**, *n.* L. *contemptus*, f. *contemnĕre*. A contemning; the mental attitude of one who contemns; dishonour, disgrace.—**Contemp'ti**BLE, *a.*—**Contemp'tib**LY,[2] *adv.*—**Contemp'tu**OUS, *a.*—**Contemp'tuous**LY,[2] *adv.*

Con'template, *vt.* L. *contemplāri*, *contemplātus*, orig. of augurs, f. CON- + *templum*, a space marked out for observation. TEMPLE.[1] To gaze upon, view; to meditate upon, study; to expect; to intend, purpose.—**Contempl**A'TION, *n.*—**Contem'plat**IVE, *a.*

Contempora'neous, *a.* L. *contemporāneus* (f. CON- + *tempus*, *temporis*, time) + -OUS. TEMPORAL.[2] Existing or occurring at the same time; covering the same space of time; of the same age.—**Contempora'neous**LY,[2] *adv.*—**Contem'por**ARY, *a.* CON- + *tempus* + -ARY. In the same senses as *contemporaneous*.—*n.* One who lives at the same time with, or is of the same age as another.

Contend', *vi.* L. *contendĕre*, *contentum*, to stretch vigorously, to contend, f. CON- + *tendĕre*, to stretch. ATTEND. To strive, fight; to dispute, argue; to vie.—**Conten'ti**ON, *n.*—**Conten'ti**OUS, *a.*—**Conten'tious**NESS, *n.*

Content', *a.* F. *content*—L. *contentus*, restrained, self-restrained, satisfied, pa.pple. of *continēre*, to CONTAIN. Satisfied with what one has; satisfied (in the sphere of action); satisfied, not unwilling *to do*; in the House of Lords, indicating an affirmative vote.—*vt.* To satisfy; to be enough for.—*v.refl.* To be satisfied; to rest satisfied *with*.—*n.*[1] Satisfaction, a contented condition.—**Content'**MENT, *n.*

Content', *n.*[2] L. *contentum*, neut. pa.pple. of *continēre*. (See prec.) In *pl.*, that which is contained; the things treated of in a book, &c. In *sing.*, containing power (of a vessel, &c.), capacity; area; volume.

Conter'minous, *a.* L. *conterminus* (f. CON- + *terminus*, boundary, TERM) + -OUS. Having a common boundary; extending equally in space, time, &c.

Contest', *vi.* F. *contester*—L. CON*testāri*, to call to witness, to bring (an action), f. *testāri*, to bear or call to witness, f. *testis*, witness. TESTAMENT. To contend, strive *with* or *against*; to vie *with*.—*vt.* To debate (a point, &c.), to dispute, controvert; to fight for.—**Con'test**, *n.* Debate; conflict, strife; competition.—**Contest'**ABLE, *a.*

Con'text, *n.* L. *contextus*, connection, f. CON*texĕre*, *contextum*, to weave together, to form. TEXT. That which precedes or follows a passage quoted and determines its meaning.—**Contex'ture**, *n.* F. *contexture*, f. *contexĕre*. A weaving together; structure, texture, composition.

Contig'uous, *a.* L. *contiguus*, touching together (f. stem *contig-* of *contingĕre*) + -OUS. CONTACT. Touching, in contact; neighbouring.—**Contigu'**ITY, *n.*

Con'tinent, *a.* F. *continent*, self-restraining, f. L. *continens*, *continentis*, continuous, self-restraining, pres.pple. of *continēre*. CONTAIN. COUNTENANCE. Self-restraining, temperate; chaste.—**Con'tin**ENCE, **Con'tin**ENCY, *nn.*—**Con'tinent**, *n.* From *continens*. One of the main continuous bodies of land on the earth.—**Continent'**AL, *a.*

Contin'gent, *a.* L. *contingens*, *contingentis*, touching on all sides, coming into connexion, happening, pres.pple. of *contingĕre*. CONTACT. Of uncertain occurrence; accidental; true only under existing conditions; dependent for occurrence or character *on* or *upon*.—*n.* A proportion furnished, esp. of troops.—**Contin'gent**LY,[2] *adv.*—**Contin'g**ENCE, -ENCY, *nn.*

Contin'ue, *vt.* F. *continuer*—L. *continuāre*, to carry on, to last, f. *continuus*, hanging together, uninterrupted, f. *continēre*, in intransitive sense 'to hang together'. CONTAIN. To carry on, persist in; to cause to last; to retain; to take up and carry on (a narrative, &c.); to prolong in space.—*vi.* To last, endure; to abide; to remain (in a state, &c.); to go on, keep on; to go on in a discourse after a pause or interruption.—**Contin'u**AL, *a.* Always going on, perpetual; very frequent.—**Contin'ual**LY,[2] *adv.*—**Contin'u**ANCE, *n.*—**Continu**A'TION, *n.*—**Continu'**ITY, *n.*—**Contin'u**OUS, *a.*—**Contin'uous**LY,[2] *adv.*

Contort', *vt.* L. CON*torquēre*, *contortum*, to twist. TORMENT. To twist, draw awry.—**Contor'ti**ON, *n.*

Con'tour, *n.* F. *contour* = It. *contorno*, a circuit, f. *contornare*, to encircle, f. CON- + L. *tornāre*, to TURN on a lathe. An outline of any figure, esp. of a coast, mountain mass, &c.

Con'traband, *n.* Sp. *contrabanda*, f. It. *contrabando*, unlawful dealing, f. CONTRA- + *bando*, Med.L. *bandum*, *bannum*, proclamation. BAN. Prohibited traffic, smuggling; smuggled goods; *contraband of war*, arms, stores, &c., forbidden to be supplied by neutrals to belligerents.—*a.* Forbidden to be imported or exported; forbidden, illegitimate.—**Con'traband**IST, *n.*

Contract', *vt.* L. CON*trahĕre*, *contractum*, to draw together, to bring about. ABSTRACT. To agree upon, enter into, esp. marriage; to betroth; to incur, become involved in; to draw together, cause to shrink, to diminish, narrow, shorten; to restrict, limit; to shorten (a word, &c.).—*vi.* To enter into an agreement; to be drawn together, become smaller.—**Con'tract**, *n.* A bargain; a writing constituting a bargain; betrothal.—**Contract'**IBLE, *a.* Capable of being drawn together.—**Contract'ile**, *a.* F. *contractile*, f. *contrahĕre*. Capable of being drawn together; pertaining to or producing contraction.—**Contrac'ti**ON, *n.*—**Contrac't**OR, *n.* One who undertakes to supply goods or execute work.

Contradict', *vt.* L. CONTRA*dīcĕre*, *contrādictum*, to speak against. DICTION. To affirm the contrary of, deny; to deny the words or statement of; to be contrary or opposed to in effect, &c.—**Contradic'tion**, *n.*—**Contradic'tory**, *a.*

Contradistin'guish, *vt.* CONTRA-. To distinguish *from* by contrast or opposition of differences.—**Contradistinc'tion**, *n.*

Contral'to, *n.* It., f. CONTRA- + ALTO. The part next above the alto; a voice, a singer with a voice of this pitch.

Con'trary, *a.* O.F. *contrarie*—L. *contrārius*, opposite, hostile, f. *contrā*, against. Opposed in nature or tendency; the opposite, the other; of wind, &c., unfavourable; opposite in position or direction.—*n.* Something the opposite of something else; *the contrary*, the exact opposite or reverse.—*adv.* In opposition or antagonism; adversely to one's well-being or wishes.—**Contrari'ety**, *n.*—**Con'trarily**,[2] *adv.*—**Con'trariwise**, *adv.* On the other hand; in the opposite way; perversely.

Contrast', *vt.* O.F. *contraster*—L.L. CONTRA*stāre*, to stand against, withstand. STATE. To place so as to bring out differences in form, colour, &c.; to set in opposition for comparison *with.*—*vi.* To show a striking difference on comparison *with.*—**Con'trast**, *n.* A placing so as to bring out differences in form, &c.; comparison, exhibition of differences, an instance of this; something which on comparison shows a striking difference.

Contravene', *vt.* F. *contrevenir*—L.L. CONTRA*venīre*, to come against, oppose. ADVENT. To transgress; to be contrary to; to dispute, contradict.—**Contraven'tion**, *n.*

Contrib'ute, *vt.* L. *contribuĕre*, *contribūtum*, to bring together, f. CON- + *tribuĕre*, to assign, bestow. ATTRIBUTE. To give or pay jointly with others; to lend (aid, &c.) towards a common result.—*vi.* To give or pay jointly; *to contribute to*, to have a part in bringing about.—**Contribu'tion**, *n.*—**Contrib'utive**, *a.*—**Contrib'utor**, *n.*—**Contrib'utory**, *a.* and *n.*

Con'trite, *a.* F. *contrit*—L. *contritus*, pa. pple. of CON*terĕre*, to rub together, grind small. TRITE. Broken in spirit by a sense of sin; displaying a spirit thus broken.—**Con'tritely**,[2] *adv.*—**Contri'tion**, *n.*

Contrive', *vt.* O.F. *controver* = It. *controvare*, f. CON- + *trovare*, O.F. *trover* (F. *trouver*), to find—L. *turbāre*, to DISTURB, stir up. TROUBADOUR. TROVER. To devise (a plan, &c.), esp. for evil; to invent, design; to succeed in bringing about, effect.—**Contriv'ance**, *n.*—**Contriv'er**, *n.*

Control', *vt.* F. *contrôler*, earlier *contreroller*, to keep a copy of a roll of accounts, oversee, f. *contrerolle*, copy of such a roll, corresp. to Med.L. CONTRA*rotulus*, f. *rotulus*, ROLL, *n.*[1] To check, verify; to regulate (payments, &c.); to check and test by comparison; to dominate, command.—*n.* The fact of controlling; domination, command; restraint, check; a check.—**Control'lable**, *a.*—**Control'ler**, *n.* One who controls; an officer of the household of a sovereign or nobleman in charge of expenditure and managing generally, an officer with similar duties in various public offices. (In the case of such officials gen. spelt erroneously *Comptroller*, the word having been in the 15th cent. spelt *countecrollour*, *countrollour*, and the first syllable having been taken for *count*=*compt*, f. F. *compter*, to count.)—**Control'ment**, *n.*

Con'troversy, *n.* L. *contrōversia*, f. *contrōversus*, turned against, disputed, f. *contrō-* = CONTRA- + *versus*, pa.pple. of *vertĕre*, to turn. VERSE. Debate, dispute; a debate or dispute.—**Controvert'**, *vt.* From an assumed **contrōvertĕre*. To debate, dispute about; to deny, contradict; to oppose, stand up against.—**Controver'sial**, *a.*—**Controver'sialist**, *n.*—**Controvert'ible**, *a.*

Con'tumacy, *n.* L. *contumācia*, f. *contumax*, *contumācis*, stubborn, prob. f. CON- + *tumēre*, to swell, to swell with pride. TUMID. Perverse resistance to authority; in law, wilful disobedience.—**Contuma'cious**, *a.*—**Contuma'ciously**,[2] *adv.*

Con'tumely, *n.* O.F. *contumelie*—L. *contumēlia*, abuse, prob. cogn. with *contumax*. (See prec.) Insolent abuse; humiliation, disgrace.—**Contume'lious**, *a.*

Contuse', *vt.* L. *contundĕre*, *contūsum*, to break to pieces, bruise, f. CON- + *tundĕre*, to beat. OBTUSE. To bruise.—**Contu'sion**, *n.*

Conun'drum, *n.* Of unknown orig. A riddle in the form of a question involving a pun in the answer.

Convalesce', *vi.* L. CON*valescĕre*, to grow strong, inceptive f. *valēre*, to be strong or well. AVAIL. To recover from sickness, regain health.—**Convales'cence**, *n.*—**Convales'cent**, *a.* and *n.*

Convene', *vi.* F. *convenir*—L. CON*venīre*, *conventum*, to come together. ADVENT. COVENANT. (See next.) To come together, assemble.—*vt.* To call together, convoke; to summon before a tribunal.—**Conven'tion**, *n.* A calling together; an assembly; an agreement, covenant; a treaty; general agreement or consent; a rule or practice based on such agreement or consent; accepted usage grown merely formal.—**Conven'tional**, *a.*—**Conven'tionally**,[2] *adv.*—**Conven'tionalism**, *n.*—**Conven'ticle**, *n.* L. *conventiculum*, in form dim. of *conventus*, an assembly. f. *convenīre*. A clandestine or illegal religious meeting; a dissenting meeting-house.

Conve'nient, *a.* L. *conveniens*, *convenientis*, agreeing, suitable, pres.pple. of *convenīre*. (See prec.) Well adapted to one's needs, favourable to one's comfort.—**Conve'niently**,[2] *adv.*—**Conve'nience**, **Conve'niency**, *nn.*

Con'vent, *n.* A.F. *covent* = O.F. *convent*—L. *conventus*, an assembly, f. *convenīre*. CONVENE. A body of monks or nuns forming a community; an institution founded to support, the building occupied by, such a community.—**Conven'tual**, *a.* Med.L. *conventuālis*. Pertaining to, characteristic of, a convent.

Converge', *vi.* L.L. *convergĕre*, to incline together, f. CON- + L. *vergĕre*, to bend, incline, VERGE, *v.* To tend to meet.—*vt.* To cause to come together.—**Conver'gence**, *n.*—**Conver'gent**, *a.*

Conversaz'ione, *n.*; *pl.* **-oni, -ones**. It., f. *conversare* = F. *converser*. (See next.) A social meeting in connexion with literature, art, or science.

Converse', *vi.* F. *converser*, to associate with—L. *conversāri*, in sim. sense, f. CON- + *versāri*, to dwell, lit., to turn oneself about, middle form of *versāre*, freq. of *vertĕre*, *versum*, to turn. VERSE. To talk *with* a person *on* or *upon* a subject.—**Con'verse**, *n.*[1] Talk, discourse.—**Convers'able**, *a.* Pleasant in or fond of conversation.—**Conversa'tion**, *n.*—**Conversa'tional**, *a.*—**Con'versant**, *a.* On familiar terms *with*; having to do *with*; versed *in*, familiarly acquainted *with*.

Convert'. *vt.* O.F. *convertir*—L. *convertĕre*,

to turn about, change, f. CON- + *vertĕre*, to turn. (See prec.) To apply *to* (another purpose); to cause to adopt a religion, an opinion, &c.; to turn to godliness; to transform; to turn *to* or *into*.—**Con'vert**, *n.* A converted person.—**Convert'**IBLE, *a.*—**Con'verse**, *a.* L. *conversus*, pa.pple. of *convertĕre*. Turned round, opposite, contrary.—*n.*[2] A statement produced by inversion or interchange of terms; something the exact opposite of another.—**Con'verse**LY,[2] *adv.*

Con'vex, *a.* L. *convexus*, arched, app. an old pa.pple. (=*convectus*) of CON*vehĕre*, to bring together. VEHICLE. Curved like the outside of a sphere, the reverse of CONCAVE.—**Convex'**ITY, *n.*

Convey', *vt.* O.F. *conveier*, f. CON- + *veie*, *voie*, L. *via*, way. CONVOY. DEVIATE. ENVOY. VIATICUM. To transport, carry; to communicate, impart; to transfer, make over.—**Convey'**ANCE, *n.*—**Convey'ancer**, *n.* One skilled in the forms of transferring property.—**Convey'ancing**, *vbl.n.* His art or profession.

Convict', *vt.* L. CON*vincĕre*, *convictum*, to overcome, hence to convict, to demonstrate. (See next.) VICTOR. To prove or declare guilty.—**Con'vict**, *n.* One proved guilty.—**Convic'**TION, *n.* A proving or declaring guilty; a being convinced, settled persuasion; an opinion or belief firmly held.

Convince', *vt.* L. *convincĕre*. (See prec.) To satisfy by argument or evidence.—**Convinc'**IBLE, *a.*

Conviv'ial, *a.* L. *convīviālis*, pertaining to a feast, f. *convīvium*, feast, f. CON- + *vīvĕre*, to live (hence, to eat). VICTUAL. VIVACITY. Festive; jovial.—**Convivial'**ITY, *n.*

Convoke', *vt.* F. *convoquer*—L. CON*vocāre*, *convocātum*, to call together. VOCABLE. To call together.—**Convoca'**TION, *n.* A calling or being called together; an assembly, esp. a provincial assembly of the clergy.

Convolve', *vt.* L. CON*volvĕre*, *convolūtum*, to roll together. VAULT. VOLUBLE. To roll together, coil, twist.—**Con'volute**, *a.*; **Con'voluted**, *ppl.a.* Rolled together, coiled.—**Convolu'**TION, *n.*—**Convol'vulus**, *n.* L., f. *convolvĕre*. A genus of plants with slender twining stems.

Convoy', *vt.* F. *convoyer*—O.F. *conveier*. CONVEY. To escort (a lady), conduct (a guest); to escort for protection, esp. of ships of war. —*n.* A convoying; an escort; a funeral train; a protecting escort, esp. of ships of war; supplies or merchant ships under armed escort.

Convulse', *vt.* L. CON*vellĕre*, *convulsum*, to pull violently, wrench, shatter. To shake or agitate violently, physically or figuratively; to affect with violent involuntary contractions of the muscles.—**Convul'**SION, *n.*—**Convul'**SIVE, *a.*—**Convul'sive**LY,[2] *adv.*

Co'ny, **Co'ney**, *n.* O.F. *conil*—L. *cunīculus*, believed to be of Spanish orig. A rabbit.

Coo, *vi.* Imitative. To make the soft sound of doves; to converse caressingly.—*n.* The sound of doves.

Cook, *n.* O.E. *coc*—L.L. *cōcus*, L. *coquus*, f. *coquĕre*, *coctum*, to cook, f. root *peq-* (orig. *pequĕre*, then *quequĕre*, then *coquĕre*), cogn. with G. *pessein* (*peq-iein*), to ripen, to cook. CONCOCT. DECOCT. KITCHEN. One who prepares food for the table.—*vi.* To act as cook; to undergo cooking.—*vt.* To prepare (food); to 'get up', concoct; to falsify, tamper with.—**Cook'**ERY, *n.*

Cool, *a.* O.E. *cól*, f. O.Teut. stem *kal-*, to be COLD. Moderately cold; causing coolness; unexcited, deliberate, calm; lacking interest or heartiness; assured, unabashed.—*n.* The cool time, place, &c.; coolness.—*vi.* To become cool; to lose passion or fervour.—*vt.* To make cool; to make less passionate or zealous; to diminish the ardour of (passion, &c.).—**Cool'**LY,[2] *adv.*—**Cool'**NESS, *n.*

Coop, *n.* M.E. *cupe*, basket, pointing to an O.E. **cúpe*, an unrecorded collateral form of *cýpe*, cask, basket, said to be f. L. *cūpa*, a tub, cask. CUP. A cage or pen for confining poultry, &c.—*vt.* To confine in a coop; to shut up within narrow limits, to cabin.—**Coop'**ER, *n.* One who makes casks and the like.—*vt.* To make or repair (casks, &c.); to furnish with hoops; to furbish *up*.—**Coop'er**AGE, *n.*

Co-op'erate, *vi.* L. CO-*operāri*, *co-operātus*, to work together. OPERATE. To work together. —**Co-opera'**TION, *n.* A working together; a combination of small capitalists for producing or dealing in goods for the joint benefit.—**Co-op'er**ATIVE, *a.*

Co-or'dinate, *a.* CO- + L. *ordinātus*, pa. pple. of *ordināre*, to arrange in order. ORDAIN. Equal in rank, degree, &c.—*n.* A co-ordinate thing.—*vt.* To place in the same rank, order, &c.; to bring into order as parts of a whole.—**Co-ordina'**TION, *n.*

Cope, *n.* M.E. *cāpe*, later *cōpe*—L.L. *cappa*, CAPE.[1] An ecclesiastical vestment like a long cloak; *the cope of heaven*, the vault of heaven; a vault or canopy.—*v.*[1]*t.* To cover (a wall, &c.) with a coping; to cover as with a coping or vault.—**Cop'ing**, *n.* The uppermost course in a wall.—**Cope'-stone**, *n.* The top stone of a building (gen. figuratively).

Cope, *v.*[2]*i.* O.F. *coper*, *couper*, *colper*, to strike, f. *cop*, *coup*, *colp*, a blow—L.L. *colpus*, L. *colaphus*, G. *kolaphos*, a blow. COPPICE. To contend *with* (often implying success).

Co'pious, *a.* L. *cōpiōsus*, plentiful, f. *cōpia*, plenty. COPY. Full of information or matter; profuse in speech; plentiful, abundant.—**Co'pious**LY,[2] *adv.*—**Co'pious**NESS, *n.*

Cop'per, *n.* O.E. *coper*, *copor*—L.L. *cuper*, L. *cuprum*, abb. f. *Cyprium aes*, Cyprian metal, f. *Cyprus*, whence the best copper came. A reddish malleable ductile metal; copper money, a copper coin; a large vessel. —*vt.* To cover with copper.—**Cop'per-plate**, **Cop'perplate**, *n.* A plate of copper for engraving; an impression therefrom; copperplate engraving.—**Cop'per-smith**, *n.* A smith who works in copper.

Cop'pice, **Copse**, *n.* O.F. *copeiz*, brushwood, f. *coper* (F. *couper*), to cut, f. *cop*, a blow. COPE, *v.*[2] A small wood of brushwood and small trees.

Cop'ula, *n.* L. *cōpula*, a band, tie, f. CO- + *apĕre*, to fasten, with dim. suff. APT. COUPLE. That part of a proposition which connects the subject and predicate; the pres. tense of *to be* used as a mere sign of predication; a connexion, link.—**Cop'ulate**, *vi.* L. *cōpulāre*, *cōpulātum*, to join, f. *cōpula*. To unite sexually.—**Copula'**TION, *n.*—**Cop'u**LATIVE, *a.* Serving to connect, esp. in grammar.—*n.* A connecting particle.

Cop'y, *n.* F. *copie*—L. *cōpia*, abundance, opportunity, power, in Med.L. transcript, f. the notion 'power (to transcribe)'. COPIOUS. A writing or a picture reproducing another; an image, imitation; something written after a model; in Eng. law, the copy of the court-roll of a manor with entries of the admissions of tenants to land held by the tenure hence called **Cop'yhold**; an example of a printed work; that from which a copy is made; matter for printing.—*vt.* To make a copy of; to imitate, follow.—**Cop'yist**, *n.*—**Cop'yright**, *n.* An exclusive right of reproducing and publishing a book or work of art.—*a.* Protected by copyright.—*vt.* To protect by copyright.

Coquet', *a.* F. *coquet*, orig. *n.* and dim. of *coq*, COCK, *n.*[1], in reference to his strutting gait and amorous characteristics. Cf. COCK, *v.*[1] Having the disposition of a coquette.—**Coquet'**, **Coquette'**, *vi.* To act the lover, flirt *with* (only of women); to trifle or dally *with*.—**Coquette'**, *n. fem.* F., fem. of *coquet*. A woman who makes a practice of trifling with the affections of men, a flirt.—**Coq'uetry**, *n.* —**Coquet'tish**, *a.*

Cor'al, *n.* O.F. *coral*—L. *corālium*, G. *korallion*, red coral. A hard calcareous marine substance produced by polyps; an ornament or toy of coral.

Cor'bel, *n.* O.F. *corbel* (F. *corbeau*), a raven, also (from the notion of a projecting beak) a corbel—L.L. *corvellus*, dim. of L. *corvus*, a raven. CORMORANT. A projection jutting out from a wall to support a weight.

Cord, *n.* F. *corde*, string of a musical instrument, cord—L. *chorda*, G. *chordē*, gut, string of an instrument. CHORD.[1] A string or small rope of several strands; a cord-like structure in the body; a rib on cloth, a ribbed fabric; a measure of cut wood.—*vt.* To bind with a cord. —**Cord'age**, *n.*—**Corduroy'**, *n.* A trade-name of Eng. invention to represent a supposed F. *corde du roi*, the king's cord (*i.e.* the fabric). A coarse thick-ribbed cotton stuff.

Cor'dial, *a.* Med.L. *cordiālis*, f. L. *cor*, *cordis*, HEART. Stimulating the heart, reviving; coming from the heart, hearty, sincere; friendly, warm.—*n.* A stimulating medicine or drink.—**Cor'dially**,[2] *adv.*—**Cordial'ity**, *n.*

Cor'don, *n.* F., f. *corde*, CORD. A line of troops, &c., to prevent passage; a guarded line; an ornamental cord or braid; a ribbon worn by members of a knightly order.

Core, *n.* Of uncertain orig. The dry horny case enclosing the seed of the apple, pear, &c.; the central or innermost part of anything.

Co-respon'dent, *n.* CO-. In a divorce suit, the man sued along with the wife.

Corin'thian, *a.* L. *Corinthius*, G. *Korinthios*, of Corinth + -AN. Of Corinth; the name of the most ornate of the three Grecian orders of architecture, characterized by capitals adorned with leaves.—*n.* A native of Corinth.

Cork, *n.* Perh. f. old Sp. (Arab.) *alcorque*, 'cork shoe', of uncertain orig. The bark of the cork-oak; a piece of cork, esp. one used as a stopper.—*vt.* To stop with a cork; to stop *up* as with a cork.—**Cork'y**, [2] *a.*

Cor'morant, *n.* F. *cormoran*, app. f. an O.F. *corp-marin* = L. *corvus marinus*, sea-raven. CORBEL. MARINE. A large and voracious sea-bird.

Corn, *n.*[1] O.E. *corn*. Common Teut. Cogn. with L. *grānum*, a GRAIN. KERNEL. A seed of one of the cereals; the fruit of the cereals, grain.—*vt.* To form into grains; to sprinkle and pickle with salt in grains.—**Corn'crake**, *n.* From *crake*, imitative of the bird's grating cry. A bird that haunts corn-fields; the landrail.

Corn, *n*[2]. O.F. *corn*—L. *cornū*, HORN. A horny excrescence on the foot or a toe.

Cor'nea, *n.* L., fem. of *corneus*, horny *cornū*. (See prec.) The horny membrane covering the fore part of the eye.

Cor'ner, *n.* A.F. *corner*—L.L. type **cornārium*, f. L. *cornū*. CORN.[2] The meeting-place of converging sides or angles; the comparatively small space included at the meeting-place; a projecting angle; an angular projection.—*vt.* To furnish with corners; to set in a corner; to drive into a position of difficulty.

Cor'net, *n.*[1] O.F. *cornet*—L. *cornū*. CORN.[2] A musical instrument of the trumpet class.

Cor'net, *n.*[2] F. *cornette*, dim. of *corne*, Med.L. *corna*, a horn, f. L. *cornua*, pl. of *cornū*, taken as fem. sing. CORN.[2] Formerly, a pennon narrowing to a point forming a cavalry standard; hence, a cavalry officer who carried the colours.

Cor'nice, *n.* F. *cornice*—It. *cornice*, of doubtful orig. *Arch.*, a horizontal moulded projection; the upper division of the entablature; an ornamental moulding along the top of the wall of a room.

Cornuco'pia, *n.* L. *cornū cōpiae*, horn of plenty. CORN.[2] COPIOUS. The figure of a horn overflowing with fruit, &c., as an emblem of plenty.

Corol'la, *n.* L., dim. of *corōna*, a CROWN, a garland. The inner envelope of a flower.

Cor'ollary, *n.* L. *corollārium*, money paid for a garland, a gratuity, a corollary, f. *corolla*. (See prec.) A geometrical proposition appended to another as following immediately from it; an inference, deduction; a result.

Cor'onal, *n.* App. A.F., f. *corune*, *coroune*, L. *corōna*, CROWN. CORONER. A coronet; a garland.

Corona'tion, *n.* O.F. *coronacion*, f. L. *corōnāre*, to crown, f. *corōna*, CROWN. The ceremony of crowning a sovereign.

Cor'oner, *n.* A.F. *coruner*, *corouner*, guardian of the pleas of the crown, f. *corune*, *coroune*. CORONAL. An officer who holds inquiries into deaths supposed to be due to violence or accident.

Cor'onet, *n.* O.F. *coronete*, dim. of *corone*, L. *corōna*, CROWN. A small or inferior crown; an ornamental band on the head; a garland.

Cor'poral, *a.* O.F. *corporal*—L. *corporālis*, f. *corpus*, *corporis*, body. Relating to the body.—**Cor'porally**,[2] *adv.*

Cor'poral, *n.* F. *corporal*, var. of *caporal*—It. *caporale*, of doubtful orig. A non-commissioned officer ranking under a sergeant.

Cor'porate, *ppl.a.* L. *corporātus*, pa.pple. of *corporāre*, to form into or furnish with a body, f. *corpus*. CORPORAL, *a.* Forming, of or belonging to, a corporation.—**Corpora'tion**, *n.* A body of persons legally authorized to act as an individual; the authorities of a city or borough.

Corpo'real, *a.* With -AL f. L. *corporeus*, bodily, f. *corpus*. CORPORAL, *a.* Of the nature of the body; material.

Corps, *n.*; *pl.* the same. F., body—L. *corpus*. CORPORAL, *a.* A body of troops.

Corpse, *n.* M.E. *corps*, a var. of earlier *cors* —O.F. *cors*, body—L. *corpus*. CORPORAL, *a.* CORSE. The dead body of a man.

Cor'pulent, *a.* F. *corpulent*—L. *corpulentus*, f. *corpus*. CORPORAL, *a.* Bulky of body, fat. —**Cor'pulence**, **Cor'pulency**, *nn.*

Cor'puscle, *n.* L. *corpusculum*, dim. of *corpus*. CORPORAL, *a.* A minute body or particle of matter.

Correct', *vt.* L. *corrigĕre*, *correctum*, to set

right, correct, f. COR- + *regĕre*, to guide, rule. REGENT. RIGHT. To set right, amend, rectify; to admonish, rebuke; to punish, chastise; to counteract, neutralize.—*a.* From *correctus*, the pa.pple., corrected, correct. Proper, exact, accurate; adhering exactly to a standard.—**Correct'**LY,[2] *adv.*—**Correc'tion**, *n.*—**Correc'tive**, *a.* and *n.*—**Correct'**NESS, *n.*

Cor'relate, *vi.* COR- + RELATE. To have a mutual relation.—*vt.* To bring into proper mutual relation.—*n.* Each of two mutually related things.—**Correla'tion**, *n.*—**Correl'ative**, *a.* and *n.*

Correspond', *vi.* Med.L. *correspondēre*, f. COR- + L. *respondēre*, to answer, RESPOND. To agree *with*, be conformable *to*; to answer or agree in regard to position, amount, &c.; to be similar *to*; to communicate *with* by letters.—**Correspon'dence**, *n.*—**Correspon'dent**, *a.* and *n.*

Cor'ridor, *n.* F. *corridor*—It. *corridore*, a long passage, f. *correre*, L. *currĕre*, to run. CURRENT. An outside connecting passage; a main passage in a building.

Corrigen'dum, *n.* Gen. in pl. **Corrigen'da**. Gerundive of L. *corrigĕre*, to CORRECT. An error noted for correction.—**Cor'rigible**, *a.* F. *corrigible*, f. *corrigĕre*. Capable of being corrected or amended, submissive to correction.

Corrob'orate, *vt.* L. COR*rōborāre*, *corrōborātum*, to strengthen, f. *rōbur*, *rōboris*, strength. ROBUST. To confirm (a legal act, &c.); to confirm, support (a statement, &c.).—**Corrobora'tion**, *n.*—**Corrob'orative**, *a.*

Corrode', *vt.* L. COR*rōdĕre*, *corrōsum*, to gnaw away. RODENT. To eat or wear away gradually.—*vi.* To become corroded.—**Corro'sion**, *n.*—**Corro'sive**, *a.* and *n.*

Cor'rugate, *vt.* L. COR*rūgāre*, *corrūgātum*, to wrinkle, f. *rūga*, wrinkle. To wrinkle; to bend into ridges.—**Corruga'tion**, *n.*

Corrupt', *vt.* L. COR*rumpĕre*, *corruptum*, to break to pieces. ABRUPT. To make rotten; to pervert, debase; to bribe.—*vi.* To putrefy, rot.—*ppl.a.* Rotten; perverted; venal.—**Corrupt'**LY,[2] *adv.*—**Corrup'tible**, *a.*—**Corruptibil'ity**, *n.*—**Corrup'tion**, *n.*

Cor'sair, *n.* F. *corsaire*—Med.L. *cursus*, *cursa*, inroad, booty, L. *cursus*, a run, march, f. *currĕre*, *cursum*, to run. COURSE. CURRENT. HUSSAR. A privateer; a pirate.

Corse, *n.* M.E. *cors*. The same as CORPSE.

Cor'set, *n.* F., dim. of O.F. *cors*, body. CORPSE. A stiffened inner bodice; stays.

Cor'uscate, *vi.* L. *coruscāre*, *coruscātum*. To glitter, sparkle.—**Corusca'tion**, *n.*

Cosmet'ic, *a.* G. *kosmētikos*, relating to adornment, f. *kosme-ein*, to arrange, adorn, f. *kosmos*, order, adornment, the universe. (See next.) Having power to beautify.—*n.* A preparation for beautifying the skin, &c.

Cos'mic, *a.* G. *kosmikos*, f. *kosmos*, the universe. (See prec.) Pertaining to the universe; pertaining to this as distinguished from the earth; characteristic of the vastness of the universe.—So **Cos'mical**, *a.*—**Cosmog'ony**, *n.* G. *kosmogonia*, f. *kosmos* + *-gonia*, as *gonē*, birth. The creation of the universe; a system or theory of this.—**Cosmop'olite**, *n.* G. *kosmopolitēs*, f. *kosmos* + *politēs*, citizen. A citizen of the world, one without national attachments or prejudices.—**Cosmopol'itan**, *a.* Free from these; belonging to all parts of the world.

Cos'set, *n.* Orig. unknown. A lamb, colt, &c., brought up by hand; a spoilt child, a pet.—*vt.* To treat as a cosset; to pet, pamper.

Cost, *vt.* O.F. *coster*, *couster*—L. *constāre*, to stand together, stand at a price, cost, f. CON- + *stāre*, to stand. CONSTANT. STATE. To be acquired or maintained for (a price, &c.); to bring on (a person) in the way of expense; to involve the expenditure, loss, &c., of.—*n.* Price; expenditure of time, labour, &c.; in *pl.*, the expenses of litigation, prosecution, &c.—**Cost'**LY,[1] *a.* Of great price or value; involving much expenditure.—**Cost'li**NESS, *n.*

Cos'tal, *a.* F. *costal*—L. *costa*, rib. COAST. Of or pertaining to the ribs.

Cos'tard, *n.* Perh. f. A.F. and O.F. *coste*, L. *costa*, rib (see prec.), in sense 'a *ribbed* apple'. A large ribbed apple.

Cos'termonger, *n.* COSTARD + MONGER. Orig., an apple-seller; now, one who sells fruit, fish, &c., in the street from a barrow.—Shortened to **Cos'ter**.

Cos'tive, *a.* O.F. *costivé*—L. *constīpātus*, pa.pple. of *constīpāre*. CONSTIPATE. Confined in the bowels; *fig.*, niggardly, stingy.

Cos'tume, *n.* F. *costume*—It. *costume*, custom, guise, manner—L. *consuētūdo*, CUSTOM. The mode of attire belonging to a nation, period, &c.; dress considered with regard to its fashion; a woman's gown.

Co'sy, **Co'sey**, *a.* Of unknown orig. Warm and sheltered; sheltering, keeping warm.—*n.* A covering on a tea-pot.—**Co'si**LY,[2] *adv.*

Cot, *n.*[1] O.E. *cot*. Cf. O.N. and Du. *kot*, cot, hut. A small house.—**Cot'tar**,[2] **Cot'ter**, *n.*—**Cote**, *n.* O.E. *cote* = *cot*. A slight building for sheep, &c.; a shed, stall.

Cot, *n.*[2] Hindī *khāt*, bedstead, hammock. A light bedstead; a sort of swinging bed on board ship; a small bed for a child.

Co'terie, *n.* F., orig. a body of peasants holding land from a lord, f. *cotier* = Med.L. *cotārius*, tenant of a *cota*, cot, f. Du. *kot*. COT.[1] An exclusive circle in society; a 'set' associated by exclusive interests, pursuits, &c.

Cotil'lion, **Cotill'on**, *n.* F. *cotillon*, lit., a petticoat, dim. of *cotte*, O.F. *cote*, COAT. The name of several dances consisting of various steps and figures.

Cot'tage, *n.* App. f. an A.F. **cotage*, found in latinized form *cotagium*, f. *cota*. COTERIE. A small house for farm-labourers, &c.; a small country or suburban house.—**Cot'tager**, *n.*

Cot'ton, *n.* F. *coton*—Arab. *qutn*, *qutun*, in Sp. Arab. *qoton*. A white fibrous downy substance clothing the seeds of the cotton-plant; the plant; thread or cloth made from cotton.—*vi.* To harmonize, agree; to fraternize; to attach oneself *to*, be drawn *to*. (The original notion in the *v.* senses is uncertain.)

Cotyle'don, *n.* G. *kotulēdōn*, a cup-shaped hollow, f. *kotulē*, a cup. The primary leaf in the embryo plant.

Couch, *vt.* F. *coucher*, earlier *colcher*, *culcher*—L. *collocāre*. COLLOCATE. ACCOUCHEMENT. To cause to lie down (only in pa.pple.); to lower (a spear, &c.) for action; to remove (a cataract) from the eye, also *to couch a person*; to put into words; to cover up (an idea, &c.) *in*, *under*, &c.—*vi.* To lie; to lie down, crouch.—*n.* A bed, a kind of sofa; a layer, stratum.—**Couch'ant**, *a.* F., pres.pple. of *coucher*. In *heraldry*, of an animal, lying with the body resting on the legs.

Cough, *vi.* M.E. *coughen*, *cowhen*—O.E. *cohhian*, found only in the derivative *cohhetan*, app. to cough, akin to M.Du. *cuchen*, Mod.

Du. and L.G. *kuchen*, to cough. All app. imitative. To expel air from the lungs with effort and a characteristic noise, generally in order to remove an obstruction.—*n.* The affection of coughing; an act of coughing.

Coun'cil, *n.* F. *concile*—L. *concilium*, an assembly called together, f. CON- + *calāre*, to summon. CONCILIATE. INTERCALATE. NOMENCLATURE. An assembly of ecclesiastics for the regulation of doctrine or discipline; a deliberative assembly; a body of advisers assisting a ruler; the administrative body of a city; a deliberative and administrative committee.—**Coun'cill**OR, *n.* A member of a ruler's or of a city, &c., council.

Coun'sel, *n.* O.F. *conseil*—L. *consilium*, deliberation, f. *consulĕre*, to CONSULT. Deliberation, consultation; advice; resolution, purpose; a secret, confidence (in phrase *to keep one's* (*own*) *counsel*); a body of legal advisers conducting a case; a single legal adviser, a barrister.—*vt.* To advise; to recommend (a course of action, &c.)—**Coun'sell**OR, *n.*

Count, *vt.* O.F. *cunter*, *conter*—L. *computāre*. COMPUTE. ACCOUNT. To reckon, calculate; to reckon in; to consider, regard to be *so and so*.—*vi.* To depend or rely *on* or *upon*; to be reckoned or accounted; to enter into the reckoning.—*n.*[1] A reckoning; the sum total; an account of moneys, an answering for conduct; estimation, consideration, regard, notice; each charge in an indictment, &c.—**Count'**LESS, *a.* Innumerable.

Count, *n.*[2] A.F. *counte* = O.F. *cunte*, *conte*, *comte*—L. *comes*, *comitis*, companion, f. COM- + *itum*, supine of *īre*, to go. CONCOMITANT. CONSTABLE. A foreign title of nobility answering to the Eng. EARL.—**Count'**ESS, *n.* The wife or widow of a count or earl; a lady holding in her own right a position equivalent to that of a count or earl.

Coun'tenance, *n.* O.F. *contenance*, *cuntenance*, manner of holding oneself, behaviour, aspect—L. *continentia*, self-restraint, in Med. L., gesture, demeanour, f. *continēre*. CONTAIN. CONTINENT. The look or expression of one's face; the face; patronage, support.—*vt.* F. *contenancer*. To patronize, support.

Coun'ter, *n.*[1] A.F. *counteour*, *countour* = O.F. *conteoir* (F. *comptoir*)—Med.L. *computātōrium*, f. *computāre*, to COUNT. Something used in keeping a reckoning, esp. at cards; an imitation coin; the table in a bank, shop, &c., on which money is paid.

Coun'ter, *a.* Arising chiefly f. combinations in COUNTER-. Opposed, opposite.—*adv.* In the opposite direction, back again; in opposition, contrary.—*n.*[2] The contrary; the curved part of the stern of a ship (the history of this sense uncertain).—*vt.* To oppose, contradict.

Counteract', *vt.* COUNTER- (1). To frustrate by contrary action.—**Counterac'**TION, *n.*

Counterbal'ance, *n.* COUNTER- (1). A weight balancing another.—*vt.* To act as a counterbalance to; to neutralize the effect of.

Coun'terfeit, *a.* O.F. *contrefet*, *contrefait*, pa.pple. of *contrefaire*, f. L. type *CONTRA-*facĕre*, to make in opposition, hence, in opposing imitation. FACT. Not genuine, sham; forged; feigned, false.—*n.* A spurious imitation; a forgery.—*vt.* To imitate (in order to deceive); to forge; to feign, pretend; to resemble.—*vi.* To feign, practise deceit.

Coun'terfoil, *n.* COUNTER- (3) + FOIL, leaf. A part of a cheque, &c., kept for reference.

Countermand', *vt.* O.F. *contremander*—Med.L. *contrāmandāre*, f. CONTRA- + L. *mandāre*, to COMMAND. To revoke, stop, prohibit by a contrary order; to order back (forces, &c.).—*n.* A contrary order.

Coun'termarch, *vi.* and *t.* COUNTER- (2). To march back.—*n.* A march back.

Coun'termine, *n.* COUNTER- (1). A mine designed to intercept one made by an enemy; a plot devised to frustrate another.—**Countermine'**, *vi.* To make a countermine.—*vt.* To frustrate by a countermine or plot.

Coun'terpane, *n.* *-Pane* = F. *pan*, L. *pannus*, cloth. Altered f. obs. *Counterpoint*—O.F. *contrepointe* = *courtepointe*, app. corruptions of *cuilte-pointe* representing L. *culcita puncta*, quilt stitched through, f. *culcita*, cushion, QUILT, and *punctus*, pa.pple. of *pungĕre*, to prick. PUNGENT. The outer covering of a bed.

Coun'terpart, *n.* COUNTER- (3). A duplicate of a lease, &c.; a thing or person that is a complement of another.

Coun'terpoint, *n.* F. *contrepoint*—Med.L. *contrāpunctum*, *cantus* CONTRA*punctus*, song or music pointed-against, an added accompaniment being indicated by points or pricks set against the notes of the melody. PUNGENT. A melody added as accompaniment to a given melody; the art of thus adding one or more melodies.

Coun'terpoise, *n.* O.F. *countrepeis* = Central F. *contrepois*, f. *contre-* (= CONTRA-) + *peis*, *pois*, L.L. *pensum*, weight. AVOIRDUPOIS. A weight balancing another; something of equivalent force; equilibrium.—*vt.* To counterbalance; to be an equivalent for; to bring into or keep in equilibrium.

Coun'terscarp, *n.* It. *contrascarpa*, f. *contra-* (CONTRA-), opposite + *scarpa*, SCARP. The outer slope of a ditch.

Coun'tersign, *n.* F. *contresigne*, f. *contre-* (= CONTRA-) + *signe*, SIGN. A sign or signal used in reply to another.—*vt.* F. *contresigner*. To sign (a document) opposite to, or in addition to another signature; to ratify.

Countervail', *vt.* A.F. *countrevaloir* = O.F. *contrevaloir*—L. *contrā valēre*, to be of strength against. CONTRA-. AVAIL. To avail against; to compensate, make up for.—*vi.* To avail *against*.

Coun'try, *n.* O.F. *cuntrée*, *contrée*—L.L. *contrāta*, a region, f. *contrā*, against, opposite, lit. 'that which fronts the view, the landscape one sees'. CONTRA-. A region, district; the territory of a nation; the land of one's birth, residence, &c.; the rural districts as distinct from the towns; the nation.—**Coun'try-dance'**. *n.* COUNTRY + DANCE. A dance of rural or native origin, esp. one in which couples stand face to face in two long lines.

Coun'ty, *n.* A.F. *counté* = O.F. *cunté*, *conté*—L.L. *comitātus* (in L., retinue, train), f. *comes*, COUNT, *n.*[2] Formerly, the domain of a count. A territorial division of the kingdom.

Coup'le, *n.* O.F. *cople*, *cuple*—L. *cōpula*. COPULA. A leash for holding two hounds together; a union of two, a pair; two of the same sort; two; a pair of equal and parallel forces acting in opposite directions.—*vt.* To tie (hounds) together in pairs; to fasten together; to join, connect; to associate, bring together.—*vi.* To come together or associate.—**Coup'ling**, *vbl.n.* The action of the *v.*; a mechanical contrivance forming a connexion.

Coup'let, *n.* F. *couplet*, dim. of *couple* = O.F. *cople*, COUPLE. A pair of lines of verse, esp. when rhyming and of the same length.

Cou'pon, *n.* F., f. *couper*, to strike, cut. COPE, *v.*[2] A separable certificate giving the bearer right to a payment of interest, &c.

Cour'age, *n.* O.F. *corage*, *curage*, answering to a L. type **corāticum*, f. *cor*, HEART. CORDIAL. Bravery, boldness, valour.—**Coura'geous**, *a.*—**Coura'geously**,[2] *adv.*

Cou'rier, *n.* F. *courier*, *courrier*—It. *corriere*, Med.L. *currerius*, a professional runner, f. It. *corre*, L. *currĕre*, to run. COURSE. A running messenger; an attendant on a traveller.

Course, *n.* F. *course*—L. *cursus*, f. *currĕre*, *cursum*, to run. COARSE. CONCUR. CORSAIR. CURRENT. Onward movement; the pursuit of game, esp. hares, with hounds; power or opportunity of running, moving, &c.; way or path; a race-course; a channel; onward progress; way, custom, practice; line of action; a fixed series of actions or proceedings, as of lectures, medicine, &c.; a division of a meal; a layer of bricks, &c.; *of course*, natural, to be expected as a natural result, naturally, obviously.—*vt.* To hunt (game, esp. hares) with hounds; to chase; to move swiftly over.—*vi.* To run or gallop about; to take one's way.—**Cours'er**, *n.* A swift horse.

Court, *n.* M.E. *court*, *curt*—O.F. *cort*, *curt*—L. *cohors*, *cohortis*, also *cors*, *cortis*. COHORT. CURTSY. An enclosed space, a yard; a section of a museum, &c.; a yard opening off a street and built round; an area in which games such as lawn-tennis, &c., are played; the residence of a sovereign, his establishment and retinue; the sovereign with his ministers as the ruling power of a state; a state assembly held by the sovereign; persons administering justice collectively, the place where they sit, a sitting of a court; homage, attention, flattery.—*vt.* To pay court to, try to win or attract; to woo; to show oneself desirous of, seek to gain.—**Cour'teous**, *a.* O.F. *corteis*, *curteis*—L. type **cortēsis*, f. *cors*. Polite, complaisant.—**Cour'teously**,[2] *adv.*—**Cour'tesy**, *n.* O.F. *cortesie*, *curtesie*. Courteous behaviour or disposition.—**Cour'tesan**, **-zan**, *n.* F. *courtisane*. A loose woman.—**Court'ier**, *n.* One who frequents a sovereign's court.—**Court'ly**,[1] *a.*—**Court'liness**, *n.*—**Court mar'tial**, *n.*; *pl.* **Courts mar'tial**. A court of naval or military officers for trying naval or military offences.—**Court'ship**, *n.* Wooing.

Cous'in, *n.* F. *cousin*—L. *consobrīnus*, *sobrīnus*, contracted f. *sorōrīnus*, a cousin by the mother's side, a cousin, f. *soror*, SISTER. The son or daughter of an uncle or aunt.

Cove, *n.* O.E. *cofa*, a small chamber, a cave. Common Teut. A sheltered recess in a coast; a concave arch or moulding.

Cov'enant, *n.* O.F. *covenant*, use as *n.* of *covenant*, *convenant*, pres.pple. of *convenir*, to come together, agree. CONVENE. A mutual agreement, a contract; a clause of an agreement.—**Covenant'**, *vi.* To enter into a covenant.—*vt.* To agree to by covenant.

Cov'er, *vt.* O.F. *cuvrir*, *covrir*, later *couvrir*—L. *cooperīre*, *coopertum*, to cover up. CURFEW. To put or spread something over (an object) for protection, concealment, &c., to serve as a covering to; to protect, shelter; to conceal, screen; to include, comprise, extend over; to traverse, pass over; to counterbalance or compensate.—*n.* That which covers; a lid; the binding of a book, one of the boards; a shelter; a screen, disguise, pretence.—**Cov'ert**, *a.* O.F. *covert*, pa.pple. of *covrir*. Hidden, secret; disguised; of a married woman, under her husband's protection.—*n.* A shelter; a place which gives shelter to game, a thicket.—**Cov'ertly**,[2] *adv.*—**Cov'erture**, *n.* Something which covers; of a married woman, the condition of being covert.

Cov'erlet, *n.* App. f. O.F. *covrir* (see prec.) + *lit*, L. *lectus*, a bed. LITTER. The uppermost covering of a bed.

Cov'et, *vt.* O.F. *cuveitier*, *coveiter*, as if a L. **cupiditāre*, f. *cupiditas*, eager desire. CUPIDITY. To desire, esp. what belongs to another.—**Cov'etous**, *a.*—**Cov'etousness**, *n.*

Cov'ey, *n.* O.F. *covée* (F. *couvée*), fem. pa.pple. of *cover* (F. *couver*), to brood, hatch—L. *cubāre*, to lie. INCUBATE. CUBICLE. A brood, esp. of partridges.

Cow, *n.* O.E. *cú*. Common Teut. and Indo-Germanic. Cogn. with G. *bous*, L. *bōs*. BEEF. BOVINE. The female of a bovine animal.—**Cow'-pox**, *n.* A vaccine disease communicated to human beings in vaccination.

Cow, *vt.* Perh. f. O.N. *kúga*, to tyrannize over. To dishearten, overawe, intimidate.

Cow'ard, *n.* O.F. *coart*, *couard*, f. *coe*, L. *cauda*, tail. Poss. from 'turning tail', or from a frightened animal's putting its tail between its legs. One who shows ignoble fear in the face of danger, pain, &c.—**Cow'ardice**, *n.* O.F. *couardise*. The quality of a coward.—**Cow'ardly**,[1] *a.*—**Cow'ardly**,[2] *adv.*

Cow'er, *vi.* Perh. of Norse orig. Cf. O.N. *kúra*, to sleep, doze, Sw. *kura*, Da. *kure*, to squat. To crouch, esp. in fear or for shelter.

Cowl, *n.* O.E. *cugele*, *cugle*—L. *cuculla*. A garment with a hood worn by monks.

Cow'slip, *n.* O.E. *cú-slyppe*, app. f. *cú*, COW + *slyppe*, slimy substance, *i.e.* cow-dung. SLOP.[2] A well-known wild flower.

Cox'comb, *n.* See COCK'S-COMB, COCKSCOMB under COCK.[1]

Cox'swain, **Cock'swain**, *n.* Lit. 'cock-lad'. COCK.[3] SWAIN. The helmsman of a boat; the person in charge of a boat and its crew.

Coy, *a.* F. *coi*, earlier *quei*, as if f. a L. **quētus* = *quiētus*, still, f. *qui-s*, QUIET. Showing (sometimes only showing modest shyness.—**Coy'ly**,[2] *adv.*—**Coy'ness**, *n.*

Coz'en, *vt.* Of uncertain orig. Often referred to COUSIN, with the notion of claiming kinship for one's own ends. Cf. F. *cousiner* in this sense. To cheat, defraud; to beguile.—**Coz'enage**, *n.*

Crab, *n.*[1] O.E. *crabba*, cogn. with L.G. *krabben*, to scratch, claw. An edible crustaceous animal with strong claws.—**Crab'bed**, *a.* From the perverse disposition supposed to be indicated by the creature's crooked gait. Perverse, wayward; irritable, ill-natured; difficult to decipher. From association with CRAB,[2] sour-tempered, morose.

Crab, *n.*[2] Of uncertain orig. A sour, harsh fruit, the wild apple.

Crack, *vi.* O.E. *cracian*. Common Teut. To make a sharp explosive noise as in breaking; to break partially.—*vt.* To cause to make a sharp noise; to break with such a noise; to break partially; to break into fissures; of the voice, to lose its clearness.—*n.* A sharp explosive noise; a fissure; a partial fracture; a flaw.—**Crack'er**, *n.* A kind of explosive firework; a small parcel of sweets, &c., containing a substance which explodes on pulling; an instrument for cracking.—**Crack'le**, *vi.* Dim. and freq. suff. *-le*. To emit slight cracks in rapid succession.—*n.* The act of crackling.—**Crack'ling**, *vbl.n.* The action of the the *v.*; the crisp skin of roast pork.

Cra'dle, *n.* O.E. *cradol*, of uncertain orig. A cot for an infant; a supporting framework. —*vt.* To lay in, or as in a cradle (often *fig.*).

Craft, *n.* O.E. *cræft*. Common Teut. Orig. sense 'strength'. Skill; skill in deceit, fraud, cunning; a trade requiring skill; a manual art; the members of a trade collectively; *collectively*, ships; with *a*, a ship.—**Crafts'man**, *n.* (I.e. *craft's man*).—**Craft'**Y,[2] *a.* Artful, cunning.—**Craft'i**LY,[2] *adv.*

Crag, *n.* App. of Celtic orig. Cf. Ir. and Gael. *creag*, rock. A steep rugged rock.

Cram, *vt.* O.E. *crammian*, to stuff. Cf. O.N. *kremja*, Sw. *krama*, to squeeze. To fill quite full or overfull; to overfeed; to thrust, force, stuff; to prepare quickly for an examination. —*n.* Such preparation; the knowledge got by it; a dense crowd.

Cramp, *n.*[1] O.F. *crampe*, f. Teut. (See next.) A painful involuntary contraction of the muscles.—*v.*[1]*t.* To affect with such a contraction.

Cramp, *n.*[2] App. f. Du. or L.G. Cf. M.Du. *krampe*, hook, Ger. f. L.G. *krampe*, cramp. Orig. the same word as prec. A bent piece of iron for holding together pieces of timber, &c.; a portable tool which can be screwed up to hold things together.—*v.*[2]*t.* To fasten with a cramp; coloured by association with *n.*[1], to shut in so as to restrict physical freedom, to restrict within narrow limits, to compress.

Cran'berry, *n.* App. adopted by the North American colonists from a L.G. source and brought to England with the fruit. The red acid fruit of a dwarf shrub growing in bogs.

Crane, *n.* O.E. *cran*. Cf. M.L.G. *krân*, *krôn*, M.Du. *crāne*. Cogn. with G. *geranos*, L. *grus*. A migratory bird with long legs, neck, and bill; a machine for raising heavy weights.—*vt.* To raise with a crane; to stretch out (the neck) like a crane.—*vi.* To lean forward with the neck stretched out.

Cra'nium, *n.* Med.L. *crānium*—G. *kranion*. MEGRIM. The skull.

Crank, *n.* M.E. *cranke*—O.E. *cranc* (only in composition), app. f. *crincan*, *cringan*, to fall in battle, app. orig., to curl oneself up. CRINGE. CRINKLE. A portion of an axis bent at right angles; a fanciful turn of speech; a whim, caprice.—*a.*[1] In a shaky condition, out of order.—**Crank'**Y,[2] *a.* Out of order; of a capricious temper, subject to whims.

Crank, *a.*[2] Of doubtful orig. Of a ship, liable to lean over or capsize.

Cran'ny, *n.* App. related to F. *cran*, a notch, cleft, of doubtful orig. CRENATE. A small narrow opening.

Crape, *n.* F. *crêpe*, earlier *crespe*, use as *n.* of *crespe*, L. *crispus*. CRISP. A wrinkled fabric of twisted material.

Crap'ulous, *a.* L. *crāpulōsus*, f. *crāpula*, intoxication—G. *kraipalē*, a drunken headache. Intemperate in drinking; suffering on account of, resulting from such intemperance. —**Crap'ul**ENCE, *n.*

Crash, *vt.* Imitative. To dash in pieces.—*vi.* To make a noise as of a hard body or of hard bodies being dashed in pieces.—*n.* Such a noise; a sudden collapse of mercantile credit.

Cra'sis, *n.* G. *krasis*, mixture, f. *kerannunai*, to mix. CRATER. The combination of the vowels of two syllables into one long vowel.

Crass, *a.* L. *crassus*, thick. GREASE. Gross, grossly stupid.

Crate, *n.* App. f. L. *crātis*, hurdle. GRILL. An open-work case for glass, &c.

Cra'ter, *n.* G. *kratēr*, bowl, f. *kerannunai*, to mix. The bowl-shaped hollow of a volcano.

Craunch, *vt.* Imitative. CRUNCH. To crush with the teeth.

Cravat', *n.* F. *cravate* = *Cravate*, Croatian, as first worn (in the 17th cent.) in imitation of Croatian mercenaries. A neckcloth.

Crave, *vt.* O.E. *crafian*. Cf. O.N. *krafa*, a demand. To ask for earnestly, beg for; to long or yearn for; to need greatly, require.

Cra'ven, *a.* Early M.E. *cravant*, beaten, or perh. owning oneself beaten, of obscure orig. Cowardly.—*n.* A confessed coward.

Crawl, *vi.* Prob. f. Norse. Cf. Da. *kravle*, to crawl, climb up, and Icelandic *krafla*, to paw with the hands; also L.G. *krabben* under CRAB.[1] SCRAWL. To move slowly by dragging the body close to the ground; to go with a slow and dragging movement; to move stealthily or abjectly.—*n.* A crawling.

Cray'fish, **Craw'fish**, *n.* M.E. *crevice*, *crevisse*—O.F. *crevice*, *escrevisse* (F. *écrevisse*), cogn. with CRAB.[1] A crustaceous animal resembling a small lobster.

Cray'on, *n.* F., f. *craie*, L. *crēta*, chalk. A pointed pencil of coloured chalk or other material; a drawing made with crayons.

Craze, *vt.* Prob. f. Norse. Cf. Sw. *krasa*, Da. *krase*, to crackle, also F. *écraser*, to break in pieces, prob. of sim. orig. To impair in health; to impair in intellect, make insane.—*vi.* To become insane.—*n.* An insane fancy, a mania.—**Cra'z**Y,[2] *a.* Full of flaws, liable to break or fall; insane; betokening insanity.

Creak, *vi.* App. imitative. To make a harsh shrill grating sound.—*n.* Such a sound.

Cream, *n.* F. *crème*, in O.F. *cresme*, fem., a popular application of *cresme*, masc., CHRISM, f. L. *chrisma*. The oily part of milk; the choice part of anything.—*vi.* Of milk, to form cream.—*vt.* To cause or allow (milk) to form cream; to skim the cream from; to take the 'cream' or choice part of.—**Cream'**Y,[2] *a.*

Crease, *n.* Orig. unknown. A mark made by folding, a fold, ridge.—*vt.* To make a crease or creases in.

Create', *vt.* L. *creāre*, *creātum*. To bring into being; to make, form, constitute; to occasion, give rise to; to invest with rank, title, &c.—**Crea'**TION, *n.*—**Crea'**TIVE, *a.*—**Crea'**TOR, *n.*—**Crea'ture**, *n.* F. *créature*—L. *creātūra*. Anything created; a living being, an animal; a human being; a result or product *of*; a dependent, a mere tool.

Cre'dence, *n.* Med.L. *crēdentia*, f. L. *crēdĕre*. (See next.) Belief, credit; a small side table on which the eucharistic elements are placed before consecration.—**Creden'ti**AL, *n.* A letter of introduction (gen. in *pl.*).

Cred'it, *n.* F. *crédit*—It. *credito*, belief, trust, reputation—L. *crēdĕre*, *crēditum*, to trust, believe. (See prec. and next.) GRANT. MISCREANT. Belief, faith, trust; good name, honour, repute; influence based on the confidence of others; honour or commendation gained; a source of honour or commendation; trust in another's ability to pay; reputation of solvency; a sum held at one's disposal; a note, bill, &c., on which money can be raised; the side of an account on which sums received are entered.—*vt.* To put faith in, believe; to enter on the credit side of an account; *to credit* (a person) *with*, to enter as due to (him); to attribute, ascribe.—

Cred'IBLE, *a.* Worthy of belief.—**Cred'**-**ib**LY,[2] *adv.*—**Credi**BIL'ITY, *n.*—**Cred'it**-ABLE, *a.* That brings honour, reputable.—**Cred'itab**LY,[2] *adv.*—**Cred'it**OR, *n.* One who gives money, &c., on credit, one to whom a debt is due.—**Cred'ulous**, *a.* L. *crēdulus* + -OUS. Apt to believe on insufficient grounds. **Credu'l**ITY, *n.*

Creed, *n.* O.E. *créda*—L. *crēdĕre*, to believe, trust. (See prec.) A form of words setting forth Christian doctrine concisely; a confession of faith; a system of belief.

Creek, *n.* M.E. *creke*—M.Du. *krēke*. Cf. O.N. *kriki*, a creek, nook. A narrow recess in a coast-line; a small harbour.

Creep, *vi.* O.E. *créopan*. Common Teut. CRIPPLE. To move with the body close to the ground; to move cautiously or slowly; to advance stealthily or imperceptibly; to move or proceed humbly or servilely; of plants, to grow on or up a surface; of the skin or flesh, to be affected with a nervous shrinking.—**Creep'**ER, *n.* One who, a plant that creeps.

Cremate', *vt.* L. *cremāre*, *cremātum*, to burn, cremate. To reduce (esp. a corpse) to ashes.—**Crem**A'TION, *n.*—**Crem'at**ORY, *n.*; also **Cremato'rium**. A place for cremating.

Cren'ate, *a.* Med.L. *crēnātus*, f. *crēna* = It. *crena*, a notch, of doubtful orig. Notched. —*vt.* To notch.—**Cren'ell**ATE,[3] *vt.* F. *créneler*, f. O.F. *crenel*, a battlement, app. in form dim. of *cren*, *cran*, notch=It. *crena*. CRANNY. To furnish with battlements or loopholes.

Cre'ole, *n.* F. *créole*—Sp. *criollo*, native to a locality, said to be a corrupted dim. of *criado*, bred, brought up, pa.pple. of *criar*, to breed, f. L. *creāre*, to CREATE. A descendant of Europeans born and living in the W. Indies.

Cre'osote, *n.* Formed to mean 'flesh-preserver' f. G. *kreas*, flesh (in comb. *kreo-*) + *sōtēr*, preserver, f. *sōzein*, to preserve. An antiseptic oily liquid obtained from wood-tar.

Crep'itate, *vi.* L. *crepitāre*, *crepitātum*, freq. of *crepāre*, to crack, crackle. CREVICE. DECREPIT. To crackle.—**Crepit**A'TION, *n.*

Crescen'do, *a.* and *adv.* It., pres.pple. of *crescere*, to increase, f. L. *crescĕre*. (See next.) *Mus.*, a direction to increase the loudness of the tone.

Cres'cent, *n.* O.F. *creissant*, pres.pple. of *creistre*, L. *crescĕre*, to grow. ACCRESCE. CONCRETE. CREW. DECREASE. The waxing moon; the figure of the moon in the first or last quarter; a figure or outline of this shape; a row of houses built in this form.—*a.* Growing, increasing; crescent-shaped.

Cress, *n.* O.E. *cresse*, *cerse*. Cogn. with O.H.G. *chresan*, to creep, as if 'creeper'. The name of various edible plants with pungent leaves.

Cres'set, *n.* O.F. *craicet*, *cresset*. A vessel to hold combustibles to be burnt for light.

Crest, *n.* O.F. *creste*—L. *crista*, tuft, plume. A tuft of feathers on an animal's head; a tuft or plume on a helmet or head-dress; in *heraldry*, a device borne above the shield, and also used separately as a cognizance; the head or top of anything; an elevated ridge.—*vt.* To furnish with a crest; to reach the summit of. —*vi.* Of waves, to rise into a crest.—**Crest'-fallen**, *pp.a.* With drooping crest; hence, cast down in spirits, abashed, dejected.

Cretonne', *n.* F., said to be f. *Creton* in Normandy, famed for linen. A stout unglazed cotton cloth with a pattern in colours.

Crevasse', *n.* F. = O.F. *crevace*. (See next.) A fissure or chasm in the ice of a glacier.

Crev'ice, *n.* O.F. *crevace*—L.L. *crepātia*, f. L. *crepāre*, to creak, crack. CREPITATE. A fissure, cleft.

Crew, *n.* O.F. *creue*, increase, use as *n.* of pa. pple. of *croistre*, L. *crescĕre*, to grow. CRESCENT. Formerly, a reinforcement. A band of armed men; a company or assemblage; a gang, mob, herd; the men manning a ship.

Crib, *n.* O.E. *crib(b)*. Common W. Germanic. A receptacle for fodder; a small house, a hovel; a child's bed; in *cribbage*, the cards thrown out from the players' hands and given to the dealer; a petty theft; a plagiarism; a literal translation.—*vt.* To confine within narrow limits; to pilfer.—**Crib'b**AGE, *n.* A game at cards characterized by the 'crib'.

Crick, *n.* Of uncertain orig. A local spasm or cramp, esp. in the neck.

Crick'et, *n.*[1] O.F. *criquet*, *crequet*, related to *criquer*, to creak, rattle, and to M.Du. *crekel*, Du. and L.G. *krekel*, cricket. All imitative. An insect which makes a characteristic chirping or creaking sound.

Crick'et, *n.*[2] Of uncertain orig. An open-air game played with a ball, bats, and wickets.

Crime, *n.* F. *crime*—L. *crīmen*, *crīminis*, judgement, accusation, offence, f. root of *cernĕre*, *crētum*, to decide, cogn. with G. *krinein*. CERTAIN. CONCERN. CRISIS. An act punishable by law; violation of law; an offence, a sin; wrong-doing.—**Crim'in**AL, *a.* and *n.*—**Crim'inal**LY,[2] *adv.*—**Criminal'**-ITY, *n.*—**Crim'in**ATE,[3] *vt.* To charge with or prove guilty of crime; to blame, condemn. —**Crim'in**OUS, *a.*

Crimp, *v.*[1]*t.* Not in O.E. Corresponds to M.Du. *crimpen*, to shrink, become wrinkled, M.H.G. *krimpfen*, to draw oneself together convulsively. To pinch with minute parallel plaits; to wrinkle or crumple minutely; to cause (the flesh of fish) to contract by gashing.

Crimp, *n.* Of uncertain orig. One who procures seamen or soldiers by decoying or entrapping them.—*v.*[2]*t.* To procure (seamen or soldiers) thus.

Crim'son, *a.* M.E. *cremosin*—O.F. *cramoisin*, Sp. *carmesí*, It. *chermisí*—Arab. *qirmazī*, f. *qirmiz*, the KERMES insect. CARMINE. Of a deep red, inclining to purple.—*n.* The colour or pigment.—*vt.* and *i.* To make or become crimson.

Cringe, *vi.* App. a modification of M.E. *crengen*, derivative (orig. trans.) of O.E. *cringan*. CRANK, *n.* To contract the muscles involuntarily, to shrink, to cower; to show base or servile deference.—*n.* A servile or deferential obeisance.

Crin'kle, *vi.* Freq. derivative f. stem of O.E. *crincan*. CRANK, *n.* To wind or twist, to wrinkle.—*vt.* To wrinkle, crimp.—*n.* A winding or twist; a wrinkle or corrugation.

Crin'oline, *n.* F., f. L. *crīnis*, hair (in sense of F. *crin*, horse-hair) + *līnum*, thread. LINE.[1] (A trade-name.) A fabric of horse-hair and thread; a hooped petticoat.

Crip'ple, *n.* M.E. *crepel*, *crupel*—O.Northumb. *crypel*, cogn. with *créopan*, to CREEP. One deprived of the use of his limbs.—*vt.* To make a cripple of; to disable or impair.

Cri'sis, *n.* L. *crisis*—G. *krisis*, decision, f. *krinein*, to decide. CRIME. CRITERION. A decisive point or stage in disease and generally.

Crisp, *a.* O.E. *crisp*, *cyrps*—L. *crispus*, curled. CRAPE. Of the hair, curly; waved or wrinkled on the surface; brittle, though somewhat firm in structure; brisk, decided.

Crite'rion, *n.*; *pl.* **-ia.** G. *kritērion*, f. *kritēs*, judge, f. *krinein.* CRISIS. A canon or standard of judgement.—**Crit'ic**, *n.* L. *criticus*—G. *kritikos*, able to discern, f. *kritēs.* One who passes judgement, esp. unfavourably, on a person or thing; a writer skilled in judging literary or artistic work or in the history of the text of particular writings.—**Crit'ic**AL, *a.* Fault-finding; relating to literary, artistic, or textual criticism; of decisive importance; involving risk; decisive.—**Crit'ical**LY,[2] *adv.*—**Crit'ic**ISM, *n.* Fault-finding; the work or function of a literary, artistic, or textual critic; a critical remark; a critique.—**Crit'ic**IZE, *vt.*—**Critique'**, *n.* F.—G. *kritikē* (*technē*), the critical (art). The art of criticism; a critical essay.

Croak, *vi.* Prob. imitative and of late formation. To emit a deep hoarse cry, as a raven or a frog; to talk dismally or despondingly.—*n.* Such a cry or such talk.—**Croak'**ER, *n.*

Cro'chet, *n.* F., dim. of *croche*, *croc*, L.L. *croccus*, hook. CROCKET. CROQUET. CROSIER, CROTCHET. Knitting done with a hooked needle.—*vi.* and *t.* To knit thus.

Crock, *n.* O.E. *croc*(*c*), *crocca.* Cf. Da. *krukke*, Sw. *kruka*, in same sense. CRUET. An earthen pot or jar.—**Crock'ery**, *n.* From obs. *crock*ER, potter + -Y.[1] Earthen vessels collectively.

Crock'et, *n.* A.F. *croket*, *croquet*=F. *crochet*, hook, crocket. CROCHET. In Gothic architecture one of the small ornaments on the inclined sides of pinnacles, pediments, &c.

Croc'odile, *n.* O.F. *cocodrille*—L. *crocodilus*—G. *krokodeilos.* A large amphibious reptile. It was fabled to shed tears to allure, or on devouring, a victim. Hence many allusions.

Cro'cus, *n.* L.—G. *krokos*, app. Semitic. A bulbous plant with yellow or purple flowers.

Croft, *n.* O.E. *croft*, of unknown orig. An enclosed piece of ground for tillage or pasture.

Crone, *n.* Prob. f. O.N.F. *caroigne*, CARRION. A withered old woman.

Cro'ny, *n.* Of unknown orig. An intimate.

Crook, *n.* M.E. *crōk*, *crōc*, app. f. O.N. *krókr*, crook, hook. Cf. M.Du. *kroke.* ENCROACH. A hook as an instrument or weapon; a shepherd's hooked staff; a crosier; a hooked appendage; a nook; a bending or curve.—*vt.* and *i.* To bend, curve.—**Crook'ed**, *a.* Bent, twisted; deformed; dishonest.

Crop, *n.* O.E. *crop*(*p*), top of a plant, bird's crop. Cf. O.N. *kroppr*, hunch on the body, Da. *krop*, a swelling. O.Teut. base *kroppo-*. Orig. sense app. 'lump' or 'mass'. CROUP.[2] GROUP. An enlargement of the gullet forming a bird's first stomach; the stock or handle of a whip; a hunting whip; the annual produce of cultivation; a cutting of the hair short, a closely cut head of hair.—*vt.* To remove the head of (a plant, tree, &c.); to gather in as a crop, to reap; to sow (land) with a crop; to cut off short, esp. of the ears and hair.—*vi.* *To crop up*, to appear or be brought into notice unexpectedly.

Cro'quet, *n.* Said to be Northern F., 'little hook', 'bent stick' = CROCHET. An open-air game played with balls, mallets, and hoops.

Cro'sier, **Cro'zier**, *n.* M.E. *croce*, *crocer*—O.F. *croce*, crosier, f. *croc*, a hook. CROCHET. A bishop's pastoral staff or crook.

Cross, *n.* Northern M.E. *cros*, f. L. *crux*, *crucis*, app. through Norse (*kross*) and O. Irish (*cros*). CRUCIAL. CRUCIFY. CRUISE. CRUSADE. A kind of gibbet, a stake with a transverse bar, esp. that on which Christ suffered; a delineation or figure of a cross; the Christian religion; an affliction; an annoyance or misfortune; any cross-shaped object; an intermixture of breeds, a breed due to this.—*vt.* To make a sign of the cross upon or over; to strike *out*, erase; to set (things) across each other; to pass across, intersect; to pass over (a line, space, &c.); to meet and pass; to thwart, oppose; to modify (a breed) by intermixture, to subject (animals) to this process.—*vi.* To intersect; to pass to the other side, pass *over.*—*a.* Transverse, passing from side to side; intersecting; contrary, opposed *to*; adverse, thwarting; ill-tempered, peevish, vexed.—**Cross'**LY,[2] *adv.*—**Cross-exam'ine**, *vt.* To examine minutely, esp. to examine a witness adduced and already examined by the other side.—**Cross-examin**A'TION, *n.*

Crotch'et, *n.* F. CROCHET. *Mus.*, a symbol for a note of half the value of a minim, in F. applied (more naturally) to the hooked symbol of the quaver (now *croche*); the note; a whim, a peculiar notion.—**Crotch'et**Y,[2] *a.*

Crouch, *vi.* Orig. doubtful. To stoop with the body drawn together; to cringe servilely.

Croup, *n.*[1] From imitative *Croup*, v., now only dialectal, to croak. A disease of the throat in children characterized by a peculiar sharp ringing cough.

Croup, *n.*[2] F. *croupe*, earlier *crope*, of Teut. orig. Cf. O.N. *kroppr.* CROP. CRUPPER. The hind-quarters of a horse.

Crou'pier, *n.* F. *croupier*, orig., one who rides on the croup (see prec.) behind another.—A raker in of money at a gaming-table; an assistant chairman at a public dinner.

Crow, *n.*[1] O.E. *cráwe*, allied to *cráwan.* CROW, *v.* A large black carrion-eating bird; an iron bar, usually beak-shaped at one end used as a lever (also **Crow'bar**).

Crow, *v.* O.E. *cráwan*, of imitative orig. Cf. Ger. *krähen.* To utter the cry of a cock; to make a loud inarticulate sound in exultation; to exult loudly, boast.—*n.*[2] A cock's crowing.

Crowd, *vi.* O.E. *crúdan.* Cf. M.Du. *crúden*, to press, push. To press or hasten on; to force one's way; to flock together, throng.—*vt.* To cram, thrust, force; to bring or pack closely together; to fill *with* a multitude; to throng (a place); to exclude by crowding or through limits of space.—*n.* A multitude; the multitude, the masses; a large collection.

Crown, *n.* A.F. *coroune*, O.N.F. *corune*, *curune*—L. *corōna*, a wreath, crown. CORONAL. CORONATION. A wreath for the head; a covering for the head worn as a symbol of sovereignty; a monarch's rule or position; a monarch; a silver coin worth five shillings; the top of the head, the head; a rounded summit; the highest part of an arch or an arched surface; the consummation or perfection of anything.—*vt.* To put a wreath or crown upon; to occupy the summit of; to complete worthily; to bring to a happy issue.

Cru'cial, *a.* F. *crucial*, f. L. *crux*, *crucis*, CROSS + -AL. From the notion of a cross as a finger-post at a parting of roads, pointing conclusively to a decision, decisive, critical.

Cru'cible, *n.* Med.L. *crucibulum*, a night-lamp, later, a melting-pot, app. in some way f. L. *crux*, *crucis*, CROSS. A melting-pot.

Cru'cify, *vt.* O.F. *crucifier*—L. *cruci figĕre*, to fix on a CROSS, f. *figere*, *fixum*, to FIX. To inflict the punishment of the cross on.—**Crucifix'**ION, *n.* The action of crucifying.

—**Cru'cifix**, *n.* O.F. *crucefix*—L. *cruci fixus*, fixed on a cross. An image of Christ upon the cross—**Cru'ciform**, *a.* Mod.L. *cruciformis*, f. L. *forma*, FORM. Cross-shaped.

Crude, *a.* L. *crūdus*, RAW. In the natural or raw state; unripe; not well thought out; lacking finish, rough.—**Crude**'LY,[2] *adv.*—**Crud**'ITY, *n.*

Cru'el, *a.* F. *cruel*—L. *crūdēlis*, cogn. with *crūdus*. (See prec.) Merciless, pitiless; causing suffering, painful.—**Cru'el**LY,[2] *adv.*—**Cru'el**TY, *n.*

Cru'et, *n.* M.E. *cruet*, *cruette*, app. representing a dim. of O.F. *cruie*, *crue*, pot, app. f. O.H.G. *kruog* (Ger. *krug*), cogn. with CROCK. A small glass bottle for vinegar, oil, &c.

Cruise, *vi.* Corresponds to Du. *kruisen*, f. *kruis*, cross, and F. *croiser*, to cross, to cruise up and down on, both f. L. *crux*, CROSS. To sail to and fro without making for a particular port.—*n.* Such a sailing.—**Cruis**'ER, *n.* A war-ship constructed for cruising for purposes of war.

Crumb, *n.* O.E. *cruma* (with excrescent *b*). Cf. M.Du. *crūme*, M.L.G. *krōme*. A small particle, as of bread; the soft part of bread.—*vt.* To reduce to or cover with crumbs.—**Crum'ble**, *vt.* and *i.* Freq. suff. *-le*. To reduce to or fall into crumbs or particles.

Crum'pet, *n.* Poss. conn. with *crump* (see next), as orig. curled up. A light muffin.

Crum'ple, *vi.* Freq. of obs. *Crump*, cogn. with CRAMP, *n.*[1] and CRIMP, *v.*[1] To shrivel up, become creased or wrinkled.—*vt.* To bend together, esp. by crushing; to crush together; to rumple; to wrinkle.

Crunch, *vt.* A recent variant of CRAUNCH.

Crup'per, *n.* O.F. *cropiere*, f. *crope*. CROUP.[2] A strap fastened to a saddle and passing under the horse's tail; the croup.

Crusade', *n.* F. *croisade*, O.F. *croisee*—Med.L. *cruciāta*, n. of action founded on pa. pple. of L. *cruciāre*, *cruciātum*, f. *crux*, CROSS, with sense 'a marking with or taking the cross'. A military expedition for the recovery of the Holy Land from the Mohammedans; a 'holy war'; an aggressive movement against some evil or fancied evil.—*vi.* To engage in a crusade.—**Crusad**'ER, *n.*

Cruse, *n.* Of uncertain orig. Sim. forms in most Teut. languages. A small earthen pot.

Crush, *vt.* O.F. *crusir*, *croissir*, *croisir*, to gnash (the teeth), smash, app. of Ger. orig. To compress so as to break; to squeeze forcibly; to subdue; to break down into small pieces.—*vi.* To become crushed.

Crust, *n.* L. *crusta*, hard surface, rind, shell, cogn. with G. *kruos*, frost. CRYSTAL. CUSTARD. The hard outer part of bread; a hard coating; the hard covering of an animal; the exterior part (of the earth).—*vt.* and *i.* To cover with, or to form or contract a crust.—**Crust**'Y,[2] *a.* Like or having a crust; short of temper.—**Crust**'ILY,[2] *adv.*—**Crusta'cea**, *n.pl.* Mod.L. *crustācea* (sc. *animālia*), f. *crusta*. A class of animals having a hard covering.—**Crusta'ce**OUS, **Crusta'ce**AN, *aa.* Of this class; the latter also as *n.*

Crutch, *n.* O.E. *crycc*. Common Teut. A staff with a cross-piece used by lame persons.

Cry, *vi.* F. *crier*—L. *quirītāre*, to wail, orig. (it is said) to implore the aid of the *Quirītes* or citizens. To call aloud, shout; to weep; of an animal, to utter its call.—*vt.* To utter loudly, call out; to proclaim.—*n.* A loud utterance; a scream, wail; a shout; an entreaty; an opinion generally expressed; a watchword, a rallying cry; a fit of weeping; the characteristic call of an animal.

Crypt, *n.* L. *crypta*, G. *kruptē*, vault, orig. fem. of *kruptos*, hidden, f. *kruptein*, to hide. APOCRYPHA. GROTTO. A chamber under the main floor of a church.—**Cryp'tic**, **Cryp'ti**CAL, *aa.* L. *crypticus*, G. *kruptikos*, fit for concealing, f. *kruptos*. Secret, mystical.

Crys'tal, *n.* O.F. *cristal*—L. *crystallum*—G. *krustallos*, clear ice, rock-crystal, f. *kruos*, frost. CRUST. A clear transparent mineral; a very clear kind of glass; glass vessels; a characteristic form, with symmetrically arranged plane faces, assumed by many substances.—*vt.* **Crys'talli**ZE, *vi.* and *t.* To assume or to cause to assume such a form.—**Crystalliza**'TION, *n.*—**Crys'tall**INE, *a.*

Cub, *n.* Orig. unknown. The young of the fox and other wild beasts.—*vt.* To bring forth (cubs).—*vi.* To bring forth cubs.

Cube, *n.* F. *cube*—L.L. *cubus*—G. *kubos*, a die, a cube. A solid figure contained by six equal squares; the product from multiplying a quantity twice by itself.—*vt.* To multiply thus.—**Cub'**IC, **Cub'**ICAL, *aa.*

Cu'bicle, *n.* L. *cubiculum*, f. *cubāre*, to lie. CONCUBINE. COVEY. A bedchamber, esp. a small separate one in a dormitory.

Cu'bit, *n.* L. *cubitum*, the elbow, the length of the forearm, conn. with *cubāre*. (See prec.) A measure of length derived from the forearm.

Cuc'koo, *n.* Imitative. Cf. G. *kokkux*, F. *coucou*. A migratory bird named from its call.

Cu'cumber, *n.* O.F. *cocombre* (F. *concombre*)—L. *cucumis*, *cucumeris*. A creeping plant with a long fleshy fruit; the fruit.

Cud, *n.* O.E. *cwidu*, cogn. with O.H.G. *chuti*, glutinous substance, O.N. *kvátha*, resin. The food which a ruminating animal brings back into its mouth to chew.

Cud'dle, *vt.* Orig. uncertain. To hug affectionately.—*vi.* To lie close and snug.

Cud'dy, *n.* Orig. uncertain. A cabin in a ship in which officers and passengers mess.

Cudg'el, *n.* O.E. *cycgel*. Orig. unknown. A short thick stick.—*vt.* To beat with a cudgel.

Cue, *n.*[1] Orig. uncertain. The end of a speech serving as a signal to another actor to enter or begin his speech; a hint how to act; the proper course to take; mood, disposition.

Cue, *n.*[2] Var. of QUEUE. A long plait of hair worn hanging down behind; the rod with which the balls are struck in billiards.

Cuff, *n.*[1] M.E. *coffe*, *cuffe*, of uncertain orig. An ornamental ending to a sleeve; a separate band worn round the wrist.

Cuff, *vt.* Of uncertain orig. Cf. Sw. *kuffa*, to thrust, push. To strike with the fist or the open hand.—*n.*[2] A blow of this kind.

Cuirass', *n.* F. *cuirasse*, formed f. *cuir*, L. *corium*, leather, after L. *coriacea*, fem. of *coriaceus*, of leather. EXCORIATE. A piece of armour for the body.

Cu'linary, *a.* L. *culīnārius*, f. *culīna*, kitchen. KILN. Of a kitchen or cookery; fit for cooking.

Cull, *vt.* O.F. *cuillir* (F. *cueillir*)—L. *colligĕre*, to COLLECT. To select; to gather, pluck.

Cul'minate, *vi.* L.L. *culmināre*, *culminātum*, f. *culmen*, *culminis*, contr. f. *columen*, summit. COLUMN. HILL. Of a heavenly body, to reach its greatest altitude; to reach the highest point.—**Culmina**'TION, *n.*

Cul'pable, *a.* O.F. *coupable*, guilty—L. *culpābilis*, blameworthy, f. *culpa*, fault, blame.

Deserving blame.—**Cul'pab**LY,[2] *adv.*—**Cul-pab**IL'ITY, *n.*

Cul'prit, *n.* Orig. in judicial formula 'Culprit, how will you be tried?' Said to have arisen from a fusion and misuse of the syllables *cul:* and *prit:* or *prist:*=O.F. *prest*, ready, used to record the formal reply in law French of the Clerk of the Crown to a plea of not guilty, '*Culpable, prest de . . .*', ('You are) guilty, (I am) ready to (proceed'). Perh. the syllables were repeated, after being recorded, as a preface to the formal question, and were used as an appellation after the real meaning had been lost sight of. Hence, the accused; one guilty of an offence.

Cult, *n.* L. *cultus*, worship, f. *colĕre*, *cultum*, to till, devote oneself to, worship. COLONY. A particular system of religious worship; devotion to a particular person or thing.—**Cul'tivate**, *vt.* L.L. *cultīvāre*, *cultīvātum*, to till, f. *colĕre*. To till; to bestow labour on (a plant, &c.); to improve, develop, refine; to devote attention to, practise, cherish.—**Cul'tiv**ABLE, *a.*—**Cultiv**A'TION, *n.*—**Cul'tivat**OR, *n.*—**Cul'ture**, *n.* L. *cultūra*, f. *colĕre*. Tillage; the rearing of a plant, &c.; improvement, development, refinement; the result of this.—*vt.* To subject to culture.—**Cul'tured**, *ppl.a.* Cultivated; refined.

Cul'vert, *n.* Recent, of obscure orig. A tunnelled drain for the conveyance of water.

Cum'ber, *vt.* Of doubtful orig. (Difficult to connect with ENCUMBER, as it occurs earlier.) To hamper, embarrass; to burden, load.—**Cum'ber**SOME, **Cum'br**OUS, *aa.*

Cu'mulate, *vt.* L. *cumulāre*, *cumulātum*, to heap, f. *cumulus*, a heap. ACCUMULATE. To gather in a heap, amass.—**Cumul**A'TION, *n.*—**Cu'mul**ATIVE, *a.* Arising from the accession of successive portions; of dividends, not contingent on yearly profits.—**Cu'mulus**, *n.*; *pl.* **-li.** The L. word. A cloud in rounded masses.

Cu'neate, *a.* L. *cuneātus*, pa.pple. of *cuneāre*, to make wedge-shaped, f. *cuneus*, wedge. COIN. Wedge-shaped. So **Cune'iform**, *a.*, applied esp., from their shape, to the characters of Persian and Assyrian inscriptions.

Cun'ning. *Vbl.n.* f. O.E. *cunnan*, to know. CAN, *v.* Dexterity, skill; skilful deceit, craft; craftiness.—*a.* Orig. pres. pple. of M.E. *cunnen*, to know, f. *cunnan*. Dexterous, skilful; skilfully contrived or executed; knowing, clever; crafty, sly.—**Cun'ning**LY,[2] *adv.*

Cup, *n.* O.E. *cuppe*, supposed to represent L.L. *cuppa* (whence F. *coupe*), gen. taken as a var. of L. *cūpa*, a tub, cask. COOP. HIVE. A small drinking-vessel; various cup-shaped formations; an ornamental vessel as a prize; a vessel for bleeding a patient; a cupful; a portion, lot (of pain, &c.).—*vt.* To bleed with a cupping-glass. —**Cup'board**, *n.* CUP + BOARD. Formerly, a table to place cups, &c., on. A closed case or recess with shelves.

Cupid'ity, *n.* F. *cupidité*—L. *cupiditas*, f. *cupidus*, longing, f. *cupĕre*, to long for. CONCUPISCENCE. COVET. Greed of gain.

Cu'pola, *n.* It., f. L. *cūpula*, dim. of *cūpa*. CUP. A dome surmounting a building.

Cur, *n.* M.E. *curre*. Cf. M.Du. *corre*, Sw. and Norw. dial. *kurre*, dog. A worthless dog; a surly ill-bred fellow.—**Cur'r**ISH, *a.*

Cu'rate, *n.* Med.L. *cūrātus*, one having a cure (of souls), orig. *a.* f. L. *cūra*. CURE. A spiritual pastor, esp. an assistant to a parish priest.—**Cu'r**ACY, *n.*—**Cura'tor**, *n.* L. *cūrātor*, f. *cūrāre*. CURE. A manager, overseer; a keeper of a museum, &c.

Curb, *vt.* F. *courber*, L. *curvāre*, to bend, f. *curvus*, bent. To restrain (a horse) with a curb; to restrain, check.—*n.* A chain on the bit for checking a horse; a restraint; the stone margin confining a footpath, a **Curb'-stone** (gen. spelt *Kerb*, *Kerb-stone*).

Curd, *n.* M.E. *crud*, *crod*, of unknown orig. Coagulated milk (often in *pl.*)—*vt.* To make into curd.—**Curd'le**, *vt.* Freq. suff. *-le*. In sim. sense.—**Curd'**Y,[2] *a.*

Cure, *n.* O.F. *cure*—L. *cūra*, care. ACCURATE. CURIOUS. SCOUR.[2] *Cure* (*of souls*), spiritual charge or oversight; a course of medical treatment; successful treatment; a remedy.—*v.* O.F. *curer*—L. *cūrāre*, to care for, cure. To heal; to remedy, rectify; to preserve (meat, &c.).—**Cu'r**ABLE, *a.*—**Cu'r**ATIVE, *a.*

Cur'few, *n.* A.F. *coeverfu* = O.F. *cuevre-fu*, f. *couvre*, imp. of *couvrir*, to COVER + *feu*, fire. A mediæval regulation requiring the covering over of fires at an hour of the evening indicated by a bell; the hour, the bell; the practice, still surviving, of ringing an evening bell.

Cu'rious, *a.* O.F. *curius*—L. *cūriōsus*, careful, inquisitive, f. *cūra*. CURE. Eager to learn, inquisitive; prying; accurate, minute; strange, singular, odd.—**Cu'rious**LY,[2] *adv.*—**Curios'**ITY, *n.* Eagerness to learn; inquisitiveness; something strange or odd.

Curl, *vt.* App. conn. with the earlier and obs. *Crull*, a., curly, corresp. to M.Du. *crul*, Fris. *kroll*, *krull*. To bend into ringlets or into a spiral or curved shape.—*vi.* To form ringlets; to take a spiral or curved shape.—*n.* A ringlet; a coil, convolution, undulation; a curling or a being curled.—**Curl'**Y,[2] *a.*

Cur'lew, *n.* Identical with O.F. *courlieus*, *corlys*, &c., said to be an imitation of the cry A snipe-like bird frequenting moors.

Cur'rant, *n.* Orig. *raisins of Corauntz* = F. *raisins de Corinthe*, raisins of Corinth. The dried fruit of a dwarf Levantine grape; the name of several shrubs allied to the gooseberry; their berries, black, red, and white.

Cur'rent, *a.* O.F. *corant*, *curant*, pres.pple. of *corre*, *curre* (F. *courir*), L. *currĕre*, to run. CONCUR. COURSE. Running, flowing; smoothly flowing; of time, running, in course of passing; of money, in circulation; generally known or reported; generally accepted.—*n.* A body of water or air in motion; the flow (of a river, &c.); the course of time or events; tendency, drift; an apparent flow of electric force.—**Cur'rent**LY,[2] *adv.*—**Cur'r**ENCY, *n.* The time during which a thing is current; the fact of money being current; money in use; prevalence, vogue.

Cur'ry, *v.*[1]*t.* O.F. *correier*, *coreer*, orig. *conreder*, *conreer*, to put in order, prepare, curry (a horse), f. *conrei*, gear, preparation, f. CON- + *rei*, *rai*, *roi*, order, of Scand. orig. and cogn. with READY. ARRAY. To rub down (a horse, &c.) with a comb; to dress (tanned leather); *to curry favour*, formerly *Favel* (=O.F. *Fauvel* f. *fauve*, fallow-coloured), 'to curry the chestnut horse', hence (it is not clear why) to seek to win favour unworthily.—**Cur'ri**ER, *n.* A dresser of tanned leather.

Cur'ry, *n.* Tamil *kari*, sauce, relish. A highly spiced preparation; a dish flavoured with this. —*v.*[2]*t.* To flavour or prepare with curry.

Curse, *n.* O.E. *curs*, with v. *cursian*, of unknown orig. ACCURSED. An utterance intended to consign (a person or thing) to evil;

a profane oath, an imprecation; a blighting affliction, a bane.—*vt.* To utter against (a person or thing) words intended to consign to evil; to rail profanely at; to swear at; to afflict.—*vi.* To utter curses.

Cur'sive, *a.* Med.L. *cursivus*, f. L. *currĕre*, to run. CURRENT. Written with a running hand.—**Cur'sory**, *a.* L. *cursōrius*, pertaining to a runner, f. *cursor*, a runner, f. *currĕre*. Hasty, hurried, passing.—**Cur'sori**LY,[2] *adv.*

Curt, *a.* L. *curtus*, cut short, short. KIRTLE. Short; brief, concise; brief to rudeness.—**Curt'**LY,[2] *adv.*—**Curtail'**, *vt.* Orig. *curtal(l)*, f. obs. *curtal*, docked—F. *courtault*, f. *court*, short, f. *curtus*. To cut short; to abridge, diminish; to deprive *of*.

Cur'tain, *n.* O.F. *cortine*, *courtine*—L.L. *cortina*, of doubtful orig. A cloth hung up as a screen; a screen in front of the stage of a theatre.—*vt.* To apply a curtain to.

Curt'sy, **Curt'sey**, *n.* Varr. of *Courtesy*. COURT. A woman's obeisance, made by bending the knees and lowering the body.—*vi.* To make a curtsy.

Curve, *a.* L. *curvus*, bent, curved. CURB. Bent.—*n.* Short for *curve-line*, &c. A bent line or outline without angles.—*vt.* To bend into a curve.—*vi.* To have or assume a curved form.—**Cur'vature**, *n.* L. *curvātūra*, f. *curvāre*, *curvātum*, to bend. A bending; curved form.—**Cur'vet**, *n.* It. *corvetta*, dim. f. *corvo*, bent, f. *curvus*. A leap of a horse in which the fore-legs are raised together and the hind-legs are raised before the fore-legs reach the ground.—*vi.* To execute a curvet.—**Curvilin'e**AL, **Curvilin'e**AR,[1] *aa.* *Curvus* + *linea*, a line. LINE.[2] Consisting of or bounded by a curved line or lines.

Cush'ion, *n.* M.E. *cusshyn*, *cushin*—F. *coussin*, earlier *cussin*—L. type *coxinum, a support for the hip, f. *coxa*, hip. A case of cloth stuffed with a soft material to support or ease the body.—*vt.* To furnish with a cushion; to set on or support with a cushion.

Cusp, *n.* L. *cuspis*, point. A point, esp. of the moon; a point at which two branches of a curve meet and stop.

Cus'tard, *n.* App. a perverted form of obs. *Crustade*, a rich pie—F. *croustade*, It. *crostata*, in same sense—L. *crustāre*, *crustātum*, to encrust, f. *crusta*, CRUST. Formerly, a kind of open pie. A dish made of eggs and milk.

Cus'tody, *n.* L. *custōdia*, f. *custos*, *custōdis*, guardian. Guardianship, safe keeping; imprisonment.—**Custo'di**AN, *n.*

Cus'tom, *n.* O.F. *custume*, *costume*—L. type **costūmen* (**costudne*) for accusative of *consuētūdo*, custom, f. *consuētus*, pa.pple. of CONSUESCĔRE, to accustom, become accustomed. COSTUME. DESUETUDE. A habit, usage, fashion; habitual doing of a thing; tribute, toll, duty (gen. in *pl.*); business patronage.—**Cus'tom**ABLE, *a.* Liable to duty.—**Cus'tom**ARY, *a.* Habitual, usual; established by custom.—**Cus'tomari**LY,[2] *adv.*—**Cus'tom**ER, *n.* One who deals regularly with a shop, a bank, &c.

Cut, *vt.* M.E. *cutten*, of unknown orig. To sever with an edged instrument, said also of the instrument; to strike with a whip, &c.; to distress deeply; to reap (corn), mow (grass), &c.; to separate or detach with an edged instrument; to divide (a pack of cards); to intersect, run into or through; to trim, clip; to curtail, reduce; to make or form by cutting; to hollow out, excavate; to perform or execute (an action, gesture, &c.); to break off connexion with, feign not to know.—*vi.* To make incision; to get or admit of being cut; to turn out *so and so* on being cut; to pass straight and rapidly.—*n.*[1] Act of cutting; a stroke with a knife, whip, &c.; a shock, blow; act of 'cutting' an acquaintance; a course or way straight across; fashion, shape; an incision, an engraving; a piece cut off; act of dividing cards.—**Cut't**ER, *n.* One who or that which cuts; a boat belonging to a ship of war; a small single-masted vessel with a straight running bowsprit.

Cut, *n.*[2] Of uncertain orig. Lot. *To draw* [*cuts*, to draw lots.

Cuta'neous, *a.* Mod. or Med.L. *cutāneus* (f. L. *cutis*, skin) + -OUS. HIDE, *n.*[1] Relating to the skin.—**Cu'ticle**, *n.* L. *cutīcula*, dim. of *cutis*. The exterior coat of the skin.

Cut'lass, *n.* F. *coutelas*, aug. of *couteau* (O.F. *coutel*), knife—L. *cultellus*, dim. of *culter*, a ploughshare, a knife. A short sword with a wide slightly curved blade.—**Cut'ler**, *n.* O.F. *coutelier*, f. *coutel*. One who makes, repairs, or deals in cutting instruments.—**Cut'l**ERY, *n.* His trade, his wares.

Cut'let, *n.* F. *côtelette*, double dim. of *côte*, O.F. *coste*, L. *costa*, rib. COAST. A small piece of meat used for broiling, &c.

Cut'tle, **Cut'tle-fish**, *n.* O.E. *cudele*, of unknown orig. A mollusc, also called ink-fish, which ejects a black fluid.

Cy'cle, *n.* L. *cyclus*—G. *kuklos*, circle, WHEEL. An orbit in the heavens; a definite recurring period; a recurrent series; a complete period, series, or set; a series of poems or romances; an abbreviation for BICYCLE.—**Cy'clic**, **Cy'cl**ICAL, *aa.*—**Cy'cl**IST, *n.* One who rides a bicycle.—**Cyclom'eter**, *n.* *Kuklos*+G.*metre-ein*, to measure. An instrument for measuring circles or for registering distance traversed, esp. by a bicycle.—**Cy'clone**, *n.* Formed f. *kuklos*, or f. *kuklo-ōn*, pres.pple. of *kuklo-ein*, to whirl. A circular storm, a tornado; a system of winds rotating round a centre of low pressure and at the same time advancing.

Cyclopæ'dia, **-pe'dia**, *n.* Shortened f. ENCYCLOPÆDIA, and in sim. sense.

Cyg'net, *n.* A dim. formed on F. *cygne* or L. *cygnus*, swan. A young swan.

Cyl'inder, *n.* L. *cylindrus*, roller, cylinder—G. *kulindros*, roller, f. *kulindein*, to roll. CALENDER. An elongated round body of uniform diameter; the chamber of a steam-engine in which the steam acts on the piston.—**Cylin'dr**IC, **Cylin'dr**ICAL, *aa.*

Cym'bal, *n.* L. *cymbalum*—G. *kumbalon*, f. *kumbē*, hollow of a vessel, cup. One of a pair of concave plates of brass or bronze struck together to produce a ringing sound.

Cyn'ic, *n.* L. *cynicus*—G. *kunikos*, dog-like, f. *kuōn*, *kunos*, dog. One of a sect of Greek philosophers marked by an ostentatious contempt of riches and the amenities of life; a sneering fault-finder.—**Cyn'**IC, **Cyn'**ICAL, *aa.*—**Cyn'ic**ISM, *n.*

Cyn'osure, *n.* L. *cynosūra*—G. *kunosoura*, lit. 'dog's tail', the Lesser Bear, f. *kuōn* (see prec.) + *oura*, tail. The constellation the Lesser Bear, which contains the pole-star; the pole-star; a centre of attraction.

Cy'press, *n.* O.F. *ciprès*—L.L. *cypressus*—G. *kuparissos*. A coniferous tree; the wood; sprigs of the tree as a symbol of mourning.

Czar, **Tsar**, *n.* Russian *tsare* (with mute *e*), ultimately representing L. *Caesar*. The title of the Emperor of Russia.—**Czar'evitch**,

Tsar'evitch, *n.* A son of a Czar. Not now in official use. The eldest son bears the differentiated title **Cesar'evitch.—Czari'na, Tsari'na**, *n.* The wife of a Czar.

D

Dab, *vt.* Of uncertain orig. Prob. imitative. To strike or cause to strike with a slight momentary pressure.—*n.*[1] A stroke of this kind; a flattish soft or moist mass.

Dab, *n.*[2] Orig. unknown. An expert, adept.

Dab, *n.*[3] Orig. unknown. A small flat-fish.

Dab'ble, *vt.* Perh. freq. of DAB. To wet, spatter, sprinkle. — *vi.* To play in shallow water; to employ oneself in a superficial way *in*.—**Dab'bl**ER, *n.*

Dab'chick, *n.* The first element app. conn. with DAB, *v.* A small diving bird.

Dace, *n.* O.F. *darz*, DART, dace. Named f. its *darting* motion. A small fresh-water fish.

Dachs'hund, *n.* Ger. = 'badger-dog'. A short-legged long-bodied dog. Also **Dachs'-hound**.

Dacoit', *n.* Hindī *dakait*. One of a band of armed robbers in India or Burmah.

Dac'tyl, *n.* L. *dactylus*—G. *daktulos*, finger, dactyl. DATE.[1] A foot consisting of a long syllable followed by two short (like the bones of a finger).—**Dactyl'**IC, *a.*

Da'do, *n.* It. *dado*, DIE, cube. The block forming the body of a pedestal; the lining, painting, &c., of the lower part of an interior wall.

Daf'fodil, *n.* Var. (with initial *d* not accounted for) of obs. *Affodill*, the Asphodel or King's Spear—Med.L. *affodillus*, L. *asphodelus*—G. *asphodelos*. Applied by confusion to a species of Narcissus also called Lent Lily.

Dag'ger, *n.* Related to F. *dague*, dagger, of unknown orig. A short edged and pointed weapon.

Daguerre'otype, *n.* F. *daguerréotype*, f. *Daguerre*, the inventor's name + *type*, TYPE. An early photographic process; a portrait produced by the process.

Dah'lia, *n.* From *Dahl*, a Swedish botanist. A genus of composite plants, natives of Mexico.

Dai'ly, *a.* O.E. *dæglic*. DAY. -LY.[1] Occurring, done, published, every day.—*adv.* -LY.[2] Every day; constantly, habitually.

Dain'ty, *n.* O.F. *deintié*, *dainté*, pleasure, tit-bit—L. *dignitas*, worthiness, excellence. DIGNITY. Anything delicious to the palate. *a.* Pleasing to the palate; delicately pretty; nice, fastidious; particular as to food, &c.—**Dain'ti**LY,[2] *adv.*—**Dain'ti**NESS, *n.*

Dai'ry, *n.* M.E. *deierie*, with *-erie* (=-ERY) f. *deie* (dial. Eng. *dey*), milk-woman—O.E. *dǽge*, corresp. to O.N. *deigja*, female servant, and cogn. with Goth. *deigan*, to knead. DOUGH. A place where milk is kept and dealt with, or where milk and its products are dealt in.

Dais, *n.* O.F. *deis*—L. *discus*, in Med.L. used in sense 'table'. DISK. Formerly, a raised table in a hall. A platform at one end of a hall, in older use often with a canopy.

Dai'sy, *n.* O.E. *dæges éage*, DAY'S EYE. A flower with a yellow disk and white or pinkish petals which close at night.

Dale, *n.* O.E. *dæl*. Common Teut. A valley.

Dal'ly, *vi.* O.F. *dalier*, to converse, chat, of Teut. orig. To act or speak sportively, to sport *with*; to trifle *with*; to loiter, delay.—**Dal'li**ANCE, *n.*

Dalmat'ic, *n.* F. *dalmatique*—L. *Dalmatica* (*vestis*), Dalmatian (garment). A vestment worn by deacons, bishops, kings, &c.

Dam, *n.*[1] Var. of DAME. A female parent.

Dam, *n.*[2] Common Teut. A barrier for confining water and raising its level.—*vt.* To confine by a dam.

Dam'age, *n.* O.F. *damage*—L. *damnum*, loss, hurt, fine + -AGE. DAMN. Injury, harm; in *pl.*, compensation in money.—*vt.* To injure.

Dam'ask, *n.* It. *damasco* (prob. through A.F.)—L. *Damascus*, the city. DAMSON. A rich silk figured fabric; a twilled linen fabric; steel with a variegated surface (all orig. made at Damascus); *damask rose*, a red variety (supposed to have come thence); the colour of the rose.—*vt.* To ornament with a variegated pattern. — **Damaskeen'**, **Damascene'**, *vvt.* To ornament with incised designs filled in with gold or silver.

Dame, *n.* O.F. *dame*, lady—L. *domina*, fem. of *dominus*, lord. DAM.[1] DAMSEL. DOMINATE. DUENNA. The legal title of the wife of a knight or baronet; a lady.

Damn, *vt.* O.F. *damner*—L. *damnāre*, *damnātum*, to condemn, fine, f. *damnum*. DAMAGE. CONDEMN. To condemn (a play) by public disapproval; to bring condemnation on, be the ruin of; to condemn to hell.—**Damna'**TION, *n.*—**Dam'nat**ORY, *a.*

Damp, *n.* Of uncertain orig. Cf. M.L.G. and Mod.Du. and Da. *damp*, vapour, steam. In coal mines, a noxious vapour; moisture, humidity; depression of spirits; a discouragement, check.—*a.* Moist, humid.—*v.* To stifle, extinguish; to dull, deaden; to discourage, check; to make moist or humid.—**Damp'**ER, *n.* Something or a person that dulls or deadens; a contrivance for controlling combustion by regulating or stopping the draught.

Dam'sel, *n.* O.F. *dameisele*, formed f. *dame*. DAME. A young unmarried woman, a girl.

Dam'son, *n.* M.E. *damascene*—L. (*prūnum*) *Damascēnum*, (plum) of Damascus. DAMASK. A small dark plum introduced from Syria; the tree bearing it.

Dance, *vi.* O.F. *dancer*, *danser*, said to be f. O.H.G. *dansôn*, to stretch out, with notion 'to form a file in dancing'. To leap or glide rhythmically; to leap or move about or up and down; to bob up and down.—*vt.* To cause to dance; to dandle.—*n.* A rhythmical leaping or gliding; a particular arrangement of such movements; a tune to which one dances; a dancing party.—**Danc'**ER, *n.*

Dandeli'on, *n.* F. *dent de lion*, lion's tooth, f. the toothed outline of the leaves—L. *dens dentis*, tooth, and *leo*, *leōnis*, lion. A well-known plant with a large yellow flower.

Dan'dle, *vt.* Of uncertain orig. Cf. It. *dandola*, a doll, a dandling, *dandolare*, to dandle, play, sport. To move lightly up and down; to pet, fondle.

Dan'druff, *n.* Orig. unknown. Scurf on the head.

Dan'dy, *n.* Orig. unknown. One who studies to dress elegantly, a fop.—*a.* Devoted to elegance in dress.—**Dan'dy**ISM, *n.*

Dan'ger, *n.* O.F. *dangier*, *danger*—L.L. **dominiārium*, f. L. *dominium*, lordship, f. *dominus*, lord. DOMINATE. Formerly, power of a lord; power to inflict injury. Liability or exposure to injury, risk; a peril, risk.—**Dan'ger**OUS, *a.*—**Dan'gerous**LY,[2] *adv.*

Dan'gle, *vi.* Of uncertain orig. Cf. Da. *dangle*,

Norw. and Sw. dial. *dangla*, varr. of Da. *dingle*, Norw. and Sw. *dingla*, to dangle. To hang loosely swaying to and fro; to hover *after* or *about* a person.—*vt.* To cause to hang loosely and swaying; to carry hanging loosely.

Dank, *a.* Orig. uncertain. Wet, wetting.

Dap'per, *a.* App. f. Flemish or other L.G. dialect, with (perh. ironical) modification of sense. Cf. M.Du. *dapper*, stout, energetic; M.L.G. *dapper*, heavy, steady, undaunted. Neat, trim, spruce; little and active.

Dap'ple, *n.* Orig. unknown. Spotting, mottled marking: an animal so marked.—*vt.* To mark with rounded spots.—*vi.* To become dappled.—*a.* Dappled.

Dare, *vi.* O.E. *dearr*, pres. of *durran*, pa. *dorste* (whence *durst*). Cogn. with G. *thrasus*, bold, *tharse-ein*, to be bold. To have boldness or courage.—*vt.* To have courage for; to defy. —**Dar'ing**, *vbl.n.* The action of the *v.*; courage, boldness.

Dark, *a.* O.E. *deorc.* (No corresp. word in the other Teut. languages.) Devoid of or deficient in light; of the moon, &c., dim, invisible; gloomy, sombre; approaching black; deep in shade; evil, wicked; gloomy, cheerless; sullen, sad; obscure in meaning; hidden, secret; reticent; unenlightened.—*n.* Absence of light; night; a dark place; dark colour or shade; the condition of being hidden or secret.—**Dark'**LY,[2] *adv.*—**Dark'**EN,[2] *vi.* To become dark; to grow gloomy or sad.—*vt.* To make dark; to cast a gloom or shadow over.—**Dark'**ISH, *a.* —**Dark'ling**, *adv.* Advbl. suff. *-ling.* In the dark.—*a.* Being, taking place, &c., in the dark; obscure, lying in darkness.—**Dark'**NESS, *n.*—**Dark'**SOME, *a.*

Dar'ling, *n.* O.E. *déorling*, f. *déore*, DEAR + -LING (2). One dearly loved or very lovable.—*a.* Dearly or best loved.

Darn, *vt.* Orig. unknown. To mend by filling-in a hole or rent with interwoven yarn or thread.—*n.* A hole or rent so mended.

Dar'nel, *n.* Orig. uncertain. Cf. Walloon dial. *darnelle* in same sense. A weed hurtful to corn.

Dart, *n.* O.F. *dart*, accus. of *darz*, of Teut. orig. DACE. A pointed missile; an act of darting.—*vt.* To throw, shoot (a dart); to send forth sharply; to cast (a glance).—*vi.* To move suddenly and rapidly.

Dash, *vt.* M.E. *daschen*, *dassen*, perh. f. Norse, or poss. imitative. To smash, break in pieces; to knock, throw, thrust *away*, *down*, &c.; to thrust, impel *against*, *upon*, &c.; to splash *with* water, &c.; to affect or qualify *with* some differing element; to destroy, frustrate (hopes, a design, &c.); to dispirit; to abash.—*vi.* To move or fall with violence; to throw oneself with violence, rush.—*n.* A violent blow or impact; a small portion (of colour, &c.); a small quantity, an infusion, tinge; a horizontal stroke (—) marking a break in sense, an omission, &c.; a sudden movement, a rush; vigour in action; a showy appearance, display, gen. in phrase *to cut a dash.*—**Dash'ing**, *ppl.a.* That dashes; spirited, lively; fashionable, showy.—**Dash'board**, *n.* A board or leather apron for preserving the interior of a vehicle from mud thrown up.

Das'tard, *n.* Orig. uncertain. Perh. *dast-* = M.E. *dased*, dull, inert. DAZE. A base coward.—*a.* Showing base cowardice.—**Das'tard**LY,[1] *a.*

Date, *n.*[1] O.F. *date* (F. *datte*)—L. *dactylus*—G. *daktulos*, finger, date. DACTYL. (Supposed to have been named from the shape. But perh. in this sense *daktulos* was a different (a Semitic) word.) The fruit of the date-palm; the palm.

Date, *n.*[2] F. *date*—L. *data*, fem. sing. (or neut. pl.) of *datus*, given, *i.e.*, of a letter, dated (at such a time and place), pa.pple. of *dăre*, to give, cogn. with G. *didonai.* DIE, *n.* DOSE. TRADITION. The specification of the time (and often of the place) of a writing; the time thus denoted; the time at which something takes place or is to take place; season, period the period to which something belongs; duration.—*vt.* To affix the date to; to ascertain the date of.—*vi.* To count the time, reckon; to bear date; to be assigned to a certain date. —**Date'**LESS, *a.* Bearing no date; endless; immemorial.—**Da'tive**, *a.* and *n.* L. *datīvus*, of or belonging to giving, f. *datus.* A noun case indicating an indirect object, as a person to whom one gives something.—**Da'tum**, *n.*; *pl.* **Da'ta.** Neut. of *datus.* Something granted and used as a basis of reasoning.

Daub, *vt.* O.F. *dauber*—L. *dealbāre* (DE- (3)), to whiten over, plaster, f. *albus*, white. ALBUM. To coat *with* plaster, &c., or dirt; to paint coarsely.—*n.* Material for daubing; a smear or patch; a coarsely painted picture.

Dau'ghter, *n.* O.E. *dohtor.* Common Teut. and Aryan. Cogn. with G. *thugatēr.* A female child or descendant; a woman in relation to her native place.—**Dau'ghter-in-law**, *n* The wife of one's son.—**Dau'ghter**LY,[1] *a.*

Daunt, *vt.* O.F. *danter*, var. of *donter* (F. *dompter*)—L. *domitāre*, freq. of *domāre*, to TAME, subdue. INDOMITABLE. To dispirit, intimidate, cause to quail.—**Daunt'**LESS, *a.*

Dau'phin, *n.* F. *dauphin*, O.F. *daulphin*, DOLPHIN. Up to 1830 the title of the eldest son of the King of France. (From the province *Dauphiné.* The name—*Dauphin*—of the lords of this is said to have been the same word as the name of the fish.)

Dav'enport, *n.* App. f. the maker's name. A kind of small writing-table with drawers.

Dav'it, *n.* Formerly also *david.* Prob. an application of the Christian name to the apparatus. Cf. JACK.[1] One of a pair of cranes on a ship for suspending or lowering a boat.

Daw, *n.* Prob. imitative. Cf. O.H.G. *tâha.* A small bird of the crow kind.

Daw'dle, *vi.* Supposed to be a var. of dial. *Daddle*, to walk unsteadily, to saunter, of obscure orig. To idle, loiter, linger.—*n.* A dawdling person; the act of dawdling.

Dawn'ing, *vbl.n.* Not in O.E. Prob. f. Norse. Known before 1300 with the earlier *dawing* (which it has superseded)—O.E. *dagung*, f. *dæg*, DAY. The beginning of daylight; first appearance, earliest beginning.—**Dawn**, *vi.* App. deduced f. *dawning.* Known f. about 1500, and has displaced the earlier *daw*—O.E. *dagian*, f. *dæg.* To begin to grow daylight; to begin to shine, appear, develop, be understood or perceived.—*n.* App. f. the *v.* Known f. about 1600. In senses sim. to those of *dawning.*

Day, *n.* O.E. *dæg.* Common Teut. The time between the rising and the setting of the sun; daylight; a period of 24 hours; this period as a point or unit of time; a specific period of 24 hours; time, era.—**Day'book**, *n.* A book for recording the transactions of the day.

Daze, *vt.* M.E. *dasen*—O.N. *dasa*, found only in refl. *dasask*, to become weary. DASTARD. To stun, stupefy, dazzle.—*n.* Stupefaction.

Daz'zle, *vt.* Freq. and dim. of DAZE. To overpower with brightness or splendour.—*n.* A brightness that dazzles the vision.

Dea'con, *n.* L. *diāconus*—G. *diakonos*, servant, in Christian use 'servant of the church'. One in the lowest degree of holy orders.

Dead, *a.* O.E. *déad.* A common Teut. a., orig. a pple. That has ceased to live; insensible, benumbed; extinct, obsolete; extinguished; lustreless; dull, muffled; lifeless, without vigour; inoperative; still, quiet; absolute, complete, entire; sure, unerring.—*n.* The time of greatest stillness, &c.; one who is dead, gen. as pl., *the dead.*—**Dead**'EN,[2] *vt.* —**Dead heat**, *n.* A 'heat' in which competitors run absolutely equally.—**Dead**'LY,[1] *a.* Mortal, fatal; to the death, implacable; death-like.—*adv.* -LY.[2] As if dead.—**Dead let'ter**, *n.* A writing taken in its bare literal sense, and hence ineffective; a statute, &c., still formally existing but which has become inoperative; a letter which cannot be delivered. —**Dead'-light**, *n.* A shutter fixed outside a ship's porthole in bad weather.—**Dead'-lock**, **Dead lock**, *n.* A complete stand-still.

Deaf, *a.* O.E. *déaf.* Common Teut. Orig. sense 'dull of perception'. Cogn. with G. *tuphlos*, blind. Lacking or defective in the sense of hearing; unwilling to hear.—**Deaf'**EN,[2] *vt.* To make deaf; to make impervious to sound.

Deal, *n.*[1] O.E. *dǽl*, a dealing, a share. Common Teut. DOLE.[1] A quantity, an amount, gen. qualified by *good, great*, &c.

Deal, *n.*[2] From L.G. Cf. M.L.G. *dele*, plank, floor. A plank of pine or fir; the wood of the pine or fir.

Deal, *vt.* O.E. *dǽlan*, f. *dǽl.* DEAL, *n.*[1] To distribute; to give (*to* a person as his share); in both senses often with *out*; to deliver *a blow*. —*vi.* To do business *with* (a person) *in* (a thing); to have to do *with* (a thing); to occupy or employ oneself *in* (a thing); *to deal with*, to act in regard to, dispose of, to handle effectively; *to deal with* or *by* (a person), to act towards (him) in a specified way.—*n.*[3] From the *v.* The distribution of cards in a game; a bargain. —**Deal'**ER, *n.* One who distributes; the player who deals the cards; a trader.

Dean, *n.* O.F. *deien, dien* (F. *doyen*)—L. *decānus*, one set over ten (*decem*), a dean. DECANAL. DECIMAL. DOYEN. The head of a body of canons; *rural dean*, a clergyman with a jurisdiction under a bishop or archdeacon; a university or college official.—**Dean'**ERY, *n.* The office or position of an ecclesiastical dean; his official residence; the jurisdiction of a rural dean.

Dear, *a.* O.E. *déore*, earlier *díore.* Common Teut. Beloved, loved; to which one is attached, of which one is fond; of a high price, expensive.—*n.* Dear one, darling.—*adv.* Also **Dear'**LY.[2] At a high price, at great cost; affectionately, fondly. — **Dear'**NESS, *n.* —

Dearth, *n.* M.E. *derthe*, dearness, dearth. Not in O.E. Formed like *warm-th*, &c. A famine; scarcity, deficiency.

Death, *n.* O.E. *déath.* Common Teut. The act or fact of dying; the state of being dead; end, extinction; cause of death.—**Death'**LESS, *a.*—**Death'**LY,[1] *a.* Death-like; deadly.

Debar', *vt.* F. *débarrer*, O.F. *desbarrer*, to unbar, f. *des-* (= DIS- (4)) + *barrer*, to bar, f. *barre*, BAR. App. adopted in the opposite sense, to exclude, shut out, prevent *from*; to prohibit, prevent, stop.

Debase', *vt.* DE- (1) (3) + obs. *Base*, to lower, debase = ABASE. To make base, degrade; to adulterate; to depreciate, esp. of coin.

Debate', *vt.* O.F. *debatre*, lit. 'to beat down', f. DE- (1) + L.L. **battĕre*, to beat. COMBAT. To dispute about, discuss.—*vi.* To engage in discussion; to consider with oneself.—*n.* Controversy, discussion; a controversy or discussion.—**Debat'**ABLE, *a.* Admitting of debate; subject to dispute.

Debauch', *vt.* F. *débaucher*, to entice from a master's service, seduce, of obscure orig. To lead away from virtue; to deprave; to vitiate.—*n.* A bout of excessive sensual indulgence; the practice of such indulgence.—**Debauched'**, *ppl.a.* Dissolute, licentious. —**Debauch**EE', *n.* A dissolute person.—**Debauch'**ERY, *n.* Sensual indulgence.

Deben'ture, *n.* Formerly *debentur*, said to be the L. *dēbentur*, there are owing, 3d. pl. pres. pass. of *dēbēre*, to owe, used as a formal beginning in certificates of indebtedness. DEBT. A bond issued by a company, &c.

Debil'itate, *vt.* L. *dēbilitāre, dēbilitātum*, f. *dēbilis*, weak. To make weak.—**Debil'ity**, *n.* F. *débilité*—L. *dēbilitas.* Weakness.

Deb'it, *n.* L. *dēbitum*, a DEBT. A sum entered as due by one; the side of an account on which sums paid out or due are entered.—*vt.* To enter on the debit side of an account; *to debit* (a person) *with*, to enter as due by (him).

Deb'onair', *a.* O.F. *debonaire*, properly a phrase, *de bon* (L. *bonus*) *aire*, of good *aire*, i.e., place, stock, race, a word of uncertain orig. Pleasant, affable, unembarrassed.

Debouch', *vi.* F. *déboucher*, to uncork, to emerge from, O.F. *desbouchier*, f. *des-* (= DIS- (1)), away + *bouche*, mouth, L. *bucca*, cheek. To issue from a narrow into a wider space; of a river, &c., to issue at a mouth or outlet.

Deb'ris, **Débris**, *n.* F. *débris*, vbl.n. f. obs. *débriser*, O.F. *debrisier*, to break in pieces, f. DE- (3) + *brisier, bruisier*, to break, BRUISE. Fragments, rubbish.

Debt, *n.* O.F. *dete, dette*—L. *dēbitum*, owed, pa.pple. of *dēbēre*, to owe, hence, a debt. DEBENTURE. DEBIT. DUE. That which is owed or due; a liability to pay or render, the condition of being under such liability.—**Debt'**OR, *n.* One who owes.

Début, *n.* F., vbl.n. f. *débuter*, to make the first stroke in billiards, &c., lead off. First appearance in public.—**Débutant**, *n.*; *fem.* **Débutante**. Pres.pple. of *débuter.* One making such a first appearance.

Dec'ade, *n.* F. *décade*—L. *decas, decadis*, G. *dekas, dekados*, a group of ten—G. *deka*, TEN. A group, set, &c., of ten; a period of ten years.

Dec'adence, *n.* F. *décadence*—Med.L. *dēcadentia*, formed f. DE- (1) + *cadēre.* DECAY. A falling away from a better state; impaired condition.—**Dec'ad**ENT, *a.*

Dec'agon, *n.* Med.L. *decagōnum*—G. *dekagōnon*, f. *deka*, TEN + *gōnia*, angle. A figure with ten angles.—**Decag'on**AL, *a.*

Dec'alogue, *n.* F. *décalogue*—L. *decalogus*—G. *dekalogos*, f. *deka*, TEN + *logos*, a saying, speech. The Ten Commandments.

Decamp', *vi.* F. *décamper*, earlier *descamper*, f. *des-* (= DIS- (1)) + *camp*, CAMP. To break up a camp; to take oneself off.

Deca'nal, *a.* L. *decānus*, DEAN + -AL. Of or pertaining to a dean or a deanery.

Decant', *vt.* F. *décanter*—Med.L. *dēcanthāre* (a word of the alchemists), f. DE- (1) + *canthus*, the lip of a cup, a transferred use of G. *kanthos* corner of the eye. To pour off (clear liquid) from the lees; to pour out (wine) into another vessel for use at the table.—**Decant'**ER, *n.* The vessel into which wine is so poured.

Decap'itate, *vt.* F. *décapiter*—L.L. *dēcapitāre*, f. DE- (6)+*caput, capitis*, head. CAPITAL. To cut off the head of.—**Decapit**A'TION, *n.*

Decasyl'lable, *n.* G. *deka*, TEN+SYLLABLE. A line of ten syllables.—**Decasyllab'**IC, *a.*

Decay', *vi.* O.F. *decair*, var. of *decaoir*, *dechaoir*, f. DE- (1)+Romanic *cadēre*, L. *cadĕre*, to fall. CADENCE. DECADENCE. To fall off, become impaired; to decline from prosperity; to wear out, become ruined; to rot; to lose health and strength.—*vt.* To rot; to cause to fail in health, &c.—*n.* A falling off from prosperity; wearing away; ruinous condition; decline in health, &c.; rotting.

Decease', *n.* F. *décès*—L. *dēcessus*, departure, death, f. *dēcēdĕre*, *dēcessum*, to depart, f. DE- (2) + *cēdĕre*, to go. CEASE. Death.—*vi.* To die.—**Deceased'**, *ppl.a.* Dead.—*n.* *The deceased*, the person (lately) dead.

Deceive', *vt.* O.F. *deceveir* (F. *décevoir*)—L. *dēcipĕre, dēceptum*, f. DE- (4) + *capĕre*, to take. CAPABLE. To lead into error, impose upon; to disappoint (expectations, &c.).—**Deceiv'**ER, *n.*—**Deceit'**, *n.* O.F. *deceite*, use as *n.* of fem. pa.pple. of *deceveir*. Deception, cheating; a trick, wile; the quality of deceiving.—**Deceit'**FUL, *a.*—**Deceit'ful**LY,[2] *a.*

Decem'ber, *n.* L., f. *decem*, ten. DECIMAL. The tenth of the Roman months; our twelfth.

Decen'nial, *a.* L. *decennis*, of ten years (f. *decem* (see prec.) + *annus*, year) + -AL. Pertaining to a period of ten years; holding office for ten years.—**Decen'nial**LY,[2] *adv.*

De'cent, *a.* L. *decens, decentis*, pres.pple. of *decēre*, to be fitting. DECORUM. Conforming to the standard of propriety, good taste, modesty, one's position, &c.; tolerable, passable.—**De'cent**LY,[2] *adv.*—**De'**CENCY, *n.*

Decen'tralize, *vt.* DE- (5). To distribute what has been concentrated.

Decep'tion, *n.* F. *déception*—L. *dēceptio*, *dēceptiōnis*, f. *dēcipĕre*, to DECEIVE. The action of deceiving; the fact or condition of being deceived; a trick.—**Decep'**TIVE, *a.*

Decide', *vt.* F. *décider*—L. *dēcīdĕre, dēcīsum*, to cut off, decide, f. DE- (2) + *caedĕre*, to cut. CONCISE. To determine, settle; to bring to a resolve.—*vi.* To settle a question; to determine, resolve. — **Decid'ed**, *ppl.a.* Settled, definite, unquestionable; resolute, determined.—**Decid'ed**LY,[2] *adv.*—**Decis'**ION, *n.* Settlement; a conclusion, judgement; a resolution; firmness of character.—**Deci'**SIVE, *a.* Deciding (a question, &c.); resolute; beyond question.—**Deci'sive**LY,[2] *adv.*

Decid'uous, *a.* L. *dēciduus*, falling down or off (f. *dēcidĕre*, f. DE- (1) (2) + *cadĕre*, to fall) + -OUS. DECAY. Of parts of plants, animals, &c., falling off periodically; of a tree, shedding its leaves every year.

Dec'imal, *a.* L. *decimus*, tenth (f. *decem*, TEN) + -AL. DEAN. Relating to tenths or ten; proceeding by tens.—**Dec'imate**, *vt.* L. *decimāre, decimātum*, f. *decem*. To select by lot and put to death one in ten; to destroy in large numbers.—**Decim**A'TION, *n.*

Deci'pher, *vt.* From CIPHER after F. *déchiffrer*, earlier *deschiffrer*, f. *des-* (= DIS- (4)) + *chiffre*, O.F. *cyfre*, CIPHER. To turn from cipher into ordinary writing; to make out the meaning of.—**Deci'pher**ABLE, *a.*

Deck, *vt.* App. f. Flemish or L.G. Cf. M.Du. *deken, decken*, Du. *dekken*, M.L.G., M.H.G. *decken*, to cover. THATCH. To clothe in rich garments, to array, attire. From the *n.*, to furnish with a deck.—*n.* Found first in English. Perh. f. the gen. sense 'covering'. A platform or floor of a ship.

Deck'le, *n.* Ger. *deckel* in same sense, properly 'little cover', dim. of *decke*, cover, conn. with prec. A contrivance for determining the size or width of the sheet in paper-making.—**Deck'le-edged**, *a.* Having a rough edge.

Declaim', *vi.* L. *dēclāmāre, dēclāmātum*, f. DE- (3) + *clāmāre*, to cry. (Formerly *declame*. Assimilated to CLAIM.) To speak rhetorically, to harangue.—*vt.* To utter rhetorically.—**Declam**A'TION, *n.*—**Declam'at**ORY, *a.*

Declare', *vt.* F. *déclarer*—L. *dēclārāre, dēclārātum*, to make evident, f. DE- (3) + *clārāre*, to make clear, f. *clārus*, CLEAR. To manifest, show; to state formally, assert, announce; to make a statement as to (goods liable to duty).—*vi.* To make known one's opinion or one's resolution to act, &c., *for* or *against*.—**Declar**A'TION, *n.*—**Declar'**ATIVE, *a.*

Decline', *vi.* F. *décliner*—L. *dēclīnāre, dēclīnātum*, to turn aside, f. DE- (2) + *-clīnāre* = G. *klinein*, to bend. LEAN, *v.* To slope downwards; to bend down, droop; of the sun, &c., to sink in the west; to decay in vigour, prosperity, &c.—*vt.* To withhold oneself from, not to engage in; not to consent to *doing* or *to do*; not to accept; to bend down; to inflect (a noun, &c.).—*n.* Gradual loss of vigour, &c., decay, deterioration; a disease sapping the bodily strength.—**Declen'sion**, *n.* Represents irregularly L. *dēclīnātio, dēclīnātiōnis*, f. *dēclīnāre*. Deviation from a standard; apostasy; decay, deterioration; case-inflexion.—**Declin'**ABLE, *a.* Admitting of case-inflexion.—**Declin**A'TION, *n.* A sloping downwards, slope; the angular distance of a heavenly body from the celestial equator; the variation of the magnetic needle from the true north-and-south line.—**Declin'at**URE, *n.* The action of declining or refusing.

Decliv'ity, *n.* L. *dēclīvitas*, f. *dēclīvis*, sloping downwards, f. DE- (1) + *clīvus*, slope, cogn. with *-clīnāre*. (See prec.) Downward slope, a downward slope.

Decoct', *vt.* L. *dēcoquĕre, dēcoctum*, to boil down, f. DE- (3) + *coquĕre*, to COOK, boil. To boil so as to extract the soluble parts.—**Decoc'**TION, *n.*

Decompose', *vt.* F. *décomposer*, f. *de-*, *des-* (= DIS (4)) + *composer*, to COMPOSE. To resolve into its elements.—*vi.* To decay, rot.—**De**COMPOSI'TION, *n.*

Dec'orate, *vt.* L. *decorāre, decorātum*, f. *decus, decoris*, grace, embellishment. (See next.) To deck with ornamental accessories; to invest with the badge of an order, with a medal, &c.—**Decor**A'TION, *n.*—**Dec'or**ATIVE, *a.*—**Dec'orat**OR, *n.* Esp., one who decorates houses, &c., with painting, &c.

Deco'rum, *n.* L. *decōrum*, use as *n.* of neut. sing. of *decōrus*, seemly, f. *decor, decōris*, what is seemly, f. *decēre*, to befit. Allied to *decus*. (See prec.) DECENT. Seemliness, propriety; polite behaviour; a requirement of polite behaviour.—**Deco'rous**, *a.* In form f. L.L. *decorōsus*, elegant, f. L. *decus* (see prec.), but in sense corresponding to *decōrus*. Characterized by decorum.—**Deco'rous**LY,[2] *adv.*

Decoy', *n.* Formed with unexplained *de-* f. obs. *Coy* in same senses—Du. *kooi*—W. Germanic *cawia, cauwia*—L. *cavea*, hollow, enclosure,

CAGE. A pond with contrivances for catching wild ducks, &c.; a bird trained to entice others into a trap; one who entices into some evil situation; an enticement, bait.—*vt.* To entice into a trap; to entice, allure.

Decrease', *vi.* O.F. *de-*, *descreistre*—L.L. *discrescĕre*, displacing L. *dēcrescĕre*, to decrease, f. DE- (1) + *crescĕre*, to grow. ACCRESCE. CRESCENT. To grow less, diminish. —*vt.* To lessen, diminish.—*n.* Lessening, diminution.—**Dec'rement**, *n.* Lessening, diminution; the amount lost by diminution.

Decree', *n.* O.F. *decré*, *decret*—L. *dēcrētum*, use as *n.* of neut. of *dēcrētus*, pa.pple. of *dēcernĕre*, to decide, f. DE- (2) + *cernĕre*, to separate, distinguish. CONCERN. An ordinance or edict; an authoritative decision.—*vt.* To order, appoint, assign; to decide or determine authoritatively.—**Decre'tal**, *a.* F. *décrétal*—L.L. *dēcrētāle*, a decree, f. *dēcrētus*. Pertaining to or containing a decree.—*n.* A papal decree.

Decrep'it, *a.* F. *décrépit*—L. *dēcrepitus*, noiseless, creeping about like the aged, decrepit, f. DE- (2), away + *crepāre*, *crepitum*, to crack, creak. CREPITATE. Old and weak.—**Decrep'itude**, *n.*

Decry', *vt.* F. *décrier*—O.F. *descrier*, to declare, publish (f. *des-* (= DIS- (1)) + *crier*, to CRY), also (with pref. = DIS- (4)), to decry (and thus in this sense the reverse of 'cry up'). DESCRY. To disparage, condemn.

Ded'icate, *vt.* L. *dēdicāre*, *dēdicātum*, to declare, proclaim, consecrate, f. DE- (1) + *dicāre*, to proclaim, conn. with *dīcĕre*, to say. ABDICATE. DICTION. To devote solemnly *to*; to give up wholly *to*; to inscribe or address (a book, &c.) *to*.—**Dedica'tion**, *n.*—**Ded'icator**, *n.*—**Ded'icatory**, *a.*

Deduce', *vt.* L. *dēdūcĕre*, *dēductum*, to lead down or away, in Med.L., to infer, f. DE- (1) (2) + *dūcĕre*, to lead. DUKE. To draw or obtain *from* (a source); to trace the course of, go through in order; to draw as a conclusion *from* something known or assumed, to infer logically.—**Deduc'ible**, *a.*—**Deduct'**, *vt.* From *dēdūcĕre*. To take away or subtract.—**Deduc'tible**, *a.*—**Deduc'tion**, *n.* Subtraction; inference; in logic, inference by reasoning from generals to particulars; an inference.—**Deduc'tive**, *a.* In logic, reasoning by deduction.—**Deduc'tively**,[2] *adv.*

Deed, *n.* O.E. *dǽd*, *déd*, f. O.Teut. vbl. stem *dǣ-*: *dō-*. DO. Something done, an act; a feat; action generally, doing, performance; a legal instrument.—**Deed'less**, *a.*—**Deed poll**, **Deed-poll**, *n.* A deed executed by one party only (so called because the edge is *polled* or cut even, not indented).

Deem, *vi.* O.E. *dǽman*, *déman*, f. *dóm*, statute, judgement. DOOM. To judge, be of opinion, consider; to judge, think, have an idea *of*.—*vt.* To judge, hold.—**Deem'ster**, *n.* Represents M.E. *dēmestre*, in form fem. of *dēmere*, O.E. *dǽmere*, judge, f. *dǽman*. Each of the two justices of the Isle of Man.

Deep, *a.* M.E. *deep*—O.E. *díop*, *déop*. Common Teut. DIP. Extending far downwards, inwards or backwards; having a (specified) dimension in these directions; far down, far back; hard to fathom, not superficial, profound; heinous, grave; affecting one profoundly; intense, very great; mighty, influential; intense from quantity of colour; low in pitch, resonant; having profound knowledge or insight; cunning, artful; much involved or implicated; immersed, engrossed.—*n.* Deep water, a deep place; *the deep*, the deep sea, the abyss of space; an abyss, cavity.—*adv.* Far down, in, &c.; profoundly, intensely, &c.—**Deep'en**,[2] *vt.* and *i.*—**Deep'ly**,[2] *adv.*

Deer, *n.* O.E. *díor*, *déor*, a wild animal. Common Teut. A family of ruminant quadrupeds with deciduous branching horns.

Deface', *vt.* Obs. F. *defacer*, orig. *desfacier*, f. *des-* (= DIS- (5)) + *face*, FACE. To mar the face or appearance of, disfigure; to blot out, efface.—**Deface'ment**, *n.*

De'falcate, *vi.* Med.L. *dēfalcāre*, *dēfalcātum*, f. DE- (1) (2) + L. *falx*, *falcis*, sickle. Formerly, to lop off, to curtail. To misappropriate property.—**Defalca'tion**, *n.* Delinquency, shortcoming; misappropriation; in *pl.*, the sum misappropriated.—**De'falcator**, *n.*

Defame', *vt.* O.F. *diffamer*—L. *diffāmāre*, to spread abroad by an ill report, defame, f. *dif-* (= DIS- (1)) + *fāma*, report, FAME. To dishonour by report or rumour, slander.—**Defama'tion**, *n.*—**Defam'atory**, *a.*

Default', *n.* O.F. *defaute*, derivative (after *faute* f. *faillir*) of *defaillir*, to fail, f. DE- (3) + *faillir*. FAIL. Want, lack; *in default of*, through the failure, in the absence, of; a defect, blemish; neglect, failure; failure to meet financial obligations.—*vi.* To be guilty of default.—*vt.* To fail to pay.—**Default'er**, *n.*

Defea'sible, *a.* A.F. *defeasible*—O.F. type **de(s)faisible*, f. *de(s)faire*, to undo, f. *des-* (= DIS- (4)) + *faire*. FEASIBLE. Capable of being made void.—**Defea'sance**, *n.*

Defeat', *vt.* O.F. *defeit*, *defait*, orig. *desfait*, pa.pple. of *desfaire* = L.L. *diffacĕre*, *disfacĕre*, to unmake, destroy, f. DIS- (4) + L. *facĕre*, to do, make. To bring to nought, frustrate; to annul; to disappoint, defraud; to vanquish, overthrow.—*n.* Frustration; overthrow.

De'fecate, *vt.* L. *dēfaecāre*, *dēfaecātum*, f. DE- (6) + *faex*, *faecis*, dregs. FÆCES. To clear from dregs or impurities; to purge away.—**Defeca'tion**, *n.*

Defect', *n.* L. *dēfectus*, defect, want, f. *dēficĕre*, *dēfectum*, to leave, fail, &c., orig., to undo, f. DE- (5) + *facĕre*, to do. DEFICIENT. The fact of falling short, deficiency; a fault, blemish; the quantity or amount by which a thing falls short.—**Defec'tive**, *a.*—**Defec'tively**,[2] *adv.*—**Defec'tion**, *n.* The action or fact of falling short, failure; desertion; apostasy.

Defend', *vt.* O.F. *defendre*—L. *dēfendĕre*, *dēfensum*, to ward off, defend, f. DE- (2) + *fendĕre* (occurring only in composition), to strike. FEND. MANIFEST. To protect, guard; to support, uphold; in law, to oppose (an action), to vindicate (oneself or one's cause), to take measures, appear, &c., in vindication of (a client).—**Defence'**, *n.* M.E. *defens*—O.F. *defens*—L. *dēfensum*, thing defended, &c., use as *n.* of neut. of *dēfensus*, pa.pple. of *dēfendĕre*. Also M.E. *defense*—O.F. *defense*—L. *dēfensa*, f. *dēfensus*. FENCE. Guarding, protection; a means of warding off attack; justification, vindication; in law, proceedings for defending oneself, &c.—**Defend'ant**, *n.* One sued in a court of law.—**Defend'er**, *n.*—**Defen'sible**, *a.*—**Defen'sive**, *a.* Protective; made or carried on for defence; of or belonging to defence; of the nature of a defence.—*n.* The position or attitude of defence.

Defer', *v.*[1]*t.* Var. of DIFFER. To put off, delay, postpone.—**Defer'ment**, *n.*

Defer', *v.*[2]*i.* F. *déférer*—L. *dēferre*, to bear down or away, to bring before one, f. DE- (1) (2) + *ferre*, to bear. CONFER. To submit in opinion or judgement *to*; to pay deference *to*. —**Def'er**ENCE, *n*. Submission in opinion, &c.; courteous regard for others.—**Deferen'**TIAL, *a*.—**Deferen'tial**LY[2], *adv*.

Defic'ient, *a*. L. *dēficiens, dēficientis*, pres. pple. of *dēficĕre*. DEFECT. Wanting or falling short *in* something; insufficient, inadequate. —**Defic'i**ENCY, *n*.—**Def'icit**, *n*. F. *déficit*—L. *dēficit*, there is wanting, 3d sing. pres. of *dēficĕre*. A falling short; excess of expenditure or liabilities over income or assets.

Defile', *v*.[1]*i*. F. *défiler*, f. *dé-* (= DIS- (1)) + *file*. FILE, *n*.[2] To march in a line, file off.—*n*. A narrow pass; a march by files.

Defile', *v*.[2]*t*. An altered form, by association with FILE, *v*.[3], of the now dial. *Defoul*, to trample down, violate, make foul, pollute—O.F. *defouler*, to trample down, violate, f. DE- (1) + *fouler*, to trample on. FOIL, *v*. To make foul or dirty, pollute; to taint, sully; to desecrate.—**Defile'**MENT, *n*.

Define', *vt*. O.F. *definer*, to end, terminate, a Romanic parallel form to L. *dēfīnīre, dēfīnītum*, to bound, end, f. DE- (3) + *fīnīre*, to bound. FINISH. Formerly, to bring to an end. To fix the limits of; to make distinct in outline or form; to lay down clearly, fix, determine; to state exactly what (a thing) is; to explain what (a word, &c.) means; to give a character to, characterize.—**Defin'**ABLE, *a*.—**Defini'**TION, *n*.—**Def'inite**, *a*. L. *dēfīnītus*, pa.pple. of *dēfīnīre*. Clearly defined, exact, precise; defining, determining.—**Def'inite**LY,[2] *adv*. —**Defin'it**IVE, *a*. Decisive, conclusive; definite, fixed, final.—**Defin'itive**LY,[2] *adv*.

Deflate', *vt*. L. *dēflāre, dēflātum*, to blow away, f. DE- (2) + *flāre*, to blow. BLOW, *v*.[1] (The prefix taken in modern use as DE- (5).) To release the air from (something inflated).—**Defl**A'TION, *n*.

Deflect', *vt*. and *i*. L. *dēflectĕre, dēflexum*, to bend downwards or aside, f. DE- (1) (2) + *flectĕre*, to bend. FLEXIBLE. To cause to turn, to turn, to one side or from a straight line.—**Deflec'**TION, **Deflex'**ION, *n*.

Deflow'er, *vt*. O.F. *desflorer*—L. *dēflōrāre*, to deprive of flowers, f. DE- (6) + *flōs, flōris*, FLOWER. To deprive of virginity; to ravage; to strip of flowers.—**Deflor**A'TION, *n*.

Deflux'ion, *n*. L. *dēfluxio, dēfluxiōnis*, f. *dēfluĕre, dēfluxum*, to flow down, f. DE- (1) + *fluĕre*, to flow. FLUENT. A flow or discharge such as that accompanying a cold.

Deforce', *vt*. A.F. *deforcer* = O.F. *deforcier*, f. *de-, des-* (= DIS- (1)) + *forcier, forcer*, to FORCE. To withhold or deprive forcibly or wrongfully.—**Deforce'**MENT, *n*.

Deform', *vt*. O.F. *deformer*—L. *dēformāre*, f. DE- (6) + *forma*, FORM, comeliness. To mar the form or shape of; to make ugly.—**Deform**A'TION, *n*.—**Deform'**ITY, *n*.

Defraud', *vt*. O.F. *defrauder*—L. *dēfraudāre*, f. DE- (3) + *fraudāre*, to cheat, f. *fraus, fraudis*, deceit, FRAUD. To cheat, beguile.

Defray', *vt*. O.F. *desfrayer*, f. *des-* (= DIS- (3)) + *fraier*, to spend, f. *frai*, gen. in pl. *frais*, expenses. Cf. L.L. *fredum*, a fine—O.H.G. *fridu*, peace, a fine for breach of the peace. AFFRAY. To pay the expense or cost of, meet, settle.—**Defray'**AL, *n*.—**Defray'**MENT, *n*.

Deft, *a*. M.E. *daft, deft*—O.E. *dæfte*, as seen in *gedæfte*, gentle, meek, primary sense 'becoming' (whence 'gentle'), 'fit' (whence 'ready, apt, deft'). Cf. Goth. *gadaban*, to befit. Skilful, dexterous; showing skill or dexterity.—**Deft'**LY,[2] *adv*.—**Deft'**NESS, *n*.

Defunct', *a*. L. *dēfunctus*, having fully performed, deceased, pa.pple. of *dēfungi*, to perform fully, f. DE- (3) + *fungi*, to perform. FUNCTION. Deceased, dead; no longer existing.—*n*. *The defunct*, the deceased.

Defy', *vt*. O.F. *desfier, defier*—Med.L. *diffīdāre*, f. *dif-* (= DIS- (4) + *fīdāre*, to trust, f. L. *fīdus*, faithful. (The sense-development seems to have been 'to renounce faith or amity with', 'to declare hostility against', 'to challenge to fight'.) To challenge to fight or to a contest, esp. to challenge to do (what the challenger is prepared to maintain cannot be done); to set at nought; to be beyond the power of.—**Defi'**ANCE, *n*.—**Defi'**ANT, *a*.

Degen'erate, *vi*. L. *dēgenerāre, dēgenerātum*, to depart from the race, f. *dēgener*, that departs from its race, f. DE- (1) + *genus, generis*, race, kind. GENUS. To fall away from the qualities proper to the race or kind, to decline in character or qualities.—*a*. Having so fallen away or declined.—**Degen'er**ACY, *n*.—**Degener**A'TION, *n*.

Degluti'tion, *n*. F. *déglutition*, f. L. *dēglūtīre*, to swallow down, f. DE- (1) + *glūtīre*, to swallow. GLUTTON. Swallowing.

Degrade', *vt*. O.F. *degrader*—L.L. *dēgradāre*, f. DE- (1) + L. *gradus*, step, degree. AGGRESSION. To reduce to a lower rank; to bring into dishonour or contempt; to debase —*vi*. To degenerate.—**Degrad**A'TION, *n*.—**Degrad'ed**, *ppl.a*. Lowered in rank, character, &c., debased.

Degree', *n*. O.F. *degre*, a step, rank (orig. a step down, as of stairs), as if f. a late Pop.L. **dēgradus*, f. DE- (1) + L. *gradus*. DEGRADE. A step or stage in a process; a step in a line of descent; relative rank, order, &c.: relative condition, state, manner, way; the relative measure, &c., of a quality, &c.; an academical rank conferred by a university; a unit of measurement of angles or of temperature; each of the stages in the comparison of an *a*. or *adv*.

Dehort', *vt*. L. *dēhortāri, dēhortātus*, to dissuade, f. DE- (2) + *hortāri*, to urge, incite. EXHORT. To dissuade *from*.—**Dehort**A'TION, *n*.—**Dehor'tat**IVE, *a*. As *n*., a dissuasive speech, &c.—**Dehor'tat**ORY, *a*.

Deic'tic, *a*. G. *deiktikos*, able to show, f. *deiktos*, vbl.a. f. *deiknunai*, to show. Directly pointing out, demonstrative.

De'ify, *vt*. F. *déifier*—L. *deificāre*, f. *deus*, god + *facĕre*, to make. To make a god of; to treat as a god.—**Dei**FICA'TION, *n*.

Deign, *vi*. O.F. *degnier*—L. *dignāre* (by-form of *dignāri*), to deem worthy, f. *dignus*, worthy. DIGNIFY. DISDAIN. To think fit, condescend. —*vt*. To condescend to give.

De'ism, *n*. L. *deus*, god + -ISM. Belief in one god with denial of revelation.—**De'**IST, *n*.—**Deis'**TIC, **Deis'**TICAL, *aa*.

De'ity, *n*. F. *déité*, earlier *deitet, deite*—L. *deitas*, f. *deus*, god. DIVINE. TUESDAY. The rank or personality of a god; the divine nature and attributes; a god.

Deject', *vt*. L. *dējicĕre, dējectum*, to throw down, f. DE- (1) + *jacĕre*, to throw. ABJECT. To depress in spirits.—**Dejec'**TION, *n*.

Delate', *vt*. L. *dēlāt-*, ppl. stem of *dēferre*, to bear or bring down, to report, to accuse, f. DE- (1) + *ferre*, to BEAR. To inform against; to give information of (an offence, &c.).

Delay', *vt*. O.F. *delaier, delayer*, answering in sense to L.L. *dīlātāre*, freq. of L. *differre*, *dīlātum*, to defer (which, however, would give *dileer*). DIFFER. To postpone, defer; to retard.—*vi.* To linger, loiter.—*n.* The action of delaying; the fact of being delayed.

Delec'table, *a.* O.F. *delectable*—L. *dēlectābilis*, f. *dēlectāre*, to DELIGHT. Delightful, pleasant.—**Delecta'tion**, *n.* Enjoyment.

Del'egate, *vt.* L. *dēlēgāre*, *dēlēgātum*, to dispatch, commit, f. DE- (2) + *lēgāre*, to depute. LEGATE. To send as a deputy, depute to act; to entrust, commit (authority, &c.).—*n.* One sent as a deputy or deputed to act.—**Delega'tion**, *n.* The action of delegating, the fact of being delegated; a body of delegates.

Delete', *vt.* L. *dēlēre*, *dēlētum*, to destroy, to delete. To strike or blot out, erase.—**Dele'tion**, *n.*

Delete'rious, *a.* Mod.L. *dēlētērius* (f. G. *dēlētērios*, f. *dēlētēr*, destroyer, f. *dēle-esthai*, to hurt) + -OUS. Hurtful, injurious.

Delf, Delft, *n.* Glazed earthenware made at *Delf* (now *Delft*) in Holland.

Delib'erate, *vt.* L. *dēlīberāre*, *dēlīberātum*, to weigh or consider well, f. DE- (3) + *lībrāre*, to weigh, f. *lībra*, a balance. EQUILIBRIUM. LEVEL. To consider carefully.—*vi.* To think carefully, take time for consideration.—*a.* Well considered; considering carefully; leisurely, slow.—**Delib'erately**,[2] *adv.*—**Delibera'tion**, *n.*—**Delib'erative**, *a.* Having the function of, or characterized by, deliberation.

Del'icate, *a.* L. *dēlicātus*, charming, tender, of uncertain orig. Pleasing to the palate; soft, slender, slight; exquisite, subtle; tender, fragile; of weak health; ticklish, critical; finely sensitive; finely skilful; sensitive to what is becoming or modest; marked by such sensitiveness.—**Del'icately**,[2] *adv.*—**Del'icacy**, *n.* The quality of being delicate; a choice piece of food a nicety, refinement.

Delic'ious, *a.* A.F. and O.F. *delicious*—L.L. *dēliciōsus*, f. L. *dēliciae*, delight, pleasure, f. *dēlicĕre*, to entice away, allure, f. DE- (2) + *lacĕre*. ELICIT. DELIGHT. Very delightful or pleasing.—**Delic'iously**,[2] *adv.*

Delict', *n.* L. *dēlictum*, fault, crime, use as *n.* of neut. sing. of pa.pple. of *dēlinquĕre*. DELINQUENT. A violation of law or right.

Delight', *vt.* M.E. *deliten*—O.F. *delitier*—L. *dēlectāre*, to charm, please, freq. of *dēlicĕre*. DELICIOUS. DELECTABLE. To please highly. —*vi.* To be highly pleased, take great pleasure.—*n.* Great pleasure; a source of this.—**Delight'ful**, *a.*—**Delight'some**, *a.*

Delim'it, *vt.* F. *délimiter*—L. *dēlimitāre*, to mark out as a boundary, f. DE- (3) + *līmitāre*, to bound, f. *līmes*, *limitis*, boundary. LIMIT. To determine the boundaries of.—**Delimita'tion**, *n.*

Delin'eate, *vt.* L. *dēlīneāre*, *dēlīneātum*, to sketch out, f. DE- (3) + *līneāre*, to draw lines, f. *līnea*, LINE. To trace the outline of, sketch out; to draw, portray; to describe.—**Delinea'tion**, *n.*—**Delin'eator**, *n.*

Delin'quent, *a.* L. *dēlinquens*, *dēlinquentis*, pres.pple. of *dēlinquĕre*, to fail, be in fault, f. DE- (3) + *linquĕre*, to leave. DELICT. RELINQUISH. Faulty, guilty.—*n.* An offender.—**Delin'quency**, *n.*

Deliquesce', *vi.* L. *dēliquescĕre*, to melt away, f. DE- (3) + *liquescĕre*, to melt, inceptive of *liquēre*, to be LIQUID or clear. To melt by absorption of moisture.—**Deliques'cence**, *n.*—**Deliques'cent**, *a.*

Delir'ium, *n.* L. *dēlīrium*, madness, f. *dēlīrāre*, to be deranged or crazy, orig., to go out of the furrow, f. DE- (2) + *līra*, ridge, furrow, in ploughing. Disorder of the mind; uncontrollable excitement.—**Delir'ious**, *a.*—**Delir'iously**,[2] *adv.*

Deliv'er, *vt.* F. *délivrer*—Late Pop. L. *dēlīberāre* (DE- (3)), used in sense of L. *līberāre*, to set free, f. *līber*, free. LIBERAL. (L. *dēlīberāre* was a different word: see DELIBERATE.) To set free, release, save; to bring (a woman) to childbirth; to give over, surrender; to hand over, transfer, distribute; to send forth, launch, discharge, throw; to give forth in words, utter. —*v.refl.* To discourse, express one's thought or opinion.—**Deliv'erance**, *n.*—**Deliv'erer**, *n.*—**Deliv'ery**,[1] *n.*

Dell, *n.* M.E. *delle*—O.E. *dell*, cogn. with *dœl*, DALE. A deep natural hollow.

Del'ta, *n.* G., the fourth letter of the alphabet (Δ). A tract of alluvial land, roughly of this shape, at the mouth of a river.—**Del'toid**, *a.* Resembling the letter, triangular.

Delude', *vt.* L. *dēlūdĕre*, *dēlūsum*, to play false, deceive, f. DE- (4) + *lūdĕre*, to play. LUDICROUS. To deceive, beguile.—**Delu'sion**, *n.*—**Delu'sive**, *a.*—**Delu'sory**, *a.*

Del'uge, *n.* F. *déluge*—L. *dīluvium*, a washing away, a flood, f. *dīluĕre*, *dīlūtum*, to wash away, dissolve, DILUTE, f. *di-* (= DIS- (1)) + *luĕre*, to wash. DILUVIAL. POLLUTE. A great flood.—*vt.* To flood, inundate.

Delve, *vt.* and *i.* O.E. *delfan*. Common West Germanic. To dig.

Demag'netize, *vt.* DE- (5). To deprive of magnetic quality.

Dem'agogue, *n.* G. *dēmagōgos*, a leader of the mob, f. *dēmos*, people + *agōgos*, leading, f. *agein*, to lead. A leader of the mob.

Demand', *vt.* F. *demander*—L. *dēmandāre*, to give in charge, entrust, in Med.L., to request, demand, f. DE- (3) + *mandāre*, to commission, order. MANDATE. To ask for as one's right or peremptorily; to call for of right or justice; to call for as necessary; to request to be told.—*n.* The action or an act of demanding; a call for a commodity; an urgent claim or requirement.—**Demand'able**, *a.*

Demarca'tion, *n.* Sp. *demarcacion*, f. *demarcar*, to mark out, f. *de-* (= DE- (3)) + *marcar*, to mark, of Teut. orig. MARK.[1] The action of marking a boundary.

Demean', *v.*[1]*refl.* O.F. *demener*, to conduct, guide, manage, *refl.*, to conduct oneself, f. DE- (3) + *mener*, to conduct—L. *mināre*, orig. (= *minārī*) to threaten, in L.L., to drive or conduct cattle, men, &c. MENACE. MIEN. PROMENADE. To behave (in a specified way).—**Demean'our**, *n.* App. of Eng. or A.F. formation. Conduct, behaviour, bearing.

Demean', *v.*[2]*t.* DE- (1) + MEAN, *a.*[1] To lower in condition, character, &c.—*v.refl.* To lower or humble oneself.

Dement', *vt.* L. *dēmentāre*, to drive mad, f. DE- (2) + *mens*, *mentis*, mind. MENTAL. To drive mad.—**Dement'ed**, *ppl.a.* Mad.—**Demen'tia**, *n.* L., n. of state. A species of insanity.

Demer'it, *n.* O.F. *demerite*, merit, also, a fault—L.L. *dēmeritum*, a fault (app. taking the prefix as privative), f. L. *dēmerērī*, *dēmeritus*, to merit well, deserve, f. DE- (3) + *merērī* in sim. sense. Formerly, merit, desert (in a good or indifferent sense). Desert (in a bad sense), censurable conduct.

Demesne', *n.* A.F. *demeyne*, later *demesne* = O.F. *demeine*, orig. a use as *n.* of *demenïe*, belonging to a lord, own, proper—L. *dominicus*, a. f. *dominus*, lord. DOMAIN. DOMINATE. Land possessed by the owner himself; the land immediately attached to a mansion; the territory of a sovereign; an estate; a region.

Dem'igod, *n.* *Demi-*, L. *dimidius*, half + GOD. A being of partly divine nature; a man raised to divine rank; a minor deity.

Dem'ijohn, *n.* Corrupted f. F. *dame-jeanne*, i.e., app., *Dame Jeanne*, 'Dame Jane', a popular appellation. A large bulging narrow-necked bottle, often cased in wicker-work.

Demise', *n.* App. of A.F. orig. Not in O.F., but *démise, desmise* would be regular as fem. n. f. pa.pple. of *démettre, desmettre*, to send away, *refl.* to resign, abdicate, f. L. *dīmittĕre*. DISMISS. Conveyance by will or lease; transference of sovereignty as on death or abdication; death.—*vt.* To convey by will or lease; to transfer (a title or dignity), esp. of sovereignty on death or abdication.—**Demit'**, *vt.* From *démettre*. To resign (an office, &c.).—**Demis'**SION, *n.*

Dem'iurge, *n.* G. *dēmiourgos*, public or skilled worker, f. *dēmios*, a. f. *dēmos*, the people + *-ergos*, working, f. **ergein*, to work. The maker or creator of the world.—**Demiur'**GIC, *a.*

Demo'bilize, *vt.* DE- (5). To disband (forces).

Democ'racy, *n.* F. *démocratie* — Med.L. *dēmocratia*—G. *dēmokratia*, f. *dēmos*, the people + *-kratia*, rule, f. *kratos*, power. Government by the people; a state so governed; the common people (in reference to their political power).—**Dem'ocrat**, *n.* F. *démocrate*. An adherent or advocate of democracy. —**Democrat'**IC, **Democrat'**ICAL, *aa.*—**Democ'rat**IZE, *vt.* and *i.*

Demol'ish, *vt.* F. *démoliss-*, lengthened stem of *démolir*, L. *dēmōlīri, dēmōlītus*, to throw down, destroy, f. DE- (5) + *mōlīri*, to build, construct, f. *mōles*, mass, massive structure. To destroy.—**Demoli'**TION, *n.*

De'mon, **Dæ'mon**, *n.* L. *daemon*—G. *daimōn*, a divinity, a tutelary deity, an evil spirit. An inferior divinity, a spirit; an attendant or indwelling spirit; an evil spirit, a devil; a fiend-like man.—**Demo'niac**, *a.* L.L. *daemoniacus*. Possessed by an evil spirit; of or pertaining to demons; of the nature of an indwelling spirit; devilish.—*n.* One possessed by an evil spirit.—**Demoni'ac**AL, *a.* Possessed by an evil spirit; of or pertaining to demons; devilish. — **Demoni'acal**LY,[2] *adv.* — **Demo'ni**AN, *a.* Relating to, of the nature of, a demon.—**Demon'**IC, **Dæmon'**IC, *a.* Devilish; relating to, of the nature of, supernatural power or genius.—**De'mon**ISM, *n.* Belief in, doctrine of, demons.—**De'mon**IZE, *vt.* To make into or like, to represent as, a demon.—**Demono**L'OGY, *n.*

Demon'etize, *vt.* F. *démonetiser*, f. DE- (5) + L. *monēta*, MONEY. To withdraw from use as money.

Dem'onstrate, *vt.* L. *dēmonstrāre, dēmonstrātum*, to point out, show, prove, f. DE- (3) + *monstrāre* in sim. sense. MONSTRANCE. To describe or explain by specimens or experiment as a method of teaching; to make evident by reasoning, prove.—*vi.* To make a show of military or naval force; to gather publicly in order to exhibit sympathy with a person or cause. — **Demon'str**ABLE, *a.* — **Demon'strab**LY,[2] *adv.* — **Demonstr**A'TION, *n.* — **Demon'str**ATIVE, *a.* Making evident; serving to do this; of a *pron.*, indicating an object; given to outward expression of the feelings, &c.—**Dem'onstrat**OR, *n.*

Demor'alize, *vt.* F. *démoraliser* (DE- (5) + MORAL, *a.* + -IZE). To deprave morally; to deprive (esp. an army) of courage and discipline (F. *moral*).—**Demoraliz**A'TION, *n.*

Demot'ic, *a.* G. *dēmotikos*, of the people, f. *dēmotēs*, one of the people, f. *dēmos*, the people. Applied to the popular form of the ancient Egyptian written character as distinguished from the hieratic.

Demul'cent, *a.* L. *dēmulcens, dēmulcentis*, pres.pple. of *dēmulcēre*, to stroke down, soothe, f. DE- (1) + *mulcēre*, to soothe. Soothing, allaying irritation.—*n.* A demulcent medicine.

Demur', *vi.* F. *demeurer*—O.F. *demourer, demorer*, to tarry, hence, to hesitate—Pop.L. *dēmorāre* = L. *dēmorāri*, to tarry, delay, f. DE- (3) + *morāri*, to delay. Formerly, to tarry, linger, wait. To make difficulties; to take exception *to*.—*n.* A demurring; an objection raised or exception taken.—**Demur'rage**, *n.* O.F. *demourage, demorage*. Detention of a ship beyond the time agreed upon; compensation for this, or for detention of railway trucks; a charge for giving gold, &c., for bullion.

Demure', *a.* Extended form of M.E. *mure*, mature, calm, demure—O.F. *meur* (F. *mûr*), ripe, discreet, &c.—L. *mātūrus*, MATURE. (The nature of the prefix is obscure.) Reserved or composed in demeanour; affectedly grave or decorous.—**Demure'**LY,[2] *adv.*

Den, *n.* O.E. *denn*, habitation of a wild beast. Cf. Early Mod. Du. *denne*, floor, cave, den. The habitation of a wild beast; a lurking-place; a small room or abode.

Denat'uralize, *vt.* DE- (5). To alter or pervert the nature of; to deprive of the rights of a subject or citizen.

Denega'tion, *n.* F. *dénégation*—L. *dēnegātio, dēnegātiōnis*, n. of action f. *dēnegāre*, to deny, f. DE- (2) + *negāre*. NEGATE. Denial.

De'nigrate, *vt.* L. *dēnigrāre, dēnigrātum*, f. DE- (3) + *nigrāre*, to blacken, f. *niger*. NEGRO. To blacken, make dark; to sully, stain, defame.—**Denigr**A'TION, *n.*

Den'izen, *n.* A.F. *deinzein*, f. *deinz* (F. *dans* —L. *dē intus*, from within), within + *-ein*, L. *-āneus*. An inhabitant; a foreigner admitted to residence and certain rights.—*vt.* To make (a person) a denizen.

Denom'inate, *vt.* L. *dēnōmināre, dēnōminātum*, to name, specify by name, f. DE- (3) + *nōmināre*, to name, f. *nōmen*. NOMINAL. To give a name to, name.—**Denomin**A'TION, *n.* Calling by a name; an appellation, designation; a class of one kind of unit in a system of numbers, weights, &c.; a class, sort, kind; a body of persons classed under a name, gen. of a religious sect. — **Denomina'tion**AL, *a.* Belonging to, or of the nature of, such a sect, sectarian.—**Denomina'tional**ISM, *n.* — **Denom'in**ATIVE, *a.* Characterized by, having the function of, naming.—**Denom'inat**OR, *n.* He who or that which denominates; the number written below the line in a fraction to show into how many parts a unit is divided.

Denote', *vt.* L. *dēnotāre*, to mark out, f. DE- (3) + *notāre*, to mark, f. *nota*, NOTE. To mark; to indicate, show; to give to understand, make known; to signify, stand for.—**Denot'**ABLE, *a.*—**Denot**A'TION, *n.* A marking; a mark, sign, indication; the signification of a term.

Dénouement, *n.* F., f. *dénouer*, to untie, f. *dé-* (=DIS- (4)) + L. *nōdāre*, to knot, f. *nōdus*, knot. NODE. The final unravelling of the plot in a drama, &c.; the solution or issue of a mystery, &c.

Denounce', *vt.* O.F. *denoncier, denuntier*—L. *dēnuntiāre, dēnuntiātum*, to give official intimation, f. DE- (3) + *nuntiāre*, to make known, f. *nuntius*, messenger. ANNOUNCE. To announce in the manner of a threat or warning; to inform against, accuse; to inveigh against; to declare (a treaty, &c.) to be at an end.—**Denounce'**MENT, *n.*—**Denunci**A'TION, *n.*—**Denun'ciat**ORY, *a.*

Dense, *a.* L. *densus*, thick. Thick, compact; stupid; of stupidity, &c., profound, intense. —**Dense'**LY,[2] *adv.*—**Dens'**ITY, *n.*

Dent, *n.* Var. of DINT. INDENT.[2] A mark, impression, or hollow caused by a blow or by pressure.—*vt.* To make a dent in.

Den'tal, *a.* Mod.L. *dentālis*, f. L. *dens, dentis*, TOOTH. INDENT.[1] Of or pertaining to the teeth; dealing with the teeth; pronounced by applying the tongue to the front upper teeth. —*n.* A dental consonant.—**Den'**TATE,[2] *a.* Having teeth or tooth-like projections on the edge.—**Den'tifrice**, *n.* F., f. L. *dentifricium*, f. *dens* + *fricāre*, to rub. A tooth-powder or tooth-paste.—**Den'**TIST, *n.* A dental surgeon. —**Denti'tion**, *n.* L. *dentitio, dentītiōnis*, a teething, f. *dentīre*, to cut teeth, f. *dens*. The production of the teeth; the system of teeth proper to an animal or to an animal at a particular age.

Denude', *vt.* L. *dēnūdāre*, to make naked, f. DE- (3) + *nūdāre* in sim. sense, f. *nūdus*, naked. NUDE. To make naked or bare; to strip, deprive *of*.—**Denud**A'TION, *n.*

Deny', *vt.* F. *dénier*—L. *dēnegāre*, to refuse, deny, f. DE- (3) + *negāre* in sim. sense. NEGATION. RENEGADE. To contradict (an assertion, &c.); to reject (a doctrine, &c.); to disown, repudiate; to refuse to give, to withhold; to refuse (a person requesting something); to refuse access to (a person visited).—**Deni'**ABLE, *a.*—**Deni'**AL, *n.*

De'odand, *n.* A.F. *deodande*—Med.L. *deōdandum*, i.e. L. *deō*, to God, dative of *deus* (DEITY) + *dandum*, neut. ger. of *dăre*, to give. A personal chattel which, having caused the death of a human being, was forfeited to the crown for pious uses.

De'odar, *n.* Hindī *dĕ'odār*—Skr. *deva-dāra*, divine tree. A species of cedar.

Deo'dorize, *vt.* DE- (5). To deprive of (offensive) odour.

Depart', *vi.* O.F. *departir*, L. *dispartīre*, to divide, f. DIS- (1)+*partīre* in sim. sense, f. *pars*, PART. To go away *from*, take one's leave; to set out, start; to diverge, deviate, desist *from*. —**Depart'**MENT, *n.* A division or part, a branch, province; a division or branch of administration.—**Department'**AL, *a.*—**Depart'**URE, *n.*

Depend', *vi.* O.F. *dependre*—L. *dēpendēre*, to hang down, f. DE- (1) + *pendēre*, to hang. IMPEND. PENDANT. To hang down; to be contingent *on* or *upon*; to rest entirely *on* or *upon* for maintenance, support, &c.; to rely, reckon *on* or *upon*; to be in suspense or undetermined.—**Depen'd**ANT, **Depen'd**ENT, *n.* One who depends on another for maintenance, &c.—**Depen'd**ENCE, *n.* The fact of depending upon something; subjection, subordination; reliance, confidence; the condition of being in suspense, &c.—**Depen'd**ENCY, *n.* The fact of depending upon something; subjection, subordination; a subordinate part, an appurtenance; a dependent territory.—**Depen'd**ENT, *a.* Hanging down; depending *on* or *upon* something or some one; subordinate, subject.—**Depen'dent**LY,[2] *adv.*

Depict', *vt.* L. *dēpingĕre, dēpictum*, to PAINT, draw, f. DE- (3) + *pingĕre* in sim. sense. To portray or figure by painting or drawing or in words.—**Depic't**ION, *n.*—**Depic't**URE, *n.*—**Depic'ture**, *vt.* DE- (3) + PICTURE, *v.* To picture, depict.

Depi'latory, *a.* As if f. a L. **dēpilātōrius*, f. *dēpilāre, dēpilātum*, to pull out the hair of, f. DE- (2) + *pilāre* in sim. sense, f. *pilus*, hair. CATERPILLAR. PELF. PILE.[3] PILL, *v.* PLUCK. PLUSH. Removing hair.—*n.* A substance which does this.

Deplete', *vt.* L. *dēplēre, dēplētum*, to empty out, draw off, f. DE- (5) + *-plēre*, to fill. COMPLETE. To empty out, exhaust; to relieve by blood-letting, &c.—**Deple'**TION, *n.*

Deplore', *vt.* L. *dēplōrāre*, to weep for bitterly, f. DE- (3) + *plōrāre*, to weep for. To weep for, regret, lament.—**Deplor'**ABLE, *a.*

Deploy', *vt.* F. *déployer* (O.F. *desployer*, to unfold)—L.L. and Med.L. *displicāre*, to unfold, f. DIS- (4) + *plicāre*, to fold. DISPLAY. COMPLEX. To spread out (troops) into a more extended line.—*vi.* To form such a line.—**Deploy'**MENT, *n.*

Depone', *vi.* L. *dēpōnĕre, dēpositum*, to lay down or aside, in Med.L., to testify, f. DE- (1) (2)+*pōnĕre*, to place. DEPOSIT. DEPOSITION. DEPOT. POSITION. To give evidence upon oath, depose.—**Depo'n**ENT, *a.* Of verbs, passive in form but active in meaning (such verbs, originally reflexive, having been regarded as having *laid aside* a passive meaning). —*n.* A deponent verb; one who depones.

Depop'ulate, *vt.* L. *dēpopulāri, dēpopulātus*, to lay waste, in Med.L., to spoil of people, f. DE- (3) + *populāri*, to lay waste, f. *populus*, PEOPLE, lit., 'to pour in a multitude over'. To deprive of inhabitants.—**Depopul**A'TION, *n.*

Deport', *v.* O.F. *deporter*, to bear, endure, *se deporter*, to forbear, quiet oneself, f. *de-* (= DE- (1) or (3)) + *porter*, L. *portāre*, to bear, carry. COMPORT. Formerly *trans*, to bear with, *refl.*, to forbear. *Refl.*, to bear or conduct oneself, behave.—*vt.* = F *déporter*, representing L. *dēportāre*, to carry away, to banish, f. DE- (2) + *portāre*. To remove, esp. into exile.—**Deport**A'TION, *n.* Removal into exile.—**Deport'**MENT, *n.* Conduct, behaviour; bearing, demeanour.

Depose', *vt.* F. *déposer*, f. DE- (1) + *poser*, to place. POSE.[1] To put down from office, esp. from sovereignty.—*vi.* To give evidence upon oath, depone.—**Deposi'tion**, *n.* O.F. *deposition*—L. *dēpositio, dēpositiōnis*, f. *dēpōnĕre*. DEPONE. In senses from the *v.*

Depos'it, *vt.* Obs. F. *depositer*—Med.L. *dēpositāre*, freq. f. L. *dēpōnĕre*. DEPONE. To set down, place in a position of rest; to give in charge for safe keeping, esp. in a bank; to pledge for the performance of a contract, &c. —*n.* Something deposited; the act of depositing; the state of being placed in safe keeping. —**Depos'it**ARY, *n.* One to whom a thing is committed for safe keeping.—**Depos'it**ORY, *n.* A place of safe keeping; a depositary.—**Depos'it**OR, *n.* One who gives in charge for safe keeping, esp. in a bank.

Dep'ot, *n.* F. *dépôt*, O.F. *depost*—L. *dēpositum*, a thing laid down or stored, neut. pa.pple. of *dēpōnĕre*. DEPONE. A place for military stores; the head-quarters of a regiment; a store-house.

Deprave', *vt.* L. *dēprāvāre*, to distort, pervert, f. DE- (3) + *prāvus*, crooked, perverse.

To deteriorate, make bad; to pervert, corrupt. —**Deprava'tion**, *n.*—**Deprav'ity**, *n.*

Dep'recate, *vt.* L. *dēprecāri, dēprecātus*, to pray away or against, f. DE- (2) + *precāri*, to PRAY. To pray against; to plead against, express disapproval of.—**Depreca'tion**, *n.* —**Dep'recative**, *a.*—**Dep'recatory**, *a.*

Depre'ciate, *vt.* L. *dēpretiāre, dēpretiātum* (in Med.L. gen. *dēpreciāre, dēpreciātum*), f. DE- (1) + *pretium*, PRICE. DISPRAISE. To lower the price or value of; to underrate, belittle.—*vi.* To fall in value.—**Deprecia'tion**, *n.*—**Depre'ciatory**, *a.*

Dep'redate, *vt.* and *i.* L. *dēpraedāri, dēpraedātus*, to plunder, f. DE- (3) + *praedāri* in sim. sense, f. *praeda*, PREY. To plunder.— **Depreda'tion**, *n.*—**Dep'redator**, *n.*

Depress', *vt.* O.F. *depresser*—L. type **dēpressāre*, freq. of *dēprimĕre, dēpressum*, to press down, f. DE- (1) + *premĕre*, to press. COMPRESS. To bring into a lower position, lower; to make weaker or less; to deject, sadden.—**Depres'sion**, *n.* The action of lowering, the process of sinking; a hollow; a being made weaker or less; a lowering of atmospheric pressure, a centre of minimum pressure; dejection.—**Depres'sible**, *a.*

Deprive', *vt.* O.F. *depriver*—L.L. **dēprīvāre*, to deprive of office, degrade, f. DE- (3) + *prīvāre*, to deprive. PRIVATE. To divest, strip, bereave *of*; to divest of office, esp. of ecclesiastical office.—**Depriva'tion**, *n.*

Depth, *n.* Not in O.E. Perh. formed, after *length*, &c., on DEEP. Distance downwards or inwards, or from front to back; the quality of being deep; profundity, abstruseness; sagacity, penetration; intensity of feelings, moral or physical qualities, &c.; a deep part of water or in the earth; an abyss; the part far from the surface or from outside; the middle (of winter, night, &c.).

Depute', *vt.* F. *députer*—L. *dēputāre, dēputātum*, to consider as, destine, allot, f. DE- (2) + *putāre*, to think, consider, &c. To commit *to* (a substitute); to appoint as one's substitute. —**Deputa'tion**, *n.* Appointment as a substitute; a body of persons sent on behalf of others.—**Dep'uty**, *n.* F. *député*, use as *n.* of pa.pple. of *députer*. A substitute, delegate.

Derac'inate, *vt.* With -ATE[3] f. F. *déraciner*, f. *dé-, des-* (= DIS- (5)) + *racine*, L.L. *rādīcina*, dim. of L. *rādix*, root. RADICAL. To tear up by the roots.

Derail', *vi.* F. *dérailler*, f. *dé-* (= DE- (2)) + *rail*, O.F. *reille*, RAIL, *n.*[1] To run off the rails. —*vt.* To cause to do this.—**Derail'ment**, *n.*

Derange', *vt.* F. *déranger*, O.F. *desrengier*, f. *des-* (= DIS- (4)) + *rengier*, to range, f. *reng*, RANK. To throw into confusion or disorder; to disorder the mind of; to disturb, interrupt. —**Derange'ment**, *n.*

Der'elict, *a.* L. *dērelictus*, pa.pple. of *dērelinquĕre*, to forsake wholly, f. DE- (3) + *relinquĕre*. RELINQUISH. Forsaken, abandoned, esp. of a ship.—*n.* Something abandoned, esp. a ship.—**Derelic'tion**, *n.* Abandonment; failure in duty, neglect.

Deride', *vt.* L. *dērīdēre, dērisum*, to laugh to scorn, f. DE- (4) + *rīdēre*, to laugh. RIDICULE. RISIBLE. To laugh to scorn.—**Deri'sion**, *n.*—**Deri'sive**, *a.*

Derive', *vt.* F. *dériver*—L. *dērīvāre, dērīvātum*, to lead off (water), divert, derive (words), f. DE- (2) + *rīvus*, brook. RIVAL. RIVULET. To draw, get, obtain *from*; to deduce, gather; to trace or show the origin of.—*vi.* and *refl.* and in *pass.* To flow, issue, arise, be descended *from*.—**Deriv'able**, *a.*—**Deriva'tion**, *n.* A drawing, obtaining, deducing; origin, descent; something derived; the tracing of the origin of a word.—**Deriv'ative**, *a.* Of derived character.—*n.* A thing of this character; a word derived from another.

Derm, **Der'ma**, *nn.* G. *derma, dermatos*, skin, f. *derein*, to flay. TEAR, *v.* Also **Der'mis**, *n.* From *derma* after *epidermis*. The true skin.—**Der'mal**, *a.* Pertaining to the skin.—**Dermatol'ogy**, *n.* The branch of science which treats of the skin.

Der'ogate, *vi.* L. *dērogāre, dērogātum*, to repeal in part, diminish, f. DE- (2) + *rogāre*, to ask, to propose a law. ABROGATE. To take away a part or detract *from*; to degenerate.— **Deroga'tion**, *n.*—**Derog'atory**, *a.*

Der'rick, *n.* From the name of a noted hangman at Tyburn, *c.* 1600. Formerly, the gallows. A contrivance for hoisting or moving heavy weights.

Der'ring do. In Chaucer (*Troilus*, v. 837) *durring don* (i.e. *durring*, vbl.n. f. *durre*, O.E. *durran*, to DARE, with *don*, M.E. pres. infinitive of DO), lit. 'the daring to do' (a thing specified); now, from a mistake of Spenser (*Shepheards Calender*, Oct., 65), spelt as above and taken in the general sense 'desperate courage, daring feats'.

Der'ringer, *n.* From the inventor's name. A small pistol with a large bore.

Der'vish, *n.* Per. *darvēsh, darvīsh*, poor, a religious beggar. (Immediately f. Turkish *dervīsh*.) A Mohammedan friar.

Des'cant, *n.* O.F. *deschant*, O.N.F. *descaunt*, *descant*—Med.L. *discantus*, part-song, refrain, f. DIS- (1) + L. *cantus*, song. CANT.[2] A melodious accompaniment to a simple musical theme; a song, a melodious strain; the art of singing or writing music in parts; an instrumental prelude; varied comment, amplification of a subject; a comment, remark; a disquisition, discourse.—**Descant'**, *vi.* To play or sing an air in harmony with a theme; to warble, sing; to make comments or remarks, discourse at large, enlarge *on* or *upon*.

Descend', *vi.* F. *descendre*—L. *dēscendĕre*, *dēscensum*, f. DE- (1) + *scandĕre*, to climb. SCAN. To come or go down, sink, fall; to slope or extend downwards; to fall violently *upon*; to stoop, condescend; to spring *from* (an ancestor, &c.) (gen. in *pass.*); to pass to an heir, to be transmitted.—*vt.* To go downwards over, along, &c.—**Descen'dant**, *a.* Descending from an ancestor.—*n.* One who is so descended, issue, offspring.—**Descen'dible**, **Descen'dable**, *aa.* Capable of transmission by inheritance; that can be gone down.—**Descent'**, *n.* F. *descente*, f. *descendre*. A coming or going down; a downward slope; a means of descending; a sudden attack; decline, sinking, fall; lineage; a generation; transmission of a title, quality, &c.

Describe', *vt.* L. *dēscrībĕre, dēscriptum*, to copy off, sketch off, mark off, f. DE- (2) + *scrībĕre*, to write. SCRIBE. To give a detailed account of; to trace out (a geometrical figure, &c.); to pass or travel over (a course or distance).—**Describ'able**, *a.*—**Descrip'tion**, *n.* In senses from the *v.*; a sort, species, kind. —**Descrip'tive**, *a.*

Descry', *vt.* O.F. *descrier*. DECRY. Formerly, to declare, publish, betray, decry. To catch sight of, esp. from a distance.

Des'ecrate, *vt.* From DE- (5) + stem of

CON-SECRATE. To take away consecrated character from, to profane; to devote *to* (evil). —**Desecra'tion**, *n.*

Desert', *n.*[1] O.F. *desert*, masc., *deserte*, fem., f. *deservir*, to DESERVE. Merit or demerit; merit, excellence, worth; an action or quality calling for reward or punishment (us. in *pl.*); that which is deserved, good or evil (us. in *pl.*).

Des'ert, *a.* O.F. *desert*—L. *dēsertus*, abandoned, left waste, pa.pple. of *dēserĕre*, to sever connexion with, abandon, f. DE- (5) + *serĕre*, to join. SERIES. Abandoned, forsaken; uninhabited, desolate; barren, waste.—*n.*[2] An uninhabited tract, a desolate barren region.—

Desert', *vt.* F. *déserter*, in O.F., to make desert—L.L. *dēsertāre*, freq. f. *dēserĕre*. To abandon, forsake, relinquish.—*vi.* To forsake one's duty, esp. of sailors and soldiers.—**Desert'er**, *n.*—**Deser'tion**, *n.*

Deserve', *vt.* O.F. *deservir*—L. *dēservīre*, to serve well, hence in late Pop.L. to merit by service, f. DE- (3) + *servīre*, to SERVE. DESERT, *n.*[1] To have a claim to, be worthy to have.—*vi.* To be worthy of reward or punishment.—**Deserved'**, *ppl.a.* Rightfully earned, merited.—**Deser'vedly**,[2] *adv.*

Des'iccate, *vt.* L. *dēsiccāre*, *dēsiccātum*, to dry thoroughly, f. DE- (3) + *siccāre*, to dry, f. *siccus*, dry. To dry, dry up.—**Desicca'tion**, *n.*

Desid'erate, *vt.* L. *dēsīderāre*, *dēsīderātum*, to miss, long for, f. -*sīderāre*, as in CONSIDER. (Perh. with pref. in sense (2) and notion of turning away from the stars and missing them.) DESIRE. To long for, want, miss.—**Desid'erative**, *a.* Of a verb, formed from another to express desire of doing the denoted act.—*n.* A desiderative verb.—**Desidera'tum**, *n.*; *pl.* **-a'ta**. Neut. pa.pple. of *dēsīderāre*. Something wanting and desired.

Design', *vt.* F. *désigner*—L. *dēsignāre*, *dēsignātum*, to mark off, DESIGNATE, contrive, f. DE- (2) + *signāre*, to mark, f. *signum*, mark, SIGN. To plan out, contrive; to purpose, intend; to establish, form, or set apart for some end; to trace the outline of, delineate; to make drawings, &c., for carrying out, to plan and execute (a structure, work of art, &c.).—*n.* A project, scheme; a purpose; an end in view; adaptation of means to ends; crafty contrivance, an instance of this; a drawing for carrying out (a work); a piece of decorative work; the art of picturesque delineation and construction.—**Design'edly**,[2] *adv.* On purpose.—**Design'ing**, *ppl.a.* Crafty, scheming.

Des'ignate, *vt.* L. *dēsignāre*. DESIGN. To point out, indicate, specify; to be an indication of; to name, style; to appoint, select, destine.—**Designa'tion**, *n.*

Desire', *vt.* O.F. *desirer*, earlier *desidrer*—L. *dēsīderāre*. DESIDERATE. To long for, crave, wish strongly; to ask for, request; to entreat, request.—*n.* Longing, craving; a wish; lust; a request; an object of desire.—**Desir'able**, *a.*—**Desirabil'ity**, *n.*—**Desir'ableness**, *n.*—**Desir'ous**, *a.*

Desist', *vi.* O.F. *desister*—L. *dēsistĕre*, f. DE- (2) + *sistĕre*, to stand still. ASSIST. To cease *from*, leave off, give over.

Desk, *n.* M.E. *deske*—Med.L. *desca*—L. *discus*, in Med.L. used in sense 'table'. DISK. An article of furniture with a sloping top to support a book or for writing upon; a case for writing materials, &c.

Des'olate, *a.* L. *dēsōlātus*, pa.pple. of *dēsōlāre*, to leave alone, forsake, f. DE- (3) + *sōlāre*, to make lonely, f. *sōlus*, alone. SOLE, *a.* Left alone, solitary; uninhabited, deserted; neglected, barren, dreary, dismal; forlorn, wretched.—*vt.* To depopulate; to lay waste; to overwhelm with grief.—**Des'olately**,[2] *adv.*—**Des'olateness**, *n.*—**Desola'tion**, *n.*

Despair', *vi.* O.F. *despeir-*, stressed stem-form of *desperer*—L. *dēspērāre*, *dēspērātum*, to be hopeless, have no hope of, f. DE- (5) + *spērāre*, to hope, f. *spēs*, hope. To give up or be without hope.—*n.* The action or condition of despairing; something causing despair.—

Des'perate, *a.* From *dēspērātus*, pa.pple. of *dēspērāre*. Leaving little or no room for hope; which there is no hope of accomplishing; reckless of consequences; marked by recklessness; hopelessly bad, extreme.—**Des'perately**,[2] *adv.*—**Despera'tion**, *n.*

Despera'do, *n.* In form identical with Old Sp. *desperado*, desperate (which, however, does not seem to occur as *n.*), pa.pple. of *desperar*, L. *dēspērāre* (see prec.). One ready for any lawless deed.

Des'picable, *a.* L. *dēspicābilis*, f. *dēspicārī*, to look down upon, despise, f. DE- (1) + -*specārī*, cogn. with *specĕre* (see next). Base, contemptible.—**Des'picably**,[2] *adv.*

Despise', *vt.* From stem *despis-* of O.F. *despire*—L. *dēspicĕre*, *dēspectum*, to look down upon, despise, f. DE- (1) + *specĕre*. SPECIES. (See next.) To look down upon, disdain.

Despite', *n.* O.F. *despit*—L. *dēspectus*, a looking down upon, f. *dēspicĕre* (see prec.). SPITE. Scorn, disdain; outrage, contumely; ill-will, malice; *in despite of*, *despite of*, in defiance of, notwithstanding.—*vt.* To treat with contempt, do despite to.—*prep.* In spite of.—**Despite'ful**, *a.*—**Despite'fully**,[2] *adv.*

Despoil', *vt.* M.E. *despuilen*—O.F. *despuillier*—L. *dēspoliāre*, *dēspoliātum*, to rob, f. DE- (3) + *spoliāre*, to strip, rob, f. *spolium*, SPOIL. To plunder, rob; to strip, deprive *of*.—**Despolia'tion**, *n.*

Despond', *vi.* L. *dēspondēre*, to promise to give, give up, *dēspondēre animum*, later *dēspondēre* simply, to lose heart, f. DE- (2) + *spondēre*, to promise. SPONSOR. To lose heart or resolution. — **Despon'dence**, -ENCY, *nn.* — **Despon'dent**, *a.*—**Despon'dently**,[2] *adv.*

Des'pot, *n.* O.F. *despot*—G. *despotēs*, master, despot. POTENT. An absolute ruler, a tyrant, oppressor.—**Despot'ic**, *a.*—**Despot'ically**, *adv.* -AL. -LY.[2]—**Des'potism**, *n.*

Des'quamate, *vi.* L. *dēsquāmāre*, *dēsquāmātum*, to remove scales from, f. DE- (2) + *squāma*, scale. To come off in the form of scales.—**Desquama'tion**, *n.*

Dessert', *n.* F. *dessert*, removal of the dishes, dessert, f. *desservir*, to remove what has been served, f. *des-* (= DIS- (4)) + *servir*, to SERVE. A course of fruit, &c., served after dinner.

Des'tine, *vt.* F. *destiner*—L. *dēstināre*, *dēstinātum*, to make firm, ordain, appoint, f. DE- (3) + obs. *stanāre*, causal deriv. of *stāre*, to STAND. To appoint or fix beforehand; to set apart, devote, intend. — **Destina'tion**, *n.* The action of destining, the fact of being destined; the intended end of a journey or course. —**Des'tiny**, *n.* O.F. *destinée*. That which is destined to happen; appointed lot; overruling necessity; the goddess of destiny.

Des'titute, *a.* L. *dēstitūtus*, pa.pple. of *dēstituĕre*, to set down, place, forsake, f. DE- (1) (2) + *statuĕre*, to place. STATUTE. Without resources, in absolute want.—**Destitu'tion**, *n.*

Des'trer, **Des'trier**, *n.* A.F. *destrer*=O.F. *destrier*—L.L. (*equus* (EQUINE)) *dextrārius*, a

f. *dextra*, right hand; so called because led by the squire with the right hand. A war-horse.

Destroy', *vt.* M.E. *destruyen*, &c.—O.F. *destruire* (F. *détruire*)—Late Pop.L. type **dēstrūgĕre* f. L. *dēstruĕre, dēstructum*, to pull down, f. DE- (5) + *struĕre*, to pile up, build. STRUCTURE. To pull down, demolish; to undo, break up, consume; to render useless, spoil; to kill, slay; to do away with, put an end to.—**Destroy'**ER, *n.* In senses f. the *v.* In full *torpedo-boat destroyer*, a small war-vessel of high speed originally designed for destroying enemy vessels fitted for discharging torpedoes. —**Destruc'**TIBLE, *a.*—**Destruc'**TION, *n.*—**Destruc'**TIVE, *a.*—**Destruc'tive**LY,[2] *adv.* —**Destruc'**TOR, *n.* One who destroys; a furnace for burning refuse.

Des'uetude, *n.* F. *désuétude*—L. *dēsuētūdo*, disuse, f. *dēsuētus*, pa.pple. of *dēsuescĕre*, to disuse, to become unaccustomed, f. DE- (5) + *suescĕre*, to become accustomed. CUSTOM. The state of disuse.

Des'ultory, *a.* L. *dēsultōrius*, of or belonging to a vaulter, superficial, f. *dēsultor*, a leaper down, vaulter, f. *dēsilīre, dēsultum*, to leap down, f. DE- (1)+*salīre*, to leap. ASSAIL. INSULT. Flitting from one thing to another; unmethodical.—**Des'ultori**LY,[2] *adv.*

Detach', *vt.* F. *détacher*, earlier *destachier*, *destacher*, f. *des-* (= DIS- (1)) + *tache*, nail. TACK. ATTACH. To unfasten, disconnect; to send off (a part from a main body) for a special purpose. — **Detach'**ABLE, *a.* — **Detach'**MENT, *n.* A detaching; a part of a main body detached; a standing apart or aloof.

Detail', *vt.* F. *détailler*, to cut in pieces, to deal with or relate minutely, f. DE- (3)+*tailler*, O.F. *taillier*, to cut. ENTAIL. To deal with or relate minutely; to appoint for a particular duty.—**De'tail**, *n.* The dealing with matters minutely; a minute account; an item, a subordinate or unimportant part; an appointing for a particular duty, a body so appointed.

Detain', *vt.* O.F. *detenir*—L. *dētinēre, dētentum*, to hold off, keep back, detain, f. DE- (2) + *tenēre*, to hold. TENABLE. To keep under restraint; to keep from proceeding or going on, stop.—**Deten'**TION, *n.*

Detect', *vt.* L. *dētegĕre, dētectum*, to uncover, disclose, f. DE- (5) + *tegĕre*, to cover. TEGUMENT. To find out (a person) as being, or as the doer of, something; to find out (something apt to escape observation).—**Detec'**TION, *n.* —**Detec'**TIVE, *a.* Having the character or function of detecting.—*n.* A police officer or private person employed to investigate cases or to watch suspected persons.

Deter', *vt.* L. *dēterrēre*, to frighten away, f. DE- (2) + *terrēre*, to frighten. TERRIBLE. To discourage, turn aside, or restrain by fear, &c.—**Deter'**MENT, *n.*—**Deter'**RENT, *a.* and *n.*

Dete'riorate, *vt.* and *i.* L. *dēteriōrāre, dēteriōrātum*, f. *dēterior*, worse, f. obs. a. *dēter*, f. *dē*, down. To make or grow worse.—**Dete'rior**A'TION, *n.*

Deter'mine, *vt.* O.F. *determiner*—L. *dētermināre, dēterminātum*, to bound, fix, settle, f. DE- (3) + *termināre*, to bound, f. *terminus*, boundary. TERM. To bring to an end; to settle, decide; to fix as known, ascertain; to decide the course of, direct; to bring to a decision (*to do* something).—*vi.* To come to an end; to give a decision, decide; to come to a decision (*to do* something); to resolve *upon* or *on*.—**Deter'min**ABLE, *a.*—**Deter'min**ANT, *a.* That determines.—*n.* Something that determines. — **Deter'min**ATE,[2] *a.* Fixed, definite; conclusive, final; resolved, resolute. —**Deter'minate**LY,[2] *adv.*—**Determin**A'TION, *n.* In senses f. the *v.*; the quality of being resolved or resolute.—**Deter'mined**, *ppl.a.* Resolute; showing determination.—**Deter'min**ISM, *n.* The theory that human action is determined by forces acting from without.—**Deter'min**IST, *n.*

Detest', *vt.* F. *détester*—L. *dētestāri*, to curse while calling down a deity to witness, to abhor, f. DE- (1) + *testāri*, to bear or call to witness, f. *testis*, a witness. TESTAMENT. To abhor, hate.—**Detest'**ABLE, *a.* Hateful.—**Detest'ab**LY,[2] *adv.*—**Detest**A'TION, *n.*

Dethrone', *vt.* DE- (6) + THRONE. To remove from the throne.—**Dethrone'**MENT, *n.*

Det'onate, *vi.* and *t.* L. *dētonāre, dētonātum*, to thunder down or forth, f. DE- (1)(2)+*tonāre*, to THUNDER. To explode or cause to explode with a loud report.—**Deton**A'TION, *n.*

Detour', **Détour**, *n.* F. *détour*, f. *dé-* (= DIS- (1)) + *tourner*, to turn—L. *tornāre*. TURN. A deviation from the direct road.

Detract', *vt.* L. *dētrahĕre, dētractum*, to draw off or away, to disparage, f. DE- (2)+*trahĕre*, to draw. ABSTRACT. To take away (a part) *from*; to disparage, belittle.—*vi.* To take away a part *from*, often implying disparagement.—**Detrac'**TION, *n.*—**Detract'**OR, *n.*

Detrain', *vt.* and *i.* DE- (2) + TRAIN. To discharge, to alight, from a railway train.

Det'riment, *n.* F. *détriment*—L. *dētrīmentum*, loss, damage, f. *dēterĕre, dētrītum*, to rub away, wear out, f. DE- (3) + *terĕre*, to rub. TRITE. Loss, damage; something causing loss or damage.—**Detrimen'**TAL, *a.*

Detri'tus, *n.* L. *dētrītus*, a rubbing away, f. *dēterĕre*. (See prec.) Matter produced by the wearing away of exposed surfaces.

Deuce, *n.*[1] F. *deux*, O.F. *deus*, L. *duo*, TWO. The two at cards or dice.

Deuce, *n.*[2] Prob. f. L.G. Cf. L.G. *de duus!* Ger. *der daus!* the deuce! Perh. (with change of gender) the same as Ger. *das daus*, the deuce or lowest throw at dice = prec. (The exclamation would thus be originally one of vexation on making this throw.) Bad luck, mischief; the devil.

Deuteron'omy, *n.* Eccles. L. *Deuteronomium*—G. *Deuteronomion*, f. *deuteros*, second + *nomos*, law. The fifth book of the Old Testament, containing a repetition, with comments, of the decalogue and of most of the laws in Exodus.

Dev'astate, *vt.* L. *dēvastāre, dēvastātum*, to lay waste, f. DE- (3) + *vastāre* in sim. sense, f. *vastus*, WASTE. VAST. To lay waste, ravage. —**Devast**A'TION, *n.*

Devel'op, *vt.* F. *développer*, O.F. *desveloper*, *desvoluper*, f. *des-* (= DIS- (4)) + the Romanic *v.* of uncertain orig. which appears in It. as *viluppare*, to fold, roll up. ENVELOP. To bring to maturity; to bring forth (something already existing in another form or condition); to bring out (the image on a photographic film), to bring out the image from (the film); to evolve as a product; to display as fully formed or in activity.—*vi.* To grow from a rudimentary into a maturer condition.—**Devel'op**MENT, *n.*

De'viate, *vi.* L. *dēviāre, dēviātum*, to turn from the way, f. DE- (2) + *via*, way. PERVIOUS. TRIVIAL. VIATICUM. To turn out of the way; to turn aside *from*; to diverge or differ *from*.—**Devi**A'TION, *n.*—**De'vi**OUS, *a.*

Lying out of the way; taking a winding or erratic course; erring, straying.

Device', *n.* M.E. *devis, devys*—O.F. *devis*, division, a devising, an invention—L. *dīvidĕre*, to DIVIDE. DEVISE. A planning or contriving; will, inclination, fancy; a project, scheme; a plot, stratagem; a mechanical contrivance; a figure or design; a cognizance.

Dev'il, *n.* O.E. *déofol* = O.H.G. *tiuval*, O.N. *djōfull*, Goth. *diabulus*—G. *diabolos*, lit., 'accuser, traducer', f. DIA*ballein*, to throw across, to set at variance, to traduce. DIABOLIC. The supreme spirit of evil; a false god, an evil or malignant spirit; applied to human beings, sometimes merely playfully or in contempt or pity; a highly-seasoned dish.—*vt.* To grill with hot condiments.—**Dev'il**ISH, *a.*—**Dev'il**RY, *n.* Diabolical art; works of the devil; extreme wickedness or cruelty; reckless exhibition of mischief, hilarity or daring.

Devise', *vt.* O.F. *deviser*, late Pop.L.**dīvisāre*, freq. of *dīvidĕre*, to DIVIDE. DEVICE. To give by will; to plan, contrive, frame; to plot, scheme.—*n.* A devising by will.

Devoid', *a.* Short for *devoided*, pa.pple. of obs. *devoid*, to empty out—O.F. *devoidier*, *desvuidier*, f. *de-*, *des-* (=DIS-(1))+*vuit*, fem. *vuide*, *voide*, empty, VOID. Empty or destitute *of*.

Dev'oir, *n.* M.E. *dever* (conformed to F. *devoir*)—O.F. *deveir*—L. *dēbēre*, to owe. DEBT. ENDEAVOUR. (One's) duty; a dutiful act of civility or respect (gen. in *pl.*).

Devolve', *vt.* L. *dēvolvĕre*, *dēvolūtum*, to roll down, f. DE- (1) + *volvĕre*, to roll. CONVOLVE. To cause (a duty, &c.) to fall *upon*.—*vi.* To pass or fall *to* or *upon*.—**Devolu'**TION, *n.*

Devote', *vt.* L. *dēvovēre*, *dēvōtum*, to vow, dedicate, f. DE- (3) + *vovēre* in sim. sense. DEVOUT. To set apart solemnly or formally; to give up or apply zealously *to* (esp. *refl.*); to curse, doom.—**Devot**EE', *n.* One zealously devoted, esp. to religion.—**Devo'**TION, *n.* Religious earnestness; religious worship or observance; dedication, consecration; addiction, application, attachment; an applying to a use or purpose.—**Devo'tion**AL, *a.*

Devour', *vt.* O.F. *devorer*—L. *dēvorāre*, to swallow down, f. DE- (1) + *vorāre*, to swallow. VORACITY. To eat voraciously or greedily; to consume, destroy.—**Devour'**ER, *n.*

Devout', *a.* O.F. *devot*—L. *dēvōtus*, pa.pple. of *dēvovēre*. DEVOTE. Pious, religious; earnest, sincere.—**Devout'**LY,[2] *adv.*

Dew, *n.* O.E. *déaw*. Common Teut. Cf. Skr. *dhāv*, to flow, run. MILDEW. Moisture from the air deposited in drops on a cool surface; moisture.—*vt.* To wet with or as with dew.—**Dew'**Y,[2] *a.*—**Dew'**INESS, *n.*

Dew'lap, *n.* The first element uncertain. The second is O.E. *læppa*, pendulous piece, skirt. Cf. Da. *doglæb*. The fold of loose skin hanging from the throat of cattle, &c.

Dex'ter, *a.* L. *dexter*, to or on the right, skilful, cogn. with G. *dexios*, Goth. *taihswa*. In *heraldry*, on the right-hand side (regarded from the point of view of the bearer of the shield).—**Dexter'**ITY, *n.* Adroitness, skill, bodily or mental.—**Dex'ter**OUS, **Dex'tr**OUS, *a.*—**Dex'terous**LY,[2] **Dex'trous**LY,[2] *adv.*

Dex'trin, *n.* F. *dextrine*, f. L. *dextra*, right hand, fem. of *dexter*. (See prec.) (So called from its property of turning the plane of polarization of light to the right.) A soluble gummy substance obtained from starch.

Dhow, Dow, *n.* Orig. language unknown. A native vessel used on the Arabian Sea.

Diabe'tes, *n.* G. *diabētēs*, lit. 'a passer through', hence, the disease, f. DIA*bainein*, to go through. BASE, *n.* A disease characterized by an immoderate discharge of urine.

Diabol'ic, *a.* F. *diabolique*—L. *diabolicus*—G. *diabolikos*, f. *diabolos*, DEVIL. Also **Diabol'**ICAL. Of or like the devil; devilish, fiendish.—**Diabol'ical**LY,[2] *adv.*

Diach'ylon, *n.* Med.L. *diachylum*, L. *diachylōn*, repg. G. *dia chulōn*, (a medicament) composed of juices, f. *dia*, through, by means of + *chulos*, juice. Formerly, a kind of ointment of vegetable juices. A kind of sticking-plaster which adheres when heated.

Diac'onal, *a.* L. *diāconālis*, f. *diāconus*, DEACON. Of or pertaining to a deacon.—**Diac'on**ATE,[1] *n.* The office, rank, period of being, a deacon; a body of deacons.

Di'adem, *n.* O.F. *diademe*—L. *diadēma*—G. *diadēma*, fillet, esp. a regal fillet, f. *diade-ein*, to bind round, f. DIA-, through, across + *de-ein*, to bind. A crown or regal fillet; a wreath for the head.

Diæ'resis, *n.* L. *diaeresis*—G. *diairesis*, f. DI- + *hairesis*, a taking, f. *haire-ein*, to take. The division of one syllable into two; the sign (¨) marking the division, or indicating that a vowel is to be pronounced separately.

Diagno'sis, *n.* G. *diagnōsis*, f. *diagignōskein*, to distinguish, f. DIA-, thoroughly, apart + *gignōskein*, to learn to KNOW. AGNOSTIC. Determination of the nature of a diseased condition; the result formally stated.—**Diagnose'**, *vt.* From the *n.* To make a diagnosis of.—**Diagnos'tic**, *a.* G. *diagnōstikos*. Of or of value for diagnosis; specifically characteristic.—*n.* Diagnosis (sometimes in *collective pl.*); a distinctive symptom.

Diag'onal, *a.* L. *diagōnālis*—G *diagōnios*, from angle to angle, f. DIA-, across + *gōnia*, angle. Extending from one angle to another, or from one corner to the opposite corner; loosely, having an oblique direction.—*n.* A diagonal line.—**Diag'onal**LY,[2] *adv.*

Di'agram, *n.* L. *diagramma*, *diagrammatis*= G. *diagramma*, something marked out by lines, f. *diagraphein*, to mark out by lines, f. DIA-, through + *graphein*, to write. GRAPHIC. A figure in lines to illustrate a definition, &c., or to aid in proving a proposition; an illustrative figure in outline; a set of lines, &c., to represent the course or results of an action or process.—**Diagrammat'**IC, -ICAL, *aa.*—**Diagrammat'ical**LY,[2] *adv.*

Di'al, *n.* Presumably f. L. *dies*, day, through Med.L. *diālis*, daily. DIURNAL. An instrument indicating the hour of the day by the sun's shadow, a **Sun'-dial**; the face of a clock, watch, &c.

Di'alect, *n.* L. *dialectus*—G. *dialektos*, discourse, way of speaking, language of a district, f. *dialegesthai*, to discourse, f. DIA-, through, across + *legein*, to speak. DIALOGUE. LEXICON. Characteristic speech or manner of speaking; a subordinate or local form of a language.—**Dialec'**TAL, *a.*

Dialec'tic, *n.*[1] O.F. *dialectique*—G. *dialektikē* (*technē*), (the art) of dialectic, fem. sing. of *dialektikos*, a. f. *dialektos*. (See prec.) The art of investigating by discussion (also in *pl.*).

Dialec'tic, *a.* G. *dialektikos*. (See prec.) Of, pertaining to, of the nature of, addicted to, logical disputation; dialectal.—*n.*[2] One skilled in dialectic.—Sim. **Dialec'**TICAL, *a.*—**Dialec'tical**LY,[2] *adv.*—**Dialect**IC'IAN, *n.* One skilled in dialectic; a student of dialects.

Di'alogue, *n.* F. *dialogue*—L. *dialogus*—G. *dialogos*, f. *dialegesthai*. DIALECT. A conversation; conversation; a book in the form of a conversation; literary composition of this kind; conversation in a novel, &c.

Diamagnet'ic, *a.* DIA-, through, across + MAGNETIC. Applied to bodies which, when freely suspended and acted on by magnetism, tend to assume a position transverse to that which a magnet tends to assume.

Diam'eter, *n.* O.F. *diametre*—L. *diametros* —G. *diametros* (*grammē*), diagonal (line), diameter of a circle, f. DIA-, through, across + *metron*, measure. A straight line passing through the centre of a circle and terminated at each end by the circumference; a straight line passing from side to side of a body through the centre; transverse measurement, thickness.—**Diamet'r**IC, **Diamet'r**ICAL, *aa.* Of or pertaining to a diameter; of opposition, &c., direct, complete.—**Diamet'rical**LY,[2] *adv.*

Di'amond, *n.* M.E. *diamant*—O.F. *diamant* —L.L. *diamas*, *diamantis*, altered f. L. *adamas*, G. *adamas*, ADAMANT. A very hard and brilliant precious stone; a diamond-shaped figure, a lozenge; in *pl.*, one of the suits at cards, marked with such a figure; in *sing.*, a card of this suit.

Diapa'son, *n.* L. *diapāsōn*, the whole octave —G. *diapasōn*, *dia pasōn*, concord of the first and last notes, octave-scale, f. *dia*, through + *pasōn*, genit. pl. fem. of *pas*, all (with *chordōn*, genit. pl. of *chordē*, string, understood). The combination of notes in a harmonious whole; a melody, a burst of harmony; the compass of a voice or instrument; the name of certain stops of an organ.

Di'aper, *n.* O.F. *diapre*, orig. *diaspre*, a fine cloth—Med.L. *diasprus*, Byzantine G. *diaspros*, pure white, f. DIA- + *aspros*, white. A linen or cotton fabric with a small diamond pattern; such a pattern; a towel, &c., of the fabric.—*vt.* To put a diaper pattern on.

Diaph'anous, *a.* With -OUS f. Med.L. *diaphanus*—G. *diaphanēs*, f. DIA-, through + *-phanēs*, appearing, f. *phainein*, to show. FANTASY. Transparent.

Di'aphragm, *n.* L. *diaphragma*—G. *diaphragma*, partition-wall, midriff, f. DIA-, apart + *phragma*, fence, f. *phrassein*, to fence in. The partition which divides the two cavities of the body, the midriff; various things resembling this.

Diarrhœ'a, *n.* L. *diarrhoea*—G. *diarrhoia*, a flowing through, the disorder, f. DIA(*r*)*rheein*, to flow through. CATARRH. Immoderate evacuation of the bowels.

Di'ary, *n.* L. *diārium*, daily allowance, later, diary, f. *dies*, day. DIURNAL. A daily record of events; a book for such a record.

Dias'tole, *n.* Med.L.—G. *diastolē*, a putting asunder, dilatation, f. DIA*stellein*, to put asunder. APOSTLE. STOLE. The dilatation of the heart or of an artery.

Diaton'ic, *a.* F. *diatonique*—L. *diatonicus*—G. *diatonikos*, f. DIA-, through, at the interval of + *tonos*, TONE. Of a musical scale, proceeding by the notes proper to the key without chromatic alteration.

Di'atribe, *n.* F. *diatribe*—L. *diatriba*, a learned discussion—G. *diatribē*, a wearing away (of time), study, discourse, f. DIA*tribein*, to rub through or away. A discourse; a bitter criticism, an invective.

Dib'ble, *n.* App. formed (with *-le* instrumental) f. *Dib*, a derivative and weakened form f. DAB. An instrument for making holes for seeds, &c.—*vt.* and *i.* To make a hole in with, to sow, &c., by means of, to use, a dibble.

Dick'y, **Dick'ey**, *n.* Orig. obscure. In the first sense perh. conn. with dial. *Dick*, leather apron, poss. an arbitrary application of the proper name *Dick*. A detached shirt-front; a seat in a carriage for the driver; a seat at the back of a carriage for servants, &c.

Dictate', *vt.* L. *dictāre*, *dictātum*, to declare, say often, dictate for writing, order, freq. of *dīcĕre*. DICTION. DITTY. INDICT. To utter (something to be written down by another); to prescribe, lay down, necessitate (a course or object of action).—**Dic'tate**, *n.* An authoritative direction.—**Dict**A'TION, *n.*—**Dicta'**TOR, *n.* An absolute ruler; one exercising absolute authority; one who dictates to a writer. —**Dictato'r**IAL, *a.*—Of an absolute ruler; overbearing.—**Dicta'tor**SHIP, *n.*

Dic'tion, *n.* L. *dictio*, *dictiōnis*, a speaking, diction, in L.L., a word, f. *dīcĕre*, *dictum*, to say, cogn. with *dicāre*, to proclaim, G. *deiknunai*, to show. ADDICT. DEDICATE. JUDGE. Choice of words and phrases, style.—**Dic'tionary**, *n.* Med.L. *dictiōnārium*, lit. 'a repertory of *dictiones*, i.e., words'. A book setting forth alphabetically the words of a language with their meanings, &c.; an alphabetical book of reference.—**Dic'tum**, *n.*; *pl.* **Dic'ta**, **Dic'tums**. L. *dictum*, thing said, neut. of *dictus*, pa.pple. of *dīcĕre*. A formal pronouncement; a maxim.

Didac'tic, *a.* G. *didaktikos*, apt at teaching, f. *didaskein*, to teach. DISCIPLE. Adapted to teach, instructive.—In *pl.* as *n.*, the science of teaching.—Sim. **Didac't**ICAL, *a.*

Did'dle, *vt.* Recent, of obscure orig. To cheat.

Die, *vi.* M.E. *dyen*, *deyen*, corresp. to O.N. *deyja*, O.S. *dóian*, O.H.G. *touwan*. (Not in O.E. Prob. lost and re-adopted from Norse.) To lose life, cease to live, come to an end; to languish, be consumed with desire; to fade away.

Die, *n.* Early M.E. *dē*, *dee*—O.F. *de*—L. *datum*, something given (app. in late Pop.L. 'something given by fortune', and so applied to dice as determining fortune), neut. of *datus*. DATE.[2] With pl. *dice*, a small cube with the faces marked with spots numbering one to six; the game played with such cubes.—With pl. *dies*, an engraved stamp for impressing a design.—**Dice**, *vi.* To play with dice.—*vt.* To cut into cubes.

Di'et, *n.*[1] O.F. *diete*—L. *diaeta* (in Med.L. *diēta*), G. *diaita*, mode of living, diet. Way of feeding; prescribed way of feeding; food.—*vt.* To prescribe or regulate the food of.—**Di'et**ARY, *n.* A prescribed course of feeding; a book prescribing such a course; an allowance of food.—*a.* Of or pertaining to diet.—**Diet**ET'IC, *a.* In *pl.* as *n.*, the branch of medicine relating to dieting.

Di'et, *n.*[2] Med.L. *diēta* (see prec.) in same sense, prob. associated with L. *dies*, day. DIURNAL. A conference or congress, esp. of the regular meetings of the estates of a realm.

Dif'fer, *vi.* F. *différer*, to differ, to defer—L. *differre*, *dīlātum*, to carry apart, to defer, to tend apart, to differ, f. *dif-* (= DIS- (1)) + *ferre*, to carry, BEAR. CONFER. DEFER.[1] To be unlike in nature, form, &c.; to disagree.—**Dif'fer**ENCE, *n.* Unlikeness; discrimination, distinction; an instance of unlikeness; the remainder left after subtraction; a diversity of opinion, a dispute; an alteration distinguishing the coat of arms of a junior branch of a family.—**Dif'fer**ENT, *a.* Unlike; not the same.—**Dif'ferent**LY,[2] *adv.*—**Differen'**TIAL, *a.* Of or relating to difference; of duties on goods, &c., differing according to circumstances; distinguishing, distinctive.—**Differen'tial**LY,[2] *adv.* Distinctively, by way of difference.—**Differen'tiate**, *vt.* Med.L. *differentiāre, differentiātum.* To make different; to constitute or to note the difference in or between, to distinguish.—*vi.* To discriminate.—**Differenti**A'TION, *n.*

Dif'ficulty, *n.* L. *difficultas* (for *difficilitas*), f. *difficilis*, hard, f. *dif-* (= DIS- (8)) + *facilis*, easy. FACILE. Hardness to be accomplished or understood; an instance of this, a hindrance, an obscure point or question, an embarrassment of affairs; unwillingness.—**Dif'ficult**, *a.* App. f. the *n.* Not easy, troublesome, hard, obscure; hard to please.

Dif'fident, *a.* L. *diffidens, diffidentis*, pres. pple. of *diffīdĕre*, to mistrust, f. *dif-* (= DIS- (4)) + *fīdĕre*, to trust, allied to *fides*, FAITH. Wanting in confidence; timid, shy.—**Dif'fident**LY,[2] *adv.*—**Dif'fid**ENCE, *n.*

Diffract', *vt.* L. *diffringĕre, diffractum*, to break in pieces, f. *dif-* (= DIS- (1)) + *frangĕre*, to break. FRACTION. To deflect and break up (a beam of light).—**Diffrac'**TION, *n.*

Diffuse', *vt.* L. *diffundĕre, diffūsum*, to pour out or away, f. *dif-* (= DIS- (1)) + *fundĕre*, to pour. CONFOUND. To spread abroad.—*a.* Spread abroad; wordy, verbose.—**Diffuse'**LY,[2] *adv.*—**Diffuse'**NESS, *n.*—**Diffu'**SION, *n.*—**Diffu'**SIVE, *a.*—**Diffu'sive**LY,[2] *adv.*

Dig, *vi.* Prob. f. F. *diguer*, to make a dike, f. *digue*, DIKE, of Teut. orig. To work with a spade.—*vt.* To turn up (the earth, &c.) with a spade; to hollow out; to get by digging; to thrust *in* or *into*.—**Dig'**GER, *n.*

Digam'ma, *n.* L.—G., f. *di-*, twice + *gamma*, the letter gamma. (So called from the shape (Ϝ), resembling two gammas (Γ) set one above the other.) A letter of the original Greek alphabet (prob. = Eng. *w*) which suffered disuse.

Digest', *vt.* L. *digerĕre, digestum*, to divide, arrange, to digest (food), f. *di-* (= DIS- (1)) + *gerĕre*, to carry. CONGEST. To arrange methodically; to ponder over; to prepare (food) in the stomach for assimilation; to endure, put up with; to prepare by boiling.—*vi.* Of food, to be digested.—**Di'gest**, *n.* L. *digesta*, orig. neut.pl. pa.pple. of *dīgerĕre*. A methodical summary; the body of the Civil Law.—**Diges'**TIBLE, *a.*—**Diges'**TION, *n.*—**Diges'**TIVE, *a.* Pertaining to or promoting digestion of food.—*n.* A digestive medicine.

Dig'it, *n.* L. *digitus*, a finger, a toe. A finger or toe; a finger's breadth; each of the numerals below ten (orig. counted on the fingers).—**Dig'it**AL, *a.*—**Digita'lis**, *n.* L. *digitālis*, a. f. *digitus* (the name having been given in allusion to the Ger. name *fingerhut*, i.e., thimble). A genus of plants including the foxglove; a medicine prepared from the foxglove.

Dig'nify, *vt.* O.F. *dignifier*—Med.L. *dignificāre*, f. L. *dignus*, worthy + *facĕre*, to make. To confer honour upon; to give a high-sounding name to.—**Dig'nified**, *ppl.a.* Stately, majestic.—**Dig'nity**, *n.* O.F. *digneté*—L. *dignitas*, f. *dignus*. Worthiness, excellence; high estimation, honour; an honourable office, title, &c.; stateliness, gravity.—**Dig'nit**ARY, *n.* One holding high office or rank.

Digress', *vi.* L. *dīgredi, dīgressus*, to go aside, f. *di-* (= DIS- (1)) + *gradi*, to go, f. *gradus*, step. AGGRESSION. To go aside from the course, esp. to deviate from the subject in writing, &c.—**Digres'**SION, *n.*—**Digres'**SIVE, *a.*

Dike, Dyke, *n.* O.E. *dīc*, ditch. Cf. M.H.G. *tīch*, pond, M.L.G. *dīk*, dam. DIG. DITCH. A ditch; an embankment; a low wall.—*vt.* To provide with a dike.

Dilap'idate, *vt.* L. *dīlapidāre, dīlapidātum*, to scatter like stones, to consume, f. *di-* (= DIS- (1)) + *lapidāre*, to throw stones at, f. *lapis, lapidis*, stone. LAPIDARY. To bring into decay or disrepair; to waste, squander.—*vi.* To fall into decay.—**Dilapid**A'TION, *n.* Esp. of impairing ecclesiastical property.

Dilate', *vt.* F. *dilater*—L. *dīlātāre, dīlātātum*, to spread out, widen, f. *dī-* (= DIS- (1)) + *lātus*, wide. LATITUDE. To expand, enlarge.—*vi.* To widen, expand; to discourse or write at large *on* or *upon*.—**Dilat'**ABLE, *a.*—**Dilat**A'TION, also (improperly) **Dila'tion**, *nn.*

Dil'atory, *a.* L. *dīlātōrius*, f. *dīlātor*, a delayer, f. *differre, dīlātum*. DIFFER. DELAY. Tending or intended to cause delay; slow, tardy.—**Dil'atori**LY,[2] *adv.*—**Dil'atori**NESS, *n.*

Dilem'ma, *n.* L. *dilemma*—G. *dilēmma*, double proposition, f. *di-*, twice + *lēmma*. LEMMA. An argument involving an opponent in the choice of two alternatives equally unfavourable; a position of doubt or perplexity.

Dilettan'te, *n.*; *pl.* **-an'ti**. It., f. *dilettare*, L. *dēlectāre*, to DELIGHT. A lover of the fine arts, gen. merely in the way of pastime.

Dil'igent, *a.* F. *diligent*—L. *dīligens, dīligentis*, diligent, orig. pres.pple. of *dīligĕre*, to esteem highly, take delight in (doing), lit. 'to choose between', f. *dī-* (= DIS- (2)) + *legĕre*, to gather, to choose. COLLECT, *v.* PREDILECTION. Constant in endeavour, industrious; actively prosecuted.—**Dil'ig**ENCE, *n.*

Dill, *n.* O.E. *dili, dile* = M.Du., Du. *dille*, O.H.G. *tilli* (Ger. *dill*). An annual yellow-flowered plant with medicinal seeds.

Dilute', *vt.* L. *dīluere, dīlūtum*, to dissolve, dilute. DELUGE. To reduce the strength of (a fluid) by admixture.—*ppl.a.* Weakened thus.—**Dilu'**TION, *n.*

Dilu'vial, *a.* L. *dīluviālis*, a. f. *dīluvium*. DELUGE. Of or belonging to a deluge or flood.

Dim, *a.* O.E. *dim(m)* = Old Fris. *dim*, O.N. *dimmr*. Faintly luminous, not clear; scarcely visible, indistinct; of colour, not bright, faint; of sound, indistinct, faint; not seeing clearly.—**Dim'**LY,[2] *adv.*—**Dim'**NESS, *n.*

Dimen'sion, *n.* F. *dimension*—L. *dīmensio, dīmensiōnis*, n. of action f. *dīmētīri, dīmensus*, to measure out, f. *dī-* (= DIS- (1)) + *mētīri*, to MEASURE. Gen. in *pl.* Measurement, size.

Dimin'ish, *vt.* *Di-* (= DIS- (1)) + MINISH, after L. *dīminuĕre, dīminūtum*, to break into pieces, f. *dī-* (= DIS- (1)) + *minuĕre*, to make smaller. To make smaller, lessen.—*vi.* To become less.—**Diminu'**TION, *n.*—**Dimin'u**TIVE, *a.* Small; minute, tiny; of a word, denoting something small.—*n.* A derivative denoting something small.

Diminuen'do. It., pres.pple. of *diminuire*, L. *dēminuĕre*, to diminish, f. DE- (3) + *minuĕre*. (See prec.) *Mus.*, a direction to decrease gradually the loudness of the tone.

Dim'ity, *n.* It. *dimito*, a kind of coarse cloth = Med.L. *dimitum*—G. *dimitos*, of double thread, a kind of cloth, f. *di-*, twice + *mitos*, a thread of the warp. A cotton fabric woven with raised stripes or fancy figures.

Dim'ple, *n.* M.E. *dympull*. Orig. uncertain. A small hollow in the surface of the body, esp. in the cheeks; any slight hollow.—*vt.* and *i.* To mark with, to break into, dimples.

Din, *n.* O.E. *dyne*, *dynn*, f. Germanic root *dun-*. Cf. Skr. *dhûni*, roaring, a torrent. A loud continued noise distressing to the ear.—*vt.* To assail with din; to repeat so as to weary.—*vi.* To make a din.

Dine, *vi.* F. *dîner*, O.F. *disner*, prob. f. L.L. **disjūnāre* for **disjējūnāre*, to break one's fast, f. DIS- (4) + L. *jējūnāre*, to fast, f. *jējūnus*, fasting. DINNER. JEJUNE. To eat the chief meal of the day.—*vt.* To give dinner to; to accommodate for dining.

Ding'hy, **Ding'ey**, *n.* Hindī *dēngī* or *dingī*, dim. of *dēngā*, *dōngā*, boat, sloop. A small ship's-boat; a pleasure boat. [wooded.

Din'gle, *n.* Of uncertain orig. A dell, gen.

Din'gy, *a.* Recent, of obscure orig. Of a dull or dirty colour or appearance.

Din'ner, *n.* From F. *dîner*, to DINE, used as *n.* The chief meal of the day.

Dint, *n.* O.E. *dynt*, a blow, cogn. with O.N. *dyntr*, *dyttr*, in same sense. DENT. The dealing of blows, force of attack; hence *by dint of*, by force of, by means of; a dent.—*vt.* To mark with dents; to drive in with force.

Di'ocese, *n.* O.F. *diocise*—Med.L. *diocēsis* for L. *diœcēsis*, a governor's jurisdiction, in Late Ecclesiastical L. a diocese—G. *dioikēsis*, house-keeping, administration, province, f. *dioike-ein*, to keep house, administer, f. DI-, through, thoroughly + *oike-ein*, to inhabit, dwell, administer, f. *oikos*, house. ECONOMY. The jurisdiction of a bishop.—**Dioc'es**AN, *a.* As *n.*, the bishop, or one of the clergy or people, of a diocese.

Diop'tric, *a.* G. *dioptrikos*, a. f. *dioptra*, an optical instrument for measuring heights, &c., f. DI- + stem *op-*, to see + instrumental suff. *-tra*. Assisting vision by means of refraction; relating to refraction.

Dip, *vt.* O.E. *dyppan*, cogn. with *díop*, *déop*, DEEP. To put partially or temporarily *in* or *into* a liquid; to immerse, involve, implicate; to lower for an instant.—*vi.* To plunge partially or temporarily *in*, *into*, *under*; to plunge one's hand, &c., into water, &c., esp. in order to take something out; to go down, sink; to slope downwards.—*n.* An act of dipping; downward slope; a hollow or depression.

Diphthe'ria, *n.* F. *diphthérie*—G. *diphthera*, piece of leather. An infectious inflammatory disease of the throat characterized by the formation of a false membrane.

Diph'thong, *n.* F. *diphthongue*—L. *diphthongus*—G. *diphthoggos*, having two sounds, as *n.*, a diphthong, f. *di-*, twice, doubly + *phthoggos*, voice, sound. A union of two vowels pronounced in one syllable.

Diplo'ma, *n.* L. *diplōma*, *diplōmatis*, a state letter of recommendation, a document conferring a privilege—G. *diplōma*, a letter of recommendation, &c., lit., 'a doubling', 'a folded paper', f. *diplo-ein*, to double, fold double, f. *diplo-os*, double. A state paper, a charter; a document conferring an honour or privilege.—**Diplo'macy**, *n.* F. *diplomatie*. The management of international relations; the art of such management, skill in this; address in negotiations or in intercourse of any kind.—**Dip'lomat**, *n.* F. *diplomate*. One engaged in official diplomacy.—So **Diplo'mat**IST, *n.* Also in sense, a shrewd or crafty person.—**Diplomat'**IC, *a.* Of official or original documents, or the management of international relations (in these senses also **Diplomat'**I-CAL); showing address in negotiations or in intercourse of any kind.—**Diplomat'ical**-LY,[2] *adv.* In senses from *diplomatic*.

Dipsoma'nia, *n.* G. *dipsa*, thirst + *mania*, madness, MANIA. A morbid craving for alcohol.—**Dipsoma'niac**, *n.* After MANIAC. One affected with dipsomania.

Dip'tych, *n.* L. *diptycha*, neut. pl. = Late G. *diptucha*, a writing-tablet of two leaves, neut. pl. of *diptuchos*, double-folded, f. *di-*, twice + **ptux*, *ptuchos*, a fold. A writing-tablet of two leaves; a picture composed of two leaves

Dire, *a.* L. *dīrus*. Dreadful, dismal, terrible—**Dire'**FUL, *a.*—**Dire'ful**LY,[2] *adv.*

Direct', *vt.* L. *dīrigĕre*, *dīrectum*, to arrange, direct, guide, f. *dī-* (= DIS- (1)) + *regĕre*, to put straight, rule. DRESS. REGENT. To write the address on (a letter, &c.); to regulate, control; to cause to move or point *to*, *towards*, &c.; to regulate the course of; to order, appoint, prescribe.—*vi.* To order, appoint.—*a.* F. *direct*—L. *dīrectus*, pa.pple. of *dīrigĕre*. Straight; of succession, lineal; going straight to the point, straightforward; without intervening agency, immediate.—**Direc'**TION, *n.* The action or function of directing; a body of directors; the address of a letter, &c.; an instruction, order; aim at a point; the course in which something moves.—**Direc'**TIVE, *a.* Having the quality or function of ruling or guiding or of directing motion.—**Direct'**LY,[2] *adv.* In a straight line; straightforwardly; completely, exactly; by a direct process or mode, immediately; straightway, at once.—**Direct'**NESS, *n.*—**Direct'**OR, *n.* One who directs, rules or guides; one of a board managing a company's affairs; a spiritual adviser.—**Direct'**RESS, **Direct'**RIX, *nn.* A female who directs.—**Direct'or**ATE,[1] *n.* A board of directors the office of a director.—**Direct'or**SHIP, *n*—**Direct'**ORY, *a.* Serving to direct, guiding—*n.* A book of rules or directions; a book containing a list of addresses.

Dirge, *n.* Orig. *dirige*, imp. of *dīrigĕre* (see prec.), the first word of the antiphon in the Office of the Dead, *Dirige, domine . . . viam meam*, Direct, O Lord . . . my way. A song of mourning or lament.

Dir'igible, *a.* L. type **dīrigibilis*, f. *dīrigĕre*, to DIRECT. That can be guided or steered.—*n.* An air-ship on the balloon principle.

Dirk, *n.* Orig. unknown. A kind of dagger.

Dirt, *n.* By metathesis f. M.E. *drit*, prob. f. O.N. *drit*, excrement. (Not in O.E.) Ordure; unclean matter, filth.—**Dirt'**Y,[2] *a.* Soiled, foul; obscene; sordid, mean.—*vt.* and *i.* To make, to become, dirty.—**Dirt'i**LY,[2] *adv.*

Disa'ble, *vt.* DIS- (6). To make unable, incapacitate, cripple, disqualify. — **Disa**BIL'-ITY, *n.* Disqualification.

Disabuse', *vt.* DIS- (4) + ABUSE, *v.* in obs. sense 'to deceive'. To undeceive.

Disadvan'tage, *n.* F. *désavantage*, f. *des-* (= DIS- (7)) + *avantage*, ADVANTAGE. An unfavourable condition or circumstance; loss, detriment.—**Disadvanta'ge**OUS, *a.*

Disaffect', *vt.* DIS- (4) + AFFECT.[1] To dislike; to alienate the affection of, make unfriendly or disloyal.—**Disaffec'**TION, *n.*

Disagree', *vi.* F. *désagréer*, f. *des-* (= DIS- (4)) + *agréer*, to AGREE. To differ, be unlike; to differ in opinion; to refuse to agree; to be at variance, quarrel; of food, &c., to be unsuitable.—**Disagree'**ABLE, *a.* Unpleasing, offensive. — **Disagree'ab**LY,[2] *adv.* — **Disagree'able**NESS, *n.*—**Disagree'**MENT, *n.*

Disallow', *vt.* O.F. *desalouer*, f. *des-* (=DIS- (4))+*alouer*, to ALLOW. To refuse to sanction; to refuse to accept as true, reasonable, &c.; to refuse to grant or accede to; to refuse to allow or permit.—**Disallow'**ANCE, *n.*

Disappear', *vi.* DIS- (4). To cease to appear or be visible; to pass away, be lost.—**Disappear'**ANCE, *n.*

Disappoint', *vt.* F. *désappointer*, f. *des-* (= DIS- (4)) + *appointer* (O.F. *apointer*), to APPOINT. To frustrate the hope or desire of; to balk, foil.—**Disappoint'**MENT, *n.*

Disapproba'tion, *n.* DIS- (7). The action or fact of disapproving, disapproval.

Disapprove', *vt.* DIS- (4). To regard with disfavour or condemnation.—*vi.* With *of* in same sense.—**Disapprov'**AL, *n.*

Disarm', *vt.* F. *désarmer*, f. *des-* (=DIS- (4)) + *armer*, to arm. ARM.[2] To deprive of arms or of a weapon; to render harmless.—**Disarm'**AMENT, *n.*

Disarrange', *vt.* DIS- (4). To throw into disorder.—**Disarrange'**MENT, *n.*

Disas'ter, *n.* F. *désastre*, f. *dés-* (=DIS- (7)) + *astre*, star, fortune, hap — L. *astrum*, G. *astron*, STAR. A calamity.—**Disas'tr**OUS, *a.*

Disavow', *vt.* F. *désavouer*, f. *des-* (=DIS- (4))+*avouer*, to AVOW. To refuse to avow or acknowledge.—**Disavow'**AL, *n.*

Disband', *vt.* Obs. F. *desbander* (now *débander*), after It. *sbandare*, f. *banda*, F. *bande*, BAND.[3] DIS- (5). Cf. Sp., Pg. *disbandar*. To dismiss (troops) from service.—*vi.* To break up, disperse.—**Disband'**MENT, *n.*

Disbar', *vt.* DIS- (5). To expel from the bar.

Disbelieve', *vt.* DIS- (4). Not to believe.—*vi.* To have no credence.—**Disbelief'**, *n.* DIS- (7). Refusal of credence.

Disbow'el, *vt.* DIS- (5). To take out the bowels of.

Disbur'den, *vt.* DIS- (5). To relieve *of* a burden; to get rid of (a burden).

Disburse', *vt.* O.F. *desbourser*, f. *des-* (=DIS- (5))+ *bourse*, Med.L. *bursa*, purse. BURSAR. To pay out (money), to pay (costs, &c.).—**Disburse'**MENT, *n.*

Discard', *vt.* DIS- (5) + CARD.[2] To throw out (a card) from the hand; to cast off, reject, give up; to cashier, dismiss.—*n.* The act of discarding a card; a card discarded.

Discern', *vt.* F. *discerner*—L. *discernĕre*, to separate, distinguish, f. DIS- (2) + *cernĕre*, to separate. CONCERN. To distinguish, see the difference between; to perceive by the intellect or the eye.—**Discern'**IBLE, *a.*—**Discern'**MENT, *n.* The act of discerning; the faculty of discerning, penetration, insight.

Discharge', *vt.* O.F. *descharger*—L.L. type **discarricāre*, f. DIS- (4) + *carricāre*, to load. CHARGE. To unload (a ship, &c.); to fire off (a firearm); to relieve *of*, release *from* (an obligation, &c.); to cashier, dismiss; to liberate from custody, to let go; to unload from a ship, &c.; to let fly (a missile); to emit; to acquit oneself of; to pay.—*n.* An unloading; a firing off, a letting fly; emission; something emitted; release, exoneration; acquittal; dismissal from service, &c.; liberation; a document importing release; payment; fulfilment.

Disci'ple, *n.* O.E. *discipul*—L. *discipulus*, learner, pupil, f. *discĕre*, to learn, cogn. with *docēre*, G. *didaskein*, to teach. DOCILE. DIDACTIC. A pupil, scholar, follower; one who follows the doctrine or example of another.—**Disci'ple**SHIP, *n.*—**Dis'cipline**, *n.* F. *discipline*—L. *disciplina*, instruction, tuition, f. *discipulus*. A course of instruction; training mental and moral; military training, the result of such training; order maintained and observed; a system of rules of conduct; a system or method of maintaining order; correction, chastisement; a scourge.—*vt.* To train; to chastise. — **Dis'ciplin**ABLE, *a.* — **Dis'ciplin**ARY, *a.*—**Disciplina'ri**AN, *n.* One who enforces discipline, esp. strictly.

Disclaim', *vi.* A.F. *des-*, *disclamer* (accented stem *des-*, *disclaime*), f. *des-*, DIS- (4) + A.F. and O.F. *clamer*, to CLAIM. To renounce a claim.—*vt.* To renounce a claim to; to repudiate or disavow.—**Disclaim'er**, *n.* A.F. *disclaimer* as *n.* An act of disclaiming.

Disclose', *vt.* O.F. *desclos-*, pres. stem of *desclore*, to unclose — Med.L. *disclaudĕre*, f. DIS- (4) + L. *claudĕre*, to CLOSE. To uncover and expose to view; to make known, reveal.—**Disclos'**URE. *n.*

Discol'our, *vt.* O.F. *descolorer*, *descoulourer*, f. *des-* (= DIS- (4)) + L. *colōrāre*, to colour, f. *color*, COLOUR. To spoil the colour of, stain; to deprive of colour.—*vi.* To become discoloured.—**Discolor**A'TION, *n.*

Discom'fit, *vt.* O.F. *desconfit*, pa.pple. of *desconfire* (F. *déconfire*), to discomfit — Late Pop.L. *disconficĕre*, f. DIS- (4) + L. *conficĕre*. COMFIT. To defeat, overthrow; to thwart, foil, disconcert.—**Discom'fit**URE, *n.*

Discom'fort, *vt.* O.F. *desconforter*, f. *des-* (= DIS- (4)) + *conforter*, to COMFORT. To make uneasy, mentally or physically.—*n.* Uneasiness of mind or body; a cause of this.

Discompose', *vt.* DIS- (4). To agitate, disquiet.—**Discompos'**URE, *n.*

Disconcert', *vt.* Obs. F. *disconcerter* (now *déconcerter*), f. DIS- (4) + *concerter*, to CONCERT. To put out of concert, disarrange, frustrate; to confuse, ruffle (a person).

Disconnect', *vt.* DIS- (4). To disjoin, separate.—**Disconnect'ed**, *ppl.a.* Incoherent.

Discon'solate, *a.* Med L. *disconsōlātus*, f. DIS- (4) + L. *consōlātus*, pa.pple. of *consōlārī*, to CONSOLE. Unhappy, comfortless.

Discontent', *a.* DIS- (8). Not content.—*vt.* DIS- (4). To make dissatisfied.—*n.* DIS- (7). Dissatisfaction.

Discontin'ue, *vt.* F. *discontinuer*—Med.L. *discontinuāre*, f. DIS- (4) + L. *continuāre*, to CONTINUE. To cease from, put a stop to; to cease to pay, receive, &c.; to leave off, give up. — **Discontin'u**ANCE, *n.* — **Discontinu'**ITY, *n.*—**Discontin'u**OUS, *a.*

Dis'cord, *n.* O.F. *des-*, *discord*, f. *des-*, *discorder*, L. *discordāre*, to be at variance, f. *discors*, *discordis*, discordant, f. DIS- (1) + *cor*, heart. CORDIAL. Absence of concord, variance, dissension; difference, diversity; disagreement of sounds. — **Discor'd**ANCE, *n.*—**Discor'd**ANT, *a.*

Discount', *vt.* O.F. *desconter*, *descompter*, to reckon back or off = Med.L. *discomputāre*, f. DIS- (4) + L. *computāre*, to COUNT, COMPUTE. Formerly, to abate, deduct. To give or receive the present value of (a bill of exchange, &c., not yet due); to detract from, lessen; to allow for exaggeration in.—**Dis'count**, *n.* A deduction made on discounting a bill, on paying an account, &c.; discounting of bills, &c.

Discoun'tenance, *vt.* Obs. F. *descontenancer*, to abash, f. *des-* (= DIS- (4)) + *contenancer*, to COUNTENANCE. To abash, disconcert. From DIS- (5) + COUNTENANCE, *n.* To withdraw countenance from, disfavour.

Discour'age, *vt.* O.F. *descoragier*, f. *des-* (= DIS- (5)) + *corage*, COURAGE. To dishearten, dispirit; to discountenance, show disapproval of.—**Discour'age**MENT, *n.*

Discourse', *n.* F. *discours*—L. *discursus*, a running to and fro, in L.L., a conversation, f. *discurrĕre, discursum*, to run to and fro, f. DIS- (1) + *currĕre*, to run. CURRENT. Conversation; a conversation; a dissertation, speech, treatise, &c.—*vi.* To converse; to speak or write a discourse.—*vt.* To treat of, tell, relate; to utter (musical sounds).

Discour'teous, *a.* DIS- (8). Rude, uncivil.—**Discour'tesy**, *n.* DIS- (7). Rudeness, incivility; an instance of this.

Discov'er, *vt.* O.F. *descovrir*—Med.L. *discooperire*, f. DIS- (4) + L. *cooperire*, to COVER. To expose to view, reveal; to make known; to display, exhibit; to obtain sight or knowledge of; to find out.—**Discov'er**ABLE, *a.*—**Discov'er**ER, *n.*—**Discov'er**Y,[1] *n.*

Discred'it, *vt.* DIS- (4). To refuse to credit; to take away confidence in; to bring into disrepute.—*n.* DIS- (7). Loss or want of reputation or of belief or confidence.—**Discred'itable**. DIS- (8). Disreputable, disgraceful.

Discreet', *a.* F. *discret*—L. *discrētus*, separate, distinct, in L.L., discreet, pa.pple. of *discernĕre*. DISCERN. Prudent, judicious; knowing when to be silent.—**Discreet'**LY,[2] *adv.*—**Discre'tion**, *n.* O.F. *des-, discrecion*—L.L. *discrētio, discrētiōnis*. Prudence, sound judgement; power of disposal.—**Discre'tion**ARY, *a.* Limited only by discretion or judgement.

Dis'crepant, *a.* L. *discrepans, discrepantis*, pres.pple. of *discrepāre*, to differ, lit., 'to sound discordantly', f. DIS- (1)+*crepāre*, to make a noise, creak. Different, inharmonious, inconsistent.—**Discrep'**ANCY, *n.*

Discrim'inate, *vt.* L. *discrīmināre, discrīminātum*, to divide, separate, f. *discrīmen, discrīminis*, division, separation, f. *discernĕre*. DISCERN. Cf. CRIME. To distinguish, differentiate; to perceive the difference in or between.—*vi.* To make a distinction; with *against*, to make an adverse distinction in regard to.—*a.* Making careful or exact distinctions.—**Discrimin**A'TION, *n.*—**Discrim'inat**IVE, *a.*

Discur'sive, *a.* L. *discurs-*, ppl. stem of *discurrĕre*+-IVE. DISCOURSE. Passing rapidly from subject to subject, rambling.

Discuss', *vt.* L. *discutĕre, discussum*, to shake to pieces, in L.L., to discuss, f. DIS- (1)+*quatĕre*, to shake. CONCUSS. To investigate by argument, debate; to try the quality of, consume (food, &c.).—**Discus'**SION, *n.*

Disdain', *vt.* O.F. *desdeignier*, representing, with *des-* for L. *dē-*, L. *dēdignāre* (by-form of *dēdignāri*), to deem unworthy, f. DE- (5)+ *dignāre*. DEIGN. To despise, scorn; to scorn (*to do* or *doing* something).—*n.* Scorn, contempt.—**Disdain'**FUL, *a.*

Disease', *n.* O.F. *desaise*, want of ease, f. *des-* (=DIS- (7))+*aise*, EASE. Formerly, want of ease. The condition of being out of health; a malady.—*vt.* To cause disease in.

Disembark', *vt.* and *i.* F. *désembarquer*, f. *des-* (=DIS- (4))+*embarquer*, to EMBARK. To put or go ashore from a ship, to land.—**Disembark**A'TION, *n.*

Disembod'y, *vt.* DIS- (4). To separate from the body; to disband (troops).

Disembogue', *vi.* and *t.* Sp. *desembocar*, to come out of the mouth of a river, f. *des-* (=DIS- (4)) + *embocar*, to run up into a creek, f. *en*, in +*boca*, mouth, L. *bucca*, cheek. Of a river, &c., to flow out, to discharge (its waters).

Disembow'el, *vt.* App. an intensive of DISBOWEL.

Disenchant', *vt.* F. *désenchanter*, f. *des-* (= DIS- (4)) + *enchanter*, to ENCHANT. To set free from enchantment or illusion.—**Disenchant'**MENT, *n.*

Disendow', *vt.* DIS- (4). To strip of endowments.—**Disendow'**MENT, *n.*

Disenfran'chise, *vt.* DIS- (4). To deprive of civil or electoral privileges.

Disengage', *vt.* DIS- (4). To detach, liberate.—**Disengaged'**, *ppl.a.* Detached; unoccupied, at liberty.—**Disengage'**MENT, *n.*

Disentail', *vt.* DIS- (4). To free from entail.—*n.* The act of disentailing.

Disentan'gle, *vt.* DIS- (4). To disengage, extricate; to unravel, untwist.—**Disentan'gle**MENT, *n.* [or right *to.*

Disenti'tle, *vt.* DIS- (4). To deprive of title

Disestab'lish, *vt.* DIS- (4). To annul the establishment of.—**Disestab'lish**MENT, *n.*

Disesteem', *vt.* DIS- (4). To slight, despise.—*n.* DIS- (7). Low estimation or regard.

Disfa'vour, *vt.* DIS- (4). To regard with disapproval.—*n.* DIS- (7). Disapproval; the condition of being unfavourably regarded.

Disfig'ure, *vt.* O.F. *desfigurer*, f. DIS- (5) + L. *figūra*, form, FIGURE. To mar the form of, deface.—**Disfigur**A'TION, *n.*—**Disfig'ure**MENT, *n.*

Disfran'chise, *vt.* DIS- (4) + obs. *Franchise* = ENFRANCHISE. The same as DISENFRANCHISE.—**Disfran'chise**MENT, *n.*

Disgorge', *vt.* O.F. *desgorger*, f. *des-* (=DIS- (5)) + *gorge*, throat. GORGE. To eject from the throat; to give up, make restitution of.

Disgrace', *n.* F. *disgrâce*—It. *disgrazia*, f. DIS- (7) + *grazia*, L. *grātia*, favour. GRACE. The state of being out of favour and honour; shame, ignominy; a cause of shame.—*vt.* To put out of favour and honour; to bring shame or discredit upon.—**Disgrace'**FUL, *a.*

Disguise', *vt.* O.F. *desguisier*, f. *des-* (=DIS- (5)) + *guise*. GUISE. To change the attire and aspect of so as to conceal identity; to misrepresent; to conceal, cloak.—*n.* The state of being disguised; a dress contrived to conceal identity; a false appearance; the act or practice of disguising.

Disgust', *vt.* Obs. F. *desgouster*, to dislike, f. *des-* (= DIS- (4)) + *gouster* (now *goûter*), L. *gustāre*, to taste, enjoy, f. *gustus*, taste. GUST.[2] Formerly, to dislike, loathe. To offend the taste or smell of; to excite aversion or repugnance in.—*n.* Loathing, aversion, repugnance.—**Disgust'**FUL, *a.*

Dish, *n.* O.E. *disc*—L. *discus*, quoit, dish, DISK. A vessel for containing food at table; a portion, a variety, of food; a dishful.—*vt.* To put into a dish to be eaten; to defeat completely, to circumvent; to present attractively (gen. with *up*). [dispirit.

Dishear'ten, *vt.* DIS- (4). To discourage,

Dishev'el, *vt.* Obs. F. *descheveler* (now *décheveler*), f. *des-* (= DIS- (5)) + *chevel* (now *cheveu*), L. *capillus*, hair. To loosen and throw abroad (the hair).—**Dishev'elled**, *ppl.a.* With the hair disordered; of the hair, in disorder; ruffled; disorderly, untidy.

Dishon'est, *a.* O.F. *deshoneste*—L. *dehonestus*, f. DE- (5) + *honestus*, honourable. HONEST. Of actions, fraudulent, knavish; of persons, wanting in honesty, disposed to cheat.—**Dishon'est**LY,[2] *adv.*—**Dishon'est**Y,[1] *n.*

Dishon'our, *n.* O.F. *deshonor* (F. *déshonneur*), f. DIS- (7) + L. *honor*, HONOUR. Ignominy, disgrace; a cause of shame; failure to honour a bill, &c.—*vt.* To treat with dishonour; to bring dishonour upon; to fail to honour (a bill, &c.).—**Dishon'our**ABLE, *a.* Involving disgrace; unprincipled, base.

Disincline', *vt.* DIS- (4). To make averse or unwilling.—**Disinclin**A'TION, *n.*

Disinfect', *vt.* DIS- (4). To cleanse from infection.—**Disinfect'**ANT, *a.* and *n.*—**Disinfec'**TION, *n.*

Disingen'uous, *a.* DIS- (8). Lacking frankness, insincere.—**Disingen'uous**LY,[2] *adv.*

Disinher'it, *vt.* DIS- (4) + INHERIT in obs. sense 'to cause to inherit'. To deprive of an inheritance.—**Disinher'it**ANCE, *n.*

Disin'tegrate, *vt.* DIS- (4). To reduce to pieces, break up; to separate, break off.—*vi.* To break up.—**Disintegr**A'TION, *n.*

Disin'terested, *ppl.a.* DIS- (8). Not influenced by personal interest, impartial.

Disjoin', *vt.* and *i.* O.F. *desjoign-*, pres. stem of *desjoindre*—L. *disjungĕre*, *disjunctum*, f. DIS- (4) + *jungĕre*, to JOIN. To separate, sever. —**Disjoint'**, *vt.* From obs. *disjoint*, ppl.a. —O.F. *desjoint*, pa.pple. of *desjoindre*. To put out of joint or orderly connexion, dislocate; to disjoin; to divide at the joints.—**Disjoint'ed**, *ppl.a.* Disjoined, separated; incoherent, disconnected.—**Disjunc'**TION, *n.*—**Disjunc'**TIVE, *a.* Separating, involving separation; of conjunctions, expressing an alternative or implying an adversative relation. —*n.* A disjunctive conjunction.

Disk, **Disc**, *n.* L. *discus*, G. *diskos*, quoit, dish, disk. DAIS. DESK. DISH. A thin circular plate; anything resembling this; the (apparently flat) surface of the sun, moon, &c.; any round luminous flat surface.

Dislike', *vt.* DIS- (4). Not to like, to disrelish.—*n.* Distaste, aversion; an aversion.

Dis'locate, *vt.* Med.L. *dislocāre*, *dislocātum*, to put out of place, f. DIS- (1) + L. *locāre*, to place, f. *locus*, place. LOCAL. To put out of place, displace; to put out of proper position, esp. of a bone; to put into disorder, disarrange. —**Disloc**A'TION, *n.*

Dislodge', *vt.* O.F. *deslogier*, to leave or cause to leave a lodging-place, f. *des-* (= DIS- (4)) + *logier*, to lodge, f. *loge*. LODGE. To displace; to drive out.—*vi.* To remove.—**Dislodge'**MENT, **Dislodg'**MENT, *n.*

Disloy'al, *a.* O.F. *desloial*, f. *des-* (= DIS- (8)) + *loial*, LOYAL. Not loyal, faithless.—**Disloy'al**LY,[2] *adv.*—**Disloy'al**TY, *n.*

Dis'mal, *a.* App. O.F. *dis mal* = L. *dies mali*, evil or unlucky days. (Treated as an *a.*, with the addition of *days*, and then used as an *a.* generally.) Disastrous, calamitous; dreary, cheerless; denoting gloom or depression.

Disman'tle, *vt.* Obs. F. *desmanteller*, to take a man's cloak off, raze (walls), f. *des-* (= DIS- (4)) + O.F. *manteler*, to cloak, f. *mantel*, cloak. MANTLE. To strip *of* (clothing, covering, &c.); to strip of equipment, furniture, &c.; to pull down, raze.—**Disman'tle**MENT, *n.*

Dismast', *vt.* DIS- (5). To deprive of masts.

Dismay', *vt.* App. represents O.F. **desmaier* = Sp. *desmayar*, to swoon, to dismay, f. *des-* (= DIS- (4)) + *mag-*, app. f. O.H.G. *magan*, to be able, cogn. with MAY, *v.*[2]. To daunt, dishearten.—*n.* Consternation.

Dismem'ber, *vt.* O.F. *desmembrer*—Med.L. *dismembrāre*, *dēmembrāre*, f. DIS- (5), DE- (6) + L. *membrum*, limb. MEMBER. To cut or tear limb from limb; to divide, partition.—**Dismem'ber**MENT, *n.*

Dismiss', *vt.* App. (with altered pref.) f. L. *dīmittĕre*, *dīmissum*, to send different ways, f. *di-* (= DIS- (1)) + *mittĕre*, to send. DEMISE. MISSION. To disperse, to disband; to send away; to remove from office, &c., discard; to put away from the mind; to treat summarily —**Dismiss'**AL, *n.*—**Dismis'**SION, *n.*

Dismount', *vi.* DIS- (4). To get down from a horse.—*vt.* To throw down from a horse; to remove (a thing) from its mounting.

Disobey', *vi.* and *t.* F. *désobéir*—Romanic *dis-*, *desobēdīre*, f. DIS- (4) + L. *obēdīre*, to OBEY. Not to obey.—**Disobe'dient**, *a.* O.F. *desobédient*, f. *des-* (= DIS- (8)) + *obēdiens*, *obēdientis*, pres.pple. of *obēdīre*. Refusing or neglecting to obey.—**Disobe'di**ENCE, *n.*

Disoblige', *vt.* F. *désobliger*, f. *dés-* (= DIS- (4)) + L. *obligāre*. OBLIGE. To refuse or neglect to oblige; to put a slight on, affront.

Disor'der, *vt.* App. a modification, after ORDER, *v.*, of earlier *desordene*, *disordeine*—O.F. *desordener*, f. *des-* (= DIS- (4)) + *ordener*, to put in order. ORDAIN. To put out of order, disarrange; to derange the functions of, to put out of health.—*n.* Confusion, confused condition; a want of order, a breach of rule, an irregularity; commotion, tumult; riot, mutiny; a disturbance of the bodily or mental functions.—**Disor'dered**, *ppl.a.* Disarranged, confused; affected with bodily or mental disorder.—**Disor'der**LY,[1] *a.* Confused, irregular; unruly, tumultuous; violating public order or morality.

Disor'ganize, *vt.* F. *désorganiser*, f. *dés-* (= DIS- (4)) + *organiser*, to ORGANIZE. To destroy the organization of, throw into confusion.—**Disorganiz**A'TION, *n.*

Disown', *vt.* DIS- (4). Not to own, to repudiate.

Dispar'age, *vt.* O.F. *desparagier*, to match unequally, later, to impose unworthy conditions on, f. *des-* (= DIS- (5)) + *parage*, L.L. *parāticum*, equality of rank, f. L. *pār*, equal. COMPARE. To bring discredit upon; to speak of or treat slightingly.—**Dispar'age**MENT, *n.*

Dis'parate, *a.* L. *disparātus*, pa.pple. of *disparāre*, to separate, f. DIS- (1) + *parāre*, to make ready. (App. influenced in sense by L. *dispar*, unequal, unlike.) PARE. Differing in kind, without relation.

Dispar'ity, *n.* F. *disparité*, f. DIS- (7) + *paritas*, PARITY. Want of equality; an instance of this; dissimilarity; an instance of this.

Dispas'sionate, *a.* DIS- (8). Free from the influence of passion; calm, composed; impartial.—**Dispas'sionate**LY,[2] *adv.*

Dispatch', **Despatch'**, *vt.* Sp. *despachar*, to dispatch, expedite, f. DIS- (4) + L. type **pactāre*, to fasten, fix, f. *pangĕre*, *pactum*, to fix. To send off in haste (a messenger, &c.); to kill; to get done, finish off, promptly or speedily; to eat up.—*n.* The sending off (of a messenger, &c.); killing; prompt or speedy accomplishment; speed; a written (esp. official) communication.

Dispeace', *n.* DIS- (7). Uneasiness of mind; [dissension.

Dispel', *vt.* L. *dispellĕre*, to drive asunder, scatter, f. DIS- (1) + *pellĕre*, to drive. COMPEL. To dissipate, disperse.

Dispense', *vt.* O.F. *dispenser*—L. *dispensāre*, to distribute by weight, manage, distribute, in Med.L., to deal with a person in accordance with ecclesiastical law, freq. of *dispendĕre*, *dispensum*, to weigh out, f. DIS- (1) + *pendĕre*, to cause to hang down, to weigh. APPEND. To deal out, distribute; to administer (justice, a sacrament, &c.); to make up (a medicine); to release *from* an obligation.—*vi.* To grant dispensations; *to dispense with*, to give special exemption or relief from, to relax the obligation of (a vow, &c.), to do away with (a requirement, &c.), to forgo, do without.—**Dispens'**ABLE, *a.*—**Dispens'**ARY, *n.* A place in which medicines are dispensed.—**Dispens**A'TION, *n.* The action of dispensing or dealing out; a provision of providence or of nature; the granting of a licence dispensing with a law, the licence.

Disperse', *vt.* F. *disperser*, f. *dispers*, L. *dispersus*, pa.pple. of *dispergĕre*, to scatter, f. DIS- (1) + *spargĕre*, to sprinkle, strew. SPARSE. To scatter; to rout; to send to, or station at, various points; to diffuse, disseminate.—*vi.* To separate.—**Disper'**SION, *n.*

Dispir'it, *vt.* Formerly also *dis-spirit*. DIS- (5). To discourage, dishearten.

Displace', *vt.* O.F. *desplacer*, f. *des-* (= DIS- (4)) + *placer*, to place, f. *place*, PLACE. To move from its place; to remove from a position, dignity, &c.; to put something else in the place of; to supplant.—**Displace'**MENT, *n.*

Display', *vt.* O.F. *despleier*—L.L. *displicāre*. DEPLOY. SPLAY. To expose to view, show; to exhibit, make manifest; to reveal unintentionally or incidentally.—*n.* An exposing to view; exhibition, manifestation; an exhibition, a show; show, ostentation.

Displease', *vi.* O.F. *desplaisir*—L. *displicēre*, f. DIS- (4) + *placēre*, to PLEASE. To be disagreeable, cause dislike.—*vt.* To offend, annoy.—**Displeas'ure**, *n.* DIS- (7). Dissatisfaction, disapproval; anger, indignation.

Disport', *v.refl.* and *i.* O.F. *se desporter*, f. *des-* (= DIS- (1)) + *porter*, L. *portare*, to carry (the notion being that of diverting the attention from serious occupations). COMPORT. SPORT. To frolic, gambol.—*n.* Relaxation.

Dispose', *vt.* O.F. *disposer*, f. DIS- (1) + *poser*, to place. POSE.[1] To arrange in a particular order or manner; to incline, make prone, *to* or *to do*; to give a tendency or inclination to.—*vi.* To ordain, appoint; *to dispose of*, to deal with definitely, get rid of, settle, finish, sell.—**Dispo'**SAL, *n.* A disposing of; control, command.—**Disposi'tion**, *n.* F. *disposition*, L. *dispositio*, *dispositiōnis*, f. *dispōnĕre*, *dispositum*, to arrange, f. DIS- (1) + *pōnĕre*, to place. POSITION. Arrangement, order; plan, preparation; condition of affairs; disposal, control; turn of mind; inclination.

Dispossess', *vt.* O.F. *despossesser*, f. *des-* (= DIS- (4)) + *possesser*, to POSSESS. To put out of possession.—**Disposses'**SION, *n.*

Dispraise', *vt.* O.F. *despreisier*—L.L. type **dispretiāre* for L. *dēpretiāre*. DEPRECIATE. To blame, censure.—*n.* Blame, censure.

Disproof', *n.* DIS- (7). Refutation.

Dispropor'tion, *n.* DIS- (7). Want of proportion or symmetry.—*vt.* To make out of due proportion.—**Dispropor'tion**ATE,[2] *a.*

Disprove', *vt.* O.F. *desprover*, f. *des-* (= DIS- (4)) + *prover*, to PROVE. To refute, rebut.

Dispute', *vi.* O.F. *desputer*—L. *disputāre*, *disputātum*, to reckon up, investigate, discuss, in L.L. to dispute, contend in words, f. DIS- (1) + *putāre*, to reckon. COMPUTE. To debate, discuss, argue.—*vt.* To debate, discuss, argue; to call in question, impugn; to oppose, resist (an action, &c.); to contend for the possession of, contest (a prize, &c.).—*n.* Debate, controversy; a debate, a controversy: a quarrel.—**Dis'put**ABLE, *a.*—**Dis'put**ANT, *n.*—**Disput**A'TION, *n.*—**Disputa'**TIOUS, *a.*

Disqual'ify, *vt.* DIS- (4). To render unqualified.—**Disquali**FICA'TION, *n.*

Disqui'et, *vt.* DIS- (4). To deprive of quietness, make uneasy.—*n.* Uneasiness, unrest.—**Disqui'**ETUDE, *n.*

Disquisi'tion, *n.* L. *disquīsitio*, *disquīsitiōnis*, f. *disquīrĕre*, *disquīsitum*, to inquire diligently, f. DIS- (3) + *quaerĕre*, to search, seek. QUEST. Diligent investigation; a learned or elaborate treatise or discourse.

Disregard', *vt.* DIS- (4). To pay no regard to.—*n.* Neglect, inattention.

Disrel'ish, *vt.* DIS- (4). To have a distaste for, dislike.—*n.* Distaste, dislike.

Disrepair', *n.* DIS- (7). The state of being out of repair.

Disrepute', *n.* DIS- (7). Ill repute, disesteem.—**Disrep'utable**, *a.* DIS- (8). Discreditable; in ill repute.

Disrespect', *n.* DIS- (7). Want of respect.—**Disrespect'**FUL, *a.*

Disrobe', *vt.* and *i.* DIS- (4). To undress.

Disrupt', *vt.* L. *disrumpĕre*, *disruptum*, to break asunder, f. DIS- (1) + *rumpĕre*, to break. ABRUPT. To break in pieces, shatter.—**Disrup'**TION, *n.*—**Disrup'**TIVE, *a.*

Dissat'isfy, *vt.* DIS- (4). To make unsatisfied, fail to satisfy.—**Dissatisfac'tion**, *n.* DIS- (7). Discontent.

Dissect', *vt.* L. *dissecāre*, *dissectum*, f. DIS- (1) + *secāre*, to cut. BISECT. To cut in pieces; to cut up (a body, &c.) for systematic examination; to examine minutely.—**Dissec'**TION, *n.*

Dissem'ble, *vt.* App. a later form of obs. *Dissimule* in sim. senses—O.F. *dissimuler*—L. *dissimulāre*, *dissimulātum*, to feign that a thing is not that which it is, f. *dissimilis*, unlike, f. DIS- (8) + *similis*, like. DISSIMULATE. SIMILAR. To cloak or disguise by a feigned appearance.—*vi.* To dissemble one's intentions, opinions, &c.—**Dissem'bl**ER, *n.*

Dissem'inate, *vt.* L. *dissēmināre*, *dissēminātum*, to spread abroad, disseminate, f. DIS- (1) + *sēmināre*, to sow, f. *sēmen*, *sēminis*, seed. SEMINARY. To scatter abroad; to spread abroad, diffuse.—**Dissemin**A'TION, *n.*

Dissent', *vi.* L. *dissentīre*, *dissensum*, f. DIS- (1) + *sentīre*, to think. ASSENT. Not to consent; to differ in opinion *from*; to differ from the doctrine, &c., of an established church.—*n.* Disagreement; disagreement with the doctrine, &c., of an established church; the dissenting section of a community.—**Dissent'**ER, *n.*—**Dissen'**SION, *n.* Disagreement; discord.—**Dissen'ti**ENT, *a.* Disagreeing, esp. with the opinion of the majority.

Dis'sertate, *vi.* L. *dissertāre*, *dissertātum*, freq. of *disserĕre*, *dissertum*, lit. 'to set forth in order', hence, to examine, to discourse, f. DIS- (1) + *serĕre*, to join. ASSERT. To discourse.—**Dissert**A'TION, *n.*

Disser'vice, *n.* DIS- (7). Injury; an injury.

Dissev'er, *vt.* O.F. *dessevrer*—L. *dissēparāre*, f. DIS- (3) + *sēparāre*, to SEPARATE. To divide, disunite.—*vi.* To separate, part.

Dis'sidence, *n.* L. *dissidentia*, f. *dissidēre*, to sit apart, disagree, f. DIS- (1) + *sedēre*, to sit. ASSESS. Disagreement, difference, dissent.—**Dis'sid**ENT, *a.*

Dissim'ilar, *a.* DIS- (8). Not similar, unlike.—**Dissimilar'**ITY, *n.*

Dissim'ulate, *vt.* and *i.* L. *dissimulāre*. = DISSEMBLE.—**Dissimul**A'TION, *n.*

Dis'sipate, *vt.* L. *dissipāre*, *dissipātum* to

scatter, f. DIS- (1) + archaic *sipāre*, to throw, throw about. To scatter; to disperse, cause to disappear; to disintegrate; to waste, squander. —*vi.* To disperse; to disappear; to disintegrate; to engage in frivolous or dissolute pleasures.—**Dissipa'**TION, *n.*—**Dis'sipated**, *ppl.a.* In senses from the *v.*; dissolute.

Disso'ciate, *vt.* L. *dissociāre, dissociātum*, f. DIS- (4) + *sociāre*, to join, unite. ASSOCIATE. To separate, sever.—**Dissocia'**TION, *n.*

Dis'solute, *a.* L. *dissolūtus*, pa.pple. of *dissolvĕre*. (See next.) Lax in morals, profligate.

Dissolve', *vt.* L. *dissolvĕre, dissolūtum*, to loosen asunder, f. DIS- (1) + *solvĕre*, to loosen. ABSOLVE. To melt in a fluid, liquefy; to destroy, undo; to break up, disperse (an assembly, &c.); to put an end to (association, connexion, &c.); to annul, abrogate.—*vi.* To vanish, disappear; to become liquefied; of an assembly, &c., to break up, disperse.—**Dis'solu**BLE, *a.*—**Dissolu'tion**, *n.*

Dis'sonant, *a.* F. *dissonant*—L. *dissonans, dissonantis*, pres.pple. of *dissonāre*, to disagree in sound, differ, f. DIS- (1) + *sonāre*, to sound. ASSONANCE. Disagreeing in sound, jarring; discordant, at variance.—**Dis'son**ANCE, *n.*

Dissuade', *vt.* L. *dissuādēre, dissuāsum*, to advise from or against, f. DIS- (1) + *suādēre*, to advise, urge. PERSUADE. SUASION. To divert *from* (a course or action) by personal influence. —**Dissua'**SION, *n.*—**Dissua'**SIVE, *a.*

Dis(s)yl'lable, *n.* After *syllable* f. F. *dissyllabe*—L. *disyllabus* = G. *disullabos*, of two syllables, f. *di-*, twice + *sullabē*, SYLLABLE. A word or metrical foot consisting of two syllables.—**Dis(s)yllab'**IC, *a.*

Dis'taff, *n.* O.E. *distæf*, supposed to be for *dis-* or *dise-stæf*. STAFF. (*Dis* or *dise* app. = L.G. *diesse*, a bunch of flax on a distaff, conn. with DIZEN.) A staff on which wool or flax was wound for spinning.

Dis'tance, *n.* O.F. *distance*—L. *distantia*, lit., 'a standing apart', hence, remoteness, f. *distans, distantis*, pres.pple. of *distāre*, to stand apart, f. *dī-* (= DIS- (1)) + *stāre*, to stand. CONSTANT. Remoteness; the extent of space between two objects; excessive reserve or dignity.—*vt.* To outstrip, excel.—**Dis'**TANT, *a.* Separate or apart in space (by a specified interval); far apart; remote; reserved in intercourse.—**Dis'tant**LY,[2] *adv.*

Distaste', *n.* DIS- (7). Disinclination, dislike.—**Distaste'**FUL, *a.* Disagreeable to the taste; causing dislike.

Distem'per, *v.*[1]*t.* Med.L. **distemperāre*, f. DIS- (4) + L. *temperāre*. TEMPER. To disorder in health or sanity.—*n.*[1] Derangement; ill health; a disease, esp. in dogs.

Distem'per, *v.*[2]*t.* O.F. *destemprer*, to dissolve, soak, f. DIS- (1) or (3) + L. *temperāre*. (See prec.) To paint in distemper.—*n.*[2] A method of painting in which the colours are mixed with size, yolk of egg, &c.

Distend', *vt.* and *i.* L. *distendĕre, distentum* (in L.L. also *distensum*), to stretch asunder, f. DIS- (1) + *tendĕre*, to stretch. ATTEND. To swell out by pressure from within, expand.—**Disten'**SIBLE, *a.*—**Disten'**SION, *n.*

Dis'tich, *n.* L. *distichon*—G. *distichon*, neut. of *distichos*, of two rows or verses, f. *di-*, twice + *stichos*, row, line of verse. A couplet.

Distil', *vi.* L. *distillāre*, more correctly *destillāre*, to drip or trickle down, f. DE- (1) + *stillāre*, to drop. STILL, *n.* To trickle down, fall, or issue forth in minute drops; to pass or condense from a still.—*vt.* To let fall or give forth in minute drops; to obtain (a substance or one of its constituents) in a state of purity by evaporation and condensation.—**Distilla'**TION, *n.*—**Distil'l**ER, *n.* One who distils, esp. one who extracts alcoholic spirit by distillation.—**Distil'l**ERY, *n.*

Distinct', *a.* L. *distinctus*, pa.pple. of *distinguĕre*. (See next.) Not identical; separate, apart; not alike; clear, definite.—**Distinct'**LY,[2] *adv.*—**Distinct'**NESS, *n.*—**Distinc'**TION, *n.* The action of distinguishing; difference, a difference; a distinguishing mark or characteristic; a treating with special consideration or honour; eminence, high quality, &c.; a distinguishing excellence.—**Distinc'**TIVE, *a.* Characteristic.

Distin'guish, *vt.* L. *distinguĕre, distinctum*, f. *dī-* (= DIS- (1)) + *stinguĕre*, orig., to prick or stick, but found only in sense 'to extinguish'. Cogn. with G. *stizein*, to prick. INSTIGATE. STIGMA. To class, classify; to make or constitute a difference in; to be a characteristic of; to draw a distinction between; to recognize, make out; to honour; to make prominent or eminent (gen. *refl.* or *pass.*).—*vi.* To draw a distinction.—**Distin'guish**ABLE, *a.*

Distort', *vt.* L. *distorquēre, distortum*, to twist different ways, f. DIS- (1) + *torquēre*, to twist. CONTORT. To put out of shape; to misrepresent, pervert.—**Distor'**TION, *n.*

Distract', *vt.* L. *distrahĕre, distractum*, to draw in different directions, f. DIS- (1) + *trahĕre*, to draw. ABSTRACT. Of the attention, &c., to turn aside, divert; to confuse, bewilder, drive mad.—**Distrac'**TION, *n.*

Distrain', *vi.* O.F. *destreindre, destraindre*, to press, vex—L. *distringĕre, districtum*, to stretch out, to detain, in L.L., to afflict, f. *dī-* (= DIS- (1)) + *stringĕre*, to bind, draw tight. ASTRINGENT. STRICT. To levy a distress.—**Distraint'**, *n.* The action of distraining.

Distraught', *ppl.a.* Altered f. obs. *distract* ppl.a. f. DISTRACT. Bewildered; crazy.

Distress', *n.* O.F. *destrece, destresse*—Late Pop. L. **districtia*, f. *districtus*, pa.pple. of *distringĕre*. DISTRAIN. Sore trouble, affliction; a sore trouble, a calamity; distressed or exhausted condition; the legal seizure and detention of a chattel.—*vt.* To put to sore straits, exhaust; to afflict.—**Distress'**FUL, *a.*

Distrib'ute, *vt.* L. *distribuĕre, distribūtum*, f. DIS- (1) + *tribuĕre*, to assign, bestow. ATTRIBUTE. To allot, apportion; to spread, scatter; to divide and arrange; to classify.—**Distrib'ut**ABLE, *a.*—**Distribu'**TION, *n.*—**Distrib'ut**IVE, *a.* Of or arising from distribution; expressing distribution or division. —*n.* A distributive word.

Dis'trict, *n.* F. *district*—Med.L. *districtus*, jurisdiction, a lord's territory, f. *distringĕre*. DISTRAIN. A portion of territory; a region.

Distrust', *n.* DIS- (7). Want of trust; doubt, suspicion.—*vt.* DIS- (4). To put no trust in; to call in question.—**Distrust'**FUL, *a.*

Disturb', *vt.* O.F. *desturber*—L. *disturbāre*, to throw into disorder, f. DIS- (3) + *turbāre*. TURBID. To trouble, agitate; to unsettle; to perplex; to interrupt, derange.—**Disturb'**ANCE, *n.*—**Disturb'**ER, *n.*

Disu'nion, *n.* DIS- (7). Separation; dissension.—**Disunite'**, *vt.* DIS- (4). To disjoin; to set at variance.—*vi.* To part.

Disuse', *n.* DIS- (7). Discontinuance of use; desuetude.—*vt.* DIS- (4). To cease to use.

Ditch, *n.* O.E. *dīc*. DIKE. A long narrow hollow dug in the ground.—*vi.* To make a ditch.—*vt.* To surround with a ditch; to dig ditches in for drainage or irrigation.

Dith'yramb, *n.* L. *dithyrambus*—G. *dithurambos*, of unknown orig. A Greek choric hymn, orig. one in honour of Bacchus; a poem similar to this; a vehement speech or writing. —**Dithyram'bic**, *a.*

Dit'tany, *n.* O.F. *ditan, ditain*—L. *dictamnus* (in Med.L. *dictamus*)—G. *diktamnon*, said to be f. *Diktē*, a mountain in Crete. A plant formerly famed for alleged medicinal virtues.

Dit'to. It. *ditto*, now *detto*—L. *dictus*, pa.pple. of *dīcĕre*. DICTION. The foresaid, the same (often abbreviated *d°, do.*).

Dittog'raphy, *n.* G. *dittos*, double + *-graphy*, G. *-graphia*, writing, f. *graphein*, to write. Unintentional repetition in copying.

Dit'ty, *n.* O.F. *dité*—L. *dictātum*, thing dictated, lesson, neut. pa.pple. of *dictāre*, to DICTATE. Formerly, a composition, treatise. A short simple song.

Diuret'ic, *a.* L. *diūrēticus*—G. *diourētikos*, f. DIoure-ein, to make water, f. *ouron*, URINE. Exciting discharge of urine.—*n.* A substance having this property.

Diur'nal, *a.* F. *diurnal*—L.L. *diurnālis* (= L. *diurnus*), of or belonging to a day, f. *dies*, day. ADJOURN. DIAL. DIARY. JOURNAL. SOJOURN. Performed in a day; daily; belonging to the day.—*n.* In the *R.C. Ch.*, a service-book containing the day-offices.

Di'vagate, *vi.* L. *dīvagāri, dīvagātus*, f. *dī-* (= DIS- (1)) + *vagāri*, to wander. VAGABOND. To wander about, stray.—**Divaga'tion**, *n.*

Divan', *n.* Turkish *divān*, orig. Per. An Oriental council of state or council-chamber; a cushioned seat against a wall; a smoking-room in a cigar-shop, a cigar-shop.

Dive, *vi.* (1) O.E. *dūfan*, strong verb, intrans., whence M.E. *dūven*; (2) the derivative causal *dýfan*, weak verb, whence M.E. *dȳven*. (This last took also an intrans. sense, and *dūven* became obs.) Cogn. with DEEP, DIP. To descend or plunge into or under water; to dart out of sight, disappear.—*n.* An act of diving; a sudden dart.—**Div'er**, *n.*

Diverge', *vi.* Mod.L. *dīvergĕre*, f. *dī-* (= DIS-(1)) + L. *vergĕre*, to bend, incline. CONVERGE. To tend to separate or part; to take different courses, differ, deviate.—*vt.* To cause to diverge.—**Diver'gence**, *n.*—**Diver'gent**, *a.*

Di'vers, *a.* O.F. *diviers, divers*—L. *dīversus*, turned different ways, different, unlike, pa.pple. of *dīvertĕre*. DIVERT. Sundry, several.

Diverse', *a.* Identical in orig. with the prec. Different, not alike; varied, diversified.—**Diverse'ly**,[2] *adv.*—**Diver'sify**, *vt.*—**Diversifica'tion**, *n.*—**Diver'sity**, *n.*

Divert', *vt.* O.F. *divertir*, to divert, alter—L. *dīvertĕre, dīversum*, to go different ways, turn aside, f. *dī-* (= DIS- (1)) + *vertĕre*, to turn. ADVERSE. DIVORCE. To turn aside, deflect; to ward off; to draw off, cause to turn, *from*; to entertain, amuse.—**Diver'sion**, *n.*

Divest', *vt.* A refashioning, after L. analogies, of earlier *Devest* in sim. senses—O.F. *desvestir, devestir*, f. *des-, de-* (= DIS- (4)) + *vestir*, L. *vestīre*, to clothe, f. *vestis*, garment. TRAVESTY. VEST. To strip *of* (clothing), unclothe; to dispossess, deprive; to free, rid.

Divide', *vt.* L. *dīvidĕre, divisum*, to separate, divide, app. f. *dī-* (= DIS- (1) or (3)) + a lost verb **vidĕre*, meaning to separate, cogn. with *viduus*, deprived, bereft. WIDOW. DEVICE. INDIVIDUAL. To split up, cleave, separate; to separate or mark out into parts or *from* (something); to class, classify; to cut off, sunder; to set at variance; to deal out, dispense; to take or have a portion of, share; to part (an assembly) into two groups for voting; *to divide* (a number) *by* (another), to ascertain how many times the latter is contained in the former. —*vi.* To become divided. —**Div'idend**, *n.* L. *dīvidendum*, use as *n.* of neut. ger. of *dīvidĕre*. A number to be divided by another; share of profit, &c.; a sum divided among a bankrupt's creditors, a creditor's share of this.—**Divis'ible**, *a.*—**Divi'sion**, *n.*—**Divi'sional**, *a.*—**Divi'sive**, *a.* Producing dissension.—**Divi'sor**, *n.* A number by which another is to be divided.

Divine', *a.* O.F. *devin*, later *divin*—L. *dīvīnus*, pertaining to a deity, cogn. with *dīvus* in sim. sense, *deus*, god. DEITY. Of, pertaining to, proceeding from God; religious, sacred; godlike, heavenly; pre-eminently excellent.—**Divine'ly**,[2] *adv.*—**Divin'ity**, *n.* The quality of being divine; a deity; theology.

Divine', *n.* O.F. *devin*, L. *dīvīnus*, soothsayer; O.F. *devin, divin*, Med.L. *dīvīnus*, theologian—all f. L. *dīvīnus*, a. (See prec.) Formerly, a soothsayer. A clergyman; a theologian.—*vt.* F. *deviner*—L. *dīvīnāre*, to foresee. To conjecture, guess; to predict, foretell. —*vi.* To practise divination; to conjecture.—**Divina'tion**, *n.*—**Divin'er**, *n.*

Divorce', *n.* F. *divorce*—L. *dīvortium*, a separation, a dissolution of marriage by consent, f. *dīvertĕre*, earlier *dīvortĕre*, in sense 'to leave one's husband'. DIVERT. Legal dissolution of marriage; complete separation, disunion.—*vt.* To dissolve the marriage of; to put away (a spouse); to separate, sever; to repudiate, put away.—**Divorce'ment**, *n.*

Divulge', *vt.* L. *dīvulgāre*, to spread abroad among the people, f. *dī-* (= DIS- (1)) + *vulgāre*, to make common, publish, f. *vulgus*, the common people. VULGAR. To tell openly, reveal.

Diz'en, *vt.* Evidently the verb belonging to *dis-, dise-* in DISTAFF. To deck out, adorn.

Diz'zy, *a.* O.E. *dysig*, foolish. A common W. Germanic adjective f. a root *dus-* found also in L.G. *dusen*, to be giddy. Giddy; mentally unsteady; causing, caused by, giddiness.—*vt.* To make dizzy; to confuse mentally.—**Diz'zily**,[2] *adv.*—**Diz'ziness**, *n.*

Do, *vt.* O.E. *dón*. Common W. Germanic (wanting in Gothic and Norse). Orig. sense 'put', 'place'. O.Teut. vbl. stem *dœ-; dô-*, cogn. with G. *the-* in *tithenai*, to put, L. *-dĕre*, in AB*dĕre*, to put away. DEED. DOOM. To bestow, confer, inflict; to perform, execute; to bring about, effect; to transact; to finish, complete; to prepare, to cook.—*vi.* To act; to contrive, manage; to perform deeds, work; to fare, get on; to answer, serve, suffice.—*v.aux.* Forms negative and interrogative sentences, and expresses emphasis.—*To do, to-do.* The dative infinitive. ADO, bustle, fuss.

Do'cile, *a.* F. *docile*—L. *docilis*, f. *docēre, doctum*, to teach. DISCIPLE. DOCTOR. Easily taught; submissive.—**Docil'ity**, *n.*

Dock, *n.*[1] O.E. *docce*. App. Common W. Germanic or O.Teut. A coarse weed.

Dock, *n.*[2] Identical with Icel. *dockr*, stumpy tail. Orig. obscure. The solid part of a tail; a cut end, a stump.—*v.*[1]*t.* To cut short, esp. of a tail; to curtail; to deprive *of*.

Dock, *n.*[3] Cf. Du. *dok*, earlier *docke*. Orig. uncertain. An excavated enclosure to receive ships for loading, unloading and repair.—*v.*[2]*t.*

To take or receive into a dock.—*vi.* To come into dock.—**Dock'yard**, *n.* An enclosure for building and repairing ships.

Dock, *n.*[4] The same as Flemish *dok*, rabbit-hutch, cage. (In Eng. prob. at first a word of rogues' cant.) The enclosure in a criminal court in which the prisoner is placed.

Dock'et, *n.* Derivation and orig. sense obscure. A list of causes for trial; an endorsement indicating the contents of a document; a warrant certifying payment of duty.—*vt.* To make an abstract of (judgements, &c.); to endorse with a note of contents.

Doc'tor, *n.* O.F. *doctor*—L. *doctor*, teacher, f. *docēre.* DOCILE. One holding the highest university degree; a medical practitioner.—*vt.* To treat medically; to adulterate; to sophisticate.—**Doctor**ATE,[1] *n.*

Doc'trine, *n.* F. *doctrine*—L. *doctrīna*, teaching, learning, f. *doctor.* (See prec.) Instruction, a body of instruction; a belief, opinion, dogma.—**Doc'trin**AL, *a.*—**Doctrinaire'**, *n.* F., f. *doctrīna.* One who seeks to apply a theory without allowing for circumstances.—**Doc'trin**ATE,[3] *vt.* To teach.

Doc'ument, *n.* O.F. *document*—L. *documentum*, a lesson, in Med.L. also a document, f. *docēre.* DOCILE. Something written or inscribed and furnishing evidence or information.—*vt.* To prove by evidence of, to furnish with, documents.—**Documen't**ARY, *a.*

Dodge, *vi.* Orig. unknown. To move to and fro, esp. in order to elude a pursuer, &c., or to gain an advantage; to play fast and loose, shuffle.—*vt.* To play fast and loose with; to elude by dodging.—*n.* A trick or artifice.

Do'do, *n.* Pg. *doudo*, simpleton. A large extinct bird with small useless wings.

Doe, *n.* O.E. *dá*, of doubtful orig. The female of the deer.

Doff, *vt.* Coalesced form of DO *off.* Cf. DON, *v.* To put off (clothes), to remove (the hat).

Dog, *n.* O.E. *docga.* Orig. unknown. A well-known domestic quadruped; applied to a person in reproach, abuse or contempt, or playfully.—*vt.* To follow pertinaciously or closely.—**Dog'ged**, *a.* Cf. CRABBED. Having the characteristics of certain dogs, pertinacious, persistent.—**Dog'ged**LY,[2] *adv.*—**Dog'**GISH, *a.*—**Dog'**GY,[2] *a.*—**Dog'-cart**, *n.* An open vehicle with two transverse seats back to back, the hinder orig. shutting up to form a box for dogs.—**Dog'-days**, *n.pl.* The days, noted as hot and unwholesome, about the time when the dog-star rises with the sun.—**Dog's-ear**, *n.* A turned-down corner of a page.—*vt.* To fill (a book) with dog's-ears.—**Dog'-star**, *n.* The star Sirius in the constellation of the Greater Dog.

Doge, *n.* Venetian *doge*—L. *dux.* DUKE. The chief magistrate of the republics of Venice and Genoa.

Dog'gerel, *a.* Perh. f. DOG used in contempt. Cf. '*dog-Latin*'. Of verse, mean, trivial.—*n.* Such verse; a piece of doggerel.

Dog'ma, *n.* L. *dogma, dogmatis*—G. *dogma*, that which seems to one, opinion, f. *doke-ein*, to seem, think. HETERODOX. ORTHODOX. A belief or principle, esp. one authoritatively laid down by a church, &c.; arrogant declaration of opinion; beliefs or principles collectively.—**Dogmat'**IC, -ICAL, *aa.* Of or pertaining to dogma or dogmas; asserting opinions arrogantly.—**Dogmat'ical**LY,[2] *adv.*—**Dog'mat**ISM, *n.* Arrogant assertion of opinion.—**Dog'mat**IST, *n.*—**Dog'mat**IZE, *vi.*

Doit, *n.* Du. *duit*, of uncertain orig. A small Dutch coin; a trifling sum.

Dol'drum, *n.* Us. in *pl.* **Dol'drums.** Perh. a derivative of DULL. For the form cf. TANTRUM. Low spirits, depression; a becalmed state of a ship; a region of light winds and calms near the equator.

Dole, *n.*[1] O.E. *dál*, a parallel form to *dǽl.* DEAL, *n.*[1] Dealing out of gifts, esp. in charity; a gift so dealt out; something sparingly given.—*vt.* To deal *out* sparingly.

Dole, *n.*[2] O.F. *doel* (F. *deuil*)—L.L. *dolium*, grief, f. L. *dolēre*, to be in pain or grief. DOLOUR. Grief, sorrow; mourning, weeping.—**Dole'**FUL, *a.*—**Dole'ful**LY,[2] *adv.*

Doll, *n.* A shortened pet-form of *Dorothy.* An image of a human being used as a toy.

Dol'lar, *n.* L.G. *daler* = H.G. *taler, thaler*, shortened f. *Joachimst(h)aler*, (coin) of the Joachimst(h)al (valley of Joachim) in Bohemia, where there were silver mines. The Eng. name for the German *thaler*, a coin of varying value; a coin of the U.S. and Canada, worth about 4*s.* 1½*d.*; various foreign coins.

Dol'man, *n.* Turkish *dōlāmān.* A Turkish robe; a kind of jacket worn by hussars; a kind of mantle worn by women.

Dol'our, *n.* O.F. *dolor, dolour*—L. *dolor*, f. *dolēre*, to grieve. DOLE.[2] Grief, sorrow.—**Dol'or**OUS, *a.*—**Dol'orous**LY,[2] *adv.*

Dol'phin, *n.* O.F. *daulphin*—Pop.L. **dalphīnus* for L. *delphīnus*—G. *delphis, delphinos.* DAUPHIN. A marine mammal resembling the porpoise; a fish celebrated for its changes of hue when dying.

Dolt, *n.* App. related to M.E. *dol, doll*, O.E. *dol*, foolish. DULL. A stupid fellow.

Domain', *n.* F. *domaine*, O.F. *demeine.* DEMESNE. In senses of *demesne*; sphere of influence, rule, &c.; field, province, scope.

Dome, *n.* In the first sense app. directly f. L. *domus*, house, home. In the second f. F. *dome* (now *dôme*)—It. *duomo*, house of God, cathedral, dome, f. *domus.* TIMBER. A stately building; a rounded vault forming a roof.

Domes'day. *Dómes*, genit. of *dóm*, DOOM + DAY. *Domesday Book*, the record of the Great Survey of William the Conqueror.

Domes'tic, *a.* L. *domesticus*, f. *domus.* DOME. Of or belonging to the house or home; not foreign, 'home'; tame; attached to home.—*n.* A household servant.—**Domes'tic**ATE,[3] *vt.* To naturalize; to attach to home; to tame.—**Domestic**A'TION, *n.*

Dom'icile, *n.* F. *domicile*—L. *domicilium*, a dwelling-place, f. *domus.* DOME. A dwelling-place; the place where one has his fixed abode; the fact of being resident.—*vt.* To settle in a fixed abode.—**Domicil'i**ARY, *a.*

Dom'inate, *vt.* L. *domināri, dominātus*, to bear rule, f. *dominus*, lord, master. DAME. DANGER. DEMESNE. DOMINION. DUNGEON. To rule, control, sway; to command, overlook, as a height.—*vi.* To bear rule, exercise control.—**Dom'in**ANT, *a.*—**Domin**A'TION, *n.*—**Domineer'**, *vi.* Du. *domineren*, to rule—F. *dominer*, f. *domināri.* To rule despotically *over*, to act imperiously.

Domin'ical, *a.* F. *dominical*—Med.L. *dominicālis*, belonging to the Lord or the Lord's day—L. *dominicus*, of or belonging to a lord, f. *dominus.* (See prec.) Of or pertaining to the Lord or the Lord's day; denoting Sundays.

Domin'ion, *n.* Obs. F. *dominion*—L. type **dominio, dominiōnis*, f. *dominium*, ownership,

f. *dominus*. DOMINATE. Rule, sway; the territory under a particular government.

Dom'ino, *n*. F. *domino*, orig. a black hood worn by priests, a mourning veil worn by women, app. derived in some way f. L. *dominus*. DOMINATE. (The pieces used in the game are said to have been named from a likeness of the backs to the garment.) A masquerade garment with a mask covering the upper part of the face; a rectangular piece of ivory, &c., with the under side black and the upper marked with pips; in *pl*., a game played with such pieces.

Don, *n*. Sp. *don*—L. *dominus*. DOMINATE. A Spanish title; a Spanish gentleman; an adept; a head, &c., of a college.

Don, *vt*. Coalesced form of DO *on*. Cf. DOFF. To put on (clothes).

Donate', *vt*. L. *dōnāre, dōnātum*, to present, f. *dōnum*, gift, f. *dăre*, to give. DATE.[2] To make a gift of.—**Don**A'TION, *n*.—**Don**'ATIVE, *a*. Of the nature of a donation.—*n*. A gift, a largess.—**Don**EE', *n*.—**Do'n**OR, *n*.

Don'jon, *n*. An archaic spelling of DUNGEON. The great tower of a castle.

Don'key, *n*. App. of dialectal or slang orig. Poss. a familiar form of *Duncan*. Cf. *Neddy* applied to the same animal. An ass.—**Don'key-en'gine**, *n*. A small subsidiary steam-engine on a ship.

Doom, *n*. O.E. *dóm*. Common Teut. Cogn. with DO. DEEM. A law; a decision or sentence; fate, destiny; destruction, ruin; the Last Judgement.—*vt*. To sentence, to condemn *to*; to destine; to decree, adjudge.—**Dooms'day**, *n*. The Judgement-day.

Door, *n*. M.E. *dure, dore*—O.E. *duru, dor*. Cf. Ger. *tür, tor*. Cogn. with Skr. *dwâr*, G. *thura*, L. *foris*. A movable barrier serving to close the entrance of a house, room, &c.

Do'ric, *a*. L. *dōricus*—G. *dōrikos*, of Doris, a division of ancient Greece. Belonging to Doris; of a dialect, broad, not refined; the name of the oldest and simplest of the three Grecian orders of architecture.

Dor'mant, *a*. O.F. *dormant*, pres.pple. of *dormir*, L. *dormīre*, to sleep. Cogn. with G. *darthanein*. Inactive as in sleep; in abeyance, not acting.—**Dor'm**ANCY, *n*.—**Dor'mer**, **Dor'mer-win'dow**, *n*. O.F. *dormeor*, L. *dormītōrium*, sleeping-room. A projecting vertical window in the slope of a roof (orig. the window of a bed-room).—**Dor'mitory**, *n*. From *dormītōrium*. A sleeping-place containing a number of beds.

Dor'mouse, *n*. Orig. obscure. The first element poss. short for North. Eng. *dorm*, to doze. Cf. O.N. *dorma*, to doze, app. f. F. *dormir* (see prec.). The second treated as MOUSE. A small hibernating rodent.

Dor'sal, *a*. Med.L. *dorsālis*, f. L. *dorsum*. ENDORSE. Of, on, near the back.

Dose, *n*. F. *dose*—Med.L. *dosis*—G. *dosis*, a giving, f. *didonai*, to give. ANTIDOTE. A quantity of medicine given or prescribed to be given at one time.—*vt*. To give doses to.

Dot, *n*. O.E. *dott*, only in sense 'head of a boil', cogn. with O.H.G. *tutto*, nipple. A minute spot or mark.—*vt*. To mark with a dot or dots; to place on a surface like dots.

Dote, *vi*. Early M.E. *doten, dotien*. Not in O.E. Corresponds to M.Du. *doten* in sim. sense. Cf. O.N. *dotta*, to nod from sleep. To be silly or weak-minded, esp. from age; to bestow excessive fondness *on* or *upon*.—**Do't**AGE, *n*.—**Do't**ARD, *n*.

Doub'le, *a*. O.F. *duble, doble* (F. *double*) = Sp. *doble*, It. *doppio*—L. *duplus*, twice as many, double, f. *duo*, TWO + *-plus*, f. root *ple-*, to fill. COMPLETE. MULTIPLE. TRIPLE. Consisting of two members, &c., forming a pair, made of two layers; folded; bent, stooping much forward; having a part double; of two kinds; ambiguous; twice as much or many; of twice the usual size, &c.; false, deceitful.—*adv*. To twice the amount or extent, in two ways or respects, twice, twice over; in a pair, two together.—*n*. A double quantity; an image or exact copy; the apparition of a living person; a sharp turn in running, an evasive turn or shift.—*vt*. To make double; to fold; to sail round (a cape or point).—*vi*. To increase twofold; to turn sharply in running, pursue a winding course.—**Doub'**LY,[2] *adv*.—**Doub'let**, *n*. F. *doublet*, something folded, a furred coat, &c., f. *double* + dim. suff. *-et*. A close-fitting body-garment formerly worn by men; one of a pair; one of two words of the same origin but different in form.—**Doubloon'**, *n*. F. *doublon* or Sp. *doblon*, aug. of *doble*. A Spanish gold coin.

Doubt, *vi*. The *b* inserted f. the L. word. M.E. *duten, douten*—O.F. *duter, douter*—L. *dubitāre*, to waver in opinion, hesitate, related to *dubius*. DUBIOUS. To waver in opinion or belief.—*vt*. To hesitate to believe, to call in question, mistrust; to suspect.—*n*. A wavering in opinion or belief; a state of affairs giving occasion for uncertainty.—**Doubt'**ER, *n*.—**Doubt'**FUL, *a*.—**Doubt'ful**LY,[2] *adv*.—**Doubt'**LESS, *a*. As *adv*., certainly, no doubt.

Douche, *n*. F. *douche*—It. *doccia*, conduit-pipe, f. *docciare*, to pour by drops—L. type **ductiāre*, f. *ductus*, leading, conduit, f. *dūcĕre*, to lead. DUKE. A stream of water, &c., applied to a part of the body.

Dough, *n*. O.E. *dáh*. Common Teut. Cf. Goth. *deigan*, to knead. Cogn. with Skr. *dih-*, to besmear, L. *fig-, fingĕre*, to handle, form. DAIRY. LADY. Flour or meal kneaded into a paste.—**Dough'**Y,[2] *a*.

Dough'ty, *a*. O.E. *dohtig*, earlier *dyhtig*, f. *dugan*, to avail, be strong. Cf. Ger. *tüchtig*. Able, worthy; valiant, stout.—**Dough'ti**LY,[2] *adv*.—**Dough'ti**NESS, *n*.

Dove, *n*. O.E. *dúfe* (only in compound form *dúfe-doppa*, f. *dúfan*, to DIVE + *doppa*, agent-n. f. *déop-* (*dop-*), to dip, and cogn. with DEEP). App. 'the diver', perh. from its habit of ducking the head. Cf. G. *kolumbis*, a diving bird, L. *columba*, dove, both f. G. *kolumbos*, diver. A bird of the pigeon family.—**Dove'cot(e)**, *n*. COT.[1] COTE. A house for doves.—**Dove'tail**, *n*. A tenon in the shape of a dove's tail spread; the corresponding mortise.—*vt*. To fit together by dovetails; to unite compactly, adjust exactly.—*vi*. To fit exactly.

Dow'ager, *n*. O.F. *douagere*, f. *douage*, dower, f. *douer*, L. *dōtāre*, to ENDOW. DOWER. DOWRY. A woman enjoying a title or property from a deceased husband.

Dow'dy, *n*. Of uncertain orig. A woman shabbily or unattractively dressed.—*a*. Shabbily dull; without brightness or smartness.

Dow'el, *n*. Poss. corresp. to M.L.G. *dovel*, M.H.G. *tübel*, Ger. *dōbel*, plug, tap. A headless pin of wood, metal, &c., for fastening together pieces of wood, stone, &c.—*vt*. To fasten with a dowel.

Dow'er, *n*. O.F. *douaire*, dower, dowry—L.L. *dōtārium* f. *dōtāre*. DOWAGER. A widow's share for life of her husband's estate;

a dowry; a talent, an endowment.—*vt.* To give a dowry to; to endow *with*.

Down, *n.*[1] O.E. *dún*, hill, prob. of Celtic orig. An open expanse of high land; a DUNE.

Down, *n.*[2] O.N. *dunn* (Icel. *dún*, Sw. *dun*, Da. *duun*). The first feathering of young birds; various substances like this.—**Down'**Y,[2] *a.*

Down, *adv.* Late O.E. *dúne*, *dún*, aphetic f. *adúne*, weakened f. *of dúne*, off the hill. A-[2]. DOWN, *n.*[1] From above; in the direction of a current, with the wind, from the capital; in a low position; into or in a fallen, sitting, &c., position; (paid) on the spot; from higher to lower in a series; to or in an inferior condition; to smaller bulk or finer consistency.—*prep.* From a higher to a lower part of; to or at what is thought of as a lower part of.—**Down'right**, *adv.* Absolutely, quite.—*a.* Directed straight downwards; straightforward, direct; absolute, positive, thorough.—**Down'**WARD, *adv.* and *a.*—**Down'**WARDS, *adv.*

Dow'ry, *n.* A.F. *dowarie* = O.F. *douaire*, DOWER. The property which a wife brings to her husband; a talent, an endowment.

Doxol'ogy, *n.* Med.L. *doxologia*—G. *doxologia*, f. *doxologos*, giving glory, f. *doxa*, glory + *-logos*, speaking, f. *legein*, to speak. DIALECT. A short formula of praise to God.

Doy'en, *n.* F. *doyen*—L. *decānus*, DEAN. The senior member of a body.

Doze, *vt.* Of doubtful orig. Cf. Da. *döse*, to make drowsy. To sleep drowsily.—*n.* A nap.

Doz'en, *n.* O.F. *dosaine*, f. *doze*, L. *duodecim* (*duo*, TWO + *decem*, TEN), twelve, with suff. *-aine* (L. *-ēna*, as in *centēna*). A set of twelve.

Drab, *n.*[1] Orig. uncertain. Evidently conn. with Ir. *drabog*, Gael. *drabag*, dirty woman. A dirty untidy woman; a harlot.

Drab, *n.*[2] F. *drap*, cloth. DRAPE. (Perh. orig. applied to cloth of the natural undyed colour.) A kind of cloth; drab colour; clothing of this colour.—*a.* Of a dull light brown or yellowish-brown; dull, wanting brightness.

Drachm, *n.* F. *drachme*—L. *drachma*—G. *drachmē*, an Attic weight and coin. Cf. G. *dragma*, as much as one can grasp, f. *drassesthai*, to grasp. DRAM. ⅛ of an ounce apothecaries' weight, $\frac{1}{16}$ avoirdupois.

Draff, *n.* Early M.E. *draf*, corresp. to M.Du. and Icel. *draf* in sim. sense. Not in O.E. Refuse, dregs; what is given to swine.

Draft, *n.* A mod. spelling of DRAUGHT. The detachment of a party for a special purpose, the party; an order for money; a demand, claim; the rough form of a writing; a design or sketch.—*vt.* To detach (a party); to make a draft of (a writing).—**Drafts'man**, *n.* One who drafts writings or makes designs.

Drag, *vt.* A derivative of O.E. *dragan* or O.N. *draga*, to DRAW. To haul along by force, pull along with difficulty; to protract tediously; to sweep with a net; to apply a drag to (a wheel).—*vi.* To lag; to trail when moving or being moved; to be tediously protracted.—*n.* A kind of vehicle; an apparatus for recovering objects from water; a net which is dragged over the bottom; an iron shoe for braking a wheel.

Drag'gle, *vt.* App. dim. and freq. of prec. Cf. WAGGLE. To wet or befoul by allowing to drag.—*vi.* To trail on the ground.

Drag'oman, *n.* F. *dragoman*—Late G. *dragoumanos*—Old Arab. *targumān*, interpreter. An interpreter, esp. in the East.

Drag'on, *n.* F. *dragon*—L. *draco*, *dracōnis*—G. *drakōn*, explained as 'the sharp-seeing', f. *drak-*, second aorist stem of *derkesthai*, to see. RANKLE. A mythical monster in reptile form, sometimes represented as breathing out fire.—**Drag'on-fly**, *n.* A preying insect with two pairs of large wings.—**Dragoon'**, *n.* F. *dragon*, a kind of carbine (as 'breathing fire'), a dragoon. A species of cavalry soldier, originally one armed with the firearm.—*vt.* To set dragoons upon; to oppress, force.

Drain, *vt.* O.E. *dréahnian*, prob. f. O.Teut. root *draug-*, to be DRY. To draw or carry (a liquid) *off* or *away*; to drink to the last drops; to withdraw water from by pipes, &c.; to empty (a vessel) by drinking; to exhaust.—*vi.* To percolate *through*, flow *off* or *away*; to become rid of moisture by percolation, &c.—*n.* A channel for draining liquid; constant outlet, expenditure, &c.—**Drain'**AGE, *n.*

Drake, *n.* M.E. *drake*. Not in O.E. Cf. Ger. dial. *draak*, *drache*. A male duck.

Dram, *n.* Phonetic spelling of and = DRACHM; also, a small draught of liquor.

Dra'ma, *n.* L.L. *drāma*, *drāmatis*—G. *drama*, deed, tragedy, f. *dra-ein*, to do, perform. Cf F. *drame*. A composition to be acted upon a stage; dramatic literature.—**Dramat'**IC, *a.*—**Dram'at**IST, *n.*—**Dram'at**IZE, *vt.*

Drape, *vt.* F. *draper*, f. *drap*, cloth—L.L. *drappus*, of unknown orig. DRAB.[2] TRAP, *v.*[2] To cover, dress, adorn; to arrange (clothes, &c.) gracefully.—**Dra'p**ER, *n.* A dealer in textile articles.—**Dra'p**ERY, *n.*

Dras'tic, *a.* G. *drastikos*, f. *drastos*, vbl.a. of *dra-ein*. DRAMA. Vigorously effective.

Draught, *n.* Early M.E. *draht*, not recorded in O.E., f. Common Teut. *dragan*, to DRAW. See also DRAFT. The action or an act of drawing; an act of drinking, the quantity drunk at once; that which is taken in a net; a dose; inhaling; the depth of water required to float a ship; a current of air; a design or sketch; in *pl.*, a game for two played with 'men' on a chess-board.—*attrib.* Of beasts, used for draught; of liquor, drawn, or ready to be drawn, from the cask.—*vt.* To make a design or sketch of.—**Draughts'man**, *n.* One who makes designs.—**Draught'**Y,[2] *a.* Abounding in currents of air.

Draw, *vt.* O.E. *dragan*. Common Teut. DRAG. To pull; to pull along; to cart, haul; to bend (a bow); to pull out of shape or place; of a ship, to require (such and such a depth of water to float her); to inhale; to attract, to entice, allure; to induce *to do*; to bring about as a result; to bring (evil, &c.) *upon*; to pull or take out; to pull (lots), to get by lot; to leave undecided; to take (water) from a well; to cause (liquid) to flow from a vessel, &c.; to receive (money, &c.); to elicit; to bring out information, &c., from; to infer; to distend, extend; to trace by drawing a pencil, &c., over a surface, to delineate; to frame, compose (a document, &c.); to frame, make (comparisons, &c.); to write out (a bill, cheque, &c.).—*vi.* To pull; to contract, shrink; to produce or admit of a current of air; to exercise attractive force; to come *together*; to practise delineation; to make a written demand for money; to make one's way, come *near*, approach; to approach in time.—*n.* An act of drawing; drawing of lots; a drawn game, &c.—**Draw'back**, *n.* An amount paid back from a charge formerly made; anything that detracts from profit or pleasure.—**Draw'**ER, *n.*[1]—**Draw'er**, *n.*[2] Cf. F. *tiroir*, f. *tirer*, to draw. A sliding box in a case.—**Draw'ers**, *n.pl.* Prob. as 'things that one draws on'. A garment for the lower part of the body and the legs.—**Draw'ing**, *vbl.n.* The action of the *v.*; the art of representing by line, a product of this.

Draw'ing-room, *n.* Shortened f. *Withdrawing-room.* A reception room to which the ladies withdraw after dinner; a formal reception by the King, &c.

Drawl, *vi.* Perh. f. Du. or L.G. App. an intensive deriv. of DRAW. To speak slowly from indolence or affectation.—*vt.* To utter thus.—*n.* Such a manner of speech.

Dray, *n.* A deriv. of O.E. *dragan*, to DRAW. Cf. Sw. *drög.* A low cart without sides.

Dread, *vt.* M.E. *dreden*, prob. aphetic f. *adreden* = O.E. *ondrǽdan*, to fear, with pref. *on-*, against, towards. A-1. The simple *drǽdan* does not occur. Cf. O.S. *andrâdan*, O.H.G. *intrâten.* To fear greatly; to venerate.—*n.* Extreme fear; reverence; anxiety; an object of dread.—*ppl.a.* To be dreaded; awful, revered.—**Dread'**FUL, *a.*—**Dread'nought**, *n.* A thick coat for very inclement weather; the woollen cloth of which such coats are made; the most powerful type of battleship (from the name of the first built).

Dream, *n.* Early M.E. *dream*, pointing to an unrecorded O.E. *dréam* = O.S., M.L.G. *drôm*, O.H.G., M.H.G. *troum* (Ger. *traum*). Poss. f. Teut. *dreug-*, *draug-*, *drug-*, to deceive. A vision during sleep; a vision of the fancy.—*vi.* To have dreams; to think *of* as possible; to indulge in fancies.—*vt.* To see in sleep; to think to be possible.—**Dream'**ER, *n.*—**Dream'**LESS, *a.*—**Dream'**Y,2 *a.*

Drear, *a.* Shortened f. and = DREARY.

Drea'ry, *a.* O.E. *dréorig*, gory, sad, f. *dréor*, gore, cogn. with O.S. *drôr*, O.H.G. *trôr.* Dismal, gloomy.—**Drea'ri**LY,2 *adv.*

Dredge, *n.* Perh. a deriv. of DRAG. An appliance for bringing up objects, mud, &c., from the bed of a river, &c.—*vt.* To bring up, to deepen, by means of a dredge.—**Dredg'**ER, *n.* A vessel constructed for dredging.

Dreg, *n.* Prob. f. Norse. Cf. Icel. *dreggjar*, pl., Sw. *drägg*, pl., in sim. sense. Gen. in *pl.* Sediment, lees; the most worthless part.

Drench, *vt.* O.E. *drencan*, causal of *drincan*, to DRINK. To make (an animal) take a draught of medicine; to wet thoroughly.—*n.* A draught, esp. one for an animal; a soaking.

Dress, *vt.* O.F. *dresser*, to arrange—L. type **drictiāre*, f. *directus*, DIRECT. To draw up (troops) in the proper line; to attire, clothe; to adorn, deck; to chastise, to reprimand; to treat (a wound); to cleanse, trim, smooth, &c.; to prepare for eating; to manure.—*vi.* To form in the proper line; to put on one's clothes.—*n.* Attire, clothing; a robe or gown.—**Dress'**ER, *n.*1—**Dress'er**, *n.*2 O.F. *dresseur* (F. *dressoir*), f. *dresser.* A kitchen sideboard.—**Dress'**Y,2 *a.* Fond of dress; stylish.

Drib'ble, *vt.* Freq. of obs. *Drib*, a formation f. DRIP or DROP, the modified consonant expressing a modification of the notion. To let drop or trickle.—*vi.* To let the spittle flow over the chin; to trickle.—*n.* A small trickling stream; a drop.—**Drib'(b)let**, *n.* From *Drib* + dim. *-let.* An inconsiderable quantity.

Drift, *n.* Early M.E. *drift*, f. O.E. *drífan*, to DRIVE. A being driven (as if by a current), a slow course or current; deviation from a ship's course; course, progress, process; meaning or purport (of a speech, &c.); a shower (of rain, &c.); things driven together by the wind; matter floating in a current.—*vi.* To move with a current or the wind; to be driven together by the wind; to be carried along in a course or *into* some condition.—*vt.* To drive along as by a current or the wind; to blow into heaps; to cover with drifts.

Drill, *v.*1*t.* Prob. f. Du. *drillen* in the same senses. Cf. M.H.G. and Ger. *drillen* also in the same senses. To bore a hole in; to train in military movements and the use of arms.—*vi.* To practise military movements, &c.—*n.*1 A boring tool; military training.

Drill, *n.*2 Of doubtful orig. A small furrow in which seed is sown; a machine for sowing in drills.—*v.*2*t.* To sow in drills.

Drill, *n.*3 App. f. the native name. A West African species of baboon.

Dril'ling. *n.*, **Drill**, *n.*4 Corr. of Ger. *drillich*—L. *trilix*, *trilīcis*, triple-twilled, f. *tri-*, three + *licium*, thrum, thread. A coarse twilled linen or cotton fabric.

Drink, *vt.* O.E. *drincan.* Common Teut. DRENCH. To swallow (liquid); to absorb.—*vi.* To swallow liquid; to take intoxicating liquor to excess.—*n.* Liquid swallowed; a beverage; excess in taking intoxicating liquor; a draught.—**Drink'**ABLE, *a.*—**Drink'**ER, *n.*

Drip, *vt.* O.E. *dryppan.* But possibly f. Norse. Cf. Da. *dryppe.* O.Teut. stem *dreup-*, &c. DROP. To let fall in drops, to let fall (drops).—*vi.* To have liquid falling off in drops; to fall in drops.—*n.* A falling, that which falls, in drops.—**Drip'ping**, *vbl.n.* The melted fat that drips from roasting meat.

Drive, *vt.* O.E. *drífan.* Common Teut. DRIFT. DROVE. To force (living beings) to move on or away; to cause to move and direct the course of (a draught-animal, a locomotive, &c.); to convey in a vehicle; to propel, to carry along; to throw, cast, impel; to fix by blows; to set going, set in motion; to incite, force.—*vi.* To guide a draught-animal, to be conveyed in a vehicle; to rush, dash; to drift; to aim *at.*—*n.* The action or an act of driving; a journey in a vehicle; a carriage road, esp. one leading to a house.—**Driv'**ER, *n.*

Driv'el, *vi.* M.E. *drevelen*—O.E. *dreflian.* Prob. cogn. with DRAFF. To slaver; to talk nonsense.—*n.* Nonsense.—**Driv'el**LER, *n.*

Driz'zle, *vi.* Poss. dim. and freq. of obs. *Drese*, O.E. *dréosan*, to fall = O.S. *driosan.* To rain or fall in fine drops.—*n.* Fine rain.

Droll, *n.* F. *drôle* (now in sense 'rascal'). Orig. doubtful. A funny fellow, a jester.—*a.* Funny; odd, queer.—**Drol'l**ERY, *n.*

Drom'edary, *n.* O.F. *dromedaire* — L.L. *dromedārius*, L. *dromas*—G. *dromas*, running, f. *dramein*, to run. A fleet kind of camel.

Drone, *n.*1 O.E. *dran*, *dræn.* Cf. M.L.G. *drâne*, *drône*, L.G. *drône*, whence Ger. *drohne.* The male of the honey-bee; a lazy idler.—*vi.* To hum or buzz; to talk in a monotonous tone; to proceed in a lazy manner.—*n.*2 App. f. the v. A deep monotonous humming or buzzing.

Droop, *vi.* M.E. *drupen*, *drowpen* — O.N. *drúpa*, to droop, hang the head, &c., f. O.Teut. stem *dreup-*, &c. DROP. To hang or sink down; to languish, flag.—*vt.* To let hang or sink down.—*n.* Drooping action or condition.

Drop, *n.* O.E. *dropa*, f. O.Teut. stem *dreup-*, *draup-*, *drup-*, to drop. DRIP. DROOP. A globule of liquid; the smallest appreciable quantity; the action or an act of dropping; part of a gallows; the distance through which a thing falls.—*vi.* To fall in drops; to fall, descend; to come to an end, lapse; to come or go casually *into*, &c.—*vt.* To let fall in drops; to let fall; to utter casually; to leave off.

Drop'sy, *n.* Aphetic f. M.E. *i-*, *ydropsy*—O.F. *i-*, *ydropisie*—L. *hydrōpisis*—G. *hudrōps*, f. *udōr*, water. A morbid accumulation of watery fluid in the body.—**Drop'**SICAL, *a.*

Dross, *n.* O.E. *drós* = M.L.G. *drôs*, M.Du. *droes*, dregs. The scum of metals; rubbish.

Drought, *n.* O.E. *drúgath*, *drúgoth*, f. *drúg-*, stem of *drýge*, DRY. Lack of rain; thirst.

Drove, *n.* O.E. *dráf*, f. *drífan*, to DRIVE. A number of beasts driven in a body, a herd. —**Drov'**ER, *n.* A driver of, a dealer in, cattle.

Drown, *vi.* M.E. *drūnen*, *drounen*, pointing to an O.E. **drúnian*. Orig. obscure. To be suffocated in water.—*vt.* To suffocate in water.

Drow'sy, *a.* Appears early in 16th c. Prob. related to O.E. *drúsian*, to sink, become slow. Inclined to sleep; lulling; dull, sluggish.—**Drow'si**LY,[2] *adv.* — **Drow'si**NESS, *n.*—

Drowse, *vi.* and *t.* App. a back-formation f. the *n.* To be or to make drowsy.

Drub, *vt.* Poss. represents Arab. *darb*, a beating, a blow, f. *daraba*, to beat. To beat.

Drudge, *n.* Of obscure orig. One kept at mean or distasteful work.—*vi.* To be kept at such work.—**Drudg'**ERY, *n.*

Drug, *n.* F. *drogue*, a Common Romanic word of uncertain orig. A medicinal substance; a commodity no longer in demand (in this sense perh. a different word).—*vt.* To mix with a drug; to give drugs to, esp. in order to stupefy.—**Drug'**GIST, *n.* A dealer in drugs.

Drug'get, *n.* F. *droguet*, of unknown orig. A coarse woollen stuff.

Dru'id, *n.* F. *druide*—Gaulish L. *Druides*, pl., of Celtic orig. An ancient Celtic priest or soothsayer.—**Druid'**IC, -ICAL, *aa.*

Drum, *n.* Corresp. to M.Du. *tromme*, M.H.G. and L.G. *trumme*. A hollow cylindrical musical instrument played with sticks; various things like it; the hollow of the middle ear.—*vi.* To beat on or as on a drum.—*vt.* To expel by beat of drum.—**Drum'm**ER, *n.*

Drunk, *ppl.a.* Pa.pple. of DRINK. Overcome by alcoholic liquor.—**Drunk'**ARD, *n.* One given to drinking.—**Drunk'en**, *ppl.a.* Earlier form of the pa.pple. Drunk; given to drinking; caused by or exhibiting intoxication.—**Drunk'en**NESS, *n.*

Drupe, *n.* L. *druppa*, *drūpa*, over-ripe, wrinkled olive = G. *druppa*. A stone-fruit.

Dry, *a.* O.E. *drýge*, corresp. to M.Du. *dröghe*, *drôghe*, L.G. *droge*, *dreuge*. O.Teut. stem *dreug-*, *draug-*, *drug-*, to be dry. DRAIN. DROUGHT. Destitute of moisture; not rainy; evaporated, dried up; not yielding water; not yielding milk; not under, in, or on water; not associated or connected with liquid; wanting in cordiality; caustically witty; meagre, plain, bare; unattractive, insipid.—*vt.* To make dry; to remove (water or moisture).—*vi.* To become dry; to disappear by evaporation, &c.—**Dry'**LY,[2] **Dri'**LY,[2] *adv.* Not cordially; frigidly; with caustic humour.—**Dry'**NESS, *n.* —**Dry'-nurse**, *n.* A nurse who does not suckle the child.—**Dry rot'**, **Dry-rot'**, *n.* A decayed condition of timber in which it crumbles to a dry powder.—**Dry'salter**, *n.* App. f. *Drysalt* (= *Dry-cure*, to cure (meat, &c.) by salting and drying) + ER. A dealer in chemical products used in the arts, formerly also in preserved meats.—**Dry'salt**ERY, *n.*

Dry'ad, *n.* L. *dryas*, pl. *dryades*—G. *druas*, f. *drus*, tree. A wood-nymph.

Du'al, *a.* L. *duālis*, containing two, f. *duo*, TWO. Of two; twofold.—**Du'al**ISM, *n.* A metaphysical system which assumes two ultimate principles or kinds of being.

Dub, *vt.* Supposed to be f. O.F. *aduber*, *adober*, *adouber*, to dub a knight, a Common Romanic word of unknown orig. To make into *a knight* by striking the shoulder with a sword; to style, nickname; to smear (leather) with fat or grease.—**Dub'bing**, *vbl.n.* Also **Dub'bin**. Grease for smearing leather.

Du'bious, *a.* L. *dubiōsus*, f. *dubius*, doubtful. DOUBT. Fraught with doubt or uncertainty; of uncertain issue; of suspected character; hesitating.—**Dubi'ety**, *n.* L.L. *dubietas*, f. *dubius*. The condition or quality of being dubious; an instance of this.

Du'cal, *a.* F. *ducal*—L.L. *ducālis*, f. L. *dux*. DUKE. Of or pertaining to a duke.

Duc'at, *n.* F. *ducat*—It. *ducato*—L.L. *ducātus*, DUCHY, also the name of a coin. A gold coin of varying value formerly in use in many European countries.

Duch'ess, *n.* F. *duchesse*—L.L. *ducissa*, f. L. *dux*. DUKE. The wife or widow of a duke. —**Duch'y**, *n.* O.F. *duché*—L.L. *ducātus*, f. *dux*. The territory of a duke.

Duck, *n.*[1] O.E. *duce*, f. **dúcan*, to DUCK. A well-known swimming bird.—**Duck'ling**, *n.* -LING (3). A young duck.

Duck, *n.*[2] App. f. Du. *doeck*, linen cloth = Ger. *tuch*. A strong untwilled fabric.

Duck, *vi.* M.E. *duken*, *douken*, corresp. to O.E. type **dúcan* = M.Du., M.L.G. *dûken*, M.H.G. *tûchen* (Ger. *tauchen*). To plunge under water and emerge again; to bend or stoop quickly.—*vt.* To plunge into water; to jerk (the head, &c.) downwards.—*n.*[3] A quick plunge; a quick bend, a jerky bow.

Duct, *n.* L. *ductus*, a leading, f. *dūcĕre*, to lead. DUKE. A channel or tube.—**Duc'tile**, *a.* F. *ductile*—L. *ductilis*, f. *dūcĕre*. Flexible, pliable; that may be drawn into wire, tough; tractable, pliant.—**Ductil'**ITY, *n.*

Dud'geon, *n.* Orig. unknown. Anger.

Due, *a.* O.F. *deü*, later *dû*, orig. pa.pple. of *devoir*, L. *dēbēre*, to owe. DEBT. DUTY. That is owing; proper to be given, inflicted, &c.; fitting, proper; adequate; to be ascribed or attributed; under engagement to be present, arrive, &c.—*adv.* Of points of the compass, straight, directly.—*n.* That which is due; a charge, fee, &c. (often in *pl.*).—**Du'**LY,[2] *adv.*

Du'el, *n.* F. *duel*—Med.L. *duellum*, an archaic form of L. *bellum*, war, appropriated to a fight between two—L. *duo*, TWO. REBEL. A fight between two persons.—**Du'ell**IST, *n.*

Duen'na, *n.* Sp. *duenna*, now *dueña*, married lady, mistress—L. *domina*. DAME. The chief lady in waiting on the Queen of Spain; an elderly woman in charge of the girls of a Spanish family; a chaperon.

Duet', *n.* It. *duetto*, dim. of *duo*, a duet—L. *duo*, TWO. A musical composition for two voices or performers.

Duf'fel, **Duff'le**, *n.* *Duffel* in Brabant. A coarse woollen cloth with a thick nap.

Duf'fer, *n.* App. conn. with slang *Duff*, to give (a thing) a new or false appearance, perh. back-formation f. slang *Duffer*, a fraudulent seller of trashy goods, of unknown orig. One who proves to be without ability; an inefficient or stupid person; a counterfeit coin, &c.

Duke, *n.* O.F. *dux*, acc. *duc*—L. *dux*, leader, f. *dūcĕre*, to lead. ABDUCT. A hereditary title of nobility ranking next below that of prince: a sovereign prince.—**Duke'**DOM, *n.*

Dul'cet, *a.* A refashioning after L. *dulcis*,

sweet, of the earlier *doucet*—F. *doucet*, dim. of *doux*, sweet, f. *dulcis*. Sweet, soothing.

Dul'cimer, *n.* O.F. *doulcemer* = obs. Sp. *dulcemele*, It. *dolcemelle*, said to represent L. *dulce melos*, sweet song. (See prec.) A stringed instrument played with two hammers.

Dull, *a.* M.E. *dul*, *dull*, pointing to an O.E. **dyl*, parallel to *dol*, foolish = O.S. *dol*, O.H.G. *tol* (Ger. *toll*). O.Teut. root *dul-*. DWELL. Stupid; insensible, inanimate; of pain, &c., not keen; sluggish; listless; tedious; blunt; not resonant; not clear or bright; of the weather, not bright, gloomy.—*vt.* and *i.* To make, to become, dull. — **Dul'**LY,[2] *adv.* — **Dull'**ARD, *n.*—**Dul(l)'**NESS, *n.*

Dumb, *a.* O.E. *dumb*. Common Teut. Orig. sense perh. 'stupid'. Incapable of speech; silent.—**Dumb'-bell**, *n.* Formerly, an apparatus for exercise like that for swinging a church-bell, but without the bell. One of a pair of weights used for exercise.—**Dumbfound'**, *vt.* *Found* in CONFOUND. To strike dumb; to confound. Also **Dumbfoun'der**, assimilated to FOUNDER.—**Dum'my**, *n.* -Y.[3] An imaginary player at whist, &c.; a counterfeit object.—**Dumb'-show**, *n.* Acting, an acting, without words.

Dum'dum (bul'let). From *Dumdum* in India, with an arsenal. A soft-nosed bullet which expands and lacerates on striking.

Dump, *n.*[1] Of obscure orig. Only in *pl.*, dejection, heaviness of spirits.—**Dump'**Y,[2] *a.*[1]

Dump, *vt.* Perh. of Norse orig. Cf. Da. *dumpe*, Norw. *dumpa*, to fall suddenly. To throw down in a mass.—*n.*[2] A heap of refuse; a place where refuse is 'dumped'; a thud.

Dump, *a.* Prob. conn. with L.G. and East Fris. *dump*, damp, moist. Of the consistence of dough. — **Dump'ling**, *n.* Prob. f. the same source, with -LING.[3] A round pudding of paste containing fruit, &c.

Dump'y, *a.*[2] Of obscure orig. Short and stout. — Hence prob. **Dump**, *n.*[3] Various dumpy objects; a small coin formerly current in Australia; a small coin or amount.

Dun, *a.* O.E. *dunn*, perh. f. Celtic. Of a dull brown colour; dark, dusky.—*n.* The colour.

Dun, *vt.* Orig. uncertain. To make persistent demands upon, esp. for money due.—*n.* One who duns; a demand for payment.

Dunce, *n.* From the name of John *Duns* Scotus, the schoolman, who died in 1308. Formerly, a dull pedant. A dullard, blockhead.

Dune, *n.* F. *dune*—O.Du. *dûna*, M.Du. *dûne* = O.E. *dún*. DOWN, *n.*[1] A mound or hill of drifted sand on the sea-coast.

Dung, *n.* O.E. *dung* = Old Fris. *dung*, O.H.G. *tunga*, manuring. Manure; the excrement of animals.—*vt.* To manure.

Dun'geon, *n.* F. *donjon*—L.L. *domnio*, *domniōnis*, f. L. *domnus* (for *dominus*), lord. DOMINATE. The great tower of a castle (now gen. DONJON); a deep dark vault.

Dun'nage, *n.* Orig. unknown. Cf. Du. *dun*, L.G. *dūn*, thin, *dūnne twige*, brushwood. Light material stowed among and beneath a cargo to prevent chafing, &c.

Duodec'imo, *n.* L., ablative of *duodecimus*, twelfth, in phrase *in duodecimo*, in a twelfth (*sc.* of a sheet). The size of a book in which each sheet is folded into twelve leaves; a book of this size.—*a.* Of this size.

Duode'num, *n.* Med.L. So called from the length = *duodēnum* (*digitōrum*), space of twelve (DIGITS or inches), f. *duodēni*, twelve each. The part of the small intestine immediately below the stomach.

Dupe, *n.* F. *dupe*, of doubtful orig. A victim of delusion.—*vt.* To delude.

Dup'lex, *a.* L. *duplex*, *duplicis*, f. *duo*, TWO + *plic-*, to fold. ACCOMPLICE. Twofold.—

Dup'licate, *vt.* L. *duplicāre*, *duplicātum*, f. *duplex*. To double; to make an exact copy of.—*a.* Twofold; that is the exact counterpart or copy of something.—*n.* One of two things exactly alike, esp. that which is made like the other.—**Duplic**A'TION, *n.*—**Duplic'**ITY, *n.* Double-dealing, deceitfulness.

Du'rance, *n.* O.F. *durance*, duration, f. *durer*. DURE. Endurance (of toil, hardship, &c.); imprisonment.

Dur'bar, *n.* Per. and Urdū *darbār*, court. The court of an Indian ruler; a public audience held by an Indian prince or by the Emperor of India or his viceroy.

Dure, *vi.* F. *durer*, L. *dūrāre*, to harden, to endure, to last, f. *dūrus*, hard. To last, continue in existence.—**Dur'**ABLE, *a.* Permanent; withstanding wear or decay.—**Dur'ably**,[2] *adv.* — **Dura**BIL'ITY, *n.* — **Dura'**TION, *n.* Continuance, length of continuance, in time.—**Dur'ing**, *prep.* In the time of.

Duress', **Duresse'**, *n.* Obs. F. *duresse*, hardness, constraint — L. *dūritia*, f. *dūrus*. (See prec.) Imprisonment; constraint.

Dusk, *a.* Orig. obscure. Dim, shadowy.—*n.* Shade, gloom; the darker stage of twilight. —**Dusk'**Y,[2] *a.*—**Dusk'**ILY,[2] *adv.*

Dust, *n.* O.E. *dúst* = Old Fris. *dûst*, M.L.G., L.G. *dust*, O.N. *dust*, all going back to an earlier *dunst*, whence Ger. *dunst*, vapour. (App. the primary notion is 'that which is blown in a cloud', like vapour, dust, &c.) Fine dry particles of earth, &c.; a cloud of dust.—*vt.* To sprinkle with dust or powder; to free from dust.—**Dust'**ER, *n.* A cloth for removing dust.—**Dust'**Y,[2] *a.*

Du'ty, *n.* A.F. *deueté*, f. *du* = O.F. *deü*. DUE. Due respect, reverence; a payment to the public revenue levied on commodities, transfers of property, &c.; that which one ought or is bound to do; moral obligation; business, office.—**Du'te**OUS, *a.*—**Du'ti**FUL, *a.*—**Du'ti**ABLE, *a.* On which a duty is levied.

Dwarf, *n.* O.E. *dweorg*, *dweorh*. Common Teut. A person much below the usual size.—*a.* Of unusually small size.—*vt.* To make dwarf; to cause to seem small by contrast or distance.—**Dwarf'**ISH, *a.*

Dwell, *vi.* O.E. *dwellan*, to mislead, delay, to go astray. O.Teut. root *dwel-*, *dwal-*, *dwol-*, (*dul-*), to be torpid, to cease, to err. DULL. Formerly, to mislead; to hinder; to tarry. To continue for a time in a place or condition; *to dwell on* or *upon*, to treat at length in speech or writing; to reside, live.—**Dwel'**LER, *n.*—**Dwel'ling**, *vbl.n.* A place of residence.

Dwin'dle, *vi.* A dim. deriv. of archaic *Dwine* in sim. sense—O.E. *dwīnan*, corresp. to O.N. *dvína*, M.L.G. and L.G. *dwinen*. To waste away, decline; to degenerate.

Dye, *n.* O.E. *déag*, *déah*. Teut. type **daugâ-*. Tinge, hue; colouring matter in solution.—*vt.* To colour; to impregnate (clothes, &c.) with a colour.—**Dy'**ER, *n.*

Dynam'ic, *a.* F. *dynamique*—G. *dunamikos*, powerful, f. *dunamis*, power, f. *dunasthai*, to be able or powerful. Of or relating to force producing motion; active, potent.—In *pl.* as *n.*, the branch of physics which treats of the action of force. Also **Dynam'**ICAL, *a.*—

Dy'namite, *n.* Coined f. *dunamis* + suff. *-ite* of scientific terms. An explosive made from nitroglycerine mixed with an inert substance.—**Dy'namo**, *n.* Abb. f. *Dynamo-electric machine.* A machine for converting mechanical into electric energy.

Dy'nasty, *n.* F. *dynastie*—L.L. *dynastia*—G. *dunasteia*, lordship, f. *dunastēs*, lord, f. *dunasthai.* (See prec.) A line of kings.—**Dynas'tic**, *a.*

Dy'sentery, *n.* O.F. *dissenterie*—L. *dysenteria*, G. *dusenteria*, f. *dus-*, pref. giving notion 'bad' + *entera*, bowels. A disorder characterized by inflammation of the large intestine.

Dyspep'sia, *n.* L., f. G. *duspepsia*, indigestion, f. *duspeptos*, hard to digest, f. *dus-* (see prec.) + *pessein, peptein*, to COOK, digest. PEPSIN. Indigestion.—**Dyspep'tic**, *a.*

E

Each, *a.* and *pron.* M.E. *elc, eche*—O.E. *ǽlc*, short for *á gelíc*, ever alike, *á*, AY + *gelíc*, LIKE. Cf. Du. *elk*, O.H.G. *eogilīh* (Ger. *jeglich*). EITHER. Every one taken separately.

Ea'ger, *a.* O.F. *aigre*, sharp, sour—L. *ācer, acris*, from root *ac-*. ACID. ACRID. Full of or characterized by keen desire.—**Ea'gerly**,[2] *adv.*—**Ea'gerness**, *n.*

Ea'gle, *n.* O.F. *egle, aigle*—L. *aquila.* A large bird of prey with keen sight.—**Eag'let**, *n.* Dim. suff. *-et.* A young eagle.

Ear, *n.*[1] O.E. *éare.* Common Teut. Cogn. with G. *ous*, L. *auris.* The organ of hearing; sensitiveness to musical sounds; listening, attention.—**Ear'wig**, *n.* O.E. *éarwicga*, f. *éar-e* + *wicga*, a kind of insect. Cf. Provincial Eng. *wiggle*, to wriggle. An insect named from the notion that it penetrates into the head through the ear.

Ear, *n.*[2] O.E. *éar* = O.H.G. *ehir*, O.N. *ax.* Cogn. with L. *acus*, chaff. A spike of corn.

Ear, *vt.* O.E. *erian.* Common Teut. Cogn. with G. *aroein*, L. *arāre.* ARABLE. To plough.

Earl, *n.* O.E. *eorl* = O.S. *erl*, warrior, O.N. *earl*, nobleman. A title of nobility giving rank next below a marquis.—**Earl'dom**, *n.*

Ear'ly, *adv.* and *a.* O.E. *árlíce*, adv. f. **ár*, positive of *ǽr*, ERE + *-líce*, -LY.[2] In the first part of the morning, life, &c.

Earn, *vt.* O.E. *earnian*, conn. with Goth. *asans*, O.H.G. *aran*, harvest, O.H.G. *esni*, hired labourer. Primary sense, 'to get for labour'. To gain by labour, &c., to merit.

Ear'nest, *n.*[1] O.E. *eornust* = O.H.G. *ernust*, M.H.G. *ernest* (Ger. *ernst*). Seriousness, serious intention, esp. in phrase, *in earnest.*—*a.* O.E. *eorneste*, f. the *n.* Serious. sincerely zealous; intense, ardent; springing from intense feeling or conviction.—**Ear'nestly**,[2] *adv.*

Ear'nest, *n.*[2] Of obscure orig. App. conn. with obs. *Erres* in same sense—O.F. *erres*, pl. (F. *arrhes*)—L. *arrha.* Money paid to bind a bargain; a foretaste, pledge.

Earth, *n.* O.E. *eorthe.* Common Teut. Cogn. with G. *era-ze*, to the ground. The ground, the soil; the dry land; land and sea as distinguished from the heaven; the planet we inhabit; soil, mould, clay.—*vt.* To cover with earth.—**Earth'en**,[1] *a.*—**Earth'enware**, *n.* Vessels, &c., of baked clay.—**Earth'ly**,[1] *a.*—**Earth'y**,[2] *a.*—**Earth'quake**, *n.* A convulsion of the earth's surface.

Ease, *n.* O.F. *eise, aise*—L.L. type **asia, *asium*, of uncertain orig. DISEASE. Comfort, convenience; freedom from annoyance; leisure; idleness, sloth; facility; freedom from awkwardness; relief, alleviation.—*vt.* To give ease of mind or body to; to relieve *of* a burden, &c.; to lighten, lessen, assuage; to relax slightly.—*vi. To ease off*, to become less burdensome.—**Ease'ful**, *a.*—**Ease'ment**, *n.* O.F. *aisement*, f. *aisier*, to put at ease. Relief, alleviation; the right of using something not one's own.—**Eas'y**, *a.* O.F. *aisié*, pa.pple. of *aisier.* Comfortable, luxurious; free from pain, annoyance, anxiety, &c.; free from awkwardness; indolent, careless; presenting few difficulties; compliant; credulous; got with ease; not burdensome; fitting loosely.—**Eas'ily**,[2] *adv.*

Ea'sel, *n.* Du. *ezel*, ass, easel = Ger. *esel*, ass. Cf. the sim. use of *horse.* A frame to support a picture which is being painted.

East, *adv.* O.E. *éast.* Cf. Du. *oost*, Ger. *ost.* O.Teut. base *aus-*, dawn. Cogn. with Skr. *ushās*, G. *auōs, ēōs*, L. *aurōra* (*ausōsa*), dawn. AURORA. In the direction of the rising sun.—*n.* The part of the sky where the sun rises; the eastern part of the world, a country, &c.—*a.* Towards or from the east.—**East'erly**,[1] *a.* Cf. NORTHERLY, &c.—**East'ern**, *a.*—**East'ward**, *adv.* and *a.*—**East'wards**, *adv.*

Eas'ter, *n.* O.E. *éastre.* Said to be f. *Eastre*, the name of a goddess whose festival fell at the vernal equinox, cogn. with EAST, and hence app. orig. the dawn-goddess. The festival commemorating Christ's resurrection.

Eat, *vt.* O.E. *etan.* Common Teut. Cogn. with Skr. *ad-*, G. *edein*, L. *edĕre.* ETCH. FRET, *v.*[2] To swallow as food; to devour, prey upon, ravage; to gnaw; to wear away.—*vi.* To take food; to have a certain consistence or flavour; to make a way by eating.—**Eat'able**, *a.*

Eaves, *n.pl.* O.E. *efes*, sing., prob. f. same root as OVER. (The final *-s* led to mistaking the word for a plural.) The edge of the roof of a building, &c., which overhangs the side.—**Eaves'drop**, *n.* The dropping of water from the eaves; the space of ground receiving the water.—*vi.* To stand within this space in order to listen to what is said in the house; hence, to listen secretly to private conversation.—**Eaves'dropper**, *n.*

Ebb, *n.* O.E. *ebba* = Old Fris. *ebba*, Du. *ebbe*, *eb.* The flowing back of the tide; decline.—*vi.* Of the tide, to flow back; to decline.

Eb'ony, *n.* M.E. *hebenyf*, app. f. L. *hebeninus* (misread *hebeniuus*), of ebony, f. *hebenus, ebenus*, G. *ebenos*, ebony, prob. of Phœnician origin. A hard black wood.

Ebri'ety, *n.* F. *ébriété*—L. *ēbrietas*, f. *ēbrius*, drunk. INEBRIATE. Drunkenness.

Ebulli'tion, *n.* L. *ēbullitio, ēbullitiōnis*, f. *ēbullire*, to bubble up. BOIL, *v.* Boiling; effervescence; a sudden outburst (of passion, &c.).—**Ebul'lience**, *n.*—**Ebul'lient**, *a.*

Ecarté, *n.* F., f. *écarter*, to discard, f. E- + *carte*, CARD.[2] (So called from a rule as to discarding.) A card-game for two.

Eccen'tric, *a.* L.L. *eccentricus*, with suff. *-icus* f. G. *ekkentros*, out of the centre, f. *ek*, out of + *kentron* (= L. *centrum*), CENTRE. Not having the axis in the centre; of motion, not circular; anomalous, irregular; odd, whimsical.—*n.* A contrivance for converting rotary into backward-and-forward motion; an eccentric person.—**Eccen'trically**, *adv.* -AL. -LY.[2]—**Eccentric'ity**, *n.*

Ecclesias'tic, *a.* Through F. and L. f. G

ekklēsiastikos, f. *ekklēsia*, church. Of or belonging to the church.—*n.* A clergyman.—Sim.
Ecclesias'tICAL, *a.*—**Ecclesiol'OGY**, *n.* The science relating to the church, esp. to church building and decoration.
Ech'elon, *n.* F. *échelon*, f. *échelle*, L. *scāla*, ladder. SCALE.[3] A formation of troops in parallel divisions each with its front clear of that in advance.
Ech'o, *n.* L. *ēchō*—G. *ēchō*, conn. with *ēchē*, sound, *ēche-ein*, to sound. CATECHIZE. A repetition of sounds by reflexion; a close imitation.—*vi.* To resound with an echo; to be repeated by echoes.—*vt.* To repeat in the manner of an echo, imitate.
Eclec'tic, *a.* G. *eklektikos*, selective, f. *eklegein*, to select, f. *ek*, out + *legein*, to choose. ECLOGUE. Borrowing or borrowed from various sources; selecting doctrines from various schools.—*n.* An Eclectic philosopher.—**Eclec'ticISM**, *n.*
Eclipse', *n.* O.F. *eclipse*—L. *eclipsis*—G. *ekleipsis*, f. *ekleipein*, to leave out, to be eclipsed, f. *ek*, out + *leipein*, to leave. ELLIPSE. An interception of the light of the sun, &c., by another body; obscurity, dimness.—*vt.* To cause to suffer eclipse; to obscure; to outshine, surpass.—**Eclip'tic**, *a.* G. *ekleiptikos*, f. *ekleipein*. Of or pertaining to an eclipse.—*n.* The apparent path of the sun, near which the moon must be to cause an eclipse.
Ec'logue, *n.* L. *ecloga*—G. *eklogē*, selection, f. *eklegein*. ECLECTIC. A short poem, esp. a pastoral dialogue.
Econ'omy, *n.* L. *oeconomia*—G. *oikonomia*, f. *oikonomos*, house-manager, f. *oikos*, house + *-nomos*, f. *nemein*, to manage. ASTRONOMY. DIOCESE. Management, administration; frugality, thrift; structure, arrangement, organization.—**Econom'IC**, *a.*—In *pl.* as *n.*, the science of the production and distribution of wealth.—**Econom'ICAL**, *a.*—**Econom'icalLY**,[2] *adv.*—**Econ'omIST**, *n.*—**Econ'omIZE**, *vt.* and *i.* To manage with prudence.
Ecru', *a.* F. *écru*. Of the colour of unbleached linen.—*n.* The colour.
Ec'stasy, *n.* O.F. *extasie*—Med.L. *extasis*—G. *ekstasis*, a standing aside, distraction of mind, f. *ek*, out + *sta-*, to STAND. Frenzy or stupor; a trance; rapture.—**Ecstat'IC**, *a.*—**Ecstat'ically**, *adv.* -AL. -LY.[2]
Ec'zema, *n.* G. *ekzema*, f. *ekze-ein*, to boil out or over, f. *ek*, out + *ze-ein*, to boil. A cutaneous eruption.
Eda'cious, *a.* L. *edax*, *edācis* (f. *edĕre*, to EAT) + -OUS. EDIBLE. Of eating; greedy.
Ed'dy, *n.* Of unknown orig. A circular current of water or air.—*vi.* and *t.* To move, to cause to move, in an eddy.
Edge, *n.* O.E. *ecg* = O.N. *egg*, O.H.G. *ekka*. From root *ak-*, *ac-* in ACID. EGG, *v.* The sharpened side of a blade; sharpness; a border. —*vt.* To give an edge or border to; to move gradually.—*vi.* To advance sideways or gradually.—**Edge'WAYS**, **Edge'WISE**, *advv.*
Ed'ible, *a.* L.L. *edibilis*, f. *edĕre*, to EAT. ESCULENT. OBESE. Eatable.
E'dict, *n.* L. *ēdictum*, f. *Edicĕre*, to say out, proclaim. ADDICT. An order or ordinance.
Ed'ifY, *vt.* F. *édifier*—L. *aedificāre*, to build, edify, f. *aedes*, house + *facĕre*, to make. -FY. To build up spiritually; to instruct, improve. —**EdificA'TION**, *n.*—**Ed'ifice**, *n.* L. *aedificium*. A building, esp. a large one.
Ed'it, *vt.* L. *ēdĕre*, *ēditum*, to put forth, f. E- + *dăre*, to give. DATE.[2] To prepare for publication; to conduct (a newspaper, &c.).—**Edi'tION**, *n.* One of the forms in which a work is published; the number of copies of a book printed at once.—**Ed'itOR**, *n.*—**Edito'RIAL**, *a.* As *n.*, a newspaper article written or inspired by the editor.—**Ed'itorSHIP**, *n.*
Ed'ucate, *vt.* L. *ēducāre*, *ēducātum*, to bring up, rear, related to *ēdūcĕre*. EDUCE. To bring up and train (young persons); to instruct. —**EducA'TION**, *n.*—**Educa'tionAL**, *a.*—**Educa'tionIST**, **Educa'tionalIST**, *nn.*—**Ed'ucATIVE**, *a.*—**Ed'ucatOR**, *n.*
Educe', *vt.* L. *Edūcĕre*, *ēductum*, to lead forth. DUKE. To bring out, develop.—**Edu'cIBLE**, *a.*—**Educ'tION**, *n.*
Eel, *n.* O.E. *ǽl*. Common Teut. A snake-like fish.
Ee'rie, **Ee'ry**, *a.* M.E. *eri*, perh., with -Y[2], f. obs. *Argh*, timid—O.E. *earg*. Common Teut. Timid, fearful; fear-inspiring.
Efface', *vt.* F. *effacer*, f. L. *ef-* (= EX-) + *facies*. FACE. To rub out, expunge, erase; to do away with; to wipe out, blot out; to reduce to insignificance.—**Efface'MENT**, *n.*
Effect', *n.* O.F. *effect* (F. *effet*)—L. *effectus*, f. *efficĕre*, *effectum*, to work out, f. *ef-* (= EX-) + *facĕre*, to make. AFFECT. A result, consequence; efficacy; operative influence; impression produced; accomplishment; in *pl.*, movable property; *in effect*, virtually, substantially.—*vt.* To bring about, accomplish.—**Effec'tIVE**, *a.* Attended with result; effectual; fit for service.—**Effec'tiveLY**,[2] *adv.*—**Effec'tual**, *a.* O.F. *effectuel*—L.L. *effectuālis* That produces the intended result.—**Effec'tualLY**,[2] *adv.*—**Effec'tuATE**,[3] *vt.* To bring about, accomplish.—**EffectuA'TION**, *n.*
Effem'inate, *a.* L. *effēminātus*, pa.pple. of *effēmināre*, to make womanish, f. *ef-* (= EX-) + *fēmina*, woman. FEMALE. Womanish, unmanly; voluptuous.—**Effem'inACY**, *n.*
Effervesce', *vi.* L. *effervescĕre*, f. *ef-* (= EX-) + *fervescĕre*, inceptive of *fervēre*, to boil. FERVENT. To give off bubbles.—**Efferves'CENCE**, *n.*—**Efferves'CENT**, *a.*
Effete', *a.* L. *effētus*, that has brought forth young, hence, worn out, f. *ef-* (= EX-) + *fētus*, pregnant. Exhausted; feeble.
Ef'ficacy, *n.* L. *efficācia*, f. *efficax*, *efficācis*, powerful, f. *efficĕre*. EFFECT. Power to produce the intended result.—**EfficA'CIOUS**, *a.*
Effic'ient, *a.* F. *efficient*—L. *efficiens*, *efficientis*, pres.pple. of *efficĕre*. EFFECT. Causing to be; adequately operative; adequately skilled. —**Effic'ientLY**,[2] *adv.*—**Effic'iENCY**, *n.*
Ef'figy, *n.* F. *effigie*—L. *effigies*, f. *ef* (= EX-)-*fingĕre*, to fashion forth. FIGURE. A likeness, image.
Effloresce', *vi.* L. *efflōrescĕre*, f. *ef-* (= EX-) + *flōrescĕre*, inceptive of *flōrēre*, to blossom, f. *flōs*, *flōris*, FLOWER. To burst into flower; to become manifest.—**Effiores'CENCE**, *n.*—**Efflores'CENT**, *a.*
Ef'fluent, *a.* L. *effluens*, *effluentis*, pres.pple. of *ef* (= EX-) *fluĕre*, to flow out. AFFLUENT. That flows forth.—*n.* A stream flowing from a larger stream, a lake, &c.—**Ef'fluENCE**, *n.* —**Efflu'vium**, *n.* L.L., f. *effluĕre*. Something flowing out invisibly; a disagreeable smell.—**Ef'flux**, *n.* From the ppl. stem. A flowing out; lapse (of time); an emanation. Sim. **Efflux'ION**, *n.*
Ef'fort, *n.* F. *effort*, f. (*s'*)*efforcer*, to endeavour—Med.L. *exfortiāre*, to use force, f. EX- + L. *fortis*, strong. COMFORT. A strenuous putting forth of power.

Effron'tery, *n.* F. *effronterie*, f. *effronté*, unblushing, app. f. *ef-* (= EX-) in sense 'lacking' + *front*, L. *frons, frontis*, forehead. FRONT. Shameless audacity, unblushing insolence.

Efful'gent, *a.* L. *effulgens, effulgentis*, f. *ef-* (= EX-) *fulgēre*, to shine forth. Brightly shining.—**Efful'gENCE**, *n.*

Effuse', *vt.* L. *ef* (= EX-) *fundĕre, effūsum*, to pour forth. CONFOUND. To pour out, shed, send forth.—**Effu'SION**, *n.* A pouring forth, a shedding; effusiveness; a literary production.—**Effu'SIVE**, *a.* Demonstratively expressed; expressing feeling demonstratively.—**Effu'siveLY**,[2] *adv.*—**Effu'siveNESS**, *n.*

Eft, *n.* O.E. *efeta*. Orig. unknown. A NEWT.

Egg, *n.* O.E. *æg*. Common Teut. The spheroidal body produced by the female of birds, &c., and containing the germ of their young.

Egg, *vt.* O.N. *eggja*, f. *egg*, EDGE. To urge *on*.

Eg'lantine, *n.* F. *églantine*, O.F. *aiglent*, prob. f. L. type **aculentus*, prickly, f. *acus*, needle. Root *ac-*. ACID. The sweet-brier.

Eg'oism, *n.* F. *égoïsme*, f. L. *ego*, I. -ISM. The belief that nothing exists but one's own mind; the theory that self-interest is the basis of morality, systematic selfishness; egotism.—**Eg'OIST**, *n.*—**Eg'otISM**, *n.* (With intrusive *t*.) The practice of talking, the vice of thinking, too much of oneself.—**Eg'otIST**, *n.*—**Egotis'tIC**, **Egotis'tICAL**, *aa.*

Egre'gious, *a.* L. *ēgregius*, f. E-, out of, hence, excelling + *grex, gregis*, the flock. AGGREGATE. Excellent; gross, flagrant.

E'gress, *n.* L. *ēgressus*, f. *ēgredi, ēgressus*, to go out, f. E- + *gradi*, to go. AGGRESSION. A going, a means of going, out.—*vi.* To go out.

E'gret, *n.* Var. of AIGRETTE. The Lesser White Heron.

Ei'der, *n.* Ultimately f. Icel. *æthar*, genit. of *æthr*, eider-duck, in the combination *æthardún*, eider-DOWN. An Arctic species of duck.

Eight, *a.* and *n.* O.E. *eahta*. Common Teut. and Aryan. Cogn. with G. *oktō*, L. *octo*. The cardinal number next after seven.

Eire'nicon, *n.* G. *eirēnikon*, neut. of *eirēnikos*, a. f. *eirēnē*, peace. A proposal tending to make peace.

Ei'ther, *a.* and *pron.* O.E. *ǽgther*, contracted f. *ǽghwæther*, f. *á*, AY + *ge-*, a prefix + *hwæther*, WHETHER. Cf. Du. *ieder*, Ger. *jeder*. EACH. One or the other; one of two; each.—*adv.* or *conj.* Used disjunctively as correlative to *or*.

Ejac'ulate, *vt.* L. EJaculāri, *ējaculātus*, to hurl forth, f. *jaculum*, dart. To say suddenly.—**EjaculA'TION**, *n.*—**Ejac'ulatORY**, *a.*

Eject', *vt.* L. *ējectāre*, freq. of *ējicĕre, ējectum*, to throw forth, f. E- + *jacĕre*, to throw. ABJECT. To throw out; to expel, drive out, evict *from*.—**Ejec'tION**, *n.*—**Eject'MENT**, *n.*

Eke, *vt.* O.E. *écan, íecan*. Teut. type **aukjan*. Cf. O.N. *auka*, Goth. *aukan*. Cogn. with G. *auxanein*, L. *augēre*. AUGMENT. To increase; *to eke out*, to supplement, to prolong, to contrive to make (a livelihood).

Eke, *adv.* O.E. *éac*. Common Teut. Also.

Elab'orate, *vt.* L. ELabōrāre, *ēlabōrātum*, to work out, f. *labor*, LABOUR. To produce; to work out in detail.—*ppl.a.* Highly finished; conducted with minuteness, minutely careful.—**ElaborA'TION**, *n.*

E'land, *n.* Du. *eland*, elk—Ger. *elen(d)*—Lithuanian *élnis*. A large S. African antelope.

Elapse', *vi.* L. ELābi, *ēlapsus*, to slip away. COLLAPSE. Of time, to slip by.

Elas'tic, *a.* Mod.L. *elasticus*, as if f. a G. **elastikos*, that drives, f. *ela-*, stem of *elaunein*, to drive. Spontaneously resuming the normal form after distortion, &c.—**Elastic'ITY**, *n.*

Elate', *vt.* L. *ef* (= EX-) *ferre, ēlātum*, to bring forth, to raise. COLLATE. To inspirit; to puff up, make proud.—**ElA'TION**, *n.*

El'bow, *n.* O.E. *elboga, elnboga*, f. *eln* (ELL) + *boga*, a bow, a bending. BOW, *n.*[1] Cf. Du. *elleboog*, Ger. *ell(en)bogen*. The outer part of the joint of the arm.—*vt.* To thrust with the elbow.—quasi-*refl.* To force one's way thus.—quasi-*trans.* To make (one's way) thus.

El'der, *n.*[1] The *d* is excrescent. M.E. *eller*—O.E. *ellen, ellærn*. Cf. M.L.G. *ellern*, Flemish *elhoren*. A low tree with much pith.

El'der, *a.* O.E. *ældra*, comp. of *ald*, OLD. Older; earlier, former.—*n.* (One's) superior in age; one of a governing body or class of old persons; an official in certain churches.—**El'derLY**,[1] *a.*—**El'dest**, *a.* O.E. *ældesta*, superl. of *ald*. Oldest; first, most ancient.

Elect', *vt.* L. *ēligĕre, ēlectum*, to pick out, f. E- + *legĕre*, to choose. COLLECT, *v.* To choose (a course of action, &c.); to choose (a person) by vote for an office or position.—*ppl.a.* Picked out, chosen; select, choice; chosen for an office, &c., but not yet acting.—**Elec'tION**, *n.*—**Electioneer'**, *vi.* Prob. formed after '*auctioneer*'. To busy oneself in (political) elections.—**Elec'tIVE**, *a.*—**Elec'tOR**, *n.*—**Elec'torAL**, *a.*—**Elec'torATE**,[1] *n.* The body of electors.

Elec'tric, *a.* Mod.L. *ēlectricus*, f. L. *ēlectrum*, G. *ēlectron*, amber. Having the property (first observed in amber) of developing electricity in certain conditions; charged with, of the nature of, pertaining to, electricity.—So, in the latter sense, **Elec'trICAL**, *a.*—**Elec'tricalLY**,[2] *adv.*—**ElectricI'AN**, *n.*—**Electric'ITY**, *n.* The force that manifests itself in lighting and many other phenomena; the branch of physical science dealing therewith.—**Elec'triFY**, *vt.* To charge with electricity, (often *fig.*)—**Electrol'ysis**, *n.* G. *lusis* as in ANALYSIS. Decomposition by electricity.—**Elec'tro-plate**, *vt.* To coat with silver by electric action.—*n.* Articles so coated.

Elec'tuary, *n.* L.L. *ēlectuārium*, perh. corr. of synonymous G. *ekleikton*, f. *ekleichein*, to LICK out. A medicinal powder, &c., mixed with honey, &c.

Eleemos'ynary, *a.* Med.L. *eleēmosynārius*, f. L.L. *eleēmosyna*. ALMS. Of or pertaining to alms; supported by, of the nature of, alms.

El'egant, *a.* F. *élégant*—L. *ēlegans, ēlegantis*, prob. a collateral form of *ēligens*, pres.pple. of *ēligĕre*, with sense 'choosing carefully'. ELECT. Tastefully ornate in attire; foppish; tastefully ornamental; graceful; characterized by refinement; refined in manners; appropriate to persons of refinement.—**El'egANCE**, *n.*

El'egy, *n.* F. *élégie*—L. *elegia*—G. *elegeia*, f. *elegos*, a mournful poem. A lament for the dead.—**Elegi'ac**, *a.* G. *elegeiakos*. Suited to elegies; plaintive; consisting of dactylic hexameters and pentameters alternately.—In *pl.* as *n.*, elegiac verses.

El'ement, *n.* O.F. *element*—L. *elementum*, a first principle. Orig. uncertain. A substance which resists chemical analysis; a constituent part; a factor or ingredient; *the four elements*, traditionally earth, water, air and fire; proper state or sphere; in *pl.* atmospheric powers, rudiments, first principles, the bread and wine used in the Eucharist.—**Elemen'tAL**, *a.*—**Elemen'tARY**, *a.*

Elen'chus, *n.* L. *elenchus*—G. *elegchos*, cross-examination. A logical refutation.

El'ephant, *n.* M.E. *olifaunt*—O.F. *olifant*, corrupted f. L. *elephantus*—G. *elephas, elephantos.* A large quadruped with long tusks and a prehensile proboscis.—**Elephanti'asis**, *n.* L.—G., f. *elephas.* A skin disease causing in the part affected a resemblance to an elephant's hide.—**Elephan'tINE**, *a.*

El'evate, *vt.* L. *Elevāre, ēlevātum*, to lift up, f. *levis*, light. ALLEVIATE. To raise, lift up; to exalt in rank; to elate.—**ElevA'TION**, *n.* In senses from the *v.*; a drawing representing a building, &c., in vertical section.—**El'evaTOR**, *n.* A machine for raising persons or weights to an upper storey.

Elev'en, *a.* and *n.* O.E. *endleofon.* A Common Teut. compound. Teut. **ain-* (**aino-*), ONE + *-lif-*, of uncertain orig. The cardinal number next after ten.

Elf, *n.*; *pl.* **Elves**. O.E. *ælf* = O.N. *álfr* (Da. *alf*). OAF. A fairy; a tricksy creature.—**El'fin**, *a.* Obscurely f. the *n.* Pertaining to elves; like an elf.—**El'fISH**, **El'VISH**, *aa.*

Elic'it, *vt.* L. *ēlicĕre, ēlicitum*, to entice out, f. E- + *lacĕre*, to entice. DELICIOUS. To draw forth, bring out, educe, evoke.

Elide', *vt.* L. *ēlīdĕre, ēlīsum*, to strike out, f. E- + *laedĕre*, to strike. COLLIDE. To omit (a vowel or syllable).—**Eli'SION**, *n.*

El'igible, *a.* F. *éligible*, as if f. a L. **ēligibilis*, f. *ēligĕre.* ELECT. Fit or qualified to be elected or chosen; desirable.—**EligiBIL'ITY**, *n.*

Elim'inate, *vt.* L. *ēlīmināre, ēlīminātum*, to thrust out of doors, f. E- + *līmen, līminis*, threshold. PRELIMINARY. To remove, expel, get rid of.—**EliminA'TION**, *n.*

Elix'ir, *n.* Med.L. *elixir*—Arab. *al-iksīr* (*al* being the definite article), in the first sense below, prob. f. Late G. *xērion*, dry powder for wounds, f. G. *xēros*, dry. A preparation by which it was sought to change metals into gold; a supposed drug prolonging life.

Elk, *n.* Prob. f. M.H.G. *elch.* Cf. O.N. *elgr* (Sw. *elg*). The largest species of deer.

Ell, *n.* O.E. *eln.* Common Teut. Orig. meaning, arm or fore-arm. Cogn. with G. *ōlenē*, L. *ulna.* ELBOW. A measure of length.

Ellipse', *n.* G. *elleipsis*, f. *elleipein*, to leave behind, to fall short, f. *en-*, in + *leipein*, to leave, cogn. with L. *linquĕre.* ECLIPSE. DELINQUENT. A curve produced by a plane cutting a cone at an angle less than that between the side and the base; an oval.—**Ellip'sis**, *n.* L. *ellīpsis*, f. the G. word. The omission of a word or words necessary to complete the grammatical construction or to express the full sense.—**Ellip'tIC**, **Ellip'tICAL**, *aa.*

Elm, *n.* O.E. *elm* = O.H.G. *elm.* Cogn. with L. *ulmus.* A well-known tree.

Elocu'tion, *n.* L. *ēlocūtio, ēlocūtiōnis*, f. *Eloqui, ēlocūtus*, to speak out. ALLOCUTE. The management of the voice and gestures in public speaking.—**Elocu'tionIST**, *n.*

E'longate, *vt.* L.L. *ēlongāre, ēlongātum*, to set at a distance, f. E- + L. *longē*, far away, f. *longus*, LONG. Formerly, to set at a distance. To lengthen.—**ElongA'TION**, *n.*

Elope', *vi.* A.F. *aloper*, perh. f. M.E. *alopen* as pa.pple. of **aleapen*, f. A- (2) + LEAP. To run away with a lover; to escape, abscond.—**Elope'MENT**, *n.*

El'oquent, *a.* F. *éloquent*—L. *ēloquens, ēloquentis*, pres.pple. of *ēloqui.* ELOCUTION. Having, marked by, fluent, forcible and apt expression.—**El'oquENCE**, *n.*

Else, *adv.* O.E. *elles*, advbl. use of genit. neut. of O.Teut. stem *aljo-* = L. *alius*, other. ALIEN. Besides; instead; otherwise.—**Else'where**, *adv.* In or to some other place.

Elu'cidate, *vt.* L.L. *ēlūcidāre, ēlūcidātum*, f. E- + L. *lūcidus*, bright. LUCID. To throw light upon, explain.—**ElucidA'TION**, *n.*

Elude', *vt.* L. *Elūdĕre, ēlūsum*, to play off, parry. ALLUDE. To escape by dexterity or artifice; to evade; to slip away from.—**Elu'SION**, *n.*—**Elu'SIVE**, *a.*—**Elu'SORY**, *a.*

Elys'ium, *n.* G. *ēlusion* (*pedion*), the Elysian (plain). See Odyssey, 4, 563. The supposed abode of the blessed dead; a delightful place or state.—**Elys'IAN**, *a.*

Ema'ciate, *vt.* L. *ēmaciāre, ēmaciātum*, f. E- + *macies*, leanness, f. *macer*, lean. MEAGRE. To make lean.—**EmaciA'TION**, *n.*

Em'anate, *vi.* L. *Emānāre, ēmānātum.* To flow forth, issue.—**EmanA'TION**, *n.*

Eman'cipate, *vt.* L. *ēmancipāre, ēmancipātum*, to set free, f. E- + *mancipāre*, to transfer property, f. *manceps, mancipis*, purchaser, lit., 'one who takes (property) in hand', f. *manus*, hand + *capĕre*, to take. MANAGE. ACCEPT. To set free.—**EmancipA'TION**, *n.*

Emas'culate, *vt.* L. *ēmasculāre, ēmasculātum*, f. E- + *masculus.* MASCULINE. To deprive of virility.—**EmasculA'TION**, *n.*

Embalm', *vt.* F. *embaumer*, f. EM-[1] (1) + *baume* (O.F. *basme*), BALM. To preserve (a corpse) with spices (often *fig.*).

Embank', *vt.* EM-[1] (1) + BANK, *n.*[1] To enclose, protect or support by a bank.—**Embank'MENT**, *n.*

Embar'go, *n.* Sp., f. *embargar*, to arrest, impede, representing L.L. **imbarricāre*, f. *im-* (= IN-[1]) + *barra*, BAR. An order stopping ships; a suspension of commerce.—*vt.* To lay an embargo on; to seize for state service.

Embark', *vt.* F. *embarquer*—L.L. *imbarcāre*, f. *im-* (= IN-[1]) + *barca*, BARK, *n.*[2] To put on board ship; to invest (money), involve (a person) *in.*—*vi.* To go on board ship; to engage *in* (a course of action, &c.).—**EmbarkA'TION**, *n.*

Embar'rass, *vt.* F. *embarrasser*, lit., 'to obstruct', f. *embarras*, obstacle, conn. with *embarrer*, to obstruct, f. EM-[1] (1) + *barre*, BAR. To involve in difficulties; to perplex; to make difficult, complicate.—**Embar'rassMENT**, *n.*

Em'bassy, *n.* A var. of (? obs.) *Ambassy*—O.F. *ambassée*—L.L. **ambactiāta*, ppl. deriv. of **ambactiāre.* AMBASSADOR. The function or office of an ambassador; his official residence; the ambassador and his retinue.

Embed', **Imbed'**, *vt.* EM-[1] (1). IN-.[1] To fix firmly in something solid; to enclose firmly.

Embel'lish, *vt.* O.F. *embelliss-*, stem of *embellir*, f. EM-[1] (2) + *bel*, L. *bellus.* BEAUTY. To adorn.—**Embel'lishMENT**, *n.*

Em'ber, *n.*[1] O.E. *æmerge*, corresp. to O.H.G. *eimuria*, O.N. *eimyrja.* A glowing cinder.

Em'ber, *n.*[2] O.E. *ymbren*, ember-day, perh a corr. of *ymbryne*, period, revolution of time, f. *ymb*, about, round (= Ger. *um*, G. *amphi*) + *ryne*, course, running, f. *rinnan*, to RUN. *Ember-days*, days appointed for fasting recurring in each of the four seasons.

Embez'zle, *vt.* A.F. *enbesiler*, to make away with, fraudulently destroy, f. EN-[1] (3) + *beseler* = O.F. *besillier*, to maltreat, destroy, app. f. L. *bis* (BI-), in L.L. used as a pref. with unfavourable sense. To appropriate (money, &c.) in breach of trust or duty.—**Embez'zleMENT**, *n.*—**Embez'zlER**, *n.*

Embit'ter, *vt.* EM-[1] (2). To make bitter, to aggravate; to make virulent.

Embla'zon, *vt.* EM-[1] (3). To portray con-

spicuously as on a heraldic shield; to adorn *with* heraldic devices, &c.; to celebrate, extol.
Em'blem, *n.* L. *emblēma, emblēmatis*, a raised ornament, mosaic work—G. *emblēma*, an insertion, f. *emballein*, to put in, f. EM-² + *ballein*, to throw. HYPERBOLA. PROBLEM. A symbolical picture; a symbol; a device.—**Emblemat'**IC, **Emblemat'**ICAL, *aa.*
Embod'y, Imbod'y, *vt.* EM-¹ (1). IN.¹ To put into, invest with, a body; to be an expression of; to incorporate; to include; to organize.—**Em-, Imbod'**IMENT, *n.*
Embol'den, Imbol'den, *vt.* EM-¹ (2), IN-¹ + BOLD + -EN.² To make bold.
Emboss', *vt.* EM-¹ (1). To put bosses on; to carve or adorn in relief.
Embouchure, *n.* F., f. *emboucher*, to put in the mouth, f. EM-¹ (1) + *bouche*. DEBOUCH. The mouth of a river or valley.
Embow'el, *vt.* O.F. *enboweler*, an alteration, with change of suffix, of *esboueler*, f. *es-* (= EX-) + *bouel*, BOWEL. To disbowel.
Embow'er, Imbow'er, *vt.* EM-¹ (1). IN-¹ + BOWER.¹ To enclose as in a bower.
Embrace', *vt.* O.F. *embracer*, f. EM-¹ (1) + *bracchium* (pl. *bracchia*), arm. BRACE. To clasp in the arms; to avail oneself of; to submit to; to adopt (a course of action, a belief, &c.); to include.—*n.* A clasping in the arms.
Embra'sure, *n.* F. *embrasure*, f. *embraser* (EM-¹ (3)) = *braser*, to slope the sides of a window, of unknown orig. An opening widening from within for the firing of a gun.
Em'brocate, *vt.* Med.L. *embrocāre, embrocātum*, f. *embrocha*, G. *embrochē*, lotion, conn. with *embrechein*, to steep, foment, f. EM-² + *brechein*, to wet. To foment.—**Embroca'**TION, *n.* The lotion used for this.
Embroi'der, *vt.* EM-¹ (3) + archaic *Broider* in same sense—F. *broder, brouder*, of unknown orig. To ornament with needlework.—**Embroi'd**ERY, *n.*
Embroil', *vt.* F. *embrouiller*, f. EM-¹ (3) + *brouiller*. BROIL.¹ To bring into disorder or discord.—**Embroil'**MENT, *n.*
Em'bryo, *n.* Med.L., corr. of G. *embruon*, gen. referred to EN-² + *bruein*, to swell or teem. Offspring before birth or breaking the egg; a thing undeveloped.
Emend', *vt.* L. *ēmendāre*. AMEND. To remove errors from.—**Emend**A'TION, *n.*
Em'erald, *n.* O.F. *emeraude, esmeraude, esmeralde*, repg. L. *smaragdus*, G. *smaragdos*. A precious stone of a bright-green colour.
Emerge', *vi.* L. *Emergĕre, ēmersum*, f. *mergĕre*, to dip. MERGE. To come up out of water, &c.; to issue; to rise into notice; to come out as a result; to arise, crop up.—**Emer'g**ENCE, *n.*—**Emer'g**ENCY, *n.* Something unforeseen demanding immediate action.—**Emer'g**ENT, *a.*—**Emer's**ION, *n.*
Emer'itus, *a.* L. *ēmeritus*, that has served his time, pa.pple. of *Emerēri*, f. *merēri*, to MERIT. Honourably discharged from service.
Em'ery, *n.* F. *émeri*, O.F. *esmeril* — L.L. *smericulum*—G. *smēris*. A hard mineral used for polishing.
Emet'ic, *a.* and *n.* G. *emetikos*, f. *eme-ein*, to VOMIT. Causing, something causing, vomiting.
Em'igrate, *vi.* L. *Emigrāre*. MIGRATE. To leave one's country in order to settle in another.—**Em'igr**ANT, *n.*—**Emigr**A'TION, *n.*
Em'inent, *a.* L. *ēminens, ēminentis*, pres. pple. of *Eminēre*, to project. (The simple *minēre* does not occur.) IMMINENT. PROMINENT. High, lofty; exalted, distinguished.—**Em'inent**LY,² *adv.*—**Em'in**ENCE, *n.*
Emir', *n.* Arab. *amīr*. ADMIRAL. An Arab prince; a descendant of Mohammed.
Emit', *vt.* L. *Emittĕre, ēmissum*, to send out. ADMIT. To send forth; to utter; to issue by authority.—**Em'iss**ARY, *n.* One sent on a mission.—**Emis's**ION, *n.*
Em'met, *n.* O.E. *æmette*. An ANT.
Emol'lient, *a.* L. *ēmolliens, ēmollientis*, pres.pple. of *Emollīre*, to soften, f. *mollis*, soft. MOLLIFY. Softening, making supple.—*n.* An emollient application.
Emol'ument, *n.* L. *ēmolumentum*, profit. Orig. uncertain. Remuneration, salary.
Emo'tion, *n.* With -ION f. L. *ēmōtus*, pa.pple. of *Emovēre*, to MOVE out. An agitation of mind.—**Emo'tion**AL, *a.* Appealing to the feelings; liable to emotion.
Empan'el, Impan'el, *vt.* EM-¹ (1). IN-¹. To enter the names of (a jury) on a panel.
Em'peror, *n.* O.F. *empereor*, oblique case of *emperere(s)*—L. *imperātor*, f. *imperāre, imperātum*, to command. IMPERATIVE. The sovereign of the Roman Empire; a title higher than that of 'king'.—*fem.* **Em'pr**ESS.—**Em'pire**, *n.* F. *empire*—L. *imperium*, conn. with *imperāre*. IMPERIAL. Imperial rule or dignity; a territory, esp. an aggregate of states, ruled by an emperor or a sovereign state.
Em'phasis, *n.* L. *emphasis* = G. *emphasis*, f. *emphainein*, to let (a thing) be seen in, exhibit, declare, f. EM-² + *phainein*, to show. DIAPHANOUS. Stress of voice; importance assigned to a fact or idea.—**Em'phas**IZE, *vt.*—**Emphat'ic**, *a.* G. *emphatikos*. Forcibly expressed; expressing oneself forcibly; strongly marked, forcible. So **Emphat'**ICAL, *a.*—**Emphat'ical**LY,² *adv.*
Empir'ic, *a.* L. *empīricus*—G. *empeirikos*, f. *empeiria*, experience, f. *empeiros*, skilled, f. EM-² + *peira*, trial. Relying, founded, on experiment, not on theory.—*n.* One who relies thus on experiment; a quack. So **Empir'**ICAL, *a.*—**Empir'ic**ISM, *n.*
Emplace'ment, *n.* F. EM-¹ (1) + PLACE + -MENT. A placing; a platform for guns.
Employ', *vt.* F. *employer*, var. of O.F. *emplier*—L. *implicāre*, to involve, in L.L., to employ, f. *im-* (= IN-¹) + *plicāre*, to fold. APPLY. IMPLY. To apply, use; to have in one's service; to find work or occupation for.—*n.* Service; an occupation.—**Employé**, *n.*; *fem.* **Employée**. Pa.pple. of *employer*. Also **Employ**EE'. One who is employed.—**Employ'**ER, *n.*—**Employ'**MENT, *n.*
Empo'rium, *n.* L. *emporium*—G. *emporion*, f. *emporos*, merchant, f. EM-² + *por-*, vbl. stem as in *poreuesthai*, to journey, cogn. with FARE. A centre of commerce; a shop.
Empow'er, *vt.* EM-¹ (1). To enable.
Emprise', Emprize', *n.* O.F. *emprinse, emprise*—L.L. **imprensa*, f. ppl. stem of **impre(he)ndĕre*, to take in hand, f. *im-* (= IN-¹) + L. *prehendĕre*. PREHENSILE. A chivalrous undertaking; chivalric enterprise.
Emp'ty, *a.* O.E. *æmetig*, f. *æmetta*, leisure, of doubtful orig. + *-ig* (= -Y²). Containing nothing; void *of*; vacant, unoccupied; frivolous, foolish; vain, meaningless.—*vt.* To make empty; to discharge, to clear *of*.—*vi.* To become empty.—**Emp'ti**NESS, *n.*
Empyr'eal, *a.* Med.L. *empyreus, empyræus* (G. *empuros* (EM-² + *pur*, FIRE), fiery) + -AL. Of or pertaining to the highest heaven or to

the sky. Sim. **Empyre'an**, *a.* -AN.—As *n.*, the highest heaven; the sky; cosmic space.
E'mu, *n.* Prob. f. Pg. *ema*, crane, ostrich. A large Australian bird.
Em'ulate, *vt.* L. *aemulāri*, *aemulātus*, to strive to equal, f. *aemulus*, rivalling. To strive to equal; to vie with, rival.—**Emul**A'TION, *n.*—**Em'ul**ATIVE, *a.*—**Em'ul**OUS, *a.*
Emul'sion, *n.* Mod.L. *ēmulsio*, *ēmulsiōnis*, f. L. E*mulgēre*, *ēmulsum*, to MILK out. A milk-like mixture or medicine.
Emunc'tory, *a.* Mod.L. *ēmunctōrius*, excretory, f. L. *ēmungĕre*, *ēmunctum*, to blow the nose, f. E- + **mungĕre* in sim. sense. Of or pertaining to nose-blowing; conveying waste matters from the body.
Ena'ble, *vt.* EN-[1] (2). To authorize; to make able.
Enact', *vt.* EN-[1] (2). To make into an act, to ordain, decree. EN-[1] (3). To perform (a play), to personate.—**Enact'**MENT, *n.*
Enam'el, *vt.* A.F. *enamayller*, *enameler*, f. EN-[1] (1) + *amayl*, O.F. *esmail*, enamel, prob. f. Teut. and cogn. with SMELT, *v.* To encrust with enamel; to variegate, adorn.—*n.* A glass-like composition applied to metal for ornament or to form a surface.
Enam'our, *vt.* O.F. *enamourer*, f. EN-[1] (1) + *amour*, L. *amor*, love. AMOROUS. To inspire with love; to charm, delight.
Encamp', *vt.* and *i.* EN-[1] (1). To lodge, to be lodged, in a camp.—**Encamp'**MENT, *n.*
Encase', **Incase'**, *vt.* EN-[1] (1). IN.[1] To put into, to surround as with, a case.
Encash', *vt.* EN-[1] (2). To convert into cash; to receive in the form of cash.
Encaus'tic, *a.* G. *egkaustikos*, f. *egkaiein*, to burn in, f. *eg-* (= EN-[2]) + *kaiein*, to burn. CAUSTIC. Pertaining to the art of ornamenting with 'burnt in' pigments.
Enceinte, *n.* F.—L.L. type **incincta*, f. *incingĕre*, *incinctum*, to gird in. IN-[1]. CINCTURE. An enclosure.—*a.* F.—L.L. *incincta*, explained as 'ungirt'. IN-[2]. Pregnant.
Enchant', *vt.* F. *enchanter*—L. IN*cantāre*, to CHANT against. To lay under a spell, bewitch; to delight, charm.—**Enchant'**ER, *n.* —**Enchant'**RESS, *n.*—**Enchant'**MENT, *n.*
Enchase', *vt.* F. *enchâsser*, to enshrine, set (gems), f. EN-[1] (1) + *châsse*, L. *capsa*, CASE.[2] To set as a jewel, to serve as a setting for; to set *with* (gems); to adorn with figures in relief or engraved work; to engrave (figures) *on*, *in*, a surface; to enshrine *in*.
Encir'cle, *vt.* EN-[1] (1). To surround.
Enclave', *n.* F., f. *enclaver*, to shut in—L.L. *inclāvāre*, f. IN-[1] + *clāvis*, key, or *clāvus*, nail. A portion of territory entirely surrounded by foreign territory.
Enclit'ic, *a.* G. *egklitikos*, f. *eg-* (= EN-[2]) + *klinein*, to lean. That leans its accent on the preceding word.—*n.* An enclitic word.
Enclose', **Inclose'**, *vt.* EN-[1] (3). IN-[1]. To surround; to fence in; to place in a cover with a letter.—**Enclos'**URE, *n.*
Enco'mium, *n.* L. *encōmium*—G. *egkōmion*, a song in honour of a conqueror, f. *eg-* (= EN-[2]) + *kōmos*, revel. COMEDY. A eulogy, panegyric.—**Enco'miast**, *n.* G. *egkōmiastēs*. A panegyrist.—**Encomias'**TIC, *a.*
Encom'pass, *vt.* EN-[1] (1). To surround.
Encore, *int.* F., still, again. Orig. doubtful. Again, once more.—*n.* A call for the repetition of a song, &c.; the repetition.—*vt.* To call for a repetition of or from.
Encoun'ter, *vt.* O.F. *encontrer*—L.L. *incontrāre*, f. IN-[1] + L. *contrā*, against. RENCONTRE. To meet in conflict; to meet with. —*n.* A meeting in conflict; a meeting.
Encour'age, *vt.* O.F. *encoragier*, f. EN-[1] (1) + *corage*, COURAGE. To inspirit; to embolden; to instigate; to countenance, patronize; to abet.—**Encour'age**MENT, *n.*
Encroach', *vi.* O.F. *encrochier*, to seize, f. EN-[1] (1) + *croc*, hook. CROCHET. Cogn. with CROOK. To intrude usurpingly.—**Encroach'**MENT, *n.*
Encrust', **Incrust'**, *vt.* EN-[1] (1). To cover with a crust.
Encum'ber, *vt.* O.F. *encombrer*, to obstruct —L.L. *incombrāre*, f. IN-[1] + *combrus*, obstacle, prob. representing L. *cumulus*, heap. To embarrass, hamper; to burden; to fill *with* (what is useless).—**Encum'br**ANCE, *n.*
Encyc'lic, *a.*; also **Encyc'lic**AL. L.L. *encyclicus*, *encyclius*—G. *egkuklios*, circular, f. *eg-* (= EN-[2]) + *kuklos*, circle. CYCLE. Sent to many persons.—*n.* An encyclical letter, esp. one issued by the Pope.
Encyclopæ'dia, **-pe'dia**, *n.* L.L. *encyclopaedia*, f. pseudo-G. *egkuklopaideia* for *egkuklios* (see prec.) *paideia*, circular or complete instruction. A book, arranged alphabetically, containing information on all branches, or on a particular branch, of knowledge.— **Encyclopæ'd**IC, **-pe'd**IC, *a.*
End, *n.* O.E. *ende*. Common Teut. A limit; an extremity; the bounding surface of an extremity; a fragment; termination, conclusion; latter part; death; event, issue; an aim, purpose.—*vt.* To put an end to.—*vi.* To come to an end; to result *in*.—**End'**LESS, *a.*— **End'**WAYS, **End'**WISE, *adv.*
Endan'ger, *vt.* EN-[1] (1). To expose to danger.
Endear', *vt.* EN-[1] (2). To make dear.— **Endear'**MENT, *n.* A caress.
Endeav'our, *vi.* EN-[1] (1) + DEVOIR. To try, make an effort.—*n.* Effort, pains.
Endem'ic, *a.* EN-[2] + G. *dēmos*, the people + -IC. DEMIURGE. DEMOTIC. Habitually existing or prevalent in a certain country.— *n.* An endemic disease. So **Endem'**ICAL, *a.*
En'dive, *n.* F. *endive*—L.L. **intibea*, fem. a. f. *intibus*, endive. A species of chicory.
En'dogen, *n.* G. *endon*, within + *-genēs*, produced, f. *gen-*, root of *gignesthai*, to come into being. A plant that grows from within.
Endorse', **Indorse'**, *vt.* M.E. *endosse* (conformed to *indorsāre* (see below))—O.F. *endosser*, corresp. to Med.L. *indorsāre*, to endorse, f. IN-[1] + L. *dorsum* (F. *dos*), back. DORSAL. REREDOS. To write, esp. to sign one's name, on the back of; to write (words) *on* (the back of).—**En-**, **Indorse'**MENT, *n.*
Endow', *vt.* EN-[1] (3) + F. *douer*, L. *dōtāre*, to endow, f. *dōs*, *dōtis*, marriage portion, allied to *dăre*, to give. DOWAGER. To provide a permanent income for; to enrich or furnish *with*.—**Endow'**MENT, *n.*
Endue', **Indue'**, *vt.* O.F. *enduire*—L. *indūcĕre*, to lead into. IN-[1]. DUKE. To put on (garments, &c.); to clothe *with* (in these senses influenced by L. *induĕre*, to put on (a garment)); to invest *with* (a quality, &c.) (in this sense influenced also by ENDOW).
Endure', *vi.* O.F. *endurer*—L. *indūrāre*, *indūrātum*, f. IN-[1] + *dūrāre*, to harden, to endure, f. *dūrus*, hard. DURE. INDURATE. To last, continue.—*vt.* To undergo, sustain, support; to be subjected to; to submit to.— **Endur'**ABLE, *a.*—**Endur'**ANCE, *n.*
En'ema, *n.* G. *enema*, f. stem of *enienai*, to send in, f. EN-[2] + *hienai*, to send. A substance passed into the rectum.

En'emy, *n.* O.F. *enemi*—L. *inimīcus*, f. IN-[2] + *amīcus*, friend. AMICABLE. INIMICAL. One that seeks to do ill to another, an adversary; an armed foe; the hostile force.

En'ergy, *n.* L.L. *energīa*—G. *energeia*, f. *energēs*, active, effective, f. EN-[2] + *ergon*, WORK. Vigour of expression or action; operation, working; capacity for exertion; power actively exerted.—**Energet'ic**, *a.* G. *energētikos*. Characterized by energy. So **Energet'**ICAL, *a.*—**Energet'ical**LY,[2] *adv.*—

Energu'men, *n.* L.L. *energūmenos* = G. *energoumenos*, pass.pple. of *energe-ein*, to work in or upon, f. EN-[2] + *ergon*. One possessed by a devil; an enthusiast or fanatic.

Ener'vate, *vt.* L. *ēnervāre*, *ēnervātum*, to take out the sinews from, weaken, f. E- + *nervus*, sinew. NERVE. To weaken, impair the vigour of.—**Enerva'**TION, *n.*

Enface', *vt.* EN-[1] (1). To write, print, &c., words on the face of (a bill, &c.); to write, print, &c. (words) thus.

Enfee'ble, *vt.* O.F. *enfeblir*, f. EN-[1] (2) + *feble*, FEEBLE. To weaken.—**Enfee'ble**MENT, *n.*

Enfeoff', *vt.* O.F. *enfeffer*, *enfieffer*, f. EN-[1] (1) + *fief*, FIEF. To invest with, to hand over as, a fief; to surrender.—**Enfeoff'**MENT, *n.*

Enfilade', *n.* F., f. *enfiler*, to thread on a string, pierce through, f. EN-[1] (1) + *fil*, L. *fīlum*, thread. FILE, *n.*[2] A fire from artillery, &c., which sweeps through a line of works or men.—*vt.* To subject to an enfilade.

Enforce', *vt.* O.F. *enforcier*—L.L. *infortiāre*, f. EN-[1] (2) + L. *fortis*, strong. COMFORT. Formerly, to strengthen. To press home, urge; to compel; to impose (a course of action, &c.); to compel the observance of; to support by force (a claim, &c.).—**Enforce'**ABLE, *a.*—**Enforce'**MENT, *n.*

Enfran'chise, *vt.* O.F. *enfranchir*, f. EN-[1] (2) + *franc*, free. FRANK. To set free; to give parliamentary representation to; to admit to the right of voting for members of parliament.—**Enfran'chise**MENT, *n.*

Engage', *vt.* F. *engager*, f. EN-[1] (1) + *gage*, pledge. GAGE. WAGE. To pledge (one's honour, &c.); to bind formally; to betroth; to hire; to bespeak; to attract, to charm; to provide occupation for; to attack; in *pass.*, to have made an appointment, promised one's presence, &c.—*vi.* To pledge oneself; to employ oneself *in* (something); to begin to fight.—**Engage'**MENT, *n.*

Engen'der, *vt.* F. *engendrer*—L. *ingenerāre*, f. IN-[1] + *generāre*, to GENERATE. To beget; to produce; to give rise to.

En'gine, *n.* O.F. *engin*—L. *ingenium*, natural capacity, f. IN-[1] + *gen-*, root of *gignĕre*, to beget. GENUS. GIN.[1] INDIGENOUS. INGENIOUS. INGENUOUS. Formerly, native talent; ingenuity; an artifice, contrivance. A mechanical contrivance, a machine, esp. one of several parts working together.—*vt.* To supply (a ship) with engines.—**Engin**EER', *n.* One who constructs military works or works of public utility; one who constructs engines; one in charge of a ship's engines.—*vt.* To construct as an engineer; to contrive.

En'glish, *a.* O.E. *Englisc*, *Ænglisc*, f. *Engle*, *Ængle*, the Angles, one of the Teutonic peoples who settled in Britain + *-isc* (-ISH). Of or pertaining to England.—*n.* The English language or people.—*vt.* To translate into English.

Engraft', **Ingraft'**, *vt.* EN-[1] (3). IN-.[1] To graft in; to incorporate, implant.

Engrain', **Ingrain'**, *vt.* EN-[1] (1), IN-[1] + GRAIN, the dye. To dye deep; to work into the texture; to implant ineradicably.

Engrave', *vt.* EN-[1] (3) + GRAVE, *v.*[1], after F. *engraver*. To carve, incise; to impress deeply; to cut on a metal plate or on a wood block for reproduction by printing.—**Engrav'**ER, *n.*—**Engrav'ing**, *vbl.n.* The action of the *v.*; the engraver's art; an impression from a plate or block.

Engross', *vt.* A.F. *engrosser*, to write in large letters, f. EN-[1] (1) + *grosse* = Med.L. *grossa*, large writing, fem. of L.L. *grossus*, thick. GROSS, *a.* To write out in large letters or in legal form.—From obs. phrase *in gross*, F. *en gros* (f. *grossus*), in the lump, by wholesale. To get or keep exclusive possession of; to occupy entirely.—**Engross'**MENT, *n.*

Engulf', **Ingulf'**, *vt.* EN-[1] (1). IN-.[1] To swallow up.

Enhance', *vt.* A.F. *enhauncer*, prob. a corr. of O.F. *enhaucer*—L.L. **inaltiāre*, f. IN-[1] + *altus*, high. ALTITUDE. To heighten, intensify; to raise (prices, &c.); to raise *in* price, value, &c.—**Enhance'**MENT, *n.*

Enig'ma, *n.* L. *aenigma*, *aenigmatis*—G. *ainigma*, f. *ainissesthai*, to speak in riddles, f. *ainos*, tale, fable. A composition the meaning of which is to be guessed; something puzzling.—**Enigmat'**IC, **Enigmat'**ICAL, *aa.*

Enjoin', *vt.* F. *enjoindre*—L. *injungĕre*, *injunctum*, to join into, to impose (a duty, &c.), f. IN-[1] + *jungĕre*, to join. ADJOIN. INJUNCTION. To order authoritatively.

Enjoy', *v.refl.* O.F. *enjoier*, to give joy to, *refl.*, to enjoy, f. EN-[1] (1) + *joie*, JOY. To be happy, find pleasure.—*vt.* To take delight in; to have the use or benefit of.—**Enjoy'**ABLE, *a.*—**Enjoy'**MENT, *n.*

Enkin'dle, *vt.* EN-[1] (3). To kindle; to inflame.

Enlarge', *vt.* O.F. *enlarger*, f. EN-[1] (2) + *large*. LARGE. To increase the size of, add to; to make more comprehensive; to set free.—*vi.* To increase or widen; to speak at large, expatiate.—**Enlarge'**MENT, *n.*

Enligh'ten, *vt.* EN-[1] (1) + LIGHT, *n.* + -EN.[2] To illuminate; to instruct, inform.—**Enligh'ten**MENT, *n.*

Enlist', *vt.* and *i.* EN-[1] (1) or (3) + LIST, *n.*[2] or *v.*[1] To engage as a soldier or as a helper.—**Enlist'**MENT, *n.*

Enli'ven, *vt.* EN[1] (1) + LIFE + -EN.[2] To animate, inspirit; to stimulate; to brighten.

En'mity, *n.* O.F. *enemistié*—L.L. **inimīcitas*, f. *inimīcus*. ENEMY. Ill-will; hostility.

Enno'ble, *vt.* F. *ennoblir*, f. EN-[1] (2) + *noble*, NOBLE. To make noble; to dignify, refine.

Ennui, *n.* F., O.F. *enui*—L. *in odio*. ANNOY. Weariness from lack of occupation or interest.

Enor'mous, *a.* L. *ēnormis* (f. E- + *norma* (NORMAL)) + -OUS. Huge, vast.—**Enor'mous**NESS, *n.*—**Enor'mi**TY, *n.* Extreme wickedness; a gross offence.

Enough', *a.* O.E. *genóg*, *genóh*. Cf. Ger. *genug*. O.Teut. root *nah* = Aryan *nak*. Cf. L. *nancisci*, *nactus*, to obtain. Sufficient.—*n.* That which is sufficient.—*adv.* Sufficiently.

Enounce', *vt.* F. *énoncer*—L. *ēnuntiāre*. ENUNCIATE. To enunciate.

Enrage', *vt.* O.F. *enrager*, f. EN-[1] (1) + *rage*. RAGE. To make furious.

Enrap'ture, *vt.* EN-[1] (1). To delight highly.

Enrich', *vt.* F. *enrichir*, f. EN-[1] (2) + *riche*, RICH, of Teut. orig. To make rich or richer.

Enrol(l)', *vt.* O.F. *enroller*, f. EN-[1] (1) + *rolle*.

ROLL, *n.*[1] To put the name of (a person) on a list; to record.—**Enrol'**MENT, *n.*

Ensconce', *vt.* EN-[1] (1) + SCONCE.[3] To place for security, concealment or comfort.

Enshrine', *vt.* EN-[1] (1). To enclose in a shrine; to serve as a shrine for.

En'sign, *n.* O.F. *enseigne*—L. *insignia*, pl. of *insigne*, badge of office, standard, neut. of *insignis*, remarkable (lit. 'with a mark on it'), f. IN-[1] + *signum*, SIGN. A badge; a naval, maritime or military flag; the bearer of the ensign, formerly the lowest commissioned infantry officer.

En'silage, *n.* F. *ensilage*, f. *ensiler*, f. Sp. *ensilar*, to put in a silo, f. EN-[1] (1) + SILO. The process of preserving fodder in a silo.

Enslave', *vt.* EN-[1] (2). To make a slave of. —**Enslave'**MENT, *n.*—**Enslav'**ER, *n.*

Ensnare', *vt.* EN-[1] (1). To catch in a snare.

Ensue', *vt.* O.F. *ensu-*, stem of *ensivre*, *ensuivre*—L.L. *insequěre*, L. *insequi*, to follow close upon, f. IN-[1] + *sequi*, to follow. CONSECUTION. SUE. To strive after, aim at.—*vi.* To be subsequent, to follow; to result.

Ensure', *vt.* A.F. *enseurer*, f. EN-[1] (2) + O.F. *seür*, SURE. INSURE. To make safe *from*, *against*; to make certain; to secure *to*, *for*.

Entab'lature, *n.* Obs. F. *entablature*—It. *intavolatura*, a planking, something laid flat, f. *intavolare*, to board, f. IN-[1] + *tavola*, L. *tabula*, plank. TABLE. *Arch.*, that which lies above a column.

Entail', *vt.* EN-[1] (2) + A.F. *taillé* = O.F. *taillié*, pa.pple. of *taillier*, to cut, hence, to fix the form of, limit—late Pop. and Med.L. *tāliāre*, *talliāre*, to cut, f. *tal(l)ia*, L. *tālea*, rod, twig, scion. DETAIL. INTAGLIO. RETAIL. TAILOR. TALLY. To settle (land, &c.) on a number of persons in succession, none of whom can dispose of it; to bestow as a possession; to impose (inconvenience, &c.) *upon*; to involve as a consequence.—*n.* The entailing of land, &c.

Entan'gle, *vt.* EN-[1] (1) and (3). To involve, to ensnare; to hamper, perplex; to twist, interlace.—**Entan'gle**MENT, *n.*

En'ter, *vi.* F. *entrer*—L. *intrāre*, conn. with *intrō*, inwards. To go or come into a place, &c.; to join a society, &c.; to begin, engage; to be a constituent element *in*.—*vt.* To go or come into (a place, &c.); to join (a society, &c.); to register.—**En'tr**ANCE, *n.*

Enter'ic, *a.* G. *enterikos*, f. *enteron*, an intestine, f. *entos*, within, f. *en*, in. EN-[2]. Of the intestines; *enteric fever*, typhoid fever.

En'terprise, *n.* O.F. *entreprise*, *-prinse*, f. pa.pple. of *entreprendre*, to take in hand—L.L. *interprenděre*, f. INTER- + L. *prenděre*, short for *prehenděre*, to lay hold of. APPRENTICE. PREHENSILE. A design, a (momentous) undertaking; engagement in such undertakings; daring spirit.—**En'terprising**, *ppl.a.* Prompt to undertake.

Entertain', *vt.* F. *entretenir*—L.L. *intertenēre*, f. INTER- + L. *tenēre*, to hold. ABSTAIN. To keep up, maintain; to engage the attention of, to amuse; to receive as a guest; to receive into the mind; to harbour, cherish. —**Entertain'**ER, *n.*—**Entertain'**MENT, *n.*

Enthral(l)', *vt.* EN-[1] (2). To enslave.—**Enthral'**MENT, *n.* [—**Enthrone'**MENT, *n.*

Enthrone', *vt.* EN-[1] (1). To seat on a throne.

Enthu'siasm, *n.* L.L. *enthūsiasmus*—G. *enthousiasmos*, f. *enthousiazein*, to be inspired, f. *entheos*, possessed by a god, f. EN-[2] + *theos*, god. ATHEISM. (Fancied) inspiration; ardent zeal, passionate eagerness.—**Enthu'siast**, *n.* G. *enthousiastēs*. One possessed by enthusiasm.—**Enthusias'**TIC, *a.*—**Enthusias'tically**, *adv.* -AL. -LY[2].

En'thymeme, *n.* L. *enthymēma* = G. *enthumēma*, an argument, a syllogism on merely probable premises, f. *enthume-esthai*, to think, infer, f. EN-[2] + *thumos*, mind. Now applied to a syllogism with one premiss suppressed.

Entice', *vt.* O.F. *enticier*, to stir up, incite, app. repg. L. type **intitiāre*, f. IN-[1] + **titius* for L. *titio*, fire-brand. To allure, attract, esp. insidiously or adroitly.—**Entice'**MENT, *n.*

Entire', *a.* O.F. *entier*—L. *integer*, whole. INTEGER. Whole; complete; thorough, total; unbroken, intact, undiminished.—**Entire'**LY,[2] *adv.*—**Enti're**TY, *n.*

Enti'tle, *vt.* A.F. *entitler*, O.F. *entiteler*—L.L. *intitulāre*, f. IN-[1] + L. *titulus*. TITLE. To give a title or designation to; to give (a person or thing) a rightful claim *to*.

En'tity, *n.* L.L. *entitas*, f. *ens*, *entis*, a neut. pres.pple. formed, after *absens*, &c., f. L. *esse*, to be. ABSENT. ESSENCE. INTEREST. Being, existence; essence; something that exists.

Entomb', *vt.* O.F. *entoumber*, f. EN-[1] (1) + *tombe*, TOMB. To bury; to serve as a tomb for.

Entomol'ogy, *n.* F. *entomologie*—G. *entoma*, insects (whose bodies are divided into segments), neut.pl. of *entomos*, cut in pieces (f. EN-[2] + *tem-*, *tom-*, stem of *temnein*, to cut) + *-logia*, -LOGY. ANATOMY. The science of insects.—**Entomol'**OGIST, *n.*

En'trails, *n.pl.* O.F. *entraille*, sing., intestines—L.L. *intrālia*, inward parts, intestines, neut.pl. of **intrālis*, inward, f. L. *inter*, between, among. The bowels, intestines.

Entrain', *vt.* and *i.* EN-[1] (1). To put, to be put, into a railway train.

Entrance', *vt.* EN-[1] (1). To throw into, to carry away as in, a trance; to transport.

Entrap', *vt.* O.F. *entraper*, f. EN-[1] (1) + *trape* TRAP. To catch in a trap (gen. *fig.*).

Entreat', *vt.* O.F. *entraitier*, f. EN-[1] (3) + *traitier*, to TREAT. Formerly, to treat, deal with; to treat *with*. To beg earnestly; to beseech, implore.—**Entreat'**Y,[1] *n.*

Entrée, *n.* F., f. *entrer*, to ENTER. The privilege of entrance, admission; a dish served between the fish and the joint.

Entrench', **Intrench'**, *vt.* EN-[1] (1). IN-[1]. To surround with trenches.—**Entrench'**MENT, **Intrench'**MENT, *n.*

Entrepôt, *n.* F.—L. type **interpositum*, neut. pa.pple. of *interpōněre*. INTERPOSITION. A storehouse for the temporary deposit of goods; a commercial centre.

Entresol, *n.* F., f. *entre*, L. *inter*, between + *sol*, L. *solum*, the ground. A storey between the ground floor and the first floor.

Entrust', **Intrust'**, *vt.* EN-[1] (1). To confide or commit *to*; to charge *with*.

En'try, *n.* F. *entrée*. ENTREE. An entering; a means of entrance; a registering.

Entwine', **Intwine'**, *vt.* EN-[1] (3). IN-[1]. To plait, interlace; to encircle *with*, to weave *about* or *round*; to clasp, embrace.

Enu'merate, *vt.* L. *ēnumerāre*, *ēnumerātum*, f. E- + *numerāre*, to count, f. *numerus*, NUMBER. To count; to mention separately; to specify.—**Enumer**A'TION, *n.*

Enun'ciate, *vt.* L. *ēnuntiāre*, *ēnuntiātum*, to tell out, make known, f. *nuntius*, messenger. ANNOUNCE. ENOUNCE. To express, to utter; to proclaim.—**Enunci**A'TION, *n.*

Envel'op, *vt.* O.F. *enveloper*, *envoluper*, f. EN-[1] (3) + the further element given under

DEVELOP. To wrap up; to serve as a wrapping for; to cover closely.—**En'velope**, *n.* F. *enveloppe.* That in which anything is enveloped; the cover of a letter.

Enven'om, *vt.* O.F. *envenimer*, f. EN-[1] (1) + *venim*, VENOM. To put poison on or in.

Envi'ron, *vt.* F. *environner*, f. *environ*, round about, f. EN-[1] (1) + O.F. **viron*, circuit, related to *virer*, to VEER. To surround.—**Envi'ron**MENT, *n.* That which environs; conditions of life or development.—**Envi'rons**, *n.pl.* F. *environs.* Outskirts.

Envis'age, *vt.* F. *envisager*, f. EN-[1] (1) + *visage*, VISAGE. To look straight at; to contemplate.

En'voy, *n.*[1] App. an alteration of F. *envoyé*, pa.pple. of *envoyer*, to send, f. EN-[1] (1) + *voie*, way. CONVEY. A diplomatic minister of the second rank; an agent or deputy.

En'voy, *n.*[2] O.F. *envoy*, orig. n. of action f. *envoiier* (F. *envoyer*). (See prec.) INVOICE. A short concluding stanza.

En'vy, *n.* F. *envie*—L. *invidia.* INVIDIOUS. Mortification and ill-will occasioned by another's superiority or success; the object of envy; a longing for advantages enjoyed by another.—*vt.* To feel envy towards or on account of.—**En'vi**ABLE, *a.*—**En'vi**OUS, *a.*

E'pact, *n.* F. *épacte*—L. *epacta*—G. *epaktē*, f. *epaktos*, vbl.a. f. *epagein*, to intercalate, f. EPI-, in addition + *agein*, to bring. The excess of the solar over the lunar year; the moon's age on the first day of the year.

Ep'aulet, Ep'aulette, *n.* F. *épaulette*, f. *épaule* (O.F. *espaule*), shoulder—L.L. *spatula*, shoulder-blade, L. *spatula.* SPATULA. ESPALIER. An ornament worn on the shoulder as part of a uniform.

Epexege'sis, *n.* G. *epexēgēsis*, f. *epexēgeesthai*, to explain besides, f. EP(I)- + *exēgeesthai.* EXEGESIS. The addition of a word or words to convey a meaning more clearly; the word or words so added.—**Epexeget'ic**, *a.* G. *epexēgētikos.* Also **Epexeget'ic**AL. Of, of the nature of, an epexegesis.

Ephem'eral, *a.* G. *ephēmeros* (f. *eph-* (= EPI-), for, during + *hēmera*, day) + -AL. Lasting only for a day; short-lived.

Ephem'eris, *n.* G. *ephēmeris*, diary, calendar, f. *ephēmeros*, in sense 'daily'. (See prec.) An astronomical almanac.

E'phod, *n.* Heb. *ēphōd*, f. *āphad*, to put on. A Jewish priestly vestment.

Ep'ic, *a.* L. *epicus*—G. *epikos*, f. *epos*, word, saying, in *pl.*, epic poetry. EPOPEE. Narrating continuously the achievements of a hero or heroes.—*n.* An epic poem.

E'picene, *a.* L. *epicoenus*—G. *epikoinos*, f. EPI- + *koinos*, common. Denoting either sex; for, having characteristics of, both sexes.

Ep'icure, *n.* L. *Epicūrus*, G. *Epikouros*, the Athenian philosopher, whose teaching has been taken to be that pleasure and pain are the chief good and evil. One who is dainty in eating and drinking.—**Epicure'**AN, *a.* Of Epicurus; devoted to refined sensuous enjoyment.—*n.* A follower of Epicurus; one with whom pleasure is the chief end.

Epidem'ic, *a.* F. *épidémique*, f. *épidémie*, an epidemic— G. *epidēmia*, prevalence of an epidemic, f. *epidēmios*, among the people, f. EPI- + *dēmos*, the people. Prevalent among a community at a special time.—*n.* An epidemic disease. So **Epidem'**ICAL, *a.*

Epider'mis, *n.* G. *epidermis*, f. EPI-, upon + *derma*, skin. DERM. The outer skin.

Ep'igram, *n.* F. *épigramme*—L. *epigramma*, *epigrammatis*—G. *epigramma*, an inscription, f. EPI*graphein*, to write upon. GRAPHIC. A short poem with a witty or satirical conclusion; a pointed saying. — **Epigrammat'**IC, *a.*—**Epigrammat'ically**, *adv.* -AL. -LY.[2]—**Epigram'mat**IST, *n.*

Ep'igraph, *n.* G. *epigraphē*, f. *epigraphein.* (See prec.) An inscription; a motto.

Ep'ilepsy, *n.* O.F. *epilepsie*—L. *epilēpsia*—G. *epilēpsia*, f. EPI*lambanein*, to seize upon. CATALEPSY. PROLEPSIS. The falling sickness.—**Epilep'**TIC, *a.*

Ep'ilogue, *n.* F. *épilogue*—L. *epilogus*, G. *epilogos*, peroration, f. EPI-, in addition + *logos*, speech. A speech or poem at the end of a play.

Epiph'any, *n.* O.F. *epiphanie* — L.L. *epiphania*, neut. pl.—Late G. *epiphania*, neut. pl. f. **epiphanios*, a. f. *epiphainein*, to manifest, f. EPI-, to + *phainein*, to show. DIAPHANOUS. The festival of the manifestation of Christ to the Magi, observed on Jan. 6th.

Epis'copal, *a.* F. *épiscopal*—L.L. *episcopālis*, f. *episcopus*, G. *episcopos*, BISHOP. Of a bishop; governed by bishops.—**Epis'cop**ACY, *n.* Government by bishops; the body of bishops.—**Episcopa'**LIAN, *a.* and *n.* Belonging, one belonging, to an episcopal church.—**Epis'cop**ATE,[1] *n.* The office, the period of office, the see, of a bishop; the body of bishops.

Ep'isode, *n.* G. *epeisodion*, orig. neut. of *epeisodios*, coming in besides, f. EPI- + *eisodos*, entering, f. *eis*, into + *hodos*, way. METHOD. In Greek tragedy, the passages of dialogue, originally subsidiary, between the choric songs; an incidental narrative or digression; an incident.—**Episod'**IC, **Episod'**ICAL, *aa.*

Epis'tle, *n.* O.F. *epistle*—L. *epistola* — G. *epistolē*, f. EPI*stellein*, to send on some occasion. APOSTLE. A letter.—**Epis'tol**ARY, *a.*

Ep'itaph, *n.* L. *epitaphium*—G. *epitaphios* (*logos*), (a speech) over or at a tomb, f. EPI- + *taphos*, tomb. An inscription on a tomb.

Epithala'mium, *n.* L. *epithalamium*—G. *epithalamios* (*humnos*), (a song) at a bridal, f. EPI- + *thalamos*, bridal chamber. A nuptial song.

Ep'ithet, *n.* L. *epitheton*—G. *epitheton*, orig. neut. of *epithetos*, attributed, f. EPI- + *the-*, to place. ANTITHESIS. THEME. An adjective indicating a characteristic quality or attribute; a significant appellation.

Epit'ome, *n.* L. *epitomē*—G. *epitomē*, f. *epitemnein*, to cut on the surface, to abridge, f. EPI- + *temnein* (stem *tem-*, *tom-*), to cut. ANATOMY. An abridgment; a condensed account.—**Epit'om**IZE, *vt.*—**Epit'om**IST, *n.*

E'poch, *n.* L.L. *epocha* — G. *epochē*, stop, pause, fixed point of time, f. *epechein*, to hold upon, to stop, f. EPI- + *echein*, to hold. SCHEME. A date; the beginning of a period; a period.

E'pode, *n.* O.F. *epode*—L. *epōdos*—G. *epōidos*, lit. 'after-song', f. *epaidein*, to sing to, f. EPI- + *aidein*, *aeidein*, to sing. ODE. The lines sung by the Greek tragic chorus after the strophe and antistrophe; a form of lyric poem invented by Archilochus and used by Horace.

Ep'onym, *n.* G. *epōnumos*, giving one's name to a person or thing, f. EPI- + *onoma* (in Æolic *onuma*), NAME. One who gives his name to a people, &c.—**Epon'ym**OUS, *a.*

E'popee, *n.* F. *épopée*—G. *epopoiia*, an epic, epic poetry, f. *epopoios*, maker of epics, f. *epos* + *-poios*, maker, f. *poie-ein*, to make. EPIC. An epic poem; epic poetry.

E'quable, *a.* L. *aequābilis*, f. *aequāre*,

EQUATE. Uniform; not easily disturbed.—**E'quab**LY,[2] *adv.*—**Equab**IL'ITY, *n.*

E'qual, *a.* L. *aequālis*, f. *aequus*, level, equal, even, fair, equitable. ADEQUATE. EQUITY. INIQUITY. Identical in amount, magnitude, &c.; having the same qualities, rank, &c.; fit or qualified; uniform in operation.—*n.* One who is equal to another.—*vt.* To be equal to.—**E'qual**LY,[2] *adv.*—**Equal'**ITY, *n.*—**E'qua-l**IZE, *vt.*—**Equaliz**A'TION, *n.*

Equanim'ity, *n.* L. *aequanimitas*, f. *aequanimis*, having an even mind, f. *aequus* (see prec.) + *animus*, mind. ANIMUS. Evenness of mind or temper.

Equate', *vt.* L. *aequāre*, *aequātum*, to make level or equal, f. *aequus*, level, EQUAL. To state the equality of (a thing) *with* or *to* (another); to treat or represent as equivalent.—**Equ**A'TION, *n.* A making equal or balancing; a formula affirming the equivalence of two quantities; a quantity added or subtracted to compensate for a known cause of error.—

Equa'tor, *n.* L.L. *aequātor*, agent-n. f. *aequāre.* A great circle of the celestial sphere whose plane is perpendicular to the earth's axis; a great circle of the earth equidistant from the poles.—**Equato'r**IAL, *a.*

Eq'uerry, *n.* F. *écurie*, earlier *escurie*, Med. L. *scūria*, stable—O.H.G. *scūr*, shed, shelter (whence Ger. *scheuer*, barn). (The form of the word is due to a supposed connexion with L. *equus*, horse.) Formerly, royal or princely stables. Short for 'gentleman of the equerry', an officer of a sovereign, &c., in charge of the horses; at the English Court, an officer in occasional attendance on the sovereign.

Eques'trian, *a.* L. *equester*, *equestris*, belonging to a horseman (f. *eques*, horseman, f. *equus*, horse) + -AN. EQUINE. Of, skilled in, horse-riding; mounted on a horse.—*n.* One who rides on horseback.

Equian'gular, *a.* EQUI-. Having equal angles.

Equidis'tant, *a.* F. *équidistant*—L.L. *aequidistans*, *aequidistantis*, f. *aequi-* (EQUI-) + L. *distans.* DISTANCE. Separated by an equal distance.

Equilat'eral, *a.* L.L. *aequilaterālis*, f. *aequi-* (EQUI-) + L. *latus*, *lateris*, side. COLLATERAL. Having all the sides equal.

Equilib'rium, *n.* L. *aequilibrium*, f. *aequi-* (EQUI-)+*libra*, balance. DELIBERATE. Equal balance between opposing forces.

E'quine, *a.* L. *equinus*, f. *equus*, horse. EQUESTRIAN. Of, pertaining to, like, a horse.

E'quinox, *n.* L. *aequinoctium*, the time of equal days and nights, f. *aequi-* (EQUI-) + *nox*, *noctis*, NIGHT. One of the two periods in the year when the sun is on the celestial equator and day and night are equal.—**Equinoc'**TIAL, *a.* As *n.*, the celestial equator.

Equip', *vt.* F. *équiper*, earlier *esquiper*, prob. f. O.N. *skipa*, to man (a vessel), fit up, prob. f. *skip* = SHIP. To fit out, furnish for service; to array, accoutre.—**Eq'uip**AGE, *n.* Outfit; a carriage and horses.—**Equip'**MENT, *n.*

E'quipoise, *n.* EQUI-. Equality or equal distribution of weight; a counterpoise.

Equipol'lent, *a.* O.F. *equipolent*—L. *aequipollens*, *aequipollentis*, f. *aequi-* (EQUI-) + *pollens*, pres.pple. of *pollēre*, to be strong. Equal in power, &c.; of the same meaning.—**Equipol'l**ENCE, **Equipol'l**ENCY, *nn.*

Eq'uity, *n.* O.F. *equité*—L. *aequitas*, f. *aequus*, EQUAL, fair. INIQUITY. Fairness, impartiality; the recourse to general principles of justice to correct or supplement the provisions of the law.—**Eq'uitable**, *a.* F. *équitable.* Fair, reasonable; in law, pertaining to, valid in, equity.—**Eq'uitab**LY,[2] *adv.*

Equiv'alent, *a.* L.L. *aequivalens*, *aequivalentis*, pres.pple. of *aequivalēre*, to have equal power, f. *aequi-* (EQUI-) + *valēre*, to be powerful. AVAIL. Equal in value; of the same meaning; tantamount; corresponding. —*n.* Something equivalent; something given by way of exchange or compensation.—**Equiv'al**ENCE, **Equiv'al**ENCY, *nn.*

Equiv'ocal *a.* L.L. *aequivocus*, ambiguous (f. *aequi-* (EQUI-) + *vocāre*, to call) + -AL. ADVOCATE. Ambiguous; of uncertain nature; doubtfully real, questionable; liable to suspicion.—**Equiv'oc**ATE,[3] *vi.* To mean one thing and express another. —**Equivoc**A'TION, *n.* — **Equiv'ocat**OR, *n.* — **Eq'uivoque**, **Eq'uivoke**, *n.* From *aequivocus.* A pun; punning; ambiguity of speech.

E'ra, *n.* L.L. *aera*, a given number, an epoch, prob. f. *aera*, counters, pl. of *aes*, bronze, money. A chronological system in which the years are numbered from a particular point; the point; a memorable date; a period.

Erad'icate, *vt.* L. *ērādicāre*, *ērādicātum*, f. E- + *rādix.* RADICAL. WORT.[1] To root out.—**Erad'ic**ABLE, *a.*—**Eradic**A'TION, *n.*

Erase', *vt.* L. *Erādĕre*, *ērāsum*, to scratch out. ABRADE. To efface, obliterate. —**Erase'**MENT, *n.*—**Eras'**URE, *n.*

Eras'tian, *a.* *Erastus* (16th c.) + -IAN. Of Erastus.—*n.* An advocate of the (supposed) doctrines of Erastus, one advocating the subordination of the church to the civil power.

Ere, *prep.* and *conj.* O.E. *ǽr*, a comp. form corresp. to O.S., O.H.G. *ēr*. EARLY. ERST. Poss. cogn. with G. *ēri*, early. Before.

Erect', *a.* L. *ērectus*, pa.pple. of *ērigĕre*, to set up, f. E- + *regĕre*, to direct. CORRECT. Upright, in an upright posture.—*vt.* To set upright; to rear, build; to form *into* (an organization, &c.).—**Erec't**ION, *n.*—**Erec'tile**, *a.* F. *érectile.* Capable of being set upright.

Er'emite, *n.* L.L. *erēmīta*—Eccles.G. *erēmitēs*, f. *erēmia*, a desert, f. *erēmos*, uninhabited. A HERMIT.

Er'got, *n.* F. *ergot*, O.F. *argot*, cock's spur, of unknown orig. A disease of the seed of rye, &c., in which the seed resembles a cock's spur; the diseased seed used as a medicine.

Er'mine, *n.* O.F. (*h*)*ermine* = Sp. *armiño*, of doubtful orig. An animal of the weasel kind, whose fur becomes white in winter; the fur.

Erode', *vt.* F. *éroder*—L. *Erōdĕre*, *ērōsum*, to gnaw away. CORRODE. To wear away; of acids, &c., to eat away.—**Ero's**ION, *n.*

Erot'ic, *a.* G. *erōtikos*, f. *erōs*, *erōtos*, (sexual) love. Of, treating of, sexual love.

Err, *vi.* F. *errer*—L. *errāre*, *errātum*, to wander, rove, mistake, cogn. with O.H.G. *irrōn* (Ger. *irren*). ABERRANT. To make mistakes, be incorrect; to sin.—**Errat'ic**, *a.* L. *errāticus*, f. *errāre.* Irregular in movement, conduct, &c.—**Erra'tum**, *n.*; *pl.* **Erra'ta**. Neut. pa.pple. of *errāre.* An error noted for correction.—**Erro'neous**, *a.* L. *errōneus*, wandering (f. *erro*, *errōnis*, vagabond, f. *errāre*) + -OUS. Incorrect, mistaken, wrong.—**Er'ror**, *n.* O.F. *error*—L. *error*, f. *errāre.* The condition of erring in opinion; a mistaken notion or belief; false beliefs collectively; a mistake; a transgression.

Er'rand, *n.* O.E. *ǽrende*, a message, corresp. to O.H.G. *ārunti*, O.N. *eyrindi.* A short journey on which one is sent to do some simple business; the business; a purpose.

Er'rant, *a.*[1] F. *errant*, pres.pple. of O.F. *errer*, *esrer*—Pop.L. *iterāre*, to journey, f. L. *iter*, journey. EYRE. Itinerant, travelling, said (after F. *chevalier errant*) of knights journeying in quest of adventures.

Er'rant, *a.*[2] L. *errans*, *errantis*, pres.pple. of *errāre*. ERR. ARRANT. Roving; erring.

Erst, *adv.* O.E. *ǽrest*, superl. of *ǽr*. ERE. Formerly in sense 'earliest'. Of old.

Eruct', *vt.* and *i.* L. Eructāre, to belch forth. To belch.—**Eruct**A'TION, *n.*

Er'udite, *a.* L. *ērudītus*, pa.pple. of *ērudīre*, to instruct, f. E- + *rudis*, unwrought, untrained. RUDE. Learned.—**Erudi'tion**, *n.*

Erupt', *vi.* and *t.* L. *ērumpĕre*, *ēruptum*, to cause to burst forth, to burst forth, f. E- + *rumpĕre*, to break, burst. ABRUPT. Of a volcano, &c., to burst, to throw, forth.—**Erup'tion**, *n.* Bursting forth; an outbreak of volcanic activity; a breaking out of a rash or of pimples.—**Erup'tive**, *a.*

Erysip'elas, *n.* G. *erusipelas*, commonly regarded as f. *erusi-* = root of *eruthros*, red + *pel-* in *pella*, skin. FELL, *n.*[1] A local febrile disease with inflammation of the skin.

Escalade', *n.* F., f. Sp. *escalada*, f. *escalar*, to scale, f. *escala*, L. *scāla*, ladder. SCALE.[3] A scaling of the walls of a fortified place.

Escallo'nia, *n.* From *Escallon*, the discoverer. A S. American flowering shrub.

Escape', *vi.* O.N.F. *escaper*, lit., 'to slip out of one's cape'—L.L. **excappāre*, f. EX- + *cappa*, CAPE.[1] To gain liberty by flight, get free; to get off safely, go unpunished; of gases, &c., to find egress.—*vt.* To be uttered inadvertently by; to elude.—*n.* The action of escaping, the fact of having escaped.—**Escapade'**, *n.* F. *escapade*—Sp. or Pg. *escapada*, f. *escapar* = *escaper*. A runaway excursion; a flighty piece of conduct.—**Escape'**MENT, *n.* In a clock or watch, the mechanism which transmits the motive power to the regulator (*i.e.* the pendulum or its equivalent), which it alternately checks and releases.

Escarp', *n.* F. *escarpe*—It. *scarpa*. SCARP. The interior slope of a ditch.—*vt.* To cut into a steep slope.—**Escarp'**MENT, *n.*

Eschatol'ogy, *n.* G. *eschatos*, last + -LOGY. The department of theology dealing with the last or final things, as death, &c.

Escheat', *n.* O.F. *eschete*, *escheoite*, n. of action (orig. fem. pa.pple.) f. *escheoir*, L.L. **excadēre*, to fall to one's share, f. EX- + *cadēre* (L. *cadĕre*), to fall. CHEAT. The lapsing of a fief to the lord on the death of a tenant without a qualified successor; property so lapsing.—*vt.* To make an escheat of; to confiscate.—*vi.* To become an escheat.

Eschew', *vt.* O.F. *eschever*, to avoid. Cf. M.H.G. *schiuhen* (Ger. *scheuen*). Cogn. with SHY, *a.* To abstain from, avoid.

Es'cort, *n.* F. *escorte*—It. *scorta*, f. *scorgere*, to conduct—L.L. **excorrigĕre*, f. EX- + L. *corrigĕre*, to set right. CORRECT. A body of armed men guarding a traveller, &c.; persons or a person accompanying a traveller, &c., as a mark of honour; attendance as an escort.—**Escort'**, *vt.* To act as escort to.

Escritoire', *n.* F. (now *écritoire*), writing-case, writing-desk—L.L. *scriptōrium*, f. *scribĕre*. SCRIBE. A writing-desk with drawers.

Es'culent, *a.* L. *esculentus*, f. *esca* (**edca*), food, f. *edĕre*, to eat. EDIBLE. Eatable.

Escut'cheon, *n.* O.N.F. *escuchon* (F. *écusson*)—L.L. **scūtio*, **scūtiōnis*, f. L. *scūtum*, shield. SCUTCHEON. ESQUIRE. The shield on which a coat of arms is depicted.

Esoter'ic, *a.* G. *esōterikos*, f. *esōterō*, comp. of *esō*, within. Taught to a select few.

Espal'ier, *n.* F., f. It. *spalliera*, something to lean the shoulder against, hence, stakes shoulder-high, f. *spalla*, shoulder—L.L. *spatula*. EPAULET. A framework on which fruit-trees, &c., are trained; a tree, &c., thus trained.

Espar'to, *n.* Sp., f. L. *spartum*—G. *sparton*, a rope made of *spartos*, either this plant or Spanish broom. A rush imported from Spain and N. Africa for manufacture into paper.

Espec'ial, *a.* O.F. *especial*. SPECIAL. Not general; pre-eminent; pertaining to a particular case.—**Espec'ial**LY,[2] *adv.*

Es'pionage, *n.* F. *espionnage*, f. *espionner*, to spy, f. *espion*, spy, prob. f. It. *spione* of Teut. orig. Cf. ESPY. The practice of playing the spy or of employing spies.

Esplanade', *n.* F., f. Sp. *esplanada*, f. *esplanar*, L. *explānāre*. EXPLAIN. A level space forming a public promenade.

Espouse', *vt.* O.F. *espouser*—L. *sponsāre*, to betroth, f. *sponsus*, pa.pple. of *spondēre*, to promise, to betroth. DESPOND. SPOUSE. To marry; to attach oneself to, embrace.—**Espous'**AL, *n.*—In *pl.*, marriage.

Espy', *vt.* O.F. *espier*, to spy upon—O.H.G. *spehôn* (Ger. *spähen*). Cogn. with G. *skeptesthai*, L. *specĕre*, to look. SCEPTIC. ASPECT. To catch sight of, discern.—**Espi'**AL, *n.*

Esquire', *n.* O.F. *esquier*, lit., 'shield-bearer—L. *scūtārius*, f. *scūtum*. ESCUTCHEON. A title of dignity next to knight.

Es'say, *n.* O.F. *essai*, var. of *assai*. ASSAY. An attempt; a short composition on any particular subject.—**Essay'**, *vt.* To try, test; to attempt.—**Es'say**IST, *n.* A writer of essays.

Es'sence, *n.* F. *essence*—L. *essentia*, f. **essens*, **essentis*, a fictitious pres.pple. of *esse*. ENTITY. An existence; foundation of being; that which constitutes the being of a thing; an extract obtained by distillation, &c., from a plant, &c.; a fragrant essence.—**Essen'**TIAL, *a.* That is such in the highest sense; of essence or intrinsic nature; necessarily belonging to a thing; important; necessary.—*n.* An indispensable element or adjunct; a chief point.

Estab'lish, *vt.* O.F. *establiss-*, stem of *establir*—L. *stabilīre*, f. *stabilis*, STABLE, *a.* To confirm, settle; to fix, institute; to found; to install, set up; to bring about, introduce; to prove.—**Estab'lish**MENT, *n.* The action of the *v.*; the conferring on a religious body of the position of a state church; the ecclesiastical system established by law; settlement in life; the full number of a regiment, &c.; an institution, house of business, &c.; a household.

Estate', *n.* O.F. *estat*—L. *status*. STATE. State, condition; rank; a class as part of the body politic; property; a landed property.

Esteem', *vt.* O.F. *estimer*—L. *aestimāre*, *aestimātum*, to value. AIM. To hold in (favourable or unfavourable) estimation; to think highly of; to account, consider, hold.—*n.* Estimation, opinion; favourable opinion.

Es'timate, *vt.* L. *aestimāre*. (See prec.) To hold in (higher or lower) esteem; to form a notion of (amounts, magnitudes, &c.); to form an opinion of.—*n.* An approximate judgement respecting amounts, &c.; the amount, &c., arrived at; a judgement respecting the qualities, &c., of persons, &c.—**Es'tim**ABLE, *a.*

Worthy of regard.—**Estima**'TION, *n.* Appreciation, esteem; opinion, judgement.

Estop', *vt.* A.F. *estopper*, f. O.F. *estoupe* (F. *étoupe*), tow—L. *stuppa*. STOP. To bar, preclude.—*n.* A stop or stoppage.—**Estop'pel**, *n.* App. f. O.F. *estouppail*, bung, cork, f. *estoupper*, to stop up, f. *estoupe*. A legal impediment or bar arising from one's own act.

Estrange', *vt.* O.F. *estranger*—L. *extrāneāre*, to treat as a stranger, f. *extrāneus*. EXTRANEOUS. STRANGE. To alienate in feeling or affection.—**Estrange**'MENT, *n.*

Es'tuary, *n.* L. *aestuārium*, a tidal channel, f. *aestus*, heat, surge, tide. The tidal mouth of a great river.

Etch, *vt.* Du. *etsen*—Ger. *ätzen*—O.Teut.**atjan*, causal of **etan*, to EAT. To engrave by eating away the surface of the plate with acids.—*vi.* To practise this art.—**Etch**'ER, *n.*—**Etch'ing**, *vbl.n.* In senses f. the *v.*; an impression from an etched plate.

Eter'nal, *a.* O.F. *eternal*—L.L. *aeternālis*, f. L. *aeternus* (**aeviternus*), everlasting, f. *aevum*, AGE. Without beginning or end; everlasting, endless; incessant, perpetual; immutable.—**Eter'nal**LY,[2] *adv.*—**Eter'ni**TY, *n.*

E'ther, *n.* L *aether*—G. *aithēr*, the clear upper air The clear sky; a substance of great elasticity supposed to permeate space; a colourless volatile liquid used as an anæsthetic.—**Ethe'real**, *a.* L. *aethereus*, G. *aitherios* + -AL. Airy, light; heavenly; impalpable.

Eth'ic, *a.* L. *ēthicus*—G. *ēthikos*, f. *ēthos*, character, in *pl.*, manners. Also **Eth'ic**AL. Relating to, treating of, morals.—**Eth'ical**LY,[2] *adv.*—**Eth'ics**, *n.pl.* The science of morals; a treatise on this; moral principles; recognized rules of conduct.

Eth'nic, *a.* G. *ethnikos*, of or for a nation, heathen, gentile, f. *ethnos*, nation, in N.T., &c., in *pl.*, the Gentiles. Heathen, pagan; pertaining to race; peculiar to a race.—**Eth'nic**AL, *a.* Of race or races or ethnology.—**Ethno**L'OGY, *n.* The science of races.

E'tiolate, *vt.* With -ATE[3] f. F. *étioler* in sim. sense, f. Norman (*s'*)*étieuler*, to grow into haulm, f. *éteule*, L. *stipula*, straw. To make pale or colourless.

Etiquette', *n.* F. *étiquette*—obs. F. *etiquet*, note, notice (from which the sense 'prescribed routine' appears to have been developed). TICKET. Prescribed ceremonial or formalities; conventional rules of personal behaviour.

Etymol'ogy, *n.* O.F. *ethimologie*—L. *etymologia*—G. *etumologia*, f. *etumon* (neut. of *etumos*, true), the true sense of a word according to its origin, its root + *-logia*, -LOGY. The tracing out of the elements of a word; an instance of this process; the facts relating to the formation of a word; the branch of philology which deals with the origin of words.—**Etymolog'**IC, **Etymolog'**ICAL, *aa.*—**Etymolog'ical**LY,[2] *adv.*—**Etymol'og**IST, *n.*—**Et'ymon**, *n.* L. *etymon*—G. *etumon*. The primary word from which a derivative comes.

Eucalyp'tus, *n.* Mod.L., as if f. a G. **eukaluptos*, to mean 'well-covered' (the bud being protected by a sort of cap), f. *eu-*, well + *kaluptos*, covered, f. *kaluptein*, to cover. A genus of Australian trees; a tree of the kind.

Eu'charist, *n.* O.F. *eucariste*—G. *eucharistia*, lit., 'a giving of thanks', f. *eucharistos*, grateful, f. *eu-*, well + stem of *charizesthai*, to offer willingly. The sacrament of the Lord's Supper; the consecrated elements.—**Eucharis'**TIC, **Eucharis'**TICAL, *aa.*

Eugen'ic, *a.* G. *eu-*, well + *gen-* (ENDOGEN) + -IC. Pertaining or adapted to the production of fine offspring.—In *pl.* as *n.*, the science dealing with such production.

Euhe'merism, *n.* L.*Euhēmerus*, G.*Euēmeros* (c. 316 B.C.), author of a work maintaining the method + -ISM. The reference of myths to an historical basis.—**Euhe'mer**IST, *n.*

Eulo'gium, *n.* Med.L., app. formed by a confusion between L. *ēlogium*, an inscription, and G. *eulogia*, praise, f. *eu*, well + *-logia*, a speaking, f. *legein*, to speak. A laudatory discourse; praise. Also in anglicized form **Eu'logy** in the same senses.—**Eu'log**IST, *n.*—**Eulogis'**TIC, *a.*—**Eu'log**IZE, *vt.*

Eu'nuch, *n.* L. *eunūchus*—G. *eunouchos*, lit., 'bed-keeper', *i.e.*, one in charge of the women, f. *eunē*, bed + *och-*, a stem of *echein*, to keep. A castrated man.

Eu'phemism, *n.* G. *euphēmismos*, the use of an auspicious for an inauspicious word, f. *euphēmizein*, to use auspicious words, f. *euphēmos*, uttering sounds of good omen, f. *eu-*, well + *phēmē*, a speech, saying. The substitution of a mild or vague expression for one which would more precisely designate what is meant; an instance of this.—**Eu'phem**IST, *n.*—**Euphemis'**TIC, *a.*

Eu'phony, *n.* F. *euphonie*—G. *euphōnia*, f. *euphōnos*, well-sounding, f. *eu-*, well + *phōnē*, voice, sound. CACOPHONY. The quality of having a pleasing sound.—**Eupho'ni**OUS, *a.*

Eu'phuism, *n.* *Euphu-es* (G. *euphuēs*, well-endowed by nature, f. *eu-*, well + *phuē*, growth, f. *phuein*, to produce), the chief character in John Lyly's works of the name + -ISM. A style like the affected style of these books.

Eura'sian, *a.* *Eur-ope* + *Asia* + -AN. Of European and Asiatic (Indian) parentage.

Euthana'sia, *n.* G. *euthanasia*, f. *eu-*, well + *thanatos*, death. A gentle and easy death.

Evac'uate, *vt.* L. *ēvacuāre*, *ēvacuātum*, to empty, f. E- + *vacuus*, empty. To empty; to quit, withdraw from; to void, discharge; to clear out, remove.—**Evacu**A'TION, *n.*

Evade', *vt.* F. *évader*—L. EVĀDĒRE, *ēvāsum*, to go out. WADE. To escape from by dexterity, to avoid, to elude; to get out of acknowledging, &c.; to defeat the intention of (a law, &c.).—**Eva'**SION, *n.*—**Eva'**SIVE, *a.*

Eval'uate, *vt.* F. *évaluer* (f. *é-* (*es-*, EX-) + *value*, VALUE) + -ATE.[3] To ascertain the value or amount of.—**Evalu**A'TION, *n.*

Evanesce', *vi.* L. EVĀNESCĒRE, to vanish away, f. *vānus*, empty, insubstantial. VAIN. To fade away, disappear, become effaced.—**Evanes'**CENCE, *n.*—**Evanes'**CENT, *a.*

Evan'gel, *n.* O.F. *evangil(l)e*—Eccles.L. *ēvangelium*—Late G. *euaggelion*, good tidings, the gospel, f. G. *euaggelos*, bringing good tidings, f. *eu-*, well + *aggellein*, to announce. The gospel.—**Evangel'**IC, *a.* Of the gospel narrative. In the following senses also **Evangel'**ICAL. Of the faith or precepts of the gospel; applied to a school of Protestants who attach exclusive importance to the doctrine of salvation by faith in the atoning death of Christ.—**Evangel'ical**, *n.* One of this school.—**Evangel'ic**ISM, *n.*—**Evan'gel**IST, *n.* One of the writers of the four Gospels; one who preaches the gospel.—**Evan'gel**IZE, *vt.* To preach the gospel to; to convert.

Evap'orate, *vt.* L. *ēvaporāre*, *ēvaporātum*, f. E- + *vapor*, steam, VAPOUR. To convert into vapour.—*vi.* To become vapour; to pass off in or like vapour.—**Evapor**A'TION, *n.*

Eve, *n.* Var. of next. Evening; the evening or day before a church festival; the time immediately preceding an event, &c.

E'ven, *n.* O.E. *æfen, éfen*, cogn. with Old Fris. *ävond*, O.H.G. *äband* (Ger. *abend*). Evening.—**E'vensong**, *n.* Evening Prayer.

E'ven, *a.* O.E. *efen, efn.* Common Teut. Flat, level; smooth; uniform throughout (in colour, &c.); free from fluctuations; equally balanced; just, impartial; divisible by 2 without remainder; containing no fractions.—*adv.* O.E. *efne.* Exactly, precisely; quite, fully; intimating the expression of an extreme case of an implied more general proposition.—*vt.* To make even; to treat as equal.

E'vening, *n.* O.E. *æfnung*, vbl.n. f. *æfnian*, to grow towards evening, f. *æfen*, EVEN, *n.* The close of the day.

Event', *n.* O.F. *event*—L. *ēventus*, f. E*venīre, ēventum*, to COME out, to happen. ADVENT. The occurrence *of*; an incident; issue.—**Event'**FUL, *a.* Rich in striking incidents; momentous.—**Even'tual**, *a.* F. *éventuel.* That will arise or happen in a particular contingency; ultimately resulting.—**Even'tual**LY,[2] *adv.* In the end.—**Eventual'**ITY, *n.* A possible event, a contingency.—**Even'tu**ATE,[3] *vi.* To result *in*; to turn out, result.

Ev'er, *adv.* O.E. *æfre.* Not in the other Teut. languages. Prob. conn. with *á*, AY. Always, in all cases; constantly, perpetually; at any time; by any chance, at all; often appended to relative pronouns, &c., giving them a generalized or indefinite force.

Ev'ery, *a.* O.E. *æfre ælc*, EVER-EACH. Each, each one; all possible; the utmost degree of.

Evict', *vt.* L. E*vincĕre, ēvictum*, to overcome completely, to succeed in proving, demonstrate. CONVICT. EVINCE. To expel by legal process, to eject.—**Evic'**TION, *n.*

Ev'ident, *a.* L. *ēvidens, ēvidentis*, f. E- + *videns*, pres.pple. of *vidēre*, to see. ADVICE. Obvious, plain.—**Ev'ident**LY,[2] *adv.*—**Ev'i-d**ENCE, *n.* A being evident; an indication, token; ground for belief, testimony; a witness (now only in *King's, &c., evidence*).—*vt.* To attest, prove, indicate.—**Eviden'**TIAL, *a.*

E'vil, *a.* M.E. *uvel*—O.E. *yfel* = M.Du. *evel*, O.H.G. *ubil, upil* (Ger. *übel*). Bad; hurtful; unpleasant, painful; unlucky, disastrous.—*n.* That which is evil; that which causes harm or mischief.—**E'vil**LY,[2] *adv.*

Evince', *vt.* L. *ēvincĕre.* EVICT. To make evident or manifest; to display, exhibit.

Evis'cerate, *vt.* L. *ēviscerāre, ēviscerātum*, f. E- + *viscera*, VISCERA. To disembowel.—**Eviscer**A'TION.

Ev'itable, *a.* L. *ēvitābilis*, f. E*vitāre*, to shun, f. *vītāre* in sim. sense. Avoidable.

Evoke', *vt.* F. *évoquer*—L. E*vocāre*, to call forth. ADVOCATE. To call forth or into being or activity.—**Evoc**A'TION, *n.*

Evolve', *vt.* L. E*volvĕre, ēvolūtum*, to roll out, unroll. VOLUBLE. To unfold, open out; to educe, deduce, develop; to give rise to, produce.—*vi.* To open out, arise, be developed.—**Evolu'**TION, *n.* An unfolding; development, growth; a movement of troops.—**Evolu'tion**AL, *a.*—**Evolu'tion**ARY, *a.*—**Evolu'tion**IST, *n.* An adherent of the doctrine of evolution or development in biology.

Ewe, *n.* O.E. *eowu.* Common Teut. and Aryan. Cogn. with Skr. *avi*, G. *ois*, L. *ovis.* A female sheep.

Ew'er, *n.* A.F. *ewer*—L. type **aquāria*, f. *aqua.* SEWER. A bedroom water-jug.

Exac'erbate, *vt.* L. EX*acerbāre, exacerbātum*, f. *acerbus.* ACERBITY. To embitter, aggravate.—**Exacerb**A'TION, *n.*

Exact', *vt.* L. *exigĕre, exactum*, to drive out, to demand, to weigh, to adjust, f. EX- + *agĕre*, to drive. ACT. EXAMINE. EXIGENT. To demand, extort; to insist upon; to require urgently.—*a.* From *exactus*, the pa. pple. Precise, rigorous; accurate in knowledge, workmanship, &c.; strictly correct, precise.—**Exact'**LY,[2] *adv.*—**Exac'ti**TUDE, *n.*—**Exact'**NESS, *n.*—**Exac'**TION, *n.*

Exag'gerate, *vt.* L. EX*aggerāre, exaggerātum*, to heap up, f. *agger*, heap. To magnify beyond the limits of truth; to intensify, aggravate.—**Exagger**A'TION, *n.*

Exalt', *vt.* L. *exaltāre, exaltātum*, f. EX- + *altus*, high. ALTAR. To raise up; to extol; to dignify, ennoble.—**Exalt**A'TION, *n.* In senses from the *v.*; elation of feeling.

Exam'ine, *vt.* F. *examiner*—L. *exāmināre*, to weigh accurately, test, f. *exāmen* (**exagmen*), *exāminis*, the tongue of a balance, f. **exag-, exigĕre.* EXACT. ASSAY. To investigate, scrutinize, check, inspect; to test (a person) by questions; to interrogate.—**Examin**A'TION, *n.*—**Exam'in**ER, *n.*

Exam'ple, *n.* O.F. *essample, example*—L. *exemplum*, a sample, f. *eximĕre.* EXEMPT. SAMPLE. A typical instance; a specimen; a warning, caution; a parallel case; action or conduct as an object of imitation.—*vt.* To furnish a pattern of, give an instance of.

Exas'perate, *vt.* L. EX*asperāre, exasperātum*, to roughen, to irritate, f. *asper*, rough. ASPERITY. To embitter, intensify; to irritate, enrage.—**Exasper**A'TION, *n.*

Ex'cavate, *vt.* L. EX*cavāre, excavātum*, to hollow out, f. *cavus*, hollow. CAVE, *n.* To hollow out; to form (a hole, &c.) by excavating; to unearth.—**Excav**A'TION, *n.*

Exceed', *vt.* F. *excéder*—L. EX*cēdĕre, excessum*, to go out, go beyond. ACCEDE. To go beyond; to be greater than; to surpass.—*vi.* To exaggerate; to be pre-eminent, to preponderate. — **Exceed'ing**LY,[2] *adv.* — **Excess'**, *n.* F. *excès*—L. *excessus.* An overstepping; intemperance; the amount by which one quantity exceeds another; superabundance; too great an amount or degree.—**Excess'**IVE, *a.*—**Excess'ive**LY,[2] *adv.*

Excel', *vi.* F. *exceller*—L. EX*cellĕre*, to rise, excel, cogn. with *celsus*, high. (The simple *cellĕre* does not occur.) To be superior *in*; to surpass others.—*vt.* To be superior to, to surpass. — **Ex'cell**ENCE, *n.* Superiority, pre-eminence; that in which a person or thing excels.—**Ex'cell**ENCY, *n.* A title of ambassadors, governors, &c.—**Ex'cell**ENT, *a.*

Except', *vt.* F. *excepter*—L. *excipĕre, exceptum*, to take out, f. EX- + *capĕre*, to take. ACCEPT. To take or leave out, to exclude.—*vi.* To make objection.—*prep.* and *conj.* From L. *exceptus*, the pa.pple. Not including, but. —**Excep'**TION, *n.*—**Excep'tion**ABLE, *a.* Open to objection.—**Excep'tion**AL, *a.*

Excerpt', *vt.* L. *excerpĕre, excerptum*, f. EX- + *carpĕre*, to pluck. CARPET. SCARCE. To cull out, extract, quote.—**Ex'cerpt**, *n.* An excerpted passage.

Exchange', *vt.* O.F. *eschangier*—L.L. EX*cambiāre.* CHANGE. To give (something) whilst receiving something else in return; to give and receive reciprocally.—*n.* The action of exchanging; a giving or receiving coin, bills, &c., in return for foreign coin, bills, &c.,

of equivalent value; the rate ruling such transactions; a building in which merchants meet for business.—**Exchange'**ABLE, *a.*

Excheq'uer, *n.* M.E. *escheker.* CHEQUER. Under the Norman and Angevin kings a department of state dealing with the revenues and determining causes relating thereto, named from the table, divided into squares, on which accounts were kept by means of counters; a court of law representing this department in its judicial capacity; the department in charge of the revenue.

Excise', *n.* App. f. M.Du. *excijs, exziis,* also *accijs,* prob. f. O.F. *acceis,* tax—L.L. *accensāre,* to tax, f. *ac-* (= AD-) + *census.* CENSUS. A duty on home goods.

Excise', *vt.* L. *excīdĕre, excīsum,* f. EX- + *caedĕre,* to cut. CONCISE. To cut out.—**Exci'**SION, *n.*

Excite', *vt.* F. *exciter*—L. EX*citāre,* to call forth, rouse up. CITE. To rouse up, awaken; to bring about; to stimulate; to stir to passion. —**Excit'**ABLE, *a.*—**Excita**BIL'ITY, *n.*—**Excite'**MENT, *n.*—**Excit**A'TION, *n.*

Exclaim', *vi.* F. *exclamer*—L. EX*clāmāre, exclāmātum,* to cry out. ACCLAIM. To cry out. —**Exclama**A'TION, *n.*—**Exclam'at**ORY, *a.*

Exclude', *vt.* L. *exclūdĕre, exclūsum,* f. EX- + *claudĕre,* to shut. CLAUSE. SLUICE. To shut out; to give no place to; not to admit of; to debar *from.*—**Exclu'**SION, *n.*—**Exclu'**SIVE, *a.* That excludes; so as to exclude; limited to an object or objects; disposed to exclude from admission to a body or from intimacy.—**Exclu'sive**LY,[2] *adv.*

Excog'itate, *vt.* L. EX*cōgitāre, excōgitātum,* to think out. COGITATE. To think out, devise.

Excommu'nicate, *vt.* Eccles. L. *excommūnicāre, excommūnicātum,* lit. 'to put out of the community', f. EX- + L. *commūnis,* COMMON. To exclude from the sacraments of the church.—**Excommunica**A'TION, *n.*

Excor'iate, *vt.* L.L. *excoriāre, excoriātum,* f. EX- + *corium.* CUIRASS. QUARRY.[1] SCOURGE. To remove skin from; to remove (the skin).

Excres'cent, *a.* L. *excrescens, excrescentis,* pres.pple. of EX*crescĕre,* to grow out. ACCRESCE. Growing out of something abnormally; redundant.—**Excres'**CENCE, *n.*

Excrete', *vt.* L. EX*cernĕre, excrētum,* to sift out. CONCERN. To separate from the vital fluids and discharge from the body.—**Ex'cre**MENT, *n.* That which is so discharged.—**Excre'**TION, *n.*—**Excre't**ORY, *a.*

Excru'ciate, *vt.* L. EX*cruciāre, excruciātum,* f. *crux, crucis,* CROSS. To torture physically or mentally.—**Excruci**A'TION, *n.*

Ex'culpate, *vt.* EX- + L. *culpa,* blame + -ATE.[3] CULPABLE. To clear *from* blame or an accusation.—**Exculp**A'TION, *n.*—**Excul'pat**ORY, *a.*

Excur'sion, *n.* L. *excursio, excursiōnis,* n. of action f. EX*currĕre, excursum,* to run out. CONCUR. A journey for the sake of pleasure or health.—**Excur'sus**, *n.* L. *excursus,* n. of action f. *excurrĕre.* A detailed discussion, often in the form of an appendix.

Excuse', *vt.* O.F. *excuser*—L. EX*cūsāre,* f. *causa,* CAUSE, process. To seek to clear from blame; to seek to remove the blame of; to obtain exemption for; to judge leniently; to condone; to exempt, set free; to remit, to dispense with.—*n.* Pardon, indulgence; a plea in extenuation or for release; that which serves to excuse.—**Excus'**ABLE, *a.*

Ex'ecrate, *vt.* L. *ex(s)ecrāri, ex(s)ecrātus,* to curse, f. EX- + *sacrāre,* in sense 'to devote to destruction'. CONSECRATE. To imprecate evil upon; to abhor.—**Ex'ecr**ABLE, *a.*—**Execr**A'TION, *n.*

Ex'ecute, *vt.* F. *exécuter*—Med.L. *execūtāre,* f. L. EX*(s)equi, ex(s)ecūtus,* to follow to the end, to perform. CONSECUTION. To follow out, perform, carry into effect; to sign (a document); to inflict capital punishment upon. —**Exec'ut**ANT, *n.* One who performs (music). —**Execu'**TION, *n.*—**Execu'tion**ER, *n.* He who carries out a death sentence.—**Exec'ut**IVE, *a.* Carrying into effect, applied esp. to the branch of the government concerned with carrying out the laws, &c.—*n.* This branch of the government.—**Exec'ut**OR, *n.* One appointed by a testator to carry his will into effect. *fem.* **Exec'u**TRIX.

Exege'sis, *n.* G. *exēgēsis,* f. *exēge-esthai,* to interpret, f. *ex-,* out + *hēge-esthai,* to guide. Explanation, interpretation.—**Exeget'ic**, *a.* G. *exēgētikos.* Explanatory; of exegesis. In the latter sense also **Exeget'ic**AL.

Exem'plar, *n.* O.F. *exemplaire*—L.L. *exemplārium,* f. L. *exemplum.* EXAMPLE. An example, model, pattern; an instance, a parallel or typical instance.—**Exem'pl**ARY, *a.* Acting as a deterrent; serving, fit to serve, as a pattern.—**Exem'plari**LY,[2] *adv.*—**Exem'plify**, *vt.* Med.L. *exemplificāre.* -FY. To illustrate by examples; to serve as an example of.—**Exempli**FICA'TION, *n.*

Exempt', *ppl.a.* F. *exempt*—L. *exemptus,* pa.pple. of *eximĕre,* to take out, f. EX- + *emĕre,* to buy, orig., to take. EXAMPLE. PEREMPTORY. PRE-EMPTION. PREMIUM. PROMPT. REDEEM. Freed, not liable, unaffected.—*vt.* To free *from.*—**Exemp'**TION, *n.*

Exequa'tur, *n.* L. *exequātur,* he may perform, 3rd sing. pres. subjunctive of *exequi.* EXECUTE. The official recognition of a consul in the country in which he is to act.

Ex'equies, *n.pl.* O.F. *exequies*—L. *ex(s)equiae,* lit. 'train of followers' (*i.e.* to the grave), f. *ex(s)equi.* EXECUTE. Funeral rites.

Ex'ercise, *n.* O.F. *exercice*—L. *exercitium,* f. *exercēre,* to keep at work, train, f. EX- + *arcēre,* to shut up, restrain. ARCH, *n.* An employing, giving effect to, exerting; habitual carrying out; practice for the sake of training; exertion with a view to health; a task prescribed for training.—*vt.* To employ, exert; to train by practice; to give employment to; to harass, afflict; to carry on or out, perform.

Exert', *vt.* L. *ex(s)erĕre, ex(s)ertum,* to put forth, f. EX- + *serĕre,* to bind. ASSERT. To bring into active operation.—**Exer'**TION, *n.*

Exfo'liate, *vi.* L.L. *exfoliāre, exfoliātum,* to strip of leaves, f. EX- + *folium,* leaf. FOIL.[1] To come off in layers, scale off; to throw off layers of bark.—**Exfoli**A'TION, *n.*

Exhale', *vt.* F. *exhaler*—L. EX*hālāre.* To breathe out; to draw up or drive off in vapour. —*vi.* To pass off into the air; to give out breath. —**Exhal**A'TION, *n.*

Exhaust', *vt.* L. EX*haurīre, exhaustum,* to draw out, to empty. To draw off (air); to use up; to account for or utilize the whole of; to empty *of;* to treat thoroughly; to weary out. —**Exhaus'**TIBLE, *a.*—**Exhaus'**TION, *n.*—**Exhaus'**TIVE, *a.*

Exhib'it, *vt.* L. *exhibēre, exhibitum,* to hold forth, present, f. EX- + *habēre,* to hold. ABLE. To administer (a medicine); to set forth, detail; to show, display.—**Exhibi'**TION, *n.* The action of the *v.,* an instance of this; an allowance to a student; a public display (of works of art, manufactures, &c.), the place where these are shown.—**Exhib'itOR**, *n.*

Exhil'arate, *vt.* L. EX*hilarāre, exhilarātum*, f. *hilaris*, cheerful. HILARITY. To gladden, enliven.—**ExhilarA'TION**, *n.*

Exhort', *vt.* L. EX*hortāri, exhortātus*, to encourage. DEHORT. HORTATIVE. To admonish earnestly, urge.—**ExhortA'TION**, *n.*

Exhume', *vt.* F. *exhumer*—Med.L. *exhumāre*, f. EX-+L. *humus*, ground. HUMBLE. To dig out or remove from beneath the ground, to unearth.—**ExhumA'TION**, *n.*

Ex'igent, *a.* L. *exigens, exigentis*, pres.pple. of *exigĕre*. EXACT. Urgent, pressing, exacting. —**Ex'igENCE, Ex'igENCY**, *nn.* Urgent need, necessity; a pressing state of circumstances.—**Ex'igIBLE**, *a.* That may be exacted.

Exig'uous, *a.* L. *exiguus* (f. *exigĕre*, to weigh strictly. EXACT) + -OUS. Scanty in measure or number.—**Exigu'ITY**, *n.*

Ex'ile, *n.* O.F. *exil*—L. *ex(s)ilium*, prob. f. EX- + *sal-* (=Skr. *sar-*, to go), root of *salīre*, to leap. ASSAIL. Expulsion from one's native land, banishment; a banished person (in this sense poss. f. the *v.*).—*vt.* To banish.

Exist', *vi.* F. *exister*—L. EX(*s*)*istĕre*, to stand out, be perceptible. ASSIST. To be, to have being; to subsist, to occur; to continue in being.—**Exist'ENCE**, *n.*—**Exist'ENT**, *a.*

Ex'it. L., 3rd sing. indicative of EX*īre*, to go out. A stage direction indicating that an actor leaves the stage.—As *n.*, the departure of an actor; death; a going out, liberty or opportunity to go out. From *exitus*, n. of action f. *exire*. A means of egress, an outlet.

Ex-li'bris, *n.* Used also as *pl.* L. *ex libris*, out of the books, from the library (of a person). A book-label bearing the owner's name, &c.

Ex'odus, *n.* L. *Exodus*—G. *exodos*, a going out, f. *ex*, out + *hodos*, way. The second book of the Old Testament relating the departure of the Israelites from Egypt; the departure; a going out or forth.

Ex'ogen, *n.* G. *exō*, without + *-genēs*. ENDOGEN. A plant that grows from without.

Exon'erate, *vt.* L. *exonerāre, exonerātum*, f. EX- + *onus, oneris*, burden. ONEROUS. To free *from*; to exculpate.—**ExonerA'TION**, *n.*

Ex'orable, *a.* L. *exōrābilis*, f. *exōrāre*, to persuade by entreaty, f. EX- + *ōrāre*, to pray. Capable of being moved by entreaty.

Exor'bitant, *a.* L.L. *exorbitans, exorbitantis*, pres.pple. of *exorbitāre*, to go out of the track, f. EX- + L. *orbita*, wheel-track. ORBIT. Excessive, immoderate, extravagant. — **Exor'bitantLY**,[2] *adv.*—**Exor'bitANCE**, *n.*

Ex'orcize, *vt.* L.L. *exorcizāre*—G. *exorkizein*, f. *ex*, out + *horkos*, oath. To expel (an evil spirit) by the use of a holy name; to clear *of* evil spirits.—**Ex'orcISM**, *n.*—**Ex'orcIST**, *n.*

Exor'dium, *n.* L., f. EX*ordīri*, to begin. PRIMORDIAL. An introductory part.

Exoter'ic, *a.* G. *exōterikos*, f. *exōterō*, comp. of *exō*, outside. Taught to the many.

Exot'ic, *a.* L. *exōticus*—G. *exōtikos*, f. *exō*, outside. Introduced from abroad, not indigenous.—*n.* An exotic plant.

Expand', *vt.* and *i.* L. EX*pandĕre, expansum*, to spread or stretch out. PACE. SPAWN. To spread or open out; to dilate, enlarge.—**Expanse'**, *n.* From *expansus*, the pa.pple. A widely extended space or area.—**Expan'sIBLE**, *a.*—**ExpansIBIL'ITY**, *n.*—**Expan'sION**, *n.*—**Expan'sIVE**, *a.*

Expa'tiate, *vi.* L. *ex(s)patiāri, ex(s)patiātus*, to wander from the course, f. EX- + *spatiāri*, to walk about, f. *spatium*, SPACE. To roam at large; to enlarge in discourse or writing.

Expa'triate, *vt.* L.L. *expatriāre, expatriātum*, f. EX- + *patria*, native land. To exile, banish.—**ExpatriA'TION**, *n.*

Expect', *vt.* L. *ex(s)pectāre*, to look out for, f. EX-+*spectāre*, to look, freq. of *specĕre*. ASPECT. To look forward to, look to, anticipate; to suppose, surmise.—**Expec'tANCY**, *n.* An expecting; a being entitled to something in the future.—**Expec'tANT**, *a.* and *n.*—**Expec'tantLY**,[2] *adv.*—**ExpectA'TION**, *n.*

Expec'torate, *vt.* L. *expectorāre, expectorātum*, to drive from the breast, f. EX- + *pectus, pectoris*, the breast. To eject (phlegm, &c.). —*vi.* To spit.—**ExpectorA'TION**, *n.*

Expe'dient, *a.* F. *expédient*—L. *expediens, expedientis*, pres.pple. of *expedīre, expedītum*, to free the feet, to help forward, to dispatch, f. EX- + *pēs, pedis*, FOOT. PEDAL. Fitting, proper or suitable to the circumstances; politic. —*n.* A contrivance or device.—**Expe'dientLY**,[2] *adv.*—**Expe'diENCE, -ENCY**, *nn.*

Ex'pedite, *vt.* L. *expedīre*. (See prec.) To help forward, hasten the progress of; to perform quickly, accomplish.—**Expedi'tION**, *n.* A warlike enterprise; a journey or voyage for a definite end; a body of persons, &c., sent on an expedition; haste, speed.—**Expedi'tionARY**, *a.*—**Expedi'tIOUS**, *a.* Speedy, prompt.

Expel', *vt.* L. EX*pellĕre, expulsum*, to drive out. APPEAL. To drive out; to eject.—**Expul'sION**, *n.*—**Expul'sIVE**, *a.*

Expend', *vt.* L. EX*pendĕre, expensum*, to weigh or pay out. COMPEND. PENDANT. SPEND. To pay out, spend; to use up, consume.—**Expen'diture**, *n.* Med.L. *expenditus*, irreg. pa.pple. of *expendĕre*+-URE. The laying out (of money, energy, &c.); the amount expended; consumption.—**Expense'**, *n.* A.F. *expense*—L.L. *expensa*, orig. fem. pa.pple. of *expendĕre*. Expenditure; cost; in *pl.*, charges, items of outlay, &c., incurred.—**Expen'sIVE**, *a.* Attended with expense, costly.

Expe'rience, *n.* F. *expérience*—L. *experientia*, f. *experīri, expertus*, to try, put to the test, f. EX- + *perīri* (found only in pa.pple. *perītus*, experienced, skilled), cogn. with G. *poros*, way, passage, *peira*, experience. FARE. PERIL. Observation of facts, &c., as a source of knowledge; a being consciously affected by an event, &c.; the event, &c.; what has been experienced; knowledge, skill, &c., gained by experience.—*vt.* To meet with, feel, suffer, undergo.—**Exper'iment**, *n.* O.F. *experiment*—L. *experīmentum*, n. of action f. *experīri*. A test, trial; a tentative procedure; an action or operation to test a hypothesis, &c.; the conducting of such operations.—*vi.* To make an experiment.—**Experimen'tAL**, *a.* Based on experience or experiment; tentative.

Expert', *a.* O.F. *expert*—L. *expertus*, pa.pple. (in active sense) of *experīri*. (See prec.) MALAPERT. Skilled, skilful. — **Ex'pert**, *n.* One who is expert; a specialist, an authority.

Ex'piate, *vt.* L. *expiāre, expiātum*, to make satisfaction for, f. EX- + *piāre*, to seek to appease (by sacrifice), f. *pius*, PIOUS. To do away with the guilt of (a sin); to pay the penalty of; to make amends for.—**Ex'piABLE**, *a.*—**ExpiA'TION**, *n.*

Expire', *vt.* F. *expirer*—L. EX(*s*)*pīrāre*, to breathe out. ASPIRE. To breathe out.—*vi.* To give out breath; to die; to end.—**ExpirA'TION**, *n.*—**Expi'rY**,[1] *n.* Close, end.

Explain′, *vt.* L. *explānāre, explānātum*, to make flat, to explain, f. EX- + *plānus*, flat. PLAIN. To give details of; to make plain or clear; to interpret; to account for.—**Explan**A′TION, *n.*—**Explan′at**ORY, *a.*

Ex′pletive, *a.* L. *explētivus*, serving to fill up, f. EX*plēre, explētum*, to fill up. COMPLETE. Serving (merely) to fill up or help out.—*n.* An expletive word or phrase; an oath or meaningless interjection.

Ex′plicate, *vt.* L. EX*plicāre, explicātum* (also *explicitum*), to unfold, display. APPLY. To develop (a notion, &c.); to explain.—**Ex**-**plic**A′TION, *n.*—**Ex′plic**ABLE, *a.*

Explic′it, *a.* F. *explicite* — L. *explicitus*, pa.pple. of *explicāre*. (See prec.) Clear, definite; express in meaning; outspoken.

Explode′, *vt.* L. EX*plōdĕre* (EX*plaudĕre*), *explōsum*, to drive out by clapping. APPLAUD. To cause to be rejected, discredit; to cause to go off with a loud noise.—*vi.* To go off thus; to fly in pieces, burst.—**Ex**-**plo′**SION, *n.*—**Explo′**SIVE, *a.* and *n.*

Exploit′, *n.* O.F. *esploit, exploit*—L. *explicitum*, neut. of *explicitus*. EXPLICIT. A deed, a feat.—*vt.* F. *exploiter*. To work, turn to account; to utilize for one's own ends.—**Exploit**A′TION, *n.*

Explore′, *vt.* F. *explorer*—L. *explōrāre*, us. explained as f. EX- + *plōrāre*, to weep (cogn. with *pluĕre*, to rain), in sense 'to make to flow'. DEPLORE. To investigate, to examine; to examine (a country, &c.) by going through it. —**Explor**A′TION, *n.*—**Explor′at**ORY, *a.*—**Explor′**ER, *n.*

Expo′nent, *n.* L. *expōnens, expōnentis*, pres. pple. of *expōnĕre*. EXPOUND. One who expounds.—**Exponen′t**IAL, *a.*

Export′, *vt.* L. EX*portāre*, to carry out. COMPORT. To send (commodities) from one country to another.—**Ex′port**, *n.* An exported article; amount exported (gen. in *pl.*); the action of exporting, an instance of this.—**Ex**-**port**A′TION, *n.*—**Export′**ER, *n.*

Expose′, *vt.* F. *exposer*, f. EX- + *poser*, to place. POSE.[1] To leave unprotected; to lay open *to*; to exhibit to public view, to display; to make known; to unmask, show up.—**Ex**-**posi′tion**, *n.* F. *exposition*—L. *expositio, expositiōnis*, f. *expōnĕre*. EXPOUND. A putting out to public view; a display; an exhibition (of works of art, &c.); a describing; explanation, an explanation.—**Expo′**SURE, *n.*

Expos′tulate, *vi.* L. EX*postulāre, expostulātum*, to demand urgently, to complain. POSTULATE. To make friendly remonstrances or representations.—**Expostul**A′TION, *n.*

Expound′, *vt.* O.F. *espondre*—L. EX*pōnĕre*, *expositum*, to put out, set forth, explain. POSITION. To explain, interpret.

Express′, *vt.* O.F. *espresser, expresser*—Med. L. *expressāre*, f. EX- + L. *pressāre*, freq. of *premĕre, pressum*, to press. COMPRESS. To press out; to emit, exude; to render, to set forth (by drawing, &c.); to represent symbolically; to manifest; to put into words; to import, signify.—*v.refl.* To put one's thoughts into words.—*a.* Truly depicted; definite, explicit; specially designed; of a messenger, specially dispatched; of a train, making few stoppages. —*adv.* Specially, on purpose; with speed.—*n.* An express messenger or train.—**Ex**-**press′**LY,[2] *adv.*—**Expres′**SIBLE, *a.*—**Expres′**SION, *n.*—**Expres′**SIVE, *a.* Serving to express; expressing much or with force.

Expro′priate, *vt.* L.L. *expropriāre, expropriātum*, f. EX- + L. *proprium*, property, neut. of *proprius*, own. APPROPRIATE. To dispossess; to take out of the owner's hands.—**Expropri**A′TION, *n.*

Expunge′, *vt.* L. *expungĕre, expunctum*, to mark for deletion by points, f. EX- + *pungĕre*, to prick. COMPUNCTION. To strike out, erase, omit.—**Expunc′t**ION, *n.*

Ex′purgate, *vt.* L. EX*purgāre, expurgātum*, to cleanse, PURGE. To free (a book, &c.) from offensive matter.—**Expurg**A′TION, *n.*

Ex′quisite, *a.* L. *exquisitus*, pa.pple. of *exquīrĕre*, to search out diligently, f. EX- + *quaerĕre*, to search, seek. ACQUIRE. Carefully chosen or devised; cultivated to a high degree of intensity; of consummate excellence, beauty, &c.; keenly felt; keenly sensitive.—*n.* A dandy.—**Ex′quisite**LY,[2] *adv.*

Exscind′, *vt.* L. EX*scindĕre*, to tear or cut out. ABSCIND. To cut out, excise.

Ex′tant, *a.* L. *ex(s)tans, ex(s)tantis*, pres. pple. of EX*(s)tāre*, to stand forth, be visible. CONSTANT. Existing; still existing.

Extem′pore, *adv.* L. phrase *ex tempore*, lit. 'out of the time'. CONTEMPORANEOUS. Without premeditation, off-hand.—*a.* Spoken, &c., without premeditation; contrived for the occasion. Sim. **Extempora′neous**, *a.* L.L. *extemporāneus* (f. *ex tempore*) + -OUS. Also **Extem′por**ARY.—**Extem′por**IZE, *vi.* To speak, &c., extempore.—*vt.* To compose offhand; to contrive for the occasion.

Extend′, *vt.* L. EX*tendĕre, extentum*, also *extensum*, to stretch out. ATTEND. To stretch out; to lengthen; to prolong in duration; to widen the area, scope, &c., of; to stretch forth; to accord, grant.—*vi.* To reach; to cover an area; to have a certain range or scope; to become larger or wider.—**Exten′**SIBLE, *a.*—**Exten′**SION, *n.*—**Exten′**SIVE, *a.* Wide in extent, large in amount; comprehensive.—**Extent′**, *n.* A.F. *extente, estente*, orig. fem. pa.pple. of *estendre*, L. *extendĕre*. Dimensions, size; scope; a space or area.

Exten′uate, *vt.* L. EX*tenuāre, extenuātum*, to make thin, diminish, f. *tenuis*, thin. ATTENUATE. To palliate.—**Extenu**A′TION, *n.*

Exte′rior, *a.* L. *exterior*, comp. of *exterus*, outside, f. *ex*, out. Outer; situated outside. —*n.* The outside; outward aspect.

Exter′minate, *vt.* L. *extermināre, exterminātum*, lit. 'to drive beyond the boundaries', f. EX- + *terminus*, boundary. DETERMINE. To extirpate.—**Extermin**A′TION, *n.*

Exter′nal, *a.* L. *externus*, outward (f. *exter* = *exterus*. EXTERIOR) + -AL. Situated outside, pertaining to the outside; outwardly perceptible; arising or acting from without; connected with what is outside.

Exterrito′rial, *a.* EX-. Outside a territory and not amenable to its laws.

Extinct′, *a.* L. *ex(s)tinctus*, pa.pple. of *ex(s)tinguĕre*. (See next.) Quenched, put out; having ceased eruption; having died out or come to an end.—**Extinc′t**ION, *n.*

Extin′guish, *vt.* L. EX*(s)tinguĕre, ex(s)tinctum*, to quench. DISTINGUISH. To quench to do away with.—**Extin′guish**ABLE, *a.*—**Extin′guish**ER, *n.* One who or that which extinguishes; a contrivance for putting out a candle, &c.—**Extin′guish**MENT, *n.*

Ex′tirpate, *vt.* L. *ex(s)tirpāre, ex(s)tirpātum*, f. EX- + *stirps*, stem, root. To pluck up by the roots; to root out, destroy, do away with. —**Extirp**A′TION, *n.*

Extol', *vt.* L. EX*tollĕre*, to lift up. TOLERATE. To praise highly.—**Extol'**MENT, *n.*
Extort', *vt.* L. EX*torquēre, extortum*, to twist out, wrench away. CONTORT. To obtain by force, intimidation, &c.—**Extor'tion**, *n.*—**Extor'tion**ATE,[2] *a.*—**Extor'tion**ER, *n.*
Ex'tra, *a.* Prob. short for EXTRAORDINARY. Beyond what is usual, due, &c., additional.—*adv.* Unusually.—*n.* Something extra.
Extract', *t.* L. EX*trahĕre, extractum*, to draw out. ABSTRACT. To copy out; to get or take out, to obtain; to obtain (constituent elements, juices, &c.).—**Ex'tract**, *n.* A preparation containing the concentrated active principle of a substance; an excerpt.—**Extract'**ABLE, *a.*—**Extrac'**TION, *n.*
Extradi'tion, *n.* F. *extradition*, f. EX- + L. *trāditio, trāditiōnis*, n. of action f. *trādĕre*, to deliver up. TRADITION. Surrender (of a fugitive criminal) by one authority to another under a treaty.—**Ex'tradite**, *vt.* Back-formation from the *n.* To surrender thus.
Extrajudic'ial, *a.* L. *extrā*, outside + *jūdicium*, judgement + -AL. Lying outside proceedings in court; not legally authorized.
Extra'neous, *a.* L. *extrāneus*, external (f. *extrā*, outside) + -OUS. STRANGE. Introduced or added from without; foreign *to* a subject; not belonging to a country, &c.
Extraor'dinary, *a.* L. *extraordinārius*, f. phrase *extrā ordinem*, outside the (usual) ORDER. Out of the usual course; appointed in addition; unusual, singular; exceeding the usual.—**Extraor'dinari**LY,[2] *adv.*
Extrav'agant, *a.* F. *extravagant*—Med.L. *extrāvagans, extrāvagantis*, pres.pple. of *extrāvagāri*, to stray outside limits, f. L. *extrā*, outside + *vagāri*, to wander. VAGABOND. Flagrantly excessive; prodigal, wasteful; exorbitant.—**Extrav'agant**LY,[2] *adv.*—**Extrav'ag**ANCE, *n.*—**Extravagan'za**, *n.* It. *estravaganza.* A fantastic composition.
Extrav'asate, *vt.* L. *extrā*, outside + *vās*, VESSEL + -ATE.[3] To force out (blood, &c.) from its proper vessel.—*vi.* To flow out.—**Extravasa'**TION, *n.*
Extreme', *a.* O.F. *extreme*—L. *extrēmus*, superl. of *exterus.* EXTERIOR. Outermost, endmost; farthest, utmost; last, latest; exceedingly great or intense; presenting a characteristic in the utmost degree; stringent, severe; going beyond moderation.—*n.* One of two things as far as possible removed from each other; the utmost, an excessive, degree.—**Extreme'**LY,[2] *adv.*—**Extrem'**ITY, *n.* The end; the utmost degree; the utmost point of need, &c.; an extreme measure (gen. in *pl.*).
Ex'tricate, *vt.* L. *extrīcāre, extrīcātum*, to disentangle, f. EX- + *trīcae*, trifles, perplexities, tricks. INTRICATE. TRICK. To disentangle, to set free *from* (difficulty, &c.).—**Ex'trica**BLE, *a.*—**Extrica'**TION, *n.*
Extrin'sic, *a.* F. *extrinsèque*—L.L. *extrinsecus*, a., f. L. *extrinsecus*, adv., on the outside, f. *extrin-* (= **extrim*, as an adverbial form of *exter.* EXTERNAL) + *secus*, by, beside, f. root of *sequi* (CONSECUTION). INTRINSIC. Lying outside of the thing under consideration; external, extraneous; accessory, adventitious.—**Extrin'sically**,[2] *adv.* -AL. -LY.[2]
Extrude', *vt.* L. EX*trūdĕre, extrūsum.* ABSTRUSE. To thrust out.—**Extru'**SION, *n.*
Exu'berant, *a.* L. *exūberans, exūberantis*, pres.pple. of EX*ūberāre*, to be fruitful, f. *ūber*, fruitful, conn. with *ūber*, UDDER. Luxuriantly fertile; growing luxuriantly; overflowing, abounding; effusive; lavish, profuse.—**Exu'berant**LY,[2] *adv.*—**Exu'ber**ANCE, *n.*
Exude', *vi.* L. EX(*s*)*ūdāre*, to sweat out. SUDATION. To ooze out like sweat.—*vt.* To give off like sweat.—**Exud**A'TION, *n.*
Exult', *vi.* F. *exulter*—L. *ex(s)ultāre*, freq. of *exsilīre*, to spring out, leap up, f. EX- + *salīre*, to leap. ASSAIL. To rejoice greatly, to triumph.—**Exult'**ANT, *a.*—**Exulta'**TION, *n.*
Eye, *n.* O.E. *éage*, corresp. to O.N. *auga*, O.S. *ōga*, O.H.G. *ouge* (Ger. *auge*). DAISY. WINDOW. The organ of sight; look, glance; observation, attention; various things resembling the eye.—*vt.* To look at; to observe narrowly.—**Eye'**LESS, *a.*—**Eye'brow**, *n.* The fringe of hair above the eye.—**Eye'lash**, *n.* The row of hairs fringing the eyelid; one of the hairs.—**Eye'lid**, *n.* The lid or cover of the eye.—**Eye'sore**, *n.* A cause of annoyance or dislike.—**Eye'-tooth**, *n.* A tooth immediately under the eye.
Eye'let, *n.* M.E. *oilet*—F. *œillet*, dim. of *œil*, L. *oculus*, eye. OCULAR. A small hole in a cloth, a sail, &c.; a loop-hole; a small eye.
Eyre, *n.* O.F. *eire*, f. *errer.* ERRANT.[1] A circuit (of judges); a circuit court.

F

Fa'bian, *a.* From Q. *Fabius* Maximus (surnamed Cunctator ('Delayer') from his cautious and dilatory tactics directed to weakening the enemy) + -AN. After the manner of Fabius.
Fa'ble, *n.* F. *fable*—L. *fābula*, a tale, a fable, f. *fāri*, to speak. AFFABLE. A fictitious narrative; a falsehood, fabrication; a short story conveying a useful lesson; the plot of a play, &c.—*vt.* To fabricate, invent (an incident, &c.)—**Fab'liau**, *n.* F., assumed sing. to O.F *fabliaux*, pl. of *fablel*, dim. of *fable.* An early French metrical tale.—**Fab'ul**IST, *n.* A writer of fables.—**Fab'ul**OUS, *a.* Given to fabling; unhistorical, legendary; incredible.
Fab'ric, *n.* F. *fabrique*—L. *fabrica*, a workshop, a skilful production, a building, f. *faber*, an artificer. FORGE, *n.* A building; a frame, structure; a woven stuff; texture, tissue.—**Fab'ric**ATE,[3] *vt.* To form, fashion; to invent (a lie, &c.); to forge (a document).—**Fabrica'**TION, *n.*—**Fab'ricat**OR, *n.*
Façade', *n.* F., f. *face*, after It. *facciata*, f. *faccia.* (See next.) The front of a building.
Face, *n.* F. *face* = It. *faccia*—Pop.L. *facia* for L. *facies*, form, visage. DEFACE. The front of the head; command of countenance; look, aspect, outward show; the surface, a surface, the principal side.—*vt.* To meet boldly or defiantly; not to shrink from; to look or front towards; to finish with a covering.—*vi.* To turn the face, look.—**Fac'et**, *n.* F. *facette*, dim. of *face.* A side of a body with many faces.—**Fa'ci**AL, *a.*
Face'tiæ, *n.pl.* L. *facētiae*, pl. of *facētia*, a jest, f. *facētus*, witty. Witticisms, pleasantries.—**Face'tious**, *a.* Jocose.
Fac'ile, *a.* F. *facile*—L. *facilis*, easy to do, affable, f. *facĕre*, to do. AFFAIR. FACULTY. Easy to do, &c.; fluent, ready; of easy temper, compliant, yielding.—**Facil'**ITY, *n.* In senses from the *a.*; in *pl.*, opportunities, favourable conditions.—**Facil'it**ATE,[3] *vt.* To give facilities for, help forward.
Facsim'ile, *n.* Orig. two words, L. *fac*, imp.

of *facĕre* (see next) + *simile*, neut. of *similis*, like. SIMILAR. An exact copy.

Fact, *n.* L. *factum*, thing done, neut. pa.pple. of *facĕre*, *factum*, to do, make. Something known to have occurred or to be true.

Fac'tion, *n.* F. *faction*—L. *factio*, *factiōnis*, a making, a faction, f. *facĕre*. (See prec.) FASHION. A party in the state, &c. (always in bad sense); dissension.—**Fac'tious**, *a.* Given to, characterized by, faction.

Facti'tious, *a.* L. *facticius* (f. *facĕre*. FACT) + -OUS. FETISH. Artificial.

Fac'titive, *a.* Mod.L. *factitivus*, f. *facĕre*. FACT. -IVE. Of a verb, expressing the notion of making a thing to be so and so.

Fac'tor, *n.* F. *facteur*—L. *factor*, agent-n. f. *facĕre*. FACT. One who buys and sells for another; one of two or more numbers, &c., which multiplied together produce a given number, &c.; a circumstance, &c., tending to produce a result.

Fac'tory, *n.* Repg. Med.L. *factōria*, f. *factor*. (See prec.) An establishment for traders in a foreign country.—Referred to type of L.L. *factōrium* (recorded in sense 'oil-press'). A manufactory, workshop.

Facto'tum, *n.* Med.L. *factōtum*, f. *fac* (FACSIMILE) + *tōtum*, the whole. TOTAL. A man-of-all-work; a confidential servant.

Fac'ulty, *n.* F. *faculté*—L. *facultas*, power, ability, f. *facilis*. FACILE. An ability or aptitude; a power of the mind; a department of a University; the members of a profession; a dispensation or licence.—**Fac'ultative**, *a.* F. *facultatif*. Optional.

Fad, *n.* Orig. unknown. A pet notion or project; a crotchet, hobby.—**Fad'dist**, *n.*

Fade, *vi.* O.F. *fader*, f. *fade*, insipid, faded, said to represent L. *vapidus*. VAPID. To wither; to grow dim or pale; to vanish.

Fæ'ces, *n.pl.* L. *faeces*, pl. of *faex*, dregs. DEFECATE. FECULENT. Sediment, dregs; excrement.—**Fæ'cal**, *a.*

Fag, *vi.* Said to be a corr. of FLAG, *v.* To toil; to act as a fag.—*vt.* To weary; to make a fag of.—*n.* Toil, drudgery; a junior schoolboy who does certain duties for a senior.

Fag-end', *n.* From obs. *Fag*, something that hangs loose (app. conn. with prec.). The last part or remnant, the extreme end.

Fag'got, **Fag'ot**, *n.* F. *fagot*, of unknown orig. A bundle of sticks bound together.—*vt.* To make into a faggot.

Fah'renheit. Gabriel Daniel *Fahrenheit* (d. 1736), the inventor of the mercurial thermometer. Denoting the thermometric scale according to which the freezing-point of water is 32° and the boiling- point 212°.

Faience, *n.* F. *faïence*, prob. f. *Faenza* in Italy. Glazed earthenware or porcelain.

Fail, *vi.* O.F. *faillir*, to be wanting, miss —Pop. L. **fallīre* (L. *fallĕre*, to deceive), to disappoint expectation, be wanting. DEFAULT. FALSE. FAULT. To be absent or wanting; to be insufficient; to become exhausted, run short; to pass away; to lose power; to be wanting at need; to be deficient *in*; to make default; to be unsuccessful; to become bankrupt. — quasi-*trans.* To disappoint, give no help to.—**Fail'ure**, *n.*

Fain, *a.* O.E. *fægen*, glad = O.S. *fagan*, O.N. *feginn*. FAWN, *v.* Glad under the circumstances; obliged, constrained.—*adv.* Gladly.

Faint, *a.* O.F. *faint*, *feint*, feigned, sluggish, cowardly, pa.pple. of *faindre*, *feindre*, to FEIGN, in early use also *refl.*, to shirk. Half-hearted, languid; dim, indistinct; inclined to swoon.—*vi.* To lose heart, give way; to swoon —*n.* A swoon.—**Faint'ly**,[2] *adv.*

Fair, *n.* O.F. *feire* (F. *foire*)—L. *fēria*, holiday. FEAST. A periodical gathering of traders.

Fair, *a.* O.E. *fæger*. Common Teut. Beautiful; attractive, specious; of complexion, &c., light; legible; unblemished; equitable, honest; expressing moderate commendation; of weather, &c., favourable; likely, promising; gentle, peaceable.—*adv.* Civilly; legibly; equitably, honestly; of striking, &c., straight.—**Fair'ish**, *a.*—**Fair'ly**,[2] *adv.*—**Fair'ness**, *n.*

Fai'ry, *n.* O.F. *faerie* (F. *férie*), fairy-land, enchantment, f. *fae*, FAY. Formerly, fairy-land, enchantment. A diminutive supernatural being with magical powers.

Faith, *n.* O.F. *feid*, *feit*—L. *fides*, f. root of *fīdĕre*, to trust, *fīdus*, trusty, cogn. with G. *peithein*, to persuade. AFFIANCE. CONFIDE. FEALTY. PERFIDY. Belief, trust; that which is or should be believed; allegiance; fidelity, loyalty. — **Faith'ful**, *a.* Loyal; steadfast; conscientious; trustworthy; accurate.—**Faith'fully**,[2] *adv.*—**Faith'less**, *a.*

Fakir', *n.* Arab. *faqīr*, lit. 'poor man'. A Mohammedan (or Hindu) religious beggar.

Fal'bala, *n.* Occurs in several Romance languages. Orig. unknown. A FURBELOW.

Fal'chion, *n.* O.F. *fauchon*—Pop.L. **falcio*, **falciōnis*—L. *falx*, *falcis*, sickle. A broad curved sword.

Fal'con, *n.* O.F. *faucon*, *falcun*—L.L. *falco*, *falcōnis*, believed to be from *falx* (see prec.) from the shape of the talons. A bird of prey which can be trained to the pursuit of other birds.—**Fal'conry**, *n.* The art of training and using such birds.

Fald'stool, *n.* Med.L. *faldistolium*—O.H.G. *faldstuol*, lit. 'folding seat', f. *faldan*, to fold (FOLD, *v.*[2]) + *stuol*, seat, chair (Ger. *stuhl*). STOOL. A bishop's armless chair; a movable desk for kneeling at; a desk at which the Litany is recited.

Fall, *vi.* O.E. *f(e)allan*. Common Teut. (Wanting in Gothic). FELL, *v.* To drop; to decline; to slope; of a stream, to issue *into*; to subside; to diminish; to come to the ground; to come to ruin; to be captured or to surrender; to sin; to have or take a certain direction; to be allotted; to come by chance; to pass *into* a condition; to become; to occur.—*n.* A dropping; a quantity falling at once or in a period; a subsidence; decline; a cascade; a slope; depreciation; a coming to the ground; capture or surrender of a fortress; a lapse into sin.

Fal'lacy, *n.* L. *fallācia*, deceit, f. *fallax*, *fallācis*, deceitful, f. *fallĕre*. FAIL. A deceptive argument; a delusive notion; delusiveness. —**Falla'cious**, *a.*—**Fal'lible**, *a.* L.L. *fallibilis*, f. *fallĕre*. Liable to err or be erroneous. —**Fal'libly**,[2] *adv.*—**Fallibil'ity**, *n.*

Fal'low, *n.* O.E. *fælging*. Cf. O.E. *fealh*, O.H.G. *felga*, harrow. Land ploughed and harrowed but not sown.—*a.*[1] In this condition.

Fal'low, *a.*[2] O.E. *fealo*, *fealu* = O.S. *falu*, O.H.G. *falo* (Ger. *falb*, *fahl*). Prob. cogn. with G. *polios*, grey, L. *pallēre*, to be PALE. Of a pale brownish- or reddish-yellow colour.—**Fal'low-deer**, *n.*

False, *a.* O.F. *fals*, *faus* (F. *faux*)—L. *falsus*, orig. pa.pple. of *fallĕre*. FAIL. Erroneous, wrong; mendacious; faithless; deceptive; counterfeit, forged. — *adv.* Faithlessly. — **False'ly**,[2] *adv.*—**False'hood**, *n.*—**Fals'-**

ITY, *n.*—**Falset'to**, *n.* It., dim. of *falso* = *fals.* A forced voice above the natural range.
Fal'sify, *vt.* F. *falsifier*—L.L. *falsificāre*, f. *falsus* (see prec.). -FY. To alter fraudulently; to misrepresent; to pervert; to fail in fulfilling. —**Falsi**FICA'TION, *n.*
Fal'ter, *vi.* Of obscure orig. To stumble; to totter; to stammer; to flinch, waver.
Fame, *n.* F. *fame*—L. *fāma*, report, fame = G. *phēmē*, f. root *pha-*, *fă-*, in G. *phanai*, L. *fāri*, to speak. AFFABLE. FABLE. FATE. PROPHET. Report; reputation; celebrity.—**Fa'mous**, *a.* Celebrated; excellent.—**Fa'mously**,[2] *adv.* Excellently.
Famil'iar, *a.* O.F. *familier*—L. *familiāris*, f. *familia.* (See next.) Intimate; well acquainted; well-known, common; unceremonious.—*n.* An intimate friend.—**Familiar'**ITY, *n.*—**Famil'iar**IZE, *vt.*
Fam'ily, *n.* L. *familia*, household, f. *famulus*, servant. Those living in a house; one's children; a group of persons nearly connected; a kindred, lineage; a race; a class.
Fam'ine, *n.* F. *famine*—L.L. type **famīna*, f. L. *fames*, hunger. Scarcity of food.—**Fam'ish**, *vt.* An alteration, after *vv.* in *-ish*, of obs. *Fame* in sim. sense, f. *fames.* To starve.—*vi.* To be very hungry.
Fan, *n.* O.E. *fann*—L. *vannus*, a basket for winnowing corn. A winnowing-machine; an instrument for cooling the face by agitation of the air; a wing; an apparatus for producing a current of air.—*vt.* To cool with or as with a fan; to drive air on (a fire).
Fanat'ic, *a.* L. *fānāticus*, inspired by a divinity, frantic, f. *fānum*, temple. FANE. Marked or influenced by excessive and mistaken enthusiasm.—*n.* An unreasoning enthusiast. So **Fanat'**ICAL, *a.*—**Fanat'ically**,[2] *adv.*—**Fanat'**ICISM, *n.*
Fan'cy, *n.* Abb. of FANTASY. Delusive imagination; aptitude for the invention of poetical imagery; an arbitrary notion; caprice, a caprice; an inclination, liking.—*vt.* To conceive, imagine; to believe without being able to prove; to have an inclination or liking for. —*a.* Ornamental; capricious; estimated by caprice; based upon or drawn from fancy. —**Fan'ci**ER, *n.* One with a liking for and good judgement in some class of curiosities, animals, &c.—**Fan'ci**FUL, *a.*
Fandan'go, *n.* Sp. Said to be of Negro orig. A lively Spanish dance; music written for it.
Fane, *n.* L. *fānum.* PROFANE. A temple.
Fan'fare, *n.* F., perh. imitative. A flourish of trumpets, &c.—**Fan'faron**, *n.* F., f. *fanfare.* A boaster or braggart.—**Fanfaronade'**, *n.* F. *fanfaronnade*, f. *fanfaron.* Boisterous or arrogant talk.
Fang, *n.* O.E. *fang*, lit., 'a seizing', f. root of O.Teut. **fanhan*, to seize, catch. Cf. Du. *vangen*, Ger. *fangen*, to seize, catch. NEWFANGLED. A long pointed tooth; a serpent's venom-tooth; the root of a tooth.
Fanta'sia, *n.* It., lit. 'fancy' = O.F. *fantasie.* (See next.) A musical composition in a style in which form is subservient to fancy.
Fan'tasy, **Phan'tasy**, *n.* O.F. *fantasie*—L. *phantasia*—G. *phantasia*, lit., 'a making visible', f. *phantazein*, to make visible, f. root *pha-*, *phan-*, of *phainein*, to show. FANCY. PANT. PHANTASM. PHASE. PHENOMENON. Imagination; a mental image; an ingenious invention or design; a visionary notion; caprice.—*vt.* To image in a visionary manner.—**Fantas'tic**, *a.* G. *phantastikos.* Perversely or irrationally imagined; capricious, extravagantly fanciful, irrational; eccentric, quaint. —**Fantas'tically**, *adv.* -AL. -LY.[2]
Far, *adv.* O.E. *feor* = O.H.G. *fer*, O.N. *fiarre.* Cogn. with G. *peran*, Skr. *paras*, beyond. FURTHER. A long way off; to a great distance; to or at an advanced point of progress; by a great interval.—*a.* Distant, remote.
Farce, *n.* F. *farce*, app. a metaphorical use of *farce*, stuffing, f. *farcir*, L. *farcīre*, to stuff. (See next.) A play aiming only at exciting laughter.—**Farc'**ICAL, *a.*
Farce, *vt.* O.F. *farsir* (F. *farcir*). (See prec.) FORCE-MEAT. Formerly, to stuff with herbs, &c. Now only *fig.*, to season, spice.
Far'cy, *n.* Var. of obs. *Farcin*—F. *farcin*—L. *farcīminum*, f. *farcīre.* FARCE, *n.* A contagious disease in horses like glanders.
Fare, *vi.* O.E. *faran.* Common Teut. Cogn. with Skr. *par*, to carry through, G. *poros*, way, passage, L. *portāre*, to carry. EXPERIENCE. FERRY. PORE, *n.* To journey, travel; to get on (well or ill); to be (well or ill) catered for. —*v.impers.* To happen, turn out.—*n.* Cost of conveyance (of a person), the person conveyed; food.—**Farewell'**, *int.* A formula of civility at parting.—*n.* Leave-taking.
Fari'na, *n.* L. *farīna*, f. *far*, spelt. Flour, meal; a preparation of maize.—**Farina'ceous**, *a.* L. *farīnāceus* (f. *farīna*) + -OUS. Consisting of, containing, flour or meal.
Farm, *n.* F. *ferme*—Med.L. *firma*, fixed payment, f. L. *firmus*, FIRM. A tract of land let for cultivation; a tract of cultivated land.—*vt.* To pay or take a fixed sum for the proceeds of (a tax, &c.); to cultivate.—**Farm'**ER, *n.*
Farra'go, *n.* L. *farrāgo*, mixed fodder, a medley, f. *far.* FARINA. A medley or mixture.
Far'rier, *n.* O.F. *ferrier*—L. *ferrārius*, smith, f. *ferrum*, iron. FERRUGINOUS. One who shoes horses or treats the diseases of horses.
Far'row, *n.* O.E. *fearh*, pig. Cf. O.H.G. *farh.* Cogn. with L. *porcus.* PORK. A litter of pigs.—*vt.* To produce (a litter).
Far'ther, *adv.* and *a.* In M.E. *ferther.* Var. of FURTHER.—**Far'thest**, *adv.* and *a.* Var. of FURTHEST.
Far'thing, *n.* O.E. *féorthing*, a quarter, f. *féortha*, fourth. A quarter of a penny.
Far'thingale, *n.* O.F. *verdugale*, *vertugalle*, corr. of Sp. *verdugado*, f. *verdugo*, young shoot, rod, f. *verde*, L. *viridis*, green. VERDANT. A petticoat distended by rods or hoops.
Fas'cinate, *vt.* L. *fascināre*, *fascinātum*, to enchant, f. *fascinum*, witchcraft. To deprive of power to escape or resist; to captivate, charm.—**Fascina**'TION, *n.*
Fascine', *n.* F. *fascine*—L. *fascīna*, faggot, f. *fascis*, bundle, faggot. A faggot in military use for filling up ditches, &c.
Fash'ion, *n.* O.F. *façon*, *fazon*—L. *factio*, a making. FACTION. Make, form; a make, form; manner, mode; a prevailing custom; conventional usage in dress, &c., esp. as observed in the upper circles of society; conformity thereto.—*vt.* To form, shape.—**Fash'ion**ABLE, *a.* Observant of the fashion in dress, &c., conformable to fashion; of, treating of, frequented by, people of fashion.
Fast, *v.* O.E. *fæstan.* Common Teut. = Goth. *fastan*, to guard, observe, fast. (See next.) To abstain from food.—*n.* An act of fasting; a season appointed for fasting.
Fast, *a.* O.E. *fæst.* Common Teut. Cogn. with Goth. *fastan.* (See prec.) Firmly fixed or attached; constant, firm; permanent; close

shut; rapid; in advance in time; dissipated.—*adv.* Firmly; tightly; very near; rapidly; in a dissipated way.—**Fas'**TEN,[2] *vt.* To attach; to make fast, secure; to fix (attention, &c.) *on* or *upon.*—*vi.* To seize *on* or *upon.*—**Fast'**NESS, *n.* In senses f. the *a.*; a fortress.

Fastid'ious, *a.* L. *fastīdiōsus*, f. *fastīdium*, loathing. Easily disgusted, over-nice.

Fat, *a.* O.E. *fǽtt*, corresp. to Old Fris. *fat*, M.Du., M.L.G. *vet* (Ger. *fett*)—O.Teut. **faitido-*, pa.pple. of **faitjan*, to fatten. Fatted; plump; containing much fat, consisting of fat; thick, substantial; fertile; slow-witted, indolent.—*n.* The fat part; the substance of which the fat parts of animal bodies are composed.—*vt.* To feed for use as food.—**Fat'**NESS, *n.*—**Fat'**TEN,[2] *vt.* and *i.*—**Fat'**TY,[2] *a.*

Fate, *n.* L. *fātum*, lit. 'that which has been spoken', neut. pa.pple. of *fāri*, to speak. FAME. FAY. PREFACE. The power supposed to predetermine events unalterably; in *pl.*, the three goddesses of fate; destiny; destruction, ruin.—*vt.* To preordain.—**Fa'**TAL, *a.* Inevitable; dealing with destiny; fraught with destiny; destructive, deadly; disastrous.—**Fa'tal**LY,[2] *adv.*—**Fa'tal**ISM, *n.* The belief in fatality.—**Fa'tal**IST, *n.*—**Fatal'**ITY, *n.* Universal subjection to fate; a calamity; a fatal accident.—**Fate'**FUL, *a.* Prophetic of, fraught with, destiny.

Fa'ther, *n.* O.E. *fæder*. Common Teut. and Aryan. Cogn. with G. *patēr*, L. *pater*. PATERNAL. PATRIARCH. PATRIOT. PATRON. REPAIR.[1] A male parent; in *pl.*, ancestors; a designer, originator; the oldest member of a society, &c.—*vt.* To beget; to bring into existence; to own oneself the father or author of; to act as father to; to fix the paternity of (a child) *on* or *upon.*—**Fa'ther**HOOD, *n.*—**Fa'ther-in-law**, *n.* The father of one's wife or husband.—**Fa'ther**LY,[1] *a.*

Fath'om, *n.* O.E. *fæthm*, the extended arms, an embrace, corresp. to O.H.G. *fadum*, cubit (Ger. *faden*). Cogn. with G. *petannunai*, to spread out, L. *patēre*, to lie open. PATENT. PETAL. A measure of 6 feet.—*vt.* To measure with a fathom line; *fig.*, to get to the bottom of.—**Fath'om**ABLE, *a.*

Fatid'ical, *a.* L. *fātidicus* (f. *fātum*, FATE + *dīcĕre*, to speak) + -AL. Having the power of prophecy.

Fatigue', *vt.* F. *fatiguer*—L. *fatīgāre*. INDEFATIGABLE. To weary.—*n.* Weariness; toil; a soldier's extra-professional duties.

Fat'uous, *a.* L. *fatuus*, foolish + -OUS. INFATUATE. Foolish, silly.—**Fatu'**ITY, *n.*

Fault, *n.* O.F. *faute*, as if f. Pop.L. **fallita*, a failing, a coming short, f. **fallitus* as pa.pple. of L. *fallĕre*. FAIL. A defect; a misdeed; culpability; a dislocation of strata.—**Fault'**LESS, *a.*—**Fault'**Y,[2] *a.*—**Fault'**ILY,[2] *adv.*

Faun, *n.* L. *Faunus*, a rural deity, also, in pl. *Fauni*, a class of such deities. One of a class of rural deities.—**Fau'na**, *n.* Mod.L., an application of *Fauna*, sister of *Faunus*. The animals of a region collectively.

Fa'vour, *n.* O.F. *favor*, *favour*—L. *favor*, f. *favēre*, to befriend, protect. Goodwill; approving disposition; exceptional kindness, an instance of this; partiality; a knot of ribbons.—*vt.* To regard with favour; to show favour to; to indulge or oblige *with*; to treat with partiality; to aid; to lend confirmation or support to; to facilitate.—**Fa'vour**ABLE, *a.*—**Fa'vourab**LY,[2] *adv.*—**Fa'vour**ER, *n.*—**Fa'vourite**, *n.* O.F. *favorit*, var. of *favori*, pa.pple. of *favorir*, to favour. A person or thing regarded with special favour; a person unduly favoured.—*a.* Beloved, chosen.—**Fa'vourit**ISM, *n.* Undue preference.

Fawn, *n.* O.F. *faon*, *feon*, as if f. Med.L. **fēto*, **fētōnis* = L. *fētus*, offspring. A young fallow-deer.—**Fawn-col'our**, *n.* A light yellowish-brown.

Fawn, *vi.* App. a var., with specialized sense, of obs. *Fain*, to rejoice—O.E. *fægnian*, f. *fægen*. FAIN. To show delight or fondness as a dog does; to court favour by a servile demeanour.

Fay, *n.* O.F. *fae*—L. *Fāta*, the Fates, *pl.* of *fātum*, FATE. A fairy.

Fe'alty, *n.* O.F. *feaute*, *feaulte*, *fealte*—L. *fidēlitas*, faithfulness, f. *fidēlis*, faithful, f. *fides*, FAITH. FIDELITY. Fidelity on the part of a vassal to his lord.

Fear, *n.* O.E. *fǽr*, a sudden peril, danger, corresp. to O.S. *fār*, ambush, O.H.G. *fāra*, ambush, danger (Ger. *gefahr*, danger). The painful emotion caused by impending danger or evil, an instance of this; a mingled feeling of dread and reverence; solicitude, anxiety.—*vi.* To be afraid.—*vt.* To regard with fear; to revere; to apprehend.—**Fear'**FUL, *a.* Dreadful, terrible; frightened, timid.—**Fear'ful**LY,[2] *adv.*—**Fear'**LESS, *a.*—**Fear'**SOME, *a.*

Fea'sible, *a.* O.F. *faisable*, *faisible*, f. *fais-*, impf. stem of *faire*, L. *facĕre*, to do. FACT. MISFEASANCE. That can be done; practicable.—**Feasib**IL'ITY, *n.*

Feast, *n.* O.F. *feste* (F. *fête*)—L. *festa*, festal ceremonies, neut.pl. of *festus*, festal (whence *festum*, neut. sing., a festivity), cogn. with *fēria*. FAIR, *n.* FESTAL. FESTIVE. FESTOON. A religious anniversary to be kept with rejoicing; a banquet.—*vi.* To fare sumptuously, regale oneself.—*vt.* To regale.

Feat, *n.* O.F. *fait*, *fet*—L. *factum*. FACT. A deed of valour; a noteworthy action.

Feath'er, *n.* O.E. *fěther*. Common Teut. Cogn. with Skr. *pat*, G *petesthai*, to fly, *pteron*, feather. FERN. One of the growths which form the covering of birds.—*vt.* To cover or provide with feathers.—*vi.* To move, float, wave, grow like a feather.—**Feath'er**Y,[2] *a.*

Fea'ture, *n.* O.F. *feture*, *faiture*—L. *factūra*, a making, f. *facĕre*, to make. FACT. Make, form; in *pl.*, the lineaments of the face; any of the parts of the face; a characteristic part of anything.—**Fea'ture**LESS, *a.*

Feb'rifuge, *n.* F. *fébrifuge*, f. L. *febris*, FEVER + *fugāre*, to drive away. A medicine adapted to drive away or reduce fever.—**Feb'rile**, *a.* F. *fébrile*—L. *febrīlis*, f. *febris*. Of or pertaining to, indicating, due to, fever.

Feb'ruary, *n.* O.F. *feverier*—L. *februārius*, f. *februa* (pl. of *februum*, purification, of Sabine orig.), a festival of purification held on the 15th of this month. The second month.

Fec'ulent, *a.* F. *féculent*—L. *faeculentus*, f. *faex*. FÆCES. Abounding with sediment; foul, fetid.—**Fec'ul**ENCE, *n.*

Fec'und, *a.* F. *fécond*—L. *fēcundus*, fruitful. Prolific, fertile.—**Fecun'd**ITY, *n.*—**Fec'und**ATE,[3] *vt.* To make fruitful; to impregnate.—**Fecund**A'TION, *n.*

Fed'eral, *a.* F. *fédéral*—L. type **foederālis*, f. *foedus*, *foederis*, treaty, covenant, cogn. with *fides*, FAITH. CONFEDERATE. Of, of the nature of, a form of government in which states unite while retaining more or less of internal independence; of the unity thus constituted.—**Fed'eral**ISM, *n.*—**Fed'eral**IST, *n.*—**Fed'**ERATE,[3] *vi.* To enter into a league.—*vt.* To league together; to unite on a federal basis.—**Feder**A'TION, *n.*

Fee, *n.* A.F. *fee, fie* = O.F. *fé, fié, fief, fiu,* prob. f. O.H.G. *fehu*, cattle, property, money, a common Teut. and Aryan word. Cogn. with L. *pecu*. FEUD.[2] PECUNIARY. A fief; a payment for services, for entrance to a public building, &c.—*vt.* To pay a fee to.

Fee'ble, *a.* O.F. *feble, fieble, foible* (F. *faible*) —L. *flēbilis*, to be wept over, f. *flēre*, to weep. FOIBLE. Weak.—**Fee'b**LY,[2] *adv.*

Feed, *vt.* O.E. *fēdan*, f. *fōda*, FOOD. To give food to; to support, supply.—*vi.* To take food. —*n.* The action or an act of feeding; fodder; an allowance of corn, &c.; a meal.

Feel, *vt.* O.E. *fēlan*. Common West Germanic. Cogn. with O.E. *folm*, G. *palamē*, L. *palma*, the PALM of the hand. To examine or try by touching; to perceive; to have an emotional conviction of.—*vi.* To use the sense of touch; to grope; to have the sensation of touch; to be consciously in a certain state; to have a certain sentiment; to have the sensibilities excited.—*n.* The sense of touch; a sensation.—**Feel'**ER, *n.* The organ of touch of certain animals; a proposal or hint to ascertain the opinions of others.

Feign, *vt.* O.F. *feindre* (pres. pple. *feignant*) —L. *fingĕre, fictum*, to form, to feign. FAINT. FICTION. FIGMENT. FIGURE. To invent, forge, imagine; to simulate.—*vi.* To pretend.

Feint, *n.* F. *feinte*, abstract n. f. *feindre*. (See prec.) A feigned attack; a pretence.—*vi.* To make a feigned attack.

Feld'spar, Fel'spar, *n.* Corr. of Ger. *feldspath*, f. *feld*, FIELD + *spath*, spar. (The second spelling due to a supposed der. f. Ger. *fels*, rock.) A crystalline white or flesh-red mineral.

Felic'itate, *vt.* L. *fēlicitāre, fēlicitātum*, to make happy, f. *fēlix, fēlicis*, happy. To reckon happy, congratulate.—**Felicit**A'TION, *n.*—**Felic'**ITY, *n.* Happiness, bliss; appropriateness of expression.—**Felic'it**OUS, *a.*

Fe'line, *a.* L. *fēlīnus*, f. *fēles*, cat. Of or pertaining to cats; cat-like.

Fell, *n.*[1] O.E. *fel, fell*. Common Teut. Cogn. with G. *pella*, L. *pellis*, skin. FILM. PELL. A skin or hide; a thick covering of hair or wool.

Fell, *n.*[2]. O.N. *fiall*, perh. cogn. with O.H.G. *felis*, Ger. *fels*, rock. A hill; a moorland ridge.

Fell, *a.* O.F. *fel*—Pop.L. *fello*. FELON. Fierce, savage; keen, piercing; deadly.

Fell, *vt.* M.E. *fellen*, &c.—O.E. *fyllan* (Mercian *fællan*), causal of *feallan* (Mercian *fallan*), to FALL. To knock down; to cut down (a tree).

Fel'lah, *n.*; *pl.* **Fel'laheen, Fel'lahs**. Arab. *fellāh*, husbandman, f. *falaha*, to till the soil. An Egyptian peasant.

Fel'loe, Fel'ly, *n.* O.E. *felg*, corresp. to M. Du. *velge*, O.H.G. *felga* (Ger. *felge*). The exterior rim of a wheel or a part thereof.

Fel'low, *n.* Late O.E. *fēolaga*—O.N. *félage*, f. *fé*, property, money (FEE) + *lag-*, to LAY. Primary sense 'one who lays down money (with others)'. A comrade; a counterpart; the like; an equal; a match; one's neighbour; another of the sort; a member; one of the incorporated members of a college; a person (in a slightly contemptuous sense).—**Fel'low**SHIP, *n.*

Fel'on, *a.* O.F. *felon*, a. and n.—Pop.L. *fello, fellōnis*, malefactor, poss. orig. 'one full of bitterness or venom', f. L. *fel*, GALL.[1] FELL, *a.* Fierce, cruel, base.—*n.* One who has committed felony.—**Fel'on**Y,[1] A crime graver than a misdemeanour.—**Felo'ni**OUS. *a.*

Felt, *n.* O.E. *felt* = M.Du. *vilt*, O.H.G. and Ger. *filz*. FILTER. A cloth or stuff made by rolling and pressure; something made of this. —*vt.* To make into felt; to cover with felt.

Feluc'ca, *n.* It. *feluc(c)a*, F. *felouque*, Mod. Arab. *falūkah*. Prob. of Arab. formation. A small Mediterranean coasting vessel propelled by oars or lateen sails.

Fe'male, *a.* M.E. *femelle*—O.F. *femelle*, n. —L. *fēmella*, dim. of *fēmina*. EFFEMINATE. Of the sex which bears offspring; of, characteristic of, this sex.—*n.* One of this sex.

Fem'inine, *a.* O.F. *feminin, -ine*—L. *fēminīnus*, f. *fēmina*. (See prec.) Of, characteristic of, women; denoting the gender to which appellations of females belong.

Fe'mur, *n.* L. *femur, femoris*, thigh. The thigh bone.—**Fem'or**AL, *a.*

Fen, *n.* O.E. *fen, fenn* = Old Fris. *fenne*, O.H.G. *fenna*, O.N. *fen*. A marsh, bog.

Fence, *n.* Shortened f. DEFENCE. The use of the sword; a defence; an enclosure, barrier; a receiver of stolen goods, his house.—*vi.* To practise the use of the sword, to use the sword scientifically.—*vt.* To put a fence round, to enclose; to deal in (stolen goods).

Fen'cible, *n.* Short for DEFENSIBLE. A soldier liable only for home defensive service.

Fend, *vt.* Shortened f. DEFEND. To defend; to ward off, turn aside.—*vi.* To provide *for oneself.*—**Fend'**ER, *n.* Something hung over a vessel's side to prevent chafing; a metal frame in front of a fire.

Fe'nian, *n.* Old Ir. *Féne*, a name of the ancient Irish people, confused with *fíann*, a supposed body of warriors in the time of Finn and other legendary Irish kings. One of an Irish league in the U.S. for the overthrow of the English Government in Ireland.

Fen'nel, *n.* O.E. *finugl, fenol*—L. *faeniculum*, orig. dim. of *faenum*, hay. A fragrant plant cultivated chiefly for use in sauces.

Fer'ment, *n.* F. *ferment*—L. *fermentum*, f. *fervēre*, to boil. EFFERVESCE. FERVENT. An agent which causes to ferment; agitation, tumult.—**Ferment'**, *vi.* To undergo a process of the nature of that resulting from the operation of leaven on dough.—*vt.* To excite, stir up.—**Ferment**A'TION, *n.*

Fern, *n.* O.E. *fearn* = M.Du. *vœren*, O.H.G. and Ger. *farn*. Cogn. with Skr. *parna*, wing, feather, leaf. Primitive sense app. 'feather'. Cf. G. *pteron*, FEATHER, *pteris*, fern. A plant producing feathery fronds.

Fero'cious, *a.* L. *ferox, ferōcis*, fierce (conn. with *ferus*. FIERCE) + -OUS. Fierce, savage. —**Feroc'**ITY, *n.*

Fer'ret, *n.* O.F. *fuiret, furet*—L.L. *fūro*, gen. identified with L.L. *fūro*, L. *fūr*, thief. A half-tamed animal employed against rabbits, rats, &c.—*vt.* To clear out or take with a ferret; to search *out.*—*vi.* To search about.

Ferru'ginous, *a.* L. *ferrūgo, ferrūginis*, iron rust (f. *ferrum*, iron) + -OUS. FARRIER. Reddish-brown; containing iron.

Fer'rule, Fer'rel, *n.* Changed (as if dim. f. L. *ferrum*, iron) f. the older *verrel, vyrelle*—O.F. *virelle, virol*—Med.L. *virola*, L. *viriola*, dim. of *viriae*, pl., bracelets. WIRE. A metal ring or cap on a stick, &c.; a ring or band.

Fer'ry, *vt.* and *i.* O.E. *ferian*, to convey across, causal of *faran*, to go. FARE. To convey, to pass, by boat over a river, &c.—*n.* A place used for, provision for, ferrying.

Fer'tile, *a.* O.F. *fertil*—L. *fertilis*, f. *ferre*, to BEAR. CONFER. Producing in abundance fruitful.—**Fertil'**ITY, *n.*—**Fer'tilize**, *vt.*—**Fertiliza'**TION.—**Fertiliz'**ER, *n.*

Fer'ule, *n.* L. *ferula*, giant fennel, a rod. A flat piece of wood used for punishment.

Fer'vent, *a.* F. *fervent*—L. *fervens, ferventis*, pres.pple. of *fervēre*, to boil. FERMENT. Burning, glowing; ardent, earnest.—**Fer'vent**LY,[2] *adv.*—**Fer'**VENCY, *n.*—**Fer'vid**, *a.* L. *fervidus.* Impassioned.—**Fer'vid**LY,[2] *adv.*—**Fer'vour**, *n.* O.F. *fervor*—L. *fervor.* Glowing condition; vehemence, zeal.

Fes'tal, *a.* O.F. *festal*, f. L. *festum* (FEAST) + -AL. Pertaining to a festivity; keeping holiday; gay, joyous.—*n.* A festivity.

Fes'ter, *n.* O.F. *festre*—L. *fistula.* FISTULA. A superficial suppuration.—*vi.* To ulcerate; to rankle; to rot.—*vt.* To cause to fester.

Fes'tive, *a.* L. *festivus*, f. *festum.* FEAST. Of a feast; mirthful, joyous; convivial, jovial.—**Fes'tiv**AL, *a.* Of or pertaining to a feast.—*n.* A festal day.—**Festiv'**ITY, *n.* Mirth, rejoicing; an occasion of feasting or rejoicing; in *pl.*, festive proceedings.

Festoon', *n.* F. *feston*—It. *festone*, believed to be f. *festa*, L. *festa* (FEAST), hence 'decoration for a feast'. A garland hung in a curved form; carved work representing this.—*vt.* To adorn with, to form into, festoons.

Fetch, *vt.* O.E. *fecc(e)an*, believed to be an altered form of *fetian* in sim. sense, of obscure orig. Poss. conn. with O.E. *fæt*, a step, pace, cogn. with *fót*, FOOT. To go for and bring; to draw forth, elicit; to realize, sell for; to attract irresistibly; to draw (breath), heave (a sigh).—*n.*[1] A fetching; a contrivance, trick.

Fetch, *n.*[2] Orig. obscure. A wraith.

Fet'id, *a.* L. *fētidus*, f. *fētēre*, to stink. Stinking.

Fet'ish, **Fet'ich**, *n.* F. *fétiche*—Pg. *feitiço*, made by art, as *n.*, charm, sorcery—L. *factīcius*, FACTITIOUS. An inanimate object worshipped by savages as having magical powers or being animated by a spirit.

Fet'lock, *n.* M.E. *fetlak, fytlok*, of obscure formation, corresp. to M.H.G. *fizlach* (Ger. *fiszloch*). The place behind a horse's pastern-joint where a tuft of hair grows; the tuft.

Fe'tor, *n.* L. *fētor*, f. *fētēre.* FETID. Stench.

Fet'ter, *n.* O.E. *feter*, f. *fót*, FOOT. Cogn. with G. *pedē*, L. *pedica*, fetter. IMPEACH. A chain or shackle for the feet; a check, restraint.—*vt.* To put fetters on.

Fet'tle, *n.* From dial. *Fettle*, to make ready, perh. f. O.E. *fetel*, girdle (= O.H.G. *fezzil* (Ger. *fessel*), chain, band, O.N. *fetill*, strap), with notion 'to gird up'. State, condition.

Fe'tus. See FŒTUS.

Feud, *n.*[1] Northern M.E. *fede* (modified in an unexplained way)—O.F. *fede, feide, faide*—O.H.G. *fêhida* (Ger. *fehde*, feud) = O.E. *fǽhth*, enmity, f. *fáh*, hostile. FOE. A state of bitter and lasting hostility; a quarrel.

Feud, *n.*[2] Med.L. *feudum*, prob. conn. (with unexplained *d*) with O.F. *fé*, &c. FEE. A fief.—**Feu'd**AL, *a.* Of, of the nature of, a fief; of the holding of land of a superior in return for service.—**Feu'dal**ISM, *n.* The feudal system of holding land.

Fe'ver, *n.* O.E. *féfor*—L. *febris.* A morbid condition characterized by a high temperature and excessive waste of the tissues, an instance of this; excitement.—*vt.* To put into a fever.—**Fe'ver**ISH, *a.*

Few, *a.* O.E. *féawe.* Common Teut. Cogn. with G. *pauros*, L. *paucus.* PAUCITY. Not many.—**Few'**NESS, *n.*

Fez, *n.* Turkish *fes*, said to be f. *Fez* in Morocco, as having been formerly chiefly made there. A Turkish cap with a tassel.

Fias'co, *n.* It. *fiasco*, bottle, FLASK, used in phrase, *far fiasco*, 'to make a bottle', hence (it is not clear why), 'to break down or fail'. A break-down, an ignominious failure.

Fi'at, *n.* L. *fiat*, let it be done, 3rd sing. pres. subj. of *fieri*, used as pass. of *facĕre*, to do, make. An authorization; a decree.

Fib, *n.* Poss. shortened f. obs. *Fible-fable*, nonsense, a reduplication of FABLE. A trivial falsehood.—*vi.* To tell a fib.

Fi'bre, *n.* F. *fibre*—L. *fibra.* FRINGE. A filament going to form animal or vegetable tissue; fibres collectively; a substance that can be spun, woven, &c.—**Fi'brous**, *a.*

Fib'ula, *n.* L. *fibula*, clasp, buckle, f. *fīgĕre*, to FIX. The long outer bone of the lower leg.

Fick'le, *a.* O.E. *ficol*, f. (*be*)*fician*, to deceive, cogn. with *fǽcne, fácne*, deceitful = O.S. *fēkni*, wicked, O.N. *feikn*, awful, monstrous. Inconstant, changeable.—**Fick'le**NESS, *n.*

Fic'tion, *n.* F. *fiction*—L. *fictio, fictiōnis*, n. of action f. *fingĕre.* FEIGN. Something imaginatively invented; a statement or narrative of this nature; novels and stories collectively; something known not to be true but conventionally accepted.—**Ficti'tious**, *a.* L. *fictīcius* + -OUS. Feigned, imaginary.

Fid'dle, *n.* M.E. *fithele*—O.E. **fithele* (implied in *fithelere*, fiddler) = M.Du. *vedel*, O.H.G. *fidula* (Ger. *fiedel*). VIOL. A musical instrument with four strings played with a bow.—*vi.* To play the fiddle; to make idle or frivolous movements, to trifle.—**Fid'dl**ER, *n.*

Fidel'ity, *n.* F. *fidélité*—L. *fidēlitas.* FEALTY. Faithfulness, loyalty.

Fid'get, *n.* From dial. *Fidge*, vi., to move about restlessly, of obscure orig. An uneasy condition inducing irregular bodily movements (gen. in *pl.*); one who fidgets or causes to fidget (in this sense f. the *v.*).—*vi.* To move restlessly to and fro; to worry.—*vt.* To trouble or worry.—**Fid'get**Y,[2] *a.*

Fidu'ciary, *a.* L. *fīdūciārius*, f. *fīdūcia*, trust, f. *fīdĕre.* FAITH. Of or pertaining to a trustee; held or given in trust.—*n.* A trustee.

Fief, *n.* F. *fief.* FEE. An estate in land held of a superior in return for service.

Field, *n.* O.E. *feld.* Common W. Germanic. A piece of land tilled or used as pasture; an enclosed piece of ground; battle-ground, the scene of warlike operations; *collect.*, those who take part in an outdoor sport; an expanse; in *heraldry*, the surface of a shield; a department.—*vi.* At cricket, &c., to stop and return the ball.—*vt.* To stop and return (the ball).—**Field'fare**, *n.* M.E. *feldefare*, perh. f. O.E. **feldefare*, f. *feld* + *faran.* FARE. (Thus lit. 'field-goer'.) A species of thrush.—**Field-mar'shal**, *n.* Ger. *feldmarschall.* A general officer of the highest rank.

Fiend, *n.* O.E. *féond*, lit. 'enemy'. Common Teut. Orig. pres.pple. of *féogian*, to hate. The devil; a devil.—**Fiend'**ISH, *a.*

Fierce, *a.* O.F. *fers, fiers*—L. *ferus*, untamed, fierce, conn. with *ferox* (FEROCIOUS) and G. *thēr* (in Æolic *phēr*), wild beast. TREACLE. Savage, raging; ardent.—**Fierce'**LY,[2] *adv.*

Fi'ery, *a.* FIRE, *n.* + -Y.[2] Consisting of, containing, fire; flaming, glowing, blazing; ardent; fiercely irritable.—**Fi'eri**LY,[2] *adv.*

Fife, *n.* Ger. *pfeife*, PIPE;[1] or corr. of F. *fifre*, fife, fifer—O.H.G. *pfīfāri* (Ger. *pfeifer*), piper, fifer. A small military wind-instrument.—*vi.* and *t.* To play on a fife.—**Fif'**ER *n.*

Fig, *n.* O.F. *fige, figue*—Pr. *figa, figua*—Pop. L. type **fica*, L. *ficus*. The fruit of a tree of the mulberry family; the tree.
Fight, *vi.* O.E. *feohtan*. Common W. Germanic. To contend in battle or single combat. —*vt.* To maintain by contention; to combat to set on to fight; to manœuvre in battle.—*n.* A battle, combat.—**Fight'**ER, *n.*
Fig'ment, *n.* L. *figmentum*, f. *fig-*, short stem of *fingĕre*. FEIGN. EFFIGY. An invented story, notion, &c.
Fig'ure, *n.* F. *figure*—L. *figūra*, f. *fig-*. (See prec.) Form, shape; a human form; a personage; appearance, conspicuous appearance, importance; image, likeness; a diagram, illustration; a space bounded by lines or planes; a numerical symbol; an amount, number; a form of expression deviating from the normal; an image, similitude. — *vt.* To represent graphically; to work or calculate *out* in figures; to imagine; to ornament.—*vi.* To use numerical figures; to make an appearance, to be conspicuous or notable; to come *out* as a result in figures.—**Fig'urative**, *a.* F. *figuratif*—L. *figūrātivus*. Emblematical; metaphorical, not literal.—**Fig'urative**LY,[2] *adv.*
Fil'ament, *n.* Med.L. *filāmentum*, f. L.L. *filāre*. FILE.[2] A thread-like body.
Fil'bert, *n.* Prob. short for *filbert-* (i.e. *Philibert-*)*nut* = dial. F. *noix de filbert*, from being ripe near St. Philibert's day, Aug. 22 (old style). The fruit of the cultivated hazel; the tree.
Filch, *vt.* Orig. unknown. To pilfer.
File, *n.*[1] O.E. *féol* (Anglian *fīl*) = M.Du., M.L.G. *vīle*, O.H.G. *fīla* (Ger. *feile*). A metal instrument for smoothing and cutting iron, &c.—*v.*[1]*t.* To apply a file to; to polish, elaborate.
File, *n.*[2] F. *fil*, L. *filum*, thread. FILIGREE. FILLET. PROFILE. A string or wire on which papers are strung, an appliance for holding papers; the papers.—From F. *file*, said to be f. L.L. *filāre*, to spin, draw out threads, f. *filum*. The number from front to rear of soldiers drawn up; a row of persons, &c., one behind the other.—*v.*[2]*t.* To put papers on or in a file.—*vi.* To march one behind the other.
File, *v.*[3]*t.* O.E. *fýlan* (in combinations) = M.Du. *vuilen*, O.H.G. *fûlen*—O.Teut. **fûlo-*. FOUL. DEFILE.[2] To taint, sully, corrupt.
Fil'ial, *a.* L.L. *filiālis*, f. *filius*, son. AFFILIATE. Of, becoming, a son or daughter.
Fil'ibuster, *n.* Sp. *filibustero*, ultimately f. Du. *vrijbuiter*, FREEBOOTER. An adventurer engaged in piracy or irregular warfare.
Fil'igree, *n.* Abb. f. obs. *Filigreen*—F. *filigrane*—It. *filigrana*, f. L. *filum*, thread (FILE[2]) + *grānum*, GRAIN, seed. Delicate work of threads and beads, usually of gold and silver.
Fill, *vt.* O.E. *fyllan*, f. *full*, FULL. Cf. O.N. *fylla*, O.H.G. *fullen* (Ger. *füllen*). To make full; to occupy completely; to hold (a position or office); to satisfy; to fulfil.—*vi.* To become full.—*n.* A full supply; enough to fill anything.
Fil'let, *n.* F. *filet*, a dim. f. L. *filum*. FILE.[2] A head-band; a strip, a fleshy portion of meat; a piece of meat rolled and tied.—*vt.* To tie up with, to make (meat, &c.) into, a fillet.
Fil'lip, *n.* Prob. imitative. Cp. FLIP. The sudden release of a finger bent against the thumb; a smart stroke thus given; a stimulus. —*vt.* To toss or strike with a fillip.
Fil'ly, *n.* Perh. f. O.N. *fylja*, conn. with *fole*, FOAL. A female foal.
Film, *n.* O.E. *filmen*, membrane, cogn. with FELL.[1] A very thin layer; a thin sensitized sheet used in photography; a fine thread; a thin veil of haze, &c.—**Film'**Y,[2] *a.*
Fil'ter, *n.* O.F. *filtre*—Med.L. *filtrum*, f. the root seen in FELT. A piece of cloth or other contrivance for straining a liquid.—*vt.* To pass through a filter.—*vi.* To percolate.—**Fil'tr**ATE,[3] *vt.* and *i.* In sim. senses.
Filth, *n.* O.E. *fýlth*, f. *fúl*, FOUL. Loathsome dirt.—**Filth'**Y,[2] *a.*—**Filth'**ILY,[2] *adv.*
Fin, *n.* O.E. *finn* = M.Du. *vinne*, M.L.G., Ger. *finne*. Prob. cogn. with L. *pinna* (*penna*), feather, fin. PEN.[2] An organ which serves a fish for propulsion and steering.
Fi'nal, *a.* F. *final*—L. *fīnālis*, f. *finis*, end. AFFINITY. FINE, *n.* FINISH. Coming at the end; ultimate; conclusive.—**Fi'nal**LY,[2] *adv.* —**Final'**ITY, *n.*—**Fina'le**, *n.* It., f. *fīnālis*. The last movement of an instrumental composition; the closing part; the conclusion.
Finance', *n.* O.F. *finance*, n. of action f. *finer*, to end, bargain for, procure, f. *fin*. FINE, *n.* The management of money; the science of revenue; in *pl.*, pecuniary resources. —*vt.* To find capital for.—*vi.* To manage monetary affairs.—**Finan'**CIAL, *a.*—**Finan'**CIER, *n.* One who is concerned with finance.
Finch, *n.* O.E. *finc* = M.Du. *vinke*, O.H.G. *fincho* (Ger. *fink*). A small singing bird.
Find, *vt.* O.E. *findan*. Common Teut. To come across, light upon; to perceive; to come to the knowledge of, discover; to discover or get by searching; to procure, get, obtain; to ascertain; to declare (a person) *guilty, &c.*; to bring in (a verdict); to supply.—*n.* An act or instance of finding; something found.
Fine, *n.* O.F. *fin*, end (used in sense 'payment by way of composition') — L. *fīnis*. FINAL. FINANCE. End (only in *in fine* finally, to sum up, in short); a sum paid as composition for rent; a sum imposed as a penalty.—*v.*[1]*t.* To punish by a fine.
Fine, *a.* F. *fin*—Common Romanic *fino*, prob. a back-formation f. *finire*, L. *fīnīre*, to FINISH. Choice; pure, clear; exquisitely fashioned; in minute particles; slender; sharp; subtle, sensitive; excellent; handsome; free from rain; showy, smartly dressed; fastidious; affectedly ornate; flattering, complimentary.—*v.*[2]*t.* To make pure or clear; to attenuate.—*vi.* To become pure, clear, attenuated.—**Fine'**LY,[2]*adv.* —**Fine'**NESS, *n.*—**Fin'**ERY, *n.* Showy dress. —**Finesse'**, *n.* F. *finesse*. Artfulness; an artifice.—*vi.* To use finesse.
Fin'ger, *n.* O.E. *finger*. Common Teut. One of the terminal members of the hand; one of these excluding the thumb; various things like a finger.—*vt.* To handle or touch with the fingers; to play upon (an instrument), to play (music), with the fingers.—*vi.* To make restless movements with the fingers.
Fin'ial, *n.* Var. of FINAL. An ornament on the apex of a roof, pediment, gable, &c.
Fin'ical, Fin'icking, Fin'ikin, *aa.* Orig. doubtful. Prob. all ultimately f. FINE, *a.* Fastidious; over-delicately wrought.
Fin'ish, *vt.* O.F. *feniss-*, lengthened stem of *fenir* (F. *finir*)—L. *fīnīre*, f. *fīnis*, end. FINE, *n.* and *a.* FINAL. To bring to an end; to dispose of; to perfect.—*vi.* To come to an end.—*n.* The end; that which perfects or finishes; the condition or quality of being perfected or finished.—**Fi'nite**, *a.* L. *fīnītus*, pa.pple. of *fīnīre*. Bounded, limited; subject to limitations or conditions

Fiord, Fjord, *n.* Norw. *fiord*—O.N. *fjörthr.* FIRTH. A long narrow arm of the sea between high cliffs, as in Norway.

Fir, *n.* M.E. *firr, firre,* perh. repg. an O.E. **fyre* or O.N. *fyri-.* Cf. O.H.G. *forha* (Ger. *föhre*). A coniferous tree.

Fire, *n.* O.E. *fýr.* Common West Germanic. Cogn. with G. *pur.* EMPYREAL. PYRE. The natural agency which operates in combustion; state of combustion; a mass of burning fuel; a conflagration; ardour, vivacity; discharge of firearms.—*vt.* To set on fire; to inspire; to bake; to supply with fuel; to explode; to discharge (a firearm); to propel from a firearm.—*vi.* To catch fire; to become excited; to discharge a firearm.—**Fire'arm,** *n.* A weapon which operates by explosion.—**Fire'-brand,** *n.* A burning piece of wood; one who kindles strife.—**Fire-new,** *a.* As if fresh from the furnace, brand-new.—**Fire'work,** *n.* A contrivance to produce a scenic effect by the combustion of gunpowder, &c.

Fir'kin, *n.* In 15th c. *ferdekyn,* app. f. a M.Du. **vierdekijn,* dim. of *vierde,* fourth. A small cask, orig. one containing a quarter of a barrel; an old measure of capacity.

Firm, *a.* O.F. *ferme*—L. *firmus.* FARM. Solid, compact; stable, steady: settled, established; resolute.—*vt.* To make firm; to solidify.—**Firm'**LY,[2] *adv.*—**Firm'**NESS, *n.*—**Firm'ament,** *n.* L. *firmāmentum,* f. *firmāre.* (See next.) The arch or vault of heaven.

Firm, *n.* It., Sp. and Pg. *firma,* signature, n. of action f. L. *firmāre,* to support, confirm, in L.L., to ratify by one's signature, f. *firmus.* (See prec.) The name under which a business is conducted; a partnership.

Fir'man, *n.* Per. *fermān* = Skr. *pramāna,* command. An order issued by an Oriental sovereign, esp. by the Sultan of Turkey.

First, *a.* O.E. *fyrst, fyrest* = O.N. *fyrstr,* O.H.G. *furist* (Ger. *fürst,* prince). Common Teut. **furisto-,* a superl. formed on the stem *fur-, for-* of FORE. Earliest in time or order, foremost in rank, position, &c.—*adv.* Before all others in time, order, &c.—**First'**LY,[2] *adv.* In the first place.—**First'ling,** *n.* -LING (2). The first product, offspring, &c.

Firth, *n.* Also in changed form **Frith.** App. f. O.N. *fjörthr.* FIORD. An arm of the sea; an estuary of a river.

Fisc, Fisk, *n.* L. *fiscus,* basket, purse, treasury. A state treasury.—**Fis'**CAL, *a.*

Fish, *n.* O.E. *fisc.* Common Teut. Cogn. with L. *piscis.* GRAMPUS. PISCATORY. A vertebrate cold-blooded animal living in the water; the flesh of fish.—*vi.* To catch or try to catch fish; to search *for* something under water.—*vt.* To try to catch fish in; to draw *up,* produce.—**Fish'**ERY, *n.* The occupation of fishing; a fishing-place; a fishing establishment.—**Fish'monger,** *n.* MONGER. One who deals in fish.—**Fish'**Y,[2] *a.*

Fis'sure, *n.* F. *fissure*—L. *fissūra,* f. *findĕre, fissum,* to cleave. A cleft.—*vt.* and *i.* To split.—**Fis'sile,** *a.* L. *fissilis.* Capable of being split; tending to split.—**Fis'**SION, *n.* Splitting; the division of a cell, &c., into new cells, &c., as a mode of reproduction.—**Fissip'arous,** *a.* *Fissi-* + L. *parĕre,* to bring forth + -OUS. Reproducing by fission; of or pertaining to such reproduction.

Fist, *n.* O.E. *fýst* = M.L.G. *fūst* (Du. *vuist*), O.H.G. *fūst* (Ger. *faust*). FOIST. The clenched hand.—*vt.* To strike with this.—**Fist'icuffs,** *n.pl.* CUFF, *n.*[2] Fighting with the fists.

Fis'tula, *n.* L. *fistula,* pipe, tube, fistula. FESTER. A long sinuous ulcer.

Fit, *n.*[1] O.E. *fitt.* Orig. uncertain. Orig. sense app. 'conflict'. A paroxysm of an ailment; a sudden seizure with convulsions or loss of consciousness; a sudden activity; a sudden transitory state; caprice, mood.—**Fit'**FUL, *a.* Spasmodic, capricious.—**Fit'ful**LY,[2] *adv.*

Fit, *a.* Of doubtful orig. Proper, appropriate; becoming, right; qualified, competent; prepared, ready; in good health.—*vt.* To be suited to, proper for; to be correctly adjusted to; to make fit or suitable; to modify, arrange; to apply, adjust, insert; to supply, furnish.—*vi.* To be correctly adjusted or adapted.—*n.*[2] Adaptation, style in which a garment fits.—**Fit'**LY,[2] *adv.*—**Fit'**NESS, *n.*

Five, *a.* and *n.* O.E. *fíf.* Common Teut. and Aryan. Cogn. with Skr. *pañca,* G. *pente,* L. *quinque.* The cardinal number next after four.—**Fifth,** *a.* -TH.[2] The corresponding ordinal number.—*n.* A fifth part.

Fix, *vt.* Ultimately f. L. *fixus,* pa.pple. of *figĕre,* to fix. Proximate orig. uncertain. AFFIX. TRANSFIX. To fasten, to make firm or stable; to set, station, establish; to decide *to do;* to appoint, assign.—*vi.* To become firm or solidified; to decide *on* or *upon;* to take up one's position.—*n.* A difficulty, dilemma.—**Fix'**ITY, *n.* Fixed state, stability.—**Fix'ture,** *n.* Altered (after *mixture*) f. obs. *Fixure*—L.L. *fixūra,* f. *figĕre.* Anything made firm or stable; a thing annexed to a house or to land; a date for a race, &c., the race, &c.

Fizz, Fizz'le, *vv.i.* Imitative. The latter with freq. suff. *-le.* To make a hissing sound.

Flab'by, *a.* Altered f. earlier *Flappy* (FLAP, *v.* + -Y[2]). Hanging loose, limp; weak, feeble.

Flac'cid, *a.* F. *flaccide*—L. *flaccidus,* f. *flaccus,* flabby. Flabby.—**Flaccid'**ITY, *n.*

Flag, *n.*[1] Orig. obscure. Cf. Du. *flag.* An aquatic plant with sword-shaped leaves.

Flag, *n.*[2] Cf. O.N. *flaga,* slab of stone. Prob. in some way conn. with FLAKE. A flat slab of stone. Also **Flag'-stone.**

Flag, *n.*[3] In all mod. Teut. languages, but app. first recorded in Eng. Cf. Da. *flag,* Du. *vlag,* Ger. *flagge.* A piece of cloth or stuff used as a standard, ensign, or signal.

Flag, *vi.* Poss. f. obs. *Flag,* a., drooping, perh. f. O.F. *flac,* L. *flaccus.* FLACCID. (The formation may be partly imitative like that of FLAP.) To droop, fade; to lose vigour.

Flag'ellate, *vt.* L. *flagellāre, flagellātum,* f. *flagellum,* dim. of *flagrum,* scourge. To scourge, whip.—**Flag'ell**ANT, *n.* One who scourges himself by way of penance or discipline.—**Flagell**A'TION, *n.*

Flag'eolet, *n.* F. *flageolet,* dim. of O.F. *flajol,* f. Pr. *flajol, flaujol,* of unknown orig. A small wind-instrument.

Flagi'tious, *a.* L. *flāgitiōsus,* f. *flāgitium,* a shameful act. Deeply criminal or wicked.

Flag'on, *n.* M.E. *flakon*—O.F. *flacon,* earlier *flascon*—Med.L. *flasco, flascōnis.* FLASK. A large bottle; a vessel for liquids.

Fla'grant, *a.* L. *flagrans, flagrantis,* pres. pple. of *flagrāre,* to burn, cogn. with G. *phlegein.* PHLEGM. Flaming into notice, glaring.—**Fla'grant**LY,[2] *adv.*—**Fla'gr**ANCY, *n.*

Flail, *n.* Late O.E. *fligel.* Cf. M.Du. *vlegel,* O.H.G., Ger. *flegel,* prob. f. L. *flagellum.* FLAGELLATE. A threshing-implement.

Flake, *n.* Of obscure orig. Prob. ultimately f. the Aryan root *plag-, plak-* (seen in G. *plēgnunai, plēssein,* to strike) = *flak-.* FLAW.[1]

A light fleecy portion; a piece of burning matter; a thin piece peeled or split off.—*vt.* To break flakes from.—*vi.* To come *away* or *off* in flakes.

Flamboy'ant, *a.* F., pres.pple. of *flamboyer*, f. *flambe*, FLAME. Marked by waved flame-like lines; florid; gorgeously coloured.

Flame, *n.* O.F. *flambe*, *flamme*—L. *flamma*. Ignited gas, a portion of ignited gas; visible combustion.—*vi.* To emit flames, to blaze.

Flamin'go, *n.* Pg. *flamengo*, Sp. *flamenco*, Pr. *flamenc*, said to be f. Romanic *flama*, L. *flamma*, FLAME + -*enc* = Teut. -*ing*. A large long-legged long-necked bird with a heavy bill and bright scarlet plumage.

Flange, *n.* Orig. obscure. A projecting flat rim or collar.—*vt.* To supply with a flange.

Flank, *n.* F. *flanc* = Pr. *flanc*, It. *fianco*—Pop.L. **flancum*, perh. f. Teut. Cf. O.H.G. *hlancha*. LINK.[1] The fleshy part of the side between the ribs and the hip; the side of anything.—*vt.* To guard or strengthen on the flank; to take in flank; to be on either side of.

Flan'nel, *n.* Orig. uncertain. Prob. Welsh, as the stuff was extensively made in Wales. An open woollen stuff, usually without a nap.

Flap, *vt.* Prob. imitative. FLAG, *v.* FLOP. To strike with something flexible and broad; to move (the wings) up and down.—*vi.* To swing or sway about loosely.—*n.* An act of flapping; anything hanging loose from one side or working on a hinge.

Flare, *vi.* Orig. unknown. To blaze with a bright unsteady flame.—*n.* The action of flaring; a bright unsteady light.

Flash, *vi.* App. imitative. Of water, to rush along, to rise and dash; of fire, &c., to break forth suddenly; to gleam; to burst into view; to make a display, show off.—*vt.* To emit (light, &c.) suddenly.—*n.* A momentary burst of light or flame; display, ostentation.—*a.* Showy, ostentatious; sham.—**Flash'**Y,[2] *a.* Brilliant but transitory; showy, ostentatious.

Flask, *n.* In nearly all Teut. and Romanic languages. Orig. uncertain. F. *flasque* was adopted in 16th c. in the first sense below. In the other senses the word is prob. f. It. *fiasco*. FIASCO. (For a Med.L. form see FLAGON.) A case to hold gunpowder; a bottle with a long narrow neck; a flat bottle for the pocket.

Flat, *n.*[1] Alteration of obs. *Flet*, floor—O.E. *flet(t)* = Old Fris. and O.N. *flet*, f. O.Teut. **flato-*, FLAT, *a.* A storey in a house; a set of rooms on one floor.

Flat, *a.* O.N. *flatr* (Sw. *flat*, Da. *flad*)—O.Teut. **flato-*. Level; at full length; level with the ground; downright, unqualified; dull, uninteresting; stupid; dejected; insipid; below the true pitch.—*n.*[2] A flat surface or portion; a level, a level expanse; a simpleton; a note half a tone below the natural pitch; the sign (♭) marking this.—**Flat'**LY,[2] *adv.*—**Flat'**NESS, *n.*—**Flat'**TEN,[2] *vt.* and *i.*

Flat'ter, *vt.* Prob. obs. *Flatter* (imitative), to float, flutter, associated with O.F. *flater* (F. *flatter*), to flatter, prob. orig. 'to flatten down, smooth', and perh. cogn. with FLAT, *a.* (An adaptation of *flater* would normally have given *flat*.) To court, fawn upon; to praise insincerely; to gratify the vanity of; to please with the idea *that*; to represent too favourably.—**Flat'ter**ER, *n.*—**Flat'tery**, *n.* F. *flatterie*. The action or practice of flattering.

Flat'ulent, *a.* F. *flatulent*—Mod.L. *flātulentus*, f. L. *flātus*, a blowing, f. *flāre*, to blow. BLOW, *v.*[1] Generating, troubled with, gases in the intestines; vain, pretentious.—**Flat'ul**ENCE, **Flat'ul**ENCY, *nn.*

Flaunt, *vi.* Orig. unknown. To wave gaily; to show oneself off.—*vt.* To show off.

Fla'vour, *n.* App. an adoption of O.F. *flaur*, *fleiur*, *fraor*, smell, of uncertain orig. The element in the taste of anything which appeals to the sense of smell; a characteristic quality; piquancy.—*vt.* To give flavour to.

Flaw, *n.*[1] Perh. f. O.N. *flaga* (recorded in sense 'slab of stone', but which may have had wider senses), f. *flah-*, *flag-*, *flak-* = *plag-*, *plak-*. FLAKE. WHITLOW. A crack, fissure; a defect, blemish.—*vt.* To make a flaw or crack in.—*vi.* To crack.—**Flaw'**LESS, *a.*

Flaw, *n.*[2] Cf. M.Du. *vlāghe*, M.L.G. *vlage*, Sw. *flaga*. A sudden burst of wind.

Flax, *n.* O.E. *fleax*. Common W. Germanic. A plant cultivated for its fibre and its seeds (linseed); the fibres.—**Flax'**EN,[1] *a.*

Flay, *vt.* O.E. *fléan*. Common Teut. Root *flah-*. FLAW.[1] To strip off the skin of.

Flea, *n.* O.E. *fléah*. Common Teut. A wingless biting insect agile in leaping.

Fleck, *n.* Cf. O.N. *flekkr*, corresp. to M.Du. *vlecke*, O.H.G. *flec(ch)* (Ger. *fleck*) in sim. senses. A mark in the skin; a spot or streak of light, &c.; a speck.—*vt.* To spot, streak, dapple.

Fledge, *vt.* From obs. *Fledge*, a., fledged—O.E. **flycge*, corresp. to M.Du. *vlugge*, M.H.G. *vlücke*, f. *flug-*, weak root of O.Teut. **fleugan*, to FLY. FLIGHT.[1] To furnish with feathers fit for flight.—**Fledge'ling**, *n.* -LING (1). A young bird just fledged.

Flee, *vi.* O.E. *fléon*. Common Teut. O.Teut. **thleuhan*. To run away, take oneself off.—*vt.* To run away from; to shun.

Fleece, *n.* O.E. *fléos*. Common W. Germanic. A sheep's wool.—*vt.* To shear; to rob heartlessly.—**Fleec'**Y,[2] *a.*

Fleer, *vi.* Perh. Scand. Cf. Norw. and Sw. dial. *flira*, Da. dial. *flire* in sim. sense. To laugh impudently or mockingly, to gibe, sneer.—*n.* Such a laugh, a gibe or sneer.

Fleet, *n.* O.E. *fléot*, a ship, or perh. ships collectively, f. *fléotan*. FLEET, *v.* A sea force.

Fleet, *a.* Cogn. with or f. O.N. *fliótr*, swift, f. root of FLEET, *v.* Swift, nimble.

Fleet, *vi.* O.E. *fléotan*, to float. Common Teut. O.Teut. **fleutan*, to float or flow. Cogn. with Skr. *plu*, *pru*, to swim, float, flow, G. *ple-ein*, to sail, L. *pluĕre*, to rain. FLIT. FLOAT. FLUTTER. To glide away, to vanish; of time, to slip away; to flit, fly.

Flesh, *n.* O.E. *flǽsc*. Common W. Germanic and Scand. The muscular parts of the body; flesh as food; the physical nature of man; the sensual appetites.—*vt.* To reward (a hound, &c.) with flesh of the game; to initiate in bloodshed; to plunge into the flesh.—**Flesh'ings**, *vbl. n.pl.* A light close-fitting flesh-coloured garment.—**Flesh'**LY,[1] *a.*—**Flesh'**Y,[2] *a.* Fat, plump; pulpy.

Fleur-de-lis, *n.* F. *fleur de lis*, flower of the lily, f. *fleur*, FLOWER, and *lis*, L.L. *līlius* = L. *līlium*, LILY. Also (corruptly) **Flow'er-de-luce**. An iris flower; the heraldic lily; the royal arms of France.

Flex'ible, *a.* F. *flexible*—L. *flexibilis*, f. *flectĕre*, *flexum*, to bend. DEFLECT. INFLECT. Bending without breaking, pliable, pliant.—**Flexi**BIL'ITY, *n.*—**Flex'**URE, *n.*

Flick, *n.* Imitative. A light blow; a jerk; a slight sharp sound.—*vt.* To strike or move with a flick.

Flick'er, *vi.* O.E. *flicorian*, imitative and freq. To flutter, hover; to quiver, vibrate; to burn unsteadily.—*n.* A flickering movement; an unsteady light or flame.

Flight, *n.*[1] O.E. *flyht* = O.S. *fluht*, f. *flug-*. FLEDGE. Manner or the action of flying with wings; swift movement; space traversed by flying; a series (of steps); things or beings flying together.—**Flight'**Y,[2] *a.* Fickle, crazy.

Flight, *n.*[2] O.E. **flyht* = O.S., O.H.G. *fluht* (Ger. *flucht*), f. *thleuh-*, weak root of **thleuhan*, to FLEE. The action of fleeing.

Flim'sy, *a.* Poss. suggested by FILM. Cf. *tipsy*. Frail; trivial; frivolous.

Flinch, *vi.* App. f. O.F. *flenchir*, *flainchir*, us. regarded as a var. of *flechir*, to bend, of obscure orig. To draw back, shrink.

Fling, *vi.* App. conn. with O.N. *flengja* (M.Sw. *flängia*, M.Da. *flænge*), to flog. To go or run hastily; to kick and plunge.—*vt.* To throw.—*n.* A passing attempt or attack; a kicking; a spell of indulgence.

Flint, *n.* O.E. *flint* = M.Du. *vlint*, conn. with O.H.G. *flins*, Da. *flint*; prob. cogn. with G. *plinthos*, brick. PLINTH. A kind of hard stone; a pebble of flint.

Flip, *vt.* Prob. imitative. Cf. FILLIP. To fillip; to move with a jerk.—*vi.* To move with a jerk; to strike smartly *at*.—*n.*[1] A fillip, a jerk.—**Flip'**PER, *n.* A limb for swimming.

Flip, *n.*[2] Perh. f. FLIP, *v.*, with the sense of 'whipping up' into froth. Beer and spirit sweetened and heated with a hot iron.

Flip'pant, *n.* App. f. FLIP, *vi.* Formerly, nimble, talkative, impertinently voluble. Displaying unbecoming levity.—**Flip'**PANCY, *n.*

Flirt, *vt.* Imitative. To throw with a jerk; to give a brisk motion to.—*vi.* To move with a jerk; to practise coquetry.—*n.* A jerk or sudden throw; one who flirts in affairs of love; one to flirt with.—**Flirt**A'TION, *n.*

Flit, *vi.* O.N. *flytja*, f. *flut-*, weak grade of the root of *flióta*. FLEET, *v.* To be gone; to pass lightly and rapidly; of time, to pass away.

Flitch, *n.* O.E. *flicce*, corresp. to O.N. *flikki*, M.L.G. *vlike*. A side of bacon.

Float, *vi.* O.E. *flotian* = M.Du. *vlôten*, O.N. *flota*, f. *flut-*, weak grade of the root of **fleutan*. FLEET, *v.* FLOTILLA. FLOTSAM. To rest on the surface of, to move on the surface of and with, a liquid; to be suspended *in* a liquid; to move gently in the air.—*vt.* Of water, &c., to support, to bear along; to get (a commercial company, &c.) started.—*n.* A floating; a floating object; a cork supporting a baited line.—**Float**A'TION, **Flot**A'TION, *n.*

Floc'culent, *a.* L. *floccus* (FLOCK[2]) + -ULENT. Resembling flocks or tufts of wool.

Flock, *n.*[1] O.E. *flocc* = O.N. *flokkr*, of obscure orig. A number of animals of a kind.—*vi.* To gather in a company or crowd.

Flock, *n.*[2] Prob. f. O.F. *floc*, L. *floccus*, lock of wool. FLOSS. A lock or tuft (of wool, &c.); in *pl.*, tufts of wool, &c., used for stuffing.

Floe, *n.* Prob. f. Norse *flo*, level piece—O.N. *fló*. A sheet of floating ice.

Flog, *vt.* Prob. imitative. To beat, whip.

Flood, *n.* O.E. *flód*. Common Teut. Aryan vbl. stem *plō-*, whence G. *plōein*, to swim, float, L. *plōrāre*, to weep. FLOW. The flowing in of the tide; a body of flowing water; an inundation; a swollen stream.—*vt.* To inundate; to cover or fill with water.

Floor, *n.* O.E. *flór*, corresp. to M.Du. *vloer*, M.H.G. *vluor* (Ger. *flur*). The under surface of a room; a set of rooms on the same level; a levelled space, esp. for threshing.—*vt.* To furnish with a floor; to knock down, defeat.

Flop, *vi.* Var. of *Flap*, to indicate a duller sound. To swing about heavily; to move clumsily.—*vt.* To throw suddenly with a bump or thud.—*n.* The action of the *v.*

Flo'ra, *n.* L. *Flōra*, goddess of flowers, f. *flōs*, *flōris*, FLOWER. The plants of a region collectively.—**Flo'**RAL, *a.* Of flowers.—**Flo'riated**, *ppl.a.* -ATE.[3] Decorated with floral ornaments.—**Flor'iculture**, *n.* *Flōs* + L. *cultūra*, tending, rearing, f. *colĕre*. CULT. The cultivation of flowers.—**Flor'id**, *a.* L. *flōridus*, flowery, f. *flōs*. Full of fine words; ornate; ruddy.—**Flor'in**, *n.* F. *florin*, f. *flōs* (the orig. florins having been stamped with the figure of a lily). Formerly applied to various gold and silver coins. An English silver coin worth two shillings.—**Flor'**IST, *n.* One who cultivates or deals in flowers.

Floss, *n.* Poss. f. some form of O.F. *flosche*, down, pile of velvet, conn. with *floc*. FLOCK.[2] Silk in fine filaments; fluff.—**Floss'**Y,[2] *a.*

Flotil'la, *n.* Sp., dim. of *flota*, O.F. *flote*, a fleet, f. *flut-*. FLOAT. A fleet of small vessels.

Flot'sam, *n.* A.F. *floteson*, f. L.L. type **flottātio*, **flottātiōnis*, f. **flottāre*, O.F. *floter* (f. *flut-*), to FLOAT. Wreckage found floating.

Flounce, *n.*[1] Alteration of earlier *Frounce*, wrinkle, fold—O.F. *fronce*, said to be f. *froncir*, to wrinkle the brow, to wrinkle, f. L. *frons*. FRONT. An ornamental appendage to a skirt.—*v.*[1]*t.* To adorn with a flounce.

Flounce, *v.*[2]*i.* Prob. imitative. Cf. Norw. *flunsa*, to hurry, Sw. dial. *flunsa*, to fall with a splash. To go with an agitated or clumsy motion; to plunge, flounder, jerk oneself.—*n.*[2] A flouncing movement.

Floun'der, *n.*[1] App. f. A.F. *floundre* = O.F. *flondre*, app. of Scand. orig. A flat-fish.

Floun'der, *vi.* Orig. obscure. To roll and tumble about, struggle along.—*n.*[2] The action.

Flour, *n.* A specific use of FLOWER. Orig., the 'flower' or finest quality of meal. Cf. F. *fleur de farine*, in sim. sense. The finer portion of meal; wheat meal; any fine powder.—*vt.* To sprinkle with flour.

Flour'ish, *vi.* O.F. *floriss-*, lengthened stem of *florir*—Pop. L. type **flōrīre*, L. *flōrēre*, f. *flōs*, FLOWER. To thrive; to be in one's bloom; to use florid language.—*vt.* To brandish; to display.—*n.* A decoration in flowing curves; a florid expression, &c.; an ostentatious waving about; a sounding (of trumpets, &c.).

Flout, *vt.* and *i.* Poss. a special use of *floute*, M.E. form of FLUTE, *vi.* Cf. Du. *fluiten*, to play the flute, to jeer. To jeer.—*n.* A jeer.

Flow, *vi.* O.E. *flówan*. Cogn. with FLOOD. To glide along as a stream; to hang loose and waving; to be poured forth, gush out; of the sea, &c., to rise and advance; to be poured out without stint.—*n.* The action or fact of flowing; the quantity that flows; that which flows; an outpouring or stream; the rise of the tide.

Flow'er, *n.* O.F. *flour*, *flur*, *flor* (F. *fleur*)—L. *flōs*, *flōris*, f. Aryan root *bhlō-*, whence BLOW, *v.*[2] EFFLORESCE. FLORA. FLOUR. FLOURISH. The coloured leaves or petals on a plant; an ornament or embellishment; the choicest.—*vi.* To bloom or blossom.—*vt.* To work flowers upon.—**Flow'er**Y,[2] *a.*

Fluc'tuate, *vi.* L. *fluctuāre*, *fluctuātum*, to undulate, f. *fluctus*, wave, f. *fluĕre*, to flow. FLUENT. To vary irregularly; to vacillate, waver.—**Fluctu**A'TION, *n.*

Flue, *n.*[1] Orig. unknown. Fluff.

Flue, *n.*[2] Orig. unknown. A passage for smoke or heated air.
Flu'ent, *a.* L. *fluens, fluentis*, pres.pple. of *fluĕre*, to flow. AFFLUENT. FLUID. SUPERFLUOUS. Flowing; flowing easily, esp. of speech, style, &c.; ready in the use of words.—**Flu'ent**LY,[2] *adv.*—**Flu'**ENCY, *n.*
Fluff, *n.* App. conn. with FLUE.[1] Light feathery stuff; a soft downy mass.
Flu'id, *a.* F. *fluide*—L. *fluidus*, f. *fluĕre*. FLUENT. Having the property of flowing, yielding to the slightest pressure.—*n.* A substance yielding thus.—**Fluid'**ITY, *n.*
Fluke, *n.*[1] O.E. *flóc*, cogn. with O.N. *flóke*, related to Ger. *flach*, flat. A flat-fish.
Fluke, *n.*[2] Poss. a transferred use of prec. from resemblance of shape. The part of an anchor which enters the ground.
Fluke, *n.*[3] Orig. unknown. A lucky stroke.
Flum'mery, *n.* Welsh *llymru*. Orig. unknown. A sweet dish of milk, flour, &c.; nonsense, empty compliments.
Flun'key, *n.* A Scotch word of uncertain orig. A male servant in livery.
Flur'ry, *n.* App. imitative. A gust or squall; a sudden commotion or excitement; perturbation, hurry. —*vt.* To bewilder, agitate.
Flush, *n.*[1] Orig. uncertain. Cf. F. *flux, flus*, obs. It. *flusso*, in same sense, app. special uses of the words repg. L. *fluxus*. FLUX. A prescribed number of cards of one suit.
Flush, *v.*[1]*i.* and *t.* Perh. imitative. To take, to cause to take, wing and fly away.—*n.*[2] A number of birds flushed at once.
Flush, *v.*[2]*i.* Orig. uncertain. Perh. conn. with FLUSH, *n.*[1] To flow suddenly or violently; to glow; of the blood, to come with a rush; of the face, &c., to redden. —*vt.* To cleanse (a drain, &c.); to make red, cause to glow; to animate, excite.—*n.*[3] A rush of water; elation, excitement; a glow of colour; a reddening of the face; freshness, vigour.—*a.* Full, swollen; plentifully supplied, esp. with money; even, level, level with the adjacent surface.
Flus'ter, *vt.* Cf. Icelandic *flaustr*, bustle, *flaustra*, to bustle. To excite with drink; to flurry.—*vi.* To bustle.—*n.* A flurry.
Flute, *n.* O.F. *fleüte, flaüte, flahute* (F. *flûte*) = Pr. *flauta* of unknown orig. FLOUT. A wind-instrument consisting of a pipe with holes or keys; a groove or channel.—*vi.* To play on a flute.—*vt.* To form flutes in.
Flut'ter, *vi.* O.E. *flotorian*, a freq. formation on *flot-*, weak grade of the root of *fléotan*. FLEET, *v.* To flap the wings rapidly without flight; to move with a quivering motion; to flit, hover; to quiver; to be excited.—*vt.* To agitate.—*n.* A fluttering; excitement.
Flu'vial, *a.* F. *fluvial*—L. *fluviālis*, f. *fluvius*, river, f. *fluĕre*. FLUENT. Of rivers.
Flux, *n.* F. *flux*—L. *fluxus*, f. *fluĕre*, to flow. FLUENT. FLUSH, *n.*[1] A morbid discharge; the flowing in of the tide; a stream, a copious flow; a succession of changes; something used to facilitate fusion.
Fly, *n.*[1] O.E. *fléoge, flýge* = M.Du. *vlieghe*, O.H.G. *flioga* (Ger. *fliege*), f. root of **fleugan*. (See next.) A two-winged insect.
Fly, *vi.* O.E. *fléogan*. Common Teut. O.Teut. **fleugan*. FLEDGE. To move through the air with wings; to pass quickly through the air; to float loosely, wave; to spring; to be forced off suddenly; to flee.—*vt.* To cause to fly; to set (a flag) flying; to flee.—*n.*[2] A flying; a vehicle let out on hire; a device for regulating the speed of machinery.—**Fly'-leaf,** *n.* A blank leaf at the beginning or end of a book.—**Fly'-wheel,** *n.* A heavy wheel to regulate motion or to accumulate power.
Foal, *n.* O.E. *fola*. Common Teut. Cogn. with G. *pōlos*, L. *pullus*. FILLY. PONY. POULT. The young of the equine kind.—*vt.* To bear (a foal).—*vi.* To bear a foal.
Foam, *n.* O.E. *fám* = O.H.G. *feim*. Minute bubbles, froth.—*vi.* To emit or gather foam.
Fob, *n.* Orig. unknown. A small pocket.
Fob, Fub, *vt.* Orig. obscure. Cf. Ger. *foppen*, to cheat. FOP. To cheat; to put *off with* (something inferior).
Fo'cus, *n.*; *pl.* **Fo'ci, Fo'cuses.** L. *focus*, hearth. FUEL. FUSIL. The point at which rays of light meet after being reflected or refracted.—*vt.* To bring to a focus.—**Fo'**CAL, *a.*
Fod'der, *n.* O.E. *fódor* = M.Du. *voeder*, O.H.G. *fuotar* (Ger. *futter*). Aryan root *pāt-*. FOOD. FORAGE. Dried food for cattle, &c.
Foe, *n.* O.E. *fáh*, hostile. Teut. type **faiho-*, referred to Aryan root *peiq-, poiq-, piq-*, whence G. *pikros*, bitter. FEUD.[1] An enemy.
Fœ'tus, Fe'tus, *n.* L. *fētus*, offspring. The young in the womb or egg when fully formed.
Fog, *n.*[1] Orig. unknown. The grass that grows after hay is cut; long grass left standing during winter. —**Fog'**GY,[2] *a.* Covered with coarse grass; thick, murky; obscure, confused.
Fog, *n.*[2] Prob. a back-formation f. FOGGY. Thick mist; obscurity due to this.
Fo'gy, Fo'gey, *n.* Poss. a use as *n.* of FOGGY in sense 'moss-grown', f. FOG[1] in dial. sense 'moss'. An old-fashioned fellow.
Foi'ble, *n.* F. *foible*, weak, obs. form of *faible*. FEEBLE. A weak point in character.
Foil, *n.*[1] O.F. *foil*, masc., f. L. *folium*, leaf, and *foille, fueille* (F. *feuille*), fem., f. *folia*, pl. of *folium*. FOLIAGE. FOLIO. PORTFOLIO. TREFOIL. A small arc or space in the tracery of a window; a thin layer, a leaf; metal in a thin sheet; a thin leaf of metal put under a gem; anything that sets off to advantage.
Foil, *n.*[2] Of obscure orig. A light pointless weapon used in fencing.
Foil, *vt.* Repg. irregularly O.F. *fuler, foler, fouler*, to full cloth, oppress—Pop.L. **fullāre*, to stamp with the feet, full, f. L. *fullo*, fuller. FULL, *v.* To defeat; to frustrate.
Foist, *vt.* Prob. f. Du. dial. *vuisten*, to take in the hand, f. *vuist*, FIST. To introduce surreptitiously *into*; to palm off *on* or *upon*.
Fold, *n.*[1] O.E. *falæd, falod*, corresp. to M.L.G. *vālt* (Du. *vaalt*), E.Fris. *folt*, enclosed space, dunghill. A pen for domestic animals.—*v.*[1]*t.* To shut up in a fold.
Fold, *v.*[2]*t.* O.E. *fealdan*. Common Teut. Cogn. with G. *di-plasios*, double. To double; to coil, wind; to lay (the arms, &c.) together; to cover or wrap up; to embrace.—*vi.* To become folded. —*n.*[2] A doubled part; a winding or sinuosity.
Fo'liage, *n.* Altered f. F. *feuillage*, f. *feuille*, leaf. FOIL, *n.*[1] Leaves collectively.
Fo'lio, *n.* L, *folio*, ablative of *folium*, leaf. FOIL.[1] The two opposite pages of an account-book; a certain number of words taken as a unit; *in folio* (orig. apprehended as a L. phrase), in the form of a sheet, made up of sheets, folded once; hence *folio* alone, a sheet folded once, a book made up of such sheets, a book of the largest size.—*a.* Of this size.
Folk, *n.* O.E. *folc* = Old Fris. *folk*, O.S., O.H.G. *folc* (Ger. *volk*). A people; people indefinitely or of a particular class (often in *pl.*).—**Folk-lore,** *n.* Popular traditional beliefs, customs, &c.; the study of these.

Fol'low, *vt.* O.E. *folgian, fylgan.* Cf. O.S. *folgôn*, O.H.G. *folgên* (Ger. *folgen*), O.N. *fylgja.* To go or come after; to keep in (a path, &c.); to succeed; to accompany, attend upon; to be consequent upon; to pursue; to strive after; to take as guide; to conform to, comply with; to engage in; to keep up with mentally.—*vi.* To go or come after; to come next, to ensue; to result.—**Fol'low**ER, *n.*

Fol'ly, *n.* O.F. *folie*, f. *fol.* FOOL.[1] Want of good sense; a foolish action, &c.

Foment', *vt.* F. *fomenter*—L.L. *fōmentāre*, f. L. *fōmentum* (for **fovimentum*), warm lotion, f. *fovēre*, to cherish, warm. To bathe with warm lotions; to foster, encourage, instigate.—**Foment**A'TION, *n.*

Fond, *a.* M.E. *fonned*, f. obs. *fon*, to lose savour, be foolish, make a fool of, of unknown orig. FUN. Foolishly credulous or sanguine; loving, tender; entertained with unreasoning affection; with *of*, having strong liking for.—**Fond'**LY,[2] *adv.*—**Fond'**NESS, *n.*

Fon'dle, *vt.* Freq. of obs. *Fond*, vt., to caress, f. prec. To handle with fondness, caress.

Font, *n.* O.E. *font*, f. a specific use in Eccles. L. of L. *fons.* FOUNT.[1] A receptacle for the water used in baptism.

Food, *n.* O.E. *fóda.* Teut. root *fad-*, *fōd-*, repg. Aryan root *păt-*, whence G. *pate-esthai*, to eat. FEED. FODDER. That which is eaten; an article of food; nutriment.

Fool, *n.*[1] M.E. *fōl*—O.F. *fol*, n. and a.—L. *follis*, bellows, in late Pop.L., empty-headed person, fool. FOLLY. One deficient in sense; a jester; a dupe.—*vi.* To act like a fool.—*vt.* To make a fool of; to dupe, delude.—**Fool'**ERY, *n.*—**Fool'hardy**, *a.* O.F. *fol hardi.* HARDY. Foolishly bold. — **Fool'hardi**NESS, *n.*—**Fool'**ISH, *a.*—**Fool'ish**LY,[2] *adv.*—**Fool's'-cap**, **Fools'cap**, *n.* A jester's cap; a dunce's cap; a 'fool's cap' used as a watermark, a size of writing- or printing-paper which formerly had this watermark.

Fool, *n.*[2] Prob. a use of prec. suggested by TRIFLE in sim. sense. A dish of fruit stewed and crushed and mixed with cream, &c.

Foot, *n.* O.E. *fót.* Common Teut. Cogn. with Skr. *pād*, G. *pous, podos*, L. *pēs, pedis.* EXPEDIENT. FETCH, *v.* FETTER. PAWN.[1] PEDAL. PEW. The lowest part of the leg; the end of a bed, &c.; foot-soldiers; a division of a verse; a measure of length, 12 inches; a base; the lowest part, bottom.—*vi.* To step, tread, dance.—*vt.* To set foot on.—**Foot'ball**, *n.* A large inflated ball; a game played with it.—**Foot'ing**, *vbl.n.* Stable position of the feet, secure position; conditions, relations.—**Foot'man**, *n.* A liveried servant.—**Foot'-pad**, *n.* PAD, *n.*[1], in obs. sense 'highwayman'. A highwayman who robs on foot.

Fop, *n.* Conn. with obs. *Fop*, v., to be a fool, to cheat, of obscure orig. Cf. Ger. *foppen.* FOB, *v.* A dandy.—**Fop'**PERY, *n.*—**Fop'**PISH, *a.*

For, *prep.* O.E. *for* = Old Fris., O.S. *for*, Goth. *faur.* Prob. a shortened form of O.Teut. **fora*, FORE. Because of; instead of, in exchange for; toward; on account of; conducing to; in favour of; toward the obtaining of; to prevent or relieve; with respect to; during; in quest of; in recompense of; in the character of. — *conj.* Because. — **Forasmuch'**, *adv.* Orig. *for as much.* With *as*, seeing that.

For'age, *n.* F. *fourrage*, f. O.F. *feurre*, fodder. Common Romanic **fodro*, of Teut. orig. Cogn. with FODDER. Fodder, esp. for horses in an army; foraging.—*vt.* To collect forage from, to pillage; to supply with forage; to get by foraging.—*vi.* To search for forage; to make a roving search *for.*

For'ay, *vt.* and *i.* Orig. obscure. Ultimately f. **fodro.* (See prec.) To pillage.—*n.* A raid.

For'bear, *n.* *For-* (= FORE-) + *beer*, obs. agent-n. f. BE. An ancestor.

Forbear', *vt.* O.E. *forberan.* FOR- (3) + BEAR, *v.* To refrain from, cease.—*vi.* To refrain; to be patient.—**Forbear'**ANCE, *n.*

Forbid', *vt.* O.E. *forbéodan.* FOR- (2) + BID. To command not to do, have, &c.; to render impossible. — **Forbid'ding**, *ppl.a.* Repellant, repulsive, uninviting.

Force, *n.* F. *force*—Pop.L. **fortia*, n. of quality f. L. *fortis*, strong. COMFORT. FORT. Strength, power; an army; a body of police; coercion; binding power, validity; import, meaning; the cause of a physical phenomenon, such causes regarded generically.—*vt.* F. *forcer.* To constrain, compel; to enter by force, to break open; to drive by force; to impose forcibly; to obtain by force; to hasten the maturity of.—**Forc'**IBLE, *a.*—**Forc'ib**LY,[2] *adv.*

Force'-meat, *n.* Obs. *Force*, v., alteration of FARCE, *v.* + MEAT. Meat chopped fine and spiced, used chiefly for stuffing.

For'ceps, *n.* L. *forceps* in same sense. An instrument for seizing and holding objects.

Ford, *n.* O.E. *ford* = O.H.G., Ger. *furt.* Cogn. with FARE. A place where a river may be crossed by wading.—*vt.* To cross by wading.—**Ford'**ABLE, *a.*

Fordo', *vt.* O.F. *fordón.* FOR- (4) + DO. To destroy; in *pa.pple.*, exhausted.

Fore, *adv.* O.E. *fore, foran*, adv., *fore*, prep. Common Teut. O.Teut. **fora* (root *fur-*, *for-*). Cogn. with G. *pro, para, peri*, L. *prō, prae, per.* FIRST. FOR. FOREMOST. FORTH. FURTHER. Now only in composition. FORE-.

Fore, *a.* This use arises from an analysis of *nn.* with FORE-, the pref. being treated as an *a.* In front.—quasi-*n.* The fore part.

Fore-and-aft, *a.* Placed in the line of a vessel's length.

Fore'arm, *n.* FORE- + ARM, *n.*[1] The arm from elbow to wrist.

Forearm', *vt.* FORE- + ARM, *v.*[2] To arm beforehand.

Forebode', *vt.* FORE-. To betoken; to have a presentiment of.

Forecast', *vt.* FORE-. To conjecture beforehand.—**Fore'cast**, *n.* A conjecture.

Fore'castle, *n.* FORE-. Formerly a short raised deck at the fore end of a ship, intended to command an enemy's decks. The sailors' quarters in the fore part of a ship.

Foreclose', *vt.* O.F. *forclos-*, stem of *forclore*, f. *for-* (L. *foris*), outside + *clore*, to CLOSE, FOREIGN. To exclude, shut out; to deprive a mortgagor of his right to redeem (the mortgage).—**Foreclo'**SURE, *n.*

Fore'father, *n.* FORE-. An ancestor.

Fore'finger, *n.* FORE-. The finger next the thumb.

Forego', *vt.* and *i.* O.E. *fore-gán.* FORE- + GO. To go before.

Fore'ground, *n.* FORE-. The part of a picture represented as in front; the most prominent position.

Fore'head, *n.* O.E. *forhéafod.* *For-* (= FORE-) + HEAD. The upper part of the face.

For'eign, *a.* O.F. *forain*—Pop.L. type **forānus*, f. L. *foris*, outside, conn. with *foris*, DOOR. FORECLOSE. FOREST. FORFEIT. Alien in character, irrelevant; introduced from outside; not in or of one's own land; relating to, connected with, other countries.—**For'eign**ER, *n.* A native of a foreign country.

Fore'land, *n.* FORE-. A cape, headland.
Fore'man, *n.* FORE-. The principal juror; one in charge of a department of work.
Fore'mast, *n.* FORE-. The forward mast.
Fore'most, *a.* O.E. *formest, fyrmest* = Old Fris. *formest*, Goth. *frumist-s*, with additional superl. suff., f. O.Teut. **formon-*, a superl. f. the root of FORE. FORMER. Most advanced in position; chief.—*adv.* In the first place.
Fore'noon, *n.* FORE-. The part of the day before noon.
Foren'sic, *a.* L. *forensis* (a. f. *forum*, FORUM) + -IC. Pertaining to, used in, courts of law; suitable or analogous to pleadings in court.
Fore-run', *vt.* FORE-. To prognosticate.
Fore'sail, *n.* FORE-. The principal sail on the foremast.
Foresee', *vt.* O.E. *foreséon*. FORE- + SEE. To have prescience of.—**Fore'sight**, *n.* Prevision; care or provision for the future.
Foreshad'ow, *vt.* FORE-. To be a type or presage of.
Fore'shore, *n.* FORE-. The part of the shore lying between high- and low-water marks.
Foreshort'en, *vt.* FORE-. To delineate (an object) so that it appears to be shortened in the directions not lying in a plane perpendicular to the line of sight.
For'est, *n.* O.F. *forest* (F. *forêt*)—Med.L. *foresta*, also *forestis* (*silva*), the outside, *i.e.* unfenced (wood), f. L. *foris*, outside. FOREIGN. An extensive wood; a woodland district set apart for hunting.—**For'ester**, *n.* O.F. *forestier*. One in charge of a forest or of growing timber.—**For'estry**, *n.* The art of planting and growing timber.
Forestall', *vt.* O.E. *foresteall*, f. FORE- + *steall*, STALL, app. in sense 'position taken up'. To be beforehand with, anticipate.
Fore'taste, *n.* FORE-. A taste beforehand.
Foretell', *vt.* FORE-. To tell of beforehand, prophesy; to indicate the approach of.
Fore'thought, *n.* FORE-. Contriving beforehand; thought for the future.
For'feit, *n.* O.F. *forfet, forfait*—Med.L. *foris factum*, trespass, fine, neut. pa.pple. of *foris facĕre*, to transgress, f. L. *foris*, outside + *facĕre*, to do. FOREIGN. Something the right to which is lost by the commission of a crime, &c.; a penalty.—*vt.* To lose the right to, to have to give up.—**For'feiture**, *n.*
Forfend', *vt.* FOR- (2) + FEND. To avert.
Forgath'er, **Foregath'er**, *vi.* FOR- (5). To assemble; to meet or associate *with*.
Forge, *n.* O.F. *forge*. Common Romanic **faurga*—L. *fabrica*. FABRIC. A smithy; a fireplace with bellows attached for heating iron, &c.; a furnace.—*v.*[1]*t.* To beat into shape; to fabricate; to make in fraudulent imitation of something; to counterfeit.—**Forg'er**, *n.*—**Forg'ery**, *n.*
Forge, *v.*[2]*i.* Orig. unknown. Of a ship, to make way.
Forget', *vt.* O.E. *forgietan*. Cf. Du. *vergeten*, Ger. *vergessen*. O.Teut. **getan* (GET) in sense 'to hold, grasp'; hence, with pref. in sense of FOR- (3), 'to lose one's hold'. To lose remembrance of; to leave behind; to omit to mention or think of.—**Forget'ful**, *a.*
Forgive', *vt.* O.E. *forgiefan*. FOR- (1) + GIVE. To remit; to pardon; to regard indulgently.—**Forgive'ness**, *n.*
Forgo', **Forego'**, *vt.* O.E. *forgán*. FOR- (3) + GO. To abstain from, let go, give up.
Fork, *n.* O.E. *forca*—L. *furca*. An implement, chiefly agricultural, with prongs; an instrument with prongs for holding food; a division into branches, the point of division, one of the branches.—*vi.* To branch.—*vt.* To make fork-shaped; to raise with a fork.
Forlorn', *a.* Pa.pple. of obs. *Forlese*, to lose —O.E. *forléosan*, f. FOR- (1) + *-léosan*, a Common Teut. v. f. root *leus-*: *laus-*: *los-*. Cf. Du. and Ger. *verloren*, lost. Prob. cogn. with G. *luein*, L. *so-lv-ĕre*, to loosen. LOOSE. LORN. LOSE. Formerly, lost, ruined. Desperate, hopeless; abandoned, forsaken; wretched.—**Forlorn hope**. Du. *verloren hoop* (HEAP), lit. 'lost troop'. Cf. F. *enfants perdus*. A storming party; a desperate enterprise.
Form, *n.* O.F. *fo(u)rme*—L. *forma*, shape. Shape; a living being, a person; nature, structure; a species, kind; a class in school; due shape; customary procedure; a fixed order of words; observance of etiquette or ceremony; a (mere) ceremony; a long seat without a back; a hare's nest.—*vt.* To put into shape, to fashion, mould; to train; to arrange, to organize; to make, bring into existence; to frame in the mind, conceive; to go to make up, compose.—*vi.* To come into existence, be produced.—**For'mal**, *a.* Explicit, definite; that is according to recognized forms, ceremonial; that is matter of routine, perfunctory; precise, stiff; stiff in design.—**For'mally**,[2] *adv.*—**For'malism**, *n.* Excessive adherence to forms.—**Formal'ity**, *n.*—**Forma'tion**, *n.* A forming; the thing formed; structure.—**For'mative**, *a.* Forming; serving to form words.
For'mer, *a.* A comp. formed (app. in the 12th c.) after *formest*, FOREMOST. Earlier in time, belonging to the past; the first mentioned of two.—**For'merly**,[2] *adv.*
For'midable, *a.* F. *formidable*—L. *formīdābilis*, f. *formīdāre*, to fear. Giving cause for fear; likely to give difficulty.
For'mula, *n.*; *pl.* **-æ**, **-as**. L. *formula*, dim. of *forma*, FORM. A form of words setting forth something or prescribed to be used; a recipe; a rule expressed in mathematical symbols; an expression of chemical composition.—**For'mulary**, *n.* A collection of formulas.—*a.* Of the nature of a formula; relating to formulas.—**For'mulate**,[3] *vt.* To reduce to a formula; to state in systematic form.
For'nicate, *vi.* L. *fornicāri*, *fornicātus*, f. *fornix*, *fornicis*, vault, brothel. To have unlawful sexual intercourse.—**Fornica'tion**, *n.*—**For'nicator**, *n.*
Forsake', *vt.* O.E. *forsacan*, to neglect, f. FOR- (3) + *sacan*, to contend, conn. with *sacu*. SAKE. To renounce; to abandon, desert.
Forsooth', *adv.* O.E. *forsóth*, f. *for*, FOR + *sóth*, SOOTH. In truth, truly (now only ironically or derisively).
Forswear', *vt.* O.E. *forswerian*, f. FOR- (3) + *swerian*, to SWEAR. To renounce on oath. —*v.refl.* To swear falsely.
Fort, *n.* F. *fort*, use as *n.* of *fort*, L. *fortis*, strong. FORCE. A fortified place.—**For'talice**, *n.* Med.L. *fortalitia*. A small fort.
Forte, *n.* F. *fort* used as *n.* (see prec.) and put (in Eng.) in fem. form. One's strong point.
For'te, *a.* and *adv.* It. *forte*, strong—L. *fortis*. FORT. *Mus.*, loud, loudly.
Forth, *adv.* O.E. *forth* = O.S. *forth*, M.H.G. *vort* (Ger. *fort*). O.Teut. type **furtho*, cogn. with FORE. Onwards in time; forward, into view; away.—**Forthwith'**, *adv.* 'Forward along with.' Immediately, at once.
For'tify, *vt.* F. *fortifier*—L. *fortificāre*, f. *fortis*, strong + *facĕre*, to make. COMFORT. -FY.

To strengthen; to corroborate; to provide with defensive works.—**Forti**FICA'TION, *n.*—**For'titude**, *n.* F. *fortitude*—L. *fortitūdo*. Resolute endurance of pain or adversity.

Fort'night, *n.* O.E. *féowertýne niht*, fourteen NIGHTS. A period of two weeks.

For'tress, *n.* O.F. *forteresse*, f. *fort*, strong. FORT. A fortified place.

Fortu'itous, *a.* L. *fortuitus*, f. *forte*, by chance (f. *fors* (see next)) + -OUS. Accidental.

For'tune, *n.* F. *fortune*—L. *fortūna*, lengthened f. *fors, fortis*, chance. Chance; the goddess of chance; luck, good or bad; good luck, prosperity; one's condition in life; position as determined by wealth: wealth, a stock of wealth.—**For'tun**ATE,[2] *a.* Lucky; auspicious, favourable.—**For'tunate**LY,[2] *adv.*

For'ty, *a.* and *n.* O.E. *féowertig*. FOUR. The cardinal number equal to four tens.

Fo'rum, *n.* L. *forum*. FORENSIC. In ancient Rome, the place of assembly for judicial and other public business; a tribunal.

For'ward, *a.* O.E. *for(e)weard*, a. and adv. FORE, *adv.* -WARD. That lies in front of one, onward; ready, prompt; precocious; presumptuous, bold.—*adv.* Towards the future; towards the front; to the front, into view; at or in the fore part of a ship; onward, so as to progress.—*vt.* To help forward; to dispatch, send.—**For'ward**LY,[2] *adv.* Presumptuously.

For'wards, *adv.* -WARDS. = FORWARD.

Fosse, *n.* F. *fosse*—L. *fossa* (sc. *terra*, earth), ditch, fem. pa.pple. of *fodĕre, fossum*, to dig. A ditch.—**Fos'sil**, *a.* F. *fossile*—L. *fossilis*, dug up, f. *fodĕre*. Of the remains of animals and plants, got by digging.—*n.* The remains of an animal or plant found in the earth.

Fos'ter-. O.E. *fóstor*, nourishment = O.N. *fóstr*, nursing, f. root *fód-*. FOOD. Hence **Fos'ter-child**, *n.* A child in relation to persons who have reared it as their own. Sim. **Fos'ter-fa'ther**, **Fos'ter-broth'er**, &c. —**Fos'ter**, *vt.* To cherish; to encourage.

Foul, *a.* O.E. *fúl* = O.H.G. *fûl* (Ger. *faul*), O.N. *fúll*—O.Teut. **fûlo-*, f. root *fu-* = Aryan *pu-* as in Skr. *pū*, to stink, G. *puon*, L. *pūs*, PUS. FILE, *v.*[3] Loathsome; dirty; muddy; charged with noxious matter; clogged, choked; abominable, detestable; obscene; disgraceful; contrary to rule or custom.—*n.* A collision; an irregular piece of play.—*vi.* To become foul. —*vt.* To make foul; to jam; to collide with.—**Foul'**LY,[2] *adv.*—**Foul'**NESS, *n.*

Found, *v.*[1]*t.* F. *fonder*—L. *fundāre*, f. *fundus*, BOTTOM. FOUNDER. To lay the base of; to establish, institute; to base, ground.—**Found**A'TION, *n.* In senses f. the *v.*; an endowed institution.—**Found'**ER, *n.*[1]

Found, *v.*[2]*t.* F. *fondre*—L. *fundĕre*. FUSE, *v.* To melt and run into a mould.—**Found'**ER, *n.*[2]—**Foun'd**RY, *n.*

Foun'der, *vi.* O.F. *fondrer*, to send to the bottom, submerge, to collapse—L. *fundus*. FOUND.[1] To fall down; of a horse, to fall lame; of a ship, to sink.—*vt.* To cause to fall lame; to sink.

Found'ling, *n.* M.E. *fundeling*, f. *funden*, pa.pple. of FIND + -LING (2). A deserted infant. [FONT. A spring, fountain.

Fount, *n.*[1] L. *fons, fontis*, spring, FOUNTAIN.

Fount, *n.*[2] F. *fonte*, f. *fondre*, to melt, cast. FOUND.[2] A complete set of type.

Foun'tain, *n.* O.F. *fontaine*—L.L. *fontāna*, fem. of L. *fontānus*, a. f. *fons*. FOUNT.[1] A spring; the source of a river; a jet of water.

Four, *a.* and *n.* O.E. *féower*. Common Teut. and Aryan. Cogn. with G. *tessares* (Doric *tetores*), L. *quattuor*. The cardinal number next after three.—**Fourth**, *a.* -TH.[2] The corresponding ordinal number.—*n.* A fourth part.—**Fourteen'**, *a.* and *n.* O.E. *féowerténe*, f. *féower* + *téne*, an inflected form of *tén*, TEN. The cardinal number composed of ten and four.—**Four-square**, *a.* Having four equal sides; in a square form.

Fowl, *n.* O.E. *fugol*, bird. Common Teut. Prob. f. *flug-*. FLEDGE. A bird; birds; a domestic cock or hen.—*vi.* To catch or shoot wildfowl.—**Fowl'**ER, *n.*

Fox, *n.* O.E. *fox*. Common Teut. VIXEN. A carnivorous animal remarkable for cunning. —*vt.* To discolour (paper).—**Fox'glove**, *n.* O.E. *foxes glófa* (? *pl.*). GLOVE. A flowering plant used in medicine.—**Fox'**Y,[2] *a.* Crafty.

Frac'tion, *n.* O.F. *fraccion*—Eccles.L. *fractio, fractiōnis*, n. of action f. L. *frangĕre, fractum*, to BREAK. INFRINGE. OSPREY. SAXIFRAGE. A breaking (of bread in the Eucharist); a fragment, scrap; a numerical quantity that is not an integer.—**Frac'tion**AL, *a.*—**Frac'-ture**, *n.* A breaking; a being broken, esp. of a bone; a crack, split.—*vt* and *i.* To break, crack.—**Frag'ile**, *a.* F. *fragile*—L. *fragilis*, f. *frag-*, root of *frangĕre*. Easily broken, perishable.—**Fragil'**ITY, *n.*—**Frag'ment**, *n.* L. *fragmentum*, f. *frag-*. A piece broken off; a small piece; a detached or incomplete part.—**Fragmen't**ARY, *a.*

Frac'tious, *a.* From FRACTION, in obs. sense 'discord, dissension', after *captious*, &c. Refractory, unruly; cross, fretful.

Fra'grant, *a.* L. *fragrans, fragrantis*, pres. pple. of *fragrāre*, to smell sweetly. Sweet-smelling.—**Fra'gr**ANCE, *n.*

Frail, *n.* O.F. *frayel*. Orig. unknown. A kind of basket made of rushes.

Frail, *a.* O.F. *fraile*—L. *fragilis*. FRAGILE. Easily broken; transient; weak; morally weak, unchaste.—**Frail'**NESS, *n.*—**Frail'**TY, *n.*

Frame, *vt.* O.E. *framian*, to be helpful or profitable, f. *fram*, a. and adv., forward. FROM. To adapt, adjust; to make, construct; to contrive, put together; to put into words; to put in a frame.—*n.* Structure, constitution; mood, condition of temper; a structure; that in which something is set or let in.—**Frame'work**, *n.* A light structure; a structure into which completing contents can be fitted.

Franc, *n.* F. *franc*, app. f. the legend on the original (a gold) coin *Francorum rex*, king of the Franks. A French silver coin = about 9½*d.*

Fran'chise, *n.* O.F. *franchise*, freedom, f. *franc*. FRANK. A legal immunity; a privilege; the right of voting at elections.

Fran'gible, *a.* O.F. *frangible*, as if f. a L. **frangibilis*, f. *frangĕre*. FRACTION. Capable of being broken.

Frank, *a.* O.F. *franc*, Med.L. *francus*, free, orig. identical with the name *Francus*, a Frank, which acquired the sense 'free' because in Frankish Gaul only the Franks, the dominant race, had freedom. ENFRANCHISE. Free in speech, candid, outspoken; open, sincere; undisguised.—*n.* The superscribed signature of a person entitled to send letters free of postage; a letter or envelope with such a signature.—*vt.* To put such a signature on.—**Frank'**LY,[2] *adv.*—**Frank'incense**, *n.* O.F. *franc* (app. in sense 'of high quality') *encens*. INCENSE, *n.* Cf. FREESTONE. An aromatic gum resin.

Fran'tic, *a.* M.E. *frentik, frantik* — O.F. *frenetique*—L.L. *phrenēticus*, delirious, a corr.

of G. *phrenitikos*, affected with *phrenitis*, delirium, f. *phrēn*, the midriff, the mind + *-itis*. -ITIS. FRENZY. PHRENETIC. PHRENOLOGY. Mad with rage, grief, &c.; displaying frenzy, wild. — **Fran'tically**, *adv.* -AL. -LY.[2]— **Fran'tic**LY,[2] *adv.*

Frater'nal, *a.* L. *frāternus* (f. *frāter*, BROTHER) + -AL. FRIAR. Of or pertaining to a brother; brotherly. —**Frater'n**ITY, *n.* The state or quality of being brotherly; an organized body of men; a body of men of the same class, &c. — **Frat'ern**IZE, *vi.* To associate *with* as a brother. — **Frat'ricide**, *n.* -CIDE(1). One who kills his brother. -CIDE (2). The killing of a brother.

Fraud, *n.* O.F. *fraude*—L. *fraus*, *fraudis*, deceit. Criminal deception; a dishonest trick. —**Fraud'**ULENT, *a.*—**Fraud'**ULENCE, *n.*

Fraught, *pa.pple.* and *ppl.a.* Pa.pple. of *Fraught*, to load (obs. except in the *pa.pple.*), f. obs. *Fraught*, freight, cargo, prob. f. M.Du. or M.L.G. *vracht*, *vrecht*, in sim. senses. FREIGHT. Laden; supplied, furnished; *fraught with*, attended with, destined to produce.

Fray, *v.*[1]*t.* Aphetic f. AFFRAY. To terrify, scare away.—*n.* A brawl, a fight.

Fray, *v.*[2]*t.* F. *frayer*—L. *fricāre*. FRICTION. To wear away.—*vi.* To become frayed.

Freak, *n.* Poss. f. dialects and cogn. with O.E. *frícian*, to dance. A capricious whim or notion; a prank or trick.—**Freak'**ISH, *a.*

Freck'le, *n.* Alteration of obs. *Frecken*—O.N. *freknur*, pl. A light-brown spot in the skin.—*vt.* and *i.* To mark, to become marked, with freckles.

Free, *a.* O.E. *fréo*. Common Teut. Orig. sense 'dear'; hence applied to those related to the head of a house as opposed to the slaves. O.Teut. **frijo-*, O.Aryan **priyo-*. FRIDAY. FRIEND. Not in bondage; having civil liberty; at liberty; unimpeded; not adhering to rules; clear, unobstructed; not fixed; acting of one's own will; ready, willing, spontaneous; liberal; abundant; frank; released or exempt; admitted to the rights *of*; allowed the use *of*; open to all traders.—*vt.* To set at liberty; to relieve or exempt *from*, rid *of* or *from*; to disengage. — **Free'**LY,[2] *adv.*—**Free'**DOM, *n.*— **Free'hand**, *a.* Drawn without guiding instruments, &c.—**Free'hold**, *n.* A tenure by which an estate is held without obligation of rent or service; an estate held thus.—**Freema'son**, *n.* A member of the fraternity called *Free and Accepted Masons*. (Why *free* is not clear.)—**Freema'son**RY, *n.* The principles, mysteries, &c., of the fraternity.

Free'booter, *n.* Du. *vrijbuiter* = Ger. *freibeuter*, f. the equivalents of FREE, *a.* and BOOTY, with -ER. FILIBUSTER. A pirate.

Free'stone, *n.* A translation of O.F. *franche pere*, 'excellent stone'. Cf. FRANKINCENSE. An easily cut stone of sand or lime.

Freeze, *vi.* O.E. *fréosan*. Common Teut. O.Teut. **freusan*. FROST. *It freezes*, the temperature of the air is such that water becomes ice; to become ice; to feel very cold.—*vt.* To change (a liquid) to a solid form by cold, to congeal; to affect with frost.

Freight, *n.* Prob. f. M.Du. or M.L.G. *vrecht*. FRAUGHT. Hire of a ship; a cargo.—*vt.* To hire, to load (a ship).—**Freight'**ER, *n.*

Fren'zy, Phren'zy, *n.* M.E. *frenesie*—O.F. *frenesie*—L.L. *phrenēsis*, a pseudo-G. formation after *phrenēticus*. FRANTIC. Delirium; fury, distraction.—**Fren'zied**, *ppl.a.*

Fre'quent, *a.* L. *frequens*, *frequentis*, crowded, frequent, cogn. with *farcīre*, to stuff. FARCE. Placed at short distances apart; often recurring.—**Frequent'**, *vt.* To resort to habitually.— **Fre'quent**LY,[2] *adv.*—**Fre'qu**ENCY, *n.*—**Frequen't**ATIVE, *a.* Of a verb, denoting repetition of an action.—*n.* Such a verb.

Fres'co, *n.* It. (See next.) A mode of painting in water-colour on freshly laid and still damp plaster; a painting executed thus.

Fresh, *a.* Prob. f. O.F. *freis*, masc., *fresche*, fem. (F. *frais*, *fraîche*) = It. *fresco*, f. O.Teut. **frisko-*. Cf. Ger. *frisch*. New; additional, other; recent; inexperienced; not salted, pickled, &c.; not salt; pure; not musty, stale, &c.; not faded or worn; not sullied, bright; looking healthy; not tired; of wind, strong.—**Fresh'**LY,[2] *adv.* —**Fresh'**EN,[2] *vi.* and *t.*—**Fresh'et**, *n.* Suff. *-et*, (orig.) dim. A stream of fresh water; a flood in a river.—**Fresh'**NESS, *n.*

Fret, *n.*[1] App. f. O.F. *frete*, trellis-work, of uncertain orig. Ornamental interlaced work; a pattern composed of combinations of straight lines generally joined at right angles.—*v.*[1]*t.* To adorn with decorative carved work.

Fret, *n.*[2] Orig. uncertain. In the guitar, &c., a bar regulating the fingering.

Fret, *v.*[2]*t.* O.E. *fretan*, f. O.Teut. *fra-* (= FOR-(4)) + **etan*, to EAT. To gnaw; to eat away; to form by wearing away; to chafe, irritate; to ruffle (water).—*vi.* To vex oneself, worry.—*n.*[3] Agitation, vexation.—**Fret'**FUL, *a.*

Fri'able, *a.* F. *friable*—L. *friābilis*, f. *friāre*, to crumble. Easily crumbled or pulverized.—**Fria**BIL'ITY, *n.*

Fri'ar, *n.* M.E. *frere*—O.F. *frere*, earlier *fredre*—L. *frāter*, brother. FRATERNAL. A member of a mendicant religious order.

Fricassee', *n.* F. *fricassée*, f. *fricasser*, to mince and cook in sauce, of unknown orig. Meat or a bird sliced and cooked with sauce.

Fric'tion, *n.* F. *friction*—L. *frictio*, *frictiōnis*, n. of action f. *fricāre*, to rub. FRAY.[2] A rubbing; resistance of a surface to the motion of a body.

Fri'day, *n.* O.E. *frigedæg*, DAY of (the Teut. goddess) Fríg, to translate L. *dies Veneris*, day of (the planet) Venus. (*Fríg* = O.N. *Frigg*, wife of *Odin*, f. **frijo-*, dear. FREE.) The sixth day of the week.—**Good Friday**. GOOD, in obs. sense 'observed as holy'. The Friday before Easter.

Friend, *n.* O.E. *fréond*, orig. pres.pple. of *fréogan*, to love, cogn. with *fréo*. FREE. One joined to another in intimacy and mutual benevolence; an acquaintance; a supporter; a Quaker.—**Friend'**LESS, *a.*—**Friend'**LY,[1] *a.* —**Friend'li**NESS, *n.*—**Friend'**SHIP, *n.*

Frieze, *n.*[1] F. *frise*, f. *friser*, to curl, to raise a nap on (cloth), of uncertain orig. FRIZZ. A kind of coarse cloth with a nap on one side. —*vt.* To cover with a nap.

Frieze, *n.*[2] F. *frise*, prob. conn. with the synonymous It. *fregio*—L. *Phrygium* (*opus*), a Phrygian (work). *Arch.*, the division of the entablature between the architrave and the cornice; a band of decoration.

Frig'ate, *n.* F. *frégate*—It. *fregata*. Orig. unknown. A war-ship less than a ship of the line.

Fright, *n.* O.E. (Northumb.) *fryhto*, var. of *fyrhto*—O.Teut. **furhtīn-*, n. of state or quality f. **furhto-*, afraid (O.H.G. *foraht*, O.E. *forht*). Sudden fear; a shocking or ridiculous person or thing.—*vt.* To terrify.—**Fright'**EN,[2] *vt.* To terrify.—**Fright'**FUL, *a.*

Frig'id, *a.* L. *frīgidus*, f. *frīgēre*, to be cold, f. *frīgus*, cold. REFRIGERATE. Very cold;

apathetic; formal, stiff; depressing; insipid, dull.—**Frig'id**LY,[2] *adv.*—**Frigid'**ITY, *n.*

Frill, *n.* Orig. uncertain. An ornamental edging.—*vt.* To decorate with a frill.

Fringe, *n.* M.E. *frenge*—O.F. *frenge*—Pop.L. **frimbia*, alteration of L. *fimbria*, fringe, conn. with *fibra*. FIBRE. An ornamental bordering of threads; anything like this.—*vt.* To put, to serve as, a fringe to.

Frisk, *vi.* From obs. *Frisk*, a., lively—O.F. *frisque*, of uncertain orig. To frolic, gambol. —*n.* A frolic.—**Frisk'**Y,[2] *a.*

Fritil'lary, *n.* L. *fritillus*, dice-box, with which the markings on the flower were app. associated. An herbaceous bulbous plant.

Frit'ter, *n.*[1] F. *friture*, fry, frying—L. *frigĕre*, to FRY. A portion of batter fried in oil, &c.

Frit'ter, *n.*[2] App. alteration (perh. due to prec.) of dial *Fitters*, fragments, f. obs. *Fitter*, to break in pieces, perh. cogn. with M.H.G. *vetze* (Ger. *fetzen*), rag. In *pl.*, fragments.—*vt.* To break in pieces; with *away*, to spend on trifles, waste.

Friv'olous, *a.* L. *frīvolus* + -OUS. Paltry, trumpery; trifling, silly.—**Frivol'**ITY, *n.*

Frizz, *v.*[1]*t.* F. *friser*. FRIEZE.[1] To curl (the hair), to form into a mass of small curls.

Frizz, *v.*[2]*i.* FRY, *v.* + imitative termination. To make a sputtering noise in frying.

Friz'zle, *v.*[1]*t.* Hardly f. FRIZZ,[1] which occurs much later. Poss. f. FRIEZE, *v.*, with freq. suff. *-le*. To curl (hair).—*n.* Frizzled hair.

Friz'zle, *v.*[2]*i.* FRIZZ[2] + freq. suff. *-le*. To frizz.—*vt.* To fry, &c., with a sputtering noise.

Fro, *adv.* M.E. *fra*—O.N. *frá*, corresp. to O.E. *fram*, FROM. Away, apart, only in TO *and fro*.

Frock, *n.* F. *froc*, of uncertain orig. A monk's outer dress; a woman's indoor dress; a coat with long skirts, a **Frock-coat**.—*vt.* To invest with the priestly office.

Frog, *n.*[1] O.E. *frogga*, cogn. with Teut. synonyms, of which there are various types. A small tailless amphibious animal.

Frog, *n.*[2] Orig. doubtful. A front-fastening for a military coat.

Frog, *n.*[3] Orig. doubtful. A horny growth in a horse's hoof.

Frol'ic, *a.* Du. *vrolijk* (= O.H.G. *frôlich* (Ger. *fröhlich*)), f. M.Du. *vrô* (= O.H.G. *frô* (Ger. *froh*)), joyous. Sportive.—*vi.* To gambol.—*n.* An outburst of mirth, a prank; merriment; a merry-making.—**Frol'ic**SOME, *a.*

From, *prep.* O.E. *fram*, *from* = O.S., O.H.G. *fram*, O.N. *frá*. Primary sense 'forward'. Cf. O.E. *fram*, a. and adv. FRAME. FRO. FURNISH. Denoting departure or moving away, source, cause, distance, &c.

Frond, *n.* L. *frons*, *frondis*, foliage. A leaf-like organ formed of stem and foliage.

Front, *n.* O.F. and F. *front* — L. *frons*, *frontis*, forehead. AFFRONT. EFFRONTERY. FLOUNCE.[1] The forehead; the face; the foremost part.—*vi.* To face, look.—*vt.* To face; to confront.—**Front'**AGE, *n.*—**Front'**AL, *a.*—**Front'al**, *n.* O.F. *frontel*. The front of a building. — **Front'ier**, *n.* O.F. *frontier*, f. *front*. The part of a country which fronts another country. — **Front'ispiece**, *n.* F. *frontispice* — Med. L. *frontispicium*, a front view, f. *frons* + *-spicium*, f. L. *specĕre*, to look. The principal front of a building; an illustration fronting the title-page of a book.—**Front'let**, *n.* O.F. *frontelet*, dim. of *frontel*. A band for the forehead.

Frost, *n.* O.E. *frost* (us. *forst*). Common Teut. From O.Teut. **freusan*, to FREEZE. The act or state of freezing; extreme cold.—*vt.* To injure with frost; to cover with rime; to give a roughened surface to; to furnish with frost-nails.—**Frost'**Y,[2] *a.*

Froth, *n.* Not in O.E. Perh. f. O.N. *frotha*. Cf. O.E. *áfrēothan* (A-[3]), to froth. The collection of small bubbles formed by agitation, &c., of a liquid; scum.—*vi.* and *t.* To throw up, to cause to throw up, froth.—**Froth'**Y,[2] *a.*

Fro'ward, *n.* Early M.E., f. *fra*, FRO + -WARD. Perverse, refractory, ungovernable.

Frown, *vi.* M.E. *froune* — O.F. *froignier*, *frongnier*, of obscure orig. To knit the brows, esp. in displeasure; to look sternly. — *n.* A knitting of the brows; a stern look.

Frow'zy, *a.* Of obscure orig. Ill-smelling, fusty; dirty, untidy, slatternly.

Fruc'tify, *vi.* F. *fructifier*—L. *fructificāre*, f. *fructus*, FRUIT + *facĕre*, to make. -FY. To bear fruit.—*vt.* To make fruitful, impregnate. —**Fructi**FICA'TION, *n.*

Fru'gal, *a.* L. *frūgālis*, f. *frūgī*, indeclinable *a.*, useful, temperate, frugal, a dat. form ('fit for food') f. *frux*, fruit of the earth, cogn. with *frui*, to enjoy. FRUIT. Sparing in the use of food, &c.; sparingly supplied or used.—**Fru'gal**LY,[2] *adv.*—**Frugal'**ITY, *n.*

Fruit, *n.* O.F. *fruit*—L. *fructus*, f. *frui*, *fructus*, to enjoy. BROOK, *v.* FRUCTIFY. FRUGAL. Vegetable products (us. in *pl.*); the edible product, the seed and its envelope, of a tree; such product collectively; produce; a result, benefit, profit.—*vi.* To bear fruit.—**Fruit'erer**, *n.* -ER doubled. A dealer in fruit.—**Fruit'**FUL, *a.*—**Fruit'**LESS, *a.*

Frui'tion, *n.* O.F. *fruition*—L. *fruitio*, *fruitiōnis*, n. of action f. *frui*. (See prec.) Enjoyment, the pleasure arising from possession.

Fru'menty, Fur'mety, *n.* O.F. *frumentee*, *fourmentee*, f. *frument*, *fourment* (F. *froment*), L. *frūmentum*, corn. Hulled wheat boiled in milk and seasoned.

Frump, *n.* Orig. unknown. A dowdy woman.

Frus'trate, *vt.* L. *frustrārī*, *frustrātus*, to deceive, disappoint, f. *frustrā*, in vain. To disappoint, baffle.—**Frustra**'TION, *n.*

Fry, *n.*[1] O.N. *frió* = Goth. *fraiw*, seed. Young fishes just produced from the spawn.

Fry, *vt.* F. *frire*—L. *frigĕre*, to roast, fry, cogn. with G. *phrugein* in sim. senses. FRITTER.[1] To cook with fat in a shallow pan.—*vi.* To be cooked thus.—*n.*[2] Fried meat.

Fuchsia, *n.* Named after the German botanist L. *Fuchs*. An ornamental shrub.

Fud'dle, *vi.* Orig. obscure. To have a drinking bout.—*vt.* To intoxicate, make tipsy.

Fu'el, *n.* O.F. *feuaile*—Pop.L. *focālia*, neut. pl. of *focālis*, a. f. *focus*, hearth. FOCUS. Material for burning.

Fug'itive, *a.* F. *fugitif*—L. *fugitīvus*, f. *fugĕre*, *fugitum*, to flee. REFUGE. That has run away from duty, &c.; flitting, shifting; evanescent.—*n.* One who flees from duty, &c.

Fugue, *n.* F. *fugue*—It. *fuga*, lit. 'flight'—L. *fuga*, conn. with *fugĕre*. (See prec.) A musical composition in which the parts seem to chase each other.

Ful'crum, *n.*; *pl.* **Ful'cra**. L. *fulcrum*, foot of a couch, f. *fulcīre*, to prop. The point upon which a lever is placed.

Fulfil', *vt.* O.E. *fullfyllan*, f. *full*, FULL + *fyllan*, to FILL. To satisfy (a desire, &c.); to carry out, execute; to obey; to satisfy the requirements of.—**Fulfil'**MENT, *n.*

Fulig'inous, *a.* L. *fūliginōsus*, f. *fūlīgo*, *fūliginis*, soot. Sooty, covered with soot.

Full, *a.* O.E. *full*. Common Teut. Cogn. with G. *plērēs*, L. *plēnus*. COMPLETE. FILL. FULFIL. PLENARY. PLETHORA. Having all it will hold; containing abundance *of*; ample, copious; complete; swelling, plump.—*n.* The highest state or degree. — *adv.* Very; completely, quite; exactly, directly. —**Ful'**LY,[2] *adv.* —**Full'**NESS, **Ful'**NESS, *n.*—**Ful'**SOME, *a.* Offending by excess, offensive to good taste.

Full, *vt.* O.F. *fuler*. FOIL, *v.* To beat cloth in order to cleanse and thicken it.—**Full'**ER, *n.*

Ful'minate, *vi.* L. *fulmināre*, *fulminātum*, to lighten, f. *fulmen*, lightning. To detonate; to 'thunder' or inveigh violently *against*.—*vt.* To 'thunder forth' (condemnation, &c.).—*n.* A substance which detonates by percussion, friction, or heat.—**Fulmina**'TION, *n.*

Fum'ble, *vi.* and *t.* Orig. obscure. Cf. Du. *fommelen*, L.G. *fummeln* in sim. senses. To grope about, to handle, awkwardly.

Fume, *n.* O.F. *fum*—L. *fūmus*, smoke. PERFUME. Smoke; odorous smoke; odour; vapour, an exhalation; a fit of anger.—*vi.* To emit fumes; to give way to anger or irritation.—**Fu'migate**, *vt.* L. *fūmigāre*, *fūmigātum*, f. *fūmus*. To apply smoke or fumes to, esp. in order to disinfect; to perfume.—**Fumiga'**TION, *n.*

Fun, *vi.* Perh. a dialectal pronunciation of obs. *Fon*. FOND. To make sport, fool.—*n.* Diversion, sport.—**Fun'**NY,[2] *a.*—**Fun'ni**LY,[2] *adv.*

Func'tion, *n.* O.F. *function*—L. *functio*, *functiōnis*, n. of action f. *fungi*, *functus*, to perform. DEFUNCT. PERFUNCTORY. Proper activity or action; an office, employment, &c.; in *pl.*, official duties; a religious or public ceremony; a quantity varying with another.—*vi.* To operate, act. — **Func'tion**AL, *a.*—**Func'tion**ARY, *n.* An official.

Fund, *n.* L. *fundus*, BOTTOM, a piece of land. PROFOUND. A permanent stock; a stock or sum of money; in *pl.*, one's pecuniary resources, the national debt.—*vt.* To convert (debt) into a permanent form; to put into a fund or stock.—**Fun'dament**, *n.* L. *fundāmentum*, foundation. The part of the body on which one sits. — **Fundamen't**AL, *a.* Going to the root of the matter; serving as a foundation or base (always *fig.*); primary.—*n.* A primary principle, rule, &c.

Fu'neral, *a.* O.F. *funeral*—Med.L. *fūnerālis*, f. L. *fūnus*, *fūneris*, a funeral. Of or pertaining to the burial of the dead.—*n.* O.F. *funeraille*. The ceremonies at the burial of a dead body.—**Fune'real**, *a.* L. *fūnereus* (f. *fūnus*) + -AL. Appropriate to a funeral, dismal.

Fun'gus, *n.*; *pl.* **Fun'gi**, **Fun'guses**. L. *fungus*, believed to be cogn. with G. *spoggos*, SPONGE. A mushroom or the like; a spongy morbid growth.—**Fun'**GOUS, *a.*

Funic'ular, *a.* L. *fūniculus* (dim. of *fūnis*, rope) + -AR.[1] Worked by a rope.

Funk, *n.* Perh. f. Flemish *fonck*, of unknown orig. Fear.—*vi.* To show fear.—*vt.* To shirk, try to evade; to be afraid of.

Fun'nel, *n.* M.E. *fonel*, app. f. O.F. **founil*, poss. f. a Pr. corr. of L. *infundibulum*, f. *infundĕre*. INFUSE. A cone-shaped vessel for pouring liquids into an opening; a tube for ventilating or for conveying smoke.

Fur, *vt.* O.F. *forrer* (F. *fourrer*), to line, sheathe, f. *fuerre*, *forre*, case, f. Teut. *fōthro-* (O.E. *fóddor*, O.H.G. *fuotar* (Ger. *futter*)). To line or cover with fur.—*n.* A lining or trimming of the dressed coat of certain animals; the soft short hair of certain animals; a coating or crust resembling this.—**Fur'r**Y,[2] *a.*—**Fur'**RIER, *n.* One who dresses or deals in fur.

Fur'below, *n.* Alteration of FALBALA. A trimming for a petticoat, &c., a flounce.

Fur'bish, *vt.* O.F. *forbiss-*, lengthened stem of *forbir*, f. O.H.G. *furban* in same sense. To burnish, polish; to rub or clean *up*.

Furl, *vt.* Prob. alteration of obs. *Furdle*, *Fardel*, to make into a bundle, f. archaic *fardel*, bundle—O.F. *fardel*, dim. of *farde*, burden, of uncertain orig. To roll up and bind (a sail).

Fur'long, *n.* O.E. *furlang*, f. *furh*, FURROW + *lang*, LONG, *a.* Orig., the length of the furrow in the common field. An eighth of a mile.

Fur'lough, *n.* Du. *verlof* (app. after Ger. *verlaub*), f. *ver-* (= FOR- (3)) + Teut. root *leub-*. LIEF. Leave of absence, esp. to a soldier.

Fur'nace, *n.* O.F. *fornaise*—L. *fornax*, *fornācis*=*furnus*, also *fornus*, cogn. with *formus*, WARM. An apparatus for the continuous application of intense heat.

Fur'nish, *vt.* O.F. *furniss-*, lengthened stem of *furnir* (also *fornir*, *fournir*)—W. Germanic **frummjan* (O.H.G. *frummen*), to promote, supply, f. **frum-*, **fram-*, forward. Cf. FROM. VENEER. To provide or supply *with*; to fit up (a house); to yield, afford.—**Fur'niture**, *n.* F. *fourniture*. Apparatus, appliances; accessories; movable articles in a house, &c.

Fur'row, *n.* O.E. *furh*. Common Teut. FURLONG. The trench made by a plough.—*vt.* To make furrows in.

Fur'ther, *a.* O.E. *furthra* = Old Fris. *fordera*, O.S. *forthoro*, O.H.G. *ford(e)ro* (Ger. *vorder*)—O.Teut. type **fur-ther-o-*, f. root of FORE + comp. suff. *-ther*. (Primary sense 'more forward, more onward'. From similarity of sense, used (with FARTHER) as comp. of FAR, displacing the regular form *farrer*.) More extended, additional, more; more distant.—*adv.* O.E. *furthor*. To or at a more advanced point, to a greater extent, more; in addition; at a greater distance. —*vt.* O.E. *fyrthr(i)an*. To help forward, promote.—**Fur'ther**ANCE, *n.* —**Fur'ther**ER, *n.*—**Fur'thermore**, *adv.* Besides, also. — **Fur'thest**, *a.* A superl. formed (app. in the 14th c.) to correspond to *further*. Most advanced; most remote.—*adv.* To or at the greatest distance.

Fur'tive, *a.* F. *furtif*, L. *furtivus*, f. *fūr*, thief. Done by stealth, secret; sly; got by theft or stealth; thievish.—**Fur'tive**LY,[2] *adv.*

Fu'ry, *n.* F. *furie*—L. *furia*, conn. with *furĕre*, to rage. INFURIATE. Wild anger; fierceness; an avenging deity.—**Fu'ri**OUS, *a.*

Furze, *n.* O.E. *fyrs*. Orig. unknown. A prickly shrub with yellow flowers, gorse.

Fuse, **Fuze**, *n.* It. *fuso* (L. *fūsus*), spindle, also, fuse (from the shape). A tube, &c., containing material by which an explosive is ignited.—**Fusee'**, **Fuzee'**, *n.* F. *fusée*, primarily, 'spindleful of tow'—Med.L. *fūsāta*, f. *fūsus*. A conical wheel on which the chain of a watch or clock is wound; a match with a large head.

Fuse, *vt.* and *i.* L. *fundĕre*, *fūsum*, to pour, melt. CONFOUND. FOUND.[2] To melt with heat.—**Fu'**SIBLE, *a.*—**Fu'**SION, *n.*

Fu'sel. Ger. *fusel*, bad brandy. *Fusel oil*, a mixture of several crude alcohols.

Fu'sil, *n.* F. *fusil*, orig., a steel for striking fire = It. *focile*—L.L. **focīle*, fire-steel, f. L. *focus*, hearth, in L.L., fire. FOCUS. A light musket. — **Fusil**IER', *n.* Orig., a soldier armed with a fusil. A member of certain infantry regiments.—**Fusillade'**, *n.* F. *fusil-*

lade. A simultaneous discharge of firearms; a wholesale execution by this means.—*vt.* To attack or shoot down by a fusillade.

Fuss, *n.* Prob. imitative. Needless or excessive bustle or concern.—*vi.* To make a fuss, be in a bustle.—**Fus'**SY,[2] *a.* -**Fus'si**LY,[2] *adv.*

Fus'tian, *n.* O.F. *fustaine*—Med.L. (*pannus*) *fustāneus*, a fustian (cloth), said to be f. *Fostat*, a cloth-manufacturing suburb of Cairo. A thick cotton cloth with a short nap; inflated language, rant. (For the development of sense cf. BOMBAST.)

Fus'tigate, *vt.* L. *fustīgāre, fustīgātum*, to cudgel to death, f. *fustis*, cudgel. To cudgel.

Fust'y, *a.* With -Y[2] f. obs. *Fust*, a wine-cask, a smell like that of a mouldy cask—O.F. *fust*, cask, primarily log, tree-trunk—L. *fustis*. (See prec.) Mouldy; smelling of damp.

Fu'tile, *a.* L. *fūtilis* (better *futtilis*), easily poured out, untrustworthy, useless, supposed to be f. *fud-*, stem of *fundĕre*. FUSE, *v.* Useless, ineffectual.—**Futil'**ITY, *n.*

Fu'ture, *a.* O.F. and F. *futur*, fem. *future*—L. *futūrus*, used as fut.pple. of *esse*, to be. That will be hereafter; of, relating to, time to come.—*n.* Time to come; what will happen in the future; prospective condition; the future tense.—**Futu'r**ITY, *n.*

Fuzz, *n.* Perh. imitative of the action of blowing away light particles. Loose volatile matter.—**Fuz'z**Y,[2] *a.* Frayed; frizzed.

G

Gab, *n.* App. imitative. Talk, twaddle; *the gift of the gab*, fluency in speaking.

Gab'ble, *vi.* Imitative. Cf. Du. *gabbeln* in sim. sense. To talk volubly, inarticulately and incoherently.—*n.* Such talk.

Ga'bion, *n.* F. *gabion*—It. *gabbione*, aug. of *gabbia*, L. *cavea*, CAGE. A basket containing earth used in fortification.

Ga'ble, *n.* Prob. f. O.F. *gable*, which is prob. f. O.N. *gafl* in same sense. The triangular upper part of the end wall of a house.

Gad, *n.* O.N. *gaddr*, spike, nail = O.H.G. *gart*. Cf. Ger. *gerte*, switch (YARD[2]). Cogn. with L. *hasta*, spear. A metal spike; a bar of iron.—**Gad'-fly**, *n.* A fly which stings cattle.

Gad, *vi.* Orig. obscure. To rove idly.

Gaff, *n.* F. *gaffe*—Sp., Pg. *gafa*, boat-hook. A barbed fishing-spear; a hooked stick for landing large fish; a spar to extend the top of a fore-and-aft sail.—*vt.* To seize with a gaff.

Gag, *vt.* App. imitative of the sound of choking. To apply a gag to.—*n.* Something put into the mouth to ensure silence.

Gage, *n.* O.F. *g(u)age*. WAGE. ENGAGE. MORTGAGE. A pledge.—*vt.* To pledge.

Gain, *vt.* F. *gagner*, O.F. *gaaignier*—O.H.G. **weidinjan*, to pasture, to forage or hunt, f. *weida* (Ger. *weide*, pasture), pasture, fodder, foraging, hunting. To obtain; to obtain as profit; to earn (a livelihood); to persuade; to reach, arrive at.—*vi.* To make a profit; to improve *in*.—*n.* Profit; an increase.

Gain'ly, *a.* With -LY[1] f. dial. *Gain*, straight—O.N. *gegn*, straight, helpful, cogn. with O.E. *gegn* (in composition). AGAIN. GAINSAY. Graceful, shapely.

Gainsay', *vt.* *Gain-* (O.E. *gegn-*, *géan-*), against. AGAIN. GAINLY. To deny; to contradict; to speak or act against, oppose.

Gait, *n.* A use of dial. *Gate*, way, path—O.N. (and Sw.) *gata*. Cf. Ger. *gasse*, lane. GAUNTLET.[2] Manner of walking.

Gai'ter, *n.* F. *guêtre* of unknown orig. A covering for the lower leg.

Ga'la, *n.* F. *gala*—It. *gala*. Conn. with GALLANT. A festive occasion.

Gal'axy, *n.* O.F. *galaxie*—L. *galaxias*—G. *galaxias*, f. *gala*, milk. The Milky Way; a brilliant assemblage or crowd.

Gale, *n.* Orig. obscure. A strong wind.

Gall, *n.*[1] O.E. *gealla*, corresp. to M.Du. *galle*, O.H.G. *galla* (Ger. *galle*). Cogn. with G. *cholē*, L. *fel*; perh. also with O.E. *geolo*, YELLOW. FELON. MELANCHOLY. Bile; the gall-bladder; bitterness of spirit, rancour.

Gall, *n.*[2] O.E. *gealla*, a sore on a horse, corresp. to Du. *gal*, M.L.G., M.H.G. *galle*. (Prob. influenced by O.F. *galler*, *galer*, to rub, scratch, gall, of unknown orig.). A sore produced by rubbing.—*vt.* To make sore or injure by rubbing; to vex, harass.

Gall, *n.*[3] F. *galle*—L. *galla*. An excrescence produced by insects on a tree, esp. on the oak.

Gal'lant, *a.* F. *galant*, pres.pple. of O.F. *galer*, to make merry, make a show, perh. f. O.H.G. *wallôn*, to wander, go on pilgrimage. GALA. Finely dressed; splendid, grand; of a ship, noble, stately; chivalrous; attentive to ladies (us. *gallant'*).—*n.* A man of fashion; one who pays court to ladies (sometimes *gallant'*).—**Gal'lant**LY[2] (also as above **Gallant'ly**) *adv.*—**Gal'lant**RY, *n.*

Gal'leon, *n.* Sp. *galeon*—Med.L. *galea*, GALLEY. A large Spanish vessel.

Gal'lery, *n.* F. *galerie* of unknown orig. A long narrow platform outside a building; a platform projecting from an inner wall; a long narrow apartment or passage; an apartment in which works of art are exhibited.

Gal'ley, *n.* O.F. *galie*—Med.L. *galea*. Orig. unknown. A low vessel propelled by sails and oars; the cooking-room in a ship.

Gal'lipot, *n.* Poss. a pot such as was imported in GALLEYS. A small glazed pot.

Gal'lon, *n.* O.N.F. *galon*, O.F. *jalon*, app. cogn. with F. *jale*, bowl, of unknown orig. A liquid measure containing four quarts.

Gal'lop, *vi.* O.F. *galoper*, of uncertain orig. To go at a gallop.—*n.* O.F. *galop*. A movement by leaps; a ride at this pace.

Gal'lows, *n.* M.E. *galwes*, pl.—O.E. *galga*, *gealga*, sing. = O.H.G. *galgo* (Ger. *galgen*). An apparatus for inflicting death by hanging.

Gal'op, *n.* F. *galop*. GALLOP. A lively dance.—*vi.* To dance a galop.

Galore', *adv.* Ir. *go leór*, to sufficiency. In abundance.—*n.* Abundance, plenty.

Galosh', *n.* F. *galoche*—G. *kalopous*, shoemaker's last, f. *kalon*, wood (only in *pl.*, logs) + *pous*, FOOT. An india-rubber over-shoe.

Gal'vanism, *n.* F. *galvanisme*, f. Luigi *Galvani* (1737-1798). Electricity developed by chemical action.—**Galvan'**IC, *a.*—**Gal'vani**ZE, *vt.* To apply galvanism to; to stimulate; to coat with metal, properly by galvanism.

Gam'bit, *n.* Sp. *gambito*—It. *gambetto*, a tripping up, f. *gamba*, leg, of doubtful orig. GAMBOL. GAMMON.[1] JAMB. A chess opening involving the loss of a pawn.

Gam'ble, *vi.* Prob. a dial. survival of a form of M.E. *gamenen*, O.E. *gamenian*, to sport, play, f. *gamen*, GAME. To play games of chance for high stakes.—**Gam'bl**ER, *n.*

Gamboge', *n.* A corr. of *Cambodia* in Assam. A gum-resin used as a yellow pigment.

Gam'bol, *n.* F. *gambade*, leap—It. *gambata*, f. *gamba*, leg. GAMBIT. A leap in dancing or sporting; a caper.—*vi.* To caper.

Game, *n.* O.E. *gamen*, sport. Common Teut. GAMBLE. Jest, fun; an amusement, pastime; a contest by way of amusement; a scheme, plan of action; wild animals or birds such as are hunted, &c.; their flesh.—*a.* Plucky, spirited. —*vi.* To gamble.—**Game**'SOME, *a.* Sportive. —**Game**'STER, *n.* A gambler.

Gam'mon, *n.*[1] O.N.F. *gambon* (F. *jambon*), ham, f. *gambe* (F. *jambe*)=It. *gamba*. GAMBIT. The bottom piece of a flitch of bacon.

Gam'mon, *n.*[2] App. orig. thieves' slang. Humbug, nonsense.—*vt.* To humbug, deceive.

Gam'ut, *n.* Med.L. *gamma* (the third Greek letter), *ut*, two musical symbols. The series of musical notes; the range of a voice, &c.

Gan'der, *n.* O.E. *ganra*, *gandra*. Cf. L.G., Du. *gander*, M.L.G. *ganre*. Cogn. with GANNET. The male of the goose.

Gang, *n.* O.E. *gang*, a going, conn. with O.E. (and Comm. Teut.) *gangan*, to go. A company, band.—**Gang**'ER, *n.* One in charge of a gang of workmen.

Gan'glion, *n.* G. *gagglion*, a tumour near tendons, used also to denote the complex nerve-centres. A knot on a nerve forming a centre for nerve fibres; a nerve-nucleus.

Gan'grene, *n.* L. *gangraena*—G. *gaggraina*. A mortification of part of the body.—*vi.* To suffer mortification.—*vt.* To cause mortification in.—**Gan'gren**OUS, *a.*

Gang'way, *n.* O.E. *gangweg*, f. *gang* (GANG) + *weg*, WAY. Formerly, a road or passage. A passage between rows of seats; a means of passing from a ship to the shore.

Gan'net, *n.* O.E. *ganot*. Cf. L.G. *gante*, Du. *gent*. Cogn. with GANDER. The solan.

Gaol, *n.* See JAIL.

Gap, *n.* O.N. *gap*, conn. with *gapa*, to GAPE. A breach or opening; a vacant space.

Gape, *vi.* O.N. *gapa* = M.Du. *gapen*, M.H.G. and Ger. *gaffen*. To open the mouth wide, yawn; to stare *at* with open mouth; to open, split.—*n.* A yawn; an open-mouthed stare.

Garage', *n.* F., f. *garer*, to shelter, of Teut. orig. Cf. O.E. *werian*, to defend, conn. with *wer*, WEIR. A shelter for motor-cars.

Garb, *n.* It. *garbo*, grace, elegance, of Teut. orig. Cf. O.H.G. *garawi*. GEAR. Fashion of dress, dress.—*vt.* To clothe, dress.

Gar'bage, *n.* Orig. obscure. Prob. f. A.F. The offal of an animal; refuse, filth.

Gar'ble, *vt.* It. *garbellare*, to sift—Arab. *gharbala*. To make selections from unfairly; to mutilate so as to misrepresent.

Gar'den, *n.* O.N.F. *gardin* (Central F. *jardin*) —Teut. **gardo-z* (O.E. *geard*, O.N. *garthr*, enclosure). Cogn. with L. *hortus*. COHORT. GARTH. ORCHARD. ORTOLAN. YARD.[1] An enclosed piece of ground used for growing flowers, vegetables, &c. — *vi.* To work in a garden.—**Gar'den**ER, *n.*

Gar'gle, *vt.* F. *gargouiller*, f. *gargouille*, throat, of doubtful orig. To wash (the mouth, &c.) with a liquid held suspended in the throat. —*n.* A liquid used for this.

Gar'goyle, *n.* O.F. *gargouille* (see prec.), app. from the water passing through the mouths of the figures. A grotesque water-spout in animal or human form.

Ga'rish, *a.* Poss. conn. with obs. *Gaure*, to stare, of doubtful orig. Showy, gaudy; glaring.

Gar'land, *n.* O.F. *garlande*, of uncertain orig. A wreath of flowers, &c.

Gar'lic, *n.* O.E. *gárléac*, 'spear-leek', f. *gár*, spear (= O.H.G. *gêr* (Ger. *ger*)) + *léac*, LEEK. A plant with a pungent smell and taste.

Gar'ment, *n.* O.F. *garniment*, equipment, vestments, f. *garnir*. GARNISH. An article of dress.

Gar'ner, *n.* O.F. *gerner*, *grenier*, storehouse —L. *grānārium*, GRANARY. A granary.

Gar'net, *n.* O.F. **gernat*, *grenat* — Med.L. *grānātum*, poss. a use (from resemblance of colour) of L. *grānātum*, POMEGRANATE. A red precious stone.

Gar'nish, *vt.* O.F. *garniss-*, lengthened stem of *garnir* (*warnir*), to fortify, to provide, prob. of Teut. orig. and cogn. with WARN. To decorate, adorn.—*n.* An embellishment added to a dish.—**Gar'niture**, *n.* F. *garniture*. Furniture, appurtenances; ornament, embellishment, trimming; apparel.

Gar'ret, *n.* O.F. *garite*, *guerite*, watch-tower (F. *guérite*, sentry-box), conn. with *garir*. (See next.) An attic.

Gar'rison, *n.* O.F. *garison*, defence, provision, f. *garir*, to defend, to furnish, of Teut. orig. A body of troops stationed in a fort or other place.—*vt.* To put a garrison in.

Gar(r)otte', *n.* Sp. *garrote* = F. *garrot*, stick (a means of tightening a cord), of obscure orig. Capital punishment or robbery by throttling. —*vt.* To put to death or rob thus.

Gar'rulous, *a.* L. *garrulus* (f. *garrire*, to chatter) + -OUS. AUGUR. Talkative.—**Garru'l**ITY, *n.*

Gar'ter, *n.* O.F. *gartier*, *jarretier* (F. *jarretière*), f. *garet*, *jaret*, the bend of the knee, perh. Celtic. A band to support a stocking.

Garth, *n.* O.N. *garthr*. GARDEN. A small piece of enclosed ground beside a house.

Gas, *n.* Invented (on the model of G. *chaos*, CHAOS) by the Dutch chemist Van Helmont. In F. *gaz*. An elastic fluid such as air; gas burnt for heating or giving light.—**Ga's**EOUS, *a.*—**Gasom'eter**, *n.* F. *gazomètre*, f. *gaz* + *mètre*, G. *metron*, measure. A tank for storing (app. orig. for measuring) gas.

Gasconade', *n.* F. *gasconnade*, f. *Gascon*, Gascon, boaster (boasting being a Gascon characteristic). Boasting.—*vi.* To boast.

Gash, *vt.* For obs. *Garse*—O.F. *garser*, to scarify, repg. *caraxāre*, L.L. form of G. *charassein*. CHARACTER. To slash.—*n.* A slash.

Gasp, *vi.* O.N. *geispa* (**geipsa*), to yawn. Cf. *geip*, idle talk. To catch the breath with open mouth.—*n.* The action or an act of gasping.

Gas'tric, *a.* G. *gastēr*, *gast(e)ros*, stomach + -IC. Of the stomach. — **Gastron'omy**, *n.* G. *gastronomia*, after *astronomia*, ASTRONOMY. The art of delicate eating.

Gate, *n.* O.E. *geat*, corresp. to Old Fris. *gat*, hole, opening, O.S. *gat*, eye of a needle. An opening in a wall; a barrier for closing it; a means of regulating the flow of water.

Gath'er, *vt.* O.E. *gad(e)rian* = M.L.G. *gadern*, M.H.G. *gatern*. Cf. O.E. *tó-gædere*, TOGETHER. To bring together; to collect, to acquire; to pucker; to infer, deduce.—*vi.* To come together, to collect; to swell and develop pus.— *n.* In *pl.*, a puckered part of a dress.

Gat'ling, *n.* From the inventor, Dr. R. J. *Gatling*. A form of machine gun.

Gaud, *n.* Perh. an A.F. n. f. *gaudir*, L. *gaudēre*, to rejoice. JOY. A showy ornament. —**Gaud'**Y,[2] *a.* Showy.—**Gaud'**ILY,[2] *adv.*

Gauge, *n.* O.N.F. *gauge*, of unknown orig. A fixed or standard measure; the distance between the rails of a railway, &c.; an instrument for measuring; a contrivance attached to a boiler, &c., to show the height of its contents; relative position (of a ship) in regard to the wind.—*vt.* To measure.

Gaunt, *a.* Orig. unknown. Very lean; desolate looking.

Gaunt'let, *n.*[1] F. *gantelet*, dim. of *gant*, glove, app. of Teut. orig. A steel glove worn with armour; a glove covering part of the arm.

Gaunt'let, *n.*[2] Corr. of *gantlope* (now rarely used)—Sw. *gatlopp*, earlier *gatu-lop*, f. *gata*, lane (GAIT) + *lopp*, course. A punishment in which the culprit had to run between two rows of men who struck at him.

Gauze, *n.* F. *gaze*, of uncertain orig. A thin transparent fabric of cotton, wire, &c.

Gavotte', *n.* F., f. Mod.Pr. *gavoto*, dance of the Gavots, *i.e.* the natives of the Alps. A lively dance; music written for it.

Gawk, *n.* Perh. f. dial. *Gawk*, left, of doubtful orig. An awkward person.—**Gawk'**Y,[2] *a.*

Gay, *a.* F. *gai*, of doubtful orig. Merry, sportive; brilliant; charming, attractive; dissipated.—**Gai'**LY,[2] *adv.*—**Gai'**ETY, *n.*

Gaze, *vi.* Orig. unknown. To look earnestly or intently.—*n.* Such a look.

Gazelle', *n.* F. *gazelle*—Arab. *ghazāl*. A small soft-eyed antelope.

Gazette', *n.* F. *gazette*, news-sheet—It. *gazzetta*, said to have been first issued at Venice, app. so called from a Venetian coin of that name, perh. the price paid for reading the news. An official newspaper.—*vt.* To be the subject of an announcement in a gazette.—**Gazett**EER', *n.* A writer in a gazette; a geographical dictionary.

Gear, *n.* M.E. *gere*, prob. f. O.N. *gervi*, apparel = O.S. *garewi*, O.H.G. *garawi*. GARB. Apparel; armour, arms; goods; apparatus; wheels working one on another; that which connects a source of power with its work.—*vt.* To connect with the work.

Gel'atin(e), *n.* F. *gélatine*—It. *gelatina*, f. *gelata*, jelly—L. *gelāta*. JELLY. The substance forming the basis of the jellies into which certain animal tissues are converted by treatment with hot water.—**Gelat'in**OUS, *a.*

Geld, *vt.* O.N. *gelda*, f. *geldr*, barren = Old Sw. *galder*, O.H.G. *galt*. To castrate.—**Geld'ing**, *n.* O.N. *geldingr*, f. *geldr*. A castrated horse.

Gel'id, *a.* L. *gelidus*, f. *gelāre*. JELLY. Very cold.

Gem, *n.* F. *gemme*—L. *gemma*, bud, gem. A precious stone, esp. when cut and polished.—*vt.* To adorn with or as with gems.

Gen'der, *n.* O.F. *gen(d)re*—L. *genus*. GENUS. A distinction in words to express differences in sex.

Geneal'ogy, *n.* O.F. *gene(a)logie*—G. *genealogia*, tracing of descent, f. *genea*, race (root *gen-*. GENUS). -LOGY. An account of one's descent from an ancestor or ancestors.—**Genealog'**ICAL, *a.*—**Geneal'og**IST, *n.*

Gen'eral, *a.* O.F. *general*—L. *generālis*, f. *genus*. GENUS. Including, affecting, all or nearly all; prevalent, usual; applicable to a variety of cases; not restricted to one department; miscellaneous; dealing with, comprising, main elements only; ranking above a colonel. —*n.* A general officer.—**Generalis'simo**, *n.* It., superl. of *generale*, general, f. *generālis*. A supreme commander.—**General'**ITY, *n.* A being general; a general principle or statement; the greater part.—**Gen'eral**IZE, *vt.* To reduce to general laws.—*vi.* To draw general conclusions. — **Generaliz**A'TION, *n.*—**Gen'eral**LY,[2] *adv.*—**Gen'eral**SHIP, *n.* The office of a general; military skill.

Gen'erate, *vt.* L. *generāre*, *generātum*, to beget, &c., f. *genus*. GENUS. ENGENDER. To bring into being, produce.—**Gener**A'TION, *n.* A bringing into being; the offspring of the same parent or parents; the body of persons born about the same time, the period covered by their lives.—**Gen'er**ATIVE, *a.*

Gener'ic, *a.* From *gener-* (stem of *genus*. GENUS) + -IC. Also **Gener'**ICAL, *a.* Belonging to, characteristic of, a genus or class, general.—**Gener'ical**LY,[2] *adv.*

Gen'erous, *a.* F. *généreux*—L. *generōsus*, of good birth, noble-minded, f. *genus*. GENUS. Noble-minded; bountiful, liberal; copious; of wine, full of strength.—**Generos'**ITY, *n.*

Gen'esis, *n.* L. *Genesis*—G. *genesis*, origin, creation, f. root *gen-*. GENUS. The first book of the Old Testament relating the Creation; origin; mode of formation or production.

Gene'va, *n.* Du. *genever*—O.F. *genevre* (F. *genièvre*)—L. *jūniperus*, JUNIPER. GIN.[2] A spirit flavoured with the juice of juniper berries, made in Holland and hence called also *Hollands*.

Ge'nial, *a.* L. *geniālis*, pertaining to generation, jovial, f. *genius*. GENIUS. Conducive to growth, mild; sympathetically cheerful, jovial.—**Genial'**ITY, *n.*—**Ge'nial**LY,[2] *adv.*

Ge'nie, *n.*; *pl.* **Ge'nii**. F. *génie* (L. *genius*, GENIUS), used, from similarity of sound and sense, to translate Arab. *jinnī*. A demon or goblin of Arabian tales.

Gen'ital, *a.* L. *genitālis*, f. *gignĕre*, *genitum*, to beget, f. root *gen-*. GENUS. PROGENITOR. Pertaining to animal generation.

Gen'itive, *a.* and *n.* L. *genetīvus*, of or belonging to birth, f. *gignĕre*. (See prec.) A noun case denoting a source, possessor, &c.

Ge'nius, *n.*; *pl.* **Ge'nii**, **Ge'niuses**. L. *genius*, tutelar deity, fondness for enjoyment, wit, talent, f. root *gen-*. GENUS. GENIAL. A tutelary deity; a demon or spirit; prevalent feeling, taste, &c.; prevailing character or spirit; quality of mind; the highest intellectual power, a man with such power.

Genteel', *a.* A re-adoption of F. *gentil*. For previous adoption see GENTLE. Elegant, fashionable (always sarcastically or playfully).

Gen'tian, *n.* L. *gentiāna*, said to be named after an Illyrian King *Gentius*. A mountain plant, usually with blue flowers.

Gen'tile, *a.* L. *gentīlis* (GENTLE), in Eccles. L. opposed to Jewish or Christian. Of a race other than the Jewish; of a word, indicating a country or nation.—*n.* One of a race other than the Jewish; a heathen.

Gen'tle, *a.* O.F. *gentil*, high-born, noble (in F., elegant, nice)—L. *gentīlis*, belonging to the same race, f. *gens*, *gentis*, race, f. root *gen-*. GENUS. GENTEEL. GENTILE. JAUNTY. Well-born; of good descent or position; noble, courteous; moderate in action, intensity, &c., mild, not rough or violent.—**Gentil'**ITY, *n.* Gentle birth; social superiority.—**Gen'tleman**, *n.* A man of gentle birth; such a person attached to the household of a sovereign, &c.; one of chivalrous instincts and fine feelings; one of high social standing or having manners indicative of this; a courteous synonym for 'man'.—**Gen'tleman**LIKE, **Gen'tleman**LY,[1] *aa.*—**Gen'tle**NESS, *n.*—**Gen'tlewoman**, *n.* A woman of gentle birth or breeding.—**Gent'**LY,[2] *adv.*—**Gent'ry**, *n.* App. alteration of obs. *Gentrice*—O.F. *genter-*

ise, var. of *gentelise*, f. *gentil*. The class immediately below the nobility; people, folks.
Genuflex'ion, *n*. Med.L. *genūflexio, genūflexiōnis*, n. of action f. *genūflectĕre*, to kneel, f. L. *genū*, knee + *flectĕre*, to bend. Kneeling.
Gen'uine, *a*. L. *genuinus*, native, natural, f. root *gen-*. GENUS. Of the true stock; not spurious; real, true; properly so called.
Ge'nus, *n*.; *pl*. **Gen'era**. L. *genus, generis*, descent, origin, race, kind = Skr. *jánas*, G. *genos*, f. Aryan root *gen-*, to produce. CONGENER. DEGENERATE. ENGINE. GENITAL. GENIUS. GENTLE. KIN. A class including subordinate classes; a kind, tribe, &c.
Geod'esy, *n*. F. *géodésie*—G. *geōdaisia*, f. *geō-*, GEO- + *daiein*, to divide. The branch of mathematics dealing with the figure and area of the earth or of large portions of it.
Geog'raphy, *n*. F. *géographie* — G. *geōgraphia*, f. *geō-*, GEO- + *-graphia*, writing, f. *graphein*, to write. GRAPHIC. The science of the external features of the earth; a treatise on this science.—**Geog'raph**ER, *n*.—**Geograph'**IC, **Geograph'**ICAL, *aa*.
Geol'ogy. *n*. GEO- and -LOGY. The science of the condition and history of the earth's crust. —**Geolog'**IC, -ICAL, *aa*.—**Geol'og**IST, *n*.
Geom'etry, *n*. F. *géométrie*—G. *geōmetria*, f. *geō-*, GEO- + *-metria*, measuring, f. *metre-ein*, to measure. The science of the relations and properties of magnitudes in space, as lines, surfaces, &c. — **Geom'eter**, *n*. G. *-metrēs*, measurer. One who studies or is skilled in geometry. — **Geomet'r**IC, **Geomet'r**ICAL, *aa*.—**Geometr**IC'IAN, *n*.
Gera'nium, *n*. L. *geranium*—G. *geranion*, f. *geranos*, crane. A genus of plants bearing a fruit resembling a crane's bill.
Germ, *n*. F. *germe* — L. *germen, germinis*, sprig, sprout. The rudiment of a new organism; a microbe; a rudiment.—**Ger'micide**, *n*. -CIDE (1). A preparation for destroying disease-germs.—**Ger'min**ATE,[3] *vi*. and *t*. To sprout, cause to sprout.—**Germin**A'TION, *n*.
Ger'man, **Ger'mane**, *a*. O.F. *germain*—L. *germānus*, having the same parents, conn. with *germen*. (See prec.) Having the same parents, or being the child of a brother- or sister-german of either of one's parents (in these senses only in *brother-, sister-, cousin-german*); relevant, pertinent (in this sense *germane*).
Ger'und, *n*. L. *gerundium*, app. f. *gerundus* = *gerendus*, to be done, gerundive of *gerĕre*. (See next.) A verbal noun.—**Gerun'd**IVE, *a*. As *n*., a verbal adjective denoting necessity or fitness.
Gest, *n*. O.F. *geste, jeste*, action, exploit, romance—L. *gesta*, actions, exploits, neut. pl. of *gestus*, pa.pple. of *gerĕre*, to carry, carry on, do. CONGEST. JEST. In *pl*. and *sing*., exploits, notable deeds; in *sing*., a story, tale.
Gesta'tion, *n*. L. *gestātio, gestātiōnis*, n. of action f. *gestāre, gestātum*, freq. of *gerĕre*. (See prec.) The carrying of young, the being carried, in the womb.
Gestic'ulate, *vi*. L. *gesticulāri, gesticulātus*, f. *gesticulus*, dim. of *gestus*, gesture, bearing, f. *gerĕre (se)*, to bear (oneself). GEST. To make lively motions with the limbs or body, esp. in speaking.—**Gesticul**A'TION, *n*.—**Ges'ture**, *n*. Med.L. *gestūra*, n. of action f. *gerĕre*, Movement of the body or limbs as an expression of feeling; such a movement.
Get, *vt*. O.N. *geta*, to get, beget = O.E. *-gitan, -gietan* (BEGET. FORGET), Goth. *(bi)gitan*. O.Teut. **getan*, cogn. with L. *pre-hendĕre*, to seize, *praeda (prae-henda)*, booty. PREHENSILE. PREY. To obtain, procure, earn, acquire; to cause to go or come; to bring into a position or state; to induce.—*vi*. To succeed in going or coming; to reach, attain; to become.
Gew'gaw, *n*. Orig. uncertain. A toy, a bauble.
Gey'ser, *n*. Icelandic *Geysir*, the name of a hot spring, conn. with *geysa*, to gush. An intermittent hot spring throwing up a column of water; an apparatus for heating water.
Ghast'ly, *a*. With -LY[1] f. obs. *Gast*, to alarm—O.E. *gǽstan*, conn. with *gást*, GHOST. AGHAST. Horrible; shocking; death-like.
Gher'kin, *n*. Du. **gurkkijn* (now *gurkje*), dim. of *gurk*, more us. *agurk*, cucumber, perh. of Slavonic orig. A small cucumber.
Ghet'to, *n*. It. *ghetto*, perh. abb. of *borghetto*, dim. of *borgo*, of Teut. orig. and = BOROUGH. A Jews' quarter in a city.
Ghost, *n*. O.E. *gást*. Common W. Germanic. Spirit; a disembodied spirit.—**Ghost'**LY,[1] *a*.
Ghoul, *n*. Arab. *ghūl*, f. a root meaning 'to seize'. A being preying on dead bodies.
Gi'ant, *n*. M.E. *geant*—O.F. *géant*—L. *gigās, gigantis*—G. *gigas, gigantos*. A human being of superhuman stature.—**Gi'ant**ESS, *n*.
Gib'ber, *vi*. Imitative. To speak rapidly and inarticulately; to talk nonsense.—**Gib'berish**, *n*. After names of languages in *-ish*. Unintelligible speech, jargon.
Gib'bet, *n*. O.F. *gibet*, gallows, in early use, staff, cudgel, dim. of *gibe*, staff, club. JIB, *n*.[2] A post with an arm from which the bodies of criminals were hung after execution.—*vt*. To execute by hanging; to hang on a gibbet.
Gib'bous, *a*. L. *gibbus*, hump + -OUS. Convex; said of the moon when the illuminated part is between a semicircle and a circle.
Gibe, **Jibe**, *vi*. Perh. f. O.F. *giber*, app. 'to handle roughly in sport'. To utter taunts, flout.—*vt*. To taunt, flout.—*n*. A taunt, flout.
Gib'let, *n*. O.F. *gibelet*, app., a stew of game. In *pl*., the portions of a goose, &c. (the liver, feet, &c.) that are removed before cooking.
Gid'dy, *a*. O.E. *gidig*, insane, var. of **gydig*, app. f. O.Teut. type **guthom*, GOD, hence 'possessed by a god'. Having a sensation of swimming in the head, dizzy; frivolous, inconstant.—**Gid'di**LY,[2] *adv*.—**Gid'di**NESS, *n*.
Gift, *n*. O.E. *gift*, conn. with *giefan*, to GIVE. A giving, bestowal; something given; a faculty, power. — *vt*. To endow or present *with*.—
Gift'ed, *ppl.a*. Well endowed by nature.
Gig, *n*. Perh. imitative. Formerly, something that whirls, as a whipping-top. A light two-wheeled carriage; a light narrow boat.
Gigan'tic, *a*. L. *gigās, gigantis*, GIANT + -IC. Like a giant in size; huge, enormous.
Gig'gle, *vi*. Imitative. Cf. Du. *giggelen*, M.H.G. *gickeln* (Ger. *kichern*). To laugh continuously in a half-suppressed way and foolishly or uncontrollably.—*n*. Such a laugh.
Gild, *vt*. O.E. *gyldan*, f. O.Teut. type **gulthom*, GOLD. To put a thin layer of gold upon. —**Gilt**, *ppl.a*. Gilded. As *n*., the layer of gold put on in gilding.
Gill, *n*.[1] Of obscure orig. The breathing organ [in fishes.
Gill, *n*.[2] O.F. *gille, gelle* (in Med.L. *gillo*), a vessel or measure for wine. A fourth of a pint.
Gil'lyflower, *n*. Corr. of O.F. *girofle, gilofre*, CLOVE.[2] The clove-scented pink.
Gim'bal, *n*. Formerly *gimmal*—O.F. *gemel*, a twin—L. *gemellus*, dim. of *geminus*, twin. In *pl*., a contrivance, usually consisting of a pair of rings, for keeping a compass, &c., suspended horizontally.

Gim'crack, *n.* Of doubtful orig. A trumpery article, a toy.—*a.* Trivial, trumpery.
Gim'let, *n.* O.F. *guimbelet*, a dim. of the word (not recorded in the Romance langs.) appearing in Eng. as WIMBLE. A boring tool terminating in a pointed screw.
Gin, *n.*[1] Shortened f. O.F. *engin*. ENGINE. A snare, trap; a kind of crane; a machine for separating cotton from its seeds.
Gin, *n.*[2] Abb. of GENEVA. A British spirit made originally in imitation of the Dutch.
Gin'ger, *n.* O.F. *gimgibre*, *gingimbre* (F. *gingembre*)—L.L. *gingiber*, earlier *zingiberi*—G. *ziggiberis*, conn. with or f. Skr. *çringa-vēra*, app. 'horn-shaped' (from the horn-like form of the root), f. *çringa*, horn + *vēra*, body. The root of a tropical plant with a hot taste.
Gin'gerly, *adv.* Poss. (with -LY[2]) f. O.F. *gensor*, comp. of *gent*, well-born, pretty, delicate (L. *genitus*, born, pa.pple. of *gignĕre*. GENITAL), used also as pos., pretty, delicate. In early use, elegantly, daintily. Cautiously; with an appearance of reluctance or distaste.
Gip'sy, **Gyp'sy**, *n.* Corrupted f. M.E. *Egypcien* (now *Egyptian*), a native of Egypt. One of a wandering race of Hindu origin formerly believed to have come from Egypt.
Giraffe', *n.* Through F. f. Arab. *zarāfah*. A ruminant quadruped with a very long neck.
Gird, *v.*[1]*t.* O.E. *gyrdan* = O.H.G. *gurten* (Ger. *gürten*), O.N. *gyrtha*. O.Teut. root *gurd-*. GIRTH. To put a belt round (the waist); to secure (clothing, &c.) thus; to encircle, enclose. —**Gird'**ER, *n.* From the *v.* in obs. sense 'to tie tightly, confine'. A main beam.—**Gir'dle**, *n.* O.E. *gyrdel*. A belt.—*vt.* To surround.
Gird, *v.*[2]*i.* Orig. unknown. To jest or gibe *at*.—*n.* A gibe.
Girl, *n.* Orig. obscure. A female child; a young unmarried woman.
Girth, *n.* O.N. *gjörth*, girdle, girth = Goth. *gairda*, girdle. O.Teut root *gerd-* = *gurd-*. GIRD.[1] A belt put round a horse to secure a saddle, &c.; measurement round an object.
Gist, *n.* O.F. *gist*, 3rd sing. pres. indic. of *gesir* (L. *jacēre*), to lie, whence *gesir en*, to depend on, consist in. JOIST. The real ground; the substance, essence.
Give, *vt.* O.E. *giefan*. Common Teut. GIFT. To bestow, confer, hand over, impart, commit, deliver; to allot, assign, attribute; to yield, supply; to cause to have; to concede.—*vi.* To yield, give way.—*n.* Yielding, elasticity.
Giz'zard, *n.* O.F. *giser*, *gezier* (F. *gésier*), said to be f. L. *gigĕria*, cooked entrails of poultry. The second stomach of birds.
Gla'cial, *a.* F. *glacial*—L. *glaciālis*, icy, f. *glacies*, ice. Icy, cold; consisting of, characterized by ice; of, produced by, glaciers.—**Glac'ier**, *n.* F. *glacier*, f. *glace*, ice, f. *glacies*. A river of ice in a high mountain valley.—**Glac'is**, *n.* F., orig., a place slippery with ice, conn. with O.F. *glacier*, to slip, f. *glacies*. The outer slope of a fortification.
Glad, *a.* O.E. *glæd* = O.S. *glad*, O.N. *glathr*, bright, joyous. Happy; marked with, imparting, joy or delight.—*vt.* To make glad.—**Glad'**LY,[2] *adv.*—**Glad'den**,[2] *vt.*—**Glad'**NESS, *n.*—**Glad'**SOME, *a.*
Glade, *n.* Orig. obscure. A clear space in a wood.
Glad'iator, *n.* L. *gladiātor*, f. *gladius*, sword. A fighter at public shows.
Gladi'olus, *n.* L., dim. of *gladius*. (See prec.) A flowering plant with sword-shaped leaves.
Glam'our, *n.* Orig. Scotch, a corr. of GRAMMAR. Cf. GRAMARYE. Magic, enchantment.
Glance, *vi.* Poss. a nasalized form of O.F. *glacier*. GLACIS. To glide off something struck; *to glance at*, *upon*, to allude to; to flash, gleam; to cast a quick look; to look quickly *over*.—*vt.* *To glance one's eye*, &c., to look quickly.—*n.* A quick look; a flash, gleam.
Gland, *n.* F. *glande*, gland, tumour, O.F. *glandre*, **glandle*—L. *glandula*, in *pl.* glands of the throat, dim. of *glans*, *glandis*, acorn. An organ which separates certain constituents from the blood.—**Glan'dul**AR,[1] *a.*—**Glan'ders**, *n.pl.* O.F. *glandre*. A disease in horses with swellings beneath the jaw.
Glare, *vi.* M.E. *glaren* = M.Du., M.L.G. *glaren*. Prob. conn. with next. To shine very brightly; to look fixedly and fiercely.—*n.* Dazzling brightness; a glaring look.
Glass, *n.* O.E. *glæs* = O.S. *glas*, *gles*, O.H.G. (and Ger.) *glas*. Perh. f. O.Teut. *glă-*, weak grade of *glō-*, to shine. GLOW. A hard transparent substance; things made of it collectively; a glass vessel; the drink contained in a glass; a lens; a telescope; a vessel for measuring time by the falling of sand; in *pl.*, spectacles.—**Glas'**SY,[2] *a.*
Glau'cous, *a.* L. *glaucus* (f. G. *glaukos*) + -OUS. Of a pale green or greyish blue colour.
Glaze, *vt.* M.E. *glasen*, f. *glas*, GLASS. To furnish with glass; to put a glaze on; to polish. —*n.* A vitreous substance applied to pottery; a transparent coating; a glossy surface. —**Gla'**ZIER, *n.* One who glazes windows.
Gleam, *n.* O.E. *glǽm*. O.Teut. root *gleim-*. GLIMMER. GLIMPSE. A subdued transient beam of light.—*vi.* To emit gleams.
Glean, *vi.* and *t.* O.F. *glener*, *glainer*—L.L. *glenāre*, of unknown orig. To gather or pick up after the reapers.—**Glean'**ER, *n.*
Glebe, *n.* L. *glaeba*, clod, soil. The soil; a portion of land assigned to a clergyman.
Glee, *n.* O.E. *glíw*, *gléo*, mirth, music = O.N. *glý*, mirth. A musical composition for three or more voices; mirth, joy.—**Glee'**FUL, *a.*—**Glee'**SOME, *a.*
Glen, *n.* Gael. *glenn* = Welsh *glyn*. A mountain valley, us. the course of a stream.
Glib, *a.* Cf. obs. *glibbery*, slippery, corresp. to Du. *glibberig*, Late M.L.G. *glibberich*. Fluent in utterance.—**Glib'**LY,[2] *adv.*
Glide, *vi.* O.E. *glídan*. Common W. Germanic. To pass smoothly and continuously or quietly and stealthily.—*n.* The act.
Glim'mer, *vi.* O.E. **glimorian*, a freq. f. *glim-*, weak grade of *gleim-*. GLEAM. To shine faintly.—*n.* A faint or wavering light.
Glimpse, *vi.* M.E. *glymsen* = M.H.G. *glimsen*, f. *glim-*. (See prec.) To glimmer.—*vt.* To catch a glimpse of.—*n.* A flash; a passing glance, a momentary view.
Glint, *vi.* Prob. altered f. dial. *Glent*, prob. of Scand. orig. To gleam.—*n.* A gleam.
Glis'ten, *vi.* O.E. *glisnian*, f. root of *glisian* in sim. sense = M.L.G. *glisen*. To glitter.
Glit'ter, *vi.* M.E. *gliteren*, prob. f. O.N. *glitra* = M.H.G., Ger. *glitzern*. To shine brightly but fitfully.—*n.* Glittering light, brilliance.
Gloa'ming, *n.* O.E. *glómung*, f. *glóm*, twilight, prob. f. *glō-*. GLOW. Evening twilight.
Gloat, *vi.* Orig. obscure. App. = M.H.G., Ger. *glotzen*, to stare. To gaze with unholy joy.
Globe, *n.* F. *globe*—L. *globus*, round body. A round body; the earth; a sphere bearing on the surface a map of the earth or the heavens. —**Glob'ule**, *n.* L. *globulus*, dim. of *globus*. A small round body; a drop; a small pill.—**Glob'ul**AR,[1] *a.* In the form of a globe.

Gloom, *vi.* M.E. *gloume.* Cf. L.G. *glum*, muddy, M.Du. *gloom*, foggy. GLUM. To look sullen or dejected; to lower; to look dark.—*n.* Darkness, obscurity; a state of depression.—**Gloom'**Y,[2] *a.*—**Gloom'**ILY,[2] *adv.*

Glo'ry, *n.* O.F. *glorie*—L. *glōria.* Merited praise, renown; a special distinction; resplendent beauty; the bliss of heaven; a state of exaltation; an aureole.—*vi.* To rejoice proudly.—**Glo'ri**FY, *vt.* To invest with glory; to extol.—**Glori**FICA'TION, *n.*—**Glo'ri**OUS, *a.*

Gloss, *n.*[1] A var. of GLOZE after L. *glossa*, G. *glōssa.* An interpretation of a word; a comment.—*v.*[1]*t.* To interpret; to comment upon; to be stated as the equivalent of (a word); to explain away.—**Glos'**SARY, *n.* A collection of glosses.

Gloss, *n.*[2] Cf. obs. Du. *gloos*, a glowing = M.H.G. *glos.* Superficial lustre.—*v.*[2]*t.* To put a gloss upon (often *fig.*).—**Glos'**SY,[2] *a.*

Glot'tis, *n.* G. *glōttis*, f. *glōtta*, var. of *glōssa*, tongue. GLOZE. The opening at the top of the windpipe.

Glove, *n.* O.E. *glóf* = O.N. *glófe.* A covering for the hand.—*vt.* To put a glove on.

Glow, *vi.* O.E. *glówan.* Cf. O.H.G. *gluoen* (Ger. *glühen*), O.N. *glóa.* O.Teut. root *glō-*, to shine. GLASS. GLOAMING. To emit light and heat without flame; to shine; to be brilliant in colouring; to be very hot; to feel bodily heat; to be ardent.—*n.* Shining heat; a sensation of bodily heat; warmth of colour; ardour.—**Glow'-worm**, *n.* An insect the female of which emits a green light.

Glow'er, *vi.* Orig. obscure. To look angrily, [scowl.

Gloze, *n.* O.F. *glose*—Med.L. *glōsa* (L. *glossa*), a difficult word, a gloss—G. *glōssa*, tongue, language, a difficult word. GLOSS.[1] POLYGLOT. A gloss; flattery, a flattering speech, &c.; a pretence.—*vi.* To comment; to talk speciously.—*vt.* To explain away.

Glue, *n.* O.F. *glu*, bird-lime—L.L. *glūs* (L. *glūten*), glue. CLAY. A substance used as a cement.—*vt.* To join with glue.

Glum, *a.* Conn. with GLOOM. Sullen, frown- [ing.

Glut, *vt.* Prob. f. O.F. *glut*, greedy. Cf. *glutun*, GLUTTON. To feed to repletion; to gratify to the full; to surfeit.—*n.* A glutting or being glutted; an excessive supply.

Glu'ten, *n.* L. *glūten*, *glūtinis*, GLUE. A viscid nitrogenous substance forming a constituent of wheat, &c.—**Glu'tin**OUS, *a.*

Glut'ton, *n.* O.F. *glutun*, *gluton*—L. *glūto*, *glūtōnis*, f. *glūtire*, to swallow. DEGLUTITION. One who eats to excess.—**Glut'ton**OUS, *a.*—**Glut'ton**Y,[1] *n.*

Glyc'erin(e), *n.* G. *glukeros*, sweet + chem. suff. *-in(e).* A sweet liquid got from fats.

Gnarled, *ppl.a.* First in Shakespeare, in a single passage (*Meas. for Meas.* II, ii, 116) for which the Folio of 1623 is the sole authority. App. a var. of (or quite possibly merely a misprint for) *knurled*, f. KNURL, *v.* Of a tree, covered with knots, distorted.

Gnash, *vi.* App. a var. of obs. *Gnast*, app. f. O.N. **gneista*, var. of *gnísta*, to gnash the teeth. To strike the teeth together.—*vt.* To strike (the teeth) together.

Gnat, *n.* O.E. *gnætt*, cogn. with Ger. dial. *gnatze.* A small two-winged fly.

Gnaw, *vt.* O.E. *gnagan*, corresp. to O.H.G. *gnagan* (Ger. *nagen*), O.N. *gnaga.* To wear away by biting; to corrode.

Gnome, *n.*[1] G. *gnōmē*, thought, opinion, in *pl.*, maxims. A pithy statement of a general truth, a maxim.—**Gno'mi**C, *a.*

Gnome, *n.*[2] F. *gnome*—Mod.L. *gnomus* (app. invented by Paracelsus). A diminutive spirit fabled to inhabit the interior of the earth.

Gno'mon, *n.* G. *gnōmōn*, one who knows, an interpreter, a gnomon, f. *gno-*, AGNOSTIC. PHYSIOGNOMY. The pin or plate which casts the shadow on a sun-dial.

Gnos'tic, *n.* G. *gnōstikos*, pertaining to knowledge, f. *gno-*. AGNOSTIC. Gen. in *pl.*, certain sects among the early Christians who claimed superior knowledge in spiritual matters.—*a.* Relating to knowledge or to the Gnostics.—**Gnos'tic**ISM, *n.*

Go, *vi.* O.E. *gán.* Common Teut. To move along; to be determined *by*; to be moving; to elapse; to turn out (well or ill), result; to depart; to break, to wear; to contribute to a result; to conduce, tend *to*; to become.—*n.* The action of going; energy, vigour.

Goad, *n.* O.E. *gád*, corresp. to Lombard *gaida*, arrow-head. A pointed rod for driving cattle.—*vt.* To prick with a goad.

Goal, *n.* Of doubtful orig. The terminal point of a race; a mark to be attained in a game; an object of effort or ambition.

Goat, *n.* O.E. *gát.* Common Teut. Cogn. with L. *haedus*, kid. A ruminant quadruped with long hair and horns.

Gob'bet, *n.* O.F. *gobet*, dim. of *gobe*, mouthful, lump, conn. with *gober*, to swallow. A lump of raw flesh or of half-digested food.

Gob'ble, *v.*[1]*t.* Prob. a vague formation on dial. *Gob*, mouthful of food, app. f. O.F. *gobe*. (See prec.) To eat hurriedly and noisily.

Gob'ble, *v.*[2]*i.* Imitative. Of a turkey-cock, to make its characteristic noise in the throat.

Gob'let, *n.* O.F. *gobelet*, dim. of *gobel*, cup, of uncertain orig. A drinking-cup.

Gob'lin, *n.* Obs. F. *gobelin*, perh. f. Med.L. *cobalus*, G. *kobalos*, rogue, in *pl.*, wicked sprites. A mischievous and ugly demon.

God, *n.* O.E. *god.* Common Teut. O.Teut. type **guthom.* GIDDY. A superhuman person; an idol; the Supreme Being.—**God'd**ESS, *n.*—**God'father (-mother)**, *nn.* A male (female) sponsor in baptism.—**God'child**, *n.* A person considered in relation to a godfather or godmother.—**God'**HEAD, *n.* The divine nature.—**God'**LESS, *a.*—**God'**LIKE, *a.*—**God'**LY,[1] *a.* Religious, pious.—**God'li**NESS, *n.*

Gof'fer, Gauf'fer, *vt.* F. *gaufrer*, to stamp figures on, f. *gaufre*, honeycomb, WAFER. To make wavy with heated irons; to emboss.

Gog'gle, *vi.* Perh. a freq. of an imitative **gog*, expressing oscillating motion. Cf. *jog.* Of the eyes, to project and roll.—*vt.* To turn (the eyes) from side to side unsteadily.—*n.* In *pl.*, a kind of spectacles to protect the eyes.—*a.* Of the eyes, protuberant and rolling.

Gold, *n.* O.E. *gold.* Common Teut. Prob. cogn. with O.E. *geolo*, YELLOW. O.Teut. type **gulthom.* GILD. A precious metal of a bright yellow colour; gold coin, wealth.—**Gold'**EN,[1] *a.*—**Gold'smith**, *n.* A worker in gold.

Golf, *n.* Doubtfully said to be f. Du. *kolf*, a club or bat. A game played over turf with a small ball driven by clubs.

Gon'dola, *n.* It. Orig. obscure. A light flat-bottomed Venetian boat.—**Gondol**IER', *n.*

Gong, *n.* Malay *gong.* Imitative. A metallic disk which resounds when struck.

Good, *a.* O.E. *gód.* Common Teut. An adjective of general commendation; commendable, excellent; right, proper; virtuous; kind; trustworthy, safe; fortunate; wholesome; efficient; adequate; valid.—*n.* That which is good;

well-being, profit; something desirable; in *pl.*, property, wares.—**Good**'LY,[1] *a.* Comely; considerable in size, &c.; admirable, excellent.—**Good**'NESS, *n.*—**Goodwill**', *n.* Favourable regard; cheerful acquiescence; heartiness; the privilege of trading as a recognized successor. —**Good**'Y,[2] *a.* Weakly or sentimentally good.

Good-bye', *int.* A contraction of *God be with you* (*ye*). Farewell.

Goose, *n.* O.E. *gós.* Common Teut. Cogn. with G. *chēn*, L. *anser* (**hanser*). A web-footed bird; a tailor's smoothing-iron. — **Goose'-step**, *n.* The action of balancing the body on either leg alternately, swinging the other.

Goose'berry, *n.* Prob. GOOSE + BERRY, though the orig. of the name is obscure. The fruit of a prickly shrub; the shrub.

Gore, *v.*[1]*t.* Doubtfully referred to *gár*, spear. GORE, *n.*[2] To pierce with the horns.

Gore, *n.*[1] O.E. *gór*, dung, dirt = M.Du. *goor*, filth, O.H.G., O.N. *gor*, slimy matter. Clotted blood.—**Gor**'Y,[2] *a.*

Gore, *n.*[2] O.E. *gára*, app. conn. with *gár*, spear (= O.H.G. *gêr* (Ger. *ger*)), from the shape of the head. A triangular piece of cloth, &c. —*v.*[2]*t.* To cut into, to shape with, a gore.

Gorge, *n.* O.F. and F. *gorge*—Pop.L. **gorga*, of unknown orig. DISGORGE. The throat; a narrow opening between hills; an act of gorging.—*vi.* To feed greedily.—*vt.* To stuff with food; to devour greedily; to fill full.

Gor'geous, *a.* O.F. *gorgias*, finely dressed, of uncertain orig. Splendid, showy.

Gorgonzo'la, *n.* From *Gorgonzola*, near Milan. An Italian ewes'-milk cheese.

Goril'la, *n.* A G. word, occurring in acc.pl. *gorillas* in the account of the Carthaginian Hanno's voyage (5th or 6th c. B.C.) as representing an alleged African name for a wild man (or rather woman), and adopted as the name of the largest of the anthropoid apes.

Gor'mandize, *n.* F. *gourmandise*, f. *gourmand.* GOURMAND. Indulgence in good eating.—*vi.* and *t.* To eat greedily.

Gorse, *n.* O.E. *gorst.* Cogn. with L. *hordeum*, barley. Cf. Ger. *gerste*, barley. Furze.

Gosh'awk, *n.* O.E. *gós-hafoc*, f. *gós*, GOOSE + *h*(*e*)*afoc*, HAWK. A large short-winged hawk.

Gos'ling, *n.* -LING (3). A young goose.

Gos'pel, *n.* O.E. *godspel*, orig. *gód spel*, good tidings (GOOD. SPELL, *n.*[1]), representing L. *ēvangelium* (EVANGEL), afterwards taken as *gŏd* (GOD) + *spel* in sense 'story', hence, 'life of Christ'. Christ's 'glad tidings', the body of Christian doctrine; the record of Christ's life, one of the books containing this.

Gos'samer, *n.* M.E. *gos*(*e*)*somer*(*e*), app. f. GOOSE + SUMMER. Poss. the word orig. denoted a 'St. Martin's summer', when geese were supposed to be in season, and was transferred to a characteristic phenomenon of the time of the year. A fine filmy substance floating in the air in calm weather, esp. in autumn.

Gos'sip, *n.* O.E. *godsibb*, f. *god*, GOD + *sib*(*b*), akin, related. A godfather or godmother; a familiar friend; an idle talker, esp. about the affairs of others; such talk.—*vi.* To talk thus.

Goth'ic, *a.* L. *gothicus*, f. *Gothi*, the Goths. Of or pertaining to the Goths; barbarous; a term for a style of architecture of which the chief characteristic is the pointed arch.

Gouge, *n.* F. *gouge*—L.L. *gubia*, *gulbia*, prob. of Celtic orig. A hollow-bladed chisel.—*vt.* To cut or to force out with or as with a gouge.

Gourd, *n.* F. *gourde*, repg. L. *cucurbita.* A fleshy fruit which when dried and hollowed out forms a vessel; the plant bearing it.

Gour'mand, *n.* F. *gourmand.* Orig. unknown. GORMANDIZE. A judge of good eating.

Gourmet, *n.* F., repg. O.F. *gourmet*, *groumet*, *gromet*, a wine-merchant's assistant, of uncertain orig. A connoisseur of table delicacies.

Gout, *n.* O.F. *goute*, *goutte*, drop, gout—L. *gutta*, drop, in Med.L. applied to diseases attributed to a flow of humours to a particular part of the body. GUTTER. A painful disease chiefly affecting the smaller joints; a drop, a splash or clot.—**Gout**'Y,[2] *a.*

Gov'ern, *vt.* O.F. *governer*—L. *gubernāre*, to steer (a ship), govern, f. G. *kuberna-ein*, to steer. To rule, direct, control, guide, influence; to serve as a precedent, &c., for; to be followed by (a grammatical case or mood).—*vi.* To hold sway.—**Gov'ern**ABLE, *a.*—**Gov'ern**ANCE, *n.*—**Gov'ern**ESS, *n.* A female teacher in a private household. — **Gov'ern**MENT, *n.* — **Governmen'**TAL, *a.*—**Gov'ern**OR, *n.*

Gown, *n.* O.F. *goune*—Med.L. *gunna*, fur garment, of obscure orig. A loose upper garment; a garment of office; a woman's frock.

Grab, *vt.* Corresponds to M.Du., M.L.G. *grabben.* Perh. a modification of the root of GRIP. To grasp, seize.—*n.* A sudden grasp.

Grace, *n.* F. *grâce*—L. *grātia*, favour, charm, f. *grātus*, pleasing, thankful. AGREE. GRATEFUL. GRATIFY. GRATIS. Attractiveness, charm; an attractive quality or feature; favour; the condition of being favoured; divine influence, the condition of being under it; virtue, a virtue; delay accorded; a short thanksgiving before a meal; a title of a duke or archbishop. —*vt.* To lend grace to, confer honour upon. —**Grace**'FUL, *a.*—**Grace**'LESS, *a.*—**Gra'**CIOUS, *a.* Having pleasing qualities; indulgent, beneficent.

Grade, *n.* F. *grade*—L. *gradus*, step, degree. AGGRESSION. DEGRADE. DEGREE. A step or stage; degree of rank, &c.; a class; a slope. —*vt.* To classify; to reduce to suitable slopes. —**Grada'tion**, *n.* L. *gradātio*, *gradātiōnis*, n. of action f. *gradus.* In *pl.*, stages, degrees; a scale or series of degrees; arrangement in grades.—**Gra'dient**, *a.* L. *gradiens*, *gradientis*, pres.pple. of *gradi*, to walk, f. *gradus.* Moving by steps.—*n.* Degree of slope.—**Grad'ual**, *a.* Med.L. *graduālis*, f. *gradus.* Taking place by degrees, advancing step by step; not steep. — **Grad'ual**LY,[2] *adv.*—**Grad'uate**, *vi.* Med.L. *graduāre*, *graduātum*, to admit to a university degree, f. *gradus.* To take a university degree.—*vt.* To divide into degrees; to arrange in gradations.—*n.* One holding a university degree.—**Gradu**A'TION, *n.*

Graft, *n.* Modification of earlier *graff*—O.F. *grafe*, a kind of pencil, a shoot for grafting (supposed to resemble a pointed pencil)—L.L. *graphium*, G. *grapheion*, a pointed instrument for writing, f. *graphein*, to write. GRAPHIC. A shoot inserted in another stock.—*vt.* To insert (a shoot) in another stock.

Grail, *n.* O.F. *grael*—Med.L. *gradālis*, cup, platter, perh. = Pop.L. **crātālis*, f. **crātus*, altered f. L. *crātēr* = G. *kratēr*, mixing-bowl. The platter used by Christ at the Last Supper.

Grain, *n.* Two words blended—(1) O.F. *grain* (F. *grain*), L. *grānum*, a seed; (2) O.F. *grain*(*n*)*e* (F. *graine*), seeds collectively—Pop.L. *grāna*, fem., orig. pl. of *grānum.* CORN.[1] FILIGREE. GRANARY. GRANGE. GRAVY. POMEGRANATE. A seed of a cereal plant; corn; a particular species of corn; a small hard particle;

the smallest English unit of weight; the scarlet grain or kermes, the dye made from it, dye in general; texture; arrangement of fibres.—*vt.* To paint in imitation of wood-fibres.

Gram'arye, *n.* O.F. **gramarye*, f. *gramaire*, GRAMMAR, which was sometimes used to denote learning in general, and hence (the occult sciences being popularly supposed to be included), magic. GLAMOUR. Magic.

Graminiv'orous, *a.* L. *grāmen*, *grāminis*, GRASS + -(*i*)*vorus*, devouring (f. *vorāre*, to devour) + -OUS. DEVOUR. Feeding on grass.

Gram'mar, *n.* O.F. *gramaire*, irregularly f. L. *grammatica*—G. *grammatikē* (sc. *technē*, art), fem. of *grammatikos*, a. f. *grammata*, literature, pl. of *gramma*, a letter, f. *graphein*, to write. GRAPHIC. GRAMARYE. An investigation of the structure and usages of a language, the system of principles and rules resulting therefrom; a book on grammar.—**Gramma'**RIAN, *n.*—**Grammat'**ICAL, *a.*

Gram'ophone, *n.* App. formed by inversion of PHONOGRAM. An instrument for recording and reproducing sounds.

Gram'pus, *n.* Formerly *graundepose*, app. alteration of *grapeys*—O.F. *grapois*, *graspeis* —L. *crassus piscis*, fat FISH. CRASS. A blowing and spouting blunt-headed sea-creature.

Gran'ary, *n.* L. *grānārium*, f. *grānum*. GRAIN. GARNER. A storehouse for grain.

Grand, *a.* O.F. *grand*—L. *grandis*, full-grown, great. Chief, main; great; splendid, solemn; gorgeously arrayed; of the 'great world'; impressive; lofty, dignified; imposing; magnificent, excellent; denoting the second degree of relationship in ascent or descent.—**Grand'**LY,[2] *adv.*—**Grandee'**, *n.* Sp., Pg. *grande*, great (person). A Spanish or Portuguese nobleman of the highest rank.—**Gran'deur**, *n.* F. *grandeur*. Eminence; nobility of character; sublimity, majesty; magnificence.—**Grand'father (-mother)**, *nn.* A father's or mother's father (mother).—**Grand'child**, *n.* The child of a son or daughter.—**Grandil'oquent**, *a.* After *eloquent* f. L. *grandiloquus*, f. *grandis* + *loqui*, to speak. ALLOCUTE. Pompous in expression.—**Grandil'oqu**ENCE, *n.*—**Gran'diose**, *a.* F. *grandiose*. Noble in plan or design; pompous.

Grange, *n.* A.F. *graunge* (F. *grange*)—Med.L. *grānea*, f. *grānum*. GRAIN. A granary; a house with farm buildings attached.

Gran'ite, *n.* It. *granito* (orig. a ppl.a. = granular) f. *grano* = O.F. *grain*. GRAIN. A granular crystalline rock used in building.

Grant, *vt.* A.F. *graunter*, *granter*, O.F. *graanter*, *greanter*, altered f. *craanter*, *creanter* —Pop.L. **crēdentāre*, f. L. *crēdens*, *crēdentis*, pres.pple. of *crēdĕre*, to entrust, believe. CREDIT. To accede to; to allow, concede; to bestow, confer; to admit, acknowledge.—*n.* The action of granting; the thing granted.—**Grant**EE', *n.*—**Grant'**ER, **Grant'**OR, *nn.*

Gran'ule, *n.* L.L. *grānulum*, dim. of *grānum*. GRAIN. A small grain; a small compact particle.—**Gran'ul**AR,[1] *a.*—**Gran'ul**ATE,[3] *vt.* To form into granules.—*vi.* To take such a form; of a wound, &c., to develop small prominences like granules.—**Granul**A'TION, *n.*

Grape, *n.* O.F. *grape*, *grappe*, bunch of grapes, prob. f. *graper*, to gather grapes with a hook, f. *grape*, hook, of Teut. orig. Cf. O.H.G. *krapfo*, hook. GRAPNEL. GRAPPLE. The fruit of the vine.

Graph'ic, *a.* L. *graphicus*—G. *graphikos*, f. *graphē*, drawing or writing, f. *graphein*, to draw or write. AUTOGRAPH. DIAGRAM. GRAMMAR. Of writing, &c., vividly descriptive.—**Graph'ically**, *adv.* -AL. -LY.[2]

Graph'ite, *n.* Ger. *graphit* — G. *graphein*. (See prec.) A form of carbon used for pencils.

Grap'nel, *n.* A.F. **grapenel*, dim. of *grapon*, in same sense, conn. with O.F. *grape*, hook. GRAPE. A hooked instrument thrown with a rope to seize an object; a small anchor with several flukes.

Grap'ple, *n.* Prob. f. O.F. **grapelle*, dim. of *grape*. (See prec.) A grapnel; the action of grappling, the state of being grappled.—*vt.* To seize with a grapnel; to grip firmly.—*vi.* To contend or deal *with*.

Grasp, *vi.* M.E. *graspen*, *grapsen*, prob. repg. O.E. **grǽpsan*, f. O.Teut. root *graip-*. GROPE. To make a clutch *at*. — *vt.* To seize firmly, grip; to comprehend.—*n.* A grasping; firm hold, mastery; mental comprehensiveness.

Grass, *n.* O.E. *græs*. Common Teut. O.Teut. root *gra-*: *grô-*, whence GREEN, GROW. Cogn. with L. *grāmen*. GRAMINIVOROUS. GRAZE.[1] Herbage; a plant grown for pasture, for covering lawns, &c.—**Grass'hopper**, *n.* A leaping insect.—**Grass'**Y,[2] *a.*

Grate, *n.* App. f. Med.L. *grāta*—It. *grate*, *grata*, grate, hurdle—L. *crātis*, hurdle. GRILL. A framework of bars (also **Grat'ing**); bars for holding fuel, a fireplace.

Grate, *vt.* O.F. *grater*, of Teut. orig. Cf. O.H.G. *chrazzôn* (Ger. *kratzen*), to scratch. To rub small with something rough.—*vi.* To have an irritating effect *on* or *upon*; to rub *against* with a harsh sound, to sound harshly.

Grate'ful, *a.* With -FUL, f. obs. *Grate*, pleasing, thankful—L. *grātus*. GRACE. Of things, pleasing, welcome; feeling gratitude, thankful.—**Grate'ful**LY,[2] *adv.*

Grat'ify, *vt.* F. *gratifier*—L. *grātificāri*, f. *grātus* (GRACE) + *facĕre*, to make. -FY. To remunerate; to do a favour to, satisfy; to indulge.—**Grati**FICA'TION, *n.*—**Grat'itude**, *n.* L.L. *grātitūdo*, f. *grātus*. A warm sense of appreciation of kindness received.

Gra'tis, *adv.* L. *grātis*, contr. f. *grātiis*, lit. 'from favour or kindness', ablative pl. of *grātia*, favour, f. *grātus*. GRACE. For nothing, without charge.—*a.* Given or done gratis.—

Gratu'itous, *a.* L. *grātuītus* (f. *grātia*) + -OUS. Bestowed or obtained without payment; unjustifiable, not called for.—**Gratu'itous**LY,[2] *adv.* — **Gratu'ity**, *n.* Med.L. *grātuītas*, f. *grātia*. A gift of money; a tip.

Grava'men, *n.* L.L. *gravāmen*, an inconvenience, in Med.L., a grievance, f. *gravis*. (See next.) A grievance; the heaviest part of an accusation.

Grave, *a.* F. *grave*—L. *gravis*, heavy, important. AGGRAVATE. GRIEVE. Weighty, important; not mirthful, staid; not showy, plain; deep in tone; *grave accent*, a mark (`) placed on vowels to give various indications. —**Grave'**LY,[2] *adv.*—**Grav'**ITY, *n.* Importance; staidness; heaviness; the force by which bodies tend to move towards each other.—**Grav'it**ATE,[3] *vi.* To move by the force of gravity; to sink, settle down.—**Gravit**A'TION, *n.*

Grave, *n.* O.E. *græf*, f. root of *grafan*. (See next.) A place in the earth for a corpse.

Grave, *v.*[1]*t.* O.E. *grafan*, to dig, to engrave. Common Teut. O.Teut. root *grab-*, *grôb-*. Cf. F. *graver*, f. Teut. ENGRAVE. GROOVE. GRUB. To engrave; to impress deeply.

Grave, *v.*[2]*t.* Poss. f. F. *grave* = *grève*. (See next.) To clean and coat a ship's bottom.

Grav'el, *n.* O.F. *gravele, gravelle*, dim. of *grave* (F. *grève*), gravel, sea-shore, of Celtic orig. Small water-worn stones; aggregations of urinary crystals, a disease thence resulting. —*vt.* To cover with gravel; to set fast (as in gravel), perplex.

Gra'vy, *n.* Prob. f. O.F. *grané* (misread as *gravé*), a kind of sauce, prob. cogn. with *grain* (GRAIN), which is quoted in sense 'anything used in cooking'. The fat and juices that come from flesh in cooking.

Gray'ling, *n.* *Gray*, GREY + -LING (2). A freshwater fish of a silvery-grey colour.

Graze, *v.*[1]*i.* and *t.* O.E. *grasian*, f. *græs*, GRASS. To feed on grass.—**Gra'**ZIER, *n.*

Graze, *v.*[2]*i.* Orig. obscure. To touch lightly in passing, esp. so as to abrade.—*vi.* To move so as to touch thus.—*n.* A grazing.

Grease, *n.* O.F. *graisse, greisse, craisse, creisse*—Pop.L. **crassia*, f. L. *crassus*, fat, thick. CRASS. Soft melted fat of animals.—*vt.* To apply grease to.—**Grea'**SY,[2] *a.*

Great, *a.* O.E. *gréat*. Common W. Germanic. GROAT. Pregnant; high in a scale of measurement or estimation; principal; important, eminent; eminently entitled to a designation; prefixed to *grand*, denoting a degree further removed in ascent or descent; *great circle*, a circle on the surface of a sphere whose plane passes through the sphere's centre.—**Great'**LY,[2] *adv.*—**Great'**NESS, *n.*

Greave, *n.* O.F. *greve*, of unknown orig. Armour for the leg below the knee (gen. in *pl.*).

Gre'cian, *a.* L. *Graecia*, Greece + -AN. Greek.—*n.* One learned in the Greek language.

Gree'dy, *a.* O.E. *grǽdig* = O.S. *grâdag*, O.H.G. *grâtag*, O.N. *gráthugr*. Orig. sense 'hungry'. Ravenous; eager for gain; eager, keen.—**Greed**, *n.* Back-formation f. the *a.* Inordinate or insatiate longing.—**Gree'di**LY,[2] *adv.*—**Gree'di**NESS, *n.*

Greek, *n.* O.E. *Crécas*, pl.—L. *Graeci*, pl.—G. *Graikoi*, pl. A native of Greece; a cunning person, a cheat.—*a.* From the *n.* Of Greece or its people; of, characteristic of, composed in, the Greek language.

Green, *a.* O.E. *gréne* = O.S. *grôni*, O.H.G. *gruoni* (Ger. *grün*). O.Teut. root *grô-*. GRASS. Of the colour of growing grass; verdant; unripe, not matured; inexperienced; easily deceived.—*n.* The colour; a piece of grassy land; in *pl.*, green vegetables. — **Green'**ERY, *n.* Verdure. — **Greengage'**, *n.* From a Sir William *Gage* (18th c.). A green kind of plum. —**Green'grocer**, *n.* A retail dealer in vegetables and fruit.—**Green'horn**, *n.* Orig. applied to an animal, app. to an ox with 'green' or young horns. A green or inexperienced person.—**Green'-room**, *n.* A room in a theatre (prob. orig. painted green) for actors when not required on the stage.

Greet, *vt.* O.E. *grǽtan*. Common W. Germanic. To accost or salute.

Grega'rious, *a.* L. *gregārius* (f. *grex, gregis*, flock) + -OUS. AGGREGATE. EGREGIOUS. Living in flocks; liking to be with others.

Grenade', *n.* F. *grenade*—Sp. *granada*, pomegranate, grenade—L. *grānātum*. POMEGRANATE. A small explosive shell.—**Grenadier'**, *n.* F. *grenadier*. Orig., a soldier who threw grenades. A member of the regiment known as the 'Grenadier Guards'.

Grey, Gray, *a.* O.E. *grǽg* = M.Du. *grau*, O.H.G. *grâo* (Ger. *grau*), O.N. *grár*. Of a colour between black and white. — *n.* The colour; grey material or clothing.

Grey'hound, *n.* O.E. *gríghund*, **grieghund* (= O.N. *greyhundr*), f. **grieg* (= O.N. *grey*, bitch), of unknown orig. + *hund*, dog. HOUND. A hunting dog with a long slender body.

Grid'dle, *n.* M.E. *gredile*, app. f. early O.F. **gredil* = *greil, grail*. GRILL. A circular iron plate for baking cakes.—**Grid'iron**, *n.* M.E. *gredire*, alteration of *gredile*, changed to *gridiron* by confusion of the termination with M.E. *ire* = *iren*, IRON. A cooking utensil formed of bars used for broiling.

Grief, *n.* O.F. *grief, gref*, vbl. n. f. *grever*, to GRIEVE. Deep sorrow; a cause of this.

Grieve, *vt.* O.F. *grever*, to burden—Pop.L. **grevāre* = L. *gravāre*, f. *gravis*, heavy. GRAVE, *a.* To affect with grief.—*vi.* To feel grief.—**Grie'**VANCE, *n.* A wrong or hardship.—**Grie'**VOUS, *a.* Having injurious effects; exciting grief; atrocious, heinous.

Grif'fin, Gryph'on, *n.* O.F. *grifoun*—L. *grȳphus* = *gryps*, G. *grups*. A monster with an eagle's head and wings and a lion's body.

Grig, *n.* Orig. obscure. A small eel; hence perh. the phrase *as merry* (or *lively*) *as a grig*.

Grill, *n.* F. *gril* (O.F. *gril(l), greil, grail*)—Pop.L. **grāticulum*, L. *crāticula*, dim. of *crātis*, hurdle. CRATE. GRATE, *n.* GRIDDLE. A gridiron; meat, &c., broiled on a gridiron.—*vt.* To broil.—*vi.* To be broiled.

Grilse, *n.* Of unknown orig. A young salmon on its first return to the river.

Grim, *a.* O.E. *grim(m)* = O.S. *grim*, O.H.G. *grim* (Ger. *grimm*). Merciless, stern; of stern or harsh aspect —**Grim'**LY,[2] *adv.*

Grimace', *n.* F. *grimace*, of uncertain orig. A distortion of the face; an affected look; affectation.—*vi.* To distort the face.

Grime, *vt.* Cf. Mod. Flemish *grijmen*, L.G. *gremen, grêmen*. To blacken, dirty.—*n.* Black particles, dirt.—**Grim'**Y,[2] *a.*

Grin, *vi.* O.E. *grennian*, cogn. with O.H.G. *grennan*, to mutter (M.H.G. *grennen*, to grin). To draw back the lips and show the teeth.—*n.* An act of grinning.

Grind, *vt.* O.E. *grindan*. Perh. cogn. with L. *frendĕre*, to gnash the teeth, to crush, bruise. GRIST. To reduce to fine particles by crushing between hard surfaces; to oppress; to make sharp or smooth; to rub gratingly.—*vi.* To perform the operation of grinding; to work or study hard; to rub gratingly.—*n.* The action of grinding; hard work or study. —**Grind'stone**, *n.* A revolving disk of stone used for sharpening or polishing.

Grip, *n.* O.E. *gripe*, f. root of GRIPE. Firm hold or grasp; the handle of a sword, &c.—*vt.* To grasp or seize firmly.

Gripe, *vt.* O.E. *grípan*. Common Teut. To grip; to oppress.—*n.* The action of griping; grip, control; in *pl.*, intestinal pains.

Gris'ly, *a.* Late O.E. *grislic*, with *-líc* (-LY[1]) f. root of **grísan*, to shudder = M.Du., M.L.G. *grisen*. Grim, ghastly.

Grist, *n.* O.E. *gríst*, f. root of *grindan*, to GRIND. Corn to be ground.

Gris'tle, *n.* O.E. *gristle* = M.L.G. *gristel*, M.H.G. *gruschel*. Cartilage.—**Gris'tl**Y,[2] *a.*

Grit, *n.* O.E. *gréot* = O.S. *griot*, O.N. *griót*, pebbles. Particles of stone or sand; coarse sandstone; spirit, pluck.—*vi.* To move with or make a grating sound.—*vt.* To grind (the teeth).—**Grit't**Y,[2] *a.*

Griz'zle, *a.* O.F. *grisel*, f. *gris*, grey—O.H.G. *gris* (Ger. *greis*) = O.S. *gris*. Grizzled.—*vt.* To make grey or grey-haired.—**Grizz'l**Y,[2] *a.*

Groan, *vi.* O.E. *grānian*. O.Teut. root *grai-*,

gri-, whence O.H.G. *grīnan* (Ger. *greinen*), to weep. To utter a low, deep sound expressive of grief or pain; to be oppressed or overburdened.—*n.* An act of groaning.

Groat, *n.* M.Du. *groot*, orig. an a. = GREAT, in sense 'thick'. Various coins formerly issued on the Continent, orig. named from the size; a former English coin equal to four pence.

Groats, *n.pl.* O.E. **grotan*, pl., cogn. with *grot*, fragment, and GRIT. Hulled, or hulled and crushed grain, chiefly oats.

Gro'cer, *n.* O.F. *grossier*—Med.L. *grossārius*, f. L.L. *grossus*. GROSS, *a.* Formerly, a wholesale dealer. A dealer in tea, sugar, spices, &c.—**Gro'**CERY, *n.* His wares (often in *pl.*).

Grog, *n.* Said to be short for GROGRAM and to have been applied as a nickname to Admiral Vernon from his grogram cloak, and transferred to the mixture which he ordered (Aug., 1740) to be served out instead of neat spirit. Spirit (orig. rum) and water.

Grog'ram, *n.* F. *gros grain*, large or coarse GRAIN. GROSS, *a.* A coarse fabric of silk, of mohair and wool, or of these mixed.

Groin, *n.* Orig. *grynde*, *grinde*, of uncertain orig. The depression on either side between the abdomen and the thigh; the edge formed by the intersection of two vaults.

Groom, *n.* Of obscure orig. A man; a serving-man; a servant in charge of horses.—*vt.* To tend as a groom; to tend carefully.

Groove, *n.* Early Mod.Du. *groeve*, f. *grōb-*, *grab-*. GRAVE, *v.*[1] A hollow cut by a tool; a piece of routine.—*vt.* To cut a groove in.

Grope, *vi.* O.E. *grápian*, f. *graip-*. GRASP. To feel about to find something.

Gross, *n.* F. *grosse*, orig. fem. of *gros*. (See next.) Twelve dozen.

Gross, *a.* F. *gros*, big, thick, coarse—L.L. *grossus*, thick. GROCER. GROGRAM. Corpulent; flagrant; total, without deductions; material, perceptible to the senses; coarse, lacking in refinement.—**Gross'**LY,[2] *adv.*

Grot, *n.* F. *grotte* = It. *grotta*. A GROTTO.

Grotesque', *n.* Early Mod.F. *crotesque*—It. *grottesca*, rude painted work suited to a grotto, orig. fem. of *grottesco*, a. f. *grotta*. (See next.) Fantastic decorative painting.—*a.* Executed in this style; fantastically extravagant or absurd.—**Grotesque'**LY,[2] *adv.*

Grot'to, *n.* It. *grotta*—L. *crypta*. CRYPT. A natural or artificial cave.

Ground, *n.* O.E. *grund*. Common Teut. The solid bottom of the sea; a reason, motive; a surface or first coating of colour for working upon; the surface of the earth; area or distance thereon; land owned or occupied; that on which one takes a stand; in *pl.*, dregs, enclosed land attached to a house.—*vt.* To establish; to instruct *in* first principles; to place on the ground.—*vi.* To run ashore.—**Ground'**-LESS, *a.* Without real cause or reason.

Ground'sel, *n.* O.E. *gundæswelg(i)æ*, perh. f. *gund*, pus + *swelgan*, to SWALLOW, absorb (from use of the plant to heal abscesses), later *grundeswylige*, app. as if 'GROUND-swallower' (referring to the rapid spread of the weed). A weed given as food to cage-birds.

Group, *n.* F. *groupe*—It. *gruppo*, prob. f. O.Teut. *kroppo-*. CROP. An artistic combination of figures; an assemblage; a class.—*vt.* To arrange in a group; to class *with*.

Grouse, *n.* Of unknown orig. A reddish game-bird; its flesh.

Grove, *n.* O.E. *gráf*. Orig. unknown. A small wood.

Grov'el, *vi.* Back-formation f. obs. *Grovelling*, adv., face downwards (taken as a pres. pple.), f. obs. (*on*) *grufe* = O.N. (*á*) *grúfu*, in same sense + *-ling*, advbl. suff. To lie face downwards, to move with the body prostrate.

Grow, *vi.* O.E. *grówan*, f. O.Teut. root *grō-*. GRASS. To increase in size by natural development; to increase gradually; to be produced; to become by degrees.—*vt.* To cause or allow to grow; to produce.—**Growth**, *n.* -TH.[1] The action, process, manner or result of growing; production; produce, product.

Growl, *vi.* Prob. imitative. To make a low, angry guttural sound; to murmur angrily.—*n.* Such a sound; an angry murmuring.

Grub, *vt.* Perh. repg. O.E. **grybban*, f. O.Teut. root *grub-*, var. of *grab-*. GRAVE, *v.*[1] To dig superficially; to root up.—*vi.* To dig; to rummage; to lead a meanly plodding life.—*n.* App. f. the *v.* The larva of an insect.

Grudge, *vt.* Alteration of dial. *Grutch*—O.F. *groucier*, to murmur, grumble, of unknown orig. To be unwilling to give or allow.—*n.* A feeling of ill-will or resentment.

Gru'el, *n.* O.F. *gruel* (F. *gruau*)—Med.L. **grūtellum*, dim. of *grūtum*, meal, of Teut. orig. A food made by boiling oatmeal in water.

Grue'some, *a.* With -SOME f. dial. *Grue*, to shudder, cogn. with O.H.G. *in-grûên* (Ger. *grauen*). Fearful, horrible, grisly.

Gruff, *a.* App. f. Du. or L.G. **grof* = O.H.G., Ger. *grob*, of uncertain orig. Rough in aspect or manner, surly.—**Gruff'**LY,[2] *adv.*

Grum'ble, *vi.* Orig. uncertain. Cf. F. *grommeler*, Provincial Ger. *grummelen*. To make dull inarticulate sounds; to murmur.—*n.* A low growl; a murmuring complaint.

Grump, *n.* Perh. suggested by GRUNT. In *pl.*, a fit of ill-humour.—**Grump'**Y,[2] *a.*

Grunt, *vi.* O.E. *grunnettan*, freq. of *grunian*, to grunt. Imitative. Cf. L. *grunnīre*. GURNARD. Of a hog, to utter its characteristic sound; to utter a similar sound, to grumble.—*n.* A hog's sound; a similar sound.

Gru'yère, *n.* A Swiss town. A cows'-milk cheese containing many cavities.

Gua'no, *n.* Sp., f. Peruvian *huanu*, dung. The excrement of sea-fowl used as manure.

Guarantee', *n.* Misused for GUARANTY. A person who makes a guaranty; guaranty, a guaranty.—*vt.* To secure *to* a person; to secure (a person) *against*, *from*, *in*.

Guar'anty, *n.* A.F. *guarantie*, f. O.F. *guarant*, *warant*. WARRANT. The action or an act of securing or warranting; a deed or writing giving security or warranty; a ground or basis of security.

Guard, *n.* F. *guarde*, *garde*. O.Teut. type **wardā*. WARD. VAN.[1] A posture of defence; a protecting; watch; a protector; a sentry; a body of soldiers engaged in protecting, watching, &c.; one in charge of a railway train; a protection, defence; in *pl.*, certain regiments of the British army.—*vt.* F. *guarder*, *garder*. REGARD. To keep in safety.—*vi.* To be on one's guard.—**Guar'dian**, *n.* A.F. *gardein*, f. *garde*. One who guards; one who has the custody of the person or property of an infant, an idiot, &c.—**Guar'dian**SHIP, *n.*

Gua'va, *n.* Sp. *guayaba*, presumably f. some S. American or W. Indian lang. A tree with an acid fruit used to make jelly, &c.; the fruit.

Gud'geon, *n.* F. *goujon*—L. *gōbio*, *gōbiōnis*. A small freshwater fish; a simpleton.

Guer'don, *n.* O.F. *guerdon*—Med.L. *wider-*

donum, repg. O.H.G. *widarlôn* = O.E. *wither-léan*, f. *wither*, again + *léan*, payment. A reward or recompense.—*vt*. To reward.

Guerril'la, **Gueril'la**, *n*. Sp. *guerrilla*, dim. of *guerra* (= F. *guerre*), WAR. An irregular war; one engaged in such warfare.

Guess, *vt*. M.E. *gessen*, cogn. with M.L.G., M.Du. *gissen*, Sw. *gissa*. To estimate by surmise, to conjecture; to conjecture rightly.—*vi*. To form conjectures.—*n*. A conjecture.

Guest, *n*. O.E. *giest*, *gæst*. Common Teut. Cogn. with L. *hostis*, a stranger (hence, an enemy). HOST.[1] One who is entertained at another's house; an inmate of an hotel.

Guffaw', *n*. Imitative. A burst of laughter.—*vi*. To laugh loudly.

Guide, *n*. F. *guide* (O.F. *guie*, *gui-s*), f. *guider* (O.F. *guier*) = It. *guidare*, to guide, prob. f. some form of the root of O.E. *witan*, to know. WIT. GUY.[1] One who shows the way; an adviser; a book of instruction or information; a contrivance for directing motion.—*vt*. To act as guide to.—**Guid'**ANCE, *n*.

Guild, **Gild**, *n*. O.N. *gildi*, payment, guild, f. O.Teut. root *geld-*, to pay, contribute. Cf. O.E. *gildan*. YIELD. An association for mutual aid and protection.

Guile, *n*. O.F. *guile*, presumably of Teut. orig. WILE. Insidious cunning, deceit, treachery.—**Guile'**FUL, *a*.—**Guile'**LESS, *a*.

Guil'lotine, *n*. F., f. J. I. *Guillotin* (died 1814), the suggester. A machine for beheading.—*vt*. To behead by the guillotine.

Guilt, *n*. O.E. *gylt*, an offence. Not elsewhere in Teut. The fact or state of having offended. — **Guilt'**LESS, *a*. — **Guilt'**Y,[2] *a*.—**Guilt'**ILY,[2] *adv*.—**Guilt'**INESS, *n*.

Guin'ea, *n*. The name of a part of the W. Coast of Africa. A former English gold coin of the value of 21*s*. first coined (with the value of 20*s*.) for a company trading with Africa: a sum of 21*s*.—**Guin'ea-fowl**, *n*. Imported from Guinea. A fowl allied to the pheasant.—**Guin'ea-pig**, *n*. The name perh. here designates vaguely a distant country. A rodent mammal originating in S. America.

Guise, *n*. O.F. *guise*, way, manner, of Teut. orig. Cf. O.H.G. *wisa* (Ger. *weise*), O.E. *wise*. WISE, *n*. Attire, garb; aspect, semblance.

Guitar', *n*. Sp. *guitarra*—G. *kithara*, lyre. A musical instrument with six strings.

Gules, *n*. O.F. *goules*, *gueules* (F. *gueules*) = Med.L. *gulæ*, pl., ermine dyed red, of doubtful orig. In *heraldry*, red.

Gulf, *n*. O.F. and F. *golfe* (in the first sense)—It.,Sp. *golfo*—Late G. *kolphos*, G. *kolpos*, bosom, hollow, bay. A partly enclosed portion of the sea; a whirlpool; a chasm or abyss.

Gull, *n*.[1] Perh. f. Welsh *gwylan*, Cornish *guilan* = Breton *goelann* (whence F. *goëland*). A long-winged web-footed sea-bird

Gull, *vt*. Perh. a transferred use of obs. *Gull*, to guzzle, to gorge, cram. Cf. Du. *gullen*, to guzzle. To dupe, cheat.—*n*.[2] A credulous person, a simpleton.—**Gull'**IBLE, *a*.

Gul'let, *n*. O.F. *goulet*, dim. of *goule*, L. *gula*, throat. The passage to the stomach.

Gul'ly, *n*. Prob. an alteration of prec. A channel or ravine worn by water.

Gulp, *vt*. Imitative. Cf. Du. *gulpen*, to guzzle. To swallow hastily.—*vi*. To gasp or choke.—*n*. A gulping; a choke.

Gum, *n*.[1] O.E. *góma*, palate = O.H.G. *guomo* (Ger. *gaumen*). The firm flesh on the jaws in which the teeth are set.

Gum, *n*.[2] O.F. *gomme*—L. *gummi*—G. *kommi*. A viscid substance issuing from certain trees.—*vt*. To fasten, &c., with gum.—**Gum'm**Y,[2] *a*.

Gun, *n*. M.E. *gunne*, *gonne*. Poss. a use coming down from old Scandinavian times (and subsequent shortening) of the O.N. female name *Gunnhildr* (both *gunn-r* and *hild-r* mean 'war') applied as a pet-name to a military engine. A weapon from which missiles are discharged by explosion. — **Gun'n**ER, *n*.—**Gun'n**ERY, *n*. The making and using of large guns.—**Gun'powder**, *n*. The explosive mixture used in guns.—**Gun'-room**, *n*. The junior officers' mess-room in a warship (orig. used by the gunner and his mates); a room in which guns are kept.—**Gun'wale**, **Gun'nel**, *n*. WALE. The upper edge of a ship's side (formerly supporting the guns).

Gur'gle, *vi*. Poss. a native imitative formation. Parallel forms are Du., M.L.G. *gorgelen*, Ger. *gurgeln*, to gargle, It. *gorgogliare*, to gargle, to bubble up. To flow in a broken current with a low intermittent noise.—*n*. The action or an act of gurgling; the noise.

Gur'nard, **Gur'net**, *n*. Prob. f. a var. of F. *grognard*, grumbler, f. *grogner*, L. *grunnire*, to GRUNT. (Thus lit. 'the grunter', from the sound the fish makes when taken out of the water.) A sea-fish furnished with spines.

Gush, *vi*. M.E. *gosshe*, *gusche*, prob. a native imitative formation. To flow out suddenly or copiously.—*n*. Such a flow.

Gust, *n*.[1] App. f. O.N. *gust-r*, conn. with *gjósa*, to gush. A sudden blast of wind; a gush, a burst, a breaking forth.—**Gust'**Y,[2] *a*.

Gust, *n*.[2] L. *gustus*, taste. CHOOSE. RAGOUT. The sense of taste; keen relish or enjoyment; savour, flavour; pleasing taste or flavour.—**Gus'to**, *n*. It., f. *gustus*. Keen relish.

Gut, *n*. O.E. *guttas*, pl., prob. conn. with *géotan*, Ger. *gieszen*, to pour. In *pl*., the bowels, intestines; a preparation of the intestines of animals used for various purposes; a narrow passage.—*vt*. To take out the guts of, to clear out the contents of.

Gutta-per'cha, *n*. Malay *getah percha*, f. *getah*, gum + *percha*, the tree. The hardened juice (like caoutchouc) of an E. Asian tree.

Gut'ter, *n*. O.F. *gutiere*, f. *goutte*, drop. GOUT. A shallow trough for carrying off rain water from a roof; a channel at the side of a street.—*vt*. To make gutters in.—*vi*. To flow in streams; of a candle, to melt away by the pouring down of the wax.

Gut'tural, *a*. Mod.L. *gutturālis*, f. L. *guttur*, throat. Of, pertaining to, produced in, the throat.—*n*. A guttural sound.

Guy, *n*.[1] O.F. *gui-s*, *guie*, GUIDE. A rope for guiding or steadying.—*v*.[1]*t*. To apply a guy to.

Guy, *n*.[2] An effigy of *Guy* Fawkes; a person of ridiculous appearance.—*v*.[2]*t*. To ridicule.

Guz'zle, *vt*. and *i*. Perh. f. O.F. *gosiller* (recorded, however, only in senses 'to vomit', 'to chatter'), conn. with *gosier*, throat, of unknown orig. To eat or drink greedily.

Gymna'sium, *n*.; *pl*. **-ia**, **-iums**. G. *gumnasion*, f. *gumnazein*, to train, lit. 'to train naked', f. *gumnos*, naked. A place for training in athletic exercises.—**Gym'nast**, *n*. G. *gumnastēs*, trainer in athletic exercises. One skilled in such exercises.—**Gymnas'**TIC, *a*. In *pl*. as *n*., the practice of athletic exercises.

Gynæcol'ogy, *n*. G. *gunē*, *gunaikos*, woman + -LOGY. The department of medicine treating of the functions and diseases of women.

Gyp'sum, *n*. L. *gypsum*—G. *gupsos*, chalk,

gypsum. The mineral from which plaster of Paris is made.

Gy'rate, *vi.* L. *gȳrāre, gȳrātum*, f. *gȳrus*, G. *guros*, circle, ring. To move in a circle, to revolve, rotate.—**Gyra'tion**, *n.*

Gyve, *n.* M.E. *give*, of obscure orig. A shackle, esp. for the leg.—*vt.* To shackle.

H

Hab'erdasher, *n.* Perh. with -ER f. obs. *Haberdash*, small wares, app.= A.F. *hapertas*, perh. the name of a fabric, of unknown orig. A dealer in small articles of dress.

Habil'iment, *n.* O.F. *habillement*, f. *habiller*, to fit out, f. *habile*, L. *habilis*, fit. ABLE. REHABILITATE. Attire; in *pl.*, vestments.

Hab'it, *n.* O.F. *habit*—L. *habitus*, n. of action f. *habēre, habitum*, to have, hold, *refl.*, to be constituted, to be. ABLE. EXHIBIT. HABITATION. Attire, a garment; bodily or mental constitution; a settled disposition or tendency. —*vt.* To dress.—**Habit'ual**, *a.* Med.L. *habituālis*, f. *habitus*. Fixed by habit, customary; customarily doing something.—**Habit'ually**,[2] *adv.*—**Habit'uate**,[3] *vt.* To accustom *to*, *to do*.—**Hab'itude**, *n.* F. *habitude*—L. *habitūdo*, condition, f. *habēre*. Manner of being; a habit.—**Habitué**, *n.* F., pa.pple. of *habituer*, to habituate. An habitual visitor, &c.

Habita'tion, *n.* F. *habitation*—L. *habitātio*, *habitātiōnis*, f. *habitāre*, to inhabit, freq. of *habēre*. (See prec.) BINNACLE. INHABIT. The act of inhabiting; a place of abode.—**Hab'itat**, *n.* 3rd sing. pres. indicative of *habitāre*. The natural home of an animal or plant.—**Hab'itable**, *a.* Fit to live in.

Hack, *v.*[1]*t.* Early M.E. *hacken*—O.E. *haccian* (in *tó-haccian*, to hack in pieces). Cf. M.H.G., M.L.G., M.Du., Ger. *hacken*. To cut irregularly, notch.—*n.*[1] A gash, a notch.

Hack, *n.*[2] Abb. of HACKNEY. A horse let out for hire; a worn-out horse; a horse for ordinary riding; a drudge.—*v.*[2]*t.* To make common or trite.

Hack'ney, *n.* O.F. *haquenée*, ambling horse or mare, of unknown orig. A horse for ordinary riding; a carriage kept for hire.—*vt.* To make common or trite.

Had'dock, *n.* Orig. uncertain. A fish like a cod.

Ha'des, *n.* G. *Haidēs*, the god of the lower world, his realm. The abode of the dead.

Hæm'orrhage, Hem'orrhage, *n.* 16th c. F. *hemorragie*—L. *haemorrhagia*—G. *haimorrhagia*, f. *haima*, blood + *-rhagia*, f. stem *rhag-* of *rhēgnunai*, to break, burst. ANÆMIA. Bleeding, esp. when profuse.

Hæm'orrhoids, Hem'orrhoids, *n.pl.* 16th c. F. *hemorrhoïdes*, through L. f. G. *haimorrhoïdes* (*phlebes*), bleeding (veins), pl. of *haimorrhoïs* = *haimorrhoos*, flowing with blood, f. *haima* (see prec.) + *-rhoos*, flowing, f. *rhe-ein*, to flow. A disease characterized by tumours of the veins about the anus, piles.

Haft, *n.* O.E. *hæft*(*e*). O.Teut. *haf-* (HEAVE) or *habē-* (HAVE). A handle.

Hag, *n.* M.E. *hagge*, perh. shortened f. O.E. *hægtis*, fury, witch = O.H.G. *hagazissa* (Ger. *hexe*). A witch; an ugly old woman.

Hag'gard, *a.* Cf. F. *hagard*, wild (orig. of a hawk), of uncertain orig. Wild-looking; gaunt.

Hag'gle, *vt.* Freq. of dial. *Hag*, to chop—O.N. *hōggva* = O.E. *héawan*, to HEW. HIGGLE. To mangle.—*vi.* To wrangle as to terms.

Hagiol'ogy, *n.* G. *hagios*, holy + -LOGY. Literature treating of the lives of saints.—**Hag'ioscope**, *n.* *Hagios* + *scope-ein*, to behold. An opening through a chancel arch or wall to enable worshippers in an aisle or side chapel to see the elevation of the host.

Ha'-ha, *n.* F. *haha*, an obstacle, a ditch behind an opening in a wall, said to be f. *ha!* of surprise. A sunk fence.

Hail, *n.*[1] O.E. *hægl*. Common Teut. Frozen vapour falling in pellets.—*v.*[1]*i.* *It hails*, hail is falling.—*vt.* To pour down as hail.

Hail, *int.* A use as *int.* of obs. *Hail*, a., hale —O.N. *heill* = O.E. *hál*. HALE. WHOLE. An exclamation of greeting.—*v.*[2]*t.* To greet, welcome; to call or shout to.—*vi.* *To hail from*, to come from.—*n.*[2] A greeting; a call or shout.

Hair, *n.* O.E. *hǽr*, *hér*. Common Teut. A filament growing from the skin of an animal; such filaments collectively.—**Hair'y**,[2] *a.*

Hake, *n.* Orig. uncertain. A fish like a cod.

Hal'berd, Hal'bert, *n.* O.F. *halebarde*—M.H.G. *helmbarde*, prob. f. *helm*, HELM[1] + *barta* (f. root of Ger. *bart*, O.E. *beard*, BEARD), broad axe, the sense being thus 'axe for smashing helmets'. A weapon consisting of an axe-blade and a spear-head mounted on a long handle.—**Halberdier'**, *n.*

Hal'cyon, *n.* L. *alcyon*, improperly *halcyon* —G. *alkuōn*. The kingfisher, fabled to charm the wind and waves to quiet in its breeding time.—*attrib.* Calm, peaceful.

Hale, *a.* The northern dial. rep. of O.E. *hál*. WHOLE. Free from infirmity, robust.

Hale, *vt.* O.F. *haler*—Old Frankish *hālon* = O.H.G. *halōn*, *holōn* (Ger. *holen*), to fetch, haul, &c. HAUL. To drag or pull.

Half, *n.*; *pl.* **Halves**. O.E. *healf*. Common Teut. Oldest sense 'side'. BEHALF. One of two equal parts.—*a.* Forming a half.—*adv.* To the extent of half. — **Half-broth'er (-sis'ter)**, *nn.* A brother (sister) by one parent only.—**Half'penny**, *n.* A coin of the value of half a penny.—**Halve**, *vt.* M.E. *halfen*, *halven*. To divide into halves.

Hal'ibut, *n.* App. (as having been commonly eaten on holy-days), f. M.E. *haly*, HOLY + *butt*, flat fish, cogn. with Du. *bot*, Ger. *butte*, flounder, of obscure orig. A large flat fish.

Hall, *n.* O.E. *heall*. Common Teut. O.Teut. root *hel-*, *hal-*, *hul-*, to cover, conceal. Cogn. with L. *cēlāre*, to CONCEAL. HELL. HELM.[1] HULL.[1] OCCULT. A large room; a squire's house; the building belonging to a guild; the entrance room of a house.—**Hall'-mark**, *n.* A mark used (orig. at Goldsmiths' Hall) for marking assayed gold or silver.

Hal'low, *vt.* O.E. *hálgian*, f. *hálig*, HOLY. To make holy, sanctify; to consecrate.

Hallu'cinate, *vt.* L. *ālūcināri* (less properly *hallūcināri*), *ālūcinātus*, to wander in mind, prob. conn. with G. *aluein*. To produce illusion in the mind of.—**Hallucina'tion**, *n.*

Ha'lo, *n.* = F. *halo*, It. *alone*—L. *halōs*—G. *halōs*, (round) threshing-floor, disk, halo. A circle of light round the sun, &c.; a similar circle put round a saint's head in a picture; ideal glory.—*vt.* To invest with a halo.

Halt, *n.* Orig. in phrase *to make halt* = Ger. *halt machen* (f. *halt*, holding, stoppage, f. *halten*, to hold, cogn. with HOLD, *v.*), adopted through one of the Romance langs. A temporary stoppage on a march or journey.—*v.*[1]*i.* To make a halt.—*vt.* To cause to halt, stop.

Halt, *a.* O.E. *halt.* Common Teut. Lame, limping.—*v.*[2]*i.* To walk unsteadily, waver.

Hal'ter, *n.* O.E. *hælftre* = O.H.G. *halftra* (Ger. *halfter*). O.Teut. root *halb-*, to hold. HELVE. A head-rope or strap for a horse; a rope for hanging.—*vt.* To put a halter on.

Hal'yard, **Hal'liard**, *n.* Orig. *halier*, f. HALE, *v.*, perverted by association with YARD.[2] A rope for raising or lowering a spar, flag, &c.

Ham, *n.* O.E. *ham(m)* = O.H.G. *hamma*, Du. *hamme.* The hollow of the knee; the back of the thigh; a hog's thigh salted and dried.—**Ham'string**, *n.* A tendon of the ham.—*vt.* To cut the hamstrings of so as to disable.

Hamadry'ad, *n.* L. *hamādryas*, pl. *hamādryades*—G. *hamadruas*, f. *hama*, together with + *drus*, tree. DRYAD. A wood-nymph whose life was fabled to depend on that of the tree to which she was attached.

Ham'let, *n.* O.F. *hamelet*, dim. of *hamel* (F. *hameau*), dim. of **ham*—W. Germanic *haim*, village, house. HOME. A small village.

Ham'mer, *n.* O.E. *hamor*, *hamer.* Common Teut. An instrument for beating, driving nails, &c.; a contrivance for exploding the charge in a gun.—*vt.* and *i.* To beat, &c., with, to deal blows with or as with, a hammer.

Ham'mock, *n.* Sp. *hamaca*, of Carib orig. A hanging bed.

Ham'per, *n.* Alteration of *Hanaper* in sim. sense—O.F. *hanapier*, a case for a *hanap* or drinking-vessel — Old Frankish **knapp-* = O.H.G. *knapf*, cup. A large covered basket.

Ham'per, *vt.* Orig. uncertain. To shackle, clog; to impede, obstruct, embarrass.

Hand, *n.* O.E. *hand*, *hond.* Common Teut. The extremity of the arm beyond the wrist; side (right or left), direction, quarter; style of writing; the cards dealt to each player; a measure of four inches.—*vt.* To lead or assist with the hand; to deliver, pass, transfer.—**Hand'cuff**, *n.* CUFF.[1] A fetter for the wrist, used in connected pairs.—*vt.* To secure with handcuffs.—**Han'dicraft**, *n.* A development after *handiwork* (see below) of obs. *Handcraft*, manual skill or work. Manual skill; a manual occupation.—**Han'diwork**, *n.* M.E. *handiwerc*—O.E. *handgeweorc*, f. *geweorc*, i.e. *weorc*, WORK, with pref. *ge-*. Work of or done by the hands; work.—**Han'dkerchief**, *n.* A small square of linen, &c., carried on the person for wiping the face, &c., or worn round the neck.—**Hand'**Y,[2] *a.* Ready to hand; easily manipulated; dexterous.

Han'dicap, *n.* Formerly, a kind of sport involving drawings from a cap, whence the name (*hand i' cap*, hand in the cap). A horse-race in which weights are carried by the horses to equalize their chances; any competition in which chances are equalized; the condition imposed for equalization; any encumbrance or disability.—*vt.* To impose a handicap on.

Han'dle, *n.* O.E. *handle*, f. HAND + instrumental suff. *-le.* A part to be grasped in the hand.—*vt.* To subject to the action of the hand; to manipulate, deal with.

Hand'sel, *n.* Perh. f. O.N. *handsal*, bargain confirmed by shaking hands = HAND-SALE. A gift on beginning or entering upon something; earnest money; first use.—*vt.* To give a handsel to; to inaugurate.

Hand'some, *a.* HAND + -SOME. Cf. *toothsome.* Formerly, easy to handle, suitable. Of a sum of money, &c., considerable; generous, magnanimous; having a fine figure.—**Hand'some**LY,[2] *adv.*—**Hand'some**NESS, *n.*

Hang, *vt.* To this *v.* and its present inflexions (pa.t. and pple. *hung* or *hanged*, the latter only of putting to death) three *vv.* have contributed, undergoing somewhat complicated modifications—(1) O.E. *hón*, trans.; (2) O.E. *hangian*, intrans.; (3) the O.N. causal v. *hengjan.* HINGE. To fasten to an object above, suspend; to suspend by way of capital punishment; to furnish *with* things suspended or *with* tapestry, wall-paper, &c.—*vi.* To be suspended from above; to lean over; to depend *on* or *upon*; to cling, to stick close.

Hank, *n.* App. f. Norse. Cf. O.N. *hönk*, hank (Sw. *hank*, string). A coil or loop.

Han'ker, *vi.* Orig. obscure. Cf. Du. *hunkeren.* With *after*, to long for.

Han'som cab, *n.* From one *Hansom*, the inventor. A kind of cab with two wheels.

Hap, *n.* O.N. *happ*, chance, good luck. Cf. O.E. *gehæp*, a., fit. PERHAPS. Fortune (good or bad), chance; something which befalls one. —*vi.* To come about, occur; to have the hap *to do.*—**Haphaz'ard**, *n.* Lit., 'hazard of chance'. Mere chance.—*a.* Random, without design.—*adv.* At random.—**Hap'**LESS, *a.* Unlucky.—**Hap'**LY,[2] *adv.* Perhaps.—**Hap'**PEN,[2] *vi.* To hap.—**Hap'**PY,[2] *a.* Having good hap; feeling great content in having it, glad; apt, dexterous; appropriate, fitting.—**Hap'pi**LY,[2] *adv.*—**Hap'pi**NESS, *n.*

Harangue', *n.* O.F. *harangue*—Med.L. *harenga*, perh. f. O.H.G. *hring*, RING,[1] in sense 'circle of hearers'. A vehement speech.—*vi.* and *t.* To make, to address in, a harangue.

Harass', *vt.* F. *harasser*, perh. f. *harer*, to set a dog on. To worry, trouble, distress.

Har'binger, *n.* O.F. *herbergere*, agent-n. f. *herbergier*, to provide lodgings for, f. *herberge*, lodgings, quarters for an army, &c.—O.H.G. and O.L.G. *heriberga*, 'shelter for an army', f. *heri* (Ger. *heer*), army + *-berga*, shelter, f. *bergan.* HARRY. BOROUGH. One sent before to purvey lodgings; one who announces an approach.—*vt.* To act as harbinger to.

Har'bour, *n.* M.E. *hereberghe*, *herberwe*, corresp. to O.E. **herebeorg*, f. *here*, army + **-beorg*, shelter. Cf. O.H.G. *heriberga*, cited under prec. Shelter, lodging; a place of shelter for ships.—*vt.* To give shelter to; to entertain in one's mind.—*vi.* To take shelter.

Hard, *a.* O.E. *heard.* Common Teut. Cogn. with G. *kratus*, strong. (See next.) Resisting force, pressure or effort; difficult to understand; hard-hearted; stingy; difficult to bear; harsh, severe; carried on with energy or persistence; applied to water containing substances making it unfit for washing.—*adv.* Vigorously; severely; with difficulty; close.—**Hard'**EN,[2] *vt.* and *i.*—**Hard'**LY,[2] *adv.* Rigorously; with trouble; barely, only just.—**Hard'**NESS, *n.*—**Hard'**SHIP, *n.* Hardness of fate, severe toil or suffering; an instance of this.—**Hard'ware**, *n.* Small ware of metal.

Har'dy, *a.* F. *hardi*, pa.pple. of O.F. *hardir*, to make hard, bold, &c., cogn. with prec. Bold, daring; robust, vigorous.—**Har'di**LY,[2] *adv.* —**Har'di**HOOD, *n.*—**Har'di**NESS, *n.*

Hare, *n.* O.E. *hara.* Common Teut. A rodent very swift quadruped with a divided upper lip.—**Hare'bell**, *n.* Perh. as growing in places frequented by hares. A plant with a slender stem and blue bell-shaped flowers.

Ha'rem, *n.* Arab. *haram*, *harīm*, lit. '(that which is) prohibited or unlawful', f. *harama*, to prohibit. The part of a Mohammedan palace or dwelling-house which is appropriated to the women; the inmates collectively.

Har'icot, *n.* F. Orig. uncertain. A ragout; a leguminous plant, the French-bean.

Hark, *vt.* Early M.E. *herkien*—O.E. type **heorcian*, corresp. to Old Fris. *herkia*, conn. with M.H.G. and Ger. *horchen.* HEARKEN. To listen to.—*vi.* To listen.

Har'lequin, *n.* F. *harlequin, arlequin*—It. *arlecchino*, a character in Italian comedy, perh. the same word as O.F. *Hellequin, Herlequin*, a devil of mediæval legend, poss. of Teut. orig. In pantomime, a mute character supposed to be invisible to the clown and pantaloon, and the rival of the clown in the affections of Columbine (It. *Colombina*, f. *colombino*, dove-like—L. *columba*, DOVE).—**Harlequinade'**, *n.* F. *arlequinade.* The part of a pantomime in which harlequin plays the chief part.

Har'lot, *n.* O.F. *harlot*, lad, base fellow, vagabond, of uncertain orig. Formerly, a vagabond, a buffoon, a 'fellow'. A prostitute.

Harm, *n.* O.E. *hearm.* Common Teut. Evil, injury.—*vt.* To do harm to.—**Harm'**FUL, *a.* —**Harm'**LESS, *a.* Unharmed; doing no harm.

Har'mony, *n.* F. *harmonie*—L. *harmonia*—G. *harmonia*, a joining, harmony, f. *harmos*, a joint, f. *ar-*, root of *arariskein*, to join, fasten. Combination and adaptation of parts so as to form an orderly or pleasing whole; agreement, concord; the combination of musical notes so as to produce a pleasing effect; melodious sound.—**Harmon'**IC, *a.* Sounding in harmony; relating to musical harmony. —*n.* A subordinate sound produced by vibration of a string, &c.—**Harmo'nious**, *a.*—**Harmo'nious**LY,[2] *adv.*—**Harmo'nium**, *n.* F. *harmonium.* A musical wind-instrument resembling a small organ.—**Har'mon**IZE, *vi.* To be in harmony, accord.—*vt.* To bring into harmony or agreement.

Har'ness, *n.* O.F. *harneis* (F. *harnais*). Orig. unknown. Armour; the tackle of a draught horse.—*vt.* To put harness on.

Harp, *n.* O.E. *hearpe.* Common Teut. A stringed musical instrument played with the fingers.—*vi.* To play on a harp: to dwell wearisomely *on* or *upon*.—**Harp'**ER, *n.*—**Harp'**IST, *n.*—**Harp'sichord**, *n.* With intrusive *s* f. obs. F. *harpechorde*, f. L.L. *harpa*, harp (of Teut. orig.) + L. *chorda*, string. CORD. A predecessor of the pianoforte.

Harpoon', *n.* F. *harpon*, cramp-iron, f. *harpe*, dog's claw, cramp-iron—L. *harpē* = G. *harpē*, sickle. A barbed spear-like missile with a rope attached.—*vt.* To strike or spear with a harpoon.—**Harpoon'**ER, *n.*

Har'py, *n.* L. *harpyiae* = G. *harpuiai*, 'snatchers', cogn. with *harpazein*, to snatch, L. *rapĕre.* RAPE, *v.* A monster with a woman's body and a bird's wings and claws.

Har'ridan, *n.* Perh. altered f. F. *haridelle*, worn-out horse, harridan. An ugly old woman.

Har'rier, *n.* App. f. HARE + -IER. A hound used in hunting the hare.

Har'row, *n.* M.E. *harwe*, corresp. to O.E. **hearwe* or **hearge*, app. conn. with M.L.G. *harke*, rake, O.N. *herfi*, harrow. A spiked frame drawn over ploughed land.—*vt.* To draw a harrow over; to distress greatly.

Har'ry, *vi.* O.E. *hergian, herian* = O.L.G. *herron*, O.H.G. *harjōn*, f. O.Teut. **harjo-*, army, whence *hari, heri*, O.E. *here.* HARBINGER. HARBOUR. To commit ravages.—*vt.* To ravage, despoil; to worry, harass.

Harsh, *a.* Northern M.E. *harsk*, corresp. to M.L.G. and Ger. *harsch.* Rough to the touch or taste; jarring; unpleasing; rigorous, severe.—**Harsh'**LY,[2] *adv.*—**Harsh'**NESS, *n.*

Hart, *n.* O.E. *heort, heorot* = O.L.G. *hirot*, O.N. *hjörtr.* A male deer.—**Harts'horn**, *n.* The aqueous solution of ammonia, orig. obtained from harts' horns.—**Hart's'-tongue**, *n.* A fern with long tongue-like fronds.

Har'vest, *n.* O.E. *hærfest* = O.H.G. *herbist* (Ger. *herbst*). Cogn. with G. *karpos*, fruit, L. *carpĕre*, to pluck. The season for gathering in the grain; the gathering in; the crop.—*vt.* To gather in.—**Har'vest**ER, *n.*

Hash, *vt.* F. *hacher*, to cut, hack, f. *hache*, axe—O.H.G. **happja.* HATCH, *v.*[2] HATCHET. To cut small for cooking.—*n.* A dish of previously cooked meat cut small and warmed up; an incongruous mixture; a bungle.

Hasp, *n.* O.E. *hæpse.* Cf. M Du. *haspe*, O.N. *hespa.* A hinged clasp for fastening a door, &c.—*vt.* To fasten with a hasp.

Has'sock, *n.* O.E. *hassuc*, of uncertain orig. A tuft of coarse grass; a kneeling-cushion.

Haste, *n.* O.F. *haste*—W. Germanic **haisti-*, in O.E. *hǽst, hést*, violence, fury = Goth. *haifsts*, strife. Speed, quickness; precipitancy; hurry.—*vi.* To come or go quickly or hurriedly. —**Has't**EN,[2] *vt.* and *i.* To haste, to cause to haste.—**Hast'**Y,[2] *a.*—**Hast'**ILY,[2] *adv.*

Hat, *n.* O.E. *hæt.* O.Teut. **hattuz*, earlier **hadnús*, f. root *had-, hōd-*, whence O.E. *hód*, HOOD. A covering for the head.—**Hat'**TER, *n.*

Hatch, *n.*[1] O.E. *hæc*, genit. *hæcce.* Cf. Du. *hek*, fence, gate, Da. *hekke*, rack in a stable. A half-door or gate; in a ship, a framework covering the openings in the deck through which cargo is lowered, such an opening.—**Hatch'way**, *n.* Such an opening.

Hatch, *v.*[1]*i.* Early M.E. *hacche(n)*—O.E. **hæccean*, conn. with M.H.G. *hecken*, Sw. *häcka.* To bring forth young birds from the egg: to come forth from the egg.—*vt.* To bring forth from the egg; to bring forth from (the egg).—*n.*[2] The action of hatching; the brood.

Hatch, *v.*[2]*t.* F. *hacher.* HASH. To engrave or draw lines on (a surface) for shading.

Hat'chet, *n.* F. *hachette*, dim. of *hache.* HASH. A small axe with a short handle.

Hatch'ment, *n.* Altered f. ACHIEVEMENT. In *heraldry*, an achievement; an armorial tablet affixed to the house of a deceased person.

Hate, *n.* O.E. *hete* (v. *hatian*, whence the *a* in the mod. n.) = O.S. *heti.* Cf. Ger. *hasz.* HEINOUS. An emotion of extreme dislike or aversion.—*vt.* To dislike very strongly.—**Hate'**FUL, *a.*—**Hat'red**, *n.* *-Red* f. O.E. *rǽden*, condition. Detestation, ill-will.

Haugh'ty, *a.* An extension of archaic *Haught*, orig. *haut*—F. *haut*, L. *altus*, high. ALTITUDE. Proud, arrogant; grand, stately.—**Haugh'ti**LY,[2] *adv.*—**Haugh'ti**NESS, *n.*

Haul, *vt.* Var. of HALE, *v.* To pull, drag.—*vi.* Of the wind, to shift, veer.—*n.* A hauling; a draught of fish; an acquisition.—**Haul'**AGE, *n.* The action of, a charge for, hauling.

Haulm, Halm, *n.* O.E. *healm* = O.S., O.H.G., Ger. *halm.* Cogn. with G. *kalamos*, L. *calamus*, reed. Stems or stalks; a stem or stalk.

Haunch, *n.* O.F. *hanche*, prob. of Ger. orig. The part between the ribs and the thigh.

Haunt, *vt.* F. *hanter*, of uncertain orig. To resort to habitually; of ghosts, &c., to visit habitually.—*n.* A place of frequent resort.

Haut'boy, *n.* F. *hautbois*, f. *haut*, high + *bois* (L.L. *boscus*), wood. HAUGHTY. BUSH. A wooden-wind instrument of high pitch.

Have, *vt.* O.E. *habban*. Common Teut. O. Teut. stem *habē-*. App. cogn. with L. *habēre*. HAFT. To hold or possess; to be possessed or affected with; to be under obligation *to do*; to carry on, engage in; to obtain.—*v.aux.* Forms the perfect and pluperfect tenses.

Ha'ven, *n.* O.E. *hæfen, hæfne* = M.Du. *haven*, M.L.G., Ger. *hafen*, O.N. *hōfn*. Gen. taken as f. root of HAVE or of HEAVE, though poss. f. O.N. *haf* = O.E. *hæf*, sea. A harbour.

Hav'ersack, *n.* F. *havresac*—Ger. *habersack*, lit., 'oat-sack', orig. a horseman's bag for carrying oats. A bag for a soldier's rations; a similar bag used by travellers.

Hav'oc, *n.* A.F. *havok*, altered f. O.F. *havot*, prob. of Teut. orig. Pillage; destruction.

Haw, *n.* Perh. short for O.E. **hægberie*, 'hedge-berry', f. *haga*, HEDGE (= M.Du. *hage*, *haghe*) + *berie*, BERRY. The fruit of the hawthorn; the hawthorn.—**Haw'thorn**, *n.* O.E. *haga-thorn*, 'hedge-thorn', f. *haga* + *thorn*, THORN. A thorny shrub used for hedges.

Hawk, *n.* O.E. *hafoc, heafoc*. Common Teut. Any bird of prey used in falconry.—*v.*[1]*i.* To engage in falconry.

Hawk, *v.*[2]*i.* Prob. imitative. To clear the throat noisily.

Haw'ker, *n.* App. f. M.L.G. *hoker* (Ger. *höker*), Du. *heuker*, in sim. sense, of obscure orig. HUCKSTER. One who goes about selling his wares.—**Hawk**, *v.*[3]*t.* App. a back-formation f. the *n.* To carry *about* for sale.

Hawse, *n.* In 16th c. *halse, haulse*, app. f. O.N. *háls*, neck, part of a ship's bow. Common Teut. Cogn. with L. *collum*. The part of the bow in which holes are cut for cables.

Haw'ser, *n.* App. A.F. *hauceour*, f. O.F. *haucier*, to hoist—L.L. type **altiāre*, f. *altus*, high. ALTITUDE. A small cable.

Hay, *n.* O.E. *híg*. Comm. Teut. O.Teut. stem *hauw-*, to HEW, cut. Grass cut and dried.

Haz'ard, *n.* O.F. *hasard*, prob. of Arab. orig. A game at dice; chance, a chance; risk, peril.—*vt.* To expose to risk; to run the risk of.—**Haz'ard**OUS, *a.*

Haze, *n.* Orig. unknown. A misty appearance in the air.—**Haz'**Y,[2] *a.* (Occurs, however, earlier than the *n.*) Misty.

Ha'zel, *n.* O.E. *hæsel* = O.H.G. *hasal* (Ger. *hasel*). Cogn. with L. *corulus* (**cosulus*). A small tree bearing nuts; the reddish-brown colour of the ripe nut.—*a.* Of this colour.

He, *pron.* O.E. *hé, he*, f. root *hi-* (orig. demonstrative, 'this'), and cogn. with Old Fris., O.S. *hi, he*. HENCE. HERE. IT. The masculine pronoun of the third person.

Head, *n.* O.E. *héafod*. Common Teut. The upper or anterior part of the body of a man or an animal; the upper or principal extremity of various things; the foremost part; a chief or leader; leadership; progress; a section or chapter.—*vt.* To furnish with a head; to lead; to get ahead of so as to turn back.—*vi.* To face, front.—**Head'**ER, *n.* One who puts a head on a cask, &c.; a plunge head foremost.—**Head'ing**, *n.* A title, &c., at the head of a page, &c.—**Head'land**, *n.* A strip of unploughed land at the border of a field; a promontory.—**Head'long**, *adv.* -LONG. Head foremost; precipitately.—*a.* Plunging head foremost; impetuous.—**Head-quar'ters**, *n.pl.* The residence of a commander-in-chief; a centre of operations.—**Head'way**, *n.* Motion ahead or forward.—**Head'**Y,[2] *a.* Impetuous, violent; intoxicating.

Heal, *vt.* O.E. *hǽlan*, f. *hál*, WHOLE, HALE. To make whole or sound; to cure; to repair, amend.—*vi.* To become whole or sound.—**Health**, *n.* O.E. *hǽlth*, f. *hál*. Soundness of body; general condition of body; a toast drunk in a person's honour.—**Health'**FUL, *a.* —**Health'**Y,[2] *a.*—**Health'**ILY,[2] *adv.*

Heap, *n.* O.E. *héap* = O.S. *hôp* (Du. *hoop*), O.H.G. *houf* (Ger. *haufe*). A collection of things lying together; a (great) quantity.—*vt.* To form into a heap; to load *with*, to bestow in large quantities *upon*.

Hear, *vi.* O.E., Anglian *héran*, early West Saxon *híeran*, late *hýran*. Common Teut. To perceive sound; to listen; to be informed, learn.—*vt.* To perceive by the ear; to listen to; to try (a case, &c.); to accede to; to get to know.—**Hear'say**, *n.* Report, rumour.—*a.* Of evidence, not based on personal knowledge.

Hear'ken, Har'ken, *vi.* O.E. *hercnian*, *heorcnian*, f. **heorcian*. HARK. To listen.

Hearse, *n.* F. *herse*—L. *(h)irpex (h)irpicis*, a kind of harrow. REHEARSE. A framework for supporting tapers, &c., over a coffin; a carriage for carrying a coffin.

Heart, *n.* O.E. *heorte*. Common Teut. Cogn. with G. *kardia*, L. *cor*. The organ which causes the blood to circulate; the mind; the soul, the spirit; the seat of love; sensibility; the seat of courage; courage; the middle; a conventional representation of a heart; in *pl.*, one of the suits at cards marked with this; in *sing.*, a card of this suit.—**Heart'**EN,[2] *vt.* To inspirit, animate.—*vi.* To be cheered.—**Heart'**LESS, *a.*—**Heart'**Y,[2] *a.* Cordial; sincere; vigorous; in sound health; satisfying the appetite.—**Heart'**ILY,[2] *adv.*

Hearth, *n.* O.E. *heorth* = O.S. *herth*, M.L.G., O.H.G. *hert*. The place where a fire is made.

Heat, *n.* O.E. *hǽtu, hǽto*. O.Teut. type **haitin-*, f. **haito-z*. HOT. The quality of being hot; the sensation of this quality; hot weather or climate; high temperature; a single course in a race; fervour, ardour, stress; sexual excitement of animals.—*vt.* To make hot; to excite.—*vi.* To become hot or excited.

Heath, *n.* O.E. *hǽth*, corresp. to M.L.G. *hêde*, M.Du. *hêde, heide*. A waste tract of land covered with dwarf shrubs; a plant or shrub found upon heaths.

Hea'then, *a.* O.E. *hǽthen* = O.S. *hêthin*, O.H.G. *heidan* (Ger. *heide*). Orig. uncertain. Neither Christian, Jewish, nor Mohammedan; pagan.—*n.* One whose religion is neither Christian, Jewish, nor Mohammedan; a pagan.—**Hea'then**ISH, *a.*—**Hea'then**ISM, *n.*

Heath'er, *n.* Orig. unknown. A low shrub growing on hill-sides and heaths.

Heave, *vt.* O.E. *hef-*, a pres. stem. of *hebban*. Common Teut. O.Teut. root *haf-*. Cogn. with L. *capĕre*, to seize. HAFT. HEAVY. To lift with effort; to utter (a sigh, &c.); to throw (something heavy).—*vi.* To bulge out; to swell up, rise; to retch.—*n.* A heaving.

Heav'en, *n.* O.E. *heofon, hefen* = M.L.G. *heven*. Orig. unknown. The expanse apparently overarching the earth, the sky (gen. in *pl.*); the abode of immortal beings; God; a state of bliss.—**Heav'en**LY,[1] *a.*

Heav'y, *a.* O.E. *hefig*, f. *hefe*, weight, f. root of *hebban*, to HEAVE. Of great weight; striking or falling with great force; clinging, impeding; intense, severe; thick, coarse; sluggish; tedious; oppressive; toilsome; sorrowful.—**Heav'**ILY,[2] *adv.*—**Heav'**INESS, *n.*

Hebdom'adal, *a.* L. *hebdomadālis*, f. *hebdomas, hebdomadis* = G. *hebdomas*, the number seven, seven days, f. *hepta*, SEVEN. Meeting, taking place, appearing, once a week.

Heb'etate, *vt.* L. *hebetāre*, *hebetātum*, f. *hebes*, *hebetis*, blunt, dull. To make dull or obtuse.—**Heb'**ETUDE, *n.*

Hec'atomb, *n.* L. *hecatombē*=G. *hekatombē*, orig. (a sacrifice of) a hundred oxen, f. *hekaton*, a hundred + *bous*, ox. COW. A great public sacrifice; a sacrifice of many victims.

Heck'le, **Hack'le**, *n.* M.E. *hechele*, *hekele*, *hakell*. Cf. M.H.G. *hechele*, *hachele* (Ger. *hechel*), M.Du. *hekele*. An instrument for combing flax or hemp; the long feathers on the neck of the cock, &c.—*vt.* To dress with a heckle; to question severely.

Hec'tic, *a.* Through F. f. L.L. *hecticus*—G. *hektikos*, habitual, consumptive, f. *hexis*, state of body, f. *hexein*, fut. of *echein*, to have, also, to be (so and so). Applied to the fever, characterized by flushed cheeks and a dry hot skin, accompanying consumption; consumptive.

Hec'tor, *n.* The name of the Homeric hero (who, however, was no bully or braggart). A bully or braggart.—*vi.* and *t.* To bully.

Hedge, *n.* O.E. **hecg*, *hegg* (corresp. to O.H.G. *hegga*, *hecka* (Ger. *hecke*)), f. same root as *haga*. HAW. A row of bushes forming a boundary. —*vt.* To surround with a hedge.—*vi.* To bet on both sides to secure oneself against loss; to shift, shuffle. — **Hedge'hog**, *n.* A small quadruped armed with spines which frequents hedges and has a pig-like snout.

He'donism, *n.* With -ISM f. G. *hēdonē*, pleasure, conn. with *hēdus*, SWEET. The ethical theory in which pleasure is regarded as the chief good.—**He'don**IST, *n.*

Heed, *vt.* O.E. *hédan* = O.S. *hôdian*, *huodian*, O.H.G. *huotan* (Ger. *hüten*). To care for; regard.—*n.* App. f. the *v.* No corresp. O.E. *n.*; but cf. O.H.G. *huota* (Ger. *hut*). Care, regard.—**Heed'**FUL, *a.*—**Heed'**LESS, *a.*

Heel, *n.* O.E. *héla*, *hǽla* (prob. contracted f. **hóh-ila*, dim. of *hóh*, heel. HOCK [1]) = Old Fris. *hêla*, M.Du. *hiele*. The hinder part of the foot; the part of a boot supporting the heel.—*v.*[1]*t.* To furnish with a heel.

Heel, *v.*[2]*i.* A corr. of earlier (now dial.) *Hield*, *Heeld*, in sim. senses—O.E. *hieldan*, to tilt, incline = M.Du., M.L.G. *helden*. Of a ship, to lean to one side.—*vt.* To cause to heel.

Hegem'ony, *n.* G. *hēgemonia*, f. *hēgemōn*, leader. Leadership, predominance.

Heg'ira, *n.* Med.L. *hegira*—Arab. *hijrah*, departure, separation. The flight of Mohammed from Mecca (622 A.D.), from which the Mohammedan era is reckoned; the era.

Heif'er, *n.* O.E. *heahfore*, of obscure orig. A young cow that has not had a calf.

Height, *n.* O.E. *híehtho*, f. *héah*, HIGH. Distance from the base upwards; the quality of being high; a high position; the top; an eminence.—**Height'**EN,[2] *vt.* To give height to; to increase, intensify.

Hei'nous, *a.* F. *haineux*, f. *haine*, hatred, f. *hair*, cogn. with HATE. Highly criminal.

Heir, *n.* O.F. *eir*, *heir*—L. *hēres*. HEREDITY. INHERIT. One who by law succeeds or is entitled to succeed to property, &c.—**Heir'**ESS, *n.*—**Heir'loom**, *n.* From LOOM, *n.*, in dial. sense 'tool, utensil'. A chattel that follows the succession to real estate or has been long in a family.—**Heir'**SHIP, *n.*

Heli'acal, *a.* L.L. *hēliacus*—G. *hēliakos*, a. f. *hēlios*, sun. Coincident with the sun's rising or setting.—**He'liograph**, *n.* From *hēlios* + *-graphos*. TELEGRAPH. An apparatus for signalling by reflecting flashes of sunlight.—**He'liotrope**, *n.* F. *héliotrope*—G. *heliotropion*, f. *hēlios* + *-tropos*, turning, f. *trepein*, to turn. A plant whose flowers turn with the sun; the purple colour of the flowers.

Hell, *n.* O.E. *hel(l)* (= O.H.G. *hella* (Ger. *hölle*), O.N. *hel*), conn. with *helan*, to cover, conceal, f. *hel-*, *hal-*, *hul-*. HALL. HOLE. The abode of the dead; this as a place of torment; a gaming-house.—**Hel'l**ISH, *a.*

Hel'lebore, *n.* L. *(h)elleborus*—G. *(h)elleboros*. A plant used by the ancients as a remedy for mental diseases, epilepsy, &c.

Helle'nic, *a.* L. *Hellēnicus*—G. *Hellēnikos*. Of or pertaining to the Hellenes or Greeks.—**Hel'len**ISM, *n.* A Greek idiom, &c.; adoption of Greek characteristics; Greek culture.

Helm, *n.*[1] O.E. *helm*. Common Teut. O.Teut. root *hel-*, *hal-*, *hul-*, to cover, conceal. HALL. HALBERD. A helmet.—**Hel'met**, *n.* Obs. F. *healmet*, *helmet*, dim. of *helme*, helm, f. O.H.G. A defensive cover for the head.

Helm, *n.*[2] O.E. *helma*. Cf. O.N. *hjálm*. The handle or wheel of a rudder.

Hel'ot, *n.* L. *hēlōtes*, pl.—G. *heilōtes* (pl. of *heilōs*), a class of serfs in Sparta. A serf.

Help, *vt.* O.E. *helpan*. Common Teut. To furnish with what is serviceable, aid; to further; to serve with food; to serve (food); to prevent; to refrain from; *to help oneself to*, to take.—*n.* Aid, assistance; an aid.—**Help'**ER, *n.*—**Help'**FUL, *a.* — **Help'**LESS, *a.* — **Help'mate**, *n.* Prob. influenced in orig. by synonymous **Help'meet**, formed by taking as one the words *help meet* in Genesis ii. 18, 20. A fitting helper, us. of a wife or husband.

Helve, *n.* O.E. *hielfe*, f. root *halb-*. HALTER. The handle of a weapon or tool.

Hem, *n.* O.E. *hem(m)*. Cf. N. Fris. *heam*, hem, edge, border. The border of a piece of cloth; such a border made by doubling the edge and sewing it down.—*vt.* To form a hem on; to shut *in*, to limit, restrain.

Hem'isphere, *n.* O.F. *emisphere*—G. *hēmisphairion*, f. *hēmi-*, HEMI- + *sphaira*, SPHERE. A half sphere; a half of the celestial sphere or of the terrestrial globe.—**Hem'istich**, *n.* G. *hēmistichion*, f. *hēmi-* + *stichos*, row, verse. Half a line of verse.

Hem'lock, *n.* O.E. *hemlic*, *hymlice*, of obscure orig. A common poisonous plant.

Hemp, *n.* O.E. *henep*, *hænep* = O.H.G. *hanaf* (Ger. *hanf*). Cogn. with G. *kannabis*, L. *cannabis*. CANVAS. A fibrous plant; the fibre.

Hen, *n.* O.E. *henn* (corresp. to O.H.G. *henna* (Ger. *henne*)), f. *hana* (cf. Ger. *hahn*), cock. The female of the domestic fowl and other birds.

Hence, *adv.* M.E. *hennes*, with advbl. genit. *-s* f. earlier *henne*—O.E. *hionan*, f. root *hi-*. HE. From this point; for this reason.

Hench'man, *n.* A corr. of a compound formed f. O.E. *hengest* = O.H.G. *hengist* (Ger. *hengst*), horse + MAN, hence app. orig. 'groom'. A squire, page; a trusty follower.

Hendi'adys, *n.* Med.L. *hendiadys*—G. *hen dia duoin*, 'one by means of two'. The expression of a single complex idea by two words connected by a conjunction.

Hepat'ic, *a.* L. *hēpaticus*—G. *hēpatikos*, a. f. *hēpar*, *hēpatos*, the liver. Of the liver.

Hep'tagon, *n.* G. *heptagōnos*, a., f. *hepta*, SEVEN + *gōnia*, angle. A figure with seven angles.—**Heptag'on**AL, *a.*

Hep'tarchy, *n.* G. *hepta*, SEVEN + *-archia*, f. *archē*, rule. A government by seven rulers; the seven ancient British kingdoms.

Hep'tateuch, *n.* G. *heptateuchos*, f. *hepta*, SEVEN + *teuchos*, implement, in Late G., book. The first seven books of the Old Testament.
Her, *pron.* O.E. *hiere, hire*, genit. of *hío, héo*, fem. of *hé*, HE. Belonging to her.
Her'ald, *n.* O.F. *heraut, herault*, prob. f. Teut. An officer charged with the duty of making royal proclamations, bearing ceremonial messages, arranging public processions, keeping the records of those entitled to armorial bearings, &c.; a messenger, envoy.—*vt.* To proclaim, announce.—**Heral'dic**, *a.*—**Her'aldry**, *n.* The art or science of a herald, esp. of blazoning and settling claims to armorial bearings; armorial bearings; heraldic pomp.
Herb, *n.* O.F. *erbe* (F. *herbe*)—L. *herba*, grass, green crops, herb. ARBOUR. A plant with a succulent stem which dies down after flowering.—**Herba'ceous**, *a.* L. *herbāceus*, grassy (f. *herba*) + -OUS. Of the nature of a herb.—**Herb'age**, *n.* Herbs collectively; grass, pasture.—**Herb'al**, *n.* A treatise on plants.—**Herb'alist**, *n.* One versed in the knowledge of plants; a dealer in medicinal herbs.—**Herba'rium**, *n.* L.L., neut. of an a. f. *herba*. A collection of dried plants.
Herd, *n.*[1] O.E. *heord*. Common Teut. A number of domestic animals of one kind kept together; a number of animals feeding or travelling together; a large company of people.
Herd, *n.*[2] O.E. *hirde, hierde*. Common Teut. Cogn. with prec. One who tends a herd.
Here, *adv.* O.E. *hér*. Common Teut. App. f. *hi-*. HE. In this place; at this point; hither.
Hered'ity, *n.* F. *hérédité*—*hērēditas*, heirship, inheritance, f. *hēres, hērēdis*, HEIR. Hereditary character; the property of an organism by which its nature and characteristics are transmitted to its descendants.—**Hered'itary**, *a.* Descending by inheritance; passing from parents to offspring or from precursors to successors. —**Hered'itarily**,[2] *adv.*—**Heredit'ament**, *n.* Med.L. *hērēditāmentum*. Something that can be inherited.
Her'esy, *n.* O.F. *eresie, heresie*—L. type **heresia* for *haeresis*, a sect, heresy—G. *hairesis*, a choosing, a set of principles, a sect, heresy, f. *haire-esthai*, to choose, middle of *haire-ein*, to take. Religious opinion, a religious opinion, contrary to orthodox doctrine; opinion, an opinion, not that generally accepted.—**Her'esiarch**, *n.* L.L. *haeresiarcha*—G. *hairesiarchēs*, f. *hairesis* + *-archēs*, ruler. A founder or leader of a heresy.—**Her'etic**, *n.* F. *hérétique*—Eccles.L. *haereticus*—G. *hairetikos*, able to choose, heretical. One holding an opinion involving heresy.—**Heret'ical**, *a.*
Her'itable, *a.* F. *héritable*, f. *hériter*, L.L. *hērēditāre*, to inherit, f. *hēres, hērēdis*, HEIR. Capable of being inherited or of inheriting.—**Her'itage**, *n.* That which has been or may be inherited; an inherited lot or portion.
Hermaph'rodite, *n.* L. *hermaphroditus*—G. *hermaphroditos*, orig. proper name of the son of Hermes and Aphrodite, fabled to have grown together with a nymph. A being combining parts characteristic of both sexes.
Hermeneu'tic, *a.* G. *hermēneutikos*, a. f. *hermēneutēs*, interpreter, f. *hermēneuein*, to interpret. Concerned with interpretation.—In *pl.* as *n.*, the art or science of interpretation.
Hermet'ic, *a.* Mod.L. *hermēticus*, irreg. f. *Hermes* (*Trismegistus*), a name given to the Egyptian god Thoth supposed to be the author of the secrets of alchemy. Relating to alchemy; *hermetic sealing*, air-tight closure of a vessel by fusion, &c. (as practised by alchemists).—**Hermet'ically**, *adv.* -AL. -LY.[2]
Her'mit, *n.* O.F. (*h*)*ermite*—L.L. *erēmīta*. EREMITE. One living alone from religious motives.—**Her'mitage**, *n.* His habitation.
Her'nia, *n.* L. Protrusion of part of an organ through the containing cavity; rupture.
He'ro, *n.* L. *hērōs*—G. *hērōs*. An illustrious warrior; one admired and venerated for his achievements and noble qualities; the chief male personage in a poem, play, &c.—**Her'oine**, *n.* L. *hērōina*—G. *hērōinē*, fem. of *hērōs*. A woman distinguished by fortitude or noble deeds; the chief female personage in a poem, &c.—**Hero'ic**, **Hero'ical**, *aa.*—**Hero'ically**,[2] *adv.*—**Her'oism**, *n.*
Her'on, *n.* M.E. *heiroun, heyron*—O.F. *hairon* (F. *héron*) = Pr. *aigron*, It. *aghirone*—O.H.G. **haiger, heiger*. (For a F. dim. see AIGRETTE.) A long-necked long-legged wading bird.
Herpetol'ogy, *n.* G. *herpeton*, reptile (f. *herpein*, to creep) + -LOGY. The study of reptiles.
Her'ring, *n.* O.E. *hǽring* = O.H.G. *hāring* (Ger. *hering*). A well-known sea fish.
Hes'itate, *vi.* L. *haesitāre, haesitātum*, to stick fast, hesitate, freq. of *haerēre*, to stick. ADHERE. INHERE. To hold back in, to speak with, indecision.—**Hes'itancy**, *n.*—**Hes'itant**, *a.*—**Hesita'tion**, *n.*
Hest, *n.* M.E. *heste, hest*, with excrescent *t* f. O.E. *hǽs*—O.Teut. type **haitan* (O.E. *hátan*), to call by name, command. Command.
Het'eroclite, *a.* L. *heteroclitus*—G. *heteroklitos*, irregularly inflected, f. *heteros*, other different + *-klitos*, f. *klinein*, to bend, inflect Irregularly declined or inflected.
Het'erodox, *a.* G. *heterodoxos*, f. *heteros* (see prec.) + *doxa*, opinion, f. *doke-ein*. DOGMA. Differing from generally accepted opinions; holding such views.—**Het'erodoxy**,[1] *n.*
Heteroge'neous, *a.* Scholastic L. *heterogeneus* (f. G. *heterogenēs*, f. *heteros* (HETEROCLITE) + *genos*, kind) + -OUS. Differing in kind or nature; composed of diverse elements. —**Heterogene'ity**, *n.*
Hew, *vi.* O.E. *héawan*. Common Teut. O. Teut. stem *hauw-*. HAGGLE. HAY. HOE. To deal blows with a cutting weapon.—*vt.* To cut, chop; to shape, &c., by cutting.
Hex'agon, *n.* G. *hexagōnos*, a., f. *hex*, SIX + *gōnia*, angle. A figure with six angles.—**Hexag'onal**, *a.*
Hexam'eter, *a.* L. *hexameter*—G. *hexametros*, f. *hex*, SIX + *metron*, measure. Consisting of six metrical feet.—*n.* An hexameter verse; *dactylic hexameter*, a line consisting of five dactyls (any of which may be replaced by a spondee) and a spondee or trochee.
Hey'-day, **Hey'day**, *n.* Orig. uncertain. Full bloom, highest stage.
Hia'tus, *n.* L. *hiātus*, opening, gap, f. *hiāre*, to gape. CHASM. YAWN. A break of continuity; a break between two vowels without an intervening consonant.
Hi'bernate, *vi.* L. *hībernāre, hībernātum*, f. *hībernus*, wintry. To pass the winter, esp. in a state of torpor.—**Hiberna'tion**, *n.*
Hic'cup, **Hic'cough**, *n.* Earlier *hicket*. Imitative. (*Hiccough* due to association with *cough*.) A spasm of the respiratory organs accompanied by a characteristic sound; a succession of such spasms.—*vi.* To have the hiccup.
Hide, *n.*[1] O.E. *hýd* = O.S., O.H.G. *hût* (Ger. *haut*), O.N. *húth*. Cogn. with G. *kutos*, L. *cutis*. The skin of an animal, raw or dressed.
Hide, *n.*[2] O.E. *híd*, earlier *hígid*, app. f.

O.Teut. *hiw-*, *hig-*, household, family. Cf. O.E. *hiwan*, *higan*, pl., members of a household, domestics. HIND, *n.*[2] An old Eng. measure of land, orig. enough to support a family.

Hide, *vt.* O.E. *hýdan*=M.Du., M.L.G. *hûden*. HOUSE. HUDDLE. To put or keep out of sight; to keep secret.—*vi.* To conceal oneself.

Hid'eous, *a.* M.E. *hidous*—A.F. *hidous* = O.F. *hidos*, *hideus*, earlier *hisdos* (F. *hideux*), f. *hisde*, *hide*, horror, fear, of doubtful orig. Revolting to the senses or feelings; odious, detestable.—**Hid'eous**LY,[2] *adv.*

Hie, *vi.* O.E. *hígian*, to strive, pant. Cf. M.Du. *higen*, to pant. To hasten, go quickly.

Hi'erarch, *n.* Med.L. *hierarcha*—G. *hierarchēs*, high priest, f. *hieros*, sacred + *-archēs*, ruling, ruler, f. *archein*, to rule. An ecclesiastical ruler.—**Hi'erarchy**, *n.* L.L. *hierarchia*—G. *hierarchia*, the power or rule of a *hierarchēs*. A division, the body, of angels; rule in ecclesiastical matters; the body of ecclesiastical rulers; a body of persons or things ranked in orders.—**Hierar'chic**, *a.*—**Hierar'chi**CAL, *a.*—**Hierat'ic**, *a.* L. *hierāticus* —G. *hierātikos*, priestly, devoted to sacred purposes, f. *hiera-esthai*, to be a priest, f. *hieros*. Of, used by, appropriate to, the priestly class; applied to a style of ancient Egyptian writing consisting of abridged hieroglyphics, and to a style of conventional religious art.—**Hieroglyph'ic**, *a.* L.L. *hieroglyphicus*—G. *hieroglup hikos*, f. *hieros* + *gluphē*, carving, f. *gluphein*, to carve. Written in or consisting of hieroglyphics; having a hidden meaning.—*n.pl.* The picture-characters used by the ancient Egyptians; a figure or device with a hidden meaning.—**Hieroglyph'ic**AL, *a.*—**Hi'eroglyph**, *n.* Back-formation f. *hieroglyphic*. A hieroglyphical character; a figure with a hidden meaning.—**Hi'erophant**, *n.* L.L. *hierophanta*—G. *hierophantēs*, f. *hieros*+ *phainein*, to bring to light. An expounder of sacred mysteries or ceremonies.

Hig'gle, *vi.* App. related to HAGGLE, with vowel-change to express a lighter action. To dispute as to terms, chaffer; to carry about wares for sale or exchange.—**Hig'**GLER, *n.*

High, *a.* O.E. *héah*, *héh*. Common Teut. HEIGHT. Extending far upwards; having a (specified) extent upwards; far up; (so far) up; of exalted rank, quality, &c.; important, grave, serious; of a road, &c., main, chief; rich in flavour or quality; slightly tainted; intense, forcible; of a season, &c., fully come; acute in pitch; haughty, arrogant; extreme in opinion; merry, hilarious.—*adv.* Far up; to a great extent, strongly; at or to a high pitch.—**High'**LY,[2] *adv.*—**High'land**, *n.* High or elevated land; in *pl.*, the mountainous northern and north-western district of Scotland.—**High'land**ER, *n.*—**High'**NESS, *n.* The quality of being high; dignity; a title of dignity.—**High Road**, **High'way**, *nn.* A main road; the ordinary route; a regular track.—**High'wayman**, *n.* A robber on the highway, esp. one on horseback.

Hilar'ity, *n.* F. *hilarité*—L. *hilaritas*, f. *hilaris*, *hilarus* = G. *hilaros*, cheerful. Cheerfulness; boisterous joy.—**Hila'ri**OUS, *a.*

Hill, *n.* O.E. *hyll* = M.Du. *hille*, *hil*, L.G. *hull*. Cogn. with G. *kolōnē*, L. *collis*, hill, L. *culmen*, summit. CULMINATE. A natural elevation less than a mountain.—**Hil'lock**, *n.* Dim. suff. *-ock*. A little hill.—**Hil'l**Y,[2] *a.*

Hilt, *n.* O.E. *hilt* = M.Du. *helt*, *hilt*, O.N. *hjalt*. The handle of a sword, &c.

Hind, *n.*[1] O.E. *hind* = O.N. *hind*. Cf. O.H.G. *hinta* (Ger. *hindin*). A female deer.

Hind, *n.*[2] With excrescent *d* early M.E. *hine*, app. developed f. *hina*, *higna*, genit. of *higan*, *hiwan*. HIDE, *n.*[2] A farm servant.

Hind, *a.* Perh. shortened f. M.E. *behind*, orig. *behindan*, f. O.E. *hindan*, adv., from behind, at the back, like *hionan*, HENCE, f. root *hi-*. HE. BEHIND. Situated in the rear.—**Hind'**ER, *a.* Perh. formed as comp. of *hind*, but used in the same sense.

Hin'der, *vt.* O.E. *hindrian* (= O.H.G. *hintarôn* (Ger. *hindern*), O.N. *hindra*), f. *hinder*, adv., backwards, conn. with *hindan*. (See prec.) To delay, impede.—**Hin'dr**ANCE, *n.*

Hinge, *n.* M.E. *heng*, *heeng*, f. O.E. *hangian*, to HANG. The movable joint by which a door, &c., hangs.—*vt.* To attach with or as with a hinge.—*vi.* To hang and turn *on*.

Hint, *n.* App. a deriv. of obs. *Hent*, to grasp —O.E. *hentan* of obscure orig. HUNT. A slight indication or suggestion.—*vt.* To give a hint of.—*vi.* To make a slight suggestion.

Hip, *n.*[1] O.E. *hype* = O.H.G. *huf* (Ger. *hüfte*), Du. *heup*. The projecting part of the thigh.

Hip, *n.*[2] O.E. *héope*, *híope*, cogn. with O.H.G. *hiufo*, thorn-bush. The fruit of the rose.

Hipped, *a.* Altered spelling of *hypt*, *hypped*, f. *hyp*, abb. of HYPOCHONDRIA. Morbidly depressed in spirits.

Hip'podrome, *n.* L. *hippodromos*—G. *hippodromos*, f. *hippos*, horse+*dromos*, race, course. A course for horse- and chariot-races; a circus.

Hippopot'amus, *n.* L.L.—G. *hippopotamos*, f. *hippos*, horse + *potamos*, river. A beast with a thick hide inhabiting African rivers.

Hire, *n.* O.E. *hýr*, corresp. to Old Fris. *hêre*, M.L.G. *hûre* (Ger. *heuer*). Payment for temporary use; wages; a hiring, a being hired.—*vt.* To take or give on hire; to employ for wages. —**Hire'ling**, *n.* -LING (1). One who serves (merely) for wages.—**Hir'**ER, *n.*

Hir'sute, *a.* L. *hirsūtus*. Hairy, shaggy.

His, *pron.* O.E. *his*, genit. of *hé*, HE. Belonging to him.

Hiss, *vi.* Imitative. To make a sharp sound like that of the letter *s*; to do so in disapproval or derision.—*vt.* To show disapproval of or dismiss with, the sound.—*n.* The sound.

Histol'ogy, *n.* G. *histos*, web + -LOGY. The study of the tissues of animals or plants.

His'tory, *n.* L. *historia*, narrative of events, account, story—G. *historia*, inquiry, narrative, f. root of *ide-ein*, to see. STORY. WIT. A narrative of events; the branch of knowledge which deals with past events; the record of the past; course of existence or life; a systematic account of phenomena.—**Histo'ri**AN, *n.*—**Histor'ic**, *a.* Esp., celebrated in history.—**Histor'i**CAL, *a.*—**Histor'ical**LY,[2] *adv.*—**Historiog'rapher**, *n.* With -ER f. G. *historiographos*, f. *historia*+*-graphos*, that writes, f. *graphein*, to write. A writer of a history; an official historian.

His'trion, *n.* L. *histrio*, *histriōnis*, stage-player. An actor.—**Histrion'**IC, *a.*

Hit, *vt.* Late O.E. *hyttan* = O.N. *hitta*, to meet with. App. f. Norse. To reach with a blow or a missile, to strike; to give (a blow, &c.); to affect injuriously; to get at, find; to imitate exactly; to suit, fit.—*vi.* To strike; to light *upon*.—*n.* A blow; a lucky stroke; an effective expression.—**Hit'**TER, *n.*

Hitch, *vt.* Orig. obscure. To move or raise with a jerk; to fasten in a temporary way.—*vi.* To walk lamely; to be caught or stopped.

—*n.* A jerk; a noose or knot for a temporary fastening; an impediment, obstruction.

Hith'er, *adv.* O.E. *hider*, f. root *hi-* of HE + suff. seen also in L. *ci-trā*, on this side. To or towards this place.—*a.* Situated on this side.—**Hith'erto**, *adv.* Up to this time.

Hive, *n.* O.E. *hýf*, prob. conn. with O.N. *húfr*, hull of a ship, L. *cūpa*, cask. CUP. A receptacle for bees.—*vt.* To gather (bees) into a hive; to store *up*.—*vi* To enter the hive; to live together like bees; to swarm *off*.

Hoar, *a.* O.E. *hár* = O.H.G. *hêr*, old, august, O.N. *hár(r)*, hoary, old. Also **Hoa'ry**.[2] Grey-haired; grey or greyish white; venerable, ancient.—**Hoar'-frost**, *n.* Frozen dew.

Hoard, *n.* O.E. *hord* = O.S. *hord*, O.H.G., Ger. *hort*, treasure. A stock of money, &c., hidden away.—*vt.* To amass and hide away.

Hoar'ding, *n.* From obs. *Hoard* in same sense, app. f. A.F. *hurdis* (mistaken for a *pl.*), palisade, a deriv. of O.F. *hurt* in same sense—O.H.G. *hurt*, HURDLE. A temporary fence round a building.

Hoarse, *a.* M.E. *hōrs, hoors*—O.E. *hás* (*hárs), corresp. to O.S. *hês*, O.H.G., O.L.G. *heis*. Rough and harsh-sounding; having a hoarse voice or sound.—**Hoarse'ly**,[2] *adv.*—**Hoarse'ness**, *n.*

Hoax, *vt.* Said to be a contracted form of HOCUS. To deceive by an amusing or mischievous fabrication.—*n.* An act of hoaxing.

Hob, *n.* Formerly also *hub*. Poss. = HUB with common notion 'protuberance'. The part of a fire-place on which things are set to warm; a peg or pin used as a mark in games. —**Hob'nail**, *n.* A nail with a large head inserted in the soles of boots.

Hob'ble, *vi.* App. cogn. with Du. *hobbelen*, to toss or rock. To walk lamely, limp.—*vt.* To tie the legs of (a horse, &c.) together.—*n.* A limping gait; a rope, &c., for hobbling.

Hob'bledehoy, Hob'badehoy, *n.* Orig. uncertain. A clumsy or awkward youth.

Hob'by, *n.* M.E. *hobyn, hoby*. Prob. the by-name *Hobin, Hobby* (= *Robin, Robbie*) for *Robert*. A small horse; a favourite occupation or topic, the pursuit of which is likened to the riding of a child's hobby-horse.—**Hob'by-horse**, *n.* A figure of a horse fastened round a performer's waist; a stick with a horse's head forming a toy for children.

Hobgob'lin, *n.* From *Hob*, familiar by-form of *Rob* (=*Robin, Robert*)+GOBLIN. (Cf. prec.) A mischievous sprite, 'Robin Goodfellow'; a terrifying apparition.

Hob'-nob, *advbl. phrase.* App. a var. of *hab-nab*, supposed to be formed f. HAVE, 'to have or not to have'. Hit or miss, at random. *Hob or nob* (prob. expressing invitation, 'take or leave'), used by two persons drinking together.—**Hob'-nob**, *vi.* To drink together; to be on familiar terms *with*.

Hock, *n.*[1], southern by-form of **Hough**—O.E. *hóh*, noted only in sense '(human) heel', but used in *hóhsinu*, hock-SINEW, in reference to a horse. HEEL. The joint in the hinder leg of a quadruped between the knee and the fetlock.—*vt.* To disable by cutting the tendons of the hock.

Hock, *n.*[2] Shortened f. *hockamore*, corr. of Ger. *Hochheimer*, f. *Hochheim* on the Main. A white wine (properly that of Hochheim).

Hock'ey, *n.* Poss. conn. with O.F. *hoquet*, shepherd's staff, crook. An outdoor game of ball played with clubs curved at one end.

Ho'cus po'cus, *n.* Orig. the appellation of a juggler of the time of James I from the sham Latin formula employed by him. HOAX. A formula of conjuring incantation; a juggler's trick; trickery, deception.—*vt.* To play tricks upon. — Hence **Ho'cus**, *vt.* To play tricks upon; to stupefy with drugs, to drug (liquor).

Hod, *n.* App. a modification of dial. *Hot*, a basket for carrying earth, &c.—O.F. *hotte*, basket, supposed to be of Ger. orig. A trough with a handle for carrying mortar, &c.

Hoe, *n.* F. *houe*—O.H.G. *houwâ* (Ger. *haue*), hoe, pickaxe, f. *houwan*, to HEW. A tool used for breaking up the ground, loosening weeds, &c.—*vt.* To break up, to weed, with a hoe.

Hog, *n.* Orig. unknown. A pig; a castrated male pig; a filthy person.—**Hogs'head**, *n.* HOG'S + HEAD. (The reason of the name is unknown.) A large cask; a liquid measure.

Hoist, *vt.* Corr. of dial. *Hoise*, of unknown orig., in 15-16th c. *hysse, hyce*, corresp. to (but cited earlier than) Norw., Sw. *hissa*, L.G., Ger. *hissen*, F. *hisser*. To raise, to set or put up.—*n.* A hoisting; an elevator.

Hold, *vt.* O.E. *haldan, healdan*. Common Teut. To keep fast, grasp; to support in or with the hand, arms, &c.; to keep (the body, &c.) in a particular position; to have capacity for; to own; to possess, occupy; to retain, to detain; to carry on, perform; to observe, celebrate; to cause (a meeting, &c.) to take place; to keep back, restrain; to believe; to entertain a specified feeling towards.—*vi.* To keep hold, cling; not to give way; to adhere or keep *to*, abide *by*; to side *with*; to maintain one's position; to last, endure; to be in force, apply; to go on, proceed; to occur, prevail. —*n.*[1] Grasp; a fortress.—**Hold'er**, *n.*

Hold, *n.*[2] Corr. of HOLE, prob. by association with prec. The cavity in a ship for cargo.

Hole, *n.* O.E. *hol*, orig. neut. of *hol*, hollow = O.S., O.H.G. *hol* (Ger. *hohl*), O.N. *holr*, perh. conn. with *helan*, to cover. HELL. A cavity; a deep place; a perforation, opening. —*vt.* To make a hole in, to perforate.

Hol'land, *n.* A linen fabric, orig. Dutch.—**Hol'lands**, *n.* See GENEVA.

Hol'low, *n.* O.E. *holh*, app. conn. with *hol*. HOLE. A cavity; an excavation or depression. —*a.* Formed in early M.E. f. the *n.* Having a cavity inside or beneath or a depression on the surface; void; not full-toned; empty, vain. —*vt.* To make hollow; to excavate.

Hol'ly, *n.* Shortened f. O.E. *holegn, holen*, conn. with O.H.G. *hulis, huls*, Du. *hulst*, also with Welsh *celyn*, Ir. *cuillean*. An evergreen shrub with prickly leaves and scarlet berries.

Hol'lyhock, *n.* From HOLY + obs. *hock*, mallow—O.E. *hoc*, of unknown orig. A tall plant bearing numerous large flowers.

Holm, *n.* O.N. *holmr*, islet, shore-meadow. A river islet; flat land by a river.

Holm'-oak, *n.* *Holm*, corr. of *holn*, O.E. *holen*, HOLLY + OAK. The evergreen oak.

Hol'ocaust, *n.* F. *holocauste*—L.L. *holocaustum*—G. *holokaustos*, burnt whole, f. *holos*, whole + *kaiein*, to burn. CAUSTIC. A sacrifice wholly burnt; a great slaughter.

Hol'ograph, *a.* L.L. *holographus*—G. *holographos*, f. *holos*, whole + *-graphos*, written, f. *graphein*, to write. Of a deed, &c., wholly written by a person.—*n.* Such a deed, &c.

Hol'ster, *n.* Corresponds to Du. *holster*. Orig. doubtful. A leather case for a pistol fixed to a horseman's saddle or belt.

Ho'ly, *a.* O.E. *hálig*, corresp. to O.S. *hêlag*, O.H.G. *heilag* (Ger. *heilig*), f. O.Teut. **hailo-*, O.E. *hál*, WHOLE, or the deriv. n. **hailoz-*, *hailiz-. HALIBUT. HALLOW. Kept inviolate from ordinary use, sacred; free from sin; divine. —**Ho'li**LY,[2] *adv.*—**Hol'iday**, *n.* O.E. *háligdæg.* DAY. A religious festival (in this sense now us. **Ho'ly-day**); a day of cessation from work.—**Ho'li**NESS, *n.* The quality of being holy; a title of the Pope.

Hol'ystone, Hol'y-stone, *n.* Orig. uncertain. A piece of sandstone for scouring a ship's decks.—*vt.* To scour with a holystone.

Hom'age, *n.* O.F. *homage*—L.L. *hominā-ticum*, f. L. *homo, hominis*, man. HUMAN. Acknowledgment of allegiance to a feudal lord; reverence, dutiful respect.

Home, *n.* O.E. *hám*, a village, a dwelling-place. Common Teut. HAMLET. A dwelling-place, house; the place of one's dwelling and nurturing with its associations; one's own country; an institution for the destitute, &c. —*a.* Of or connected with home or one's home; domestic; treating of domestic affairs; that strikes home, to the point, direct.—*adv.* To one's home; to the point, directly, effectively. —**Home'**LESS, *a.*—**Home'**LY,[1] *a.* Fitting for a home, plain, not fine; not comely.—

Home'spun, *a.* Spun at home; made of homespun; plain, homely.—*n.* Cloth made of homespun yarn; anything plain or homely.—

Home'stead, *n.* O.E. *stede*, place. STEAD. A home or dwelling; a house with its dependent buildings.—**Home'**WARD, *adv.* and *a.*—**Home'**WARDS, *adv.*

Hom'icide, *n.* L. *homicīda*, f. *homo*, man + -CIDE (1). One who kills a man. -CIDE (2). The killing of a man.—**Homici'd**AL, *a.*

Hom'ily, *n.* O.F. *omilie*—Eccles.L. *homīlia*—G. *homilia*, converse, f. *homilos*, throng. A sermon.—**Homilet'ic**, *a.* G. *homilētikos*, affable, conversable, f. *homile-ein*, to consort. Of sermons.—In *pl.* as *n.*, the art of preaching.

Homœop'athy, *n.* G. *homoios*, like + *pathos*, suffering. The curing of a diseased action by inducing a similar action.—**Homœopath'**IC, *a.*—**Homœopath'ically**, *adv.* -AL. -LY.[2] —**Homœop'ath**IST, *n.*

Homoge'neous, *a.* Scholastic L. *homogeneus* (f. G. *homogenēs*, f. *homos*, same + *genos*, kind) + -OUS. Of the same kind or nature; composed of elements of the same kind.—**Homogene'**ITY, *n.*

Homol'ogate, *vt.* Med.L. *homologāre, homologātum*, aft. G. *homologe-ein*, to acknowledge, f. *homologos*, agreeing, f. *homos*, same + *logos*, discourse, ratio, analogy. To acknowledge, confirm.—**Homol'ogous**, *a.* From *homologos*. Having the same relation, &c.

Homon'ymous, *a.* G. *homōnumos*, of the same name, f. *homos*, same + *onoma* (in Æolic *onuma*), NAME. Of words, identical in sound but differing in sense; having the same name. —**Hom'onym**, *n.* From the neut. of the G. *a.* An homonymous word; a person or thing having the same name as another.

Homun'cule, *n.* L. *homunculus*, dim. of *homo*, man. HUMAN. A diminutive man.

Hone, *n.* O.E. *hán*, a stone = O.N. *hein.* A whetstone.—*vt.* To sharpen on a hone.

Hon'est, *a.* O.F. *honeste*—L. *honestus*, honourable, f. *honor*, HONOUR. A vague epithet of praise; dealing fairly and uprightly; ingenuous; free from fraud; unadulterated.—**Hon'est**LY,[2] *adv.*—**Hon'est**Y,[1] *n.*

Hon'ey, *n.* O.E. *hunig* = O.H.G. *honag* (Ger. *honig*), O.N. *hunang.* The sweet viscid fluid collected by the bee, &c.—**Hon'eycomb**, *n.* O.E. *hunigcamb.* COMB. The structure of wax containing hexagonal cells in which honey is stored.—*vt.* To fill with cells or perforations (often *fig.*).—**Hon'ey-dew**, *n.* A sweet sticky substance found on plants, formerly thought to be akin to dew.—**Hon'eymoon**, *n.* The first month after marriage (orig. from a comparison of wedded love to the changing moon); the holiday taken together by a newly-married pair.—**Hon'eysuckle**, *n.* M.E. *hunisuccle*, app. extended f. *hunisuce*—O.E. *hunigsúce*, f. *hunig* + *súcan*, to SUCK. Formerly applied to various flowers yielding honey. A climbing shrub with fragrant yellowish flowers.

Hon'our, *n.* O.F. *honor*—L. *honor.* HONEST. High respect or esteem; renown, reputation; a fine sense of what is due or right; chastity, purity; exalted rank or position; a position or title of rank; a source or cause of honour; one of the highest of a suit of cards; in *pl.*, civilities rendered, special distinction in an examination.—*vt.* To hold in honour; to treat with honour; to accept or pay (a bill, &c.) when due.—**Honora'rium**, *n.* L.L. *honōrārium*, a gift made on admission to an office. A fee for professional services.—**Hon'or**ARY, *a.* Conferred merely for the sake of honour; holding a position without pay or the usual duties; giving services without pay.—**Honorif'**IC, *a.* Conferring honour.—**Hon'our**ABLE, *a.*—**Hon'ourab**LY,[2] *adv.*

Hood, *n.* O.E. *hód* = O.H.G. *huot* (Ger. *hut*, hat). HAT. A covering for the head and neck; a badge worn over the gown by university graduates.—*vt.* To put a hood on.—**Hood'wink**, *vt.* To blindfold; to deceive.

Hoof, *n.* O.E. *hóf.* Common Teut. The horny growth on the feet of the horse, &c.

Hook, *n.* O.E. *hóc* = M.L.G. *hôk*, M.Du. *hoec.* A bent piece of metal, &c., for catching hold, hanging up, &c.; a curved cutting instrument.—*vt.* To catch or secure with a hook.

Hoop, *n.*[1] Late O.E. *hóp* = Old Fris. *hôp*, M.Du. *hoop.* A circular band of metal or other material; a circle of flexible elastic material for expanding a woman's skirt; a crinoline.—*v.*[1]*t.* To bind with a hoop or hoops.

Hoop, *v.*[2]*i.* F. *houper.* WHOOP. To whoop. —*n.*[2] A whoop.—**Hoop'ing-cough**, *n.* A contagious disease with short coughs and a long sonorous inspiration (the hoop).

Hoo'poe, *n.* App. an alteration (with partial assimilation to the L. word) of earlier *hoop*—F. *huppe*, in O.F. also *pupu*—L. *upupa.* A crested bird with variegated plumage.

Hoot, *vi.* Prob. imitative. Cf. Da. *huie*, to shout, F. *huer*, to hoot. HUE.[2] To utter loud sounds of disapproval; to cry, as an owl.—*vt.* To assail or dismiss with hoots.—*n.* A cry of disapproval; the cry of an owl.

Hop, *n.*[1] M.Du. *hoppe* = late O.H.G. *hopfo* (Ger. *hopfen*), of obscure orig. In *pl.*, the cones of a climbing plant used to give a bitter taste to malt liquors; the plant.

Hop, *vi.* O.E. *hoppian*, corresp. to O.N. *hoppa.* Cf. Ger. *hüpfen.* Of animals, to spring with all the feet at once; of a person, to spring with one foot.—*n.*[2] The action or an act of hopping.—**Hop'p**ER, *n.* One who hops; a receiver (orig. with a shaking or hopping motion) through which grain passes to be ground; a boat which conveys away dredged matter.

Hope, *n.* Late O.E. *hopa*, corresp. to M.L.G., M.Du. *hope*, M.H.G., Ger. *hoffe.* Expectation of something desired; something that gives, an object of, hope.—*vi.* To feel hope.—*vt.* To expect with desire.—**Hope'**FUL, *a.*—**Hope'fulLY**,[2] *adv.*—**Hope'**LESS, *a.*

Horde, *n.* Ultimately (app. through F. *horde*) f. Turkish *hordā*, camp. A tribe or troop of nomads; a rabble.—*vi.* To live as in a horde.

Hore'hound, Hoar'hound, *n.* O.E. *hāre hūne*, f. *hār*, HOAR + *hūne*, used also by itself as the name of the plant, of uncertain orig. A herb with whitish leaves the juice of which is used as a remedy for coughs, &c.

Hori'zon, *n.* O.F. *orizon*—L.L. *horizōn*, *horizontis*—G. *horizōn* (*kuklos*), the bounding (circle), horizon, pres.pple. of *horizein*, to bound. APHORISM. The boundary line of the part of the earth's surface visible from a given point.—**Horizon'**TAL, *a.* Parallel to the plane of the horizon, level.

Horn, *n.* O.E. *horn.* Common Teut. Cogn. with G. *keras*, L. *cornū*. A hard projection on the head of certain animals; the substance of which horns consist; various things made of it or resembling a horn; a wind instrument, orig. made of a horn.—**Horn'pipe**, *n.* An obsolete wind instrument; a lively and vigorous sailors' dance.—**Horn'**Y,[2] *a.*

Hor'net, *n.* O.E. *hyrnet*, corresp. to O.H.G. *hornuz* (Ger. *hornisse*). A large kind of wasp.

Hor'ologe, *n.* O.F. *orloge*—L. *hōrologium*—G. *hōrologion*, instrument for telling the hour, f. *hōra*, hour + *-logion*, f. *legein*, to tell. A dial, hour-glass or clock.—**Horol'og**IST, *n.*—**Horol'ogy**, *n.* G. *hōra* + -LOGY. The art or science of making horologes.

Hor'oscope, *n.* F. *horoscope*—L. *hōroscopus*—G. *hōroskopos*, caster of nativities, horoscope, f. *hōra*, hour + *skopos*, watcher. BISHOP. A scheme showing the position of the planets at a particular moment, esp. at the moment of a person's birth.

Hor'rible, *a.* O.F. (*h*)*orrible*, L. *horribilis*, f. *horrēre*, to bristle, to quake with fear. ABHOR. ORDURE. Exciting or fitted to excite horror, hideous, frightful.—**Hor'rib**LY,[2] *adv.*—**Hor'rid**, *a.* L. *horridus*, f. *horrēre*. Bristling; causing horror or aversion, detestable; offensive.—**Hor'rid**LY,[2] *adv.*—**Hor'ri**FY, *vt.* To move to horror.—**Horri**F'IC, *a.*—**Hor'ror**, *n.* O.F. *orror*, (*h*)*orrour*—L. *horror*, f. *horrēre*. Aversion mingled with dread; intense dislike; something horrifying.

Horse, *n.* O.E. *hors.* Common Teut. WALRUS. A well-known quadruped used for draught and for riding upon; the adult male; cavalry; a frame for support.—*vt.* To provide with a horse or horses; to carry or support on the back.—**Horse-chest'nut**, *n.* (Said to be so called from alleged use in the East as a medicine for horses.) A large nut like a chestnut; the tree bearing it.—**Horse-pow'er**, *n.* The rate of work of a horse in drawing; hence, a unit for measuring the rate of work of an engine, &c.—**Horse-rad'ish**, *n.* From *horse* used to denote a strong or coarse kind. A plant with a pungent root.—**Hors'**Y,[2] *a.* Having to do with horses; affecting the dress, &c., of a groom or jockey.

Hor'tative, *a.* L. *hortātivus*, f. *hortārī*, *hortātus*, to urge, incite. DEHORT. Tending or serving to exhort.—Sim. **Hor'tat**ORY, *a.*

Hor'ticulture, *n.* L. *hortus*, GARDEN + *cultūra.* ARBORICULTURE. The art of cultivating gardens.—**Horticul'tur**AL, *a.*

Hose, *n.* O.E. *hosa* = O.H.G. *hosa* (Ger. *hose*), trousers, O.N. *hosa*, stocking. An article of clothing for the lower part of the body and legs, now (in collective pl. *hose*) stockings reaching to the knee; a flexible tube for conveying water.—**Ho'**SIER, *n.* A dealer in stockings, underclothing, &c.—**Ho'si**ERY, *n.*

Hos'pitable, *a.* L. type **hospitābilis*—Med. L. *hospitāre*, to receive as a guest, f. *hospes*, *hospitis*, HOST,[2] guest. Giving welcome and entertainment to strangers or guests.—**Hos'pitab**LY,[2] *adv.*—**Hos'pital**, *n.* O.F. *hospital*—Med.L. *hospitāle*, place of reception for guests, neut. sing. of L. *hospitālis*, hospitable, f. *hospes*. An asylum for the destitute or infirm; an institution for the sick or wounded.—**Hospital'**ITY, *n.* The practice of being hospitable; an instance of this.—**Hos'tel**, *n.* O.F. (*h*)*ostel* (F. *hôtel*)—Med.L. *hospitāle*. An inn or hotel; a house of residence for students.—**Hos'tel**RY, *n.* An inn or hotel.—(**H**)**ost'ler**, *n.* Shortened f. archaic *Hosteler*, innkeeper—O.F. *hostelier*, f. *hostel*. Now applied to a man who attends to horses at an inn.

Host, *n.*[1] O.F. *ost*, *host*—L. *hostis*, stranger, enemy, in Med.L., army. GUEST. An army; a multitude.—**Hos'tile**, *a.* L. *hostīlis*, f. *hostis*. Of, pertaining to, characteristic of, an enemy; unfriendly; contrary, antagonistic.—**Hostil'**ITY, *n.* The state or fact of being hostile; hostile action; in *pl.*, hostile acts.

Host, *n.*[2] O.F. *oste*, *hoste* (F. *hôte*)—L. *hospes*, *hospitis*. HOSPITABLE. One who entertains another at his house or table; one who keeps an inn or hotel.—**Host'**ESS, *n.*

Host, *n.*[3] O.F. *oiste*, *hoiste*—L. *hostia*, victim, sacrifice. The bread of the Eucharist.

Hos'tage, *n.* O.F. *ostage*, *hostage*—Pop.L. type **obsidāticum* (-AGE), f. L.L. *obsidātus*, n. of state or quality f. *obses*, *obsidis*, hostage. A person taken or given as a pledge.

Hot, *a.* O.E. *hát.* Common Teut. O.Teut. type **haito-z.* HEAT. Producing a well-known sensation caused by nearness to fire, &c.; having this sensation; pungent; ardent; wrathful; intense, severe.—**Hot'**LY,[2] *adv.*

Hotch'pot, *n.*; also (in the first sense) **Hotch'potch**. F. *hochepot*, f. *hocher*, to shake, shake together + *pot*, POT. A dish of many ingredients; a blending together of properties to secure equality of division.

Hotel', *n.* F. *hôtel.* HOSTEL (under HOSPITABLE). An inn of a superior kind.

Hough. See HOCK.[1]

Hound, *n.* O.E. *hund.* Common Teut. Supposed to be cogn. with G. *kuōn*, L. *canis*. CANINE. KENNEL.[1] POODLE. A hunting dog.—*vt.* To chase with hounds; to set (a person, &c.) *at* (another, &c.); to urge *on*.

Hour, *n.* O.F. *ore*, *hore* (F. *heure*)—L. *hōra*—G. *hōra*, season, hour. The twenty-fourth part of a day; the 'time of day'; an appointed time; in *pl.*, prayers for stated times of the day, a book containing these.—**Hour'**LY,[1] *a.* Happening every hour; frequent.—**Hour'**LY,[2] *adv.* Every hour; frequently.

House, *n.* O.E. *hús.* Common Teut. Perh. f. root of *hýdan*, to HIDE. HUSBAND. A building for habitation or for various other purposes; an inn; a legislative or deliberative assembly; a business establishment or firm; a household; a lineage, race.—*vt.* To receive or put into, to furnish with, a house.—*vi.* To dwell or take shelter.—**House'breaker**, *n.* A burglar; one whose business it is to demolish houses.—**House'hold**, *n.* The inmates of a house collectively.—*a.* Of or belonging to a house, domestic; familiar.—**House'hold**ER, *n.* One who occupies a house as the dwelling of his household; the head of a household.—

House'keeper, *n.* A woman managing the affairs of a household. — **House'wife**, *n.* M.E. *hus(e)wif*, f. *hús* + *wíf*, woman, WIFE. The mistress of a household; a pocket-case for needles, scissors, &c.

Hou'sing, *n.* From archaic *House*, to cover with a *house* (=*housing*), f. O.F. *huche*, *houce* (F. *housse*), perh. of Arab. orig. A covering put on a horse for defence or ornament (gen. in *pl.*).

Hov'el, *n.* Of uncertain orig. An open shed; a miserable dwelling-place.

Hov'er, *vi.* Perh. an iterative deriv. of obs. *Hove* in sim. senses of unknown orig. To remain suspended in the air; to linger *about*; to be in a state of suspense or indecision.

How, *adv.* O.E. *hú*. O.Teut. **hwô*, f. the interrog. pron. stem *hwa-*. WHO. In direct questions, in what way or manner? by what means? in what condition? to what extent or degree?—In dependent questions, in what way or manner; by what means; in what condition; to what extent or degree.—**Howev'er**, *adv.* EVER. In whatever manner; by whatever means; to whatever extent.—*conj.* Nevertheless, notwithstanding.

How'itzer, *n.* Formed f. obs. *Howitz*, *Haubitz*, in same sense—Ger. *haubitze*, earlier *haufnitz*—Bohemian *houfnice*, stone-sling. A short gun for firing shells.

Howl, *vi.* Imitative. M.E. *houlen* = M.Du. *hûlen*, Ger. *heulen*. Cf. G. *hula-ein*, L. *ululāre*. To utter a prolonged, loud and doleful cry.—*n.* Such a cry; a savage yell.

Hoy, *n.* App. f. M.Du. *hoei*, var. of *hoede*, &c., of unknown orig. A small coasting vessel.

Hoy'den, *n.* Of uncertain orig. A rude or ill-bred girl or woman.—**Hoy'den**ISH, *a.*

Hub, *n.* Of unknown orig. HOB. The nave of a wheel; a central point of activity, &c.

Hub'bub, *n.* Prob. repg. some Ir. expression. A confused noise or din; an uproar or riot.

Huck'ster, *n.* In form a deriv. with -STER of obs. *Huck*, to chaffer (corresp. to Ger. dial. *hocken*, *hucken*), which, however, occurs later. Cf. M.Du. *hokester*, *hockster*, *huckster*, M.L.G. *hoker* (HAWKER), app. also later. (The orig. of all these words is obscure.) A hawker.—*vi.* To higgle.—*vt.* To deal in in a petty way.

Hud'dle, *vt.* Poss. f. the root of *hýdan*, to HIDE. To heap together confusedly; to contract (oneself) together; to thrust in a disorderly way *into*, &c.; to put *on* (clothes) hurriedly; to finish *up* in haste.—*vi.* To nestle *together*.—*n.* A confused mass; confusion.

Hue, *n.*[1] O.E. *hiew*, *hiw*. Cf. Goth. *hiwi*, form, appearance, Sw. *hý*, skin, complexion. Complexion; colour.

Hue, *n.*[2] O.F. *hu*, n. of action f. *huer*, to HOOT. *Hue and cry*, outcry after a criminal.

Huff, *vi.* Imitative of a blast of air through an orifice. Formerly, to blow, puff; to puff or swell with pride. To take offence.—*vt.* To bully; to offend.—*n.* A fit of petulance.

Hug, *vt.* Orig. unknown. To clasp tightly; to cherish, cling to; to keep close to.—*v.refl.* To congratulate oneself.—*n.* A close embrace.

Huge, *a.* M.E. *huge*, *hoge*, app. aphetic f. O.F. *ahuge*, *ahoge*, of unknown orig. Very great or large, immense.—**Huge'**LY,[2] *adv.*

Hug'ger-mug'ger, *n.* Orig. unknown. Secrecy, confusion.—*a.* Secret; confused.

Hulk, *n.* O.E. *hulc*—Med.L. *hulcus*, *hulca*, perh. f. G. *holkas*, trading vessel, lit. 'ship that is towed', f. *helkein*, to draw. A big unwieldy vessel; the body of a dismantled ship.—**Hulk'ing**, *a.* Big, unwieldy.

Hull, *n.*[1] O.E. *hulu*, f. O.Teut. *hul-*. HALL. A shell, husk.—*v.*[1]*t.* To remove the hull of.

Hull, *n.*[2] Poss. the same as prec. A ship's frame.—*v.*[2]*t.* To send a shot into the hull of.

Hum, *vi.* Imitative. To make a low continuous sound, as a bee; to make a low inarticulate sound with the voice.—*vt.* To sing with closed lips.—*n.* A humming sound.

Hu'man, *a.* F. *humain*—L. *hūmānus*, cogn. with *homo*, man, which is cogn. with O.E. *guma*, man. BRIDEGROOM. HOMAGE. Of, belonging to, characteristic of, of the nature of, man.—**Hu'man**LY,[2] *adv.*—**Humane'**, *a.* An earlier spelling now restricted to the following senses. Kind, benevolent; of studies, &c., tending to refine, as the ancient classics, &c.—**Hu'man**ISM, *n.* A system of thought or action concerned with merely human interests or with those of humanity in general, the 'Religion of Humanity'; devotion to humane studies.—**Hu'man**IST, *n.* A student of human affairs or of human nature; a classical scholar.—**Human'**ITY, *n.* The quality of being human; man in the abstract; kindness, benevolence; in *pl.* with *the*, humane studies or literature.—**Humanit**A'RIAN, *n.* One who professes the 'Religion of Humanity'; a philanthropist (in derision).—**Hu'man**IZE, *vt.* To make human; to civilize, refine.

Hum'ble, *a.* O.F. *(h)umble*—L. *humilis*, low, mean, base, f. *humus*, ground, earth. EXHUME. HUMILIATE. Not proud; unpretentious, modest.—*vt.* To bring low, abase.—**Humb'**LY,[2] *adv.*—**Humb'le**NESS, *n.*

Humb'le-bee, *n.* App. f. obs. *Humble*, to hum, app. cogn. with M.H.G., Ger. *hummeln*. A large bee with a loud hum, a bumble-bee.

Humb'le pie. From obs. *Humbles*, *Numbles*, the inwards of a deer—O.F. *numbles*, pl., loin of veal, fillet of venison, &c., app. repg. L. *lumbulus*, dim. of *lumbus*, LOIN. *To eat humble pie*, to be very submissive, to apologize humbly (by association with HUMBLE, *a.*).

Hum'bug, *n.* A slang or cant word of unknown orig. A fraud, sham; deception; nonsense; an impostor.—*vt.* To delude.

Hum'drum, *a.* App. a reduplicating formation f. HUM. Monotonous, dull.

Hu'mid, *a.* L. *(h)ūmidus*, f *(h)ūmēre*, to be moist. Moist, damp.—**Humid'**ITY, *n.*

Humil'iate, *vt.* L.L. *humiliāre*, *humiliātum*, f. L. *humilis*. HUMBLE. To lower the dignity of, to mortify.—**Humili**A'TION, *n.*—**Humil'**ITY, *n.* Humbleness; humble state.

Hum'mock, *n.* Orig. obscure. A low knoll.

Hu'mour, *n.* A.F. *(h)umour*, F. *(h)umor* (now *humeur*)—L. *(h)ūmor*, moisture, conn. with *(h)ūmēre*. HUMID. A fluid of an animal or plant; one of the four chief fluids of ancient and mediæval physiology supposed to determine one's constitution; temperament; mood; a whim, caprice; the quality (less purely intellectual than wit) of writing, speech, &c., which excites amusement, the faculty of perceiving or expressing what is amusing or ludicrous.—*vt.* To indulge; to adapt or accommodate oneself to.—**Hu'mor**IST, *n.*—**Hu'mor**OUS, *a.*—**Hu'morous**LY,[2] *adv.*—**Hu'mour**SOME *a.* Capricious; peevish.

Hump, *n.* Orig. obscure. A protuberance on the body.—*vt.* To make hump-shaped.

Hump'back, Hump'-back, *n.* A back having a hump; a person with such a back.

Hunch, *vt.* Orig. obscure. App. conn. with prec. To thrust *out* or *up*, to bend, so as to form a hump.—*n.* A hump; a thick piece.—

Hunch'back, Hunch'-back, *n.* = HUMPBACK.

Hun'dred, *a.* and *n.* O.E. *hundred* = Late O.H.G., Ger. *hundert*, corresp. to Goth. type **hunda-rath*, 'the number of 100', f. *-rath*, related to *rathjan*, to reckon. (The simple *hund*, cogn. with G. *hekaton*, L. *centum*, was used in O.E. in sense 'hundred'.) The cardinal number equal to ten times ten; a subdivision of a county. — **Hun'dredweight**, *n.* A weight of 112 pounds (prob. orig. of 100).

Hun'ger, *n.* O.E. *hungor* = O.H.G. *hungar* (Ger. *hunger*), O.N. *hungr*. The sensation caused by want of food.—*vi.* To feel this.—**Hun'gr**Y,[2] *a.* Feeling this.

Hunk, *n.* = W. Flem. *hunke*. A thick piece.

Hunks, *n.* Orig. unknown. A stingy man.

Hunt, *vi.* O.E. *huntian*, app. f. *hunta*, hunter, prob. f. the same root as *hentan*, to grasp. HINT. To go in pursuit of wild animals or game.—*vt.* To pursue (wild animals or game); to do this over (a district); to use in hunting. —*n.* The act of hunting; a hunting association, their district.—**Hunt'**ER, *n.* One who hunts; a horse used in hunting.—**Hunt'r**ESS, *n.*—**Hunts'man**, *n.* A hunter; a man in charge of a pack of hounds.

Hur'dle, *n.* O.E. *hyrdel*, deriv. of a primitive repd. by Goth. *haurds*, door, O.H.G. *hurt* (Ger. *hürde*), hurdle. Cf. G. *kurtia*, wickerwork, L. *crātis*, hurdle. HOARDING. A portable frame used to form temporary fences, &c.

Hurl, *vt.* Akin to L.G. *hurreln*, to toss, dash. No doubt to be traced back to an imitative *hurr* expressing rapid motion. HURRY. To drive, impel, fling; to utter vehemently.—*n.* The action or an act of hurling.—**Hur'ly-bur'ly**, *n.* From *hurling* in obs. sense 'strife, commotion', with initially-varied repetition. Commotion, a commotion.

Hur'ricane, *n.* Sp. *huracan*—Carib *huracan*. A violent storm or tempest.

Hur'ry, *n.* Prob. founded on *hurr*. HURL. Immoderate haste; urgency of action through want of time.—*vt.* To convey or cause to go with great haste; to impel (to action, &c.) impetuously; to urge to greater speed.—*vi.* To move or act with great haste. — **Hur'ry-scur'ry**, *adv.* App. a reduplication like HURLY-BURLY. In disorderly haste.—*a.* Characterized by such haste.—*n.* Such haste.—*vi.* To move with hurry-scurry.

Hurt, *vt.* App. f. O.F. *hurter* (F. *heurter*), to bring into violent collision, of obscure orig. To cause injury or harm to; to vex, offend.—*n.* Injury, harm; a wound.—**Hurt'**FUL, *a.*—**Hurt'le**, *vt.* App. a dim. and iterative of *hurt* in obs. sense 'to strike with a shock'. To dash, dart.—*vi.* To meet in shock; to clatter, rattle; to dart, rush with noise.

Hus'band, *n.* Late O.E. *húsbonda*, *húsbunda*, master of a house, f. *hús*, HOUSE + *bonda*, *bunda*, O.N. *bóande*, *búande*, husbandman, yeoman. BOND, *a.* A man married to a woman; a manager.—*vt.* To till (the soil); to manage prudently.—**Hus'bandman**, *n.* A tiller of the soil.—**Hus'band**RY, *n.* Agriculture; prudent management.

Hush, *vt.* App. a back-formation f. archaic *Husht*, silent (taken as a pa.pple.), f. the imitative int. *husht*! (now *hush*!), be silent. To silence; to lull.—*vi.* To be silent.

Husk, *n.* Late M.E. *huske* of uncertain orig. Poss. conn. with *hús*, HOUSE. The dry covering of certain fruits and seeds.—*vt.* To remove the husk from.—**Husk'**Y,[2] *a.* Consisting of husks; dry as a husk; dry in the throat.

Hussar', *n.* Hungarian *huszar*, light horseman, orig., freebooter—Old Servian *husar*, *kursar*, freebooter—It. *corsaro*, *corsare* = F. *corsaire*, CORSAIR. A member of a light cavalry regiment.

Hus'sy, *n.* A reduction of HOUSEWIFE. A woman of improper behaviour; a pert girl.

Hus'ting, *n.* O.E. *hústing*, council — O.N. *hús-thing*, house-assembly, select council, f. *hús*, HOUSE + *thing*, assembly, THING. In *sing.* or *pl.*, a court held in the Guildhall of London; in *pl.*, a temporary platform from which parliamentary candidates were nominated and addressed the electors.

Hust'le, *vt.* Du. *husselen*, *hutselen*, to toss, freq. of *hutsen*, M.H.G. *hutzen*. To push about roughly, jostle.

Hut, *n.* F. *hutte*—M.H.G., Ger. *hütte*, perh. f. root of O.E. *hýdan*, to HIDE. A small rude dwelling; a wooden shelter for troops.

Hutch, *n.* F. *huche*—Med.L. *hūtica*, referred by some to Ger. *hut*. HEED. A chest or coffer; a box for rabbits, &c.; a box-like truck.

Hy'acinth, *n.* L. *hyacinthus*, G. *huakinthos*, a plant not certainly identified, a blue precious stone (prob. the sapphire). JACINTH. A reddish-orange precious stone; a bulbous plant with bell-shaped flowers.—**Hyacin'th**INE, *a.* Of the colour of the gem or of the flower.

Hy'brid, *n.* L. *hibrida*, *hybrida*. The offspring of two animals or plants of different species, a mongrel.—*a.* Mongrel.

Hy'drant, *n.* Irreg. f. G. *hudōr*, water + -ANT. A means of drawing water from a main.

Hydrau'lic, *a.* L. *hydraulicus*—G. *hudraulikon* (*organon*), water (-organ), f. *hudōr*, water + *aulos*, flute, pipe. Pertaining or relating to the conveyance of water, worked by water-power.—In *pl.* as *n.*, the science of the conveyance of water and of water-power.

Hy'drogen, *n.* F. *hydrogène* — G. *hudōr*, water + *-gen*, root of *genna-ein*, to beget. A colourless gas, with oxygen forming water.

Hydrog'raphy, *n.* F. *hydrographie* — G. *hudōr*, water + *-graphia*, writing, f. *graphein*, to write. The description of the waters of the earth.—**Hydrog'raph**ER, *n.*—**Hydrograph'**IC, **Hydrograph'**ICAL, *aa.*

Hydrop'athy, *n.* Formed on G. *hudōr*, water, after *allopathy*, &c. Medical treatment by application of water.—**Hydropath'**IC, *a.* —*n.* A hydropathic establishment.

Hydropho'bia, *n.* L. *hydrophobia* — G. *hudrophobia*, f. *hudōr*, water + *phobos*, dread. Rabies, esp. when transmitted to man (characterized by an aversion to water).

Hye'na, Hyæ'na, *n.* L. *hyaena*—G. *huaina*, f. *hus*, hog, SOW (app. from a supposed likeness to the hog). A carnivorous quadruped allied to the dog.

Hy'giene, *n.* F. *hygiène*—G. *hugieinē* (*technē*), (art) of health, fem. of *hugieinos*, healthy, f. *hugiēs* in sim. sense. The principles of health. —**Hygien'**IC, *a.* Sanitary.

Hygrom'eter, *n.* G. *hugros*, moist + *metre-ein*, to measure. An instrument for measuring the humidity of the air.

Hymene'al, *a.* With -AL f. G. *humenaios*, of marriage, as *n.*, wedding, wedding-song, f. *Humēn*, god of marriage. Of marriage.—*n.* A wedding-song; in *pl.*, a wedding.

Hymn, *n.* L. *hymnus*—G. *humnos*, an ode. A song of praise to God; an ode or song of praise.—*vt.* To praise in song.—**Hym'n**AL, *a.* Of hymns.—*n.* A book of hymns.—**Hym'nody**, *n.* Med.L. *hymnōdia*—G. *humnōidia*, singing of songs, f. *humnos* + *ōidē*, song, ODE. The singing or composition of hymns; hymns collectively.—**Hymno**L'OGY, *n.*

Hyper'bola, *n.* G. *huperbolē*, lit., excess, f. *huperballein*, to exceed, f. *huper-* (HYPER-) + *ballein*, to throw. EMBLEM. A double curve produced by a plane cutting a double cone at an angle greater than that between the side and the base.

Hyper'bole, *a.* G. *hyperbolē* (see prec.), in sense 'exaggeration'. Exaggeration, an instance of this.—**Hyperbol'**ICAL, *a.*

Hyperbor'ean, *a.* L.L. *hyperboreānus*, L. *hyperboreus*—G. *hyperboreos*, *-boreios*, f. *huper-* (HYPER-) + *boreios*, northern, f. *boreas*, the north wind. Of the far north.—*n.* An inhabitant of the far north (in Greek fable one of a race dwelling beyond the north wind).

Hypercrit'ical, *a.* HYPER-. Extremely or unduly critical.—**Hypercrit'ic**ISM, *n.*

Hy'phen, *n.* L.L. *hyphen*—G. *huphen*, use as n. of *huphen*, adv., together, f. *hupo* (HYPO-) + *hen*, one. A short line (-) indicating that two words or syllables are to be connected.

Hypnot'ic, *a.* F. *hypnotique*—L.L. *hypnōticus*—G. *hupnōtikos*, sleepy, f. *hupnos*, sleep. Inducing sleep; of hypnotism.—**Hyp'not**ISM, *n.* The artificial production of a sleep-like state; the state.—**Hyp'not**IZE, *vt.*

Hypochon'dria, *n.* L.L. *hypochondria*, neut.pl. = G. (*ta*) *hupochondria*, (the) soft parts below the costal cartilages, neut.pl. of *hupochondrios*, a., f. *hupo-* (HYPO-)+*chondros*, cartilage. HIPPED. Morbid depression of spirits (formerly connected with the viscera as the supposed seat of melancholy).—**Hypochon'driac**, *a.* G. *hupochondriakos*, affected in the *hupochondria*. Affected or characterized by hypochondria. Sim. **Hypochondri'ac**AL, *a.*

Hypoc'risy, *n.* O.F. *ypocrisie* (F. *hypocrisie*) —G. *hupokrisis*, the acting of a part, feigning, f. *hupokrinesthai*, to answer, play a part, f. *hupo-* (HYPO-) in somewhat undetermined sense, 'thereat' + *krinein*, to decide. CRISIS. The assuming of a feigned appearance of goodness with dissimulation of real character, pretence.—**Hyp'ocrite**, *n.* G. *hupokritēs*, actor, pretender, f. *hupokrinesthai*. One who practises hypocrisy.—**Hypocrit'**ICAL, *a.*

Hypoder'mic, *a.* From HYPO- + G. *derma*, skin + -IC. DERM. Pertaining to the use of remedies introduced beneath the skin.

Hypot'enuse, *n.* G. *hupoteinousa* (*grammē*), lit. '(line) stretching under', fem. pres.pple. of *hupoteinein*, to stretch under, f. *hupo-* (HYPO-) + *teinein*, to stretch. The side of a right-angled triangle opposite the right angle.

Hypoth'ecate, *vt.* Med.L. *hypothēcāre*, *hypothēcātum*—G. *hupothēkē*, a pledge, f. *hupo-* (HYPO-) + *the-*, stem of *tithenai*, to place. To pledge, mortgage.—**Hypothec**A'TION, *n.*

Hypoth'esis, *n.* G. *hupothesis*, base, basis of an argument, supposition, f. *hupo-* (HYPO-) + *thesis*, a placing, f. *the-*. (See prec.) A proposition as a basis for reasoning; a supposition, assumption.—**Hypothet'**ICAL, *a.*

Hys'sop, *n.* L. *hyssōpus* = G. *hussōpos*. A small bushy aromatic herb.

Hyster'ic, *a.* L. *hystericus*—G. *husterikos*, suffering in the womb, hysterical, f. *hustera*, womb. Also **Hyster'**ICAL. Of, affected or characterized by, hysteria.—**Hyste'ria**, *n.* Formed as abstract *n.* to *hysteric*. A nervous affection (attacking chiefly women, and formerly thought to be due to a disturbance of the womb), with convulsive fits of laughing, &c., and perversion of the moral and intellectual faculties. (Also called *hysterics*.)

I

I, *pron.* O.E. *ic* = Goth., O.L.G. *ik*, O.H.G. *ih* (Ger. *ich*). Cogn. with Skr. *ahám*, G. *egō*, L. *ego*. The pronoun of the first person.

Iam'bus, *n.* G. *iambos*, f. *iaptein*, to assail (the iambic metre having been first used by satiric writers). A metrical foot, a short followed by a long syllable.—**Iam'b**IC, *a.*

I'bex, *n.* L. *ibex*. A kind of wild goat.

I'bis. L. *ībis*—G. *ibis*. A stork-like bird, an object of veneration to the ancient Egyptians.

Ice, *n.* O.E. *īs*. Common Teut. Frozen water; a frozen confection.—*vt.* To cover with ice; to cover with sugar; to cool in ice.—**Ice'berg**, *n.* Formed with Du., Ger., &c., *berg*, hill. A floating mass of ice.—**I'cicle**, *n.* O.E. **īs-gicel*, *īses gicel*, f. *īses*, genit. of *īs* + *gicel*—O.N. *jökull*, dim. of *jaki*, piece of ice. A pendent piece of ice produced by the freezing of successive drops of water.—**Ic'**Y,[2] *a.*

Ichneu'mon, *n.* G. *ichneumōn*, f. *ichneuein*, to track, f. *ichnos*, track. A small Egyptian quadruped which hunts out crocodiles' eggs.

I'chor, *n.* G. *ichōr*. The blood of the gods.

Ichthyol'ogy, *n.* G. *ichthus*, fish + -LOGY. The part of zoology which treats of fishes.

I'con, *n.* L.L. *īcōn* = G. *eikōn*, image. A sacred picture, &c., honoured in the Eastern Church.—**Icon'oclast**, *n.* Late G. *eikonoklastēs*, f. *eikōn* + *-klastēs*, breaker, f. *kla-ein*, to break. A destroyer of images (often *fig.*).

Ide'a, *n.* L.L. *idea*—G. *idea*, look, form, kind, f. *id-*, root of *ide-ein*, to see. WIT. A supposed archetype of a class; a governing conception or principle; a conception; a thought or way of thinking; a supposition, impression.—**Ide'**AL, *a.* Existing as an idea; answering to one's highest conception; fancied, visionary. —*n.* A perfect type.—**Ide'al**LY,[2] *adv.*—**Ide'al**ISM, *n.* A system of thought in which the objects of perception are held to consist of ideas; imaginative treatment.—**Ide'al**IST, *n.* —**Ideal'**ITY, *n.*—**Ide'al**IZE, *vt.* To represent or regard as an ideal.

Iden'tity, *n.* F. *identité*—L.L. *identitas*, formed f. *identi-* = L. *idem*, same + *-tas*. (-TY.) Absolute sameness; individuality, personality. —**Iden't**ICAL, *a.* The very same.—**Iden'tical**LY,[2] *adv.*—**Iden'ti**FY, *vt.* To treat as identical *with*; to associate inseparably *with*; to ascertain who or what a thing or a person is.—**Identi**FICA'TION, *n.*

Id'iom, *n.* L. *idiōma*—G. *idiōma*, *idiōmatos*, a peculiarity, a peculiarity of language, f. *idios*, own, private. One's language; a dialect; the manner of expression natural, a form of expression peculiar, to a language.—**Idiomat'ic**, *a.* G. *idiōmatikos*. Peculiar to a language; given to, marked by, the use of idioms.—**Idiomat'ically**, *adv.* -AL. -LY.[2]

Idiosyn'crasy, *n.* G. *idiosugkrasia*, f. *idios* (see prec.) + *sun-* (SYN-) + *krasis*, mixture. CRASIS. Individual bent of mind.

Id'iot, *n.* F. *idiot*—L. *idiōta*, ignorant person—G. *idiōtēs*, private (hence unskilled or ill-informed) person, f. *idios*. IDIOM. A person mentally incapacitated.—**Id'iocy**, *n*. App. formed on *idiot* after *prophet, prophecy*, &c. The state of being an idiot.—**Idiot'**IC, *a*.—**Idiot'ically**, *adv*. -AL. -LY.[2]

I'dle, *a*. O.E. *idel*, empty, useless = O.S. *īdal*, O.H.G. *ītal* (Ger. *eitel*). Ineffective, vain, frivolous; groundless; useless; doing nothing; not in operation; lazy.—*vi*. and *t*. To be idle, to pass (time) *away* in idleness.—**I'dLY**,[2] *adv*. —**I'dle**NESS, *n*.—**I'dl**ER, *n*.

I'dol, *n*. O.F. *idole*—L.L. *īdōlum*—G. *eidōlon*, image, idol, f. *eidos*, form, shape. An image of a deity set up to be worshipped; a phantom. —**Idol'atry**, *n*. O.F. *idolatrie*, repg. a Comm. Romanic *īdōlatrīa* shortened f. Eccles.L. *īdōlolatrīa*—G. *eidōlolatreia*, f. *eidōlon* + *latreia*, service, worship. The worship of idols. —**Idol'ater**, *n*. F. *idolatre* (now *idolâtre*)—Eccles.L. *īdōlolatrēs* (shortened in Romanic to *idolatra*)—G. *eidōlolatrēs*. A worshipper of idols.—**Idol'atr**ESS, *n*.—**Idol'atr**OUS, *a*.—**I'dol**IZE, *vt*. To adore to excess.

I'dyll, I'dyl, *n*. L. *īdyllium*—G. *eidullion*, dim of *eidos*. (See prec.) A short poem describing a picturesque (gen. rustic) scene or incident.—**Idyl'l**IC, *a*. Of the nature of an idyll; full of natural or picturesque charm.

If, *conj*. O.E. *gif*. Cf. O.N. *ef*, if, O.H.G. *ibu* (Ger. *ob*), whether, if. Granted that; whether.

Ig'nis fat'uus, *n*. Mod.L. Lit. 'foolish fire', f. *ignis*, fire + *fatuus*, foolish. FATUOUS. A phosphorescent light flitting over marshy ground, called also Will-o'-the-wisp. — **Ig'neous**, *a*. L. *igneus* (a. f. *ignis*) + -OUS. Fiery; resulting from the action of fire.—

Ignite', *vt*. L. *ignīre, ignītum*, f. *ignis*. To set on fire.—*vi*. To take fire.—**Igni't**ION, *n*.

Igno'ble, *a*. F. *ignoble*—L. *ignōbilis*, f. *i*- (= IN-[2]) + *gnōbilis, nōbilis*, NOBLE. Of low birth; base, sordid.—**Igno'b**LY,[2] *adv*.

Ig'nominy, *n*. F. *ignominie*—L. *ignōminia*, f. *i*- (= IN-[2]) + **gnōmen, nōmen*, NAME, reputation. Disgrace, infamy; base conduct.—**Ignomin'i**OUS, *a*.

Ignore', *vt*. L. *ignōrāre*, not to know, disregard, f. *i*- (= IN-[2]) + **gnōrāre*, f. root *gno*- as in *gnoscĕre, noscĕre*, to get to know, G. *gnōnai*, to KNOW. Of a grand jury, to reject (an indictment); to disregard, leave out of account. —**Ignora'mus**, *n*. 1st pl. pres. indic. of *ignōrāre*, 'we disregard (it)', formerly endorsed on an indictment rejected by a grand jury. An ignorant person (app. f. the use of the word as a proper name in works written to expose the ignorance of lawyers).—**Ig'nor**ANCE, *n*. Lack of knowledge.—**Ig'nor**ANT, *a*. Lacking knowledge.—**Ig'norant**LY,[2] *adv*.

Ill, *a*. Early M.E. *ill*—O.N. *illr*, of unknown orig. Morally evil; of repute, &c., implying evil; marked by evil intent; hurtful; offensive, disagreeable; unlucky, disastrous; difficult; faulty; inefficient; improper; of health, &c., disordered; not well, sick.—*n*. Evil; harm; a calamity.—*adv*. Unkindly; unfortunately; not well; imperfectly, scarcely.—**Ill'**NESS, *n*.

Illa'tive, *a*. L.L. *illātīvus*, f. *inferre, illātum*. INFER. Introducing or stating an inference.

Ille'gal, *a*. Med.L. *illēgālis*, f. *il*- (= IN-[2]) + L. *lēgālis*, LEGAL. Contrary to law.—**Ille'gal**LY,[2] *adv*.—**Illegal'**ITY, *n*.

Illeg'ible, *a*. *Il*- (= IN-[2]). Not legible.—**Illeg'ib**LY,[2] *adv*.—**Illegib**IL'ITY, *n*.

Illegit'imate, *a*. After *legitimate* f. L. *illēgitimus*, unlawful, f. *il*- (= IN-[2]) + *lēgitimus*. LEGITIMATE. Not authorized by law; not born in wedlock; incorrectly deduced.—**Illegit'imate**LY,[2] *adv*.—**Illegit'im**ACY, *n*.

Illib'eral, *a*. F. *illibéral*—L. *illīberālis*, f. *il*- (= IN-[2]) + *līberālis*, LIBERAL. Sordid; narrow-minded.—**Illiberal'**ITY, *n*.

Illic'it, *a*. F. *illicite*—L. *illicitus*, f. *il*- (= IN-[2]) + *licitus*. LICIT. Unlawful, forbidden.

Illim'itable, *a*. *Il*- (= IN-[2]). Boundless.

Illit'erate, *a*. L. *illitterātus*, f. *il*- (= IN-[2]) + *litterātus*. LITERATE. Uneducated; unable to read.—**Illit'er**ACY, *n*.

Illog'ical, *a*. *Il*- (= IN-[2]). Devoid of or contrary to logic.—**Illog'ical**LY,[2] *adv*.

Illude', *vt*. L. *illūdĕre, illūsum*, to make sport of, f. *il*- (= IN-[1]) + *lūdĕre*, to play. ALLUDE. To trick.—**Illu's**ION, *n*. Deception; a deceptive appearance, &c.; perception involving false belief or conception, an instance of this.—**Illu'sion**IST, *n*. A conjuror.—**Illu's**IVE, *a*.—**Illu's**ORY, *a*.

Illu'minate, *vt*. L. *illūmināre, illūminātum*, f. *il*- (= IN-[1]) + *lūmen*, light. LUMINARY. To light up; to enlighten; to decorate with lights; to decorate in gold and colours.—**Illumin**A'TION, *n*.—**Illu'min**ATIVE, *a*.—

Illumina'ti, *n.pl*. Pl. of L. *illūminātus*, pa.pple. of *illūmināre*. Applied to various societies claiming special enlightenment.—

Illu'mine, *vt*. F. *illuminer*. To light up.

Il'lustrate, *vt*. L. *illustrāre, illustrātum*, to light up, elucidate, f. *il*- (= IN-[1]) + *lustrāre*. LUSTRE.[1] To elucidate; to explain by examples; to furnish (a book, &c.) with drawings or pictures. — **Illustra't**ION, *n*. — **Illus'tr**ATIVE, *a*. — **Il'lustrat**OR, *n*. — **Illus'trious**, *a*. L. *illustris*, bright, famous + -OUS. Famous, renowned.

Im'age, *n*. F. *image*—L. *imāgo, imāginis*, likeness, statue, conception, &c., app. f. same root as *imitārī*, to IMITATE. A sculptured figure; an optical appearance of an object produced by reflection or refraction of rays of light; semblance, likeness; a counterpart, copy; a typical example; a conception; a figure of speech.—*vt*. To delineate; to reflect, mirror; to represent *to oneself*.—**Im'ag**ERY, *n*. Carved figures; the use of rhetorical figures.—**Imag'ine**, *vt*. F. *imaginer*—L. *imāgināre*, to form an image of, in middle *imāginārī*, to imagine, f. *imāgo*. To picture to oneself; to conjecture; to think, suppose.—**Imag'in**ABLE, *a*.—**Imag'in**ARY, *a*. Existing only in fancy.—**Imagin**A'TION, *n*.—**Imag'in**ATIVE, *a*.

Im'becile, *a*. F. *imbécile*—L. *imbēcillus*. Weak in mind or body; inane, absurd.—*n*. A person of weak mind.—**Imbecil'**ITY, *n*.

Imbibe', *vt*. L. *imbibĕre*, to imbibe (opinions, &c.), later in lit. sense, to drink in, f. *im*- (= IN-[1]) + *bibĕre*, to drink. BEVERAGE. BIBULOUS. To 'drink in', assimilate (opinions, knowledge, &c.); to drink (liquid); to absorb.

Imbro'glio, *n*. It. *imbroglio*, an entangling, &c., f. *im*- (= IN-[1]) + *broglio*, confusion. BROIL.[1] A confused heap; a complicated situation.

Imbrue', *vt*. O.F. *embreuver, emb(e)uvrer, embev(e)rer*, to moisten, dye, f. EM-[1] + *-bevrer*, L. type **biberāre*, L. *bibĕre*, to drink. IMBIBE. To stain or dye *in, with* (blood, &c.).

Imbue', *vt*. L. *imbuĕre*, to wet, tinge, app. (with *im*- = IN-[1]) a causal form conn. with *bibĕre*. (See prec.) To saturate, dye, inspire, *with*.

Im'itate, *vt*. L. *imitārī, imitātus*. IMAGE. To take as one's model; to mimic, copy, simulate.—**Im'it**ABLE, *a*.—**Imit**A'TION, *n*. Often *attrib*.—**Im'it**ATIVE, *a*.—**Im'itat**OR, *n*.

Immac'ulate, *a.* L. *immaculātus*, f. *im-* (= IN-[2])+*maculātus*. MACULATE. Spotless.

Im'manent, *a.* L.L. *immanens, immanentis*, pres.pple. of *im*(= IN-[1])*manēre*, to dwell in. MANOR. Abiding *in*, inherent.

Immate'rial, *a.* Med.L. *immāteriālis*, f. *im-* (= IN-[2]) + *māteriālis*, MATERIAL. Not consisting of matter, incorporeal; unimportant.

Immature', *a.* L. *immātūrus*, f. *im-* (= IN-[2]) + *mātūrus*, MATURE. Not perfect or completed, unripe.—**Immatur**'ITY, *n.*

Immeas'urable, *a.* *Im-* (= IN-[2]). Not to be measured.—**Immeas'urab**LY,[2] *adv.*

Imme'diate, *a.* Med.L. *immediātus*, f. *im-* (= IN-[2]) + L.L. *mediātus*, MEDIATE. In or involving actual contact or direct relation; nearest, next; of time, present or just coming; done or happening at once, instant; having a direct bearing.—**Imme'diate**LY,[2] *adv.*

Immemo'rial, *a.* Med.L. *immemoriālis*, f. *im-* (= IN-[2]) + L. *memoriālis*, of or belonging to memory, f. *memoria*, MEMORY. Beyond living memory.—**Immemo'rial**LY,[2] *adv.*

Immense', *a.* F. *immense*—L. *immensus*, immeasurable, f. *im-* (= IN-[2]) + *mensus*, pa. pple. of *mētīri*, to MEASURE. Vast, huge.—**Immense'**LY,[2] *adv.* Immeasurably; very greatly.—**Immens'**ITY, *n.*

Immerse', *vt.* L. *im*(= IN-[1])*mergĕre*, *immersum*, to dip or plunge into. EMERGE. To dip or plunge into a liquid; to embed, involve.—**Immer'**SION, *n.*

Immethod'ical, *a.* *Im-* (= IN-[2]). Lacking method.

Im'migrate, *vi.* L. *im*(= IN-[1])*migrāre*, *immigrātum*, to remove into. MIGRATE. To settle in a country.—*vt.* To bring in as settlers.—**Im'migr**ANT, *n.*—**Immigr**A'TION, *n.*

Im'minent, *a.* L. *imminens, imminentis*, pres.pple. of *imminēre* (*im-* = IN-[1]), to project, impend. EMINENT. Close at hand.—**Im'minent**LY,[2] *adv.*—**Im'min**ENCE, *n.*

Immo'bile, *a.* F. *immobile*—L. *immōbilis*, f. *im-* (= IN-[2]) + *mōbilis*, MOBILE. Fixed, stable; motionless.—**Immobil'**ITY, *n.*—**Immo'bil**IZE, *vt.*

Immod'erate, *a.* L. *immoderātus*, f. *im-* (= IN-[2]) + *moderātus*, MODERATE. Excessive.—**Immod'erate**LY,[2] *adv.*

Immod'est, *a.* L. *immodestus*, f. *im-* (= IN-[2]) + *modestus*, MODEST. Not modest.—**Immod'est**LY,[2] *adv.*—**Immod'est**Y,[1] *n.*

Im'molate, *vt.* L. *immolāre*, *immolātum*, to sprinkle with sacrificial meal, to sacrifice, f. *im-* (= IN-[1]) + *mola*, millstone, sacrificial meal. MILL. To sacrifice.—**Immol**A'TION, *n.*

Immor'al, *a.* *Im-* (= IN-[2]). Vicious.—**Immor'al**LY,[2] *adv.*—**Immoral'**ITY, *n.*

Immor'tal, *a.* L. *immortālis*, f. *im-* (= IN-[2]) + *mortālis*, MORTAL. Not subject to death; imperishable.—**Immor'tal**LY,[2] *adv.*—**Immortal'**ITY, *n.*—**Immor'tal**IZE, *vt.* To exempt from death; to cause to be ever remembered.—**Immortelle'**, *n.* F., fem. of *immortel*, L. *immortālis*. A flower which retains its colour after being dried.

Immo'vable, *a.* *Im-* (= IN-[2]). That cannot be moved; motionless; unalterable; steadfast, unyielding.—**Immo'vab**LY,[2] *adv.*

Immune', *a.* L. *immūnis*, exempt, orig. from a public service, f. *im-* (= IN-[2]) + *mūnis*, ready to be of service, conn. with *mūnus*. MUNICIPAL. Proof against hurtful influences.—**Immun'**ITY, *n.* Exemption from a service, &c., privilege; a privilege; freedom, exemption; the condition of being immune.

Immure', *vt.* Med.L. *immūrāre*, f. *im-* (= IN-[1]) + L. *mūrus*, wall. MURAL. To imprison.

Immu'table, *a.* L. *immūtābilis*, f. *im-* (= IN-[2]) + *mūtābilis*, MUTABLE. Unchangeable.—**Immuta**BIL'ITY, *n.*

Imp, *vt.* O.E. *impian*, to graft = O.H.G. *impfôn* (Ger. *impfen*, to inoculate), prob. in some way f. G. *emphuein*, to implant. To fit (a wing) *with* fresh feathers.—*n.* A 'child of the devil', a little devil; a mischievous child.

Im'pact, *n.* L. type **impactus*, f. *impingĕre*, *impactum*. IMPINGE. The act of impinging.

Impair', *vt.* M.E. *empeiren*—O.F. *empeirer*—L. type **impējōrāre*, to make worse, f. *im-* (= IN-[1]) + *pējor*, worse. To lessen injuriously, to damage, injure.—**Impair'**MENT, *n.*

Impale', *vt.* F. *empaler*—Med.L. *impālāre*, f. *im-* (= IN-[1]) + L. *pālus*, stake. PALE, *n.* To put to death by fixing on a pointed stake; to combine (two coats of arms) by placing them side by side separated by a vertical line.

Impal'pable, *a.* Med.L. *impalpābilis*, f. *im-* (= IN-[2]) + L.L. *palpābilis*, PALPABLE. Imperceptible to the touch.

Impart', *vt.* O.F. *impartir*—L. *impartīre*, f. *im-* (= IN-[1]) + *partīre*, to share, f. *pars*, PART. To give a share of, to communicate.

Impar'tial, *a.* *Im-* (= IN-[2]). Not partial, fair.—**Impar'tial**LY,[2] *adv.*—**Impartial'**ITY, *n.*

Impas'sable, *a.* *Im-* (= IN-[2]). Impossible to traverse.

Impas'sible, *a.* Eccles.L. *impassibilis*, f. *im-* (= IN-[2]) + L. *passibilis*, capable of feeling, f. *pati*. PASSION. Incapable of suffering or of feeling.—**Impassi**BIL'ITY, *n.*

Impas'sion, *vt.* It. *impassionare*, f. *im-* (= IN-[1]) + *passione* = F. *passion*, PASSION. To stir the feelings of.—**Impas'sioned**, *ppl.a.* Having the feelings deeply moved.

Impas'sive, *a.* *Im-* (= IN-[2]) + PASSIVE in obs. sense 'suffering, liable to suffer'. Incapable of suffering; apathetic; serene.

Impa'tient, *a.* O.F. *impatient*—L. *impatiens*, *impatientis*, f. *im-* (= IN-[2]) + *patiens*, PATIENT. Not willingly enduring pain, &c.; irascible.—**Impa'tient**LY,[2] *adv.*—**Impa'ti**ENCE, *n.*

Impeach', *vt.* O.F. *empechier*, *empescher* (F. *empêcher*), to hinder—L.L. *impedicāre*, to catch, entangle, f. *im-* (= IN-[1]) + L. *pedica* (f. *pēs*, *pedis*, FOOT), FETTER. PEACH, *v.* To discredit, disparage; to bring a charge against, esp., to accuse of treason; to censure.—**Impeach'**MENT, *n.*—**Impeach'**ABLE, *a.*

Impec'cable, *a.* L.L. *impeccābilis*, f. *im-* (= IN-[2]) + L. *peccāre*, to sin. Incapable of sin.

Impecu'nious, *a.* *Im-* (= IN-[2]). Penniless.

Impede', *vt.* L. *impedīre*, lit., to entangle the feet, f. *im-* (= IN-[1]) + *pēs*, *pedis*, FOOT. To hinder, obstruct.—**Imped'i**MENT, *n.*

Impel', *vt.* L. *impellĕre*, *impulsum*, f. *im-* (= IN-[1]) + *pellĕre*, to drive. COMPEL. IMPULSE. To constrain, urge.

Impend', *vi.* L. *impendēre*, f. *im-* (= IN-[1]) + *pendēre*. DEPEND. To be imminent.

Impen'etrable, *a.* F. *impénétrable*—L. *impenetrābilis*, f. *im-* (= IN-[2]) + *penetrābilis*, PENETRABLE. That cannot be penetrated; inscrutable.—**Impenetra**BIL'ITY, *n.*

Impen'itent, *a.* L. *impaenitens*, *impaenitentis*, f. *im-* (= IN-[2]) + *paenitens*, PENITENT. Not penitent, obdurate.—**Impen'it**ENCE, *n.*

Imper'ative, *a.* L. *imperātīvus*, of or proceeding from a command, f. *imperāre*, to command. EMPEROR. Expressing command; peremptory; urgent.—*n.* The imperative mood.

Impercep'tible, *a.* F. *imperceptible*—Med. L. *imperceptibilis*, f. *im-* (= IN-[2]) + L. *perceptibilis*, PERCEPTIBLE. That cannot be perceived.—**Impercep'tib**LY,[2] *adv.*

Imper'fect, *a.* F. *imparfait*—L. *imperfectus*, f. *im-* (= IN-[2]) + *perfectus*, PERFECT. Incomplete; defective; expressing past uncompleted action.—*n.* The imperfect tense. — **Imper'fect**LY,[2] *adv.*—**Imperfec'**TION, *n.*

Impe'rial, *a.* O.F. *imperial*—L. *imperiālis*, f. *imperium*, EMPIRE. Of an empire, a sovereign state, or an emperor; majestic.—*n.* A small part of the beard left growing below the lower lip (after the Emperor Napoleon III).—**Impe'ri**OUS, *a.* Domineering; urgent.

Imper'il, *vt.* *Im-* (= IN-[1]). To bring into peril.

Imper'ishable, *a.* *Im-* (= IN-[2]). Indestructible.

Imper'meable, *a.* L.L. *impermeābilis*, f. *im-* (= IN-[2]) + L. *permeābilis*, PERMEABLE. That cannot be passed through or traversed.

Imper'sonal, *a.* L.L. *impersonālis*, f. *im-* (= IN-[2]) + L. *personālis*, PERSONAL. Applied to verbs used only in the third person singular; having no personal reference or connexion; not endowed with personality.

Imper'sonate, *vt.* *Im-* (= IN-[1]) + L. *persōna*, PERSON + -ATE.[3] To typify; to play the part of.—**Imperson**A'TION, *n.*

Imper'tinent, *a.* L. *impertinens*, *impertinentis*, not belonging, in Med.L., unsuitable, absurd, f. *im-* (= IN-[2]) + *pertinens*, PERTINENT. Irrelevant; insolent, saucy. — **Imper'tinent**LY,[2] *adv.*—**Imper'tin**ENCE, *n.*

Impertur'bable, *a.* L.L. *imperturbābilis*, f. *im-* (= IN-[2]) + **perturbābilis*, PERTURBABLE. Not liable to be agitated, calm.

Imper'vious, *a.* L. *impervius* (f. *im-* (= IN-[2]) + *pervius*, PERVIOUS) + -OUS. Not to be passed through; not open *to* (argument, &c.).

Im'petrate, *vt.* L. *impetrāre*, *impetrātum*, f. *im-* (= IN-[1]) + *patrāre*, to bring about, effect. To get by request or entreaty.

Im'petus, *n.* L. *impetus*, an attack, vehemence, f. *impetĕre*, to attack, f. *im-* (= IN-[1]) + *petĕre*, to seek. APPETITE. Energy of motion; stimulus, impulse.—**Impet'u**OUS, *a.* Moving rapidly and forcibly; vehement, ardent. — **Impet'uous**LY,[2] *adv.*—**Impetuos'**ITY, *n.*

Impinge', *vi.* L. *impingĕre*, to strike at or into, f. *im-* (= IN-[1]) + *pangĕre*, to fasten, drive in. COMPACT, *ppl.a.* IMPACT. To strike or dash; to infringe or encroach *on* or *upon*.

Im'pious, *a.* L. *impius* (f. *im-* (= IN-[2]) + *pius*, PIOUS) + -OUS. Wicked, profane. — **Im'piously**LY,[2] *adv.* — **Impi'ety**, *n.* L. *impietas*. Irreligion; want of reverence.

Implac'able, *a.* F. *implacable*—L. *implācābilis*, f. *im-* (= IN-[2]) + *plācābilis*, PLACABLE. Not to be appeased.—**Implac'ab**LY,[2] *adv.*

Implant', *vt.* F. *implanter*, f. *im-* (= IN-[1]) + *planter*, to plant, f. *plante*, L. *planta*. PLANT. To insert; to instil (an opinion, &c.).

Im'plement, *n.* App. f. L. *implēmentum*, a filling up, in sense 'that which serves to stock (a house, &c.)', f. *implēre* (*im-* = IN-[1]), to fill up. COMPLETE. An article of furniture; a tool.

Im'plicate, *vt.* L. *im*(= IN-[1])*plicāre*, *implicātum*, to fold in, entangle. APPLY. IMPLY. To entwine; to involve, imply; to involve *in* (a charge, &c.). — **Implic**A'TION, *n.* — **Implic'it**, *a.* L. *implicitus*, pa.pple. of *implicāre*. Implied though not plainly expressed; unquestioning.—**Implic'it**LY,[2] *adv.*

Implore', *vt.* L. *implōrāre*, to entreat with tears, implore, f. *im-* (= IN-[1]) + *plōrāre*, to weep. DEPLORE. To entreat earnestly.

Imply', *vt.* O.F. *emplier*, to entwine—L. *implicāre*. IMPLICATE. EMPLOY. To involve as a consequence; to insinuate.

Impol'icy, *n.* *Im-* (= IN-[2]). Bad policy.—**Impol'itic**, *a.* *Im-* (= IN-[2]). Inexpedient.

Im'polite', *a.* L. *impolītus*, unpolished, f. *im-* (= IN-[2]) + *polītus*, POLITE. Uncivil.

Impon'derable, *a.* *Im-* (= IN-[2]). Having no appreciable weight.

Import', *vt.* L. *im*(= IN-[1])*portāre*, to carry in, in Med.L., to be of consequence. COMPORT. To bring (commodities) into one country from another; to involve, imply; to signify, mean; to express, state; to be of consequence to, concern.—**Im'port**, *n.* An imported article; amount imported (gen. in *pl.*); the action of importing, an instance of this; meaning; consequence, importance.—**Import**A'TION, *n.*—**Import'**ER, *n.*—**Impor'tant**, *a.* Of consequence, momentous; consequential, pompous. — **Impor'**TANCE, *n.* Consequence, moment; pompousness.

Importune', *vt.* F. *importuner*—Med.L. *importūnāri*, to worry, f. L. *importūnus*, unsuitable, troublesome, orig., 'hard of access', f. *im-* (= IN-[2]) + *portus*, entrance, harbour. PORT, *n.*[1] To solicit pressingly.—**Impor'tun**ATE,[2] *a.* Pressing in solicitation.—**Impor'tunate**LY,[2] *adv.*—**Importu'n**ITY, *n.*

Impose', *vt.* F. *imposer*, f. *im-* (= IN-[1]) + *poser*, to place. POSE.[1] To lay or set *on* or *upon*; to inflict, to levy or enforce.—*vi.* To be striking or impressive; to practise deceit *on* or *upon*.—**Imposi'tion**, *n.* L. *impositio*, *impositiōnis*, f. *im* (= IN-[1]) *pōnĕre*, *impositum*, to place upon. DEPONE. The action of laying on, inflicting, &c.; something levied; the action of deceiving, an instance of this.—**Impos'tor**, *n.* F. *imposteur*—L.L. *impostor*, agent-n. f. *impōnĕre*. A deceiver, one who assumes a false character.—**Impos'**TURE, *n.*

Impos'sible, *a.* F. *impossible*—L. *impossibilis*, f. *im-* (= IN-[2]) + *possibilis*, POSSIBLE. Not possible.—**Impossi**BIL'ITY, *n.*

Im'post, *n.*[1] O.F. *impost* (F. *impôt*)—Med.L. *impostus*—L. *impositus*, *impostus*, pa.pple. of *impōnĕre*. IMPOSITION. A tax, duty, tribute.

Im'post, *n.*[2] F. *imposte*—It. *imposta*—L. *impostus*. (See prec.) The upper (and frequently projecting) course of a pillar, &c.

Im'potent, *a.* F. *impotent*—L. *impotens*, *impotentis*, f. *im-* (= IN-[2]) + *potens*, POTENT. Powerless, ineffective; without bodily strength; wholly lacking sexual power.—**Im'potent**LY,[2] *adv.*—**Im'pot**ENCE, **Im'pot**ENCY, *nn.*

Impound', *vt.* *Im-* (= IN-[1]) + POUND, *n.*[2] To shut up in or as in a pound; to take legal and formal possession of.

Impov'erish, *vt.* O.F. *empoveriss-*, lengthened stem of *empov(e)rir*, f. EM-[1] + *povre*, POOR. To make poor or weak.

Imprac'ticable, *a.* *Im-* (= IN-[2]). That cannot be effected, carried out, traversed; intractable.—**Impracticab**BIL'ITY, *n.*

Im'precate, *vt.* L. *imprecāri*, *imprecātus*, f. *im-* (= IN-[1]) + *precāri*, to PRAY. To invoke or call down (evil) *upon*.—**Impreca'**TION, *n.*

Impreg'nable, *a.* Corr. of *impreignable*, *imprenable*—F. *imprenable*, f. *im-* (= IN-[2]) + *prenable*, able to be taken, f. *prendre*, L. *prehendĕre*. PREHENSILE. Proof against attack.—**Impregna**BIL'ITY, *n.*

Impreg'nate, *vt.* L.L. *impraegnāre*, *impraegnātum*, f. *im-* (= IN-[1]) + *praegnāre*, to be pregnant, f. L. *praegnans*, PREGNANT. To make pregnant; to fill, saturate. imbue.—**Impregna**'TION, *n*.

Impress', *v.*[1]*t*. L. *imprimĕre, impressum*, f. *im-* (= IN-[1]) + *premĕre*, to press. PRESS.[1] IMPRINT. To produce (a mark) by pressure, to mark (a thing) by pressure; to influence or affect deeply.—**Im'press**, *n*. The act of impressing, a mark impressed; a characteristic mark.—**Impres'**SIBLE, *a*. Liable to be easily impressed or influenced.—**Impres'**SION, *n*. The action or process of impressing; an impressed mark; a printed copy, an engraving; the aggregate of copies printed at once; an effect produced on a thing or on the mind, &c.; an indistinct notion. — **Impres'sion**ABLE, *a*. Impressible. — **Impres'sion**ISM, *n*. A method of painting, &c., so as to give a general effect without elaboration of detail. — **Impres'sion**IST, *n*.—**Impres'**SIVE, *a*. Making a deep impression, exciting deep feeling.

Impress', *v.*[2]*t*. *Im-* (= IN-[1]) + PRESS.[2] = PRESS.[2]—**Impress'**MENT, *n*.

Imprint', *vt*. M.E. *emprinten*, &c.—O.F. *empreinter*, to print—Pop.L. *impremĕre*, for L. *imprimĕre*. IMPRESS.[1] To impress (a mark) *on* or *in*; to impress *with* a mark.—**Im'print**, *n*. A mark impressed; the publisher's name, &c., with the date, or the printer's name, &c., printed in a book.—**Imprima'tur**, *n*. 'Let it be printed', 3d sing. pres. subjunctive pass. of *imprimĕre* in Mod.L. sense, to print. A licence to print; sanction.

Impris'on, *vt*. O.F. *emprisoner*, f. EM-[1] + *prison*, PRISON. To put in prison; to confine, shut up.—**Impris'on**MENT, *n*.

Improb'able, *a*. L. *improbābilis*, f. *im-* (= IN-[2]) + *probābilis*, PROBABLE. Not likely to be true.—**Improba**BIL'ITY, *n*.

Impromp'tu, *adv*. and *a*. L. *in promptu*, in readiness, f. *promptus*, readiness, f. *prōmĕre*. PROMPT. Extempore.—*n*. Something composed or said impromptu.

Improp'er, *a*. *Im-* (= IN-[2]). Irregular, wrong; unsuitable; unseemly, indecent.—**Improp'er**LY,[2] *adv*. — **Impropri'ety**, *n*. L. *improprietas*. PROPRIETY. The quality of being improper; an instance of this.

Impro'priate, *vt*. Med.L. *impropriāre, impropriātum*, f. *im-* (= IN-[1]) + *proprius*. PROPER. To place (church property) in lay hands.

Improve', *vt*. A.F. *en-, emprower, enprouwer, emprover*, to be of advantage to, f. EN-[1], EM-[1] + O.F. *pro, prou, preu*, oblique case of *pros*, advantage, profit, poss. formed in some way f. L. *prōdesse*, to benefit. PROUD. To make good use of; to make better.—*vi*. To become better. — **Improv'**ABLE, *a*. — **Improve'**MENT, *n*.—**Improv'**ER, *n*. In senses f. the *v*.; one who works at a trade for low or no wages to improve his knowledge or skill.

Improv'ident, *a*. *Im-* (= IN-[2]). Heedless; thriftless.—**Improv'id**ENCE, *n*.

Improvise', *vt*. F. *improviser*—It. *improv(v)isare*, f. *impro(v)viso*, L. *imprōvisus*, unforeseen, f. *im-* (= IN-[2]) + *prōvisus*, pa.pple. of *prōvidēre*. PROVIDE. To utter or perform extempore; to contrive for the occasion.

Impru'dent, *a*. L. *imprūdens, imprūdentis*, f. *im-* (= IN-[2]) + *prūdens*. PRUDENT. Not prudent, heedless, incautious. — **Impru'dent**LY,[2] *adv*.—**Impru'd**ENCE, *n*.

Im'pudent, *a*. L. *impudens, impudentis*, shameless, impudent, f. *im-* (= IN-[2]) + *pudens*, modest, orig. pres.pple. of *pudēre*, to feel shame. Insolently disrespectful. — **Im'pudent**LY,[2] *adv*.—**Im'pud**ENCE, *n*.—**Impudic'ity**, *n*. F. *impudicité*—L. type **impudicitas* for *impudicitia*, f. *impudīcus*, shameless, f. *impudens*. Shamelessness, immodesty.

Impugn', *vt*. F. *impugner*—L. *impugnāre*, to assail, f. *im-* (= IN-[1]) + *pugnāre*, to fight. PUGNACIOUS. To call in question, dispute.

Im'pulse, *n*. L. *impulsus*, f. *impellĕre*, to IMPEL. A sudden application of force, motion thereby caused; incitement; sudden inclination to act.—Sim. **Impul'**SION, *n*.—**Impul'**SIVE, *a*. Given to acting without premeditation.—**Impul'sive**LY,[2] *adv*.

Impu'nity, *n*. L. *impūnitas*, f. *impūnis*, unpunished, f. *im-* (= IN-[2]) + *poena*, penalty. PAIN. Freedom from penalty.

Impure', *a*. L. *impūrus*, f. *im-* (= IN-[2]) + *pūrus*, PURE. Dirty; ceremonially unclean; defiled by sin; contaminated, adulterated.—**Impure'**LY,[2] *adv*.—**Impur'**ITY, *n*.

Impute', *vt*. F. *imputer*—L. *imputāre*, to bring into the reckoning, f. *im-* (= IN-[1]) + *putāre*, to reckon. COMPUTE. To set to the account of, ascribe.—**Imput**A'TION, *n*.

In, *prep*. O.E. *in, inn*. Common Teut. Cogn. with G. *en*, L. *in*. INN. Indicating a being within limits of place, time, circumstances, &c.—*adv*. O.E. *inn, in*. In some place, state, &c.—*vt*. O.E. *innian*. To get in, esp. grain, &c.—**In'**LY,[2] *adv*. Within, in the heart; intimately, closely.—**In'ning**, *vbl.n*. Getting in, esp. of grain, &c.; in *pl*., at cricket, the part of the game during which either side is 'in' or batting, a player's turn of batting.—**In'**WARD, *adv*. and *a*.—In *pl*. as *n*., the entrails. —**In'**WARDS, *adv*. —**In'ward**LY,[2] *adv*.

Inabil'ity, *n*. IN-[2]. Want of ability.

Inacces'sible, *a*. F. *inaccessible*—L.L. *inaccessibilis*, f. IN-[2] + *accessibilis*, ACCESSIBLE. That cannot be reached or entered.

Inac'curate, *a*. IN-[2]. Inexact, incorrect.—**Inac'curate**LY,[2] *adv*.—**Inac'cur**ACY, *n*.

Inac'tion, *n*. IN-[2]. Absence of action or activity.—**Inac'**TIVE, *a*.—**Inactiv'**ITY, *n*.

Inad'equate, *a*. IN-[2]. Not sufficient.—**Inad'equate**LY,[2] *adv*.—**Inad'equ**ACY, *n*.

Inadmis'sible, *a*. IN-[2]. Not to be admitted or allowed.—**Inadmissi**BIL'ITY, *n*.

Inadver'tence, **Inadver't**ENCY, *nn*. Scholastic L. *inadvertentia*, f. IN-[2] + *advertentia*, ADVERTENCE. Failing to pay attention; an oversight.—**Inadver't**ENT, *a*.

Inadvi'sable, *a*. IN-[2]. Not advisable.

Ina'lienable, *a*. IN-[2] + *Alien*, earlier equivalent of ALIENATE + -ABLE. That cannot be alienated or transferred.

Inane', *a*. L. *inānis*, empty, useless. Empty, void; silly, senseless.—*n*. Infinite void space. —**Inane'**LY,[2] *adv*.—**Inan'**ITY, *n*.—**Inani'tion**, *n*. L. *inānītio, inānītiōnis*, emptiness, f. *inānīre*, to make empty, f. *inānis*. A being empty, esp. exhaustion through want of food.

Inan'imate, *a*. L.L. *inanimātus*, f. IN-[2] + L. *animātus*, ANIMATE. Lifeless; spiritless.

Inap'plicable, *a*. IN-[2]. Not applicable.

Inappre'ciable, *a*. IN-[2]. Imperceptible.

Inappro'priate, *a*. IN-[2]. Unsuitable.

Inapt', *a*. IN-[2]. Unsuitable; unskilful.—**Inapt'**LY,[2] *adv*.—**Inap'ti**TUDE, *n*.

Inartic'ulate, *a*. L. *inarticulātus*, f. IN-[2] + *articulātus*, ARTICULATE. Not articulate.

Inartis'tic, *a*. IN-[2]. Not in accordance with the rules of art; lacking appreciation of art.

Inasmuch', *adv*. Orig. three words. *Inasmuch as*, in so far as, seeing that, since.

Inatten'tion, *n.* IN-[2]. Failure to attend or take heed, neglect.—**Inatten'**TIVE, *a.*

Inau'dible, *a.* L. *inaudibilis*, f. IN-[2] + **audibilis*, AUDIBLE. That cannot be heard. —**Inau'dib**LY,[2] *adv.*

Inau'gurate, *vt.* L. *inaugurāre*, *inaugurātum*, to take omens from the flight of birds, to consecrate by doing this, f. IN-[1] + *augurāre*, to take such omens, f. *augur*, AUGUR. To consecrate, install; to commence or bring into use with a ceremony; to enter upon.—**Inau'gur**AL, *a.*—**Inaugur**A'TION, *n.*

Inauspic'ious, *a.* IN-[2]. Of ill omen.

In'born, *ppl.a.* IN, *adv.* Implanted by nature.

Incal'culable, *a.* IN-[2]. Beyond calculation.—**Incal'culab**LY,[2] *adv.*

Incandes'cent, *a.* L. *incandescens*, *incandescentis*, pres.pple. of *incandescĕre*, to glow, f. IN-[1] + *candescĕre*, inceptive of *candēre*, to glisten. CANDID. Glowing or white with heat.—**Incandes'**CENCE, *n.*

Incanta'tion, *n.* F. *incantation*—L. *incantātio*, *incantātiōnis*, f. *incantāre*, to enchant, f. IN-[1] + *cantāre*. CHANT. Magic; a spell.

Inca'pable, *a.* Med.L. *incapābilis*, f. IN-[2] + L.L. *capābilis*. CAPABLE. Not susceptible *of* or admitting; unable; incompetent; not qualified.—**Incapa**BIL'ITY, *n.*

Incapac'ity, *n.* F. *incapacité*, f. IN-[2] + *capacité*, CAPACITY. Want of capacity; disqualification, a disqualification.—**Incapac'it**ATE,[3] *vt.* To make incapable; to disqualify.

Incar'cerate, *vt.* Med.L. *incarcerāre*, *incarcerātum*, f. IN-[1] + L. *carcer*, prison. To put in prison.—**Incarcer**A'TION, *n.*

In'carnate, *vt.* L. *incarnāre*, *incarnātum*, f. IN-[1] + *caro*, flesh. CARNAGE. To embody in flesh.—**Incar'n**ATE,[2] *a.* Embodied in flesh. —**Incarn**A'TION, *n.*

Incau'tious, *a.* IN-[2]. Wanting in caution, heedless.—**Incau'tious**LY,[2] *adv.*

Incen'diary, *a.* L. *incendiārius*, setting on fire, f. *incendium*, conflagration, f. *incendĕre*, *incensum*, to set on fire, f. IN-[1] + **candĕre*, to cause to glow. Cf. *candēre*. CANDID. (See next.) Of, guilty of, arson; tending to stir up strife.—*n.* One who commits arson; one who stirs up strife.—**Incen'diar**ISM, *n.*

In'cense, *n.* O.F. *encens*—Eccles.L. *incensum*, neut. pa.pple. of *incendĕre* (see prec.), lit. 'that which is set on fire'. A substance used to produce a sweet smell when burned; the smoke of this.—*v.*[1]*t.* To perfume with incense.

Incense', *v.*[2]*t.* O.F. *incenser*—L. *incendĕre*. INCENDIARY. To stir to rage, exasperate.

Incen'tive, *a.* L. *incentīvus*, setting the tune, inciting, f. *incinĕre*, to blow or sound, f. IN-[1] + *canĕre*, to sing. CANT.[2] Arousing to feeling or action.—*n.* Something that does this.

Incep'tion, *n.* L. *inceptio*, *inceptiōnis*, f. *incipĕre*, *inceptum*, to take in hand, to begin, f. IN-[1] + *capĕre*, to take. ACCEPT. Beginning. —**Incep'**TIVE, *a.* Beginning; expressing the beginning of action.—*n.* An inceptive verb.

Incer'titude, *n.* F. *incertitude*—L. type **incertitūdo*, f. IN-[2] + *certitūdo*, CERTITUDE. Uncertainty; hesitation; insecurity.

Inces'sant, *a.* F. *incessant*—L.L. *incessans*, *incessantis*, f. IN-[2] + *cessans*, pres.pple. of *cessāre*, to CEASE. That does not cease, continual.

In'cest, *n.* L. *incestus*, f. IN-[2] + *castus*, CHASTE. Sexual intercourse of kindred within forbidden degrees.

Inch, *n.* O.E. *ynce*—L. *uncia*, a twelfth, the twelfth of a pound or of a foot. OUNCE.[1] QUINCUNX. UNCIAL. The twelfth of a foot.

In'choate, *a.* L. *inchoātus*, pa.pple. of *inchoāre*, to begin. Just begun, imperfect.

In'cident, *a.* L. *incidens*, *incidentis*, pres. pple. of *incidĕre*, to fall into or upon, to happen, f. IN-[1] + *cadĕre*, to fall. CADENCE. Appertaining or attaching; falling or striking *upon*. —*n.* A subordinate event; an event.—**In'cid**ENCE, *n.* A falling upon or affecting; extent of influence.—**Inciden'**TAL, *a.* Casual, subsidiary.—**Inciden'tal**LY,[2] *adv.*

Incip'ient, *a.* L. *incipiens*, *incipientis*, pres. pple. of *incipĕre*. INCEPTION. Beginning.

Incise', *vt.* F. *inciser*—L. *incidĕre*, *incīsum*, to cut into, f. IN-[1] + *caedĕre*, to cut. CÆSURA. To cut into; to engrave.—**Inci'**SION, *n.* A cutting into; a cut.—**Inci'**SIVE, *a.* Cutting, penetrating.—**Inci'**SOR, *n.* A cutting tooth.

Incite', *vt.* F. *inciter*—L. *incitāre*, f. IN-[1] + *citāre*. CITE. To urge.—**Incite'**MENT, *n.*

Incivil'ity, *n.* F. *incivilité*—L.L. *incīvīlitas*, f. *incīvīlis*, uncivil, f. IN-[2] + L. *cīvīlis*, CIVIL. Uncivil conduct; an uncivil act.

Inclem'ent, *a.* L. *inclēmens*, *inclēmentis*, f. IN-[2] + *clēmens*, CLEMENT. Of weather, &c., severe, extreme.—**Inclem'**ENCY, *n.*

Incline', *vt.* F. *incliner*—L. *inclīnāre*, to bend or be bent in any direction, f. IN-[1] + *-clīnāre*. DECLINE. To bend or turn (*lit.* and *fig.*).—*vi.* To be disposed; to slope; to have an oblique position or direction; to tend *to* some quality, &c.—**Inclin**A'TION, *n.*

Include', *vt.* L. *inclūdĕre*, *inclūsum*, to shut in, f. IN-[1] + *claudĕre*, to shut. CONCLUDE. To comprise, comprehend; to reckon in an enumeration, &c.—**Inclu'**SION, *n.*—**Inclu'**SIVE, *a.*—**Inclu'sive**LY,[2] *adv.*

Incog'nito, *a.* It. *incognito*, unknown, disguised—L. *incognitus*, unknown, f. IN-[2] + *cognitus*, pa.pple. of *cognoscĕre*. COGNITION. Whose identity is concealed or not avowed.—*adv.* With one's identity concealed or not avowed.—*n.* The condition of being incognito.

Incohe'rent, *a.* IN-[2]. Not coherent; inconsistent; disjointed, rambling.—**Incohe'rent**LY,[2] *adv.*—**Incohe'r**ENCE, *n.*

Incombus'tible, *a.* Med.L. *incombustibilis*, f. IN-[2] + L.L. *combustibilis*, COMBUSTIBLE. That cannot be burnt or consumed by fire.—**Incombusti**BIL'ITY, *n.*

In'come, *n.* IN, *adv.* + COME. The annual produce of one's work, investments, &c.

Incommen'surable, *a.* Med.L. *incommensūrābilis*, f. IN-[2] + *commensūrābilis*, COMMENSURABLE. Having no common measure; not comparable; disproportioned.

Incommode', *vt.* F. *incommoder*—L. *incommodāre*, f. *incommodus*, inconvenient, f. IN-[2] + *commodus*. COMMODE. To inconvenience, trouble.—**Incommo'di**OUS, *a.*

Incommu'nicable, *a.* IN-[2]. That cannot be imparted, shared, or uttered.

Incom'parable, *a.* F. *incomparable*—L. *incomparābilis*, f. IN-[2] + *comparābilis*, COMPARABLE. With which there is no comparison, matchless.—**Incom'parab**LY,[2] *adv.*

Incompat'ible, *a.* Med.L. *incompatibilis*, f. IN-[2] + *compatibilis*, COMPATIBLE. Discordant; inconsistent.—**Incompati**BIL'ITY, *n.*

Incom'petent, *a.* F. *incompétent*—L.L. *incompetens*, *incompetentis*, f. IN-[2] + *competens*, COMPETENT. Of inadequate ability; not qualified.—**Incom'pet**ENCE, -ENCY, *nn.*

Incomplete', *a.* L.L. *incomplētus*, f. IN-[2] + *complētus*, COMPLETE. Imperfect, defective, unfinished.—**Incomplete'**LY,[2] *adv.*

Incomprehen'sible, *a.* L. *incomprehen-*

sibilis, f. IN-[2] + *comprehensibilis*, COMPREHENSIBLE. Boundless; unintelligible.—**Incomprehensi**BIL'ITY, *n.*

Inconcei'vable, *a.* IN-[2]. That cannot be conceived.—**Inconcei'vab**LY,[2] *adv.*

Inconclu'sive, *a.* IN-[2]. Not decisive or convincing.—**Inconclu'sive**LY,[2] *adv.*

Incondite', *a.* L. *inconditus*, disordered, f. IN-[2] + *conditus*, pa.pple. of *condĕre*, to put together. RECONDITE. Ill-constructed, rude.

Incon'gruous, *a.* With -OUS f. L. *incongruus*, f. IN-[2] + *congruus*, CONGRUOUS. Not accordant; absurd.—**Incongru'**ITY, *n.*

Incon'sequent, *a.* L. *inconsequens*, *inconsequentis*, f. IN-[2] + *consequens*, CONSEQUENT. Irrelevant; involving false reasoning; illogical; disconnected.—**Incon'sequ**ENCE, *n.*

Inconsid'erable, *a.* F. *inconsidérable*, f. IN-[2] + *considérable*, CONSIDERABLE. Of small importance, value, &c.

Inconsid'erate, *a.* L. *inconsīderātus*, f. IN-[2] + *considerātus*, CONSIDERATE. Thoughtless, rash, indiscreet; without regard for others.

Inconsis'tent, *a.* IN-[2]. Not agreeing or according; lacking harmony between its parts; not constant in thought or action.—**Inconsis'tent**LY,[2] *adv.*—**Inconsis'ten**CY, *n.*

Inconsol'able, *a.* L. *inconsōlābilis*, f. IN-[2] + *consōlābilis*, CONSOLABLE. Not admitting of consolation; disconsolate.

Inconspic'uous, *a.* With -OUS f. L.L. *inconspicuus*, f. IN-[2] + *conspicuus*, CONSPICUOUS. Not readily seen.

Incon'stant, *a.* F. *inconstant*—L. *inconstans*, *inconstantis*, f. IN-[2] + *constans*, CONSTANT. Fickle; irregular, variable.—**Incon'stant**LY,[2] *adv.*—**Incon'stan**CY, *n.*

Incontest'able, *a.* F. *incontestable*, f. IN-[2] + *contestable*, CONTESTABLE. That cannot be disputed.—**Incontest'ab**LY,[2] *adv.*

Incon'tinent, *a.* L. *incontinens*, *incontinentis*, f. IN-[2] + *continens*, CONTINENT. Lacking self-restraint, not chaste; unable to retain or keep back.—**Incon'tin**ENCE, *n.*

Incon'tinent, *adv.* F. *incontinent*—L.L. *in continenti* (*tempore*), in continuous (time), without an interval. CONTINENT. Straightway. Sim. **Incon'tinent**LY.[2]

Incontrovert'ible, *a.* IN-[2]. Indisputable.

Inconve'nient, *a.* F. *inconvénient*—L. *inconveniens*, *inconvenientis*, not accordant, not befitting, f. IN-[2] + *conveniens*. CONVENIENT. Not convenient.—**Inconve'nient**LY,[2] *adv.* —**Inconve'ni**ENCE, *n.* Whence **Inconve'nience**, *vt.* To cause inconvenience to.

Incor'porate, *vt.* L.L. *incorporāre*, *incorporātum*, f. IN-[1] + *corporāre*. CORPORATE. To unite into one body; to embody, include; to form into a legal society.—*vi.* To unite.—**Incorpor**A'TION, *n.*

Incorpo'real, *a.* With -AL f. L. *incorporeus*, f. IN-[2] + *corporeus*. CORPOREAL. Not of the nature of the body, immaterial.

Incorrect', *a.* L. *incorrectus*, f. IN-[2] + *correctus*. CORRECT. Containing errors; faulty; inaccurate.—**Incorrect'**LY,[2] *adv.*

Incor'rigible, *a.* F. *incorrigible*, f. IN-[2] + *corrigible*, CORRIGIBLE. Incurably bad.

Incorrupt'ible, *a.* L.L. *incorruptibilis*, f. IN-[2] + *corruptibilis*, CORRUPTIBLE. That cannot decay; that cannot be bribed.

Increase', *vi.* A. F. *encres*(*s*)-=O.F. *encreis*(*s*)-, stem of *encreistre*—L. *increscĕre*, f. IN-[1] + *crescĕre*, to grow. ACCRESCE. INCREMENT. To become greater in size, number, &c.—*vt.* To make greater or more numerous.—**In'crease**, *n.* Increasing, growth; procreation, breeding; an increased amount.

Incred'ible, *a.* L. *incrēdibilis*, f. IN-[2] + *crēdibilis*, CREDIBLE. Beyond belief.—**Incred'ib**LY,[2] *adv.*—**Incredi**BIL'ITY, *n.*

Incred'ulous, *a.* With -OUS f. L. *incrēdulus*, f. IN-[2] + *crēdulus*, CREDULOUS. Withholding belief.—**Incredu'l**ITY, *n.*

In'crement, *n.* L. *incrēmentum*, f. *increscĕre*, to INCREASE. Increase, growth; profit.

Incrim'inate, *vt.* Med.L. *incrīmināre*, *incrīminātum*, f. IN-[1] + L. *crīmināre*, *-āri*, to CRIMINATE. To involve in an accusation.

Incrust', *vt.* IN-.[1] Var. of ENCRUST.—**Incrust**A'TION, *n.* An encrusting; a facing of marble, &c.; a hard coating; a scab.

In'cubate, *vt.* L. *incubāre*, *incubātum* (more us. *incubitum*), to lie in or upon, sit upon eggs, f. IN-[1] + *cubāre*. CONCUBINE. To hatch (eggs). —*vi.* Of disease germs, to pass through the phase between contagion, &c., and the appearance of the first symptoms.—**Incub**A'TION, *n.*—**In'cubat**OR, *n.* An apparatus for artificial hatching.—**In'cubus**, *n.* L.L. = L. *incubo*, nightmare, f. *incubāre*. An evil spirit fabled to descend on sleepers; the nightmare.

In'culcate, *vt.* L. *inculcāre*, *inculcātum*, lit., to tread in, f. IN-[1] + *calcāre*. CAULK. To impress on the mind.—**Inculc**A'TION, *n.*

In'culpate, *vt.* L. *inculpāre*, *inculpātum*, f. IN-[1] + *culpāre*, to blame, f. *culpa*. CULPABLE. To incriminate.—**Inculp**A'TION, *n.*

Incum'bent, *a.* L. *incumbens*, *incumbentis*, pres.pple. of *incumbĕre*, to lie upon, f. IN-[1] + **cumbĕre*, to lie, allied to *cubāre*. CONCUBINE. SUCCUMB. Lying; resting *upon* as a duty or obligation.—*n.* The holder of an office, esp. of a benefice.—**Incum'ben**CY, *n.*

Incu'nable, *n.* F. *incunable*—L. **incūnābulum*, sing. of *incūnābula*, swaddling-bands, childhood, f. IN-[1] + *cūnābula* = *cūnae*, cradle. A book printed before 1500. So **Incunab'ula**, *pl.*, with *sing.* **Incunab'ulum**.

Incur', *vt.* L. *incurrĕre*, *incursum*, to run into, f. IN-[1] + *currĕre*, to run. CONCUR. To fall into, bring upon oneself.—**Incur'**SION, *n.* An invasion or sudden attack.

Incu'rable, *a.* O.F. *incurable*—L.L. *incurābilis*, f. IN-[2] + *curābilis*, CURABLE. That cannot be cured.—*n.* One suffering from an incurable disease.—**Incu'rab**LY,[2] *adv.*

Incu'rious, *a.* L. *incūriōsus*, f. IN-[2] + *cūriōsus*, CURIOUS. Showing no curiosity.

Indebt'ed, *ppl.a.* O.F. *endetté*, pa.pple. of *endetter*, to involve in debt, f. EN-[1] (1) + *dette*, DEBT. Owing.—**Indebt'ed**NESS, *n.*

Inde'cent, *a.* L. *indecens*, *indecentis*, f. IN-[2] + *decens*, DECENT. Unseemly; obscene.—**Inde'cent**LY,[2] *adv.*—**Inde'c**ENCY, *n.*

Indeci'pherable, *a.* IN-[2]. Not capable of being deciphered or made out.

Indeci'sion, *n.* F. *indécision*, f. IN-[2] + *décision*, DECISION. Irresolution, hesitation.—**Indeci'**SIVE, *a.* Not decisive; irresolute.

Indeclin'able, *a.* F. *indéclinable*—L. *indēclīnābilis*, f. IN-[2] + *dēclīnābilis*, DECLINABLE. Not admitting of case-inflexion.

Indeco'rum, *n.* L. *indecōrum*, use as *n.* of neut. sing. of *indecōrus*, unseemly, f. IN-[2] + *decōrus*. DECORUM. An unbeseeming act; lack of decorum.—**Indeco'r**OUS, *a.*

Indeed', *adv.* IN, *prep.* + DEED. Really; in reality; in fact; it must be admitted.

Indefati'gable, *a.* Obs. F. *indéfatigable*—L. *indēfatīgābilis*, f. IN-[2] + *dēfatīgāre*, f. DE- (3) + *fatīgāre*, to FATIGUE. Untiring.

Indefea'sible, *a.* IN-2. Not defeasible.

Indefen'sible, *a.* IN-2. Admitting of no defence; inexcusable, unjustifiable.

Indef'inite, *a.* L. *indēfīnītus*, f. IN-2 + *dēfīnītus*, DEFINITE. Vague; unlimited; not defining.—**Indef'inite**LY,2 *adv.*

Indel'ible, *a.* L. *indēlēbilis*, f. IN-2 + *dēlēbilis*, that may be blotted out, f. *dēlēre*, to DELETE. That cannot be deleted or effaced, permanent.—**Indel'ib**LY,2 *adv.*

Indel'icate, *a.* IN-2. Wanting in delicacy, unrefined, coarse; wanting in tact.—**Indel'icate**LY,2 *adv.*—**Indel'ic**ACY, *n.*

Indem'nity, *n.* F. *indemnité*—L.L. *indemnitas*, n. of condition f. *indemnis*, unhurt, f. IN-2 + *damnum*, loss, DAMAGE. Security against loss; exemption from penalties, &c.; compensation, a sum paid for this.—**Indem'ni**FY, *vt.* To give an indemnity to; to compensate.—**Indemni**FICA'TION, *n.*

Indent', *v.*1*t.* F. *endenter*, to notch—L. type **indentāre*, f. IN-1 + **dentāre*, to furnish with teeth, f. *dens.* DENTAL. To notch, give a zigzag outline to; to constitute a deep recess in; to sever in a zigzag line for identification (copies of a document drawn up between two or more parties).—*vi.* To make out an order with a counterfoil: to make a requisition *upon* (a person) *for* (a thing).—*n.*1 A notch; a deep recess; a requisition. — **Indent**A'TION, *n.* The action of indenting, a notch; a deep recess; something with an indented outline; the forming of a dent, a dent (in this sense f. INDENT, *v.*2).—**Inden'**TURE, *n.* An indented document, a deed between two or more parties in general; a contract of apprenticeship.—*vt.* To bind by indenture.

Indent', *v.*2*t.* IN-1 + DENT, *v.* To form as a dent; to dent.—**In'dent**, *n.*2 A dent.

Indepen'dent, *a.* IN-2. Self-governing; not contingent; not dependent on another or on something else; not requiring to earn a livelihood; sufficient for independence; thinking or acting for oneself.—*n.* A Congregationalist. —**Indepen'dent**LY,2 *adv.* — **Indepen'**DENCE, *n.*—**Indepen'**DENCY, *n.* Independence; Congregationalism.

Indescrib'able, *a.* IN-2. Not admitting of, beyond, description.

Indestruc'tible, *a.* IN-2. That cannot be destroyed.

Indeter'minate, *a.* L. *indēterminātus*, f. IN-2 + *dēterminātus*, DETERMINATE. Not fixed; left uncertain: indefinite.

In'dex, *n.*; *pl.* **In'dexes**, **In'dices**. L. *index*, the forefinger, a sign, a list, f. *indicāre*, *indicātum*, to point out, indicate, f. IN-1 + *dicāre*, to make known. ABDICATE. The forefinger; a pointer; a sign, token; an alphabetical list of names, &c., occurring in a book; a list of books forbidden to Roman Catholics (short for *index librorum prohibitorum*); a figure showing to what power a quantity is raised.—*vt.* To provide (a book) with an index; to insert in an index.—**In'dicate**, *vt.* From *indicāre.* To point out; to betoken; to state briefly.—**Indic**A'TION, *n.*—**Indic'**ATIVE, *a.* That indicates; suggestive *of*; applied to the mood of a verb which expresses relations of fact.—*n.* The mood; a verb in the mood.—**In'dicat**OR, *n.* A person or thing that points out; a recording instrument.

In'dia-rub'ber, *n.* Caoutchouc (as being used to rub out pencil marks, &c.).

Indict', *vt.* A.F. *enditer*, to indict, corresp. to O.F. *enditer*, to indicate, write, inform, &c. —L. type **indictāre*, f. IN-1 + *dictāre.* DICTATE. To accuse, esp. by legal process.—**Indict'**ABLE, *a.* Liable, causing liability, to be indicted.—**Indict'**MENT, *n.*

Indif'ferent, *a.* L. *indifferens*, *indifferentis*, careless, neither good nor evil, f. IN-2 + *differens*, DIFFERENT. Impartial; careless, unconcerned; neither good nor bad; not very good, rather bad; unimportant. — **Indif'ferent**LY,2 *adv.*—**Indif'fer**ENCE, *n.*

Indig'enous, *a.* With -OUS f. L.L. *indigenus*, native, f. L. *indigena*, a native, f. *indi-* (*indu-*), ancient form of *in-* (IN-1) + *gen-*, root of *gignĕre*, to beget. ENGINE. Born or naturally produced in a country.

In'digent, *a.* F. *indigent*—L. *indigens*, *indigentis*, pres.pple. of *indigĕre*, to be in need, f. *indu-* (see prec.) + *egēre*, to be needy. Wanting, deficient; needy, poor.—**In'dig**ENCE, *n.*

Indiges'tible, *a.* L. *indīgestibilis*, f. IN-2 + *dīgestibilis*, DIGESTIBLE. Not easily digested.—**Indiges'**TION, *n.* Difficulty in digesting; an attack of indigestion.

Indig'nant, *a.* L. *indignans*, *indignantis*, pres.pple. of *indignāri*, to consider as unworthy, be indignant, f. *indignus*, unworthy, f. IN-2 + *dignus*, worthy. DIGNIFY. Provoked to wrath, scornful.—**Indig'nant**LY,2 *adv.*—**Indign**A'TION, *n.* — **Indig'ni**TY, *n.* Unworthy treatment; a slight or insult.

In'digo, *n.* L. *indicum*—G. *indikon*, neut. of *Indikos*, Indian. A blue dye obtained from an Indian plant; the plant.

Indirect', *a.* F. *indirect*, f. IN-2 + *direct*, DIRECT. Not straight or straightforward; not levied directly.—**Indirect'**LY,2 *adv.*

Indiscreet', *a.* L.L. *indiscrētus*, f. IN-2 + *discrētus*, DISCREET. Imprudent, injudicious. —**Indiscreet'**LY,2 *adv.*—**Indiscret'**ION, *n.*

Indiscrim'inate, *a.* IN-2. Done with, making, no distinctions.

Indispens'able, *a.* Med.L. *indispensābilis*, f. IN-2 + *dispensābilis*, DISPENSABLE. Necessary.—**Indispens'ab**LY,2 *adv.*

Indispose', *vt.* IN-2. To put out of proper condition or health; to disincline.—**Indisposed'**, *ppl.a.* Not well; disinclined.—**Indisposi'**TION, *n.* Illness; disinclination.

Indis'putable, *a.* L.L. *indisputābilis*, f. IN-2 + *disputābilis*, DISPUTABLE. That cannot be disputed.—**Indis'putab**LY,2 *adv.*

Indis'soluble, *a.* L. *indissolūbilis*, f. IN-2 + *dissolūbilis*, DISSOLUBLE. Not to be dissolved or annulled.—**Indis'solub**LY,2 *adv.*

Indistinct', *a.* L. *indistinctus*, f. IN-2 + *distinctus*, DISTINCT. Not clearly defined or discerned; blurred.—**Indistinct'**LY,2 *adv.*

Indistin'guishable, *a.* IN-2. That cannot be distinguished; imperceptible.

Indite', *vt.* O.F. *enditer.* INDICT. To write.

Individ'ual, *a.* Med.L. *indīviduālis*, f. L. *indīviduus*, undivided, indivisible, f. IN-2 + *dīviduus*, divisible, f. *dīvidĕre*, to DIVIDE. Single; striking; of a single person or thing.—*n.* A single person or thing; a person.—**Individ'ual**LY,2 *adv.*—**Individual'**ITY, *n.* Separate existence; individual character.—**Individ'ual**ISM, *n.* Egoism; the social theory advocating the free action of the individual.—**Individ'ual**IST, *n.*

Indivis'ible, *a.* L.L. *indīvīsibilis*, f. IN-2 + *dīvīsibilis*, DIVISIBLE. Not capable of division or distribution.—**Indivisi**BIL'ITY, *n.*

Indoc'trinate, *vt.* L. type **indoctrīnāre*, **indoctrīnātum*, f. IN-1 + *doctrīnāre.* DOCTRINATE. To teach; to instruct *in*, imbue *with.*

In'dolent, *a.* L.L. *indolens*, *indolentis* f.

IN-2 + L. *dolens*, pres.pple. of *dolēre*. DOLE.[2] Causing no pain; lazy.—**In'dol**ENCE, *n.*

Indom'itable, *a.* L.L. *indomitābilis*, f. IN-2 + *domitāre*. DAUNT. Not to be subdued, unyielding.—**Indom'itab**LY,[2] *adv.*

In'door, *a.* Within, used, &c., within, doors. —**Indoors'**, *adv.* In or into a house, &c.

Indu'bitable, *a.* L. *indubitābilis*, f. IN-2 + *dubitābilis*, doubtful, f. *dubitāre*. DOUBT. Not to be doubted.—**Indu'bitab**LY,[2] *adv.*

Induce', *vt.* L. *indūcĕre*, *inductum*, to lead into, f. IN-1 + *dūcĕre*. DUKE. To lead on, prevail upon; to bring about; to infer.—**Induce'**MENT, *n.* A motive or incentive.—

Induct', *vt.* From *indūcĕre*. To introduce into office, install; to initiate *into*, introduce *to*.—**Induc'**TION, *n.* Initiation; a preface, preamble; installation; the inferring of a general law from particular instances, an instance of this, the result.—**Induc'**TIVE, *a.* Of reasoning, &c., proceeding by induction.

Indulge', *vt.* L. *indulgēre*, to be tender to, to give oneself up to. To gratify by compliance; to give free course to, to entertain, cherish.—*vi.* To take one's pleasure freely *in*. —**Indul'gent**, *a.*—**Indul'gent**LY,[2] *adv.*—**Indul'gence**, *n.* In senses from the *v.*; in the *R. C. Church*, a remission of punishment still due to sin after absolution.

In'durate, *vt.* and *i.* L. *indūrāre*. ENDURE. To harden (*lit.* and *fig.*).—**Indur**A'TION, *n.*

In'dustry, *n.* L. *industria*, diligence, assiduity. Diligence, assiduity; systematized production; a trade. —**Indus'tri**AL, *a.*—**Indus'tri**OUS, *a.* Diligent, assiduous.

Ine'briate, *vt.* L. *inēbriāre*, *inēbriātum*, f. IN-1 + *ēbriāre*, to intoxicate, f. *ēbrius*, drunk. EBRIETY. To intoxicate.—*a.* Drunken.—*n.* An habitual drunkard.—**Inebri**A'TION, *n.*—**Inebri'ety**, *n.* IN-1. Drunkenness.

Ined'ited, *a.* IN-2. Not published.

Inef'fable, *a.* F. *ineffable*—L. *ineffābilis*, f. IN-2 + *effābilis*, that may be uttered, f. *effāri*, to utter, f. *ef-* (= EX-) + *fāri*, to speak. AFFABLE. Unspeakable.—**Inef'fab**LY,[2] *adv.*

Ineffec'tive, *a.* IN-2. Not effective.

Ineffec'tual, *a.* IN-2. Not effectual.

Inef'ficacy, *n.* L.L. *inefficācia*, f. *inefficax*, ineffectual, f. IN-2 + *efficax*. EFFICACY. Want of efficacy.—**Ineffic**A'CIOUS, *a.* [c'IENCY, *n.*

Ineffic'ient, *a.* IN-2. Not efficient.—**Ineffi-**

Inel'egant, *a.* F. *inélégant*—L. *inēlegans*, *inēlegantis*, f. IN-2 + *ēlegans*, ELEGANT. Wanting in refinement.—**Inel'egant**LY,[2] *adv.*—**Inel'eg**ANCE, **Inel'eg**ANCY, *nn.*

Inel'igible, *a.* IN-2. Unfit or unqualified to be elected or chosen.—**Ineligi**BIL'ITY, *n.*

Inept', *a.* L. *ineptus*, f. IN-2 + *aptus*. APT. Out of place; absurd.—**Inep'ti**TUDE, *n.*

Inequal'ity, *n.* O.F. *inequalité*—Med.L. *inaequālitas*, f. L. *inaequālis*, uneven, unequal, f. IN-2 + *aequālis*. EQUAL. Want of equality; uneven distribution, an instance of this; an irregularity of surface, &c.

Ineq'uitable, *a.* IN-2. Not equitable, unjust, unfair.—**Ineq'uitab**LY,[2] *adv.*

Inerad'icable, *a.* IN-2. Not capable of being eradicated.—**Inerad'icab**LY,[2] *adv.*

Inert', *a.* L. *iners*, *inertis*, unskilled, inactive, f. IN-2 + *ars*, ART. Without active properties, inanimate; sluggish, slow.—**Inert'**LY,[2] *adv.*—**Inert'**NESS, *n.*—**Iner'tia**, *n.* L. *inertia*, want of skill, inactivity, f. *iners*. The property of matter in virtue of which it tends to continue in its existing state of rest or of motion in a straight line; sluggishness.

Ines'timable, *a.* F. *inestimable*—L. *inaestimābilis*, f. IN-2 + *aestimābilis*, ESTIMABLE. That cannot be estimated or computed; invaluable, priceless.—**Ines'timab**LY,[2] *adv.*

Inev'itable, *a.* L. *inēvitābilis*, f. IN-2 + *ēvitābilis*, EVITABLE. Unavoidable, not to be escaped.—**Inev'itab**LY,[2] *adv.*

Inexact', *a.* IN-2. Not exact.—**Inexact'**LY,[2] *adv.*—**Inexac'ti**TUDE, *n.*

Inexcu'sable, *a.* L. *inexcūsābilis*, f. IN-2 + *excūsābilis*, EXCUSABLE. Not to be excused or justified.—**Inexcu'sab**LY,[2] *adv.*

Inexhau'stible, *a.* IN-2. Not capable of being exhausted.—**Inexhau'stib**LY,[2] *adv.*

Inex'orable, *a.* L. *inexōrābilis*, f. IN-2 + *exōrābilis*, EXORABLE. Not to be moved by entreaty, relentless.—**Inex'orab**LY,[2] *adv.*

Inexpe'dient, *a.* IN-2. Not expedient, impolitic.—**Inexpe'di**ENCY, *n.*

Inexpen'sive, *a.* IN-2. Cheap.

Inexpe'rience, *n.* F. *inexpérience*—L.L. *inexperientia*, f. IN-2 + L. *experientia*, EXPERIENCE. Want of experience.

Inexpert', *a.* O.F. *inexpert*—L. *inexpertus*, without experience, untried, f. IN-2 + *expertus*. EXPERT. Unskilled.—**Inexpert'**LY,[2] *adv.*

Inex'piable, *a.* L. *inexpiābilis*, f. IN-2 + *expiāre*. EXPIATE. Unpardonable; implacable.

Inex'plicable, *a.* F. *inexplicable*—L. *inexplicābilis*, f. IN-2 + *explicābilis*, EXPLICABLE. That cannot be explained.

Inexpres'sible, *a.* IN-2. That cannot be expressed. —**Inexpres'sib**LY,[2] *adv.* —**Inexpres'sive**, *a.* IN-2. Not expressive.

Inexpug'nable, *a.* F. *inexpugnable*—L. *inexpugnābilis*, f. IN-2 + *expugnābilis*, that may be taken, f. *expugnāre*, to take by storm, f. EX- + *pugnāre*, to fight. PUGNACIOUS. Impregnable. [be extinguished.

Inextin'guishable, *a.* IN-2. That cannot

Inex'tricable, *a.* L. *inextrīcābilis*, f. IN-2 + *extrīcāre*. EXTRICATE. Not to be escaped from or untied.—**Inex'tricab**LY,[2] *adv.*

Infal'lible, *a.* Med.L. *infallibilis*, f. IN-2 + L.L. *fallibilis*, FALLIBLE. Not liable to err or to be erroneous; not liable to fail, certain. —**Infal'lib**LY,[2] *adv.*—**Infalli**BIL'ITY, *n.*

In'famous, *a.* Corresponds to O.F. *infameux*, Med.L. *infāmōsus* = L. *infāmis*, f. IN-2 + *fāma*, FAME. Notoriously bad or vile.—**In'famous**LY,[2] *adv.*—**In'fam**Y,[1] *n.*

In'fant, *n.* O.F. *enfant*—L. *infans*, *infantis*, use as *n.* of *infans*, unable to speak, f. IN-2 + *fans*, pres.pple. of *fāri*. AFFABLE. A very young child; a minor.—**In'f**ANCY, *n.*—**Infan'ticide**, *n.* F. *infanticide*—L.L. *infanticīda*. -CIDE (1). One who kills an infant.—-CIDE (2). The killing of an infant; the custom of killing new-born infants. — **In'fantile**, *a.* L.L. *infantilis*. Also **In'fan**TINE. Of an infant or infancy.

In'fantry, *n.* F. *infanterie*—It. *infanteria*, f. *infante*, youth, foot soldier—L. *infans*. (See prec.) Foot soldiers collectively.

Infat'uate, *vt.* L. *infatuāre*, *infatuātum*, f. IN-1 + *fatuus*. FATUOUS. To affect with folly or a foolish passion.—**Infatu**A'TION, *n.*

Infect', *vt.* L. *inficĕre*, *infectum*, to dye, taint, f. IN-1 + *facĕre*, to make, put. AFFECT. To make noxious; to affect with disease. — **Infec'**TION, *n.*—**Infec'**TIOUS, **Infec'**TIVE, *aa.*

Infelic'ity, *n.* L. *infēlīcitas*, f. *infēlix*, *infēlīcis*, unhappy, f. IN-2 + *fēlix*. FELICITATE. Unhappiness; a misfortune; inaptness, an inaptness, of expression.—**Infelic'itous**, *a.*

Infer′, *vt.* L. *inferre*, to bring in, in Med.L., to infer, f. IN-[1] + *ferre.* DEFER. To deduce by reasoning; to imply.—**In′fer**ENCE, *n.*—**Inferen′tial**, *a.*—**Inferen′tial**LY,[2] *adv.*

Infe′rior, *a.* L. *inferior*, comp. of *inferus*, low. Lower; comparatively bad. —*n.* One lower in rank, &c.—**Inferior′**ITY, *n.*

Infer′nal, *a.* F. *infernal*—L. *infernālis*, of the lower regions, f. *infernus*, lying below, conn. with *inferus.* (See prec.) Of the world below; hellish.—**Infer′nal**LY,[2] *adv.*

Infest′, *vt.* L. *infestāre*, f. *infestus*, hostile. To molest in swarms; to harass.

In′fidel, *n.* O.F. *infidele*—L. *infidēlis*, unfaithful, infidel, f. IN-[2] + *fidēlis.* FEALTY. One who is not of the speaker's religion; one who does not believe in religion; an unbeliever. —*a.* Unbelieving; adhering to a false religion. —**Infidel′**ITY, *n.* Religious unbelief; unfaithfulness, an instance of this.

Infil′trate, *vt.* IN-[1]. To cause to pass through pores; to pass through the pores of.—*vi.* To percolate.—**Infiltra′**TION, *n.*

In′finite, *a.* L. *infīnītus*, boundless, f. IN-[2] + *fīnītus.* FINITE. Without limit or end; immense, vast. — **In′finite**LY,[2] *adv.* — **Infinites′imal**, *a.* Mod.L. *infinitesimus* (f. *infīnītus*) + -AL. Infinitely or extremely small. —**Infin′it**IVE, *a.* Applied to that form of a verb which expresses the notion of the verb without reference to any particular subject.—*n.* The infinitive mood; a verb in this mood. —**Infin′**ITY, *n.*

Infirm′, *a.* L. *infirmus*, not strong, f. IN-[2] + *firmus*, FIRM. Weak; weak in body; irresolute. — **Infir′mary**, *n.* Med.L. *infirmāria.* A hospital.—**Infir′m**ITY, *n.*

Inflame′, *vt.* O.F. *enflammer*—L. *inflammāre*, f. IN-[1] + *flamma*, FLAME. To set on fire; to excite; to raise (a part of the body) to a morbid heat; to exacerbate. —*vi.* To catch fire; to become inflamed.—**Inflam′m**ABLE, *a.* Easily set on fire; excitable.—**Inflamma′**TION, *n.*—**Inflam′mat**ORY, *a.*

Inflate′, *vt.* L. *inflāre*, *inflātum*, f. IN-[1] + *flāre*, to blow. BLOW, *v.*[1] To distend with air; to puff up *with* pride, &c.; to raise above the proper value, &c.—**Infl**A′TION, *n.*

Inflect′, *vt.* L. *inflectĕre*, *inflexum*, f. IN-[1] + *flectĕre*, to bend. DEFLECT. To bend inwards; to vary the form of (a word) to express different grammatical relations; to modulate (the voice). —**Inflex′**ION, **Inflec′t**ION, *n.*

Inflex′ible, *a.* L. *inflexibilis*, f. IN-[2] + *flexibilis*, FLEXIBLE. Not to be bent (*lit.* and *fig.*). —**Inflex′ib**LY,[2] *adv.*—**Inflexi**BIL′ITY, *n.*

Inflict′, *vt.* L. *inflīgĕre*, *inflictum*, to strike on, inflict, f. IN-[1] + *flīgĕre*, to strike. AFFLICT. PROFLIGATE. To lay on, impose, cause to be borne.—**Inflic′t**ION, *n.*

In′fluence, *n.* F. *influence*, emanation from the stars = L.L. *influentia*, f. L. *influens*, *influentis*, pres.pple. of *influĕre*, *influxum*, to flow in, f. IN-[1] + *fluĕre*, to flow. AFFLUENT. The supposed flowing from the stars of a fluid affecting men and things; agency or power invisibly or insensibly serving to modify, affect, &c.; ascendancy; credit with those in power.—*vt.* To exert influence upon. — **Influen′ti**AL, *a.* Exerting influence; having great influence.—**Influen′za**, *n.* It. *influenza*, influence, epidemic, influenza, f. *influentia.* A contagious febrile disorder with prostration and catarrh.—**In′flux**, *n.* L.L. *influxus*, f. *influĕre.* A flowing in or into.

Inform′, *vt.* O.F. *enformer*—L. *informāre.* *informātum*, to give form to, to instruct, f. IN-[1] + *forma*, FORM. To inspire, animate; to tell (one) *of*, apprise.—*vi.* To bring a charge or complaint *against.* — **Infor′m**ANT, *n.* One who tells or apprises.—**Informa′**TION, *n.*— **Infor′mat**IVE, **Infor′mat**ORY, *aa.*—**Infor′m**ER, *n.* One who brings a charge.

Infor′mal, *a.* IN-[2]. Not formal; not in prescribed form, irregular; unofficial; unceremonious. — **Informal′**ITY, *n.* — **Infor′mal**LY,[2] *adv.*

Infran′gible, *a.* IN-[2]. That cannot be [broken.

Infre′quent, *a.* L. *infrequens*, *infrequentis*, f. IN-[2] + *frequens*, FREQUENT. Seldom happening; not plentiful. — **Infre′quent**LY,[2] *adv.*—**Infre′qu**ENCY, *n.*

Infringe′, *vt.* L. *infringĕre*, *infractum*, to break, lessen, make void, f. IN-[1] + *frangĕre*, to break. FRACTION. REFRACT. REFRAIN, *n.* To contravene, transgress.—**Infrac′t**ION, *n.*—**Infringe′**MENT, *n.*

Infu′riate, *vt.* Med.L. *infuriāre*, *infuriātum*, to madden, f. IN-[1] + L. *furiāre*, in sim. sense, f. *furia*, FURY. To fill with fury, enrage.

Infuse′, *vt.* L. *infundĕre*, *infūsum*, to pour in, f. IN-[1] + *fundĕre*, to pour. CONFOUND. To pour in; to instil; to steep in order to extract soluble properties.—**Infu′s**ION, *n.*

Inge′nious, *a.* F. *ingénieux*—L. *ingeniōsus*, clever, ingenious, f. *ingenium.* ENGINE. Clever at contriving or constructing; cleverly contrived or constructed.—**Inge′nious**LY,[2] *adv.*

Ingen′uous, *a.* L. *ingenuus*, native, free born, noble, frank (f. IN-[1] + *gen-.* ENGINE) + -OUS. Frank; guileless.—**Ingenu′**ITY, *n.* Cleverness in contrivance, &c. (by confusion with prec.).—**Ingen′uous**LY,[2] *adv.*

Inglo′rious, *a.* L. *inglōriōsus*, without repute, f. IN-[2] + *glōriōsus*, GLORIOUS. Shameful, ignominious.—**Inglo′rious**LY,[2] *adv.*

In′got, *n.* Of uncertain orig. A mass of cast metal, esp. of gold or silver.

Ingrate′, *a.* L. *ingrātus*, f. IN-[2] + *grātus.* GRACE. Ungrateful.—*n.* An ungrateful person.—**Ingrat′itude**, *n.* F. *ingratitude*—L.L. *ingrātitūdo.* Want of gratitude.

Ingra′tiate, *v.refl.* App. f. It. *ingratiare*, to put in grace, refl. *ingratiarsi*, to ingratiate oneself, f. *in grazia*, L. *in grātiam*, into favour. GRACE. To get oneself into favour.

Ingre′dient, *n.* L. *ingrediens*, *ingredientis*, pres.pple. of *ingredi*, *ingressus*, to enter, f. IN-[1] + *gradi*, to go. AGGRESSION. Something that enters into the composition of a thing.—**In′gress**, *n.* L. *ingressus*, f. *ingredi.* Entering; right or means of entering.

In′guinal, *a.* L. *inguinālis*, f. *inguen*, *inguinis*, the groin. Pertaining to the groin.

Inhab′it, *vt.* O.F. *enhabiter*—L. *inhabitāre*, f. IN-[1] + *habitāre.* HABITATION. To dwell in.—**Inhab′it**ABLE, *a.*—**Inhab′it**ANT, *n.*—**Inhab′it**ER, *n.*—**Inhabit**A′TION, *n.*

Inhale′, *vt.* L. *inhālāre*, to breathe upon, f. IN-[1] + *hālāre*, to breathe. To breathe in (being taken as the opposite of *exhale*).—*vi.* To draw in breath.—**Inhal**A′TION, *n.*

Inharmo′nious, *a.* IN-[2]. Not harmonious.

Inhere′, *vi.* L. *inhaerēre*, to stick in, f. IN-[1] + *haerēre*, to stick. ADHERE. To exist as a quality, &c., *in*; to be vested *in.*—**Inhe′r**ENCE, **Inhe′r**ENCY, *nn.*—**Inhe′r**ENT, *a.*

Inher′it, *vt.* O.F. *enheriter*, to put (one) in possession as heir, f. EN-[1] (3) + *heriter*, to make (one) heir—L.L. *hērēditāre*, to inherit, f. *hēres*, HEIR. To take as heir; to derive from progenitors.—*vi.* To succeed as heir.—**Inher′i-**

TANCE, *n.*—**Inher'it**OR, *n.*—**Inher'itr**ESS, **Inher'i**TRIX, *nn.*

Inhib'it, *vt.* L. *inhibēre, inhibitum*, to hold in, restrain, f. IN-[1] + *habēre*, to hold. ABLE. To forbid, esp. in ecclesiastical law; to hinder, stop.—**Inhibi'**TION, *n.*—**Inhib'it**ORY, *a.*

Inhos'pitable, *a.* O.F. *inhospitable*—Med. or Mod.L. *inhospitābilis* (= L. *inhospitālis*). IN-[2]. HOSPITABLE. Not hospitable; not affording shelter, bleak.—**Inhospital'**ITY, *n.*

Inhu'man, *a.* L. *inhūmānus*, f. IN-[2] + *hūmānus*, HUMAN. Lacking natural kindness and pity, cruel, barbarous.—**Inhuman'**ITY, *n.*—**Inhu'man**LY,[2] *adv.*

Inhume', *vt.* L. *inhumāre*, f. IN-[1] + *humus*. EXHUME. To bury.—**Inhum**A'TION, *n.*

Inim'ical, *a.* L.L. *inimīcālis*, f. L. *inimīcus*, unfriendly. ENEMY. Hostile; hurtful.

Inim'itable, *a.* L. *inimitābilis*, f. IN-[2] + *imitābilis*, IMITABLE. Surpassing imitation; peerless.—**Inim'itab**LY,[2] *adv.*

Iniq'uity, *n.* O.F. *iniquité*—L. *inīquitas*, f. *inīquus*, unfair, f. IN-[2] + *aequus*. EQUITY. Sin; gross injustice.—**Iniq'uit**OUS, *a.*

Init'ial, *a.* L. *initiālis*, f. *initium*, beginning. COMMENCE. Of or pertaining to a beginning; standing at the beginning of a word, &c.—*n.* An initial letter; in *pl.*, the initials of a name.—*vt.* To put one's initials to (a writing, &c.).—**Init'i**ATE,[3] *vt.* To originate, give rise to; to admit (esp. formally) to a society or to knowledge of secrets, &c.—**Initi**A'TION, *n.*—**Init'i**ATIVE, *a.* As *n.*, a taking the first step or lead, origination; the right or function of originating.—**Init'iat**ORY, *a.*

Inject', *vt.* L. *injicĕre, injectum*, to throw in, f. IN-[1] + *jacĕre*, to throw. ABJECT. To drive (a fluid) into a cavity, &c., esp. of medicines introduced into the cavities, &c., of the body; to fill by injecting.—**Injec'**TION, *n.*

Injudic'ious, *a.* IN-[2]. Unwise, imprudent, indiscreet.—**Injudic'ious**LY,[2] *adv.*

Injunc'tion, *n.* L.L. *injunctio, injunctiōnis*, f. *injungĕre*. ENJOIN. An enjoining; an authoritative order or admonition.

In'jury, *n.* L. *injūria*, wrong, damage, f. *injūrius*, wrongful, f. IN-[2] + *jūs, jūris*, right. JURY. Wrongful action or treatment, a wrongful act; damage.—**In'jure**, *vt.* Back-formation f. the *n.* To do wrong or damage to.—**Inju'ri**OUS, *a.*—**Inju'rious**LY,[2] *adv.*

Injus'tice, *n.* F. *injustice*—L. *injustitia*, f. *injustus*, unjust, f. IN-[2] + *justus*. JUST. Unjust action, an instance of this.

Ink, *n.* O.F. *enque* (F. *encre*)—L.L. *encaustum*, G. *egkauston*, the purple ink used by the later Emperors for their signatures, f. *egkaiein*. ENCAUSTIC. The fluid used in writing; the viscous paste used in printing.—*vt.* To mark or smear with ink.—**Ink'**Y,[2] *a.*

Ink'ling, *n.* From obs. *Inkle*, to whisper, hint at, of unknown orig. A hint, slight suggestion; a vague notion or suspicion.

In'land, *n.* IN, *adv.* The interior part of a country.—*a.* Of or pertaining to this; carried on, operating, within a country.—*adv.* In or towards the interior of a country.

Inlay', *vt.* IN, *prep.* To embed; to ornament *with* something embedded in the surface.

In'let, *n.* IN, *adv.* An entrance; a creek.

In'mate, *n.* IN, *adv.* (or perh. orig. INN, in obs. sense 'dwelling-place'.) One who dwells with others; an inhabitant.

Inn, *n.* O.E. *inn*, dwelling-place, f. *inn*, IN, *adv.* Cf. O.N. *inne, inni*, inn. A house for the entertainment of travellers; *Inns of Court*, the buildings belonging to the four societies entitled to admit to practice at the bar.

In'nate, *a.* L.L. *innātus*, f. IN-[1] + L. *nātus*, pa.pple. of *nasci*. AGNATE. Inborn.

In'ner, *a.* O.E. *inne(r)ra*, a., comp. of *inn*, IN, adv. Lying within; mental, spiritual.

Inner'vate, *vt.* IN-[1] + L. *nervus* (NERVE) + -ATE.[3] To supply with nerve-force, stimulate.—**Innerv**A'TION, *n.*

In'nocent, *a.* F. *innocent*—L. *innocens, innocentis*, f. IN-[2] + *nocens*, pres.pple. of *nocēre*, to hurt. NOXIOUS. Doing, knowing, no evil; free from guilt; simple, unsuspecting; artless, ingenuous.—*n.* A young child; an idiot.—**In'nocent**LY,[2] *adv.*—**In'noc**ENCE, *n.*—**Innoc'uous**, *a.* L. *innocuus* (f. IN-[2] + *nocuus*, hurtful, f. *nocēre*) + -OUS. Harmless.

In'novate, *vi.* L. *innovāre, innovātum*, to renew, alter, f. IN-[1] + *novāre*, to make new, f. *novus*. NOVEL. To make changes.—**Inno**VA'TION, *n.*—**In'novat**OR, *n.*

Innuen'do, *n.* L., 'by nodding to or intimating', ablative gerund of IN[1]*nuĕre*, to nod to, intimate. An oblique hint or suggestion.

Innu'merable, *a.* L. *innumerābilis*, f. IN-[2] + *numerābilis*, f. *numerāre*, to number, f. *numerus*, NUMBER. Numberless, countless.

Innutri'tious, *a.* IN-[2]. Not nutritious.

Inoc'ulate, *vt.* L. *inoculāre, inoculātum*, to engraft, f. IN-[1] + *oculus*, eye, bud. OCULAR. To impregnate with the germs of a disease, generally in order to secure immunity from its ordinary attacks.—**Inocul**A'TION, *n.*

Inoffen'sive, *a.* IN-[2]. Not offending.

Inop'erative, *a.* IN-[2]. Not operating.

Inopportune', *a.* L.L. *inopportūnus*, unfitting, f. IN-[2] + *opportūnus*, OPPORTUNE. Unseasonable.—**Inopportune'**LY,[2] *adv.*

Inor'dinate, *a.* L. *inordinātus*, disordered, irregular, f. IN-[2] + *ordinātus*, pa.pple. of *ordināre*, to regulate, ORDAIN. Ill-regulated; immoderate.—**Inor'dinate**LY,[2] *adv.*

Inorgan'ic, *a.* IN-[2]. Not having the organization proper to living beings; not occurring in organized beings; extraneous.

In'quest, *n.* O.F. *enqueste*—Med.L. *inquesta*, use as *n.* of fem. of *inquestus*, pa.pple. of **inquærĕre*. INQUIRE. A judicial inquiry; a jury holding an inquest.

Inquire', **Enquire'**, *vt.* M.E. *enquere(n)*—O.F. *enquerre* (F. *enquérir*)—Late Pop.L. type **inquērĕre* for *inquaerĕre* (L. *inquīrĕre, inquīsītum*), f. IN-[1] + L. *quaerĕre*, to ask. QUEST. To ask about, ask to be told.—*vi.* To make search or investigation; to ask.—**Inquir'**ER, **Enquir'**ER, *n.*—**Inquir'**Y,[1] **Enquir'**Y,[1] *n.*—**Inquisi'**TION, *n.* Investigation, an investigation; in the *R.C. Church*, a tribunal for the suppression of heresy.—**Inquis'it**OR, *n.* An official investigator; an officer of the Inquisition.—**Inquisito'r**IAL, *a.* Of, having the office of, an inquisitor; prying.—**Inquis'it**IVE, *a.* Given to inquiry; curious, prying.

In'road, *n.* IN, *adv.* + ROAD in obs. sense 'a riding'. A raid; an encroachment.

Insalu'brious, *a.* L. *insalūbris* (f. IN-[2] + *salūbris*, SALUBRIOUS) + -OUS. Unfavourable to health.—**Insalu'br**ITY, *n.*

Insane', *a.* L. *insānus*, f. IN-[2] + *sānus*, SANE. Mentally deranged; idiotic, senseless; appropriated to insane persons.—**Insane'**LY,[2] *adv.*—**Insan'**ITY, *n.*

Insan'itary, *a.* IN-[2]. Hurtful to health.

Insa'tiable, *a.* L. *insatiābilis*, f. IN-[2] + *satiāre*, to SATIATE. That cannot be satisfied.—**Insatia**BIL'ITY, *n.*—**Insa'tiab**LY,[2] *adv.*

—**Insa'tiate**, *a.* L. *insatiātus*, f. IN-[2] + *satiātus*, pa.pple. of *satiāre*. Insatiable.

Inscribe', *vt.* L. *inscrībĕre*, *inscriptum*, to write in or upon, f. IN-[1] + *scrībĕre*. SCRIBE. To write, &c., in or on something; to enroll; to dedicate.—**Inscrip'tION**, *n.*

Inscru'table, *a.* L.L. *inscrūtābilis*, f. IN-[2] +L. *scrūtāri*. SCRUTINY. Entirely mysterious. —**Inscrutab**IL'ITY, *n.*

In'sect, *n.* L. *insectum*, lit., 'thing cut into', neut. of *insectus*, pa.pple. of *insecāre*, to cut into, f. IN-[1] + *secāre*, to cut. SAW.[1] A small invertebrate animal usually having a body divided into segments. — **Insec'ticide**, *n.* -CIDE (1). A preparation for destroying insects.

Insecure', *a.* Med.L. *insēcūrus*, f. IN-[2] + *sēcūrus*, SECURE. Not safe; not firm.—**Insecure'**LY,[2] *adv.*—**Insecu'r**ITY, *n.*

Insen'sate, *a.* L.L. *insensātus*, f. IN-[2] + *sensātus*, gifted with sense, f. L. *sensus*, SENSE. Without sensation; unfeeling; foolish.

Insen'sible, *a.* L. *insensibilis*, f. IN-[2] + *sensibilis*, SENSIBLE. Not perceptible; unconscious; unmoved, indifferent; callous.—**Insen'sib**LY,[2] *adv.*—**Insensib**IL'ITY, *n.*

Insen'sitive, *a.* IN-[2]. Not sensitive.

Insen'tient, *a.* IN-[2]. Incapable of feeling.

Insep'arable, *a.* L. *insēparābilis*, f. IN-[2] + *sēparābilis*, SEPARABLE. Not separable.

Insert', *vt.* L. *inserĕre*, *insertum*, to put into, f. IN-[1] + *serĕre*. SERIES. To put or introduce *in* or *into*.—**Inser'tION**, *n.*

Inset', *vt.* IN, *adv.* To insert.—**In'set**, *n.* Something extra inserted in a book, &c.

In'shore, *adv.* IN, *adv.* Near the shore.

Inside, *n.* IN, *adv.* (used *attrib.*). The inner side, surface or part.—*a.* On, in, of, the inside. —*adv.* In or into the inside.—*prep.* On the inner side of, in the inner part of.—**Insid'**ER, *n.* A member of a set, party, &c.

Insid'ious, *a.* L. *insidiōsus*, deceitful, f. *insidiae*, pl., an ambush, artifice, f. *insidēre*, to sit in, f. IN-[1] + *sedēre*, to sit. ASSESS. Stealthy, crafty.—**Insid'ious**LY,[2] *adv.*

In'sight, *n.* IN, *adv.* A seeing beneath the surface, the power of thus seeing.

Insig'nia, *n.pl.* L., *pl.* of *insigne*, mark, badge of office, f. *insignis*, marked, remarkable, f. IN-[1] + *signum*. SIGN. Badges or emblems of office, honour, &c.

Insignif'icant, *a.* IN-[2]. Meaningless; trivial, trifling; contemptible, petty. —**Insignif'ic**ANCE, **Insignif'ic**ANCY, *nn.*

Insincere', *a.* L. *insincērus*, f. IN-[2]+*sincērus*. SINCERE. Disingenuous. —**Insincere'**LY,[2] *adv.* — **Insincer'**ITY, *n.*

Insin'uate, *vt.* L. *insinuāre*, *insinuātum*, f. IN-[1] + *sinuāre*, to curve, bend, f. *sinus*. SINUOUS. To introduce or instil indirectly or by imperceptible degrees; to hint obliquely. — *v.refl.* To make one's way sinuously into a place or into favour, &c.—**Insinu**A'TION, *n.*

Insip'id, *a.* L.L. *insipidus*, f. IN-[2] + *sapidus*, SAPID. Tasteless; uninteresting, dull, lifeless.—**Insipid'**ITY, *n.*

Insist', *vi.* L. *insistĕre*, f. IN-[1] + *sistĕre*, to cause to stand, to stand. ASSIST. To dwell *upon*; with *upon*, to maintain, demand persistently.—**Insis't**ENCE, *n.*

In'solent, *a.* L. *insolens*, *insolentis*, unusual, insolent, f. IN-[2] + *solens*, pres.pple. of *solēre*, to be accustomed. Impertinently insulting.— **In'solent**LY,[2] *adv.*—**In'sol**ENCE, *n.*

Insol'uble, *a.* L. *insolūbilis*, that cannot be loosed, f. IN-[2] + *solūbilis*. SOLUBLE. Not soluble.—**Insolub**IL'ITY, *n.*

Insol'vent, *a.* IN-[2]. Not able to pay one's debts; relating to insolvents.—*n.* An insolvent person.—**Insol'**VENCY, *n.*

Insom'nia, *n.* L., f. *insomnis*, sleepless, f. IN-[2] + *somnus*, sleep. Sleeplessness.

Insomuch', *adv.* Orig. three words. *Insomuch that*, to such an extent that.

Inspect', *vt.* L. *inspectāre*, freq. of *inspicĕre*, to look into, f. IN-[1]+*specĕre*, to look. ASPECT. To examine closely or officially. — **Inspec'tION**, *n.*—**Inspect'**OR, *n.* One who inspects; a supervising officer.

Inspire', *vt.* O.F. *inspirer*—L. *inspīrāre*, to breathe into, f. IN-[1] + *spīrāre*. ASPIRE. To inhale; to animate; to influence or actuate *with* a feeling, &c.; of the feeling, &c., to influence, actuate; to impart supernaturally; to arouse, awaken (a feeling, &c.). — *vi.* To draw in breath.—**Inspir**A'TION, *n.*

Inspir'it, *vt.* IN-[1]. To animate; to incite.

Insta'ble, *a.* L. *instabilis*, f. IN-[2] + *stabilis*, STABLE. Not stable.—**Instab**IL'ITY, *n.*

Install', *vt.* Med.L. *installāre*, f. IN-[1] + *stallum*, O.H.G. *stal*, standing-place, sitting-place. STALL. To invest with an office, &c., by seating in a stall or with due ceremony; to establish; to put in position for use.—**Install**A'TION, *n.*—**Instal'**MENT, *n.*[1]

Instal'ment, *n.*[2] From obs. *Install*, to pay by instalments (app. f. IN-[1] + STALL, *v.*, in obs. sense 'to arrange (a payment)') + -MENT. A part of a debt paid before the rest.

In'stance, *n.* F. *instance*, urgency, suit—L. *instantia*, a being near, urgency, a pleading in a suit, in Med.L., an instance to the contrary, f. *instans*, *instantis*, pres.pple. of *instāre*, to stand in or upon, to urge, f. IN-[1] + *stāre*, to STAND. Instigation, suggestion; an illustrative example; place in a series.—*vt.* To cite as an example.—**In'stant**, *a.* F. *instant*—L. *instans*. Pressing, urgent; belonging to the current month; close at hand; immediate.—*n.* Point of time; a point of time, a moment.— **Instanta'neous**, *a.* L. type **instantāneus* (f. *instans*) + -OUS. Done or happening in an instant. — **Instanta'neous**LY,[2] *adv.* — **Instan'ter**, *adv.* L. *instanter*, urgently, earnestly, in L.L., at once. At once.—**In'stant**LY,[2] *adv.* At once.

Instead', *adv.* *In* STEAD=*in place*. In place *of*; as a substitute or alternative.

In'step, *n.* App. in some way f. IN + STEP. The upper surface of the foot.

In'stigate, *vt.* L. *instigāre*, *instigātum*, f. IN-[1] + **stigāre*, to prick. Cf. G. *stizein* (root *stig-*), to prick. STIGMA. STICK. To incite; to foment, bring about.—**Instig**A'TION, *n.*

Instil(l)', *vt.* L. *instillāre*, f. IN-[1] + *stillāre*, to let fall in drops. DISTIL. To put in by drops (often *fig.*).—**Instill**A'TION, *n.*

In'stinct, *n.* L. *instinctus*, incitement, f. *instinguĕre*, *instinctum*, to incite, f. IN-[1] + *stinguĕre*. DISTINGUISH. Innate impulse, esp. in animals; unconscious skill. — **Instinct'**, *ppl.a.* From *instinctus*, the *pa.pple*. Imbued or inspired *with*.—**Instinc'tIVE**, *a.*

In'stitute, *vt.* L. *instituĕre*, *institūtum*, f. IN-[1] + *statuĕre*, to set up, establish. CONSTITUTE. To establish; to bring into use, set in operation; to invest with a benefice.—*n.* L. *institūtum*. A scientific, &c., society, the building occupied by it; in *pl.*, the elements of a subject.—**Institu'tION**, *n.* The action of instituting; an established law, custom, &c.; an association or organization for the promotion of some object, the building occupied by it.

Instruct', *vt.* L. *instruĕre, instructum*, to build in or into, to equip, fit out, to instruct, f. IN-[1] + *struĕre*, to pile up, build. CONSTRUCT. To teach, to inform; to give directions to, to order.—**Instruc'**TION, *n.*—**Instruc'**TIVE, *a.*—**Instruct'**OR, *n.*

In'strument, *n.* L. *instrūmentum*, a tool, a document, f. *instruĕre*. (See prec.) That by means of which a purpose is effected; a tool or implement; a contrivance for producing music; a formal writing. — **Instrumen'**TAL, *a.* Serving as, of, denoting, an instrument; of music, performed on an instrument.—**Instrumental'**ITY, *n.* A being instrumental; a means.—**Instrumenta'tion**, *n.* F. *instrumentation.* The composition of music for instruments; instrumentality.

Insubor'dinate, *a.* IN-[2]. Not obedient to orders.—**Insubordin**A'TION, *n.*

Insubstan'tial, *a.* Med.L. *insubstantiālis*, f. IN-[2] + *substantiālis*, SUBSTANTIAL. Not real; not of stout or solid substance.

Insuf'ferable, *a.* IN-[2]. Not to be endured, intolerable.—**Insuf'ferab**LY,[2] *adv.*

Insuffic'ient, *a.* L.L. *insufficiens, insufficientis*, f. IN-[2] + L. *sufficiens*, SUFFICIENT. Inadequate.—**Insuffic'i**ENCY, *n.*

In'sular, *a.* L. *insulāris*, f. *insula*, island. ISLE. Of, composing, an island; of islanders, narrow-minded.—**Insular'**ITY, *n.*—**In'sulate**, *vt.* -ATE.[3] To make into an island; to set or place apart; to prevent the passage of electricity from.—**Insul**A'TION, *n.*—**In'sulat**OR, *n.* A substance that prevents the passage of electricity; a contrivance for supporting and insulating telegraph-wires.

Insult', *vt.* L. *insultāre*, to leap upon, insult, freq. of *insilīre*, to leap upon, f. IN-[1] + *salīre*, to leap. ASSAIL. EXILE. To assail contemptuously in speech or action.—**In'sult**, *n.* The action or an act of insulting.

Insu'perable, *a.* L. *insuperābilis*, f. IN-[2] + *superābilis*, SUPERABLE. That cannot be surmounted.—**Insu'perab**LY,[2] *adv.*

Insuppor'table, *a.* Eccles.L. *insupportābilis*, f. IN-[2] + L. *supportāre*. SUPPORT. Not to be endured.—**Insuppor'tab**LY,[2] *adv.*

Insure', *vt.* Var. of ENSURE with IN-[1]. To secure the payment of (a sum of money) in the event of loss, death, &c.; to secure this in the event of the loss, &c., of; to make safe *from, against*; to make certain.—**Insur'**ABLE, *a.*—**Insur'**ANCE, *n.*—**Insur'**ER, *n.*

Insur'gent, *a.* L. *insurgens, insurgentis*, pres.pple. of *insurgĕre, insurrectum*, to rise upon or to, f. IN-[1] + *surgĕre*, to rise. SURGE. Rising in active revolt.—*n.* A rebel.—**Insurrec'**TION, *n.*

Insurmount'able, *a.* IN-[2]. That cannot be surmounted.

Insuscep'tible, *a.* IN-[2]. Not liable to be affected.—**Insusceptib**IL'ITY, *n.*

Intact', *a.* L. *intactus*, f. IN-[2] + *tactus*, pa. pple. of *tangĕre*. ATTAIN. Unimpaired.

Intag'lio, *n.* It., engraved work, f. *intagliare*, to engrave, f. IN-[1] + *tagliare* (= O.F. *taill(i)er*), to cut. ENTAIL. A figure engraved in stone, &c.; such engraving; an engraved gem.

Intan'gible, *a.* Med.L. *intangibilis*, f. IN-[2] + L. *tangibilis*, TANGIBLE. Impalpable.

In'teger, *n.* L. *integer*, untouched, entire, f. IN-[2] + *tag-, teg-*, root of *tangĕre*. INTACT. ENTIRE. A whole number as distinguished from a fraction.—**In'tegr**AL, *a.* Of a whole; not fractional.—**In'tegr**ATE,[3] *vt.* To combine into a whole; to complete.—**Integr**A'TION, *n.*—**Integ'r**ITY, *n.* Completeness; original perfect state; uprightness, honesty.

Integ'ument, *n.* L. *integumentum*, f. IN-[1] + *tegumentum*, TEGUMENT. A covering.

In'tellect, *n.* L. *intellectus*, perception, intellect, f. *intelligĕre*. (See next.) The faculty by which one knows and reasons.—**Intellec'tual**, *a.* L. *intellectuālis*. Of, appealing to, the intellect; having a powerful intellect.

Intel'ligent, *a.* L. *intelligens, intelligentis*, pres.pple. of *intelligĕre, intellectum*, to perceive, understand, f. *intel-* (= INTER-), between, within + *legĕre*, to bring together, pick out, read. COLLECT. Possessing intellect; quick to understand. — **Intel'ligent**LY,[2] *adv.*—**Intel'lig**ENCE, *n.* Intellect; quickness of understanding; information, news.—**Intel'ligenc**ER, *n.* A spy; a bringer of news.—**Intel'lig**IBLE, *a.* That can be understood.—**Intel'ligib**LY,[2] *adv.*—**Intelligi**BIL'ITY, *n.*

Intem'perate, *a.* L. *intemperātus*, f. IN-[2] + *temperātus*, TEMPERATE. Not temperate; immoderate; addicted to drinking.—**Intem'perate**LY,[2] *adv.*—**Intem'per**ANCE, *n.*

Intend', *vt.* F. *entendre*—L. *intendĕre, intentum* and *intensum*, to stretch towards, turn one's attention, intend, f. IN-[1] + *tendĕre*, to stretch. ATTEND. To signify by one's words; to purpose, design, destine. — **Intent'**, *n.* O.F. *entente*, f. *entendre*. Purpose.—*a.* L. *intentus*, pa.pple. of *intendĕre*. Having the mind bent on something; earnest, eager.—**Intent'**LY,[2] *adv.*—**Intent'**NESS, *n.*—**Inten'**TION, *n.* Purpose.—**Inten'tion**AL, *a.*

Intense', *a.* F. *intense*—L. *intensus*, pa.pple. of *intendĕre*. (See prec.) Very strong or acute; having a quality in a high degree. — **Intense'**LY,[2] *adv.*—**Inten's**IFY, *vt.* and *i.*—**Intens**IFICA'TION, *n.* — **Inten's**ION, *n.* Notable degree; strenuous exertion. — **Inten's**ITY, *n.* — **Inten's**IVE, *a.* Expressing intensity, giving emphasis; aiming at increasing productiveness.—*n.* An intensive word or prefix.

Inter', *vt.* O.F. *enterrer*—Pop.L. *interrāre*, f. IN-[1] + *terra*. TERRESTRIAL. To bury.

Interact', *vi.* INTER-. To act on each other. —**Interac'**TION, *n.* Reciprocal action.

Inter'calate, *vt.* L. *intercalāre, intercalātum*, to proclaim the insertion of a day, &c., to intercalate, f. INTER- + *calāre*, to proclaim. COUNCIL. To insert (an additional day, &c.) in the calendar; to interpolate.—**Inter'cal**ARY, *a.*—**Intercal**A'TION, *n.*

Intercede', *vi.* L. INTER*cēdĕre, intercessum*, to go or come between, in Med.L., to intercede. ACCEDE. To interpose on behalf of another. —**Interces's**ION, *n.*—**Interces's**OR, *n.*

Intercept', *vt.* L. *intercipĕre, interceptum*, f. INTER- + *capĕre*, to take. ACCEPT. To seize when on the way; to stop the passage of; to check, prevent.—**Intercep'**TION, *n.*

Interchange', *vt.* O.F. *entre-changier*, f. *entre-* (= INTER-) + *changier, changer*, to CHANGE. To exchange with each other; to transpose; to alternate.—**In'terchange**, *n.* The act of interchanging; transposition; alternation.—**Interchange'**ABLE, *a.*

Intercommu'nicate, *vi.* Anglo-L. INTER*commūnicāre, intercommūnicātum.* COMMUNICATE. To have mutual intercourse.—**Intercommunic**A'TION, *n.*

In'tercourse, *n.* O.F. *entrecours*, exchange, commerce, f. *entrecorre*, L. INTER*currĕre*, to run between. CONCUR. Mutual dealings; social familiarity.

In'terdict, *n.* O.F. *entredit*—L. *interdictum*, f. INTER*dicĕre*, *interdictum*, to speak between, interpose by speaking, forbid. ADDICT. A prohibition; a sentence debarring from ecclesiastical functions or privileges.—**Interdict'**, *vt.* To prohibit; to lay under an interdict.—**Interdic'**TION *n.*—**Interdic'**TORY, *a.*

In'terest, *n.* Alteration (app. aft. F. *interest*, now *intérêt*) of obs. *Interess*—A.F. *interesse*—Med.L. *interesse*, compensation for loss, use as *n.* of L. INTER*esse*, to be between, make a difference, concern. ENTITY. A being concerned *in* something, the something; persons having a common interest; selfish pursuit of one's own ends; personal influence; a feeling of concern or curiosity; money paid for the use of money lent.—*vt.* To cause to have a concern or interest in a thing or person; to excite the attention or curiosity of.

Interfere', *vi.* O.F. *s'entreferir*, to strike each other, f. *entre-* (= INTER-) + *ferir*, L. *ferire*, to strike. To collide, clash; to meddle *with*; to interpose.—**Interfer'**ENCE, *n.*

In'terim, *n.* L. *interim*, in the meantime. The meantime.—*a.* Provisional, temporary.

Inte'rior, *a.* L. *interior*, comp. f. *inter.* INTER-. Lying within or more within; inland; domestic; mental, spiritual.—*n.* The inside; the inland parts; inner nature or being.

Interject', *vt.* L. *interjicĕre*, *interjectum*, to throw between, f. INTER- + *jacĕre*, to throw. ABJECT. To interpose, insert; to remark parenthetically or by way of interruption.—**Interjec'**TION, *n.* The utterance of ejaculations, an ejaculation; a natural ejaculation as a part of speech.—**Interjec'tion**AL, *a.*

Interlace', *vt.* F. *entrelacer*, f. *entre-* (= INTER-) + *lacer*, to LACE. To entangle, involve; to weave together; to intersperse or mingle *with*.—*vi.* To cross as if woven together.

Interleave', *vt.* INTER- + LEAF (pl. *leaves*). To insert (blank) leaves in (a book).

Interline', *vt.* Med.L. *interlineāre*, f. INTER- + L. *līnea*, LINE. To insert words between the lines of; to insert (words) thus.—**Interline**A'TION, *n.*

Interloc'utor, *n.* L. type **interlocūtor*, agent-n. f. INTER*loqui*, to speak between. ALLOCUTE. One who takes part in a dialogue.

Interlope', *vi.* From INTER- + *lope*, dial. form of LEAP. To intrude within the domain or sphere of another.—**Interlop'**ER, *n.*

In'terlude, *n.* Med. (Anglo-) L. *interlūdium*, f. INTER- + L. *lūdus*, a play, f. *lūdĕre*, to play. ALLUDE. An interval in a play, something filling it up; an interval.

Intermar'ry, *vi.* INTER-. To form a connexion by marriage.—**Intermar'riage**, *n.*

Intermed'dle, *vi.* A.F. *entremedler* = O.F. *entremesler*, f. *entre-* (= INTER-) + *mesler*. MEDDLE. To meddle, interfere.

Interme'diate, *a.* Med.L. *intermediātus*, f. L. INTER*medius*. MID. Interposed, intervening.—**Interme'di**ARY, *a.* Intermediate. —*n.* A go-between.—**Intermedi**A'TION, *n.* —**Intermez'zo**, *n.* It. = *intermedio*, f. L. *intermedius*. A short light performance between the acts of a play or opera.

Inter'minable, *a.* L.L. *interminābilis*, f. IN-[2] + L. *termināre*, to TERMINATE. Endless.

Intermin'gle, *vt.* INTER-. To mingle together; to mix *with*.—*vi.* To mingle together.

Intermit', *vt.* and *i.* L. *intermittĕre*, *intermissum*, f. INTER-, between + *mittĕre*, to send, let go, put. ADMIT. To stop for a time.—**Intermis'**SION, *n.*—**Intermit'**TENT, *a.*

Intermix', *vt.* and *i.* App. f. *Intermixt*, ppl.a. (as if a pa.pple.)—L. *intermixtus*, pa.pple. of INTER*miscēre*, to MIX among. To mix together.—**Intermix'**TURE, *n.*

Intern', *vt.* F. *interner*, f. *interne*, L. *internus*, internal, f. *in*, in. (Cf. *externus*, EXTERNAL.) To confine within prescribed limits.—

Inter'nal, *a.* Late Med.L. *internālis*. Of, in, the inside; of the inner nature; of domestic affairs.—**Inter'nal**LY,[2] *adv.*

Interna'tional, *a.* INTER-. Existing or carried on between different nations; pertaining to the relations between nations.

Interne'cine, *a.* L. *internecīnus*, deadly, destructive, f. *internecium*, utter slaughter, f. *internecāre*, to kill, f. INTER-, in intensive sense + *necāre*, to put to death. Deadly, destructive; in modern use, mutually destructive (taking the prefix improperly).

Interpel'late, *vt.* L. *interpellāre*, *interpellātum*, to interrupt by speaking, f. INTER- + *pellāre* = *pellĕre*, to drive. APPEAL. In the French or other Chamber, to interrupt the proceedings and ask an explanation from (a Minister).—**Interpell**A'TION, *n.*

Inter'polate, *vt.* L. *interpolāre*, *interpolātum*, to furbish up, alter. f. INTER- + -*polāre*, conn. with *polire*, to POLISH. To insert new (and misleading) matter in; to insert (spurious matter).—**Interpol**A'TION, *n.*

Interpose', *vt.* F. *interposer*, f. INTER- + *poser*, to place. POSE.[1] To place between; to say as interrupting; to put forth or introduce as intervening.—*vi.* To stand in the way; to intervene, interfere.—**Interposi'tion**, *n.* F. *interposition* — L. *interpositio*, *interpositiōnis*, n. of action f. INTER*pōnĕre*, to place between. APPOSITE. In senses from the *v.*

Inter'pret, *vt.* L. *interpretāri*, f. *interpres*, *interpretis*, agent, explainer, interpreter, f. INTER- + root corresp. to Skr. *prath-*, to spread abroad. To expound the meaning of, explain, translate; to explain or take in a specified way; to bring out the artistic meaning of.—**Interpret**A'TION, *n.*—**Inter'pret**ER, *n.* One who interprets, esp. in a conversation.

Interreg'num, *n.* L., f. INTER- + *regnum*, REIGN. An interval between reigns.

Inter'rogate, *vt.* L. *interrogāre*, *interrogātum*, f. INTER-, between, at intervals + *rogāre*, to ask. ABROGATE. To ask questions of, examine by questions.—**Interroga**A'TION, *n.* —**Interrog'at**IVE, *a.* Of, of the nature of, questioning; used in asking a question.—*n.* An interrogative word.—**Interrog'at**ORY, *a.* Interrogative.—*n.* A question.

Interrupt', *vt.* L. *interrumpĕre*, *interruptum*, f. INTER- + *rumpĕre*, to break. ABRUPT. To break off, stop the course of; to cause to stop in speaking.—**Interrup'**TION, *n.*

Intersect', *vt.* L. *intersecāre*, *intersectum*, f. INTER- + *secāre*, to cut. SAW.[1] To cross; of a line, &c., to pass through or across.—*vi.* To cross each other.—**Intersec'**TION, *n.*

Intersperse', *vt.* L. *interspersus*, pa.pple. of **interspergĕre*, f. INTER- + *spargĕre*, to scatter. ASPERSE. To place here and there; to furnish *with* things placed here and there.—**Intersper'**SION, *n.*

Interstel'lar, *a.* INTER-. Between the stars.

Inter'stice, *n.* L. *interstitium*, f. *intersistĕre*, **interstitum*, to stand still between, f. INTER- + *sistĕre*, to stand. ASSIST. An intervening space, a crevice.—**Intersti'**TIAL, *a.*

In'terval, *n.* F. *intervalle*—L. *intervallum*, space between ramparts, interval, f. INTER-

+ *vallum*, rampart. WALL. A pause; an intervening time or space; difference of pitch.

Intervene′, *vi.* L. *intervenīre*, f. INTER- + *venīre*, to come. ADVENT. To happen in the meantime; to interpose; to be placed, extend, come in, *between*.—**Interven′**TION, *n.*

In′terview, *n.* F. *entrevue*, vbl.n. f. *entrevoir*, to have a glimpse of, *refl.*, to see each other, f. *entre-* (= INTER-) + *voir*, L. *vidēre*, to see. ADVICE. A formally arranged meeting; a meeting to obtain statements for publication.—*vt.* To have an interview with.—**In′terview**ER, *n.*

Interweave′, *vt.* INTER-. To weave together.

Intes′tate, *a.* L. *intestātus*, f. IN-[2] + *testātus*, TESTATE. That has left no will; not disposed of by will.—*n.* An intestate person.—**Intes′ta**CY, *n.*

Intes′tine, *a.* L. *intestīnus*, internal, f. *intus*, within. Domestic, not foreign.—*n.* L. *intestīnum*, neut. of *intestīnus*. The alimentary canal (gen. in *pl.*).—**Intes′tin**AL, *a.*

In′timate, *vt.* L. *intimāre*, *intimātum*, to bring into, to intimate, f. *intimus*, inmost, close in friendship, f. *intus*. (See prec.) To announce; to indicate.—**Intima′**TION, *n.*

In′timate, *a.* After prec. f. F. *intime*, f. *intimus*. Most inward; closely personal; closely united in friendship; of knowledge, &c., due to familiarity.—*n.* A close friend.—**In′tim**ACY, *n.*—**In′timate**LY,[2] *adv.*

Intim′idate, *vt.* Med.L. *intimidāre*, *intimidātum*, f. IN-[1] + *timidus*, TIMID. To force or deter by threats.—**Intimida′**TION, *n.*

In′to, *prep.* Orig. two words. O.E. *in tó*, IN, *adv.*, and TO. In and to, denoting inward motion, direction or change of condition.

Intol′erable, *a.* L. *intolerābilis*, f. IN-[2] + *tolerābilis*, TOLERABLE. That cannot be borne, unendurable.—**Intol′erab**LY,[2] *adv.*

Intol′erant, *a.* L. *intolerans*, *intolerantis*, f. IN-[2] + *tolerans*, pres.pple. of *tolerāre*. TOLERATE. Unable or unwilling to endure; not tolerating differences of opinion or practice.—**Intol′erant**LY,[2] *adv.*—**Intol′er**ANCE, *n.*

In′tonate, *vt.* Med.L. *intonāre*, *intonātum*, to intone, f. IN-[1] + L. *tonus*, TONE. To intone; to pronounce with a particular tone.—**Intona′**TION, *n.*—**Intone′**, *vt.* From *intonāre*. To recite in a singing voice, to chant.

Intox′icate, *vt.* Med.L. *intoxicāre*, *intoxicātum*, f. IN-[1] + L. *toxicāre*, to smear with poison, f. *toxicum*, poison. TOXIC. To make drunk; to excite beyond self-control.—**Intox′ic**ANT, *n.*—**Intoxica′**TION, *n.*

Intrac′table, *a.* L. *intractābilis*, f. IN-[2] + *tractābilis*, TRACTABLE. Not tractable.

Intran′sitive, *a.* L. *intransitīvus*, not passing over, f. IN-[2] + *transīre*, to pass over. TRANSIENT. Of a verb, expressing action which does not pass over to an object.

Intrep′id, *a.* L. *intrepidus*, f. IN-[2] + *trepidus*, alarmed. TREPIDATION. Undaunted.—**Intrep′id**LY,[2] *adv.*—**Intrepid′**ITY, *n.*

In′tricate, *a.* L. *intrīcātus*, pa.pple. of *intrīcāre*, to entangle, f. IN-[1] + *tricae*, perplexities. EXTRICATE. Involved, complicated.—**In′tricate**LY,[2] *adv.*—**In′tric**ACY, *n.*

Intrigue′, *n.* F. *intrigue*—It. *intrigo*, *-ico*, f. *intrigare*, *-care*, to entangle, entrap—L. *intrīcāre*. (See prec.) Underhand plotting; an underhand plot; clandestine illicit intimacy between a man and a woman.—*vi.* To carry on an intrigue.—**Intrig′u**ER, *n.*

Intrin′sic, *a.* F. *intrinsèque*—L.L. *intrinsecus*, a., f. L. *intrinsecus*, adv., on the inside, f. *intrin-* (= **intrim*, conn. with *intrā*, within) + *secus*. EXTRINSIC. Inherent, essential.—**Intrin′sically**, *adv.* -AL. -LY.[2]

Introduce′, *vt.* L. *intrōdūcĕre*, *intrōductum*, to lead or bring in, originate, f. *intrō*, within + *dūcĕre*, to lead. DUKE. To insert; to usher in, present formally; to bring in, add; to bring into use or notice; to make (a person) known to another.—**Introduc′**TION, *n.*—**Introduc′**TORY, *a.* Preliminary.

Introspect′, *vi.* L. *intrōspicĕre*, *intrōspectum*, to look into, examine, f. *intrō*, within + *specĕre*. ASPECT. To examine one's own mind.—**Introspec′**TION, *n.*—**Introspec′**TIVE, *a.*

Intrude′, *vt.* L. *intrūdĕre*, *intrūsum*, f. IN-[1] + *trūdĕre*, to thrust. ABSTRUSE. To force *into*, *on*, *upon*.—*v.refl.* and *i.* To thrust oneself in without right or invitation.—**Intrud′**ER, *n.*—**Intru′**SION, *n.*—**Intru′**SIVE, *a.*

Intui′tion, *n.* F. *intuition*—L.L. *intuitio*, *intuitiōnis*, n. of action f. *intuēri*, *intuitus*, to look upon, consider, f. IN-[1] + *tuēri*, to watch. TUITION. Immediate or direct apprehension or insight, an instance of this.—**Intu′it**IVE, *a.*—**Intu′itive**LY,[2] *adv.*

In′undate, *vt.* L. *inundāre*, *inundātum*, f. IN-[1] + *undāre*, to rise in waves, f. *unda*, wave. ABOUND. To overflow.—**Inunda′**TION, *n.*

Inure′, **Enure′**, *vt.* IN-[1], EN-[1] (1) + obs. *Ure*, work, operation, f. F. *œuvre*, L. *opera*, work. OPERA. To habituate.—*vi.* To take effect.

Inutil′ity, *n.* F. *inutilité*—L. *inūtilitas*, f. IN-[2] + *ūtilitas*, UTILITY. Uselessness.

Invade′, *vt.* L. *invādĕre*, *invāsum*, f. IN-[1] + *vādĕre*, to go. EVADE. To enter with hostile intent; to encroach on, violate.—**Invad′**ER, *n.*—**Inva′**SION, *n.*

Inval′id, *a.* L. *invalidus*, weak, inefficient, f. IN-[2] + *validus*. VALID. Of no legal force.—**Inval′id**ATE,[3] *vt.*—**Invalid′**ITY, *n.*[1]

Invalid′, *n.* From as prec. with stress modified after F. *invalide*. An infirm or sickly person.—*vt.* To treat, to send *home*, &c., as an invalid.—**Invalid′**ITY, *n.*[2]

Inval′uable, *a.* IN-[2]. Beyond price.

Inva′riable, *a.* IN-[2]. Unchangeable, unchanging, constant.—**Inva′riab**LY,[2] *adv.*

Inveigh′, *vi.* L. *invehĕre*, *invectum*, to carry into, *refl.* and *pass.*, to assail, f. IN-[1] + *vehĕre*, to carry. VEHICLE. To give vent to loud censure.—**Invec′tive**, *n.* F. *invective*—Med. L. *invectīva* (sc. *ōrātio*, speech), f. *invehĕre*. Loud censure; a violent attack in words.

Invei′gle, *vt.* Formerly *envegle*, app. a corr. of **avegle*—F. *aveugler*, to blind, f. *aveugle*, late Pop.L. *aboculus*, blind, f. AB-, away from, without + *oculus*, eye. INOCULATE. To entice, seduce.—**Invei′gle**MENT, *n.*

Invent′, *vt.* L. *invenīre*, *inventum*, to come upon, discover, contrive, f. IN-[1] + *venīre*, to come. ADVENT. To fabricate, feign; to devise, originate.—**Inven′**TION, *n.*—**Inven′**TIVE, *a.*—**Invent′**OR, *n.*

In′ventory, *n.* Med.L. *inventōrium*, L. *inventārium*, lit., a list of what is found, f. *invenīre*. (See prec.) A detailed list; a catalogue.

Invert′, *vt.* L. *invertĕre*, *inversum*, f. IN-[1] + *vertĕre*, to turn. ADVERSE. To turn in an opposite direction or upside down; to reverse the relations of.—**Inverse′**, *a.* L. *inversus*, pa.pple. of *invertĕre*. Inverted.—**Inverse′**LY,[2] *adv.*—**Inver′**SION, *n.*

Inver′tebrate, *a.* IN-[2]. Having no spine.

Invest′, *vt.* L. *investīre*, *investītum*, f. IN-[1] + *vestīre*, to clothe. DIVEST. To clothe, to endue; to form a covering to; to besiege: to lay out (money) in order to gain interest or profits. — **Inves'titure**, *n.* The action or ceremony of clothing or enduing.—**Invest'ment**, *n.*—**Invest'or**, *n.*

Inves'tigate, *vt.* L. *investigāre, investigātum*, f. IN-[1] + *vestigāre*, to trace out, conn. with *vestigium*. VESTIGE. To inquire into systematically.—**Investiga'tion**, *n.*

Invet'erate, *a.* L. *inveterātus*, pa.pple. of *inveterāre*, to give age or duration to, f. IN-[1] + *vetus*. VETERAN. Long-established; deep-seated; obstinate.—**Invet'eracy**, *n.*

Invid'ious, *a.* L. *invidiōsus*, f. *invidia*, ENVY. Entailing or fitted to excite ill will; giving offence.—**Invid'iously**,[2] *adv.*

Invig'orate, *vt.* IN-[1] + *vigor*, VIGOUR + -ATE.[3] To give vigour to, animate.

Invin'cible, *a.* F. *invincible*—L. *invincibilis*, f. IN-[2] + *vincibilis*, that may be conquered, f. *vincĕre*. VICTOR. Unconquerable. —**Invin'cibly**,[2] *adv.*—**Invincibil'ity**, *n.*

Invi'olate, *a.* L. *inviolātus*, unhurt, f. IN-[2] + *violātus*, pa.pple. of *violāre*, to VIOLATE. Unhurt, unprofaned, unbroken, intact.—**Invi'olable**, *a.* Not to be violated.—**Invi'olably**,[2] *adv.*—**Inviolabil'ity**, *n.*

Invis'ible, *a.* F. *invisible*—L. *invīsibilis*, f. IN-[2] + *vīsibilis*, VISIBLE. That cannot be seen; imperceptible.—**Invis'ibly**,[2] *adv.*—**Invisibil'ity**, *n.*

Invite', *vt.* F. *inviter*—L. *invītāre*. VIE. To ask to come *to*, *into*, &c., or *to do*; to ask for; to allure, attract.—**Invita'tion**, *n.*

In'voice, *n.* App. orig. = *Invoyes*, pl. of obs. *Invoy*, an invoice—O.F. *envoy*. ENVOY.[2] A list of goods sent, with prices, &c.—*vt.* To make an invoice of, enter in an invoice.

Invoke', *vt.* F. *invoquer*, L. *invocāre*, f. IN-[1] + *vocāre*, to call. VOCABLE. To call upon in prayer or as a witness.—**Invoca'tion**, *n.*

Invol'untary, *a.* L. *involuntārius*, f. IN-[2] + *voluntārius*. VOLUNTARY. Independent of the will.—**Invol'untarily**,[2] *adv.*

Involve', *vt.* L. *involvĕre*, to roll upon, envelop, f. IN-[1] + *volvĕre*, to roll. CONVOLVE. To envelop; to make intricate; to entangle *in* (trouble, &c.); to implicate *in* (a charge, &c.); to include, imply.—**In'volute**, *a.* L. *involūtus*, pa.pple. of *involvĕre*. Intricate; rolled or curved up spirally.—**Involu'tion**, *n.*

Invul'nerable, *a.* L. *invulnerābilis*, f. IN-[2] + *vulnerābilis*, VULNERABLE. Incapable of being injured or effectively assailed.

I'odine, *n.* With chemical suff. *-ine* f. F. *iode*, iodine, f. G. *iōdēs*, violet-coloured (f. *ion*, violet + *-eidēs*, like, f. *eidos*, form), from the colour of the vapour. A non-metallic element used in medicine.

Ion'ic, *a.* L. *Iōnicus*—G. *Iōnikos*, of Ionia. The name of one of the three Grecian orders of architecture characterized by the two lateral volutes of the capital.

Io'ta, *n.* G. *iōta*. JOT. The name of the smallest Greek letter; a very small quantity.

Ipecacuan'ha, *n.* Pg., f. Tupi-guarani (Brazilian) *ipe-kaa-guéne*. The root of a S. American plant with emetic and purgative properties; the plant.

Ire, *n.* O.F. *ire*—L. *īra*. Anger, wrath.—**Ire'ful**, *a.*—**Iras'cible**, *a.* F. *irascible*—L. *īrascibilis*, f. *īrasci*, *īrātus*, to be angry, f. *īra*. Prone to anger.—**Irascibil'ity**, *n.*—**Irate'**, *a.* L. *īrātus*, f. *īrasci*. Angry.

I'ris, *n.* L. *īris*, *īridis*—G. *iris*, *iridos*. A rainbow; a circular membrane in the eye containing the pupil; a genus of plants with sword-shaped leaves.—**Irides'cent**, *a.* Adjectival suff. *-escent*. Displaying colours like those of the rainbow; flashing with changing colours.—**Irides'cence**, *n.*

Irk, *vt.* M.E. *irken*, *yrken*, of uncertain orig. To weary, trouble, disgust.—**Irk'some**, *a.*

I'ron, *n.* M.E. *iren*, *ire*—O.E. *īren*, also *īsern*, *īsen*=O.S. *īsarn*, O.H.G. *īsarn* (Ger. *eisen*), O.N. *īsarn*. The most abundant and useful of the metals; various instruments, tools, &c., of iron; an implement for smoothing cloth, &c.; in *pl.*, shackles, fetters.—*a.* Of or like iron; inflexible, harsh, severe.—*vt.* To furnish with iron; to shackle; to smooth with an iron.—**I'ronmonger**, *n.* MONGER. A dealer in hardware.—**I'ronmongery**, *n.* His wares.

I'rony, *n.* L. *īrōnīa*—G. *eirōneia*, dissimulation, f. *eirōn*, a dissembler. A figure of speech in which the intended meaning is the opposite of that expressed by the words used.—**Iron'ical**, *a.*—**Iron'ically**,[2] *adv.*

Irra'diate, *vt.* L. *irradiāre*, *irradiātum*, f. *ir-* (= IN-[1]) + *radiāre*. RADIATE. To shine upon, to illumine (often *fig.*).—**Irradia'tion**, *n.* The action or the result of irradiating; the apparent enlargement of a brightly illuminated object.—**Irra'diance**, *n.*

Irra'tional, *a.* L. *irratiōnālis*, f. *ir-* (=IN-[2]) + *ratiōnālis*, RATIONAL. Not endowed with reason; unreasonable, absurd; of a quantity, that cannot be expressed in the natural numbers.—**Irra'tionally**,[2] *adv.*

Irreclaim'able, *a.* *Ir-* (= IN-[2]). That cannot be reclaimed.—**Irreclaim'ably**,[2] *adv.*

Irreconci'lable, *a.* *Ir-* (=IN-[2]). That cannot be made friendly; inconsistent, incompatible.—**Irreconci'lably**,[2] *adv.*

Irrecov'erable, *a.* *Ir-* (= IN-[2]). That can not be got back or remedied.—**Irrecov'erably**,[2] *adv.*

Irredeem'able, *a.* *Ir-* (= IN-[2]). That can not be redeemed; that cannot be converted into cash.—**Irredeem'ably**,[2] *adv.*

Irredu'cible, *a.* *Ir-* (= IN-[2]). That cannot be reduced or brought *to* a desired form.

Irref'ragable, *a.* L.L. *irrefrāgābilis*, f. *ir-* (= IN-[2]) + L. *refrāgāri*, to oppose. That cannot be refuted.—**Irref'ragably**,[2] *adv.*

Irref'utable, *a.* L. *irrefūtābilis*, f. *ir-* (= IN-[2]) + *refūtābilis*, REFUTABLE. That cannot be refuted.—**Irref'utably**,[2] *adv.*

Irreg'ular, *a.* O.F. *irreguler*—Med.L. *irrēgulāris*, f. *ir-* (= IN-[2]) + L. *rēgulāris*. REGULAR. Not in accordance with rule or principle; disorderly, lawless; not of regular form; not regular in occurrence or continuance; inflected not in the usual way.—**Irreg'ularly**,[2] *adv.*—**Irregular'ity**, *n.*

Irrel'evant, *a.* *Ir-* (= IN-[2]). Not to the purpose, that does not apply.—**Irrel'evantly**,[2] *adv.*—**Irrel'evance**, -ANCY, *nn.*

Irrelig'ion, *n.* L. *irreligio*, *irreligiōnis*, f. *ir-* (= IN-[2]) + *religio*, RELIGION. Want of or hostility to religion.—**Irrelig'ious**, *a.*

Irreme'diable, *a.* L. *irremediābilis*, f. *ir-* (= IN-[2]) + *remediābilis*, REMEDIABLE. Not to be remedied.—**Irreme'diably**,[2] *adv.*

Irremis'sible, *a.* F. *irrémissible*—L. *irremissibilis*, f. *ir-* (= IN-[2]) + *remissibilis*, REMISSIBLE. Unpardonable; perpetually binding.—**Irremis'sibly**,[2] *adv.*

Irremov'able, *a.* *Ir-* (= IN-[2]). Not removable.

Irrep'arable, *a.* F. *irréparable*—L. *irreparābilis*, f. *ir-* (= IN-[2]) + *reparābilis*, REPARABLE. Not reparable.—**Irrep'arably**,[2] *adv.*

Irrepres'sible, *a.* *Ir-* (= IN-[2]) + REPRESS

+-IBLE. Not to be repressed.—**Irrepres'sibly**,[2] *adv.*

Irreproach'able, *a.* F. *irréprochable*, f. *ir-* (= IN-[2]) + *reprochable*, REPROACHABLE. Not open to reproach or blame. — **Irreproach'ably**,[2] *adv.*

Irresist'ible, *a.* L.L. *irresistibilis*, f. *ir-* (= IN-[2]) + *resistĕre*, to RESIST. That cannot be withstood.—**Irresist'ibly**,[2] *adv.*

Irres'olute, *a.* L. *irresolūtus*, f. *ir-* (= IN-[2]) + *resolūtus*. RESOLUTE. Undecided; wanting in resolution.—**Irres'olutely**,[2] *adv.*—**Irresolu'tion**, *n.*

Irrespec'tive, *a.* *Ir-* (= IN-[2]). Without taking account *of*.—**Irrespec'tively**,[2] *adv.*

Irrespon'sible, *a.* *Ir-* (= IN-[2]). Not answerable for conduct, exempt from responsibility. — **Irrespon'sibly**,[2] *adv.* — **Irresponsibil'ity**, *n.*

Irrespon'sive, *a.* *Ir-* (= IN-[2]). Not responsive.

Irretrie'vable, *a.* *Ir-* (= IN-[2]). Not to be retrieved.—**Irretrie'vably**,[2] *adv.*

Irrev'erent, *a.* L. *irreverens*, *irreverentis*, f. *ir-* (= IN-[2]) + *reverens*, pres.pple. of *reverēri*, to REVERE. Wanting in reverence or respect. —**Irrev'erently**,[2] *adv.*—**Irrev'erence**, *n.*

Irrev'ocable, *a.* L. *irrevocābilis*, f. *ir-* (= IN-[2]) + *revocābilis*, REVOCABLE. Beyond recall; unalterable.—**Irrev'ocably**,[2] *adv.*

Ir'rigate, *vt.* L. *irrigāre*, *irrigātum*, f. *ir-* (= IN-[1]) + *rigāre*, to wet. To water by means of channels or streams.—**Irriga'tion**, *n.*

Ir'ritate, *vt.* L. *irrītāre*, *irrītātum*, to incite, stimulate, irritate. To excite to anger; to excite to morbid action or to an abnormal condition.—**Ir'ritable**, *a.* Easily excited to anger; morbidly excitable.—**Irritabil'ity**, *n.*—**Ir'ritant**, *a.* Irritating.—*n.* An irritant substance.—**Irrita'tion**, *n.*

Irrupt', *vi.* L. *irrumpĕre*, *irruptum*, f. *ir-* (= IN-[1]) + *rumpĕre*. ABRUPT. To break or rush in.—**Irrup'tion**, *n.*—**Irrup'tive**, *a.*

I'singlass, *n.* Said to be a corr. of obs. Du. *huisenblas* (= Ger. *hausenblase*), isinglass, lit., 'sturgeon's bladder'. A gelatinous substance obtained from certain fishes, esp. the sturgeon.

I'sland, *n.* O.E. *ígland*, *íland*, f. *íeg*, *íg* (= O.N., Old Fris. *ey*), isle + LAND. A piece of land completely surrounded by water.—**I'slander**, *n.* A dweller on an island.

Isle, *n.* O.F. *isle*, *ile* (F. *île*)—L. *insula*. INSULAR. ISOLATED. An island.—**Is'let**, *n.* F. dim. *islette* (now *îlette*). A little island.

Isoch'ronal, *a.* G. *isochronos* (f. *isos*, equal + *chronos*, time) + AL. Equal in time; vibrating uniformly. Sim., **Isoch'ronous**, *a.*

I'solated, *ppl.a.* Formerly *isolé*, *isolé'd*. F. *isolé*—It. *isolato*—L. *insulātus*, made into an island, f. *insula*. ISLE. Placed or standing apart or alone.—**I'solate**, *vt.* Back-formation f. the *ppl.a.* To place or set apart or alone.—**Isola'tion**.

Isos'celes, *a.* L.L. *īsosceles*—G. *isoskelēs*, equal-legged, f. *isos*, equal + *skelos*, leg. Of a triangle, having two of its sides equal.

I'sotherm, *n.* F. *isotherme*, f. G. *isos*, equal + *thermē*, heat. A line passing through points of equal temperature.—**Isother'mal**, *a.*

Is'sue, *n.* O.F. *issue*, *eissue*, &c. — Pop.L. **exūta*, f. fem. of **exūtus* for L. *exitus*, pa.pple. of *exīre*. EXIT. A going or passing out; a discharge from the body; a way out; a child or children, progeny; outcome, event, result; a point or matter in contention; a sending or giving out officially or publicly.—*vi.* To go or pass out; to take origin, arise; to result *in*.—*vt.* To emit or discharge; to send or give out officially or publicly.

Isth'mus, *n.* L. *isthmus*—G. *isthmos*, neck, neck of land. A neck of land.

It, *pron.* O.E. *hit*, neut. f. *hi-*, HE. The neuter pronoun of the third person.—**Its**, *pron.* Formed with *'s* of the genit. case, and orig. written *it's*. Belonging to it.

Ital'ic, *a.* L. *Italicus*, Italian, f. *Italia*, Italy. Applied to a species of type which slopes to the right, first used at Venice in 1501 in an edition of Virgil dedicated to Italy.—*n.pl.* Italic letters.—**Ital'icize**, *vt.* To put in italics.

Itch, *vi.* O.E. *gicc(e)an*. W. Germanic **jukkjan* (O.H.G. *jucchen*, Ger. *jucken*). To be affected by a sensation causing a desire to scratch.—*n.* Such a sensation; a disease characterized by such a sensation.—**Itch'y**.[2] *a.*

I'tem, *adv.* L. *item*. Likewise, also.—*n.* An article or unit in an enumeration; a detail.

It'erate, *vt.* L. *iterāre*, *iterātum*, f. *iterum*, again. To repeat.—**Itera'tion**, *n.*—**It'erative**, *a.* Characterized by repetition; frequentative.—*n.* A frequentative verb.

Itin'erate, *vi.* L.L. *itinerāri*, *itinerātus*, to travel, f. L. *iter*, *itineris*, journey. To travel from place to place.—**Itin'erant**, *a.*—**Itin'erary**, *n.* L. *itinerārium*, use as *n.* of neut. of *itinerārius*, a. f. *iter*. A record of travel; a line of travel; a guide-book for travellers.

I'vory, *n.* O.F. *yvoire*, Norman F. *ivurie*—L. *eboreus*, a. f. *ebur*, *eboris*, ivory. The white elastic substance forming the main part of the tusks of the elephant, &c.

I'vy, *n.* O.E. *ífig*, conn. with O.H.G. *ebahewi* (Ger. *epheu*). A climbing evergreen shrub.

J

Jab'ber, *vi.* App. imitative with freq. form. To talk rapidly and indistinctly.—*vt.* To utter thus.—*n.* Rapid, indistinct talk.

Jac'inth, *n.* O.F. *iacinte*—L. *hyacinthus*. = HYACINTH (the precious stone).

Jack, *n.*[1] A familiar equivalent of *John*. A sailor (also **Jack-tar**); a knave at cards; a machine for turning a spit; a machine for lifting weights; various mechanical appliances; at bowls, the smaller bowl, placed as a mark; in names of animals signifying *male*, as **Jack'ass**, or *small*, as **Jack'daw** = DAW.

Jack, *n.*[2] Prob. an application of prec. Said of things smaller than the normal. A ship's flag smaller than the ensign.

Jack, *n.*[3] F. *jaque* of uncertain orig. A strengthened coat; a vessel for liquor.

Jack'al, *n.* Turkish *chakāl*—Per. *shagāl*. A wild animal of the dog kind.

Jack'anapes, *n.* Orig. *Jack Napes*, poss. a playful name for a tame ape. An ape; a pert impertinent fellow; a pert child.

Jack'-boot, *n.* Sense of *jack* uncertain. A large boot coming above the knee.

Jack'et, *n.* O.F. *jaquet*, *jacquet*, dim. of *jaque*. JACK.[3] A sleeved outer garment.

Jacobe'an, *a.* L.L. *Jacōbaeus*, f. *Jacōbus*, James. Pertaining to the time of James I.—**Jac'obin**, *n.* F., f. Med.L. *Jacōbinus*, a. f. *Jacōbus*. A friar of the order of St. Dominic (from the church in Paris of St. *Jacques* (Jacobus) near which the French members built their first convent); one of a French democratic club established in 1789 in the convent; an extreme radical.—**Jac'obite**, *n.* Suff. *-ite*, denoting an adherent. An adherent of James II after his abdication, or of his son.

Jade, *n.*[1] Orig. unknown. A sorry horse; applied (sometimes playfully) to a woman.—*vt.* To make a jade of (a horse); to fatigue, weary.

Jade, *n.*[2] F. *le jade* for *l'ejade*—Sp. (*piedra de*) *ijada*, lit. 'colic (stone)', f. *ijada*, L. *īle*, the flank. A light-green or bluish mineral.

Jag, *n.* App. imitative. A protruding bristle or point.—*vt.* To make ragged or uneven.

Jag'uar, *n.* Tupi-guarani (Brazilian) *jaguara.* A large carnivorous quadruped.

Jail, **Gaol**, *n.* Old Parisian F. *jaiole, jaile*, Norman F. *gaiole, gaole*—Pop.L. **gaviōla* for **caveola*, dim. of L. *cavea.* CAGE. A place of confinement, a prison.—**Jail'**ER, **Jail'**OR, **Gaol'**ER, *n.* The keeper of a jail.

Jal'ap, *n.* F. *jalap*—Sp. *jalapa*, f. *Jalapa*, *Xalapa*, a city of Mexico, A purgative drug.

Jam, *vt.* App. imitative. CHAMP. To squeeze; to cause to stick and become unworkable; to pack or force together, to thrust; to block.—*vi.* To stick and become unworkable.

Jam, *n.* Perh. f. prec. in sense 'to bruise or crush'. Fruit boiled with sugar.

Jamb, *n.* F. *jambe*, leg, jamb = It. *gamba*, leg. GAMBIT. A side piece of a door, &c.

Jan'gle, *vi.* O.F. *jangler* of uncertain orig. To wrangle; to sound harshly or discordantly. —*vt.* To cause to sound thus.—*n.* Such a sound; contention.

Jan'itor, *n.* L. *jānitor*, f. *jānua*, door. A door-keeper.

Jan'izary, **Jan'issary**, *n.* Turkish *yeñi-tsheri*, f. *yeñi*, new + *tsheri*, soldiery. One of a former bodyguard of the Sultan of Turkey.

Jan'uary, *n.* L. *Jānuārius* (sc. *mensis*, month), the month of the god *Jānus*, conn. with *jānua.* JANITOR. The first month.

Japan', *n.* A very hard varnish, orig. from *Japan.*—*vt.* To cover with japan.

Jape, *n.* Orig. obscure. A joke.—*vi.* To joke.

Jar, *n.*[1] F. *jarre*—Arab. *jarrah*, earthen water-vessel. A vessel of various forms.

Jar, *vi.* Prob. imitative. To make a discordant sound; to grate *on* or *upon* (the feelings, &c.); to vibrate; to be at variance.—*vt.* To cause to sound harshly or to vibrate.—*n.* A grating sound; a shock; variance; a quarrel.

Jar'gon, *n.* O.F. *jargon*, sound of birds, prattle, of uncertain orig. The twittering of birds; meaningless talk; a barbarous language.

Jargonelle', *n.* F. *jargonelle*, as being gritty, dim. of *jargon*, It. *giargone*, a Ceylonese mineral, of obscure orig. A variety of pear.

Jas'mine, *n.* = F. *jasmin*, Sp. *jazmin*, Ger. *jasmin.* Also **Jes'samine** = obs. F. *jas(s)emin, jessemin.* All f. Arab. *yās(a)mīn*—Per. *yāsmīn.* A fragrant flowering shrub.

Jas'per, *n.* O.F. *jaspre*, var. of *jaspe*—L. *iaspis*- G. *iaspis*, of Oriental orig. A precious stone, usually red, yellow, or brown.

Jaun'dice, *n.* F. *jaunice*, lit., 'yellowness', f. *jalne, jaune*, L. *galbus*, yellow. A disease characterized by yellowness of the skin, &c.

Jaunt, *vi.* Orig. obscure. To make a short pleasure journey.—*n.* Such a journey.

Jaunt'y, *a.* Orig. *jantee, janty*, repg. F. *gentil.* GENTLE. Easy and sprightly in manner; lively, brisk.—**Jaunt'i**LY,[2] *adv.*

Jav'elin, *n.* F. *javeline*, perh. of Celtic orig. A light spear thrown with the hand.

Jaw, *n.* Orig. uncertain. One of the bones in which the teeth are set.

Jay, *n.* O.F. *jay* (F. *geai*), of uncertain orig. A chattering bird with beautiful plumage.

Jeal'ous, *a.* O.F. *gelos* (F. *jaloux*)—L.L. *zēlōsus*, f. *zēlus*, G. *zēlos*, emulation, jealousy. ZEAL. Suspiciously vigilant; distrustful of the faithfulness of wife, husband, &c.; envious. —**Jeal'ous**LY,[2] *adv.*—**Jeal'ous**Y,[1] *n.*

Jeer, *vi.* Orig. unknown. To scoff *at* derisively. —*vt.* To deride.—*n.* A scoff or flout.

Jeho'vah, *n.* Heb. *Yahōvāh*, properly *Yahweh.* God, the Almighty.

Jejune', *a.* L. *jējūnus*, fasting, barren. DINE. Unsatisfying to the mind, uninteresting, dry.

Jel'ly, *n.* F. *gelée*, frost, jelly—L. *gelāta*, fem. pa.pple. of *gelāre*, to freeze (used as *n.* in Romanic) f. *gelu*, frost. COLD. GELATIN. GELID. A soft stiff semi-transparent article of food; anything of the consistence of this.—**Jel'ly-fish**, *n.* A gelatinous marine animal.

Jem'my, *n.* Pet-form of *James.* A crowbar used by burglars.

Jen'ny, *n.* Pet-form of *Janet* or *Jane.* A machine for spinning.

Jeop'ardy, *n.* M.E. *iuparti*, &c.—O.F. *iu parti*, lit., 'divided game', hence, 'uncertain chance', in Med.L. *jocus partītus*, f. *jocus*, JOKE + pa.pple. of *partīre* (DEPART). Peril, danger.—**Jeop'ard**, *vt.* Back-formation f. the *n.* Also **Jeop'ard**IZE. To put in jeopardy.

Jeremi'ad, *n.* F. *jérémiade*, f. *Jérémie*, Jeremiah, referring to the 'Lamentations' in the O.Testament. A doleful complaint.

Jerk, *n.* App. imitative. A quick suddenly arrested movement.—*v.*[1]*t.* To throw, &c., with a jerk.—*vi.* To give a jerk.—**Jerk'**Y,[2] *a.*

Jerk, *v.*[2]*t.* Corr. of American Sp. *charquear*, f. *charque*, Peruvian *ccharqui*, dried unsalted flesh in strips. To cure (meat) by drying it in the sun in long thin slices.

Jer'kin, *n.* Orig. unknown. A close-fitting jacket.

Jer'ry-build'er, *n.* App. in some way f. *Jerry*, contraction of *Jeremiah.* A speculative builder of unsubstantial houses.

Jer'sey, *n.* From the knitting industry of *Jersey.* A close-fitting knitted jacket.

Jest, *n.* Var. of GEST. A taunt; a piece of banter; a joke; sport, fun; an object of derision.—*vi.* To scoff, jeer; to trifle; to joke.—**Jest'**ER, *n.* A professional buffoon or fool.

Jes'uit, *n.* Mod.L. *Jēsuīta*, f. *Jēsus*, Jesus. One of the Society of Jesus, founded by Ignatius Loyola in 1533; a dissembling person. —**Jesuit'**ICAL, *a.*—**Jes'uit**ISM, *n.*

Jet, *n.*[1] O.F. *jaiet, jayet* (F. *jai*)—L. *gagātēs*—G. *gagatēs*, f. *Gagai*, a town in Lycia. A hard black mineral taking a brilliant polish.

Jet, *vt.* and *i.* F. *jeter*, to throw—L. *jactāre*, freq. of *jacĕre, jactum*, to throw. ABJECT. JETTISON. JETTY. JUT. To emit, to come forth, in a jet.—*n.*[2] A stream of liquid, gas, &c., from a small orifice; a nozzle for emission.

Jet'sam, *n.* Orig. *jetson*, shortened f. *jetteson* = JETTISON. Goods thrown overboard to lighten a ship (and afterwards washed ashore).

Jet'tison, *n.* A.F. *getteson*, O.F. *getaison*—L. *jactātio, jactātiōnis*, n. of action f. *jactāre.* JET, *v.* A throwing of goods overboard to lighten a ship.—*vt.* To throw overboard thus.

Jet'ty, *n.* O.F. *getee, jetee*, a throwing, a jetty, use as *n.* of fem. pa.pple. of *jeter.* JET, *v.* A structure projecting into the sea, a river, &c.

Jew'el, *n.* A.F. *juel, jeual* = O.F. *joel* (F. *joyau*), of disputed orig. A personal ornament containing a precious stone; a precious stone, a gem.—*vt.* To furnish with jewels.—**Jew'ell**ER, *n.* A dealer in jewels.—**Jew'ell**ERY, **Jew'el**RY, *nn.* Jewels collectively.

Jib, *n.*[1] Orig. uncertain. The foremost sail of a ship, triangular in shape.

Jib, *n.*[2] App. abb. of GIBBET. The arm of a crane.
Jib, *v.*[1]*t.* Orig. obscure. To pull (a sail) from one side of a vessel to the other.—*vi.* Of a sail, to shift or swing round.
Jib, *v.*[2]*i.* Orig. uncertain. Of a horse, &c., to stop and refuse to go on, to move restively.
Jig, *n.* Orig. uncertain. A lively dance; the music; various mechanical contrivances.—*vi.* To dance a jig; to make jerky motions.
Jilt, *vt.* Orig. unknown. To cast off (a lover) capriciously.—*n.* One who does this.
Jin'gle, *vi.* Imitative. To give forth mingled ringing sounds.—*vt.* To cause to do this. —*n.* A jingling sound.
Jin'go. App. orig. conjuror's gibberish. *By jingo*, a slight oath.—*n.* From this expression in the refrain of an effusively patriotic music-hall song (1878). A bellicose patriot.
Job, *n.* Orig. obscure. A piece of work; a public trust turned to personal or party advantage.—*v.*[1]*i.* To do odd pieces of work; to make a job of a trust; to deal in stocks.—*vt.* To hire or let out on hire (a horse, &c.).—**Job'**BER, *n.*—**Job'**BERY, *n.*—**Job'master**, *n.* One who jobs horses, &c.
Job, *v.*[2]*t.* App. imitative. To stab, prod; to thrust (something sharp) into something.
Jock'ey, *n.* Dim. of *Jock*, Scotch for JACK.[1] A professional rider in races.—*vt.* To trick.
Jocose', *a.* L. *jocōsus*, f. *jocus*, JOKE. Full of jokes; said or done in joke.—**Jocose'**LY,[2] *adv.*—**Jocose'**NESS, *n.*—**Jocos'**ITY, *n.*
Joc'ular, *a.* L. *joculāris*, f. *joculus*, dim. of *jocus*, JOKE. JUGGLE. Jocose.—**Joc'ular**LY,[2] *adv.*—**Jocular'**ITY, *n.*
Joc'und, *a.* O.F. *jocond*, *jocund*—L.L. *jōcundus*, modification (after *jocus*, JOKE) of L. *jūcundus*, pleasant, f. *juvāre*, to help, to please. ADJUTANT. Mirthful, merry.—**Joc'und**LY,[2] *adv.*—**Jocun'**DITY, *n.*
Jog, *vt.* App. imitative. To move or push with a jerk.—*vi.* To move unsteadily; to go with a jolting pace.—*n.* A jogging.—**Jog'gle**, *vt.* and *i.* App. with freq. suff. *-le.* To jog continuously or repeatedly.—*n.* A joggling.
Join, *vt.* O.F. *joign-*, stem of *joindre*—L. *jungĕre*, *junctum*. Root *yug-*. YOKE. JUNCTION. To put together so as to become one; to connect by something intervening; to combine, unite; to unite or attach oneself to; to become one with; to adjoin.—*vi.* To become one; to combine; to be in contact.—*n.* A joining or being joined; a place of joining.—**Join'er**, *n.* A.F. *joignour*, O.F. *joigneor.* A worker in wood who does lighter work than a carpenter.—**Joint**, *n.* O.F. *joint*, use as *n.* of pa.pple. of *joindre.* The arrangement by which two bones or two pieces of a structure or mechanism are fitted together; a portion of a carcass consisting of a bone or bones with the meat thereon.—**Joint**, *a.* From the F. pa.pple. Joined; united or sharing; held, done, &c., by two or more together.—**Joint**, *vt.* From the *n.* To connect by a joint; to divide at the joints.—**Joint'**LY,[2] *adv.*—**Joint'-stock**, *a.* Having a stock or capital owned by a number jointly.—**Join'ture**, *n.* F. *jointure*—L. *junctūra*, a joint, f. *jungĕre.* Property settled on a wife for her use on the husband's death (orig., the holding of property by husband and wife jointly as a provision for the wife on survivance).
Joist, *n.* O.F. *giste*, a beam of a bridge, f. *gesir.* GIST. A large beam of a floor, &c.
Joke, *n.* App. f. L. *jocus*, joke, pastime. JEOPARDY. JOCOSE. JOCULAR. Something intended to cause, something causing, laughter; something not earnest or serious.—*vi.* To make jokes.—*vt.* To banter.—**Jok'**ER, *n.*
Jol'ly, *a.* O.F. *jolif*, *joli*, gay, lively, festive, handsome, &c., of uncertain orig. Joyous; festive; delightful.—**Jolli**FICA'TION, *n.* A making merry, merriment.—**Jol'l**ITY, *n.*
Jol'ly-boat, *n.* Orig. uncertain. A ship's boat with a bluff bow and wide stern.
Jolt, *vt.* Orig. obscure. To shake with a jolt.—*vi.* To move with jerks.—*n.* An abrupt shock or jerk throwing up to fall again.
Jon'quil, *n.* = Sp. *junquillo*, dim. of *junco*, L. *juncus*, rush. JUNKET. The rush-leaved daffodil.
Jo'rum, *n.* Orig. uncertain. A large drinking-bowl.
Jos'tle, **Jus'tle**, *vi.* JUST, *v.* + freq. suff. *-le.* To knock *against*, contend *with*.—*vt.* To knock or push against; to shove.
Jot, *n.* L. *iōta* (read as *jōta*)—G. *iōta.* IOTA. A very small quantity.—*vt.* App. f. the *n.*, and orig. in sense 'to make the smallest mark with a pen, &c.'. To write *down* briefly.
Jour'nal, *n.* O.F. *journal*, daily, as *n.*, a day, a day's work—L.L. *diurnālis.* DIURNAL. A daily record; a newspaper or periodical publication; the part of a shaft resting on the supports.—**Jour'nal**ISM, *n.* Editing or writing in a journal; the journals collectively.—**Jour'nal**IST, *n.*—**Journalis'**TIC, *a.*
Jour'ney, *n.* O.F. *jornee*, *journee*, day, day's travel, travel—Pop.L. *diurnāta*, orig. fem. pa.pple. of L.L. *diurnāre*, to SOJOURN. Distance travelled; a course of going or travelling, an expedition.—*vi.* To travel.
Jour'neyman, *n.* From prec. in obs. sense 'a day's labour'. One who has learned a trade and works at it for days' wages.
Jo'vial, *a.* F. *jovial*—It. *gioviale*, born under (the planet) Jupiter (regarded as the source of joy)—L. *joviālis*, of Jupiter, f. *Jovis*, used as genit. of *Jūpiter.* Heartily mirthful, jolly.—**Jo'vial**LY,[2] *adv.*—**Jovial'**ITY, *n.*
Jowl, **Jole**, *n.* M.E. *chavel*, *chawl*—O.E. *ceafl*, jaw, corresp. to Mod. Flemish *kavel*, Du. *kevel*, gum. The cheek, a cheek.
Joy, *n.* O.F. *joie*, *joye*—Pop.L. **gaudia*, fem. for L. *gaudia*, pl. of *gaudium*, joy, f. *gaudēre.* GAUD. Exultation of spirit, delight; an instance or kind of this; a source of joy.—*vi.* O.F. *joir.* To feel or show joy; to delight *in.* —*vt.* To fill with joy.—**Joy'**FUL, *a.*—**Joy'ful**LY,[2] *adv.*—**Joy'**LESS, *a.*—**Joy'**OUS, *a.*
Ju'bilate, *vi.* L. *jūbilāre*, *jūbilātum*, to shout for joy, f. *jūbilum*, a shout. To rejoice, exult.—**Ju'bil**ANT, *a.*—**Jubil**A'TION, *n.*
Ju'bilee, *n.* F. *jubilé*—L.L. *jūbilaeus*, orig. an *a.* after G. *iōbēlaios*, a. f. *iōbēlos*, Heb. *yōbēl*, jubilee, app. orig. ram, hence, ram's horn, with which the jubilee was proclaimed. (The L.L. word assimilated to *jūbilum.* (See prec.)) Among the Jews, a year of emancipation kept every fifty years; a fiftieth anniversary; a season of general rejoicing; general rejoicing.
Judge, *n.* O.F. *juge*—L. *jūdex*, *jūdicis*, f. *jūs*, law + *-dicus*, saying, f. *dicĕre*, to say. JURYDICTION. An officer appointed to administer the law; one who decides, an arbiter, umpire; one qualified to pronounce an opinion.—*vt.* O.F. *jugier*—L. *jūdicāre.* To sit in judgement upon; to decide, determine; to form or pronounce an opinion upon; to infer, consider, suppose.—*vi.* To act as judge; to arbitrate: to form an opinion.—**Judge'**MENT, **Judg'**MENT, *n.* The action of trying a cause; a judicial decision; the forming or pronouncing

of an opinion; censure; the faculty of judging; good judgement, discernment.
Jud'icature, *n.* Med.L. *jūdicātūra*, f. *jūdicāre*. (See prec.) Administration of justice; a legal tribunal, such tribunals collectively.
Judic'ial, *a.* L. *jūdiciālis*, f. *jūdicium*, judgement, f. *jūdex*, JUDGE. PREJUDICE. Pertaining to the administration of justice; proper to a court of law; resulting from a legal judgement; having the function of judging.—**Judic'ial**LY,[2] *adv.*—**Judic'iary**, *a.* L. *jūdiciārius*, f. *jūdicium*. Pertaining to courts of law.—*n.* Legal tribunals collectively.—**Judic'ious**, *a.* F. *judicieux*, f. *jūdicium*. Having or showing good judgement, discreet.—**Judic'ious**LY,[2] *adv.*
Jug, *n.* Poss. a transferred use of *Jug*, pet-form of *Joan* or *Joanna*. A deep vessel for liquids; a jug and its contents, the contents.—*vt.* To cook (esp. a hare) in a jug or jar.
Jug'gle, *vi.* O.F. *jogler*, *jugler*—L.L. *joculāre* for L. *joculāri*, to jest, f. *joculus*. JOCULAR. To play conjuring tricks; to practise deceit *with*.—*vt.* To trick or cheat *out of*.—*n.* A juggling.—**Jug'gl**ER, *n.*—**Jug'gl**ERY, *n.*
Jug'ular, *a.* Med.L. *jugulāris*, f. L. *jugulum*, collar-bone, neck. Of or in the neck or throat.
Juice, *n.* F. *jus*—L. *jūs*, broth, soup. VERJUICE. The liquid part of vegetables, fruits, or animal bodies.—**Juic'**Y,[2] *a.*
Ju'jube, *n.* F. *jujube*, Med.L. *jujuba*, altered f. G. *zizuphon*, the jujube tree of Per. orig. The fruit of a shrub; the shrub; a lozenge flavoured with, or in imitation of, the fruit.
Ju'lep, *n.* F. *julep*—Arab. *julāb*—Per. *gul-āb*, rose-water, f. *gul*, rose + *āb*, water. A sweet drink of various kinds.
July', *n.* A.F. *julie*—L. *Jūlius*, named after C. *Julius* Caesar. The seventh month.
Jum'ble, *vi.* Prob. imitative. To move about in disorder.—*vt.* To mingle *together*, mix *up*, in confusion.—*n.* A confused mixture.
Jump, *vi.* App. imitative. To throw oneself upward, forward, &c.—*vt.* To pass by jumping; to seize upon.—*n.* A jumping.
Junc'tion, *n.* L. *junctio*, *junctiōnis*, n. of action f. *jungĕre*, to JOIN. The action or place of joining; the fact of being joined.—**Junc'**TURE, *n.* Junction, a junction; a particular time or state of affairs.
June, *n.* F. *juin*—L. *Jūnius*. The sixth month.
Jun'gle, *n.* Hindī *jangal*, desert. Orig., waste ground. Land covered with underwood, long grass, &c.; a tract of such land.
Ju'nior, *a.* L. *jūnior*, comp. of *juvenis*, young. JUVENILE. The younger; of lower standing or position.—*n.* A junior person.—**Junior'**ITY, *n.*
Ju'niper, *n.* L. *jūniperus*. GENEVA. A shrub yielding berries used to flavour gin.
Junk, *n.*[1] Orig. obscure. Pieces of old rope; salt meat used on long voyages.
Junk, *n.*[2] App. f. Javanese *djong*, ship. The native sailing vessel of the Chinese seas.
Junk'et, *n.* App. f. O.N.F. **jonket* or *jonquette*, rush-basket, f. *jonc*, L. *juncus*, rush. JONQUIL. Formerly, a cream-cheese (orig. made in a rush-basket). Curds sweetened and flavoured; a feast.—*vi.* To feast.
Jun'ta, *n.* Sp. *junta*, It. *giunta*—L. *juncta*, fem. pa.pple. (used as *n.* in Romanic) of *jungĕre*, to JOIN. In Spain and Italy, a deliberative or administrative council.—Erroneously **Jun'to**. A self-elected council or committee.
Ju'piter, *n.* L. *Jūpiter*. The supreme deity of the Romans; the largest of the planets.
Jurid'ical, *a.* L. *jūridicus* (f. *jūs*, *jūris*, law + *-dicus*) + -AL. JUDGE. Relating to the administration of law, legal.
Jurisconsult', *n.* L. *jūrisconsultus*, f. *jūs*, *jūris*, law + *consultus*, well considered, skilful, ppl.a. f. *consulĕre*, to CONSULT. JURY. One skilled in law.—**Jurisdic'tion**, *n.* O.F. *jurisdiction*—L. *jūrisdictio*, *jūrisdictiōnis*, f. *jūs* + *dictio*. DICTION. Administration of justice; rule, control; extent or territory of this.—**Jurispru'dence**, *n.* L. *jūrisprūdentia*, f. *jūs* + *prūdentia*, knowledge, skill, f. *prūdens*. PRUDENT. Skill in law; the science, a system, of law.—**Ju'rist**, *n.* F. *juriste*—Med.L. *jūrista*, f. *jūs*. One skilled in law.
Ju'ry, *n.* A.F. *juree* = O.F. *jurée*, oath, inquest—Med.L. *jūrāta*, n. f. fem. pa.pple. of L. *jūrāre*, to swear, f. *jūs*, *jūris*, right, law. CONJURE. INJURY. JUDGE. JURISCONSULT. JUST, *a.* A body of men sworn to render a true answer on a question submitted to them; a body selected to award prizes; *grand jury*, a jury which inquires into indictments; *petty jury*, a jury which tries a final issue of fact.—**Ju'ror**, *n.* A.F. *jurour* = O.F. *jureor*—L. *jūrātor*, agent-n. f. *jūrāre*. One of a jury (also **Ju'ryman**); one who takes an oath.
Ju'ry-mast, *n.* Orig. unknown. A temporary mast put up instead of a broken one.
Just, Joust, *vi.* O.F. *juster*, *jouster*—Late Pop.L. *juxtāre*, to approach, meet, f. L. *juxtā*, near together. JOSTLE. To engage in a just.—*n.* A combat with lances between two knights on horseback.
Just, *a.* F. *juste*—L. *justus*, f. *jūs*. JURY. Righteous; upright, equitable; consonant with equity, fair; deserved; well-founded; proper, correct; true.—*adv.* Exactly, precisely; precisely now or then; no more than, barely.—**Just'**LY,[2] *adv.*—**Just'**NESS, *n.*—**Jus'tice**, *n.* O.F. *justice*—L. *justitia*, f. *justus*. The quality of being just, just conduct; conformity to right or truth; requital of desert; the administration of law; a judicial officer; *justice of the peace*, an inferior magistrate in counties and towns charged with the preservation of the peace and other duties.—**Justic'iary**, *n.* Med.L. *justiciārius*, judge, f. *justitia*. An administrator of justice.—*a.* Of the administration of justice.—**Jus'ti**FY, *vt.* To show to be in the right or innocent; to exculpate; to adduce grounds for.—**Justifi'**ABLE, *a.*—**Justi**FICA'TION, *n.*—**Jus'tificat**ORY, *a.*
Jut, *vi.* Var. of JET, *v.* To project.—*n.* A jutting out; something that juts out.
Jute, *n.* Bengāli *jhōto*, *jhuto*. A fibre imported from Bengal; the plant furnishing it.
Ju'venile, *a.* L. *juvenīlis*, f. *juvenis*, YOUNG. JUNIOR. Young; characteristic of, suited to, the young.—*n.* A young person.—**Juvenil'**ITY, *n.*—**Juvenes'cent**, *a.* L. *juvenescens*, *juvenescentis*, pres.pple. of *juvenescĕre*, to reach the age of youth, f. *juvenis*. Becoming young.—**Juvenes'**CENCE, *n.*
Juxtapose', *vt.* F. *juxtaposer*, f. L. *juxtā*, near + F. *poser*. POSE.[1] To place side by side or near.—**Juxtaposi'**TION, *n.*

K

Kale, *n.* Northern form of COLE. Cabbage.
Kalei'doscope, *n.* G. *kalos*, beautiful + *eidos*, form + *skope-ein*, to behold. An optical instrument exhibiting a succession of coloured figures.—**Kaleidoscop'**IC, *a.*

Kangaroo', *n.* Said to have been the name in an Australian language. An Australian mammal with abnormally developed hind-legs.
Keel, *n.* Prob. f. O.N. *kjölr*. The lowest longitudinal timber (or line of iron plates) of a ship.—*vt.* To turn up the keel of, to upset.—**Ke(e)l'son**, *n.* Orig. of second element unknown. = Du. *kolzwijn*, Ger. *kielschwein*. A line of timber or plates above the keel.
Keel'haul, *vt.* Du. *kielhalen*, f. *kiel*, keel, orig. ship, boat, and = O.E. *céol*, O.N. *kjóll* (not conn. with O.N. *kjōlr* (see prec.)) + *halen* = Ger. *holen*. HALE, *v.* To haul (a person) under the keel of a ship by way of punishment.
Keen, *a.* O.E. *céne*. Common Teut. Formerly, wise, brave, fierce. Sharp; vivid; causing acute pain; acute, intense; eager; highly sensitive; sharp-witted.—**Keen**'LY,[2] *adv.*
Keep, *vt.* O.E. *cépan*, of unknown orig. Orig. sense perh. 'to lay hold' with the hands or the mind. To stand to (a promise, &c.); to celebrate, solemnize; to take care of; to maintain, support; to employ; to retain; to cause to continue (in some state, &c.); to restrain; to reserve; to continue to have or hold; to carry on, manage.—*vi.* To remain, stay; to continue, go on; to remain in good condition.—*n.* The central tower of a castle; food, maintenance.—**Keep**'ER, *n.*—**Keep'ing**, *vbl.n.* In senses from the *v.*; agreement, harmony.—**Keep'sake**, *n.* Something kept for the sake of the giver.
Keg, *n.* Earlier *Cag* = O.N. *kaggi*. A small cask.
Kelp, *n.* Orig. unknown. Large seaweeds which are burnt for their ashes; the ashes.
Ken, *n.* From *Ken* (now archaic or Scottish), to know—O.E. *cennan*, causal form of *cunnan*. CAN, *v.* Range of vision; perception.
Ken'nel, *n.*[1] App. f. O.N.F. **kenil* = F. *chenil* —Pop.L. *canīle*, f. L. *canis*, dog. CANINE. A shelter for a dog.
Ken'nel, *n.*[2] Obs. *Cannel* = CHANNEL. A street-gutter.
Kerb, Kerb'-stone. See CURB.
Ker'chief, *n.* O.F. *cuevrechief*, f. *cuvrir*, *covrir*, to COVER + *chief*, *chef*, head. CHIEF. A cloth for covering the head or neck.
Ker'mes, *n.* = F. *kermès*, Sp. *carmes*—Arab. *qirmiz*. CRIMSON. An insect used for dyeing found on oak-trees in S. Europe and N. Africa.
Ker'nel, *n.* O.E. *cyrnel*, dim. of *corn*, seed, grain. CORN.[1] Formerly, a seed or pip. The soft part of a nut or stone-fruit.
Ker'osene, *n.* G. *kēros*, wax + chemical suff. *-ene*. A kind of lamp-oil.
Ker'sey, *n.* Poss. f. *Kersey* in Suffolk. A kind of coarse woollen cloth, usually ribbed.
Ker'seymere, *n.* Corr. of *Cassimere* = CASHMERE, by confusion with prec. A twilled cloth of fine wool.
Ketch, *n.* Later form of obs. *Catch*, perh. f. CATCH, *n.* in obs. sense 'chase, pursuit'. A two-masted coasting vessel.
Ketch'up, *n.* App. f. Chinese *kôe-chiap* or *kê-tsiap*, brine of pickled fish. A sauce made from the juice of mushrooms, &c.
Ket'tle, *n.* O.E. *cetel*. Common Teut. Prob. f. L. *catillus*, dim. of *catinus*, dish, pot. A metal vessel for boiling water.—**Ket'tle-drum**, *n.* A drum made of a brass or copper vessel covered with parchment.
Key, *n.* O.E. *cǽg* = Old Fris. *kei*, *kay*. An instrument for moving the bolt of a lock; a system of definitely related musical notes; each of the levers by which the organ, &c., are played.—**Key'board**, *n.* The set of such levers.—**Key'stone**, *n.* The top stone of an arch, which locks the whole together.
Kha'ki, *a.* Urdū (Per.) *khākī*, dusty, f. *khāk*, dust. Of a dull brownish yellow.—*n.* A fabric of the colour, used for military uniforms.
Kick, *vi.* M.E. *kike*, *kyke*, of unknown orig. To strike out with the foot; to be recalcitrant; of firearms, to recoil.—*vt.* To strike with the foot.—*n.* A blow with the foot; recoil.
Kid, *n.* Perh. f. O.N. *kith*, conn. with Ger. *kitze*. A young goat; leather of kid-skin.
Kid'nap, *vt.* From prec. in obs. sense 'an indentured servant in the American colonies' + cant *nap*, to seize. Cf. Sw. *nappa*, Da. *nappe*. Orig., to carry off as a 'kid'. To steal (a child), to abduct (a person).—**Kid'napp**ER, *n.*
Kid'ney, *n.* Orig. obscure. One of the pair of organs which secrete the urine; kind, sort.
Kill, *vt.* Orig. obscure. To deprive of life.
Kiln, *n.* O.E. *cylene*, &c.—L. *culīna*, kitchen. CULINARY. A furnace for burning, drying, &c.
Kilt, *vt.* App. Scand. Cf. Da. *kilte*, to tuck up, O.N. *kilting*, skirt. To tuck up (the skirts). —*n.* A short skirt worn by Highlanders.
Kin, *n.* O.E. *cyn(n)*. Common Teut. O.Teut. root *kin-*, *kan-*, *kun-*. Cogn. with GENUS. KING. A family or clan; one's relatives collectively; *of kin*, related by blood.—**Kind**, *n.* O.E. *gecynd*, nature, with pref. *ge-* f. *kun-*. Natural disposition; generic nature; a genus, a sort or variety; *in kind*, in goods, not in money.—**Kind**, *a.* O.E. *gecynde*, f. *gecynd*. Having a good or sympathetic nature; showing, arising from, a kind disposition.—**Kind**'LY,[1] *a.* Kind; genial; pleasant.—**Kind'li**NESS, *n.*—**Kind**'LY,[2] *adv.*—**Kind'**NESS, *n.*—**Kin'dred**, *n.* With excrescent *d* f. *kin* + *-red* as in HATRED. The being of kin; one's relatives collectively.—*a.* Of kin; of like nature, cognate.—**Kin**'SHIP, *n.*—**Kins'man**, *n.* Early M.E., f. *kinnes*, genit. of *kin* + MAN. A man of one's own kin.
Kin'dergarten, *n.* Ger., lit., 'children's garden'. A school in which young children are taught by means of games, toys, &c.
Kin'dle, *vt.* App. f. O.N. *kynda*, with freq. suff. *-le*. To set on fire.—*vi.* To catch fire.
Kinemat'ic, *a.* G. *kinēma*, *kinēmatos*, a motion (f. *kine-ein*, to move) + -IC. Relating to pure motion.—In *pl.* as *n.*, the science of pure motion.—**Kine'matograph, Cinemat'ograph**, *n.* F. *cinématographe*, f. *kinēma* + *-graphe*, G. *-graphia*, writing, drawing, f. *graphein*. GRAPHIC. A contrivance for projecting pictures on a screen in rapid succession so as to give the effect of motion.
Kinet'ic, *a.* G. *kinētikos*, of or for putting in motion, f. *kine-ein*. (See prec.) Of, relating to, due to, motion.—In *pl.* as *n.*, the branch of dynamics which deals with the relations between motions and forces.
King, *n.* O.E. *cyning*. Common Teut. App. in some way conn. with *cyn(n)*, KIN. Perh. 'scion of a (noble) race'. The ruler of an independent state; the chief piece in chess; a card in each suit bearing the representation of a king.—**King**'DOM, *n.* A state ruled by a king; his territory; a realm, region, sphere.—**King'fisher**, *n.* A small bird with a long beak and brilliant plumage feeding on fish.—**King**'LY,[1] *a.*—**King**'SHIP, *n.*
Kink, *n.* Prob. f. Du. *kink*, twist = Da., Sw. *kink*. A short twist in a rope, &c.—*vi.* To form a kink.—*vt.* To cause to kink.
Kip'per, *n.* Orig. uncertain. A male salmon at spawning time; a kippered fish, esp. a

kippered herring (in this sense f. the *v.*).—*vt.* App. f. the *n.* To cure by rubbing with salt, pepper, &c., and drying.

Kir'tle, *n.* O.E. *cyrtel* = O.N. *kyrtill*, tunic, app. dim. forms and f. L. *curtus*, short. CURT. A man's tunic or coat; a woman's gown.

Kiss, *n.* O.E. *coss* (the mod. *i* due to the *v.*) = O.H.G. *chus* (Ger. *kuss*), O.N. *koss*. A touch or pressure with the lips.—*vt.* O.E. *cyssan*. To give a kiss to.—*vi.* To exchange kisses.

Kit, *n.* App. f. M.Du. *kitte*, hooped wooden vessel, of uncertain orig. A circular hooped wooden vessel; an outfit, personal effects.

Kit'chen, *n.* O.E. *cycene* = O.H.G. *chuhhīna* (Ger. *küche*)—Pop.L. *cucīna*, *cocīna*, varr. of L. *coquīna*, f. *coquĕre*, to COOK. The part of a house in which food is cooked.

Kite, *n.* O.E. *cýta*, of unknown orig. A bird of prey; a light frame flown in a strong wind.

Kith, *n.* O.E. *cýth*, native land, relationship, f. *cúth*, known. UNCOUTH. *Kith and kin*, one's friends and relatives.

Kit'ten, *n.* A.F. **kitoun*=O.F. *chitoun*, var. of *chaton*, f. *chat*, L. *catus*, CAT. A young cat.—*vi.* To bring forth kittens.

Kleptoma'nia, *n.* G. *kleptein*, to steal + MANIA. An irresistible tendency to steal.

Knack, *n.* Orig. obscure. A trick; a faculty of doing something cleverly and successfully.

Knack'er, *n.* Orig. unknown. One who buys up worn-out horses or old houses, ships, &c.

Knap'sack, *n.* L.G. *knapsack*. *Knap-* gen. taken as L.G. *knappen*, to nibble. A bag or case for necessaries carried on the shoulders.

Knave, *n.* O.E. *cnafa*, boy = O.H.G. *knabo* (Ger. *knabe*). A servant-boy, a male servant; a base and crafty rogue; a card in each suit bearing the representation of a soldier or servant.—**Knav'**ERY, *n.*—**Knav'**ISH, *a.*

Knead, *vt.* O.E. *cnedan*=O.S. *knedan*, O.H.G. *chnetan* (Ger. *kneten*). To work up into dough; to operate on (muscles, &c.) as if kneading.

Knee, *n.* O.E. *cnéow*, *cnéo*. Common Teut. Cogn. with Skr. *jānu*, G. *gonu*, L. *genu*. The joint in the middle of the leg.—**Knee-breech'es**, *n.pl.* Breeches reaching to the knee.—**Knee'-cap**, *n.* A protective covering for the knee; the convex bone in front of the knee, called also the **Knee'-pan**.

Kneel, *vi.* Early M.E. *cneolen*—O.E. *cnéowlian*, f. *cnéow*, KNEE. To remain supported on the bended knees or on one of them.

Knell, *vi.* O.E. *cnyllan*, to knock, beat noisily. Cf. M.H.G. *knüllen*, to beat. Of a bell, to ring for a death.—*n.* O.E. *cnyll*. The sound of a bell rung thus.

Knick'erbocker, *n.* The pretended author of W. Irving's *History of New York*. In *pl.*, knee-breeches fitting close to the knee (app. as resembling the breeches of Dutchmen in Cruikshank's illustrations to the book).

Knick'-knack, Nick'-nack, *n.* Reduplication of KNACK in obs. sense 'toy, trinket'. A trinket, a pleasing trifle.

Knife, *n.*; *pl.* **Knives**. Late O.E. *cníf* = M.L.G. *kníf*, Ger. *kneif*, O.N. *knífr*. A cutting blade fixed in a handle.

Knight, *n.* O.E. *cniht*, youth, servant. Common W. Germanic. A military follower; one of an honourable military rank; one of a non-hereditary rank giving the right to prefix *Sir* to one's name.—*vt.* To create (one) a knight.—**Knight'**HOOD, *n.*—**Knight'**LY,[1] *a.*

Knit, *vt.* O.E. *cnyttan*, to knot, f. *cnotta*, a KNOT. To form (a fabric, &c.) by putting together a series of loops of yarn, &c.; to contract in folds or wrinkles; to make compact.—*vi.* To become compact or closely united.

Knob, *n.* = M.L.G. *knobbe*, knot, knob, &c., Flemish *knobbe(n)*, lump (of bread, &c.). A small rounded lump, esp. at the end or on the surface of anything.—**Knob'**BY,[2] *a.*

Knock, *vi.* and *t.* Late O.E. *cnocian*. Cf. O.N. *knoka*. Prob. imitative. To strike, hit.—*n.* A sounding blow; a stroke.—**Knock'**ER, *n.* A metal appliance for knocking on a door.—**Knock'-kneed**, *a.* Having knees that knock together in walking.

Knoll, *n.*[1] O.E. *cnoll*, hill-top, hillock, cogn. with Du. *knolle*, *knol*, ball, turnip, Ger. *knollen*, bulb. A small rounded hill.

Knoll, *vt.* From same root as KNELL. To ring a knell for; to summon by bell.—*n.*[2] The sound of a large bell.

Knot, *n.* O.E. *cnotta* = Du. *knot*, Ger. *knoten*. KNIT. A twisting together of cords, &c., for fastening; a bow or cockade; a measure of the rate of motion of a ship (so called from the pieces of knotted string attached as marks to the log-line); a nautical mile; a difficult point; a lump; a thickened part; a small group.—*vt.* To tie in, secure with, a knot.—**Knot'**TY,[2] *a.* Full of knots; intricate, puzzling.

Knout, *n.* Russian *knut*. A kind of whip formerly used in Russia as an instrument of punishment.—*vt.* To flog with the knout.

Know, *vt.* O.E. *(ge)cnáwan*. Common Teut. and Aryan. Cogn. with O.E. *cunnan* (CAN, *v.*), Skr. *jnā-*, G. *gignōskein*, *gnōnai*, L. *(g)noscĕre*. COGNITION. DIAGNOSIS. IGNORE. To perceive and identify; to recognize, distinguish; to be acquainted with; to have experience of; to be aware or informed of; to be conversant with; to comprehend, understand.—*vi.* To have knowledge or understanding.—**Know'**ABLE, *a.*—**Know'ing**, *ppl.a.* That knows; well-informed; shrewd, cunning.—**Know'ing**LY,[2] *adv.* Consciously, intentionally.—**Know'ledge**, *n.* M.E. *knaulage*, *knowleche*. (The second element obscure.) The fact of knowing; acquaintance; perception, apprehension; erudition; the sum of what is known.

Knuck'le, *n.* M.E. *knokel* = M.Du. *knōkel*, M.H.G. *knuchel* (Ger. *knöchel*), app. dim. of a word for 'bone' as seen in M.H.G. *knoche* (Ger. *knochen*). A bone at a finger-joint, esp. at the root of a finger.—*vi.* To put one's knuckles on the ground in playing at marbles; fig., *to knuckle down* or *under*, to give in, submit.—*vt.* To strike with the knuckles.

Knur(r), *n.* =M.H.G. *knorre* (Ger. *knorren*). A knot on a tree; a hard concretion.

Knurl, *n.* App. f. prec. A knot or knob; a small ridge.—*vt.* To make knurls on.

Koran', *n.* Arab. *qurān*, *qorān*, f. *qara-a*, he read. The Mohammedan sacred book.

Kotow', *n.* Chinese *k'o-t'ou*, f. *k'o*, knock + *t'ou*, head. A Chinese obeisance effected by touching the ground with the forehead.—*vi.* To perform the kotow.

L

La'bel, *n.* O.F. *label*, a label (in heraldry), a shred, of obscure orig. In *heraldry*, a band distinguishing an eldest son; a strip carrying the seal of a document; a slip of paper, &c., attached to an object and bearing its name, destination, &c.—*vt.* To attach a label to.

La'bial, *a.* Med.L. *labiālis*, f. L. *labium*.

LIP. Of the lips; pronounced chiefly by the lips.—*n.* A labial sound.

La'bour, *n.* O.F. *labor, labour*—L. *labor.* Painful or compulsory exertion of the body or mind; an instance of this; industrial labourers collectively; the pains of childbirth.—*vt.* F. *labourer*—L. *labōrāre.* To spend labour upon; to elaborate.—*vi.* To strive; to be troubled or distressed; of a ship, to be tossed heavily.—**Lab'oratory**, *n.* Med.L. *labōrātōrium.* A place set apart for scientific, esp. for chemical, investigations.—**Labo'r**IOUS, *a.*—**Labo'ri-ous**LY,[2] *adv.*—**La'bour**ER, *n.*

Labur'num, *n.* L. A small tree bearing a profusion of bright yellow flowers.

Lab'yrinth, *n.* L. *labyrinthus*—G. *laburinthos*, prob. of foreign orig. A structure containing many passages intricately arranged.—**Labyrin'th**INE, *a.*

Lac, *n.*[1] Hindustani *lākh*—Skr. *lākshā.* A resinous incrustation found on certain trees.

Lac, *n.*[2], **Lakh**. Hindustani *lākh*—Skr. *laksha.* A hundred thousand (gen. of rupees).

Lace, *n.* O.F. *laz, las*—L. *laqueus*, noose, snare. LASSO. LATCHET. A cord serving to draw opposite edges together; ornamental braid; a fine fabric of interlaced threads.—*vt.* O.F. *lacier* (F. *lacer*). To fasten with a lace; to embroider; to mingle (*with* spirits).

Lac'erate, *vt.* L. *lacerāre, lacerātum*, f. *lacer*, mangled, torn. To mangle, tear; to afflict, distress.—**Lacer**A'TION, *n.*

La'ches, *n.* O.F. *laschesse*, f. *lasche*, negligent—L. *laxus.* LAX. Negligence, delay.

Lach'rymal, *a.* Med.L. *lacrimālis*, f. L. *lacrima*, a TEAR. Of, secreting, tears.—**Lach'-rym**OSE, *a.* Tearful, given to tears.

Lack, *n.* Early M.E. *lac* = M.Du. *lac*, M.L.G. *lak.* Deficiency, want; an instance of this.—*vt.* To be without or deficient in.

Lack'ey, **Lac'quey**, *n.* F. *laquais*, of obscure orig. A man-servant.—*vt.* To be lackey to.

Lacon'ic, *a.* G. *Lakōnikos*, Laconian, Spartan. Of Spartan brevity in speech; brief, concise.—**Lacon'ically**, *adv.* -AL. -LY.[2]

Lac'quer, *n.* Obs. F. *lacre*, sealing-wax—Pg. *lacca*, LAC.[1] A gold-coloured varnish; articles coated with it.—*vt.* To coat with it.

Lac'teal, *a.* L. *lacteus* (f. *lac, lactis*, milk) + -AL. LETTUCE. Pertaining to, consisting of, milk.—**Lacta'tion**, *n.* L. *lactāre*, to suckle. -ATION. Suckling.—**Lac'tic**, *a.*

Lacu'na, *n.* L. *lacūna*, hole, pool, f. *lacus*, LAKE.[1] A blank, missing portion; a gap.

Lacus'trine, *a.* As if f. a L. **lacuster*, **lacustris* (a. f. *lacus* (see prec.)) + -INE. Of or pertaining to a lake.

Lad, *n.* M.E. *ladde.* Orig. obscure. A boy, [youth.

Lad'der, *n.* O.E. *hlǣd(d)er*, corresp. to M.Du. *lēdere*, O.H.G. *leitara* (Ger. *leiter*). Cogn. with LEAN, *v.*, and G. *klimax.* CLIMAX. An appliance for ascending a height consisting of a series of bars fixed between two supports.

Lade, *vt.* O.E. *hladan.* Common Teut. To load; to ship (goods); to take up (a liquid).—**La'dle**, *n.* O.E. *hlædel*, f. *hladan* + suff. *-el*, of names of instruments. An implement for lading liquids.—*vi.* To lift out with a ladle.

La'dy, *n.* O.E. *hlǣfdīge*, f. *hlāf*, bread, LOAF + (prob.) root *dig-*, as in Goth. *deigan*, to knead. DOUGH. LORD. Formerly, the mistress of a household. A female ruler; the Virgin Mary; a woman of high position in society or of good breeding; part of the customary designation of certain women of high rank.—**La'dy-bird**, *n.* Our Lady('s) bird. A small British beetle.—**La'dy Day**, *n.* Our Lady('s) day. The Feast of the Annunciation, 25th March.—**La'dy**LIKE, *a.*—**La'dy**SHIP, *n.* The being a lady; with possessive pronouns, a title given to certain women of high rank.

Lag, *vi.* Orig. obscure. To slacken one's pace, to fall behind.—**Lag'**GARD, *n.* One who lags, a loiterer.—*a.* Hanging back, loitering, slow.

Lagoon', *n.* F. *lagune*—It. and Sp. *laguna*—L. *lacūna.* LACUNA. A shallow stretch of water connected with the sea.

La'ic, *a.* Eccles.L. *lāicus*—G. *laikos*, f. *laos*, the people. LAY, *a.* Of a layman or the laity.—**La'ic**IZE, *vt.* To make lay.

Lair, *n.* O.E. *leger*, f. root *leg-*. LIE, *v.*[1] LEAGUER. The resting-place of an animal.

La'ity, *n.* LAY, *a.* + -ITY. Laymen collectively; unprofessional people.

Lake, *n.*[1] O.F. *lac*—L. *lacus*, tank, pond, lake. A body of water surrounded by land.

Lake, *n.*[2] Var. of LAC.[1] A red pigment, originally obtained from lac.

Lamb, *n.* O.E. *lamb.* Common Teut. The young of the sheep.—*vi.* To bring forth a lamb.

Lam'bent, *a.* L. *lambens, lambentis*, pres. pple. of *lambĕre*, to lick, lap. LAP, *v.*[2] Playing lightly on a surface; softly radiant.

Lame, *a.* O.E. *lama*, corresp. to O.S. *lamo*, O.H.G. *lam* (Ger. *lahm*). Crippled in a limb; of the limb, crippled; defective; unsatisfactory.—*vt.* To make lame.—**Lame'**LY,[2] *adv.*

Lament', *n.* L. *lāmentum.* An expression of grief; a song of grief.—*vi.* and *t.* L. *lāmentāri.* To express or feel sorrow (for).—**Lam'ent**ABLE, *a.*—**Lament**A'TION, *n.*

Lam'mas, *n.* O.E. *hlāfmæsse*, f. *hlāf*, bread, LOAF + *mæsse*, MASS.[1] The 1st of August, formerly observed as a harvest festival.

Lamp, *n.* F. *lampe*—L. *lampas*—G. *lampas*, torch, lamp, f. *lampein*, to shine. A vessel holding oil to be burnt at a wick; various vessels enclosing sources of light.—**Lamp'-black**, *n.* A pigment made of soot.

Lampoon', *n.* F. *lampon*, said to be f. *lampons*, let us drink, imp. of *lamper*, to 'toss off' liquor. A virulent satire on an individual.—*vt.* To make a lampoon on.—**Lampoon'**ER, *n.*

Lam'prey, *n.* O.F. **lampreie* (O.F. and F. *lamproie*)—Med.L. *lamprēda*, perh. = *lampetra*, explained as f. L. *lambĕre*, to lick + *petra*, stone, the fish clinging to stones by a sucker. LIMPET. An eel-like scaleless fish.

Lance, *n.* F. *lance*—L. *lancea*, said to be of Sp. orig. A weapon consisting of a wooden shaft with a steel head.—*vt.* O.F. *lancier.* LAUNCH, *v.* To fling, throw; to pierce with a lance or a lancet.—**Lanc'er**, *n.* F. *lancier.* A soldier armed with a lance.—**Lan'cet**, *n.* F. *lancette*, dim. of *lance.* A surgical instrument for bleeding, opening abscesses, &c.

Lan'cinate, *vt.* L. *lancināre, lancinātum.* Cf. *lacer.* LACERATE. To tear, pierce.

Land, *n.* O.E. *land.* Common Teut. Cogn. with Ir. *land, lann*, enclosure, Welsh *llan*, enclosure, church. LAWN.[2] The solid part of the earth's surface; ground, soil; a country; property consisting in land (often in *pl.*).—*vt.* To set on shore; to bring to a place or into a position.—*vi.* To go ashore.—**Land'-ing**, *vbl.n.* The act of landing; a level part at the top of stairs or between two flights of stairs.—**Land'lord**, **Land'lady**, *nn.* One who lets land, a house, &c.; the master or mistress of an inn, &c.—**Land'mark**, *n.* O.E. *landmearc.* MARK.[1] Something marking a boundary; an object in the landscape serving as a guide, esp. to sailors.—**Land'-rail**, *n.* RAIL, *n.*[2] The corn-crake.—**Land'-scape**, *n.* Du. *landschap*, f. *land* + *-schap* = -SHIP. A picture of natural scenery on land; a view or prospect of such scenery.

Lan'dau, *n.* From *Landau* in Germany, as first made there. A four-wheeled carriage with a top which can be closed or thrown open.

Lane, *n.* O.E. *lane, lone* = O.Fris. *lana, lona*, Du. *laan*. A narrow road or street.

Lan'guage, *n.* F. *langage*—Pop.L. type **linguāticum*, f. L. *lingua*, tongue, language. LINGUAL. The body of words used by a nation, tribe, &c., or in a branch of knowledge; any mode of expressing thought, &c.; manner or style of expression.

Lan'guish, *vi.* F. *languiss-*, a stem of *languir*—Pop.L. **languīre* for L. *languēre*. LAX. To grow or be weak or faint; to be in a state of suffering; to pine *for*; to assume a languid look.—**Lan'guid**, *a.* L. *languidus*. Faint, weak; spiritless, apathetic; wanting in force; sluggish, dull.—**Lan'guid**LY,[2] *adv.*—**Lan'-guor**, *n.* O.F. *languor*—L. *languor*. Faintness, weariness; want of energy; tenderness of mood.—**Lan'guor**OUS, *a.*

Lank, *a.* O.E. *hlanc*. Cf. Ger. *lenken*, to bend. Lean and tall; not plump; without curl.—**Lank'**Y,[2] *a.* Awkwardly lean and long.

Lan'tern, *n.* F. *lanterne*—L. *lanterna*, said to be f. G. *lamptēr*, f. *lampein*. LAMP. A transparent case for holding a light; an erection on a dome, &c., to admit light.

Lan'yard, *n.* F. *lanière*, thong, of doubtful orig. A short rope for various purposes.

Lap, *n.*[1] O.E. *lappa, læppa* = M.Du. *lappe*, O.H.G. *lappa*. The loose lower part of a garment; the sitting body from the waist to the knees with its covering garments. From the *v.*, a single round of the course in racing.—*v.*[1]*t.* Prob. f. the *n.* in sense 'fold, piece of cloth'. To fold, wrap (a garment, &c.) *round*, &c.; to wrap up, clothe, bind up; to surround, fold in.—**Lapel'**, *n.* Dim. suff. *-el*. The part of the front of a coat which is folded over towards either shoulder.—**Lap'pet**, *n.* Dim. suff. *-et*. A loose part of a garment, &c.

Lap, *v.*[2]*t.* O.E. *lapian* = M.Du. *lapen*, O.H.G. *laffan*. Cogn. with G. *laptein*, L. *lambĕre*. LAMBENT. To take up with the tongue; to beat upon with a rippling sound.—*vi.* To move with such a sound.—*n.*[2] A lapping.

Lap'idary, *a.* L. *lapidārius*, f. *lapis, lapidis*, stone. Concerned with stones; engraved on stone.—*n.* One who cuts and polishes gems.

Lapse, *n.* L. *lapsus*, slip, fall, f. *lābi, lapsus*, to slip, fall. COLLAPSE. A slip (of the memory, &c.); a falling from rectitude; the lapsing of a right, &c.; the passing away (of time), a period elapsed.—*vi.* To fall away or pass gradually; to pass away, terminate, &c., through some failure; to glide; to sink, subside.

Lap'wing, *n.* O.E. *hléapewince*, f. *hléapan*, to LEAP + **wince-*, to totter, waver. Cf. O.E. *wincian*, to WINK. (Named from its flight. Popularly conn. with LAP, *v.*[1] and WING, from the rapid folding and opening of the wings.) A bird of the plover family, the pewit.

Lar'board, *n.* M.E. *lad(d)eborde, latheborde* (assimilated to STARBOARD), f. an unknown component + O.E. *bord*, ship's side. BOARD. The left-hand (now the port) side of a ship.—*a.* Belonging to or on this side.

Lar'ceny, *n.* App., with -Y[1], f. A.F. *larcin*, O.F. *larrecin*—L. *latrōcinium*, robbery, f. *latro*, robber. Theft of personal goods.

Larch, *n.* Ger. *lärche*—L. *larix, laricis*. A coniferous tree with tough and durable wood.

Lard, *n.* O.F. *lard*, bacon—L. *lāridum, lardum*, lard. Prepared pig's fat.—*vt.* To insert strips of bacon in; to intersperse or garnish (writing, &c.).—**Lar'der**, *n.* O.F. *lardier*—Med.L. *lardārium*. A store-room for meat, &c.

Large, *n.* F. *large*—L. *larga*, fem. of *largus*, copious, abundant. Wide in range or capacity; great in size, number, &c.—**Large'**LY,[2] *adv.*—**Lar'gess(e)**, *n.* F. *largesse*—L.L. **largitia*. Bountiful bestowal of gifts; a gift.

Lar'go, *a.* and *adv.* It. = broad. *Mus.*, slow, and with a broad dignified treatment.

Lark, *n.*[1] O.E. *láferce*, corresp. to Du. *leeuwerik*, O.H.G. *lêrahha* (Ger. *lerche*). A well-known singing-bird. [*n.*[2] A frolic.

Lark, *vi.* Poss. conn. with prec. To frolic.—

Lar'va, *n.*; *pl.* **Lar'væ**. L., a ghost, a mask. An insect in the caterpillar state.

Lar'ynx, *n.* G. *larugx*. The upper part of the wind-pipe.

Lascar', *n.* App. an erroneous use of Urdu *lashkar*, army, camp. An East Indian sailor.

Lasciv'ious, *a.* L.L. *lasciviōsus*, f. L. *lascivia*, n. of quality f. *lascīvus*, sportive, lustful. Inclined or inciting to lust.

Lash, *v.*[1]*i.* Orig. obscure. To dash, rush; to make a dash, aim a blow *at*.—*vt.* To strike with a whip, &c.—*n.* A stroke with a whip, &c.; the flexible part of a whip.

Lash, *v.*[2]*t.* Perh. f. O.F. *lachier*, dial. var. of *lacier*. LACE, *v.* To fasten with a cord, &c.

Lass, *n.* M.E. *lasce, lasse*, perh. f. O.N. **lasqa*, fem. of **lasqar*, unmarried. A girl.

Las'situde, *n.* F. *lassitude*—L. *lassitūdo*, f. *lassus*, weary. Weariness.

Las'so, *n.* Sp. *lazo* = O.F. *laz*. LACE. A long rope with a noose.—*vt.* To catch with a lasso.

Last, *n.* O.E. *lást*, footstep, *lǽst*, boot, *lǽste*, last, cogn. with O.H.G. *leist* (Ger. *leisten*), last, O.N. *leistr*, foot, sock. A model of the foot for shaping boots, &c.

Last, *a.* O.E. *latost*, Northumb. *lætest*, superl. of *læt*, LATE, *a.*, *late*, LATE, *adv.* Following all others; most recent; lowest in rank, &c.; the only remaining; final; utmost, extreme.—*adv.* After all others; most recently; in the last place.—**Last'**LY,[2] *adv.*

Last, *vi.* O.E. *lǽstan*, orig., 'to follow in the track of', f. *lást*, footstep. LAST, *n.* To continue; to hold out, remain undecayed, &c.

Latch, *n.* Perh. f. O.F. *lache*, vbl. n. f. *lachier* = *lacier*. LACE, *v.* A fastening for a door or gate.—*vt.* To fasten with a latch.

Lat'chet, *n.* O.F. *lachet*, dial. var. of *lacet*, dim. of *laz, las*. LACE. A shoe-lace.

Late, *a.* O.E. *læt*. Common Teut. Cogn. with L. *lassus*, weary. LATTER. LAST. LET. Coming, &c., after the proper time; advanced in time; belonging to an advanced stage of development; recently dead; that was recently, but is not now (something); recent in date.—*adv.* O.E. *late*. After the proper time; at or till a late hour; recently (but not now).—**Late'**LY,[2] *adv.* Not long since, recently.

Lateen', *a.* F. *latine* in *voile latine*, 'Latin sail', so named from its use in the Mediterranean. *Lateen sail*, a triangular sail suspended from a yard at an angle of 45° to the mast.

La'tent, *a.* L. *latens, latentis*, pres.pple. of *latēre*, to be hidden. Present or existing but not visible or developed.—**La'**TENCY, *n.*

Lat'eral, *a.* L. *laterālis*, f. *latus, lateris*, side. COLLATERAL. Of or at the side.

Lath, *n.* O.E. *lætt* = M.Du., Ger. *latte*. Cf.

F. *latte* f. Teut. A thin strip of wood to support plaster, &c.—*vt.* To put laths on.

Lathe, *n.* Cf. Da. *dreje-lad*, turning-lathe. A machine for cutting into a round form.

Lath'er, *n.* O.E. *léathor*. Cf. O.N. *lauthr*, foam. Teut. root *lau-*, to wash. Cogn. with G. *loutron*, bath, L. *lavāre*. LAVE. LYE. Froth of soap and water; sweat, esp. of a horse.—*vt.* and *i.* To cover with, to form, lather.

Lat'in, *a.* L. *Latinus*, a. f. *Latium*, the portion of Italy which included Rome. Of the ancient Romans; of, characteristic of, composed in, their language; speaking a language descended from theirs.—*n.* Their language.—**Latin**'ITY, *n.* Manner of writing Latin.

Lat'itude, *n.* L. *lātitūdo, lātitūdinis*, breadth, width, f. *lātus*, broad. Freedom from restrictions; distance of a place on its meridian north or south of the equator; in *pl.*, regions, climes. —**Latitudin**A'RIAN, *a.* Allowing, showing, latitude in thought or action.—*n.* One allowing or showing such latitude.

Latrine', *n.* F. *latrine*—L. *lātrīna, lavātrīna*, bath, privy, f. *lavāre*, to wash. LAVE. A privy, esp. in a camp, a hospital, &c.

Lat'ter, *a.* O.E. *lætra*, comp. of *læt*, LATE, *a.* Later; the second mentioned of two.—**Lat'ter**LY,[2] *adv.* At the end of a period; lately.

Lat'tice, *n.* O.F. and F. *lattis*, f. *latte*. LATH. A structure of crossed strips of wood, &c., with spaces between; a window, &c., so made.

Laud, *n.* O.F. *laude*—L. *laus, laudis*, praise. Praise; a hymn of praise; in *pl.*, a service of the Church the Psalms of which end with Psalms called *Laudes*.—*vt.* L. *laudāre, laudātum*. ALLOW. To praise.—**Laud'**ABLE, *a.* —**Laud**A'TION, *n.*—**Laud'at**ORY, *a.*

Lau'danum, *n.* Formed (perhaps arbitrarily) by Paracelsus as the name of a marvellous drug. The alcoholic tincture of opium.

Laugh, *vi.* O.E. (Anglian) *hlæhhan*. Common Teut. Prob. imitative. To make the noise and movements forming the instinctive expression of mirth or of a sense of the ludicrous; to mock *at*.—*vt.* To affect by laughing; *to laugh to scorn*, to deride utterly.—**Laugh'**ABLE, *a.* —**Laugh'ing-stock**, *n.* An object of laughter.—**Laugh'ter**, *n.* O.E. *hleahtor*. The action of laughing. [A large boat.

Launch, *n.*[1] Sp. *lancha*, perh. of Malay orig.

Launch, *vt.* O.N.F. *lancher* = O.F. *lancier*. LANCE, *v.* To hurl (a threat, &c.); to set afloat; to start, set on foot.—*vi.* To enter upon a course.—*n.*[2] The launching of a vessel.

Laun'der, *vt.* From obs. *Launder*, one who washes linen, contraction of *lavender*—O.F. *lavandier*—L.L. *lavandārius*, f. L. *lavāre*. LAVE. To wash and 'get up' (linen).—**Laun'dr**ESS, *n.* A woman who does this. —**Laun'dry**, *n.* Altered f. obs. *Lavendry*—O.F. *lavanderie*. A place where this is done.

Lau'rel, *n.* F. *laurier*, O.F. *lor*—L. *laurus*. The bay tree; in *pl.*, a wreath of laurel as an emblem of victory, &c.—**Lau'reate**, *a.* L. *laureātus*, f. *laurea*, laurel crown, fem. of *laureus*, a. f. *laurus*. Crowned with laurel; *poet laureate*, an officer of the Royal Household with the duty of writing court-odes, &c.

La'va, *n.* It. (f. *lavare*, L. *lavāre* (see next)), orig., a stream caused by sudden rain. Fluid volcanic matter; this when solidified.

Lave, *vt.* F. *laver*—L. *lavāre* = G. *louein*. LATHER. LATRINE. LAUNDER. POLLUTE. To wash; to flow along.—**Lav'atory**, *n.* L. *lavātōrium*. A place for washing the hands and face.

Lav'ender, *n.* A.F. *lavendre*—Med.L. *lavendula*, of uncertain orig. A small aromatic shrub; the colour of the flowers, pale blue with a trace of red.

Lav'ish, *a.* From obs. *Lavish*, profusion—O.F. *lavasse, lavache*, deluge of rain. Spending or giving profusely; abundant, profuse.—*vt.* To spend or give profusely.

Law, *n.* Late O.E. *lagu*—O.N. **lagu*, law, *pl.* of *lag*, something laid or fixed, *e.g.* layer, fixed price. O.Teut. root *lag-*. LAY, *v.* OUTLAW. The body of rules binding on a community; one of the rules; a general principle deduced from particular facts.—**Law'**FUL, *a.* Permitted or recognized by law. —**Law'giver**, *n.* One who makes laws.—**Law'**LESS, *a.* Regardless of, uncontrolled by, law.—**Law'yer**, *n.* *-Yer* = -ER. One versed in law; a member of the legal profession.

Lawn, *n.*[1] *Laon* in France. A fine linen.

Lawn, *n.*[2] Later form of obs. *Laund*—O.F. *launde*, wooded ground, f. Celtic. Cogn. with LAND. A glade; a piece of ground covered with carefully tended grass.—**Lawn-ten'nis**, *n.* A modification of the game of TENNIS.

Lax, *a.* L. *laxus*, loose, cogn. with *languēre*, to LANGUISH. LACHES. LEASH. SLACK. Of the bowels, acting easily; loose, slack; not strict or severe; vague.—**Lax'ative**, *a.* F. *laxatif*—L. *laxātīvus*, a. f. *laxāre, laxātum*, to loose, f. *laxus*. LEASE. Opening the bowels. —*n.* A laxative medicine.—**Lax'**ITY, *n.*

Lay, *n.*[1] O.F. *lai* = Pr. *lais, lays*, prob. f. Teut. VIRELAY. A short poem to be sung.

Lay, *a.* F. *lai* (now *laïque*)—Eccles.L. *lāicus*. LAIC. LAITY. Not clerical; not professional —**Lay'man**, *n.* A lay person.

Lay, *vt.* O.E. *lecgan* = O.S. *leggian* (Du. *leggen*), O.H.G. *lecken, legen* (Ger. *legen*). O.Teut. root *lag-*, var. of *leg-*. LIE, *v.*[1] FELLOW. LAW. To bring or cast down from an erect position; to cause to subside; to place, deposit; to bring forth (an egg); to stake, wager; to put, apply; to put into some condition; to bring forward (a claim, charge, &c.); to impose (a burden, &c.); to place in position; to arrange, devise.—*vi.* To deal blows.—*n.*[2] A share in a venture.—**Lay'**ER, *n.* One who lays; a thickness of matter spread on a surface; one of a series of such thicknesses, a stratum; a shoot or twig fastened down to strike root.

Lay fig'ure, *n.* From **lay*, abstracted f. obs. *lay-man* in sim. sense—Du. *leeman*, **ledenman*, f. *led*, limb, joint + *man*, MAN. A jointed figure of the body used by artists.

Laz'ar, *n.* Med.L. *lazarus*, an application of *Lazarus* (Luke, xvi, 20). A leper.—**Lazaret'to**, *n.* It. *lazzareto*, f. *lazzaro* = *lazarus*. A hospital for lepers; a quarantine station.

La'zy, *a.* Orig. obscure. Averse to effort, slothful.—**La'zi**LY,[2] *adv.*—**La'zi**NESS, *n.*

Lea, *n.* O.E. *léa(h)*, app. cogn. with L. *lūcus*, grove. A tract of open ground.

Lead, *n.*[1] O.E. *léad* = Du. *lood*, Ger. *lot*. A soft heavy metal; a plummet for sounding; short for BLACK-LEAD; in *pl.*, strips of lead on a roof, lead frames in a window.—*v.*[1]*t.* To cover, &c., with lead.—**Lead'**EN,[1] *a.*

Lead, *v.*[2]*t.* O.E. *lǽdan*. Common Teut. (Not in Goth.) O.Teut. **laidjan*, f. **laidâ*, road, journey. LOAD. To conduct, guide; to induce, persuade; to serve as a way or passage for; to go through (life); to have the first place in; to play (the first card in a trick).—*vi.* To go first; to play the first card in a trick. —*n.*[2] Example, precedent; the front place; the action or privilege of leading at cards.—

Lead'ER, *n.* One who leads; an article expressing editorial opinion.—**Lead'er**SHIP, *n.*

Leaf, *n.*; *pl.* **Leaves**. O.E. *léaf* = O.N. *lauf*, O.H.G. *loup* (Ger. *laub*). LODGE. An expanded growth of a plant; a part of a book, &c., containing two pages; a thin sheet; one of the parts of a double door; a flap at the side of, a movable addition to, a table.—**Leaf'let**, *n.* Dim. suff. *-let*. A small leaf; a folded unstitched sheet of paper containing printed matter.—**Leaf'**LESS, *a.*—**Leaf'**Y,[2] *a.*

League, *n.*[1] App. f. It. *lega*, f. *legare*, L. *ligāre*, to bind. ALLY. An agreement for mutual assistance; the body of states or persons so united.—*vt.* To form into, to cause to join, a league.—*vi.* To form a league.

League, *n.*[2] L.L. *leuga*, *leuca*, said to be of Gaulish orig. A measure of about 3 miles.

Lea'guer, *n.* Du. *leger*, corresp. to O.E. *leger*. LAIR. A camp for a siege; a siege.

Leak, *vi.* From or cogn. with O.N. *leka* = M.Du. *leken*, to leak, drip. To pass *out, away*, &c., by a leak; to allow fluid to pass through a leak.—*n.* Perh. f. Du. or L.G. A hole or fissure by which a fluid passes into or out of something.—**Leak'**AGE, *n.* A leaking; diminution due to gradual escape or waste.—**Leak'**Y,[2] *a.* [Faithful, true.

Leal, *a.* O.F. *leial*, *leal* (F. *loyal*). LOYAL.

Lean, *a.* O.E. *hlǽne*, of doubtful orig. Wanting in flesh; poor, meagre; containing little fat.—*n.* The lean part of meat.

Lean, *vi.* O.E. *hleonian*, *hlinian*, corresp. to O.S. *hlinôn*, O.H.G. (*h*)*linên* (Ger. *lehnen*). Cogn. with G. *klinein* (CLIMAX), L. *-clīnāre* (DECLINE). To incline the body for support; to bend or incline; to tend *towards, to*; to incline in mind.—*vt.* To cause to lean, to prop.

Leap, *vi.* O.E. *hléapan*. Common Teut. LAPWING. To spring from the ground.—*vt.* To pass over by leaping.—*n.* An act of leaping.—**Leap'-year**, *n.* Perh. so called because in such a year each fixed festival (after Feb.) 'leaps' to the next week-day but one to that on which it fell in the preceding year, not to the next as usual. A bissextile year, the day now intercalated being Feb. 29.

Learn, *vt.* O.E. *leornian* = O.S. *linôn*, O.H.G. *lirnên*, *lernên* (Ger. *lernen*), f. *lis-*, weak grade of O.Teut. root *lais-*. LORE. To gain knowledge of or skill in.—*vi.* To gain knowledge or skill.—**Learn'ed**, *ppl.a.* Having much knowledge gained by study, erudite.—**Learn'ed**LY,[2] *adv.*—**Learn'ing**, *vbl.n.* The action of the *v.*; knowledge gained by study.

Lease, *vt.* A.F. *lesser*, a specific use of O.F. *lesser*, *laissier* (F. *laisser*), to let go—L. *laxāre*. LAXATIVE. To give the use of by a lease; to take or hold on lease.—*n.* A contract by which the use of lands, &c., is given on specified terms; the instrument embodying the contract.—**Lease'hold**, *n.* A holding by lease; land, &c., so held.—**Less**EE', *n.*—**Les'**SOR, *n.*

Leash, *n.* O.F. *lesse*, *laisse*—L.L. *laxa*, thong, loose rope, fem. of *laxus*. LAX. A thong or line in which hounds are held; a set of three.

Least, *a.* O.E. *lǽsest*, *lǽst*, superl. f. O.Teut. **laisiz-*, LESS. Used as superl. of LITTLE.—*adv.* In the least degree.

Leath'er, *n.* O.E. *lether* (in compounds) = O.N. *lethr*, O.H.G. *ledar* (Ger. *leder*). Skin prepared for use.—**Leath'ern**, *a.* -EN.[1]—**Leath'er**Y,[2] *a.*

Leave, *n.* O.E. *léaf* = O.H.G. **louba*, f. Teut. root *leub-*. LIEF. Permission; permission to be absent from duty, the period of such absence; *to take* (*one's*) *leave of*, to bid farewell to.

Leave, *vt.* O.E. *lǽfan*, corresp. to O.N. *leifa*, O.H.G. *leiben*. Teut. root *laib-* = *lib-* (LIFE. LIVE, *v.*), to remain, continue, app. f. a primary sense 'to adhere, be sticky', as in the cogn. Skr. *lip-*, to smear, adhere to, G. *lipos*, grease. To have remaining after one's death or as a consequence, &c., after removal or cessation; to transmit *to* successors; to allow to remain; to suffer to be done, &c., by another; to deposit, give in charge; to go away from, quit.

Leav'en, *n.* F. *levain*—L. *levāmen*, means of raising, f. *levāre*, to raise, f. *levis*, light. LEVER. Yeast.—*vt.* To treat with leaven.

Lech'er, *n.* O.F. *lecheor*, *lecheur*, agent-n. f. *lechier* (F. *lécher*, to lick), to live in debauchery or gluttony—O.H.G. *leckôn*, to LICK. A lewd man.—**Lech'erous**, *a.* O.F. *lecheros*. Addicted to, marked by, lechery.—**Lech'**ERY, *n.*

Lec'tern, *n.* O.F. *lettrun*—L.L. *lectrum*, pulpit, f. root of L. *legĕre*. (See next.) A reading-desk in a church.

Lec'tion, *n.* O.F. *lectiun*—L. *lectio*, *lectiōnis*, n. of action f. *legĕre*, *lectum*, to choose, read. COLLECT. LEGEND. LESSON. A reading of a text in a particular copy or edition.—**Lec'tionary**, *n.* Eccles.L. *lectiōnārium*. A book containing the lessons to be read in church.—

Lec'ture, *n.* L.L. *lectūra*, commentary. A discourse before an audience; a speech by way of reproof.—*vi.* To deliver a lecture.—*vt.* To reprove.—**Lec'turer**ER, *n.*

Ledge, *n.* Poss. a M.E. formation f. *legge*, to LAY. A narrow surface on the top of a structure or projection; a ridge of rocks.

Led'ger, *n.* Cf. Du. *legger* (f. *leggen*, to LAY), properly 'a book laid always ready'. The principal account-book of merchants, &c.

Lee, *n.*[1] O.E. *hléo*, shelter, cogn. with O.S. *hleo*, shelter, O.N. *hlé*, lee (in the nautical sense). Shelter, protection; the side of a ship, &c., turned away from the wind.—**Lee'**WARD, *a.* On the lee side.—**Lee'-way**, *n.* The drift of a ship in the leeward direction.

Lee, *n.*[2] F. *lie*—Gaulish L. *lia*, perh. of Celtic orig. In *pl.*, the sediment of wine, &c.

Leech, *n.*[1] O.E. *lǽce*, corresp. to O.H.G. *lâhhi*, M.Sw. *läkir*. A physician.

Leech, *n.*[2] O.E. *lǽce*, Kentish *lýce* = M.Du. *lake*, *lieke*. A blood-sucking worm.

Leek, *n.* O.E. *léac* = M.Du. *looc*, O.H.G. *louh* (Ger. *lauch*). GARLICK. A culinary herb allied to the onion.

Leer, *vi.* Perh. f. obs. *Leer*, cheek (with notion 'to glance over one's cheek')—O.E. *hléor* = O.S. *hleor*. To cast a sly, immodest or malign side glance.—*n.* Such a glance.

Left, *a.* O.E. *left*, *lyft*, app. in sense 'weak, worthless', like E.Fris. *luf*, Du. dial. *loof*. Cf. M.Du. *luft*, *lucht*, left. Denoting the hand which is normally the weaker and the other parts on the same side.—*n.* The left side or part.—*adv.* On or towards the left side.

Leg, *n.* O.N. *leggr*. One of the organs by which an animal body is supported and moves; a leg-like support.—**Leg'ging**, *n.* Gen. in *pl.* An extra covering for the leg.

Leg'acy, *n.* O.F. *legacie*, legateship—Med. L. *lēgātia*, legate's district, f. *lēgātus*, LEGATE, *n.* Formerly, a legateship; a bequeathing. (Cf. LEGATE, *v.*) Anything given by will.

Le'gal, *a.* L. *lēgālis*, f. *lex*, *lēgis*, law. LEGISLATOR. LEGITIMATE. LOYAL. PRIVILEGE. Of, appointed or permitted by, law.—**Le'gal**LY,[2] *adv.*—**Legal'**ITY, *n.*—**Le'gal**IZE, *vt.* To make legal, authorize, sanction.

Leg'ate, *n.* O.F. *legat*—L. *lēgātus*, pa.pple. of *lēgāre*, to depute, to bequeath. ALLEGE. LEGACY. An ambassador, esp. of the pope.—**Leg'ate**SHIP, *n.*—**Lega'**TION, *n.* The sending of a legate; his mission, his residence, his office; a diplomatic minister and his suite.

Legate', *vt.* L. *lēgāre.* (See prec.) To bequeath.—**Legat**EE', *n.*

Lega'to, *a.* and *adv.* It., pa.pple. of *legare*, L. *ligāre*, to bind. *Mus.*, without breaks.

Leg'end, *n.* F. *lègende*—Med.L. *legenda*, lit., 'what is read', fem. vbl.n. f. L. *legĕre*, to gather, choose, read. LECTION. LEGIBLE. LEGION. SACRILEGE. An unauthentic traditional story; an inscription.—**Leg'end**ARY, *a.*

Legerdemain', *n.* F. *léger de main*, light of hand. Jugglery, conjuring tricks.

Leg'ible, *a.* L.L. *legibilis*, f. *legĕre.* LEGEND. Easily read.—**Legi**BIL'ITY, *n.*

Le'gion, *n.* O.F. *legion*—L. *legio*, *legiōnis*, f. *legĕre*, to choose, levy (an army). LEGEND. A body of infantry in the Roman army; applied to some modern military bodies; a vast multitude.—**Le'gion**ARY, *a.* Of or belonging to a legion.—*n.* A legionary soldier.

Leg'islator, *n.* L. *lēgis-lātor*, f. *lex* (LEGAL) + *lātor*, agent-n. f. *ferre*, *lātum*, to BEAR, bring. A lawgiver.—**Leg'islate**, *vi.* Back-formation f. the *n.* To make laws.—**Legis-la'**TION, *n.*—**Leg'islat**IVE, *a.*—**Leg'isla**TURE, *n.* A body that makes laws.

Legit'imate, *a.* Med.L. *lēgitimātus*, pa.pple. of *lēgitimāre*, to declare to be lawful, f. L. *lēgitimus*, lawful, f. *lex.* LEGAL. Born in wedlock; sanctioned by law or by the laws of reasoning.—*vt.* To make legitimate.—**Legit'im**ACY, *n.*—**Legitima'**TION, *n.*—**Legit'imat**IZE, *vt.*—**Legit'im**IST, *n.* A supporter of an hereditary monarchical title.

Leg'ume, *n.* F. *légume*—L. *legūmen*, *legūminis*, pulse, f. *legĕre*, to gather. LEGEND. The edible part of a leguminous plant; the pod; an edible vegetable.—**Legu'min**OUS, *a.* Of, pertaining to, of the nature of pulse.

Leis'ure, *n.* O.F. *leisir* (F. *loisir*), use as n. of *leisir*, L. *licēre.* LICENCE. Freedom from occupation; free time.—**Leis'ure**LY,[1] *a.* Deliberate.—**Leis'ure**LY,[2] *adv.*

Lem'ma, *n.* G. *lēmma*, something taken, an assumption, f. root of *lambanein*, to take. CATALEPSY. A subsidiary proposition assumed or demonstrated.

Lem'on, *n.* F. *limon* (now restricted to the lime), conn. with *lime*, LIME,[2] and prob. of Oriental orig. Cf. Arab. *laimūn*, Per. *limūn.* A fruit with an acid juice; its colour, pale yellow.—**Lemonade'**, *n.* F. *limonade.* A drink made from lemon-juice.

Lend, *vt.* O.E. *lǽnan*, f. *lǽn*, LOAN. To give the temporary use of; to give, impart.—*v.refl.* To adapt oneself *to*, to be adapted *to.*

Length, *n.* O.E. *lengthu*, conn. with *lang*, LONG. The quality of being long; extent from end to end; a long stretch; a piece of a certain length.—**Length'**EN,[2] *vt.* and *i.*—**Length'**WISE, *adv.* and *a.*—**Length'**Y,[2] *a.*

Le'nient, *a.* L. *lēniens*, *lēnientis*, pres. pple. of *lēnire*, *lēnītum*, to soothe, f. *lēnis*, mild. Gentle, mild.—**Le'ni**ENCE, -ENCY, *nn.*—**Le'nient**LY,[2] *adv.*—**Len'**ITY, *n.*—**Len'i**TIVE, *a.* Soothing.—*n.* A lenitive drug.

Lens, *n.* L. *lens*, LENTIL. A lentil-shaped piece of glass with one or both surfaces curved.

Len'ten, *a.* O.E. *lencten*, spring = M.Du. *lentin*, app. a deriv. or compound of the shorter synonym appearing as M.L.G., M.Du., Du. *lente*, O.H.G. *lenzo* (Ger. *lenz*), perh. conn. with LONG, *a.*, and referring to the lengthening days. Formerly, the spring; Lent. Now only *attrib.* or as *a.*, of, appropriate to Lent.—**Lent**, *n.* Contr. f. *lenten.* The period of fasting from Ash-Wednesday to Easter-eve.

Len'til, *n.* F. *lentille*—L. *lenticula*, dim. of *lens*, *lentis*, lentil. LENS. The seed of a leguminous plant; the plant.

Len'to, *a.* and *adv.* It. *Mus.*, slow.

Le'onine, *a.*[1] L. *leōnīnus*, f. *leo*, LION. Like a lion, that of a lion.

Le'onine, *a.*[2] L. *leōnīnus*, f. *Leo.* A kind of rhyming Latin verse prob. named from some mediæval poet called Leo.

Leop'ard, *n.* O.F. *leopard*—L.L. *leopardus*—Late G. *leopardos*, f. *leōn*, LION + *pardos*, PARD. A spotted carnivorous quadruped, the panther.

Lep'er, *n.* App. orig. *a.*, f. attrib. use of obs. *Leper*, leprosy—O.F. *lepre*—L. *lepra*—G. *lepra*, orig. fem. of *lepros*, scaly, f. *lepos*, scale. One affected with leprosy.—**Lep'rous**, *a.* O.F. *leprous*—L.L. *leprōsus.* Affected with leprosy.—**Lep'rosy**, *n.* App. f. Med.L. **leprōsia*, f. *leprōsus.* A foul disease which forms scales on the skin and slowly eats away the body.

Lepidop'terous, *a.* G. *lepis*, *lepidos*, scale + *pteron*, wing + -OUS. Having wings covered with scales.

Lese-maj'esty, *n.* F. *lèse-majesté*—L. *laesa mājestas*, violated majesty (*sc.* of the sovereign people), f. *laesa*, fem. pa.pple. of *laedĕre* (COLLIDE) + *mājestas*, MAJESTY. Treason.

Le'sion, *n.* F. *lésion*—L. *laesio*, *laesiōnis*, n. of action f. *laedĕre.* COLLIDE. Injury.

Less, *a.* O.E. *lǽssa* = O.Fris. *lēssa.* O.Teut. type **laisizon-*, f. **laisiz*, f. **laiso-* + comp. suff. *-iz.* LEAST. Used as comp. of LITTLE.—*adv.* O.E. *lǽs* = O.Fris. *lēs*, f. **laisiz.* To a smaller extent, in a lower degree.—**Les's**EN,[2] *vi.* and *t.*—**Les'ser**, *a.* Double comp. f. *less.*

Les'son, *n.* O.F. *lecon*—L. *lectio.* LECTION. A portion of Scripture read in church; something to be studied by a pupil; a portion of a course of instruction.—*vt.* To teach.

Lest, *conj.* O.E. phrase (*thý*) *lǽs the* (becoming *les te* in M.E.), lit., 'whereby less', f. *thý*, instrumental of the dem. and rel. pron. + *lǽs*, LESS, *adv.* + *the*, rel. particle. That . . . not, for fear that; after *vv.* of fearing, often = that.

Let, *v.*[1]*t.* O.E. *lǽtan.* Common Teut. Cogn. with LATE. Primary sense app. 'to let go through weariness'. To allow (blood, &c.) to escape; to lease; to permit, allow; to cause (only in *to let* (one) *know*).—*vi.* To be leased.

Let, *v.*[2]*t.* O.E. *lettan* (conn. with *læt*, LATE) = O.N. *letja.* To hinder.—*n.* Hindrance; an impediment. [Deadly.

Le'thal, *a.* L. *lēt(h)ālis*, f. *lēt(h)um*, death.

Leth'argy, *n.* L. *lēthargia*—G. *lēthargia*, f. *lēthargos*, forgetful, f. *lēthē*, forgetfulness. Morbid drowsiness, torpor.—**Lethar'g**IC, *a.*

Let'ter, *n.* O.F. *lettre*—L. *littera*, a letter of the alphabet, in *pl.*, an epistle, a document, records, learning. LITERAL. A symbol representing a sound; a written message; in *pl.*, literature, learning.—*vt.* To mark with letters.—**Let'tered**, *ppl.a.* Learned, literate.—**Let'terpress**, *n.* Matter printed from types.

Let'tuce, *n.* M.E. *letuse*, conn. with O.F. *laituë*—L. *lactūca*, f. *lac*, milk (as having a milky juice). LACTEAL. A herb used as a salad.

Levant', *vi.* Perh. f. Sp. *levantar*, to lift (as in *levantar el campo*, to break up the camp), f. *levar*, L. *levāre.* LEVER. To abscond.

Lev'ee, *n.* F. *levé*, var. of *lever*, rising, use as *n.* of *lever*, to rise. A reception on rising; a reception for men held by the sovereign.

Lev'el, *n.* O.F. *livel* (F. *niveau*)—L. *lībella*, dim. of *lībra*, balance, level. DELIBERATE. An instrument indicating a horizontal line; an imaginary horizontal line; social, moral, &c., position or standard; a level surface or tract; a horizontal passage in a mine.—*a.* Even in surface; horizontal; of even quality, style, &c.—*vt.* To make level; to bring to the same level; to lay low, raze; to point (a gun, &c.). —*vi.* To aim with a gun, &c.

Le'ver, *n.* O.F. **levere*, *leveour*, agent-n. f. *lever*, L. *levāre*, to raise, f. *levis*, light. LEVANT. LEVITY. LEVY. A bar used to overcome resistance at one of its ends by means of force applied at the other.—**Le'ver**AGE, *n.* The action of a lever; its power.

Lev'eret, *n.* O.F. *levrete*, dim. of *levre*, L. *lepus*, *leporis*, hare. A young hare.

Levi'athan, *n.* Heb. *livyāthān*. The name in Hebrew poetry of some sea-monster.

Lev'in, *n.* Orig. unknown. Lightning.

Le'vite, *n.* L. *levīta*—G. *leuitēs*, f. *Leui*, Levi. One of the tribe of Levi; one of the portion of the tribe who assisted the priests in the Jewish temple-worship.—**Levit'ical**, *a.* L.L. *levīticus* (a. f. *levīta*) + -AL. Of the Levites or their ritual.—**Levit'icus**, *n.* L.L. *Levīticus* (sc. *liber*, book). The third book of the Old Testament dealing with the Levitical law and ritual.

Lev'ity, *n.* O.F. *levité*—L. *levitas*, f. *levis*, light. ALLEVIATE. ELEVATE. LEAVEN. LEVER. Unseasonable jocularity; fickleness.

Lev'y, *n.* F. *levée*, f. *lever*. LEVER. The act of collecting taxes, &c., or enrolling troops; the troops enrolled (also in *pl.*); a call of so much per head.—*vt.* To collect (taxes, &c.); to enrol (troops); to make (war).

Lewd, *a.* O.E. *lǽwede*, of obscure orig. Lustful.—**Lewd**'LY,[2] *adv.*—**Lewd**'NESS, *n.*

Lex'icon, *n.* G. *lexikon* (*biblion*), word(-book), f. *lexikos*, of or for words, f. *lexis*, a speaking, a word, f. *legein*, to speak. DIALECT. A word-book or dictionary.—**Lexicog'raphy**, *n.* G. *-graphia*, f. *graphein*, to write. The art of writing dictionaries.—**Lexicog'rapher**, *n.*

Li'able, *a.* Perh. f. A.F. **liable* = Med.L. **ligābilis*, that can be bound, f. *ligāre*, to bind. ALLY. Subject *to*, answerable; likely to suffer (from something), exposed *to*.—**Lia**BIL'ITY, *n.*

Libate', *vt.* L. *lībāre*, *lībātum*. To pour (wine, &c.) in honour of a god.—**Liba**'TION, *n.*

Li'bel, *n.* O.F. *libel*—L. *libellus*, dim. of *liber*, book. LIBRARY. Formerly, a little book, a short treatise. A published statement damaging to a person's reputation.—*vt.* To publish a libel against.—**Li'bell**OUS, *a.*

Lib'eral, *a.* O.F. *liberal*—L. *līberālis*, befitting a free man, bountiful, f. *līber*, free. DELIVER. Suitable to those of good social station; bountiful, generous; made without stint; open-minded; of a political party, favouring changes tending towards democracy.—*n.* One of such a party.—**Lib'eral**ISM, *n.*—**Liberal'**ITY, *n.*—**Lib'eral**LY,[2] *adv.*

Lib'erty, *n.* F. *liberté*—L. *lībertas*, f. *līber*. (See prec.) The state or condition of being free; free opportunity, leave, permission; an overstepping of rules.—**Lib'erate**, *vt.* L. *līberāre*, *līberātum*. To set free.—**Libera'**TION, *n.*—**Lib'erat**OR, *n.*—**Lib'ertine**, *n.* L. *lībertīnus*, a freedman. One who follows his own inclinations; a dissolute man.—*a.* Dissolute.—**Lib'ertin**ISM, *n.*

Libid'inous, *a.* L. *libīdinōsus*, f. *libīdo*, *libīdinis*, lust. Lustful, lewd.

Li'brary, *n.* F. *librairie* (now only 'bookseller's shop')—L. *librārium*, bookcase, neut. of *librārius*, a. f. *liber*, book. LIBEL. A place set apart for books; the books therein.—**Libra'ri**AN, *n.* One in charge of a library.

Libret'to, *n.* It., dim. of *libro*, L. *liber*, book. (See prec.) The words of an opera, &c.

Li'cence, *n.* F. *licence*—L. *licentia*, f. *licēre*, to be lawful. LEISURE. LICIT. Leave, permission; a formal permission, the document giving it; liberty of action; excessive liberty; dissoluteness; deviation from rule.—**Li'cense**, **Li'cence**, *vt.* To grant a licence to.—**Licen'ti**ATE,[2] *n.* One licensed to practise an art or profession.—**Licen'tious**, *a.* Disregarding rules; dissolute.—**Licen'tious**LY,[2] *adv.*

Li'chen, *n.* L. *lichēn*—G. *leichēn*. A leafless plant growing on rocks, trees, &c.

Lich'-gate, **Lych'-gate**, *n.* From obs. *Lich*, corpse—O.E. *līc*, form, body = O.N. *līk*, O.H.G. *līh* (Ger. *leiche*, corpse). LIKE, *a.* The roofed gate of a churchyard under which a corpse is placed to await the clergyman.

Lic'it, *a.* L. *licitus*, pa.pple. of *licēre*, to be lawful. LICENCE. Lawful, permitted.

Lick, *vt.* O.E. *liccian* = O.H.G. *leckōn* (Ger. *lecken*). Cogn. with Skr. *lih*, G. *leichein*, L. *lingěre*. LECHER. To pass the tongue over; to thrash; to excel.—*n.* An act of licking.

Lick'erish, *a.* Altered (with -ISH) f. obs. *Lickerous* — A.F. **likerous* = O.F. *lecheros*, LECHEROUS. Fond of dainty fare; lewd.

Lid, *n.* O.E. *hlid* = Du. *lid*, O.H.G. *hlit*. A movable cover; the cover of the eye.

Lie, *v.*[1]*i.* O.E. *licgan*. Common Teut. O.Teut. root *leg-*. Cogn. with G. *lechos*, L. *lectus*, bed. LAIR. LAY, *v.* LOW, *a.* To be placed horizontally or at rest; to be situated; to exist, be set or arranged; to be incumbent *upon*; of an action at law, to be sustainable.—*n.* Direction, position; state (of affairs, &c.).

Lie, *v.*[2]*i.* O.E. *léogan*. Common Teut. To tell a lie.—*n.* O.E. *lyge*. A false statement intended to deceive.—**Li**'AR,[2] *n.*

Lief, *a.* O.E. *léof*, *líof* = O.N. *liúfr*, O.H.G *liub*, *lieb* (Ger. *lieb*), f. Teut. root *leub-*, to like. From one grade (*laub-*) of the root come BELIEVE, FURLOUGH, LEAVE, *n.*; from another (*lub-*) comes LOVE. Dear.—*adv.* Gladly.

Liege, *a.* O.F. *liege*, prob. an adoption of O.H.G. *ledig*, free (with change of sense perh. due to the influence of L. *ligātus*, bound). Entitled to, bound to render, feudal service. —*n.* The lord; the vassal; a loyal subject.

Li'en, *n.* F. *lien*—L. *ligāmen*, bond, tie, f. *ligāre*, to bind. ALLY. A right to retain property until a claim is satisfied.

Lieu, *n.* F. *lieu*, L. *locus*, place. LOCAL. *In lieu of*, instead of.—**Lieuten'ant**, *n.* F., f. *lieu* + *tenant*, holding. TENANT. A substitute; a junior officer in the navy and army.

Life, *n.*; *pl.* **Lives**. O.E. *līf*, corresp. to O. Fris. *līf*, life, body, O.H.G. *līb*, life (Ger. *leib*, body). Teut. root *lib-*. LEAVE, *v.* Animate existence; vivacity; living things collectively; the period from birth to death; one's life-history; manner of living.—**Life'**LESS, *a.*

Lift, *vt.* O.N. *lypta* = M.H.G. Ger. *lüften*, f. O.Teut. **luftus* (O.N. *loft*), air, sky. LOFT. To raise to a higher position.—*vi.* To rise.—*n.* The action or an act of lifting; an elevator.

Lig'ament, *n.* L. *ligāmentum*, f. *ligāre*, to bind. ALLY. LIEN. OBLIGE. A bond of union; one of the bands of tissue which bind the bones together. — **Lig'ature**, *n.* L. *ligātūra*, a binding. A thread used to tie up an artery.

Light, *a.*[1] O.E. *léoht, līht* = O.Fris. *li(u)cht*, O.H.G. *līht(i)* (Ger. *leicht*). Cogn. with G. *elaphros.* LUNG. Of little weight; not laden; lightly armed; lightly constructed; gentle, not violent; easily digested; trivial; frivolous, unthinking; nimble, quick; easy to bear; easy to accomplish; requiring little mental effort.—*adv.* In a light manner.—**Light'**EN,[2] *v.*[1]*t.* To reduce or remove the load of; to mitigate.—**Light'**LY,[2] *adv.*—**Light'**NESS, *n.*—**Lights**, *n.pl.* The lungs (from their lightness).

Light, *v.*[1]*i.* O.E. *līhtan*, to make light, to relieve of a burden, conn. with prec. To descend *from* a horse or vehicle; to alight; to come by chance *on* or *upon.*—**Light'**ER, *n.* A large boat used in unloading ships.

Light, *n.* O.E. *léoht*, corresp. to O.Fris. *liacht*, O.H.G. *lioht* (Ger. *licht*). Cogn. with G. *leukos*, white, L. *lux*, light. LUCIFER. LUCUBRATE. The natural agent by which objects become visible; a source or means of admission of light; daylight; the state of being visible; mental illumination; a part of a picture represented as lighted up.—*a.*[2] Not dark; pale in hue.—*v.*[2]*t.* O.E. *līhtan.* To set burning; to give light to; to brighten *up* (the eyes, &c.).—*vi.* To take fire; of the eyes, &c., to brighten *up.* —**Light'**EN,[2] *v.*[2]*t.* To give light to; to light up (the face, &c.).—*vi.* Of the face, &c., to light up; to shine; to flash lightning.—**Light'ning**, *n.* Alteration of *lightening.* A visible atmospheric discharge of electricity.—**Light'house**, *n.* A tower bearing a light.—**Light'**SOME, *a.* Radiant; well-lighted, bright.

Lig'neous, *a.* L. *ligneus* (f. *lignum*, wood)+ -OUS. Of the nature of wood; wooden.

Like, *a.* Early M.E. *līch, lik*, shortened form of O.E. *gelic* (lit., 'having the same form', f. pref. *ge-* + *līc*, form, body) = O.N. *glíkr*, O.H.G. *gilih* (Ger. *gleich*). EACH. LICH-GATE. -LY.[1] Resembling, similar; such as.—*adv.* (quasi-*prep.*). In or after the manner of, as in the case of.—**Like'**LY,[1] *a.* Having an appearance of truth, probable; apparently suitable; promising, hopeful.—*adv.* Probably.—**Like'li**HOOD, *n.* — **Lik'**EN,[2] *vt.* To compare.— —**Like'**NESS, *n.* The fact or quality of being like; a portrait.—**Like'wise**, *adv.* Abb. f. *in like wise.* In the like manner; moreover.

Like, *vi.* O.E. *līcian*, to please, orig., to be like or suitable for, conn. with prec. To be pleasing. —*vt.* To find agreeable; to find it agreeable *to do* or *be.*—**Like'**ABLE, *a.*

Li'lac, *n.* F. *lilac* (now *lilas*)—Sp. *lilac*—Arab. *līlak*, conn. with *nīl*, indigo. ANILINE. A shrub with pale violet flowers; the colour of the flowers.—*a.* Of the colour.

Lilt, *vt.* and *i.* M.E. *lulte*, perh. cogn. with Du., L.G. *lul*, pipe. To sing merrily.—*n.* The rhythmical cadence of music or verse.

Lil'y, *n.* O.E. *lilie*—L. *līlium*—G. *leirion.* A bulbous plant with bright flowers.

Limb, *n.*[1] O.E. *lim* = O.N. *limr.* An arm or leg; a branch of a tree.—*vt.* To dismember.

Limb, *n.*[2] L. *limbus*, border, edge. The edge of the disk of the sun or moon.

Lim'ber, *n.* Orig. obscure. The detachable fore part of a gun-carriage.—*vt.* To attach the limber to (a gun).

Lim'ber, *a.* Orig. obscure. Flexible, pliant.

Lim'bo, *n.* Ablative sing. of L. *limbus* (LIMB[2]), in Med.L. in first sense below, in such phrases as *in* or *e* (in or out of) *limbo.* A supposed region on the border of Hell, the abode of the just who died before Christ's coming and of unbaptized infants; prison, confinement.

Lime, *n.*[1] O.E. *līm*, adhesive substance = O.N. *līm*, O.H.G. *līm* (Ger. *leim*). Cogn. with L. *līmus*, mud. LOAM. A viscous substance used for catching birds, birdlime; the alkaline earth forming the chief constituent of mortar. —*vt.* To smear, to catch, with birdlime; to treat (land) with lime.—**Lime'stone**, *n.* A rock which yields lime when burnt.

Lime, *n.*[2] F. *lime.* LEMON. A fruit smaller and more acid than the lemon.

Lime, *n.*[3] App. alteration of *line* = *lind.* LINDEN. A common ornamental tree.

Lim'it, *n.* F. *limite*—L. *līmes, līmitis.* A boundary; a restriction; utmost extent, duration, &c.—*vt.* L. *līmitāre.* To bound, restrict. —**Lim'it**ABLE, *a.*—**Limit**A'TION, *n.*

Limn, *vt.* Alteration of obs. *Lumine*, to illuminate (manuscripts, &c.).—O.F. *luminer*—Med.L. *lūmināre*, f. L. *lūmen*, light. LUMINARY. To paint (a picture); to depict.

Limp, *a.* Orig. obscure. Wanting in firmness or stiffness.—**Limp'**LY,[2] *adv.*

Limp, *vi.* Cogn. with M.H.G. *limphin.* To walk lamely.—*n.* A limping gait.

Lim'pet, *n.* O.E. *lempedu*—Med.L. *lamprēda*, limpet, also LAMPREY. A mollusc which adheres tightly to its rock.

Lim'pid, *a.* L. *limpidus*, prob. conn. with *lympha.* LYMPH. Clear.—**Limpid'**ITY, *n.*

Linch'-pin, *n.* Obs. *Linch* in same sense (O.E. *lynis* = O.S. *lunisa*, Ger. *lünse*) + PIN. A pin to keep a wheel on the axle-tree.

Lin'den, *n.* Use as *n.* of obs. *Linden*, a. f. obs. *lind, line*, the linden—O.E. *lind* = O.H.G. *linda* (Ger. *linde*). LIME.[3] The lime-tree.

Line, *n.*[1] O.E. *līn*, flax = O.H.G. *līn.* Cogn. with G. *linon*, L. *līnum.* CRINOLINE. LINEN. Linen thread or cloth.—*v.*[1]*t.* To cover inside.

Line, *n.*[2] In sense 'cord' O.E. *līne* = M.Du. *līne*, O.H.G. *līna*—L. *līnea*, linen thread, line, orig. fem. of *līneus*, a. f. *līnum*, flax. (See prec.) In the other senses f. F. *ligne*, f. *līnea.* A cord or string (and hence, a fishing-line, a telegraph wire); a stroke made with a pen, &c.; the equator; the twelfth part of an inch; a limit; a row of persons or things; a trench or rampart; *ship of the line*, one able to take part in a main attack; *the line*, the regular and numbered troops; a series of persons in chronological succession; lineage; course (of action, life, &c.): a department of activity.—*v.*[2]*t.* To mark with a line or lines; to bring into a line; to set a line (of troops, &c.) along.—**Lin'eage**, *n.* O.F. *lignage.* Lineal descent from, the descendants of, an ancestor.—**Lin'**EAL, *a.* Of, consisting of lines; in the direct line of descent.—**Lin'eament**, *n.* F. *linéament* — L. *līneāmentum.* A distinctive feature, esp. of the face.—**Lin'**EAR,[1] *a.*

Lin'en, *a.* O.E. *līnen*, f. *līn.* LINE.[1] Made of flax or linen.—*n.* Cloth woven from flax; linen articles collectively.

Ling, *n.* Cf. O.N. *langa*, Ger. *leng.* Prob. conn. with LONG, *a.* A long slender fish.

Lin'ger, *vi.* Northern M.E. *lenger*, freq. of obs. *Leng*, to prolong, linger—O.E. *lengan*, to prolong, conn. with *lang*, LONG, *a.* To loiter, tarry; to remain long in sickness, &c.

Lin'gual, *a.* Med.L. *linguālis*, f. L. *lingua*, TONGUE. LANGUAGE. Of the tongue or language; formed by the tongue.—*n.* A lingual sound.—**Lin'gu**IST, *n.* One skilled in languages.—**Linguis'**TIC, *a.* Of languages.—In *pl.* as *n.*, the science of languages.

Lin'iment, *n.* L. *linimentum*, f. *linire*, to smear, anoint. An embrocation.

Link, *n.*[1] O.N. **hlenkr*, cogn. with O.H.G. *hlancha*, bend of the body, FLANK, Ger. *gelenk*, joint, link. A ring of a chain.—*vt.* and *i.* To join, to be joined, with or as with a link.

Link, *n.*[2] Of obscure orig. A torch.

Lin'net, *n.* O.F. *linette* (F. *linotte*), f. *lin*, L. *linum*, flax, as feeding on the seeds. LINE.[1] A well-known song-bird.

Lin'seed, *n.* M.E. *lin*, O.E. *lín*, flax (LINE[1]) + SEED. The seed of flax.

Lin'sey-wool'sey, *n.* From *Linsey* in same sense (perh. f. LINE[1] + SAY, *n.*[1]) + WOOL, with jingling ending. WINCEY. A material of coarse wool woven on a cotton warp.

Lint, *n.* M.E. *linnet*, in some way conn. with LINE.[1] Soft material for dressing wounds.

Lin'tel, *n.* O.F. *lintel*—Pop.L. **līmitellus*, dim. f. *līmes*, *līmitis*, LIMIT, confused with *līmen*, *līminis*, threshold, lintel. The horizontal top piece of a door or window.

Li'on, *n.* A.F. *liun* (F. *lion*)—L. *leo*, *leōnis* = G. *leōn*. LEONINE.[1] LEOPARD. A large carnivorous quadruped; a person of note.—**Li'on**ESS, *n.*—**Li'on**IZE, *vt.* To treat as a 'lion'.

Lip, *n.* O.E. *lippa*, corresp. to M.L.G., M.Du., Ger. *lippe*. Cogn. with L. *labium*. LABIAL. Either of the edges of the mouth; a margin or edge.—*vt.* To touch with the lips.

Liqueur', *n.* F. = O.F. *licur*. LIQUOR. An alcoholic liquor sweetened and flavoured.

Liq'uid, *a.* O.F. *liquide*—L. *liquidus*, liquid, bright, f. *liquēre*, to be liquid. PROLIX. Fluid, not solid or gaseous; bright; of sound, clear, not harsh.—*n.* A liquid substance.—**Liq'ue**FY, *vt.* and *i.*—**Lique**FAC'TION, *n.*—**Liques'cent**, *a.* L. *liquescens*, *liquescentis*, pres.pple. of *liquescĕre*, to become liquid. Tending to become liquid.—**Liq'uid**ATE,[3] *vt.* To pay (a debt): to arrange the affairs of and dissolve (a company, &c.).—**Liquid**A'TION, *n.*—**Liq'uidat**OR, *n.*—**Liquid'**ITY, *n.*

Liq'uor, *n.* O.F. *licur*—L. *liquor*, liquidity, a liquid, cogn. with prec. A liquid (in technical senses); liquid, esp. alcoholic, for drinking.

Liq'uorice, *n.* A.F. *lycorys*, O.F. **licorice*—L.L. *liquirītia*—G. *glukurrhiza*, f. *glukus*, sweet + *rhiza*, root. The root of a plant; a preparation made from it; the plant.

Lisp, *vi.* O.E. **wlispian*, f. *wlisp*, lisping. Imitative. Cf. Ger. *lispeln*. To speak with imperfect pronunciation of the sibilant letters; to speak falteringly.—*vt.* To utter lispingly.—*n.* A lisping.

Lis'som, *a.* Var. of LITHESOME. Supple, agile.

List, *n.*[1] O.E. *líste* = M.Du. *lijste*, O.H.G. *līsta* (Ger. *leiste*). The border or edge of a cloth; a strip of cloth, &c.; in *pl.*, the barriers enclosing a space for tilting (in this sense as = O.F. *lisse* (F. *lice*), of doubtful orig.).

List, *n.*[2] Perh. = prec., the sense being developed from that of 'strip (of paper)'. A roll or catalogue.—*v.*[1]*t.* To set down in a list.

List, *n.*[3] Orig. obscure. Inclination of a ship to one side.—*v.*[2]*i.* To incline thus.

List, *v.*[3]*i.* O.E. *lystan* = O.H.G. *lusten* (Ger. *lüsten*). LUST. To desire—*n.*[4] Desire.

List, *v.*[4]*t.* and *i.* O.E. *hlistan*, f. *hlyst*, hearing = O.N., O.S. *hlust*. Cogn. with LOUD and G. *kluein*, L. *cluēre*. To listen.

Lis'ten, *vt.* O.Northumb. *lysna*, corresp. to M.H.G. *lüsenen*. Cogn. with prec., and deriving the *t* from association therewith. To give ear to.—*vi.* To give ear.

List'less, *a.* LIST, *n.*[4] + -LESS. Languidly indifferent.—**List'less**LY,[2] *adv.*

Lit'any, *n.* Med.L. *litania*—G. *litaneia*, prayer, f. *litaneuein*, to pray. A form of prayer in which the clergy lead and the people respond.

Lit'eral, *a.* O.F. *literal*—L. *litterālis*, f. *littera*, LETTER. Of letters; verbally exact; according to the sense of the actual wording, not figurative.—**Lit'eral**LY,[2] *adv.*—**Lit'er**ARY, *a.* Of, versed in, literature.—**Lit'er**ATE,[2] *a.* Versed in literature, educated.—**Litera'tim**, *adv.* L. *litterātim*. Letter for letter.—**Lit'erature**, *n.* L. *litterātūra*. The activity or profession of a writer of books; a body of writings; writings of merit collectively.

Lithe, *a.* O.E. *líthe*, gentle, soft = O.H.G. *lindi* (Ger. *lind*). Cogn. with L. *lentus*, pliant, slow. Supple.—**Lithe'**SOME, *a.* Lissom.

Lithog'raphy, *n.* F. *lithographie*, f. G. *lithos*, stone + *graphein*, to write. GRAPHIC. The making of a drawing, &c., on stone and taking impressions in ink.—**Lith'ograph**, *n.* App. a back-formation. A print produced thus.—*vt.* To produce thus.—**Lithog'raph**ER, *n.*—**Lithograph'**IC, *a.*

Lithot'omy, *n.* G. *lithotomia*, f. *lithos*, stone + -*tomia*, cutting, f. *temnein*, to cut. ATOM. Cutting for stone in the bladder.

Lit'igate, *vi.* L. *lītigāre*, *lītigātum*, f. *lis*, *lītis*, lawsuit. To go to law.—*vt.* To go to law about.—**Lit'ig**ANT, *a.* and *n.* **Litig**A'TION, *n.*—**Litig'**IOUS, *a.* Fond of going to law.

Lit'mus, *n.* M.Du. *leecmos*, f. the Du. equivalent of LAC[1] + *moes*, pulp. A blue colouring matter turned red by acids.

Lit'ter, *n.* A.F. *litere*, O.F. *litiere*—Med.L. *lectāria*, f. L. *lectus*, bed. COVERLET. A portable bed; straw, &c., serving as bedding for animals; fragments lying about, untidiness; the young produced at a birth.—*vt.* To strew with litter; to scatter in disorder *on*, &c.; to lie littered upon; to bring forth (young).

Lit'tle, *a.* O.E. *lýtel*, *lytel*, corresp. to O.S. *luttil*, O.H.G. *luzzil*. Prob. conn. with *lútan*, to LOUT. Small; paltry; not much.—*n.* A small quantity, &c.—*adv.* But slightly.

Lit'toral, *a.* L. *littorālis*, better *lītorālis*, f. *lītus*, *lītoris*, shore. Pertaining or adjacent to the shore.—*n.* A littoral district.

Lit'urgy, *n.* Med.L. *līturgia*—G. *leitourgia*, public duty, service of the gods, liturgy, f. **leitos*, public + *ergon*, WORK. A form of public worship.—**Litur'g**ICAL, *a.*

Live, *a.* Attrib. use of M.E. *live* (O.E. *life*, dat. sing. of *líf*, LIFE) in *in*, *on live*, alive. Living; full of life, active; flaming, glowing.

Live, *vi.* O.E. *libban*. Common Teut. Teut. root *lib-*. LEAVE, *v.* To have life; to feed, subsist; to pass one's life; to continue in life; to dwell.—**Liv'ing**, *vbl.n.* The action of the *v.*; livelihood; a benefice.

Live'lihood, *n.* O.E. *líflád*, f. *líf*, LIFE + *lád*, course. LOAD. Means of living.

Live'long, *a.* Orig. two words, LIEF, *a.* and LONG, *a.* Of *day*, &c., intensive of *long*.

Live'ly, *a.* O.E. *líflic*, f. *líf*, LIFE + -*lic*, -LY[1]. Brisk; vivid.—**Live'li**NESS, *n.*

Liv'er, *n.* O.E. *lifer* = O.N. *lifr*, Ger. *leber*. The organ which secretes the bile.

Liv'ery, *n.* A.F. *liveré*, F. *livrée*, orig. fem. pa.pple. of *livrer*, to hand over, f. L. *līberāre*. DELIVER. The dispensing of food, &c., to servants, &c.; allowance of food for horses, hence, *at livery*, kept for the owner at a fixed charge; distinctive raiment of servants, members of a company, &c.—**Liv'ery-man**, *n.*

A member (and entitled to wear the 'livery') of one of the London guilds. — **Liv'ery-sta'ble**, *n.* A stable where horses are kept at livery or hired out. [colour.

Liv'id, *a.* L. *līvidus.* Of a bluish leaden

Liz'ard, *n.* O.F. *lesarde* (= Sp. *lagarto*)—L. *lacerta.* ALLIGATOR. A four-footed reptile.

Lla'ma, *n.* Sp., f. Peruvian. A S. American ruminant quadruped allied to the camel.

Load, *n.* O.E. *lád*, way, course, corresp. to O.N. *leith.* O.Teut. **laidā.* LEAD, *v.*[2] LIVELIHOOD. LODE. (Influenced by association with LADE.) A burden; the amount usually loaded at once.—*vt.* To put a load on or in, to put a cargo in; to put as a load or cargo; to charge (a firearm); to weigh down, oppress.

Load'stone, Lode'stone, *n.* From prec. Lit. 'way-stone', as guiding mariners. A magnetic ore of iron, a magnet.—**Load'star, Lode'star**, *n.* The pole star.

Loaf, *n.*; *pl.* **Loaves**. O.E. *hláf.* Common Teut. LADY. LAMMAS. LORD. A mass of bread as baked; a conical mass of sugar.

Loaf, *vi.* Orig. obscure. To spend time idly.

Loam, *n.* O.E. *lám* = Du. *leem*, Ger. *lehm.* Cogn. with LIME.[1] A very fertile soil.

Loan, *n.* O.N. *lán* = O.E. *lǽn*, M.Du. *lêne.* Cogn. with G. *leipein*, L. *linquĕre*, to leave. LEND. A thing lent; the action of lending.

Loath, Loth, *a.* O.E. *láth*, hostile, hateful. Common Teut. Reluctant, unwilling. — **Loath'**LY,[1] *a.* Disgusting.—**Loath'**SOME, *a.* Noisome; disgusting. [To abhor.

Loathe, *vt.* O.E. *láthian*, conn. with prec.

Lob'by, *n.* Med.L. *lobia.* LODGE. A passage or corridor into which rooms open.

Lobe, *n.* L.L. *lobus*—G. *lobos*, lobe of the ear, &c. A round projection.—**Lob'ule**, *n.* Mod. L. *lobulus*, dim. of *lobus.* A small lobe.

Lob'ster, *n.* O.E. *loppestre*, corr. of L. *locusta*, lobster, LOCUST. A large marine crustacean.

Lo'cal, *a.* F. *local*—L. *locālis*, f. *locus*, place. ALLOCATE. LIEU. Pertaining to place; belonging to or existing in a particular place or district.—**Local'**ITY, *n.* Place, situation; a district.—**Lo'cal**IZE, *vt.*—**Lo'cal**LY,[2] *adv.*—**Locate'**,[3] *vt.* To attribute to a place; to find the place of.—**Loca'**TION, *n.* The action of placing; situation.—**Loc'at**IVE, *a.* and *n.* A noun case denoting 'place where'.

Loch, *n.* Gael. A lake; an arm of the sea.

Lock, *n.*[1] O.E. *loc* = O.N. *lokkr*, O.H.G. *loc* (Ger. *locke*). A portion of the hair, a tress.

Lock, *n.*[2] O.E. *loc*, corresp. to O.N. *lok*, lid, O.H.G. *loh* (Ger. *loch*), hole. O.Teut. root *lūk-*, to close, enclose. An appliance for fastening a door, lid, &c.; the mechanism by which a firearm is discharged; an enclosure in a canal or river for transferring boats from one level to another; a close crowd of vehicles.—*vt.* To fasten with a lock; to join firmly; to embrace closely.—*vi.* To become fixed; to unite closely. —**Lock'**ER, *n.* A small cupboard with a lock. —**Lock'-jaw**, *n.* Alteration of *locked jaw.* A spasmodic rigidity of the jaws.

Lock'et, *n.* O.F. *locquet*, dim. of *loc*, lock = LOCK.[2] Formerly, a fastening of a necklace, &c. A small case worn as an ornament.

Lo'comotive, *a.* As if f. Mod.L. *locōmōtīvus*, f. L. *locō*, ablative of *locus*, place + Med.L. *mōtīvus*, MOTIVE. Of, having the power of, movement from place to place.—*n.* A steam engine moving from place to place by its own power.—**Locomo'tion**, *n.* From *locō*+*mōtio*, MOTION. Locomotive action or power.

Lo'cust, *n.* O.F. *locuste*—L. *locusta.* LOBSTER. A destructive insect; the fruit of a tree (the carob); the tree. — **Lo'cust-tree**, *n.* The locust; certain American trees (app. f. resemblance of their fruit to that of the locust).

Locu'tion, *n.* L. *locūtio*, *locūtiōnis*, f. *loqui*, to speak. ALLOCUTE. OBLOQUY. A phrase.

Lode, *n.* Var. of LOAD. A vein of ore.

Lodge, *n.* O.F. *loge*, arbour, hut—Med.L. *laubia*, *lobia*, covered walk—O.H.G. **laubja*, shady place, booth (Ger. *laube*, arbour), cogn. with LEAF. LOBBY. A house occupied for hunting or shooting; a cottage at an entrance gate; the meeting-place of a branch of freemasons, &c., the branch.—*vt.* To house; to deposit; to place *with* or *in the hands of*; to throw so as to be arrested at a particular point; to beat down (crops).—*vi.* To live in another's house at a fixed charge; of something thrown, to be lodged.—**Lodg'**ER, *n.*—**Lodg(e)'**MENT, *n.* A lodging or being lodged; a making good one's position on hostile ground.

Loft, *n.* Late O.E. *loft*—O.N. *loft*, *lopt*, air, sky, upper room. LIFT. An attic; a room over a stable; a gallery in a church, &c.—**Loft'**Y,[2] *a.* Of great height; haughty; elevated, sublime.—**Loft'i**LY,[2] *adv.*

Log, *n.* Late M.E. *logge*, of obscure orig. Prob. imitative, to express the notion of something massive. An unhewn portion of a felled tree; an apparatus for ascertaining a ship's speed; a journal kept on a ship, a **Log'-book**.

Log'arithm, *n.* G. *logos*, perh. in sense 'calculation' + *arithmos*, number. One of a class of arithmetical functions tabulated for use in calculations.—**Logarith'mi**C, -ICAL, *aa.*

Log'gerhead, *n.* Dial. *Logger*, horse-clog (cf. LOG) + HEAD. A blockhead; *at loggerheads*, quarrelling (this use of obscure orig.).

Log'ic, *n.* F. *logique*—Med.L. *logica*—G. *logikē* (*technē*), logical (art), fem. of *logikos*, a. f. *logos*, reasoning. The art of reasoning.—**Log'ic**AL, *a.* Of or pertaining to logic; according to right reasoning; able to reason rightly.—**Log'ical**LY,[2] *adv.*—**Logic'**IAN, *n.*

Logom'achy, *n.* G. *logomachia*, f. *logos*, word + *-machia*, fighting, f. *mache-esthai*, to fight. Contention, a contention, about words.

Loin, *n.* O.F. *loigne*, var. of *longe*—Med.L. **lumbea*, fem. of **lumbeus*, a. f. L. *lumbus.* LUMBAR. The part of the body on either side between the ribs and the hip-bone.

Loi'ter, *vi.* M.Du. *loteren*, to wag about (like a loose tooth). Cf. E.Fris. *lōteren* in sim. sense. To waste time on the way, to dawdle.

Loll, *vi.* App. imitative of swinging. To lie idly; of the tongue, to hang out.—*vt.* To let (the tongue) hang out.

Lol'lipop, *n.* Orig. obscure. In *pl.*, sweetmeats.

Lone, *a.* Aphetic f. ALONE. Solitary; isolated; unfrequented. — **Lone'**LY,[1] *a.* Lone; feeling sadness from being solitary.—**Lone'li**NESS, *n.*—**Lone'**SOME, *a.* Lonely.

Long, *a.* O.E. *lang*, *long.* Common Teut, Cogn. with L. *longus.* FURLONG. LENGTH. LING. LINGER. LUNGE. Having a great extent from end to end; too long; of a vowel, having the greater of the two recognized measures of duration.—*adv.* For or during a long time; at, from, to a distant point of time.

Long, *vi.* O.E. *langian*, impersonal = O.S. *langōn*, impersonal, O.N. *langa*, impersonal and personal. Conn. with prec. Formerly, *impersonal* with acc., *me longs*, I long. To have an earnest desire *for* or *to do.*

Longe'val, *a.* L. *longaevus* (f. *longus*, LONG.

a. + *aevum*, AGE) + -AL. Existing long.—**Longev'**ITY, *n.* Long existence.

Lon'gitude, *n.* L. *longitūdo, longitūdinis*, f. *longus*, LONG, *a.* Length; distance of a place east or west measured by the angle which its meridian makes with a standard meridian.—**Longitu'din**AL, *a.* Of length or longitude; in the direction of the length.

Loo, *n.* Abb. f. *Lanterloo*, the name of an older form of the game—F. *lantur(e)lu*, orig. an unmeaning refrain. A game of cards.

Loo'by, *n.* Cf. LUBBER. A clumsy person.

Loo'fah, *n.* Egyptian Arab. *lūfah*, a plant. The fibrous pod used as a sponge, &c.

Look, *vi.* O.E. *lócian* = O.S. *lôcon*. To apply one's sight; to direct one's eyes with a particular expression; to take care, make sure; to front or be turned *to*, &c.; to seem; to hope or be on the watch *for*.—*n.* A looking; appearance, aspect.—**Look'ing-glass**, *n.* A glass in which to look to see one's face, &c., reflected, a mirror.—**Look-out**, *n.* A being on the watch; a place for watching; a watchman.

Loom, *n.* M.E. *lome*, tool, utensil (a sense still surviving in dialects)—O.E. *gelóma*, of obscure orig. HEIRLOOM. A machine for weaving yarn or thread into cloth; the part of an oar that is within the boat in rowing.

Loom, *vi.* Poss. orig. to come slowly towards. Cf. E.Fris. *lômen*, Sw. dial. *loma*, to move slowly. To appear indistinctly and enlarged.

Loop, *n.*[1] Of obscure orig. The doubling of a part of a piece of string, &c.; the part doubled. —*vt.* To form into a loop; to fasten by means of a loop.—*vi.* To form a loop.

Loop, *n.*[2] Prob. conn. with M.Du. *lûpen* (Du. *luipen*), to lie in wait. An opening for looking through or for discharging missiles.—Sim. **Loop'-hole**. Also, a means of escape.

Loose, *a.* M.E. *lôs*—O.N. *lauss*, loose, corresp. to O.E. *léas*, destitute of (-LESS), false. Common Teut. General senses 'loose', 'destitute of', 'loose in conduct', 'worthless'. Teut. root *laus-*. FORLORN. Free from restraint; not attached; not fastened together; not securely attached; slack; not fitting closely; not close in structure or arrangement; of the bowels, relaxed; inaccurate, vague; dissolute. —*vt.* To set free; to unfasten; to detach; to make slack, relax. — *vi.* To shoot, let fly.—**Loose'**LY,[2] *adv.*—**Loos'**EN,[2] *vt.* To set free; to unfasten; to detach; to make slack, relax; to make less compact, sever into particles; to relax, relieve costiveness of (the bowels).—*vi.* To become loose.—**Loose'**NESS, *n.*

Loot, *n.* Hindī *lūt*. Plunder; illicit gains; looting.—*vt.* To plunder; to carry off as loot.

Lop, *n.* Orig. obscure. The smaller branches of trees, faggot-wood.—*v.*[1]*t.* To cut away the branches of (a tree); to cut away (the branches).

Lop, *v.*[2]*i.* Perh. imitative. To hang limply; to slouch; to dawdle.—**Lop-si'ded**, *a.* That leans to one side; too heavy on one side.

Loqua'cious, *a.* L. *loquax, loquācis* (f. *loqui*, to speak) + -OUS. ALLOCUTE. Given to much talking.—**Loquac'**ITY, *n.*

Lord, *n.* O.E. *hláford, hláfweard*, f. *hláf*, bread, LOAF + *weard* WARD. LADY. Formerly, the head of a household. One holding dominion over others; an owner; a feudal superior; God; a title of Christ; part of the customary designation of a peer, &c.—*vi.* To domineer *over*.—**Lord'ling**, *n.* -LING (3). A petty lord.—**Lord'**LY,[1] *a.*—**Lord'li**NESS, *n.* —**Lord'**SHIP, *n.* The dignity and functions of a lord; his domain; with possessive pronouns, a title given to peers, &c.

Lore, *n.* O.E. *lár* = O.S., O.H.G. *lêra* (Ger. *lehre*). O.Teut. root *lais-*. LEARN. What is taught or learned, learning, erudition.

Lorgnette', *n.* F., f. *lorgner*, to squint. Eye-glasses with a handle; an opera-glass.

Lorn, *a.* Pa.pple. of obs. *Lese*, to lose—O.E. *-léosan*. FORLORN. Abandoned, desolate.

Lose, *vt.* O.E. *losian*, gen. intrans., to perish, be lost, f. *los*, dissolution, destruction (occurring only in dative, and app. not the source of LOSS), corresp. to O.N. *los*, breaking up of an army. From *lus-*, weak grade of *laus-*. FORLORN. To be deprived of; to fail to retain; to become unable to find; to deviate from (the way); to waste; to let slip; to fail to get; to be too late for (a train, &c.); to be defeated in; to cause the loss of.—*vi.* To suffer loss.

Loss, *n.* Perh. a back-formation f. *lost*, pa. pple. of LOSE. Destruction; being deprived of, failure to retain (something); being defeated; failure to take advantage, to make good use, to obtain; something lost; detriment.

Lot, *n.* O.E. *hlot*, conn. with *hléotan*, O.S. *hliotan*, O.N. *hlióta*, to cast lots, get by lot. (F. *lot*, lot, It. *lotto*, a game of chance, are f. Teut.) ALLOT. LOTTERY. An object used in deciding disputes, &c., by an appeal to chance or to a supposed divine influence; the casting or drawing of lots; one's destiny or portion; an item at an auction; a number or collection; a large number or quantity.

Lo'tion, *n.* L. *lōtio, lōtiōnis*, washing, f. *lavāre, lōtum*, to wash. A liquid applied to wounds, &c., or used for beautifying the skin.

Lot'tery, *n.* It. *lotteria*, f. *lotto*. LOT. A distribution of prizes by chance.

Lo'tus, *n.* L. *lōtus*—G. *lōtos*. A plant supposed to yield a fruit producing forgetfulness (Odyssey 9, 93); a tree with hard black wood; the lily of the Nile; some kind of clover.

Loud, *a.* O.E. *hlúd*. Common W. Germanic. Cogn. with LIST, *v.*[4] Strongly audible; making a loud sound; clamorous; of colour, &c., vulgarly obtrusive.—**Loud'**LY,[2] *adv.*

Lounge, *vi.* Perh. suggested by obs. *Lungis*, an awkward fellow, a laggard—O.F. *longis*—L. *Longinus*, the traditional name of the centurion who pierced Christ's body (popularly associated with L. *longus*, long). To move indolently; to loll; to idle.—*vt.* To pass (time) *away* in lounging.—**Loung'**ER, *n.*

Lour, Low'er, *vi.* M.E. *louren*, of obscure orig., perh. repg. an O.E. **lūrian*. To frown, scowl; to look dark and threatening.

Louse, *n.*; *pl.* **Lice**. O.E. *lús*. Common Teut. A parasitic insect.—**Lous'**Y,[2] *a.*

Lout, *vi.* O.E. *lútan*, corresp. to O.N. *lúta*. LITTLE. To bend, bow.

Lout, *n.* Perh. of dial. orig. and conn. with prec. An awkward ill-mannered fellow.

Love, *n.* O.E. *lufu* = O.H.G. *luba*, f. Teut. root *leub-*. LIEF. Warm affection; strong liking; attachment based upon difference in sex; sexual passion; a sweetheart; no score, nothing.—*vt.* O.E. *lufian*. To bear love to; to have a strong liking for.—*vi.* To be in love. —**Lov'**ABLE, *a.*—**Love'-bird**, *n.* A small bird of the parrot kind remarkable for its affection for its mate.—**Love'**LESS, *a.*—**Love'-lorn**, *a.* Forsaken by one's love; pining for love. —**Love'**LY,[1] *a.* Exquisitely beautiful; excellent, delightful.—**Lov'**ER, *n.*

Low, *a.* Early M.E. *lāh*—O.N. *lágr* = O.Fris. *lêge, lêch*, M.Du. *lage, laech*. Cogn. with LIE.[1]

Not tall; not elevated in position; of a river, &c., containing less water than usual; of humble rank or estimation; commonplace, mean; undignified; abject, base; coarse, vulgar; lacking bodily vigour, weak; dejected, dispirited; not high in amount or in degree of intensity; of a sound, produced by slow vibrations; of a voice, not loud.—**Low'er**, *vt.* From *lower*, comp. of *low*. To cause or allow to descend; to make lower; to diminish in amount, price, quality, &c.; to degrade, dishonour.—**Low'land**, *n.* Low land; in *pl.*, the less mountainous part of Scotland lying south and east of the Highlands.—**Low'lander**, *n.*—**Low'ly**,[1] *a.* Humble, modest, unpretending.—**Low'liness**, *n.*

Low, *vi.* O.E. *hlówan*. Common Teut. Cogn. with G. *kiklēskein*, to call, L. *clāmāre*, to shout. To utter the cry of cattle.—*n.* The cry.

Loy'al, *a.* F. *loyal*, O.F. *loial*—L. *lēgālis*. LEAL. LEGAL. True to obligations; faithful to the sovereign or to authority; devoted to the person of the sovereign.—**Loy'alist**, *n.*—**Loy'ally**,[2] *adv.*—**Loy'alty**, *n.*

Loz'enge, *n.* O.F. *losenge*, perh. a deriv. of the word appearing as Pr. *lausa*, Sp. *losa*, Pg. *lousa*, slab, tombstone—L.L. **lapidea*, f. L. *lapis*, stone. LAPIDARY. A figure having four equal sides and two acute and two obtuse angles; a small cake of prepared sugar.

Lub'ber, *n.* Poss. in form an adoption of O.F. *lobeor*, swindler, parasite, f. *lober*, to deceive, to sponge upon, and altered in sense by association with dial. *Lob*, a bumpkin, lout, of uncertain orig. A big, clumsy, stupid fellow; a clumsy seaman.—**Lub'berly**,[1] *a.*

Lu'bricate, *vt.* L. *lūbricāre*, *lūbricātum*, f. *lūbricus*, slippery, cogn. with SLIP, *v.* To make slippery or smooth; to apply oil to (a machine).—**Lu'bricant**, *n.* A material for lubricating machinery.—**Lubrica'tion**, *n.*—**Lu'bricator**, *n.* One who lubricates; a lubricant; a contrivance for lubricating machinery.—**Lubric'ity**, *n.* Slipperiness; lewdness.

Lucern(e)', *n.* F. *luzerne*—Mod.Pr. *luzerno*, of unknown orig. A plant resembling clover.

Lu'cid, *a.* L. *lūcidus*, f. *lūcēre*, to shine. ELUCIDATE. Bright; pellucid; easily understood; sane.—**Lucid'ity**, *n.*—**Lu'cidly**,[2] *adv.*—**Lu'cent**, *a.* Bright; pellucid.

Lu'cifer, *n.* L. *lūcifer*, light-bringing, as *n.*, the morning-star, f. *lux*, *lūcis*, LIGHT + *-fer*, bearing, f. *ferre*, to BEAR. The morning-star; the planet Venus when she appears before sunrise; the rebel archangel; a match for producing fire (orig. *lucifer match*).

Luck, *n.* L.G. *luk*, shortened form of *geluk* (M.H.G. *gelücke*, Ger. *glück*), of unknown orig. Fortune, good or bad; chance; good fortune.—**Luck'less**, *a.* Unfortunate.—**Luck'y**,[2] *a.* Having good luck.—**Luck'ily**,[2] *adv.*

Lu'cre, *n.* L. *lucrum*, cogn. with G. *apolauein*, to enjoy. Gain or profit as a motive.—**Lu'crative**, *a.* L. *lucrātivus*, f. *lucrāri*, *lucrātus*, to gain, f. *lucrum*. Yielding gain.

Lu'cubrate, *vi.* L. *lūcubrāre*, *lūcubrātum*, to work by lamp-light, f. *lux*, *lūcis*, LIGHT. To produce lucubrations.—**Lucubra'tion**, *n.* Nocturnal study, study; the product of nocturnal study, an elaborate literary work.

Lu'dicrous, *a.* L. *lūdicrus*, that serves for sport, done in sport (f. *lūdĕre*, to play) + -OUS. ALLUDE. PRELUDE. Laughably absurd, droll, ridiculous.—**Lu'dicrously**,[2] *adv.*

Luff, *n.* M.E. *lof*, *loof*, app. f. O.F. *lof*, some contrivance for altering the course of a ship (the earliest sense in Eng., now obsolete). Cf. Du. *loef*, weather-gauge, luff. ALOOF. The weather part of a fore-and-aft sail, *i.e.* the part next the mast.—*vt.* and *i.* To bring the head of (a ship) nearer to the wind.

Lug, *vi.* Prob. of Scand. orig. Cf. Sw. *lugga*, to pull a person's hair, f. *lugg*, forelock. To pull, tug.—*vt.* To drag with effort.—*n.*[1] An act of lugging.—**Lug'gage**, *n.* The necessaries which a traveller takes with him.

Lug, *n.*[2] Cf. Du. *log*, slow, heavy. A marine worm used as bait.

Lug'-sail, *n.* Of uncertain orig. A four-cornered sail fixed upon a yard which hangs obliquely on the mast.—**Lug'ger**, *n.* App. formed f. *lug-*. A small vessel with such sails.

Lugu'brious, *a.* L. *lūgubris*, of mourning (f. *lūgēre*, to mourn) + -OUS. Mournful.

Luke'warm, *a.* From dial. *Luke*, in sim. senses (app. f. O.E. **hlēow* = O.N. *hlýr*, warm, mild) + WARM, *a.* Moderately warm, tepid; lacking enthusiasm or ardour, indifferent.

Lull, *vt.* Imitative of the repetition of *lu*, *lu*, or similar sounds. Cf. Sw. *lulla*, Da. *lulle*; also L. *lallāre*. To soothe with sounds, to sing to rest; to make quiescent.—*vi.* To become quiescent.—*n.* A brief period of quiescence.—**Lul'laby**, *int.* From *lull* + *-by*. Cf. '*bye-bye*', child's word for sleep, bed. A soothing refrain.—*n.* A song that soothes to rest.

Lum'bar, *a.* Mod.L. *lumbāris*, f. L. *lumbus*, LOIN. Of, belonging to, situated in, the loins.—**Lumba'go**, *n.* L. *lumbāgo*, f. *lumbus*. A rheumatic affection in the lumbar region.

Lum'ber, *v.*[1]*i.* M.E. *lomere*, poss. a freq. formation on *lome*, LAME. To move heavily.

Lum'ber, *n.* Prob. f. prec., perh. associated with obs. *Lumber* = *Lombard* in obs. sense 'a pawnbroker's establishment'—F. *Lombard*, a Lombard—It. *Lombardo*—L.L. *Longobardus* (the Lombards having been noted bankers and brokers). Disused furniture, useless and cumbrous material; roughly prepared timber.—*v.*[2]*t.* To obstruct, burden uselessly.

Lu'minary, *n.* F. *luminaire*—Med. L. *lūminārium*, f. L. *lūmen*, *lūminis*, light. ILLUMINATE. LIMN. A celestial body giving light.—**Lu'minous**, *a.* L. *lūminōsus*. Shining, bright; well lighted.—**Luminos'ity**, *n.*

Lump, *n.* Of uncertain orig. Cf. L.G. *lump*, coarse, heavy, Da. *lump(e)*, lump. A shapeless piece or mass; a swelling; *lump sum*, a sum covering a number of items.—*vt.* To throw together in one mass, sum, or group.—*vi.* To move heavily.—**Lump'ish**, *a.* Heavy and clumsy; stupid, sluggish.—**Lump'y**,[2] *a.*

Lu'nar, *a.* L. *lūnāris*, f. *lūna*, the moon. Of, pertaining to, measured by, the moon.

Lu'natic, *a.* L.L. *lūnāticus*, f. *lūna*. (See prec.) Insane (recurring insanity having been supposed to depend on the changes of the moon).—*n.* A lunatic person.—**Lu'nacy**, *n.*

Lunch, *n.* Perh. evolved f. LUMP. Formerly, a thick piece, a hunk. A meal taken in the early afternoon. (In this sense the word is a contraction of **Lun'cheon**, which appears to be in some way related to it.)

Lunette', *n.* F., dim. of *lune*, L. *lūna*. LUNAR. An arched opening in a concave ceiling; a small fort with an angular front.

Lung, *n.* O.E. *lungen* = O.H.G. *lungun* (Ger. *lunge*), O.N. *lunga*. Cogn. with LIGHT, *a.*[1] (the lungs having been named from their lightness). Each of the two organs of respiration.

Lunge, *n.* Aphetic var. of obs. *Allonge* in same sense—F. *allonge*, f. *allonger*, to lengthen, lunge, f. *à*, to + *long*, L. *longus*, LONG, *a*. A thrust with a sword, &c.—*vi*. To make a lunge.

Lu'pus, *n*. L. *lupus*, WOLF. An eating disease of the skin.—**Lu'pine**, *a*. L. *lupīnus*, f. *lupus*. Having the nature and qualities of a wolf.

Lurch, *n*.[1] F. *lourche*, an old game like backgammon, of uncertain orig. Formerly, the game. A concluding state of the score at various games in which one player is much ahead of the other; hence, *to leave in the lurch*, to abandon in a position of difficulty.

Lurch, *n*.[2] Orig. obscure. A sudden leaning over to one side.—*v*.[1]*i*. To make a lurch.

Lurch, *v*.[2]*t*. App. a var. of LURK. To cheat. —**Lurch'**ER, *n*. A petty thief or cheat; a mongrel dog much used by poachers.

Lure, *n*. O.F. *leurre*, *loerre* = Pr. *loire*, cogn. with It. *logoro*, bait, prob. of Teut. orig. Cf. Ger. *luder*, bait. An apparatus for recalling a hawk; something which entices or tempts. —*vt*. Cf. F. *leurrer*. To recall (a hawk) by means of the lure; to entice, tempt.

Lu'rid, *a*. L. *lūridus*. Pale and dismal in colour; shining in darkness with a red glare.

Lurk, *vi*. App. f. *lur* = LOUR, in obs. sense 'to lurk', with freq. suff. To lie hidden; to remain furtively about a spot; to be latent.

Lus'cious, *a*. Of obscure orig. Sweet, highly pleasant; sweet to excess, cloying.

Lust, *n*. O.E. *lust*, pleasure, delight. Common Teut. Cogn. with LIST, *v*.[3], and G. *lilaiesthai*, to desire. Formerly, pleasure; inclination, appetite. Sexual or passionate desire.—*vi*. To have a passionate desire.—**Lust'**FUL, *a*.—**Lust'**Y,[2] *a*. Formerly, merry; pleasing. Healthy, vigorous.—**Lust'i**LY,[2] *adv*.

Lus'tre, *n*.[1] F. *lustre*—L. *lustrāre*, to illumine. ILLUSTRATE. Refulgence, gloss; brilliancy; splendour of renown, glory; a thin glossy dress material.—**Lus'tr**OUS, *a*.

Lus'tre, *n*.[2] L. **Lustrum** (also used unchanged), among the Romans, a purificatory sacrifice made every five years, app. f. the root of *luĕre*, to wash. A period of five years.—**Lus-tr**ATE',[3] *vt*. To purify by sacrifice.—**Lus'tr**AL, *a*.—**Lustr**A'TION, *n*.

Lute, *n*. F. *lut*—Arab. *al-'ūd* (where *al* is the definite article). A stringed musical instrument played with the fingers.

Lux'ate, *vt*. L. *luxāre*, *luxātum*, f. *luxus*, dislocated—G. *loxos*, slanting. To dislocate, put out of joint.—**Luxa'**TION, *n*.

Lux'ury, *n*. O.F. *luxurie*—L. *luxuria*, luxuriance, riotous living, f. *luxus*, abundance, sumptuous enjoyment. Habitual indulgence in what is choice and costly; something not indispensable conducing to enjoyment; abundance of appliances for comfort.—**Luxu'ri**OUS, *a*.—**Luxu'rious**LY,[2] *adv*.—**Luxu'ri**ATE,[3] *vi*. To grow rank; to indulge in luxury, to feast, revel; to take great delight *in*.—**Luxu'ri**ANT, *a*. Growing profusely; abundant, profuse.—**Luxu'ri**ANCE, *n*.

Lyd'dite, *n*. From *Lydd* in Kent, as first used there + suff. *-ite* of scientific terms. A powerful explosive.

Lye, *n*. O.E. *léag*, *lēah* = O.H.G. *louga* (Ger. *lauge*). Prob. f. Teut. root *lau-*. LATHER. Alkaline water for washing clothes.

Ly'ing-in', *n*. The being in childbed.

Lymph, *n*. L. *lympha*, water. LIMPID. Clear water; a colourless animal fluid.—**Lymphat'ic**, *a*. L. *lymphāticus*, distracted, frenzied (cf. *hydrophobia*), in Mod.L. used in sense 'of lymph'. Of lymph; flabby, pale and sluggish (a state formerly supposed to result from an excess of lymph in the system).—*n*. A vessel in the body conveying lymph.

Lynch law, *n*. In early use *Lynch's* (*Linch's*) *law*. Orig. uncertain. The expression has been associated (app. erroneously) with the name of Charles *Lynch*, a Virginian justice of the peace, who in 1780 illegally fined and imprisoned certain tories. The practice of condemning to death by a self-constituted court. —**Lynch**, *vt*. To put to death by lynch law.

Lynx, *n*. L. *lynx*—G. *lugx*, prob. conn. with *leussein*, to see. OUNCE.[2] An animal of the cat kind noted for the keenness of its sight.

Lyre, *n*. F. *lyre*—L. *lyra*—G. *lura*. A stringed instrument of the harp kind.—**Lyr'**IC, **Lyr'**ICAL, *aa*. Of or pertaining to the lyre; meant to be sung; characteristic of song; applied to short poems expressing the poet's own thoughts and feelings, also to a poet who writes such poems.—**Lyr'ic**, *n*. A lyric poem.—**Lyr'**IST, *n*. A player on the lyre; a lyric poet.

M

Macad'am, *n*. From John Loudon *McAdam*, the inventor. A kind of roadway constructed of successive layers of stone broken to pieces of a nearly uniform size (only *attrib*.); the material used.—**Macad'am**IZE, *vt*. To make or repair (a road) according to McAdam's system.

Macaro'ni, *n*. It. *maccaroni*, pl., of obscure orig. An Italian paste of wheat made into small tubes and dried; an exquisite who affected Continental tastes.—**Macaron'**IC, *a*. Applied to a kind of verse in which vernacular words are used in a Latin (or Greek) context and with Latin (or Greek) terminations.—

Macaroon', *n*. F. *macaron*—It. *maccarone*, sing. of *maccaroni*. A small sweet cake or biscuit containing ground almonds.

Macaw', *n*. Pg. *macao*, of obscure orig. A long-tailed bird of the parrot kind.

Mace, *n*.[1] O.F. *masse*, *mace* = It. *mazza*, Sp. *maza*, of doubtful orig. A staff or club of metal or with a metal (often spiked) head; a staff of office borne before certain officials.

Mace, *n*.[2] M.E. *macis* (taken as a *pl*.)—F. *macis*, of unknown orig. A spice made from the dried outer covering of the nutmeg.

Mac'erate, *vt*. L. *mācerāre*, *mācerātum*, perh. cogn. with G. *massein*, to knead. To soften by steeping; to cause (the body) to waste away esp. by fasting.—**Macer**A'TION, *n*.

Machine', *n*. F. *machine*—L. *māchina*—G. *mēchanē*, f. *mēchos*, a means, expedient. O. Aryan root *magh-*. MAY, *v*.[2] MECHANIC. A fabric; a vehicle; an apparatus for applying mechanical power.—*vt*. To make or operate upon by a machine.—**Mach'in**ATE,[3] *vi*. To lay plots, scheme.—**Machin**A'TION, *n*.—**Machin'**ERY, *n*. Machines; the parts of a machine collectively.—**Machin'**IST, *n*. One who makes or works machines.

Mack'erel, *n*. O.F. *makerel* (F. *maquereau*), of unknown orig. A well-known sea-fish.

Mack'intosh, *n*. From Charles *Macintosh*, the inventor of the material. *Attrib*., to designate a coat, &c., of a material consisting of two or more layers of cloth cemented with india-rubber; also short for *Mackintosh coat*, &c.

Mac'rocosm, *n*. F. *macrocosme*—Med.L. *macrocosmus*, formed f. G. *makros*, great + *kosmos*, world. The great world or universe, as distinguished from the MICROCOSM.

Mac'ulate, *vt.* L. *maculāre, maculātum*, f. *macula*, spot, mesh. MAIL.[1] TRAMMEL. To spot, stain.—*ppl.a.* L. *maculātus*, the *pa.pple.* Spotted, stained.—**Macul**A'TION, *n.*

Mad, *a.* Contr. representative of O.E. *gemǣd(e)d*, pa. pple. of *gemǣdan*, to make insane, f. *gemād*, insane, corresp. to O.S. *gimēd*, foolish, O.H.G. *gameit*, foolish, vain. (The pref. *ge-*, *gi-*, *ga-* is unessential.) Indogermanic root *mei-*, to change. Cf. L. *mūtāre*. COMMUTE. Suffering from mental disease, frenzied, furious; suffering from rabies; wildly excited or foolish.—*vt.* To make mad.—**Mad'-cap**, *n.* A reckless, flighty, or wildly impulsive person.—**Mad'd**EN,[2] *vi.* and *t.* To become, to make, mad.—**Mad'**LY,[2] *adv.*—**Mad'-man**, *n.* One who is mad.—**Mad'**NESS, *n.*

Mad'am, *n.* O.F. *ma dame*, my lady. DAME. A respectful or polite form of address to ladies.

Mad'der, *n.* O.E. *mædere*. Cf. Sw. *madra*, Norw. *modra*. A climbing plant; the root, used as a source of colouring matter; the dye-stuff or pigment prepared from this.

Madei'ra, *n.* White wine of *Madeira*.

Madon'na, *n.* It., orig. two words = F. *ma dame*. MADAM. The Virgin Mary; a picture of the Virgin Mary.

Mad'rigal, *n.* It. *madrigale*, perh. f. *mandria*, herd (L. *mandra*, stall, stable), and thus orig. 'pastoral song'. A short amatory lyrical poem; a part song for three or more voices without instrumental accompaniment.

Mæ'nad, *n.* L. *maenas, maenadis*—G. *mainas*, f. *mainesthai*, to rave. A votaress of Bacchus.

Maesto'so, *a.* and *adv.* It. = majestic. *Mus.*, in a majestical manner.

Magazine', *n.* F. *magasin*, It. *magazzino*, Sp. *magacen*—Arab. *makhāzin*, pl. of *makhzan*, storehouse, f. *khazana*, to store up. A warehouse; a place for gunpowder or other military stores; a periodical publication; a chamber in a rifle, &c., containing a supply of cartridges.

Magen'ta, *n.* A brilliant crimson aniline dye, discovered shortly after the date of the battle of *Magenta* (1859).—*a.* Of the colour.

Mag'got, *n.* App. connected with obs. *Maddock* in same sense—Early M.E. *mathek*, corresp. to or f. O.N. *mathkr*, M.L.G. *medeke*, dims. of the word appearing in O.E. as *mathu*, *matha*, worm; or poss. f. an O.E. **mathuc*, dim. of these words. MAWKISH. Larva, a grub; a whimsical fancy.—**Mag'got**Y,[2] *a.*

Magi, Magic, &c. See MAGUS.

Mag'istrate, *n.* L. *magistrātus*, the office of a magistrate, a magistrate, f. *magister*, MASTER. A civil officer administering the law.—**Magiste'rial**, *a.* Med.L. *magisteriālis*—L.L. *magisterius*, f. *magister*. Of or pertaining to a master or magistrate; authoritative; dictatorial. — **Mag'istr**ACY, *n.* The office of a magistrate; magistrates collectively.

Magnan'imous, *a.* L. *magnanimus* (f. *magnus*, great + *animus*, mind) + -OUS. MAGNIFICENT. Great-souled, above petty resentment or jealousy.—**Magnanim'**ITY, *n.*

Mag'nate, *n.* L.L. *magnas, magnātis*, f. L. *magnus*. (See prec.) An eminent man.

Magne'sia, *n.* Med.L. *magnēsia*—G. *Magnēsia* (*lithos*), (stone) of Magnesia, designating the loadstone and some silverlike stone. A white earthy powder used in medicine, a compound of **Magne'sium** (formed f. *magnesia*), a metallic chemical element.

Mag'net, *n.* O.F. *magnete*—L. *magnes, magnētis*—G. *Magnēs* (*lithos*), (stone) of Magnesia. (Cf. prec.) Loadstone, an ore of iron which attracts iron and steel; a piece of loadstone; a bar of iron or steel to which the characteristic property of loadstone has been imparted, and which, when freely suspended, tends to assume a position approximately north and south.—**Magnet'**IC, *a.* — **Magnet'ically**, *adv.* -ICAL. -LY.[2] — **Mag'net**ISM, *n.* Magnetic phenomena and their laws; the agency producing these phenomena; attractive influence, charm.—**Mag'net**IZE, *n.* To impart magnetic properties to; to attract, charm.

Magnif'icent, *a.* O.F. *magnificent*—L. *magnificent-*, altered stem of *magnificus*, lit., 'doing great things', f. *magnus*, great + *-ficus*, f. *facĕre*, to do. FACT. MAGNANIMOUS. MAGNITUDE. Living in splendour; imposing; excellent.—**Magnif'ic**ENCE, *n.* — **Magnif'icent**LY,[2] *adv.* — **Mag'ni**FY, *vt.* To extol; to make greater; to exaggerate; to increase the apparent size of (as with a lens, &c.).

Magnil'oquent, *a.* L. *magniloquus* (f. *magnus* (see prec.) + *-loquus*, speaking, f. *loqui*, to speak (ALLOCUTE)) + -ENT. Speaking loftily.—**Magnil'oqu**ENCE, *n.*

Mag'nitude, *n.* L. *magnitūdo*, f. *magnus*. MAGNIFICENT. Greatness, size, importance.

Magno'lia, *n.* From Pierre *Magnol*, botanist. A tree with beautiful foliage and flowers.

Mag'num, *n.* Neut. sing. of L. *magnus*. MAGNIFICENT. A bottle holding two quarts.

Mag'pie, *n.* From *Mag*, short for *Margaret* + PIE.[1] A bird which can be taught to speak.

Ma'gus, *n.*; *pl.* **Ma'gi**. L.—G. *magos*—Old Per. *magus*. One of the ancient Persian priestly class; a magician or sorcerer; one of the 'wise men of the East' who brought offerings to the infant Christ.—**Mag'ic**, *a.* F. *magique*—L. *magicus*—G. *magikos*, a. f. *magos*. Of, working or produced by, magic: like magic in effect.—*n.* The pretended art of producing effects by superhuman means. — **Mag'**ICAL, *a.*—**Mag'ical**LY,[2] *adv.*—**Magic'**IAN, *n.*

Mahog'any, *n.* Orig. unknown. The wood of a tropical American tree; the tree.

Mahout', *n.* Hindī *mahāut*, *mahāwat*. An elephant-driver.

Mai'den, *n.* O.E. *mægden* = O.H.G. *magatīn*, a dim. formation f. the word meaning maiden appearing in O.E. as *mægeth*, *mægth*, and in O.H.G. as *magad* (Ger. *magd*, maidservant). A young unmarried woman; a virgin.—*a.* Unmarried; of, befitting, a maiden; that has yielded no results; the first of its kind, made, &c., for the first time.—**Maid**, *n.* Shortened f. *maiden*. A young unmarried woman, a virgin; a female servant.—**Mai'denhair**, *n.* A fern with hairlike stalks and delicate fronds.—**Mai'den**HEAD, *n.* Virginity.—**Mai'den**-HOOD, *n.*—**Mai'den**LY,[1] *a.*

Mail, *n.*[1] F. *maille*—L. *macula*, spot, mesh of a net. MACULATE. Formerly, one of the rings or plates composing mail-armour. Armour of interlaced rings or overlapping plates.

Mail, *n.*[2] O.F. *male* (F. *malle*), bag, of Teut. orig. Cf. O.H.G. *malha*, M.Du. *male*. A bag of letters; the letters conveyed on one occasion; a person or vehicle conveying letters; the official dispatch of letters.

Maim, *vt.* O.F. *mahaignier*, *mayner*, &c., of uncertain orig. MANGLE, *v.*[2] To mutilate, cripple.—*n.* A mutilation, a mutilating wound.

Main, *n.* O.E. *mægen* = O.H.G. *magan*, *megin*, O.N. *magn*, *megn*, *megin*, f. root *mag-*. MAY, *v.*[2] Strength, power (in phrase *with might and main*).—The open ocean, the chief matter (in phrase *in the main*, for the most part), a principal pipe, &c. (in these senses f. MAIN, *a.*).

Main, *a.* Prob. partly repg. O.E. *mægen* (see prec.) in compounds, and partly f. the cogn. O.N. *megenn*, *megn*, strong, powerful. Of strength, exerted to the full (in phrase *by main force*); chief in size or extent, principal, leading.—**Main'land**, *n.* The continuous stretch of land which forms the main part of a country.—**Main'**LY,[2] *adv.*—**Main'mast**, *n.* The principal mast in a ship.—**Main'sail**, *n.* In a square-rigged ship, a sail attached to the main-yard; in one rigged fore-and-aft, a sail set on the after part of the mainmast.

Maintain', *vt.* F. *maintenir*—L. *manū tenēre*, to hold in the hand (*manū*, ablative of *manus*, hand; *tenēre*, to hold). MANAGE. ABSTAIN. To carry on (a contest, &c.); to continue in (a condition, &c.); to preserve; to support (one's position in life, &c.), to sustain (life); to provide with livelihood; to keep supplied; to defend, support; to affirm.—**Maintain'**ABLE, *a.*—**Main'ten**ANCE, *n.*

Maize, *n.* Sp. *maiz*, a Cuban word. An American cereal plant; the grain it yields.

Maj'esty, *n.* F. *majesté*—L. *mājestas*, conn. with *mājor*. MAJOR. The dignity of a sovereign; with possessive pronouns, a royal and imperial title; kingly bearing.—**Majes'tic**, **Majes'tical**, *aa.*—**Majes'tical**LY,[2] *adv.*

Maiol'ica, *n.* It. *maiolica*, said to be f. *Majolica*, early form of *Majorca*, as having been best made there. Fine glazed Italian pottery.

Ma'jor, *n.*[1] F. *major* (L. *mājor* (see next)), short for *sergent-major*, sergeant-major (now the highest non-commissioned officer, but orig. denoting a much higher rank). An officer in the army ranking next above a captain.—**Major'**ITY, *n.*[1] The rank of a major.

Ma'jor, *a.* L. *mājor*, used as comp. of *magnus*, great. MAYOR. Greater; out of (one's) minority.—*n.*[2] One out of minority.—**Major'**ITY, *n.*[2] The state of being a major; the greater number; the larger party voting together in an assembly; the excess of votes on one side.—**Ma'jor-do'mo**, *n.* Sp. *mayordomo*—Med. L. *mājor domūs* (*mājor* used as *n.*; *domūs*, genit. of *domus*, house). The head servant of a princely or wealthy household.—**Majus'cule**, *a.* F.—L. *mājuscula* (sc. *littera*, letter), fem. of *mājusculus*, dim. of *mājor*. Of a letter, large.—*n.* A large letter.

Make, *vt.* O.E. *macian*. Common W. Germanic. Teut. root *mako-*, app. orig. meaning 'fit, suitable'. MATCH.[1] To bring into being, produce, construct; to establish; to appoint; to cause to come into a specified condition; to amount to, count as; to gain, earn; to cause to do something; to accomplish (a distance), to reach (a place).—*vi.* To tend, to contribute; of the tide, to rise.—*n.* Style of construction, form, structure.—**Mak'**ER, *n.*

Mal'achite, *n.* F. *malachite*—L. **malachītēs*, *molochītēs*—G. **malachitēs*, *molochitēs*, a stone (perh. malachite) of the colour of the leaf of the mallow, f. *malachē*, *molochē*, the MALLOW. A green mineral taking a high polish.

Maladjust'ment, *n.* MAL- (1). Faulty adjustment.

Maladministra'tion, *n.* MAL- (1). Faulty administration.

Mal'adroit, *a.* F. *maladroit*, f. MAL- (2) + *adroit*, ADROIT. Awkward, clumsy.

Mal'ady, *n.* F. *maladie*, f. *malade*, sick—L.L. *male habitus* (L. *male*, ill (MAL-); *habitus*, pa.pple. of *habēre*, to have (ABLE)). A disease.

Mal'apert, *a.* O.F. *malapert*, the contrary of *apert* = *espert*, clever, L. *expertus*, EXPERT. PERT. Suff. thus MAL- (2), but app. apprehended as MAL- (1). Impudent, saucy.

Mala'ria, *n.* It. *mal' aria*, for *mala aria* (*mala*, L. *malus*, bad; *aria* = F. *air*, AIR). An unwholesome atmospheric state caused by exhalations from marshes; a class of fevers formerly supposed to be due to this cause.—**Mala'ri**AL, *a.*—**Mala'ri**OUS, *a.*

Mal'content, *a.* O.F. *malcontent*, f. MAL- (2) + *content*, CONTENT, *a.* Actively discontented.—*n.* A malcontent person.

Male, *a.* O.F. *male*, *masle* (F. *mâle*), earlier *mascle*—L. *masculus*, MASCULINE. Of the begetting sex.—*n.* A male person or animal.

Maledic'tion, *n.* L. *maledictio*, *maledictiōnis*, n. of action f. *maledīcĕre*, to speak evil of, f. *male* (MAL-), ill + *dīcĕre*, to speak. DICTION. MALISON. A curse.

Mal'efactor, *n.* L. *malefactor*, agent-n. f. *malefacĕre*, to do wrong, f. *male* (MAL-), ill + *facĕre*, to do. FACT. A criminal.—**Malef'icent**, *a.* L. *maleficent-*, altered stem of *maleficus*, evil-doing, f. *male* + *-ficus*, f. *facĕre*. Baleful, hurtful.—**Malef'ic**ENCE, *n.*

Malev'olent, *a.* O.F. *malivolent*—L. *mali-*, *malevolens*, *mali-*, *malevolentis*, f. *male* (MAL-), ill + *volens*, pres.pple. of *velle*, to wish. VOLITION. Entertaining, indicative of, ill-will.—**Malev'ol**ENCE, *n.*

Malforma'tion, *n.* MAL- (1). Faulty formation.

Mal'ice, *n.* F. *malice*—L. *malitia*, f. *malus*, bad. Active ill-will.—**Malic'**IOUS, *a.*

Malign', *a.* O.F. *maligne* (F. *malin*)—L. *malignus*, f. *malus*, bad. Malevolent; baleful.—**Malig'nant**, *a.* L. *malignans*, *malignantis*, pres.pple. of *malignāre*, to do with malice, f. *malignus*. Of a disease, very virulent: feeling intense ill-will.—**Malig'n**ANCY, *n.*—**Malig'nant**LY,[2] *adv.*—**Malig'n**ITY, *n.*

Maling'er, *vi.* F. *malingre*, sickly, of obscure orig. To feign illness in order to escape duty.—**Maling'er**ER, *n.*

Mal'ison, *n.* O.F. *maleison*—L. *maledictio*, [MALEDICTION. A curse.

Mall, *n.* A special application of MAUL, *n.*, to represent senses of F. *mail*. The mallet used in a game called *pall-mall* (O.F. *pallemaille*—It. *pallamaglio*, lit., 'ball-mallet', f. *palla*, *balla*, BALL,[1] of Teut. orig. + *maglio*, mallet, L. *malleus*, hammer); the game; a place where the game was played; a sheltered walk.

Mal'lard, *n.* O.F. *mallart*, of obscure orig. The male of the wild duck.

Mal'leable, *a.* O.F. *malleable*—L. **malleābilis*, f. *malleāre*, to hammer, f. *malleus*, hammer. MAUL. Capable of being hammered into shape.—**Mallea**BIL'ITY, *n.*

Mal'let, *n.* F. *maillet*, dim. of *mail*. MAUL. A hammer, generally of wood.

Mal'low, *n.* O.E. *mealuwe*—L. *malva*, app. conn. with G. *malachē*. MALACHITE. MAUVE. A wild plant bearing reddish-purple flowers.

Malm'sey, *n.* Med.L. *malmasia*, a corr. of *Monemvasia* in the Morea. A strong sweet wine orig. from Monemvasia.

Malo'dorous, *a.* MAL- (1). Evil-smelling.

Malprac'tice, *n.* MAL- (1). Wrong-doing.

Malt, *n.* O.E. *mealt*. Common Teut. Cogn. with MELT. Grain prepared for brewing, &c.—*vt.* To make into malt.—**Malt'**STER, *n.*

Maltreat', *vt.* F. *maltraiter*, f. MAL- (1) + *traiter*, to TREAT. To treat ill, abuse, handle roughly.—**Maltreat'**MENT, *n.*

Malversa'tion, *n.* F. *malversation*, f. *malverser*, to be guilty of malversation—L. *male versāri* (*male* (MAL-), ill; *versāri*, to conduct

oneself, pass. freq. of *vertĕre*, to turn). Corrupt behaviour in a position of trust.
Mamma′, Mama′, *n.* A reduplication of *ma*, an infantine syllable. Mother.
Mamma′lia, *n.pl.* Neut.pl. of L.L. *mammālis*, a. f. L. *mamma*, breast. A class of animals the females of which suckle their young.—**Mamma′li**AN, *a.*—**Mam′mal**, *n.* Orig. in *pl.* as = *mammalia*. A mammalian animal.
Mam′mon, *n.* L.L. *mam(m)ōna*—G. *mamōnas*—Aramaic *māmōnā*, riches. The devil of covetousness; wealth as an evil influence.
Mam′moth, *n.* Russian *mammot*, of obscure orig. A large extinct species of elephant.
Man, *n.*; *pl.* **Men**. O.E. *man(n)*, human being, man. Common Teut. WOMAN. An adult human male; such a one having the qualities proper to a man; a person; the human race collectively; a manservant; one of the pieces used in chess, &c.—*vt.* To furnish with men.—**Man′**FUL, *a.* Brave, resolute.—**Man′ful**′LY,[2] *adv.*—**Man′hole**, *n.* An opening through which a man may pass.—**Man′**HOOD, *n.*—**Man′ikin**, *n.* Du. *manneken*, dim. of *man*. A little man; a model of the human body.—**Mankind′**, *n.* Human beings in general.—**Man′**LIKE, *a.*—**Man′**LY,[1] *a.*—**Man′li**NESS, *n.*—**Man′**NISH, *a.* Manlike.—**Man′slaughter**, *n.* Homicide committed unintentionally or under provocation.
Man′acle, *n.* O.F. *manicle*—L. *manicula*, little hand, in Med.L., gauntlet, dim. of *manus*, hand. MANAGE. A fetter for the hand.—*vt.* To fetter (the hands); to handcuff.
Man′age, *vt.* Prob. f. It. *maneggiare*, to handle, to train horses—L. type **manidiāre*, f. *manus*, hand. AMANUENSIS. MAINTAIN. MANACLE. MANIFEST. MANUAL. To wield (a weapon, &c.); to conduct, carry on; to succeed in accomplishing; to induce to consent.—*vi.* To conduct affairs.—**Man′age**ABLE, *a.*—**Man′age**MENT, *n.*—**Man′ag**ER, *n.*
Man′darin, *n.* Pg. *mandarim*—Malay *mantrī*—Hindī *mantrī*—Skr. *mantrin*, counsellor, f. *mantra*, counsel, f. root *man*, to think. A Chinese official.
Man′date, *n.* L. *mandātum*, use as *n.* of neut. pa.pple. of *mandāre*, to commit, COMMAND. COMMEND. A command or order; the instruction or commission given by electors to their member or to a parliament.—**Man′dat**ARY, *n.* One to whom a mandate is given.—**Man′dat**ORY, *a.* Of, relating to, conveying, a mandate.—*n.* A mandatary.
Man′dible, *n.* L.L. *mandibula*, L. *mandĕre*, to chew. A jaw.—**Mandib′ul**AR,[1] *a.*
Man′dolin(e), *n.* F. *mandoline*—It. *mandolino*, dim. of *mandola* = *pandora*. BANJO. A musical instrument of the lute kind.
Man′drake, *n.* M.E. *mandrag(g)e*, contr. f. *mandragora*—L.L. *mandragora*—G. *mandragoras*. A plant with narcotic properties.
Man′drill, *n.* App. f. MAN + DRILL.[3] The largest and most ferocious of the baboons.
Man′ducate, *vt.* L. *mandūcāre*, *mandūcātum* = *mandĕre*. MANDIBLE. MANGE. MANGER. To chew.—**Manduc**A′TION, *n.*
Mane, *n.* O.E. *manu* = M.Du. *mane*, O.H.G. *mana* (Ger. *mähne*). Primary sense 'neck'. Cf. L. *monīle*, necklace. The long hair on the back of the neck of a horse, lion, &c.
Man′ganese, *n.* F. *manganèse*—It. *manganese*, corr. of Med.L. *magnēsia*. MAGNESIA. A black mineral used in glass-making; the metallic element of which this is the oxide.
Mange, *n.* O.F. *manjue*, itch, f. *manjuer* = *mangier* (F. *manger*), to eat—L. *mandūcāre*. MANDUCATE. Cf. F. *démanger*, to itch. A skin disease of dogs, &c.—**Mang′**Y,[2] *a.*
Man′gel-wur′zel, Man′gold-wur′zel, *n.* Ger. *mangold-wurzel*, f. *mangold*, beet + *wurzel*, root. A variety of beet.
Man′ger, *n.* F. *mangeoire*—Pop.L. type **mandūcātōria*, f. *mandūcāre*. MANDUCATE. A trough from which horses and cattle eat.
Man′gle, *n.* Du. *mangel*, app. short for *mangelstok*, f. *mangelen*, to mangle, f. M.Du. *mange*, a mangle, also a mangonel (an obs. engine of war), ultimately f. G. *magganon*, an engine of war. A machine for rolling washed linen, &c.—*v.*[1]*t.* To pass through a mangle.
Man′gle, *v.*[2]*t.* A.F. *mangler*, *mahangler*, app. freq. of O.F. *mahaignier*. MAIM. To hack.
Man′go, *n.* Pg. *manga*—Malay *manggā*—Tamil *mān-kāy* (*mān*, the tree + *kāy* = fruit). The fruit of an Indian tree; the tree.
Man′grove, *n.* Perh. ultimately f. Malay *manggi-manggi*. A tropical sea-shore tree.
Ma′nia, *n.* L. *mania*—G. *mania*. Cogn. with G. *menos*, rage, L. *mens*, MIND. Mental derangement with excitement and violence; great enthusiasm.—**Ma′niac**, *a.* L.L. *maniacus*. Of, affected with, marked by, mania.—*n.* A maniac person.—**Mani′ac**AL, *a.*
Man′icure, *n.* F. *manicure*, f. L. *manus*, hand + *cūra*, care. One who undertakes the treatment of the hands; such treatment.
Man′ifest, *a.* L. *manifestus*, believed to be f. *manus*, hand + **festus*, struck, f. root seen in *dēfendĕre*, to DEFEND. (The orig. sense would thus be 'that can be struck with the hand, palpable'.) MANUAL. Clearly revealed.—*vt.* F. *manifester*—L. *manifestāre*. To make manifest; to show.—*n.* F. *manifeste*. The list of a ship's cargo.—**Manifest**A′TION, *n.*—**Manifes′to**, *n.* It. *manifesto*. A public declaration or proclamation.
Man′ifold, *a.* O.E. *manigfeald*. MANY. -FOLD. Diverse; numerous and varied.
Manipula′tion, *n.* F. *manipulation*, as if f. a L. **manipulāre*, f. *manipulus*, handful, f. *manus*, hand + *pl-*, *plē-*, to fill, as in *plēnus*, FULL. MANUAL. Handling of objects; operating upon or managing, esp. with skill.—**Manip′ulate**, *vt.* App. a back-formation f. *manipulation*. To handle, operate upon, manage, esp. with skill.—**Manip′ulat**OR, *n.*
Man′na, *n.* L. *manna*—G. *manna*—Heb. *mān*. The food miraculously supplied to the Israelites in the Wilderness.
Man′ner, *n.* A.F. *manere* (O.F. *maniere*, F. *manière*)—Pop.L. type **man(u)āria*, app. an absolute use of the fem. of L. *manuārius*, a. f. *manus*, hand. MANUAL. (The orig. sense would thus be 'mode of handling'.) The way in which something is done or takes place; custom, usage; deportment, bearing; kind, sort; in *pl.*, behaviour in social intercourse, good manners.—**Man′ner**ISM, *n.* Addiction to a distinctive method of treatment, esp. in art and literature; an instance of this.—**Man′ner**LY,[1] *a.* Having good manners.
Manœu′vre, *vi.* F. *manœuvrer*, to handle, to manœuvre—L.L. *manoperāre*, for L. *manū* (ablative of *manus*) *operārī*, to work with the hand. MANUAL. OPERATE. MANURE. To perform manœuvres; to employ stratagems, scheme.—*vt.* To cause to perform manœuvres.—*n.* A regulated movement of troops or ships of war; an expedient or artifice.
Man′or, *n.* O.F. *manoir*, dwelling, use as *n.* of *manoir*, to dwell—L. *manēre*, *mansum*, to

remain. IMMANENT. REMAIN. A unit of English territorial organization.—**Mano'r**IAL, *a.*

Man'sion, *n.* O.F. *mansion*—L. *mansio, mansiōnis*, n. of action f. *manēre*. (See prec.) MENAGERIE. MENIAL. A stately residence.

Mansuete', *a.* L. *mansuētus*, pa.pple. of *mansuescĕre*, to tame, lit. 'to accustom to the hand', f. *manus*, hand + *suescĕre*, to accustom. MANUAL. CUSTOM. MASTIFF. Tame; gentle, mild.—**Man'sue**TUDE, *n.*

Man'tel, *n.* Var. of next. Also **Man'telpiece**. The structure of wood, &c., about a fireplace; the projecting upper part of this.

Man'tle, *n.* O.F. *mantel*, a cloak, the piece of timber or stone supporting the masonry above a fireplace (F. *manteau*, cloak)—L. *mantēlum*, cloth, cloak. A loose sleeveless cloak; a covering.—*vt.* To cover; to conceal, obscure.—*vi.* To become covered with scum; of the blood, to suffuse the cheeks; of the face, to glow.

Man'ual, *a.* L. *manuālis*, a. f. *manus*, hand. MANAGE. MANIPULATION. MANNER. MANŒUVRE. Of the hand; done with the hands; of a signature, autograph (chiefly in *sign manual*).—*n.* A concise treatise (L.L. *manuāle*); the key-board of an organ.

Manufac'ture, *n.* F. *manufacture*—Med.L. **manufactūra*, f. L. *manū facĕre* (*manū*, ablative of *manus*, hand; *facĕre*, to make). (See prec.) FACT. The making of things by hand or mechanical power; a branch of manufacturing industry; something manufactured.—*vt.* To work up (material); to make from material.—**Manufac't**ORY, *n.* A place where things are manufactured. — **Manufac'tur**ER, *n.* The owner of a manufactory.

Manumit', *vt.* L. *manūmittĕre, manūmissum*, ante-classical *manū ēmittĕre*, lit. 'to send forth from one's hand'. (See prec.) EMIT. To free from slavery.—**Manumis'**SION, *n.*

Manure', *vt.* A.F. *maynoverer*, to work with the hands = O.F. *manouvrer* (F. *manœuvrer*). MANŒUVRE. Formerly, to occupy (land); to till. To enrich (land) with manure.—*n.* Dung, &c., applied to land to fertilize it.

Man'uscript, *a.* Med.L. *manūscriptus*, f. L. *manū* (MANUFACTURE) + *scriptus*, pa.pple. of *scrībĕre*, to write. SCRIBE. Written with the hand.—*n.* A manuscript document, &c.

Man'y, *a.* O.E. *manig*. Common Teut. Denoting great indefinite number.

Map, *n.* L. *mappa*, NAPKIN, in Med.L. *mappa mundi*, map of the world. A representation on the flat of the earth's surface or of the heavens.—*vt.* To make a map of.

Ma'ple, *n.* O.E. *mapel* (*tréow*), maple (TREE), of unknown orig. A tree of the sycamore kind, a variety of which yields sugar.

Mar, *vt.* O.E. *merran*, to hinder, mar. Common Teut. To spoil, impair.

Maraud', *vi.* and *t.* F. *marauder*, f. *maraud*, rogue, vagabond, of obscure orig. To make a raid in order to plunder.—**Maraud'**ER, *n.*

Mar'ble, *n.* F. *marbre*—L. *marmor*, f. or cogn. with G. *marmaros*, sparkling stone, later, marble. A form of limestone capable of taking a polish; a slab of marble; a small ball used in a game called *marbles*.—*vt.* To colour so as to resemble variegated marble.

March, *n.*[1] A.F. *marche*, O.F. *march(e)* (F. *mars*)—L. *Martius* (sc. *mensis*, month), the month of MARS. The third month.

March, *n.*[2] F. *marche*, f. Teut. Cf. O.S. *marka*, O.H.G. *marcha*. MARK.[1] A border or frontier (often in *pl.*).—*v.*[1]*i.* To border *upon*, be conterminous *with*.

March, *v.*[2]*i.* F. *marcher*, of disputed orig. To walk with a military step; to start on a march; to go.—*vt.* To cause to march or go.—*n.*[3] The action of marching; orderly forward movement; the distance covered in a day's march; a tune intended to accompany marching.

Mar'chioness, *n.* Med.L. *marchiōnissa*, fem. of *marchio*, a captain of the marches, f. *marca*. MARQUIS. The wife or widow of a marquis.

March'pane, Mar'zipan, *n.* F. *marcepain* (now *massepain*), Ger. *marzipan*. Orig. obscure. A sweetmeat of pounded almonds, &c.

Mare, *n.* O.E. *mere* (fem. of *mearh* (O.Teut. **marho-z*), horse) = O.N. *merr*, O.H.G. *meriha* (Ger. *mähre*, jade). MARSHAL. The female of an equine animal, esp. of the horse.

Mar'garine, *n.* F., misuse of *margarine*, a compound of *acide margarique*, a fatty acid named f. G. *margaron*, pearl, in allusion to its lustre. An imitation of butter.

Mar'gin, *n.* L. *margo, marginis*. MARK.[1] A border or edge; time, material, &c., allowed for contingencies; the blank part of a page.—*vt.* To annotate in the margin; to provide with a margin.—**Mar'gin**AL, *a.*

Mar'guerite, *n.* F. (= the Eng. female name *Margaret*)—L.L. *Margarita*, f. L. *margarīta*, pearl. The ox-eye daisy.

Mar'igold, *n.* *Mary* (the Virgin Mary) + obs. *gold*, marigold—O.E. *golde*, app. conn. with GOLD. A garden plant with yellow flowers.

Marine', *a.* F. *marin* (fem. *marine*)—L. *marīnus*, f. *mare*, sea. MERE, *n.* ROSEMARY. Of the sea or shipping; used at sea.—*n.* The collective shipping of a country; a soldier serving on a warship.—**Mar'iner**, *n.* A.F. *mariner*—Med.L. *marīnārius*. A sailor.

Mariol'atry, *n.* G. *Maria*, Mary + *latreia*, worship. Worship of the Virgin Mary.

Marionette', *n.* F. *marionnette*, f. *Marion*, dim. of *Marie*, Mary. A puppet.

Mar'ital, *a.* L. *marītālis*, f. *marītus*, husband. MARRY. Of a husband or marriage.

Mar'itime, *a.* L. *maritimus*, f. *mare*, sea. MARINE. Bordering upon the sea; relating to or dealing with navigation.

Mar'joram, *n.* O.F. *majorane* (F. *marjolaine*), of obscure orig. An aromatic herb.

Mark, *n.*[1] O.E. *mearc*, boundary, landmark, sign = O.S. *marka*, O.H.G. *marcha* (Ger. *mark*), boundary. Cf. F. *marque*, f. Teut. MARCH, *n.*[2] DEMARCATION. MARQUETRY. App. cogn. with L. *margo*, MARGIN. Formerly, a boundary, a boundary-stone. Something set up to be aimed at; a goal; a sign or token; a distinctive feature; a device, inscription; a visible trace or impression; a line, dot, scar, or the like.—*vt.* O.E. *mearcian*. Cf. F. *marquer*. To trace *out* boundaries for; to make a mark on; to indicate; to be a distinguishing feature of; to observe, watch.—*vi.* To take notice, consider.—**Marks'man**, *n.* *Mark's man*. One skilled in shooting at a mark.

Mark, *n.*[2] O.E. *marc*, a weight. Com. Teut. and Romanic. A former money of account = 13*s.* 4*d.* (orig. the value of a mark of silver).

Mar'ket, *n.* Late O.E. *market*—O.N.F. *market* (F. *marché*) = Sp. Pg. *mercado*, It. *mercato*—L. *mercātus*, f. *mercāri*, to trade. MERCHANT. MART. A periodical assembly for buying and selling; a place where goods, &c., are sold; demand (for a commodity); a place or seat of trade.—*vt.* To sell in a market; to bring to market.—**Mar'ket**ABLE, *a.*

Marl, *n.* O.F. *marle* (F. *marne*)—L.L. *margila*, dim. of L. *marga*, marl. A clayey soil used as a fertilizer.—*vt.* To fertilize with marl.

Mar'malade, *n.* F. *marmelade*—Pg. *marmelada,* f. *marmelo,* quince—L. *melimēlum* = G. *melimēlon,* 'honey-apple', an apple grafted on a quince, f. *meli,* honey + *mēlon,* apple. MELLIFLUOUS. A preserve of fruit (orig. quinces, now us. oranges) boiled with sugar.

Marmo'real, *a.* L. *marmoreus* (f. *marmor,* MARBLE) + -AL. Like, made of, marble.

Maroon', *n.*[1] F. *marron,* chestnut, the colour—It. *marrone,* chestnut, of unknown orig. A brownish-crimson colour.—*a.* Of the colour.

Maroon', *n.*[2] F. *marron,* said to be a corr. of Sp. *cimarron,* wild. One of a class of negroes (orig. fugitive slaves) living in the wild parts of the W. Indies; one who is marooned. —*vt.* To leave on a desolate island.

Marque, *n.* F.—Pr. *marca,* vbl.n. f. *marcar* (Med.L. *marcāre*), to seize as a pledge. *Letters of marque,* a licence authorizing a private person to capture enemy merchant shipping.

Marquee', *n.* Assumed sing. f. *marquise,* F. *marquise* (orig. fem. of *marquis,* MARQUIS). A large tent (app. orig. one for a marchioness).

Mar'quetry, *n.* F. *marqueterie,* f. *marqueter,* to variegate, f. *marque,* mark, f. Teut. MARK.[1] Inlaid work.

Mar'quis, -quess, *n.* F. *marquis,* O.F. *marchis,* f. com. Romanic *marca* (= F. *marche,* MARCH, *n.*[2]) + suff. = L. *-ensis* forming aa. f. place-names. MARCHIONESS. A noble ranking next below a duke.—**Mar'quis**ATE,[1] *n.*

Mar'row, *n.* O.E. *mearg, mearh.* Common Teut. The fatty substance contained in bones.

Mar'ry, *vt.* F. *marier*—L. *marītāre,* f. *marītus.* MARITAL. To join as husband and wife; to take as husband or wife.—*vi.* To take a husband or wife.—**Mar'riage,** *n.* F. *mariage.* The condition of being married; the action or an act of marrying.—**Mar'riage**ABLE, *a.*

Mars, *n.* L. MARCH, *n.*[1] The Roman god of war; one of the seven planets.

Marsh, *n.* O.E. *merse, merise* = M.Du. *mersch(e),* M.L.G., Ger. *marsch.* O.Teut. **mari-.* MERE, *n.* MORASS. A tract of lowlying wet land.—**Marsh-mal'low,** *n.* A herb growing near marshes.—**Marsh mar'igold,** *n.* A plant with yellow flowers growing in moist meadows.—**Marsh'**Y,[2] *a.*

Mar'shal, *n.* O.F. *mareschal,* farrier, marshal —Frankish L. *mariscalcus*—O.H.G. *marahscalh,* 'horse-servant'—O.Teut. **marho-z,* horse: **skalko-z,* servant. MARE. Formerly, a farrier. A high officer of state, the *Earl Marshal;* a general officer of the highest rank, called *Field Marshal;* an officer who arranges ceremonies.—*vt.* To arrange in due order; to conduct or usher ceremoniously.

Mart, *n.* Du. *markt,* f. Romanic. MARKET. A market-place or market hall; an emporium.

Martel'lo tow'er, *n.* Corr. of Cape *Mortella* in Corsica, where the English fleet captured a tower of this kind in 1793. A small round fort to prevent landing on a coast.

Mar'ten, *n.* O.F. *martrine,* marten fur, fem. of *martrin,* a. f. *martre,* the marten, of Teut. orig. An animal yielding a valuable fur.

Mar'tial, *a.* F. *martial*—L. *martiālis,* a. f. *Mars,* MARS. Pertaining to war; warlike.

Mar'tin, *n.* App. a use of the Christian name *Martin.* A species of swallow.

Mar'tinet, *n.* From General *Martinet* (temp. Louis XIV). A strict disciplinarian.

Mar'tingale, *n.* F. *martingale,* of obscure orig. A strap to prevent a horse from rearing.

Mar'tinmas, *n.* *Martin* + MASS.[1] The feast of St. Martin of Tours, 11th November.

Mar'tyr, *n.* O.E. *martyr*—Eccles.L. *martyr* —G. *martur,* martyr, Æolic and late form of *martus,* witness. One put to death for refusal to renounce the Christian faith; one who suffers in some cause; one in constant suffering.—*vt.* To make a martyr of; to torment.—**Mar'tyr**DOM, *n.*—**Mar'tyr**IZE, *vt.*—**Martyrol'**OGY, *n.* A list or history of martyrs; the histories of martyrs collectively.

Mar'vel, *n.* O.F. *merveille*—L. *mīrābilia,* neut.pl. of *mīrābilis,* wonderful, f. *mīrāri,* to wonder. ADMIRE. A wonderful thing.—*vi.* To wonder.—**Mar'vell**OUS, *a.*

Mas'cot, *n.* Provincial F. *mascotte,* perh. conn. with Mod.Pr. *masco,* witch. Something supposed to bring good luck.

Mas'culine, *a.* F. *masculin*—L. *masculinus,* f. *masculus,* in form dim. f. *mās,* a. and n., MALE. Pertaining or peculiar to males; manly, vigorous; mannish; denoting the gender to which appellations of males belong.

Mash, *n.* O.E. *máx(-wyrt),* mash(-WORT[2]), corresp. to late M.H.G., Ger. *meisch,* crushed grapes, infused malt. Perh. conn. with O.E. *miscian,* to MIX. Malt mixed with warm water to form wort; a warm food for horses, &c.—*vt.* To convert (malt) into wort; to beat into a soft mass.

Mask, *n.* F. *masque,* of disputed orig., prob. not conn. with Sp. *máscara.* MASQUERADE. A covering for the face for disguise or protection; a disguise, pretence.—*vt.* To cover with a mask; to hide; to disguise.

Ma'son, *n.* O.F. *masson, maçon*—Med.L. *macio,* of obscure orig. A worker in stone; a freemason.—**Mason'**IC, *a.* Of freemasonry. —**Ma'son**RY, *n.* Stonework; freemasonry.

Masque, *n.* Var. of MASK. A masquerade; a form of amateur histrionic performance (such as Milton's *Comus*) once popular.

Masquerade', *n.* Sp. *mascarada,* f. *máscara* (= It. *maschera*), MASK, of disputed orig. A masked ball.—*vi.* To go about in disguise.

Mass, *n.*[1] O.E. *mæsse*—Pop.L. *messa*—Eccles. L. *missa,* religious service, the Eucharist (f. *missus,* pa.pple. of L. *mittěre,* to send, dismiss), supposed by many to have orig. denoted the formula '*ite, missa est*', 'go, (the congregation) is dismissed', at the end of a service. MISSAL. The Eucharistic service; in form *-mas,* with the name of a saint, &c., a feast-day, as in CHRISTMAS, LAMMAS, &c.

Mass, *n.*[2] F. *masse*—L. *massa,* prob. f. G. *maza,* barley-cake. AMASS. A body of matter; a dense collection of bodies; a large quantity or amount, *the masses,* the populace.—*vt.* and *i.* To gather or form into a mass.—**Mas'**SIVE, *a.* Having great size and weight; solid, substantial.—**Mas'**SY,[2] *a.* Solid, weighty.

Mas'sacre, *n.* F. *massacre.* Orig. unknown. Indiscriminate killing; a general slaughter.—*vt.* To make a massacre of; to murder cruelly.

Massage', *n.* F. *massage,* f. *masser,* to massage, perh. f. Pg. *amassar,* to knead, f. *massa,* dough = MASS.[2] Curative friction and kneading.—*vt.* To apply massage to.—**Masseur', Masseuse',** *nn.* F., agent-nn., f. *masser.* A man, a woman, who practises massage.

Mast, *n.*[1] O.E. *mæst.* Common Teut. Cogn. with L. *mālus.* A pole for supporting sails.

Mast, *n.*[2] O.E. *mæst.* Common W. Germanic. Prob. f. Aryan root *med-,* to be fat, to flow, and cogn. with L. *madēre,* to be wet. MEAT. Collectively, the fruit of the beech, &c.

Mas'ter, *n.* O.F. *maistre* (F. *maître*)—L. *magister*. MAGISTRATE. MISTRESS. One who employs another; the head of a household; an owner; one in control; a victor; the captain of a merchant ship; a teacher; an artist of eminent skill; prefixed as a title of courtesy to the name of a boy, and (contracted to *Mr.* and pronounced mis'ter) to that of a man.—*vt.* To overcome; to tame; to acquire complete knowledge of or skill in.—**Mas'ter**FUL, *a.* Imperious, self-willed.—**Mas'ter**LY,[1] *a.* Skilfully done or exercised.—**Mas'ter**Y,[1] *n.* Authority; victory; intellectual command.

Mas'tic, *n.* F. *mastic*—L. *mastichē*—G. *mastichē*. A gum got from certain trees.

Mas'ticate, *vt.* L. *masticāre*, *masticātum*. To chew.—**Mastic**A'TION, *n.*

Mas'tiff, *n.* O.F. *mastin* (F. *mâtin*)—Pop.L. type **mansuētinus*, f. L. *mansuetus*. MANSUETE. A large dog, useful as a watch-dog.

Mas'todon, *n.* G. *mastos*, breast + *odous*, *odontos*, TOOTH. A large extinct mammal with nipple-like projections on its molar teeth.

Mat, *n.* O.E. *matt*—L.L. *matta*. An article of plaited rushes, straw, &c., for lying, sitting, or kneeling upon, for protecting floors, &c., or for wiping shoes upon: a thick tangled mass.—*vt.* and *i.* To form into such a mass.

Match, *n.*[1] O.E. *gemæcca*, *gemecca*, f. Teut. root *mako-*. MAKE. One able to contend as an equal with another; a person or thing that equals or exactly corresponds to another; a trial of skill; a marriage; a person viewed with regard to his or her eligibility for marriage.—*vt.* To join in marriage; to encounter with equal power; to place in conflict *with*, pit *against*; to pair or assort; to equal or correspond to; to get something corresponding to (a colour, pattern, &c.).—*vi.* To correspond.—**Match'**LESS, *a.* Without an equal.

Match, *n.*[2] O.F. *mesche*, *meiche* (F. *mèche*), wick, match for a gun, of obscure orig. A slow-burning wick or cord for firing a gun, igniting gunpowder, &c.; a slender body tipped with a substance which ignites by friction.

Mate, *n.*[1] O.F. *mat* in *eschec mat*, CHECKMATE. Checkmate.—*vt.* To checkmate.

Mate, *n.*[2] App. f. M.L.G. *mate* = O.H.G. *gimazzo*, meat-companion (*gi-* implying participation). Cf. Goth. *mats*, MEAT. A comrade; a husband or wife; an officer in a merchant ship immediately under the master.—*vt.* To marry.—*vi.* To keep company *with*.

Mate'rial, *a.* L.L. *māteriālis*, f. L. *māteria*, MATTER. Of matter or body; concerned with things of the body, unspiritual; important, considerable; pertinent or essential *to*.—*n.* The matter from which a thing is made; the elements or substance of a thing; a stuff or fabric.—**Mate'rial**ISM, *n.* The opinion that nothing exists but matter.—**Mate'rial**IST, *n.*—**Materialis'**TIC, *a.*—**Mate'rial**IZE, *vt.* To make or represent as material.—*vi.* To come into perceptible existence.—**Mate'rial**LY,[2] *adv.*

Mater'nal, *a.* F. *maternel*—L. *māternus*, f. *māter*, MOTHER. Of, related through, a mother.—**Mater'n**ITY, *n.* Motherhood.

Mathemat'ics, *n.pl.* Pl. of *Mathematic*, sometimes used in the same sense — O.F. *mathematique*—L. *mathēmatica* (*ars*), G. *mathēmatikē* (*technē*), the mathematical (art), f. G. *mathēma*, something learned, a science (esp. mathematical), f. root of *manthanein*, to learn. The science of space and number.—**Mathemat'ic**AL, *a.*—**Mathemat**IC'IAN, *n.*

Mat'ins, *n.pl.* F. *matines*—Eccles.L. *mātūtīnae*, fem. pl. of L. *mātūtīnus*, belonging to the morning. MATUTINAL. One of the canonical hours, properly a midnight office, but sometimes recited at daybreak; morning prayer in the Church of England.

Ma'tricide, *n.* L. *matricida*, f. *māter*, MOTHER + -CIDE (1). A killer of his mother. -CIDE (2). The killing of one's mother.

Matric'ulate, *vt.* Med.L. **matrīculāre*, **matrīculātum*, f. L.L. *matrīcula*, register, dim. of L. *matrix* (MATRIX), in L.L. used in same sense. To enter on a college or university register.—*vi.* To enter one's name on such a register.—**Matricul**A'TION, *n.*

Mat'rimony, *n.* O.F. *matremoine*—L. *matrimōnium*, lit., 'motherhood', f. *māter*, MOTHER. Marriage.—**Matrimo'ni**AL, *a.*

Ma'trix, *n.*; *pl.* **Ma'trixes**, **-ices**. L. *mātrix*, breeding-animal, in L.L. womb, app. f. *māter*, MOTHER. MATRICULATE. The womb; an embedding mass; a mould for casting.

Ma'tron, *n.* F. *matrone*—L. *matrōna*, f. *māter*, MOTHER. A married woman; a woman in charge of the domestic arrangements of a hospital, &c.—**Ma'tron**LY,[1] *a.*

Mat'ter, *n.* O.F. *matere*—L. *māteria*. MATERIAL. The substance of which a thing is made up; any substance; pus; physical or corporeal substance in general; the substance of a book, &c.; ground, reason; a thing or affair.—*vi.* To discharge pus; to be of importance.

Mat'tock, *n.* O.E. *mattuc*. Orig. unknown. A tool for loosening hard ground.

Matt'ress, *n.* O.F. *materas*—It. *materasso*, prob. f. Arab. (*al-*)*matrah*, (the) place where something is thrown, in mod. use also mat, cushion, f. root *taraha*, to throw. A stuffed canvas case used as or under a bed; a frame with stretched wires for supporting a bed.

Mature', *a.* L. *mātūrus*, ripe. DEMURE. Complete in development or growth; careful, carefully considered.—*vt.* To bring to maturity.—*vi.* To come to maturity; of a bill, &c., to become due.—**Matur'**ITY, *n.*

Matuti'nal, *a.* L. *mātūtīnālis*, f. *mātūtīnus*. MATINS. Of, happening in, the morning.

Maud'lin, *a.* From attrib. use (in allusion to pictures representing the Magdalen weeping) of *Maudlin*—O.F. *Madelaine*—L. *Magdalēna*, (Mary) Magdalen. Weakly sentimental; shedding tears of drunkenness.

Maul, **Mall**, *n.* F. *mail*—L. *malleus*, hammer. MALL. MALLEABLE. MALLET. A heavy hammer, generally of wood.—**Maul**, *vt.* To beat, bruise; to handle roughly, shatter.

Maul'stick, *n.* Du. *maalstok*, f. *malen*, to paint + *stok*, stick. A light stick used by artists to support the hand in painting.

Maun'der, *vi.* Of obscure orig. Perh. imitative. To move or act in a dreamy or inconsequent way; to wander in one's talk, to drivel.

Mausole'um, *n.* L. *mausōlēum*—G. *mausōleion*, the magnificent tomb of Mausolus, King of Caria (4th c. B.C.). A stately edifice erected as a place of burial.

Mauve, *n.* F. *mauve*—L. *malva*, MALLOW. A bright purple aniline dye; the colour of the dye.—*a.* Of the colour.

Maw, *n.* O.E. *maga*. Common Teut. The stomach.

Mawk'ish, *a.* Obs. *Mawk*, maggot (f. O.N. *mathkr*, MAGGOT) + -ISH. Having a faint sickly flavour; feebly sentimental.

Maxil'la, *n.* L. A jaw, esp. the upper jaw.—**Maxil'l**ARY, *a.*

Max'im, *n.*[1] F. *maxime*—L. *maxima*, fem. of *maximus*, greatest, used elliptically. A short proposition expressing a general truth; a rule or principle of conduct.

Max'im, *n.*[2] From the inventor, Sir H. *Maxim*. A form of machine gun.

Max'imum, *n.* L., neut. of *maximus*. MAXIM.[1] The highest magnitude or quantity.—*a.* That is a maximum.

May, *n.* F. *mai*—L. *Māius* (sc. *mensis*, month), of obscure orig. The fifth month; blossoms of the hawthorn; the hawthorn.—*v.*[1]*i.* To take part in the festivities of May-day (May 1st).

May, *v.*[2] *aux.* O.E. *magan*, pres.t. *mæg*. Common Teut. O.Teut. root *mag-*, O.Aryan *magh-*. Primary sense, to be strong or able. DISMAY. MACHINE. MAIN. MIGHT. Used to express possibility, opportunity, permission, wish, &c.

May'or, *n.* F. *maire*—L. *mājor*. MAJOR. The head of a municipal corporation.—**May'or**AL, *a.*—**May'oral**TY, *n.* His office, his period of office.—**May'or**ESS, *n.* His wife.

Maze, *vt.* Orig. uncertain. Poss. f. an O.E. **masian*. Cf. O.E. *ámasod*, amazed. To bewilder, perplex.—*n.* A labyrinth.—**Maz'**Y,[2] *a.*

Mazur'ka, *n.* Polish *mazurka*, lit., a woman of the province Mazovia. A lively Polish dance; music written for it.

Mead, *n.*[1] O.E. *meodu*. Common Teut. and Aryan. Cogn. with Skr. *mádhu*, honey, sweet drink, G. *methu*, wine. An alcoholic liquor made from honey and water.

Mead, *n.*[2] O.E. *mǽd*, f. root *mē-*. MOW. A meadow.—**Mead'ow**, *n.* O.E. *mǽdwe*, oblique case of *mǽd*. A piece of grass land.

Mea'gre, *a.* O.F. *megre*, *maigre*—L. *macer*. EMACIATE. Lean, thin; poor, scanty.

Meal, *n.*[1] O.E. *melo* (stem *melw-*). Common Teut. Cogn. with G. *mulē*, mill, L. *mola*, millstone, *molĕre*, to grind. MILL. MOULD.[1] Grain (gen. excluding wheat) ground to a powder.—**Meal'**Y,[2] *a.*

Meal, *n.*[2] O.E. *mǽl*, mark, fixed time, meal. Common Teut. A regular or any occasion of taking food; the food taken.

Mean, *a.*[1] App. repg. obs. *I-mene*, common to two or more—O.E. *gemǽne* = O.H.G. *gimeini* (Ger. *gemein*). Cogn. with L. *commūnis*, COMMON. Formerly, common to two or more. Hence (through the senses 'ordinary', 'not very good'), inferior in ability, &c.; shabby; small-minded.—**Mean'**LY,[2] *adv.*

Mean, *a.*[2] O.F. *men*, *meien* (F. *moyen*)—L.L. *mediānus*, a. f. *medius*, middle. MID. MIZEN. Intermediate in time, quality, &c.—*n.* That which is intermediate; in *pl.* (often treated as *sing.*), that by which something is brought about; in *pl.*, one's pecuniary resources.—**Mean'time**, **Mean'while**, *nn.* The time between one period or event and another.—*adv.* During or within this time.

Mean, *vt.* O.E. *mǽnan*. Common W. Germanic. To purpose, design, intend, destine; to signify; to import.—*vi.* To be disposed or intentioned in a specified way.—**Mean'ing**, *vbl.n.* Sense, import; significance.—*ppl.a.* Expressive, significant.—**Mean'ing**LY,[2] *adv.*

Mean'der, *n.* L. *maeander*—G. *maiandros*, f. the winding Phrygian river *Maiandros*. In *pl.*, windings; a circuitous journey (gen. *pl.*).—*vi.* To flow in meanders; to wander aimlessly.

Mea'sles, *n.pl.* M.E. *maseles*, cogn. with Du. *mazelen*. Teut. root *mas-*, *mǽs-*, spot, excrescence. An infectious disease with red pustules.—**Mea'sl**Y,[2] *a.* Of measles; contemptible.

Meas'ure, *n.* F. *mesure*—L. *mensūra*, n. of action f. *mētīri*, *mensus*, to measure. COMMENSURABLE. IMMENSE. MENSURATION. Ascertained size or quantity; a vessel, rod, line, &c., for measuring; a unit of measurement; that by which something is estimated; a limit; a quantity or proportion bestowed; poetical rhythm; a metrical group or period; an air, tune; musical time; a stately dance; a plan or course of action; a law.—*vt.* To ascertain the size or quantity of; to have a measurement of (so much); to estimate; to bring into competition *with*.—**Meas'ur**ABLE, *a.*—**Meas'ured**, *ppl.a.* Having a marked rhythm; carefully considered.—**Meas'ure**MENT, *n.*

Meat, *n.* O.E. *mete* = Goth. *mats*, O.N. *matr*. Perh. f. root *med-*. MAST.[2] MATE.[2] Food the flesh of animals used as food.

Mechan'ic, *a.* L. *mēchanicus*, mechanical—G. *mēchanikos*, f. *mēchanē*. MACHINE. Of the nature of, pertaining to, a machine.—*n.* One employed in a manual occupation; a skilled workman.—*n.pl.* The branch of science which deals with motion and tendencies to motion.—**Mechan'ic**AL, *a.* Concerned with machines; concerned with manual operations; worked or produced by or as by a machine; like a machine, lacking spontaneity; pertaining to mechanics.—**Mechan'ical**LY,[2] *adv.*—**Mechan**IC'IAN, *n.*—**Mech'an**ISM, *n.* The structure of a machine; a piece of machinery.

Med'al, *n.* F. *médaille*—It. *medaglia*—Pop.L. type **metallea*, f. *metallum*, METAL. A piece of metal in the form of a coin bearing an inscription or device and used as a memento or a reward.—**Medal'lion**, *n.* F. *médaillon*—It. *medaglione*, aug. of *medaglia*. A large medal; various things resembling this used in decorative work.—**Med'all**IST, *n.* One who makes medals; the winner of a medal.

Med'dle, *vi.* O.F. *medler*, *mesdler*, varr. of *mesler* (F. *mêler*), to mix—Pop.L. **misculāre* f. L. *miscēre*, to MIX. MEDLEY. PELL-MELL. Formerly, to mix. To concern oneself interferingly.—**Med'dle**SOME, *a.*

Mediæ'val, **Medie'val**, *a.* L. *medius*, middle (MID) + *aevum*, AGE + -AL. Of, pertaining to, characteristic of the Middle Ages.—**Mediæ'val**ISM, **Medie'val**ISM, *n.*

Me'diate, *vi.* L.L. *mediāre*, *mediātum*, to be in the middle, f. *medius*, middle. MID. To be between; to intervene in order to reconcile.—*vt.* To effect by mediation.—*a.* Not immediate, connected indirectly; involving or depending on something intermediate.—**Media**'TION, *n.*—**Me'diat**OR, *n.*

Med'icine, *n.* O.F. *medicine*—L. *medicīna*, the healing art, a remedy, f. *medicus*, physician, f. *medēri*, to heal. MEDITATE. REMEDY. The art of healing by means of remedies and the regulation of diet, &c.; a remedy.—**Med'ic**AL, *a.*—**Med'ical**LY,[2] *adv.*—**Medic'ament**, *n.* F. *médicament*—L. *medicāmentum*, f. *medicāri*, *medicātus*, to heal, f. *medicus*. A remedy.—**Med'icate**, *vt.* From *medicāri*. To treat medically; to impregnate with a medicinal substance.—**Med'ic**ABLE, *a.*—**Medica**'TION, *n.*—**Med'icat**IVE, *a.* Curative.—**Medic'in**AL, *a.* Having healing properties.

Me'diocre, *a.* F. *médiocre*—L. *mediocris*, f. *medius*, middle. MID. Neither bad nor good.—**Medioc'r**ITY, *n.*

Med'itate, *vt.* L. *meditāri*, *meditātus*. Cogn. with G. *medesthai*, to be mindful of, L. *medēri*, to heal. MEDICINE. METE. To reflect upon, ponder; to plan or design.—*vi.* To engage in thought or contemplation.—**Medita**'TION, *n.*—**Med'itat**IVE, *a.*—**Med'itative**LY,[2] *adv.*

Me'dium, *n.*; *pl.* **-ia**, **-iums**. L. *medium*,

neut. of *medius.* MID. A middle quality, degree, &c.; an intervening substance conveying force; environment; an agency, means, &c. —*a.* Between two qualities, degrees, &c.

Med'lar, *n.* O.F. *medler,* the tree, f. *medle, var. of *mesle,* the fruit—L. *mespilum*—G. *mespilon.* A tree bearing a fruit like a small apple, eaten when decayed; the fruit.

Med'ley, *n.* O.F. *medlee,* var. of *meslee* (F. *mêlée*)—Pop.L. *miscu*lāta,* f. *misc*ulāre,* to mix. MEDDLE. MELEE. Combat, esp. hand-to-hand; a heterogeneous mixture.

Medul'la, *n.* L. Marrow.—**Medul'l**ARY, *a.*

Meed, *n.* O.E. *méd* = O.S. *mêda,* O.H.G. *mêta* (Ger. *miete*). Cogn. with Skr. *mīdhá,* prize, contest, G. *misthos,* wages. Formerly, wages, recompense. A reward; a merited portion.

Meek, *a.* Early M.E. *meoc*—O.N. *miúkr,* soft, pliant (Sw. *mjuk,* Da. *myg*). Piously humble; tamely submissive.—**Meek'**LY,[2] *adv.*

Meer'schaum, *n.* Ger., lit. 'sea-foam', f. *meer,* sea + *schaum,* foam. MERE. SCUM. A soft white clay-like substance used for making bowls of tobacco-pipes.

Meet, *a.* M.E. *mēte,* prob. repg. O.E. (Anglian) *gemēte = O.E. *gemǽte,* f. *mæt-,* var. of *met-,* root of METE. Etymological sense thus 'commensurate'. Suitable, fit.—**Meet'**LY,[2] *adv.*

Meet, *vt.* O.E. *mētan,* (conn. with *mót,* MOOT), corresp. to O.S. *mōtian,* O.N. *mǿta.* To come face to face with; to go to welcome; to encounter in combat, to cope with; to come into conformity with; to satisfy, to pay.—*vi.* To come face to face; to assemble; to come into contact; *to meet with,* to light upon, to experience or undergo.—*n.* A meeting for a hunt.—**Meet'ing,** *vbl.n.* An assembly.

Megalith'ic, *a.* G. *megas,* great + *lithos,* stone + -IC. Consisting of great stones.

Megaloma'nia, *n.* *Megalo-,* combining form of G. *megas,* great + MANIA. The passion for great things.—**Megaloma'niac,** *a.* and *n.*

Meg'aphone, *n.* G. *megas,* great + *phōnē,* sound, voice. An instrument for carrying sound to a great distance.

Megilp', *n.* Of obscure orig. A preparation used as a vehicle for oil colours.

Me'grim, *n.* F. *migraine*—L. *hēmicrānia*—G. *hēmikrania,* f. *hēmi-,* HEMI- + *kranion,* skull. CRANIUM. A headache affecting one side of the head; a whim or fancy; in *pl.,* low spirits.

Mel'ancholy, *n.* O.F. *melancolie*—L. *melancholia*—G. *melagcholia,* lit., 'condition of having black bile', f. *melas,* black + *cholē,* bile. CHOLER. GALL.[1] Gloom or dejection; pensive sadness.—*a.* Gloomy, dejected; pensive; dismal, saddening.—**Melancho'lia,** *n.* The L. word. A mental disease marked by gloom and depression.—**Melanchol'**IC, *a.*

Mêlée, *n.* F. MEDLEY. A mixed fight.

Me'liorate, *vt.* and *i.* L.L. *meliōrāre, meliōrātum,* f. L. *melior,* better. To make, to grow, better.—**Melior**A'TION, *n.*

Mellif'luous, *a.* L. *mellifluus* (f. *mel* = G. *meli,* honey + *fluĕre,* to flow) + -OUS. MARMALADE. MOLASSES. AFFLUENT. Sweet as honey.—**Mellif'lu**ENT, *a.* In same sense.—**Mellif'lu**ENCE, *n.*

Mel'low, *a.* Perh. developed f. an attrib. use of O.E. *melo* (*melw-*), M.E. *melowe.* MEAL.[1] Soft, juicy; mature; partly intoxicated.—*vt.* and *i.* To make, to become, mellow.

Melo'deon, Melo'dion, *n.* Perh. f. MELODY after ACCORDION. A kind of accordion.

Mel'odrama, *n.* Alteration after DRAMA of earlier *Melodrame*—F. *mélodrame,* f. G. *melos,* song + F. *drame,* DRAMA. In earlier use, a play with songs interspersed. A play ending happily characterized by sensational incidents.—**Melodramat'**IC, *a.*

Mel'ody, *n.* O.F. *melodie*—L.L. *melōdia*—G. *melōidia,* a singing, f. *melōidos,* singing songs, f. *melos,* song + *ōid-* = *aoid-,* f. *aeidein,* to sing. Sweet music; beauty of sound; a series of musical notes arranged in an expressive succession; the arrangement of notes thus.—**Melo'di**OUS, *a.*—**Mel'od**IST, *n.* A singer; a composer of melodies.

Mel'on, *n.* F. *melon*—L.L. *mēlo, mēlōnis,* app. shortened f. *mēlopepo* = G. *mēlopepōn,* an apple-shaped melon not eaten till over-ripe, f. *mēlon,* apple + *pepōn,* ripe. A name applied to various kinds of gourds.

Melt, *vi.* Orig. two *vv.,* O.E. *meltan,* intrans., and *mieltan, myltan,* causal of this. Cogn. with G. *meldein,* to melt, L. *mollis,* soft. MALT. SMELT, *v.* To become liquid by heat; to be dissolved; to become softened by pity, &c.; to pass imperceptibly *into;* to waste *away.*—*vt.* To make liquid by heat; to dissolve; to soften.

Mem'ber, *n.* F. *membre*—L. *membrum,* limb. A limb; a part of a complex structure; each of the individuals forming a body; a division of a sentence.—**Mem'ber**SHIP, *n.*

Mem'brane, *n.* L. *membrāna,* f. *membrum.* (See prec.) A thin flexible tissue in the body or in a plant.—**Mem'bran**OUS, *a.*

Memen'to, *n.* Imp. of L. *meminisse,* to remember. Something serving to remind.

Mem'oir, *n.* F. *mémoire,* masc., specialized use of *mémoire,* fem., MEMORY. A record of events; an autobiographical record (often in *pl.*); a biography; a dissertation.

Mem'orable, *a.* L. *memorābilis,* f. *memorāre,* to bring to mind, recount, f. *memor.* MEMORY. Worthy of remembrance.—**Mem'orab**LY,[2] *adv.*—**Memorabil'ia,** *n.pl.* Neut.pl. of *memorābilis.* Memorable things.—**Memoran'dum,** *n.* Neut. sing. of ger. of *memorāre.* A note to help the memory; a note of the terms of a contract; an informal letter.

Mem'ory, *n.* O.F. *memorie, memoire* (F. *mémoire*)—L. *memoria,* f. *memor,* mindful. REMEMBER. The faculty of remembrance; recollection, remembrance; a recollection; the length of time over which one's memory extends.—**Memo'ri**AL, *a.* Of memory; preserving the memory of something.—*n.* Something doing this; a record; a statement of facts in a petition, &c.—**Memo'rial**IZE, *vt.* To commemorate; to petition.—**Memo'rial**IST, *n.* A petitioner; a writer of memorials.—**Mem'or**IZE, *vt.* To record.

Men'ace, *n.* O.F. *menace*—L. *mināciа,* f. *minax, minācis,* a. f. *minārī,* to threaten. AMENABLE. COMMINATE. DEMEAN.[1] MINATORY. A threat.—*vt.* To threaten.

Menag'erie, *n.* F. *ménagerie,* orig., a place for domestic animals, f. *ménage,* household—L. *mansio.* MANSION. MESSUAGE. A collection of wild animals kept for exhibition.

Mend, *vt.* Aphetic f. AMEND. To rectify, put right, correct; to repair.—*vi.* To improve; to regain health.—*n.* A repaired hole.

Menda'cious, *a.* L. *mendax, mendācis* (f. root of *mentīre,* to lie) + -OUS. Lying, untruthful.—**Mendac'**ITY, *n.*

Men'dicant, *a.* L. *mendīcans, mendīcantis,* pres.pple. of *mendīcāre,* to beg, f. *mendīcus,* beggar. Begging.—*n.* A beggar.—**Men'di**CANCY, *n.*—**Mendic'**ITY, *n.*

Me'nial, *a.* A.F. *menial,* f. *meiniee* = O.F.

meyné, mesnie, household—L. *mansio*. MANSION. Of a servant, attached to the house; servile, sordid.—*n*. A menial servant.

Men'ses, *n.pl.* L. (*pl.* of *mensis*, month). The monthly discharge of a woman.

Men'struate, *vi.* L. *menstruāre*, *menstruātum*, f. *menstrua*, the menses. To discharge the menses.—**Menstrua**'TION, *n*.

Mensura'tion, *n*. L.L. *mensūrātio*, *mensūrātiōnis*, f. L. *mensūrāre*, to measure, f. *mensūra*. MEASURE. Measuring.

Men'tal, *a*. F. *mental*—L.L. *mentālis*, f. L. *mens,mentis*, MIND. DEMENT. REMINISCENCE. Of or pertaining to, performed by, the mind. —**Mental**'ITY, *n*.—**Men'tal**LY,[2] *adv*.

Men'tion, *n*. F. *mention*—L. *mentio*, *mentiōnis*, f. root of *mens*. (See prec.) A referring to or remarking upon (a person or thing).—*vt*. To make mention of.—**Men'tion**ABLE, *a*.

Men'tor, *n*. The name of the Ithacan noble whose person Athene assumed when acting as the guide and adviser of Telemachus (Odyssey 2, 267, &c.); hence, a sage and trusted adviser.

Menu, *n*. F. *menu* (L. *minūtus*, MINUTE), small, as *n*., small matters, detailed list, menu. A list of dishes to be served.

Mer'cantile, *a*. F. *mercantile*—It. *mercantil*, f. *mercante* = *mercatante*, MERCHANT. Of, belonging to, engaged in, trade.

Mer'cenary, *a*. L. *mercēnārius*, f. *merces*. MERCY. Working (merely) for reward or gain; of soldiers, hired.—*n*. A hired soldier.

Mer'cer, *n*. F. *mercier*—Pop.L. **merciārius*, f. *merx*. (See next.) A dealer in textile fabrics, esp. silks, &c.—**Mer'**CERY, *n*. His wares.

Mer'chant, *n*. O.F. *marchand* = It. *mercatante*—Pop.L. **mercātans*, **mercātantis*, pres. pple. of **mercātāre*, freq. of L. *mercāri*, to trade, f. *merx*, *mercis*, merchandise. MARKET. MERCANTILE. (And see prec.) A wholesale trader. —**Mer'chandise**, *n*. F. *marchandise*, f. *marchand*. The commodities in which he deals.—**Mer'chant**ABLE, *a*. Marketable.—**Mer'chantman**, *n*. A trading ship.

Mer'cury, *n*. L. *Mercurius*, prob. (as orig. the god of commerce), f. *merx*. (See prec.) The Roman god of eloquence and skill, and the messenger of the gods; the planet nearest to the sun; a white metal, liquid at ordinary temperatures, quicksilver.—**Mercu'ri**AL, *a*. Pertaining to the planet; sprightly, volatile (orig. referring to birth under the planet, supposed to confer the qualities of the god); pertaining to or containing quicksilver.

Mer'cy, *n*. F. *merci*—L. *merces*, *mercēdis*, fee, reward, in Christian L., compassion. MERCENARY. Forbearance and compassion; a gift of God.—**Mer'ci**FUL, *a*.—**Mer'ci**LESS, *a*.

Mere, *n*. O.E. *mere*, sea, lake, corresp. to O.N. *marr*, O.H.G. *meri*, *marī* (Ger. *meer*), sea. O.Teut. **mari-*, sea, lake. Cogn. with L. *mare*, sea. MARINE. MARSH. A lake.

Mere, *a*. L. *merus*, undiluted, pure. Of no greater extent, value, &c., than the designation implies.—**Mere'**LY,[2] *adv*.

Meretric'ious, *a*. L. *meretricius* (f. *meretrix*, *meretrīcis*, harlot, fem. agent-n. f. *merēre*. MERIT) + -OUS. Of, like, befitting, a harlot.

Merge, *vt.* and *i*. L. *mergĕre*, to dip, plunge. EMERGE. IMMERSE. To cause to lose, to lose, identity.—**Mer'ger**, *n*. Law F. *merger*. Extinction of a right, &c., by absorption.

Merid'ian, *a*. O.F. *meridien*—L. *merīdiānus*, f. *merīdies*, earlier *medīdies*, noon, f. *medius*, middle + *dies*, day. MID. DIURNAL. Of or pertaining to noon, or to the position, aspect, or power of the sun at noon; pertaining to or characteristic of a period of greatest splendour. —*n*. Noon; the highest point attained by a star, &c.; a period of greatest splendour; an imaginary circle in the heavens passing through the celestial poles and the zenith of any place on the earth; a similar circle of the earth in the plane of this and passing through the poles and a place.—**Merid'ion**AL, *a*.

Meri'no, *n*. Sp., the distinctive epithet of a particular breed of sheep, repg. L.L. *mājōrīnus*, of a larger kind, f. L. *mājor*, greater. MAJOR. A variety of sheep; a soft material originally made of merino wool.

Mer'it, *n*. O.F. *merite*—L. *meritum*, neut. pa.pple. of *merēre*, *merēri*, to deserve, to earn as pay. Cogn. with G. *meros*, share. MERETRICIOUS. The quality of deserving well; excellence, worth; an excellence; in *pl*., intrinsic excellences or defects. — *vt*. To deserve.—**Merito'rious**, *a*. L. *meritōrius* (bringing in money) + -OUS. Well-deserving.

Mer'maid, *n*. MERE, *n*. + MAID. An imaginary marine being having the upper part like a woman and the lower like a fish.

Mer'ry, *a*. O.E. *myr(i)ge*, pleasing, merry, prob. conn. with O.Teut. **murgjo-*, short (hence, 'making the time short', 'cheering'), and cogn. with G. *brachus*, short. MIRTH. Joyous, hilarious.—**Mer'ri**LY,[2] *adv*.—**Mer'ri**MENT, *n*.—**Mer'ry-go-round**, *n*. A revolving machine with cars or wooden horses.—**Mer'rythought**, *n*. The forked bone between the neck and breast of a bird.

Mesh, *n*. Cogn. with O.E. *max*, net, O.N. *mōskve*, mesh. One of the open spaces of a net.—*vt*. To catch in the meshes of a net.

Mes'merism, *n*. The name of F. A. *Mesmer*, an Austrian physician + -ISM. Mesmer's system of inducing an hypnotic state by influence exercised over a patient.—**Mesmer'**IC, *a*.—**Mes'mer**IST, *n*.—**Mes'mer**IZE, *vt*.

Mess, *n*. O.F. *mes*, a serving of food, a dish of food (F. *mets*, viand, dish)—L.L. *missum*, neut. pa.pple. of L. *mittĕre*, to send, in L.L. to put. ADMIT. A portion of partly liquid or pulpy food; a state of confusion or untidiness; a company of persons who regularly take their meals together.—*vi*. To take one's meals thus; to put things into confusion or an untidy state, to busy oneself vaguely.—*vt*. To make a mess of, to muddle.—**Mess'mate**, *n*. A companion at meals; one of a mess.

Mes'sage, *n*. F. *message*—Pop.L. **missāticum*, f. L. *mittĕre*. (See prec.) A communication from one person to another.—**Mes'senger**, *n*. With intrusive *n* (cf. PASSENGER) f. F. *messager*. One who takes a message.

Messi'ah, *n*. Alteration of *Messias*—L. *Messīās*—G. *Messias*—Heb. *māshiākh*, anointed, f. *māshakh*, to anoint. The promised deliverer of the Jewish nation; Christ.

Mes'suage, *n*. A.F. *messuage*, prob. corr. of O.F. *mesnage* = F. *ménage*. MENAGERIE. A house with its outbuildings and land.

Met'al, *n*. O.F. *metal*—L. *metallum*, mine, metal—G. *metallon*, mine, app. in some way conn. with *metalla-ein*, to inquire about. METTLE. An elementary substance, such as gold, &c., having a characteristic lustre and generally fusible and malleable; broken stone used in macadamizing roads.—**Metal'l**IC, *a*. —**Met'allurgy**, *n*. G. **metallourgia*, f. *metallourgos*, miner, f. *metallon* + *-ergos*, worker, f. *ergon*, WORK. The art of smelting and refining metals.—**Met'allurg**IST, *n*

Metamor'phosis, *n.* L. *metamorphōsis*—G. *metamorphōsis*, n. of action f. *metamorphoein*, to transform, f. META- + *morphē*, form. MORPHOLOGY. Change of form, substance, circumstances, character, &c.—**Metamor'phose**, *vt.* F. *métamorphoser*, f. *métamorphose*, n., f. L. To change, transform.

Met'aphor, *n.* F. *métaphore*—L. *metaphora*—G. *metaphora*, f. *metapherein*, to transfer, f. META- + *pherein*, to BEAR. A figure of speech in which a term is transferred to something to which it does not literally apply; an instance of this.—**Metaphor'**ICAL, *a.*

Metaphys'ics, *n.pl.* Med.L. *metaphysica*, neut.pl.—Med.G. *ta metaphusika* (alteration of *ta meta ta phusika*, 'the (works) coming after the Physics'), the title applied to the portion of Aristotle's works dealing with ontology from its position in the received arrangement of his writings. The theoretical philosophy of being and knowing. Also in form **Metaphys'ic**, repg. Scholastic L. *metaphysica*, fem. sing.—**Metaphys'ic**AL, *a.*—**Metaphys**IC'IAN, *n.*

Metath'esis, *n.* G. *metathesis*, transposition, f. META- + *thesis*. THESIS. Transposition.

Mete, *vt.* O.E. *metan*. Common Teut. O. Teut. root *met-*, pre-Teut. *med-*. MEET, *a.* Cogn. with G. *medimnos*, a measure of capacity, L. *modus*, measure, *meditāri*, to MEDITATE. MODE. To measure.—**Met'**ER, *n.* An instrument for measuring gas, &c.

Metempsycho'sis, *n.* G. *metempsuchōsis*, formed f. META- + *en*, in + *psuchē*, soul. PSYCHIC. Transmigration of the soul.

Me'teor, *n.* G. *meteōra*, atmospheric phenomena, neut.pl. of *meteōros*, raised from the ground, f. META- + *eōr-*, var. of the root of *aeirein*, to raise. Any atmospheric phenomenon; a luminous body appearing temporarily in the sky.—**Meteor'**IC, *a.*—**Me'teorite**, *n.* Scientific suff. *-ite*. Also **Me'teorolite**. F. *météorolithe*, f. G. *meteōro-* + *lithos*, stone. A fallen meteor, an aerolite.—**Meteorol**'OGY. The science that treats of the phenomena of the atmosphere.—**Meteorolog'**ICAL, *a.*—**Meteorol'og**IST, *n.*

Methinks, *v.impers.* O.E. *mē thyncth*, it seems to me, f. *thyncean*, to seem, conn. with *thanc*, a thought (THANK), and *thenc(e)an*, to THINK. It seems to me.

Meth'od, *n.* F. *méthode*—L. *methodus*—G. *methodos*, a following after, pursuit of knowledge, mode of investigation, f. *meth-* (= META-) + *hodos*, way. EPISODE. PERIOD. SYNOD. A mode of procedure; orderly arrangement of ideas; orderliness and regularity.—**Method'**ICAL, *a.*—**Meth'od**IST, *n.* (App. as advocating a particular 'method' of belief.) A member of any of several religious bodies originating from the labours of J. and C. Wesley and G. Whitefield.—**Meth'od**ISM, *n.*—**Meth'od**IZE, *vt.* To reduce to order.

Meth'yl, *n.* F. *méthyle*, back-formation f. *méthylène*, a sim. substance, f. G. *methu*, wine + *hulē*, wood. The base of wood spirit.—**Meth'yl**ATE,[3] *vt.* To mix with methyl.

Metic'ulous, *a.* L. *meticulōsus*, timid, f. *metus*, fear. Over-scrupulous about details.

Meton'ymy, *n.* G. *metōnumia*, f. *met-* (= META-) + *onoma* (in Æolic *onuma*), NAME. The substitution of the name of an attribute of a thing for the name of the thing.

Me'tre, *n.*[1] O.F. *metre*—L. *metrum*—G. *metron*, a measure, metre. Any form of poetical rhythm; metrical arrangement; composition in metre.—**Met'r**ICAL, *a.*

Me'tre, *n.*[2] F. *mètre*—G. *metron*. (See prec.) A unit of length = 39·37 inches.—**Met'r**IC, *a.* Of the system of weights and measures of which the metre is the fundamental unit.

Metrop'olis, *n.* L. *mētropolis*—G. *mētropolis*, mother-state, chief city, f. *mētēr*, mother + *polis*, city, state. POLICY.[1] The seat of a metropolitan; a chief city.—**Metropol'itan**, *a.* Med.L. *mētropolitānus*—G. *mētropolitēs*. Of or constituting a metropolis.—*n.* A bishop set over the bishops of a province.

Mett'le, *n.* Var. of METAL. Quality of disposition; spirit, courage.—**Mett'le**SOME, *a.*

Mew, *n.*[1] O.E. *mǣw*, corresp. to O.S. *mēu* (Du. *meeuw*, Ger. *möwe*). A sea-gull.

Mew, *v.*[1]*i.* F. *muer*—L. *mūtāre*, to change. MUTABLE. Of a hawk, to moult.—*vt.* From the *n.* To put (a moulting hawk) in a mew; to confine, to shut *up*.—*n.*[2] A cage for moulting hawks.—**Mews**, *n.pl.* (but gen. used as sing.). Orig., the royal stables at Charing Cross, built on the site of the old royal mews. A set of stables round an open space.

Mew, *v.*[2]*i.* Imitative. Of a cat, to utter its characteristic sound.—*n.*[3] The sound.

Mez'zo-sopra'no. It. *mezzo*, middle, half—L. *medius*. MID. A voice intermediate between soprano and contralto; the part for this voice; a singer with a voice of this pitch.

Mez'zotint, *n.* It. *mezzotinto*, f. *mezzo* (see prec.) + *tinto*, tint, f. *tingere*, to tint—L. *tingĕre*, to dye. TINCTURE. A half-tint; a method of engraving in which the lights and half-lights are produced by scraping a roughened surface; a print thus produced.—*vt.* To engrave in mezzotint.

Mias'ma, *n.* G. *miasma*, *miasmatos*, pollution. Noxious emanations.—**Miasmat'**IC, *a.*

Mi'ca, *n.* L. *mica*, grain, crumb (prob. associated with *micāre*, to shine). A mineral occurring in glittering plates or scales.

Mich'aelmas, *n.* *Michael* + MASS.[1] The feast of St. Michael the Archangel, 29th Sept.

Mi'crobe, *n.* F. *microbe*—G. *mikros*, small + *bios*, life. A minute being, esp. of bacteria.

Mi'crocosm, *n.* F. *microcosme*—Med.L. *microcosmus*, formed f. G. *mikros*, small + *kosmos*, world. The little world of human nature; man as an epitome of the MACROCOSM.

Mi'crophone, *n.* G. *mikros*, small + *phōnē*, sound. An instrument for magnifying small sounds.—**Mi'croscope**, *n.* *Mikros* + G. *skopein*, to look. SCEPTIC. An instrument by which details of objects are magnified and rendered visible.—**Microscop'**IC, *a.* Microscopical; so small as to be invisible save through a microscope.—**Microscop'**ICAL, *a.* Pertaining or relating to the microscope.

Mic'turate, *vi.* Incorrectly in form and sense f. L. *micturīre*, desiderative of *mingĕre*, to make water. To make water.—**Micturi'**TION, *n.* The desire to do this; doing this.

Mid, *a.* O.E. *midd*, middle. Common Teut. and Indo-Germanic. Cogn. with Skr. *madhya*, G. *messos*, *mesos*, L. *medius*, middle. MEAN, *a.*[2] MEDIATE. MEDIOCRE. MERIDIAN. MIDDLE. MOIETY. (The) middle of (the) (often with hyphen or joined to the qualified word).—**Mid'day**, *n.* Noon.—**Mid'land**, *n.* The middle part of a country; in *pl.*, the middle counties of England.—*a.* In the middle of the land.—**Mid'night**, *n.* 12 o'clock at night.—**Mid'shipman**, *n.* So called from being stationed amidships when on duty. Denoting a naval rank immediately below that of the lowest commissioned officer.—

Mid'summer, *n.* 24th June.—**Mid'way**, *a.* and *adv.* In the middle of the way; half-way.

Mid'dle, *a.* O.E. *middel*, a. and n. = O.Fris. *middel*, a., O.H.G. *mittil*, a. (Ger. *mittel*, a. and n.). Cogn. with MID. Equidistant from extremities; intermediate between two extremes, medium; of a Greek verb, denoting reflexive or reciprocal action or action viewed as affecting the subject.—*n.* The middle point or part.—**Mid'dleman**, *n.* A trader through whom goods pass from producer to consumer.

Mid'dling, *a.* Prob. f. MID + adj. suff. *-ling*. Moderately good.—*adv.* Moderately.

Midge, *n.* O.E. *mycg* = O.H.G. *mucca* (Ger. *mücke*). A small gnat-like insect.

Mid'riff, *n.* O.E. *midhrif*, f. *midd*, MID + *hrif*, belly. The diaphragm.

Midst, *n.* M.E. *middes* (as in *on-middes*, altered form of O.E. *on middan*, AMID) with addition of *t*. The position of being in the middle, among, &c.—*prep.* In the midst of.

Mid'wife, *n.* Prob. f. obs. *Mid*, with (O.E. *mid*. Common Teut. Cogn. with G. *meta*. META-) + WIFE, in older sense 'woman'; hence 'one with the mother at the birth'. A woman who assists women in childbed. — **Mid'wif**ERY, *n.* The art or practice of doing this.

Mien, *n.* Prob. aphetic f. obs. *Demean*, demeanour, f. DEMEAN,[1] partly assimilated in sense and form to F. *mine*, expression of face, look, appearance, of uncertain orig. Air or manner as expressive of character or mood.

Might, *n.* O.E. *miht* = O.S., O.H.G. *maht* (Ger. *macht*), f. root *mag-*. MAY, *v.*[2] Ability to do one's will; power, strength.—**Might'**Y,[2] *a.* Powerful, strong.—**Might'**ILY,[2] *adv.*

Mignonette', *n.* F. *mignonnette*, fem. dim. of *mignon*. MINION. A fragrant plant.

Mi'grate, *vi.* L. *migrāre*, *migrātum*. EMIGRATE. IMMIGRATE. TRANSMIGRATE. To move from one place to another.—**Mi'gr**ANT, *a.* and *n.*—**Migra'**TION, *n.*—**Mi'grat**ORY, *a.*

Milch, *a.* M.E. *mielch*, *milche*, repg. O.E. **milce*, conn. with MILK. Cf. Ger. *melk(-kuh)*, milch(-cow). Giving milk, kept for milking.

Mild, *a.* O.E. *milde*. Common Teut. Cogn. with G. *malthakos*, soft, mild. Merciful, indulgent, gentle; operating gently; soft to the palate; of beer, not strongly flavoured with hops.—**Mild'**LY,[2] *adv.*—**Mild'**NESS, *n.*

Mil'dew, *n.* O.E. *meledēaw*, *mildēaw* (= O.H.G. *militou* (Ger. *meltau*)), f. *mele*, *mil*, conn. with L. *mel*, honey + *dēaw*, DEW. MELLIFLUOUS. Formerly, honey-dew. A destructive fungous growth.—*vt.* and *i.* To taint, to become tainted, with mildew.

Mile, *n.* O.E. *mīl* = M.Du. *mīle*, O.H.G. *mīla* (Ger. *meile*)—L. *mīlia*, *millia*, pl. of *mille*, a thousand, whence *mille* (*passuum*), a thousand (paces), a Roman mile. MILLENARY. In modern English use, a measure of length = 1760 yards.—**Mile'**AGE, *n.* Distance in miles.

Mil'itary, *a.* F. *militaire*—L. *mīlitāris*, f. *mīles*, *mīlitis*, soldier. Pertaining to, used or done by, befitting, soldiers; belonging to, connected with, the army.—*n.* Soldiers collectively.—**Mil'itar**ISM, *n.* The prevalence of military feeling among a people; predominance of a military class.—**Mil'itar**IST, *n.*—

Mil'itate, *vi.* L. *mīlitāre*, *mīlitātum*, to serve as a soldier, f. *mīles*. To have force *against*.—**Mil'it**ANT, *a.* Warring; combative.—**Mili'tia**, *n.* L. *mīlitia*, military service. A citizen army; a branch of the English military service enrolled for home defence.

Milk, *n.* O. Mercian *milc* = West Saxon *meolc*, *meoluc*, corresp. to O.N. *miolk*, O.H.G. *miluh* (Ger. *milch*). Cogn. with G. *amelgein*, L. *mulgēre*, to milk. The white fluid secreted by female animals and serving as nourishment for their young.—*vt.* To draw milk from.—

Milk'sop, *n.* An effeminate man or youth.—**Milk'**Y,[2] *a.* *Milky Way*, a band of stars not separately visible encircling the heavens.

Mill, *n.* O.E. *mylen*—L.L. *molinum*, *molina*, mill, L. *mola*, millstone. MEAL.[1] IMMOLATE. MOLAR. A building fitted, an apparatus designed, for grinding corn, &c.; a building in which an industry is carried on; a machine for fulling cloth; a machine for stamping coins.—*vt.* To pass through a mill; to stamp (coins) in a mill, esp. so as to produce regular markings on the edges.—**Mil'l**ER, *n.*—**Mill'-race**, *n.* A current of water driving a mill-wheel; its channel.—**Mill'stone** *n.* One of a pair of circular stones used for grinding.

Mil'lenary, *a.* L. *millēnārius*, containing a thousand, f. *millēni*, a thousand each, f. *mille*. MILE. Of, consisting of, a thousand.—*n.* A thousand years.—**Millena'ri**AN, *a.* Of, believing in, the millennium.—*n.* A believer in the millennium.—**Millen'nium**, *n.* L. *mille* + *annus*, year, after L. *biennium*, &c. A thousand years; the period of a thousand years during which (according to some) Christ is to reign on earth.—**Millen'ni**AL, *a.*—

Milles'imal, *a.* L. *millēsimus*, thousandth. Thousandth; consisting of thousandths.

Mil'let, *n.* F. *millet*, dim. of *mil* in same sense—L. *milium*. The minute grain of a cereal plant, a native of India; the plant.

Mil'liard, *n.* F., f. L. *mille*, a thousand. MILE. A thousand millions.

Mil'liner, *n.* *Milan* + -ER. Formerly, a vendor of Milanese wares. A person who makes up female apparel.—**Mil'lin**ERY, *n*

Mil'lion, *n.* F., f. L. *mille*, a thousand + aug. suff. MILE. A thousand thousands.—

Millionaire', *n.* F. *millionnaire*. One possessed of a million of money; a very rich person.

Milt, *n.* O.E. *milte*, spleen = M.Du. *milte*, spleen, milt of fish, O.H.G. *milzi* (Ger. *milz*), spleen. Perh. f. the root of MELT, referring to supposed digestive functions of the spleen. The spleen; the roe of the male fish, the soft roe (in this sense prob. confused with MILK, the older name for the soft roe).

Mime, *n.* L. *mimus*, G. *mimos*, an actor in a kind of farcical drama, such a drama, f. *mimeesthai*, to imitate. A mimic, jester; the kind of drama mentioned above.—**Mimet'ic**, *a.* G. *mimētikos*. Of, addicted to, clever at, imitation.—**Mimet'ically**, *adv.* -ICAL. -LY.[2]—**Mim'ic**, *a.* L. *mimicus*, G. *mimikos*. Of, of the nature of, imitation; imitative, as opposed to real.—*n.* One skilled in ludicrous imitation.—*vt.* To imitate ludicrously or minutely; to resemble closely.—**Mim'ic**RY, *n.*

Min'aret, *n.* Arab. *manārat*, lamp, lighthouse, minaret, f. root of *nār*, fire. A tall slender tower connected with a mosque.

Mi'natory, *a.* O.F. *minatoire*—L.L. *minātōrius*, f. L. *minārī*, to MENACE. Menacing.

Mince, *vt.* O.F. *mincier*, *minchier*—Pop.L. **minūtiāre*—L. *minūtia*, smallness, fineness, f. *minūtus*, MINUTE. MINISH. To cut or chop small; to utter with affected elegance.—*vi.* To walk in an affected manner.—*n.* Minced meat.—**Mince'meat**, *n.* Altered f.

minced meat. A mixture of currants, sugar, suet, &c., and sometimes minced meat.—**Mince'-pie**, *n.* Altered f. *minced-pie.* A pie containing mincemeat.

Mind, *n.* M.E. *mynd*, repg. O.E. *gemynd* = O.H.G. *gimunt*, Goth. *gamunds*, memory. Cogn. with Skr. *manas*, mind, G. *menos*, rage, L. *mens*, mind. COMMENT. MANIA. MENTAL. Remembrance; one's opinion or purpose; wish, inclination; temper or mood of a specified kind; the seat of consciousness or volition; the intellectual powers.—*vt.* To bear in mind; to give heed to; to apply oneself to; to care for, trouble oneself about; to dislike.—**Mind'**FUL, *a.* Taking thought or care; keeping remembrance.

Mine, *n.* F. *mine*, of doubtful orig. An excavation for digging out ores, coal, &c.; an underground gallery to contain an explosive for blowing up fortifications, &c., the charge; a receptacle containing an explosive placed in the sea, &c., to destroy ships.—*vt.* F. *miner.* To dig from a mine; to burrow in; to undermine; to lay mines under or in.—*vi.* To make or work in a mine.—**Min'**ER, *n.*—**Min'eral**, *a.* F. *minéral.* Got by mining; impregnated with mineral substances; inorganic.—*n.* A substance got by mining; each of the species of inorganic substances.—**Mineral**'OGY, *n.* The science of minerals.—**Mineralog'**ICAL, *a.*—**Mineral'og**IST, *n.*

Mine, *pron.* O.E. *mín.* Common Teut. Conn. with *me*, acc. and dat. of the pron. of the first person. My; belonging to me.

Min'gle, *vt.* and *i.* Late M.E. *mengel*, freq. f. *meng*, O.E. *mengan*, to mix = O.N. *menga*, O.H.G., Ger. *mengen*, conn. with O.E. *gemang*, *mang*, mixture. AMONG. MONGREL. To mix; to unite or join in company or association.

Min'iature, *n.* It. *miniatura* — Med.L. *miniātūra*, f. L. *miniāre*, to colour with red-lead, f. *minium*, red-lead. A picture in an illuminated manuscript; hence (such pictures being usually small), a portrait or representation on a small scale.—*a.* Small-scale.

Min'im, *n.* L. *minimus*, smallest. *Mus.*, a note having half the length of a semibreve; a creature or thing of the least size or importance; the smallest fluid measure.—**Min'i**MIZE, *vt.* To reduce to, estimate at, the smallest possible amount, &c.—**Min'imum**, *n.* L., neut. of *minimus.* The lowest magnitude or quantity.—*a.* That is a minimum.

Min'ion, *n.* F. *mignon.* MIGNONETTE. A favourite, esp. an unworthy favourite.

Min'ish, *vt.* and *i.* O.F. *menusier*, *menuisier* —Pop.L. **minūtiāre.* MINCE. To diminish.

Min'ister, *n.* O.F. *ministre*—L. *minister*, servant. One administering a department of the state; a political agent in a foreign state; a clergyman.—*vt.* O.F. *ministrer*—L. *ministrāre.* To furnish, supply.—*vi.* To serve, give tendance; to be serviceable, to contribute. —**Min'istr**ANT, *a.* and *n.*—**Ministra'**TION, *n.*—**Min'istr**ATIVE, *a.*—**Min'istry**, *n.* L. *ministerium*, service, f. *minister.* The action of ministering; the functions, the office, of a clergyman; agency, instrumentality; the body of ministers administering the state.—**Ministe'rial**, *a.* F. *ministériel*—L.L. *ministeriālis*, ministering, f. *ministerium.* MINSTREL. Of, entrusted with, the administration of the law; instrumental; of the functions or character of a clergyman; of a minister of state; supporting the ministers of the day.—**Ministe'rial**IST, *n.* Such a supporter.

Min'now, *n.* Prob. repg. O.E. **mynwe* = O.H.G. *munewa*, *munua*, some kind of fish. A small freshwater fish.

Mi'nor, *a.* L. *minor*, used as comp. of *parvus*, small. Cogn. with G. *minuthein*, L. *minuĕre*, O.E. *minsian*, to diminish. MINUS. MINUTE. Lesser; comparatively small or unimportant; under age, not yet 21 years old.—*n.* A person under age.—**Minor'**ITY, *n.* The state of being a minor; the lesser number; the smaller party voting together in an assembly.

Min'ster, *n.* O.E. *mynster*—Eccles.L. *monastērium*, MONASTERY. Cf. O.H.G. *munistri* (Ger. *münster*). The church of a monastery; a cathedral church.

Min'strel, *n.* O.F. *menestral*, *ministral*—L.L. *ministeriālis*, one having an official duty. MINISTERIAL. In early use, one who entertained his patrons with singing, jesting, &c. A mediæval singer or musician; a bard or poet.—**Min'strelsy**, *n.* O.F. *menestralsie.* The minstrel's art; minstrels; minstrel poetry.

Mint, *n.*[1] O.E. *mynet*, repg. W. Germanic **munita*—L. *monēta*, MONEY. A place where money is coined.—*vt.* To make (coin).

Mint, *n.*[2] O.E. *minte* = O.H.G. *minza* (Ger. *münze*)—L. *menta*, *mentha*, G. *minthē.* An aromatic plant.

Minuet', *n.* F. *menuet*, use as *n.* of *menuet*, dim. of *menu.* MENU. A slow stately dance; music for it.

Mi'nus, quasi-*prep.* L. *minus*, neut. of *minor*, less. MINOR. Indicating (gen. by the symbol −) that a second expression is to be subtracted from a first; with the deduction of.

Minus'cule, *n.* F.—L. *minuscula* (sc. *littera*, letter), fem. of *minusculus*, dim. of *minor.* MINOR. Of a letter, small.—*n.* A small letter.

Minute', *a.* L. *minūtus*, pa.pple. of *minuĕre*, to make small, diminish. MENU. MINCE. MINOR. Very small; very precise or particular.—**Min'ute**, *n.* F. *minute*—L. *minūta* (*pars*, part), fem. of *minūtus.* The sixtieth part of an hour or of an angular degree; a moment; a point of time; a rough draft, a memorandum; a record of proceedings (gen. in *pl.*).—*vt.* To make a minute of, to record in minutes.—**Minute'**LY,[2] *adv.*—**Minu'tiæ**, *n.pl.* L. *minūtiae*, trifles, pl. of *minūtia*, smallness, f. *minūtus.* Precise details; trifles.

Minx, *n.* Poss., with added *s*, corr. of dial. *Minikin*, lass — Early Mod.Du. *minneken*, f. *minne*, love, with dim. suff. A pert girl.

Mir'acle, *n.* O.F. *miracle*—L. *mīrāculum*, a wonder, in Eccles.L., a miracle, f. *mīrārī*, to wonder at, conn. with *mīrus*, wonderful. ADMIRE. MARVEL. MIRAGE. A supernatural event; a marvel.—**Mir'acle play**, *n.* A mediæval play based on the lives of Christ and the saints.—**Mirac'ul**OUS, *a.*

Mirage', *n.* F., f. (*se*) *mirer*, to look at oneself in a mirror, be reflected, f. Pop.L. **mīrāre*, to look at, L. *mīrārī.* (See prec.) MIRROR. An optical illusion, esp. an illusory appearance of distant water.

Mire, *n.* O.N. *mýrr*, f. O.Teut. root *meus-*, var. of *mus-.* MOSS. A piece of swampy ground; mud, dirt.—*vt.* To set fast in the mire; to defile with mire.—**Mir'**Y,[2] *a.*

Mir'ror, *n.* O.F. *mirour*, earlier *miradoir* (F. *miroir*)—Pop.L. **mīrātōrium*, f. **mīrāre.* MIRAGE. A polished surface reflecting images of objects.—*vt.* To reflect an image of.

Mirth, *n.* O.E. *myr(i)gth*, conn. with *myr(i)ge*, MERRY. Merriment.—**Mirth'**FUL, *a.*

Misadven'ture, *n.* O.F. *mesavcnture*, f.

mes- (MIS-[2]) + *aventure, auenture.* ADVENTURE. Bad luck; a mishap or misfortune.

Misalli'ance, *n.* MIS-[1]. (After F. *mésalliance.*) An improper or degrading marriage.

Mis'anthrope, *n.* G. *misanthrōpos*, f. *mise-ein*, to hate + *anthrōpos*, man. A hater of mankind. —**Misanthrop**'IC, -ICAL, *aa.* — **Misan'thropist**, *n.*—**Misan'thropy**,[1] *n.*

Misapply', *vt.* MIS-[1]. To apply erroneously or to a wrong object.—**Misapplic**A'TION, *n.*

Misapprehend', *vt.* MIS-[1]. Not to understand rightly.—**Misapprehen'**SION, *n.*

Misappro'priate, *vt.* MIS-[1]. To appropriate wrongly.—**Misappropri**A'TION, *n.*

Misbecome', *vt.* MIS-[1]. To suit ill.

Misbegot'ten, *ppl.a.* MIS-[1]. Bastard.

Misbehave', *vi.* and *refl.* MIS-[1]. To conduct oneself improperly.—**Misbeha'viour**, *n.*

Misbelieve', *vi.* MIS-[1]. To hold an erroneous belief.—**Misbelief'**, *n.*

Miscal'culate, *vt.* MIS-[1]. To calculate or estimate wrongly.—**Miscalcul**A'TION, *n.*

Miscall', *vt.* MIS-[1]. To call by a wrong name.

Miscar'ry, *vi.* MIS-[1]. To fail; to be delivered prematurely *of* a child; of a letter, not to be delivered.—**Miscar'ri**AGE, *n.*

Miscella'neous, *a.* L. *miscellāneus* (f. *miscellus*, mixed, f. *miscēre*, to MIX) + -OUS. Of mixed composition or character.—**Miscel'lany**, *n.* App. f. F. *miscellanées*, fem. pl.—L. *miscellānea*, neut. pl. of *miscellāneus*. A collection of writings in one book; a medley.

Mischance', *n.* O.F. *mesch(e)ance.* MIS-[2]. CHANCE. Bad luck; a misfortune.

Mis'chief, *n.* O.F. *meschief*, vbl.n. f. *meschever*, to be unfortunate, f. *mes-* (MIS-[2]) + *chever*, to succeed, f. *chef*, head. CHIEF. Harm; an injury; a source of harm or of annoyance; annoying conduct.—**Mis'chievous**, *a.* A.F. *meschevous*, f. *meschever.* Having harmful effects; disposed to petty annoyance.

Misconceive', *vi.* MIS-[1]. To form a false conception.—*vt.* To form such a conception of, misapprehend.—**Misconcep'**TION, *n.*

Miscon'duct, *n.* MIS-[1]. Bad management; improper conduct.—**Misconduct'**, *vt.* To mismanage.—*v.refl.* To misbehave.

Miscon'strue, *vt.* MIS-[1]. To mistake the meaning of.—**Misconstruc'**TION, *n.*

Miscount', *vt.* MIS-[1]. To reckon wrongly.—*n.* A wrong reckoning.

Mis'creant, *a.* O.F. *mescreant*, f. *mes-* (MIS-[2]) + *creant*, believing, pres.pple. of *creire*, L. *crēdĕre*, to believe. CREDIT. RECREANT. Infidel; depraved.—*n.* An infidel; a villain.

Misdeal', *vi.* MIS-[1]. To make a mistake in dealing cards.—*n.* A wrongly made deal.

Misdeed', *n.* O.E. *misdǽd.* MIS-[1]. DEED. A wrong action, an offence or crime.

Misdemean', *v.refl.* MIS-[1]. To misbehave. —**Misdemean'our**, *n.* Misconduct; an offence less grave than a felony. —**Misdemean'**ANT, *n.* One convicted of a misdemeanour; one guilty of misconduct.

Misdirect', *vt.* MIS-[1]. To direct wrongly.—**Misdirec'**TION, *n.*

Misdoubt', *vt.* MIS-[1] (intensifying the notion of uneasy feeling). To be mistrustful of; to have misgivings as to; to suspect.

Mi'ser, *n.* L. *miser*, wretched. Formerly, a wretched person. One who lives miserably to hoard wealth; a niggard.—**Mis'erable**, *a.* F. *misérable*—L. *miserābilis*, pitiable, f. *miserāri*, to pity, f. *miser.* Very unhappy; causing wretchedness; despicable. — **Mis'erab**LY,[2] *adv.* — **Mi'ser**LY,[1] *a.* — **Mis'ery**, *n.* O.F. *miserie*—L. *miseria*, f. *miser.* A state of unhappiness; a source of wretchedness.

Misfea'sance, *n.* O.F. *mesfaisance*, f. *mesfaisant*, pres.pple. of *mesfaire*, to do wrongly, f. *mes-* (MIS-[2]) + *faire*, to do. FEASIBLE. The wrongful exercise of lawful authority.

Misfit', *n.* MIS-[1] + FIT, *n.*[2] A garment that fits badly.

Misfor'tune, *n.* MIS-[1]. Bad fortune; an instance of this.

Misgive', *vt.* (orig. with dat.). MIS-[1] + GIVE in obs. sense 'to suggest (to one)'. Of one's heart, &c., to suggest doubt or apprehension to.

Misgov'ern, *vt.* MIS-[1]. To mismanage the government of.—**Misgov'ern**MENT, *n.*

Misguide', *vt.* MIS-[1]. To guide wrongly.

Mishap', *n.* MIS-[1]. Bad luck; a misfortune.

Misinform', *vt.* MIS-[1]. To give wrong information to.—**Misinform**A'TION, *n.*

Misinter'pret, *vt.* MIS-[1]. To interpret erroneously.—**Misinterpret**A'TION, *n.*

Misjudge', *vt.* MIS-[1]. To judge wrongly.

Mislay', *vt.* MIS-[1]. To put (a thing) where it cannot readily be found.

Mislead', *vt.* O.E. *mislǽdan.* MIS-[1]. LEAD, *v.*[2] To lead astray or into error.

Misman'age, *vt.* MIS-[1]. To manage badly or wrongly.—**Misman'age**MENT, *n.*

Misname', *vt.* MIS-[1]. To name wrongly.

Misno'mer, *n.* O.F. *mesnom(m)er*, inf. used as n., f. *mes-* (MIS-[2]) + *nommer*, L. *nōmināre*, to name, f. *nōmen.* NOMINAL. The use of a wrong name or term; a wrong name or term.

Misog'amy, *n.* G. *misogamos*, hating marriage (f. *mise-ein*, to hate + *gamos*, marriage) + -Y.[1] Hatred of marriage.—**Misog'am**IST, *n.*

Misog'ynist, *n.* G. *misogunēs* (f. *mise-ein*, to hate + *gunē*, woman) + -IST. A hater of women.—**Misog'yn**Y,[1] *n.*

Misplace', *vt.* MIS-[1]. To place wrongly.

Misprint', *vt.* MIS-[1]. To print incorrectly. —*n.* A mistake in printing.

Mispri'sion, *n.*[1] O.F. *mesprision*, mistake, wrong action, f. *mes-* (MIS-[2]) + L. *prensio, prensiōnis.* PRISON. A wrong action or omission; *misprision of treason*, &c., orig., an offence akin to treason, &c., now, concealment of knowledge of treason, &c.

Misprize', *vt.* O.F. *mesprisier* (F. *mépriser*), f. *mes-* (MIS-[2]) + *prisier.* PRIZE, *v.*[2] To despise; to fail to appreciate.—**Mispri'**SION, *n.*[2]

Mispronounce', *vt.* MIS-[1]. To pronounce incorrectly.—**Mispronunci**A'TION, *n.*

Misquote', *vt.* MIS-[1]. To quote incorrectly. —**Misquot**A'TION, *n.*

Misreport', *vt.* MIS-[1]. To report incorrectly. —*n.* An incorrect report.

Misrepresent', *vt.* MIS-[1]. To represent wrongly.—**Misrepresent**A'TION, *n.*

Misrule', *vt.* MIS-[1]. To rule badly.—*n.* Bad rule; a state of disorder or rebellion.

Miss, *n.*[1] Contr. f. MISTRESS. A title of an unmarried woman or girl; a girl.

Miss, *vt.* O.E. *missan* = M.Du., Du. *missen*, O.H.G. *missan* (Ger. *missen*). Cogn. with MIS-[1]. To fail to hit, meet, or light upon; to fail to obtain or receive; to let slip; not to be in time for; to fail to see, hear, apprehend; to omit; to discover the absence of; to feel the want of. —*n.*[2] Failure to hit or obtain.

Mis'sal, *n.* Eccles.L. *missāle*, neut. sing. of *missālis*, a. f. *missa*, MASS.[1] A mass-book.

Mis'sel-thrush, *n.* Obs. *Missel*, O.E. *mistel*, *mistil*, MISTLETOE = O.H.G. *mistil* (Ger. *mistel*). A thrush which feeds on mistletoe-berries.

Mis'sile, *a.* L. *missilis*, f. *mittĕre.* (See next.)

Capable of being thrown.—*n.* L. *missile*, neut. of *missilis*. A missile object or weapon.
Mis'sion, *n.* L. *missio, missiōnis*, n. of action f. *mittĕre, missum*, to send. ADMIT. DISMISS. MESS. SURMISE. A sending or being sent on some service; a sending forth to preach a religion; a body of persons sent; the business or function of one sent; one's vocation in life.—**Mis'sion**ARY, *a.* Of religious missions.—*n.* One who goes on a religious mission.
Mis'sive, *a.* Med.L. *missivus*, f. *mittĕre*. (See prec.) *Letter missive*, one from a superior conveying a command, &c.—*n.* A letter.
Misspell', *vt.* MIS-1. To spell incorrectly.
Misspend', *vt.* MIS-1. To spend amiss.
Misstate', *vt.* MIS-1. To state erroneously; to misrepresent.—**Misstate'**MENT, *n.*
Mist, *n.* O.E. *mist* = M.L.G., M.Du. *mist*. O.N. *mistur*. Cogn. with Skr. *mih, mēgha*, G. *omichlē*. Vapour of water condensed into fine drops.—**Mist'**Y,2 *a.*—**Mist'i**LY,2 *adv.*
Mistake', *vt.* O.N. *mistaka*, to take in error, f. MIS-1 + *taka*, to TAKE. To misunderstand the meaning, intention, &c., of; to substitute in thought or perception (one thing) *for* (another).—*vi.* To be in error.—*n.* An error in thought or action.—**Mistak'**ABLE, *a.*
Mis'ter, *n.* See MASTER.
Mis'tletoe, *n.* O.E. *mistiltán* (= O.N. *mistilteinn*) f. *mistil* (MISSEL-THRUSH) + *tán*, twig. A parasitic plant growing on various trees.
Mistranslate', *vt.* To translate incorrectly. —**Mistransl**A'TION, *n.*
Mis'tress, *n.* O.F. *maistresse* (F. *maîtresse*), f. *maistre*, MASTER + *-esse* (= -ESS). MISS, *n.*1 A woman who employs other persons; the female head of a household; a female owner; a woman with power to control or use; a female teacher; a sweetheart; one who occupies a wife's place illicitly; a title of a married woman (contracted to *Mrs.*).
Mistrust', *vt.* MIS-1. Not to trust.—*n.* Lack of trust.—**Mistrust'**FUL, *a.*
Misunderstand', *vt.* MIS-1. To understand wrongly. — **Misunderstand'ing**, *vbl.n.* Failure to understand; a disagreement.
Misuse', *vt.* MIS-1. To use improperly; to maltreat.—*n.* Improper use; an improper use.
Mite, *n.*1 O.E. *mite* = M.Du., M.L.G. *mite* (Du. *mijt*). A very small insect, now gen. restricted to the cheese-mite.
Mite, *n.*2 M.Du. *mite* = M.L.G. *mite*. Prob. the same as prec. Orig., a very small Flemish copper coin. A very small coin or thing.
Mit'igate, *vt.* L. *mītigāre, mītigātum*, f. *mītis*, mild, gentle. To appease; to alleviate; to make less severe.—**Mitig**A'TION, *n.*
Mi'tre, *n.* F. *mitre*—L. *mitra*, G. *mitra*, a head-band. A bishop's head-dress.
Mit'ten, *n.* F. *mitaine*, of obscure orig. A glove with a division for the thumb only.
Mix, *vt.* Back-formation f. obs. ppl.a. *Mixt* = *mixed* — F. *mixte*—L. *mixtus*, pa.pple. of *miscēre*, to mix, cogn. with G. *misgein*, and cogn. with (or the source of) O.E. *miscian* (which did not survive into M.E.). MEDDLE. MISCELLANEOUS. PROMISCUOUS. To put together so as to produce common diffusion of particles or members, to mingle, blend.—*vi.* To be mixed; to associate.—**Mix'**TURE, *n.*
Mi'zen, *n.* F. *misaine* (now foresail), prob. f. It. *mezzana*, orig. fem. of *mezzano*, middle—L.L. *mediānus*. MEAN, *a.*2 A fore-and-aft sail set on the after side of the mizen-mast.—**Mi'zen-mast**, *n.* The aftermost mast of a three-masted ship.
Miz'zle, *vi.* Cf. dial. Du. *miezelen*. To drizzle. —*n.* A drizzle.
Mnemon'ic, *a.* G. *mnēmonikos*, f. *mnēmōn*, mindful, f. *mna-esthai*, to remember. AMNESTY. Of, intended to aid, the memory.—In *pl.* as *n.*, the art of improving the memory.
Moan, *n.* App. repg. an O.E. **mán*, conn. with *mǽnan*, to lament, of unknown orig. A prolonged low murmur indicative of suffering.—*vt.* To bewail.—*vi.* To utter a moan.
Moat, *n.* M.E. *mote, mot*, app. identical with obs. *Mote*, mound, embankment—O.F. *mote, motte*, clod, mound, castle, supposed to be of Teut. orig. (For the change of sense cf. DIKE.) A deep wide ditch surrounding a town or building.—*vt.* To surround with a moat.
Mob, *n.* Abb. of obs. *Mobile*, shortened form of L. *mōbile vulgus*, the movable or excitable crowd. MOBILE. The disorderly part of the population; a disorderly crowd; the populace; a promiscuous assemblage.—*vt.* To attack in a mob, to crowd round and molest.
Mob-cap, *n.* = obs. *Mob*, of doubtful orig. An indoor cap formerly worn by women.
Mo'bile, *a.* F. *mobile*—L. *mōbilis*, f. *movēre*, to MOVE. MOB. Capable of movement; easily changing in expression fickle.—**Mobil'**ITY, *n.*—**Mo'bil**IZE, *vt.* To prepare (an army) for active service.—**Mobiliz**A'TION, *n.*
Moc'casin, *n.* N. Amer. Indian *mockasin*. The foot-gear of the N. American Indians.
Mock, *vt.* O.F. *mocquer* (F. *se moquer de*), perh. repg. a Pop.L. **muccāre*, to wipe the nose (as a gesture of contempt), f. L. *mūcus, muccus*, MUCUS. To hold up to ridicule; to defy; to delude, disappoint; to ridicule by imitation.—*vi.* To use ridicule.—*n.* An act or the action of mocking; a thing to be derided.—*a.* Counterfeit.—**Mock'**ER, *n.*—**Mock'**ERY, *n.*
Mode, *n.* L. *modus*, a measure, measure, manner, musical mode. METE. MODERN. MODICUM. MODIFY. MODULATE. MOOD.2 A scheme or system of musical sounds; way, manner, method.—From F. *mode*, f. *modus*. A prevailing fashion; conventional usage in dress, manners, &c.—**Mo'd**ISH, *a.* According to, conforming to, the prevailing fashion.
Mod'el, *n.* O.F. *modelle* (F. *modèle*)—It. *modello*, dim. of *modo*, L. *modus*. (See prec.) A solid representation of an object; design, pattern, build; an exemplar; a person serving as an artist's pattern.—*vt.* To form, frame, fashion; to form *on*, &c., a model.
Mod'erate, *vt.* and *i.* L. *moderāri, moderātus*, f. *moder-, modes-* (whence *modestus*, MODEST), a stem parallel with *modo-, modus*, MODE. To render, to become, less intense, violent, &c. — *a.* L. *moderātus*, the pa.pple. Not going to extremes, temperate; fairly large or good.—**Moder**A'TION, *n.*
Mod'ern, *a.* L. *modernus*, f. *modo*, just now, orig. ablative of *modus*. MODE. Of, characteristic of, our own or recent times.—**Mod'ern**ISM, *n.* An expression or peculiarity characteristic of modern times; modern character or views.—**Mod'ern**IZE, *vt.* To give a modern character or appearance to.
Mod'est, *a.* F. *modeste*—L. *modestus*, keeping due measure, MODERATE, modest. Not bold or forward; decorous, chaste; not importunate; unpretentious.—**Mod'est**Y,1 *n.*
Mod'icum, *n.* L., neut. sing. of *modicus*, moderate, f. *modus*. MODE. A small or moderate quantity or portion.
Mod'ify, *vt.* F. *modifier*—L. *modificāre*, to regulate, control, f. *modus*, MODE + *facĕre*, to

make. To make less severe, &c.; to make partial changes in.—**Modi**FICA'TION, *n.*
Mod'ulate, *vt.* L. *modulāri, modulātus*, to regulate, f. *modulus*, dim. of *modus*, MODE. MOULD.[2] To regulate, adjust, temper; to vary (the voice) in tone.—*vi.* To change the key of music.—**Modul**A'TION, *n.*
Mo'hair, *n.* Ultimately (prob. associated with *hair*) f. Arab. *mukhayyar*, cloth of goats' hair, lit. 'select, choice', pa.pple. of *khayyara*, to choose. MOIRE. A fine cloth made from the hair of the Angora goat; the hair.
Moham'medan, *a.* *Mohammed* (repg. Arab. *Muhammad*) + -AN. Of Mohammed or his religion.—**Moham'medan**ISM, *n.*
Moi'ety, *n.* O.F. *moité, moitié*, earlier *meité, meitiet*—L. *medietas*, middle point, in L.L. half, f. *medius*. MID. A half; a part.
Moil, *vt.* O.F. *moillier*, to wet—Pop.L. **molliāre*, f. L. *mollis*, soft. MOLLIFY. To wet.—*vi.* To toil.—*n.* Toil; turmoil, confusion.
Moiré, *a.* F., pa.pple. of *moirer*, to make like *moire*, a watered fabric, orig. mohair, now us. silk, said to be an adoption of some form of MOHAIR. Watered.—*n.* A variegated appearance like that of watered silk.
Moist, *a.* O.F. *moiste* (F. *moite*), of disputed orig. Slightly wet, damp.—**Mois't**EN,[2] *vt.*—
Moist'ure, *n.* O.F. *moistour*. Liquid diffused or condensed in small quantity.
Mo'lar, *a.* L. *molāris*, f. *mola*. MILL. Serving to grind food.—*n.* A molar tooth.
Molas'ses, *n.* Pg. *melaço*—L.L. *mellāceum*, must, neut. of **mellāceus*, a. f. *mel*, honey. MELLIFLUOUS. The uncrystallized juice drained from raw sugar; treacle.
Mole, *n.*[1] O.E. *māl*, spot, corresp. to O.H.G. *meil*. A small dark prominence on the skin.
Mole, *n.*[2] M.E. *molle*, corresp. to M.Du., M.L.G. *mol*. A burrowing animal with very small eyes.—**Mole'skin**, *n.* Its fur; a strong soft fustian; in *pl.*, garments made of this.
Mole, *n.*[3] F. *môle*—L. *mōles*, a mass, a mole. A pier or breakwater.
Mol'ecule, *n.* F. *molécule*—Mod.L. *mōlēcula*, dim. of *mōles*. (See prec.) One of the extremely small particles of which matter is conceived to consist.—**Molec'ul**AR,[1] *a.*
Molest', *vt.* O.F. *molester*—L. *molestāre*, to trouble, f. *molestus*, troublesome, perh. conn. with *mōles*, mass, difficulty. MOLE.[3] To interfere or meddle with so as to injure or annoy or with hostile intent.—**Molest**A'TION, *n.*
Mol'lify, *vt.* F. *mollifier*—L. *mollificāre*, f. *mollis*, soft + *facĕre*, to make. EMOLLIENT. MOIL. To appease.—**Molli**FICA'TION, *n.*
Mol'lusc, *n.* F. *mollusque*—L. *mollusca*, a kind of soft nut, f. *mollis*. (See prec.) A soft-bodied and (usually) hard-shelled animal.
Mo'ment, *n.* L. *mōmentum*, movement, short time, importance, f. *movēre*, to MOVE. A very brief space of time, an instant; importance.—**Mo'ment**ARY, *a.* Lasting only a moment.—**Mo'mentari**LY,[2] *adv.*—**Moment'**OUS, *a.* Important.—**Moment'um**, *n.* The L. word. The force of a moving body; impetus.
Mon'achism, *n.* L. *monachus*, MONK + -ISM. The monastic system.
Mo'nad, *n.* L. *monas, monadis*, G. *monas*, a unit, f. *monos*, alone. Unity, a unit.
Mon'arch, *n.* L. *monarcha*, G. *monarchēs*, a sole ruler, f. *mon-* (MONO-) + *archein*, to rule. The sovereign of a state.—**Monar'ch**AL, *a.*—**Mon'arch**Y,[1] *n.* A state ruled by a monarch; his rule.—**Monar'ch**IC, -ICAL, *aa.*—**Mon'arch**IST, *n.* A supporter of monarchy.

Mon'astery, *n.* Eccles.L. *monastērium*—Late G. *monastērion*, f. *monazein*, to dwell alone, f. *monos*, alone. MINSTER. MONK. The house of a religious order.—**Monas'tic**, *a.* Med.L. *monasticus*—Late G. *monastikos*. Of monks, nuns, or monasteries.—*n.* A monk.—**Monas'tic**ISM, *n.* Monachism.
Mon'day, *n.* O.E. *mōnandæg*, day of the moon, f. *mōnan*, genit. of *mōna*, MOON + *dæg*, DAY. (A translation of L.L. *lūnae dies*.) The second day of the week.
Mon'ey, *n.* O.F. *moneie*—L. *monēta*, a mint, money, orig. the name of a goddess *Monēta* (identified with Juno) in whose temple at Rome money was coined. MINT.[1] Current coin; any medium of exchange.—**Mon'et**ARY, *a.*—**Mon'et**IZE, *vt.* To put into circulation as money.
Mon'ger, *n.* O.E. *mangere*, agent-n. f. *mangian*, to traffic = O.S. *mangôn*, O.N. *manga*—L. *mango*, trafficker. A dealer or trafficker.
Mon'goose, *n.* Marathi *mangūs*. An Indian ichneumon which kills snakes unharmed.
Mon'grel, *n.* App. f. root *meng-, mang-, mong-* of MINGLE + dim. and depreciatory suff. *-rel*. An animal, esp. a dog, of a mixed breed.—*a.* That is a mongrel.
Mo'nial, *n.* O.F. *monial* (F. *meneau*) of unknown orig. MULLION. A mullion.
Mo'nism, *n.* G. *monos*, single + -ISM. A doctrine assuming a single principle of being.
Moni'tion, *n.* L. *monitio, monitiōnis*, n. of action f. *monēre, monitum*, to remind, warn, admonish. ADMONISH. MONSTER. MONUMENT. SUMMON. Warning; a warning.—**Mon'it**OR, *n.* One who gives warning or advice; a senior pupil charged with special duties; a kind of war-ship of shallow construction but armed with heavy guns.—**Mon'it**ORY, *a.*—**Mon'itr**ESS, *n.*
Monk, *n.* O.E. *munuc*—Pop.L. **monicus*, for L. *monachus*, Late G. *monachos*, use as *n.* of *monachos*, single, solitary, f. *monos*, alone (the word thus meaning orig. a hermit). MONACHISM. MONASTERY. One of a community of men living apart under vows.—**Monk'**ISH, *a.*
Mon'key, *n.* Perh. f. a M.L.G. or M.Du. source and repg. a dim. of some form of the Romanic word appearing as early Mod.F. *monne*, It. *monna*, Sp., Pg. *mona*, female ape, of unknown orig. A mammal allied to man.
Mon'ochord, *n.* F. *monocorde* — Med.L. *monochordos, -on*—G. *monochordon*, neut. of *monochordos*, having a single string, f. MONO- + *chordē*, string. CORD. A musical instrument having a single string.
Mon'ochrome, *n.* Med.L. *monochrōma, monochrōmatis*—G. *monochrōmatos*, of one colour, f. MONO- + *chrōma, chrōmatos*, colour. CHROMATIC. A painting executed in different tints of one colour. From F. *monochrome*—G. *monochrōmos* = *monochrōmatos*. Representation in one colour.—*a.* Executed in one colour; of only one colour.—**Monochromat'**IC, *a.*
Mon'ody, *n.* L. *monōdia*, G. *monōidia*, solo, lament, f. *monōidos*, singing alone, f. *mon-*, MONO- + *ōid-* = *aoid-*, f. *aeidein*, to sing. COMEDY. A poem bewailing a death.
Monog'amy, *n.* F. *monogamie*—Eccles.L. *monogamia*—G. *monogamia*, f. *monogamos*, marrying only once, f. MONO- + *gamos*, marriage. The custom of being married to only one person at a time.—**Monog'am**IST, *n.*
Mon'ogram, *n.* Med.L. *monogramma*, neut. pl., formed after Late G. *monogrammon*, neut

sing. of *monogrammos*, a., f. MONO- + *gramma*, letter. Two or more letters interwoven.
Mon'ograph, *n.* MONO- + G. *graphein*, to write. A separate treatise on a single subject.
Mon'olith, *n.* L. *monolithus*, G. *monolithos*, of one stone, f. MONO- + *lithos*, stone. A pillar, &c., of a single block of stone.
Mon'ologue, *n.* F. *monologue*—G. *monologos*, speaking alone, f. MONO- + *logos*, discourse. A dramatic composition for a single performer; a soliloquy.
Monoma'nia, *n.* MONO- + G. *mania*, MANIA. Insanity in regard to a single subject.—**Monoma'niac**, *n.* After *maniac*. A sufferer from monomania.—**Monomani'ac**AL, *a.*
Monomet'allism, *n.* MONO- + METAL + -ISM. A system of currency based on a single metal.—**Monomet'all**IST, *n.*
Monop'oly, *n.* L.L. *monopōlium*—G. *monopōlion*, f. MONO- + *pōle-ein*, to sell. Exclusive possession of a trade; an exclusive privilege of trading; exclusive possession, control, or exercise. — **Monop'ol**IST, *n.* — **Monop'o**IIZE, *vt.* To gain exclusive possession, &c., of.
Monosyl'lable, *n.* L.L. *monosyllabus*—G. *monosullabos*, of one syllable, f. MONO- + *sullabē*, SYLLABLE. A word of one syllable.—**Monosyllab'**IC, *a.*
Mon'otheism, *n.* MONO- + G. *theos*, god + -ISM. The doctrine or belief that there is only one God.—**Mon'othe**IST, *n.*
Mon'otone, *a.* Late G. *monotonos*, f. MONO- + *tonos*, TONE. Continuing on one note.—*n.* A continuing on one note; sameness of style. —**Monot'on**OUS, *a.* Monotone; lacking variety.—**Monot'on**Y,[1] *n.*
Monsoon', *n.* Early Mod.Du. *monssoen*—Pg. *monção*, believed to be f. Arab. *mausim*, lit. 'season'. The trade-wind of the Indian Ocean.
Mon'ster, *n.* O.F. *monstre*—L. *monstrum*, portent, monster, f. *monēre*. MONITION. An animal or plant deviating from the normal; a very wicked person; a huge animal or thing.—*a.* Huge.—**Mon'str**OUS, *a.*—**Mon'strous**LY,[2] *adv.*—**Monstros'**ITY, *n.*
Mon'strance, *n.* O.F. *monstrance*—Med.L. *monstrantia*, f. L. *monstrans*, *monstrantis*, pres.pple. of *monstrāre*, to point out, show. DEMONSTRATE. MUSTER. An open or transparent vessel in which the host is exposed.
Month, *n.* O.E. *mónath*. Common Teut. O.Teut. **mænōth-*, conn. with **mænon-*, MOON. One of the twelve portions into which the year is divided.—**Month'**LY,[1] *a.* Occurring, appearing, payable, every month.—*n.* A magazine published once a month.—**Month'**LY,[2] *adv.* Once a month, in every month.
Mon'ument, *a.* L. *monumentum*, f. *monēre*, to remind. MONITION. A written record; anything that commemorates, esp. a structure commemorating a person, event, &c.—**Monument'**AL, *a.* Pertaining to, serving as, like, a monument; vast, stupendous.
Mood, *n.*[1] O.E. *mód*, mind, courage, pride, corresp. to O.Fris. *môd*, mind, thought, intention, O.H.G. *muot*, mind, thought, courage (Ger. *mut*, spirit, courage, anger), O.N. *móthr*, anger, grief. Cogn. with G. *maiesthai*, to seek. One's disposition at a particular time.—**Mood'**Y,[2] *a.* Melancholy, gloomy, sullen.
Mood, *n.*[2] Alteration of MODE. Any of the forms of the syllogism; a group of forms serving to indicate the function of a verb.
Moon, *n.* O.E. *móna*. Common Teut. O.Teut. **mænon-*. Cogn. with G. *mēnē*, moon, *mēn*, L. *mensis*, MONTH. MONDAY. The satellite of the earth; a satellite of a planet.—**Moon'stone**, *n.* A gem, so named from its lustre.
Moor, *n.* O.E. *mór* = M.Du. *moer*, O.H.G. *muor*. A tract of unenclosed waste land; a tract of land preserved for shooting.—**Moor'cock**, **Moor'-fowl**, *nn.* The red grouse.
Moor, *vt.* Prob. repg. O.E. **márian* = M.Du. *māren*. To secure (a ship, &c.) with chains or ropes.—*vi.* To secure one's ship, &c., thus.
Moot, *n.* O.E. *mót* = O.N. *mót*. MEET, *v.* An assembly of people.—*vt.* To raise or bring forward for discussion.—*a.* From attrib. use of the *n.* in obs. sense 'argument, discussion'. That can be argued, not decided, doubtful.
Mop, *n.* Earlier *mappe*, poss. an adoption of L. *mappa*, NAPKIN. A bundle of cloth or yarn fastened to a handle and used for cleaning.—*vt.* To rub, to wipe *up*, with a mop.
Mope, *vi.* Cf. Sw. dial. *mopa*, to sulk, Da. *maabe*, to be stupid or unconscious. To be dull or listless.—*n.* One who mopes.
Moraine', *n.* F. *moraine*, of uncertain orig. Debris deposited by a glacier.
Mor'al, *a.* L. *mōrālis*, f. *mōs*, *mōris*, custom. MOROSE. Of or pertaining to the distinction between right and wrong; of good moral conduct; not admitting of reasonable doubt.—*n.* The practical lesson (of a fable, &c.); condition (of troops, &c.) with respect to discipline, spirit, &c. (in this sense an adoption of F. *moral*); in *pl.*, habits in regard to right and wrong.—**Mor'al**IST, *n.* A teacher or student of morals. —**Moral'**ITY, *n.* A species of drama inculcating a moral lesson, in which the chief characters personified abstract qualities; moral science; a system of morals; good moral conduct.—**Mor'al**IZE, *vt.* To interpret morally; to improve morally.—*vi.* To indulge in moral reflections.—**Mor'al**LY,[2] *adv.*
Morass', *n.* Du. *moeras*, earlier *moerasch*, altered form (after *moer*, MOOR, *n.*) of *marasch*; *maras*—O.F. *maresc*, *marais*, f. Teut. and cogn. with MARSH. A bog or marsh.
Mor'bid, *a.* L. *morbidus*, f. *morbus*, disease, conn. with *mori*, *mortuus*, to die. MORIBUND. MORTAL. MORTMAIN. Unwholesome, sickly. —**Morbif'**IC, *a.* Causing disease.
Mor'dant, *a.* F. *mordant*, pres.pple. of *mordre*, L. *mordēre*, to bite. MORSEL. REMORSE. Biting, caustic.—*n.* A substance used for fixing dyes, &c.
More, *a.* O.E. *mára*. Common Teut. Greater in quantity, number or degree.—*adv.* To a greater extent, in a greater degree; in addition.—**Moreo'ver**, *adv.* The *adv.* + OVER, *adv.* Besides, further.
Morganat'ic, *a.* Mod.L. *morganāticus*, evolved f. Med.L. *matrimōnium ad morganāticam*, morganatic marriage, where *morganāticam* prob. = *morganāticum*, morning-gift, a gift by the husband to the wife on the morning after the marriage (this being all that wife or issue can claim in the case of a morganatic marriage), f. O.H.G. *morgan*, MORN, in **morgangeba* = M.H.G. *morgengâbe*, morning-gift. Applied to a marriage with a woman of inferior rank, who remains in her rank, the issue not inheriting from their father.
Mor'ibund, *a.* L. *moribundus*, f. *mori*. MORBID. In a dying state.
Morn, *n.* M.E. *morwen*—O.E. *morgen*. Common Teut. MORROW. TO-MORROW. The morning.—**Mor'ning**, *n.* M.E. *morwening*, *morning*, f. *morwen* after EVENING. The early part of the day.
Moroc'co, *n.* A goatskin leather originally produced in *Morocco*.

Morose′, *a.* L. *mōrōsus*, capricious, f. *mōs*, custom, self-will. MORAL. Sullen, unsocial.

Mor′phia, (and with chem. suff. *-ine*) **Mor′phine**, *nn.* From *Morpheus*, Ovid's god of dreams, as f. G. **Morpheus*, f. *morphē*. (See next.) A narcotic prepared from opium.

Morphol′ogy, *n.* G. *morphē*, form + -LOGY. METAMORPHOSIS. The science of form, esp. in connection with biology and grammar.

Mor′ris, *n.* Use as *n.* of *Morys*, obs. var. of *Moorish*. A dance by persons in fancy costume usually representing characters in the Robin Hood legend.

Mor′row, *n.* M.E. *morwe*, shortened f. *morwen*, MORN. (The) following day.

Mor′sel, *n.* O.F. *morsel* (F. *morceau*), dim. of *mors*, a bite—L. *morsum*, neut. pa.pple. of *mordēre*. MORDANT. A mouthful; a fragment.

Mor′tal, *a.* L. *mortālis*, f. *mors*, *mortis*, death, conn. with *mori*, to die. MORBID. Cogn. with G. (*m*)*brotos*, mortal. AMBROSIA. MORTGAGE. MORTIFY. MURDER. Subject to death; causing death.—*n.* A mortal being.—**Mortal′**ITY, *n.* Mortal nature; great loss of life; death-rate.—**Mor′tal**LY,[2] *adv.*

Mor′tar, *n.*[1] In the first sense perh. repg. O.E. *mortere* — L. *mortārium*, a vessel for pounding; or perh. wholly f. F. *mortier*, f. *mortārium*. A vessel in which substances are pounded with a pestle; a short cannon for throwing shells at high angles.

Mor′tar, *n.*[2] F. *mortier*—L. *mortārium* (see prec.), mortar for building, this being gen. taken as a transferred sense through the sense 'trough for making mortar'. Lime and sand mixed with water used as a cement in building.

Mort′gage, *n.* O.F. *mortgage*, lit. 'dead pledge' (the property pledged becoming 'dead' to the pledger on his failing to make due repayment), f. *mort*, dead (f. *mort*, L. *mors*, death. MORTAL)+*gage*, GAGE. A conveyance of real or personal property by a debtor (the **Mortgag**OR′ or **Mort′gag**ER) to a creditor (the **Mortgag**EE′) as security for money lent, the property to be reconveyed on repayment within a specified time; the deed effecting the transaction.—*vt.* To convey by mortgage.

Mor′tify, *vt.* F. *mortifier*—L. *mortificāre*, to kill, f. *mors*, death +*facĕre*, to make. MORTAL. To subdue (the body, &c.) by self-denial, &c.; to humiliate, to chagrin.—*vi.* Of a part of the body, to become dead while the rest is living.—**Morti**FICA′TION, *n.*

Mor′tise, *n.* F. *mortaise*, of unknown orig. A cavity to receive a tenon.—*vt.* To fasten by mortise and tenon; to cut a mortise in.

Mort′main, *n.* O.F. *mortemain*, 'dead hand', *i.e.* impersonal ownership—L. *mortua*, fem. of *mortuus*, dead (f. *mori*. MORBID); *manus*, hand. MANAGE. Ownership by a corporation without power to alienate.

Mort′uary, *a.* L. *mortuārius*, f. *mortuus*. (See prec.) Of burial or death.—*n.* A place in which dead bodies are kept for a time.

Mosa′ic, *a.* F. *mosaïque*—Med.L. *mosaicus*, *mūsaicus*, as if f. a G. **mousaikos* = *mouseios*, a. f. *mousa*, MUSE, *n.*[1] Cf. Late G. *mouseion*, mosaic work. Of a process of producing pictures, &c., by joining together minute pieces of coloured glass, &c.; produced thus.—*n.* The process; a piece of mosaic work.

Mosque, *n.* F. *mosquée*—It. *moschea*—Arab. *masgid*, f. *sagada*, to worship. A Mohammedan place of worship.

Mosqui′to, *n.* Sp. and Pg. *mosquito*, dim. of *mosca*, L. *musca*, fly. A gnat the female of which stings and sucks blood.

Moss, *n.* O.E. *mos*, bog, corresp. to M.Du., O.H.G. *mos* (Ger. *moos*), bog, also, the plant. O.Teut. root *mus-*, whence prob. F. *mousse*, the plant. MIRE. MUSHROOM. A bog or swamp; a small plant covering a surface in crowded masses; such plants massed together.—*vt.* To cover with moss.—**Moss′**Y,[2] *a.*

Most, *a.* O.E. *mǽst*. Common Teut. Greatest in quantity or degree.—*n.* The greatest quantity or degree.—*adv.* In the greatest degree.—**Most′**LY,[2] *adv.* For the most part.

Mote, *n.* O.E. *mot*, perh. cogn. with Du. *mot*, sawdust, grit, L.G. *mut*, dust, grit. Poss. conn. with SMUT. A particle of dust.

Moth, *n.* O.E. *moththe*, *mohthe*, corresp. to M.Du., Ger. *motte*. A small nocturnal insect.

Moth′er, *n.* O.E. *módor*. Common Teut. and Indo-Germanic. (Wanting in Gothic.) Cogn. with Skr. *mātar-*, G. *mētēr*, L. *māter*. MATERNAL. MATRIMONY. MATRIX. MATRON. A female parent; the head of a female religious community.—*attrib.* Inherited or learned from one's mother, inborn.—*vt.* To be the mother of; to tend as a mother.—**Moth′er**HOOD, *n.*—**Moth′er-in-law**, *n.* The mother of one's wife or husband.—**Moth′er**LY,[1] *a.*—

Mother of pearl, *n.* Cf. Ger. *perlmutter*. An iridescent substance forming the inner layer of some shells.

Mo′tion, *n.* F. *motion*—L. *mōtio*, *mōtiōnis*, n. of action f. *movēre*, to MOVE. The process or an instance or kind of moving, the condition of a moving body; a proposal made in an assembly; an application to a court or judge.—*vt.* To direct by a sign.—*vi.* To make a sign by way of direction.—**Mo′tion**LESS, *a.*

Mo′tive, *a.* O.F. *motif* or Med.L. *mōtīvus*, f. L. *movēre*, to MOVE. Causing motion.—*n.* That which induces a person to act in a particular way; the dominant idea of an artistic work.

Mot′ley, *a.* Orig. obscure. MOTTLE. Variegated, chequered; heterogeneous.—*n.* A motley colour; the motley-coloured dress of a jester.

Mo′tor, *n.* L. *mōtor*, agent-n. f. *movēre*, to MOVE. That which imparts motion; a machine supplying motive power.—**Mo′tor-car**, *n.* A carriage propelled by a motor.

Mot′tle, *n.* Prob. a back-formation f. MOTLEY, *a.* A blotch on a surface; an arrangement of blotches.—*vt.* To mark with blotches.

Mot′to, *n.* It. *motto*—Pop.L. **mottum*, altered f. *muttum*, uttered sound, cogn. with L. *muttīre*, to mutter. A maxim adopted as a rule of conduct; a short inscribed sentence; in *heraldry*, a word or sentence accompanying a crest, &c.

Mould, *n.*[1] O.E. *molde* = O.H.G. *molta*, O.N. *mold*. Cogn. with MEAL.[1] Loose earth; the surface soil.—**Moul′der**, *vi.* App. f. the *n.* with freq. suff. *-er*. To decay to dust.

Mould, *n.*[2] M.E. *mold*(*e*)—O.F. *modle* (F. *moule*)—L. *modulus*. MODULATE. A pattern for shaping; a hollow form in which metal is cast; native character; form, shape.—*vt.* To form, shape, fashion.—**Mould′ing**, *vbl.n.* The action of the *v.*; a moulded object; an ornamental variety of contour.

Mould, *n.*[3] Perh. developed f. obs. *Mould*, a., orig. ppl., mouldy, with -(*e*)*d* f. obs. *Moul*, to make or grow mouldy—Early M.E. *muwle*, f. or cogn. with O.N. **mugla* (Sw. *mōgla*, Norw. *mugla*). A woolly or furry growth caused by dampness.—**Mould′**Y,[2] *a.*

Moult, *vi.* M.E. *mouten*—O.E. *mútian*—L.

mūtāre, to change. MUTABLE. To shed feathers, integument, &c.—*vt.* To shed (feathers, &c.).—*n.* The action of moulting.

Mound, *n.* Of obscure orig. An artificial elevation of earth or stones; a hillock.

Mount, *n.*[1] F. *mont*—L. *mons, montis*, mountain. AMOUNT. MOUNTAIN. A hill.

Mount, *vi.* O.F. *monter*—Pop.L. **montāre*, f. L. *mons*. (See prec.) To go upwards, ascend; to get on horseback; to rise in amount. —*vt.* To ascend, climb; to get upon the back of; to set upon an elevation; to furnish with a horse; to fit on or in a mount.—*n.*[2] That on which anything is fitted, supported or placed; a horse; an opportunity of riding.

Mount'ain, *n.* O.F. *montaigne*—Pop.L. **montānea*, mountain region, app. a use as *n.* of fem. of *montāneus*, a. f. L. *mons*. MOUNT, *n.*[1] A natural elevation of considerable size.—**Mountain**EER', *n.* A dweller among mountains; one skilled in climbing mountains.—**Mount'ain**OUS, *a.*

Mount'ebank, *n.* It. *montambanco, montimbanco*, contracted f. *monta in banco*, lit. 'mount-on-bench' (*monta*, imp. of *montare* = O.F. and F. *monter* (MOUNT, *v.*); *banco* = *banca*, bench (BANK[2])). One who mounted a platform in a public place and told stories, performed conjuring tricks, &c.; a charlatan.

Mourn, *vi.* O.E. *murnan*. Common Teut. Prob. cogn. with G. *merimna*, care. To feel sorrow, lament; to wear the customary garb of sorrow. — *vt.* To grieve for, lament. — **Mourn'**ER, *n.*—**Mourn'**FUL, *a.*—**Mourn'ful**LY,[2] *adv.*—**Mourn'ing**, *vbl.n.* The action of the *v.*; the conventional manifestation of grief for a death: the garb of a mourner.

Mouse, *n.*; *pl.* **Mice**. O.E. *mús*. Common Teut. and Indo-Germanic. Cogn. with G. *mus*, L. *mūs*. MUSCLE. REARMOUSE. A small rodent quadruped.—*vi.* To catch mice.

Moustache', *n.* F. *moustache*—It. *mostaccio* —G. *mustax, mustakos*. Hair on the upper lip.

Mouth, *n.* O.E. *múth*. Common Teut. Cogn. with L. *mentum*, chin. The orifice in the head; the opening of anything hollow; the outfall of a river, the entrance of a harbour, &c.—*vt.* To declaim; to take into the mouth.—*vi.* To declaim. — **Mouth'piece**, *n.* A terminating part intended to be put between the lips; one who speaks for others.

Move, *vt.* A.F. *mover*, O.F. *movoir, mouvoir* —L. *movēre, mōtum*. COMMOTION. MOBILE. MOMENT. MOTION. MOTIVE. MUTINY. To change the position of; to set or keep in motion; to stir the feelings of; to stir (the feelings, &c.); to actuate, impel; to make formal application to; to propose (a resolution, &c.). —*vi.* To change place or posture; to go forward, proceed; to take action.—*n.* A moving; an action calculated to gain some end.—**Mov'**ABLE, *a.* That can be moved; of property, personal; changing its date every year. —*n.* An article that may be removed from a house, &c.; in *pl.*, personal property.—**Move'**MENT, *n.* The action or process of the *v.* (in the intrans. senses); the moving parts of a mechanism; a principal division of a musical work; a course of endeavour.

Mow, *vt.* O.E. *máwan*. Common W.Germanic. Cogn. with G. *ama-ein*, to reap. O. Teut. root *mæ-*, pre-Teut. *mē-*. AFTERMATH. MEAD.[2] To cut (grass, &c.); to cut the grass, &c., in (a field, &c.).—*vi.* To cut grass, &c.

Much, *a.* Early M.E. *muche*, &c., shortened f. *muchel*, &c.—O.E. *micel, mycel*. Common Teut. Cogn. with G. *megas* (lengthened stem *megal-*). Existing in great quantity.—quasi-*n.* A great deal; an important point or matter. —*adv.* In a great degree; pretty nearly.

Mu'cilage, *n.* F. *mucilage*—L.L. *mūcilāgo, mūcilāginis*, a mouldy juice, f. L. *mūcus*, MUCUS. A viscous substance obtained from plants.—**Mucilag'in**OUS, *a.*

Muck, *n.* Early M.E. *muk*, prob. of Scandinavian orig. Cf. O.N. *myki*, dung. The dung of cattle; unclean matter.—**Muck'**Y,[2] *a.*

Mu'cus, *n.* L. *mūcus*, mucus of the nose. Conn. with *ē-mungěre*, G. *mussesthai*, to blow the nose. MUCILAGE. A viscid substance secreted by the mucous membrane.—**Mu'**COUS, *a.*—**Mu'cous mem'brane**. The internal skin coated with mucus.

Mud, *n.* M.E. *mode, mudde*, cogn. with M.L.G. *mudde*, mud, Du. *modden*, to dabble in mud. Wet and soft earth.—*vt.* To make turbid; to cover with mud.—**Mud'dle**, *vt.* Freq. suff. *-le*. To make muddy; to bewilder, esp. with drink; to confuse *together*, mix up; to mismanage, bungle.—*vi.* To busy oneself in a confused ineffective way.—*n.* Disorder, confusion, bewilderment. — **Mud'd**Y,[2] *a.* — **Mud'dy**, *vt.* To make muddy.

Muff, *n.*[1] Prob. f. Du. *mof*—F. *moufle*, mitten, O.F. *mofle, moufle*, Med.L. *muffula*, thick glove. Orig. unknown. MUFFLE. A cylindrical covering for keeping the hands warm.

Muff, *n.*[2] Poss. an application of prec., 'one who keeps his hands in a muff'. One without skill or practical sense, a duffer.

Muf'fin, *n.* Perh. in some way conn. with O.F. *moufflet*, soft bread. A light flat circular cake.

Muf'fle, *vt.* App. f. O.F. *mofle, moufle*. MUFF.[1] To wrap up; to envelop so as to deaden sound; to deaden (sound).—**Muf'fl**ER, *n.* A covering for the neck and throat.

Muf'ti, *n.* Arab. *muftī*, pple. of *aftā*, to decide a point of law. A Mohammedan priest or expounder of law; perh. hence (poss. alluding to the attire of a mufti of the stage) plain clothes as distinguished from uniform.

Mug, *n.* Cogn. with L.G. *mokke, mukke*, Sw *mugg*. A drinking-vessel.

Mug'gy, *a.* Dial. *Mug*, a fog or mist (cf. O.N. *mugga*, mist, drizzle, perh. the source) + -Y.[2] Damp, close, stifling.

Mulat'to, *n.* Sp. *mulato*, young mule, mulatto, f. *mulo*, L. *mūlus*, MULE. The offspring of a European and a Negro.

Mul'berry, *n.* Prob. f. M.H.G. *mûlbere* (Ger. *maulbeere*), O.H.G. *mûlberi*, altered form of *mûr-beri, mōr-beri*, f. L. *mōrum*, mulberry + O.H.G. *beri*, BERRY. The fruit of a tree on the leaves of which silk-worms feed; the tree.

Mulch, *n.* Prob. use as *n.* of obs. *mulch*, soft = dial. *melch, melsh*—O.E. *melsc*. Wet straw, leaves, &c., spread to protect the roots of newly planted trees, &c. — *vt.* To protect with mulch.

Mulct, *n.* L. *multa, mulcta*. A fine; a penalty.—*vt.* To fine; to deprive or divest *of*.

Mule, *n.* O.F. *mul*, masc., *mule*, fem.—L. *mūlus*. MULATTO. The offspring of a he-ass and a mare, or of a horse and a she-ass; a stupid, obstinate person.—**Muleteer'**, *n.* F. *muletier*, f. *mulet*, mule (in form dim. of *mul*). A mule-driver.—**Mul'**ISH, *a.*

Mull, *vt.* Orig. obscure. To heat (wine, &c.) with sugar, spices, &c.

Mul'let, *n.* O.F. *mulet*, dim. f. L. *mullus*, red mullet. The name of two genera of fishes, the red and the grey mullet.

Mulligataw'ny, *n.* Tamil *milagu-tannir*, 'pepper-water'. An Indian curry-soup.
Mul'lion, *n.* Prob. alteration of *muniall* = MONIAL. A vertical dividing bar in a window or in screen-work.
Multifa'rious, *a.* L.L. *multifārius* (f. *multus*, many) + -OUS. Much diversified.
Mul'tiform, *a.* L. *multiformis*, f. *multi-*, combining form of *multus*, many + *forma*, FORM. Of many and various forms or kinds.
Mul'tiple, *a.* F. *multiple*—L.L. *multiplus*, f. *multi-* (see prec.) + *-plus*, f. root *ple-*, to fill. COMPLETE. DOUBLE. Manifold, having many parts, elements, &c.—*n.* A quantity which contains another an exact number of times.
Mul'tiplex, *a.* L. *multiplex*, *multiplicis*, f. *multi-* (MULTIFORM) + *plic-*, to fold. ACCOMPLICE. Manifold.—**Multiplic**'ITY, *n.* Manifold variety; an instance of this.
Mul'tiply, *vt.* O.F. *multiplier*—L. *multiplicāre*, f. *multiplex*. (See prec.) To substitute for (a number) a number equal to any given number of times its value; to adduce in large numbers. — *vi.* To increase in number or amount.—**Multiplica**'TION, *n.*
Mul'titude, *n.* L. *multitūdo*, *multitūdinis*, f. *multus*, many. Great number; a great number; a throng.—**Multitu'dinous**, *a.* Very numerous; existing in many forms.
Mum, *vi.* From *mum!* int. (See next.) To act in dumb-show.—**Mum'mer**, *n.*—**Mum'mery**, *n.* A performance in dumb-show; ridiculous ceremonial; an instance of this.
Mum'ble, *vi.* M.E. *momele*, a freq. f. imitative int. **Mum!** silence! To speak indistinctly.—*vt.* To chew softly; to utter indistinctly.
Mum'my, *n.* F. *momie*—Med.L. *mumia*—Arab. *mūmiyā*, f. *mūm*, wax. An embalmed body.—**Mum'mi**FY, *vt.*
Mump, *n.* Imitative. Formerly, a grimace. In *pl.* (treated as *sing.*). a contagious disease characterized by swelling of the salivary glands; also in *pl.*, a fit of sulks.—*vi.* To sulk.
Munch, *vt.* App. imitative. To chew audibly.
Mun'dane, *a.* F. *mondain*—L. *mundānus*, f. *mundus*, world. Pertaining to this world or to the universe.
Munic'ipal, *a.* L. *mūnicipālis*, f. *mūniceps*, *mūnicipis*, an inhabitant of a *mūnicipium* or free town, lit. 'one who undertakes offices', f. *mūnia*, official duties (conn. with *mūnus*, service, duty, present) + root of *capĕre*, to take. IMMUNE. REMUNERATE. Pertaining to the internal affairs of a state or to the government of a city or town.—**Municipal**'ITY, *n.* A city or town having local self-government; the governing body.
Munif'icent, *a.* L. *mūnificent-*, altered stem of *mūnificus*, lit. 'making presents', f. *mūnus* (see prec.) + *-ficus*, f. *facĕre*, to make. Splendidly generous.—**Munif'ic**ENCE, *n.*
Mu'niment, *n.* O.F. *muniment*—L. *mūnimentum*, a defence, in Med.L., a title-deed, f. *mūnire*, to fortify. A title-deed, a charter.
Muni'tion, *n.* F. *munition*—L. *mūnitio*, *mūnitiōnis*, n. of action f. *mūnire*. (See prec.) In *sing.* and *pl.*, military stores.
Mu'ral, *a.* F. *mural*—L. *mūrālis*, f. *mūrus*, wall. IMMURE. Of, resembling, on, a wall.
Mur'der, *n.* O.E. *morthor* = Goth. *maurthr*. Cogn. with MORTAL. The unlawful and premeditated killing of a human being.—*vt.* To kill (a human being) thus.—**Mur'der**ER, *n.*—**Mur'der**ESS, *n.*—**Mur'der**OUS, *a.*
Murk, *a.* O.E. *mirce* = O.S. *mirki*, O.N. *myrkr*. Obscure, dark.—*n.* Darkness; thick vapour.—**Murk'**Y,[2] *a.*
Mur'mur, *vi.* F. *murmurer*—L. *murmurāre*, f. *murmur*, a murmuring (a reduplicated imitative form). Cf. G. *mormurein*, to boil and roar. To emit a low continuous sound; to mutter complaint.—*vt.* To utter in a low voice.—*n.* An act or sound of murmuring.
Mur'rain, *n.* F. *morine*, gen. regarded as a deriv. of L. *mori*. MORTAL. A cattle-plague.
Mus'cadine, *n.* Prob. formed in Eng. on Pr. *muscat*. (See next.) A musk-flavoured kind of grape.
Mus'cat, *n.* F. *muscat*, a. and n.—Pr. *muscat*, a. = It. *moscato*, musk-flavoured—L.L. **muscātus*, f. *muscus*, MUSK. The muscadine grape; a strong sweet wine made from it. Sim. **Muscatel'**, **Muscadel'**, *n.* O.F. *muscatel*, *muscadel*—Pr. **muscadel*, dim. of *muscat*.
Mus'cle, *n.* L. *musculus* (also in sense 'a MUSSEL'), dim. of *mūs*, MOUSE, certain muscles being thought to resemble a mouse. A fibrous band producing movement in the body by contraction; the part of the body which is composed of muscles.—**Mus'cul**AR,[1] *a.*
Muse, *n.*[1] F. *muse*—L. *mūsa*—G. *mousa*. MOSAIC. MUSIC. In *mythology*, one of the nine sister-goddesses the inspirers of learning and the arts.—**Muse'um**, *n.* L. *mūsēum*—G. *mouseion*, a seat of the Muses, f. *mousa*. A repository for objects illustrating antiquities, the arts, &c.
Muse, *vi.* F. *muser*, to stand idling, in O.F. also to muse, prob. conn. with O.F. *muse*, MUZZLE, the primary notion being that of a dog sniffing the air when in doubt as to the scent. AMUSE. To be lost in thought; to gaze meditatively.—*n.*[2] A fit of musing.
Mush'room, *n.* F. *mousseron*, prob. a deriv. of *mousse*, MOSS. An edible fungus.
Mu'sic, *n.* F. *musique*—L. *mūsica*—G. *mousikē* (*technē*), (the art) of the Muse (f. *mousa*, MUSE), applied to any art, also esp. to music. The art which deals with the combination of sounds in beautiful form and so as to express emotion; the science of the laws of the art; musical sounds; musical composition; such composition graphically represented.—**Mu'si**CAL, *a.*—**Mu'sical**LY,[2] *adv.*—**Musi**'CIAN, *n.*
Musk, *n.* F. *musc*—L.L. *muscus*—Late G. *moschos*, prob. f. Pers. *musk*, perh. f. Skr. *mushka*, testicle. MUSCAT. NUTMEG. A scent secreted in a gland near the testicles of the **Musk'-deer**; various plants with a musky scent.—**Musk'**Y,[2] *a.*
Mus'ket, *n.* F. *mousquet*—It. *moschetto*, orig. a small kind of hawk, of disputed orig. A military hand-gun. — **Musket**EER', *n.*—**Mus'ket**RY, *n.* Muskets collectively; troops armed with, the art of using, muskets.
Mus'lin, *n.* F. *mousseline*—It. *mussolina*, f. *Mosul* in Kurdistan, where muslin was formerly made. A fine cotton fabric.
Mus'sel, *n.* O.E. *muscle* = M.Du. *mosscele*, O.H.G. *muscula* (Ger. *muschel*)—L.L. *muscula* = L. *musculus*. MUSCLE. A bivalve shell-fish.
Must, *n.* L. *mustum*, orig. neut. (sc. *vīnum*, wine) of *mustus*, new, fresh. MUSTARD. Unfermented wine.
Must, *v.aux.*, *pres.* or *pa.* O.E. *mōste*, pa.t. of preterite-pres. *mōt*, may, must. Cf. Du. *moet*, Ger. *muss*, must. Primary sense app. that of Goth. *ga-mōt*, (it) has room. Am (&c.) obliged to, resolved to, certain to.
Mus'tard, *n.* O.F. *moustarde*, *mostarde* (F *moutarde*), f. Com. Romanic *mosto*, L. *mustum*

MUST, *n.*, the condiment having been orig. prepared by mixing with must. The ground seeds of a plant, forming a condiment when made into a paste; the plant.

Mus'ter, *n.* O.F. *mostre, moustre,* vbl.n. f. Com. Romanic *mostrare,* L. *monstrāre,* to show. MONSTRANCE. Formerly, a showing or display. An assembling of men for inspection, exercise, &c.; an assembly.—*vt.* To assemble or collect.—*vi.* To come together.

Mus'ty, *a.* Orig. obscure. Prob. (with -Y[2]) in some way conn. with MOIST. Mouldy, fusty.

Mu'table, *a.* L. *mūtābilis,* f. *mūtāre,* to change. COMMUTE. MEW, *v.*[1] MOULT. MUTUAL. Liable to change.—**Muta**'TION, *n.*

Mute, *a.* L. *mūtus.* Not emitting sound, silent; dumb; of a consonant, produced by complete closure of the organs of the mouth.—*n.* A dumb person; a hired mourner; a mute consonant.—**Mute**'LY,[2] *adv.*

Mu'tilate, *vt.* L. *mutilāre, mutilātum,* f. *mutilus,* maimed. To deprive of a limb or organ; to make imperfect.—**Mutila**'TION, *n.*

Mu'tiny, *n.* With -Y[1] (perh. after *felony*), f. obs. *Mutine,* mutineer—F. *mutin,* mutineer, also, formerly, mutiny—Pop.L. **movita,* vbl.n. f. L. *movēre,* to MOVE. Revolt against constituted authority, esp. against the officers of a disciplined body.—*vi.* To commit mutiny.—**Mutin**EER', *n.*—**Mu'tin**OUS, *a.*

Mut'ter, *vi.* Prob. imitative with freq. suff. *-er.* To speak with the mouth nearly closed; to complain in low indistinct tones.—*vt.* To utter in such tones.—*n.* An act of muttering.

Mut'ton, *n.* O.F. *moton* (F. *mouton*), sheep, mutton — Med.L. *multo, multōnis,* prob. f. Gaulish. The flesh of sheep used as food.

Mu'tual, *a.* F. *mutuel*—L. *mūtuus,* borrowed, reciprocal, conn. with *mūtāre.* MUTABLE. Possessed, performed, &c., by each (of two) towards or with regard to the other; pertaining to both, common.—**Mu'tual**LY,[2] *adv.*

Muz'zle, *n.* O.F. *musel, muzel* (F. *museau*)—Med.L. *mūsellum,* dim. of *mūsum* (whence O.F. *muse*), of uncertain orig. MUSE, *v.* The projecting mouth and nose of an animal; something put over a muzzle; the open end of a firearm.—*vt.* To put a muzzle on.

My, *pron.* Early M.E. *mī,* reduced f. *mīn,* O.E. *mín,* MINE, *pron.* Belonging to me.

Myo'pia, *n.* G. *muōpia,* f. *muōps,* short-sighted, f. *muein* (MYSTERY)+*ōps,* eye. Shortsightedness.—**Myop'**IC, *a.*

Myoso'tis, *n.* L. *myosōtis*—G. *muosōtis,* f. *mus, muos,* MOUSE + *ous, ōtos,* EAR, *n.*[1] A small plant with blue, pink, or white flowers.

Myr'iad, *n.* G. *murias, muriados,* f. *murios,* countless, ten thousand. Ten thousand; in *pl.,* countless numbers.—*a.* Countless.

Myr'midon, *n.* L. *Myrmidones,* G. *Murmidones,* the followers of Achilles to Troy. Formerly, a faithful follower. A base servant.

Myrrh, *n.* O.E. *myrre* = O.H.G. *myrrâ* (Ger. *myrrhe*)—L. *murra*—G. *murra,* of Semitic orig. An aromatic gum-resin.

Myr'tle, *n.* O.F. *myrtille,* myrtle-berry—Pop.L. **myrtilla,* dim. of L. *myrta,* myrtle—G. *murtos.* An evergreen shrub with white aromatic flowers.

Mys'tery, *n.* A.F. **misterie* (O.F. *mistere,* F. *mystère*)—L. *mystērium*—G. *mustērion,* secret doctrine, secret, f. *mustēs,* one initiated, f. *mue-ein,* to initiate, f. *muein,* to be closed, to close the eyes. MYOPIA. A divinely revealed truth; a religious rite; an obscure or secret thing; the condition of being a mystery: a miracle play.—**Myste'ri**OUS, *a.*—**Myste'rious**LY,[2] *adv.*—**Mys'tic,** *a.* O.F. *mystique*—L. *mysticus*—G. *mustikos,* f. *mustēs.* Spiritually allegorical; of hidden meaning; awe-inspiring.—*n.* One who seeks union with the Deity by contemplation or self-surrender, or believes in spiritual apprehension of truths beyond the understanding. Sim. **Mys'ti**CAL, *a.*—**Mys'tic**ISM, *n.*—**Mys'tify,** *vt.* F. *mystifier,* irreg. f. *mystère* or *mystique.* To bewilder; to involve in mystery.—**Mysti**FICA'TION, *n.*

Myth, *n.* L.L. *mythos*—G. *mūthos.* A fictitious narrative usually involving supernatural persons or events; a fictitious person or object.—**Myth'**IC, **Myth'**ICAL, *aa.* Of the nature of, consisting of, based on, a myth; fictitious.—**Mythol**'OGY, *n.* Myths collectively; a body of myths; the science of myths.—**Mytholog'**IC, -ICAL, *aa.*—**Mythol'**OGIST, *n.*

N

Nab, *vt.* Orig. obscure. To catch, arrest.

Na'bob, *n.* Urdū *nawwāb,* deputy governor. A deputy governor in the Mogul Empire; a rich retired Anglo-Indian.

Na'dir, *n.* = F., Sp., Pg., It. *nadir*—Arab. *nazīr,* opposite to, in full *nazīr es-semt,* opposite to the ZENITH. The point opposite to the zenith.

Nag, *n.* Orig. obscure. A small riding horse.

Nag, *vi.* and *t.* Prob. of Scand. orig. Cf. Sw. and Norw. *nagga,* to gnaw, to irritate. To be worrying, to worry, by persistent fault-finding.

Nai'ad, *n.* L. *nāïas, nāïadis*—G. *naïas,* conn. with *naein,* to flow. A river-nymph.

Nail, *n.* O.E. *nægel, nægl* = O.H.G., Ger. *nagel,* O.N. *nagl.* Cogn. with G. *onux,* L. *unguis.* The horny covering on the ends of the fingers and toes; a claw; a small metal spike used for fixing or as a peg; a cloth-measure = 2¼ inches.—*vt.* To fix with a nail.

Naïve, Naive, *a.* F. *naïve,* fem. of *naïf*—L. *nātīvus,* NATIVE. Unaffected, simple, natural.

Na'ked, *a.* O.E. *nacod* = M.Du. *naket,* O.H.G. *nakot* (Ger. *nackt*). Cogn. with L. *nūdus.* Having no clothes on; exposed to view or to injury; bare, mere.—**Na'ked**LY,[2] *adv.*

Nam'by-pam'by, *a.* Formed on *Ambrose* Philips, a pastoral poet ridiculed by Pope. Weakly sentimental, affectedly simple.

Name, *n.* O.E. *nama* = O.S., O.H.G. *namo* (Ger. *name*). Cogn. with Skr. *nāman,* G. *onoma,* L. *nōmen.* ANONYMOUS. EPONYM. IGNOMINY. NOMINAL. NOUN. SYNONYM. That by which a person, thing, &c., is designated; reputation; one's repute.—*vt.* To give a name to; to give the right name to; to call by some title; to appoint; to mention.—**Name'**LESS, *a.*—**Name'**LY,[2] *adv.*—That is to say.—**Name'sake,** *n.* Perh. from two persons being mentioned together 'for the *names' sake*'. A person having the same name as another.

Nankeen', *n.* A yellow cotton cloth originally made at *Nankin* in China.

Nap, *n.*[1] M.Du. or M.L.G. *noppe* (Ger. *noppe*), of uncertain orig. A roughish surface on cloth produced by projecting fibres.

Nap, *vi.* O.E. *hnappian, hnæppian,* app. conn. with O.H.G. *(h)naffezan.* To take a short sleep.—*n.*[2] A short sleep.

Nape, *n.* Orig. obscure. The back of the neck.

Naph'tha, *n.* L. *naphtha*—G. *naphtha.* An inflammable volatile liquid.

Nap'kin, *n.* App., with dim. suff. *-kin*, f. F. *nappe*, table-cloth—L. *mappa*, napkin. APRON. MAP. MOP. A square piece of linen used for wiping the lips or fingers at meals.

Narcis'sus, *n.* L. *narcissus*—G. *narkissos*, said to be named f. *narkē*, numbness, on account of narcotic properties. A bulbous plant bearing a scented white flower.

Narcot'ic, *n.* Med.L. *narcōticum*—G. *narkōtikon*, neut. of *narkōtikos*, benumbing, f. *narko-ein*, to benumb, f. *narkē*. (See prec.) A substance inducing sleep or insensibility.—*a.* Inducing sleep or insensibility.

Nard, *n.* L. *nardus*—G. *nardos*, of Oriental orig. An aromatic substance known also as SPIKENARD; the plant yielding it.

Narrate', *vt.* L. *narrāre*, *narrātum*, app. conn. with *gnārus*, knowing, conn. with *gnoscĕre*. COGNITION. To relate, give an account of.—**Narra**'TION, *n.*—**Nar'rat**IVE, *a.* As *n.*, an account or story.—**Narra'to**R, *n.*

Nar'row, *a.* O.E. *nearu*, *nearo* = O.S. *naru*, of doubtful orig. Of little breadth; small, confined; restricted; limited in amount; prejudiced; careful, precise.—*n.* A narrow part of a strait, &c.—*vi.* and *t.* To become, to make, narrow.—**Nar'row**LY,[2] *adv.*

Nar'whal, *n.* Da. or Sw. *narhval*, f. *hval* = O.E. *hwæl*, WHALE. Cf. O.N. *náhvalr*, perh. f. *ná-r*, corpse, referring to the colour of the skin. A sea animal with horns developed from one or both of its two teeth.

Na'sal, *a.* Med.L. **nāsālis*, f. L. *nāsus*, nose. Of or pertaining to the nose; of sounds, produced by the nose.—*n.* A nasal sound.—**Na'sal**IZE, *vt.* To make nasal in sound.

Nas'cent, *a.* L. *nascens*, *nascentis*, pres.pple. of *nasci*, to be born. NATAL. In the act of being born or of coming into existence.

Nastur'tium, *n.* L., lit. (it is said) 'nose-wring', from its pungency, f. *nāsus*, nose + *torquēre*. TORMENT. A genus of plants including the watercress; a garden plant with orange-coloured flowers.

Nas'ty, *a.* Orig. obscure. Cf. Du. *nestig*, dirty. Dirty, foul; nauseous; disagreeable; troublesome.—**Nas'ti**LY,[2] *adv.*—**Nas'ti**NESS, *n.*

Na'tal, *a.* L. *nātālis*, f. *nasci*, *nātus*, to be born. AGNATE. COGNATE. NASCENT. NATION. NATIVE. NATURE. PUISNE. RENASCENT. Of or pertaining to one's birth.

Nata'tion, *n.* L. *natātio*, *natātiōnis*, f. *natāre*, freq. of *nāre*, to swim. Swimming.

Na'tion, *n.* F. *nation*—L. *nātio*, *nātiōnis*, f. *nasci*. NATAL. A body of persons organized as a state.—**Nat'ion**AL, *a.*—**Nat'ional**IST, *n.* An advocate of national rights.—**National**'ITY, *n.* National quality; national feeling; the fact of belonging to a particular nation; a nation.—**Nat'ional**IZE, *vt.* To convert into the property of the nation.

Na'tive, *a.* L. *nātīvus*, f. *nasci*. NATAL. NAÏVE. Inborn; that was the place of one's birth; occurring in a pure state; born or produced in a particular place.—*n.* One born in a place; an oyster reared in an artificial bed.—**Nativ**'ITY, *n.* Birth; a horoscope.

Nat'ty, *a.* Of obscure orig. Neatly smart, spruce.—**Nat'ti**LY,[2] *adv.*—**Nat'ti**NESS, *n.*

Na'ture, *n.* F. *nature*—L. *nātūra*, f. *nasci*. NATAL. The essential qualities of a thing; innate character; kind, class; the inherent power underlying the physical and mental activities; the vital functions; the physical power underlying all phenomena; treatment of a subject with fidelity to nature.—**Nat'ur**AL, *a.* Based upon innate moral feeling; not unusual or miraculous; not due to accident, violence, &c.; not artificial; free from affectation; innate; normally connected or pertaining; illegitimate; of the study of nature.—*n.* A half-witted person.—**Nat'ural**IST, *n.* One who studies animals or plants.—**Nat'ural**IZE, *vt.* To admit to citizenship; to acclimatize.—**Naturaliza**'TION, *n.*—**Nat'ural**LY,[2] *adv.*

Naught, *n.* O.E. *náwiht*, *náht*, f. *ná*, no + *wiht*, a whit. NO, *adv.* WIGHT. Nothing.—*a.* Worthless, bad.—**Naught'**Y,[2] *a.* Wayward, bad (only in mild or playful censure).—**Naught'i**LY,[2] *adv.*—**Naught'i**NESS, *n.*

Nau'sea, *n.* L. *nausea*—G. *nausia*, sea-sickness, f. *naus*. (See next.) A feeling of sickness; disgust.—**Nau'se**ATE,[3] *vt.* To reject (food, &c.) with nausea; to loathe; to affect with nausea.—*vi.* To feel nausea.—**Nau'se**OUS, *a.*

Nau'tical, *a.* L. *nauticus* (= G. *nautikos*, f. *nautēs*, sailor, f. *naus*, ship) + -AL. NAVY. Pertaining to seamen or navigation.

Nau'tilus, *n.* L. *nautilus*—G. *nautilos*, sailor, nautilus, f. *nautēs*. (See prec.) A shell-fish furnished with a sail-like membrane.

Nave, *n.*[1] O.E. *nafu*, *nafa* = M.Du. *nave*, O.H.G. *naba* (Ger. *nabe*). Cogn. with Skr. *nābhi*, *nābha*, nave, navel. AUGER. NAVEL. The central block of a wheel, a hub.

Nave, *n.*[2] = Sp., It. *nave*—L. *nāvis*, ship. NAVY. The main part or body of a church.

Na'vel, *n.* O.E. *nafela* = M.Du. *navel(e)*, O.H.G. *nabalo* (Ger. *nabel*), app. f. stem of NAVE.[1] A depression on the abdomen at the point where the umbilical cord was attached

Nav'igate, *vi.* L. *nāvigāre*, *nāvigātum*, f. *nāvis*, ship + *agĕre*, to drive, guide. NAVY. To sail.—*vt.* To sail over; to direct or manage (a ship).—**Nav'ig**ABLE, *a.*—**Naviga**'TION, *n.*—**Nav'igato**R, *n.* One who navigates; one employed in making a canal or in similar earthwork (cf. *navigation* in dial. sense 'canal').—**Nav'vy**, *n.* Abb. of *navigator* in the second sense.

Na'vy, *n.* O.F. *navie*—L. *nāvis* = G. *naus*, ship. NAUTICAL. NAUTILUS. NAVE.[2] NAVIGATE. A fleet; the war-ships of a country collectively.—**Na'v**AL, *a.*

Nay, *adv.* O.N. *nei*, f. *ne*, not + *ei* = O.E. *á*, AY. Expressing negation, refusal, &c.

Neap, *a.* O.E. *nép* (in *népflód*, neap-FLOOD), of obscure orig. *Neap-tide*, the low tide which occurs at the first and third quarters of the moon.

Near, *adv.* O.N. *nǽr*, properly comp. of *ná-* = O.E. *néah*, NIGH, but also used as positive. At or to a short distance, in or into proximity.—*prep.* Close to.—*a.* Closely related; very intimate; close at hand; of parts of horses, vehicles, &c., left; stingy.—*vi.* and *t.* To approach.—**Near'**LY,[2] *adv.*—**Near'**NESS, *n.*

Neat, *n.* O.E. *néat* = O.H.G. *nōz*, O.N. *naut*. O.Teut. root *neut-*, *naut-*, to enjoy or possess. An animal of the ox kind; cattle.

Neat, *a.* F. *net*, clean, pure—L. *nitidus*, f. *nitēre*, to shine. NET, *a.* Undiluted, pure; elegantly made or proportioned; cleverly expressed; cleverly contrived or executed; tidy.—**Neat'**LY,[2] *adv.*—**Neat'**NESS, *n.*

Neb, *n.* O.E. *nebb* = O.N. *nef*, conn. with M.Du., M.L.G. *nebbe*. NIB. A bird's beak.

Neb'ula, *n.* L. *nebula*, mist, vapour, cogn. with G. *nephelē*, O.H.G. *nebul* (Ger. *nebel*). A cloud-like cluster of stars, a luminous patch of supposed stellar matter.—**Neb'ul**AR,[1] *a.*—**Neb'ul**OUS, *a.* Cloud-like; hazy, vague.

Nec'essary, *a.* L. *necessārius*, f. *necesse*, unavoidable. Needful, requisite; inevitably happening.—*n.* That which is necessary, a requisite.—**Nec'essari**LY,[2] *adv.*—**Neces'si**TY, *n.* Constraint arising from the constitution of things; a constraining state of things; an imperative need; a being indispensable; an indispensable thing; poverty.—**Neces'sit**ATE,[3] *vt.* To make necessary.—**Neces'sit**OUS, *a.* Poor, needy.

Neck, *n.* O.E. *hnecca* = M.Du. *necke*, M.H.G. *nacke* (Ger. *nacken*). The narrow part below the head; the narrow part of a bottle; a narrow piece of land.—**Neck'erchief**, *n.* A kerchief for the neck.—**Neck'lace**, *n.* An ornament for the neck.—**Neck'let**, *n.* Suff. *-let* of articles of attire. An ornament or piece of fur for the neck.

Nec'romancy, *n.* O.F. *nygromancie*, Med. L. *nigromantia*, alteration, by association with L. *niger*, black ('the black art'), of L. *necromantia*—G. *nekromanteia*, f. *nekros*, corpse + *manteia*, divination, prophecy. The pretended art of divination by communication with the dead; magic.—**Nec'romanc**ER, *n.*

Necrop'olis, *n.* G. *nekropolis*, f. *nekros*, corpse + *polis*, city. A cemetery.

Necro'sis, *n.* G. *nekrōsis*, deadness, f. *nekroein*, to make dead, f. *nekros*, corpse. The death of a portion of animal tissue.

Nec'tar, *n.* L. *nectar*—G. *nektar*. The drink of the gods; the honey of a flower.—**Necta'r**EAN, **Necta'r**EOUS, *aa.*—**Nec'tar**INE, *a.* As *n.*, a variety of peach.

Need, *n.* O.E. *nied* (*nýd*, *néd*) = O.S. *nôd*, O.H.G. *nôt* (Ger. *not*). Necessity; an exigency or emergency; poverty; something in respect to which want is felt.—*vi.* To be under a necessity or obligation.—*vt.* To be in need of, require.—**Need'**FUL, *a.*—**Need'**LESS, *a.*—**Needs**, *adv.* O.E. *nýdes*, *nédes*. Of necessity, necessarily.—**Need'**Y,[1] *a.* Poor, indigent.

Need'le, *n.* O.E. *nǽdl* = O.S. *nâdla*, O.H.G. *nâdela* (Ger. *nadel*). An instrument for passing thread through cloth; a knitting pin; the piece of magnetized steel in a compass.

Nefa'rious, *a.* L. *nefārius* (f. *nefas*, sin, crime) + -OUS. Wicked, iniquitous.

Negate', *vt.* L. *negāre*, *negātum*, to DENY. To deny; to deny the existence of; to nullify.—**Nega'**TION, *n.*—**Neg'at**IVE, *a.* Expressing or implying denial; lacking distinctive attributes; the opposite of positive.—*n.* A negative statement or word; in *photography*, a print made by the direct action of light in which the lights and shadows are reversed.—*vt.* To reject, set aside; to disprove.

Neglect', *vt.* L. *negligĕre*, *neglectum*, f. *neg-*, not + *legĕre*, to gather, pick up. COLLECT. To disregard, slight; to fail to pay due attention to; to fail to perform; to omit through carelessness *to do*.—*n.* The fact of neglecting; the fact or condition of being neglected.—**Neglect'**FUL, *a.*—**Neg'lig**ENCE, *n.*—**Neg'lig**ENT, *a.*—**Neg'lig**IBLE, *a.*

Nego'tiate, *vi.* L. *negōtiāri*, *negōtiātus*, f. *negōtium*, a business, f. *neg-*, not + *ōtium*, leisure. To hold communication or confer with a view to arranging some matter.—*vt.* To arrange thus; to transfer (a bill, &c.); to get over (a fence, &c.).—**Nego'ti**ABLE, *a.*—**Negoti**A'TION, *n.*—**Nego'tiat**OR, *n.*

Ne'gro, *n.* Sp. or Pg. *negro*—L. *niger*, black. NIELLO. NIGRESCENT. A man of the African or black race.—**Ne'gr**ESS, *n.*

Ne'gus, *n.* After the inventor, Colonel Francis *Negus*. A mixture of wine and hot water sweetened and flavoured.

Neigh, *vi.* O.E. *hnǽgan* = M.Du. *neyen*, M.H.G. *nêgen*. Imitative. Of a horse, to utter its characteristic sound.—*n.* The sound.

Neigh'bour, *n.* O.E. *néahgebúr*, f. *néah*, NIGH + *gebúr*, dweller, f. *búr*, dwelling. BOWER.[1] One who lives, sits, stands, &c., near another.—*vi.* To lie close *upon*.—*vt.* To lie close to, adjoin.—**Neigh'bour**HOOD, *n.* Vicinity, near situation; those livir near a certain place; a district.—**Neigh'bour**LY,[1] *adv.* Befitting, inclined to act as, a good neighbour.

Nei'ther, *a.* and *pron.* M.E., alteration after EITHER of *nauther* (O.E. *nawther*, *nauther*, contracted f. *náhwæther*, f. *ná*, not + *hwæther*, WHETHER), *nouther* (O.E. *nowther*, contracted f. *ne*, not + *ó*, ever + *hwæther*). NOR. Not the one or the other.—*adv.* or *conj.* Used disjunctively as correlative to *nor*.

Nem'esis, *n.* G. *Nemesis*, f. *nemein*, to deal out, give what is due. The goddess of retribution; one who avenges; retributive justice.

Neolith'ic, *a.* G. *neos*, NEW + *lithos*, stone + -IC. Of the later stone age.

Neol'ogy, *n.* F. *néologie*, f. G. *neos*, NEW + *logos*, discourse. The use of new terms; a new term.—**Neol'og**ISM, *n.*

Ne'ophyte, *n.* Eccles.L. *neophytus*—G. *neophutos*, lit., 'newly planted', f. *neos*, NEW + *phuton*, plant. A new convert; a novice.

Nepen'the(s), *n.* L. *nēpenthes*—G. *nēpenthes*, epithet in Homer of a soothing drug, neut. of *nēpenthēs*, f. *nē-*, not + *penthos*, grief. A drug supposed to bring forgetfulness of care.

Neph'ew, *n.* O.F. *neveu*—L. *nepos*, *nepōtis*, grandson, nephew, cogn. with O.E. *nefa*, Ger. *neffe*, nephew. A brother's or sister's son.

Nephri'tis, *n.* G. *nephritis*, f. *nephros*, kidney + -ITIS. Inflammation of the kidneys.

Nep'otism, *n.* It. *nepotismo*, f. *nepote*, L. *nepos*. NEPHEW. Favouritism (orig. on the part of Popes) to nephews or other relatives.

Nep'tune, *n.* L. *Neptūnus*, god of the sea. The most remote of the planets.

Ner'eid, *n.* L. *nērēis*, *nērēidos*—G. *nērēis*, f. *Nēreus*, a sea-god. A sea-nymph.

Nerve, *n.* L. *nervus*, app. conn. with the synonymous G. *neuron*, sinew, nerve. ENERVATE. NEURALGIA. A sinew or tendon; vigour, energy; a fibre or bundle of fibres connected with the brain, spinal cord, &c., and serving to convey impulses of sensation or motion.—*vt.* To give vigour to; to embolden.—**Nerve'**LESS, *a.*—**Nerv'**OUS, *a.* Vigorous; of, affecting, the nerves; disordered in the nerves, timid, easily agitated; agitating.—**Nerv'ous**LY,[2] *adv.*—**Nerv'ous**NESS, *n.*

Nes'cient, *a.* L. *nesciens*, *nescientis*, pres. pple. of *nescīre*, to be ignorant, f. *ne*, not + *scīre*, to know. SCIENCE. NICE. Ignorant.—**Nes'ci**ENCE, *n.*

Ness, *n.* O.E. *næs* = O.N. *nes*, conn. with O.E. *nasu*, nose. A promontory or cape.

Nest, *n.* O.E. *nest* = M.Du., O.H.G., Ger. *nest*. Cogn. with L. *nīdus*. The place in which a bird lays and hatches its eggs; an animal's lair or breeding place.—*vi.* To make or have a nest.—**Nest'le**, *vi.* O.E. *nestlian*. To settle down snugly; to press oneself affectionately *close to* or *to*.—*vt.* To press or rest snugly or affectionately.—**Nest'**LING, *n.* -LING (1). A bird too young to leave the nest.

Net, *n.* O.E. *net*(*t*). Common Teut. An open fabric of mesh-work.—*v.*[1]*t.* To cover with net; to catch in a net.

Net, *a.* F. *net.* NEAT, *a.* Free from deduction.—*v.*[2]*t.* To gain as clear profit.

Neth'er, *a.* O.E. *neothera*, *nithera*, comp. forms of *nither*, down, itself a comp. f. *ni-*, down + comp. suff. BENEATH. Lower.

Net'tle, *n.* O.E. *netele*, *netle.* Common Teut. A plant with stinging leaf-hairs.—*vt.* To irritate, provoke.—**Net'tle-rash**, *n.* An eruption like the result of the sting of a nettle.

Neural'gia, *n.* G. *neuron*, NERVE + *algos*, pain. A painful affection of a nerve.—**Neural'gic**, *a.*

Neurasthe'nia, *n.* G. *neuron*, NERVE + *astheneia*, lack of strength, f. *asthenēs*, weak, f. A-[4] + *sthenos*, strength. Nervous debility. —**Neurasthen'ic**, *a.*

Neurot'ic, *a.* G. type **neurōtikos*, f. *neuron*, NERVE. Of the nature of, characterized by, nervous disorder; having disordered nerves.

Neu'ter, *a.* L. *neuter*, neither, of the neuter gender, f. *ne*, not + *uter*, either. Neither masculine nor feminine; of verbs, neither active nor passive.—*n.* A neuter word.—**Neu'tral**, *a.* Taking the side of neither party; belonging to a neutral power; belonging to neither of two categories.—*n.* A state, a subject of a state, which remains neutral.—**Neutral'ity**, *n.*—**Neu'tralize**, *vt.* To counterbalance, make ineffective.

Névé, *n.* F.—Alpine dial. *nevé*—L. *nix*, *nivis*, SNOW. Snow on the upper part of a glacier not yet formed into ice; a field of snow.

Nev'er, *adv.* O.E. *næfre*, f. *ne*, not + *æfre*, EVER. At no time; in no way.—**Neverthe-less'**, *adv.* Notwithstanding.

New, *a.* O.E. *níwe*, *néowe.* Common Teut. Cogn. with G. *neos*, L. *novus.* NOVEL. Not existing or known before; unfamiliar; fresh, further; other than the old; that has not existed long; lately made; unimpaired; but lately come into a certain state; inexperienced. —*adv.* (Always hyphened.) Recently, freshly. —**Newfan'gled**, *a.* With *-ed* f. M.E. *newefangel*, f. *newe* + *-fangel*, repg. O.E. **fangol*, inclined to take, f. root of FANG. Fond of novelty; new-fashioned.—**New'ly**,[2] *adv.*—**New'ness**, *n.*—**News**, *n.pl.* After O.F. *noveles*, pl. of *novel*, L. *novus.* The report of recent events, tidings (often treated as *sing.*). —**News'monger**, *n.* MONGER. One who collects and spreads news.—**News'paper**, *n.* A periodical publication containing news.

New'el, *n.* O.F. *nouel* (F. *noyau*), kernel, newel—L. *nux*, nut. NUTMEG. The pillar from which the steps of a winding stair radiate; the post at the bottom or top of a stair.

Newt, *n.* For *ewt* (with *n* transferred from the indefinite article *an*), var. of *evet* = O.E. *efeta*, EFT. For the form cf. NICKNAME. A small tailed amphibious creature, an eft.

Next, *a.* O.E. *néahst*, *néhst*, superl. of *néah*, *néh*, NIGH. Nearest; immediately succeeding. —*adv.* On the first future occasion.

Nib, *n.* App. a later spelling of NEB. The point of a pen; a separate pen-point.

Nib'ble, *vt.* Corresponds to L.G. *nibbelen* = Du. *knibbelen.* To take little bites of.—*vi.* To take little bites.—*n.* A little bite.

Nice, *a.* O.F. *nice*, ignorant, foolish—L. *nescius*, ignorant, f. *nescire.* NESCIENT. Formerly, foolish, senseless. Fastidious, hard to please; careful, scrupulous; difficult to decide; minute, subtle; precise; appetizing; delightful. —**Nice'ly**,[2] *adv.*—**Nic'ety**, *n.*

Niche, *n.* F. *niche*—It. *nicchia*, of doubtful orig. A recess in a wall.

Nick, *vt.* Orig. obscure. To make a notch in to indent; to hit or catch exactly.—*n.* A notch; the exact point of time.

Nick'el, *n.* Abb. of Ger. *kupfernickel*, a copper-coloured ore from which nickel was first got, f. *kupfer*, copper + *nickel*, a mischievous demon (the ore being deceptive and yielding no copper). A hard white metal.

Nick'name, *n.* Later form (with transferred *n* as in NEWT) of *eke-name*, f. *eke*, O.E. *éaca*, an addition, conn. with EKE, *v.* An additional name, gen. given in ridicule or jest.—*vt.* To misname; to give a nickname to.

Nic'otine, *n.* F., f. Jacques *Nicot*, who introduced tobacco into France + chem. suff. *-ine.* The essential principle of tobacco.

Nid'ify, *vi.* L. *nidificāre*, f. *nidus*, NEST. -FY. To build a nest.—**Nidifica'tion.**

Niece, *n.* F. *nièce*—Pop.L. *neptia* for L. *neptis*, granddaughter, niece, conn. with *nepos*. NEPHEW. A brother's or sister's daughter.

Niel'lo, *n.* It.—L. *nigellus*, dim. of *niger*, black. NEGRO. A black compound used for filling in engraved designs; work, a specimen of work, produced by applying niello.

Nig'gard, *n.* Orig. obscure. A mean stingy person.—*a.* Mean, stingy.—**Nig'gardly**,[1] *a.* —**Nig'gardly**,[2] *adv.*

Nig'ger, *n.* Alteration of earlier *neger*—F. *nègre*—Sp. *negro*, NEGRO. A negro.

Nig'gle, *vi.* App. of Scand. orig. Cf. Norw. *nigla.* To work or to move *along* in a trifling or ineffective way; to be over-precise.

Nigh, *adv.*, *prep.*, and *a.* O.E. *néah*, *néh.* Com. Teut. NEAR. NEIGHBOUR. NEXT. Near.

Night, *n.* O.E. *niht*, *neaht.* Common Teut. Cogn. with Skr. *nákta*, G. *nux*, L. *nox.* The daily period of darkness; the end of daylight. —**Night'ingale**, *n.* Earlier *nightegale*—O.E. *nihtegale*, f. *gale*, a singer, f. *galan*, to sing, conn. with *gellan.* YELL. A bird the male of which sings by night.—**Night'ly**,[1] *a.* Happening or done by night or every night; pertaining to the night.—**Night'ly**,[2] *adv.* Every night; by night.—**Night'mare**, *n.* Obs. *Mare*, incubus, nightmare—O.E. *mare* = M.Du. *mare*, O.H.G. *mara.* An incubus; a feeling of suffocation or distress during sleep; a bad dream.—**Night'shade**, *n.* O.E. *nihtscada*, app. f. *night* + SHADE, *n.*, referring to the narcotic or poisonous properties of the berries. A plant of the potato family.

Nigres'cent, *a.* L. *nigrescens*, *nigrescentis*, pres.pple. of *nigrescĕre*, to grow black, from *niger*, black. NEGRO. Somewhat black.—**Nigres'cence**, *n.* A becoming black; blackness.—**Ni'gritude**, *n.* Blackness.

Ni'hilism, *n.* L. *nihil*, nothing + -ISM. Negative doctrines; the principles of an extreme Russian revolutionary party.—**Ni'hilist**, *n.*

Nim'ble, *a.* O.E. *numol*, *numel*, f. *num-*, ppl. stem of *niman*, to take = M.Du. *nemen*, O.H.G. *neman*, *nemen* (Ger. *nehmen*), prob. cogn. with G. *nemein.* NEMESIS. NUMB. Agile, active, alert.—**Nim'bly**,[2] *adv.*

Nim'bus, *n.* L. *nimbus*, cloud. A cloud or cloud-like splendour imagined as investing a person or thing; a halo.

Nin'compoop, *n.* Prob. a fanciful formation. A fool.

Nine, *a.* and *n.* O.E. *nigon*, &c. = O.S., O.Fris. *nigun*, &c. Cogn. with Skr. *náva(n)*, G. *ennea*, L. *novem.* The cardinal number next after eight.—**Nine'-pins**, *n.pl.* A game in which nine 'pins' are set up to be knocked down by a ball; the pins; in *sing.*, one of the pins.

Nin'ny, *n.* Perh. abb. of *innocent*, an idiot, with transferred *n* as in NEWT. A fool.

Nip, *vt.* App. a var. of the stem *nip-* seen in Du. *nijpen* (M.Du., M.L.G. *nīpen*), to nip. To pinch, squeeze sharply; to sever or take *off* by nipping; to check or destroy the growth of. —*n.* A pinch; a check to growth, sharp coldness of weather.—**Nip'p**ERS, *n.pl.* Pincers.

Nip'ple, *n.* Orig. uncertain. The small prominence terminating a breast.

Nirva'na, *n.* Skr., lit., 'blowing out, extinction', f. *nirvā*, to blow. In Buddhist theology, the extinction of individual existence by absorption in the supreme spirit.

Nit, *n.* O.E. *hnitu* = M.Du. *nete*, O.H.G. *niz* (Ger. *nisse*). The egg of a louse, &c.

Ni'tre, *n.* F. *nitre*—L. *nitrum*, G. *nitron*, native soda. Saltpetre, a compound of potassium, nitrogen and oxygen, a constituent of gunpowder.—**Ni'trogen**, *n.* F. *nitrogène*, f. *nitro-*, *nitron* + *gen-* as in HYDROGEN. A gas without colour, taste or smell forming about four-fifths of the atmosphere.—**Nitrog'en**OUS, *a.*—**Nitroglyc'erine**, *n.* An explosive liquid obtained by adding glycerine to certain acids containing nitrogen and sulphur.

No, *a.* Reduced f. *nān*, *nōn*, NONE, *a.* Not any.—**No'body**, *n.* No person, no one; a person of no importance.—**Noth'ing**, *n.* Not anything; a thing or person of no importance; a cipher.—*adv.* Not at all, in no way.

No, *adv.* O.E. *ná*, f. *ne*, not + *á*, ever, AY. NAUGHT. Expressing a negative reply to a question or request.

No'ble, *a.* F. *noble*—L. *nōbilis*, well-known, high-born, excellent, f. root (*g*)*no-* of (*g*)*noscĕre*. KNOW. Distinguished by character, deeds, rank or birth; of a lofty character; impressive; excellent.—*n.* One of a class distinguished by rank or birth; also **No'bleman**.—**Nobil'**ITY, *n.* The being noble; the nobles; a noble class. —**No'b**LY,[2] *adv.*

Noctur'nal, *a.* L.L. *nocturnālis*, f. L. *nocturnus*, a. f. *nox*, *noctis*, NIGHT. Of, active in, the night; done or happening by night.—**Noc'turne**, *n.* F. *nocturne*, f. *nocturnus*. A dreamy piece of music; a night-scene.

Nod, *vi.* Orig. obscure. To make a quick inclination of the head in assent, command, &c.; to let the head fall forward when sleepy; to bend downward or forward.—*vt.* To incline (the head); to signify thus.—*n.* A nodding.

Nod'dle, *n.* Orig. obscure. The head.

Node, *n.* L. *nōdus*. DENOUEMENT. A knot or knob; one of the two points at which a planet's orbit cuts the ecliptic.—**Nod'ule**, *n.* L. *nōdulus*, dim. of *nōdus*. A small node; a small round lump.—**Nod'ul**AR,[1] *a.*

Noise, *n.* F. *noise*, of uncertain orig. Loud outcry or din; a loud or harsh sound; a sound. —*vt.* To report, rumour.—**Noise'**LESS, *a.*— **Nois'**Y,[2] *a.*—**Nois'i**LY,[2] *adv.*

Noi'some, *a.* Obs. *Noy*, aphetic f. ANNOY + -SOME. Harmful; ill-smelling; offensive.

No'mad, *n.* L. *Nomas*, pl. *Nomades*—G. *nomas*, roving for pasture, f. *nemein*, to pasture. One who lives a roving life.—**Nomad'**IC, *a.*

No'menclature, *n.* L. *nōmenclātūra*, f. *nōmen*, NAME + *calāre*, to call. COUNCIL. A system of names; the terminology of a science.

Nom'inal, *a.* L. *nōminālis*, f. *nōmen*, *nōminis*, NAME. DENOMINATE. MISNOMER. RENOWN. Of a name or names; existing in name only.—**Nom'inal**LY,[2] *adv.*—**Nom'in**ATE,[3] *vt.* To appoint to an office; to propose as a candidate.—**Nomin**A'TION, *n.*—**Nom'inat**IVE, *a.* and *n.* A noun case indicating the subject, or connection with the subject, of a verb.—**Nom'inat**OR, *n.*—**Nomin**EE', *n.*

Non-. Of the derivatives in NON-, which are numerous and for the most part self-explanatory, only a few are here recorded. Examples are given in the List of Prefixes.

Non'age, *n.* A.F. *nounage* = O.F. *nonage*, f. NON- + *age*, *aäge*, AGE. Minority.

Nonagena'rian, *a.* L. *nōnāgēnārius* (f. *nōnāgēni*, ninety each, f. *nōnāginta*, ninety) + -AN. Between ninety and a hundred years old.—*n.* One of such an age.

Nonce. Orig. in M.E. phrase *to* (**for*) *than anes*, 'to (for) THEN ONCE', coming, by transference of *n* as in NEWT, to be *for the nanes*. *For the nonce*, for the time being; for the present occasion.

Non'chalant, *a.* F., pres.pple. of *nonchaloir*, f. NON- + *chaloir*, L. *calēre*, to be warm. Indifferent, unconcerned.—**Non'chal**ANCE, *n.*

Nonconfor'mist, *n.* NON- + CONFORM + -IST. One who does not conform to an established church.—**Nonconfor'm**ITY, *n.*

Non'descript, *a.* NON- + obs. *descript*, ppl.a. —L. *dēscriptus*, pa.pple. of *dēscrībĕre*, to DESCRIBE. Not easily described or classified.— *n.* A nondescript person or thing.

None, *pron.* O.E. *nán*, f. *ne*, not + *án*, ONE. No one, not any; no part or amount.—*a.* No. —*adv.* In no way; by no amount.

Nonen'tity, *n.* NON-. Non-existence; a non-existent thing, a figment; a person or thing of no importance.

Non-ju'ror, *n.* NON-. One of the clergy who refused to take the oath of allegiance to William and Mary.

Nonpareil', *a.* F. *nonpareil*, f. NON-+*pareil*, like—Pop.L. **pāriculus*, dim. of L. *pār*, equal. Unequalled.—*n.* Something unequalled.

Non'plus, *n.* L. *nōn plūs*, not more. A state in which no more can be done or said.—*vt.* To bring to a nonplus.

Non'sense, *n.* NON-. That which is not sense; senseless action.—**Nonsen'**SICAL, *a.*

Non'suit, *n.* A.F. *no*(*u*)*nsute*. NON-. SUIT. The stopping of a suit by the judge.—*vt.* To subject to a nonsuit.

Nood'le, *n.* Orig. obscure. A simpleton.

Nook, *n.* M.E. *nōk*, prob. of Scand. orig. A corner; a secluded or sheltered place.

Noon, *n.* O.E. *nón* = O.N. *nón*, M.Du. *noen*— L. *nōna* (*hōra*), ninth (hour), fem. of *nōnus*, f. *novem*, NINE. The ninth hour by Roman reckoning (about 3 p.m.). Now, midday.

Noose, *n.* Poss. f. Pr. *nous*, noose—L. *nōdus*, knot. NODE. A running loop tightening on pulling.—*vt.* To catch by a noose.

Nor, *conj.* Prob. contraction of *nouther*, *nother*, NEITHER. Continuing the force of a negative; as correlative to *neither*; and not.

Norm, *n.* L. *norma*, carpenter's square, rule, pattern. ENORMOUS. A standard, model, pattern.—**Nor'mal**, *a.* L. *normālis*. Perpendicular; constituting, conforming to, the common type.—*n.* A perpendicular.

North, *adv.* O.E. *north*. Common Teut. Towards the part of the heavens opposite to the midday sun.—*n.* The cardinal point opposite to the midday sun; the northern part of the world, a country, &c.—*a.* Towards or from the north.—**North'er**LY,[1] *a.* Cf. EASTERLY, &c.—**North'**ERN, *a.*—**North'**WARD, *adv.* and *a.*—**North'**WARDS, *adv.*— **North-east'** (**-west'**), *adv.* In the direction midway between north and east (west).—*n.*

The direction thus midway.—*a.* Blowing from, lying in or towards, the north-east (-west).

Nose, *n.* O.E. *nosu* = M.Du., M.L.G. *nose.* NOSTRIL. The organ of smell, used also in breathing and speech; the sense of smell.—*vt.* To perceive the smell of, detect.—*vi.* To smell.—**Nose'gay,** *n.* GAY in obs. use as *n.*, a toy. A bunch of sweet-smelling flowers.

Nosol'ogy, *n.* G. *nosos,* disease + -LOGY. Systematic classification of diseases.

Nostal'gia, *n.* G. *nostos,* return home + *algos,* pain. Home-sickness.

Nos'tril, *n.* O.E. *nosthyrl,* f. stem of *nosu,* NOSE + *thýrel,* orifice, f. *thurh,* THROUGH. One of the orifices of the nose.

Nos'trum, *n.* L., neut. of *noster,* our. A quack medicine prepared by the seller.

Not, *adv.* Abb. f. NOUGHT, *adv.* The ordinary adverb of negation.

Not'able, *a.* F. *notable*—L. *notābilis,* f. *nota,* NOTE. Worthy of note, remarkable, eminent. —*n.* An eminent person.—**Nota**BIL'ITY, *n.* The quality of being notable; an eminent person.—**Not'ab**LY,[2] *adv.*

Not'ary, *n.* L. *notārius,* secretary, clerk, f. *nota,* NOTE. One authorized to attest documents, protest bills, &c.—**Nota'ri**AL, *a.*

Nota'tion, *n.* L. *notātio notātiōnis,* n. of action f. *notāre,* to note, f. *nota,* NOTE. The process of representing numbers, &c., by a system of signs; the signs.

Notch, *n.* App., with transferred *n* as in NEWT, f. older F. *oche* (F. *hoche*). in same sense, of unknown orig. A V-shaped incision or indentation.—*vt.* To make notches in.

Note, *n.* L. *nota,* mark, perh. conn. with *nōtus.* (See next.) ANNOTATE. DENOTE. A symbol representing a musical sound; a single tone of definite pitch; a mark, sign, token; an abstract or brief record or memorandum; an annotation; a short letter; a written or printed promise to pay; distinction, fame; regard, attention.—*vt.* To observe; to give attention to; to set down in writing.—**Not'ed,** *ppl.a.* Well known, celebrated.—**Note'worthy,** *a.* Worthy of note, remarkable.

Not'ice, *n.* F. *notice*—L. *nōtitia,* a being known, a knowing, f. *nōtus,* pa.pple. of *noscĕre.* KNOW. NOTION. Intimation, warning; note, attention; a short review of a book, &c.—*vt.* To make mention of; to perceive, observe; to treat with attention.—**Not'ice**ABLE, *a.*

Not'ify, *vt.* F. *notifier*—L. *nōtificāre,* f. *nōtus.* (See prec.) -FY. To make known, give notice of; to give notice to.—**Noti**FICA'TION, *n.*

No'tion, *n.* L. *nōtio, nōtiōnis,* f. *nōtus.* NOTICE. An idea or concept; an opinion or belief; an inclination or fancy.

Noto'rious, *a.* Med.L. *nōtōrius* (f. L. *nōtus.* NOTICE) + -OUS. Well known; noted *for* some bad practice, quality, &c.—**Notori'**ETY, *n.*

Notwithstand'ing, *prep.* NOT + pres.pple. of WITHSTAND. In spite of.—*adv.* Nevertheless.—*conj.* Although.

Nought, *n.* O.E. *nówiht,* f. *ne,* not + *ówiht,* var. of *āwiht, āht,* AUGHT. NOT. Nothing; a cipher.—*adv.* In no way, not at all.

Noun, *n.* A.F. *noun,* O.F. *nun, nom*—L. *nōmen,* NAME. A word denoting a person or thing.

Nour'ish, *vt.* O.F. *noris(s)-, nuris(s)-,* lengthened stem of *norir, nurir* (F. *nourrir*), L. *nūtrīre, nūtrītum,* to suckle, nourish. NURSE. NURTURE. NUTRIENT. To supply with food; to foster, cherish.—**Nour'ish**MENT, *n.*

Nov'el, *a.* O.F. *novel*—L. *novellus,* dim. of *novus,* NEW. INNOVATE. NOVICE. New, strange.—*n.* It. *novella,* f. *novellus.* A fictitious prose narrative of real life.—**Nov'el**IST, *n.* A writer of novels.—**Nov'el**TY, *n.*

Novem'ber, *n.* L., f. *novem,* NINE. The ninth of the Roman months; our eleventh.

Nov'ice, *n.* O.F. *novice*—L. *novīcius,* new, f. *novus.* NOVEL. A candidate for admission to a religious order; one new to anything.—**Novi'ci**ATE,[1] **Novi'ti**ATE,[1] *n.*

Now, *adv.* O.E. *nú,* as in all the older Teut. languages. Cogn. with Skr. *nu, nú,* G. *nun,* L. *nunc.* At the present time; under the present circumstances; immediately; just before this time; at the time spoken of.—**Now'adays,** *adv.* *Now* + A-[1] + *day's,* genit. of DAY. At the present day, in these times.

Nox'ious, *a.* L. *noxius* (f. *noxa,* hurt, f. *nocēre,* to hurt) + -OUS. INNOCENT. NUISANCE. Hurtful, harmful; unwholesome.

Noz'zle, *n.* NOSE + instrumental suff. *-le.* A spout or projecting aperture.

Nu'bile, *a.* L. *nūbilis,* f. *nūbĕre,* to marry. NUPTIAL. Of a woman, marriageable.

Nu'cleus, *n.* L. *nucleus,* kernel, f. *nux, nucis,* nut. NUTMEG. A kernel or centre.

Nude, *a.* L. *nūdus.* DENUDE. Naked, bare; unclothed.—**Nu'di**TY, *n.*

Nudge, *vt.* Poss. conn. with Norw. dial. *nugga, nyggja,* to push, rub. To touch slightly with the elbow.—*n.* Such a touch.

Nu'gatory, *a.* L. *nūgātōrius,* f. *nūgāri, nūgātus,* to trifle. Trifling; futile.

Nug'get, *n.* App. a deriv. of s.w. dial. *nug,* a lump. A rough lump of native gold.

Nui'sance, *n.* O.F. *nuisance,* f. *nuis-,* stem of *nuire,* L. *nocēre,* to hurt. NOXIOUS. Something injurious, offensive, or annoying.

Null, *a.* O.F. *nul*—L. *nullus,* none, f. *ne,* not + *ullus,* any. ANNUL. Of no effect, invalid; ineffective.—**Nul'li**FY, *vt.*—**Nul'li**TY, *n.*

Numb, *a.* Pa.pple. of archaic *Nim,* O.E. *niman.* NIMBLE. Deprived of feeling or movement by cold.—*vt.* To make numb.

Num'ber, *n.* O.F. *nombre, numbre*—L. *numerus.* ENUMERATE. INNUMERABLE. SUPERNUMERARY. (See next.) A sum or aggregate; in *pl.*, the fourth book of the Old Testament containing a census of the Israelites; a symbol or symbols representing a sum; a (numbered) part of a periodical, &c.; a collection or company; in *pl.*, a multitude; a consideration of things as units to be separated or combined; a form of a word to denote one, two, or more persons or things; rhythm; in *pl.*, metrical feet, lines, verses.—*vt.* To count, to enumerate; to class or reckon; to assign a number to; to comprise, to amount to.—**Num'ber**LESS, *a.* That cannot be numbered.

Nu'meral, *a.* L.L. *numerālis,* f. L. *numerus.* (See prec.) Of or expressing number.—*n.* A word or symbol denoting a number.—**Nu'mer**ATE,[3] *vt.* To number, count.—**Nu'mer**ABLE, *a.*—**Numer**A'TION, *n.*—**Nu'merator,** *n.* He who or that which numbers; the number written above the line in a fraction showing how many parts of a unit are taken. —**Numer'**ICAL, *a.* Of number; in respect of numbers.—**Nu'mer**OUS, *a.* Abundant; many.

Numismat'ic, *a.* F. *numismatique*—L. *numisma, numismatis* = G. *nomisma,* current coin, f. *nomizein,* to have in use. Of coins.—In *pl.* as *n.*, the study of coins.—**Numis'mat**IST, *n.*

Num'skull, *n.* NUMB. *a.* A dolt; the pate.

Nun, *n.* O.E. *nunne* = O.H.G., O.N. *nunna*—Eccles.L. *nonna,* fem. of *nonnus,* monk. A

member of a community of women living apart under vows.—**Nun'ne**RY, *n.* A convent.
Nun'cio, *n.* Earlier It. *nuncio*—L. *nuntius*, messenger. ANNOUNCE. DENOUNCE. A representative of the Pope at a foreign court.
Nun'cupative, *a.* Med.L. *nuncupātivus*, f. L. *nuncupāre*, to name. Of a will, oral.
Nup'tial, *a.* L. *nuptiālis*, f. *nuptiae*, pl., a marriage, f, *nūbĕre*, *nuptum*, to marry. CONNUBIAL. NUBILE. Of or pertaining to marriage or a marriage.—*n.pl.* A marriage.
Nurse, *n.* M.E. *norice*, *nurice*—O.F. *norice*, *nurice*, *nourrice*—L.L. *nūtricia*, orig. fem. of *nūtricius*, a. f. *nūtrix*, *nūtrīcis*, nurse, f. *nūtrīre*. NOURISH. A woman employed to suckle or to attend to a child; one who attends to the sick.—*vt.* To act as nurse to.—**Nurs'**ERY, *n.* A room for children and their nurse; a piece of ground in which plants are reared.—**Nurs'ling**, *n.* -LING (1). An infant.
Nur'ture, *n.* O.F. *nurture*, *nourture* (F. *nourriture*)—L.L. *nūtritūra*, a nursing, f. *nūtrīre*. NOURISH. Nourishment; bringing-up, rearing.—*vt.* To nourish; to bring up.
Nut, *n.* O.E. *hnutu*. Common Teut. WALNUT. A fruit consisting of a hard shell and a kernel; a small block with a grooved hole to be screwed on a bolt.—*vi.* To gather nuts.
Nuta'tion, *n.* L. *nūtātio*, *nūtātiōnis*, n. of action f. *nūtāre*, to nod. A nodding; a slight oscillation of the earth's axis.
Nut'meg, *n.* A.F. or O.F. **nois mugue*, var. of O.F. *nois mug(u)ede*, &c., f. *nois*, L. *nux*, nut+L.L. *muscus*, MUSK. NEWEL. NUCLEUS. The aromatic seed of an E. Indian tree.
Nu'trient, *a.* L. *nūtriens*, *nūtrientis*, pres. pple. of *nūtrīre*. NOURISH. Nourishing.—**Nu'tri**MENT, *n.* Food.—**Nutri'**TION, *n.* A supplying or receiving of nutriment; nutriment.—**Nutri'**TIOUS, *a.*—**Nu'triti**VE, *a.*
Nux vom'ica, *n.* Med.L., f. L. *nux*, nut + fem. of **vomicus*, a. f. *vomĕre*, to VOMIT. The seed of an E. Indian tree yielding strychnia.
Nuz'zle, *vi.* NOSE + vbl. suff. *-le*. To burrow with the nose; to poke with the nose *into*; to press the nose *against*; to nestle, lie snug. —*vt.* To touch or rub with the nose.
Nymph, *n.* F. *nymphe*—L. *nympha*—G. *numphē*, bride, nymph. A semi-divine female being inhabiting rivers, woods, &c.; a damsel. —**Nymph'olepsy**, *n.* After *epilepsy*, f. G. *numpholēptos*, caught by nymphs, f. *numphē*+ *lambanein*, to take. An ecstasy of emotion.

O

Oaf, *n.* Var. of obs. *Auf*—O.N. *álfr*, ELF. An elf's child, a changeling; a dolt.
Oak, *n.* O.E. *ác*. Common Teut. A well-known forest tree.—**Oak'**EN,[1] *a.*
Oak'um, *n.* O.E. *ácumbe*, *ǽcumbe*, tow, lit. 'off-combings', f. *ǽ-*, away, off + stem of *cemban*, to comb, conn. with *camb*, COMB. Loose fibre got by picking old ropes.
Oar, *n.* O.E. *ár*, cogn. with O.N. *ár*, and perh. with G. *eretmon*. A wooden lever used to propel a boat.—*vt.* and *i.* To row.
Oa'sis, *n.*; *pl.* **-ses**. L. *oasis*—G. *oasis*, app. of Egyptian orig. A fertile spot in a desert.
Oast, *n.* O.E. *ást*, kiln, corresp. to M.L.G. *eist*, Du. *eest*. Cogn. with G. *aithos*, L. *aestus*, heat. ESTUARY. A kiln for drying hops.
Oat, *n.* O.E. *áte*, of obscure orig. In *pl.*, the grains of a cereal; the plant (gen. in *pl.*).
Oath, *n.* O.E. *áth*. Common Teut. A solemn appeal to something held in reverence in witness that a statement is true or that a promise shall be kept; a piece of profanity in speech.
Ob'durate, *a.* L. *obdūrātus*, pa.pple. of *obdūrāre*, f. OB- (4) + *dūrāre*. ENDURE. Hardened in sin; stubborn.—**Ob'dur**ACY, *n.*
Obe'dient, *a.* O.F. *obedient*—L. *obēdiens*, *obēdientis*, pres.pple. of *obēdīre*, to OBEY. Submissive to authority.—**Obe'di**ENCE, *n.*
Obeis'ance, *n.* F. *obéissance*, obedience, f. *obéissant*, pres.pple. of *obéir*, to OBEY. Formerly, obedience. A bow or curtsy.
Ob'elisk, *n.* L. *obeliscus*—G. *obeliskos*, dim. of *obelos*, spit, obelisk. A rectangular tapering column of stone with a pyramidal apex; a mark (— or ÷) used in ancient manuscripts to indicate a spurious, doubtful, or superfluous word or passage (in this sense also **Ob'elus** = G. *obelos*); a reference mark (†) in printing. —**Ob'el**IZE, *vt.* To mark as spurious, &c., with the obelus or obelisk.
Obese', *a.* L. *obēsus*, 'that has eaten himself fat', pa.pple. middle of *obedĕre* (OB- (4)), to EAT away. Very fat.—**Obe'**SITY, *n.*
Obey', *vt.* F. *obéir*—L. *obēdīre*, f. OB- (1) + *audīre*. AUDIBLE. OBEDIENT. OBEISANCE. To do the bidding of; to be actuated by.
Obfus'cate, *vt.* L. *obfuscāre*, *obfuscātum*, f. OB- (3) + *fuscāre*, to darken, f. *fuscus*, dark. To darken the understanding of, to stupefy.
Obit'uary, *n.* Med.L. *obituārius*, f. *obitus*, a going down, death, f. *obīre*, to go down, to die, f. OB- (3) + *īre*, to go. POST-OBIT. A record or announcement of a death or deaths.—*a.* Relating to or recording a death or deaths.
Object', *vt.* L. *objicĕre*, *objectum*, to throw towards, cast in the way, f. OB- (1) + *jacĕre*, to throw. ABJECT. To state in opposition; to lay to one's charge.—*vi.* To state an objection; to have an objection *to*.—**Ob'ject**, *n.* Med.L. *objectum*, lit. 'thing thrown before (the eyes, &c.)', neut. pa.pple. of *objicĕre*. Something presented to one of the senses; an object exciting disdain, pity, &c.; that to which action, thought, &c., is directed; an end or purpose; a word, &c., dependent on a verb or preposition.—**Objec'**TION, *n.*—**Objec'tion**ABLE, *a.*—**Objec'**TIVE, *a.* Presented to consciousness treating of outward things rather than of thoughts or feelings.—*n.* An object or aim. —**Objectiv'**ITY, *n.*—**Objec'**TOR, *n.*
Ob'jurgate, *vt.* L. *objurgāre*, *objurgātum*, f. OB- (2) + *jurgāre*, to chide. To rebuke severely, chide.—**Objurg**A'TION, *n.*
Oblate', *a.* Mod.L. *oblātus*, f. OB-, with obscure force + L. *lātus*, pa.pple. of *ferre*, to BEAR. Flattened at the poles.
Obla'tion, *n.* O.F. *oblation*—L.L. *oblātio*, *oblātiōnis*, n. of action f. L. *offerre*, to OFFER. A sacrificing; a sacrifice or offering.
Ob'ligate, *vt.* L. *obligāre*. (See next.) To bind or compel.—**Oblig**A'TION, *n.* A binding oneself, a promise; a legal agreement; moral or legal constraint; one's duty; a debt of gratitude; a service or favour.—**Ob'ligat**ORY, *a.* Binding; creating an obligation.
Oblige', *vt.* O.F. *obliger*—L. *obligāre*, *obligātum*, to bind to, make liable, f. OB- (1) + *ligāre*. LIGAMENT. To bind morally or legally; to do a service to; to compel.
Oblique', *a.* L. *oblīquus*, f. OB- (1) + *līqu-*, *līc-*, for which cf. *licinus*, bent upwards. Having a slanting or sloping direction or position; indirect, indirectly stated; mentally or morally perverse; applied to any grammati-

cal case except the nominative and vocative.—**Oblique'**LY,[2] *adv.*—**Obliq'u**ITY, *n.*

Oblit'erate, *vt.* L. *oblit(t)erāre, oblit(t)erātum*, f. OB- (2) + *lit(t)era*, LETTER. To blot out; to wipe out, efface.—**Oblitera**'TION, *n.*

Obliv'ion, *n.* O.F. *oblivion*—L. *oblīvio, oblīviōnis*, f. *oblīvisci*, to forget, of uncertain orig. A forgetting or being forgotten; overlooking of offences.—**Obliv'i**OUS, *a.*

Ob'long, *a.* L. OB*longus*, rather LONG, oblong. (The force of the *ob-* is obscure.) Rectangular with the adjacent sides unequal.—*n.* An oblong figure.

Ob'loquy, *n.* L. *obloquium*, a contradiction, f. *obloqui*, to speak against. OB- (2). LOCUTION. Detraction, abuse; evil fame, disgrace.

Obnox'ious, *a.* L. *obnoxiōsus*, f. *obnoxius*, subject, liable, f. OB- (1) + *noxa*. NOXIOUS. Subject, liable; odious, offensive.

O'boe, *n.* It. *oboe*—F. *hautbois*. = HAUTBOY.

Obscene', *a.* L. *obscēnus*, ill-omened, disgusting, indecent, of doubtful orig. Offensive; indecent, lewd.—**Obscen'**ITY, *n.*

Obscure', *a.* O.F. *obscur*—L. *obscūrus*, lit., 'covered over', f. OB- (3) + *scur-*, f. root *scu-*, Skr. *sku-*, to cover. Cogn. with G. *skutos*, hide, L. *scūtum*, shield. Dark, gloomy; hidden, retired; inconspicuous; humble, lowly; doubtful, uncertain; hard to understand.—*vt.* To dim the lustre of; to conceal; to make unintelligible.—**Obscur'**ANT, *n.* One who opposes enlightenment or reform.—**Obscur'ant**ISM, *n.*—**Obscur'**ITY, *n.*

Ob'secrate, *vt.* L. *obsecrāre, obsecrātum*, to entreat (in the name of something sacred), f. OB- (5) + *sacrāre*, to consecrate. SACRAMENT. To entreat; to beg (a thing).—**Obsecra**'TION, *n.* Entreaty; any one of the prayers in the Litany beginning with 'by'.

Ob'sequies, *n.* Pl. of obs. *Obsequy*—A.F. *obsequie* = O.F. *obsèque*—Med.L. *obsequiae*, pl., app. a mixture of L. *exsequiae*, funeral (f. EX- + *sequi*, to follow), and *obsequium*. (See next.) Funeral rites.

Obse'quious, *a.* L. *obsequiōsus*, obedient, f. *obsequium*, obedience, f. *obsequi*, to submit to, f. OB- (1) + *sequi*, to follow. SEQUEL. Servilely compliant; fawning, cringing.

Observe', *vt.* F. *observer*—L. *observāre*, to watch, attend to, f. OB- (1) + *servāre*, to keep safe, PRESERVE. To follow, adhere to, hold to; to celebrate duly; to watch; to note systematically; to notice, perceive; to mention, remark.—*vi.* To make a remark.—**Observ'**ABLE, *a.* Perceptible; worthy of notice.—**Observ'ab**LY,[2] *adv.* Perceptibly.—**Observ'**ANCE, *n.* Due regard, paying attention, keeping; a customary rite; an ordinance; notice, watching.—**Observ'**ANT, *a.* Paying due regard; heedful; quick to notice.—**Observa**'TION, *n.* The action, habit or practice of observing; perception; a remark.—**Observ'at**ORY, *n.* A building for observing natural phenomena.—**Observ'**ER, *n.*

Obsess', *vt.* L. *obsidēre, obsessum*, to sit down before, besiege, f. OB- (1) (2) + *sedēre*, to sit. ASSESS. To haunt, harass.—**Obses'**SION, *n.*

Obsid'ian, *n.* L. *obsidiānus*, erroneously for *obsiānus*, f. *Obsius*, the finder in Ethiopia of a stone resembling this. A dark-coloured vitreous volcanic rock.

Ob'solete, *a.* L. *obsolētus*, old, worn out, ppl.a. f. *obsolescĕre, obsolētum*, to grow old, wear out, of doubtful orig. No longer in use.—**Obsoles'**CENT, *a.* Passing out of use.

Ob'stacle, *n.* O.F. *obstacle*—L. *obstāculum*, f. *obstāre*, to STAND near or against. OB- (1) (2). A hindrance, impediment.

Obstet'ric, *a.* Mod.L. *obstetricus* for L. *obstetrīcius*, f. *obstetrix, obstetrīcis*, midwife, f. *obstāre*. (See prec.) Of midwifery.—In *pl.* as *n.*, midwifery.—**Obstet'r**ICAL, *a.*

Ob'stinate, *a.* L. *obstinātus*, ppl.a. f. *obstināre, obstinātum*, to persist, lengthened f. *obstāre*. OBSTACLE. Self-willed, stubborn.—**Ob'stin**ACY, *n.*—**Ob'stinate**LY,[2] *adv.*

Obstrep'erous, *a.* L. *obstreperus*, clamorous (f. *obstrepĕre*, to make a noise against) + -OUS. OB- (2). Clamorous; turbulent, unruly.

Obstruct', *vt.* L. *obstruĕre, obstructum*, to build against, block up. OB- (2). STRUCTURE. To block up; to hinder.—**Obstruc't**ION, *n.*—**Obstruc'tion**IST, *n.*—One who hinders systematically.—**Obstruc't**IVE, *a.* and *n.*

Obtain', *vt.* F. *obtenir*—L. *obtinēre*, to keep, possess, to obtain, f. OB- (2) + *tenēre*. to hold. CONTAIN. To acquire, get.—*vi.* To be prevalent or customary, to exist.—**Obtain'**ABLE, *a.*

Obtest', *vt.* L. *obtestāri*. OB- (5). TESTAMENT. To call to witness; to beg earnestly, entreat, implore.—**Obtest**A'TION, *n.*

Obtrude', *vt.* L. *obtrūdĕre, obtrūsum*, to thrust against. OB- (2). INTRUDE. To thrust forth; to thrust forward unduly, force *on* or *upon*.—**Obtrus'**ION, *n.*—**Obtrus'**IVE, *a.*

Obtuse', *a.* L. *obtūsus*, blunt, dull, pa.pple. of *obtundĕre*, to beat against, blunt. OB- (2). CONTUSE. Not sharp or pointed; greater than a right angle; dull, stupid.—**Obtuse'**LY,[2] *adv.*

Ob'verse, *n.* L. *obversus*, pa.pple. of *obvertĕre*, to turn towards. OB- (1). VERSE. The side of a coin bearing the head or chief design.

Ob'viate, *vt.* L. *obviāre, obviātum*, to meet, withstand, f. OB- (2) + *via*, way. DEVIATE. To get out of the way, to prevent.—**Ob'vious**, *a.* L. *obvius*, in the way, meeting (f. *ob-* + *via* as above) + -OUS. Clear, manifest.

Occa'sion, *n.* L. *occāsio, occāsiōnis*, falling down (of things towards each other), occasion, f. *occidĕre, occāsum*, to fall down, to go down, set, f. *oc-* (= OB- (3)) + *cadĕre*, to fall. CADENCE. An opportunity; a reason, ground; a cause; a subsidiary cause; need, necessity; the time, a time, at which something happens.—*vt.* To cause, bring about.—**Occa'sion**AL, *a.* Made for, arising out of, a special occasion; happening or met with now and then.

Oc'cident, *n.* F. *occident*—L. *occidens, occidentis*, orig. pres.pple. of *occidĕre*. (See prec. The quarter of the setting sun; western countries, the West.—**Occident'**AL, *a.*

Oc'ciput, *n.* L. *occiput, occipitis*, f. *oc-* (= OB (2)) + *caput*, head. CAPITAL. The back of the head.—**Occip'it**AL, *a.*

Occlude', *vt.* L. *occlūdĕre, occlūsum*, f. *oc* (= OB- (3)) + *claudĕre*, to CLOSE. To shut or stop up; to shut in or out.—**Occlu'**SION, *n.*

Occult', *a.* L. *occultus*, pa.pple. of *occulĕre*, to cover up, conceal, f. *oc-* (= OB-)(3)) + **celĕre*, to hide, conn. with *cēlāre*. HALL. Secret; mysterious; magical, mystical.—*vt.* L. *occultāre*, freq. of *occulĕre*. To hide, cut off from view.—**Occult**A'TION, *n.*

Oc'cupy, *vt.* O.F. *occuper*—L. *occupāre*, to seize, f. *oc-* (= OB- (2)) + *capĕre*, to take. CAPABLE. To take possession of (a place); to hold possession of; to inhabit; to take up (space or time), to be in or at; to employ busy.—**Oc'cup**ANCY, *n.* The fact of occupying; residence.—**Oc'cup**ANT, *n.*—**Occupa'**TION, *n.* Seizure; possession; employment; an employment.—**Oc'cupi**ER, *n.*

Occur', *vi.* L. *occurrĕre*, to run to, run to meet, to occur, f. *oc-* (= OB- (1) (2)) + *currĕre*, to run. CONCUR. To present itself; to come into one's mind; to happen.—**Occur'**RENCE, *n.*

O'cean, *n.* F. *océan*—L. *ōceanus*—G. *ōkeanos*, orig. the great river supposed to encompass the earth. The great body of water on the globe; a main region of this.—**Ocean'**IC, *a.*

O'chre, *n.* F. *ocre*—L. *ōchra*—G. *ōchra*, yellow ochre, f. *ōchros*, pale yellow. A light yellow, orange or brown pigment.

Oc'tagon, *n.* L. *octăgōnus* = G. *oktagōnos*, eight-cornered, f. *okta-* for *oktō*, EIGHT + *gōnia*, angle. A figure with eight angles.—**Octag'on**AL, *a.*

Oc'tave, *n.* F. *octave*—L. *octāva*, fem. of *octāvus*, eighth (sc. *dies*, day). The eight days beginning with the day of a festival; a group of eight lines of verse; the first eight lines of a sonnet; a note eight degrees above or below a given note, this interval.—**Octa'vo**, *n.* L., ablative of *octāvus* in phrase *in octāvo*, in an eighth (*sc.* of a sheet). The size of a book in which each sheet is folded into eight leaves; a book of this size.—*a.* Of this size.

Octo'ber, *n.* L. *Octōber*, f. *octo*, EIGHT. The eighth of the Roman months; our tenth.

Octogena'rian, *a.* L. *octōgēnārius* (f. *octōgēni*, eighty each, f. *octōginta*, eighty) + -AN. Of the age of eighty years.—*n.* One of this age.

Octo'pus, *n.* G. *oktōpous*, eight-footed, f. *oktō*, EIGHT + *pous*, FOOT. A mollusc having eight arms furnished with suckers.

Oc'ular, *a.* L. *oculāris*, f. *oculus*, eye. BINOCULAR. EYELET. INOCULATE. INVEIGLE. Of the eye or the sense of sight, visual.—**Oc'ular**LY,[2] *adv.*—**Oc'ul**IST, *n.* A surgeon who treats diseases of the eye.

O'dalisque, *n.* F. *odalisque*—Turkish *ōdaliq*, f. *ōdah*, chamber, hall + *-liq*, denoting function. A female slave in a harem, esp. in the seraglio of the Sultan of Turkey.

Odd, *n.* M.E. *odde*—O.N. *odda-* (as in *oddatala*, odd number), f. *oddi*, point, angle, triangle, whence the notion 'third or odd number'. Cogn. with O.H.G. *ort*, angle, point, place (Ger. *ort*, place), O.E. *ord*, point, origin. That is one in addition to a pair or pairs; of a number, not even; not part of a regular set, casual; strange; peculiar, queer.—**Odd'**ITY, *n.* The quality of being odd or peculiar; an odd or peculiar person or thing.—**Odd'**MENTS, *n.pl.* Odds and ends.—**Odds**, *n.pl.* Difference; dissension; balance of advantage; an allowance to a weaker competitor; an advantage conceded in betting; balance of probability; *odds and ends*, odd fragments or remnants.

Ode, *n.* F. *ode*—L.L. *ōdē*—G. *ōidē*, song, contracted f. *aoidē*, f. *aeidein*, to sing. COMEDY. PALINODE. PROSODY. THRENODY. TRAGEDY. A lyric poem in an exalted style.

O'dium, *n.* L. *odium*, f. *ōdisse*, to hate. Hatred; opprobrium.—**O'dious**, *a.*

O'dour, *n.* A.F. *odour*, O.F. *odor*, *odur*—L. *odor*. Scent, smell.—**Odorif'erous**, *a.* L. *odōrifer* (f. *-fer*, bearing, f. *ferre*, to BEAR) + -OUS. Diffusing fragrance.—**O'dor**IZE, *vt.* To fill with an odour, scent.—**O'dor**OUS, *a.*—**O'dour**LESS, *a.*

Œcumen'ical, *a.* L. *oecūmenicus* (f. G. *oikoumenikos*, of (*hē*) *oikoumenē* (*gē*), (the) inhabited (earth), pres. pple. pass. of *oike·ein*, to inhabit) + -AL. Of or representing the whole world.

Œsoph'agus, *n.* G. *oisophagos*, of uncertain orig. The gullet.

Of, *prep.* O.E. *of*, weak form of *æf*, orig. *af*, corresp. to O.H.G. *aba*, *ab* (Ger. *ab*), O.N. *af*, away. AFTER. OFF. Denoting source, cause, motive, possession or ownership, attribute, quality, material; concerning, relating to.

Off, *adv.* Var. of prec. Away; so as to be out of position, not on, or no longer going on.—*prep.* Away from, down or up from; not on; disengaged from.—*a.* More distant; of parts of horses, vehicles, &c., right; denoting suspension of a usual course.—**Off-hand'**, *adv.* At once; without premeditation.—**Off'-hand**, *a.* Done or made off-hand.

Of'fal, *n.* OFF, *adv.* + FALL, *n.* The parts cut off in dressing a carcass for food; refuse.

Offend', *vi.* O.F. *offendre*—L. *offendĕre*, *offensum*, to strike against, commit a fault, displease, f. *of-* (= OB- (2)) + *fendĕre*. DEFEND. To do amiss.—*vt.* To displease, to excite personal annoyance or resentment in.—**Offence'**, *n.* F. *offense*—L. *offensa*, f. *offendĕre*. Attack; the act or fact of offending; wounded feeling, displeasure, resentment; a sin or fault.—**Offend'**ER, *n.*—**Offen'**SIVE, *a.* As *n.*, the position or attitude of attack.

Of'fer, *vt.* O.E. *offrian* = O.Fris. *offria*, O.S. *offrôn*—L. *offerre*, *oblātum*, to bring before, present, in Eccles.L., to offer to God, sacrifice, f. *of-* (= OB- (1)) + *ferre*, to BEAR. OBLATION. PROFFER. To present for acceptance or refusal; to propose; to attempt to inflict (violence, &c.) or to make (resistance, &c.); to try *to do*.—*vi.* To present itself, occur.—*n.* An offering; a bid.—**Of'ferer**, *n.*—**Of'fertory**, *n.* Eccles.L. *offertōrium*—L.L. *offert-*, ppl. stem (for *oblāt-*) of *offerre*. The part of the Communion Service at which offerings are made; the collection of offerings; the gifts offered.

Of'fice, *n.* A.F. and O.F. *office*—L. *officium*, a service, a duty, an appointment, in Med.L., a Church Service, prob. f. *of-* (= OB- (1)) + *-ficium*, f. *facĕre*, to do. FACT. A service, kindness; a duty, task, function; a position of authority, &c.; official position; a prescribed form of worship; a place for doing business; a corporation, &c., carrying on business; in *pl.*, the parts of a house devoted to household work.—**Of'fic**ER, *n.* One who holds an office or post; one in command in the navy or army.—*vt.* To furnish with officers.—**Offic'ial**, *a.* Of or holding an office; authorized, authoritative.—*n.* One holding an office.—**Offic'ial**ISM, *n.* Excessive official routine.—**Offic'i**ATE,[3] *vi.* To discharge the office of a priest; to perform a duty or service.—**Offic'i**OUS, *a.* Meddlesome, interfering.

Off'ing, *n.* OFF, *adv.* + *-ing*. The part of the sea distant from the shore; position at a distance from the shore.

Off'set, *n.* OFF, *adv.* A set-off; an offshoot.

Off'shoot, *n.* OFF, *adv.* A lateral shoot.

Off'spring, *n.* O.E. *ofspring*, f. *of*, OF, OFF + *springan*, to SPRING. Progeny, issue.

Oft, *adv.* O.E. *oft*. Common Teut. Many times. Gen. in extended form **Of'ten**.

Ogee', *n.* App. worn down f. F. *ogive*, OGIVE. A moulding showing in section a continuous double curve (app. as being the usual moulding employed in ogives).

O'give, *n.* F. *ogive*, of uncertain orig. The diagonal rib of a vault; a pointed arch.

O'gle, *vi.* and *t.* App. f. Du. or L.G. Cf. L.G. *oegeln*, freq. of *oegen*, to look at. To cast, to eye with, amorous or insinuating glances.—*n.* Such a glance.

O'gre, *n.* F. *ogre*, of unknown orig. A man-eating giant.—**O'gr**ESS, *n.*

Oil, *n.* O.F. *oile* (F. *huile*)—L. *oleum*, olive

oil, f. *olea* = G. *elaia*, OLIVE. PETROLEUM. A viscid unctuous inflammable liquid lighter than water.—*vt.* To apply oil to.—**Oil'**Y,[2] *a.*

Oint'ment, *n.* O.F. *oignement*—L. type **ungu(i)mentum* for *unguentum*, UNGUENT. An unctuous preparation to apply to the body.

Old, *a.* O.E. *ald.* Common Teut. Orig. 'grown up', f. O.Teut. vbl. stem *al-*, cogn. with L. *alĕre*, to nourish. ALDERMAN. ELDER. Having lived or existed long; of (a specified) age; ancient; of an earlier period.—**Old'en**, *a.* Obs. *Old*, old age (Early M.E. *ald*, app. f. O.N. *öld*, age, conn. with O.E. *ald*) + -EN.[1] Ancient, old.—**Old-fash'ioned**, *a.* Antiquated; fond of old fashions or ways.

Oleag'inous, *a.* F. *oléagineux*—L. *oleāginus*, a. f. *olea.* OIL. Oily, greasy.

Olean'der, *n.* Med.L. *oleander*, conjectured to be a corr. of *lorandrum*, itself a corr. of RHODODENDRON. An evergreen Levantine flowering shrub called also *rose-bay*.

Olfac'tory, *a.* L. **olfactōrius*, f. *olfacĕre*, *olfactum*, to smell at, f. *olēre*, to emit a smell + *facĕre*, to make. REDOLENT. Of smell.

Ol'igarch, *n.* G. *oligarchēs*, f. *oligos*, few + *archein*, to rule. One of a few holding power. —**Oligar'ch**IC, -ICAL, *aa.*—**Ol'igarch**Y,[1] *n.* Government by a few; the ruling few.

Ol'ive, *n.* F. *olive*—L. *oliva* = G. *elaia*, olive-tree, olive. OIL. An evergreen tree; its fruit, which yields an oil; an olive-branch as an emblem of peace.—*a.* Of the colour of the fruit, a yellowish green.

Olym'piad, *n.* F. *Olympiade*—L. *Olympias*, *Olympiadis*—G. *Olumpias*, f. *Olumpios*, of Olympia. The period of four years between the celebrations of the games at Olympia, used by the ancient Greeks in computing time.

Om'elet, **Om'elette**, *n.* F. *omelette*, earlier *amelette*, app. changed f. *alemette* = *alemelle*, blade, lit. 'thin plate' (the omelet being thus named from its thin flat shape), app. f. *lamelle*, L. *lāmella*, dim. of *lāmina*, plate. A dish of eggs seasoned and fried.

O'men, *n.* L. *ōmen*, *ōminis.* ABOMINABLE. A prophetic sign or token; prognostication.—*vt.* To prognosticate, presage.—**Om'in**OUS, *a.* Of the nature of an omen; of ill omen.

Omit', *vt.* L. *omittĕre*, *omissum*, to let go, disregard, f. *o-* (= OB- (1)) + *mittĕre*, to send. MISSION. To leave out; to pass over, to neglect. —**Omis'**SION, *n.*

Om'nibus, *n.* F. *omnibus*—L. *omnibus*, 'for all', dat. pl. of *omnis*, all. A public vehicle.

Omnip'otent, *a.* F. *omnipotent*—L. *omnipotens*, *omnipotentis*, f. OMNI- + *potens*, POTENT. All-powerful.—**Omnip'ot**ENCE, *n.*

Omnipres'ent, *a.* Med. Scholastic L. *omnipraesens*, *omnipraesentis*, f. OMNI- + L. *praesens*, PRESENT. Present everywhere at the same time.—**Omnipres'**ENCE, *n.*

Omnis'cient, *a.* OMNI- + L. *sciens.* SCIENCE. All-knowing.—**Omnis'ci**ENCE, *n.*

Omniv'orous, *a.* L. *omnivorus* (f. OMNI- + *vorāre*, to DEVOUR) + -OUS. Feeding on all kinds of food (often *fig.*).

On, *prep.* O.E. *an*, *on* = O.H.G. *ana*, *an* (Ger. *an*), O.N. *á.* Cogn. with G. *ana.* Above and touching; so as to meet the surface of; at, near; expressing reliance, dependence, &c.; immediately after and as a result; in reference to; toward or so as to affect; among the staff of; denoting a state, occupation, &c.—*adv.* So as to be on; in progression; forward; continuously.—**On'**WARD, *adv.* and *a.*—**On'**WARDS, *adv.*

Once, *adv.* M.E. *ānes*, *ōnes*, genit. of *ān*, *ōn* ONE. NONCE. One time only; ever, at all, only; formerly.

One, *a.* M.E. *ān*, *ōn*, &c.—O.E. *án.* Common Teut. Cogn. with L. *ūnus.* A. ANON. ELEVEN. NONE. ONCE. The lowest cardinal number; a single; a united; the same; uniformly the same; identical; in harmony; a particular.—*n.* A single person or thing; the symbol denoting unity.—*pron.* A person; any one whatever.—**One'**NESS, *n.* The being one or the only one; unity; unchangingness, harmony.

On'erous, *a.* O.F. *onereus*—L. *onerōsus*, f. *onus*, *oneris.* EXONERATE. Burdensome.

On'ion, *n.* F. *oignon*—L. *ūnio*, *ūniōnis*, oneness, also, a kind of single onion. UNION A bulb with a pungent flavour; its plant.

Only, *a.* O.E. *ánlíc.* ONE. -LY.[1] Single, sole, one.—*adv.* M.E. *ōnliche*, f. *ōnlich* (O.E. *ánlíc*) + advbl. *-e.* Solely, merely, exclusively. —*conj.* Excepting that, but, were it not that.

Onomatopœ'ia, *n.* L. *onomatopoeïa*—G. *onomatopoiïa*, f. *onoma*, *onomatos*, NAME + *poie-ein*, to make. POEM. The formation of a word by imitation of a sound associated with an object, &c.—**Onomatopœ'**IC, *a.* Also (after *poetic*) **Onomatopoet'ic.**

On'set, *n.* ON, *adv.* + SET. An attack; a start.

On'slaught, *n.* Poss. repg. (after *draught*, &c.) Du. *aanslag*, Ger. *anschlag*, striking at, attempt. An onset, attack.

Ontol'ogy, *n.* *Onto-*, combining form of G. *ōn*, *ontos*, pres.pple. of *einai*, to be + -LOGY. The science or study of being.

On'yx, *n.* L. *onyx*—G. *onux.* A variety of quartz much used for cameos.

Ooze, *n.*[1] O.E. *wáse*, cogn. with O.N. *veisa* stagnant pool, puddle. Wet mud or slime.—**Ooz'**Y,[2] *a.*[1] Muddy; composed of or like ooze.

Ooze, *vi.* M.E. *wōsen*, f. *wōse*, O.E. *wós*, juice, sap. Cf. M.L.G. *wos(e)*, scum. Of moisture, to pass gradually through a body, to percolate; to exude moisture.—*vt.* To emit (moisture, &c.) gradually.—*n.*[2] Exudation; that which oozes.—**Ooz'**Y,[2] *a.*[2] Exuding moisture.

O'pal, *n.* L. *opalus.* Cf. G. *opallios.* A gem of changing hues.—**Opales'cent**, *a.* *-Escent*, repg. pres.pple. of L. inceptives in *-escĕre.* Showing changing hues like the opal.

Opaque', *a.* L. *opācus*, shady, darkened (the present spelling being after F. *opaque*). Not transparent.—**Opac'**ITY, *n.*

O'pen, *a.* O.E. *open.* Common Teut. App. f. root of UP. Of a door, &c., not shut; not shut up, unenclosed; without a lid, roof, &c.; bare, exposed; not folded, unfolded; unobstructed; acting without concealment; not restricted, generally available; accessible.—*n.* A clear space.—*vt.* To set open; to give access to; to unfold; to make a hole or incision in; to lay bare, disclose; to begin, set in action.—*vi.* To become open; to become disclosed; to begin.—**O'pen**LY,[2] *adv.*

Op'era, *n.* It. *opera*—L. *opera*, work, f. *opus.* (See next.) INURE. A musical dramatic performance or composition; a theatre for operas. —**Operat'**IC, *a.* (After *dramatic.*)

Op'erate, *vi.* L. *operārī*, *operātus*, to work, to have effect, f. *opus*, *operis*, work. MANŒUVRE. OPUSCULE. To act, work; to subject the body to some surgical process.—*vt.* To bring about, accomplish.—**Opera'**TION, *n.*—**Op'erat**IVE, *a.* As *n.*, an artisan or mechanic.—**Op'erat**OR, *n.*

Oph'icleide, *n.* F. *ophicléide*, f. G. *ophis*, serpent + *kleis*, *kleidos*, key. A brass wind-instrument with keys, a development of the ancient serpent.

Ophthal'mia, *n.* L.L.—G. *ophthalmia*, f. *ophthalmos*, eye, conn. with *ops*. OPTIC. Inflammation of the eye.—**Ophthal'mic**, *a.* Of, treating disorders of, the eye.

O'piate, *a.* Med.L. *opiātus*, pa.pple. of **opiāre*, to form or treat with OPIUM. Made with or containing opium; narcotic.—*n.* A narcotic.

Opine', *vi.* L. *opīnāri*. To think, suppose; to express an opinion.—**Opin'ion**, *n.* F. *opinion*—L. *opinio, opīniōnis*, f. *opīnāri*. What one thinks; a judgement or belief; an estimate of character, &c.—**Opin'ionated**, *a.* -ATE.[3] *-Ed.* Obstinate in opinion; self-willed. Sim. **Opin'ionative**.

O'pium, *n.* L. *opium*—G. *opion*, dim. of *opos*, vegetable juice. OPIATE. The solidified juice of a species of poppy.

Opos'sum, *n.* American Indian (Virginian). A small American mammal.

Oppon'ent, *a.* L. *oppōnens, oppōnentis*, pres.pple. of *oppōnĕre*. OPPOSITE. Opposing, adverse.—*n.* An adversary or antagonist.

Opportune', *a.* F. *opportun, -une*—L. *opportūnus*, f. *op-* (= OB- (1)) + *portus*, entrance, harbour. PORT, *n.*[1] Fit, suitable; seasonable, well-timed.—**Opportun'ism**, *n.* The policy of doing in politics what is expedient at the time without regard to principle.—**Opportun'ist**, *n.*—**Opportun'ity**, *n.* A favourable time or condition of things.

Oppose', *vt.* F. *opposer*, f. *op-* (= OB- (2)) + *poser*, to place. POSE.[1] To set over against; to contrast; to set as an obstacle or antagonist; to withstand, resist.—**Oppos'er**, *n.*—**Op'posite**, *a.* F. *opposite*—L. *oppositus*, pa.pple. of *oppōnĕre*, to set against, f. *op-* (= OB- (2)) + *pōnĕre*, to place. POSITION. Lying over against; contrary; diametrically different.—**Opposi'tion**, *n.* The relative position of two heavenly bodies when exactly opposite to each other; contrast; resistance; a political party opposed to that in office.

Oppress', *vt.* O.F. *oppresser*—Med.L. *oppressāre*, freq. of L. *opprimĕre, oppressum*, to press against, f. *op-* (= OB- (2)) + *premĕre*, to PRESS.[1] To weigh down; to tyrannize over.—**Oppres'sion**, *n.*—**Oppres'sive**, *a.*—**Oppres'sor**, *n.*

Oppro'brium, *n.* L., f. *opprobrāre*, to reproach, f. *op-* (= OB- (2)) + *probrum*, disgrace. Disgrace, infamy; a cause of disgrace.—**Oppro'brious**, *a.*—**Oppro'briously**,[2] *adv.*

Oppugn', *vt.* L. *oppugnāre*, to fight against, f. *op-* (= OB- (2)) + *pugnāre*, to fight. PUGNACIOUS. To oppose, call in question, controvert.—**Oppug'nant**, *a.*

Opta'tive, *a.* F. *optatif, -ive*—L.L. *optātīvus*, f. *optāre*, to wish. OPTION. Applied to a mood of a verb expressing wish.—*n.* The optative mood; a verb in this mood.

Op'tic, *a.* F. *optique*—Med.L. *opticus*—G. *optikos*, of or pertaining to sight, f. *optos*, seen, f. *op-* as in *ops*, eye, *opsomai*, I shall see. AUTOPSY. OPHTHALMIA. Pertaining to or connected with the eye or sight.—In *pl.* as *n.*, the science of sight or of light.—*n.* The eye (gen. in *pl.*).—**Op'tical**, *a.*—**Opti'cian**, *n.* A maker of or dealer in optical instruments.

Op'timism, *n.* F. *optimisme*—L. *optimus*, best. -ISM. The view that good must ultimately prevail; disposition to hope for the best.—**Op'timist**, *n.*—**Optimis'tic**, *a.*

Op'tion, *n.* F. *option*—L. *optio, optiōnis*, f. *optāre*, to choose, wish. ADOPT. OPTATIVE. Choice; something chosen; power of choice.—**Op'tional**, *a.* That is a matter of choice.

Op'ulent, *a.* L. *opulentus*, f. **ops, opis*, power, riches. Rich.—**Op'ulence**, *n.*

Opus'cule, *n.* F. *opuscule*—L. *opusculum*, dim. of *opus*. OPERATE. A small work.

Or, *n.* F. *or*—L. *aurum*, gold. AUREOLA. In *heraldry*, gold.

Or, *conj.*[1] Reduced from obs. *Other*, of doubtful orig., which took the place of O.E. *odde*, earlier *odda* = O.S. *oththo*, O.H.G. *eddo, odo* (Ger. *oder*). Indicating an alternative; often correlative to *either* or *whether*; if not.

Or, *conj.*[2] O.E. *ár*. Cf. O.N. *ár*, O.E. *ǽr*, ERE. *Or ever* (*e'er*), before.

Or'acle, *n.* F. *oracle*—L. *ōrāculum*, f. *ōrāre*, to speak, pray (f. *ōs, ōris*, mouth) with suff. of material instrument. ORATION. ORIFICE. OSCULATE. A place where divine utterances were supposed to be given; a divine response, decision or message.—**Orac'ular**,[1] *a.*

O'ral, *a.* L. *ōs, ōris* + -AL. (See prec.) By word of mouth, spoken.—**O'rally**,[2] *adv.*

Or'ange, *n.* O.F. *orange* = Sp. *naranja*—Arab. *nāranj*, Per. *nārang*. The fruit of an Eastern tree; the tree; the colour of the fruit, a reddish yellow.—*a.* Of the colour.

Orang'-outang, **Orang'-utan**, *n.* Malay *ōrang-ūtan*, 'man of the woods'. A large ape.

Ora'tion, *n.* L. *ōrātio, ōrātiōnis*, n. of action f. *ōrāre*. ORACLE. ORISON. A formal speech.—**Or'ator**, *n.*—**Orator'ical**, *a.* Pertaining to an orator or to oratory; given to oratory.—**Or'atory**, *n.*[1] L. *ōrātōrium* (sc. *templum*), place of prayer. A small chapel.—**Or'atory**,[1] *n.*[2] The art of public speaking; eloquence.

Orato'rio, *n.* It. *oratorio* (from musical services held at the oratory of St. Philip Neri in Rome)—L. *ōrātōrium*. ORATORY.[1] A semi-dramatic sacred musical composition.

Orb, *n.* L. *orbis*, ring, disk, circle. A sphere or globe; a heavenly body.—*vt.* To encircle; to make circular or globular.—**Or'bit**, *n.* L. *orbita*, wheel-track, circuit, f. *orbis*. EXORBITANT. The cavity containing the eye; the path of a heavenly body.

Or'chard, *n.* O.E. *ort-geard*. YARD.[1] *Ort* app. = L. *hortus*, GARDEN. An enclosure for the cultivation of fruit-trees.

Or'chestra, *n.* L. *orchestra*—G. *orchēstra*, the space in the theatre on which the chorus danced, f. *orche-esthai*, to dance. The part of a theatre, &c., assigned to musicians; a company of musicians.—**Orches'tral**, *a.*—**Or'chestrate**,[3] *vt.* To compose or arrange for an orchestra.—**Orchestra'tion**, *n.*

Or'chis, *n.* L. *orchis*—G. *orchis*, testicle, the plant (from the shape of the tubers). A genus of flowering plants.—**Or'chid**, *n.* Botanical suff. *-id.* Any plant of the genus.

Ordain', *vt.* O.F. *ordener*, L. *ordināre*, to set in order, f. *ordo*, ORDER. DISORDER. COORDINATE. To admit to the orders of deacon or priest; to decree, destine; to enact.—**Ordain'ment**, *n.*—**Or'dinance**, *n.* That which is ordained; a decree. command; a religious observance.—**Ordina'tion**, *n.*

Ord'eal, *n.* A mod. rep. of O.E. *ordál, ordǽl*, f. *or-*, out + *dál, dǽl*. DOLE.[1] DEAL, *n.*[1] A mode of trial by subjection to a dangerous physical test; a trying experience.

Or'der, *n.* O.F. *ordre*—L. *ordo, ordinis*, row, rank. ORDAIN. A rank, social division; a class, group; in *pl.*, the status of an ordained clergyman; a monastic society; succession of acts or events; methodical arrangement; prescribed mode of procedure; law-abiding state; state, condition; a command; a pass for admission.—*vt.* To arrange; to regulate, conduct; to command, direct; to give an order for.—**Or'der**LY,[1] *a.* Regular, methodical; well-conducted.—*n.* A non-commissioned officer or private soldier attending a superior to carry orders; a male attendant in a military hospital. — **Or'derli**NESS, *n.* — **Or'dinal**, *a.* L.L. *ordinālis.* Marking position in a series.—

Or'dinal, *n.* Med.L. *ordināle*, use as *n.* of neut. of *ordinālis.* A service-book.—**Or'din**ARY, *a.* Usual; somewhat inferior.—*n.* One holding ecclesiastical jurisdiction of his own right; a public meal at a fixed price.

Ord'nance, *n.* Syncopated var. of ORDINANCE (see under ORDAIN), which formerly denoted battle-array, a host in array. Formerly, military stores. Cannon; *ordnance survey*, the official survey of the kingdom, orig. under the direction of the Master-General of the [Board of] Ordnance, a board formerly charged with the supply of military stores.

Or'dure, *n.* F. *ordure*, f. O.F. *ord*, filthy—L. *horridus.* HORRID. Excrement, dung.

Ore, *n.* M.E. *ōr*, answering phonetically to O.E. *ár*, *ǽr*, brass (=M.Du. *eer*, O.H.G. *êr*—L. *aes, aeris*), identified in sense with O.E. *óra*, ore (corresp. to Du. *oer*, L.G. *ûr*). A native mineral from which metals are obtained.

O'read, *n.* L. *orēas*, pl. *orēades*—G. *oreias*, f. *oros*, mountain. A mountain-nymph.

Or'gan, *n.* L. *organum*—G. *organon*, an instrument, conn. with *ergon*, WORK. The largest musical wind-instrument; a member of an animal or plant body discharging a particular function; a means of action or operation; a newspaper serving as the mouthpiece of a party, &c.—**Organ'**IC, *a.* Of a disease, involving alteration in the structure of an organ; having an organized physical structure; forming a constituent of animals and plants; organized, systematic.—**Organ'ically**, *adv.* -ICAL. -LY.[2]—**Or'gan**ISM, *n.* An organized system or body. — **Or'gan**IST, *n.* One who plays an organ.—**Or'gan**IZE, *vt.* To furnish with organs; to give a definite structure to; to get up, put into working order.—**Organ-iz**A'TION, *n.*—**Or'ganiz**ER, *n.*

Or'gasm, *n.* G. type **orgasmos*, f. *orga-ein*, to swell with moisture, to be excited. Immoderate excitement; a paroxysm.

Or'gy, *n.* Chiefly in *pl.* **Or'gies**. F. *orgies*, pl.—L. *orgia*, G. *orgia*, pl., secret rites, a nocturnal Bacchic festival. Secret rites or observances; wild or dissolute revels.

O'riel, *n.* O.F. *oriol*, porch, corridor, of unknown orig. A large recess with a window; the window.

O'rient, *n.* F. *orient*—L. *oriens, orientis*, orig. pres.pple. of *orīri*, to arise. ABORT. ORIGIN. The quarter of the rising sun; eastern countries, the East; a brilliant pearl.—*a.* Eastern; brilliant; of the sun, rising.—**Orient'**, *vt.* To place so as to face the east; to place or adjust.—**Orient**A'TION, *n.*—**Orient'**AL, *a.* Of, in, characteristic of, the East.—*n.* A native of the East.—**Orient'al**IST, *n.* One versed in Eastern languages.

Or'ifice, *n.* F. *orifice*—L.L. *ōrificium*, f. *ōs, ōris*, mouth + *facĕre*, to make. ORACLE. FACT. An opening or aperture.

Or'igin, *n.* App. f. F. *origine*—L. *origo, originis*, f. *orīri*, to arise. ORIENT. ABORIGINAL. Beginning, rise, source; descent, parentage.—**Orig'in**AL. *a.* That has always belonged to a person or thing, primary, innate; of a thing in relation to a copy or reproduction; not derivative or dependent; novel fresh; inventive, creative.—*n.* A writing in relation to a copy or translation; a picture in relation to a reproduction; a singular or eccentric person.—**Original'**ITY, *n.*—**Orig'inal**LY,[2] *adv.*—**Orig'in**ATE,[3] *vt.* To bring into existence.—*vi.* To come into existence.—**Origin**A'TION, *n.*—**Orig'inat**OR, *n.*

Or'ison, *n.* O.F. *oreison*, *orison* (F. *oraison*)—L. *ōrātio.* ORATION. A prayer.

Or'molu, *n.* F. *or moulu*, lit. 'ground gold'. A gold-like alloy of copper, zinc, and tin.

Or'nament, *n.* O.F. *ornement*—L. *ornāmentum*, equipment, embellishment, f. *ornāre*, to equip, embellish. ADORN. SUBORN. A decoration, embellishment; decoration.—*vt.* To adorn, embellish.—**Ornamen't**AL, *a.*—**Ornament**A'TION, *n.*—**Ornate'**, *a.* L. *ornātus*, pa.pple. of *ornāre.* Highly embellished.

Ornithol'ogy, *n.* G. *ornis, ornithos*, bird + -LOGY. The science of birds.—**Ornitholo-g'**ICAL, *a.*—**Ornithol'og**IST, *n.*

Orog'raphy, *n.* G. *oros*, mountain+*-graphia*, writing, f. *graphein*, to write. OREAD. GRAPHIC. The science of mountains.—**Oro-graph'**IC, **Orograph'**ICAL, *aa.*

Or'phan, *n.* L.L. *orphanus*—G. *orphanos*, orphaned. A child bereaved of a parent or parents.—*a.* That is an orphan.—*vt.* To make orphan.—**Or'phan**AGE, *n.* The being an orphan; an institution for orphans.

Or'piment, *n.* F. *orpiment*—L. *auripigmentum*, 'gold pigment', f. *aurum*, gold + *pigmentum*, PIGMENT. Yellow arsenic.

Or'rery, *n.* After Charles Boyle, Earl of *Orrery*, who had a machine of the sort constructed. A mechanism representing the motions of the solar system.

Or'ris, *n.* App. a corr. of IRIS. A plant of the genus *Iris*, the fleur-de-lis.

Or'thodox, *a.* G. *orthodoxos*, right in opinion, f. *orthos*, right + *doxa*, opinion. HETERODOX. In accordance with general opinion; holding such views.—**Or'thodox**Y,[1] *n.*

Or'thoepy, *n.* G. *orthoepeia*, correctness of diction, f. *orthos*, right + *epos*, word. EPIC. The art of correct pronunciation.

Orthog'raphy, *n.* O.F. *ortographie*—L. *orthographia*—G. *orthographia*, f. *orthos*, right + *graphein*, to write. Correct spelling.

Or'tolan, *n.* F. *ortolan*—It. *ortolano*, gardener, ortolan (lit. 'garden-bird')—L. *hortulānus*, gardener, f. *hortulus*, dim. of *hortus*, GARDEN. A small bird of delicate flavour.

Os'cillate, *vi.* L. *oscillāre, oscillātum.* To swing to and fro.—**Oscill**A'TION, *n.*

Os'culate, *vt.* and *i.* L. *osculāri, osculātus*, f. *osculum*, little mouth, kiss, dim. of *ōs.* ORACLE. To kiss.—**Oscul**A'TION, *n.*

O'sier, *n.* F. *osier*, app. conn. with 9th c. L. *ausāria. osāria*, willow-bed. A species of willow; one of its pliant shoots.

Os'prey, *n.* App. repg. L. *ossifraga*, lit. 'bone-breaker', f. *os* (see next) + *frag-*, base of *frangĕre.* FRACTION. A fish-eating bird.

Os'seous, *a.* L. *osseus* (f. *os, ossis*, bone, conn. with G. *osteon*) + -OUS. OSTEOLOGY. Of or like bone.—**Os'si**FY, *vi.* and *t.* To change into bone.—**Ossi**FICA'TION, *n.*

Osten'sible, *a.* F. *ostensible*—L. type **ostensibilis*, f. *ostendĕre, ostensum*, to stretch before one, show, f. *os-* (for **ops-* = OB- (1)) + *tendĕre*, to stretch. TEND.[2] Merely professed, pretended.—**Osten'sib**LY,[2] *adv.*—**Ostenta'-**

tion, *n.* F. *ostentation*—L. *ostentātio, ostentātiōnis*, n. of action f. *ostentāre*, freq. of *ostendĕre*. Pretentious display.—**Ostenta'**TIOUS, *a.*—**Ostenta'tious**LY,² *adv.*

Osteol'ogy, *n.* G. *osteon*, bone + -LOGY. OSSEOUS. The science of bones.

Ost'ler, *n.* See HOSTLER under HOSPITABLE.

Os'tracize, *vt.* G. *ostrakizein*, to banish temporarily by voting with potsherds, f. *ostrakon*, earthen vessel, potsherd. To exclude from society, privileges, &c.—**Os'trac**ISM, *n.*

Os'trich, *n.* O.F. *ostruce, ostruche* (F. *autruche*)—Pop.L. *avistrūthio*, f. L. *avis*, bird + L.L. *strūthio*, G. *strouthiōn*, ostrich, f. *strouthos*, sparrow, also, the large bird, *i.e.*, the ostrich. AUSPICE. The largest of birds.

Oth'er, *a.* O.E. *óther*, other, second. Common Teut. Cogn. with Skr. *ántara-s*. The remaining (person, thing, &c.) of two; not this, not the same, further, additional.—*pron.* The remaining of two.—**Oth'er**WISE, *adv.* Differently; if not, else; in other respects.

O'tiose, *a.* L. *ōtiōsus*, f. *ōtium*, leisure. At leisure; lazy; nugatory, futile, superfluous.

Ot'ter, *n.* O.E. *otor*. Common Teut. WATER. An aquatic carnivorous mammal.

Ot'toman, *n.* From *Ottoman*, Turkish (of the dominions of the Sultan), f. *Othman*, the founder of the present Turkish dynasty. A cushioned seat without back or arms.

Ought, *n., adv.* Var. of AUGHT.

Ought, *v.aux.* O.E. *áhte*, pa.t. of *ágan*. OWE. Expressing duty or obligation, or what is befitting, advisable, to be expected, &c.

Ounce, *n.*¹ O.F. *unce* (F. *once*)—L. *uncia*. INCH. The twelfth of a pound Troy; the sixteenth of a pound avoirdupois.

Ounce, *n.*² O.F. *once*, said to have arisen f. treating as the definite article (*l'*) the *l* of earlier *lonce* = It. *lonza*, ultimately f. L. *lynx*, LYNX. An Asiatic feline beast (orig. the lynx).

Our, *pron.* O.E. *úre*, genit. of *wé*, WE. Belonging to us.

Oust, *vt.* A.F. *ouster* = O.F. *oster* (F. *ôter*), to remove. Orig. uncertain. To eject, expel.

Out, *adv.* O.E. *út*. Common Teut. ABOUT. BUT. UTMOST. UTTER. Expressing motion or direction from within, from among others, &c.; away, to a distance; not in or within; not in place; no longer concealed; extinguished; not in employment or office; into extinction; to an end or to completion, to exhaustion; loudly, plainly; in error; at a loss; introduced into society.—**Out'ing**, *vbl.n.* A pleasure excursion.—**Out'**WARD, *adv.* and *a.*—**Out'**WARDS, *adv.*—**Out'ward**LY,² *adv.*

Outbid', *vt.* OUT-. To bid more than.

Out'break, *n.* OUT-. A breaking out, a sudden manifestation of passion, disease, &c.

Out'cast, *ppl.a.* OUT-. Cast out, homeless. —*n.* A homeless person.

Out'come, *n.* OUT-. Result, effect.

Out'cry, *n.* OUT-. An excited exclamation or shout; loud clamour.

Outdo', *vt.* OUT-. To excel, surpass.

Out'-door, Out'door, *a.* OUT-. Done, existing, used, out of doors; relieved or administered apart from residence in a workhouse, &c. —**Outdoors'**, *adv.* Out of doors.

Out'er, *a.* Comp. of OUT. Further out than another; on the outside, external.

Out'fall, *n.* OUT-. The mouth of a river, &c.

Out'fit, *n.* OUT-. A fitting out; equipment. —**Out'fitt**ER, *n.*

Outflank', *vt.* OUT-. To get beyond the flank [of.

Out'house, *n.* OUT-. A subsidiary building.

Out'land, *n.* OUT-. A foreign land.—*a.* Foreign.—**Outland'**ISH, *a.* Foreign; foreign-looking, odd; out-of-the-way, remote.

Out'law, *n.* Late O.E. *útlaga*—O.N. *útlagi*, f. *útlagr*, outlawed, f. *út*, OUT + **lagu*. LAW. One put outside the protection of the law; an exile.—*vt.* To declare an outlaw.—**Out'law**RY, *n.* The condition of an outlaw; the action or legal process of outlawing.

Out'lay, *n.* OUT-. A laying out, expenditure.

Out'let, *n.* OUT-. An opening at which anything is let out; a letting out, discharge.

Out'line, *n.* OUT-. In *pl.*, the lines bounding a figure, main features, general principles; in *sing.*, the contour of a figure, a sketch without shading, a general description.—*vt.* To draw the outlines of; to describe generally.

Outlive', *vt.* OUT-. To survive.

Outnum'ber, *vt.* OUT-. To exceed in num- [ber.

Out'post, *n.* OUT-. A post at a distance from an army; a detachment occupying it.

Out'put, *n.* OUT-. Quantity produced.

Out'rage, *n.* O.F. *ultrage*, outrage, &c.—Romanic type **ultragium*, f. L. *ultrā*, beyond. Violent injury or harm; a deed of violence; an indignity.—*vt.* To insult, to violate.—**Outra'geo**US, *a.* Excessive; violent, furious; grossly offensive or abusive.

Out'rider, *n.* OUT-. A mounted servant.

Out'rigger, *n.* OUT, *adv.* + RIG + -ER. A boom or framework outside a ship's gunwale; a bracket at the side of a rowing boat bearing a rowlock at the outer edge; a rowing boat fitted with outriggers.

Out'right, *adv.* OUT, *adv.* Altogether, en- [tirely.

Outri'val, *vt.* OUT-. To outdo, excel.

Outrun', *vt.* OUT-. To run faster or further than; to run or go beyond.

Out'set, *n.* OUT-. Start, beginning.

Out'side, *n.* OUT-. The outer side, surface or part; the position close to the outer side, &c.—*a.* On, in, belonging to, the outside.—*adv.* In or into the outside.—*prep.* On or in the outside of.—**Outsid'**ER, *n.* One not belonging to a set, party, &c.

Out'skirts, *n.pl.* OUT-. The outer border.

Outspo'ken, *ppl.a.* From *speak out*, the pa.pple. having a resultant force. Cf. '*well read*'. Direct in speech, candid, frank.

Outstand'ing, *ppl.a.* OUT-. Projecting; conspicuous, eminent; remaining unsettled.

Outstrip', *vt.* OUT- + STRIP, in obs. sense to run swiftly, speed. To outrun; to surpass.

Outwit', *vt.* OUT-. To be too clever for.

Out'work, *n.* OUT-. An outer defence.

O'val, *a.* Prob. f. Mod.L. *ōvālis*, f. L. *ōvum*, egg. Egg-shaped, elliptical.—*n.* An oval figure. —**O'vary**, *n.* Mod.L. *ōvārium*. The female organ in which ova or eggs are produced.

Ova'tion, *n.* L. *ovātio, ovātiōnis*, a lesser triumph, lit. 'rejoicing', f. *ovāre*, to rejoice. A burst of enthusiastic applause.

Ov'en, *n.* O.E. *ofn, ofen*. Common Teut. Cf. Skr. *ukhá-s*, cooking pot, G. *ipnos*, furnace, oven. A chamber for baking or cooking.

O'ver, *adv.* O.E. *ofer*, adv. and prep. Common Teut. Cogn. with Skr. *upari*, G. *huper*, L. *super*. Comp. formation f. Teut. *ufa-, uf-*, whence *ufan* in ABOVE. EAVES. Above; passing above and beyond, going beyond, exaggeration; over the edge; from the erect position; turning an upper surface forward and down; from side to side, traversing space; from one side to another; on the other side; remaining, left; in excess or addition; excessively; from beginning to end; expressing repetition; past, gone by, at an end.—*prep.* Above; expressing purpose, occupation, consideration, &c.; on, upon; throughout; above in authority, &c.; in preference to, more than; in excess of; across; from side to side of, to the other side of, along; on the other side of; during.—*a.* The upper; upper, outer.

Overawe′, *vt.* OVER- (4). To intimidate.

Overbal′ance, *vt.* OVER- (1) and (3). To do more than balance; to destroy the equilibrium of.—*vi.* To lose one's balance.

Overbear′, *vt.* OVER- (1). To overthrow; to overcome, overpower; to surpass in weight, &c.—**Overbear′ing**, *ppl.a.* Domineering.

O′verboard, *adv.* OVER, *prep.* Over or beyond a ship's side.

Overbur′den, *vt.* OVER- (2). To burden to [excess.

Overcome′, *vt.* O.E. *ofercuman*, f. *ofer*, OVER + *cuman*, to COME. To get the better of, overpower; to surmount, recover from.

Overdo′, *vt.* OVER- (2). To exaggerate; to cook too much; to fatigue, exhaust.

Overdraw′, *vt.* OVER- (2). To draw in excess of what is at one's credit; to exaggerate.

O′verdue, *a.* OVER- (3). More than due.

Overflow′, *vt.* O.E. *oferflówan*, f. *ofer*, OVER + *flówan*, to FLOW. To flow over; to flood.—*vi.* To flow over; to be too full.—**O′verflow**, *n.* Overflowing; superabundance.

Overgrow′, *vt.* OVER- (1). To grow over; to choke by overgrowing.—*vi.* OVER- (5). To grow too large.

Overhaul′, *vt.* OVER- (1). To examine thoroughly, esp. in order to repair; to overtake (for the sense cf. OVERTAKE).—**O′verhaul**, *n.* A thorough examination, esp. for repair.

Overhear′, *vt.* OVER- (app. with sense 'over or beyond the intended reach of the voice'). To hear what is not intended to be heard.

Overlap′, *vt.* OVER- (1) + LAP, *v.*[1] To extend over and cover part of; to coincide partly with; to cover and extend beyond.

Overlook′, *vt.* OVER- (1). To look over the top of; to look over and beyond and so fail to see, to take no notice of; to look down upon; to afford a view of; to superintend.

O′verlord, *n.* OVER- (6). A supreme lord.

Overmas′ter, *vt.* OVER- (4). To master completely, overcome, overpower.

Overmatch′, *vt.* OVER- (3). To do more than match, excel.—**O′vermatch**, *n.* A person or thing more than a match for another.

Overpow′er, *vt.* OVER- (7). To subdue; to make ineffective or imperceptible by greater intensity; to overwhelm.

Overreach′, *v.refl.* OVER- (5). To strain oneself by reaching too far.—*vt.* OVER- (7). To circumvent, outwit.

Override′, *vt.* O.E. *oferrídan*, f. *ofer*, OVER + *rídan*, to RIDE. To ride over or across; to set at nought, set aside.

Overrule′, *vt.* OVER- (4). To control, modify or set aside by higher authority; to reject (a plea, &c.); to prevail over (a person).

Oversee′, *vt.* O.E. *ofersēon*, f. *ofer*, OVER + *sēon*, to SEE. To look down upon, overlook; to superintend.—**O′verseER**, *n.*

Overshad′ow, *vt.* OVER- (1). To cast a shadow over; to shelter; to cast into the shade.

O′vershot, *a.* OVER- (1). Driven by water shot over from above.

O′versight, *n.* OVER- (1). Superintendence; failure, a failure, to see or notice.

Overstep′, *vt.* O.E. *ofersteppan*, f. *ofer*, OVER + *steppan*, to STEP. To step or pass over or beyond.

Overt′, *a.* O.F. *overt*, pa.pple. of *ovrir* (F. *ouvrir*), to open, of disputed orig. OVERTURE. Open, unconcealed.—**Overt′LY**,[2] *adv.*

Overtake′, *vt.* Perh. f. OVER- (1) with sense 'to take by getting *over* the intervening space'. To come up with in pursuit; to work off, get through.

Overtask′, *vt.* OVER- (2). To task too heavily.

Overthrow′, *vt.* OVER- (1). To upset, to knock down; to defeat, ruin, bring to nought.—**O′verthrow**, *n.* Defeat, ruin.

O′vertime, *n.* OVER- (1). Time worked beyond the usual hours.

Overtop′, *vt.* OVER- (1). To rise over the top of, tower above; to excel, surpass.

O′verture, *n.* O.F. *overture*, f. *overt*. OVERT. An opening of negotiations, a proposal; the introduction to an opera, &c.

Overturn′, *vt.* OVER- (1). To overthrow, upset; to subvert, destroy.—*vi.* To capsize.

Overwee′ning, *ppl.a.* OVER- (2). Thinking too much of oneself, arrogant; excessive.

Overwhelm′, *vt.* OVER- (1). To submerge completely, to bring to ruin; to overcome completely in mind or feeling; to 'deluge' with.

O′vine, *a.* L. *ovīnus*, f. *ovis*, sheep. Of, pertaining to, of the nature of, sheep.

Ovip′arous, *a.* L. *ōviparus* (f. *ōvum*, egg + *parĕre*, to bring forth) + -OUS. OVAL. Producing young by means of eggs expelled from the body and subsequently hatched.

O′vum, *n.*; *pl.* **O′va**. L. *ōvum*. OVAL. The female reproductive cell which when fertilized may become a new individual.

Owe, *vt.* O.E. *ágan*, to possess. Common Teut. OUGHT. OWN, *a.* To be under obligation to repay, pay or render; to be indebted for.—**Ow′ing**, *ppl.a.* Owed, due; *owing to*, caused by, in consequence of.

Owl, *n.* O.E. *úle*. Common Teut. Pointing to an O.Teut. imitative root *uwwā*. Cf. L. *ulula*. A nocturnal bird of prey.—**Owl′et**, *n.* Dim. suff. *-et*. A young owl; an owl.

Own, *a.* O.E. *ǽgen*, *ágen*, orig. pa.pple. of *ágan*, to possess. OWE. OWN, *v.* Emphasizing a possessive case or adjective; that which is (one's) own.

Own, *vt.* O.E. *ágnian*, f. *ágen*, OWN, *a.* To have as one's own, possess; to acknowledge, admit.—*vi.* To confess *to*.—**Own′ER**, *n.*—**Own′erSHIP**, *n.*

Ox, *n.*; *pl.* **Ox′en**. O.E. *oxa*. Common Teut. The domestic bovine quadruped; the male castrated or reared for food.—**Ox′-eye**, *n.* The corn marigold; a large kind of daisy.—**Ox′lip**, *n.* O.E. *oxan-slyppe*, f. *oxan*, genit. sing. of *oxa* + *slyppe* as in COWSLIP. A hybrid between the cowslip and the primrose.

Oxal′ic, *a.* F. *oxalique*—L. *oxalis* = G. *oxalis*, wood sorrel, f. *oxus*, sour. Of, derived from, wood sorrel; *oxalic acid*, a highly poisonous acid occurring in wood sorrel and other plants.

Ox′ide, *n.* F. *oxide* (now *oxyde*), f. *oxy-gène*, OXYGEN + *-ide* after *acide*, acid. A compound of oxygen.—**Ox′idIZE**, *vt.* To convert into an oxide; to coat with oxide; to make rusty.—*vi.* To combine with oxygen; to rust.

Ox′ygen, *n.* F. *oxygène*, intended to mean 'acidifying (principle)' (oxygen having been held to be the essential principle of acids), f. G. *oxus*, sharp, sour + *-gen* as in HYDROGEN. A non-metallic element, a colourless gas.

Oxymo′ron, *n.* G. *oxumōron*, neut. of *oxumōros*, 'sharply foolish', f. *oxus*, sharp + *mōros*, foolish. A witty saying gaining its point from being in terms absurd or paradoxical; a contradiction in terms.

Ox'ytone, *a.* G. *oxutonos*, having the acute accent, from *oxus*, sharp + *tonos*, TONE. In *Greek grammar*, having the acute accent on the last syllable.—PAR*oxytone* and PRO*paroxytone* words have this accent on the penultimate and the antepenultimate respectively.

Oy'er. A.F. *oyer* = O.F. *oir*, *oyr*, L. *audīre*, to hear. AUDIBLE. Short for *oyer and terminer* (L. *termināre*, to TERMINATE), 'hearing and determining', a criminal trial under the writ so called directed to judges on circuit.

Oyez', **Oyes'**, *int.* O.F. *oiez*, *oyez*, imp.pl. of *oir*. (See prec.) A call by a public crier or court officer to command silence and attention.

Oy'ster, *n.* O.F. *oistre*, *uistre*, *huistre* (F. *huître*)—L. *ostrea*, *ostreum*—G. *ostreon*. A bivalve mollusc esteemed as a delicacy.

Ozone', *n.* F. *ozone*, f. G. *ozein*, to smell + chem. suff. *-one*. An altered condition of oxygen with a pungent and refreshing odour.

P

Pace, *n.* O.F. *pas*—L. *passus*, f. *pandĕre*, *passum*, to stretch. EXPAND. COMPASS. PASS. A step; the length of a step; gait; an amble; rate of stepping; speed.—*vi.* To step; to amble. —*vt.* To traverse with, to measure by, steps; to set the pace for.—**Pac'**ER, *n.*

Pachyder'matous, *a.* G. *pachus*, thick + *derma* (DERM) + -OUS. Thick-skinned.

Pacif'ic, *a.* L. *pācificus*, f. *pax*, *pācis*, PEACE + *-ficus*. -FIC. Tending to peace; peaceable; tranquil.—**Pac'i**FY, *vt.* To calm; to establish peace in.—**Paci**FICA'TION, *n.*

Pack, *n.* M.E. *packe*, *pakke*, corresp. to M.Du., M.L.G. *pak*, late M.H.G., Ger. *pack*. Orig. unknown. A bundle; a set of persons, a gang; a collection or lot of things; a company of hounds, also of wolves, &c.; a set of playing-cards; a large area of floating ice.—*v.*[1]*t.* To make into a bundle, to put together in a box, &c.; to crowd together; to fill (a box, &c.) with things packed in; to order off summarily.—*vi.* To take oneself off.—**Pack'**AGE, *n.* A bundle of things packed up; a case for packing. —**Pack'**ER, *n.*—**Pack'et**, *n.* Dim. suff. *-et*. A small package or parcel; a mail-boat (in full **Pack'et-boat**).—**Pack'-horse**, *n.* A horse that carries packs of goods.—**Pack'-saddle**, *n.* A saddle suited to a pack-horse.

Pack, *v.*[2]*t.* App. in some way conn. with next. Formerly, to plot. To make up (a jury, &c.) so as to secure a partial decision.

Pact, *n.* O.F. *pact*—L. *pactum*, use as *n.* of neut. pa.pple. of *pacisci*, to agree. COMPACT, *n.* A covenant or compact.

Pad, *n.*[1] Du. or L.G. *pad* = O.H.G. *pfad*, cogn. with PATH. FOOTPAD. A path; an easy-paced horse.—*v.*[1]*i.* To travel on foot.

Pad, *n.*[2] Orig. obscure. A stuffed saddle; a cushion; sheets of paper forming a block.—*v.*[2]*t.* To furnish with padding.—**Pad'ding**, *vbl.n.* The action of the *v.*; material for stuffing.

Pad'dle, *n.* Orig. obscure. A short oar with a broad blade; one of the boards of a paddle-wheel.—*v.*[1]*i.* To move by means of paddles; to row gently.—*vt.* To propel by means of paddles.—**Pad'dle-wheel**, *n.* A wheel fitted with boards on the circumference for propelling a steamship.—**Pad'dle-box**, *n.* The casing over the upper part of this.

Pad'dle, *v.*[2]*i.* Orig. obscure. To dabble with the feet in shallow water; to toddle.

Pad'dock, *n.* App. alteration of dial. *Parrock*—O.E. *pearroc*, *pearruc*, fence, enclosed space, corresp. to O.H.G. *pfarrih* in sim. sense, M.Du. *perc*, *parc*, pen. Cf. O.F. *parc*, PARK. A small field; an enclosure.

Pad'lock, *n.* Orig. of *pad* doubtful. A detachable lock.—*vt.* To secure with a padlock.

Pæ'an, *n.* L. *paean*—G. *paian*, a chant, orig. one to Apollo as *Paian*, the healer. PEONY. A song or shout of triumph, joy, &c.

Pa'gan, *n.* L. *pāgānus*, villager, in Eccles.L., pagan, f. *pāgus*, district, the country. PAYNIM. PEASANT. A heathen.—*a.* Heathen; heathenish.—**Pa'gan**ISM, *n.*

Page, *n.*[1] O.F. *page* = It. *paggio*, Med.L. *pagius*. Orig. doubtful. A boy servant.

Page, *n.*[2] F. *page*—L. *pāgina*, f. stem *pag-* of *pangĕre*, to fasten, fix together. COMPACT, *ppl.a.* One side of a leaf of a book, &c.—*vt.* To paginate.—**Pag'in**ATE,[3] *vt.* To number the pages of.—**Pagin**A'TION, *n.*

Pag'eant, *n.* M.E. *pagyn*, *padgin* (with *t* added). Orig. obscure. A brilliant spectacle. —**Pag'eant**RY, *n.* Splendid display.

Pago'da, *n.* Pg. *pagode*, app. a corr. of an Indian word. An Eastern temple.

Pail, *n.* Orig. uncertain. Cf. O.E. *pægel*, wine-measure; also O.F. *paelle*, *paielle*, &c., frying-pan, brazier, &c., f. L. *patella*, dim. of *patina*, pan. A vessel for carrying liquids.

Paillasse', **Pal'liasse**, *n.* F. *paillasse*, f. *paille*, L. *palea*, straw. A straw mattress.

Pain, *n.* O.F. *peine*—L. *poena*, penalty, pain IMPUNITY. PENAL. PINE.[1] PUNISH. Penalty, suffering, distress; in *pl.*, trouble taken.—*vt.* To inflict pain upon.—**Pain'**FUL, *a.*—**Pain'**LESS, *a.*—**Pains'taking**, *a.* Assiduous.

Paint, *vt.* O.F. *peindre* (pa.pple. *peint*)—L. *pingĕre*. DEPICT. PICTURE. To delineate in colours; to adorn with a painting; to cover with paint, colour.—*n.* Colouring matter.—**Paint'**ER, *n.*[1]—**Paint'ing**, *vbl.n.* The action of the *v.*; something painted, a picture.

Paint'er, *n.*[2] Orig. uncertain. A rope for fastening the bow of a boat to a ship, &c.

Pair, *n.* F. *paire*—L. *paria*, neut. pl. of *pār*, equal, taken as fem. sing. COMPARE. COMPEER. A set of two; two voters on opposite sides who agree not to vote.—*vt.* To join in a pair or pairs.—*vi.* To come together in a pair or pairs; of two voters, to agree as above.

Pal'ace, *n.* O.F. *palais*—L. *palātium*, the imperial palace on the hill at Rome called the *Palātium*, a palace. The official residence of an emperor, king, bishop, &c.—**Pala'ti**AL, *a.*

Pal'adin, *n.* F. *paladin*—It. *paladino*—L. *palātīnus*, PALATINE, f. *palātium*. (See prec.) One of Charlemagne's peers; a knightly hero.

Palæog'raphy, *n.* G. *palaios*, old + *graphein*, to write. The study of ancient writing.

Palæolith'ic, *a.* G. *palaios*, old + *lithos*, stone + -IC. Of the early stone age.

Palæontol'ogy, *n.* G. *palaios*, old + ONTOLOGY. The study of extinct organized beings.

Palanquin', **Palankeen'**, *n.* Pg. *palanquin*, of Indian orig. Cf. Pali *pallanko*. A covered litter or conveyance used in India, &c.

Pal'ate, *n.* L. *palātum*. The roof of the mouth; the sense of taste.—**Pal'at**ABLE, *a.* Agreeable to the palate.—**Pal'at**AL, *a.* Of the palate; produced by placing the tongue against the palate.—*n.* A palatal sound.

Pal'atine, *a.* F. *palatin*, *-ine*—L. *palātīnus*. PALADIN. Of a palace; having royal privileges; *Count Palatine*, one having sovereign jurisdiction; *County Palatine* (also **Palat'i**NATE[1]), his territory.

Pala'ver, *n.* Pg. *palavra*, word, speech—L. *parabola.* PARABLE. A parley or conference; idle talk; talk meant to cajole.—*vi.* To talk idly or flatteringly.—*vt.* To cajole.

Pale, *n.* F. *pal*—L. *pālus.* IMPALE. PALISADE. PEEL, *n.*[1] POLE.[1] TRAVAIL. A stake; a limit or boundary; a particular territory or district.—**Pal'ing**, *vbl.n.* A fence (gen. in *pl.*).

Pale, *a.* O.F. *pale*—L. *pallidus*, f. *pallēre*, to be pale. APPAL. FALLOW, *a.*[2] PALLID. Of a whitish appearance, wan; faintly coloured; dim.—*vi.* and *t.* To grow, to make, pale.

Pal'etot, *n.* F. Orig. uncertain. A loose coat.

Pal'ette, *n.* F., dim. of *pale*, shovel, oar-blade—L. *pāla*, spade. A painter's colour-board.

Pal'frey, *n.* O.F. *palefreid*, *palefrei*—L.L. *palafrēdus*, *parafrēdus*, *paraverēdus*, f. PARA-, beside, extra + *verēdus*, light horse, said to be of Celtic orig. A small saddle-horse.

Pal'impsest, *n.* L. *palimpsēstus*—G. *palimpsēstos*, scraped again, in neut., palimpsest, f. *palin*, again + *psēstos*, vbl.a. f. *psa-ein*, to rub smooth. A manuscript containing a later writing written over an effaced earlier.

Pal'inode, *n.* L. *palinōdia*—G. *palinōidia*, a singing over again, a palinode (orig. applied to an ode of Stesichorus recanting an attack), f. *palin*, again + *ōidē.* ODE. A recantation.

Palisade', *n.* F. *palissade*, f. *palisser*, to enclose with pales, f. *palis* = *pal*, PALE, *n.* A fence of stakes for enclosure or defence.

Pall, *n.* O.E. *pæll*, costly robe—L. *pallium*, covering, Greek cloak. PALLIATE. An altar-cloth; a cloth spread over a coffin.

Pall, *vi.* App. aphetic f. APPAL, formerly used in this sense. To become insipid.—*vt.* To satiate, cloy.

Palla'dium, *n.* L. *palladium*—G. *palladion*, an image of Pallas on which the safety of Troy was supposed to depend. A safe-guard.

Pal'let, *n.* M.E. *paillet.* Cf. dial. F. *paillet*, heap of straw, f. *paille.* PAILLASSE. A straw bed, a mean bed.

Pal'liate, *vt.* From obs. *Palliate*, cloaked—L. *palliātus*, f. *pallium.* PALL, *n.* To relieve temporarily; to extenuate, excuse.—**Pallia'**TION, *n.*—**Pal'liat**IVE, *a.* Serving to palliate.—*n.* Something that palliates.

Pal'lid, *a.* L. *pallidus.* PALE, *a.* Pale.—**Pal'lor**, *n.* L. *pallor.* Paleness.

Palm, *n.*[1] O.E. *palm* = O.H.G. *palma*, O.N. *pálmr*—L. *palma.* (See next.) A tropical tree; a leaf of the tree as a symbol of victory, &c.—**Pal'm**ARY, *a.* Worthy to bear the palm, pre-eminent.—**Palm'er**, *n.* A.F. *palmer*—Med.L. *palmārius.* A pilgrim bearing a palm-leaf as having been to the Holy Land; an itinerant monk vowed to poverty.—**Palm Sun'day**, *n.* The Sunday before Easter, so called from observance by processions bearing palm-leaves. — **Palm'**Y,[2] *a.* Abounding in palms, palm-like; flourishing.

Palm, *n.*[2] M.E. *paume*—F. *paume*—L. *palma*, palm of the hand, palm-tree. (See prec.) FEEL. The flat of the hand.—*vt.* To conceal in the palm; to pass *off* by trickery.—**Palm'istry**, *n. Paume* + an obscure element. Divination from the palm.—**Palm'**IST, *n.* Back-formation f. *palmistry.* One who practises palmistry.

Pal'pable, *a.* L.L. *palpābilis*, f. L. *palpāre*, to stroke, touch softly. That may be touched or felt; easily perceptible.—**Pal'pab**LY,[2] *adv.*

Pal'pitate, *vi.* L. *palpitāre*, *palpitātum*, freq. of *palpāre.* (See prec.) To throb; to tremble, quiver.—**Palpita'**TION, *n.*

Pal'sy, *n.* M.E. *parlesie*, *palesie*, &c.—O.F. *paralysie*—L. *paralysis*—G. *paralusis*, f. *paraluein*, to loose from beside, disable, f. PARA- + *luein*, to loose. Paralysis.

Pal'ter, *vi.* Orig. unknown. To deal evasively; to shuffle; to play fast and loose.

Pal'try, *a.* Perh. attrib. use of dial. *Paltry*, rubbish, trash, app. a deriv. in -RY of a n. *palt*, exemplified in Northamptonshire *palt* in same sense, perh. identical with Fris. *palt*, rag, M.Du. *palt*, fragment. Worthless, petty.

Pam'pa, *n.* Sp.—Peruvian *bamba*, plain. A treeless plain in southern S. America.

Pam'per, *vt.* Corresp. to W. Flemish *pamperen*, and to dial. Ger. *pampen*, to cram (of which it is in form a freq.). To over-indulge.

Pamph'let, *n.* App. a generalized use of *Pamphilet* or *Panflet*, familiar name of the 12th-c. poem or comedy *Pamphilus, seu de Amore.* A small treatise, stitched but not bound.—**Pamphlet**EER', *n.*

Pan, *n.* O.E. *panne* = O.H.G. *pfanna* (Ger. *pfanne*). A broad shallow vessel.—**Pan'cake**, *n.* A thin cake of fried batter.—**Pan'tile**, *n.* A curved roofing tile; a paving tile.

Panace'a, *n.* L. *panacēa*—G. *panakeia*, f. *panakēs*, all-healing, f. *pan*, neut. of *pas* all + *ake-esthai*, to heal. A universal remedy.

Pan'creas, *n.* G. *pagkreas*, *pagkreatos*, f. *pan*, neut. of *pas*, all + *kreas*, flesh (app. from its softness). A gland near the stomach.—**Pancreat'**IC, *a.*

Pandemo'nium, *n.* G. *pan*, neut. of *pas*, all + *daimōn*, divinity, DEMON. Hell.

Pan'der, *n.* L. *Pandarus*, G. *Pandaros*, fabled by Boccaccio to have procured for Troilus the love of Chryseis. A pimp or procurer.—*vi.* To play the pander.

Pane, *n.* F. *pan*, skirt, pane, &c.—L. *pannus*, a cloth. COUNTERPANE. PANEL. The piece of glass in a compartment of a window.

Panegyr'ic, *n.* F. *panégyrique*—L. *panēgyricus*—G. *panēgurikos*, fit for a public assembly, f. *panēguris*, f. *pan*, neut. of *pas*, all + *aguris* = *agora*, assembly. PAREGORIC. A laudatorydiscourse;eulogy.—**Panegyr'ic**AL, *a.*—**Pan'egyr**IST, *n.*—**Pan'egyr**IZE, *vt.*

Pan'el, *n.* O.F. *panel*, piece of cloth, saddle-cushion = Med.L. *pannellus*, dim. of *pannus.* PANE. The pad of a saddle; a slip of parchment containing a list of jurors; the jury; a compartment of a door, &c.; a compartment below or above a general level; a thin board on which to paint.—*vt.* To fit with panels.

Pang, *n.* Orig. uncertain. A sudden pain.

Pan'ic, *a.* F. *panique*—G. *panikos*, of or for the god Pan. *Panic fear, terror*, &c., sudden fear, &c., such as was attributed to the action of Pan.—*n.* A sudden and excessive fear.—**Pan'-pipe**, *n.* A musical instrument made of reeds graduated in length, the invention of which was ascribed to Pan.

Pan'nier, *n.* F. *panier*—L. *pānārium*, bread-basket, f. *pānis*, bread. COMPANION. A basket for a beast's back or a man's shoulders.

Pan'nikin, *n.* PAN + dim. suff. *-kin.* A small metal drinking-vessel.

Pan'oply, *n.* G. *panoplia*, f. *pan*, neut. of *pas*, all + *hopla*, arms. A full suit of armour.

Panora'ma, *n.* G. *pan* (see prec.) + *horama*, view, f. *hora-ein*, to see. A picture arranged round a spectator or unfolded before him; a complete survey.—**Panoram'**IC, *a.*

Pan'sy, *n.* F. *pensée*, a fanciful application

of *pensée*, thought, f. *penser*, to think. PENSIVE. A variety of violet.

Pant, *vi.* App. shortened f. O.F. *pantoisier*, said to be f. Pop.L. *phantasiāre*, to have nightmare, pant, f. L. *phantasia*, FANTASY. To gasp for breath; to yearn.—*n.* A gasp.

Pantaloon′, *n.* F. *pantalon*—It. *pantalone*, a buffoon in Italian comedy representing the Venetian, of whom *Pantalone* was a nickname, said to be f. *San Pantaleone*, a favourite Venetian saint. In pantomime, a foolish old man, the butt of the clown; in *pl.*, trousers (app. orig. of a fashion imitated from the stage).

Pan′theist, *n.* G. *pan*, neut. of *pas*, all + *theos*, God + -IST. One who believes that God and the universe are identical.—**Pan′the**ISM, *n.*—**Pantheis′**TIC, *a.*—**Panthe′on**, *n.* L. *panthēon*—G. *pantheion*, f. *pan* + *theios*, a. f. *theos*. A temple to all the gods; the deities of a people collectively.

Pan′ther, *n.* O.F. *pantère* (F. *panthère*)—L. *panthēra*—G. *panthēr*. The leopard.

Pant′omime, *n.* L. *pantomimus*, actor in dumb show, ballet-dancer—G. *pantomimos*, lit. 'imitator of all', f. *panto-* (*pas*, *pantos*, all) + *mimos*, mimic. MIME. A Christmas dramatic entertainment; dumb show.

Pan′try, *n.* A.F. *panetrie* = O.F. *paneterie*, bread-room—Med.L. *pānetārius*, baker, f. L. *pānis*, bread. COMPANION. A room for bread and other provisions, plate, linen, &c.

Pap, *n.*[1] M.E. *pappe*, app. f. Scand. and imitative of the sound made by an infant in opening and closing the lips. A teat or nipple.

Pap, *n.*[2] = M.L.G. *pappe*, Du. *pap*. App. formed like prec. Soft food for infants, &c.

Papa′, *n.* F. *papa*—L. *pāpa*, in Eccles.L., bishop—G. *papas* = *pappas*, a child's word for father, in Eccles.G., bishop. POPE. Father.

Pa′pacy, *n.* Med.L. *pāpātia*, f. *pāpa*, POPE. The office of pope; the papal system.—**Pa′p**AL, *a.* Of or pertaining to the pope.—**Pa′p**IST, *n.*—**Papis′t**IC, **Papis′t**ICAL, *aa.*

Pa′per, *n.* A.F. *papir* = O.F. *papier*—L. *papyrus*, the paper-reed of the Nile, writing-material made from it—G. *papuros*, the reed. A substance in the form of a thin flexible sheet used for writing, printing or drawing on, for wrapping things up, &c.; a sheet of paper written or printed on; in *pl.*, documents, &c.; bills of exchange collectively; a newspaper; an essay or article.—*vt.* To enclose in or cover with paper.—**Pap′ier mâché**, *n.* F. *papier* + *mâché*, chewed, pa.pple. of *mâcher*, L. *masticāre*, to chew. MASTICATE. Paper-pulp shaped by moulding and dried hard.

Par, *n.* L. *pār*, equal, that which is equal, equality. COMPARE. COMPEER. PEER, *n.* UMPIRE. Equality of value or standing; equality between market and nominal value.—**Par′**ITY, *n.* Equality; likeness, analogy.

Parab′asis, *n.* G. *parabasis*, lit. 'a going aside, a digression', f. PARAbainein, to go aside. In Greek comedy, a part sung by the chorus in the poet's own name.

Par′able, *n.* F. *parabole*—L. *parabola*, a comparison, a parable, a speech—G. *parabolē*, a placing beside or comparing, a parable, a parabola, f. PARA- + *bolē*, a throw, f. *ballein*, to throw. PALAVER. PARLOUR. PAROLE. A narrative setting forth moral or spiritual relations typically.—**Parab′ola**, *n.* 16th-c. L. *parabola*. A curve formed by the intersection of a cone with a plane parallel to its side.

Par′achute, *n.* F., f. *para-* (It. *para*, imp. of *parare*, to defend, cover from, orig., to prepare—L. *parāre*. PARE) + *chute*, fall. A contrivance serving to check a fall through the air.

Par′aclete, *n.* F. *paraclet*—Eccles.L. *paraclētus*—G. *paraklētos*, intercessor, f. PARA*kalein*, to call to one's side. The Holy Spirit.

Parade′, *n.* F. *parade*—It. *parata*, a showy setting forth, f. L. *parāre*. PARE. Show, display; a muster of troops; a parade-ground.—*vt.* To muster (troops); to make a display of.—*vi.* To march with display.

Par′adigm, *n.* F. *paradigme*—L. *paradīgma*—G. *paradeigma*, f. PARA*deiknunai*, to show beside or side by side. A pattern, example; a table of the inflexions of a verb, &c.

Par′adise, *n.* F. *paradis*—L. *paradīsus*—G. *paradeisos*, orig. park or pleasure-ground, of Per. orig. The garden of Eden; heaven.

Par′ados, *n.* F. *parados*, f. PARA- + *dos*, L. *dorsum*, back. ENDORSE. A protecting elevation behind a fortified place or a trench.

Par′adox, *n.* L. *paradoxum*, neut. of *paradoxus*, G. *paradoxos*, contrary to received opinion or to expectation, f. PARA- + *doxa*, opinion. HETERODOX. A statement apparently absurd though it may prove to be well-founded.—**Paradox′**ICAL, *a.*

Par′affin, *n.* L. *parum*, too little + *affinis*, having AFFINITY (from its neutral quality). A fatty substance, also an oil (**Par′affin oil**), obtained by distillation from coal, &c.

Par′agon, *n.* O.F. *paragon*—It. *paragone*, of uncertain orig. A pattern of excellence.

Par′agraph, *n.* F. *paragraphe*—L.L. *paragraphus*—G. *paragraphos*, a stroke denoting a break in the sense, a passage so marked, f. PARA, beside + *graphein*, to write. A symbol (¶) denoting the beginning of a section; a section of a chapter or book; a short article.

Par′akeet, **Par′oquet**, *n.* O.F. *paroquet*, said to be f. It. *parrochetto*, dim. of *parroco*, parson. Cf. F. *moineau*, sparrow, dim. of *moine*, monk. A small bird of the parrot kind.

Par′allax, *n.* F. *parallaxe*—G. *parallaxis*, alternation, parallax, f. *parallassein*, to make alternate, f. PAR- + *allassein*, to change. The angle between two straight lines drawn to an object from different points of view.

Par′allel, *a.* F. *parallèle*—L. *parallēlus*—G. *parallēlos*, f. PAR-, beside + **allēlos*, one another. At a continuously equal distance; analogous, corresponding.—*n.* A parallel line; one of the lines indicating degrees of latitude; something agreeing or analogous; a comparison.—*vt.* To bring into comparison, liken; to match.—**Par′allel**ISM, *n.* A being parallel.—**Parallel′ogram**, *n.* F. *parallélogramme*—L. *parallēlogrammum*—G. *parallēlogrammon*, neut. of *parallēlogrammos*, bounded by parallel lines, f. *parallēlos* + *grammē*, line. A four-sided figure with the opposite sides parallel.

Paral′ysis, *n.* L. *paralysis*. PALSY. A nervous affection producing incapacity of motion or feeling.—**Par′alyse**, *vt.* F. *paralyser*, f. *paralysie*. PALSY. To affect with paralysis.—**Paralyt′ic**, *a.* F. *paralytique*—L. *paralyticus*—G. *paralutikos*, f. *paraluein*. PALSY. Affected with, of the nature of, paralysis.—*n.* One affected with paralysis.

Par′amount, *a.* A.F. *paramont*, f. O.F. *par*, by + *amont*, *à mont*, adv., up above—L. *ad montem*. AMOUNT. Supreme.

Par′amour, *n.* O.F. *par amour*, by or through love, f. L. *per* (PER-) and *amor* (AMOROUS). The illicit partner of a married man or woman.

Par′apet, *n.* F. *parapet* or It. *parapetto*, f.

para (PARACHUTE) + *petto*, L. *pectus*, breast. A defence breast-high; a low wall.

Paraphernaʹlia, *n.pl.* Med.L., neut.pl. of L.L. *paraphernālis*, a. f. *parapherna*, pl., articles brought by a wife besides the dowry and remaining under her control—G. *parapherna*, pl., f. PARA- + *phernē*, dowry. Articles which the law allows a wife to keep as her own; personal belongings, articles of equipment.

Parʹaphrase, *n.* F. *paraphrase*—L. *paraphrasis*—G. *paraphrasis*, f. *paraphrazein*, to tell a thing in other words, f. PARA-, besides + *phrazein*, to tell. PHRASE. An expression in other words of the meaning of a passage, &c.; a free translation.—*vt.* To express the meaning of in other words; to translate freely.

Parʹasite, *n.* L. *parasītus*—G. *parasitos*, lit. 'one who eats at another's table', f. PARA- + *sitos*, food. A toady or hanger-on; an animal or plant which lives in or on another organism. — **Parasitʹ**IC, **Parasitʹ**ICAL, *aa.*

Parasolʹ, *n.* F. *parasol*—It. *parasole*, f. *para* (PARACHUTE) + *sole*, L. *sōl*, SUN. A small umbrella for keeping off the sun's rays.

Parʹboil, *vt.* O.F. *parboillir*—L.L. PER-*bullīre*, to BOIL thoroughly. To boil partially (the suff. having been identified with *part*).

Parʹbuckle, *n.* Orig. unknown. A device for handling a heavy object by means of a rope both ends of which pass round it.—*vt.* To raise or lower by means of a parbuckle.

Parʹcel, *n.* F. *parcelle*—L. type **particella*, dim. of *particula*, dim. of *pars*, PART. A part or portion; a package; a quantity or lot.—*vt.* To divide into parcels; to make up in a parcel.

Parch, *vt.* and *i.* Orig. unknown. To make, to become, very hot and dry.

Parchʹment, *n.* F. *parchemin*—L. *pergamēna*, use as *n.* of fem. of *Pergamēnus*, of Pergamus in Mysia, where parchment was invented. The skin of the sheep, &c., prepared for writing; a document on parchment.

Pard, *n.* O.F. *pard*—L. *pardus*—G. *pardos*, f. *pardalis*. CAMELOPARD. The leopard.

Parʹdon, *vt.* O.F. *pardoner* (F. *pardonner*)—L.L. *perdōnāre*, to grant, remit, f. PER- + *dōnāre*. DONATE. To forgive; to excuse.—*n.* Forgiveness; excuse.—**Parʹdon**ABLE, *a.*

Pare, *vt.* F. *parer*, to prepare, trim, pare—L. *parāre*, *parātum*, to make ready, PREPARE. APPARATUS. DISPARATE. PARACHUTE. PARADE. PARRY. REPAIR.[2] SEPARATE. VITUPERATE. To trim, smooth or reduce by cutting; to cut or shave *off* or *away*.

Paregorʹic, *a.* L.L. *parēgoricus*—G. *parēgorikos*, encouraging, soothing, f. *parēgoros*, consoling, soothing, f. PARA-, beside + *-agoros*, speaking, f. *agora*, assembly. PANEGYRIC. Soothing.—*n.* A soothing medicine.

Paʹrent, *n.* O.F. *parent*, kinsman—L. *parens*, *parentis*, parent, ancestor, f. *parĕre*, to bring forth. PARTURIENT. REPERTORY. A father or mother.—**Paʹrent**AGE, *n.* Lineage, birth. —**Parenʹ**TAL, *a.*

Parenʹthesis, *n.*; *pl.* **-theses**. Med.L.—G. *parenthesis*, f. PAR- + EN-[2] + *thesis*. THESIS. An inserted explanatory clause, &c.; in *pl.*, the marks ( ) used to include a parenthesis.—**Parenthetʹ**IC, -ICAL, *aa.* G. agent-suff. *-et-*. Of, of the nature of, a parenthesis.

Parʹget, *vt.* O.F. *pargeter*, *parjeter*, to fill up the joints of stones with mortar or plaster, f. *par-* = PER-, through, all over + *jeter*, to throw. JET, *v.* To cover with plaster; to adorn with plaster-work.—*n.* Plaster used for covering; ornamental plaster-work.

Parheʹlion, *n.* L. *parēlion*—G. *parēlion*, f. PAR-, beside + *hēlios*, sun. A mock sun.

Parʹiah, *n.* Tamil *paraiyar*, pl. of *paraiyan*, name of the largest of the lower castes in S. India, lit. 'drummer', f. *parai*, a drum beaten at certain festivals. One of the caste above referred to or of any low Hindoo caste; a social outcast.

Parʹish, *n.* O.F. *paroisse*—Pop.L. **parocia* for *parochia*, substituted for Eccles.L. *paroccia*, G. *paroikia*, an ecclesiastical district (perh. orig. applied to colonies of Jews in Alexandria, &c.), f. *paroikos*, dwelling beside, in Christian use, sojourning, f. PAR- + *oikos*, house. An ecclesiastical district under a priest; a subdivision of a county. — **Parishʹioner**, *n.* Obs. *Parishen*, *Parishion* in same sense (O.F. *paroissien*) + -ER. An inhabitant of a parish.

Park, *n.* O.F. *parc*. PADDOCK. PARQUET. An enclosed space for beasts of the chase; a large ornamental piece of ground attached to a mansion; a piece of ground laid out for public recreation; a space allotted to, an equipment of, artillery, stores, &c.

Parʹlance, *n.* A.F. and O.F. *parlance*, f *parler*, Med.L. *parlāre*, to speak. PARLOUR. PARLIAMENT. Mode of speech.

Parʹley, *n.* F. *parler* as *n.* (See prec.) Speech, discourse; an informal conference with an enemy.—*vi.* To discourse; to hold a parley.

Parʹliament, *n.* O.F. *parlement*, speaking, supreme court, f. *parler*. PARLANCE. The supreme legislature of the United Kingdom. —**Parliamentʹ**ARY, *a.*

Parʹlour, *n.* A.F. *parlur*, O.F. *parleor*, *parleour* = Med.L. *parlātōrium*, f. *parlāre*, *parōlāre*, *parabolāre*, to speak, f. L. *parabola*. PARABLE. PARLANCE. A room in a monastery for conversation; a sitting-room.

Paroʹchial, *a.* O.F. *parochial*—Eccles.L. *parochiālis*, f. *parochia*. PARISH. Of a parish or parishes; narrow, provincial.

Parʹody, *n.* Ultimately (perh. through L. or F.) f. G. *parōidia*, burlesque poem or song, f. PAR-, beside, mock- + *ōidē*, song. ODE. A burlesque imitation of a work.—*vt.* To ridicule by imitation.—**Parʹod**IST, *n.*

Paroleʹ, *n.* F. *parole*, word, word of honour —L. *parabola*. PARABLE. An undertaking by a prisoner of war not to attempt escape or to refrain from taking up arms.—*a.* Oral.

Parʹoxysm, *n.* F. *paroxysme*—Med.L. *paroxysmus*—G. *paroxusmos*, f. *paroxunein*, to irritate, f. PAR- + *oxunein*, to sharpen, f. *oxus*, sharp. A violent access of disease, &c.

Parquetʹ, *n.* F. *parquet*, O.F. *parchet*, part of a park, &c., wooden flooring, dim. of *parc*, PARK. A flooring of pieces of wood arranged in a pattern. Also **Parʹquet**RY.

Parʹricide, *n.* F. *parricide*—L. *parricīda*, said to be for **patricīda*, f. *pater*, father + -CIDE (1). One who kills his father or a near relative.— -CIDE (2). His crime.

Parʹrot, *n.* Conjectured to be = F. *Perrot*, dim. of *Pierre*, Peter. One of an order of birds some of which can be taught to speak.

Parʹry, *vt.* App. f. F. *parer*, It. *parare*, in this sense—L. *parāre*. PARE. To ward off.

Parse, *vt.* App. f. L. *pars*, PART. To resolve (a sentence) into its component parts of speech.

Parʹsimony, *n.* L. *parsimōnia*, f. *parcĕre*, *parsum*, to be sparing. Undue carefulness in the use of money, &c.—**Parsimoʹni**OUS, *a.*

Parsʹley, *n.* App. a corr. of O.F. *peresil* (F. *persil*)—L.L. *petrosīlium* for L. *petroselīnum*—G. *petroselinon*, 'rock-parsley', f. *petra*, rock

+ *selinon*, parsley. CELERY. A plant used for seasoning and garnishing.

Pars'nip, *n.* M.E. *passenep, pasnep(e)*, ultimately repg. L. *pastināca*, conn. with *pastināre*, to dig, *pastinum*, two-pronged digging-fork. A culinary vegetable; its root.

Par'son, *n.* M.E. *persone*—A.F. and O.F. *persone*—L. *persōna*, PERSON, in Med.L., 'rector of a parish'. A rector; a clergyman. —**Par'son**AGE, *n.* His benefice or house.

Part, *n.* F. *part*—L. *pars, partis.* DEPART. PARCEL. PARSE. PORTION. A portion, share, section, region; interest, concern; function, duty; the character assigned to an actor; the melody assigned to a voice or instrument in concerted music; in *pl.*, abilities, talents; side in a contest, &c.; *part of speech*, each of the grammatical classes of words.—*vt.* F. *partir* —L. *partīre.* To divide, sever, separate; to distribute.—*vi.* To divide, break; to quit one another's company; to depart.—**Partak'er**, *n.* *Part*, n. + *taker*. One who takes a part or share.—**Partak'ing**, *vbl.n.* The taking of a part or share.—**Partake'**, *vt.* Back-formation f. the two prec. To take a part in.—*vi.* To take or have a part or share; to have something *of*.—**Part'**LY,[2] *adv.*

Parterre', *n.* F., f. phrase *par terre*, on or over the ground. A level space with flower-beds; part of the floor of a theatre.

Par'thian, *a.* -AN. Of Parthia; often used in allusion to a characteristic backward discharging of missiles by Parthian horsemen in real or pretended flight.

Par'tial, *a.* F. *partial*—L.L. *partiālis*, f. L. *pars*, PART. Prejudiced, unfair; with *to*, fond of; involving or constituting a part only.—**Partial'**ITY, *n.*—**Par'tial**LY,[2] *adv.*

Partic'ipate, *vt.* and *i.* L. *participāre, participātum*, f. *particeps, participis*, partaking, f. *pars*, PART + *capĕre*, to take. To partake.—**Particip**A'TION, *n.*—**Partic'ipat**OR, *n.*

Par'ticiple, *n.* O.F. *participle*, by-form of *participe*—L. *participium*, f. *particeps.* (See prec.) A word partaking of the nature of an *a.* and a *v.*, a verbal *a.*—**Particip'**IAL, *a.*

Par'ticle, *n.* L. *particula*, dim. of *pars*, PART. A very small part or quantity; a minor part of speech.—**Partic'ul**AR,[1] *a.* Not general, special; individual, separate; more than ordinary, marked; detailed, minute; exacting in regard to details, fastidious.—*n.* A detail or item; in *pl.*, a detailed account.—**Particular'**ITY, *n.* — **Partic'ular**IZE, *vt.* To mention in detail.—**Partic'ular**LY,[2] *adv.*

Par'ti-coloured, *a.* PARTY, *a.* Variegated in colour; varied, diversified.

Par'tisan, **Par'tizan**, *n.* F. *partisan*, f. an It. dial. form = Tuscan *partigiano*, f. *parte*, L. *pars*, PART. One who takes part with another, esp. a blind or unreasoning adherent.

Parti'tion, *n.* F. *partition*—L. *partītio, partītiōnis*, f. *partīre.* PART. A dividing, distribution; a division-wall; a division.—*vt.* To divide.—**Par'tit**IVE, *a.* Denoting a part only.

Part'ner, *n.* Formerly *partener*, app. an alteration (under the influence of PART) of *Parcener* (now only in law)—A.F. *parcener* = O.F. *parçonier* = Med.L. *partiōnārius* for *partītiōnārius*, f. *partītio*. (See prec.) An associate, esp. in business.—**Part'ner**SHIP, *n.*

Part'ridge, *n.* M.E. *pertrich, partrich.* Cf. O.F. *perdriz*, alteration of *perdiz*—L. *perdix*—G. *perdix*. A well-known game-bird.

Partu'rient, *a.* L. *parturiens, parturientis*, pres.pple. of *parturīre*, desiderative of *parĕre*. PARENT. About to give birth, in travail.—**Parturi**'TION, *n.* Childbirth.

Par'ty, *n.* F. *partie*—L. *partīta*, fem. of *partītus*, pa.pple. of *partīre.* PART. Those on one side in a contest, &c.; the system of taking sides on public questions; a company of persons; a gathering for social pleasure; each of two or more litigants, contracting persons, &c.—**Par'ty**, *a.* F. *parti*, L. *partītus*. Divided; parti-coloured; now only in *heraldry*, of a shield, divided into parts.—**Par'ty-wall**, *n.* *Party*, a. A common wall.

Pas'chal, *a.* F. *pascal*—L.L. *paschālis*, f. *pascha*, the Passover—G. *pascha*—Aramaic *paskhā*. Of the Passover or Easter.

Pash'a, **Pach'a**, *n.* Turkish *pāshā*, app. = *bāshā*, f. *bāsh*, head, chief. A Turkish officer of high rank.

Pasquinade', *n.* It. *pasquinata*, f. *Pasquino*, the name (of doubtful orig.) of a statue in Rome on which lampoons were fixed. A lampoon.

Pass, *n.*[1] Orig. the same as PACE. A narrow passage through a mountainous region.

Pass, *vi.* F. *passer*—Pop.L. **passāre*, f. L. *passus*, PACE. To go, go on, move, proceed: to be current; to be accepted as adequate or qualified; to be sanctioned; to undergo transition; to die; to happen.—*vt.* To go by; to cross; to reach the standard of; to be sanctioned by; to go beyond, exceed; to move, draw, push; to spend (time, &c.); to agree to, declare correct, sanction; to hand, transfer; to put into circulation; to pledge (one's word, &c.); to discharge from the body; to utter.—*n.*[2] A critical position; leave to pass or travel, a document giving this.—**Pass'**ABLE, *a.* In senses f. the *v.*; tolerable, fairly good.—**Pass'**ABLY,[2] *adv.*—**Pass'age**, *n.* F. *passage*, f. *passer*. The action of passing; opportunity of passing, leave to pass; a crossing by sea; a way, an entrance or exit; a gallery or corridor; a part of a book, &c.—**Pass'ant**, *a.* F. *passant*, pres. pple. of *passer*. In *heraldry*, of a beast, walking and looking to the dexter side.—**Pass'enger**, *n.* M.E. *passager*—F. *passager*, use as *n.* of *passager*, passing, f. *passage*. (For the intrusive *n.* cf. MESSENGER, SCAVENGER.) A passer by or through; a traveller in a public conveyance. —**Pass'ing-bell**, *n.* A bell rung at the hour of, or just after death.—**Pass'over**, *n.* A Jewish feast commemorating the 'passing over' of the houses of the Israelites when the first-born of the Egyptians were slain; the lamb sacrificed.—**Pass'port**, *n.* F. *passeport*, f. *passe*, imp. of *passer* + *port*, PORT, *n.*[1] A document granting permission to travel.

Pas'sion, *n.* O.F. *passion*—L. *passio, passiōnis*, n. of action f. *pati, passus*, to suffer. IMPASSIBLE. PATIENT. The sufferings of Christ; a strong emotion; an outburst of anger; angry feeling; love; an ardent predilection, an object of this.—**Pas'sion**ATE,[2] *a.* Irascible; wrathful; ardently desirous; impassioned; vehement; swayed by the emotions.—**Pas'sion Sun'day**, *n.* The fifth Sunday in Lent.—**Pas'sion Week**, *n.* The week before Easter, in which Christ's passion is commemorated.—**Pas'**SIVE, *a.* That is the object of action; in *grammar*, of the voice in which the object of action is made the grammatical subject; submissive; quiescent.—**Pas'sive**LY,[2] *adv.*

Past, *ppl.a.* Pa.pple. of PASS. Gone by in time; expressing past action or state.—*n.* Past time; that which happened in the past.—*prep.* After; beyond.—*adv.* So as to pass or go by.

Paste, *n.* O.F. *paste* (F. *pâte*) — Common Romanic *pasta*, supposed to be f. G. *pasta*, pl., barley-porridge, f. *pastos*, sprinkled (with salt), f. *passein*, to sprinkle. Dough for pastry; boiled flour and water as a cement; a soft plastic composition; a hard vitreous composition.—*vt.* To fasten with paste.—**Paste'board**, *n.* A stiff substance of pasted paper.—**Past'**RY, *n.* Articles made of paste, pies, tarts, &c.—**Pas'ty**, *n.* O.F. *pastée* (F. *pâté*). A meat-pie.—**Pas'ty**,[2] *a.* Like paste, pale and dull.

Pas'tel, *n.* F. *pastel*—It. *pastello*, a plant yielding a dye, the dye, dim. of *pasta* (see prec.), the name having been applied to the colouring matter got by pulping and thence to the plant. A paste used as a crayon or for making crayons; a drawing in pastel.

Pas'tern, *n.* O.F. *pasturon*, deriv. of *pasture*, shackle for the pastern-joint, pastern, said to be the same as *pasture*, PASTURE, transferred to the shackle and thence to the joint. A horse's foot between the fetlock and the hoof.

Pas'til, **Pastille'**, *n.* F. *pastille*—L. *pastillus*, little loaf, lozenge, a dim. of uncertain orig. app. associated in Romanic with *pasta*, PASTE. A small roll of prepared paste burnt as a disinfectant, &c.; a sugared confection.

Pas'time, *n.* PASS + TIME. Cf. F. *passe-temps*. Recreation, diversion; a sport, a game.

Pas'tor, *n.* O.F. *pastor*, *pastur*—L. *pastor*, shepherd, agent-n. f. *pascĕre*, *pastum*, to feed. PESTER. REPAST. The minister in charge of a church.—**Pas'tor**AL, *a.* Of shepherds; used for pasture; portraying the life of shepherds or of the country; of a pastor.—*n.* A pastoral poem; pastoral poetry; a letter from a bishop to his clergy or people.—**Pas'tor**ATE,[1] *n.* The office, the tenure of office, of a pastor; pastors collectively.—**Pas'ture**, *n.* O.F. *pasture*—L.L. *pastūra*. PASTERN. Grass land; a piece of grass land; the growing grass eaten by cattle.—*vi.* To graze.—*vt.* To put to pasture.—**Pas'tur**AGE, *n.* Grazing; grass land; a piece of grass land; growing grass.

Pat, *n.* Prob. imitative. PATTER.[2] A gentle stroke; a small mass formed by patting.—*vi.* and *t.* To strike lightly.—*adv.* Appositely, aptly, in the nick of time.—*a.* Apposite, apt.

Patch, *n.* M.E. *pasche*, *patche*, of unknown orig. A piece of cloth, &c., covering a hole; a small piece of black silk, &c., worn on the face; a piece of ground.—*vt.* To put a patch on; to mark as with patches.—**Patch'**Y,[2] *a.*

Pate, *n.* Orig. unknown. The head, the skull.

Patel'la, *n.* L. *patella*, dim. of *patina*. (See next.) The knee-pan or knee-cap.

Pat'en, *n.* O.F. *patène*—L. *patena*, *patina*, pan, f. *patēre*. (See next.) The plate on which the eucharistic bread is laid.

Pa'tent, *a.* F. *patent*—L. *patens*, *patentis*, pres.pple. of *patēre*, to lie open. FATHOM. *Letters patent*, an open document conferring a right, title, &c., esp. the sole right in an invention; protected by letters patent.—Directly f. L. Open; clear, manifest.—*n.* Letters patent; a patented invention.—*vt.* To obtain a patent for.—**Patent**EE', *n.*

Paterfamil'ias, *n.* L., f. *pater*, FATHER + *familias*, archaic genit. of *familia*, FAMILY. The father or head of a family.

Pater'nal, *a.* L. *paternālis*, f. *paternus*, fatherly, f. *pater*, FATHER. Fatherly; derived from, related through, a father.—**Pater'n**ITY, *n.* Fatherhood; paternal origin.

Pat'ernos'ter, *n.* L. *pater noster*, our FATHER, beginning the Lord's Prayer in Latin. PATTER.[1] The Lord's Prayer; every eleventh bead in a rosary; a rosary.

Path, *n.* O.E. *pæth*. Common W. Germanic. A track or footway; way, course.

Pa'thos, *n.* G. *pathos*, suffering, feeling. APATHY. SYMPATHY. The quality in writing, music, &c., which excites pity or sadness.—**Pathet'ic**, *a.* L.L. *pathēticus*—G. *pathētikos*. Full of pathos.—Sim. **Pathet'ic**AL.—**Pathet'ical**LY,[2] *adv.*—**Patho**L'OGY, *n.* The science of diseases.—**Pathol'og**IST, *n.*

Pa'tient, *a.* O.F. *pacient*, *patient*—L. *patiens*, *patientis*, pres.pple. of *pati*, to suffer. PASSION. Enduring with composure; diligent, unwearied.—*n.* One under medical treatment.—**Pa'tient**LY,[2] *adv.*—**Pa'ti**ENCE, *n.*

Pat'ina, *n.* F. *patine*, perh. f. L. *patina*. PATEN. An incrustation on old bronze.

Pat'ois, *n.* F. Orig. unknown. A dialect.

Pa'triarch, *n.* O.F. *patriarche*—L. *patriarcha*—G. *patriarchēs*, f. *patria*, family + *archein*, to rule. The head of a family or tribe; certain bishops in the Eastern and Western Churches.—**Patriarch'**AL, *a.*

Patric'ian, *n.* L. *patricius*, of the rank of the *patres*, the FATHERS or senators of Rome + -AN. A Roman noble; a noble.—*a.* Noble.

Pat'rimony, *n.* F. *patrimoine*—L. *patrimōnium*, f. *pater*, FATHER. A paternal inheritance.—**Patrimo'ni**AL, *a.*

Pat'riot, *n.* F. *patriote*—L.L. *patriōta* = G. *patriōtēs*, fellow-countryman, f. *patrios*, of one's fathers, f. *patēr*, FATHER. A lover of his country.—**Patriot'**IC, *a.*—**Pat'riot**ISM, *n.*

Patris'tic, *a.* L. *pater*, G. *patēr*, FATHER + -IST + -IC. Of the study of the writings of the Fathers of the Church; of the Fathers.

Patrol', *vi.* F. *patrouiller*, orig., to paddle in the mud, earlier *patouiller*. Orig. uncertain. To go the rounds in a camp or garrison.—*vt.* To go the rounds of.—*n.* The action of patrolling; a patrolling detachment.

Pa'tron, *n.* M.E. *patroun*—O.F. *patrun*, *patron*—L. *patrōnus*, protector, defender, f. *pater*, FATHER. PATTERN. A protector; one who lends influential support to a person, cause, &c.; the holder of an advowson; a guardian saint.—**Pat'ron**AGE, *n.*—**Pa'tron**ESS, *n.*—**Pat'ron**IZE, *vt.* To act as a patron towards; to support by expenditure or one's custom; to treat condescendingly.

Patronym'ic, *a.* L. *patrōnymicus*—G. *patrōnumikos*, f. *patrōnumos*, named from the father, f. *patēr*, FATHER + *onoma* (in Æolic *onuma*), NAME. Derived from the name of a father or ancestor.—*n.* A name so derived.

Pat'ten, *n.* F. *patin*, perh. conn. with *patte*, paw. A kind of shoe worn under an ordinary shoe to raise it out of wet or mud.

Pat'ter, *v.*[1]*t.* From *Pater* in PATERNOSTER. To repeat (prayers, &c.) glibly and mechanically.—*vi.* To talk glibly.—*n.*[1] The cant or jargon of beggars, &c.; chatter; rapid speech in the course of a song.

Pat'ter, *v.*[2]*i.* Dim. and freq. of PAT, *v.* To make a rapid succession of light taps; to run with quick sounding steps.—*n.*[2] A pattering.

Pat'tern, *n.* M.E. *patron*—F. *patron*, patron, pattern. PATRON. An excellent example; a model; a sample; a decorative design.

Pat'ty, *n.* F. *pâté*. PASTY. A little pie.

Pau'city, *n.* L. *paucitas*, f. *paucus*, FEW, conn. with *pauper*, POOR. Fewness; smallness of quantity.

Pau'lo-post-fu'ture, *a.* and *n.* Mod.L. *paulo post futūrum*, to translate G. *ho met* *oligon mellōn*, the future after a little. In *Greek grammar*, a passive tense expressing that an event will take place immediately.

Paunch, *n.* O.N.F. *panche* = O.F. *pance* (F. *panse*)—L. *pantex, panticis*. The belly.

Pau'per, *n.* L. *pauper*, POOR. One dependent on charity or on poor-law relief.—**Pau'per**ISM, *n.* The existence of a pauper class. —**Pau'per**IZE, *vt.* To make a pauper of.

Pause, *n.* F. *pause*—L. *pausa*—G. *pausis*, a ceasing, f. *pauein*, to cease. A short cessation; intermission, delay.—*vi.* From the *n.*, or f. F. *pauser* or L. *pausāre*. To make a pause; to hesitate; to dwell or linger *upon*.

Pave, *vt.* F. *paver*, f. L. *pavire*, to beat, to ram or tread down, or back-formation f. *pavement* (see below). To lay with a pavement.—**Pave'ment**, *n.* F. *pavement*—L. *pavimentum*, beaten or rammed floor, f. *pavire*. A solid covering for a floor, street, &c.; a paved footway by the side of a street.—**Pav'iour**, *n.* App. alteration of **Pav'**ER. One who paves.

Pavil'ion, *n.* F. *pavillon*—L. *pāpilio, pāpiliōnis*, a butterfly, also (app. from likeness to the wings), a tent. A large tent; a light ornamental building.

Paw, *n.* O.F. *powe, poue*, varr. of *poe*, app. of Frankish orig. Cf. M.Du. *pôte*, H.G. *pfote*. The foot of a beast having claws.—*vt.* To touch or strike with the paw.—*vi.* To scrape the ground with the hoofs.

Pawl, *n.* Poss. = F. *pal*, stake. PALE, *n.* A bar to prevent recoil of a capstan, &c.

Pawn, *n.*[1] A.F. *poun*, O.F. *poon, paon*, varr. of *peon*, earlier *pehon, pedon*, foot-soldier, pawn—Med.L. *pedo, pedōnis*, foot-soldier, f. L. *pēs, pedis*, FOOT. PIONEER. A piece of the smallest value in chess.

Pawn, *n.*[2] O.F. *pan*, app. the same as M.Du. *pant*, M.H.G. *pfant* (Ger. *pfand*). A pledge; state of being pledged.—*vt.* To pledge.—**Pawn'broker**, *n.* One who lends on pledges.

Pax, *n.* L. *pax*, PEACE. The kiss of peace; a tablet bearing a representation of a sacred subject kissed at mass by the priests and passed to the congregation to be kissed.

Pay, *vt.* F. *payer*, in O.F. also, to appease, satisfy—L. *pācāre*, to make peaceful, pacify, in Med.L. also, to pay, f. *pax*, PEACE. To give to (a person) money due to him; to reward, requite; to give (money, &c.) as due; to give money in discharge of; to render, bestow (attention, respect, &c.); to let *out* (a rope).—*vi.* To be profitable.—*n.* A paying or being paid; wages.—**Pay'**ABLE, *a.*—**Pay**EE', *n.*—**Pay'master**, *n.* An official who pays troops, &c.—**Pay'**MENT, *n.*

Pay'nim, *n.* O.F. *paienime*, earlier *paienisme*, L.L. *pāgānismus*, PAGANISM. A pagan.

Pea, *n.*; *pl.* **Pease**, **Peas**. O.E. *pise* (L. *pisa*, late form of *pisum*, G. *pisos, pison*), whence M.E. *pēse*, pl. *pēsen*; 16th c. *pease*, pl. *paesen, peses, pease*. From the last form arose *pea* as a new sing. The round seed of a climbing annual plant; the plant.—**Pease'cod**, **Peas'cod**, *n.* COD.[2] A pea-pod.

Peace, *n.* O.F. *pais* (F. *paix*)—L. *pax, pācis*. APPEASE. PACIFIC. PAY. Freedom from war; a treaty for cessation of war; public order and security; tranquillity.—**Peace'able**, *a.* O.F. *paisible*. Avoiding strife; free from disturbance.—**Peace'**FUL, *a.*

Peach, *n.* F. *pêche*, O.F. *pesche*—L.L. *persica* for L. *persicum*, short for *Persicum mālum*, Persian apple. A stone-fruit; its tree.

Peach, *vi.* Aphetic f. obs. *Appeach*, to hinder, to accuse, repg. earlier **anpeche*, Eng. or A.F. form f. O.F. *empechier*. IMPEACH. To inform against an accomplice.

Pea'cock, *n.* O.E. *pēa*, peacock (L. *pāvo*) + COCK.[1] A bird with gorgeous plumage and a strutting gait.—**Pea'hen**, *n.* The female.

Pea'-jacket, *n.* Late M.Du. *pie*, now *pij, pije*, coat of coarse woollen stuff, of obscure orig. + JACKET. A short stout outer coat.

Peak, *n.* Var. of PIKE.[1] The projecting part of the brim of a cap; the upper outer corner of an extended sail; a pointed hill-top.

Peak, *vi.* Orig. uncertain. To look sickly.

Peal, *n.* Perh. aphetic f. APPEAL. The loud ringing of a bell or of a set of bells; a set of bells; a loud outburst of sound.—*vi.* To sound forth in a peal.—*vt.* To utter loudly.

Pear, *n.* O.E. *pere, peru* = M.Du., M.L.G. *pere*—L.L. *pira, pēra*, fem. sing. for L. *pira*, pl. of *pirum*. PERRY. A fruit; its tree.

Pearl, *n.* F. *perle*, of uncertain orig. A concretion in the shell of various bivalve molluscs, valued as a gem.—*vt.* To adorn with pearls or with mother of pearl.—**Pearl'**Y,[2] *a.*

Peas'ant, *n.* A.F. *paisant*, O.F. *paisent, païsant, paysant* (F. *paysan*), f. *païs, pays*, country—L.L. *pāgensis* (*ager*), (territory) of a *pāgus*. PAGAN. A worker on the land; a rustic. —**Peas'antr**Y, *n.* Peasants collectively.

Peat, *n.* Poss. conn. with stem *pette-*, which gave O.F. *pece, piece*, PIECE (the first sense below being the earlier). A piece of decomposed vegetable matter cut into shape for fuel; such matter, often forming large bogs.

Peb'ble, *n.* O.E. *papol-stán*, pebble-STONE Orig. unknown. A stone rounded by water; a kind of rock-crystal used for spectacle-lenses.

Peccadil'lo, *n.* Sp. *pecadillo*, dim. of *pecado*, L. *peccātum*, sin, f. *peccāre*. (See next.) A small or venial fault or sin.

Pec'cant, *a.* L. *peccans, peccantis*, pres.pple. of *peccāre*, to sin. Sinning; morbid, corrupt.

Peck, *n.*[1] M.E. *pek* = O.F. *pek*. Orig. unknown. The fourth part of a bushel.

Peck, *vt.* App. a collateral form of PICK. To indent or pierce with the beak; to take (food) with the beak.—*n.*[2] An act of pecking.

Pec'toral, *n.* O.F. *pectoral*—L. *pectorāle*, breast-plate, neut. of *pectorālis*, a. f. *pectus, pectoris*, the breast. EXPECTORATE. An ornament on the breast, esp. that worn by the Jewish High Priest.—*a.* Of, pertaining to, in, upon, good for, the chest.

Pec'ulate, *vt.* and *i.* L. *pecūlāri, pecūlātus*, to embezzle, f. *pecūlium*, private property, orig. in cattle, f. *pecu*, cattle, money. PECUNIARY. To embezzle.—**Pecul**A'TION, *n.*

Pecu'liar, *a.* L. *pecūliāris*, f. *pecūlium*. (See prec.) That belongs to or characterizes an individual; special; strange.—**Peculiar'**ITY, *n.* The quality of being characteristic of an individual or unlike others; a distinguishing characteristic.—**Pecu'liar**LY,[2] *adv.*

Pecu'niary, *a.* L. *pecūniārius*, f. *pecūnia*, money, f. *pecu*. PECULATE. FEE. Of, consisting of, money.—**Pecu'ni**OUS, *a.* Wealthy.

Ped'agogue, *n.* O.F. *pedagogue*—L. *paedagōgus*—G. *paidagōgos*, a slave who took boys to school, f. *pais, paidos*, boy + *agōgos*, leading, f. *agein*, to lead. A schoolmaster, teacher.

Pedal, *n.* App. f. F. *pedale* in senses 'feet', 'trick with the feet', 'organ-pedals'—It. *pedale*, foot—L. *pedālis*, a. f. *pēs, pedis*, FOOT. A lever worked by the foot.

Ped'ant, *n.* F. *pédant* or its source It. *pedante*, schoolmaster, pedant, of uncertain orig. (The first element app. the same as in PEDAGOGUE.) One who overrates book-learning or lays undue stress on details of knowledge or adherence to formal rules.—**Pedan'**TIC, -ICAL, *aa.*—**Ped'antr**Y, *n.*

Ped'dle, *vi.* In first sense app. back-formation f. *pedler*, PEDLAR. In second app. alteration of PIDDLE. To be a pedlar; to trifle.

Ped'estal, *n.* F. *piédestal*—It. *piedestallo*, i.e. *pie di stallo*, foot of a stall, f. *piè*, *piede*, L. *pēs*, *pedis*, FOOT + *stallo*, O.H.G. *stal*, STALL. The base of a pillar, statue, &c.

Pedes'trian, *a.* L. *pedester*, on foot (f. *pēs*, *pedis*, FOOT) + -AN. On foot.—*n.* A walker.

Ped'igree, *n.* Formerly *pedegru*, *pee-de-grew*, &c., app. A.F. forms = F. *piè* (*pied*, L. *pēs*, FOOT) *de grue* (L. *grus*, CRANE), 'crane's foot', so called from a three-line mark like a bird's claws used to denote succession in pedigrees. A genealogical table; lineage, descent.

Ped'iment, *n.* Alteration of *periment*, *peremint*, said to be a workmen's term, of obscure orig. The triangular part crowning the front of a building in the Grecian style.

Ped'lar, *n.* Orig. obscure. Much earlier than PEDDLE. A travelling seller of small goods.

Peel, *n.*[1] O.F. *pel*, *piel* (F. *pieu*), L. *pālus*, stake. PALE, *n.* Formerly, a stake, a palisade. A small tower in the border counties of England and Scotland (prob. orig. *peel-house*, 'palisaded house').

Peel, *vt.* Var. of PILL, *v.*, now dial. in this sense. To strip of integument; to strip *off* (the integument).—*vi.* To become bare of bark, skin, &c.—*n.*[2] The rind of a fruit.

Peep, *v.*[1]*i.* Orig. unknown. To look through a narrow aperture; to look furtively or slyly; to begin to appear.—*n.*[1] An act of peeping.

Peep, *v.*[2]*i.* M.E. *pēpen*, earlier *pīpen*, *pypen*, to PIPE. To make the weak shrill sound of young birds, mice, &c.—*n.*[2] The sound.

Peer, *n.* O.F. *per*, *peer* (F. *pair*)—L. *pār*, equal. PAR. One's equal; a member of one of the degrees of nobility, a noble.—**Peer'**AGE, *n.* The body of peers; the rank of a peer; a book containing a list of peers.—**Peer'**ESS, *n.*—**Peer'**LESS, *a.* Matchless.

Peer, *vi.* Orig. uncertain. To look narrowly; to peep out; to come in sight. [fretful.

Pee'vish, *a.* Orig. unknown. Querulous,

Peg, *n.* App. f. L.G. Cf. L.G. *pigge*, dial. Du. *peg*. A pin or bolt.—*vt.* To fix with a peg; to mark *out* with pegs.—*vi.* To work *away* persistently.

Pe'jorate, *vt.* L. *pējōrāre*, *pējōrātum*, f. *pējor*, worse. To make worse, to depreciate.—**Pe'jor**ATIVE, *a.*

Pel'erine, *n.* F. *pèlerine*, 'pilgrim's cape', fem. of *pèlerin*, PILGRIM. A woman's long narrow cape or tippet.

Pelf, *n.* O.N.F. **pelfe*, var. of O.F. *pelfre*, booty, spoil, perh. conn. with L. *pilāre*, in sense 'to pillage', F. *piller*. DEPILATORY. PILFER. Money, wealth (in contempt).

Pel'ican, *n.* L.L. *pelicānus*—G. *pelekan*, perh. f. *peleka-ein*, to hew with an axe (f. *pelekus*, axe), from the appearance or action of the bill. A water-bird with a large bill.

Pelisse', *n.* F.—L. *pellicia* (*vestis*), (coat) of skins, f. *pellis*, skin. FELL, *n.*[1] PILLION. PELL. SURPLICE. A long mantle; a child's coat.

Pell, *n.* O.F. *pel* (F. *peau*), L. *pellis*, skin. (See prec.) A skin or roll of parchment.

Pel'let, *n.* F. *pelote*, dim. f. L. *pila*, ball. PLATOON. A small ball; a globule of shot.

Pell-mell, *adv.* F. *pêle-mêle*, in O.F. *meslemesle*. *Pesle-* uncertain. *-Mesle* app. the stem of *mesler*, to mix. MEDDLE. In confusion.

Pellu'cid, *a.* L. *pellūcidus*, f. *pel-*, PER*lūcēre*, to shine through. LUCID. Transparent.

Pelt, *n.*[1] App. conn. with PELL. A raw hide.

Pelt, *vt.* Orig. uncertain. To assail with missiles.—*vi.* To aim *at* with missiles; of rain, &c., to beat violently.—*n.*[2] An act of pelting.

Pel'vis, *n.* L. *pelvis*, basin. The basin-shaped cavity formed by the haunch-bones.

Pem'mican, *n.* N. Amer. Indian *pimecan*, f. *pime*, fat. Dried and pressed meat and fat.

Pen, *n.*[1] O.E. *penn*. Orig. uncertain. A small enclosure.—*v.*[1]*t.* To shut up in a pen.

Pen, *n.*[2] O.F. *penne*—L. *penna*, feather, in L.L. pen. FIN. PENNON. PINION.[1] An instrument for writing with ink.—*v.*[2]*t.* To write, to compose.

Pe'nal, *a.* F. *pénal*—L. *pēnālis*, *poenālis*, a. f. *poena*, G. *poinē*, penalty. PAIN. SUBPOENA. Of or relating to punishment; punishable.—**Pe'nal**IZE, *vt.* To make punishable; to subject to a penalty.—**Pen'al**TY, *n.* A punishment, fine; suffering or loss due to a fault, &c.

Pen'ance, *n.* O.F. *peneance*, *pennance*—L. *paenitentia*, penitence, f. *paenitens*, PENITENT. Discipline imposed upon a penitent.

Pen'cil, *n.* O.F. *pincel* (F. *pinceau*)—L. *pēnicillus*, dim. of *pēniculus*, brush, dim. of *pēnis*, tail. PENIS. A small paint-brush used by artists; an instrument, gen. of black-lead, for writing, drawing, &c.; a set of converging or diverging rays of light.—*vt.* To mark with a pencil; to draw or write with a pencil.

Pen'dant, *n.* F. *pendant*, use as *n.* of pres pple. of *pendre*, L. *pendēre*, to hang, conn with *pendĕre*, *pensum*, to cause to hang, to weigh, to pay. APPEND. DEPEND. EXPEND. PENSILE. PENSION. PENSIVE. A hanging ornament; a tapering nautical flag (in this sense app. a corr. of PENNON).—**Pen'dent**, *a.* F. *pendant*. Hanging.—**Pend'ing**, *ppl.a.* After F. *pendant*. Remaining undecided.—*prep.* During; until.—**Pen'dulous**, *a.* L *pendulus*, hanging down (f. *pendēre*) + -OUS. Pendent; vibrating.—**Pen'dulum**, *n.* Mod. L., use as *n.* of neut. of *pendulus*. A body suspended so as to swing, esp. as a part of a clock.

Pen'etrate, *vt.* L. *penetrāre*, *penetrātum*, conn. with *penitus*, in the inside. To make one's (or its) way into; to permeate; to find out, understand.—*vi.* To gain entrance or access.—**Pen'etr**ABLE, *a.*—**Penetr**A'TION, *n.*—**Pen'etrat**IVE, *a.*

Pen'guin, *n.* Orig. obscure. App. first applied to the great auk (still called in F. *grand pingouin*). A southern sea-bird.

Penin'sula, *n.* L. *paeninsula*, f. *paene*, almost+*insula*. ISLE. A piece of land nearly surrounded by water.—**Penin'sul**AR,[1] *a.*

Pe'nis, *n.* L. *pēnis*, tail, penis. PENCIL. The male organ of generation.

Pen'itent, *a.* O.F. *penitent*—L. *paenitens*, *paenitentis*, pres.pple. of *paenitēre*, to repent. PENANCE. REPENT. That repents with purpose to amend.—*n.* One who repents; one doing penance; one under the direction of a confessor.—**Pen'it**ENCE, *n.*—**Peniten'**TIAL, *a.*—**Peniten'ti**ARY, *a.* Of, doing, administering penance.—*n.* An ecclesiastical officer dealing with penitents; a prison.

Pen'nant, *n.* App. a compromise between PENNON and PENDANT. A pennon.

Pen'non, *n.* O.F. *pennon*, feather of an arrow, pennon, prob. f. L. *penna*. PEN.[2] A streamer attached to a lance: a pendant.

Pen'ny, *n.*; pl. **Pen'nies**, **Pence**. O.E. *pening*, *penig* = O.S. *penning*, O.H.G. *pfenning* (Ger. *pfennig*). A coin of the value of 1/12 of a shilling.—**Pen'ni**LESS, *a.* Destitute.—**Pen'nyweight**, *n.* 1/20 of an ounce Troy.

Pen'sile, *a.* L. *pensilis*, f. **pens-*, *pendĕre*. PENDANT. Suspended, hanging down.

Pen'sion, *n.* F. *pension*—L. *pensio*, *pensiōnis*, payment, f. *pendĕre*. PENDANT. An annuity in consideration of past services.—*vt.* To grant a pension to.—**Pen'sion**ARY, *a.* In receipt of, consisting in, a pension.—*n.* A pensioner. **Pen'sion**ER, *n.* One in receipt of a pension.

Pen'sive, *a.* F. *pensif*, *-ive*, f. *penser*, to think —L. *pensāre*, freq. of *pendĕre*. PENDANT. PANSY. POISE. PREPENSE. Thoughtful; sad.

Pent, *pa.pple.* and *ppl.a.* Pa.pple. of *Pend*, obs. var. of PEN, *v.*[1] Shut up, confined.

Pent'agon, *n.* G. *pentagōnon*, f. *penta-*, combining form of *pente*, FIVE + *gōnia*, angle. A figure having five angles and five sides.—**Pentag'on**AL, *a.*—**Pentam'eter**, *n.* L. *pentameter*—G. *pentametros*, a., f. *penta-* + *metron*, measure. A verse consisting of five feet; *dactylic pentameter*, a line composed of two halves, the first consisting of two dactyls (either or both of which may be replaced by a spondee) and a long syllable, the second of two dactyls and a long or short syllable.

Pent'ateuch, *n.* L. *pentateuchus*—G. *pentateuchos*, orig. a., 'of five books', f. *penta-* (see prec.) + *teuchos*, implement, in late G., book. The first five books of the Old Testament.

Pent'ecost, *n.* Eccles.L. *pentēcostē*—G. *pentēkostē* (*hēmera*), lit. 'fiftieth (day)'. A Jewish festival on the fiftieth day after the Passover; Whitsunday.

Pent'house, *n.* Corr. of M.E. *pentis*, *pendis*, app. aphetic f. O.F. *apentis*, *apendis*—L. *appendicium*, appendage, conn. with *appendĕre*. APPEND. Associated with F. *pente*, slope. A subsidiary structure serving as an outhouse, &c.; a sloping roof.

Penul'timate, *a.* L. *paene*, almost. The last but one.—*n.* The last syllable but one.

Penum'bra, *n.* L. *paene*, almost + *umbra*, shadow. UMBRAGE. The partial shadow surrounding the total shadow in an eclipse.

Pen'ury, *n.* L. *pēnūria*, want, need. Poverty. —**Penu'ri**OUS, *a.* Parsimonious, stingy.

Pe'ony, *n.* O.E. *peonie*—L.L. *peōnia*, L. *paeōnia*—G. *paiōnia*, f. *Paiōn* = *Paian*. PÆAN. A plant with large globular flowers formerly used in medicine.

Peo'ple, *n.* O.F. *pople*, *peuple*, &c.—L. *populus*. DEPOPULATE. POPULACE. PUBLIC. Persons forming a community; lieges, subjects, followers; the common people; persons indefinitely.—*vt.* To fill with people; to inhabit.

Pep'per, *n.* O.E. *pipor* = M.Du. *peper*, M.H.G., Ger. *pfeffer*—L. *piper* = G. *peperi*, of Oriental orig. A pungent condiment prepared from the berries of a plant; the plant.—*vt.* To season with, to sprinkle like, pepper.—**Pep'permint**, *n.* A species of mint; its pungent essential oil; a lozenge flavoured with this.—**Pep'pery**,[2] *a.* Pungent; hot-tempered.

Pep'sin, *n.* G. *pepsis*, digestion (f. *pessein*, *peptein*, to COOK, digest) + chem. suff. *-in*. DYSPEPSIA. The active principle of gastric juice.—**Pep'ti**C, *a.* Of, promoting, digestion.

Peram'bulate, *vt.* L. PER*ambulāre*, *perambulātum*. AMBLE. AMBULANCE. To walk through, over, or about; to survey.—**Perambul**A'TION, *n.*—**Peram'bulat**OR, *n.* A hand-carriage for a child.

Perceive', *vt.* O.F. **perceivre*, northern form of *perçoivre* (F. *percevoir*)—L. *percipĕre*, *perceptum*, to seize, to perceive, f. PER-, thoroughly + *capĕre*, to take. CAPABLE. To apprehend with the mind or one of the senses.—**Perceiv'**ABLE, *a.*—**Per'cept**, *n.* From neut. of *perceptus*, pa.pple. of *percipĕre*. The object of perception; the mental result of perceiving. —**Percep'ti**BLE, *a.*—**Percep'tib**LY,[2] *adv.* —**Percep'ti**ON, *n.* —**Percep'ti**VE, *a.*— **Percip'i**ENT, *a.* Perceiving, conscious.

Percent'age, *n.* *Per cent* (CENT) + -AGE. A rate or proportion per cent.

Perch, *n.*[1] F. *perche*—L. *perca*—G. *perkē*, so called from its dusky colour. Cf. *perknos*, dark coloured. A freshwater fish.

Perch, *n.*[2] F. *perche*—L. *pertica*, pole. A horizontal bar for a bird to rest upon; as a measure, a pole.—*vi.* and *t.* To alight or rest, to set, upon or as upon a perch.

Perchance', *adv.* A.F. *par chance*, f. O.F. *par* (L. *per*), by + *cheance*, *chance*, CHANCE. By any chance; perhaps.

Per'colate, *vt.* L. PER*cōlāre*, *percōlātum*, f. *cōlum*, strainer, conn. with *cōlāre*. COLANDER. To filter or ooze through.—*vi.* To ooze. —**Percol**A'TION, *n.*

Percus'sion, *n.* L. *percussio*, *percussiōnis*, n. of action f. *percutĕre*, *percussum*, to strike through, strike, f. PER- + *quatĕre*, to shake, strike. CONCUSS. Striking; a stroke.

Perdi'tion, *n.* O.F. *perdicion* (F. *perdition*) —L. *perditio*, *perditiōnis*, n. of action f. *perdĕre*, to destroy, f. PER- + *dăre*, to give, put. Destruction; eternal death.

Per'egrinate, *vi.* L. *peregrīnāri*, *peregrīnātus*, f. *peregrīnus*. (See next.) To travel, journey.—**Peregrin**A'TION, *n.*

Per'egrine, *a.* L. *peregrīnus*, f. *peregre*, abroad, from or to abroad, f. PER-, through + *ager*, field, land. ACRE. PILGRIM. Foreign.

Per'emptory, *a.* A.F. *peremptorie* (F. *péremptoire*)—L. *peremptōrius*, destructive, decisive, f. PER*imĕre*, *peremptum*, to take away entirely, destroy, f. *emĕre*. EXEMPT. Precluding debate, settled; decisive; positive, dogmatic.—**Per'emptori**LY,[2] *adv.*

Peren'nial, *a.* L. *perennis* (f. PER + *annus*, year) + -AL. Lasting through the year; permanent, everlasting.—*n.* A plant which lives for a number of years.—**Peren'nial**LY,[2] *adv.*

Per'fect, *a.* M.E. *parfit*—O.F. *parfit* (F. *parfait*)—L. *perfectus*, pa.pple. of *perficĕre*, to complete, accomplish, f. PER- + *facĕre*, to do. FACT. Thoroughly versed or skilled; complete, faultless; precise; unqualified; mere, sheer; of a tense, expressing completed action. —*vt.* To make perfect, to bring to completion. —**Perfec'ti**BLE, *a.*—**Perfecti**BIL'ITY, *n.*— **Perfec'ti**ON, *n.*—**Per'fect**LY,[2] *adv.*

Perfer'vid, *a.* PER-. Very fervid or ardent.

Per'fidy, *n.* F. *perfidie*—L. *perfidia*, f. *perfidus*, that breaks faith, f. PER- + *fides*, FAITH. Treachery.—**Perfid'i**OUS, *a.* Treacherous.

Per'forate, *vt.* L. *perforāre*, *perforātum*, f. PER- + *forāre*, to BORE. To make a hole or rows of holes through.—**Perfor**A'TION, *n.*

Perforce', *adv.* O.F. *par force*, by FORCE. Of necessity; compulsorily.

Perform', *vt.* O.F. *par-*, *performer*, f. *par-* (= PER-) + *forme*, FORM, 'to carry through in due form'; or perh. alteration of *parfournir*, to achieve, complete, f. *par-* + *fournir*, to FURNISH. To carry into effect; to accomplish, execute, do, make; to go through or execute (a duty, a play, &c.), act (a part, &c.).—*vi.* To do one's part; to act in a play, perform music, &c.—**Perform'**ANCE, *n.*—**Perform'**ER, *n.*

Perfume', *vt.* F. *parfumer*, lit. 'to smoke thoroughly', f. *par-* (= PER-) + L. *fūmāre*, to smoke, reek, f. *fūmus*, smoke, FUME. To impart a sweet scent to.—**Per'fume**, *n.* A sweet scent; a substance emitting a sweet scent.—**Perfum'**ER, *n.* One who makes or sells perfumes.—**Perfum'**ERY, *n.* His business; his place of business; his wares.

Perfunct'ory, *a.* Late Law L. *perfunctōrius*, lit. 'in the manner of one who wishes to get through with a matter', f. *perfunctor*, agent-n. f. PER*fungi*, *perfunctus*, to perform, get through with. FUNCTION. Done merely as a matter of duty or for form's sake.

Per'gola, *n.* It.—L. *pergula*, projecting shed, vine-arbour, f. *pergĕre*, to go on, proceed, f. PER- + *regĕre*. REGENT. An arbour of plants on trellis-work; a covered walk thus formed.

Perhaps', *adv.* L. *per*, by + *happes*, *haps*, pl. of *happe*, HAP. It may be, possibly.

Pe'ri, *n.* Per. *parī*, *perī*. In Persian mythology, a good (orig. an evil) fairy or genie.

Pericar'dium, *n.* G. *perikardion*, neut. of *perikardios*, round the heart, f. PERI- + *kardia*. CARDIAC. The membrane enclosing the heart.

Per'igee, *n.* PERI- + G. *gē*, the earth. The point of the moon's or a planet's orbit nearest the earth.—**Perihe'lion**, *n.* G. *hēlios*, sun. The point of a planet's orbit nearest the sun.

Per'il, *n.* F. *péril*—L. *periculum*, experiment, peril, f. root of *experiri* (EXPERIENCE) + *-culum*, suff. naming instruments. Danger, risk.—*vt.* To put in peril.—**Per'il**OUS, *a.*

Perim'eter, *n.* L. *perimetros*—G. *perimetros*, f. PERI- + *metron*, measure. Circumference.

Pe'riod, *n.* F. *période*—L. *periodus*—G. *periodos*, lit. 'way round', f. PERI- + *hodos*, way. METHOD. The time of revolution of a heavenly body; an indefinite or a specified portion of time; end; a complete sentence; the point (.) marking the end of this.—**Period'**IC, **Period'**ICAL, *aa.* Of or proper to the revolution of a heavenly body; recurring at intervals.—The latter also, published regularly each week, month, &c.; and as *n.*, a periodical magazine.—**Period'ical**LY,[2] *adv.*

Peripatet'ic, *a.* F. *péripatétique*—L. *peripatēticus*—G. *peripatētikos*, given to walking about, applied to Aristotle, who taught while walking, and his followers, f. PERI- + *pate-ein*, to walk. Of or relating to Aristotle's philosophy or followers; going about, itinerant.

Periph'ery, *n.* O.F. *peripherie*—L.L. *peripheria*—G. *periphereia*, f. PERI- + *pherein*, to carry, BEAR. Circumference.

Periph'rasis, *n.* L.—G. *periphrasis*, f. PERI- + *phrasis*. PHRASE. A roundabout way of speaking; a roundabout expression.—**Periphrast'**IC, *a.*

Per'iscope, *n.* PERI- + G. *skope-ein*, to look. An optical contrivance, used on submarines and in trench warfare, for giving a view of objects as they appear from a higher point.

Per'ish, *vi.* O.F. *periss-*, lengthened stem of *perir*—L. PER*īre*, to pass away, perish, f. *īre*, to go. To cease to exist.—**Per'ish**ABLE, *a.*

Perispo'menon, *a.* G. *perispōmenon*, neut. pres.pple. pass. of *perispa-ein*, to draw or pull round, mark with the circumflex, f. PERI- + *spa-ein*, to draw, pull. In *Greek grammar*, having the circumflex accent on the last syllable. — A PRO*perispomenon* word has this accent on the penultima'e.

Per'istyle, *n.* F. *péristyle*—L. *peristȳlum*—G. *peristulon*, neut. of *peristulos*, having pillars all round, f. PERI- + *stulos*, pillar. A row of surrounding columns; the space surrounded.

Peritone'um, -æ'um, *n.* L.—G. *peritonaion*, neut. of *peritonaios*, a. f. *peritonos*, stretched round, f. PERI- + *-tonos*, stretched, f. *teinein*. TONE. The membrane lining the cavity of the abdomen.—**Periton**I'TIS, *n.*

Per'iwig, *n.* Corr. of *perwyke*, alteration of *perruck*—F. *perruque*, PERUKE. A wig.

Per'iwinkle, *n.*[1] O.E. *peruince*—L. *pervinca*. An evergreen trailing plant with blue flowers.

Per'iwinkle, *n.*[2] A late and corrupt form, perh. by association with prec. See under WINKLE. A bivalve edible mollusc.

Per'jure, *v.refl.* O.F. *parjurer*—L. PER*jūrāre*, f. *jūrāre*, to swear. JURY. To forswear oneself.—**Per'jur**ER, *n.*—**Per'jur**Y,[1] *n.*

Perk, *a.* Orig. uncertain. Pert, saucy.—*vi.* To carry oneself, lift one's head, briskly or jauntily. — *vt.* To smarten *up*; to hold *up* briskly or jauntily.—**Perk'**Y,[2] *a.* Perk.

Per'manent, *a.* L. *permanens*, *permanentis*, pres. pple. of PER*manēre*, to stay to the end. MANOR. Continuing or meant to continue indefinitely, lasting.—**Per'man**ENCE, *n.*—**Per'man**ENCY, *n.* The quality of being permanent; a permanent thing, position, &c.

Per'meate, *vt.* L. PER*meāre*, *permeātum*, to go or pass through. CONGEE. To pass or spread itself through.—**Per'me**ABLE, *a.*—**Perme**A'TION, *n.*

Permit', *vt.* L. PER*mittĕre*, *permissum*, to let go through, permit, f. *mittĕre*, to send. MISSION. To allow.—**Per'mit**, *n.* A written permission.—**Permis'**SIBLE, *a.*—**Permis'**SION, *n.*—**Permis'**SIVE, *a.*

Permute', *vt.* L. PER*mūtāre*, to change thoroughly, interchange. MUTABLE. To subject to permutation.—**Permut**A'TION, *n.* A changing of the order of a set of things; each of the ways in which the things can be arranged.

Pernic'ious, *a.* F. *pernicieux*—L. *perniciōsus*, f. *pernicies*, destruction, ruin, f. PER- + *nex*, *necis*, death, conn. with *necāre*, to kill. INTERNECINE. Deadly, ruinous.

Per'orate, *vi.* L. PER*ōrāre*, *perōrātum*. ORACLE. To speak at length; to utter a peroration.—**Peror**A'TION, *n.* A rhetorical conclusion to a speech.

Perpendic'ular, *a.* O.F. *perpendiculer*—L. *perpendiculāris*, f. *perpendiculum*, plummet, f. PER- + *pendĕre*, to hang + *-culum*, suff. of instruments. PENDANT. At right angles to a plane, &c.—*n.* A perpendicular line; erect position.—**Perpendic'ular**LY,[2] *adv.*

Per'petrate, *vt.* L. *perpetrāre*, *perpetrātum*, to carry through, perform, f. PER- + *patrāre*, in sim. sense. To commit (an evil deed).—**Perpetr**A'TION, *n.*—**Per'petrat**OR, *n.*

Perpet'ual, *a.* F. *perpétuel*—L. *perpetuālis*, universal, f. *perpetuus*, perpetual, app. f. PER- + *petĕre*. PETITION. Lasting or meant to last for ever; continuous.—**Perpet'ual**LY,[2] *adv.*—**Perpet'u**ATE,[3] *vt.*—**Perpetu**A'TION, *n.*—**Perpetu'**ITY, *n.*

Perplex', *vt.* Formed under the influence of obs. *Perplex*, a., puzzled, intricate (L. *perplexus*, intricate, f. PER- + *plexus*, pa.pple. of *plectĕre*, to plait, conn. with *plicāre*, to fold (PLAIT)), and of *Perplexed*, ppl. a. (itself app. an alteration of the a.). To puzzle, bewilder; to make intricate.—**Perplex'**ITY, *n.*

Per'quisite, *n.* L. *perquīsītum*, neut. pa.pple. of *perquīrĕre*, to seek for diligently (f. PER- +

quaerĕre. ACQUIRE), in Med.L., an acquisition. A casual emolument, a gratuity.

Per'ry, *n.* O.F. *peré*—L.L. type **pērātum*, f. *pēra*, PEAR. The fermented juice of pears.

Per'secute, *vt.* F. *persécuter*—L. PER*sequi*, *persecūtus*, to pursue. SEQUEL. To oppress for the holding of an opinion; to harass, vex. —**Persecu'tion**, *n.*—**Per'secutor**, *n.*

Persevere', *vi.* F. *persévérer*—L. *persevērāre*, to abide by strictly, persevere, f. PER*sevērus*, very strict. SEVERE. To continue steadfastly in a course of action.—**Persever'ance**, *n.*

Persist', *vi.* L. *persistĕre*, f. PER- + *sistĕre*, to stand. ASSIST. To continue steadfastly in a course of action, a state, an opinion, &c.; to last, endure.—**Persist'ence**, -ENCY, *nn.* —**Persist'ent**, *a.*—**Persist'ently**,[2] *adv.*

Per'son, *n.* O.F. *persone* (F. *personne*)—L. *persōna*, an actor's mask, a character or part, a person, perh. conn. with *personāre*, to sound through. ASSONANCE. PARSON. A character sustained or assumed; an individual human being; bodily frame or figure; one of the three modes of being constituting the Trinity; each of the three classes of pronouns, &c., denoting the person referred to. — **Per'sonable**, *a.* Having a well-formed person.—**Per'sonage**, *n.* A person of note; a person.—**Per'sonal**, *a.* One's own; done, held, &c., by oneself; of one's person or body; directed or referring to a particular person; *personal property*, property excluding land and the interests in land that pass to the heir; of or denoting a grammatical person.—**Personal'ity**, *n.* The being a person; distinctive personal character; a person; the being directed to a particular person; a personal remark, &c.—**Per'sonally**,[2] *adv.*—**Per'sonalty**, *n.* Personal property.—**Per'sonate**,[3] *vt.* To play the part of; to pass oneself off as.—**Persona'tion**, *n.* —**Person'ify**, *vt.* To figure or represent as a person; to typify.—**Personifica'tion**, *n.* —**Personnel'**, *n.* F. The body of persons engaged in a service.

Perspec'tive, *n.* Med.L. *perspectīva* (*ars*), (the science) of optics, fem. of *perspectīvus*, optical, f. *perspicĕre*, *perspectum*, to look or see through, view, f. PER- + *specĕre*, to look. SPECIES. The art of so delineating objects on a plane surface that they appear to have their actual relative positions and magnitudes; a drawing in perspective; a scene or view.

Perspic'uous, *a.* L. *perspicuus*, transparent, manifest (f. *perspicĕre* (see prec.)) + -OUS. Clearly expressed; clear in expression.—**Perspicu'ity**, *n.*—**Perspica'cious**, *a.* Of quick discernment.—**Perspicac'ity**, *n.*

Perspire', *vi.* L. PER*spīrāre*, etymologically to breathe through, but only in senses 'to breathe everywhere', 'to blow constantly'. ASPIRE. To sweat.—**Perspira'tion**, *n.*

Persuade', *vt.* L. PER*suādēre*, *persuāsum*. DISSUADE. To bring to believe something, convince; to induce to an act.—**Persua'sion**, *n.*—**Persua'sive**, *a.*

Pert, *a.* Aphetic f. archaic *Apert*, open, unconcealed (formerly also clever, pert)—O.F. *apert*, open, clever—L. *apertus*, pa.pple. of *aperire*, to open. APERIENT. MALAPERT. Forward in speech and behaviour.

Pertain', *vi.* O.F. *partenir*—L. *pertinēre*, to reach, extend, belong, f. PER- + *tenēre*, to hold. TENANT. To belong; to be appropriate; to relate.—**Per'tinent**, *a.* To the point, apposite.—**Per'tinence**, -ENCY, *nn.*

Pertina'cious, *a.* L. *pertinax*, *pertinācis*, very tenacious, pertinacious (f. PER- + *tenax*, TENACIOUS) + -OUS. Persistent, obstinate.—**Pertinac'ity**, *n.*

Perturb', *vt.* O.F. *perturber*—L. PER*turbāre*. TURBID. To disturb greatly, to agitate. —**Perturb'able**, *a.*—**Perturba'tion**, *n.*

Peruke', *n.* F. *perruque*—It. *perruca*, of obscure orig. PERIWIG. A wig.

Peruse', *vt.* App. PER- + USE, *v.*, with notion of 'going through'. To examine in detail; to read thoroughly; to read.—**Perus'al**, *n.*

Pervade', *vt.* L. PER*vādĕre*, *pervāsum*, to go or spread through. EVADE. To permeate. —**Perva'sion**, *n.*—**Perva'sive**, *a.*

Pervert', *vt.* F. *pervertir*—L. PER*vertĕre*, to overturn, ruin, corrupt. VERSE. To turn from the right course, use, &c.; to corrupt.—**Per'vert**, *n.* An apostate.—**Perver'sion**, *n.*—**Perver'sive**, *a.*—**Per'verse**, *a.* F. *pervers*—L. *perversus*, pa.pple. of *pervertĕre*. Wicked; persistent in what is wrong; froward; petulant.—**Perver'sity**, *n.*

Per'vious, *a.* L. *pervius* (f. PER- + *via*, way) + -OUS. DEVIATE. Permeable.

Pes'simism, *n.* L. *pessimus*, worst + -ISM, after *optimism*. The doctrine that everything tends to evil; tendency to expect the worst.—**Pes'simist**, *n.*—**Pessimis'tic**, *a.*

Pest, *n.* F. *peste*—L. *pestis*. A pestilence; a noxious or troublesome thing or person.—**Pestif'erous**, *a.* L. *pestifer* (f. *-fer*, bearing, f. *ferre*, to BEAR) + -OUS. Bringing plague, deadly; noxious.—**Pes'tilent**, *a.* L. *pestilens*, *pestilentis*, a ppl. deriv. f. *pestis*. Deadly; noxious; troublesome.—**Pes'tilence**, *n.* A deadly epidemic.—**Pestilen'tial**, *a.*

Pes'ter, *vt.* App. short for obs. *Empester*, *Impester*, to entangle (O.F. *empestrer* (F. *empêtrer*), formed f. EM-[1] (1) + L.L. *pastōrium*, tether for a horse, f. *pascĕre*, to feed); or perh. for the O.F. word. PASTOR. To trouble persistently with petty vexations.

Pest'le, *n.* O.F. *pestel*—L. *pistillum*, dim. of **pistrum*, f. *pinsĕre*, *pistum*, to pound. PISTIL. PISTON. An instrument for pounding in a mortar.—*vt.* To pound with a pestle.

Pet, *n.*[1] Orig. unknown. An animal kept as a favourite; a darling.—*vt.* To treat as a pet.

Pet, *n.*[2] Orig. unknown. Offence at being (or feeling) slighted; a fit of ill-humour from this cause.—**Pet'tish**, *a.* Subject to pets.

Pet'al, *n.* F. *pétale*—Mod.L. *petalum*, in L., metal plate—G. *petalon*, leaf, f. root of *petannunai*, to spread out. FATHOM. A flower leaf.

Petard', *n.* F. *pétard*, f. *péter*, to break wind, f. *pet*, L. *pēditum*, a doing so, neut. pa.pple. of *pēdĕre*, to do so. A small engine of war for blowing in a gate, &c.

Pe'ter, *vi.* From U.S. Orig. unknown. *To peter out*, to disappear gradually, die out, fail.

Peti'tion, *n.* F. *pétition*—L. *petitio*, *petitiōnis*, n. of action f. *petĕre*, to aim at, seek. APPETITE. COMPETE. PERPETUAL. PETULANT. REPEAT. An asking or humbly requesting; a formal application or request in writing.—*vt.* To address or present a petition to.—**Peti'tionary**, *a.*—**Peti'tioner**, *n.*

Pet'rel, *n.* Perh. f. St. *Peter* (as seeming to walk on the sea). A small sea-bird.

Pet'rify, *vt.* F. *pétrifier*, f. L. *petra*, G. *petra*, rock + *-ficāre*. -FY. SALTPETRE. To convert into stone (often *fig.*).—**Petrifac'tion**, *n.*

Petro'leum, *n.* Med.L., f, *petra* (see prec.) + L. *oleum*, OIL. A mineral oil found in rocks or floating on water.—**Pet'rol**, *n.* F. *pétrole*, f. Med.L. *petroleum*, Refined petroleum.

Pet'ticoat, *n.* Orig. two words, PETTY, in obs. sense 'small', and COAT. Formerly, a small coat. A woman's skirt or under-skirt.

Pet'tifogger, *n.* PETTY + (poss.) *Fugger*, the name of the celebrated mercantile family of Augsburg. An attorney in petty and sharp practice.—**Pet'tifog**, *vi.* App. back-formation f. the *n.* To act as a pettifogger.

Pet'ty, *a.* Late M.E. *pety*, phonetic spelling of obs. *petit*—F. *petit*, small, of uncertain orig. Inconsiderable, trifling; non-commissioned.

Pet'ulant, *a.* F. *pétulant*—L. *petulans, petulantis*, pert, pres.pple. of **petulāre*, dim. of *petĕre*. PETITION. (App. influenced by PETTISH.) Pettish, peevish.—**Pet'ul**ANCE, *n.*

Pew, *n.* Late M.E. *puwe, pywe, pewe*, app. orig. identical in form with O.F. *puye, puie*, parapet, balcony—L. *podia*, pl. of *podium*, elevated place, balcony—G. *podion*, base, pedestal, dim of *pous*, FOOT. Formerly, a raised standing-place, now, a fixed bench, in a church.

Pe'wit, Pee'wit, *n.* Imitative of the cry. Cf. Du. *kieviet*, M.L.G. *kivit*. The lapwing.

Pew'ter, *n.* O.F. *peutre, peautre*, later also *espeautre*; in Du. *piauter, spiauter*, Ger. *spiauter*. Orig. unknown. SPELTER. An alloy of tin and lead; pewter ware; a pewter pot.

Phae'ton, *n.* G. *Phaethōn*, 'the shiner', son of Helios, the sun, and driver of his chariot. A light four-wheeled open carriage.

Phal'anx, *n.* L. *phalanx* — G. *phalagx*. Heavy-armed infantry (esp. Macedonian) in close order; a compact body of persons, &c.

Phan'tasm, *n.* F. *fantasme*—L. *phantasma* —G. *phantasma*, appearance, image, f. *phantazein*. FANTASY. An illusion; a phantom.—**Phantas'm**AL, *a.*—**Phantasmago'ria**, *n.* App. f. G. *phantasma* + *agora*, assembly. An exhibition of optical illusions (ofen *fig.*).—**Phan'tasy**, *n.* See FANTASY.—**Phan'tom**, *n.* O.F. *fantosme*, f. L. *phantasma*. An apparition or spectre; a mental illusion.

Pharisa'ic, *a.* L. *pharisaïcus*—G. *pharisaïkos*, f. *pharisaios*, a Pharisee, one of a Jewish sect distinguished by strict observance of the law, lit. 'one who separates himself', f. Heb. *pārūsh*, separated. Of the Pharisees; hypocritical (in this sense also **Pharisa'ic**AL).

Pharmaceu'tic, *a.* L. *pharmaceuticus*—G. *pharmakeutikos*, f. *pharmakeutēs* = *pharmakeus*, druggist, f. *pharmakon*, drug. Relating to pharmacy.—In *pl.* as *n.*, the science of pharmacy.—**Pharmaceu'tic**AL, *a.* Relating to or engaged in pharmacy.—**Pharmacopœ'ia**, *n.* G. *pharmakopoiia*, the art of making drugs, f. *pharmakon* + *poie-ein*, to make. An official book of drugs.—**Phar'macy**, *n.* O.F. *farmacie*—L.L. *pharmacīa*—G. *pharmakeia*, the art of the *pharmakeus*. The art of preparing and dispensing drugs.

Phase, *n.* G. *phasis*, f. *pha-*. FANTASY. An aspect of the moon or of a planet according to its illumination; a stage of change.

Pheas'ant, *n.* A.F. *fesant*—O.F. *fesan* (F. *faisan*)—L. *phāsiānus*—G. *phāsiānos* (*ornis*), (the bird) of the Phasis, a river of Colchis. A well-known game-bird.

Phenom'enon, *n.*; *pl.* **-mena**. L. *phaenomenon*—G. *phainomenon*, pres.pple. pass. of *phainein*. FANTASY. Any thing that appears or is observed; something remarkable.—**Phenom'en**AL, *a.* Of the nature of a phenomenon; relating to phenomena; remarkable.

Phial. See VIAL.

Philan'der, *vi.* From obs. *Philander*, n., one given to making love (used in story, &c., as a proper name, esp. for a lover, being app. taken as = a loving man)—G. *philandros*, a., loving men, f. *phile-ein*, to love + *anēr, andros*, man. To make love in a trifling manner.

Philan'thropy, *n.* L.L. *philanthrōpia*—G. *philanthrōpia*, f. *philanthrōpos*, loving men, f. *phile-ein*, to love + *anthrōpos*, man. Love to mankind, practical benevolence.—**Philanthrop'**IC, *a.*—**Philan'throp**IST, *n.*

Philat'ely, *n.* F. *philatélie* —G. *phile-ein*, to love + *atelēs*, free from tax, f. A-[4] + *telos*, tax. The practice of collecting postage stamps and other devices for prepaying letters, &c.

Philharmon'ic, *a.* F. *philharmonique*, after It. *filarmonico*, f. G. *phile-ein*, to love + *harmonikos*, HARMONIC. Fond of music.

Philip'pic, *n.* L. *Philippicus* = G. *Philippikos*, a. f. *Philippos*, Philip. Each of the orations of Demosthenes against Philip of Macedon; a bitter invective.

Phil'istine, *n.* F. *philistin*—L.L. *Philistīni*, pl.—Late G. *Philistinoi*, pl., prob. repg. the native name. A warlike people who harassed the Israelites; 'the enemy'; one lacking culture or taste.—**Phil'istin**ISM, *n.*

Philol'ogy, *n.* F. *philologie*—L. *philologia* —G. *philologia*, abstract n. f. *philologos*, fond of speech or of literature, f. *phile-ein*, to love + *logos*, discourse. Love of literature; the science of language.—**Philol'og**ER, *n.*—**Philolog'**ICAL, *a.*—**Philol'og**IST, *n.*

Philos'ophy, *n.* O.F. *philosophie*—L. *philosophia*—G. *philosophia*, n. of condition f. *philosophos*, lover of wisdom, philosopher, f. *phile-ein*, to love + *sophos*, skilful, wise, *sophia*, skill, wisdom. SOPHIST. The love of wisdom; the department of knowledge dealing with the general causes and principles of things; a philosophical system; one's system of life; serenity, calmness of temper.—**Philos'opher**, *n.* O.F. *philosophe*—L. *philosophus*—G. *philosophos*. One versed in, or regulating his life by, philosophy.—**Philosoph'**IC, -ICAL, *aa.* — **Philosoph'ical**LY,[2] *adv.* — **Philos'oph**IZE, *vi.* To play the philosopher.

Phil'tre, Phil'ter, *n.* F. *philtre*—L. *philtrum*—G. *philtron*, f. *phile-ein*, to love + *-tron*, suff. of instruments. A love-charm.

Phlebot'omy, *n.* O.F. *flebothomie*—L. *phlebotomia*—G. *phlebotomia*, f. *phleps, phlebos*, vein + *tom-*. EPITOME. Blood-letting.

Phlegm, *n.* O.F. *fleume, flemme* (F. *flegme*)—L. *phlegma, phlegmatis*—G. *phlegma*, inflammation, clammy humour (due to heat), f. *phlegein*, to burn, blaze. FLAGRANT. Mucus; apathy; calmness.—**Phlegmat'**IC, *a.*

Phœ'nix, *n.* O.E. and O.F. *fenix*—L. *phoenix* —G. *phoinix*. A bird fabled to be the only one of its kind, and, after living for five or six centuries, to burn itself to ashes and emerge with renewed youth.

Phonet'ic, *a.* G. *phōnētikos*, a. f. *phōnētos*, to be spoken, f. *phōne-ein*, to speak, f. *phōnē*, sound. ANTHEM. CACOPHONY. SYMPHONY. Representing, relating to, consisting of, vocal sounds.—In *pl.* as *n.*, the science of, vocal sounds.—**Phonet'ically**, *adv.* -AL. -LY.[2]

Pho'nogram, *n.* G. *phōnē* (see prec.) + *-gram*, after TELEGRAM. A symbol representing a spoken sound; a sound-record made by a phonograph.—**Pho'nograph**, *n.* *Phōnē* + *-graphos*, as in TELEGRAPH. An instrument for recording and reproducing sounds.

Phos'phorus, *n.* G. *phōsphoros*, bringing light, f. *phōs, phōtos*, light + *-phoros*, bringing, f. *pherein*, to BEAR. A non-metallic element luminous in the dark.—**Phosphoresce′**, *vi.* Suff. *-esce* aft. *-escĕre* of L. inceptives. To be luminous like phosphorus.—**Phosphores′**CENCE, *n.*—**Phosphores′**CENT, *a.*

Pho′tograph, *n.* G. *phōs* (see prec.) + *-graphos*, drawn, f. *graphein*, to draw. A picture or likeness obtained by the action of light on a sensitized film. — *vt.* To take a photograph of. — **Photog′raph**ER, *n.* — **Photograph′**IC, *a.*—**Photog′raphy**,[1] *n.*—**Photogravure′**, *n.* F., f. *gravure*, f. *graver*. GRAVE, *v.*[1] A process of engraving by the action of light; a picture thus produced.

Phrase, *n.* L.L. *phrasis*—G. *phrasis*, speech, way of speaking, f. *phrazein*, to point out, tell. PARAPHRASE. PERIPHRASIS. Manner of expression, diction; a small group of words expressing a single notion; a short or pithy expression. — *vt.* To express in words. — **Phraseol′**OGY, *n.* Manner of expression.

Phrenet′ic, *a.* O.F. *frenetike*—L.L. *phrenēticus*. FRANTIC. Fanatic; frantic.

Phrenol′ogy, *n.* G. *phrēn* (FRANTIC) + -LOGY. The doctrine that the degree of development of individual mental powers is indicated by the configuration of the skull.

Phthi′sis, *n.* G. *phthisis*, a wasting, f. *phthinein*, to decay, waste away. Consumption of the lungs.—**Phthi′**SICAL, *a.*

Phylac′tery, *n.* L. *phylactērium*—G. *phulaktērion*, guarded post, phylactery, f. *phulaktēr*, a guard, f. *phulassein*, to guard. PROPHYLACTIC. A small leather box containing Hebrew texts on vellum worn by Jews as a reminder to keep the law; an amulet.

Phylloxe′ra, *n.* G. *phullon*, leaf + *xēros*, dry. A genus of destructive plant-lice.

Phys′ic, *n.* M.E. *fisike*—O.F. *fisique*—L. *physica*—G. *phusikē* (*epistēmē*), (knowledge) of nature, f. *phusikos*, a. f. *phusis*, nature. The healing art; medicine.—In *pl.*, the science of the properties of matter and energy.—*vt.* To dose with medicine.—**Phys′ic**AL, *a.* Of matter; of, in accordance with, the laws of nature; of physics; corporeal.—**Phys′ical**LY,[2] *adv.*—**Phys**IC′IAN, *n.* A practiser of the healing art.—**Phys′ic**IST, *n.* A student of physics.

Physiogn′omy, *n.* O.F. *phisonomie*—Med. L. *physionomia*—G. *phusiognōmonia*, f. *phusis*, nature + *gnōmōn*. GNOMON. The art of judging of the character by the features; the face. —**Physiogn′om**IST, *n.*

Physiog′raphy, *n.* G. *phusis*, nature + *-graphia* as in GEOGRAPHY. A description of nature; the science of the natural features of the earth.—**Physiog′raph**ER, *n.*

Physiol′ogy, *n.* L. *physiologia*—G. *phusiologia*, natural science, f. *phusis*, nature + *-logia*. -LOGY. The science of the normal phenomena of living things.—**Physiol′og**IST, *n.*

Physique′, *n.* F., use as *n.* of *physique*, L. *physicus*, G. *phusikos*, physical. PHYSIC. Bodily structure and development.

Piac′ular, *a.* L. *piāculāris*, f. *piāculum*, propitiatory sacrifice, f. *piāre*, to propitiate, f. *pius*, PIOUS. Making expiation; sinful.

Pia′no, *a.* and *adv.* It.—L. *plānus*, flat, in L.L., soft, low. PLAIN. *Mus.*, in a low tone or voice.—**Pianofor′te**, *n.* It., earlier *piano e forte* (L. *fortis*. FORCE), soft and strong, used in the descriptive name of a harpsichord capable of gradation of tone. Also in shortened form **Pia′no**. A stringed musical instrument, in which tones are produced by hammers worked from a keyboard.—**Pi′an**IST, *n.* A player on the pianoforte.

Piaz′za, *n.* It. — Common Romanic type **plattia*—L. *platea*, broad street, courtyard—G. *plateia* (*hodos*), broad (street), fem. of *platus*, broad, flat. PLACE. PLAICE. PLANE, *n.*[1] PLATE. A public square or market-place.

Picaresque′, *a.* Sp. *picaresco*, roguish, f. *picaro*, rogue, of doubtful orig. Applied to fiction dealing with the adventures of rogues.

Pick, *n.*[1] App. a collateral form of PIKE.[1] A mattock.—Also **Pick′axe**—M.E. *pickoys*, *picois* (altered by confusion of the suff. with *axe*)—O.F. *picois*, Med.L. *picosium*, conn. with O.F. *pic*, in sense 'pickaxe'. PIKE.[1]

Pick, *vt.* O.E. **pician* or **pícan*, to puncture. Orig. doubtful. (In the first sense evidently conn. with prec.) PECK, *v.* To pierce, break the surface of; to form by picking; to clean (the teeth, &c.) by applying something pointed; to gather, cull; to take up (small bits of food); to choose *out*, select carefully; to seek and find an occasion of; to rifle the contents of.—*n.*[2] An act of picking; the choicest portion.

Pick′et, *n.* F. *piquet*, with dim. suff. f. *piquer*. PIKE.[3] A pointed stake; a body of troops or a soldier on watch; men stationed by a trade-union in a strike to dissuade or deter men willing to work (gen. in *pl.*).—*vt.* To enclose or secure with pickets; to post as a picket; to beset (non-strikers) with pickets.

Pick′le, *n.* App. f. M.Du. *pekel*(*e*) or M.L.G. *pēkel* (Ger. *pökel*). A salt or acid liquor for preserving flesh, vegetables, &c.; in *pl.*, pickled vegetables; a disagreeable plight; a troublesome child.—*vt.* To preserve in pickle.

Pic′nic, *n.* F. *pique-nique*, of obscure orig. A pleasure party including a repast out of doors.—*vi.* To hold or take part in a picnic.

Pic′ture, *n.* L. *pictūra*, f. *pingĕre*, *pictum* to PAINT. PIGMENT. A painting or drawing —*vt.* To represent in or as in a picture.—**Picto′rial**, *a.* L.L. *pictōrius* (f. L. *pictor*, agent-n. f. *pingĕre*) + -AL. Of, expressed in of the nature of, a picture; illustrated; graphic. —**Picto′rial**LY,[2] *adv.*—**Picturesque′**, *a* F. *pittoresque*—It. *pittoresco*, f. *pittore*, L *pictor*. Cf. STATUESQUE. Like, fit to be the subject of, a picture; graphic.

Pid′dle, *vi.* Orig. obscure. PEDDLE. To trifle, dally.

Pie, *n.*[1] O.F. *pie*—L. *pica*. The magpie.—**Pie′bald**, *a.* BALD in sense 'streaked with white'. Irregularly marked with white and black or other dark colour (like a magpie's plumage); parti-coloured.—**Pied**, *ppl.a.*, as if pa.pple. of a v. **pie*. Parti-coloured.

Pie, *n.*[2] Orig. obscure. A dish of meat, fruit, &c., covered with paste and baked.

Pie, *n.*[3] Poss. transferred use of prec., referring to a pie of miscellaneous contents. A mass of type mingled in confusion.

Piece, *n.* O.F. *pece*, *piece* (F. *pièce*). Orig. obscure. PEAT. A separate portion or fragment; a length in which cloth is woven; a cask, gen. = two hogsheads; a single object; an example; a gun; each of the pieces of ivory, &c., with which chess, &c., are played; a coin; a literary composition, a play.—*vt.* To repair; to join.—**Piece′meal**, *adv.* M.E. *pece-mele*. MEAL.[2] By pieces; into or in pieces.

Pier, *n.* Orig. *per*—Med.L. *pera*, of unknown orig. A support of a bridge; a structure projecting into the sea as a landing-place, &c.

Pierce, *vt.* O.F. *percer*, of uncertain orig. To penetrate as a sharp instrument does, to prick, perforate; to force one's way through or into.

Pi′ety, *n.* O.F, *piete*—L. *pietas*, f. *pius*, PIOUS.

PITY. Godliness, devoutness; dutifulness.—**Pi'et**ISM, *n.* A movement in the 17th c. for the revival of piety in the Lutheran Church; emotional or exaggerated piety.—**Pi'et**IST, *n.*

Pig, *n.* M.E. *pigge*, of obscure orig. A well-known domestic animal; an oblong mass of smelted metal. — *vi.* To lodge together like pigs.—**Pig'g**ERY, *n.* A place for pigs; pig-like condition. — **Pig'g**ISH, *a.* — **Pig'tail**, *n.* A plait of hair hanging from the back of the head.

Pig'eon, *n.* O.F. *pijon*, young bird, young dove, dove (F. *pigeon*)—L.L. *pipio*, *pipiōnis*, young chirping bird, f. *pipire*, to chirp, conn. with *pīpāre*. PIPE.[1] A well-known bird; a dupe or gull.—**Pig'eon-hole**, *n.* A hole for the passage of pigeons; a recess for pigeons to nest in; a compartment for papers.

Pig'ment, *n.* L. *pigmentum*, f. *pingĕre*. PICTURE. ORPIMENT. A paint or dye.

Pike, *n.*[1] O.E. *piic*, *pic* = O.F. *pic* (which, however, occurs later), of disputed orig. PEAK, *n.* PICK, *n.*[1] A sharp point, a spike.

Pike, *n.*[2] App. short for *pike-fish*. (See prec.) A freshwater fish with a long slender snout.

Pike, *n.*[3] F. *pique*, conn. with *piquer*, to pierce, prick, irritate, and *pic*. PIKE.[1] PICKET. PIQUE. A weapon consisting of a long wooden shaft with a pointed head of iron or steel.

Pilas'ter, *n.* F. *pilastre*—It. *pilastro* (the suff. expressing incomplete resemblance)—L. *pīla*. PILE.[2] A square pillar partly projecting from a wall.

Pilau', **Pilaw'**, *n.* Per. *pilāw*. An Oriental dish of rice boiled with meat, spices, &c.

Pil'chard, *n.* Orig. obscure. A small sea fish.

Pile, *n.*[1] O.E. *pīl*, dart, pointed stake=M.Du. *pīl*, O.H.G. *pfīl* (Ger. *pfeil*), dart, arrow—L. *pīlum*, pestle, javelin. A heavy beam driven into the ground to serve as a foundation.

Pile, *n.*[2] F. *pile*, heap, pier of a bridge, &c.—L. *pīla*, pillar. PILASTER. PILLAR. A heap; a high mass of masonry; an electric battery.—*vt.* To heap up; to cover *with* things heaped.

Pile, *n.*[3] L. *pilus*, hair. DEPILATORY. Fine short hair, wool; a nap upon cloth.

Pile, *n.*[4] L. *pila*. PILL. In *pl.*, hæmorrhoids.

Pil'fer, *vt.* App. f. O.F. *pelfrer*, to rob, f. *pelfre*. PELF. To steal in small quantities.

Pil'grim, *n.* O.F. **pelegrin*, later *pèlerin*—L. *peregrīnus*, foreign, a foreigner. PEREGRINE. A wanderer; one who journeys to a sacred place as an act of devotion.—**Pil'grim**AGE, *n.*

Pill, *n.* L *pilula*, dim. of *pila*, ball. PILE.[4] Cf. Ger. *pille*, F. *pilule*. A small ball of medicinal substance; any small round body.

Pill, *vt.* O.E, **pilian*, prob. f. L. *pilāre*, in sense 'to pillage'. DEPILATORY. To pillage.—**Pil'lage**, *n.* F. *pillage*, f. *piller*. PELF. Plunder, spoliation.—*vt.* To plunder, spoil.

Pil'lar, *n.* O.F. *piler* (F. *pilier*)—Late Pop. L. *pilāre*—L. *pila*. PILE.[2] A column.

Pill'ion, *n.* App. f. Celtic. Cf. Ir. *pillín*, Gael. *pillin*, ultimately f. L. *pellis*, skin. PELL. A woman's light saddle; a pad or cushion behind a saddle for a second rider.

Pil'lory, *n.* O.F. *pillori*, &c. Orig. uncertain. A wooden framework contrived to confine the head and hands of an offender.—*vt.* To set in the pillory; to expose to ridicule or abuse.

Pil'low, *n.* O.E. *pyle*, *pylu* = M.Du. *pöluwe*, O.H.G. *pfuliwi* (Ger. *pfühl*) — L. *pulvīnus*, cushion. A support for the head in sleeping.

Pi'lot, *n.* Early Mod.F. *pillotte* (now *pilote*)—It. *pilota*, supposed to be altered f. *pedota*, poss. f. late G. **pēdōtēs*, steersman, f. *pēdon*, oar. One who directs the course of a ship in waters where local knowledge is needed; a guide or leader.—*vt.* To conduct as pilot; to guide, lead.—**Pi'lot**AGE, *n.* [small pill.

Pil'ule, *n.* F. *pilule*. PILL, *n.* A pill; a

Pimp, *n.* Orig. obscure. One who provides means for the gratification of lust.

Pim'ple, *n.* Orig. unknown. A small solid tumour of the skin.—**Pim'ply**,[2] *a.*

Pin, *n.* Late O.E. *pinn* = M.L.G. *pinne*, *pin*, M.Du. *pinne*, app. f. L. *pinna*, pinnacle, applied also to points of various kinds (perh. to be distinguished from *penna*, *pinna*, feather). PINION.[2] PINNACLE. A small piece of wood, &c., to serve as a fastening, for hanging something on, &c.; a sharpened piece of wire for holding together parts of dress, papers, &c., for securing the hair, a hat, &c., or for ornament.—*vt.* To fasten with a pin; to seize and hold fast.—**Pin'afore**, *n.* The *v.* + *afore*, in front. A-[1]. A covering worn in front by children, &c.—**Pin'-money**, *n.* An annual sum settled on a wife for her private expenditure.

Pin'cers, *n.pl.* M.E. *pinsours*, &c., app. A.F. agent-n. f. *pincier*, *pincer*. (See next.) A double instrument for grasping objects.

Pinch, *vt.* O.N.F. **pinchier* = O.F. *pincier* (F. *pincer*), of obscure orig. To nip, squeeze; to straiten or stint.—*n.* A pinching; stress; an exigency; as much as can be taken up with the tips of finger and thumb.

Pinch'beck, *n.* The name of the inventor. An alloy of copper and zinc resembling gold.

Pine, *n.*[1] Early M.E. *pīne*—O.E. **pīn*—L. *poena*. PAIN. Grief.—*vi.* O.E. *pīnian*, to torment. To languish; to long eagerly.

Pine, *n.*[2] F. *pin*—L. *pīnus*. An evergreen coniferous tree; a pine-apple.—**Pine'-apple**, *n.* Formerly, a pine-cone. The juicy fruit (like a pine-cone) of a tropical plant; the plant.

Pin'ion, *n.*[1] O.F. *pignon* = *penon*, *pennon* = It. *pennone*, orig. 'plume', aug. of L. *penna*. PEN.[2] A wing; the part of a cooked bird's wing corresponding to the fore-arm.—*vt.* To disable (a bird's wings), to disable thus; to bind (the arms), to disable thus.

Pin'ion, *n.*[2] F. *pignon*, specific application of O.F. *pignon*, battlement (the teeth of a wheel resembling the indentations of a battlement), aug. of L. *pinna*. PIN. A small cog-wheel fitting into a larger.

Pink, *n.* Orig. obscure. A garden plant; the height of excellence.—*a.* Of a pale rose-colour.

Pink, *vt.* Cf. L.G. *pinken*, to strike, peck. To pierce; to ornament with perforations.

Pin'nace, *n.* F. *pinasse*, *pinace*, of unknown orig. A light vessel, a boat.

Pin'nacle, *n.* O.F. *pinacle*, *pinnacle*—L.L. *pinnāculum*, dim. of *pinna*. PIN. A small turret; a peak; the highest point or pitch.

Pint, *n.* F. *pinte*, a liquid measure = It., Sp., Pg. *pinta*, M.Du., M.H.G., Ger. *pinte*. A liquid measure equal to half a quart.

Pioneer', *n.* F. *pionnier*, O.F. *paonier*, *peonier*, orig. 'foot-soldier', f. *peon*. PAWN.[1] One of a body of soldiers who prepare the way for the main body.—*vt.* To prepare (a way, &c.); to act as pioneer or leader to.

Pi'ous, *a.* L. *pius* + -OUS. EXPIATE. Devout.

Pip, *n.*[1] App. f. M.Du. *pippe* = M.L.G. *pip* (Ger. *pipps*)—Pop.L. *pīpīta*, app. alteration of L. *pītuīta*. A disease of fowls.

Pip, *n.*[2] Orig. unknown. A spot on playing-cards, dice or dominoes. [of fruit.

Pip, *n.*[3] App. shortened f. PIPPIN. A seed

Pipe, *n.*[1] O.E. *pīpe* = M.Du. *pīpe*, O.H.G. *pfīfa* (Ger. *pfeife*)—L.L. **pīpa*, f. *pīpāre*, to pipe, chirp. PIGEON. FIFE. A musical wind-instrument; the voice in singing, the note of a bird; a tube; a sound-tube in an organ; a tube fitted with a bowl for smoking tobacco.—*vi.* To play on a pipe; to whiz.—*vt.* To play on a pipe; to summon by a pipe.—**Pip'**ER, *n.*—**Pipe'-clay**, *n.* A kind of clay used for making tobacco-pipes and for cleaning white cloth.—*vt.* To whiten with pipe-clay.

Pipe, *n.*[2] O.F., F. *pipe*, of the same origin as prec., with special sense 'a cylindrical vessel'. A cask = two hogsheads. [ware pot.

Pip'kin, *n.* Orig. doubtful. A small earthen-

Pip'pin, *n.* O.F. *pepin*, pip. Orig. obscure. A kind of apple raised from seed.

Pi'quant, *a.* F., pres.pple. of *piquer*. PIKE.[3] Pungent, stimulating.—**Pi'qu**ANCY, *n.*

Pique, *vt.* F. *piquer*. PIKE.[3] To irritate, wound the pride of; to stimulate, excite to action.—*n.* Ill-feeling, enmity; offence taken.

Piquet', *n.* F., of uncertain orig. A card-game for two with 32 cards.

Pi'rate, *n.* L. *pīrāta*—G. *peiratēs*, f. *peiraein*, to attempt, attack. A sea-robber; an infringer of copyright.—*vt.* To publish in infringement of copyright. — **Pi'r**ACY, *n.* — **Pirat'**ICAL, *a.*—**Pirat'ical**LY,[2] *adv.*

Pir'ouette, *n.* F. *pirouette*, spinning top, pirouette. Orig. unknown. A spinning round on the toe.—*vi.* To make a pirouette.

Pis'catory, *a.* L. *piscātōrius*, a. f. *piscātor*, fisher, f. *piscāri*, to fish, f. *piscis*, FISH. PORPOISE. Of, addicted to, fishing.

Pisci'na, *n.* L. *piscīna*, fishpond, in Med.L., piscina, f. *piscis*. (See prec.) A perforated stone basin for carrying off water used in rinsing the chalice and the hands of the priest.

Pis'til, *n.* F. *pistil*—L. *pistillum*, PESTLE. The female organ of a flower.

Pis'tol, *n.* Obs. F. *pistole*, app. shortened f. *pistolet*, dagger, pistol, in It. *pistoletto*, app. dim. f. stem of *pistolese*, short sword, use as *n.* of *Pistolese*, of Pistoia. A small firearm.—*vt.* To shoot with a pistol.

Pis'ton, *n.* F. *piston*—It. *pistone*, var. of *pestone*, great pestle, aug. f. stem of *pestello*, L. *pistillum*, PESTLE. A disk fitting into and driven up and down in a cylinder.

Pit, *n.* O.E. *pytt* = M.Du. *putte*, O.H.G. *pfuzzi*—L. *puteus*, well, pit. A hole in the ground; an enclosure in which animals were set to fight; the shaft of a coal-mine, the mine; a hollow in the body; the part of the floor of a theatre behind the stalls.—*vt.* To put in a pit; to set to fight or in rivalry; to mark with small scars.—**Pit'fall**, *n.* O.E. *fealle*, falling trap-door, f. *feallan*, to FALL. A concealed pit for catching animals or men.

Pitch, *n.*[1] O.E. *pic*—L. *pix*, *picis* = G. *pissa*. A dark tenacious substance obtained from tar.—*v.*[1]*t.* To smear with pitch.—**Pitch'**Y,[2] *a.* Full of, smeared with, dark as, pitch.

Pitch, *v.*[2]*t.* M.E. *piche(n)*, *picche(n)*. Orig. obscure. To set, fix, place, set up; to set in battle array (now only in *pa.pple.*); to cast or throw.—*vi.* To fix or decide *upon*; to fall headlong; of a ship, to plunge with the head into the sea.—*n.*[2] An act of pitching; one's station; highest point or degree; height, level; degree of acuteness of tone; slope.—**Pitch'fork**, *n.* A fork for lifting and pitching hay, &c.—*vt.* To throw with or as with a pitchfork.

Pit'cher, *n.* O.F. *pichier* (F. *pichet*)—Med.L. *picārium*, *bicārium*, referred to G. **bikarion*, dim. of *bikos*, drinking-bowl. A large earthenware vessel.

Pith, *n.* O.E. *pitha*, corresp. to M.Du. *pitte*, M.L.G. *pit*. The spongy cellular tissue in the stems and branches of certain plants; essence, spirit; force, vigour.—**Pith'**Y,[2] *a.* Consisting of pith; terse, sententious.—**Pith'i**LY,[2] *adv.*

Pit'tance, *n.* O.F. *pitance*, *-ence*, app. the same word as *pitance*, *pietance*, pity (f. L. type **pietantia*, deriv. of *pietas*, PIETY), recorded also in sense 'pittance'. A donation to provide additional food, &c.; the allowance; a remuneration or stipend; a (small) allowance.

Pit'y, *n.* O.F. *pitet*, *pité*, *pitié*—L. *pietas*, PIETY, in L.L., pity. Compassion, sympathy; a cause for pity or regret.—*vt.* To feel pity for.—**Pit'eous**, *a.* O.F. *pitos*, *piteus*, A.F. *pitous*—L. type **pietōsus*, f. *pietas*. Exciting or deserving pity.—**Pit'i**ABLE, *a.*—**Pit'iab**LY,[2] *adv.*—**Pit'i**FUL, *a.* Full of pity; piteous; contemptible, despicable.—**Pit'i**LESS, *a.*

Piv'ot, *n.* F. *pivot*. Orig. obscure. A short shaft or pin on which something turns.—*vt.* and *i.* To furnish with, to turn as on, a pivot.

Pix'y, Pix'ie, *n.* Orig. obscure. A fairy.

Plac'ard, *n.* O.F. *plaquard*, *placard*, f. *plaquier*, to lay flat, plaster — M. Flemish *placken*, to plaster, coat with something sticky. A notice to be posted up.—*vt.* To set up placards on; to advertise by placards.

Placate', *vt.* L. *plācāre*, *plācātum*. To appease or pacify.—**Plac'**ABLE, *a.*

Place, *n.* F. *place*, f. **plattia*. PIAZZA. An open space in a city; a particular part or spot position; a mansion; rank; an office or employment.—*vt.* To put in a particular place.

Plac'id, *a.* L. *placidus*, f. *placēre*, to PLEASE Calm, serene.—**Placid'**ITY, *n.*

Pla'giary, *n.* L. *plagiārius*, kidnapper, plagiarist. One who purloins literary, artistic, &c., work; the doing this; something so purloined.—**Pla'giar**ISM, *n.*—**Pla'giar**IST, *n.* —**Pla'giar**IZE, *vt.* and *i.*

Plague, *n.* O.F. *plage*, *plague*, stroke, wound (F. *plaie*)—L. *plāga* = G. *plēgē*. PLAINT. An affliction; something causing trouble or annoyance; a pestilence.—*vt.* To trouble or annoy.—**Pla'gu**Y,[2] *a.*—**Pla'gui**LY,[2] *adv.*

Plaice, *n.* O.F. *plaïz*, *plaïs*—L.L. *platessa*, app. f. root of G. *platus*. PIAZZA. A flat-fish.

Plaid, *n.* The same as Gael. *plaide*, Ir. *plaid*, blanket. Orig. uncertain. A long piece of woollen cloth, often with a tartan pattern.

Plain, *a.* O.F. *plain*—L. *plānus*. EXPLAIN. PIANO. PLAN. PLANE, *a.* and *v.* Flat, level; of sight, &c., unobstructed; manifest; sheer, mere; easily understood; not intricate; unembellished; straightforward; ordinary, common; simple in manners, dress, &c.; not beautiful.—*n.* A tract of level ground.—*adv.* Straightforwardly; clearly.—**Plain'**LY,[2] *adv.*

Plaint, *n.* O.F. *pleint*, *plaint*—L. *planctus*, f. *plangĕre*, *planctum* (COMPLAIN), conn. with *plāga*. PLAGUE. Lamentation; a complaint. —**Plain'tive**, *a.* O.F. *plaintif*, *-ive*. Mournful, sad.—**Plain'tiff**, *n.* O.F. *plaintif* as *n.* One who sues in a court of law.

Plait, *n.* O.F. *pleit*, later *ploit*, fold, manner of folding, condition—L.L. **plictum*, f. *plicitum*, neut. pa.pple. of L. *plicāre*, to fold. APPLY. IMPLICATE. PERPLEX. PLIGHT.[2] A fold or crease; a braid of hair, a plaited band of straw, &c.—*vt.* To form into plaits.

Plan, *n.* F. *plan*, plane surface, plan, use as *n.* of *plan*, flat, learned form of *plain*. PLAIN. A drawing representing a building, &c., in horizontal section; a large-scale map of a small region; a scheme of arrangement; a project, design; method, way of proceeding.—*vt.* To make a plan of; to devise, contrive.

Plane, *n.*[1] F. *plane*—L. *platanus*—G. *platanos*, f. *platus*. PIAZZA. PLANTAIN.[2] A forest tree with broad leaves.

Plane, *a.* L. *plānus*. PLAIN. Perfectly flat or level.—*n.*[2] A plane surface; an imaginary horizontal plane.

Plane, *vt.* F. *planer*—L. *plānāre*, f. *plānus*. PLAIN. To make smooth or level; to smooth with a plane.—*n.*[3] A tool for smoothing wood.

Plan'et, *n.* O.F. *planete*—L. *planētae*, pl. = G. *planētai*, pl., wandering stars, planets, f. *plana-ein*, to lead astray. A heavenly body revolving round the sun and apparently moving among the fixed stars.—**Plan'et**ARY, *a.*

Plan'gent, *a.* L. *plangens*, *plangentis*, pres. pple. of *plangĕre*, to strike noisily. Loud.

Plank, *n.* O.N.F. *planke* = F. *planche*—L. *planca*. A long flat piece of sawn timber.

Plant, *n.* O.E. *plante*—L. *planta*, sprout, shoot, sole of the foot. (See next.) PLANTIGRADE. SUPPLANT. A member of the lower of the two kingdoms of living beings, a vegetable; the machinery, &c., used in carrying on an industrial process.—*vt.* O.E. *plantian*—L. *plantāre*. To set in the ground to grow; to set firmly; to stock with plants.—**Planta**'TION, *n.* A planting; a wood of planted trees; a tropical or sub-tropical estate on which cotton, tobacco, &c., are cultivated.—**Plant'**ER, *n.* The owner of such an estate.

Plan'tain, *n.*[1] O.F. *plantain*—L. *plantāgo*, *plantāginis*, app. f. *planta*, sole (see prec.), referring to the broad flat leaves. A low herb.

Plan'tain, *n.*[2] In 16th c. *platan*, *plantan(e)*—Sp. *plátano*, *plántano*, identical in form with *plátano*, *plántano*, L. *platanus*, PLANE.[1] A tree-like tropical plant; its fleshy fruit.

Plan'tigrade, *a.* F. *plantigrade*, f. L. *planta*, sole + *-gradus*, going, f. *gradi*, to go. PLANT. AGGRESSION. Walking on the soles of the feet.

Plash, *n.*[1] O.E. *plæsc*, cogn. with M.Du. *plasch*, and app. with next. A pool or puddle.

Plash, *vt.* and *i.* Cf. M.Du. *plassen*, Ger. *plätschern*. App. conn. with prec. and imitative. SPLASH. To splash.—*n.*[2] A splash.

Plas'ter, *n.* O.E. *plaster*, in the first sense—Pop.L. *plastrum*, shortened f. L. *emplastrum*—G. *emplastron*, var. of *emplaston*, f. *emplastos*, daubed on, f. *emplassein* (EM-[2]), f. *plassein*, to form, mould, to apply as a plaster. (In the other senses reinforced by O.F. *plastre* (F. *plâtre*).) An external curative application; a mixture of lime, sand, &c., for covering walls, &c.; *plaster of Paris*, a preparation of Paris gypsum.—*vt.* To apply a plaster to; to cover with plaster.—**Plas'ter**ER, *n.*

Plas'tic, *a.* L. *plasticus*—G. *plastikos*, that may be moulded, of moulding, f. *plastos*, vbl. a. f. *plassein*. (See prec.) Moulding formless matter; produced by moulding; easily moulded.—**Plastic'**ITY, *n.*

Plat, *n.* Var. of PLOT. A small piece of ground.

Plate, *n.* O.F. *plate*, plate of metal, &c., orig. fem. of *plat*, Late and Med. L. *plattus*, flat, perh. f. G. *platus*. PIAZZA. PLATINUM. PLATITUDE. PLATTER. A flat thin sheet of metal, &c.; a piece of steel or iron going to compose armour; a sheet of copper or steel engraved to print from, an engraving; utensils of gold or silver; a shallow circular vessel from which food is eaten.—*vt.* To cover with a thin coating of gold or silver.—**Plateau'**, *n.* F. *plateau*, O.F. *platel*, flat piece, dim. f. *plat*. An elevated tract of level land.—**Plate'-layer**, *n.* From *plate* in local sense 'metal wheel-track, rail'. One who attends to the rails of a railway.

Plat'form, *n.* F. *plateforme*, flat form, plane figure, plan, f. *plat* (see prec.) + *forme*, FORM. A raised level surface or flooring; a basis of policy on which persons unite.

Plat'inum, *n.* Altered f. the earlier name *platina*—Sp. *platina*, dim. f. *plata*, silver, in form = O.F. *plate*. PLATE. A white, heavy, malleable metal.—**Plat'inotype**, *n.* A process of photographic printing in which platinum is used; a print produced by the process.

Plat'itude, *n* F. *platitude*, f. *plat*. PLATE. Commonplaceness; a commonplace remark.—**Platitu'dinous**, *a.* (Cf. *multitudinous*.)

Platoon', *n.* F. *peloton*, little ball, platoon, dim. of *pelote*. PELLET. A small body of foot-soldiers operating as a unit.

Plat'ter, *n.* A.F. *plater*, deriv. of *plat*, dish, f. *plat*, flat. PLATE. A flat dish for food.

Plau'dit, *n.* Shortened f. L. *plaudite*, imp. pl. of *plaudĕre*, to APPLAUD. An act of applauding. — **Plau'**SIBLE, *a.* Apparently worthy of acceptance or trust, fair-seeming; fair-spoken.—**Plausi**BIL'ITY, *n.*

Play, *vi.* O.E. *plegian*, *plagian*, *plœgian*, corresp. to M.Du. *pleyen*, *pleien*, *playen*, to dance, rejoice. Cf. Du. *plegen*, Ger. *pflegen*, to take care of. Primary sense 'to bestir or busily occupy oneself'. To move lightly with alternating or irregular motion, to flicker, ripple, &c.; to move in its proper motion; to discharge water, &c., *on*; to amuse oneself; to engage in a game; to perform on a musical instrument.—*vt.* To actuate or work (an instrument); to engage in (a game); to contend against in a game; to put down (a card) in one's turn; to perform (music), to perform on (an instrument); to act (a drama, &c.); to act the part of; to represent (a part).—*n.* A wielding lightly; brisk alternating or irregular motion; activity; free movement, room for movement; amusement, sport; gambling; a dramatic piece or performance.—**Play'**ER, *n.*—**Play'**FUL, *a.*—**Play'thing**, *n.* A toy.—**Play'wright**, *n.* A composer of plays.

Plea, *n.* M.E. *plaid*, *plai*—O.F. *plaid*, decision, law-court, law-suit—L. *placitum*, decision, decree, &c., neut. pa.pple. of *placēre*, to PLEASE. A suit at law; a statement by or for a defendant or prisoner; a pretext or excuse.—**Plead**, *vi.* O.F. *plaidier*, to sue, plead, f. *plaid*. To state a litigant's case; to make earnest appeal.—*vt.* To allege as a plea or pretext or in excuse; to state (a case).

Pleach, *vt.* O.F. **plechier*, dial. form of *plessier*—L. *plectĕre*. COMPLEX. To entwine, esp. of boughs in a hedge, &c.

Please, *vt.* M.E. *plaise*, *pleise*, *plese*—O.F. *plaisir* (F. *plaire*)—L. *placēre*, to be pleasing. COMPLACENT. PLACID. PLEA. To be agreeable to, gratify; in *pass.*, to like, think proper.—*vi.* To like, think proper.—**Pleas'ance**, *n.* O.F. *plaisance*, f. *plaisir*. Joy, delight; a pleasure-ground.—**Pleas'ant**, *a.* O.F. *plaisant*, properly pres.pple. of *plaisir*. Pleasing, agreeable.—**Pleas'ant**LY,[2] *adv.*—**Pleas'ant**RY, *n.* Jocularity, facetiousness; a joke.—**Pleas'ure**, *n.* O.F. *plaisir*, use as *n.* of the inf. Enjoyment, gratification; sensual gratification; will, choice.—**Pleas'ur**ABLE, *a.* Affording, capable of affording, pleasure.

Plebei'an, *n.* L. *plēbeius*, of the *plebs* or common people + -AN. One of the common people.—*a.* Of low birth; vulgar.—**Pleb'is-**

cite, *n.* F. *plébiscite*—L. *plēbiscitum*, a decree of the people, f. *plēbis*, genit. of *plebs* + *scitum*, decree, neut. pa.pple. of *sciscĕre*, to seek to know, decree, inceptive of *scire*, to know. A direct vote of all the electors.

Plec'trum, *n.* L. *plectrum*—G. *plēktron*, f. *plēssein*, to strike. APOPLEXY. An instrument for plucking the strings of a lyre, &c.

Pledge, *n.* O.F. *plege*—Early Frankish L. *plevium*, *plibium*, Med.L. *plivium*, app. f. Med.L. *plevire*, *plebire*, to warrant, prob. repg. some form of W. Germanic *plegan*. PLIGHT.[1] Anything handed over as security; a toast; a promise.—*vt.* To hand over as a pledge; to plight (one's word, &c.); to drink a toast to.

Plei'ad, *n.*; *pl.* **Plei'ads**, **Plei'ades**. L. *Plēias*, pl. *Plēiades*—G. *Pleiades*, pl., prob. f. *ple-ein*, to sail, their rising marking the beginning of the sailing-season. In *pl.*, a cluster of small stars in the constellation Taurus; in *sing.*, a brilliant group.

Ple'nary, *a.* L.L. *plēnārius*, f. *plēnus*, FULL. PLUS. (See next.) Complete, entire.—**Plenipoten'tiary**, *a.* Med.L. *plēnipotentiārius*, f. L. type **plēnipotentia*, n. of quality f. L.L. *plēnipotens*, *plēnipotentis*, having full power, f. *plēnus* + L. *potens*, POTENT. Having full power. — *n.* A person, esp. an ambassador, having full power.—**Plen'i**TUDE, *n.* Fullness, completeness; abundance.

Plen'ty, *n.* O.F. *plentet*, *plenté*—L. *plēnitas*, fullness, f. *plēnus*. (See prec.) Abundance; a time of abundance.—**Plen'teous**, *a.* M.E. *plentifous*, *plentivous* — O.F. *plentivous*, extended f. *plentif*, a. f. *plenté*. Abundant, copious.—**Plen'ti**FUL, *a.* Abundant.

Ple'onasm, *n.* L. *pleonasmus*—G. *pleonasmos*, f. *pleonazein*, to be redundant, f. *pleōn*, more. The use of redundant words; a redundant word or phrase.—**Pleonas'tic**, *a.* G. type **pleonastikos*. Redundant.

Pleth'ora, *n.* Med.L. *plēthōra*—G. *plēthōrē*, fullness, plethora, f. *plēthein*, to be full, conn. with *plērēs*, FULL. An excess of red corpuscles in the blood; an excess.—**Plethor'**IC, *a.*

Pleu'risy, *n.* O.F. *pleurisie*—L.L. *pleurisis* for *pleuritis*—G. *pleuritis*, f. *pleura*, side, rib + -ITIS. Inflammation of the pleura (f. G. *pleura*), the membrane enveloping the lungs.

Pli'able, *a.* F. *pliable*, f. *plier*, to bend. PLY, *n.* Easily bent or influenced.—**Pliabil'**ITY, *n.*—**Pli'ant**, *a.* F. *pliant*, pres.pple. of *plier*. Pliable.—**Pli'**ANCY, *n.*—**Pli'**ERS, *n.pl.* Small pincers.

Plight, *n.*[1] O.E. *pliht*, risk, f. *pleón*, to risk the loss of, or W. Germanic *plegan*, to be responsible for. PLEDGE. Undertaking (of a risk or obligation).—*vt.* To engage (one's troth, faith, &c.); to engage (oneself).

Plight, *n.*[2] M.E. *plit*, *plyt* (altered by association with prec.) — A.F. *plit*, O.F. *ploit*. PLAIT. Condition, state (gen. evil).

Plinth, *n.* L. *plinthus*—G. *plinthos*, brick, squared stone. FLINT. The square base of a column or pedestal; a pedestal.

Plod, *vi.* App. imitative. To walk heavily, trudge; to work in a laborious stolid way.

Plot, *n.* Orig. unknown. A small piece of ground; the plan or scheme of a play, novel, &c.; a secret evil project planned in concert (in this sense prob. influenced by (or short for) *complot* (now rare), in same sense—F. *complot*, of uncertain orig.).—*vt.* To make a plan or map of; to contrive (in evil sense).

Plough, *n.* Late O.E. *plóh* = O.N. *plógr*. Cf. O.Fris. *plōch*, O.H.G. *pfluog* (Ger. *pflug*). An implement for turning up the soil.—*vt.* To turn up with a plough; to furrow.

Plov'er, *n.* O.F. *plovier*—L.L. **pluvārius*, a. f. L. *pluvia*, rain. (The connexion with rain variously explained.) PLUVIAL. The name of several birds, including the lapwing.

Pluck, *vt.* Late O.E. *ploccian*, *pluccian*. Com. W. Germanic. By some referred to a Pop.L. **piluccāre* (inferred f. It. *piluccare*), f. **pilucca*, tuft of hair, f. L. *pilus*. DEPILATORY. To pull or pick off, gather; to give a pull at; to strip of feathers, &c.; to reject in an examination.—*n.* A plucking; the heart, &c., of a beast as used for food; courage, spirit.—**Pluck'**Y,[2] *a.*—**Pluck'**ILY,[2] *adv.*

Plug, *n.* App. f. M.Du. *plugge*, Cf. M.L.G. *plugge*, Sw. *plugg*. A piece of wood, &c., for stopping a hole; a piece of tobacco for chewing.—*vt.* To stop with or as with a plug.

Plum, *n.* O.E. *plúme*, corresp. to M.L.G. *plūme*, O.H.G. **phlūma* (Ger. *pflaume*)—L.L. *prūna for* L. *prūnum*—Late G. *prounon* for G. *proumnon*. PRUNE. A well-known stone-fruit; the tree bearing it; a raisin.

Plumb, *n.* F. *plomb*—L. *plumbum*, lead. PLUMMET. PLUNGE. A plummet; the perpendicular.—*a.* Perpendicular.—*adv.* Perpendicularly; exactly.—*vt.* To sound with a plummet; to set perpendicularly.—**Plum'ber**, *n.* O.F. *plummier* — L. *plumbārius*. One who works in lead, &c.—**Plumb'-line**, *n.* A cord with a plummet attached.

Plumba'go, *n.* L. *plumbāgo*, a species of lead ore, f. *plumbum*. (See prec.) Black-lead.

Plume, *n.* O.F. *plume* — L. *plūma*, small feather, down. A feather; a feather or feathers as an ornament.—*vt.* To furnish with plumes. —*v.refl.* To dress the feathers; to pride oneself *on*.—**Plu'**MAGE, *n.* Feathers collectively.

Plum'met, *n.* O.F. *plombet*, *plommet*, dim. of *plomb*. PLUMB. A ball of lead attached to a cord and used for sounding, &c.

Plump, *a.* Corresp. to M.Du. *plomp*, blunt, dull in mind, M.L.G. *plump*, *plomp*, unshapen, blunt, of obscure orig. Formerly, blunt, dull. Hence (app. through the sense 'rounded, not angular'), of rounded form, moderately fat.

Plump, *vi.* = M.Du. *plompen*, M.L.G. *plumpen*. Prob. imitative. To drop with abruptly arrested motion; to give all one's votes *for* (a single candidate).—*vt.* To drop or throw abruptly.—*n.* A heavy fall.—*adv.* With a sudden drop or impact; directly, in plain terms.

Plun'der, *vt.* Late M.H.G., Ger. *plündern*, lit. 'to rob of household effects', f. M.H.G. *blunder*, *plunder*, household stuff. Cf. Ger. *plunder*, lumber. To rob systematically; to take by robbery.—*n.* Spoliation; spoil, booty.

Plunge, *vt.* O.F. *plung(i)er*, &c. (F. *plonger*), said to be f. L.L. **plumbicāre*, to heave the lead, f. L. *plumbum*. PLUMB. To put forcibly *into* (a liquid, &c.); to force *into* (a state, &c.). —*vi.* To throw oneself *into* (a liquid, &c.); to enter abruptly *into* (a place, &c.); to throw oneself violently forward.—*n.* A plunging.

Pluper'fect, *a.* Contr. f. *plus-quam-perfect*, L. *plus quam perfectum*, more than PERFECT. Of a tense, expressing action completed prior to a past point of time.

Plus, quasi-*prep.* L. *plūs*, *plūris*, more. cogn. with *plēnus*. PLENARY. Indicating (gen. by the symbol +) that a second expression is to be added to a first; with the addition of.—

Plu'ral, *a.* L. *plūrālis*, f. *plūs*. Denoting more than one person or thing; more than one.—*n.* A word in its plural form.—**Plu'-**

ralIST, *n.* One who holds more than one benefice at once.—**Plu'ralISM**, *n.* Such holding; a doctrine assuming more than one principle of being.—**Plural'ITY**, *n.* The state of being plural or a pluralist; a benefice held with another or others; a multitude; the greater number.

Plush *n.* F. *pluche*, contr. f. *peluche*, shag, plush--L.L. type **pilūceus*, hairy, f. *pilus*. DEPILATORY. A fabric with a long soft nap.

Plutoc'racy, *n.* G. *ploutokratia*, f. *ploutos*, riches + *-kratia*, rule, f. *kratos*, power. Government by the rich; this ruling class.—**Plu'tocrat**, *n.* After *aristocrat*, &c. One of the class.—**Plutocrat'IC**, *a.*

Plu'vial, *a.* L. *pluviālis*, f. *pluvia*, rain. PLOVER. Of or pertaining to rain; rainy.

Ply, *n.* F. *pli*, f. *plier*, to fold, bend—L. *plicāre*. APPLY. COMPLEX. PLIABLE. A fold.

Ply, *vt.* M.E. *plye*, aphetic f. *aplye*, APPLY. To wield, handle, employ; to apply oneself to, work at; to assail; to supply persistently *with*. —*vi.* To sail, go, take one's stand, regularly.

Pneumat'ic, *a.* L. *pneumaticus*—G. *pneumatikos*, a. f. *pneuma*, *pneumatos*, wind, breath, f. *pne-ein*, to blow. Of, acting by means of, wind or air; inflated with compressed air.

Pneumo'nia, *n.* G. *pneumonia*, f. *pneumōn*, lung. Inflammation of the lungs.

Poach, *v.*[1]*t.* O.F. *pochier*, to put in a bag, to poach, f. *poche*, bag. Cf. Icel. *poki*, early Mod. Flemish *poke*. POCKET. POUCH. To cook (an egg) by dropping it without the shell into boiling water (app. from the yolk being thus enclosed in the white as in a bag).

Poach, *v.*[2]*t.* App. var. of POKE. To cut up (the ground) with the hoofs; to take (game) illegally.—*vi.* Of ground, to be cut up; to trespass in order to steal game.—**Poach'ER**, *n.*

Pock, *n.* O.E. *poc* = M.Du., M.L.G., Ger. *pocke*. SMALL-POX. A pustule.

Pock'et, *n.* Anglo-Norman *pokete*, dim. of O.N.F. *poke* = F. *poche*. POACH.[1] A small bag in a garment; a cavity filled with gold or other ore.—*vt.* To put into one's pocket.

Pod, *n.* Orig. unknown. A long seed-vessel. —*vi.* To bear pods.—*vt.* To strip of pods.

Pod'gy, *a.* A parallel form of PUDGY.

Po'em, *n.* F. *poème*—L. *poēma*—G. *poēma*, var. of *poiēma*, f. *poe-ein*, var. of *poie-ein*, to make. A work of a poet.—**Po'esy**, *n.* O.F. *poesie*—L. *poēsis*—G. *poēsis*, var. of *poiēsis*, f. *poe-ein*, *poie-ein*. POSY. Poetry.—**Po'et**, *n.* O.F. *poete*—L. *poēta*—G. *poētēs*, var. of *poiētēs*, f. *poe-ein*, *poie-ein*. A writer (gen. in verse) of high power of imagination and expression.—**Poetas'ter**, *n.* *-Aster*, suff. expressing contempt. A paltry poet. — **Po'etESS**, *n.* — **Poet'IC**, **Poet'ICAL**, *aa.* — **Poet'icalLY**,[2] *adv.* — **Po'etry**, *n.* O.F. *poetrie* — Med.L. *poetria*, f. *poēta*. The poet's art; the product of the art.

Poi'gnant, *a.* O.F. *poignant*, pres.pple. of *poindre*, L. *pungĕre*. PUNGENT. Pungent, keen, piercing.—**Poi'gnANCY**, *n.*

Point, *n.* In senses (A) f. F. *point* — L. *punctum*, prick, small mark, point in space or time, neut. pa.pple. of *pungĕre*. PUNGENT. APPOINT. In senses (B) f. F. *pointe*—Com. Romanic and Med.L. *puncta*, a piercing, a sharp extremity, ppl.n. f. *pungĕre*. PUNCHEON.[1] (A) A small dot or mark; a punctuation mark; an item, detail, particular; in *pl.*, odds; a unit of value; that which has position but no magnitude; position, stage, degree; the precise moment; a characteristic; the essential thing; one's object. (B) A sharp end; a promontory; a movable rail for directing a train from one set of rails to another (gen. in *pl.*); one of the 32 direction-marks of a compass; salient feature, effective part; effectiveness, pungency. (C) From the *v.* Of a dog, an act of pointing.—*vt.* O.F. *pointer*, f. *point* and *pointe*. To sharpen; to give point to (words, &c.); to fill the joints of with mortar; to direct or aim *at*.—*vi.* To extend the finger in order to make an indication; to direct attention; of a dog, to indicate the position of game by standing and looking towards it.—**Point-blank**, *a.* App. f. the *v.* + BLANK, *n.*, in sense 'white spot in the centre of a target'. Aimed horizontally.—*adv.* With such an aim. —**Point'ER**, *n.* A rod for pointing; an index-hand or indicator; a dog trained to point.—**Point'LESS**, *a.* Blunt; ineffective.

Poise, *vt.* O.F. *pois-*, earlier *peis-*, stem of *peser*, late Pop.L. *pēsāre* for L. *pensāre*, to weigh. PENSIVE. To place or hold in equilibrium.—*vi.* To be so held.—*n.* O.F. *pois* (F. *poids*), earlier *peis*. AVOIRDUPOIS. Equilibrium; carriage (of the body, &c.).

Poi'son, *n.* O.F. *poison*—L. *pōtio*. POTION. A substance which kills or injures when introduced into a living organism. — *vt.* To give poison to; to taint, corrupt.—**Poi'sonOUS**, *a.*

Poke, *vt.* M.E. *pōken* = Late M.Du., M.L.G. *poken*. POACH.[2] To thrust or push with the hand, a stick, &c.; to thrust forward, esp. obtrusively. — *vi.* To go prying. — *n.* An act of poking. — **Pok'ER**, *n.* An instrument for stirring a fire.—**Pok'Y**,[2] *a.* Petty in size.

Pole, *n.*[1] O.E. *pál* = O.H.G. *phāl* (Ger. *pfahl*), O.N. *páll*—L. *pālus*. PALE, *n.* A long cylindrical piece of wood; a measure of length, 5½ yards; a measure of area, 30¼ square yards. —*vt.* To push or propel with a pole.

Pole, *n.*[2] L. *polus*—G. *polos*, pivot, pole. f. *pelein*, to be in motion. PULLEY. Each of the two points about which the stars seem to revolve; each of the extremities of the axis of the earth; each of the opposite points of a magnet.—**Pol'AR**,[1] *a.*—**Polar'ITY**, *n.* The quality of being polar or of possessing magnetic poles. — **Pol'arize**, *vt.* F. *polariser*, formed f. *pôle*, L. *polus*. So to affect light that the vibrations are restricted to one plane. *Polar* + -IZE. To give magnetic polarity to.—**PolarizA'TION**, *n.*

Pole'-axe, *n.* M.E. *pol(l)ax* (= M.Du. *pol(l)-aex*, M.L.G. *pol(l)exe*), f. POLL + AXE. (An axe with a particular kind of head, or one for cutting off or splitting the head.) A battle-axe; a halberd; a butcher's axe.

Pole'cat, *n.* Perh. f. O.F. *pole*, *poule*, hen + CAT (as preying on hens). POULT. A small quadruped of the weasel family.

Polem'ic, *a.* G. *polemikos*, a. f. *polemos*, war. Controversial.—*n.* Aggressive controversy; in *pl.*, the practice of this.—Sim. **Polem'ICAL**, *a.*

Police', *n.* F. *police* — Med.L. *polītia*, L. *polītia*. (See next.) Civil administration; public order; the department of government, the civil force, charged with the maintenance of public order.—*vt.* To keep in order.

Pol'icy, *n.*[1] O.F. *policie*, civil administration—L. *polītia*—G. *politeia*, citizenship, government, f. *politēs*, citizen, f. *polis*, city, state. METROPOLIS. POLITIC. (See prec.) Political sagacity; prudent or expedient procedure; sagacity; cunning; a course of action adopted.

Pol'icy, *n.*[2] F. *police* = It. *polizza*, writing, bond, &c., said to be f. Med.L. *apodissa*, *apo-*

dixa, receipt or security for money, altered f. L. *apodixis*, G. *apodeixis*, a making known, proof, f. APO*deiknunai*, to show. A document containing a contract of insurance.

Pol'ish, *vt.* F. *poliss-*, lengthened stem of *polir*, L. *polīre*. INTERPOLATE. To make smooth and glossy; to refine.—*n.* An act of polishing; smoothness and glossiness; refinement; a substance used in polishing.—**Polite'**, *a.* L. *polītus*, properly pa.pple. of *polīre*. Refined, elegant; of refined manners, courteous. —**Polite'**LY,[2] *adv.*—**Polite'**NESS, *n.*

Pol'itic, *a.* F. *politique*—L. *politicus*, G. *politikos*, a. f. *politēs*. POLICY.[1] Sagacious, shrewd; expedient, judicious; cunning.—In *pl.* as *n.*, the science and art of government; political affairs or principles; political life.—**Polit'ic**AL, *a.* Public, civil; having an organized government; relating to or concerned with politics.—**Politic**'IAN, *n.* One engaged in politics.—**Pol'ity**, *n.* Obs. F. *politie*—L. *politia*. POLICY.[1] Civil order or government; a form of government; a state.

Pol'ka, *n.* F. and Ger. *polka*, of uncertain orig. Poss. corr. of Czech *pulka*, half, from the characteristic short half steps. A dance of Bohemian origin; music written for it.

Poll, *n.* = obs. Du., L.G. *polle*. POLE-AXE. TADPOLE. The head, the top of the head; the counting of voters; the action or time and place of voting, the votes recorded.—*vt.* To cut off the top of; to take the votes of; to receive (votes).—*vi.* To vote.—**Poll'**ARD, *n.* An animal which has cast its horns; a tree which has been polled so as to produce a rounded mass of young branches; bran sifted from flour.—*vt.* To make a pollard of (a tree).

Pol'len, *n.* L. *pollen*, fine flour. The fertilizing dust or male element of flowers.

Pollute', *vt.* L. *polluĕre*, *pollūtum* f. *pol-*, *por-* (= PRO-), forth + *luĕre* = G. *louein*, to wash. ABLUTION. ALLUVIUM. LAVE. To make foul; to desecrate, sully.—**Pollu'**TION, *n.*

Po'lo, *n.* Baltī *polo*. A game like hockey of Eastern origin played on horseback.

Polonaise', *n.* F. *polonaise*, properly fem. of *polonais*, Polish. A bodice with a skirt open from the waist downwards (suggested by the dress of Polish women); a slow Polish dance; music written for it.

Poltroon', *n.* F. *poltron*—It. *poltrone*, sluggard, coward, f. *poltro*, lazy, app. f. **poltro*, couch, bed, referred to O.H.G. *polstar*, pillow, BOLSTER. A spiritless coward.

Polyan'dry, *n.* G. *poluandria*, n. of state f. *poluandros*, full of men, having many husbands, f. *polu-* (POLY-) + *anēr*, *andros*, man. Plurality of husbands.

Polyan'thus, *n.* POLY- + G. *anthos*, flower. ANTHOLOGY. A cultivated form of primrose.

Pol'ychrome, *a.* F. *polychrome*—G. *poluchrōmos*, f. *polu-* (POLY-) + *chrōma*, *chrōmatos*, colour. CHROMATIC. Many-coloured; executed in many colours.—*n.* A work of art so executed.—**Polychromat'**IC, *a.*

Polyg'amy, *n.* F. *polygamie* — Eccles.G. *polugamia*, f. *polugamos*, often married, f. *polu-* (POLY-) + *gamos*, marriage. The custom of being married to several persons at a time. —**Polyg'am**IST, *n.*

Pol'yglot, *a.* G. *poluglōttos*, f. *polu-* (POLY-) + *glōtta*, *glōssa*. GLOZE. Speaking, writing, written in, several languages.

Pol'ygon, *n.* L. *polygōnum*—G. *polugōnon*, properly neut. of *polugōnos*, polygonal, f. *polu-* (POLY-) + *gōnia*, angle. A figure having many angles or sides.—**Polyg'on**AL, *a.*—**Polyhe'dron**, *n.* G. *poluedron*, properly neut. of *poluedros*, many-sided, f. *polu-* + *hedra*, base A solid figure contained by many faces.

Pol'yp(e), *n.* F. *polype*—L. *polypus*, G. *polupous*, cuttle-fish, polypus in the nose, f. *polu-* (POLY-) + *pous*. FOOT. A coral-insect. —**Pol'ypus**, *n.* L. *polypus*. A ramified tumour.

Polysyl'lable, *n.* Med.L. *polysyllaba* (sc. *vox*, word), fem. of *polysyllabus*, G. *polusullabos*, of many syllables, f. *polu-* (POLY-) + *sullabē*, SYLLABLE. A word of many syllables. —**Polysyllab'**IC, *a.*

Polytech'nic, *a.* F. *polytechnique*—G. *polutechnos*, skilled in many arts, f. *polu-* (POLY-) + *technē*, art. TECHNIC. Dealing with various arts.—*n.* A school for teaching various arts.

Pol'ytheism, *n.* F. *polythéisme*, f. G. *polutheos*, of or belonging to many gods, f. *polu-* (POLY-) + *theos*, god. The doctrine or belief that there are many gods.—**Pol'ythe**IST, *n.*

Pomade', *n.* F. *pommade* = Sp. *pomada*, It. *pomata*—L. *pōmum*, fruit, apple (apples being said to have been orig. an ingredient). POMICULTURE. POMMEL. A scented ointment.—Sim. **Poma'tum**. Mod.L. *pōmātum*.

Pome'granate, *n.* O.F. *pome grenate*, f. *pome* (F. *pomme*), L. *pōmum* (see prec.) + *grenate* (F. *grenade*), L. *grānātum*, pomegranate, lit. '(apple) with many seeds', f. *grānātus*, having many seeds, f. *grānum*. GRAIN. GARNET. GRENADE. The fruit of a N. African and W. Asiatic tree; the tree.

Po'miculture, *n.* L. *pōmum* + *cultūra*. POMADE. ARBORICULTURE. Fruit-growing.

Pom'mel, *n.* O.F. *pomel* (F. *pommeau*)—L.L. type **pōmellum*, dim. of *pōmum*. POMADE. A rounded knob; the knob terminating the hilt of a sword; the upward projecting front part of a saddle.—*vt.* To beat repeatedly.

Pomp, *n.* F. *pompe*—L. *pompa*—G. *pompē*, a sending, a procession, pomp, f. *pempein*, to send. Splendid display, magnificence.—**Pomp'**OUS, *a.* Splendid, magnificent; consequential; inflated, turgid.—**Pompos'**ITY, *n.*

Pond, *n.* M.E. *ponde*, app. var. of POUND, *n.*[2] in sense (now dial.) 'pond, esp. a body of water held up by a dam'. A small body of still water artificially formed.

Pon'der, *vt.* O.F. *ponderer*, L. *ponderāre*, to weigh, f. *pondus*, *ponderis*, weight. POUND, *n.*[1] PREPONDERATE. To weigh mentally. — *vi.* To meditate.—**Pon'der**ABLE, *a.* Having appreciable weight.—**Pon'der**OUS, *a.* Heavy.

Pon'iard, *n.* F. *poignard*, f. *poing*, L. *pugnus*, fist. PUGILISM. A dagger.—*vt.* To stab, esp. to stab to death, with a poniard.

Pont'iff, *n.* F. *pontife*—L. *pontifex*, *pontificis*, high-priest. The Pope; a bishop; a chief priest. — **Pontif'ic**AL, *a.* — *n.pl.* The vestments of a bishop or priest.—**Pontif'ic**ATE,[1] *n.* The office or period of office of the Pope.

Pontoon', *n.* F. *ponton*—L. *ponto*, *pontōnis*, Gallic transport, punt, also pontoon, in the last sense referred to *pons*, *pontis*, bridge. PUNT. A boat supporting a temporary bridge.

Po'ny, *n.* Scotch *powney*, prob. f. O.F. *poulinet*, dim. of *poulain*, *polain*, foal—L. *pullus*, FOAL, chicken. PULLET. A small horse.

Poo'dle, *n.* Ger. *pudel*, short for *pudelhund*, f. L.G. *pud(d)eln*, to splash in water + *hund*, dog, HOUND (being a water-dog). Cf. Ger. dial. *pudel*, PUDDLE. A pet dog.

Pool, *n.*[1] O.E. *pōl* = M.L.G. *pōl*, Du. *poel*. A small body of still water (usually natural); a deep place in a river.

Pool, *n.*[2] F. *poule*, hen, pool (at first perh. in slang sense 'booty'). POULT. The collective amount of the stakes and fines of the players in certain games; the receptacle containing these; a variety of billiards; a combination of capitalists to avoid competition.—*vt.* To throw into a common fund.

Poop, *n.* O.F. *pupe*, *pope* (F. *poupe*)—L. *puppis*. The stern of a ship; a high deck at the stern.—*vt.* To break over the stern of; to ship (a wave) over the stern.

Poor, *a.* M.E. *pōre*—O.F. *povre*, *poure* (F. *pauvre*)—L. *pauper*. IMPOVERISH. PAUCITY. PAUPER. POVERTY. Destitute of material possessions, indigent; scanty; paltry, insignificant; hapless, unfortunate.—**Poor'**LY,[2] *adv.* —**Poor'**LY,[1] *a.* Not in good health.

Pop, *vi.* Imitative. To make a small, quick, explosive sound; to go or come suddenly.—*vt.* To put or place suddenly; to put (a question) abruptly.—*n.* An act of popping.

Pope, *n.* O.E. *pápa*—Eccles.L. *pāpa* (whence It. *papa*, F. *pape*). PAPA. PAPACY. The bishop of Rome as head of the Roman Catholic Church.—**Pope'**DOM, *n.*—**Pop'**ERY, *n.* The papal ecclesiastical system.—**Pop'**ISH, *a.*

Pop'injay, *n.* O.F. *papegai*, *papingay* = Sp. *papagayo*, Pg. *papagaio*, M.H.G. *papagey*. Cf. Med.G. *papagas*, Arab. *babaghā*, these prob. repg. the earliest form f. imitation of the cry in some barbarian language. A parrot; a figure of a parrot as a mark to shoot at.

Pop'lar, *n.* O.F. *poplier* (F. *peuplier*)—L. *populus*. A well-known tree.

Pop'lin, *n.* F. *popeline*, earlier *papeline*—It. *papalina*, fem. of *papalino*, PAPAL (because made at the papal town of Avignon). A fabric of silk and worsted.

Pop'py, *n.* O.E. *papoeg*, *popæg*, app. repg. W.Germanic **papāg*, **popāg*, f. Pop.L. **papāvum* for L. *papāver*. A plant yielding opium.

Pop'ulace, *n.* F. *populace*—It. *popolaccio*, with depreciatory suff. *-accio* f. *popolo*, L. *populus*, PEOPLE. The common people; the rabble.—**Pop'ul**AR,[1] *a.* Of, carried on by, the people; adapted to, finding favour with, the common people; common, general.—**Popular'**ITY, *n.*—**Pop'ular**IZE, *vt.* To make popular; to extend to the common people; to present in a popular form.—**Pop'ular**LY,[2] *adv.*—**Pop'ul**ATE,[3] *vt.* To form the inhabitants of; to furnish with inhabitants.—**Popul**A'TION, *n.* The state of a country with respect to inhabitants; the body of inhabitants.—**Pop'ul**OUS, *a.* Full of inhabitants.

Por'celain, *n.* F. *porcelaine*—It. *porcellana*, a kind of shell, the dense polished substance thereof, and (from resemblance to this) chinaware, deriv. of *porcella*, dim. of *porca*, shell, of uncertain orig. A fine kind of earthenware.

Porch, *n.* F. *porche*—L. *porticus*, colonnade, porch, f. *porta*, gate. PORT, *n.*[2] PORTICO. A covered approach to the entrance of a building.

Por'cine, *a.* F. *porcin*, *-ine*—L. *porcīnus*, a. f. *porcus*. PORK. Of, like, a pig or pigs.

Por'cupine, *n.* M.E. *porkepyn*—O.F. *porc espin*—L. **porcus spīnus* (? for *spīnōsus*), f. *porcus*, pig, and *spīna*, thorn. PORK. SPINE. (F. *porc-épic* is f. *épi*—L. *spīcus*=*spīca*, SPIKE.[1]) A rodent quadruped covered with spines.

Pore, *n.* F. *pore*—L. *porus*—G. *poros*, passage, pore. FARE. A minute opening, esp. in the skin. — **Por'**OUS, *a.* Full of pores. — **Poros'**ITY, *n.*

Pore, *vi.* M.E. *pūren*, *pouren*, of obscure orig. To look or meditate intently.

Pork, *n.* F. *porc*—L. *porcus*, pig. FARROW. PORCINE. PORCUPINE. PORPOISE. Pig's flesh as food.—**Pork'**ER, *n.* A pig bred for food.

Pornog'raphy, *n.* G. *pornographos*, writing of harlots (f. *pornē*, harlot + *-graphos*, f. *graphein*, to write) + Y.[1] Obscene literature.

Por'phyry, *n.* L.L. **porphyrius* (sc. *lapis*), purple stone—G. *porphureos*, purple, f. *porphura*. PURPLE. A hard reddish Egyptian rock.

Por'poise, *n.* O.F. *porpeis*, *porpois*—L. type **porcus piscis*, pig-fish. PORK. PISCATORY. A marine mammal about five feet long.

Por'ridge, *n.* Altered form of POTTAGE. Oatmeal stirred into boiling water.—**Por'ring**ER, *n.* (For the *n* cf. PASSENGER.) A small dish for porridge, &c.

Port, *n.*[1] O.E. *port* (reinforced in M.E. by O.F. *port*)—L. *portus*. IMPORTUNE. OPPORTUNE. PASSPORT. A harbour or haven.

Port, *n.*[2] F. *porte*—L. *porta*, door, gate. PORCH. PORTE. A city gate; an opening in the side of a ship (also **Port'-hole**).—**Por'tal**, *n.* Obs. F. *portal*—Med.L. *portāle*, orig. neut. of *portālis*, a. f. *porta*. A stately door or gate.—**Portcul'lis**, *n.* O.F. *porte coleïce*, f. *porte* + *col(e)ïce*, *couleïce*, fem. of *couleïs*, flowing, sliding—L. type **cōlātīcius*, f. *cōlātus*, pa.pple. of *cōlāre*, to strain, in Romanic (F. *couler*), to flow. COLANDER. A grating constructed to slide up and down in a gateway.—**Port'**ER, *n.*[1] A door-keeper.

Port, *n.*[3] and *a.* Perh. to be referred to PORT, *n.*[1] (With the old steering apparatus on the starboard side, it would, to keep this free, be convenient, in entering port, to have the port on the larboard.) Has now replaced LARBOARD.—*v.*[1]*t.* To put (the helm) to port.

Port, *n.*[4] Shortened f. *Oporto wine*, f. *Oporto* (Pg. *O Porto*, lit. 'the Port', f. L. *portus*. PORT, *n.*[1]). A red Portuguese wine.

Port, *v.*[2]*t.* F. *porter*—L. *portāre*, to bear, carry. COMPORT. To carry (a rifle) slanting upwards towards the left.—*n.*[5] Mien, demeanour.—**Port'**ABLE, *a.* Easily carried.—**Port'**AGE, *n.* A carrying or transporting.—**Port'**ER, *n.*[2] A bearer of burdens.—**Port'er**, *n.*[3] Short for *porter's beer* (app. as orig. drunk chiefly by porters). A dark-brown kind of beer.—**Port'er**AGE, *n.* The carriage of goods, &c.; the charge for this.—**Port'fire**, *n.* Aft. F. *porte-feu*, f. *porte*, imp. of *porter* + *feu*, fire. A device for firing rockets, &c., and for igniting explosives.—**Portfo'lio**, *n.* Orig. *porto folio*—It. *portafogli*, f. *porta*, imp. of *portare*, L *portāre* + *fogli*, pl. of *foglio*, leaf, sheet of paper—L. *folium*. FOIL.[1] A case for sheets of paper, &c.—**Port'**LY,[1] *a.* Of dignified bearing; large in person.—**Portman'teau**, *n.* F. *portemanteau*, f. *porte*, imp. of *porter* + *manteau*, MANTLE. A travelling bag.

Porte, *n.* F. *Porte*, in full *la Sublime Porte*, translating Turkish (Arabic) *Babi Ali*, lit. 'lofty gate' (f. *bāb*, gate + *'aliy*, high), the central office of the Turkish government. PORT, *n.*[2] The Turkish court or government.

Portend', *vt.* L. *portendĕre*, *portentum* (archaic form, with *por-* for PRO-, of *prōtendĕre*, to stretch forth. TENSE, *a.*). To presage; to give warning of.—**Por'tent**, *n.* L. *portentum*. An omen; a marvel.—**Portent'**OUS, *a.*

Por'tico, *n.* It. *portico*—L. *porticus*. PORCH. A covered walk; a colonnade.

Por'tion, *n.* O.F. *portion*—L. *portio*, *portiōnis*, conn. with *pars*, PART. A part or share; one's lot or destiny.—*vt.* To distribute.

Portray', *vt.* O.F. *pourtraire*—L. PROtrahĕre,

to draw forth, reveal, in Med.L., to portray. TREAT. To delineate, depict.—**Por'trait**, *n.* F. *portrait*, f. *portrait*, pa.pple. of obs. *portraire* = *pourtraire*. A likeness. — **Por'traitURE**, *n.*—**Portray'AL**, *n.*

Pose, *v.*[1]*t.* F. *poser*—L. *pausāre*, to halt, cease, PAUSE, in L.L., to rest, which acquired also, through confusion with *pōnĕre*, to place (POSITION), the sense 'to lay to rest, put or set down, place'. COMPOSE, DEPOSE, DISPOSE, &c. To lay down (an assertion, claim, &c.); to propound, propose; to place in an attitude. —*vi.* To assume an attitude; to give oneself out *as*; to attitudinize.—*n.* An attitude; an attitude assumed for effect.

Pose, *v.*[2]*t.* Short for OPPOSE. To puzzle, nonplus.—**Pos'ER**, *n.* A puzzling question.

Pos'it, *vt.* L. *posit-*, ppl. stem of *pōnĕre*. POSITION. To place; to lay down, assume.

Posi'tion, *n.* F. *position*—L. *positio*, *positiōnis*, n. of action f. *pōnĕre*, *positum*, to put, place, set. APPOSITE. COMPOUND. DEPONE. OPPOSITE. POSE.[1] POSIT. POST. POSTURE. REPOSE.[1] (See next.) Affirmative assertion; an assertion; attitude; situation, site; condition; rank; a situation or employment.

Pos'itive, *a.* F. *positif*, *-ive*—L. *positīvus*, settled, positive (in grammar), f. *positus*, pa. pple. of *pōnĕre*. (See prec.) Formally laid down; not admitting of question; definite; confident in opinion; applied to the primary form of an *a.* or *adv.* expressing simple quality; nothing less than; dealing only with matters of fact and experience; having real existence. —*n.* The positive degree of an *a.* or *adv.*; in *photography*, a print in which the lights and shadows are as in nature.—**Pos'itiveLY**,[2] *adv.*—**Pos'itivISM**, *n.* A system of philosophy recognizing only matters of fact and experience.—**Pos'itivIST**, *n.*

Pos'se, *n.* L. *posse*, in Med.L. as *n.*, power, armed force. POTENT. A body (of constables).

Possess', *vt.* O.F. *possessier*, *possesser* (F. *posséder*)—L. *possidēre*, *possessum*, f. old prep. *port* = G. *proti*, *pros*, at, on + *sedēre*, to SIT. To hold, own, have; of an evil spirit, to occupy and dominate; with *with*, to cause to feel or entertain; in *pass.*, to be in possession *of*.—*v.refl.* To take possession *of*.—**Posses'SION**, *n.*—**Posses'SIVE**, *a.* and *n.* A noun case denoting possession.—**Posses'SOR**, *n.*

Pos'set, *n.* M.E. *poshote*, *possot*, of unknown orig. Hot milk curdled with wine, &c.

Pos'sible, *a.* L. *possibilis*, f. *posse*. POTENT. That may or can exist, be done or happen.—**PossiBIL'ITY**, *n.*—**Pos'sibLY**,[2] *adv.*

Post, *n.*[1] O.E. *post*—L. *postis*, conn. with *pōnĕre*. POSITION. A stout pole set upright. —*v.*[1]*t.* To affix to a post, stick *up* in a public place.—**Post'ER**, *n.* A placard posted up.

Post, *n.*[2] F. *poste*—It. *posta*, orig. the same as *posta*, station, stand—L.L. *posta*, f. *postus* = *positus*. POSITIVE. Formerly applied to men with horses stationed at intervals along roads to carry letters. One who travels with letters; a dispatch of letters, the letters; the official conveyance of letters; a place for postal business.—*v.*[2]*i.* To travel with relays of horses; to hasten.—*vt.* To put into a post office for transmission; to transfer (entries) to a ledger; to inform fully.—**Post'AGE**, *n.* The charge for carrying a letter.—**Post'AL**, *a.*—**Post'master**, *n.* An official in charge of a post office.—**Post'master Gen'eral**, *n.* The head of the postal system.

Post, *n.*[3] F. *poste*—It. *posto*, a post, station, employment—L. *postum*, contr. f. *positum*, neut. of *positus*. (See prec.) The place where a soldier is stationed; a position taken; a fort; an office or situation.—*v.*[3]*t.* To place, station.

Post-date', *vt.* L. *post*, after + DATE, *v.* To assign a date later than the actual date to.

Poste'rior, *a.* L. *posterior*, comp. of *posterus*, coming after, behind, f. *post*, after. PREPOSTEROUS. Later; coming after; hinder. —*n.pl.* The hinder parts.—**Poster'ITY**, *n.* Descendants; all succeeding generations.

Post'ern, *n.* O.F. *posterne*, altered f. *posterle*—L.L. *posterula*, a dim. formed f. *posterus*. (See prec.) A back or private door.

Pos'thumous, *a.* L. *postumus* (in L.L. *posthumus*), superl. f. *post*, after. Born after the father's death; published after the author's death; occurring or continuing after death.

Postil'ion, **Postil'lion**, *n.* F. *postillon*—It. *postiglione*, post-rider, f. *posta*. POST.[2] A rider on the near leading horse of a carriage and four or on the near horse of a pair.

Postmerid'ian, *a.* L. *postmerīdiānus*, f. *post*, after + *merīdies*, noon. MERIDIAN. Pertaining to the afternoon.

Post-mor'tem, *a.* L. *post mortem*, after death. MORTAL. Taking place after death.

Post-o'bit, *n.* L. *post obitum*, after death, f. *post*, after + *obitus*, death. OBITUARY. A bond to take effect on a death.

Postpone', *vt.* L. *postpōnĕre*, f. *post*, after + *pōnĕre*. POSITION. To put off to a later time; to subordinate.—**Postpone'MENT**, *n.*

Postpran'dial, *a.* L. *post*, after + *prandium*, luncheon + -AL. After-dinner.

Post'script, *n.* L. *postscriptum*, neut. pa. pple. of *postscrībĕre*, to write after, f. *post*, after + *scrībĕre*, to write. SCRIBE. An addition to a letter or book.

Pos'tulate, *vt.* L. *postulāre*, *postulātum*. To require, demand, claim; to take for granted. —*n.* Something taken for granted.

Pos'ture, *n.* F. *posture*, earlier *positure*—L. *positūra*, f. *pōnĕre*. POSITION. Attitude, pose; a state (of affairs, &c.).

Po'sy, *n.* Shortened f. POESY. A motto on a ring, &c.; a bunch of flowers.

Pot, *n.* Late O.E. or early M.E. *pott*, cogn. with M.Du. *pot(t)*, M.L.G. *pot*, *put*, F. *pot*. Orig. unknown. HOTCHPOT. POTTAGE. POTTLE. A rounded vessel; a potful.—*vt.* To put or plant in a pot; to preserve (meat, &c.); to shoot (game) for cooking; to shoot.—*vi.* To shoot *at*. —**Pot'TER**, *n.* A maker of earthenware.—**Pot'TERY**, *n.* His workshop; his art; his products collectively.

Po'table, *a.* F. *potable*—L.L. *pōtābilis*, f. L. *pōtāre*, to drink. POTION. Drinkable.—**PotA'TION**, *n.* Drinking; a drinking, a drink.

Pot'ash, *n.* Orig. *pot-ashes*, app. f. Du. *potasschen*. Cf. F. *potasse*. Also **Potass'**, f. F. *potasse*. An alkaline substance orig. got by treating vegetable matter in iron pots.—**Potas'sium**, *n.* The basis of potash.

Pota'to, *n.* Sp. *patata*, var. of *batata* (the Haitian name), applied to the tubers of a plant (and to the plant) app. first seen by the Spaniards in the W. Indies (now distinguished as the *sweet* or *Spanish potato*). A S. American plant grown for its tubers; the tubers.

Po'tent, *n.* L. *potens*, *potentis*, pres.pple. of *posse*, to be able, have power, short for *potis esse*, f. *potis*, able, cogn. with Skr. *pati-*, master, lord, G. *posis*, husband, *des-potēs*, DESPOT. POSSE. POSSIBLE. POWER. PUISSANT. Powerful.—**Po'tENCY**, *n.*—**Po'tentATE**,[1] *n.* A ruler. — **Poten'ti**AL, *a.* Possible; latent. — **Potential'**ITY, *n.*—**Po'tent**LY,[2] *adv.*

Poth'er, *n.* Orig. unknown. A choking smoke or cloud of dust; turmoil; a din. —*vt.* To worry, perplex.—*vi.* To make a fuss.

Po'tion, *n.* O.F. *potion*—L. *pōtio, pōtiōnis,* draught, also, poison, f. *pōtāre, pōtum,* to drink, cogn. with Skr. *pā*, G. *pinein* (perf. *pepōkenai*). POISON. POTABLE. A dose; a draught.

Pot'sherd, *n.* POT + SHARD.[1] A broken piece of earthenware.

Pot'tage, *n.* F. *potage,* lit. 'that which is put in a POT'. PORRIDGE. A dish of vegetables, &c., boiled to softness in water.

Pot'ter, *vi.* App. freq. (with shortened vowel) of dial. *Pote,* to push, thrust—O.E. *potian,* of uncertain orig. To work or act in a feeble or unsystematic way; to saunter or dawdle.

Pot'tle, *n.* O.F. *potel,* dim. of *pot,* POT. A former liquid measure; a pot containing this.

Pouch, *n.* O.N.F. *pouche* = O.F. *poche.* POACH.[1] A small bag.—*vt.* To put into a pouch; to pocket, take.

Poult, *n.* M.E., contr. f. *polet, poullet*—F. *poulet,* dim. of *poule,* hen—L.L. *pulla,* hen, fem. of L. *pullus,* young animal, FOAL, chicken. POLECAT. POOL.[2] PULLET. A chicken. — **Poult'erer,** *n.* -ER doubled. A dealer in poultry.—**Poult'**RY, *n.* Domestic fowls.

Poul'tice, *n.* Orig. *pultes,* pl. (soon taken as sing.)—L. *pultes,* pl. of *puls* (= G. *poltos*), pap made of meal, PULSE, &c. A soft mass applied to the skin.—*vt.* To put a poultice on.

Pounce. *n.*[1] App. conn. with PUNCHEON.[1] The claw of a bird of prey.—*vi.* To seize *upon* suddenly; to spring unexpectedly *upon.*—*n.*[2] From the *v.* An act of pouncing.

Pounce, *n.*[3] F. *ponce,* pumice, pounce—L. *pūmex,* PUMICE. A fine powder used to prevent ink from spreading.

Pound, *n.*[1] O.E. *pund* = O.N. *pund,* O.H.G. *phunt* (Ger. *pfund*)—L. *pondo,* orig. instrumental ablative of **pondus, *pondi* = *pondus, ponderis.* PONDER. 12 ounces Troy, 16 avoirdupois; a money of account (orig. a pound of silver) equal to 20 shillings.—**Pound'**AGE, *n.* A payment of so much per pound (money); a charge of so much per pound (weight).

Pound, *n.*[2] O.E. *pund* (only in combination). Orig. unknown. POND. An enclosure for stray cattle.—*v.*[1]*t.* To shut up in a pound.

Pound, *v.*[2]*t.* O.E. *pûnian.* Cf. L.G. *pūn,* chips of stone, Du. *puin,* rubbish. To reduce to powder; to beat severely.

Pour, *vt.* M.E. *pouren.* Doubtfully referred to O.F. *purer,* to purify, cleanse, in Norman, to drip—L. *pūrāre,* to purify (with religious rites), f. *pūrus,* PURE. To emit in or as in a stream.—*vi.* To flow or run in a stream.

Pout, *vi.* Perh. f. O.E. **pútian,* f. vbl. stem **put-,* to swell. To thrust out the lips in displeasure; to protrude.—*vt.* To protrude.—*n.* An act of pouting.—**Pout'**ER, *n.* A breed of pigeon with great power of inflating the crop.

Pov'erty, *n.* O.F. *poverté* (F. *pauvreté*)—L. *paupertas,* f. *pauper,* POOR. The condition of being poor; lack, dearth.

Pow'der, *n.* F. *poudre,* earlier *poldre, puldre* —L. *pulvis, pulveris.* PULVERIZE. Matter in a state of minute division; a medicine, &c., in the form of powder; gunpowder.—*vt.* To apply powder to; to scatter like powder; to reduce to powder.—**Pow'der**Y,[2] *a.*

Pow'er, *n.* A.F. *poër* = O.F. *poër, poeir* (whence *povoir,* F. *pouvoir*), inf. used as *n.*—Late Pop.L. *potēre* for *posse.* POTENT. Ability to do or act; might; rule; authority given; legal capacity or authority; an influential person, &c.; a state or nation as having authority or influence; the product of multiplying a number by itself a specified number of times.— **Pow'er**FUL, *a.*—**Pow'er**LESS, *a.*

Prac'tical, *a.* Obs. F. *practique* (var. of *pratique,* practical—L.L. *practicus* = G. *praktikos,* fit for action, f. *prassein,* to do, act) + -AL. PRAGMATIC. Relating to action; actually useful; engaged in an occupation; devoted or inclined to action; that is so and so in effect though not in name.—**Prac'tical**LY,[2] *adv.*—**Prac'tic**ABLE, *a.* That can be done or effected; that can be traversed or used.— **Practica**BIL'ITY, *n.*—**Prac'tise,** *vt.* O.F. *practiser,* f. *practiquer,* Med.L. *practicāre.* To do habitually; to carry out in action; to work at (an occupation, &c.); to exercise oneself in; to train.—*vi.* To exercise a profession; to exercise oneself.—**Prac'tice,** *n.* Formerly *practyse, practize.* App. f. the *v.* Habitual doing; action as distinguished from theory; a habit; exercise in an art, &c.; the exercise of a profession.—**Practi'**CIAN, *n.* A practitioner.—**Practi'tion**ER, *n.* Erroneously extended f. **practitian* = *practician,* as if f. a *n.* in *-ition.* One engaged in a profession, &c.

Præ'tor, Pre'tor, *n.* L. *praetor,* contr. f. **prae-itor,* 'one who goes before', f. *prae-* (PRE-) + **itor,* agent-n. f. *ire, itum,* to go. A Roman magistrate; a chief magistrate.

Pragmat'ic, *a.* = F. *pragmatique*—L. *pragmaticus,* skilled in business = G. *pragmatikos,* f. *pragma,* deed, affair, f. *prassein.* PRACTICAL. Of the affairs of a state, &c.; officiously meddling; dogmatic. — Sim. **Pragmat'**ICAL. — **Prag'mat**ISM, *n.* Officiousness; pedantry; matter-of-fact treatment of things; the testing of the value of an assertion by its practical consequences.—**Prag'mat**IST.

Prai'rie, *n.* F. *prairie,* meadow, prairie— Romanic type **prātāria*—L. *prātum,* meadow. An extensive grassy plain.

Praise, *vt.* O.F. *preisier,* to put a value on, to praise—L.L. *pretiāre, preciāre,* to value, f. L. *pretium,* PRICE. To proclaim the excellence of, laud, extol.—*n.* Praising; the fact or condition of being praised; that for which praise is given or deserved. — **Praise'-worthy,** *a.* Worthy of praise.

Prance, *vi.* Orig. unknown. Of a horse, to spring and bound; to move or walk in an elated or arrogant way.—*n.* A prancing.

Prank, *n.* Orig. unknown. A trick or frolic.

Prank, *vt.* Cogn. with Du. *pronk,* Ger. *prunk,* show, parade. To deck showily.

Prate, *vi.* = M.Du. *prāten, praeten,* M.L.G. *praten.* App. imitative. To talk idly, chatter. —*vt.* To utter in a prating way.—*n.* Chatter. —**Prat'tle,** *vi.* and *t.* Dim. and freq. To talk, to utter, childishly.—*n.* Childish chatter.

Prat'ique, *n.* F. *pratique,* practice, intercourse, pratique. PRACTICAL. Leave granted to a ship to communicate with the shore.

Prawn, *n.* M.E. *prayne, prane.* Orig. unknown. An edible marine crustacean.

Pray, *vt.* and *i.* O.F. *preier*—L.L. *precāre,* L. *precāri.* DEPRECATE. To supplicate devoutly or earnestly.—**Pray'er,** *n.* O.F. *preiere* (F. *prière*)—Med.L. *precāria,* fem., orig. neut. pl. of L. *precārius,* got by prayer, f. *precāri.* PRECARIOUS. An earnest entreaty, esp. to God; the action or practice of praying to God.

Preach, *vi.* F. *prêcher,* O.F. *prechier*—L. *praedicāre, praedicātum,* to proclaim publicly state, in Eccles.L. to preach, f. *prae-* (PRE-) + *dicāre*, to proclaim. ABDICATE. PREDICATE. To deliver a sermon.—*vt.* To set forth in a religious discourse.—**Preach'**ER, *n.*

Pre'amble, *n.* F. *préambule*—Med.L. *praeambulum*, orig. neut. sing. of *praeambulus*, going before, f. L. *praeambulāre*, to walk before. PRE-. AMBLE. An introductory part.

Preb'end, *n.* O.F. *prebende*—Med.L. *praebenda*, orig. neut. pl. ger. of L. *praebēre*, to offer, supply, for *praehibēre*, f. *prae-* (PRE-) + *habēre*, to hold. PROVENDER. A canon's share of the revenues of a cathedral, &c.—**Preb'end**ARY, *n.* The holder of a prebend.

Preca'rious, *a.* L. *precārius*, got by PRAYER, depending on favour, uncertain + -OUS. Uncertain; insecure, unstable; perilous.

Precau'tion, *n.* F. *précaution*—L.L. *praecautio*, *praecautiōnis*, f. L. *praecavēre*, to guard against beforehand. PRE-. CAUTION. Caution beforehand; an instance of this.

Precede', *vt.* F. *précéder*—L. *praecēdĕre*, to go before, to excel. PRE-. CEASE. To go before; to come before in rank, order, time, &c. —*vi.* To go or come before.—**Prece'd**ENCE, -ENCY, *nn.*—**Prece'd**ENT, *a.*—**Prec'ed**ENT, *n.* A previous case taken as a rule.—**Preces'sion**, *n.* L.L. *praecessio*, *praecessiōnis*, a going before, f. *praecēdĕre*. *Precession of the equinoxes*, the earlier occurrence of the equinoxes in each successive sidereal year.

Precent'or, *n.* L.L. *praecentor*, f. L. *praecinĕre*, *praecentum*, to sing before, f. *prae-* (PRE-) + *canĕre*. CANT.[2] A leader of singing.

Pre'cept, *n.* L. *praeceptum*, properly neut. pa.pple. of *praecipĕre*, to take beforehand, give rules to, f. *prae-* (PRE-) + *capĕre*. CAPABLE. A command or injunction.—**Precept'**OR, *n.* A teacher.—**Precept'**RESS, *n.*

Pre'cinct, *n.* Med.L. *praecinctum*, properly neut. pa.pple. of L. *praecingĕre*, to gird in front, encircle. PRE-. CINCTURE. An enclosed space; environs; a boundary or limit.

Prec'ious, *a.* O.F. *precios* (F. *précieux*)—L. *pretiōsus*, f. *pretium*, PRICE. Of great price or worth; affected, over-refined.—**Prec'ious**LY,[2] *adv.*—**Prec'ious**NESS, *n.*

Prec'ipice, *n.* F. *précipice*—L. *praecipitium*, f. *praeceps*, *praecipitis*, headlong, steep, f. *prae-* (PRE-) + *caput*. CAPITAL. A very steep face of rock, &c.—**Precip'it**ANCE, -ANCY, *nn.* Headlong speed; hastiness.—**Precip'i**TATE,[3] *vt.* To throw headlong; to hurry; to hasten the occurrence of; *chem.*, to cause to be deposited in solid form from solution; to condense from vapour.—*a.* -ATE.[2] Rushing headlong; very sudden; rash.—*n.* A substance or moisture chemically precipitated.—**Precip'itate**LY,[2] *adv.*—**Precipit**A'TION, *n.*—**Precip'it**OUS, *a.*

Précis, *n.* F., use as *n.* of *précis*, cut short. (See next.) An abstract.

Precise', *a.* F. *précis*, *-ise*—L. *praecīsus*, pa.pple. of *praecīdĕre*, to cut off in front, cut short, f. *prae-* (PRE-) + *caedĕre*. CÆSURA. Strictly expressed; exact; punctilious, scrupulous; over-exact; (the) exact, (the) very.—**Precise'**LY,[2] *adv.*—**Preci'**SIAN, *n.* A punctilious person.—**Preci'**SION, *n.*

Preclude', *vt.* L. *praeclūdĕre*, f. *prae-* (PRE-) + *claudĕre*, to CLOSE. To exclude, prevent.

Preco'cious, *a.* L. *praecox*, *praecocis*, early ripe, precocious (f. *prae-* (PRE-) + *coquĕre*, to COOK, ripen) + -OUS. APRICOT. Bearing blossom early; prematurely developed; indicating such development.—**Precoc'**ITY, *n*

Preconceive', *vt.* PRE-. To conceive beforehand.—**Preconcep'**TION, *n.*

Preconcert', *vt.* PRE-. To concert or arrange beforehand.

Precur'sor, *n.* L. *praecursor*, agent-n. f. *praecurrĕre*, to run before. PRE-. CURRENT. One who or that which goes before.

Preda'cious, *a.* L. type **praedax*, **praedācis* (f. *praedāri*, to plunder, f. *praeda*, PREY) + -OUS. Preying on other animals.—**Pred'atory**, *a.* L. *praedātōrius*, f. *praedātor*, agent-n. f. *praedāri*. Of, relating to, plundering; addicted to plunder; predacious.

Predecease', *vt.* PRE-. To die before.—*n.* Death before.—**Predeces'sor**, *n.* F. *prédécesseur*—L.L. *praedēcessor*, f. *prae-* (PRE-) + *dēcessor*, agent-n. f. *dēcēdĕre*. DECEASE. One who has preceded another in an office, &c.

Predes'tine, *vt.* L. *praedēstināre*. PRE-. DESTINE. To appoint or ordain beforehand. —**Predestin**A'TION, *n.* Esp., the doctrine that God has foreordained whatever happens and the lot of all men in and after life.

Predeter'mine, *vt.* Eccles.L. *praedēterminăre*. PRE-. DETERMINE. To fix or decide beforehand.—**Predetermin**A'TION, *n.*

Pre'dial, *a.* Med.L. *praediālis*, f. L. *praedium*, farm. Consisting of land; agrarian.

Pred'icate, *vt.* L. *praedicāre*. PREACH. To affirm, assert.—*n.* That which is predicated; in *grammar*, the statement made about a subject.—**Pred'ic**ABLE, *a.* and *n.*—**Predic'a**MENT, *n.* A category; a condition or situation, esp. a trying or dangerous situation. —**Predica**'TION, *n.*—**Predic'ative**, *a.*

Predict', *vt.* L. *praedīcĕre*, *praedictum*. PREDICTION. To foretell.—**Predic'tion**, *n.*

Predilec'tion, *n.* F. *prédilection*—L. type **praedīlectio*, **praedīlectiōnis*, n. of action f. Med.L. *praedīligĕre*, *praedilectum*. PRE-. DILIGENT. A preference or partiality.

Predispose', *vt.* PRE-. To dispose (a person, &c.) beforehand; to make liable or subject *to* something.—**Predisposi'tion**, *n.*

Predom'inate, *vi.* Med.L. **praedomināre*. PRE-. DOMINATE. To have controlling power *over*; to be the main or leading element.—**Predom'in**ANCE, *n.*—**Predom'in**ANT, *a.*

Pre-em'inent, *a.* L. *prae-ēminens*. PRE-. EMINENT. Excelling others.—**Pre-em'inent**LY,[2] *adv.*—**Pre-em'in**ENCE, *n.*

Pre-emp'tion, *n.* Med.L. **prae-emptio*, **prae-emptiōnis*, n. of action f. **prae-emere*, to buy beforehand. PRE-. EXEMPT. Purchase, the right to purchase, before an opportunity is given to others.

Preen, *vt.* App. var. of obs. *Prune*—M.E. *prune*, *pruyne*, *proyne*, app. of F. orig. To trim (the feathers) with the beak.

Pre-exist', *vi.* and *t.* PRE-. To exist before. —**Pre-exist'**ENCE, *n.*—**Pre-exist'**ENT, *a.*

Pref'ace, *n.* F. *préface*, app. f. Med.L. *prefātia* for L. *praefātio*, n. of action f. *praefāri*, to say beforehand. PRE-. FATE. An introduction to a book, &c.—*vt.* To furnish with a preface; to introduce (a speech, &c.) *with*.—**Pref'at**ORY, *a.*

Pre'fect, *n.* O.F. *prefect* (F. *préfet*)—L. *praefectus*, orig. pa.pple. of *praeficĕre*, to place in authority, f. *prae-* (PRE-) + *facĕre*, to make. FACT. A chief administrative official.

Prefer', *vt.* F. *préférer*—L. *praeferre*, to BEAR or put before. PRE-. PRELATE. To put forward in rank, &c., promote; to present, submit; to like better, choose rather.—**Pref'er**ABLE, *a.*—**Pref'erab**LY,[2] *adv.*—**Pref'-**

ERENCE, *n.* — **Preferen'tial**, *a.* Med.L. *praeferentia*, preference + -AL. Giving or receiving a preference.—**Prefer'**MENT, *n.*

Prefix', *vt.* O.F. *prefixer* — L. *praefigĕre*. PRE-. FIX. To put by way of introduction or title; to place before a word in combination. —**Pre'fix**, *n.* A prefixed verbal element.

Preg'nant, *a.* L. *praegnans*, *praegnantis*, gen. explained as a ppl. form f. *prae-* (PRE-) + root *gna-* of *(g)nasci*, *(g)nātus*, to be born. AGNATE. IMPREGNATE. With child; full of meaning.—**Preg'n**ANCY, *n.*

Prehen'sile, *a.* F. *préhensile*—L. *prehendĕre* (earlier *praehendĕre*), *prehensum*, to grasp, seize, f. *prae-* (PRE-) + **handĕre*, cogn. with G. *chandanein*, to take in, hold. APPREHEND. EMPRISE. ENTERPRISE. GET. IMPREGNABLE. PRISON. PRIZE, *n.*[1] REPRIEVE. SURPRISE. Having the capacity of grasping.

Prehistor'ic, *a.* PRE-. Relating to a period anterior to historical accounts.

Prej'udice, *n.* F. *préjudice*—L. *praejūdicium*, preceding judgement, damage, f. *prae-* (PRE-) + *jūdicium*. JUDICIAL. Injury by some judgement or action; preconceived opinion, prepossession (us. unfavourable); an instance of this. —*vt.* To injure; to cause to entertain a prejudice.—**Prejudic'i**AL, *a.*

Prel'ate, *n.* O.F. *prelat*—Med.L. *praelātus*, use as *n.* of pa.pple. of L. *praeferre*. PREFER. An ecclesiastical dignitary. — **Prel'**ACY, *n.* His office or rank; prelates collectively; government by prelates.—**Prelat'**IC, -ICAL, *aa.*

Prelect', *vi.* L. *praelegĕre*, *praelectum*, to read to others. PRE-. LECTION. To give a lecture.—**Prelec't**ION, *n.* A lecture.

Prelim'inary, *n.* F. *préliminaire*, f. L. *prae-* (PRE-) + *līmen*. ELIMINATE. An introductory or preparatory step, statement, &c.— *a.* Introductory, preparatory.

Prel'ude, *vt.* L. *praelūdĕre*, to play beforehand, prelude. PRE-. LUDICROUS. To introduce, foreshadow.—*vi.* To give or form a prelude *to*.—*n.* A preliminary performance, &c.

Prem'ature, *a.* L. *praemātūrus*. PRE-. MATURE. Too early; over-hasty.

Premed'itate, *vt.* PRE-. To plan or contrive previously.—**Premedit**A'TION, *n.*

Prem'ier, *a.* F. *premier*, first—L. *prīmārius*. PRIMARY. Chief.—*n.* The Prime Minister.

Prem'ise, **Prem'iss**, *n.* F. *prémisse*—Med.L. *praemissa*, orig. fem. pa.pple. of *praemittĕre*, to put before. PRE-. MISSION. A previous statement from which another is inferred; *the premises*, what has just been mentioned, the preliminary part of a deed, the subject of a conveyance, &c., as therein expressed, a house with its adjuncts. — **Premise'**, *vt.* To state by way of introduction.

Pre'mium, *n.* L. *praemium*, booty, profit, reward, f. *prae-* (PRE-) + *emĕre*. EXEMPT. A reward; a sum paid for insurance; a bonus; excess over nominal value.

Premon'ish, *vt.* L. *praemonēre*, after ADMONISH. PRE-. To warn beforehand.—**Premoni't**ION, *n.*—**Premon'it**ORY, *a.*

Preoc'cupy, *vt.* PRE-. To occupy or engross to the exclusion of other things; to take possession of beforehand. — **Preoccup**A'TION, *n.* Occupation beforehand; occupation taking precedence of all other, first business; mental absorption. [hand.

Pre-ordain', *vt.* PRE-. To ordain before-

Prepare', *vt.* F. *préparer*—L. *praeparāre*, to make ready beforehand, prepare. PRE-. PARE. To make ready; to get ready by study; to make or compound.—*vi.* To get ready.—**Prepar**A'TION, *n.*—**Prepar'at**IVE *a.* and *n.*—**Prepar'at**ORY, *a.*

Prepay', *vt.* PRE-. To pay (a charge) beforehand; to pay a charge for beforehand.—**Prepay'**MENT, *n.*

Prepense', *a.* Earlier *prepenst*, *perpensed*, *purpensed*, f. obs. *purpense* to premeditate—O.F. *purpenser*, f. *pur-*, *pour-* (PRO-, forth) + *penser*. PENSIVE. Premeditated, intentional.

Prepon'derate, *vi.* L. *praeponderāre*, *praeponderātum*. PRE-. PONDER. To be of greater weight; to exceed or be superior.—**Prepon'der**ANT, *a.*—**Prepon'der**ANCE, *n.*

Preposi'tion, *n.* L. *praepositio*, *praepositiōnis*, a putting before, a preposition, f. *praepōnĕre*. PRE-. POSITION. PROVOST. A particle marking a relation between two words.—**Preposi'tion**AL, *a.*

Prepossess', *vt.* PRE-. To inspire or affect beforehand; to impress favourably beforehand.—**Preposses's**ION, *n.*

Prepos'terous, *a.* L. *praeposterus*, reversed, absurd (f. *prae*, before (PRE-) + *posterus*, after (POSTERIOR)) + -OUS. Utterly absurd.

Prerog'ative, *n.* F. *prérogative*—L. *praerogātiva*, preference, privilege (properly, as epithet of *tribus*, denoting the TRIBE first called on to vote), fem. of *praerogātīvus*, asked first, f. *praerogāre*, to ask first. PRE-. ROGATION. The pre-eminence of the sovereign; a peculiar right or privilege.

Pre'sage, *n.* F. *présage*—L. *praesāgium*, f. *praesāgīre*, to perceive beforehand. PRE-. SAGACIOUS. An omen; a presentiment.—**Presage'**, *vt.* To portend; to predict.

Presbyo'pia, *n.* G. *presbus* (see next) + *-ōpia*, f. *ōps*, eye. A form of long-sightedness incident to old age.—**Presbyop'**IC, *a.*

Pres'byter, *n.* L.L. *presbyter*—G. *presbuteros*, properly comp. of *presbus*, old man. PRIEST. An elder in a church; a priest.—**Pres'bytery**, *n.* O.F. *presbiterie*, priest's house. A priest's house (in the *R.C. Church*); a part of a church reserved for the clergy; in certain churches, a body of ministers and elders forming a church court; the district they represent.—**Presbyte'ri**AN, *a.* and *n.*

Pre'scient, *a.* F. *prescient*—L. *praesciens*, *praescientis*, pres.pple. of *praescīre*, to know before. PRE-. SCIENCE. Having foreknowledge.—**Pre'sci**ENCE, *n.*

Prescribe', *vt.* L. *praescrībĕre*, *praescriptum*, to write before, to order, appoint. PRE-. SCRIBE. To order, appoint; to order the use of (a medicine). — **Prescrip't**ION, *n.* Prescribing, that which is prescribed; loss of a right by lapse of time; acquirement of a right by long use.—**Prescrip't**IVE, *a.*

Pres'ent, *a.* O.F. *present*—L. *praesens*, *praesentis*, pres.pple. of *prae-esse*, to be before, be at hand, f. *prae-* (PRE-) + *esse*, to be. That is here (or there); in hand, being dealt with; that is so now; expressing present action or state. —*n.*[1] The present time.—**Pres'ent**LY,[2] *adv.* Soon.—**Pres'**ENCE, *n.*

Present', *vt.* O.F. *presenter*—L. *praesentāre*, to place before, hold out, in Late and Med.L. to present as a gift, f. *praesens*. (See prec.) To introduce (a person) formally; to name for institution *to* a benefice; to show, exhibit; to set forth, to submit; to point or aim (a weapon); to give, offer, deliver.—**Pres'ent**, *n.*[2] O.F. *present*. A gift. — **Present'**ABLE, *a.* That can be presented; fit to be seen.—**Presenta'**TION, *n.*—**Present'**MENT, *n.*

Present′iment, *n.* Obs. F. *presentiment.* PRE-. SENTIMENT. A foreboding.

Preserve′, *vt.* F. *préserver*—L.L. *praeservāre*, f. *prae-* (PRE-) + *servāre*, to keep safe. CONSERVE. To keep from harm; to maintain, to retain; to keep (fruit, &c.) from decomposition; to keep (game, ground, &c.) for one's own shooting, &c.—*n.* Preserved fruit; a preserved piece of ground, &c.—**Preserva′**TION, *n.*—**Preser′vat**IVE, *a.* and *n.*

Preside′, *vi.* F. *présider*—L. *praesidēre*, to sit before, preside over, f. *prae-* (PRE-) + *sedēre*, to SIT. To occupy the seat of authority in an assembly; to exercise superintendence.—**Pres′id**ENT, *n.* The head of a body of persons, a council, &c.; one who presides over a meeting; the head of a republic.—**Pres′id**ENCY, *n.*—**Presiden′t**IAL, *a.*

Press, *v.*[1]*t.* O.F. *presser*—L. *pressāre*, freq. of *premĕre*, *pressum.* COMPRESS, DEPRESS, IMPRESS,[1] &c. To exert a steady force against; to bear heavily upon; to urge on, impel; to solicit earnestly.—*vi.* To bear heavily *upon*; to crowd.—*n.* A throng; the act of pressing; an instrument for compressing; a machine for printing; a printing office: the work or function of the press; newspapers, &c., collectively; a large cupboard.—**Pres′s**URE, *n.*

Press, *v.*[2]*t.* Altered f. obs. *Prest*, f. *prest* (also obs.), a loan, wages in advance—O.F. *prest* (F. *prêt*), vbl. n. f. *prester* (F. *prêter*), to furnish, lend—L. *praestāre*, to STAND before, furnish, in Late and Med.L., to lend. PRE-. IMPRESS.[2] To force to serve in the navy or army (orig., to engage with earnest-money).

Prestidig′itator, *n.* F. *prestidigitateur*, f. *preste*, nimble (It. *presto*, L.L. *praestus*, ready. PRESTO) + L. *digitus*, finger, DIGIT + agent-suff. A conjurer.—**Prestidigita′**TION, *n.*

Prestige′, *n.* F. *prestige*—L. *praestigium*, an illusion, for **praestrigium*, f. *praestringĕre*, to bind fast, blindfold. PRE-. STRICT. Reputation from previous character, success, &c.

Pres′to, *adv.* It. *presto*—L.L. *praestus*, a., L. *praestō*, adv., at hand, superl. forms f. *prae.* PRE-. Immediately, at once.—*a.* Ready, rapid. —*Mus.* (*a.* and *adv.*), in quick time, fast.

Presume′, *vt.* L. *praesūmĕre*, *praesumptum*, to take before, in L.L. to take for granted, dare. PRE-. ASSUME. To take upon oneself, make bold, *to do*; to take for granted.—*vi.* To take liberties; to rely *upon* presumptuously.—**Presum′**ABLE, *a.*—**Presum′ab**LY,[2] *adv.* —**Presump′t**ION, *n.*—**Presump′t**IVE, *a.* Warranting inferences; based on inference.—

Presump′tuous, *a.* O.F. *presumptuoux* (F. *présomptueux*)—L.L. *praesumptuōsus*, var. of *praesumptiōsus.* Unduly bold, presuming.—**Presump′tuous**LY,[2] *adv.*

Presuppose′, *vt.* F. *présupposer.* PRE-. To take for granted beforehand; to imply, involve. —**Presupposi′t**ION, *n.*

Pretend′, *vt.* L. *praetendĕre*, to stretch forth, pretend. PRE-. TENSE, *a.* To feign *to be* or *to do*; to feign (a quality); to allege with intent to deceive.—*vi.* To lay claim *to*; to feign.—**Pret**ENCE′, *n.*—**Pretend′**ER, *n.* One who makes a baseless claim.—**Preten′s**ION, *n.* A claim; ostentation.—**Preten′ti**OUS, *a.*

Pret′erite, **Pret′erit**, *a.* F. *prétérit*—L. *praeteritus*, pa.pple. of *praeterīre*, to go by or past, f. *praeter*, past + *īre*, to go. Past; expressing past action or state.

Pretermit′, *vt.* L. *praetermittĕre*, to let pass, omit, f. *praeter*, past + *mittĕre*, to send. MISSION. To omit; to take no notice of.

Preternat′ural, *a.* Med.L. *praeternātūrālis*, f. L. *praeter nātūram*, beyond NATURE. Out of the ordinary course of nature.

Pre′text, *n.* L. *praetextus*, display, pretext, f. *praetexĕre*, to weave in front, to pretend. PRE-. TEXT. An excuse or pretence.

Pret′ty, *a.* O.E. *prættig*, deceitful, cunning, clever, f. *prætt*, trick, craft. Orig. obscure. Cf. M.Du. *parte*, Icel. *prettr*, crafty trick. Formerly, cunning; clever. A general epithet of commendation; attractive in appearance.—*adv.* Moderately.—**Pret′ti**LY,[2] *adv.*

Prevail′, *vi.* L. *praevalēre.* PRE-. AVAIL. To be superior, get the better; to succeed; to predominate, to be in general use or practice. —**Prev′al**ENCE, *n.*—**Prev′al**ENT, *a.*

Prevar′icate, *vi.* L. *praevārīcārī*, *praevārīcātus*, to walk crookedly, to collude, f. *prae-* (PRE-) + *vārīcāre*, to straddle, f. *vāricus*, straddling, f. *vārus*, knock-kneed. To shuffle, equivocate.—**Prevarica′**TION, *n.*

Prevent′, *vt.* L. *praevenīre*, *praeventum*, to come before, hinder. PRE-. ADVENT. To hinder.—**Prevent′**ABLE, -IBLE, *aa.*—**Preven′t**ION, *n.*—**Preven′t**IVE, *a.* and *n.*

Pre′vious, *a.* L. *praevius*, going before (f. *prae-* (PRE-) + *via*, way) + -OUS. DEVIATE. Antecedent, preceding.—**Pre′vious**LY,[2] *adv.*

Previ′sion, *n.* L. *type* **praevīsio*, **praevīsiōnis*, n. of action f. *praevidēre*, to foresee. PRE-. VISION. Foresight.

Prey, *n.* O.F. *preie* (F. *proie*), earlier **preide* —L. *praeda.* DEPREDATE. GET. PREDACIOUS. Booty; an animal killed by another. —*vi.* To take booty; with *on*, *upon*, to seize as prey; to have a baneful influence *on*, *upon.*

Pri′apism, *n.* L.L. *priāpismus* = G. *priapismos*, f. *priapizein*, to be lewd, f. *Priapos*, god of procreation. Licentiousness.

Price, *n.* O.F. *pris* (F. *prix*)—L.L. *precium*, L. *pretium.* APPRAISE. DEPRECIATE. PRAISE. PRIZE.[2] That for which a thing is bought or sold.—*vt.* To fix or ask the price of.—**Price′**LESS, *a.* Invaluable.

Prick, *n.* O.E. *prica*, *pricca* = Du. *prik*, sharp point, L.G. *prik*, dot, spot. An impression made by pricking; the act of pricking, the fact of being pricked.—*vt.* O.E. *prician.* To pierce slightly with a sharp point; to mark by a prick; to erect (the ear).—**Prick′le**, *n.* O.E. *pricel*, earlier *pricels*, f. stem *pric-* of *prician* + instrumental suff. *-els.* A pointed process, a spine.—*vt.* and *i.* To cause to tingle, to tingle, as if pricked.—**Prick′l**Y,[2] *a.*

Prick′et, *n.* App. f. Med. (Anglo-) L. *priket-tus*, f. *prike*, PRICK, *n.* + dim. suff. *ettus.* A buck in its second year having straight unbranched horns.

Pride, *n.* O.E. *prýte*, f. *prút*, *prúd*, PROUD. An unduly high opinion of oneself; arrogance; a feeling of elation or satisfaction, something giving rise to this; the prime, the flower.—*v.refl.* To take pride, take credit to oneself.

Priest, *n.* O.E. *préost* = O.H.G. *prést*, *priast*, O.N. *prestr*—L.L. *presbyter.* PRESBYTER. An official minister of religion; a clergyman in orders above those of a deacon and below those of a bishop.—**Priest′**ESS, *n.*—**Priest′**HOOD, *n.*—**Priest′**LY,[1] *a.*

Prig, *n.* Rogues' cant of obscure orig. A thief; one who affects superior culture, morality, &c. (perh. in this sense a different word).—*vt.* To steal.—**Prig′g**ISH, *a.*

Prim, *a.* Orig. obscure. App. orig. slang. Consciously or affectedly strict or precise.

Pri′mage, *n.* Med.L. *primāgium*, an allowance made by custom to the master and crew of a ship for the loading and care of the cargo. Orig. obscure. A sum *per cent* paid by custom in addition to the freight of a vessel.

Pri'mal, *a.* Med.L. *prīmālis*, f. *prīmus*. PRIME, *a.* Of the earliest age; chief, fundamental.—**Pri'mary**, *a.* L. *prīmārius*. Chief, fundamental; of the first stage, division, &c.—**Pri'mari**LY,[2] *adv.* — **Prim'er**, *n.* From *prīmārius*. An elementary school-book.

Pri'mate, *n.* F. *primat*—L.L. *prīmas*, *prīmātis*, of the first rank, in Med.L., a primate, f. *prīmus*. (See next.) An archbishop.—**Pri'ma**CY, *n.* Pre-eminence; a primate's office.

Prime, *a.* = F. *prime*—L. *prīmus*, first. First in time, rank, &c.; of the best quality; not divisible by any other number; *Prime Minister*, the leader of the government.

Prime, *n.* O.E. *prīm*—L. *prīma* (*hōra*), the first (HOUR). (See prec.) An office for the first hour of the day; the first hour of the day; the stage or state of greatest perfection.

Prime, *vt.* Orig. uncertain. (Poss. conn. with L. *prīmus* (PRIME, *a.*), priming being for the most part a *first* operation.) To supply (a gun) with powder for firing the charge; to furnish fully *with* information for subsequent use; to give a first coat of paint to.

Prime'val, **Primæ'val**, *a.* L. *primaevus*, in earliest life (f. *prīmus* (PRIME, *a.*) + *aevum*, AGE) + -AL. Of the first age of the world.

Prim'itive, *a.* F. *primitif*—L. *prīmitīvus*, f. *prīmus*. PRIME, *a.* Early, ancient; original.

Primogen'iture, *n.* Med.L. *prīmogenitūra*, f. L. *prīmo*, adv., first (f. *prīmus* (PRIME, *a.*)) + *genitūra*, a begetting, f. root *gen-* of *gignĕre*. GENITAL. The rule by which real estate passes to an intestate's eldest son.

Primor'dial, *a.* L.L. *prīmordiālis*, f. *prīmordium*, beginning, f. *prīmus* (PRIME, *a.*) + *ordīri*, to begin. EXORDIUM. Primeval.

Prim'rose, *n.* History obscure. Corresponds in form to O.F. *primerose* (Med.L. *prīma rosa*, first (PRIME, *a.*) ROSE), of uncertain meaning. App. applied to the primula, and restricted later to the primrose. A spring plant bearing pale-yellow flowers; one of the flowers.

Prim'ula, *n.* Med.L. *prīmula* (orig. *prīmula vēris*, 'little firstling of spring'), fem. of L. *prīmulus*, dim. of *prīmus*. PRIME, *a.* VERNAL. App. formerly applied to various plants. A genus of plants including the primrose.

Prince, *n.* F. *prince*—L. *princeps*, *principis*, first, the first or chief person, f. *prīmus* (PRIME, *a.*) + *-cip-*, f. *capĕre*, to take. A ruler; the chief, the greatest; a son of a king or queen.—**Prince'**LY,[1] *a.*—**Prin'**CESS, *n.*

Prin'cipal, *a.* = F. *principal*—L. *principālis*, f. *princeps*. (See prec.) First in importance, &c.; of money, that is the sum invested or lent and yielding interest.—*n.* A chief or head; a principal sum.—**Principal'**ITY, *n.* The position or dignity of a prince; his territory.—**Prin'cipal**LY,[2] *adv.* —**Prin'cip**ATE,[1] *n.* The territory of a prince.

Prin'ciple, *n.* After *participle*, &c., f. L. *principium*, beginning, in *pl.*, elements, principles, f. *princeps*. PRINCE. An ultimate basis; a fundamental quality, law, truth, motive, or reason of action; uprightness.

Print, *n.* O.F. *priente*, *preinte*, impression of a seal, &c., f. *prient*, *preint*, pa.pple. of *preindre*, L. *premĕre*, to press. PRESS.[1] An impression; a printed cotton fabric; the state of being printed; printed lettering; an impression from an engraved plate.—*vt.* To impress; to produce (a book, &c.) by the application of inked types to paper, &c.; to stamp (a fabric) with a design.—**Print'**ER, *n.*

Pri'or, *n.* L. *prior*, former, superior, in Med.L., a prior. Earlier, former.—*adv.* Previously *to*.—*n.* A superior officer of a religious house or order.—**Pri'or**ESS, *n.*—**Prior'**ITY, *n.*—**Pri'or**Y,[1] *n.* A monastery or nunnery under a prior.

Prism, *n.* L.L. *prisma*, *prismatis*—G. *prisma*, thing sawn, prism, f. *prizein*, to saw. A solid figure or body of which the ends are two similar, equal, and parallel rectilineal figures, and the sides parallelograms; a transparent prism of triangular section by which a beam of light can be decomposed.—**Prismat'**IC, *a.*

Pris'on, *n.* O.F. *prison*, a taking, a prison, earlier *preson*—L. *prensio*, *prensiōnis*, for *prehensio*, n. of action f. *prehendĕre*. PREHENSILE. MISPRISION.[1] A jail.—**Pris'on**ER, *n.* One kept in prison; one captured in war.

Pris'tine, *a.* L. *pristinus*. Original, primitive.

Pri'vate, *a.* L. *prīvātus*, deprived of office, peculiar to oneself, pa.pple. of *prīvāre*, to DEPRIVE. PRIVY. Not holding public office; of a soldier, without any rank; secret; not open to the public; one's own; non-official; personal; confidential; secluded.—*n.* A private soldier.—**Pri'**VACY, *n.*—**Privat**EER', *n.* A privately owned armed vessel authorized by a government to be used in war.—**Pri'vate**LY,[2] *adv.*—**Priva'**TION, *n.* The action of depriving; lack of comforts or necessaries.—**Priv'**ATIVE, *a.* Expressing privation or negation.

Priv'et, *n.* Orig. unknown. A bushy evergreen shrub much used for hedges.

Priv'ilege, *n.* L. *prīvilēgium*, a law relating to an individual, a privilege, f. *prīvus*, single, peculiar + *lex*. LEGAL. An exceptional right, immunity, &c.—*vt.* To give a privilege to.

Priv'y, *a.* F. *privé*, private—L. *prīvātus*. PRIVATE. One's own (in **Privy coun'cil**, a body of advisers selected by the sovereign); in the secret; clandestine.—*n.* A private place of ease.—**Priv'i**LY,[2] *adv.*—**Priv'**ITY, *n.* A being privy to something; mutual interest.

Prize, *n.*[1] F. *prise*, a taking or capture, a captured ship—Early Romanic *prēsa*, *prensa*, f. pa.pple. of L. *prehendĕre*. PREHENSILE. A legal capture at sea; property thus captured.—*v.*[1]*t.* To seize as prize.

Prize, *n.*[2] Var. of M.E. *prīs*, *prise*, now PRICE. A reward of victory or superiority.—*v.*[2]*t.* O.F. *prisier*. To value highly.

Prize, *n.*[3], **Prise**. F. *prise*, a taking hold. PRIZE.[1] The act of prizing.—**Prize**, *v.*[3]*t.*, **Prise**. To force up or force open by leverage.

Prob'able, *a.* L. *probābilis*, that may be proved, probable, f. *probāre*. PROVE. Likely, credible.—**Proba**BIL'ITY, *n.*—**Prob'ab**LY,[2] *adv.* — **Pro'bate**, *n.* L. *probātum*, thing proved, neut. pa.pple. of *probāre*. The proving of a will; the document certifying this.—**Proba'**TION, *n.* The testing of a candidate for membership, &c.; a releasing during good behaviour of an offender.—**Proba'tion**ER, *n.* A candidate on trial. — **Pro'bat**IVE, *a.* Affording proof.—**Probe**, *n.* L.L. *proba*, a proof, in Med.L., an examination, f. *probāre*. An instrument for examining a wound, &c.—*vt.* To examine with a probe.

Pro'bity, *n.* L. *probitas*, f. *probus*. PROVE. Honesty, uprightness, rectitude.

Prob'lem, *n.* F. *problème*—L. *problēma*, *problēmatis*—G. *problēma*, lit. 'something thrown forward'; f. *proballein*, to throw forward, f *pro-*, before + *ballein*. EMBLEM. A difficult or doubtful question; a geometrical proposition in which something is required to be done. —**Problemat'**IC, **Problemat'**ICAL, *aa.*

Probos'cis, *n.* L. *proboscis*—G. *proboskis*, lit. 'a means of providing food', f. *pro-*, before + *boskein*, to feed. A trunk or snout.

Proceed', *vi.* F. *procéder*—L. PROcēdĕre, *prōcessum*. CEASE. To go forward, go on, advance; to go to law; to be carried on.—**Proce'd**URE, *n.* The fact or manner of proceeding; conduct.—**Pro'ceeds**, *n.pl.* Price, profit.—**Pro'cess**, *n.* F. *procès*—L. *prōcessus*. Course; a course or method of action; the proceedings in an action at law, an action; a projection from a main body.—**Proces'**SION, *n.* The marching of a body of persons in a formal way; the body so marching; an issuing from a source.—**Proces'sion**AL, *a.*

Proclaim', *vt.* L. PROclāmāre, to call out. CLAIM. To make official or public announcement of.—**Proclama'**TION, *n.*

Proclit'ic, *a.* With *pro-*, before, after G. *egklitikos*, ENCLITIC. That is closely attached in pronunciation to the following word, and has no accent of its own.—*n.* A proclitic word.

Procliv'ity, *n.* L. *prōclivitas*, f. *prōclivis*, sloping downwards, f. PRO- + *clivus*. DECLIVITY. An inclination or tendency.

Procras'tinate, *vi.* L. *prōcrastināre*, *prōcrastinātum*, f. PRO- + *crastinus*, of to-morrow, f. *crās*, to-morrow. To put off action from day to day, delay.—**Procrastina'**TION, *n.*

Pro'create, *vt.* L. PROcreāre, *prōcreātum*. CREATE. To beget.—**Procrea'**TION, *n.*

Procrus'tean, *a.* G. *Prokroustēs*, 'the stretcher-out' (f. *prokrouein*, to beat out, to stretch, f. *pro-*, forward + *krouein*, to beat), a fabulous Greek robber said to have stretched or mutilated his captives to fit the same bed + -AN. Aiming at uniformity by violent methods.

Proc'tor, *n.* Shortened form of PROCURATOR. A practitioner in an ecclesiastical court; a university disciplinary officer.

Procure', *vt.* F. *procurer*—L. PROcūrāre, *prōcūrātum*, to care for, attend to. CURE, *v.* To bring about; to obtain, get.—**Procur'**ABLE, *a.*—**Procura'**TION, *n.* The appointment of a procurator; his authority.—**Pro-c'urat**OR, *n.* One who manages another's affairs.—**Procure'**MENT, *n.*—**Procur'**ER, *n.* A pimp.—Sim. **Procur'**ESS, *n.*

Prod, *vt.* Perh. imitative. To prick or poke with something pointed.—*n.* A prodding.

Prod'igal, *a.* Obs. F. *prodigal*—L.L. **prōdigālis*, f. L. *prōdigus*, wasteful, f. *prōdigĕre*, to drive forth, squander, f. *prod-* (= PRO-) + *agĕre*, to drive. ACT. Wastefully lavish.—*n.* A prodigal person.—**Prodigal'**ITY, *n.*

Prod'igy, *n.* L. *prōdigium*, of doubtful orig. A marvel; a person of marvellous gifts.—**Prodig'i**OUS, *a.*—**Prodig'ious**LY,[2] *adv.*

Produce', *vt.* L. PROdūcĕre, *prōductum*, to lead forth, produce. DUKE. To bring into view, present; to extend in length; to bring into being, to yield, to make.—**Prod'uce**, *n.* That which is yielded or made.—**Produc'**ER, *n.*—**Produc'**IBLE, *a.*—**Prod'uct**, *n.* L. *prōductum*, neut. of the pa.pple. The number resulting from multiplication; the result of an action or operation.—**Produc'tion**, *n.*—**Produc'**TIVE, *a.*—**Productiv'**ITY, *n.*

Pro'em, *n.* O.F. *proeme*—L. *prooemium*—G. *prooimion*, f. *pro-*, before + *oimos*, way, road. A preface or exordium.

Profane', *a.* F. *profane*—L. *profānus*, lit., before (*i.e.* outside) the temple, f. PRO- + *fānum*. FANE. Not sacred, secular; blasphemous, ribald, impious.—*vt.* F. *profaner*—L. *profānāre*. To violate, desecrate.—**Profana'**TION, *n.*—**Profan'**ITY, *n.*

Profess', *vt.* L. PROfitēri, *professus*, to CONFESS openly, declare publicly. To affirm, avow; to lay claim to; to make protestation of, pretend to; to make (something) one's profession or business; to teach (a subject) as a professor. —**Profess'ed**LY,[2]*adv.* Avowedly; ostensibly. —**Profes'**SION, *n.* Professing; an occupation, such as medicine, &c., in which one professes skill; the body of persons engaged in a profession.—**Profes'sion**AL, *a.* As *n.*, one who makes a profession of a pastime. — **Profes'**SOR, *n.* A teacher of the highest rank in a university, &c.—**Professo'**RIAL, *a.*—**Professo'ri**ATE,[1] *n.* Professors; the office of professor.—**Profes'sor**SHIP, *n.*

Prof'fer, *vt.* O.F. *poroffrir*, *proffrir*, f. *por-* (= PRO-) + *offrir*, L. *offerre*, to OFFER. To offer, tender.—*n.* An offer.

Profic'ient, *a.* L. *prōficiens*, *prōficientis*, pres.pple. of *prōficĕre*, *prōfectum*, to make progress, accomplish, f. PRO- + *facĕre*, to make. FACT. PROFIT. Skilled, expert.—*n.* One who is proficient.—**Profic'i**ENCY, *n.*

Pro'file, *vt.* Obs. It. *profilare*, to draw in outline, f. *pro-* (= PRO-) + *filare*, to spin, draw a line—L.L. *filāre*. FILE, *n.*[2] To draw in profile.—*n.* Obs. It. *profilo*, outline. A drawing in side outline, esp. of the face; the side outline, esp. of the face.

Prof'it, *n.* O.F. *profit*—L. *prōfectus*, progress profit, f. *prōficĕre*. PROFICIENT. Benefit gained; proceeds, returns.—*vt.* and *i.* To benefit.—**Prof'it**ABLE, *a.* Yielding benefit, lucrative.—**Prof'it**LESS, *a.*

Prof'ligate, *a.* L. *prōflīgātus*, miserable, profligate, pa.pple. of *prōflīgāre*, to dash to the ground, f. PRO- + *-flīgāre* for *flīgĕre*. INFLICT. Dissolute, licentious; recklessly prodigal.—**Prof'lig**ACY, *n.*

Profound', *a.* O.F. *profund*, *profond*—L. *profundus*, f. PRO- + *fundus*, bottom. FUND. Deep; very learned; marked by great learning; abstruse; intense.—**Profund'**ITY, *n.*

Profuse', *a.* L. *profūsus*, properly pa.pple. of PROfundĕre, to pour forth. FUSE, *v.* Prodigal; abundant.—**Profu'**SION, *n.*

Progen'itor, *n.* Obs. F. *progeniteur*—L. *prōgenitor*, agent-n. f. PROgignĕre, to beget. GENITAL. An ancestor.—**Prog'eny**, *n.* Obs. F. *progenie*—L. *prōgenies*. Descendants.

Progno'sis, *n.* L.L. *prognōsis*—G. *prognōsis*, f. *progignōskein*. (See next.) Forecasting, a forecast of, the probable course of disease.

Prognos'tic, *n.* O.F. *pronostique*—L. *prognōsticon*—G. *prognōstikon*, use as *n.* of neut. sing. of *prognōstikos*, foreknowing, f. *progignōskein*, to foreknow, f. *pro-*, before + *gignōskein*. AGNOSTIC. An omen; a prediction.—**Prognos'tic**ATE,[3] *vt.* To foretell; to betoken.—**Prognostica'**TION, *n.*

Pro'gramme, *n.* F. *programme*—L.L. *programma*=G. *programma*, proclamation, notice, f. *prographein*, to write in public, f. *pro-*, before + *graphein*. GRAPHIC. A descriptive notice of a series of events; a plan or scheme.

Pro'gress, *n.* F. *progrès*—L. *prōgressus*, f. PROgredi, *prōgressus*, to go forward. AGGRESSION. A state journey; onward movement, course; development, improvement.—**Progress'**, *vi.* To go forward; to advance.—**Progres'**SION, *n.*—**Progres'**SIVE, *a.*

Prohib'it, *vt.* L. PRO*hibēre*, *prohibitum*, to hold in front, hinder, prohibit. INHIBIT. To forbid; to prevent.—**Prohibi'tion**, *n.*—**Prohib'itive**, *a.*—**Prohib'itory**, *a.*

Project', *vt.* L. PRO*jicĕre*, *prōjectum*, to throw forth. ABJECT. To throw; to plan, contrive; to cause to appear *on* or *against* a background.—*vi.* To jut out.—**Proj'ect**, *n.* A plan.—**Projec'tile**, *a.* Mod.L. *prōjectilis.* Impelling; capable of being thrown.—*n.* A missile.—**Projec'tion**, *n.*—**Project'or**, *n.*

Pro'late, *a.* L. *prōlātus*, pa.pple. of PRO*ferre*, to BEAR forward, prolong. Lengthened towards the poles; widely spread.

Prolegom'enon, *n.*; *pl.* **Prolegom'ena**. G. *prolegomenon*, neut. pres.pple. pass. of *prolegein*, to say beforehand, f. *pro-*, beforehand + *legein*, to say. A preliminary discourse.

Prolep'sis, *n.* L. *prolepsis*—G. *prolēpsis*, a preconception, f. *prolambanein*, to take before, f. *pro-*, before + *lambanein*, to take. EPILEPSY. Anticipation; a figure of speech by which a thing to follow as a result is represented as already done.—**Prolep'tic**, *a.* G. *prolēptikos*, anticipative. Of prolepsis.

Proleta'riate, *n.* F. *prolétariat*—L. *prōlētārius*, one able to serve the state only by begetting children, f. *prōles*, offspring, app. f. PRO- + *olēre*. ADULT. The lowest class of the community.—**Proleta'rian**, *a.* and *n.*

Prolif'ic, *a.* Med.L. *prōlificus*, f. *prōles*. (See prec.) -FIC. Fertile; fruitful.

Pro'lix, *a.* L. *prōlixus*, long, prolix, app. 'that has flowed forth', f. PRO- + **lixus*, pa.pple. of *liquēre*. LIQUID. Wordy, tedious.—**Prolix'ity**, *n.*

Pro'locutor, *n.* L. *prōlocūtor*, agent-n. f. PRO*loqui*, to speak out. ALLOCUTE. A spokesman; the chairman of an assembly.

Pro'logue, *n.* F. *prologue*—L. *prōlogus*—G. *prologos*, f. *pro-*, before + *logos*, speech. A preface; a speech before a play.

Prolong', *vt.* O.F. *prolonguer*—L.L. *prōlongāre*, f. PRO- + *longus*, LONG. PURLOIN. To lengthen out.—**Prolonga'tion**, *n.*

Promenade', *n.* F. *promenade*, f. *promener*, to lead forth, cause to walk, *refl.*, to walk—L.L. PRO*mināre*, to drive (a beast) onward. DEMEAN.[1] A leisurely walk; a place for promenading.—*vi.* To make a promenade.

Prom'inent, *a.* L. *prōminens*, *prōminentis*, pres.pple. of PRO*minēre*, to jut out. EMINENT. Projecting; conspicuous, distinguished.—**Prom'inence**, *n.*

Promis'cuous, *a.* L. *prōmiscuus* (f. PRO- + *miscēre*, to MIX) + -OUS. Mixed in disorder; indiscriminate.—**Promiscu'ity**, *n.*

Prom'ise, *n.* L. *prōmissum*, use as *n.* of neut. pa.pple. of PRO*mittĕre*, to send forth, to promise. MISSION. An undertaking to do or give something; a ground of expectation.—*vt.* To make promise of; to afford expectation of.—*vi.* To make a promise.—**Prom'issory**, *a.* *Promissory note*, a document containing a promise to pay a specified sum.

Prom'ontory, *n.* Med.L. *prōmontōrium*, alteration (after *mons*, *montis*, MOUNT) of L. *prōmunturium*, perh. to be referred to *prōminēre*. PROMINENT. A point of high land jutting out into the sea.

Promote', *vt.* L. PRO*movēre*, *prōmōtum*, to MOVE forward. To raise to higher rank; to further; to take steps towards the passing of (a private act) or the formation of (a company).—**Promot'er**, *n.*—**Promo'tion**, *n.*

Prompt, *a.* L. *promptus*, properly pa.pple. of *prōmĕre*, to take forth, f. PRO- + *emĕre*. EXEMPT. IMPROMPTU. Ready and willing; done, given, &c., at once.—*vt.* To incite or instigate; to suggest; to help (a speaker or actor) when at a loss.—**Prompt'er**, *n.*—**Prompt'itude**, *n.*—**Prompt'ly**,[2] *adv.*

Prom'ulgate, *vt.* L. *prōmulgāre*, *prōmulgātum*, of unknown orig. To proclaim or publish.—**Promulga'tion**, *n.*

Prone, *a.* L. *prōnus*. Lying face downwards, lying flat, prostrate; inclined, liable.

Prong, *n.* Orig. obscure. A forked instrument; a spike of a fork.

Pronom'inal, *a.* L.L. *prōnōminālis*, f. *prōnōmen*, *prōnōminis*, pronoun, f. PRO- + L. *nōmen*. NOUN. Of the nature of a pronoun.

Pro'noun, *n.* PRO-. A word used to represent a noun.

Pronounce', *vt.* O.F. *pronuncier*—L. PRO*nuntiāre*, to make known publicly, utter. ANNOUNCE. To declare, affirm; to utter.—*vi.* To give an opinion or decision.—**Pronounce'able**, *a.*—**Pronounced'**, *ppl.a.* Strongly marked, decided.—**Pronuncia'tion**, *n.*

Proof, *n.* O.F. *prueve*, &c.—L.L. *proba*, f. *probāre*. PROVE. Something which proves; demonstration; test; the standard of strength of spirits; a trial impression from type; an early impression from an engraved plate.—*a.* Impenetrable, invulnerable.

Prop, *n.* = M.Du. *proppe*. Orig. uncertain. A pole, &c., as a support.—*vt.* To support.

Propagan'da, *n.* It., f. L. *Congregatio de propaganda fide*, a body of cardinals in charge of the propagation of the faith. (See next.) An association, &c., for propagating a doctrine, &c.—**Propagan'dist**, *n.*

Prop'agate, *vt.* L. *prōpāgāre*, *prōpāgātum*, to fasten down, to propagate by slips, to extend, prob. f. PRO- + root *pag-* of *pangĕre*. COMPACT, *ppl.a.* To reproduce or breed; to increase; to disseminate, diffuse; to transmit.—*vi.* To breed; to increase.—**Propaga'tion**, *n.*

Propel', *vt.* L. PRO*pellĕre*, *prōpulsum*. COMPEL. To cause to move forward. — **Propel'ler**, *n.* An appliance in screw form for propelling a steamer.—**Propul'sion**, *n.*

Propen'sity, *n.* L. *prōpensus*, hanging forward, disposed (pa.pple. of PRO*pendēre*. PENDANT) + -ITY. Inclination, tendency.

Prop'er, *a.* F. *propre*—L. *proprius*, one's own. APPROPRIATE. IMPROPRIATE. One's (or its) own; special, individual, peculiar; of a noun, denoting an individual person, &c.; strict, accurate; strictly so called; fit; becoming.—**Prop'erly**,[2] *adv.*—**Prop'erty**, *n.* O.F. *proprieté*—L. *proprietas*, n. of quality f. *proprius*. PROPRIETARY. The being owned, the fact of owning; that which one owns; a piece of land; an article of furniture, costume, &c., used on the stage; a quality.

Proph'et, *n.* F. *prophète*—L. *propheta*—G. *prophētēs*, one who speaks for a god and interprets his will, a prophet, f. *pro-*, for + *-phētēs*, speaker, f. *phanai*. FAME. One who foretells future events.—**Proph'etess**, *n.*—**Proph'ecy**, *n.* O.F. *prophecie*—Eccles.L. *prophētia*—G. *prophēteia*, divine interpretation. Foretelling; an instance of this.—**Proph'esy**, *vi.* O.F. *prophecier*. To utter predictions.—*vt.* To foretell.—**Prophet'ic**, -ICAL, *aa.*

Prophylac'tic, *a.* G. *prophulaktikos*, f. *prophulassein*, to keep guard before, f. *pro-*, before + *phulassein*. PHYLACTERY. That defends from or tends to ward off disease.—*n.* A prophylactic medicine or measure.

Propin'quity, *n.* Obs. F. *propinquité*—L. *propinquitas*, f. *propinquus*, a., near, f. *prope*, adv., near. APPROACH. Nearness.

Propi'tious, *a.* O.F. *propicius*—L. *propitius*, of doubtful orig. Favourable; boding well.—**Propi'ti**ATE,[3] *vt.* To appease.—**Propiti**A'TION, *n.*—**Propi'tiat**ORY, *a.*

Propor'tion, *n.* F. *proportion*—L. *prōportio, prōportiōnis*, comparative relation, app. f. phrase *prō portiōne*, for (his or its) share. PRO-. PORTION. A share, a part; comparative relation; relation, comparison, analogy; relative size; form, shape; a rule for finding a fourth number bearing the same ratio to a third as a second does to a first; in *pl.*, dimensions.—*vt.* To adjust in due proportion; to form, shape.—**Propor'tion**ABLE, *a.* In due proportion.—**Propor'tion**AL, *a.* Of proportion; proportionable; having the same ratio.—**Propor'tional**LY,[2] *adv.*—**Propor'tion**ATE,[2] *a.* Proportionable.

Propose', *vt.* F. *proposer*, f. PRO- + *poser*, to place. POSE.[1] PURPOSE. To put forward for consideration or imitation, or as something to be attained; to offer; to nominate for a position; to intend.—*vi.* To make an offer of marriage.—**Propos'**AL, *n.*—**Propos'**ER, *n.* —**Proposi'tion**, *n.* F. *proposition*—L. *prōpositio, prōpositiōnis*, n. of action f. PRO*pōnĕre, prōpositum*, to set forth. POSITION. An assertion; the action of proposing something to be done; something so proposed.—**Propound'**, *vt.* With excrescent *d* f. *prōpōnĕre*. To propose for consideration.

Propri'etary, *n.* L.L. *proprietārius*, a., proprietary, as n., an owner, f. *proprietas*. PROPERTY. A body of owners; ownership.—*a.* In private ownership; owning property; relating to ownership.—**Propri'etor**, *n.* Irregularly formed, and substituted for *proprietary*, formerly used in this sense. An owner.—**Propri'et**RESS, **Propri'e**TRIX, *nn.*—**Propri'ety**, *n.* F. *propriété*, f. *proprietas*. Fitness, appropriateness; becomingness, decency.

Prorogue', *vt.* F. *proroger*—L. *prōrogāre*, app. lit., to ask publicly, hence, to prolong (a term of office), f. PRO- + *rogāre*, to ask. ABROGATE. To discontinue the meetings of without dissolution.—**Proroga**'TION, *n.*

Proscribe', *vt.* L. PRO*scrībĕre, prōscriptum*, to write in front of, to declare publicly to be banished. SCRIBE. To outlaw; to condemn as dangerous.—**Proscrip'**TION, *n.*

Prose, *n.* F. *prose*—L. *prōsa* (*ōrātio*), lit., straightforward (discourse), fem. of *prōsus*, contr. f. *prorsus*, contr. f. *prōversus*, pa.pple. of PRO*vertĕre*, to turn forwards. VERSE. Speech or writing not in verse.—*vi.* To talk or write prosily.—**Prosa'ic**, *a.* Med.L. *prōsaicus*. Commonplace, dull.—**Pro'sy**,[2] *a.* Dull, tedious.—**Pro'si**LY,[2] *adv.*

Pros'ecute, *vt.* L. PRO*sequi, prōsecūtus*, to follow forth, attend, go on with. SEQUEL. To persevere in; to carry on; to institute legal proceedings against.—**Prosecu'**TION, *n.*—**Pros'ecut**OR, **Prosecu'**TRIX, *nn.*

Pros'elyte, *n.* L.L. *prosēlytus*—G. *prosēlutos*, having come, one who has come to a place, a convert, f. *prosēluth-*, 2nd aorist stem of *proserchesthai*, to come to, f. *pros-*, to + *erchesthai*, to come. A convert.—**Pros'elyt**IZE, *vt.*

Pros'ody, *n.* L. *prosōdia*, tone of a syllable —G. *prosōidia*, a song to music, tone of a syllable, f. *pros-*, to + *ōidē*. ODE. The science of versification.—**Pros'od**IST, *n.*

Prosopopœ'ia, *n.* L. *prosōpopoeia*—G. *prosōpopoiia*, personification, f. *prosōpon*, face + *poie-ein*, to make. A rhetorical figure by which an inanimate thing is personified or by which an absent person is represented as speaking, &c.

Pros'pect, *n.* L. *prōspectus*, a look-out, view. f. PRO*spicĕre, prospectum*, to look forward, ASPECT. An extensive view; a mental looking forward; that which one can look forward to. —*vi.* and *t.* To explore for gold, &c.—**Prospec'**TIVE, *a.* Future.—**Prospec'tive**LY,[2] *adv.*—**Prospec'tus**, *n.* From *prōspectus*. A description of a proposed work or enterprise.

Pros'per, *vi.* F. *prospérer*—L. *prosperāre*, to cause to succeed, f. *prosper*, favourable, fortunate, f. PRO- + *sper-*, root of *spērāre*. DESPAIR. To thrive, do well.—*vt.* To promote the prosperity of.—**Prosper'**ITY, *n.* Good fortune, well-being.—**Pros'per**OUS, *a.*

Pros'titute, *n.* L. *prōstitūta*, orig. fem. pa.pple. of PRO*stituĕre*, to place before, expose publicly. CONSTITUTE. A woman who sells her favours.—*vt.* To make a prostitute of; to sell basely; to corrupt.—**Prostitu'**TION, *n.*

Pros'trate, *a.* L. *prōstrātus*, pa.pple. of PRO*sternĕre*, to strew before, to throw down. STRATUM. Lying face down; lying flat; overcome; exhausted.—*vt.* To lay flat; to overcome; to reduce to exhaustion.—**Prostra**'TION, *n.*

Prot'asis, *n.* G. *protasis*, lit. 'a stretching forward', f. *pro-*, forward + *tasis*, n. of action f. *teinein*, to stretch. The clause of a conditional sentence expressing the condition, the consequence being expressed in the **Apod'osis** (G. *apodosis*, lit., 'a giving back', f. *apodidonai*, to give back, f. APO- + *didonai*, to give).

Pro'tean, *a.* With -AN f. *Prōteus*, a sea-god who could assume various forms (Odyssey 4, 385 and foll.). Taking various forms.

Protect', *vt.* L. PRO*tegĕre, prōtectum*, to cover in front, defend. DETECT. To defend or guard; to guard (a home industry) against foreign competition.—**Protec'**TION, *n.*—**Protec'tion**IST, *n.*—**Protec'**TIVE, *a.*—**Protec'**TOR, *n.* One who protects; a regent; the title of Oliver Cromwell and his son Richard.—**Protec'**TRESS, **Protec'**TRIX, *nn.* —**Protec'tor**ATE,[1] *n.* The office of a Protector of a state; the relation of a power to a territory under its suzerainty; such a territory.

Protest', *vt.* F. *protester*—L. PRO*testāri*, to declare in public, protest. TESTAMENT. To affirm formally; to make a written declaration of non-payment or non-acceptance of (a bill). —*vi.* To make formal affirmation; to make a formal declaration *against* an action, proposal, &c.—**Pro'test**, *n.* A formal affirmation; a written declaration as to a bill not paid or not accepted; a formal declaration of objection.—**Prot'est**ANT, *n.* One of a church repudiating the papal authority.—*a.* Of Protestants.—**Prot'estant**ISM, *n.*—**Protest**A'TION, *n.*

Pro'tocol, *n.* O.F. *prothocole* (F. *protocole*)—Med.L. *prōtocollum*—G. *prōtokollon*, a first leaf, an index leaf glued on the case of a manuscript, f. *prōtos*, first + *kolla*, glue. A signed note of points agreed upon to be embodied in a treaty; a formal or official statement.

Pro'toplasm, *n.* Ger. *protoplasma*—G. *prōtos*, first + *plasma*, thing formed, f. *plassein*, to form. A substance supposed to constitute the physical basis of life.—**Pro'toplast**, *n.* L.L. *prōtoplastus*—G. *prōtoplastos*, first-formed, f. *prōtos* + *plastos*, formed, f. *plassein*. The first man; the original or model.

Pro'totype, *n.* F. *prototype*—Mod.L. *prōtotypon*—G. *prōtotupon*, properly neut. of *prōto-*

tupos, primitive, f. *prōtos*, first + *tupos*, TYPE. The first or primary type of anything.

Protract', *vt.* L. PRO*trahĕre*, *prōtractum*, to draw forth, lengthen. TREAT. To lengthen, prolong; to draw to scale.—**Protrac'**TION, *n.*

Protrude', *vt.* and *i.* L. PRO*trūdĕre*, *prōtrūsum*. ABSTRUSE. To stick out. — **Protru'**SION, *n.*—**Protru'**SIVE, *a.*

Protu'berant, *a.* L.L. *prōtūberans*, *prōtūberantis*, pres.pple. of *prōtūberāre*, to swell out, f. PRO- + *tūber*. TRUFFLE. Swelling out, prominent.—**Protu'ber**ANCE, *n.*

Proud, *a.* O.E. *prút*, *prúd*, proud = O.N. *prúthr*, brave, magnificent, both prob. f. O.F. *prud*, *prod*, *pro*, *prou* (F. *preux*), valiant—L.L. **prōdis*, useful, profitable, app. conn. with *prōd-* in L. *prōdesse*, to benefit. IMPROVE. PRIDE. PROWESS. PRUDE. Feeling or displaying pride; feeling high satisfaction; feeling lofty self-respect; that is a cause of pride; of high degree; stately.—**Proud'**LY,[2] *adv.*

Prove, *vt.* O.F. *prover* (F. *prouver*)—L. *probāre*, f. *probus*, good. PROBABLE. PROBITY. PROOF. REPROBATE. To test; to demonstrate; to establish the validity of (a will).—*vi.* To turn out *to be*, &c.

Prov'enance, *n.* F. *provenance*, f. *provenant*, pres.pple. of *provenir*, L. PRO*venire*, to come forth, arise. ADVENT. Origin, derivation; place of origin.

Prov'ender, *n.* O.F. *provendre*, var. of *provende*—Romanic type **provenda* for L. *praebenda*. PREBEND. Dry food for horses, &c.

Prov'erb, *n.* F. *proverbe*—L. *prōverbium*, f. PRO- + *verbum*, WORD (as if 'a (recognized) set of words put forth'). A short pithy saying; a byword.—**Prover'b**IAL, *a.*

Provide', *vi.* L. PRO*vidēre*, *prōvīsum*, to see forwards, be cautious, see to. ADVICE. IMPROVISE. PRUDENT. PURVEY. To exercise foresight, make preparation; to stipulate.—*vt.* To supply, afford; to equip, fit out.—**Prov'id**ENT, *a.* Foreseeing; economical, thrifty.—**Prov'id**ENCE, *n.* Foresight; economy; applied to the Deity as exercising prescient power for the benefit of man.—**Providen'**TIAL, *a.*—**Providen'tial**LY,[2] *adv.*—**Prov'ident**LY,[2] *adv.*—**Provi'**SION, *n.* The action of providing; something provided; an arrangement or measure; in *pl.*, food; a proviso. — *vt.* To supply with food. — **Provi'sion**AL, *a.* Temporary.—**Provi'so**, *n.* Ablative sing. neut. of pa.pple. of *prōvidēre* as in Med.L. legal phrase *prōviso* (*quod*), provided (that). A stipulation or condition.

Prov'ince, *n.* F. *province*—L. *prōvincia*, of uncertain orig. A division of a country; a part of a country outside the capital; sphere of action, &c.—**Provin'**CIAL, *a.* Of a province; lacking the manners and culture of the capital. — **Provin'cial**ISM, *n.* Provincial character; a provincial turn of speech.

Provoke', *vt.* O.F. *provoker* (F. *provoquer*) —L. PRO*vocāre*, to call forth, challenge. CONVOKE. To incite; to irritate; to bring about. —**Provoca'**TION, *n.*—**Provoc'at**IVE, *a.*

Prov'ost, *n.* Corresp. to O.E. *profost*, O.F. *provost*—Med.L. *prōpositus*=*praepositus*, prefect, president, use as *n.* of pa.pple. of *praepōnĕre*. PREPOSITION. The head of certain colleges; in Scotland=a mayor.—**Prov'ost-mar'shal**. A head of military police.

Prow, *n.* F. *proue*, prob. ultimately f. L. *prōra*, G. *prōira*. The fore-part of a ship.

Prow'ess, *n.* O.F. *proec(c)e* (F. *prouesse*), f. *pro*, *prou*. PROUD. Bravery, valour.

Prowl, *vi.* M.E. *prollen*. Orig. unknown. To roam stealthily, esp. for prey.—*n.* The act.

Prox'imate, *a.* L.L. *proximātus*, pa.pple. of *proximāre*, to approach, f. L. *proximus*, nearest, superl. form conn. with *prope*. PROPINQUITY. Next, nearest; soon approaching; immediate. —**Proxim'**ITY, *n.*—**Prox'imo**, *a.* Ablative sing. masc. (sc. *mense*, month) of *proximus*. Belonging to next month.

Prox'y, *n.* Shortened f. obs. *procur*ACY, the office of a PROCURATOR. The action of a deputy; a writing authorizing a person to vote for another; a deputy.

Prude, *n.* F. *prude*—O.F. *prude*, *prode*, good, virtuous, prob. a fem. form of *prud*, *prod*. PROUD. A woman who affects great propriety.—**Pru'd**ERY, *n.*—**Pru'd**ISH, *a.*

Pru'dent, *a.* L. *prūdens*, *prūdentis*, foreseeing, skilled, judicious, contr. f. *prōvidens*, pres.pple. of *prōvidēre*. PROVIDE. JURISPRUDENCE. Circumspect, discreet.—**Pru'd**ENCE, *n.*—**Pruden'**TIAL, *a.*

Prune, *n.* F. *prune*, plum—L.L. *prūna*. PLUM. A dried plum.

Prune, *vt.* Formerly *prouyne*, *proine*—O.F. *proōing(n)ier*, *proignier*, of uncertain orig. To lop off superfluous twigs from; to lop off.

Pru'rient, *a.* L. *prūriens*, *prūrientis*, pres. pple. of *prūrīre*, to itch, be wanton. Given to lewd thoughts.—**Pru'ri**ENCE, -ENCY, *nn.*

Prus'sic, *a.* F. *prussique*, f. *Prusse*, Prussia. Cf. SPRUCE. Of or derived from Prussian blue; *prussic acid*, a deadly poison.

Pry, *vi.* M.E. *prien*. Orig. unknown. To look closely or curiously.

Psalm, *n.* Eccles.L. *psalmus*—G. *psalmos*, a twitching with the fingers, a song sung to the harp, a psalm, f. *psallein*, to twitch. A sacred song.—**Psalm'**IST, *n.* A writer of psalms.—**Psalm'ody**, *n.* L.L. *psalmōdia*—G. *psalmōidia*, a singing to the harp, f. *psalmos* + *ōidē*. ODE. The art or practice of singing sacred music. — **Psal'ter**, *n.* M.E. *sauter*—A.F. *sauter* = O.F. *sautier*, *saltier*—L. *psaltērium*, psaltery, psalter—G. *psaltērion*, psaltery, f. *psallein*. The Book of Psalms; a copy of the Psalms.—**Psal'tery**, *n.* L. *psaltērium*. An ancient stringed instrument played by plucking.

Pseu'donym, *n.* G. *pseudōnumos*, bearing a false name, f. PSEUDO- + *onoma* (in Æolic *onuma*), NAME. A false name.—**Pseudon'ym**OUS, *a.*

Psy'chic, *a.* G. *psuchikos*, a. f. *psuchē*, soul. METEMPSYCHOSIS. Also **Psy'chic**AL. Of the soul; of phenomena beyond the domain of physical law.—**Psychol**'OGY, *n.* The science of the soul or mind.—**Psycholog'**ICAL, *a.*—**Psychol'og**IST, *n.*

Ptar'migan, *n.* = Gael. *tarmachan*. Orig. unknown. (The *p* app. inserted after Greek words.) The white grouse.

Pto'maine, *n.* It. *ptomaina*, f. G. *ptōma*, fallen body, corpse, f. *piptein*, to fall. An alkaloid substance, often poisonous, occurring in putrefying animal and vegetable matter.

Pu'berty, *n.* F. *puberté*—L. *pūbertas*, f. *pūber*, grown up, conn. with *pūbes*. (See next.) The state of being capable of procreation.

Pubes'cent, *a.* L. *pūbescens*, *pūbescentis*, pres.pple. of *pūbescĕre*, to attain puberty, f. *pūbes*, the hair on the groin marking puberty. (See prec.) Attaining or having attained puberty; downy.—**Pubes'c**ENCE, *n.*

Pub'lic, *a.* F. *public*—L. *publicus*, earlier *poplicus*, f. *poplus*, later *populus*, PEOPLE. Not private; of or concerning the whole community; open to all; open to general observation; of or engaged in the affairs of the community.—*n.* The community.—**Pub'lican,** *n.* L. *publicānus*, one who farmed the taxes, a tax-gatherer. One who keeps a public-house. —**Publica'tion,** *n.* L. *publicātio*, *publicātiōnis*, n. of action f. *publicāre*, to seize to the public use, to make known. A making publicly known; the issue of a book, &c., for sale; a book, &c., so issued.—**Public-house,** *n.* A place for the sale and consumption of alcoholic liquors.—**Pub'lic**IST, *n.* One versed in 'public' or international law; a writer on current public topics. — **Public'**ITY, *n.* — **Pub'lic**LY,[2] *adv.*—**Pub'lish,** *vt.* O.F. *publier*, f. *publicāre*. To make publicly known; to issue (a book, &c.) for sale.—**Pub'lish**ER, *n.*

Puce, *a.* F. *puce*, n.—L. *pūlex*, flea. Flea-coloured, brownish purple.—*n.* The colour.

Puck'er, *vi.* and *t.* A freq. prob. conn. with POCKET, the contractions being thought of as bag-like. To contract with wrinkles.—*n.* A wrinkle or a collection of wrinkles.

Pud'ding, *n.* M.E. *poding*, *puddyng*, a kind of sausage. Prob. conn. with F. *boudin*, of uncertain orig. A dish of flour, eggs, &c.

Pud'dle, *n.* M.E. *podel*, *puddel*, app. dim. f. O.E. *pudd*, ditch. Cf. Ger. dial. *pudel*, *pfudel*, puddle. POODLE. A small muddy pool; clay, &c., used as a water-tight lining.—*vi.* To dabble about in dirt.—*vt.* To line with puddle; to make (molten iron) malleable.

Pud'gy, *a.* With -Y[2] f. dial. *Pudge*, anything pudgy, of obscure orig. PODGY. Short and thick or fat.

Pu'erile, *a.* L. *puerīlis*, a. f. *puer*, boy. Boyish, childish; immature.—**Puer'peral,** *a.* L. *puerperus*, bearing children (f. *puer* + *parĕre*. PARENT) + -AL. Of parturition.

Puff, *vi.* M.E. *puffen*—O.E. **puffian*. Imitative. Cf. M.Du. *puffen*. To blow abruptly; to breathe hard.—*vt.* To drive or emit by puffing; to blow *out*; to inflate; to commend extravagantly.—*n.* A puffing; a piece of light pastry; extravagant commendation, an instance of this.—**Puf'f**Y,[2] *a.* Tumid; flabby.

Puf'fin, *n.* M.E. *poffin*, *pophyn*, *puffyn*. Orig. unknown. A sea-bird of the auk family.

Pug, *n.* Orig. unknown. A dwarf dog.—**Pug nose, Pug'-nose,** *n.* A snub nose.

Pu'gilism, *n.* L. *pugil*, boxer (f. root *pug-* as in *pugnus*, fist, and *pugnāre* (see next)) + -ISM. PONIARD. Boxing.—**Pu'gil**IST, *n.* A boxer.—**Pugilis'**TIC, *a.*

Pugna'cious, *a.* L. *pugnax*, *pugnācis*, combative (f. *pugnāre*, to fight (see prec.)) + -OUS. IMPUGN. INEXPUGNABLE. REPUGNANT. Given to fighting.—**Pugnac'**ITY, *n.*

Pui'sne, *a.* O.F. *puisne* (F. *puîné*). f. *puis*, L. *postea*, after + *né*, L. *nātus*, born, pa.pple. of *nasci*. NATAL. PUNY. Junior.

Pu'issant, *a.* F. *puissant*, earlier *possant*—Romanic **possens*, **possentis*, as pres.pple. of L. *posse*. POTENT. Powerful.—**Pu'iss**ANCE, *n.*

Puke, *vi.* Orig. unknown. To vomit.

Pule, *vi.* From or parallel to F. *piauler*, of imitative orig. To whine.

Pull, *vt.* O.E. *pullian*, to pluck. Orig. uncertain. To pluck up by the root; to tug at; to draw or haul; to draw (an oar); to propel or convey by rowing.—*vi.* To row.—*n.* Pulling; a long draught of liquor.

Pul'let, *n.* F. *poulet*. POULT. A young fowl.

Pul'ley, *n.* O.F. *polie* (F. *poulie*), prob. f. G. **polidion*, little pivot or axis, dim. of *polos*. POLE.[2] A wheel grooved for a cord.

Pul'lulate, *vi.* L. *pullulāre*, *pullulātum*, f. *pullulus*, dim. of *pullus*. POULT. To sprout; to spring up abundantly, teem, swarm.

Pul'monary, *a.* L. *pulmōnārius*, f. *pulmo*, *pulmōnis*, lung, conn. with G. *pneumōn*, *pleumōn*. PNEUMONIA. Pertaining to or affecting the lungs; consumptive.

Pulp, *n.* L. *pulpa*, fleshy part. Soft, moist animal or vegetable matter.—*vt.* To reduce to pulp.—**Pulp'**Y,[2] *a.*

Pul'pit, *n.* L. *pulpitum*, a stage, esp. one for actors, in Med.L., a pulpit. An elevated structure for a preacher.

Pul'sate, *vi.* L. *pulsāre*, *pulsātum*, freq. of *pellĕre*, *pulsum*, to beat, drive. APPEAL. COMPEL. PUSH. To throb; to quiver.—**Puls**A'TION, *n.*—**Pulse,** *n.*[1] M.E. *pous*—O.F. *pous*—L. *pulsus*, f. *pellĕre*. The beating of the arteries, esp. in the wrist.—*vi.* To pulsate.

Pulse, *n.*[2] O.F. *pols*, *pouls*—L. *puls*. POULTICE. Peas, beans, &c.; plants yielding pulse.

Pul'verize, *vt.* L.L. *pulverizāre*, f. *pulvis*, POWDER. To reduce to powder.

Pu'ma, *n.* Sp.—Peruvian *puma*. A large American feline quadruped.

Pum'ice, *n.* O.F. *pumis*—L. *pūmex*. POUNCE.[3] A light spongy stone.

Pum'mel, *vt.* Altered f. and = POMMEL, *v.*

Pump, *n.*[1] Late M.E. *pumpe*, *pompe* = Early Mod.Du. *pompe*, L.G., Ger. *pumpe*. Orig. obscure. A device for raising water, extracting air, &c.—*vi.* To work a pump.—*vt.* To raise or remove, to free from water, with a pump; to question artfully or persistently.

Pump, *n.*[2] Orig. obscure. A dancing-shoe.

Pump'kin, *n.* Earlier *pumpion* (obs. F. *pompon*, *popon*—L. *pepo*, *peponis* = G. *pepōn*) + dim. suff. *-kin*. A large egg-shaped or globular fruit; the plant bearing it.

Pun, *n.* Orig. unknown. A play on words.—*vi.* To make puns.—**Pun'**STER, *n.*

Punch, *n.*[1] App. a collateral form of POUNCE,[1] or shortened f. PUNCHEON.[1] An instrument for perforating or stamping; a blow with the fist.—*vt.* To pierce or perforate in the manner of a punch; to strike with the fist.

Punch, *n.*[2] Orig. uncertain. A beverage of spirits with hot water, lemons, &c.

Punch, *n.*[3] Orig. uncertain. A draught horse with a short thick body and short legs.

Punch, *n.*[4] Abb. of *Punchinello*, earlier *Polichinello*, app. f. Neapolitan *Polecenella* = It. *Pulcinella*, a character of the puppet theatre. Orig. uncertain. The principal character in the puppet-show 'Punch and Judy'.

Pun'cheon, *n.*[1] O.F. *poinçon*, *poinchon*, &c. —L.L. **punctio*, **punctiōnis*, f. *puncta*, POINT. POUNCE.[1] PUNCH.[1] A tool for piercing.

Pun'cheon, *n.*[2] In form identical with prec. in O.F. and Eng., but believed to be a different word. A large cask.

Punctil'io, *n.* It. *puntiglio*, Sp. *puntillo*, dim. of *punto*, L. *punctum*, point, f. *pungĕre*. PUNGENT. A minute detail of action or conduct.—**Punctil'i**OUS, *a.* Attentive to punctilios.—**Punct'u**AL, *a.* In good time, not late.—**Punctual'**ITY, *n.*—**Punct'ual**LY,[2] *adv.*—**Punct'u**ATE,[3] *vt.* To insert punctuation-marks in.—**Punctu**A'TION, *n.* The inserting of marks in writing or printing to aid the sense.—**Punct'**URE, *n.* An act of pricking; a hole made by pricking.—*vt.* To prick.

Pun'dit, *n.* Hindī *pandit*—Skr. *pandita*, learned, a learned man. A learned Hindu.

Pun'gent, *a.* L. *pungens*, *pungentis*, pres pple. of *pungĕre*, *punctum*, to pierce, prick.

COMPUNCTION. COUNTERPANE. COUNTERPOINT. POIGNANT. POINT. PUNCTILIO. Incisive, biting; irritant. — **Pun'g**ENCY, *n.*

Pun'ish, *vt.* F. *puniss-*, extended stem of *punir*—L. *pūnīre* (earlier *poenīre*), *pūnītum*, f. *poena*. PAIN. To cause to suffer for an offence; to punish on account of (an offence). —**Pun'ish**ABLE, *a.* — **Pun'ish**MENT, *n.* — **Pu'nit**IVE, *a.* Inflicting punishment.

Pun'ka(h), *n.* Hindī *pankhā*, fan—Skr. *pakshaka*, f. *paksha*, wing. A large swinging fan used in the E. Indies for freshening hot air.

Punt, *n.* O.E. *punt*—L. *ponto*. PONTOON. A shallow flat-bottomed boat.—*vt.* To convey in a punt; to propel with a pole.

Pu'ny, *a.* Var. of PUISNE. Small; weakly.

Pup, *n.* and *vi.* Shortened f. and = PUPPY.

Pu'pa, *n.* L. *pūpa*, girl, doll, fem. of *pūpus*. (See next.) PUPPET. PUPPY. A chrysalis.

Pu'pil, *n.*[1] F. *pupille*—L. *pūpillus*, orphan boy, ward, dim. of *pūpus*, boy. (See prec.) A minor orphan; a scholar.—**Pu'pil(l)**AGE, *n.*

Pu'pil, *n.*[2] O.F. *pupille*—L. *pūpilla*, orphan girl, ward, pupil of the eye, fem. of *pūpillus*. (See prec.) The aperture of the eye.

Pup'pet, *n.* Earlier *poppet*, app. f. F. *poupette*, dim. f. L. *pūpa*. PUPA. A human figure with jointed limbs moved by wires.

Pup'py, *n.* Corresp. in form to F. *poupée*, doll (whence app. in Eng. 'a toy dog'), app. f. Romanic *puppa* for L. *pūpa*. PUPA. A young dog.—*vi.* To bring forth puppies.

Pur'blind, *a.* Perh. *pure* (*i.e.* entirely) *blind*; or with O.F. *pur-*, *pour-*, intensive. Formerly, quite blind. Partially blind; dim-sighted.

Pur'chase, *vt.* A.F. *purchacer* = O.F. *por-*, *purchacier*, to seek for, f. *por-*, *pur-* (= PRO-), for + *chacier*. CHASE.[1] To buy.—*n.* Buying; what is bought; advantageous position for applying power.—**Pur'chas**ER, *n.*

Pure, *a.* O.F. *pur*, fem. *pure*—L. *pūrus*. PURGE. Unmixed, clean; clear, spotless; mere, simple; sheer, utter; faultless, correct; innocent, untainted. — **Pure'**LY,[2] *adv.* — **Pu'r**IFY, *vt.* and *i.* — **Puri**FICA'TION, *n.* —**Pu'rificat**ORY, *a.*—**Pu'r**ISM, *n.* Excessive attention to correctness of language.—**Pu'r**IST, *n.* — **Pu'r**ITY, *n.* — **Pu'rit**AN, *n.* One of those who called for further 'purification' of the Church after the reformation under Elizabeth; one strict in religion or morals.—*a.* Of the Puritans.—**Puritan'**IC, -ICAL, *aa.* Marked by the strictness of Puritans.

Purée, *n.* F., of uncertain orig. A soup of vegetables, meat, &c., boiled to a pulp.

Pur'fle, *vt.* O.F. *porfiler* = It. *profilare*. PROFILE. To border; to adorn with a border; to adorn, ornament.—*n.* O.F. *porfil*. A border, esp. an ornamental border.

Purge, *vt.* O.F. *purgier*—L. *purgāre*, earlier *pūrigāre*, to make clean, f. *pūrus*, PURE. To make clean; to clear *away*, *off*, &c.; to empty (the bowels); to exculpate; to get free from (a sentence).—*n.* Purging; an aperient medicine. —**Purg**A'TION, *n.* — **Pur'gat**IVE, *a.* and *n.* —**Pur'gat**ORY, *a.* As *n.*, in Roman Catholic belief, a state in which souls of the dead undergo a cleansing.

Purl, *n.*[1] App. orig. *pyrl(e)*, f. archaic and dial. *pyrl(e)*, *pirl*, to whirl, twist, of unknown orig. Thread of twisted gold or silver; a small twist or loop (or a series of such twists or loops) ornamenting the edge of lace, &c.; in knitting, an inversion of the stitches (in this sense perh. a different word). — *v.*[1]*t.* To ornament with purls.—*vi.* In knitting, to invert stitches.

Purl, *v.*[2]*i.* Poss. conn. with *pyrl(e)*. (See prec.) Cf. Norw. *purla*, to bubble up, Sw. dial. *porla*, to purl. To flow with a whirling motion and a murmuring sound.—*n.*[2] The action or sound.

Pur'lieu, *n.* App. altered f. *purley*, shortened f. *puraley*, *puralé*, a perambulation to settle the boundaries of a royal forest, hence, a purlieu—A.F. *purale(e)* = O.F. *por-*, *puralee*, a going through, f. *por-*, *puraler* (PRO-), interchanging with *paraler* (PER-), to go through, f. *aler* (F. *aller*), to go, of uncertain orig. ALLEY. A tract of land on the border of a forest; one's bounds; in *pl.*, the outskirts.

Purloin', *vt.* A.F. *purloigner* = O.F. *porloigner*, to put far away, f. *por-* (PRO-) + *loing*, *loin*, L. *longē*, far, f. *longus*. PROLONG. Formerly, to put far away. To pilfer, filch.

Pur'ple, *n.* M.E. *purpre*, *purper* = O.F. *purpre* (F. *pourpre*) — L. *purpura* — G. *porphura*, the Tyrian shell-fish yielding purple (actually crimson) dye, the dye. PORPHYRY. A colour composed of red and blue; a purple robe, the dress of emperors, &c. — *a.* Of the colour.—*vt.* and *i.* To make or become purple.

Purport', *vt.* O.F. *por-*, *purporter* to embody, extend—Late Pop.L. *PRO*portāre*, to carry forth. PORT, *v.*[2] To mean, imply.—

Pur'port, *n.* Meaning, sense.

Pur'pose, *vt.* O.F. *por-*, *purposer*, f. *por-*, *pur-* (PRO-) + *poser*. PROPOSE. To intend.—*n.* O.F. *por-*, *purpos*. An aim; intention; the matter in question, the point at issue.—**Pur'pose**LESS, *a.*—**Pur'pose**LY,[2] *adv.*

Purr, *n.* Imitative. The sound of a cat when pleased.—*vi.* To make the sound.

Purse, *n.* O.E. *purs*, app. f. Med.L. *bursa*. BURSAR. A small bag for money.—*vt.* To put into one's purse; to pucker (like the drawn-in mouth of an old-fashioned purse).—**Purs'**ER, *n.* A ship-officer who keeps the accounts.

Pursue', *vt.* A.F. *pursuer* = O.F. *porsuire*, *porsivre*, &c. (F. *poursuivre*)—L.L. PRO*sequĕre*. SUE. To follow with intent to overtake; to seek after, aim at; to go on with, carry out; to engage in, carry on.—*vi.* To go in pursuit; to go on (in speech). — **Pur'su**ANCE, *n.* — **Pur'su**ANT, *a.* As quasi-*adv.* Pursuantly.—**Pur'suant**LY,[2] *adv.* In a way that is consequent, accordantly.—**Pursu'**ER, *n.*—**Pursuit'**, *n.* A.F. *purseute*, *pursute*. The action of pursuing; that which one engages in.—

Pur'suivant, *n.* O.F. *porsivant*, properly pres.pple. of *porsivre*. An officer of the College of Arms ranking below a herald; an attendant.

Purs'y, *a.* Later form of archaic *Pursive*, prob. f. A.F. *porsif*, app. = O.F. *polsif* (F. *poussif*), f. *polser*, in sense 'to breathe with difficulty'. PUSH. Short-winded; fat.

Pu'rulent, *a.* L. *pūrulentus*, f. *pūs*, *pūris*, PUS. Consisting of or like pus; suppurating.—**Pu'rul**ENCE, **Pu'rul**ENCY, *nn.*

Purvey', *vt.* A.F. *purveier* = O.F. *porveeir* (F. *pourvoir*)—L. *prōvidēre*, to PROVIDE. To furnish, supply.—**Purvey'**OR, *n.*

Pur'view, *n.* A.F. *purview* (*est*), (it is) provided = O.F. *porveu*, pa.pple. of *porveeir*. (See prec.) The body of a statute, beginning with the words 'Be it enacted'; scope, range.

Pus, *n.* L. *pūs*. FOUL. PUSTULE. SUPPURATE. Yellowish viscid matter from a wound.

Push, *vt.* F. *pousser*, O.F. *polser*, *poulser*—L. *pulsāre*. PULSATE. PURSY. To press against with force; to move thus; to urge. — *vi.* To make one's way, go *on* (against opposition, &c.). —*n.* An act of pushing; persevering energy.

Pusillan'imous, *a.* Eccles.L. *pusillanimis*

(f. L. *pusillus*, very small + *animus*. ANIMUS) + -OUS. Cowardly.—**Pusillanim'**ITY, *n.*

Puss, *n.* Perh. orig. a call to attract a cat. Sim. forms in various Teut. languages. A cat; a hare.—Sim. **Pus'sy**. Dim. suff. *-y*.

Pus'tule, *n.* L. *pustula*, f. *pūs*, PUS. A pimple.

Put, *vt.* Early M.E. *pūten*—Late O.E. *putian*. Orig. obscure. To throw (a stone, &c.) from the shoulder; to place, set, to cause to be in a place, &c.; to express *in*, turn *into* words or writing; to place *in*, bring *into*, a state.

Pu'tative, *a.* L.L. *putātivus*, f. L. *putāre*, to reckon. COMPUTE. Reputed, supposed.

Pu'trid, *a.* L. *putridus*, f. *putrēre*, to rot, f. *puter*, rotten. Rotten.—**Pu'trefy**, *vt.* and *i.* F. *putréfier*—L. *putrefacĕre*, to make rotten, f. *putrēre* + *facĕre*, to make. FACT. To make, to become, putrid. — **Putrefac'tion**, *n.* — **Putrefac'tive**, *a.*—**Putres'cent**, *a.* L. *putrescens*, *putrescentis*, pres.pple. of *putrescĕre*, inceptive of *putrēre*. Becoming putrid.—**Putres'**CENCE, *n.*—**Putrid'**ITY, *n.*

Put'tee, *n.* Hindī *pattī*, band, bandage. A strip of cloth worn round the lower leg.

Put'ty, *n.* F. *potée*, in the first sense, orig. 'a potful', f. *pot*, POT. Calcined tin for polishing; a cement of whiting and oil.—*vt.* To fix or fill up with putty.

Puz'zle, *vt.* Orig. obscure. To perplex; to make *out* by ingenuity and patience.—*vi.* To be bewildered, to ponder in perplexity.—*n.* The being puzzled; a puzzling question; a toy or problem exercising ingenuity and patience.

Pyæ'mia, *n.* G. *puon* = L. *pūs*, PUS + *haima*, blood. Blood-poisoning with fever.

Pyg'my, *n.* L. *pygmaeus*—G. *pugmaios*, a. and n., f. *pugmē*, a measure of length from the elbow to the knuckles. A dwarf.—*a.* Dwarf.

Pyja'mas, *n.pl.* Pers. *pāē jāmah*, foot (or leg) garment. Loose drawers; a sleeping-suit.

Pyr'amid, *n.* App. after F. *pyramide*, f. L. *pyramis*, *pyramidis* — G. *puramis*, prob. of Egyptian orig. A monumental structure with sloping sides meeting at an apex; a solid figure of this shape.—**Pyram'id**AL, *a.*

Pyre, *n.* L. *pyra*—G. *pura*, f. *pur*, FIRE. A pile of wood for burning a dead body.—**Py'rotechny**, *n.* G. *pur* + *technē*, art. The art of making and using fireworks.

Py'thon, *n.* L. *Pythōn*, G. *Puthōn*, the serpent slain by Apollo near Delphi. A genus of large non-venomous serpents.

Pyx, *n.* L. *pyxis*, BOX. A vessel in which the host is kept; a box at the Mint in which specimens of gold and silver coins are placed to be tested at the annual 'Trial of the Pyx'.

Q

Quack, *n.*,[1] and in full **Quack'salver**. Du. *quacksalver*, app. f. *quacken*, to QUACK about (*i.e.* to boast about the virtues of) + *salf*, *zalf*, SALVE. An ignorant pretender to medical skill.—**Quack'**ERY, *n.*

Quack, *vi.* Imitative. Of a duck, to utter its characteristic sound.—*n.*[2] The sound.

Quadrages'ima, *n.* Med.L. *quadrāgēsima* (sc. *dies*, day), fem. of L. *quadrāgēsimus*, fortieth. Formerly, the forty days of Lent. The first Sunday in Lent.

Quad'rangle, *n.* F. *quadrangle*—L.L. *quadrangulum*, neut. of *quadrangulus*, four-cornered, f. *quadr-* (= QUADRI-) + *angulus*, ANGLE. A figure having four angles and four sides; a square in a building.—**Quadran'gul**AR,[1] *a.*—**Quad'rant**, *n.* L. *quadrans*, *quadrantis*, fourth part, f. *quadr-*. A quarter of the circumference or area of a circle; an instrument with a graduated arc equal to a fourth of a circle for measuring angular distances.—**Quadrate'**, *vt.* L. *quadrāre*, *quadrātum*, f. *quadr-*. QUARRY.[2] SQUARE. To make square. —*vi.* To square or agree *with*.—**Quad'**RATE,[2] *a.* Square.—**Quadrat'**IC, *a.* Of an equation, involving the square of an unknown quantity. —**Quad'rat**URE, *n.* The action or process of squaring; the position of one heavenly body relative to another when they are 90° apart.—**Quadrilat'eral**, *a.* L.L. *quadrilaterus*, four-sided (f. QUADRI- + *latus* (LATERAL)) + -AL. Four-sided.—*n.* A four-sided figure.

Quadrille', *n.* F. *quadrille*—Sp. *cuadrilla*, It. *quadriglia*, a band or troop, app. f. *cuadra*, *quadra*, L. *quadra*, square, conn. with *quadr-*. (See prec.) A square dance; music for it.

Quadroon', *n.* Sp. *cuarteron*, f. *cuarto*, a quarter—L. *quartus*, fourth. The offspring of a white person and a mulatto.

Quad'ruped, *n.* L. *quadrupēs*, *quadrupedis*, f. *quadru-* (= QUADRI-) + *pēs*, FOOT. An animal which has four feet.

Quad'ruple, *a.* F. *quadruple*—L. *quadruplus*, f. *quadru-* (= QUADRI-) + *-plus*. DOUBLE. Fourfold.—*vt.* and *i.* To make or become four times as great or as many.

Quaff, *vi.* Orig. obscure. To drink deeply.—*vt.* To drink copiously; to drain (a cup, &c.).

Quag, *n.* Conn. with dial. *Quag*, to shake. Imitative. A marshy place covered with yielding or shaking turf. Also **Quag'mire**.

Quail, *n.* O.F. *quaille* (F. *caille*), prob. Teut. Cf. imitative M.Du., M.L.G. *quackele*, O.H.G. *quatala*. A bird allied to the partridge.

Quail, *vi.* Orig. unknown. To flinch.

Quaint, *a.* O.F. *cointe*, *queinte*—L. *cognitus*, known, pa.pple. of *cognoscĕre*. COGNITION. Formerly, skilled; skilfully made. Unusual or uncommon, with an old-fashioned daintiness or prettiness.—**Quaint'**LY,[2] *adv.*

Quake, *vi.* O.E. *cwacian*, not found in the cogn. langs. QUAVER. To shake or tremble. —*n.* The act of quaking.—**Quak'**ER, *n.* (App. f. attributed shaking in religious ecstasy.) One of the Society of Friends.—**Quak'er**ESS, *n.*

Qual'ify, *vt.* Med.L. *quālificāre*, to attribute a quality to, f. L. *quālis*, of such a kind. -FY. To describe in a certain way, to characterize *as*; to make competent or legally capable; to modify; to moderate or mitigate. — *vi.* To make oneself competent or legally capable.—**Quali**FICA'TION, *n.*—**Qual'ity**, *n.* F. *qualité*—L. *quālitas*. A property or characteristic; kind; degree of excellence; high rank.—**Qual'it**ATIVE, *a.* Relating to quality.

Qualm, *n.* Orig. obscure. Cf. dial. Ger. *qualm*, swoon. A sudden feeling of sickness; a scruple of conscience.

Quanda'ry, *n.* Orig. unknown. A state of perplexity.

Quan'tity, *n.* F. *quantité*—L. *quantitas*, f. *quantus*, how much, how great. Size; amount, sum; length or shortness of metrical sounds; the property of things which can be determined by measurement; a (specified or indefinite) amount or number.—**Quan'tit**ATIVE, *a.* Relating to quantity. — **Quan'tum**, *n.* L., neut. of *quantus*. A share; an amount.

Quar'antine, *n.* Prob. f. It. *quarantina*, f. *quaranta*, L. *quadrāginta*, forty. A period (orig. of forty days) of isolation of suspected persons in order to prevent the spread of disease; the fact or practice of such isolation.

Quar'rel, *n.* O.F. *querele, querelle*—L. *querēla*, complaint, f. *queri*, to complain. QUERULOUS. A ground of complaint; an angry contention.—*vi.* To make complaint or protest; to contend angrily.—**Quar'rel**SOME, *a.*

Quar'ry, *n.*[1] O.F. *cuirée, curée*, f. *cuir*, L. *corium*, hide. EXCORIATE. Formerly, parts of a deer put on the hide and given to the hounds. The object of the chase.

Quar'ry, *n.*[2] Med.L. *quareia*, var. of *quareria, quadrāria*, f. L. *quadrāre*, to square (stones). QUADRATE. An excavation from which stone is obtained.—*vt.* To obtain from a quarry; to form a quarry in.

Quart, *n.* F. *quarte*—L. *quarta*, a fourth, fem. of *quartus*, fourth. A liquid measure, one-fourth of a gallon or two pints; a quart-pot.—**Quar'ter**, *n.* O.F. *quarter, quartier*—L. *quartārius*, a fourth part (of a measure), f. *quartus*. The fourth part of anything; one of the four divisions of an heraldic shield; 8 bushels; 28 pounds; the fourth part of a year; the region about a point of the compass, the point; region, district; a division of a town; dwelling-place, lodgings (gen. in *pl.*); assigned or appropriate position; clemency to one who surrenders.—*vt.* To divide into quarters; to add (another coat) to one's hereditary arms; to station or lodge.—**Quar'ter-deck**, *n.* Orig. a deck covering about a quarter of the vessel. The part of the upper deck between the after-mast and the stern.—**Quar'ter**LY,[1] *a.* Taking place, done, &c., every quarter, relating to a quarter.—*n.* A review, &c., published every quarter.—**Quar'ter**LY,[2] *adv.* Every quarter, once a quarter.—**Quar'termaster**, *n.* An officer attached to a regiment who provides quarters for the soldiers, looks after the rations, &c.; a petty officer who attends to the steering of a ship, stowing, &c. (app. in this sense f. *quarter* in the sense 'assigned or appropriate position'). — **Quar'tern**, *n.* A.F. *quartrun*, O.F. *quart(e)ron*, f. *quart(e)*, fourth, fourth part. A quarter of a stone or peck.—**Quar'tern-loaf**, *n.* A four-pound loaf (made of a quartern of flour).

Quartet', Quartette', *n.* F. *quartette*—It. *quartetto*, f. *quarto*, L. *quartus*, fourth + dim. suff. *-etto*. A composition for four voices or instruments; a set of four singers or players.

Quar'to, *n.* L., ablative of *quartus*, fourth, in phrase *in quarto*, in a fourth (*sc.* of a sheet). The size of a book in which each sheet is folded into four leaves; a book of this size.—*a.* Of this size.

Quartz, *n.* Ger. *quarz*, of uncertain orig. A [pure variety of silica.

Quash, *vt.* O.F. *quasser* = *casser*—L. *quassāre*, freq. of *quatĕre*. CASHIER. CASK. CONCUSS. SQUASH. To annul; to crush, suppress.

Quas'sia, *n.* From the name of a negro who discovered the virtues of the root. The wood, bark, or root of a S. American tree; a medicinal decoction prepared therefrom; the tree.

Quat'rain, *n.* F. *quatrain*, f. *quatre*, L. *quattuor*, FOUR. A set of four lines rhyming alternately.

Qua'ver, *vi.* With freq. suff. *-er* f. obs. *Quave*, to shake—M.E. *cwavien*, prob. repg. an O.E. **cwafian*, parallel with *cwacian*, to QUAKE. Prob. imitative like QUIVER, *v.* To vibrate, tremble; to use trills in singing.—*vt.* To sing with trills.—*n.* *Mus.*, a note having half the length of a crotchet; a trill; a trembling in the voice; a tremulous movement.

Quay, *n.* Altered (after F. *quai*) f. *kay, key*—O.F. *kay, cay*, cogn. with Sp. *cayo*, reef, perh. of Celtic orig. An artificial landing-place.

Quean, *n.* O.E. *cwene*, woman = O.S. *quena*, Goth. *qino*. Cogn. with G. *gunē*. QUEEN. An impudent or ill-behaved woman.

Quea'sy, *a.* Orig. obscure. Prob. f. F. Causing, inclined to, sickness; over-scrupulous.

Queen, *n.* O.E. *cwén*, wife (app. applied only to a king's wife), cogn. with *cwene*. QUEAN. The wife of a king; a female sovereign; the perfect female of bees, &c.; in chess, the piece with the greatest freedom of movement; a card in each suit bearing the representation of a queen.—**Queen'**LY,[1] *a.*

Queer, *a.* Orig. doubtful. Strange, odd; out of sorts, ill, faint.—**Queer'**LY,[2] *adv.*

Quell, *vt.* O.E. *cwellan*, to kill, causal of *cwelan*, to die = O.S. *quelan*, O.H.G. *quelen*. To crush, suppress.

Quench, *vt.* M.E. *cwenken, quenchen*—O.E. **cwencan*, causal corresp. to *cwincan*, to be extinguished = Fris. *kwinka*. To extinguish; to suppress; to slake (thirst) completely.

Quer'ulous, *a.* L.L. *querulōsus*, f. L. *querulus*, complaining, f. *queri*. QUARREL. Complaining, full of complaints.

Que'ry, *n.* L. *quaere*, imp. of *quaerĕre*. (See next.) Used to introduce a question; a question; a mark (?) to indicate a doubt.—*vt.* To ask, inquire; to put a query against.

Quest, *n.* O.F. *queste*—Pop.L. **questa*, pa.pple. of *quērĕre*, L. *quaerĕre*, to seek, to INQUIRE. ACQUIRE. CONQUER. Search or pursuit.—*vi.* To search or seek.

Ques'tion, *n.* O.F. *question*—L. *quaestio, quaestiōnis*, n. of action f. *quaerĕre*. (See prec.) The action of inquiring or asking; a problem, a difficult subject; a subject of discussion, debate, or strife; an interrogation, inquiry.—*vt.* To interrogate; to doubt, hold uncertain; to dispute.—**Ques'tion**ABLE, *a.* Open to dispute; of doubtful nature.

Queue, *n.* F. *queue*, O.F. *coue, cue, coe*—L. *cauda*, tail. CAUDAL. CUE.[2] A long plait of hair worn behind; a line of waiting persons.

Quib'ble, *n.* App., with dim. suff. *-le*, f. obs. *Quib* in the second sense—L. *quibus*, dat. and ablative pl. of *qui*, who, which, and as a common word in law papers associated with legal equivocations. A pun; an equivocation or evasion.—*vi.* To evade the point by a quibble.

Quick, *a.* O.E. *cwicu, cwic*. Common Teut. Cogn. with G. *bios*, life, L. *vīvus*, living. WHITLOW. Living; growing, alive; of fire, burning strongly; strongly felt, keen; keen in perception; mentally active; rapid, swift.—*n.* Sensitive flesh.—*adv.* Quickly.—**Quick'**EN,[2] *vt.* To give life to; to stir up, rouse; to hasten. —*vi.* To become living; to become faster.—**Quick'lime**, *n.* Lime burned but not yet slaked with water. — **Quick'**LY,[2] *adv.*—**Quick'sand**, *n.* From the *a.* in sense 'shifting, yielding to pressure'. A bed of loose wet sand which swallows up objects.—**Quick'set**, *n.* Live slips set to grow, esp. for hedges; a quickset hedge.—**Quick'silver**, *n.* O.E. *cwic seolfor*. SILVER. Mercury.

Quid, *n.* Var. of CUD. A lump of tobacco kept in the mouth and chewed.

Quid'dity, *n.* Scholastic L. *quidditas*, f. L. *quid*, what? The essence of a thing; a quibble, a quirk; subtlety (of wit).

Quid'nunc, *n.* L. *quid*, what? + *nunc*, now. One greedy of news, a gossip.

Qui'et, *n.* L. *quies, quiētis*. Absence of disturbance, noise or agitation.—*vt.* and *i.* To make, to become, quiet.—**Qui'et**, *a.* L. *quiētus*, pa.pple. of *quiescĕre*, to rest, be still, conn. with *quies*. ACQUIESCE. ACQUIT. COY. QUIT. At rest; gentle; not active; making no noise; not obtrusive; free from disturbance, noise or agitation.—**Qui'et**LY,[2] *adv.*—**Quies'**CENT, *a.* At rest.—**Quies'**CENCE, *n.*—**Qui'**ETUDE, *n.*—**Quie'tus**, *n.* Med.L. *quiētus (est)*, (he is) quit. A receipt; death.

Quill, *n.* Orig. obscure. Cf. L.G. *quiele*, Ger. *kiel*. The tube of a feather; one of the sharp spines of a porcupine.

Quil'let, *n.* Perh. short for obs. *Quillity*, perh. altered f. QUIDDITY. A quibble, a quirk.

Quilt, *n.* O.F. *cuilte*—L. *culcita*, stuffed sack, cushion. COUNTERPANE. A padded bed-cover.—*vt.* To stitch (two pieces of cloth) with padding between.

Quince, *n.* Properly pl. of obs. *quine* = *coyn*—O.F. *cooin* (F. *coing*)—L. *cotōneum*, var. of *cydōnium*, neut. of *cydōnius*, of *Cydōnia*, G. *Kudōnia*, Canea in Crete. The fruit of a tree of the pear family; the tree.

Quin'cunx, *n.* L. *quincunx*, five-twelfths, f. *quinque*, FIVE + *uncia*. INCH. An arrangement of five objects one at each corner and one at the centre of a rectangle (app. from the use of five dots thus arranged to denote five-twelfths of the Roman coin an as).

Quinine', *n.* From *quina*, Sp. spelling of Peruvian *kina*, bark + chem. suff. *-ine*. An alkaloid found in the bark of certain trees and used as a febrifuge, &c.

Quinquages'ima, *n.* Med.L. *quinquāgēsima* (sc. *dies*, day), fem. of L. *quinquāgēsimus*, fiftieth. App. formed on the analogy of QUADRAGESIMA, the succeeding Sunday. The Sunday before Lent, Shrove Sunday.

Quin'sy, *n.* Med.L. *quinancia*—G. *kunagchē*, dog-quinsy, sore throat, f. *kuōn*, *kunos*, dog + *agchein*, to throttle. Inflammation of the throat; suppuration of the tonsils.

Quintes'sence, *n.* Med.L. *quinta essentia*, 'fifth ESSENCE', supposed to be latent in all things. The most essential part or feature.

Quintet', **Quintette'**, *n.* F. *quintette*—It. *quintetto*, f. *quinto*, L. *quintus*, fifth + dim. suff. *-etto*. A composition for five voices or instruments; a set of five singers or players.

Quip, *n.* Var. of obs. *Quippy*, perh. f. L. *quippe*, indeed, forsooth (with sarcastic force). A sharp sarcastic remark; an equivocation.

Quire, *n.*[1] O.F. *quaer*, *quaeir*—Pop.L. **quaternum*, f. L. *quaterni*, a set of four, f. *quattuor*, FOUR. Four sheets doubled to form eight leaves; twenty-four sheets of writing-paper.

Quire, *n.*[2] Var. of CHOIR.

Quirk, *n.* Orig. obscure. An equivocation or quibble; a clever or witty remark.

Quit, *a.* O.F. *quitte*, earlier *quite*—L. *quiētus*, QUIET. QUITE. REQUITE. Free, rid.—*vt.* To renounce; to go away from; to make a return for; to pay up.—*v.refl.* To do one's part, bear oneself.—**Quits**, *a.* The *s* unexplained. Equal or even (*with* another).—**Quit'**TANCE, *n.* Release; discharge; a receipt.

Quite, *adv.* From *quite*, QUIT, *a.* Completely, entirely; actually, really, positively.

Quiv'er, *n.*[1] A.F. *quivier*, O.F. *quivre*, *coivre*, app. f. Teut. Cf. O.H.G. *kohhar* (Ger. *köcher*), O.E. *cocer*. A case for arrows.

Quiv'er, *vi.* App. imitative. Cf. QUAVER. To shake or tremble slightly and rapidly.—*n.*[2] An act of quivering.

Quixot'ic, *a.* The name of the hero of Cervantes's romance + -IC. Characterized by or displaying enthusiasm for visionary ideals.

Quiz, *n.* Orig. obscure. One who quizzes; a hoax; the act or practice of quizzing.—*vt.* To make fun of; to look at mockingly.

Quoit, *n.* Orig. obscure. App. f. F. A ring of iron thrown at a mark; in *pl.* the sport of throwing the quoit.—*vt.* To throw like a quoit.

Quo'rum, *n.* L., lit. 'of whom', f. the wording of commissions '*quorum vos . . . unum* (*duos, &c.*) *esse volumus*', 'of whom we will that you . . . be one (two, &c.)'. Orig. applied to certain justices of the peace whose presence was necessary to constitute a court. A fixed number of any body whose presence is necessary for the valid transaction of business.

Quo'ta, *n.* Med.L. *quota* (sc. *pars*, part), 'how great a part', fem. of L *quotus*, f. *quot*, how many. A part or share to be contributed.

Quote, *vt.* Med.L. *quotāre*, to mark by numbers for reference, f. L. *quot*. (See prec.) To copy out or repeat passages from; to copy out or repeat (a passage); to adduce, allege; to state the price of.—**Quot'**ABLE, *a.* Suitable for quoting.—**Quot**A'TION, *n.*

Quoth, *vt.* Pa.t. of obs. *Quethe*, to say—O.E. *cwethan* = O.H.G. *quedan*, *chweden*, O.N. *kvetha*. BEQUEATH. Said.

Quotid'ian, *a.* L. *quotīdiānus*, f. *quotīdie*, daily, f. *quot*, how many + *dies*, day. Daily; recurring every day; commonplace, ordinary.

Quo'tient, *n.* L. *quotiens*, how many times (f. *quot*, how many), taken as a pres.ppl. with stem in *-ent-*. The number resulting from dividing one number by another.

R

Rab'bet, *n.* O.F. *rab(b)at*, a beating down, a recess in a wall, f. *rabatre*, to beat back or down. REBATE. A groove or slot in a piece of wood, stone, &c., to receive an edge, &c., of another piece.—*vt.* To join or fix by a rabbet; to form a rabbet in.

Rab'bi, *n.* Heb. *rabbī*, 'my master', f. *rabh*, master + pronominal suff. A Jewish doctor of the law.—**Rab'bin**, *n.* F. *rabbin*, Med.L. *rabbīnus* (the *n* having perh. come f. a supposed pl. (**rabbin*) of the Heb. word). A rabbi.—**Rabbin'**ICAL, *a.*

Rab'bit, *n.* App. of Northern F. orig. Cf. Flemish *robbe*. A burrowing rodent.—*Welsh rabbit*, a dish of toasted cheese = RAREBIT.

Rab'ble, *n.* Poss. (with root-notion that of hurry and confusion) conn. with obs. *Rabble*, v., to speak in a rapid confused manner = Du. *rabbelen*, L.G. *rabbeln*. A tumultuous crowd, a mob; the low or disorderly part of the populace.—**Rab'ble**MENT, *n.* Such part of the populace; confusion, tumult.

Ra'bies, *n.* L. *rabies*, madness, f. *rabĕre*, to rage, rave. RAGE. Canine madness.—**Rab'id**, *a.* L. *rabidus*, mad. Raging; having a feeling, view, &c., in a violent degree.

Race, *n.*[1] O.N. *rás*, running, race, rush (of water), &c. = O.E. *rǣs*, in sim. senses, M.L.G. *rās*, current. The course of life; a strong current; a running, riding, &c., in competition.—*vi.* To run a race; to run, &c., swiftly.—*vt.* To run a race with; to cause to run a race or to move swiftly.

Race, *n.*[2] F. *race*—It. *razza* = Sp. *raza*, of obscure orig. A group of persons, &c., having

a common origin; a breed or stock of animals; a group having a common feature.—**Ra'**CIAL, *a.*—**Ra'**CY,[2] *a.* Having a distinctive quality.
Race, *n.*[3] O.F. *rais, raiz*—L. *rādix.* RADICAL. A root (of ginger).
Rack, *n.*[1] Perh. Scandinavian. Cf. Norw. and Sw. dial. *rak*, wreck, wreckage, f. O.N. *reka*, to drive. Clouds driven before the wind.
Rack, *n.*[2] App. f. M.Du. *rec* or M.L.G. *rek(ke)* (Ger. *recke*, a frame for stretching leather, &c.), prob. f. *recken.* RACK, *v.*[1] A frame with upright bars to hold fodder; a framework for holding articles; a bar with teeth on the side or edge.
Rack, *n.*[3] Var. of WRACK. Destruction.
Rack, *v.*[1]*t.* Prob. f. M.Du. or M.L.G. *recken*, to stretch. RACK, *n.*[2] To torture by stretching; to inflict pain on; to injure by straining, &c.; to task severely, strain; to raise (rent) too high; to oppress by exactions, esp. of excessive rent.—*n.*[4] Prob. formed f. the *v.* in Eng. An instrument for torturing by stretching.
Rack, *v.*[2]*t.* Pr. (Gascon) *arracar*, f. *raca*, the stems, &c., of grapes, thick dregs. To draw off (wine, &c.) from the lees.
Rack'et, *n.*[1], **Rac'quet**. F. *raquette*, of uncertain orig. A bat used in tennis, &c.; in *pl.*, a game of ball.
Rack'et, *n.*[2] Prob. imitative. Loud noise, uproar; a loud noise; a trying situation.—*vi.* To make a noise; to live a gay life.
Ra'diate, *vi.* L. *radiāre, radiātum*, to furnish with rays, to emit rays, f. *radius*, ray. RADIUS. To emit rays of light or heat; to issue in rays.—*vt.* To emit (light or heat) in rays. — **Radi**A'TION, *n.* — **Ra'di**ANCE, *n.* Brightness.—**Ra'di**ANT, *a.* Bright.—**Ra'diat**OR, *n.* That which radiates; a small heated chamber warming a room, &c.—**Ra'dium**, *n.* Formed after *sodium*, &c. A rare metal with great power of *radiating* energy.
Rad'ical, *a.* L.L. *rādīcālis*, f. L. *rādix, rādīcis*, root. ERADICATE. RACE.[3] Of a root; fundamental; primary; going to the root, thorough.—*n.* A word which cannot be analysed into simpler elements; an advocate of 'radical reform'.—**Rad'ical**ISM, *n.*
Rad'ish, *n.* F. *radis*—Pr. *raditz*—L. *rādix.* (See prec.) A pungent root; its plant.
Ra'dius, *n.* L. *radius*, staff, spoke, ray. RADIATE. RAY. The thicker and shorter of the two bones of the forearm; a straight line from the centre of a circle or sphere to the circumference.
Raff, *n.* App. the second member in *riff and raff.* RIFF-RAFF. The rabble.—**Raf'f**ISH, *a.* Disreputable, vulgar.
Raf'fia, *n.* Malagasy. A kind of palm; fibre used for tying up plants, &c.
Raf'fle, *n.* F. *rafle*, a game of dice, of uncertain orig. A kind of lottery.—*vi.* and *t.* To take part in, to dispose of by, a raffle.
Raft, *n.* O.N. *raptr*, RAFTER. A beam; a collection of logs joined together in the water.
Raft'er, *n.* O.E. *ræfter* = M.L.G. *rafter*, conn. with O.N. *raptr.* RAFT. A main roof-beam.
Rag, *n.* M.E. *ragge*, poss. representing an O.E. **ragg*, f. O.N. *rögg*, strip of fur. RUG. A fragment of cloth; a scrap, bit.—**Rag'ged**, *a.* Shaggy; of a rough or irregular form; faulty, imperfect; rent, torn; wearing clothes in rags.
Rag'amuffin, *n.* Prob. f. RAG with a fanciful ending. A ragged dirty man or boy.
Rage, *n.* F. *rage*—L. *rabies.* RABIES. Violent anger; fury; a violent feeling or passion; excitement, violence.—*vi.* To act or speak furiously; to be violent or boisterous; to be widely and virulently prevalent.
Ragout, *n.* F. *ragoût*, f. *ragoûter*, to revive the taste of, f. RE- (9) + *à*, to + *goût*, taste, f. L. *gustus.* GUST.[2] A dish of meat cut small, stewed with vegetables, and highly seasoned.
Raid, *n.* Scotch form of O.E. *rád.* ROAD. A hostile incursion; a rush, attack.—*vi.* To go upon a raid.—*vt.* To make a raid on.
Rail, *n.*[1] O.F. *reille*—L. *rēgula.* RULE. A horizontal bar; such a bar as part of a fence; a fence; a bar or line of bars of iron or steel to bear and guide wheels.—*v.*[1]*t.* To enclose with rails.—**Rail'ing**, *vbl.n.* A fence.—**Rail'way**, *n.* A road with lines of rails on which vehicles run.
Rail, *n.*[2] F. *râle.* Orig. uncertain. A family [of birds.
Rail, *v.*[2]*i.* F. *railler*, of uncertain orig. RALLY.[2] To utter abusive language.—**Rail'lery**, *n.* F. *raillerie.* Good-humoured ridicule, banter.
Rai'ment, *n.* Aphetic f. obs. *Array*MENT. ARRAY. Clothing, apparel.
Rain, *n.* O.E. *regn, rén.* Common Teut. Condensed moisture falling through the air in drops; the fall of such drops.—*vi. It rains*, rain is falling.—*vt.* To pour down like rain.—**Rain'bow**, *n.* O.E. *rénboga.* BOW, *n.*[1] An arch showing the prismatic colours formed opposite to the sun in rain-drops.—**Rain'**Y,[2] *a.*
Raise, *vt.* O.N. *reisa* (= O.E. *rǽran*, to REAR), causal f. *rais-*, var. of *rīs-*, to RISE. To set on end; to lift up; to breed; to bring into existence or action; to levy, collect; to put an end to (a siege); to increase the amount of.
Rai'sin, *n.* O.F. *raisin*, a grape—Pop.L. **racīmus*, L. *racēmus*, cluster of grapes. A partially dried grape.
Ra'ja(h), *n.* Hindī *rājā*, Skr. *rājan*, king, f. *rāj*, to rule. Cogn. with L. *rex.* REGAL. An Indian king, ruler, or noble; a Malay or Javanese ruler or chief.
Rake, *n.*[1] O.E. *raca* = M.L.G., M.Du. *rāke*, conn. with O.H.G. *rehho, recho* (Ger. *rechen*). An implement for drawing together hay, &c., or for breaking the surface of the ground, &c. —*v.*[1]*t.* O.N. *raka* = (M.)L.G., (M.)Du. *raken.* To draw together with a rake; to apply a rake to so as to make smooth, &c., or so as to find something; to sweep with shot.
Rake, *n.*[2] Abb. of archaic *Rake-hell*, i.e., 'such a man as you must rake hell to find'. A dissolute man of fashion.—**Rak'**ISH, *a.*
Rake, *v.*[2]*i.* Orig. obscure. Of a ship's timbers, masts, &c., to have a slope or inclination. —*n.*[3] Such slope or inclination.
Ral'ly, *v.*[1]*t.* F. *rallier*, f. RE- (9) + *alier, allier*, to ALLY. To bring together again (a scattered army, &c.); to bring together to one's aid; to revive, rouse.—*vi.* To come together again; to recover vigour.—*n.* An act of rallying.
Ral'ly, *v.*[2]*t.* F. *railler.* RAIL, *v.*[2] To assail with banter, make fun of.
Ram, *n.* O.E. *ram(m)* = M.Du., M.L.G., M.H.G. *ram.* A male sheep; a swinging beam for battering down walls (also **Bat'tering-ram**); a beak projecting from the bows of a war-ship; an automatic water-raising machine. —*vt.* To beat down (earth); to cram, stuff, thrust; to strike (another ship) with the ram.—**Ram'rod**, *n.* A rod for ramming down the charge of a muzzle-loading gun.
Ram'ble, *vi.* Orig. obscure. To go about without aim or direction; to talk incoherently. —*n.* An aimless walk.—**Ram'bl**ER, *n.* One who rambles; a rose which climbs freely.
Ram'ify, *vi.* F. *ramifier*—Med.L. *rāmifi-*

cāre, f. L. *rāmus*, branch. -FY. To form branches, spread in branches.—*vt.* To cause to do this.—**Rami**FICA'TION, *n.*

Ramp, *vi.* O.F. *ramper*, to creep, climb, of uncertain orig. ROMP. To stand on the hind legs; to storm or rage.—**Ram'p**ANT, *a.* Standing on the hind legs; violent, unrestrained.

Ramp, *n.* F. *rampe*, f. *ramper*. (See prec.) A slope; an upward bend in a stair-rail.

Rampage', *vi.* Perh. based on RAMP, *v.* To storm or rage; to rush wildly.—*n.* The action of rampaging; a state of excitement.

Ram'part, *n.* F. *rempart*, f. *remparer*, to fortify, f. RE- (8) + *emparer*, to take possession of, f. ANTE- + L. *parāre*. PARE. A mound for defence.—*vt.* To fortify with a rampart.

Ram'shackle, *a.* Var. of *ramshackled*, perh. = *rans(h)ackled* f. obs. *ransackle*, f. RANSACK + freq. suff. *-le* (as if 'wrecked by plundering'). Loose, crazy.

Ranch, *n.* Sp. *rancho*, a company eating together. A cattle-breeding establishment in the U.S.—*vi.* To conduct a ranch.

Ran'cid, *a.* L. *rancidus*, stinking. Tasting or smelling like stale fat.—**Rancid'**ITY, *n.*—**Ran'cour**, *n.* O.F. *rancour*—L. *rancor*, rancidity, bitter grudge. Inveterate and bitter ill-feeling.—**Ran'corous**, *a.*

Ran'dom, *n.* O.F. *randon*, f. *randir*, to run fast, gallop. *At random*, a haphazard, heedlessly.—*a.* Made, done, &c., at random.

Rank, *n.* F. *ranc*, obs. var. of *rang*, us. supposed to be f. O.H.G. *hrinc*, *hring*, RING, *n.*[1] ARRANGE. RINK. A row or line; soldiers drawn up in a line; line, order; an order of the community; (one's) social position; high social position; relative position or place; in *pl.*, common soldiers.—*vt.* To draw up in a rank; to classify. — *vi.* To have rank or place.—**Rank'**ER, *n.* A commissioned officer who has risen from the ranks.—**Range**, *n.* O.F. *range*, row, rank, f. *ranger*, to range, f. *rang*. A row or line; sphere of operation; the distance to which a gun can send a bullet; the distance of an object aimed at; a place for practising shooting; a kitchen grate.—*vt.* O.F. *ranger*. To set in a row; to traverse in all directions. —*vi.* To extend; to rove; to vary.—**Rang'**ER, *n.* One who ranges; a forest officer.

Rank, *a.* O.E. *ranc*, proud, strong = (M.)L.G. *rank*, long and thin, O.N. *rakkr*, slender, bold. Growing too luxuriantly; offensive in smell; of smell, offensively strong; coarse, indecent; absolute, downright.—**Rank'**LY,[2] *adv.*

Rank'le, *vi.* O.F. *rancler*, *raoncler*, *draoncler*, f. *rancle*, *raoncle*, *draoncle*, festering sore = Med.L. *dranculus*, *dracunculus*, in form dim. of L. *draco*, DRAGON. To fester painfully; to continue to cause painful or bitter feelings.

Ran'sack, *vt.* O.N. *rannsaka*, f. *rann*, house + *-saka*, var. of *sœkja*, to SEEK. To search thoroughly.

Ran'som, *n.* O.F. *raençon*, *rançon*, *ranson*—L. *redemptio*, f. *redimĕre*. REDEEM. Release from captivity by payment; the sum paid.—*vt.* To pay a ransom for.

Rant, *vi.* Obs. Du. *randten*, *ranten*, to rave. Cf. Ger. *ranzen*, to frolic. To speak in an extravagant high-flown way.—*n.* Such speech.

Ranun'culus, *n.* L. *rānunculus*, little frog, a plant (perh. ranunculus), dim. of *rāna*, frog. A genus of plants including the buttercup.

Rap, *n.*[1] Prob. imitative. Cf. Da. *rap*, Sw. *rapp*. A sharp smart blow; a knock.—*v.*[1]*t.* To give a rap to.—*vi.* To give a rap.

Rap, *n.*[2] Orig. obscure. A small counterfeit coin current in Ireland in the 18th c.; a type of the smallest coin; an atom, the least bit.

Rapa'cious, *a.* L. *rapax*, *rapācis*, grasping (f. *rapĕre* (RAPE, *v.*)) + -OUS. Inordinately greedy.—**Rapac'**ITY, *n.*

Rape, *n.*[1] L. *rāpum*, *rāpa*, turnip, rape. A plant the seeds of which yield an oil.

Rape, *vt.* Prob. f. L. *rapĕre*, to seize. HARPY. RAPACIOUS. RAPID. RAPINE. RAPT. RAVISH. SURREPTITIOUS. To take by force; to commit rape on.—*n.*[2] The act of carrying away a woman by force; carnal knowledge of a woman against her will, an instance of this.

Rap'id, *a.* L. *rapidus*, f. *rapĕre*. (See prec.) Very quick.—*n.* A part of a river with a swift current.—**Rapid'**ITY, *n.*—**Rap'id**LY,[2] *adv.*

Ra'pier, *n.* F. *rapière*. Orig. unknown. A light sharp-pointed sword for thrusting.

Rap'ine, *n.* L. *rapina*, f. *rapĕre*. RAPE, *v.* RAVIN. Plunder, pillage, robbery.

Rapt, *pa.pple.* and *ppl.a.* L. *raptus*, pa.pple. of *rapĕre*. RAPE, *v.* Snatched away from earth, ordinary thoughts, &c.; absorbed, intent.—**Rap**, *v.*[2]*t.* App. back-formation f. the pa.pple. To affect with rapture.—**Rap'**TURE, *n.* Ecstatic delight; an instance of this; the expression of this.—**Rap'tur**OUS, *a.*

Rare, *a.* L. *rārus*. Of a loose texture, not dense; not frequent; uncommon; of uncommon excellence.—**Rare'bit**, *n.* Formed to account for and = WELSH RABBIT.—**Rar'**EFY, *vt.* To lessen the density of.—**Rare**FAC'TION, *n.*—**Rare'**LY,[2] *adv.*—**Rar'**ITY, *n.*

Ras'cal, *n.* O.F. *rascaille* (F. *racaille*), the rabble. Orig. uncertain. A mean or dishonest fellow.—Sim. (app. fanciful formations) **Rascal'lion**, **Rapscal'lion**.—**Ras'cal**LY,[1] *a.*—**Rascal'**ITY, *n.*

Rase, *vt.* F. *raser*—Pop.L. **rāsāre*, f. L. *rādĕre*, *rāsum*, to scrape. ABRADE. ERASE. RAZE. To scrape out, erase.

Rash, *n.* Perh. f. O.F. *rache*, *rasche*, in sim sense. An eruption on the skin.

Rash, *a.* = M.Du. *rasch*, O.H.G. *rasc* (Ger. *rasch*), active, quick. Impetuous, hasty.

Rash'er, *n.* Poss. f. obs. *Rash*, to slice, var. of RASE. A thin slice of bacon or ham.

Rasp, *vt.* O.F. *rasper* (F. *râper*), perh. of Teut. orig. Cf. O.H.G. *raspôn*, to scrape together. To scrape with a rasp; to grate upon. —*vi.* To scrape; to make a grating sound.—*n.* A coarse kind of file.

Rasp'berry, *n.* From *Rasp* (now dial.), raspberry (perh. back-formation f. obs. *raspis*, in same sense, of doubtful orig.) + BERRY. The fruit of a well-known plant; the plant.

Rat, *n.* O.E. *ræt* = Du. *rat*, M.H.G. *rat* (Ger. *ratz*), F. *rat*, Sp., Pg. *rato*. Ultimate orig. uncertain. A small rodent; one who deserts his party (as rats are said to leave a sinking ship).—*vi.* To hunt rats; to desert one's party. —**Rats'bane**, *n.* Rat-poison.

Ratafi'a, *n.* F. *ratafia*. Orig. unknown. A cordial flavoured with the kernels of certain fruits; a biscuit, &c., flavoured with this.

Rat'chet, *n.* F. *rochet*, blunt lance-head, spool, ratchet = It. *rocchetto*, spool, ratchet. Cf. It. *rocchetta*. ROCKET. A set of teeth on a wheel; a wheel with such teeth.

Rate, *n.* O.F. *rate*—Med.L. *rata*, f. L. (*pro*) *rata* (*parte*), (according to the) proportional (share or PART), fem. pa.pple. of *rēri*, to reckon, calculate. RATIFY. RATIO. Proportion between two things; standard of reckoning; a fixed charge; an amount assessed on property for local purposes; degree of speed, &c.—*v.*[1]*t.* To estimate the value of; to value *at*, to reckon; to value for assessment. —**Rate'**ABLE, *a.* That can be rated, proportional; liable to payment of rates.—**Rate'-payer**, *n.* One who pays rates.—**Rat'ing**, *vbl.n.* The action of the *v.*; position held on a ship's books; in *pl.*, men of a certain rating.

Rate, *v.*[2]*t.* Orig. obscure. To scold angrily.

Ra'ther, *adv.* Comp. of obs. *Rathe*, quickly, soon—O.E. *hrathe* = O.H.G. (*h*)*rado*. More correctly; to some extent; in preference.

Rat'ify, *vt.* F. *ratifier*—Med.L. *ratificāre*, f. L. *ratus*, pa.pple. of *rēri*. RATE, *n.* -FY. To confirm.—**Rati**FICA'TION, *n.*

Ra'tio, *n.* L. *ratio*, *ratiōnis*, a reckoning, a cause, the understanding or reason, f. *rēri*. RATE, *n.* ARRAIGN. REASON. Proportion.—**Ratioc'inate**, *vi.* L. *ratiōcināri*, *ratiōcinātus*, f. *ratio*. To reason.—**Ratiocin**A'TION, *n.*—**Rat'ion**, *n.* A fixed daily amount of food. —*vt.* To supply with rations.—**Rat'ional**, *a.* L. *ratiōnālis*. Endowed with reason; sensible, sane; reasonable, not foolish.—**Rationa'le**, *n.* L., neut. of *ratiōnālis*. A statement of reasons; the fundamental reason.—**Rat'ional**ISM, *n.* The principle of regarding reason as the chief or only guide in investigations.—**Rat'ional**IST, *n.*—**Rational'**ITY, *n.* The power of reasoning; the fact of being agreeable to reason.—**Rat'ional**LY,[2] *adv.*

Rat'lin(e), **Rat'ling**, *n.* Orig. obscure. Perh. the same as O.F. *raalingue*, cordage strengthening the edge of a sail. Gen. in *pl.*, lines fixed horizontally on a ship's shrouds.

Rattan', *n.* Malay *rōtan*. An E. Indian climbing palm; a stick of rattan.

Rat'tle, *vi.* = M.Du., L.G. *ratelen*, Ger. *rasseln*. Prob. imitative. To give out short sharp sounds; to chatter.—*vt.* To cause to rattle.—*n.* An instrument for making a rattling noise; a set of rattling rings in the tail of the **Rat'tlesnake**; a rattling sound; a chatterer.

Rau'cous, *a.* L. *raucus* + -OUS. Hoarse.

Rav'age, *n.* F. *ravage*, f. *ravir*, to RAVISH. Destruction, devastation; in *pl.*, depredations. —*vt.* To devastate, lay waste.

Rave, *vi.* O.F. *raver*, app. a var. of *rêver*, to dream, rave, of obscure orig. REVERIE. To talk deliriously or with enthusiasm.

Rav'el, *vi.* App. f. Du. *ravelen*, to tangle, fray out, unweave. Cf. L.G. *reffeln*. To fray *out*.—*vt.* To entangle; to disentangle.

Ra'ven, *n.*[1] O.E. *hræfn*. Common Teut. A black bird of prey of the crow kind.

Rav'in, *n.*, **Rav'en**, *n.*[2] F. *ravine* (obs. in this sense)—L. *rapīna*, RAPINE. (See next.) Robbery, rapine; voracity.—**Rav'en**, *vi.* To plunder; to feed greedily.—*vt.* To devour.—**Rav'en**OUS, *a.* Voracious; very hungry.

Ravine', *n.* F. *ravine*, violent rush (of water), ravine. (See prec.) The bed of a torrent.

Rav'ish, *vt.* F. *raviss-*, lengthened stem of *ravir*—Pop.L. **rapīre*, L. *rapĕre*. RAPE, *v.* RAVAGE. To carry off; to rape (a woman); to fill with ecstasy.—**Rav'ish**MENT, *n.*

Raw, *a.* O.E. *hréaw*. Common Teut. Conn. with G. *kreas*, raw flesh, L. *cruor*, blood, *crūdus*, raw. CRUDE. Uncooked; not manufactured; crude; inexperienced; with the flesh exposed; chilly, bleak.

Ray, *n.*[1] O.F. *rai*, *ray*, acc. (nom. *rais*, *raiz*, &c.)—L. *radius*. RADIUS. A line of light; one of a system of lines diverging from a centre.—*vi.* To issue in rays.

Ray, *n.*[2] F. *raie*—L. *raia*. A flat-fish.

Raze, *vt.* Var. of RASE. To wound slightly; to efface, destroy.—**Ra'zor**, *n.* O.F. *rasor*, f. *raser*. An instrument for shaving.

Reach, *vt.* O.E. *rǽcan* = M.Du. *reiken*, O.H.G., Ger. *reichen*. To stretch *out* (the hand, &c.); to hand *to*; to succeed in touching or grasping; to come to, arrive at.—*vi.* To stretch out the hand, &c.; to extend.—*n.* An act of reaching; power of touching or grasping; range, scope; a portion of a river, &c., between two bends.

React', *vi.* RE- (1) (2) (9). To act in return or in turn; of a chemical agent, to act on another; to act in opposition; to return towards a former condition.—**Reac'**TION, *n.*—**Reac'tion**ARY, *a.* Of, characterized by, inclined to, reaction.—*n.* One inclined to reaction.—**Rea'gent**, *n.* A chemical substance used to determine the presence of another by reaction.

Read, *vt.* O.E. *rǽdan*, to counsel, consult, interpret, read. Common Teut. RIDDLE.[1] To make out or expound the meaning of (a riddle, &c.); to scan and understand (something written, printed, &c.), to peruse; to adopt or give (a particular word in or form of a passage); to learn by reading; to read and utter.—*vi.* To be engaged in perusal, to study; to find mention *of* in reading; to turn out *so and so* when read.—*ppl.a.* Versed *in* by reading; learned. —**Read'**ABLE, *a.* Legible; pleasant to read.—**Read'**ER, *n.* One who reads; one who corrects proofs in a printing-office; a book containing passages for exercise in reading.

Read'y, *a.* Early M.E. *readi*, *redi*, app. (with suff. = -Y[2]) f. O.E. *rǽde*, f. Teut. stem *raid-*, to put in order, prepare, whence O.F. *rai*, &c. ARRAY. CURRY, *v.*[1] Prepared, in order; willing; prompt; quick to plan, &c.; *ready money*, actual coin, payment on the spot.—**Read'i**LY,[2] *adv.*—**Read'i**NESS, *n.*

Re'al, *a.* O.F. *real*, *reel* (F. *réel*), or L.L. *reālis*, f. *rēs*, thing. REPUBLIC. Actually existing, present or happening; genuine; (the) actual (thing, &c.); of property, consisting in immovable things, as land and houses.—**Re'al**ISM, *n.* A tendency to regard things as they actually are; resulting artistic treatment. —**Re'al**IST, *n.*—**Realis'**TIC, *a.*—**Real'**ITY, *n.* Real existence; what is real; a real thing, &c.—**Re'al**IZE, *vt.* To make real; to understand clearly; to convert into money; to acquire (profits, &c.).—**Realiz**A'TION, *n.*—**Re'al**LY,[2] *adv.*—**Re'al**TY, *n.* Real property.

Realm, *n.* O.F. *reaume*, *realme* (F. *royaume*) —Pop.L. **rēgālimen*, f. L. *rēgālis*, REGAL. A kingdom; a sphere, domain, province.

Ream, *n.* M.E. *rēm*, *rīm* = Du. *riem*, O.F. *rayme*, &c. (F. *rame*), Sp. *resma*—Arab. *rizmah*, bale, bundle. A quantity of paper = 20 quires.

Reap, *vi.* O.E. *reopan*, also *rīpan* or *ripan*, *rypan*. Not in the cogn. langs. To cut grain. —*vt.* To cut (grain); to cut the crop of.—**Reap'**ER, *n.*

Rear, *n.* Shortened f. ARREAR. The hindmost part (of an army or fleet); the back or back part.—**Rear'-guard**, *n.* O.F. *rereguarde*, shortened f. *arere-guarde*. ARREAR. GUARD. Troops protecting the rear.

Rear, *vt.* O.E. *rǽran*. RAISE. To set on end, lift up; to build up; to breed, bring up, grow.—*vi.* To rise on the hind feet.

Rear'mouse, **Rere'mouse**, *n.* O.E. *hreremús*, f. *mús*, MOUSE. The first element may represent O.E. *hréran*. UPROAR. The bat.

Rea'son, *n.* O.F. *reison*, &c. (F. *raison*)—L. *ratio*. RATIO. A ground or motive; the mental power employed in directing thought or action; sanity; a sensible view of a matter; the being agreeable to the reason.—*vi.* To employ the reason in forming conclusions; to employ argument *with.*—*vt.* To persuade *into,* &c., by reasoning.—**Rea'son**ABLE, *a.* Sensible; moderate in demands; agreeable to the reason; not excessive; inexpensive; suitable.

Reassure', *vt.* RE- (9). To restore to confidence.—**Reassur'**ANCE, *n.*

Réaumur. René A. F. de *Réaumur* (d. 1757), the introducer. Denoting the thermometric scale according to which the freezing point of water is 0° and the boiling point 80°.

Reave, *vi.* O.E. *réafian.* Common Teut. Orig. sense app. 'to break'. Cf. L. *rumpěre.* ROB. ROVE. To plunder.—*vt.* To despoil *of*; to take forcibly.

Rebate', *vt.* O.F. *rabatre,* f. RE- (5) + *abatre.* ABATE. To lessen; to blunt.—*n.* A discount.

Reb'el, *a.* F. *rebelle,* a. and n.—L. *rebellis,* rebellious, f. RE- (2) + *bellum,* war. DUEL. REVEL. In arms against the ruling power; contumacious.—*n.* One in arms against the ruling power or resisting authority.—**Rebel'**, *vi.* To take arms as a rebel; to resist authority. —**Rebel'l**ION, *n.*—**Rebel'l**IOUS, *a.*

Rebound', *vi.* O.F. *rebondir.* RE- (1). BOUND, *v.*[2] To bound back on impact, recoil. —*n.* The act of rebounding.

Rebuff', *n.* Obs. F. *rebuffe*—It. *ribuffo,* f. *ri-* (= RE-(2)) + *buffo,* puff, app. of imitative orig. A peremptory check, a blunt refusal.—*vt.* To subject to a rebuff.

Rebuke', *vt.* A.F. and O.N.F. *rebuker* = O.F. *rebuch(i)er,* f. RE- (5) + *bucher,* to strike. To find fault with sharply.—*n.* The action.

Re'bus, *n.* L. *rēbus,* ablative pl. of *rēs,* thing. A representation by way of enigma of the syllables of a name, &c., by pictures, &c.

Rebut', *vt.* O.F. *reboter, rebuter,* f. RE- (9) + *boter, buter.* BUTT.[3] To force back; to refute.

Recal'citrate, *vi.* L. *recalcitrāre, recalcitrātum,* to kick back, be disobedient, f. RE- (2) + *calcitrāre,* to kick, f. *calx,* heel. CAULK. To be refractory.—**Recal'citr**ANT, *a.*

Recall', *vt.* RE- (9). To summon or bring back; to remember: to revoke, annul.—*n.* The act or possibility of recalling.

Recant', *vt.* L. *recantāre* f. RE- (8) + *cantāre,* to sing, CHANT. Cf. PALINODE. To retract, esp. formally, as erroneous.—*vi.* To make recantation.—**Recant**A'TION, *n.*

Recapit'ulate, *vt.* L.L. *recapitulāre, -ātum,* f. RE- (8) + *capitulāre.* CAPITULATE. To state again briefly.—**Recapitul**A'TION, *n.*

Recap'ture, *vt.* RE- (9). To recover by capture.—*n.* Recovery by capture.

Recast', *vt.* RE- (8). To fashion anew.—*n.* The action; something recast.

Recede', *vi.* L. *recēdere,* f. RE- (5) + *cēděre,* to go. CEASE. RECESS. To go back, withdraw.

Receipt', *n.* O.N.F. *receite, receyte* = O.F. *reçoite,* var. of *recete*—L. *recepta,* fem. pa.pple. of *recipěre,* to RECEIVE. A recipe; that which is received; a receiving, a being received; a written acknowledgment of payment, &c.—*vt.* To write a receipt on (an account).

Receive', *vt.* O.N.F. *receivre, receyvre* = O.F. *reçoivre* (F. *recevoir*)—L. *recipěre, receptum,* to take back, to take, receive, f. RE- (9) + *capěre.* CAPABLE. RECEIPT. RECEPTACLE. RECIPE. To take; to reset (stolen goods); to accept; to admit; to greet; to get; to experience. —**Receiv'**ABLE, *a.*—**Receiv'**ER, *n.* One who receives; a receptacle; an official in charge of a bankruptcy, a liquidation, &c.

Recense', *vt.* L. *recensēre,* f. RE- (8) + *censēre.* CENSOR. To revise (a text).—**Recen'**SION, *n.*

Re'cent, *a.* L. *recens, recentis.* That has lately happened, been made, &c.—**Re'c**ENCY, *n.*—**Re'cent**LY,[2] *adv.*

Recep'tacle, *n.* L. *receptāculum,* f. *recipěre,* to RECEIVE. A containing vessel, place, &c. —**Recep'**TION, *n.* Receiving; manner of receiving, a formal receiving of guests.—**Recep'**TIVE, *a.*—**Receptiv'**ITY, *n.*

Recess', *n.* L. *recessus,* f. *recēděre.* RECEDE. The act of receding; a time of cessation from work, &c.; a retired place; an indentation, a niche or alcove.—**Reces'**SION, *n.*

Recid'ivist, *n.* F. *récidiviste*—L. *recidivus,* falling back, f. *reciděre,* to fall back, f. RE- (9) + *caděre,* to fall. ACCIDENT. CADENCE. One who relapses into crime.

Rec'ipe, *n.* L. *recipe,* imp. of *recipěre,* to take, RECEIVE. A prescription; directions for cooking a dish.—**Recip'i**ENT, *a.* That receives or can receive.—*n.* One who receives.

Recip'rocal, *a.* L. *reciprocus* (app. f. **re-co-,* backwards (f. RE- (9)), and **pro-co-,* forwards (f. PRO-)) + -AL. In return; mutual; corresponding, complementary.—**Recip'rocal**LY,[2] *adv.*—**Recip'roc**ATE,[3] *vi.* To move backwards and forwards.—*vt.* To give, &c., in return; to give and receive mutually.—**Reciproc**A'TION, *n.*—**Reciproc'**ITY, *n.*

Recite', *vt.* L. *recitāre,* f. RE- (8) + *citāre.* CITE. To repeat aloud, esp. to an audience; to state.—**Recit'**AL, *n.*—**Recit**A'TION, *n.*—**Recitative'**, *n.* It. *recitativo,* f. ppl. stem of *recitāre.* Musical utterance between singing and speech.—**Recit'**ER, *n.* One who recites; a book containing passages for recitation.

Reck, *vi.* O.E. *reccan.* Common Teut. To pay heed, care.—**Reck'**LESS, *a.*

Reck'on, *vt.* O.E. *(ge)recenian* = M.L.G., M.Du. *rekenen,* O.H.G. *rechenôn* (Ger. *rechnen*). To count; to include in a class; to estimate; to consider, regard.—*vi.* To settle accounts.

Reclaim', *vt.* O.F. *reclamer*—L. *reclāmāre,* to cry out against. RE- (2). CLAIM. To bring back *from* wrong *to* right; to tame; to make fit for cultivation; to demand or take back.—**Reclaim'**ABLE, *a.*—**Reclam**A'TION, *n.*

Recline', *vt.* O.F. *recliner*—L. *reclīnāre,* f. RE- (9) + *-clīnāre.* DECLINE. To cause to lie down or incline, to rest.—*vi.* To lean or repose.

Recluse', *a.* F. *reclus,* pa.pple. of *reclure,* L. *reclūděre,* to shut up, f. RE- (4) + *clauděre,* to shut, CLOSE. Shut up, secluded.—*n.* One secluded from the world, a monk or hermit.

Rec'ognize, *vt.* O.F. *reconuiss-, recognoiss-,* &c., stem of *recon(n)oistre* (F. *reconnaître*)—L. *recognoscěre,* to know again, to inspect. RE- (8). COGNITION. RECONNOITRE. To know again; to identify; to treat as valid; to take notice of.—**Recogni'**TION, *n.*—**Re'cogniz**ABLE, *a.*—**Recog'niz**ANCE, *n.* A bond entered into before a court.

Recoil', *vi.* O.F. *reculer,* f. RE- (9) + *cul,* L. *cūlus,* the posteriors. To draw or spring back; to rebound; of a gun, to spring back on being fired.—*n.* The act of recoiling.

Recollect', *vt.* L. *recolligěre,* to gather again. RE- (8). COLLECT. To call back to mind, remember.—**Recollec'**TION, *n.*

Recommend', *vt.* Med.L. *recommendāre.* RE- (5). COMMEND. To commit, entrust; to present or introduce as worthy of favour, &c.; to make acceptable.—**Recommend**A'TION, *n.*

Rec'ompense, *vt.* O.F. *recompenser*—L.L. *recompensāre.* RE- (1). COMPENSATE. To reward, repay; to compensate; to make up for. —*n.* Compensation; reward, return.

Rec'oncile, *vt.* L. *reconciliāre.* RE- (9). CONCILIATE. To bring back into friendship or concord; to bring into acquiescence or submission; to adjust, settle, to make consistent or accordant.—**Rec'oncil**ABLE, *a.*—**Rec'oncile**MENT, *n.*—**Reconcili**A'TION, *n.*

Rec'ondite, *a.* L. *reconditus*, pa.pple. of *recondĕre*, to put away, hide, f. RE- (4) + CON*dĕre*, to put together. DO. ABSCOND. Abstruse, obscure.

Reconnoi'tre, *vt.* F. *reconnoître* (now *reconnaître*). RECOGNIZE. To make a reconnaissance of.—*vi.* To make a reconnaissance. —**Recon'naissance**, *n.* F., f. *reconnaiss-*, stem of *reconnaître.* A military or naval survey of a tract of country, a coast, &c.

Record', *vt.* O.F. *recorder*—L. *recordāre* (classical *recordāri*), to call to mind, remember, f. RE- (8) + *cor.* ACCORD. To put down in writing.—**Rec'ord**, *n.* The being recorded; a written account or report; the best recorded achievement.—**Record'**ER, *n.* One who records; a city or borough magistrate.

Recount', *vt.* O.N.F. and A.F. *reconter*, f. RE- (8) + *conter*, to COUNT. To tell in detail.

Recoup', *vt.* F. *recouper*, to cut back, &c., f. RE- (5) + *couper.* COPPICE. To deduct, keep back; to recompense, compensate.

Recourse', *n.* F. *recours*—L. *recursus*, a running back, f. *recurrĕre*, to run back, return. RE- (9). COURSE. RECUR. A betaking of oneself *to* (a person or thing) for aid, &c.; the person or thing.

Recov'er, *vt.* A.F. *recoverer*, O.F. *recov(e)rer*, *recuvrer* (F. *recouvrer*)—L. *recuperāre* (*reciperāre*), to get again, to revive, restore, f. RE- (9) + *capĕre.* CAPABLE. RECUPERATE. To get or win back; to get by legal process; to bring back to life or health; to get over, get better from. —*vi.* To get well again.—**Recov'er**ABLE, *a.*—**Recov'er**Y,[1] *n.*

Rec'reant, *a.* O.F. *recreant*, (one) who yields, pres.pple. of *recroire*, to yield in a trial by combat = Med.L. *recrēdĕre*, to surrender (oneself), f. RE- (6) + L. *crēdĕre*, to entrust. CREDIT. MISCREANT. Cowardly, craven; apostate.—*n.* A craven; an apostate.

Rec'reate, *vt.* L. *recreāre*, to make anew, restore, refresh. RE- (8). CREATE. To restore, refresh; to enliven, amuse.—*vi.* To take recreation.—**Recre**A'TION, *n.*—**Rec're**ATIVE, *a.*

Recrim'inate, *vi.* Med.L. *recrīmināri*, *-ātus*, f. RE- (1) + L. *crīmināri*, to accuse, f. *crīmen.* CRIME. To retort a charge.—**Recrimin**A'TION, *n.*—**Recrim'inat**ORY, *a.*

Recrudesce', *vi.* L. *recrūdescĕre*, f. RE- (8) + *crūdescĕre*, inceptive f. *crūdus*, raw. CRUDE. To break out again.—**Recrudes'**CENCE, *n.*

Recruit', *n.* Obs. F. *recrute*, a raising of troops = F. *recrue*, f. *recrû*, pa.pple. of *recroître*, L. *recrescĕre*, to grow again. RE- (8). CRESCENT. A newly enlisted soldier.—*vt.* To enlist as a recruit; to strengthen or reinforce; to refresh or re-invigorate. —*vi.* To enlist fresh soldiers; to recover health or strength.

Rec'tangle, *n.* L. *rectiangulum*, a right-angled triangle, f. *rectus* (see next) + *angulus*, ANGLE. A four-sided figure having all its angles right angles.—**Rectan'gul**AR,[1] *a.*

Rec'tify, *vt.* F. *rectifier*—L.L. *rectificāre*, f. L. *rectus*, straight, correct, orig. pa.pple. of *regĕre.* REGENT. -FY. To put right, correct; to purify or refine.—**Recti**FICA'TION, *n.*

Rectilin'eal, *a.* L.L. *rectilīneus* (f. *rectus* (see prec.) + L. *līnea*, LINE[2]) + -AL. Also **Rectilin'**EAR.[1] In a straight line; formed or characterized by straight lines.

Rec'titude, *n.* F. *rectitude*—L.L. *rectitūdo*, f. L. *rectus.* RECTIFY. Goodness, integrity.

Rec'to, *n.* L., ablative neut. of *rectus.* RECTIFY. The right-hand page of a book; the front of a leaf.

Rec'tor, *n.* L. *rector*, agent-n. f. *regĕre.* REGENT. An incumbent of a parish who holds the tithes; the head of certain colleges, &c. — **Recto'r**IAL, *a.* — **Rec't**ORY, *n.* The benefice or residence of a rector.

Rec'tum, *n.* L. *rectum* (sc. *intestīnum*), neut. of *rectus*, straight. RECTIFY. INTESTINE. The final section of the large intestine.

Recum'bent, *a.* L. *recumbens, recumbentis*, pres.pple. of *recumbĕre*, to lie down again, lie down. RE- (9). INCUMBENT. Lying down.

Recu'perate, *vt.* From ppl. stem of L. *recuperāre.* RECOVER. To restore to health, &c. —*vi.* To recover.—**Recuper**A'TION, *n.*

Recur', *vi.* L. *recurrĕre.* RECOURSE. To return in thought, &c.; to come back to the mind, &c.; to happen or appear again.—**Recur'r**ENCE, *n.*—**Recur'r**ENT, *a.*

Recurve', *vt.* and *i.* L. *recurvāre*, f. RE- (9) + *curvāre.* CURVATURE. To bend backwards.

Rec'usant, *n.* L. *recūsans, recūsantis*, pres. pple. of *recūsāre*, to make objection, refuse, f. RE- (2) + *causa*, CAUSE. One who refused to attend the services of the Church of England; one refusing submission or compliance. —*a.* Dissenting, refusing submission or compliance.—**Rec'us**ANCE, **Rec'us**ANCY, *nn.*

Red, *a.* O.E. *rēad.* Common Teut. Cogn. with G. *eruthros*, L. *ruber.* ROUGE. RUBICUND. RUBRIC. RUDDY. Of the colour of blood.—*n.* The colour.—**Red'breast**, *n.* The robin.—**Red'd**EN,[2] *vt.* and *i.*—**Red-lead**, *n.* A red oxide of lead used as a pigment.

Redac'tion, *n.* F. *rédaction*, f. L. *redigĕre*, *redactum*, to bring back, collect, f. *red-* (= RE- (8)) + *agĕre*, to drive. ACT. Preparing for publication; revision; a new edition.—**Redact'**, *vt.* Back-formation f. *redaction.* To prepare for publication; to draw up, frame.

Redeem', *vt.* L. *redimĕre, redemptum*, to buy back. *Red-* = RE- (8). EXEMPT. To buy back, regain, recover; to fulfil (a promise, &c.); to ransom, free; to free from sin and its consequences; to make up for.—**Redeem'**ABLE, *a.*—**Redeem'**ER, *n.*—**Redemp'**TION, *n.*

Redin'tegrate, *vt.* L. *redintegrāre.* *Red-* = RE- (9). INTEGRATE. To make whole again, renew, restore.—**Redintegr**A'TION, *n.*

Red'olent, *a.* L. *redolens, redolentis*, pres. pple. of *redolēre*, to emit a scent. *Red-* = RE- (6). OLFACTORY. Sweet-smelling; odorous or smelling *of* or *with.*—**Red'ol**ENCE, *n.*

Redoub'le, *vt.* and *i.* F. *redoubler*, f. RE- (6) + *doubler*, to double, f. *double*, DOUBLE. To make, to grow, twice as great or as much.

Redoubt', *n.* F. *redoute*—It. *ridotto*—Med.L. *reductus*, secret place, refuge, f. L. *reductus*, retired, pa.pple. of *redūcĕre.* REDUCE. A species of outwork.

Redoubt', *vt.* F. *redouter*, f. RE- (6) + *douter*, to DOUBT. To dread.—**Redoubt'**ABLE, *a.*

Redound', *vi.* F. *redonder*—L. *redundāre*, to overflow, f. *red-* (= RE- (6)) + *undāre*, to rise in waves, f. *unda.* UNDULATE. To contribute or turn *to* (one's advantage, &c.); to result or accrue *to.*—**Redun'd**ANT, *a.* Superfluous.—**Redun'd**ANCE, -ANCY, *nn.*

Redress', *vt.* F. *redresser.* RE- (8). DRESS.

To set right, to amend, reform.—*n.* Reparation, compensation.

Reduce′, *vt.* L. *redūcĕre, reductum,* to lead or draw back. RE- (9). DUKE. REDOUBT, *n.* To replace (a dislocated, &c., part); to bring *to* (order, form, &c.); to turn *to*, convert *into*; to subdue, capture; to degrade; to diminish. —**Reduc′**IBLE, *a.*—**Reduc′tion**, *n.*

Redup′licate, *vt.* Med.L. *reduplicāre, reduplicātum.* RE- (6). DUPLICATE. To redouble; to repeat (a letter or syllable) to form a tense, &c.—**Reduplica**′TION, *n.*

Re-ech′o, *vi.* RE- (6). To echo, to resound. —*vt.* To echo back.—*n.* An echo.

Reed, *n.* O.E. *hrēod.* Common W. Germanic. The tall straight stem of certain plants; a rustic musical pipe; a part of certain musical instruments producing sound.—**Reed′**Y,[2] *a.* Full of reeds; like a reed-instrument in tone.

Reef, *n.*[1] = Du. *reef, rif,* Ger. *reff*—O.N. *rif,* prob. transferred sense of *rif,* RIB. A part of a sail which can be rolled up to reduce the sail-area.—*vt.* To take in a reef of.

Reef, *n.*[2] = Du. *rif,* Ger. *riff*—O.N. *rif,* prob. as in prec. A ridge of rocks lying near the surface of the sea, &c.; an auriferous lode.

Reek, *n.* O.E. *rēc.* Common Teut. Dense smoke; vapour; a strong fume or smell.—*vi.* To smoke; to emit vapour; to stink.

Reel, *n.*[1] O.E. *hrēol.* Not in the cogn. langs. An appliance on which thread, a fishing line, &c., can be wound.—*v.*[1]*t.* To wind on a reel.

Reel, *v.*[2]*i.* Poss. conn. with prec. To be dizzy; to stagger, sway.—*n.*[2] An act of reeling.

Reel, *n.*[3] Perh. the same as the *n.*[2] A lively Scotch dance; music for it.

Reeve, *n.* O.E. *gerēfa,* magistrate. Orig. uncertain. SHERIFF. A minor local official.

Reeve, *vt.* Orig. obscure. To pass (a rope) through a hole, a block, &c.

Refash′ion, *vt.* RE- (8). To fashion anew.

Refec′tion, *n.* F. *réfection*—L. *refectio, refectiōnis,* n. of action f. *reficĕre,* to make again, refresh, f. RE- (8) + *facĕre.* FACT. Refreshment with food or drink; a meal.—**Refec′**TORY, *n.* A room for meals.

Refer′, *vt.* O.F. *referer* (F. *référer*)—L. *referre.* RE- (9). FERTILE. RELATE. To trace back, ascribe; to submit for decision, &c.; to send *to* (a person, &c.) for information, &c.—*vi.* To have relation, be directed; to allude.—**Ref′er**ABLE, *a.*—**Referee′**, *n.* An umpire.—**Ref′er**ENCE, *n.*—**Referen′dum**, *n.* Neut. ger. of *referre.* The submitting of a question to the whole body of voters.

Refine′, *vt.* RE- (6) + FINE, *v.*[2] To purify; to make elegant or cultured.—*vi.* To become pure; to indulge in subtle language, &c.—**Refine′**MENT, *n.*—**Refin′**ER, *n.*—**Refin′**ERY, *n.* A place where sugar, &c., is refined.

Reflect, *vt.* L. *reflectĕre, reflexum,* to turn away or back. RE- (5) (9). DEFLECT. To throw or send back; to bring (discredit, &c.) *on.*—*vi.* To meditate *on*; to cast blame, &c., *on.*—**Reflec′**TION, **Reflex′**ION, *n.*—**Reflec′**TIVE, *a.*—**Reflec′**TOR, *n.* A polished surface for reflecting light, &c.—**Re′flex**, *n.* L.L. *reflexus.* Reflection; a reflected image.—*a.* From the pa.pple. Reflected; bent back; of muscular action, &c., involuntary.—**Reflex′**IVE, *a.* Characterized by or denoting action directed on the subject of a clause or sentence.

Re′flux, *n.* RE- (9). A flowing back.

Reform′, *vt.* L. *reformāre.* RE- (8). CONFORM. To amend or improve; to put an end to (an abuse, &c.); to bring from wrong courses to right.—*vi.* To leave wrong courses for right. —*n.* Amendment; an instance of this; the removal of an abuse.—**Reforma**′TION, *n.* Esp., the movement in the 16th century for reforming the Church of Rome.—**Refor′ma**TORY, *a.* As *n.*, an institution for the reformation of juvenile offenders.—**Reform′**ER, *n.*

Refract′, *vt.* L. *refringĕre, refractum,* to break up. RE- (5). INFRINGE. To break the course of (light, &c.).—**Refrac′**TION, *n.*—**Refrac′**TIVE, *a.*—**Refrac′tory**, *a.* Var. of obs. *Refractary*—L. *refractārius,* f. *refringĕre.* Stubborn, unmanageable; difficult to treat or work.—**Refran′**GIBLE, *a.*

Refrain′, *n.* O.F. *refrain*—Pop.L. **refrangĕre,* to break again. RE- (8). INFRINGE. A burden or chorus.

Refrain′, *vt.* O.F. *refrener*—L. *refrēnāre,* to curb, f. RE- (9) + *frēnum,* bridle, curb. To restrain, to put a check upon.—*vi.* To abstain.

Refresh′, *vt.* O.F. *refrescher,* f. RE- (9) + *fresche.* FRESH. To impart freshness or fresh vigour to.—**Refresh′**ER, *n.* One who or that which refreshes; an extra fee paid to counsel in prolonged cases.—**Refresh′**MENT, *n.*

Refrig′erate, *vt.* L. *refrīgerāre, refrīgerātum,* f. RE- (9) + *frīgerāre,* to make cool, f. *frīgus.* FRIGID. To make cool; to freeze.—**Refrigera**′TION, *n.*—**Refrigera′tor**, *n.* An apparatus for cooling or freezing.

Ref′uge, *n.* F. *refuge*—L. *refugium,* f. *refugĕre,* to take refuge, f. RE- (4) + *fugĕre,* to flee. FUGITIVE. Shelter, protection; something affording refuge.—**Refugee′**, *n.* F. *réfugié,* pa.pple. of (*se*) *réfugier,* to take refuge. One who seeks refuge in a foreign country.

Reful′gent, *a.* L. *refulgens, refulgentis,* pres.pple. of *refulgēre,* to shine brightly, f. RE- (6) + *fulgēre,* to shine. Shining brightly, radiant.—**Reful′**GENCE, *n.*

Refund′, *vt.* L. *refundĕre,* to pour back RE- (9). FUSE, *v.* (See next.) To pay back; to reimburse (a person).

Refuse′, *vt.* O.F. *refuser*—Pop.L. **refūsāre,* f. L. *refundĕre.* (See prec.) To decline to take, accept, submit to; to decline *to do*; to decline to give or grant.—*vi.* To make refusal.—**Ref′use**, *a.* App. f. O.F. *refuse,* pa.pple. of *refuser.* Discarded, useless.—*n.* Refuse matter.—**Refus′**AL, *n.*

Refute′, *vt.* L. *refūtāre,* to drive back, refute. RE- (9). CONFUTE. To disprove.—**Ref′ut**ABLE, *a.*—**Refuta**′TION, *n.*

Regain′, *vt.* F. *regagner.* RE- (9). GAIN. To recover possession of; to get back to.

Re′gal, *a.* L. *rēgālis,* f. *rex, rēgis,* king, conn. with *regĕre.* REGENT. RAJA. REALM. ROYAL. Of, befitting, like, a king.—**Rega′lia**, *n.pl.* L., neut. pl. of *rēgālis.* The insignia of royalty. —**Regal′**ITY, *n.*—**Re′gal**LY,[2] *adv.*

Regale′, *vt.* F. *régaler,* It. *regalare,* Sp. and Pg. *regalar.* Orig. obscure. To feast or entertain choicely.—*n.* A choice repast.

Regard′, *vt.* F. *regarder.* RE- (6). GUARD, *v.* REWARD. To look at; to give heed to; to consider or look on *as*; to concern or relate to.—*n.* A look; respect, point, particular; heed; esteem; in *pl.*, an expression of goodwill.—**Regard′**FUL, *a.*—**Regard′**LESS, *a.*

Regat′ta, *n.* Venetian *regatta,* orig., a strife. Orig. unknown. A series of yacht-races.

Regen′erate, *vt.* L. *regenerāre, regenerātum.* RE- (8). GENERATE. To cause to be 'born again' spiritually; to reform completely. —*ppl.a.* 'Born again'; reformed.—**Regen′er**ACY, *n.*—**Regenera**′TION, *n.*

Re'gent, *a.* L. *regens, regentis*, pres.pple. of *regĕre, rectum*, to rule, guide. CORRECT. RECTIFY. RECTOR. REGAL. REGION. REIGN. RIGHT, *a.* RULE. SURGE. Holding the position of regent.—*n.* One who rules a kingdom during the minority, absence, &c., of the sovereign.—**Re'**GENCY, *n.*—**Régime, Regime'**, *n.* F. *régime*—L. *regimen*, rule, government, f. *regĕre*. A system of government; a prevailing system of things.—**Reg'imen**, *n.* L., see above. Rule; a prescribed course of diet, &c.—**Reg'iment**, *n.* L. *regimentum*, f. *regĕre*. Rule; an organized body of troops forming a unit of an army.—**Regimen't**AL, *a.* In *pl.* as *n.*, military uniform.

Reg'icide, *n.* L. *rex* (REGAL) + -CIDE (1). One who kills a king.— -CIDE (2). The crime of a regicide.

Re'gion, *n.* A.F. *regiun* (F. *région*)—L. *regio, regiōnis*, direction, limit, territory, f. *regĕre*. REGENT. A tract, area, division.

Reg'ister, *n.* F. *registre*, Med.L. *regestrum, registrum*, f. L.L. *regesta*, things recorded, neut. pa.pple. of L. *regerĕre*, to carry back, to record. RE- (8). GEST. A written record; a stop in an organ; the compass of a voice or instrument; a registering device.—*vt.* To set down formally in writing, to enter in a register. — **Reg'istr**AR,[2] *n.* The keeper of a register. — **Registr**A'TION, *n.* — **Reg'istr**Y, *n.* Registering; a place for registers.

Reg'nal, *a.* Med.L. *regnālis*, f. L. *regnāre*, to REIGN. Of a reign or reigns; of a kingdom or a king; *regnal day*, the anniversary of a king's accession.—**Reg'n**ANT, *a.* Reigning.

Regrate', *vt.* O.F. *regrater*, perh. f. RE- (8) + *grater*. GRATE, *v.* To buy up (goods) in order to retail at a profit; to retail.

Re'gress, *n.* L. *regressus*, f. *regredi, regressus*, to go back. RE- (9). EGRESS. A going or coming back.

Regret', *vt.* F. *regretter*, of uncertain orig. To grieve for the loss of or on account of.—*n.* Grief for something lost, done, left undone, &c.—**Regret'**FUL, *a.*—**Regret't**ABLE, *a.*

Reg'ular, *a.* L. *rēgulāris*, a. f. *rēgula*, RULE. Of clergy, living under a religious rule; symmetrical, uniform; habitual; adhering, done according, to rule; belonging to the standing army.—*n.* A member of the standing army.—**Regular'**ITY, *n.*—**Reg'ul**ATE,[3] *vt.* To subject to rule; to adjust. — **Regul**A'TION, *n.* Regulating; a rule.—**Reg'ulat**OR, *n.*

Regur'gitate, *vi.* Med.L. *regurgitāre, regurgitātum*, f. RE- (9) + L.L. *gurgitāre*, to engulf, f. L. *gurges, gurgitis*, whirlpool. To gush back.—*vt.* To pour or cast out again, esp. from the stomach.—**Regurgit**A'TION, *n.*

Rehabil'itate, *vt.* Med.L. *rehabilitāre, rehabilitātum*, f. RE- (9) + *habilitāre*, to make fit, enable, f. L. *habilis*. HABILIMENT. To restore to a former position or reputation.

Rehearse', *vt.* O.F. *rehercer*, app. f. RE- (8) + *hercer, herser*, to harrow, f. *herce, herse*, harrow. HEARSE. To repeat aloud; to say over again; to recount in order; to practise (a play, &c.) in private.—**Rehears'**AL, *n.*

Reign, *n.* O.F. *regne, reigne*, &c. (F. *règne*)—L. *regnum*, f. *regĕre*. REGENT. INTERREGNUM. Royal power; the period of a sovereign's rule. — *vi.* O.F. *regner* — L. *regnāre*. REGNANT. To be king; to hold sway, prevail.

Reimburse', *vt.* RE- (9) + obs. *Imburse*, to put into a purse — Med.L. *imbursāre*, f. *im-* (= IN-[1]) + *bursa*. BURSAR. To pay back; to recompense.—**Reimburse'**MENT, *n.*

Rein, *n.* O.F. *rene* (F. *rêne*), gen. taken as repg. a Com. Romanic **retina*, f. L. *retinēre*. RETAIN. One of two straps attached to the bridle for controlling a horse.—*vt.* To check with the reins.—*vi.* To submit to the reins.

Rein'deer, *n.* Ultimately repg. O.N. *hreindýri*, f. *hreinn*, reindeer + *dýr*, DEER. A deer of the sub-arctic regions.

Reinforce', *vt.* RE- (8) + *inforce* = ENFORCE. To strengthen (an army, &c.) by adding men; to strengthen.—**Reinforce'**MENT, *n.*

Reins, *n.pl.* O.F. *reins*—L. *rēnes*. The kidneys; the loins.

Reinstate', *vt.* RE- (9) + obs. *Instate*, to install, establish, f. IN-[1] + STATE. To reinstall or re-establish; to restore, replace.

Reinsure', *vt.* RE- (8). To insure with another (a risk undertaken by oneself).

Reit'erate, *vt.* L. *reiterāre*. RE- (6). To repeat.—**Reiter**A'TION, *n.*—**Reit'er**ATIVE, *a.*

Reject', *vt.* L. *rejicĕre, rejectum*. RE- (5). ABJECT. To refuse to have, take, grant, agree to, submit to, &c.—**Rejec'**TION, *n.*

Rejoice', *vt.* O.F. *rejoiss-*, lengthened stem of *rejoir* (F. *réjouir*). RE- (6). JOY. To make joyful.—*vi.* To be full of joy.

Rejoin', *v.*[1]*t.* F. *rejoindre*, to join again. RE- (9). JOIN. To say in answer. (The sense app. developed in A.F. legal use.)—**Rejoin'der**, *n.* *Rejoindre* as *n.* An answer.

Rejoin', *v.*[2]*t.* RE- (9). To reunite; to join (a person, a company, &c.) again.

Reju'venate, *vt.* RE- (9) + L. *juvenis* (JUVENILE) + -ATE.[3] To restore to youth.—**Rejuvenesce'**, *vi.* L.L. *rejuvenescĕre*, f. RE- (9) + *juvenis*. To grow young again.—**Rejuvenes'**CENCE, *n.*—**Rejuvenes'**CENT, *a.*

Relapse', *vi.* L. *relābi, relapsus*, to fall back. RE- (9). LAPSE. To fall back into evil or illness, or *into* a state, &c.—*n.* A relapsing.

Relate', *vt.* L. *referre, relātum*. REFER COLLATE. To narrate; to bring into relation *to*, to connect.—*vi.* To have reference or relation *to*.—**Rela'tion**, *n.* Narration; a narrative; connexion, correspondence, association; mode of connexion; connexion by blood or marriage; a person thus connected.—**Rela'tion**SHIP, *n.*—**Rel'at**IVE, *a.* In *grammar*, referring to an antecedent term; comparative; dependent on relation to something else, not absolute; having reference or relation *to*.—*n.* A relative word; one connected by blood or marriage.—**Rel'ative**LY,[2] *adv.*

Relax', *vt.* L. *relaxāre*, to widen again, loosen, mitigate, f. RE- (9) + *laxāre*, to loosen, f. *laxus*. LAX. RELEASE. RELISH. To make loose or slack; to mitigate; to abate.—*vi.* To become relaxed; to grow more friendly.—**Relax**A'TION, *n.* A relaxing; recreation.

Relay', *n.* O.F. *relais*, of obscure orig. A set of horses stationed on a road to relieve others; a relief-gang of men.

Release', *vt.* O.F. *relesser* — L. *relaxāre*. RELAX. To give up, resign, surrender; to set free.—*n.* Releasing; a written discharge.

Rel'egate, *vt.* L. *relēgāre, relēgātum*, to send away, to banish. RE- (5). LEGATE. To banish; to consign, refer, commit, to hand over.

Relent', *vi.* Ultimately f. RE- (9) + L. *lentus*, pliant, easy, calm. Cf. F. (*se*) *ralentir*. To soften in temper, depart from a harsh intention or inclination.—**Relent'**LESS, *a.*

Rel'evant, *a.* Med.L. *relevans, -antis*, pres. pple. of *relevāre*. RELIEVE. Bearing on the matter in hand.—**Rel'ev**ANCE, -ANCY, *nn.*

Rel'ic, *n.* F. *relique*—L. *reliquiae*, pl., remains, f. *relinquĕre*. RELINQUISH. RELIQUARY. Something remaining as a memorial of a saint, &c.; a surviving trace or memorial; in *pl.*, that which remains, the body of one deceased.—**Rel'ict**, *n.* Med.L. *relicta*, properly fem. pa.pple. of *relinquĕre*. A widow.

Relief', *n.*[1] F. *relief* = It. *rilievo*, raised or embossed work, f. *rilevare*, to raise = F. *relever*. (See next.) The projection of a design from a plane surface; distinctness, prominence.

Relieve', *vt.* O.F. *relever*—L. *relevāre*, to lift up, to free from (evil), assist, to mitigate. RE- (9). ELEVATE. RELEVANT. To assist in trouble; to raise the siege of; to free from fear, &c.; to give (a person) ease from pain, &c.; to mitigate; to make less monotonous, &c.; to release from duty; to cause to be prominent. —**Relief'**, *n.*[2] O.F. *relief*, f. *relever*. Alleviation; aid; assistance given to a pauper; release from duty; one who relieves another.

Relig'ion, *n.* L. *religio*, *religiōnis*, piety, perh. conn. with *religāre*, to bind up or back. RE- (9). LIGAMENT. RELY. A state of life under monastic vows; a system of faith and worship; practical piety.—**Relig'ious**, *a.*—**Relig'ious**NESS, *n.*—**Religios'**ITY, *n.* Religiousness; affected religiousness.

Relin'quish, *vt.* O.F. *relinquiss-*, lengthened stem of *relinquir*—L. *relinquĕre*, to leave behind, forsake, f. RE- (3) + *linquĕre*, to leave. DELINQUENT. DERELICT. RELIC. To give up; to resign, surrender.

Rel'iquary, *n.* F. *reliquaire*, f. *relique*. RELIC. A case or shrine for a relic.

Rel'ish, *n.* Orig. *reles*, aftertaste, taste—O.F. *reles*, that which is left behind, var. of *relais*, f. *relaisser*, to leave behind—L. *relaxāre*. RELAX. Taste or flavour; a trace or tinge; a savoury taste; something savoury; liking.—*vt.* To give a pleasing taste to; to enjoy, to like.—*vi.* To have a taste or trace *of*; to have a specified taste.

Reluc'tant, *a.* L. *reluctans*, *reluctantis*, pres.pple. of *reluctāri*, to struggle against, f. RE- (2) + *luctāri*, to wrestle, struggle. Unwilling.—**Reluc'tance**, *n.*

Rely', *vi.* O.F. *relier*, to bind up or together —L. *religāre*. RELIGION. Formerly, to gather (soldiers, &c.) together; to retire *to* one's friends, &c. To depend *on* or *upon*.—**Reli'**ABLE, *a.* Trustworthy.—**Reli'**ANCE, *n.*

Remain', *vi.* A.F. *remeyn-*, *remayn-*, a stem of O.F. *remanoir* (also *remenoir*, *remaindre*)—L. *remanēre*, to stay behind. RE- (3). MANOR. REMNANT. To be left; to abide, stay; to continue; to be still in existence.—**Remain'der**, *n.* *Remaindre* as *n.* A further interest in property coming into effect on the determination of an interest; the residue, the rest; the number remaining after subtraction.

Remand', *vt.* L.L. *remandāre*, recorded in sense 'to send back word'. RE-(9). MANDATE. To commit again, send back, esp. into custody.

Remark', *vt.* F. *remarquer*. RE- (6). MARK. To take notice of; to say.—*vi.* To make a remark *on*.—*n.* Observation, comment; a comment.—**Remark'**ABLE, *a.* Noteworthy.

Rem'edy, *n.* A.F. *remedie*, *remedy* (= O.F. *remede* (F. *remède*))—L. *remedium*, f. RE- (9) + *med-*, stem of *medēri*. MEDICINE. Something which cures, counteracts or removes evil; reparation, redress.—*vt.* To cure; to put right, rectify.—**Reme'di**ABLE, *a.*—**Reme'di**AL, *a.*

Remem'ber, *vt.* O.F. *remembrer*—L.L. *rememorāri*, to call to mind, f. RE- (9) + *memor*. MEMORY. To retain in or recall to the memory; to fee, reward; to mention as sending greeting.—*vi.* To have in mind, to recall to the mind.—**Remem'br**ANCE, *n.*—**Remem'brancer**, *n.* One who or that which reminds; the name of various officials.

Remind', *vt.* RE- (8). MIND, *v.* Formerly, to remember. To put in mind *of*.—**Remind'**ER, *n.* Something which reminds.

Reminis'cence, *n.* F. *réminiscence*—L.L. *reminiscentia*, f. L. *reminisci*, to remember, f. RE- (9) + root of *mens*. MENTAL. Remembering; a remembrance; in *pl.*, a record of one's remembrances.—**Reminis'**CENT, *a.* Of, having, reminiscence; reminding.

Remiss', *a.* L. *remissus*, pa.pple. of *remittĕre*. (See next.) Negligent.—**Remiss'**LY,[2] *adv.*

Remit', *vt.* L. *remittĕre*, *remissum*, to slacken, to yield, forgive. RE- (5). MISSION. To forgive; not to exact the carrying out of (a sentence) or payment of; to give up; to allow to slacken; to refer for consideration, &c.; to send (money).—*vi.* To slacken, abate.—**Remis'**SIBLE, *a.*—**Remis'**SION, *n.*—**Remit'**TANCE, *n.* A sending of money; money sent.

Rem'nant, *n.* Contr. f. obs. *Remenant*—O.F. *remenant*, pres.pple. of *remenoir*, to REMAIN. A small remaining piece, &c.

Remon'strate, *vi.* Med.L. *remonstrāre*, *remonstrātum*, to demonstrate, f. RE- (2). MONSTRANCE. Formerly, to demonstrate, to protest against. To protest *against*; to expostulate *with*; to urge.—**Remon'str**ANCE, *n.*

Remorse', *n.* O.F. *remors* (F. *remords*)—L.L. *remorsus*, vbl. n. f. L. *remordēre*, to bite again, vex. RE- (8). MORDANT. A feeling of regret and repentance.—**Remorse'**FUL, *a.*—**Remorse'**LESS, *a.* From *remorse* in obs. sense 'pity'. Pitiless.

Remote', *a.* L. *remōtus*, pa.pple. of *removēre*. REMOVE. Far away, distant; widely different; secluded; slight, faint.—**Remote'**LY,[2] *adv.*

Remount', *vt.* O.F. *remonter*. RE- (9). MOUNT, *v.* To set on horseback again; to mount again; to provide with fresh horses.—*vi.* To mount again.—*n.* A fresh horse.

Remove', *vt.* O.F. *remouvoir*—L. *removēre*, to put aside, remove. RE- (4). MOVE. REMOTE. To put aside, take off or away; to put out of office.—*vi.* To depart, to change residence.—**Remov'**ABLE, *a.*—**Remov'**AL, *n.*

Remu'nerate, *vt.* L. *remūnerāri*, *remūnerātus*, f. RE- (1) + *mūnus*. MUNICIPAL. To requite, reward.—**Remunera'**TION, *n.*—**Remu'ner**ATIVE, *a.*

Renas'cent, *a.* L. *renascens*, *renascentis*, pres.pple. of *renasci*, to be born again. RE- (8). NATAL. Springing up afresh.—**Renas'**CENCE, *n.* Rebirth, revival; the revival of art and letters in the 14th to 16th centuries, the period of this (in this sense also in F. form **Renais'sance**, f. *renaître*, L. *renasci*).

Rencon'tre, *n.* F., vbl. n. f. *rencontrer*, to meet. RE- (without appreciable force). ENCOUNTER. Also in Eng. form **Rencoun'ter**. A battle or conflict; a duel; a meeting.

Rend, *vt.* O.E. *rendan* = O.Fris. *renda*. Not in the other Teut. langs. RENT.[2] To tear *off*, *from*, &c., or in pieces.—*vi.* To split or tear.

Ren'der, *vt.* O.F. *rendre*—Pop.L. **rendĕre* = L. *reddĕre*, to give back, f. *red-* (= RE- (9)) + *dăre*, to give. DATE.[2] RENT.[1] SURRENDER. To give back; to give in return; to depict; to perform (music); to translate; to hand over, give, surrender; to send in (an account); to give, pay, show; to do (a service); to cause to become; to clarify.—**Ren'dezvous**, *n.* F., use as *n.* of *rendez vous*, present yourselves, imp. of *rendre*. A place of meeting.—*vi.* To assemble at a rendezvous; to meet, come together.—**Rendi'**TION, *n.* Surrender.

Ren'egade, Renega'do, *n.* Sp. *renegado*—Med.L. *renegātus*, orig. pa.pple. of *renegāre*, to deny, renounce, f. RE- (9) + L. *negāre*, to DENY. RUNAGATE. An apostate.

Renew', *vt.* RE- (9) + NEW, *a.* To get again; to repair, restore; to begin again; to keep fresh, full, &c.; to grant anew.—**Renew'**AL, *n.*

Ren'net, *n.* From *renne*, obs. form of RUN, in sense (now dial.) 'to coagulate, form curd'. A preparation for curdling milk.

Renounce', *vt.* F. *renoncer*—L. *renuntiāre*, to bring back word, to proclaim, to give up. RE- (9) (5). ANNOUNCE. To give up, abandon; to cast off, repudiate.—*vi.* At cards, to fail to follow suit.—**Renuncia'**TION, *n.*

Ren'ovate, *vt.* L. *renovāre*, *renovātum*, f. RE- (9) + *novāre*, to make new, f. *novus*, NEW. To repair, restore.—**Renova'**TION, *n.*

Renown', *n.* A.F. *renoun* = O.F. *renon*, f. *renomer*, to make famous, f. RE- (8) + L. *nōmināre*, to name, f. *nōmen*. NOMINAL. Fame.—*vt.* To make famous.

Rent, *n.*[1] O.F. *rente*, revenue, income—Pop. L. **rendita*, fem. pa.pple. of **rendĕre*. RENDER. A payment made for the use of land or a house.—*vt.* To hold as tenant; to let out.—**Rent'**AL, *n.* A rent-roll; rents received.

Rent, *n.*[2] Obs. *Rent*, var. of REND. A tear.

Rep(p), *n.* F. *reps*. Orig. unknown. A fabric with a corded surface.

Repair', *v.*[1]*i.* O.F. *repairer*, earlier *repadrer*—L.L. *repatriāre*, to return to one's country, f. RE- (9) + *patria*, fatherland, f. *pater*, FATHER. REPATRIATE. To betake oneself; to resort.

Repair', *v.*[2]*t.* O.E. *reparer*—L. *reparāre*, f. RE- (9) + *parāre*, to make ready. PARE. To restore to good condition, to mend.—*n.* A restoring to good condition; condition or good condition.—**Rep'ar**ABLE, *a.* That can be made good.—**Repara'**TION, *n.* A repairing or being repaired; amends, compensation.

Repartee', *n.* F. *repartie*, fem. pa.pple. of *repartir*, to set out again, to reply promptly. RE- (8). PART. A ready or witty reply; the faculty of making such replies.

Repast', *n.* O.F. *repast* (F. *repas*), f. *repaistre*, to feed—L.L. *repascĕre*, to feed again. RE- (8). PASTOR. A meal.—*vi.* To feed, feast.

Repa'triate, *vt.* From ppl. stem of L.L. *repatriāre*. REPAIR.[1] To restore to his own country.

Repay', *vt.* O.F. *repaier*, f. RE- (9) + *payer*, to PAY. To pay back; to pay (a person) back; to make a return for, requite.—**Repay'**ABLE, *a.*—**Repay'**MENT, *n.*

Repeal', *vt.* A.F. *repel(l)er* = O.F. *rapeler* (F. *rappeler*). RE- (9). APPEAL. To revoke, annul.—*n.* The act, an act, of repealing.

Repeat', *vt.* F. *répéter*—L. *repetĕre*, *repetitum*, to seek again, recommence. RE- (8). PETITION. To say or do again; to say over; to strike (the last hour, &c.) again.—**Repeat'ed**LY,[2]*adv.* Frequently.—**Repeat'**ER, *n.*—**Repeti'**TION, *n.* Repeating.

Repel', *vt.* L. *repellĕre*, *repulsum*. RE- (2). COMPEL. REPULSE. To drive or force back; to reject as unfounded; to reject (a suitor, &c.); to affect with aversion.—**Repel'l**ENT, *a.*

Repent', *vi.* F. *repentir*, f. RE- (3) + L. *paenitēre*. PENITENT. To feel regret for something done or left undone.—*vt.* To feel regret for.—**Repent'**ANCE, *n.*—**Repent'**ANT, *a.*

Repercus'sion, *n.* L. *repercussio*, *repercussiōnis*, n. of action f. *repercutĕre*, to drive back. RE- (2). PERCUSSION. Recoil; echo.

Rep'ertory, *n.* L. *repertōrium*, list, catalogue, f. *reperīre*, *repertum*, to find, f. RE- (8) + *parīre* = *parĕre*. PARENT. A place where something may be found, a storehouse; a repertoire.—**Rep'ertoire**, *n.* F. *répertoire*, f. *repertōrium*. A stock of plays, songs, &c.

Repine', *vi.* App. f. RE- (6) + PINE, *v.* To show discontent, to murmur, complain.

Replace', *vt.* RE- (9). To put back in the former place; to take the place of; to fill the place of *with* or *by* a substitute.

Replen'ish, *vt.* O.F. *repleniss-*, lengthened stem of *replenir*, f. RE- (9) + *plenir*, to fill—L. *plēnus*, full. COMPLETE. To fill up again.

Replete', *a.* L. *replētus*, pa.pple. of *replēre*, to fill up. RE- (6). COMPLETE. Filled; sated; fully supplied.—**Reple'**TION, *n.*

Rep'lica, *n.* It. *replica*, f. *replicare*, L. *replicāre*. REPLY. A copy of a picture, &c., made by the original artist.

Replica'tion, *n.* O.F. *replication*—L. *replicātio*, *replicātiōnis*, n. of action f. *replicāre*. (See next.) Reply; a reply; reverberation, echo.

Reply', *vi.* O.F. *replier*, L. *replicāre*, to fold back, reply. RE- (9). APPLY. To answer.—*vt.* To say in answer.—*n.* Answer; an answer.

Report', *vt.* A.F. and O.F. *reporter*—L. *reportāre*, to bring back, to report. RE- (9). COMPORT. To relate, narrate, tell; to take down in writing; to take down the words of; to prepare or give in an account or statement of; to name as an offender.—*vi.* To prepare or give in a report.—*n.* A rumour; repute, fame; an account or statement; the noise of the discharge of a gun, &c.—**Report'**ER, *n.*

Repose', *v.*[1]*t.* After *depose*, *dispose*, &c., f. L. *repōnĕre*, *repositum*, to replace, to place, put. RE- (9). POSITION. To put (trust, &c.) *in*.—**Repos'**AL, *n.*—**Repos'it**ORY, *n.* A place where things are stored or offered for sale.

Repose', *v.*[2]*refl.* F. *reposer*. RE- (5). POSE.[1] To lay oneself down to rest.—*vt.* To afford rest to.—*vi.* To take rest.—*n.* Rest.

Reprehend', *vt.* L. *reprehendĕre*, *reprehensum*, to restrain, reprehend. RE- (2). PREHENSILE. To find fault with, rebuke.—**Reprehen'**SIBLE, *a.*—**Reprehen'**SION, *n.*

Represent', *vt.* L. *repraesentāre*. RE- (8). PRESENT, *v.* To give out *as*, declare *to be*; to exhibit, depict; to perform (a play); to symbolize; to stand in place of; to act as deputy for; to serve as an example of.—**Representa'**TION, *n.*—**Represen'**TATIVE, *a.* and *n.*

Repress', *vt.* L. *reprimĕre*, *repressum*, f. RE- (2) + *premĕre*. PRESS.[1] REPRIMAND. To check, restrain, suppress.—**Repres'**SION, *n.*—**Repres'**SIVE, *a.*

Reprieve', *vt.* First in *repryed*, pa.pple., sent back to prison, app. f. A.F. and F. *repris*, pa.pple. of *reprendre*, to take back again, f. RE- (9) + *prendre*, to take—L. *prehendĕre*. PREHENSILE. REPRISAL. (The *-ve* not accounted for.) To suspend the execution of.—*n.* A reprieving; a warrant granting a reprieve.

Rep'rimand, *n.* F. *réprimande*, f. *reprimer*, to repress, reprove—L. *reprimĕre*. REPRESS. A sharp rebuke.—*vt.* To rebuke sharply.

Reprint', *vt.* RE- (8). To print again.—*n.* A new impression of a book without alteration.

Repri'sal, *n.* O.F. *reprisaille*, f. *repris*. REPRIEVE. Seizure from an enemy in retaliation; an act of retaliation.

Reproach', *vt.* F. *reprocher*, perh. to be referred to a Romanic *reprobicare, f. L. reprobāre. (See next.) To rebuke, to upbraid with.—n. A source of disgrace or discredit; disgrace; blame; an expression of blame.—**Reproach'**ABLE, a.—**Reproach'**FUL, a.

Rep'robate, vt. L. reprobāre, reprobātum, f. RE- (7) + probāre, to test, to approve of. PROVE. REPROVE. (See prec.) To disapprove of, condemn, reject.—a. -ATE.[2] Depraved; rejected by God.—n. One so rejected; a depraved person.—**Reprob**A'TION, n.

Reproduce', vt. RE- (8). To create or form anew; to bring (new individuals) into existence; to bring about or present anew.—**Reproduc'**TION, n.—**Reproduc'**TIVE, a.

Reprove', vt. O.F. reprover (F. réprouver)—L. reprobāre. REPROBATE. To blame, rebuke.—**Reproof'**, n. O.F. reprove. Blame, rebuke; an expression of blame or rebuke.

Rep'tile, a. L.L. reptilis, f. L. rēpĕre, reptum, to creep. Creeping, crawling.—n. A creeping or crawling animal.—**Reptil'i**AN, a.

Repub'lic, n. L. respublica, the state, f. rēs, thing, affair (REAL)+publica, fem. of publicus, PUBLIC. A state in which the supreme power is vested in the people and their elected representatives.—**Repub'lic**AN, a. and n.

Repu'diate, vt. L. repudiāre, repudiātum, to divorce, to reject, f. repudium, divorce, poss. f. RE- (5) + pudēre. IMPUDENT. To put away, cast off, disown, reject.—**Repudi**A'TION, n.

Repugn', vi. and t. F. répugner—L. repugnāre, f. RE- (2) + pugnāre. IMPUGN. To resist.—**Repug'n**ANT, a. Contrary, inconsistent; distasteful.—**Repug'n**ANCE, n.

Repulse', vt. From ppl. stem of L. repellĕre, to REPEL. To drive or force back; to reject, rebuff.—n. A repulsing, a being repulsed; rejection, rebuff.—**Repul'**SION, n. Repulsing; distaste, aversion.—**Repul'**SIVE, a.

Repute', vt. L. reputāre. RE- (6). PUTATIVE. To consider, reckon.—n. Reputation; distinction, credit.—**Rep'ut**ABLE, a. Of good reputation.—**Reput**A'TION, n. Common or general estimate; distinction, credit; one's good name; credit or estimation of having, &c.—**Reput'ed**LY,[2] adv. In general estimation.

Request', n. A.F. requeste. RE- (6). QUEST. The act or an act of asking (a favour, &c.); a petition; the being in demand.—vt. To ask.

Re'quiem, n. L. (acc. of requies, rest), the first word of the mass. A mass for the repose of the souls of the dead.

Require', vt. O.F. requer-, requier-, stem of requerre—L. requīrĕre, f. RE- (6) + quaerĕre. QUEST. To claim, demand; to need, want.—**Require'**MENT, n.—**Req'uisite**, a. L. requisitus, pa.pple. of requīrĕre. Necessary.—n. Something necessary.—**Requisi'**TION, n. A demand; an order for the furnishing of military supplies; the state of being put into service or use.—vt. To make requisition for or upon; to press into service.

Requite', vt. RE- (1) + quite, var. of QUIT, v. To repay; to retaliate on.—**Requit'**AL, n.

Rer'edos, n. A.F. *reredos, f. rere = REAR, n. + dos. ENDORSE. A facing or screen covering the wall behind an altar.

Rescind', vt. L. rescindĕre, rescissum. RE- (5). ABSCIND. To annul.—**Rescis'**SION, n.

Re'script, n. L. rescriptum, neut. pa.pple. of rescrībĕre, to write in reply. RE- (1). SCRIBE. A decretal epistle from the pope; an edict.

Res'cue, vt. O.F. rescoure—Romanic type *re-excutĕre, f. RE- (9) + EX- + L. quatĕre. CONCUSS. To deliver, save.—n. Rescuing.

Research', n. Obs. F. recerche (F. recherche), f. RE- (6) + cerche, vbl. n. f. cerchier, to SEARCH. A careful inquiry; inquiry, investigation.

Resem'ble, vt. O.F. resembler (F. ressembler). RE- (1). SEMBLANCE. To be like; to compare or liken.—**Resem'bl**ANCE, n.

Resent', vt. F. ressentir, to feel, f. RE- (6) + L. sentīre. SENSE. To feel injured or insulted by.—**Resent'**FUL, a.—**Resent'**MENT, n.

Reserve', vt. O.F. reserver (F. réserver)—L. reservāre. RE- (3). PRESERVE. To keep for future use; to postpone the discussion, &c., of; to keep to or for oneself; to set apart.—n. Something stored up, kept on hand, or set apart; in pl., troops retained for support; a part of the army, &c., liable to be called out only in emergency; limitation of belief, &c.; reticence, want of cordiality.—**Reserva'**TION, n. In senses from the v.; a limitation or exception, expressed or tacit.—**Reserved'**, ppl.a. Reticent.—**Reserv'**IST, n. One serving in the reserve.—**Res'ervoir**, n. F. réservoir. An artificial pond for storing water.

Reset', vt. O.F. receter—L. receptāre, freq. of recipĕre. RECEIVE. To receive (stolen goods).

Reside', vi. L. residēre, to remain behind. RE- (3). ASSESS. To have one's abode, dwell; to be vested in.—**Res'id**ENCE, n.—**Res'id**ENCY, n. The official residence of the English representative in a native Indian state.—**Res'id**ENT, a. and n.—**Residen'ti**AL, a. Suitable for or containing houses of the better class; connected with residence.

Res'idue, n. F. résidu—L. residuum, neut. of residuus, remaining, f. residēre. (See prec.) That which is left; what remains of an estate after paying debts, legacies, &c.—**Resid'u**AL, a.—**Resid'u**ARY, a.—**Resid'uum**, n. L., see above. A residue.

Resign', vt. O.F. resigner—L. resignāre, to unseal, annul. RE- (7). SIGNATURE. To give up, surrender, yield up.—vi. To give up an office, &c.—**Resign**A'TION, n.—**Resigned'**, ppl.a. Submissive, acquiescent.

Resile', vi. L. resilīre, to leap back. RE- (9). ASSAIL. To draw back from one's word, &c.; to shrink, recoil; to rebound; to manifest elasticity.—**Resil'i**ENCE, n. Rebound; elasticity.—**Resil'i**ENCY, n. Tendency to rebound; elasticity.—**Resil'i**ENT, a. Rebounding; elastic.

Res'in, n. F. résine—L. rēsina. ROSIN. An adhesive substance exuding from trees and plants, esp. the fir and pine.—**Res'in**OUS, a.

Resist', vt. F. résister—L. resistĕre. RE- (2). ASSIST. To withstand the action of; to oppose.—vi. To offer resistance.—**Resist'**ANCE, n.—**Resist'**ANT, -ENT, aa.—**Resist'**IBLE, a.—**Resist'**LESS, a. Irresistible; unresisting.

Resolve', vt. L. resolvĕre, resolūtum, to loosen, to separate, set free. RE- (5). SOLVE. To separate into its component parts; to convert or transform; to solve, answer; to determine or decide.—vi. To separate into component parts; to make up one's mind.—n. A determination; firmness of purpose.—**Res'olute**, a. L. resolūtus, pa.pple. of resolvĕre. Determined, firm.—**Resolu'**TION, n. Separation into component parts; conversion; a determination; a fixed resolve; firmness of purpose.

Res'onant, a. L. resonans, -antis, pres.pple. of resonāre, to sound again, f. RE- (8) + sonāre, to sound, f. sonus, SOUND, n.[1] Resounding; prolonging sound.—**Res'on**ANCE, n.

Resort', vi. O.F. resortir, to go out again, rebound, retire, &c., f. RE- (8) + sortir, to go out, of obscure orig. To have recourse to; to repair *to* habitually.—*n.* Recourse; that to which one has recourse; a frequented place.

Resound', *vi.* RE- (8) + SOUND, *v.*[1], after L. *resonāre.* RESONANT. To ring, re-echo, to go on sounding.—*vt.* To proclaim (praises, &c.).

Resource', *n.* F. *ressource*, f. O.F. *re(s)-sourdre*, to rise again, f. RE- (9) + *sourdre.* SOURCE. A means of supplying a want, &c.; an expedient or device; in *pl.*, means of support, &c., collectively.—**Resource'**FUL, *a.*

Respect', *vt.* L. *respicĕre, respectum*, to look behind, to consider. RE- (3). ASPECT. RESPITE. To refer or relate to; to treat with esteem, deference, or consideration.—*n.* Reference, relation; a point or particular; a consideration; esteem, deference. — **Respect'**ABLE, *a.* Worthy of respect; of moderately good standing; moderately good.—**Respecta**BIL'ITY, *n.* — **Respect'**FUL, *a.* — **Respec'**t'IVE, *a.* Relating severally each to each, several, separate.—**Respect'ive**LY,[2] *adv.*

Respire', *vi.* and *t.* L. *respīrāre*, to breathe back, breathe. RE- (9). ASPIRE. To breathe. —**Res'pir**ABLE, *a.* — **Respir**A'TION, *n.* — **Res'pirat**OR, *n.* A means of avoiding cold, dust, &c., in breathing.—**Res'pirat**ORY, *a.*

Res'pite, *n.* O.F. *respit* (F. *répit*)—L. *respectus*, consideration, regard, f. *respicĕre.* RESPECT. Delay; a reprieve; temporary cessation.—*vt.* To grant a respite to.

Resplend', *vi.* L. *resplendēre.* RE- (6). SPLENDID. To shine brightly.—**Resplen'**-**d**ENT, *a.*—**Resplen'd**ENCE, -ENCY, *nn.*

Respond', *vi.* L. *respondēre, responsum*, to promise in return, to answer. RE- (1). SPONSOR. To answer; to act in response *to.*—**Respon'd**ENT, *a.* Making reply. — *n.* One who answers; a defendant.—**Response'**, *n.* L. *responsum*, f. *respondēre.* Answer; an answer; a feeling answering to some influence; a part of the liturgy said by the people answering the priest.—**Respon's**IBLE, *a.* Liable to be called to account; of good credit and repute.—**Responsi**BIL'ITY, *n.* — **Respon'**-SIVE, *a.* Answering; responding readily.

Rest, *n.*[1] O.E. *ræst(e)*, *rest(e)* = M.Du. *reste*, O.H.G. *resta.* Cessation from activity; freedom from exertion; absence or cessation of motion; in *music*, a pause; a supporting appliance.—*v.*[1]*i.* To take rest; to be supported.—*vt.* To give (one) rest; to lay *upon* something for support.—**Rest'**FUL, *a.*—**Rest'**LESS, *a.*

Rest, *v.*[2]*i.* F. *rester*—L. *restāre*, to stop behind, remain. RE- (3). STATE. ARREST. RESTIVE. To remain, be left.—*n.*[2] The remainder, the others.

Rest, *n.*[3] Shortened from *arest*, ARREST, *n.* —O.F. *arest*, f. *arester.* A contrivance for holding the butt-end of a lance.

Res'taurant, *n.* F., use as *n.* of pres.pple. of *restaurer.* RESTORE. A place where meals, &c., are supplied.—**Restaurateur**, *n.* F., agent-n. f. *restaurer.* A restaurant-keeper.

Res'titute, *vt.* L. *restituĕre, restitūtum*, to set up again, to give back. RE- (9). CONSTITUTE. To restore, refund.—**Restitu'**TION, *n.*

Res'tive, *a.* Altered f. *restif(f)*—O.F. *restif* (F. *rétif*)—Pop.L. **restivus*, f. L. *restāre.* REST, *v.*[2] Stubborn, resisting control.

Restore', *vt.* O.F. *restorer* (F. *restaurer*)—L. *restaurāre*, to rebuild. RE- (9). STORE. RESTAURANT. To build up again; to repair, renew; to bring back to a normal state; to re-establish, reinstate; to give back.—**Restor**A'TION, *n.*—**Restor'**ATIVE, *a.* As *n.*, a strengthening medicine. &c.

Restrain', *vt.* O.F. *restrai(g)n-*, stem of *restraindre*—L. *restringĕre, restrictum*, to bind fast, restrain. RE- (6). STRICT. To check, hold back; to confine.—**Restraint'**, *n.* O.F. *restrainte.* A restraining; a means of restraining; being restrained.—**Restrict'**, *vt.* From the ppl. stem of *restringĕre.* To limit, bound. —**Restric'**TION, *n.*—**Restric'**TIVE, *a.*

Result', *vi.* L. *resultāre*, freq. of *resilīre*, to leap back. RE- (9). EXULT. To arise as an effect or consequence; to end or conclude.—*n.* Effect; issue, outcome.—**Result'**ANT, *a.*

Resume', *vt.* O.F. *resumer* (F. *résumer*)—L. *resūmĕre, resumptum*, to take again. RE- (8). ASSUME. To take to oneself anew; to begin again; to recapitulate, summarize. — **Résumé**, *n.* F., pa.pple. of *résumer.* A summary. —**Resump'**TION, *n.*—**Resump'**TIVE, *a.*

Resurge', *vi.* L. *resurgĕre, resurrectum.* RE- (9). SURGE. To rise again.—**Resur'g**ENT, *a.*—**Resurrec'**TION, *n.* Christ's rising again; the festival commemorating this; the rising again at the Last Day; revival, restoration.—**Resurrect'**, *vt.* Back-formation f. *resurrection.* To restore to life.

Resus'citate, *vt.* and *i.* L. *resuscitāre, resuscitātum.* RE- (9). *Sus-* = SUB- (1). CITE. To revive.—**Resuscit**A'TION, *n.*

Re'tail, *n.* O.F. *retail*, a piece cut off, f. *retaillier*, to cut off. RE- (5). ENTAIL. Sale in small quantities.—**Retail'**, *vt.* To sell by retail; to recount in detail.

Retain', *vt.* O.F. *retenir*—L. *retinēre, retentum*, to hold or keep back. RE- (3). ABSTAIN. REIN. RETINUE. To keep under control; to keep in one's service; to engage (a barrister); to keep in possession or in mind.—**Retain'**ER, *n.* A fee to engage a barrister; a follower.—**Reten'**TION, *n.*—**Reten'**TIVE, *a.*

Retal'iate, *vt.* L. *retāliāre, retāliātum*, f. RE- (1) + *tālis*, such-like. To repay in kind.—*vi.* To make requital.—**Retali**A'TION, *n.*

Retard', *vt.* L. *retardāre*, f. RE- (3) + *tardus*, slow. TARDY. To make slow, delay, hinder. —**Retard**A'TION, *n.*

Retch, *vi.* Var. of obs. *Reach*—O.E. *hrǽcan* = O.N. *hrǽkja*, to spit, f. O.E. *hráca*, O.N. *hráki*, spittle. To make efforts to vomit.

Ret'icent, *a.* L. *reticens, reticentis*, pres.pple. of *reticēre*, to be silent, to keep secret, f. RE- (4) + *tacēre.* TACIT. Reserved, disinclined to speak.—**Ret'ic**ENCE, *n.*

Retic'ulate, *a.* L. *rēticulātus*, f. *rēticulum*, dim. of *rēte*, net. Also **Retic'ulated**. Constructed or arranged like a net.—**Retic'ulate**, *vt.* and *i.* Back-formation f. *reticulated.* To make, to be, like network. —**Reticul**A'TION, *n.*—**Ret'icule**, *n.* F. *réticule*, f. *rēticulum.* A small bag used by ladies.

Ret'ina, *n.* Med.L. *rētina*, perh. f. L. *rēte.* (See prec.) The sensitive coating at the back of the eye.

Ret'inue, *n.* O.F. *retenue*, orig. fem. pa.pple. of *retenir.* RETAIN. A band of attendants.

Retire', *vi.* F. *retirer*, f. RE- (4) + *tirer*, to draw. TIER. To withdraw; to seek shelter or seclusion; to give up office, &c.—*vt.* To order to retire; to withdraw (a bill, &c.) from currency. —**Retired'**, *ppl.a.* Secluded; having given up office, &c.—**Retire'**MENT, *n.*—**Retir'ing**, *ppl.a.* Unobtrusive, unsociable.

Retort', *vt.* L. *retorquēre, retortum*, to twist or cast back. RE- (9). CONTORT. To repay in kind; to hurl back (a charge, &c.); to say in repartee.—*n.*[1] An incisive reply; a repartee.

Retort', *n.*[2] F. *retorte*—Med.L. *retorta*, orig.

fem. pa.pple. of *retorquēre*. (See prec.) A vessel with a bent neck for distilling.

Retract', *v.*[1]*t.* L. *retrahĕre, retractum*, to draw back. RE- (4). TREAT. RETREAT. To draw back or in.—**Retrac'**TION, *n.*[1] (Also = RETRACTATION.)

Retract', *v.*[2]*t.* L. *retractāre*, to handle again, reconsider, to refuse, f. RE- (8) + *tractāre*, freq. of *trahĕre*. (See prec.) To withdraw, recall, revoke.—*vi.* To make withdrawal.—**Retrac**TA'TION, *n.*

Retreat', *n.* O.F. *retret, retrete*, varr. of *retrait, retraite*, f. pa.pple. of *retraire*, L. *retrahĕre*. RETRACT.[1] The signal to retire; a retiring; a place of seclusion.—*vi.* To retire.

Retrench', *vt*, Obs. F. *retrencher*. RE- (5). TRENCH. To cut down, curtail.—*vi.* To reduce expenses.—**Retrench'**MENT, *n.*

Ret'ribute, *vt.* L. *retribuĕre, retribūtum*. RE- (1). TRIBUTE. To give in return; to make return for, repay.—**Retribu'**TION, *n.*—**Retrib'u**TIVE, *a.*—**Retrib'u**TORY, *a.*

Retrieve', *vt.* O.F. *retroev-*, stressed stem of *retrover*. RE- (8). TROVER. Of a dog, to find (game) again, to bring in killed game; to restore, revive; to make good, repair.—**Retriev'**ABLE, *a.* — **Retriev'**AL, *n.* — **Retriev'**ER, *n.* A dog trained to retrieve.

Ret'rocede, *v.*[1]*i.* L. *retrōcēdĕre, retrōcessum*. RETRO-. ACCEDE. To go back, retire.—**Retroces'**SION, *n.*[1]

Retrocede', *v.*[2]*t.* F. *rétrocéder*, f. RETRO- + *céder*, to CEDE. To cede (territory) back again.—**Retroces'**SION, *n.*[2]

Ret'rograde, *a.* L. *retrōgradus*, f. RETRO- + *gradus*, step. GRADE. Of a planet, apparently moving from east to west (*i.e.* contrary to the order of the signs); retiring, retreating; tending to revert to a worse condition.—*vi.* L. *retrōgradi, retrōgressus*. RETRO-. AGGRESSION. To seem to move from east to west; to retire; to revert to a worse condition.—**Retrogres'**SION, *n.*—**Retrogres'**SIVE, *a.*

Ret'rospect, *n.* L. type **retrōspectus*, f. *retrōspicere, retrōspectum*, to look back at. RETRO-. ASPECT. A view or survey of past time.—**Retrospec'**TION, *n.*—**Retrospec'**TIVE, *a.*

Return', *vi.* O.F. *retorner, retourner*, f. RE- (9) + *torner, tourner*—L. *tornāre*. TURN. To come or go back.—*vt.* To send or give back; to report officially; to report as having been elected; to elect.—*n.* Returning; being returned; recurrence; profit; an official report.

Reu'nion, *n.* = F. *réunion*. RE- (9). UNION. A reuniting or being reunited; a social gathering.—**Reunite'**, *vt.* and *i.* Med.L. *reūnīre*. RE- (9). UNITE. To unite again.

Reveal', *vt.* O.F. *reveler*—L. *revēlāre*, f. RE- (7) + *vēlum*. VEIL. To disclose in a supernatural manner; to make known, show.—**Revel**A'TION, *n.*

Reveil'le, *n.* F. *réveillez*, imp. pl. of *réveiller*, to awaken, f. RE- (9) + *veiller*, L. *vigilāre*, to keep watch, f. *vigil*. VIGIL. A morning signal to waken soldiers.

Rev'el, *vi.* O.F. *reveler*, to rebel, to make noise—L. *rebellāre*, to rebel, conn. with *rebellis*. REBEL. To make merry; to take great delight *in*.—*n.* Noisy mirth; a merry-making.—**Rev'eller**, *n.*—**Rev'elry**, *n.*

Revenge', *v.refl.* Obs. F. *revenger*, f. RE- (1) + *venger*. VENGEANCE. To avenge oneself.—*vt.* To inflict punishment for; to avenge (a person).—*n.* Revenging.—**Revenge'**FUL, *a.*

Rev'enue, *n.* O.F. *revenue*, orig. fem. pa.pple. of *revenir*, to come back, f. RE- (9) + *venir*. L. *venīre*, to come. ADVENT. Income.

Rever'berate, *vt.* L. *reverberāre, reverberātum*, to strike back, f. RE- (9) + *verberāre*, to beat, f. *verber*, scourge. To return (a sound), reflect (light, &c.).—*vi.* To re-echo; to be reflected.—**Reverber**A'TION, *n.*

Revere', *vt.* L. *reverēri*, f. RE- (6) + *verēri*, to fear. WARE, *a.* To hold in deep respect or veneration.—**Rev'er**ENCE, *n.* Deep respect or veneration; an obeisance.—*vt.* To regard with veneration; to hold in high respect.—**Rev'erend**, *a.* L. *reverendus*, ger. of *reverēri*. Worthy of reverence; a respectful epithet applied to the clergy.—**Rev'er**ENT, *a.* Feeling or showing due reverence.—**Reveren'**TIAL, *a.* Inspired or marked by reverence.

Rev'erie, *n.* F. *rêverie*, f. *rêver*. RAVE. A fantastic idea; a fit of musing.

Reverse', *vt.* F. *reverser*—L.L. *reversāre*, to turn round, f. RE- (5) + *versāre*, freq. of *vertĕre*, to turn. ADVERSE. To turn upside down or the other way; to annul; to change completely.—*n.* O.F. *reverse*, f. ppl. stem of L. *revertĕre*, to turn back, return, f. RE- (9) + *vertĕre*. The opposite or contrary; the side opposite to the obverse; a disaster or defeat.—*a.* L. *reversus*, pa.pple. of *revertĕre*. Opposite, contrary.—**Rever'**SAL, *n.*—**Rever'**SIBLE, *a.*—**Rever'**SION, *n.* The return of an estate to a grantor on the expiry of the grant; the right to succeed to an estate, an office, &c., upon a death, &c.; a returning to a condition, &c.—**Rever'sion**ER, *n.* One entitled to succeed in reversion.—**Revert'**, *vi.* O.F. *revertir*—L. *revertĕre*. To return to a former possessor; to return to a condition, &c.; to return in discourse or thought.

Revet', *vt.* F. *revêtir*, O.F. *revestir*—L.L. *revestīre*, to clothe again, f. RE- (8) + *vestīre*. DIVEST. To face (a wall, &c.) with masonry, &c.—**Revet'**MENT, *n.* A wall supporting a rampart, &c.; a facing of masonry, &c.

Review', *n.* Older F. *reveue* (F. *revue*), vbl. n. f. *revoir*, to see again, f. RE- (8) + *voir*, L. *vidēre*. ADVICE. Revision of a sentence, &c.; a formal inspection of troops, &c.; an inspection or survey; a critique of a book, &c.; a periodical publication containing critiques, articles on current topics, &c.—*vt.* RE- (8) + VIEW, *v.* To view again; to submit (a sentence, &c.) to revision; to survey; to inspect (troops, &c.) formally; to write a review of.—**Review'**ER, *n.* A writer of reviews.

Revile', *vt.* O.F. *reviler*, f. RE- (6) + *vil*, VILE. To assail with abusive language.

Revise', *vt.* F. *réviser*, f. RE- (8) + *viser*, to have in view, f. L. *visĕre*, freq. of *vidēre*. ADVICE. To look over for correction; to examine again for amendment or alteration.—*n.* A proof showing corrections carried out.—**Revi'**SAL, *n.*—**Revi'**SION, *n.*

Revive', *vi.* F. *revivre*—L. *revīvĕre*, to live again. RE- (8). VIVACITY. To come back to life; to assume fresh vigour.—*vt.* To restore to life; to give fresh vigour to; to bring again into use, knowledge, &c.—**Revi'**VAL, *n.*

Reviv'ify, *vt.* L.L. *revīvificāre*. (See prec.) -FY. To restore to life or vigour.

Revoke', *vt.* O.F. *revoquer*—L. *revocāre*, to call back, to annul. RE- (9). VOCABLE. To annul.—*vi.* At cards, to neglect to follow suit.—*n.* At cards, an act of revoking.—**Rev'oc**ABLE, *a.*—**Revoca'**TION, *n.*

Revolt', *vi.* F. *révolter*, f. RE- (2) + L. *volūtāre*, freq. of *volvĕre*, to roll. VOLUBLE. To cast off allegiance; to feel disgust. —*vt.* To affect with disgust.—*n.* A rebellion.

Revolve', *vt.* L. *revolvĕre, revolūtum*, to roll back, to meditate upon. RE- (9). VOLUBLE. To meditate upon; to rotate.—*vi.* To rotate.—**Revolu'**TION, *n.* Rotation or turning round; an act of rotation; a great change; an overthrow of government.—**Revolu'tion**ARY, *a.*—**Revolu'tion**IST, *n.*—**Revolu'tion**IZE, *vt.*—**Revolv'**ER, *n.* A repeating pistol with revolving cartridge-chambers.

Revul'sion, *n.* L. *revulsio, revulsiōnis*, n. of action f. *revellĕre, revulsum*, to pluck away, f. RE- (5) + *vellĕre*, to pluck. CONVULSE. A drawing away; a violent change of feeling.

Reward', *vt.* O.N.F. *rewarder* = O.F. *reguarder, regarder*. REGARD. To repay, recompense; to make return for.—*n.* A recompense or return; recompense, retribution.

Rhab'domancy, *n.* L.L. *rhabdomantia*—G. *rhabdomanteia*, f. *rhabdos*, rod + *manteia*, divination, prophecy. Divination by means of a rod, esp. the art of discovering water, &c., by means of a rod.

Rhap'sody, *n.* L. *rhapsōdia*, a book of an epic poem—G. *rhapsōidia*, the recitation of epic poems, a portion of such a poem for recitation, conn. with *rhapsōidos*, a reciter of epic poems, f. *rhaptein*, to stitch + *ōidē*, song. ODE. An epic poem, a part of one; a disconnected and extravagant speech, &c.—**Rhapsod'**IC, -ICAL, *aa.*—**Rhap'sod**IST, *n.* A reciter of epic poems; a user of rhapsodical language.

Rhet'oric, *n.* L. *rhētorica*—G. *rhētorikē* (*technē*), (the art) of public speaking, fem. of *rhētorikos*, pertaining to public speaking, f. *rhētōr*, public speaker. The art of speaking effectively (often in depreciatory sense).—**Rhetor'**ICAL, *a.*—**Rhetori**C'IAN, *n.*

Rheum, *n.* O.F. *reume*—L. *rheuma*—G. *rheuma, rheumatos*, a flux, rheum, f. *rheu-*, root of *rhe-ein*, to flow. RHYME. Watery matter secreted by the mucous glands or membrane; a cold.—**Rheu'matism**, *n.* L.L. *rheumatismus*, rheum, catarrh—G. *rheumatismos*, a flux, f. *rheumatizein*, to have a flux, f. *rheuma*. Inflammation and pain of the joints (formerly supposed to be caused by a defluxion of rheum).—**Rheumat'**IC, *a.*

Rhinoc'eros, *n.* L.L. *rhīnocerōs*—G. *rhinokerōs*, f. *rhis, rhinos*, nose + *keras*, HORN. A quadruped with a horn (or two) on the nose.

Rhododen'dron, *n.* L.L. *rhododendron*, G. *rhododendron*, the OLEANDER, lit. 'rose-tree', f. *rhodon*, ROSE + *dendron*, tree. A flowering shrub, a native of the Caucasus.

Rhomb, **Rhom'bus**, *n.* L. *rhombus*, G. *rhombos*. A four-sided figure with all the sides, but only the opposite angles, equal.

Rhu'barb, *n.* O.F. *reubarbe*—Med.L. *r(h)eubarbarum*, altered (by assoc. with *rhēum*, G. *rhēon* = *rha*) f. *rha barbarum*, 'foreign *rha*', G. *rha*, rhubarb, said to be f. the ancient name *Rha* of the Volga. An Eastern plant the root of which is used in medicine; a plant the stalks of which are used as food.

Rhyme, *n.* Var. of **Rime**[1]—O.F. *rime*, earlier **ridme, *ritme*—L. *rhythmus*, rhythm—G. *rhuthmos*, measured motion, time, rhythm, f. *rhe-ein*, to flow. RHEUM. (See next.) A poem showing agreement in the terminal sounds of words or lines; verse showing such agreement; such agreement; an instance of this.—*vi.* To make rhymes; to end in sounds that form a rhyme. —*vt.* To put into rhyming form.—**Rhym'**ER, *n.*—**Rhyme'**STER, *n.*

Rhyth'm, *n.* L. *rhythmus*. (See prec.) A measured recurring emphasis; the measured flow of words or phrases. —**Rhyth'm**IC, **Rhyth'm**ICAL, *aa.*

Rib, *n.* O.E. *rib, ribb*. Common Teut. REEF.[1] One of the curved bones springing in pairs from the spine; a ridge on cloth, &c.—*vt.* To furnish with ribs; to mark with ridges.

Rib'ald, *n.* O.F. *ribaut, ribaud*, orig., a menial, of obscure orig. One who jests or jeers irreverently.—*a.* Wantonly irreverent, scurrilous.—**Rib'ald**RY, *n.*

Ribbon, *n.* Later form of *riban, riband*—O.E. *riban, ruban*, of obscure orig. A narrow band of silk, satin, &c.

Rice, *n.* M.E. *rys*, &c.=Du. *rijst*, M.H.G. *rîs* (Ger. *reis*)—O.F. *ris* (F. *riz*)—It. *riso*, repg. L. **orizum*, var. of *oriza, oryza*—G. *oruza* (also *oruzon*), prob. of Oriental orig. The seeds of an Eastern plant; the plant.

Rich, *a.* O.E. *rîce*, powerful, rich. Common Teut. Believed to represent Celtic *rix* = L. *rex*. REGAL. Having abundant possessions or resources; fertile; costly, splendid; containing much of such ingredients as fat, eggs, &c.; mellow; abundant; very amusing.—**Rich'es**, *n.pl.* Var. of obs. *Richesse*, sing.—O.F. *richesse*, f. *riche*, rich, of Teut. orig. Abundant possessions or resources.—**Rich'**LY,[2] *adv.*

Rick, *n.* O.E. *hréac* = M.Du. *rooc, roke*, O.N. *hraukr*. A stack of hay, &c.

Rick'ets, *n.pl.* Orig. doubtful. A disease of children marked by softening of the bones. —**Rick'et**Y,[2] *a.* Suffering from this; shaky.

Ric'ochet, *n.* F., of unknown orig. A method of firing in which the projectile skips along a surface.—*vi.* Of a projectile, to skip thus.

Rid, *vt.* O.N. *rythja*. Orig. unknown. To clear (land); to make free *of*.—**Rid'd**ANCE, *n.*

Rid'dle, *n.*[1] O.E. *rǽdels, rǽdelse*, counsel, conjecture, a riddle, f. *rǽdan*, to READ. A puzzling question.—*v.*[1]*i.*—To speak in or propound riddles.—*vt.* To interpret (a riddle).

Rid'dle, *n.*[2] O.E. *hriddel*, earlier *hrider, hridder*, f. a stem *hrid-*, to shake. Cogn. with L. *cribrum*, conn. with *cernĕre*. CONCERN. A coarse sieve.—*v.*[2]*t.* To pass through a riddle; to pierce with holes like those of a riddle.

Ride, *vi.* O.E. *rîdan*. Common Teut. BED-RID. ROAD. To go on horseback or in a vehicle; to lie at anchor.—*vt.* To traverse on horseback; to sit or be carried upon.—*n.* An excursion on horseback or in a vehicle; a road for riding on horseback.—**Rid'**ER, *n.* One who rides; a supplementary clause or addition.

Ridge, *n.* O.E. *hrycg*, back, spine. Common Teut. The top or crest; a range of hills; a raised part between furrows; a narrow raised part on a surface.—*vt.* To form into ridges.

Rid'icule, *n.* F. *ridicule*—L. *rīdiculum*, neut. of *rīdiculus*, laughable, f. *rīdēre*. DERIDE. An absurdity; absurd nature or character; the act or practice of ridiculing.—*vt.* To treat with mockery, deride.—**Ridic'ul**OUS, *a.*

Rid'ing, *n.* Late O.E. type **thrithing* or **thriding*—O.N. *thrithjungr*, third part, f. *thrithi*, THIRD. An administrative division, esp. one of the three divisions of Yorkshire.

Rife, *a.* Late O.E. *rýfe* = M.Du. *rive, rijf*, O.N. *rífr*. Prevalent, current, abundant.

Riff-raff, *n.* Formerly *riff and raff*—O.F. *rif et raf*. Disreputable persons; the rabble.

Rif'le, *v.*[1]*t.* O.F. *rifler*, to graze, scratch, plunder, &c., of obscure orig. To despoil.

Rif'le, *v.*[2]*t.* Ultimately repg. F. *rifler*. (See

prec.) To form spiral grooves in (a gun).—*n.* One of a set of such grooves; a firearm with the bore thus grooved.

Rift, *n.* Scand. Cogn. with RIVE. Cf. Da., Norw. *rift.* A cleft or fissure.—*vt.* To split.

Rig, *vt.* Orig. obscure. Cf. Norw. *rigga*, to bind up. To make (a ship) ready; to dress, clothe; to fit up. — *n.* The arrangement of masts, sails, &c., on a ship; costume, style of dress.—**Rig'ging**, *n.* The ropes, &c., supporting masts and used in working sails, &c.

Right, *n.* O.E. *riht, ryht*, conn. with the *a.* What is just or due; justice; legally or morally just claim; one's due; the right side or part.—*a.* O.E. *reht, riht, ryht.* Common Teut. Conn. with L. *rectus*, f. root *reg-* of *regĕre.* CORRECT. Straight; *right angle*, an angle of 90 degrees; just, equitable; correct, proper; true; correct in opinion, &c.; real, genuine; denoting the hand which is normally the stronger and the other parts on the same side.—*vt.* O.E. *rehtan, rihtan, ryhtan.* To bring back to a straight or vertical position; to do justice to, to vindicate.—*vi.* To come back to a vertical position.—*adv.* O.E. *rehte, rihte, ryhte.* Straight; in a straight course; very; properly; accurately; on or towards the right side.—**Right'eous**, *a.* O.E. *rihtwis, ryhtwis*, f. *riht, ryht* (the *n.*) + *wis*, WISE, *a.*, 'wise as to what is right'. Just, upright.—**Right'**FUL, *a.*—**Right'**LY,[2] *adv.*

Rig'id, *a.* L. *rigidus*, f. *rigēre*, to be stiff. Stiff, not flexible; harsh; strict; exact, precise.—**Rigid'**ITY, *n.*—**Rig'id**LY,[2] *adv.*—**Rig'or**, *n.* L. *rigor*, numbness, stiffness, conn. with *rigēre.* A sudden chill with shivering.—**Rig'our**, *n.* O.F. *rigour*, f. *rigor.* Harshness, severity; an instance of this; the strict terms, &c., *of* a law, &c.—**Rig'or**OUS, *a.*

Rig'marole, *n.* App. alteration of obs. *Ragman roll*, a list or catalogue, f. *ragman*, in sim. sense, of obscure orig. + ROLL, *n.*[1] A succession of incoherent statements.

Rill, *n.* = Du., L.G. *ril.* A small stream.

Rim, *n.* O.E. *rima* = O.N. *rime, rimi*, raised strip of land, ridge. The outer ring of a wheel; edge.—*vt.* To furnish with a rim; to edge.

Rime, *n.*[1] and *vi.* and *t.* See RHYME.

Rime, *n.*[2] O.E. *hrim* = M.Du. *rijm*, O.N. *hrím.* Hoar-frost.

Rind, *n.* O.E. *rind* = M.Du. *rinde*, O.H.G. *rinda.* The coating of trees, &c.; the skin of fruits, &c.; an outer crust or integument.

Rin'derpest, *n.* Ger. *rinderpest*, f. *rinder*, pl. of *rind*, ox + *pest* = PEST. Cattle-plague.

Ring, *n.*[1] O.E. *hring.* Common Teut. CIRCLE. HARANGUE. RANK, *n.* A small circle of gold, &c., worn on the finger; a circle of persons (whence, from obs. phrase *to lead the ring*, to take the lead, **Ring'leader**, *n.*, a leader of a mutiny, &c.); various things like a ring.—*v.*[1]*t.* To encircle.—**Ring'let**, *n.* Dim. suff. *-let.* A small ring; a curly lock of hair.

Ring, *v.*[2]*i.* O.E. *hringan* = O.N. *hringja.* Perh. imitative. To emit a clear resonant sound; to resound, re-echo.—*vt.* To cause (a bell) to sound.—*n.*[2] A set of bells; a ringing sound; an act of ringing.

Rink, *n.* From O.F. *renc*, var. of *ranc*, RANK, with change of sense. Formerly, a space prepared for a combat, &c. A sheet of ice for skating; a floor prepared for roller-skating.

Rinse, *vt.* F. *rincer*, of unknown orig. To clean by putting in and emptying out water; to drench with or agitate in water.

Ri'ot, *n.* O.F. *riote*, debate, dispute, &c., of unknown orig. Unrestrained mirth; disorder, tumult; an outbreak of disorder.—*vi.* To revel.—**Ri'ot**ER, *n.*—**Ri'ot**OUS, *a.*

Rip, *vt.* Orig. obscure. Cf. Fris. *rippe*, to rip, tear, Flemish *rippen*, to rip, strip off roughly. To cut or tear away; to cut or tear apart; to slash or open *up.*—*n.* A rent or tear.

Ripa'rian, *a.* L. *ripārius*, a. f. *ripa*, bank (RIVER) + -AN. Of or on the banks of a river.

Ripe, *a.* O.E. *ripe* = M.Du. *ripe*, O.H.G. *rifi, rife* (Ger. *reif*). Poss. conn. with O.E. *ripan*, to REAP. Ready for reaping or gathering; mature; ready or fit.—*vi.* and *t.* To mature.—**Rip'**EN,[2] *vi.* and *t.*

Rip'ple, *vi.* Orig. obscure. To be covered with little waves; to flow in ripples.—*vt.* To form little waves upon.—*n.* A slight ruffling of the surface; a sound as of rippling water.

Rise, *vi.* O.E. *rísan.* Common Teut. RAISE. To get up from lying, sitting, &c.; to make insurrection *against*; to adjourn; to appear above the horizon; to ascend; to slope or extend upwards; to swell up; to reach a higher level of thought, rank, &c.; to increase; to occur; to come into existence.—*n.* The rising of the sun, &c.; ascent; elevation; a piece of rising ground; an increase; a beginning.

Ris'ible, *a.* L.L. *risibilis*, f. ppl. stem of *ridēre.* DERIDE. Of laughter; inclined to laugh; laughable.—**Risi**BIL'ITY, *n.*

Risk, *n.* F. *risque*—It. *risco, rischio*, of uncertain orig. Hazard, danger.—*vt.* To hazard; to venture upon.—**Risk'**Y,[2] *a.*

Ris'sole, *n.* F. *rissole*, perh. repg. Pop.L. **russeola*, f. L. *russeolus*, reddish, dim. f. *russus.* RUSSET. A cake of meat, &c., chopped up with bread-crumbs, &c., and fried.

Rite, *n.* L. *ritus.* A religious ceremony; a formal custom or practice; the general practice of a country, &c., in religion or worship.—**Rit'u**AL, *a.* As *n.*, a prescribed order of religious service; a book containing this; the performance of ritual acts.—**Rit'ual**ISM, *n.* The practice, esp. the practice regarded by some as excessive, of ritual.—**Rit'ual**IST, *n.*

Ri'val, *n.* L. *rivālis*, orig. 'one using the same brook as another', f. *rivus*, brook. DERIVE. One who pursues the same object as another, or disputes distinction with another.—*a.* In the position of a rival.—*vt.* To vie with.—*vi.* To act as a rival.—**Ri'val**RY, *n.*

Rive, *vt.* O.N. *rífa* = O.Fris. **rīva.* RIFT. To tear, rend, split.—*vi.* To split, cleave.

Riv'er, *n.* O.F. *rivere, riviere* (F. *rivière*)—Pop.L. *ripāria*, f. *ripa*, bank. ARRIVE. RIPARIAN. A large stream of water.

Riv'et, *n.* O.F. *rivet*, f. *river*, to fix, clench, of uncertain orig. A bolt for fastening metal plates together, the end being beaten out after insertion.—*vt.* To make fast with rivets.

Riv'ulet, *n.* Perh. f. It. *rivoletto*, dim. of *rivolo*, dim. of *rivo*, L. *rivus*, brook. DERIVE. A small stream.

Roach, *n.* O.F. *roche.* Orig. uncertain. A small freshwater fish of the carp family.

Road, *n.* O.E. *rád* (f. *rídan*, to RIDE), a riding, a raid, a roadstead. INROAD. RAID. A roadstead; a line of regular communication between places; direction, way.—**Road'stead**, *n.* *Road* + STEAD. A place where ships may lie at anchor near the shore.—**Road'**STER, *n.* A horse suited for the road.

Roam, *vi.* Orig. unknown. To wander, rove.—*vt.* To wander over or through.

Roan, *a.* O.F. *roan, rouen* (F. *rouan*). Orig. unknown. Having a coat the prevailing colour of which is mingled with another, esp. chestnut or bay mixed with white or grey.—*n.*[1] Such a colour; a roan animal.

Roan, *n.*[2] Poss. f. *Roan*, old form of *Rouen*. A flexible leather made of sheepskin.

Roar, *vi.* O.E. *rárian*=M.Du. *reeren*, O.H.G. *rêrên*. Prob. imitative. To utter a loud and deep or hoarse cry; to make a loud noise.—*vt.* To utter loudly, to shout *out*.—*n.* A roaring.

Roast, *vt.* O.F. *rostir* (F. *rôtir*), of Teut. orig. Cf. O.H.G. *rôsten* (Ger. *rösten*), Du. *roosten*. ROSTER. To cook by exposure to fire; to treat or prepare by heat.—*vi.* To be roasted.—*n.* O.F. *rost* (F. *rôt*). A piece of meat roasted or for roasting. From the *v.*, roast meat; a roasting. —*ppl.a.* Obs. pa.pple. of the *v.* Roasted.

Rob, *vt.* O.F. *rober*, *robber*, *rouber*, &c., of Teut. orig. The stem *roub-* = that of REAVE. ROBE. To despoil, to plunder, to deprive *of*.—**Rob'ber**, *n.*—**Rob'bery**, *n.*

Robe, *n.* O.F. *robe*, *robbe*, *roube*, conn. with *rober*, to ROB. Orig. sense 'spoil, booty'. A long outer garment; a form of lady's dress.—*vt.* To dress.—*vi.* To put on robes or vestments.

Rob'in, *n.* O.F. *Robin*, dim. or familiar form of *Robert*. Also **Rob'in red'breast**. A red-breasted bird.

Robust', *a.* L. *rōbustus*, f. *rōbur*. CORROBORATE. Sturdy, hardy, vigorous.

Roch'et, *n.* O.F. *rochet*, dim. of the Teut. word seen in O.H.G. (*h*)*roch* (Ger. *rock*), coat. A linen vestment worn by a bishop.

Rock, *n.* O.F. *roke*, *roque*, &c. (F. *roche*). Orig. unknown. A large rugged mass of stone; hard and massive stone; a hard sweetmeat.—**Rock'ery**, *n.* An artificial mound of stones and soil for ferns, &c.—**Rock'y**,[2] *a.*

Rock, *vt.* O.E. *roccian*, app. f. Teut. stem *rukk-* seen in M.Du. *rucken*, O.H.G. *rucchen* (Ger. *rücken*), to tug, pull. To move (a child) gently to and fro to send it to sleep; to cause to sway to and fro.—*vi.* To sway to and fro.—**Rock'er**, *n.* A curved piece on which a cradle, &c., rocks.

Rock'et, *n.* It. *rocchetta*, app. a dim. of *rocca*, distaff (referring to the form), perh. of Teut. orig. Cf. M.Du. *rocke*, O.H.G. *rocco* (Ger. *rocken*). RATCHET. A projectile firework.

Roco'co, *a.* F. *rococo*, said to be a fanciful formation on stem of *rocaille*, pebble- or shell-work. Like workmanship of the time of Louis XIV and XV as shown in conventional shell- and scroll-work, &c.; old-fashioned.

Rod, *n.* O.E. *rodd*, corresp. in sense to M.Du. *ro(o)de*, O.H.G. *rouda* (Ger. *rute*). Prob. conn. with O.N. *rudda*, club. ROOD. A straight slender stick; as a measure, a pole.

Ro'dent, *a.* L. *rōdens*, *rōdentis*, pres.pple. of *rōdĕre*, to gnaw. CORRODE. ERODE. Gnawing.—*n.* A gnawing animal.

Rodomontade', *n.* F. *rodomontade*—It. *rodomontata*, f. *Rodomonte*, the boastful Saracen in Ariosto's *Orlando Furioso*. A boastful saying; boastful language.

Roe, *n.*[1] O.E. *ráha*, *ráa*, *rá*. Common Teut. A small species of deer.

Roe, *n.*[2] Cf. M.Du. *roch*, O.H.G. *rogo*. A mass [of fish-eggs.

Roga'tion, *n.* L. *rogātio*, *rogātiōnis*, n. of action f. *rogāre*, to ask, propose. ABROGATE. PREROGATIVE. PROROGUE. Solemn prayers (us. in *pl.*).

Rogue, *n.* A cant word. Orig. unknown. An idle vagrant; a rascal (often used playfully). —**Ro'guery**, *n.*—**Ro'guish**, *a.*

Rois'ter, *n.* F. *rustre* in sim. sense, var. of *ruste*, a rustic—L. *rusticus*, RUSTIC. A swaggering fellow.—*vi.* To play the roister.

Rôle, *n.* F. *rôle*. (See next.) Orig. the 'roll' containing an actor's part. A part or character played or assumed.

Roll, *n.*[1] O.F. *roolle*, *rolle*, *role*, &c. (F. *rôle*)—L. *rotulus*, orig. dim. of *rota*, wheel. CONTROL. ENROL. ROTARY. ROULEAU. (See prec. and next.) A piece of paper, &c., rolled up; a list or catalogue; a small loaf.

Roll, *vt.* O.F. *roller*, *roler*, *rouler* (F. *rouler*) —Pop.L. **rotulāre*, f. L. *rotula*, dim. of *rota*. (See prec.) To move by turning over and over; to utter with a full sound; to wind round upon itself; to spread out, to smooth, level.—*vi.* To move by turning over and over; to move or sweep along; to turn over and over; to re-echo; of a ship, to swing from side to side.—*n.*[2] An act of rolling; a rolling sound or motion.—**Rol'ler**, *n.* A cylinder put under something to be moved; a cylinder for smoothing the ground, crushing, &c.; that on which something is rolled up; a long swelling wave.

Rol'lick, *vi.* Orig. unknown. To move in a joyous careless way; to revel *in*.

Ro'ly-po'ly, *n.* App. a fanciful formation on ROLL, *v.* Jammed paste rolled into a pudding.

Ro'man, *a.* L. *Rōmānus*, f. *Rōma*, Rome. Of or connected with Rome or the Church of Rome; applied to the ordinary upright species of type representing most closely the letters of Roman inscriptions and manuscripts.

Romance', *n.* O.F. *romanz*, *romans*—Pop.L. **rōmānice*, adv. f. *Rōmānicus* = *Rōmānus*. (See prec.) The languages descended from Latin; a tale of chivalry; a narrative of events remote from those of ordinary life; romantic fiction; romantic character or associations.—*vi.* To speak after the fashion of romances.—**Roman'ic**, *a.* L. *Rōmānicus*. Descended from Latin.—**Roman'tic**, *a.* F. *romantique*, f. *romant* (now *roman*), romance, novel, later form of *romanz*, &c. Like romances; fictitious fantastic; readily influenced by, appealing to, the imagination; characterized by romance.

Ro'many, *n.* Gipsy *Romani*, fem. and pl. of *Romano*, a. f. *Rom*, man, husband, gipsy. A gipsy; the gipsy language.

Romp, *vi.* Perh. a modification of RAMP. To frolic boisterously.—*n.* One who romps; a boisterous frolic.

Ron'del, *n.* Older F., f. *rond*, ROUND. Also **Ron'deau**. F., later form of *rondel*. A short poem with two rhymes and with the opening words used twice as a refrain.

Rood, *n.* O.E. *ród*, corresp. to O.Fris. *rôde*, O.S. *ruoda*, cross. Cogn. with ROD. The cross; a crucifix; 40 square poles.—**Rood'-screen**, *n.* A screen (properly surmounted by a rood) between the nave and the choir of a church.

Roof, *n.* O.E. *hróf* = O.Icel. *hróf*, boat-shed, Du. *roef*, cabin. The outside upper covering of a building; a ceiling; the top of a coach, &c. —*vt.* To provide with a roof; to be a roof over.

Rook, *n.*[1] O.E. *hróc* = M.Du. *roec*, O.N. *hrókr*. A bird of the crow kind; a cheat or swindler.—*vt.* To cheat.—**Rook'ery**, *n.* A colony of rooks; a cluster of mean houses.

Rook, *n.*[2] O.F. *roc*(*k*), *rok*, &c., ultimately f. Per. *rukh*. Orig. sense doubtful. A piece at chess called also a castle.

Room, *n.* O.E. *rúm*. Common Teut. Space; sufficient space; opportunity, scope; a division of a house.—**Room'y**,[2] *a.* Spacious.

Roost, *n.* O.E. *hróst* = M.Du. *roest*. A perch for fowls.—*vi.* To settle on a roost.

Root, *n.* O.E. *rót*—O.N. *rót*. Orig. stem *wrōt-*, conn. with O.E. *wyrt*, WORT.[1] The part of a plant below the earth's surface; source, origin; an ultimate element of a language.—*v.*[1]*t.* To furnish with roots; to pull *up* or *out* by or as by the roots.

Root, *v.*[2]*i.* Later form of obs. *Wroot*—O.E. *wrótan*. Cf. O.E. *wrót*, Ger. *rüssel*, swine's snout. ROUT, *v.*[2] To grub with the snout.—*vt.* To dig *up* thus; to search *out*, hunt *up*.

Rope, *n.* O.E. *ráp*. Common Teut. A thick cord or line.—*vt.* To secure with a rope; to mark off with a rope.—*vi.* To be drawn out into a filament.—**Rop'**Y,[2] *a.* Sticky and stringy.

Ro'sary, *n.* L. *rosārium*, rose-garden, f. *rosa*. (See next.) A rose-garden; a prescribed set of devotions; a string of beads to assist the memory in reciting the rosary.

Rose, *n.* O.E. *rose*, *róse*—L. *rosa*, prob. f. G. *rhodea*, rose-bush, f. *rhodon*, rose. RHODODENDRON. (See prec.) A well-known flower; a rose-bush; a perforated nozzle; a delicate red or light crimson colour.—*a.* Of the colour. —**Ro'seate**, *a* L. *roseus*, a. f. *rosa* + -ATE.[2] Rose-coloured; rosy.—**Ro'**SERY, *n.* A rose-garden.—**Rosette'**, *n.* F., dim. of *rose*, L. *rosa*. A bunch of ribbons, &c., like a rose; a rose-shaped architectural ornament.—**Rose'-wood**, *n.* A fragrant wood. — **Ro'**SY,[2] *a.* Rose-coloured; bright, hopeful.

Rose'mary, *n.* Alteration (as if for 'rose of Mary') of obs. *Rosmarine*—L. *rōs marīnus*, lit. 'sea-dew' (app. in reference to the plant's growing near the sea). MARINE. An evergreen shrub with fragrant leaves.

Ros'in, *n.* Alteration of RESIN. Resin in a solid state.—*vt.* To smear or rub with rosin.

Ros'ter, *n.* Du. *rooster*, table, list, transferred use of *rooster*, gridiron, f. *roosten*, to ROAST, referring to parallel lines on the paper. A list showing the order of service of officers, regiments, &c.

Ros'trum, *n.* L. *rostrum*, beak, in pl., *rostra*, a platform for speakers in the Roman Forum adorned with the beaks of captured ships. A platform, &c., for public speaking.

Rot, *vi.* and *t.* O.E. *rotian*. Common Teut. To undergo, to affect with, natural decomposition.—*n.* App. f. Scand. Cf. Icel., Norw. *rot*, obs. Da. *rodt*. Decay, putrefaction; a disease of sheep; nonsense.—**Rot'ten**, *a.* O.N. *rotinn*, a pa.pple. in form and cogn. with O.E. *rotian*. Decomposed; corrupt

Ro'tary, *a.* L.L. *rotārius*, f. L. *rota*, wheel. BAROUCHE. ROLL. ROTUND. ROUE. Of motion, circular.—**Rot**ATE',[3] *vi.* and *t.* To move, to cause to move, round a centre.—**Rot**A'TION, *n.* Motion round a centre; a recurring series or period; recurring succession.—**Ro'tat**ORY, *a.*

Rote, *n.* Orig. unknown. Formerly, custom, habit. *By rote*, by mere memory without understanding or reflection.

Rotund', *a.* L. *rotundus*, conn. with *rota*. ROTARY. ROUND. Round, rounded; plump. —**Rotun'da**, *n.* Var. of earlier *rotonda*, It., orig. fem. of *rotondo*, L. *rotundus*. A circular building or hall.—**Rotun'd**ITY, *n.*

Roué, *n.* F., orig. pa.pple. of *rouer*, to break on the wheel, f. *roue*, L. *rota*. ROTARY. ROWEL. A debauchee (as deserving the punishment).

Rouge, *n.* F. *rouge*, red, rouge—L. *rubeus*, red, conn. with *ruber*, RED. RUBY. A red powder used as a cosmetic.—*vt.* To colour with rouge.—*vi.* To use rouge.

Rough, *a.* O.E. *rúh*, *rúg* = M.Du. *ruuch*, O.H.G. *ruuh* (Ger. *rauh*). Not even or smooth; stormy; violent; harsh, rude; wanting grace, rugged; lacking refinement; approximately accurate; in a preliminary form.—*vt.* To make rough; to plan *out* roughly.—*n.* A disorderly fellow. — **Rough'-cast**, *ppl.a.* From CAST, in obs. sense 'to cover by casting (mortar, &c.) on'. Roughly coated with a mixture of lime and gravel.—*n.* Such a mixture.—*vt.* To coat with rough-cast.—**Rough'**EN,[2] *vt.* and *i.* — **Rough'-hew**, *vt.* To shape out roughly.— **Rough'**LY,[2] *adv.*

Rouleau', *n.* F., repg. O.F. *rolel* (pl. *roleaux*), f. *role*, ROLL, *n.*[1] Gold coins made up into a cylindrical packet.

Roulette', *n.* F., dim. of *rouelle*, O.F. *rouele*. ROWEL. A game of chance played on a table with a revolving centre.

Round, *a.* O.F. *rund-*, *rond-*, *round-*, &c. (F. *rond*)—L. *rotundus*. RONDEL. ROTUND. RUNLET. Spherical; circular; approximately correct; of a sum of money, large; sonorous; plain, straightforward.—*n.* Something round; a step of a ladder; movement in a circle; a recurring series of duties, &c.; the circuit performed by sentries; a military patrol; a customary circuit or course; a charge for a firearm.—*adv.* With a circular course; in a circle; throughout; on all sides; in the opposite direction; to a different opinion.—*prep.* So as to encircle or include; about; on all sides of.—*vt.* To make round; to encircle.—*vi.* To become round; to make a turn.—**Round'about**, *n.* A circuitous course; a merry-go-round.—*a.* Circuitous, indirect.—**Roun'del**, *n.* F. *rondel*. RONDEL. A small circular object; a rondel.—**Roun'delay**, *n.* F. *rondelet*, dim. of *rondel*, with ending assimilated to LAY, *n.*[1] A short simple song with a refrain.—**Round'head**, *n.* From the custom of wearing the hair cut close. An adherent of the Parliament in the Civil War. —**Round'**LY,[2] *adv.* Outspokenly, frankly; without qualification; sharply, severely. — **Round rob'in**, *n.* Orig. a sailors' term. App. a use of *Robin*. ROBIN. A petition, &c., having the subscribers' names in a circle so that it may not be known who signed first.

Rouse, *n.* Prob. shortened f. CAROUSE, *to drink carouse* being taken as *to drink a rouse*. A bumper; a bout of drinking, a carousal.

Rouse, *vt.* Orig. obscure. Prob. f. A.F. or O.F. as being originally a hawking and hunting term. To cause (game) to rise or issue from cover; to awaken from sleep, &c.; to stir up.—*vi.* To waken up; to bestir oneself.

Rout, *n.*[1] A.F. *rute*, O.F. *route*—L. *rupta*, fem. pa.pple. of *rumpĕre*, to break. Orig. sense 'division, detachment'. RUPTURE. ROUTE. A band or troop; a disorderly or disreputable crowd; a large evening party.

Rout, *n.*[2] Obs. F. *route*, f. L. *rupta*. (See prec.) Disorderly retreat; an instance of this. —*v.*[1]*t.* To put to rout.

Rout, *v.*[2]*i.* and *t.* Var. of and = ROOT, *v.*[2] Also, to force or fetch *out*.

Route, *n.* F. *route*—L. *rupta* (sc. *via*, way), *i.e.* a way cut through a forest, &c. ROUT.[1] A way, road, course.—**Routine'**, *n.* F., dim. of *route*. A regular course; regular procedure.

Rove, *vi.* Poss a Midland form of obs. *Rave*, to wander, app. of Scand. orig. (cf. Icel. *ráfa* in same sense), and influenced by obs. *Rove*, to practise piracy—M.L.G. or M.Du. *roven*, to rob, conn. with REAVE. To wander about.—*vt.* To wander over.—**Ro'ver**, *n.* M.L.G. or M.Du. *rover*, f. *roven*. A pirate.

Row, *n.*[1] ?O.E. *ráw*, var. of *rǽw*, poss. conn. with M.Du. *rīe*, M.H.G. *rīhe* (Ger. *reihe*). A number of objects in a straight line.

Row, *n.*[2] Slang, of obscure orig. A noisy disturbance or dispute; noise, din.—*v.*[1]*t.* To rate or scold.—*vi.* To make a row.

Row, *v.*[2]*i.* O.E. *rówan* = M.Du. *royen*, O.N. *róa*. Cogn. with O.E. *róther* (RUDDER) and G. *eretmon*, L. *rēmus*, oar. To propel a boat by oars.—*vt.* To propel by oars; to convey by rowing.—*n.*[3] A spell of rowing.

Row'an, *n.* Scand., prob. corresp. to Norw. *raun*. The mountain ash; its berry.

Row'dy, *n.* American, of obscure orig. A disorderly fellow, a rough.—*a.* Disorderly.

Row'el, *n.* O.F. *rouel*, masc., or *rouele*, fem., dim. of *roue*, wheel. ROUE. ROULETTE. A small wheel with sharp points on a spur.

Row'lock, *n.* Prob. altered f. *oarlock*—O.E. *árloc*, f. *ár*, OAR + *loc*, LOCK.[2] An oar-rest.

Roy'al, *a.* O.F. *roial* (F. *royal*)—L. *rēgālis*, REGAL. Of, founded by, befitting, a king; majestic, munificent.—**Roy'al**IST, *n.* A monarchist. — **Roy'al**TY, *n.* Royal dignity or power; royal persons; a payment to a landowner for the right to work minerals, or to an inventor for use of the invention; a payment to an author, &c., depending on sales.

Rub, *vt.* M.E. *rubben* = L.G. *rubben*, of obscure orig. To pass over the surface of with friction; to polish, clean, &c., by rubbing; to remove by rubbing.—*vi.* To come with friction into contact; to become frayed or worn with friction. — *n.* A rubbing; an inequality of ground diverting a bowl from its course; such diversion; an impediment.—**Rub'b**ER, *n.*[1]

Rub'ber, *n.*[2] Orig. unknown. Three games at whist, &c.; two games won out of three.

Rub'bish, *n.* App. conn. with next. Refuse material, trash.—**Rub'bish**Y,[2] *a.*

Rub'ble, *n.* Orig. unknown. Waste fragments of stone; undressed pieces of stone.

Ru'bicund, *a.* L. *rubicundus*, f. *rubēre*, to be red, conn. with *ruber*, RED. Ruddy.

Ru'bric, *n.* L. *rubrīca*, f. *ruber*, RED. A heading of a chapter, &c., a direction in a liturgy (properly one in red).—**Ru'bric**ATE,[3] *vt.* To mark, write, or print in red; to furnish with rubrics.—**Rubric**A'TION, *n.*

Ru'by, *n.* O.F. *rubi*, *rubis*—Romanic stem *rubin-*, obscurely related to L. *rubeus*. ROUGE. A red gem; the colour.—*a.* Of the colour.

Ruck, *n.*[1] App. of Scand. orig. = Norw. *ruka*, perh. conn. with O.N. *hraukr*, RICK. A heap of fuel; a crowd; the undistinguished crowd.

Ruck, *n.*[2] O.N. *hrukka*. A crease or wrinkle. —*vi.* and *t.* To become, to make, creased.

Ruck'le, *vi.* Scand. Cf. Norw. dial. *rukla*. To make a rattling or gurgling sound, esp. in the throat.—*n.* Such a sound.

Rud'der, *n.* O.E. *róther*, steering oar = M.Du. *roder*, O.H.G. *ruadar* (Ger. *ruder*). ROW, *v.*[2] The flat piece of wood, &c., by which a ship is steered.

Rud'dle, *n.* Conn. with dial. *rud*, red colour—O.E. *rudu*, conn. with *réad*, RED. Red ochre.—*vt.* To mark or paint with ruddle.

Rud'dy, *a.* O.E. *rudig*, conn. with *réad*, RED. RUST. Of a healthy red; ruddy-faced.

Rude, *a.* L. *rudis*, unwrought, imperfect, uneducated, &c. ERUDITE. Uneducated; unrefined; uncivil; violent; roughly made.— **Rude**'LY,[2] *adv.*—**Ru'diment**, *n.* L. *rudīmentum*, beginning, first principle, f. *rudis*. In *pl.*, first principles or elements, imperfect beginnings.—**Rudimen't**ARY, *a.*

Rue, *n.*[1] F. *rue*, earlier *rude*—L. *rūta*—G. *rutē*. A plant with bitter strong-smelling leaves.

Rue, *vt.* O.E. *hréowan* = M.Du. *rouwen*, O.H.G. (*h*)*riuwan* (Ger. *reuen*). RUTH. To repent of, to wish undone.—*vi.* To be repentant or regretful.—*n.*[2] O.E. *hréow*. Repentance, regret.—**Rue**'FUL, *a.*

Ruff, *n.*[1] Poss. f. ROUGH, *a.* A plaited collar.

Ruff, *n.*[2] Older F. *roffle*, *rouffle*, earlier *romfle*, *ronfle* = It. *ronfa*, a card game. Perh. corrupted f. F. *triomphe*, It. *trionfo*. TRIUMPH. Formerly, a card game. The act of trumping. —*vt.* To trump.

Ruf'fian, *n.* O.F. *rufyen*, *ruffian*, &c. = Sp. *rufian*, It. *ruffiano*. Orig. obscure. A low brutal fellow.—**Ruf'fian**LY,[1] *a.*

Ruf'fle, *v.*[1]*t.* Orig. doubtful. Cf. L.G. *ruffelen*, to crumple, curl, O.N. *hrufla*, to scratch. To disorder, make uneven or rough; to furnish with ruffles; to annoy, trouble.—*n.*[1] Perturbation; something plaited used as a frill.

Ruf'fle, *v.*[2]*i.* Orig. unknown. To contend; to swagger; to bluster.—*n.*[2] A contention.

Rug, *n.* Perh. Scand. Cf. Norw. dial. *rugga*, coarse coverlet, Sw. *rugg*, ruffled or coarse hair. App. conn. with O.N. *rögg*. RAG. A large piece of woollen stuff used as a covering; a mat for the floor.—**Rug'ged**, *a.* App. of sim. orig. Rough; broken, uneven; furrowed; rude, uncultivated; rough and sturdy.

Ru'in, *n.* O.F. *ruyne*, *ruine*—L. *ruīna*, f. *ruĕre*, to fall. A giving way and falling; the state of having done so; in *pl.*, the remains of something decayed and fallen; a ruined building, &c.; downfall, decay, destruction, something causing this.—*vt.* To reduce to ruins; to destroy; to bring to poverty; to spoil.— **Ruin**A'TION, *n.*—**Ru'in**OUS, *a.*

Rule, *n.* O.F. *riule*, *rule*, &c.—L. *rēgula*, straight stick, pattern, &c., f. *regĕre*. REGENT. RAIL, *n.*[1] REGULAR. A principle of conduct, &c.; a precept or law; a criterion or canon; what is normally the case; government; a strip of wood, &c., for measuring length.—*vt.* To govern; to decree; to mark with parallel lines by means of a ruler.—*vi.* To hold sway; to be prevalent; to decide.—**Rul'**ER, *n.* One who rules; a piece of wood, &c., for guiding a pen, &c., in making straight lines.

Rum, *n.* Perh. abb. f. earlier *rumbullion*, *rumbustion*. Orig. unknown. A spirit distilled from products of sugar-cane.

Rum, *a.* Orig. unknown. Odd, queer.

Rum'ble, *vi.* M.E. *romblen*, *rumblen* = M.Du. *rommelen*, *rummelen*, Da. *rumle*. Imitative. To make a low continuous sound.—*n.* Such a sound; a seat for servants behind a carriage.

Ru'minate, *vt.* L. *rūmināri*, *rūminātus*, to chew the cud, to think over, f. *rūmen*, *rūminis*, gullet. To think over.—*vi.* To chew the cud; to meditate.—**Rumin**A'TION, *n.*— **Ru'min**ANT, *a.* and *n.*

Rum'mage, *vt.* and *i.* From the *n.* in obs. sense 'the arranging of casks, &c., in a ship's hold'—Older F. *arrumage* (F. *arrimage*), of doubtful orig. To search thoroughly.—*n.* In this sense f. the *v.* A thorough search.

Rum'mer, *n.* = Du. *romer*, Ger. *römer*. Perh. 'Roman glass'. A large drinking-glass.

Ru'mour, *n.* O.F. *rumur*, *rumour* (F. *rumeur*)—L. *rūmor*. General talk, hearsay; a current and unauthenticated statement.—*vt.* To circulate by way of rumour.

Rump, *n.* Prob. Scand. Cf. Da. *rumpe*, Sw. *rumpa*. The buttocks.

Rum'ple, *n.* M.Du. *rompel* or M.L.G. *rumpel*(*e*), deriv. of M.Du. *rompe*, M.L.G. *rumpe*, wrinkle. A wrinkle or crease.—*vt.* To wrinkle or crease; to disorder.

Run, *vi.* M.E. *rinne(n)*, *renne(n)*—O.E. *rinnan*=O.N. *rinna*, *renna*, M.Du. *rinnen*, O.H.G. *rinnan*. (The M.E. forms prob. due mainly to O.N.) EMBER.[2] To go with quick movements of the legs; to move rapidly; to compete in a race; to flee; to revolve; to go on, continue; to have a certain purport.—*vt.* To traverse by running; to expose oneself, to be exposed, to (danger, &c.); to cause to run; to land (smuggled goods).—*n.* An act or spell of running; a spell or course; a rush of demands on a bank, &c.; course, direction, tendency.—**Run'**NER, *n.* One who runs; a creeping stem thrown out by the strawberry, &c., and taking root; a piece on which a sledge, &c., slides.

Run'agate, *n.* Alteration of obs. *Renegate*—Med.L. *renegātus*. RENEGADE. A deserter, a fugitive; a vagabond.

Rune, *n.* O.N. and Icel. *rún*, cogn. with O.E. *rún*, whisper, mystery, M.Du. *rune*, whisper, secret counsel. A character of the earliest Teutonic alphabet.—**Ru'n**IC, *a.*

Rung, *n.* O.E. *hrung*=M.Du. *rong(h)e*, O.H.G. *runga*. A cross-bar or spoke.

Run'let, *n.* O.F. *rondelet*, dim. of *rondelle*, little barrel, f. *rond-*, ROUND. A cask of varying capacity.

Run'nel, *n.* Altered (after *run*) f. obs. *rinel*—O.E. *rinnelle*, *rynele*, f. stem of RUN. A small stream or channel; a gutter.

Rupee', *n.* Urdū *rūpiyah*, f. Skr. *rūpya*, wrought silver. The Indian monetary unit; a silver coin = 1*s.* 4*d.*

Rup'ture, *n.* L. *ruptūra*, a fracture, f. *rumpĕre*, *ruptum*, to break. ABRUPT. ROUT, *n.*[1] and [2]. ROUTE. A breach of friendly relations; abdominal hernia; a breaking or bursting; a break.—*vt.* To break or burst; to affect with hernia.—*vi.* To break or burst.

Ru'ral, *a.* L. *rūrālis*, f. *rūs*, *rūris*, country. RUSTIC. Of or pertaining to the country.

Ruse, *n.* F. *ruse*, vbl.n. f. *ruser*. RUSH, *v.* An artifice, trick, stratagem.

Rush, *n.*[1] O.E. *risc*, *risce*, corresp. to M.Du. *risch*, M.L.G. *risch(e)*. A plant with straight stems or stalks growing in damp places; a stem or stalk of this.—**Rush'**Y,[2] *a.*

Rush, *vt.* A.F. *russher*, var. of *russer* = O.F. *re(h)usser*, *ruser*, &c., to drive back, to retreat, of doubtful orig. RUSE. To impel, drag, &c., violently; to take by sudden assault.—*vi.* To move violently or rapidly.—*n.*[2] Rushing.

Rusk, *n.* Sp. or Pg. *rosca*, twist, twisted roll of bread. A hard crisp cake of bread.

Rus'set, *n.* O.F. *rousset*, dim. of *rous* (F. *roux*), reddish—L. *russus*, red. RISSOLE. A woollen cloth of a reddish-brown or similar colour; the colour; a variety of apple.—*a.* Of the colour; made of russet; rustic, simple.

Rus'sia (leath'er), *n.* A durable leather used in bookbinding.

Rust, *n.* O.E. *rúst* = M.Du. *roest*, O.H.G. and Ger. *rost*. Cogn. with RUDDY. The coating formed on iron, &c., by the action of air or moisture; a disease in plants.—*vi.* and *t.* To contract, to affect with, rust.—**Rust'**Y,[2] *a.*

Rus'tic, *a.* L. *rusticus*, f. *rūs*. RURAL. ROISTER. Of, living in, characteristic of, the country; lacking elegance or refinement.—*n.* A peasant. —**Rus'tic**ATE,[3] *vi.* To live a country life.—*vt.* To banish from a university.—**Rustic**A'TION, *n.*—**Rustic'**ITY, *n.*

Rus'tle, *vi.* Imitative. Cf. Du. *ridselen*, *ritselen*. To emit on movement a succession of light rapid sounds.—*n.* Such a succession.

Rut, *n.*[1] O.F. *rut*, var. of *ruit*—L. *rugītus*, a roaring, f. *rugīre*, to roar. The annual sexual excitement of the male of deer and other animals.—*v.*[1]*i.* To be under the influence of this.

Rut, *n.*[2] Orig. obscure. A furrow made by a wheel; a settled habit or course of life.—*v.*[2]*t.* To mark with ruts.—**Rut't**Y,[2] *a.*

Ruth, *n.* M.E. *reuthe*, *rewthe*, f. *rewen*, to RUE. Pity.—**Ruth'**LESS, *a.* Pitiless.

Rye, *n.* O.E. *ryge* = O.N. *rugr*. A kind of grain; the plant yielding it.

Rye'-grass, *n.* Alteration of earlier *Raygrass*, f. obs. *ray*, rye-grass, of obscure orig. A kind of grass cultivated for fodder.

Ry'ot, *n.* Urdū *raiyat* of Arab. orig. An Indian peasant or husbandman.

S

Sab'bath, *n.* L. *sabbatum*—G. *sabbaton*—Heb. *shabbāth*, f. root *shābath*, to rest. Among the Jews, the seventh day of the week; in Christian use, Sunday.—**Sabbat**A'RIAN, *n.* A strict observer of Sunday.—*a.* Having relation to the tenets of Sabbatarians.—**Sabbat'**IC, **Sabbat'**ICAL, *aa.*

Sa'ble, *n.* O.F. *sable*, sable fur, prob. f. Slavonic. Cf. Icel. *safal*, the animal. A small arctic and sub-arctic quadruped; its fur; black; in *pl.*, mourning garments.—*a.* Black.

Sa'bre, *n.* F., altered f. *sable*—Ger. *sabel* (now *säbel*), prob. f. some Oriental language. A cavalry sword.—*vt.* To strike with a sabre.—**Sa'bretache**, *n.* F.—Ger. *säbeltasche*, f. *tasche*, pocket. A satchel suspended from a cavalry officer's sword-belt.

Sac, *n.* F. *sac*, or L. *saccus*. SACK.[1] A bag-like cavity in an animal or vegetable body.

Sac'charine, *a.* L. *saccharum* or G. *sakchar*, *sakcharon*, SUGAR, of Oriental orig. + chemical suff. *-ine*. Sugary; composed of sugar.

Sacerdo'tal, *a.* L. *sacerdōtālis*, f. *sacerdos*, *sacerdōtis*, priest. Of priests or priesthood; ascribing supernatural powers to priests.—**Sacerdo'tal**ISM, *n.*

Sack, *n.*[1] O.E. *sacc*—L. *saccus*, G. *sakkos*, prob. of Oriental orig. SAC. SATCHEL. A large bag; a sackful.—*v.*[1]*t.* To put into a sack.—**Sack'cloth**, *n.* A coarse fabric used in making sacks.

Sack, *n.*[2] F. *sac*—It. *sacco*, of doubtful orig. Plundering.—*v.*[2]*t.* To plunder.

Sack'but, *n.* F. *saquebute*, presumably = (though the change in sense has not been accounted for) O.N.F. *saqueboute*, explained as 'a hooked lance for pulling men off their horses'. (The first element is O.N.F. *saquier*, to pull, draw. The second is by some connected with *bouter*. BUTT.[3]) An obsolete wind-instrument of the trumpet kind.

Sac'rament, *n.* F. *sacrement*—L. *sacrāmentum*, an engagement, oath, in L.L., a sacrament, f. *sacrāre*, to consecrate, f. *sacer*, sacred, f. base *sac-* of *sancīre*. SAINT. (And see next.) The name common to certain ceremonies of the Christian Church, applied esp. to the Eucharist.—**Sacramen'**TAL, *a.*

Sa'cred, *a.* From obs. *Sacre* (F. *sacrer*—L. *sacrāre* (see prec.), to CONSECRATE) + *-ed*. Dedicated, consecrated; inviolable.—**Sa'cred**LY,[2] *adv.*—**Sac'rifice**, *n.* F. *sacrifice*—L. *sacrificium*, f. *sacrificus*, sacrificial, f. *sacer* (see prec.) + *-ficus*, -FIC. The making of an offering to a deity; the thing offered; the giving up of something in order to gain an end; the loss thus entailed.—*vt.* To offer as a sacrifice; to give up in order to gain an end; to permit thus injury to (a person or his interests).—*vi.* To offer sacrifice.—**Sacrifi'**CIAL, *a.*—**Sac'rist**, *n.* O.F. *sacriste*—L. *sacrista*, f. *sacer*. Also **Sac'ristan**. Med.L. *sacristānus*, f. *sacrista*. SEXTON. An official in charge of sacred vessels, &c.—**Sac'risty**, *n.* F. *sacristie*—Med.L. *sacristia*, f. *sacrista*. The repository for such vessels, &c.—**Sac'rosanct**, *a.* L. *sacrōsanctus*, f. *sacrō*, ablative of *sacrum*, holy rite (neut. of *sacer*) + *sanctus*, pa.pple. of *sancīre*. SAINT. Secured from violation by religious sanction, sacred.

Sac'rilege, *n.* O.F. *sacrilege*—L. *sacrilegium*, f. *sacrilegus*, a stealer of sacred things, f. *sacer* (SACRAMENT) + *legĕre*, to gather. Robbery or profanation of sacred things.—**Sacrileg'i**OUS, *a.*

Sa'crum, *n.* L. (*os*) *sacrum*, sacred (bone), neut. of *sacer*, sacred, so called from sacrificial use. SACRAMENT. The bone forming the back of the pelvis.

Sad, *a.* O.E. *sæd*, sated. Common Teut. Cogn. with L. *satis*, enough. SATE. Sorrowful; expressive of or causing sorrow; deplorably bad; of colour, dull, sober.—**Sad'**LY,[2] *adv.*—**Sad'd**EN,[2] *vt.* and *i.*

Sad'dle, *n.* O.E. *sadol*, *sadul*. Common Teut. A seat for a rider; the part of the harness of a shaft-horse which bears the shafts; a joint of mutton, &c. including the two loins.—**Sad'dl**ER, *n.*—**Sad'dl**ERY, *n.*

Sad'ducee, *n.* L.L. *saddūcaeus*—Late G. *saddoukaios*—Late Heb. *caddūqī*, app. f. the personal name *Caddūq* (Zadok, prob. the high-priest of David's time). One of a Jewish sect or party who denied the resurrection of the dead and the obligation of the traditional law.—**Sadduce'**AN, *a.*

Safe, *n.* M.E. *sauf*, *sāf*—F. *sauf*—L. *salvus*. SAVE. Unharmed; not exposed to danger; affording security; not involving risk; secured, not dangerous; trustworthy; cautious.—*n.* A receptacle for safe storage.—**Safe'**LY,[2] *adv.*—**Safe'**TY, *n.*—**Safe-con'duct**, *n.* F. *sauf-conduit*, f. *sauf* + *conduit*, L.L. *conductus*. CONDUCT, *n.* A permit securing safe passage.—**Safe'-guard**, *n.* F. *sauve-garde*, f. *sauve* (fem. of *sauf*) + *garde*, GUARD, *n.* A safe-conduct; a protection.—*vt.* To protect.

Saf'fron, *n.* F. *safran*—Arab. *za'farān*. An orange-red colouring matter got from the crocus; the colour.—*a.* Of the colour.

Sag, *vi.* M.E. *saggen*. Not in O.E. Cf. Du. *zakken*, Sw. *sacka*, to subside. To subside gradually; to droop; to bend downwards in the middle.

Sa'ga, *n.* O.N. and Icel. *saga*, narrative, story, corresp. to O.E. *sagu*. SAW.[2] An Icelandic or Norwegian mediæval narrative composition in prose.

Saga'cious, *a.* L. *sagax*, *sagācis* (f. *sāgīre*, to discern acutely) + -OUS. PRESAGE. SEEK. Acute in mind, shrewd; showing sagacity.—**Saga'cious**LY,[2] *adv.*—**Sagac'**ITY, *n.*

Sage, *n.*[1] F. *sauge*—L. *salvia*, f. its supposed healing virtues, f. *salvāre*, to heal, f. *salvus*, SAFE. An aromatic culinary herb.

Sage, *a.* F. *sage*—L. *sapĕre*, to be wise. SAPID. Wise, discreet; based on sound judgement.—*n.*[2] A man of deep wisdom.—**Sage'**LY,[2] *adv.*

Sa'go, *n.* Malay *sāgū*. A starch got from several palms and used as food; the tree.

Sail, *n.* O.E. *segl*, *segel*. Common Teut. A piece of canvas attached to a ship's mast to catch the wind; an apparatus on a windmill for this purpose; collective *sing.*, sailing-vessels; an act of sailing, a voyage (in this sense f. the *v.*).—*vi.* To travel by water; of a ship, to move through the water; to start on a voyage.—*vt.* To navigate.—**Sail'**OR, *n.*

Sain'foin, *n.* F. *sainfoin*, app. f. *sain*, health-giving, L. *sānus* (SANE) + *foin*, L. *faenum*, hay. A low-growing herb used as fodder.

Saint, *a.* O.F. *saint*—L. *sanctus*, pa.pple. of *sancīre*, to render sacred. SACRAMENT. SANCTIFY. Holy; prefixed to the name of a canonized person.—*n.* One of the dead in heaven; one canonized.—*vt.* To canonize.—**Saint'ed**, *ppl.a.* Canonized; of holy life; sacred.—**Saint'**LY,[1] *a.*—**Saint'li**NESS, *n.*

Sake, *n.* O.E. *sacu*, strife, law-suit, affair. Cf. Icel. *sōk*, charge, crime, Du. *zaak*, matter. FORSAKE. In phrases *for* (one's, a thing's) *sake*, *for the sake of.* Out of consideration for (a person), on (a person's) account; on account of, in order to attain (something).

Salaam', *n.* Arab. *salām* = Heb. *shālōm*, peace. The Oriental salutation, 'Peace (be upon you)'; a ceremonious bow.—*vt.* To make a salaam to.—*vi.* To make a salaam.

Sala'cious, *a.* L. *salax*, *salācis* (f. root of *salīre*, to leap) + -OUS. SALIENT. Lustful, lecherous.—**Salac'**ITY, *n.*

Sal'ad, *n.* O.F. *salade*—O.It. *salata*, salad of herbs, pa.pple. fem. of *salare*, to salt, f. *sale*, L. *sal*, SALT. A seasoned dish of uncooked herbs, &c.; a herb, &c., used for such a dish.

Sal'amander, *n.* F. *salamandre*—L. *salamandra*—G. *salamandra*, a kind of lizard, of Eastern orig. A lizard-like animal fabled to live in fire; a tailed amphibious creature.

Sal'ary, *n.* A.F. *salarie*—L. *salārium*, orig. money to buy salt, f. *sal*, SALT. Fixed payment for non-manual or non-mechanical work.—*vt.* To pay a salary to.

Sale, *n.* O.E. *sala*, prob. f. O.N. *sala*, fem., *sal*, neut. O.Teut. **salā*, gift, delivery, **saljan*, to SELL. A selling; an auction.

Sal'ic, *a.* F. *salique*, belonging to the Salii, a Frankish tribe. *Salic law*, a law excluding females from dynastic succession.

Sa'lient, *a.* L. *saliens*, *salientis*, pres.pple. of *salīre*, to leap. ASSAIL. INSULT. SALACIOUS. SALLY. Of an angle, pointing outward; jutting out; prominent.—**Sa'li**ENCE, *n.*

Sa'line, *a.* L. *salīnus* (as in *salīnae*, salt-pits), f. *sal*, SALT. Impregnated with salt, salty.

Sali'va, *n.* L. *saliva*. A colourless liquid which assists mastication.—**Sal'iv**ARY, *a.*—**Sal'iv**ATE,[3] *vt.* and *i.* To cause to have, to have, an unusual flow of saliva.

Sal'low, *a.* O.E. *salo*. Cf. O.H.G. *salo*, dark-coloured, whence F. *sale*, dirty. Of a sickly yellow colour.

Sal'low, *n.* O.E. *sealh*. Cogn. with L. *salix*, willow. A kind of willow.

Sal'ly, *vi.* F. *saillir*, to leap, to issue forth, f. L. *salīre*. SALIENT. To issue suddenly, esp. from a fort; to set out.—*n.* A rush out; a setting out; an outburst; a witticism.

Sal'mon, *n.* A.F. *samoun*—L. *salmo*, *salmōnis*. Perh. f. *salīre*. SALIENT. A large fish with pink flesh prized for food and sport.

Saloon', *n.* F. *salon*, large room, *salle*, room—O.H.G. *sal* (Ger. *saal*), abode, hall, room. Cf. Du. *zaal*, hall. A large apartment or public room; a large cabin in a ship.

Salt, *n.* O.E. *sealt.* Common Teut. Cogn. with G. *hals*, L. *sal.* SALAD. SALARY. SALINE. SAUCE. SAUCER. SAUSAGE. A substance used for seasoning and preserving food (often *fig.*); a chemical compound formed by the union of an acid and a metal.—*a.* Impregnated or preserved with salt; tasting like salt; pungent.—*vt.* To preserve with salt; to make pungent. — **Salt'**ISH, **Salt'**Y,[2] *aa.* — **Salt'**NESS, *n.*—**Salt'-cellar**, *n.* Corrupted from A.F. *saler*, salt-holder (the *salt* being thus superfluous)—L.L. *salārium*, in same sense, f. *sal.* A small vessel for salt.—**Saltpe'tre**, *n.* O.F. *salpetre*—Med.L. *salpetra*, prob. for *sal petrae*, salt of the rock. PETRIFY. Nitre.

Sal'tire, *n.* O.F. *saut(e)oir, saultoir*, &c., orig., a triangular stirrup—L.L. *saltātōrium*, stirrup, f. *saltātōrius*, a. f. *saltātor*, leaper, f. *saltāre*, *saltātum*, freq. of *salīre*, to leap. SALIENT. In *heraldry*, a St. Andrew's cross.

Salu'brious, *a.* With -OUS f. L. *salūbris*, f. *salus, salūtis*, health, cogn. with *salvus*, SAFE. Favourable to health.—**Salu'bri**TY, *n.*

Sal'utary, *a.* L. *salūtāris*, f. *salus* (see prec.). Conducive to health or well-being; wholesome.

Salute', *vt.* L. *salūtāre*, to wish health to, greet, f. *salus.* SALUBRIOUS. To greet in words or with a gesture; to kiss; in mil. and naval use, to pay respect to (a superior) in a prescribed way.—*n.* An utterance or gesture by which one salutes another; a kiss; in mil. and naval use, a paying of respect to a superior.—**Saluta'**TION, *n.*

Sal'vage, *n.* L.L. *salvāgium*, f. *salvāre*, to SAVE. A payment due for saving a ship from peril; the action of saving a ship or other property from peril or fire; property so saved. —**Salve**, *v.*[1]*t.* Back-formation f. *salvage.* To save from peril, &c.—**Salva'**TION, *n.* The saving of the soul; preservation from mishap; a means of salvation.

Salve, *n.* O.E. *sealf.* Cf. Du. *zalf*, Ger. *salbe.* A healing ointment.—*v.*[2]*t.* To anoint with salve (often *fig.*).

Sal'ver, *n.* Formed on F. *salve*, a tray for presenting things to a king—Sp. *salva*, a tray on which a cup was placed after tasting for poison, f. *salvo*, L. *salvus*, SAFE. A tray for handing refreshments, presenting letters, &c.

Sal'vo, *n.* Orig. *salva*—It. *salva*, salutation, salvo, perh. formed on L. *salvē!* hail! imp. of *salvēre*, to be well, f. *salvus*, SAFE. A simultaneous discharge of firearms, properly by way of a salute.

Sal volat'ile, *n.* Mod.L. *sal volātile*, 'VOLATILE SALT'. An aromatic preparation of ammonia applied in fainting fits, &c.

Same, *a.* M.E. *same*—O.N. *same, samr*, a Common Teut. word not found in O.E. Cogn. with G. *homos*, same, and also with G. *hama*, L. *simul*, together. ANOMALOUS. SIMULATE. Not different, identical.—**Same'**NESS, *n.* The quality of being the same; monotony.

Sam'phire, *n.* Formerly *sampere, sampire*—F. (*herbe de*) *Saint Pierre*, lit. 'St. Peter's HERB'. A plant growing on rocks by the sea the leaves of which are used in pickles.

Sam'ple, *n.* M.E. *sample*, aphetic f. O.F. *essample*, EXAMPLE. A specimen.—*vt.* To take or present a sample of.—**Sam'pler**, *n.* Aphetic f. O.F. *essamplaire, exemplaire*, EXEMPLAR. A beginner's exercise in embroidery.

San'ative, *a.* Med.L. *sānātīvus*, f. *sānāre*, *sānātum*, to heal, f. *sānus*, whole, healthy. SANE. Healing, curative; pertaining to healing.—Sim. **San'at**ORY.—**Sanato'rium**, *n.* Mod.L. *sānātōrium*, f. *sānāre.* An establishment for invalids; a health resort.

Sanc'tify, *vt.* O.F. *saintifier*—Eccles.L. *sanctificāre*, to make holy, f. *sanctus*, holy + *facĕre*, to make. SAINT. To set apart as holy; to purify from sin; to give religious sanction to. —**Sancti**FICA'TION.—**Sanc'timony**, *n.* L. *sanctimōnia*, holiness, f. *sanctus.* Assumed or outward saintliness.—**Sanctimo'ni**OUS, *a.*—**Sanc'tity**, *n.* L. *sanctitas*, f. *sanctus.* Saintliness; inviolability; in *pl.*, sacred obligations or objects.—**Sanc'tuary**, *n.* L. *sanctuārium*, a shrine, f. *sanctus.* A holy place; a place affording immunity to a fugitive from justice; such immunity, the privilege of affording it.—**Sanc'tum**, *n.* Neut. of *sanctus.* A sacred place or shrine.

Sanc'tion, *n.* L. *sanctio, sanctiōnis*, a rendering sacred, f. *sancīre.* SAINT. A penalty for breaking, a reward for observing, a law; binding force given to an oath; solemn ratification; permission; countenance.—*vt.* To ratify; to permit; to countenance.

Sand, *n.* O.E. *sand.* Common Teut. Cogn. with G. *amathos.* Fine particles of rock; in *pl.*, tracts of sand.—*vt.* To cover or mix with sand.—**Sand'stone**, *n.* A rock composed of sand.—**Sand'**Y,[2] *a.*

San'dal, *n.*[1] L. *sandalium*—G. *sandalion*, sandal, dim. of *sandalon* in same sense, of unknown orig., prob. Persian. A shoe consisting of a sole with straps.

San'dal, *n.*[2] Also **San'dalwood**. Med.L *sandalum*, app. ultimately f. Skr. *chandana* A scented wood obtained from several species of trees.

Sand'wich, *n.* Said to be named f. the 4th Earl of *Sandwich*, who once spent twenty-four hours at the gaming-table eating only some slices of cold beef placed between slices of toast. An article of food like this, made of meat, &c., and bread.—*vt.* To insert between two other and widely different things.

Sane, *a.* L. *sānus*, healthy, sane. SAINFOIN. SANATIVE. Of sound mind; rational, sensible. —**San'**ITY, *n.*—**San'it**ARY, *a.* Relating to the conditions affecting health; free from injurious influences.—**Sanit**A'TION, *n.* The improving of sanitary conditions.

San'guine, *a.* F. *sanguin*—L. *sanguineus*, f. *sanguis, sanguinis*, blood. CONSANGUINEOUS. Blood-red; disposed to hopefulness or confidence; hopeful or confident.—**San'guin**ARY, *a.* Bloody; bloodthirsty.

San'hedrim, San'hedrin, *n.* Late Heb *sanhedrin*—G. *sunedrion*, council, lit., 'a sitting together', f. *sun* (SYN-) + *hedra*, seat. The highest court of justice and supreme council at ancient Jerusalem.

Sap, *n.*[1] O.E. *sæp.* Common W. Germanic. The vital juice of plants.—**Sap'**LESS, *a.*—**Sap'ling**, *n.* -LING (1). A young tree.

Sap, *n.*[2] F. *sappe* (now *sape*)—It. *zappa*, spade, spadework, of uncertain orig. A constructing of covered trenches for approaching a besieged place; such a trench.—*vi.* To construct such trenches.—*vt.* To undermine; to destroy insidiously.—**Sap'per**, *n.*

Sap'id, *a.* L. *sapidus*, f. *sapĕre*, to taste, also, to be wise. INSIPID. SAGE, *a.* SAVOUR. Savoury; having taste or flavour.—**Sapid'**ITY, *n.*—**Sa'pient**, *a.* L. *sapiens, sapientis*, pres.pple. of *sapĕre.* Wise (generally used ironically).—**Sa'pi**ENCE, *n.*

Sapona'ceous, *a.* Mod.L. *sāpōnāceus* (f. L.

sāpo, sāpōnis, SOAP) + -OUS. Like or containing soap.

Sapph'ire, *n.* O.F. *safir*—L. *sapphīrus*—G. *sappheiros*, prob. Semitic. A blue gem.

Sar'aband, *n.* F. *sarabande*—Sp. *zarabanda*, prob. of Oriental orig. A slow stately Spanish dance; music written for it.

Sar'casm, *n.* L.L. *sarcasmus*—G. *sarkasmos*, f. *sarkazein*, to tear flesh, bite the lips in rage, sneer, f. *sarx*, flesh. A bitter or cutting expression; such language.—**Sarcas'tic**, *a.*—**Sarcas'tically**, *adv.* -AL. -LY.[2]

Sarcoph'agus, *n.*; *pl.* **-ph'agi**. G. *sarkophagos*, flesh-consuming, hence, a kind of limestone, f. *sarx* (see prec.) + *phagein*, to eat. A stone coffin.

Sardine,' *n.* F. *sardine*—L. *sardīna*, f. *sarda*, G. *sardē*, prob. the sardine. A small fish of the herring family.

Sardon'ic, *a.* F. *sardonique*, as if f. a L. **sardonicus*—G. *sardanios* or *sardonios*, first in Odyssey, 20, 302 (neut. sing. as *adv.*) of inward smiling. Orig. and real meaning unknown. Of laughter or a smile, bitter, scornful; applied also to persons.

Sarsaparil'la, *n.* Sp. *zarzaparrilla*, f. *zarza*, bramble + (it is said) **parrilla*, dim. of *parra*, vine, the plant being a climbing one and the berries having some resemblance to grapes. A tropical-American plant; the dried roots used as a tonic, &c.

Sar'senet, **Sar'cenet**, *n.* A.F. *sarzinett*, prob., with meaning 'Saracen cloth', a dim. of *Sarzin*, L.L. *Saracēnus*, G. *Sarakēnos*, Saracen, of uncertain orig. A fine silk material.

Sarto'rial, *a.* L. *sartōrius* (f. *sartor*, patcher, f. *sarcīre*, *sartum*, to patch) + -AL. Pertaining to a tailor.

Sash, *n.*[1] F. *châssis*, window-frame—L. *capsa*, CASE.[2] A frame forming a window.

Sash, *n.*[2] Orig. *shash*—Arab. *shāsh*, muslin, turban-'sash'. A scarf for the body.

Sa'tan, *n.* L. *satan*—G. *satan*—Heb. *sātān*, adversary. The Devil.—**Satan'ic**, *a.*

Sat'chel, *n.* O.F. *sachel*—L. *saccellus*, dim. of *saccus*, SACK.[1] A small bag.

Sate, *vt.* App. alteration, after L. *satis*, enough, *satur*, full, of obs. *Sade* in same sense—O.E. *sadian*. Cf. O.E. *sæd*, sated. SAD. SATIRE. SATISFY. SATURATE. To satisfy or indulge to the full; to surfeit. Sim. **Sa'tiate**, *vt.* L. *satiāre*, *satiātum*, f. *satis*.—**Sa'tiable**, *a.*—**Sati'ety**, *n.* A being surfeited; disgust, weariness.

Sateen', *n.* From SATIN after *velveteen*. A cotton or woollen fabric resembling satin.

Sat'ellite, *n.* F. *satellite*—L. *satelles*, *satellitis*, attendant, guard. One of the retinue of a person of importance; a small planet revolving round a larger.

Sat'in, *n.* F. *satin*, prob. f. L.L. (*pannus*) *sētīnus*, silken (cloth), f. *sēta*, silk, L. *saeta*, *sēta*, bristle. A glossy silk fabric.

Sat'ire, *n.* F. *satire*—L. *satira*, earlier *satura* (f. *satura* (*lanx*), full (dish), fem. of *satur*, full), a medley, hence, a discursive poem, a poem assailing prevalent follies or vices. SATE. A poem or prose composition of this nature; satirical composition; the employment of sarcasm, &c.—**Satir'ic**, **Satir'ical**, *aa.*—**Sat'irist**, *n.*—**Sat'irize**, *vt.*

Sat'isfy, *vt.* O.F. *satisfier*—L. *satisfacĕre*, *satisfactum*, lit., 'to make enough', f. *satis* (SATE) + *facĕre*, to make. To pay off, fulfil; to content; to convince; to solve (a doubt, &c.).—**Satisfac'tion**, *n.*—**Satisfac'tory**, *a.*

Sat'rap, *n.* L. *satrapa*—G. *satrapēs*—Old Per. *khsatra-pāvā*, guardian of a province, f. *khsatra*, province + *pā-*, to protect. The governor of an ancient Persian province.

Sat'urate, *vt.* L. *saturāre*, *saturātum*, f. *satur*, full. SATE. To soak thoroughly *with*; to cause to dissolve the maximum amount.—**Satura'tion**, *n.*

Sat'urn, *n.* L. *Sāturnus*. An Italic god; the most remote of the seven planets.—**Sat'urday**, *n.* O.E. *Sætern*(*es*)*dæg*, a translation of L. *Sāturni dies*, the DAY of (the planet) Saturn. The seventh day of the week.—**Satur'nine**, *a.* O.F. *saturnin*. Born under the malignant influence of the planet; hence, sluggish, cold, gloomy.

Sat'yr, *n.* L. *satyrus*—G. *saturos*. A woodland god, part man, part beast, of the train of Bacchus.—**Satyr'ic**, *a.*

Sauce, *n.* F. *sauce*—Pop.L. *salsa*, a thing salted, fem. of L. *salsus*, salted, f. *sal*, SALT. A liquid preparation for giving a relish to food.—*vt.* To prepare with sauces.—**Sau'cy**,[2] *a.* Impertinent, rude (often not seriously used, and implying sprightliness or piquancy).—**Sau'cer**, *n.* O.F. *saussier*, sauce-dish, f. *sauce*. A shallow vessel under a cup.

Saun'ter, *vi.* Orig. unknown. To walk in a leisurely way.—*n.* A leisurely walk or gait.

Sau'rian, *a.* G. *saura*, *sauros*, lizard. Of the lizard order.—*n.* A reptile of the order.

Sau'sage, *n.* O.N.F. *saussiche*—L.L. *salsīcia*, use as *n.* of fem. of **salsīcius*, a. f. *salsus*, salted. SAUCE. Minced meat stuffed into a prepared intestine of an ox, &c.

Sav'age, *a.* F. *sauvage*—L. *silvāticus*, wild, woodland, f. *silva*, a wood. SILVAN. Wild, untamed; unpolished; uncivilized; ferocious; enraged.—*n.* An uncivilized person.—**Sav'agely**,[2] *adv.*—**Sav'agery**, *n.*

Savan'nah, *n.* Sp. *zavana*, app. a Carib word. A treeless plain, esp. in tropical America.

Savant, *n.* F., use as *n.* of early pres.pple. (now *sachant*) of *savoir*, to know—L. *sapĕre*. SAPID. A man of learning or science.

Save, *vt.* O.F. *salver*, *sauver*—L.L. *salvāre*, f. L. *salvus*, SAFE. SALVAGE. To deliver from peril; to deliver from sin and its consequences; to give immunity *from* hurt or annoyance; to guard from hurt; to keep intact; to be in time for; to set apart, lay by; to store up by economy; to avoid spending or consuming; to use or consume sparingly.—**Sav'ing**, *vbl.n.* The action of the *v.*; an instance of this; money saved (gen. in *pl.*).—*prep.* and *conj.* Except.—**Sav'iour**, *n.* O.F. *sauveour*—L.L. *salvātor*, f. *salvāre*. One who saves, esp. of Christ.

Sav'eloy, *n.* Corr. of F. *cervelas*, O.F. *cervelat*—It. *cervellata*, f. *cervello*, brain (L. *cerebellum*, dim. of *cerebrum*. CEREBRAL); so called as having originally been made of pigs' brains. A highly seasoned cooked and dried sausage.

Sa'vory, *n.* Ultimately f. L. *saturēia*. Proximate source uncertain. A herb used for flavouring ingredients in cooking.

Sa'vour, *n.* O.F. *savur*, *savour*—L. *sapor*, f. *sapĕre*, to taste. SAPID. Quality in relation to taste; agreeable taste; smell, perfume.—*vi.* To be *well* or *ill* pleasing; *to savour of*, to show traces of, have characteristics of.—*vt.* To taste; to relish, like.—**Sa'voury**,[2] *a.* As *n.*, a dish served as a stimulant or digestive.

Saw, *n.*[1] O.E. *sagu*, lit. 'cutter', f. root *seg-*, *sek-*, to cut. Cf. L. *secāre*, to cut. INSECT.

SCYTHE. SECTION. SEDGE. SICKLE. A toothed cutting instrument.—*vt.* To cut or form with a saw.—**Saw'yer**, *n.* Altered form of **Saw'**ER. A workman who saws.

Saw, *n.*[2] O.E. *sagu*, a saying. Cf. O.E. *secgan*, to SAY. A pithy saying, a proverb.

Sax'ifrage, *n.* O.F. *saxifrage*—L. *saxifraga* (sc. *herba.* HERB), f. *saxum*, rock + *frag-*, root of *frangěre*, to break. FRACTION. App. so named because many species grow in the clefts of rocks. Applied to various kinds of Alpine and rock plants with tufted foliage and white, yellow, or red flowers.

Say, *n.*[1] F. *saie*—L. *saga*, pl. of *sagum*, military cloak. LINSEY-WOOLSEY. A fine cloth like serge.

Say, *vt.* O.E. *secgan*, prob. cogn. with G. *enepein* (*en-seq-*), L. *inquam* (*in-squ-*). To utter, pronounce; to make known, state, declare; to recite, repeat.—*vi.* To make a statement.—*n.*[2] A voice in a matter; what one has to say.—**Say'ing**, *vbl.n.* The action of the *v.*; a proverb.

Scab, *n.* O.N. *skabbr, corresp. to O.E. *sceabb*, f. which comes SHABBY. Cf. Sw. *skabb*, Da. *skab.* A skin-disease; a disease of plants; the crust which forms over a wound; a mean, low fellow.—**Scab'**BY,[2] *a.*

Scab'bard, *n.* A.F. *escauberc* (found only in pl. *escaubers*), of doubtful orig. (*-Berc* is prob. f. Teut. *bergan*, to protect. BOROUGH.) The sheath of a sword or dagger.

Sca'bious, *n.* Med.L. *scabiōsa* (sc. *herba.* HERB), fem. of L. *scabiōsus*, a. f. *scabies*, the itch, f. *scaběre*, to scratch, scrape, prob. conn. with O.E. *sceafan.* SHAVE, *v.* A plant with blue, pink, or white flowers formerly held efficacious for the cure of certain skin-diseases.

Scaffold, *n.* O.F. *schaffaut*, *eschaffaut*, of doubtful orig. A temporary platform for workmen; a platform on which a criminal is executed.—**Scaffolding**, *vbl.n.* A framework of platforms and their supports for workmen.

Scald, *n.*[1], **Skald**. O.N. *skáld*, of unknown orig. An ancient Scandinavian poet.

Scald, *vt.* O.N.F. *escalder*—L.L. *excaldāre*, to wash in hot water, f. EX- + L. *caldus*, *calidus*, hot. CAULDRON. To injure with hot liquid or steam; to cleanse with boiling water.—*n.*[2] An injury or a cleansing as above.

Scale, *n.*[1] O.N. *skál*, bowl, in pl., weighing scales, f. Teut. root *skel-*, *skal-*, *skul-*, *skæl-*, to separate, divide. (See next.) SHALE. SHELL. SHOAL.[2] SKILL. One of the pans of a balance; in *pl.*, a weighing instrument; in *sing.* in same sense.—*v.*[1]*t.* To weigh in scales; to have a weight of.

Scale, *n.*[2] O.F. *escale*—O.H.G. *scala*, f. Teut. *skal-.* (See prec.) One of the small thin outgrowths protecting fishes and reptiles; a thin flake separating from the skin; a flake generally.—*v.*[2]*t.* To remove the scales from (fish, &c.).—*vi.* To come *off* or *away* in scales.

Scale, *n.*[3] L. *scāla*, ladder, f. *scanděre*, to climb. ASCEND. ESCALADE. SCAN. A series of musical notes with fixed intervals; a series of degrees or graduations; a graduated measuring instrument; a system of representing objects in a smaller or larger size; degree, proportion; a standard of measurement, &c.—*v.*[3]*t.* To attack with ladders; to climb.

Scalene', *a.* L. *scalēnus*—G. *skalēnos*, uneven, unequal. Of a triangle, having three unequal sides.

Scal'lop, **Scol'lop**, *n.* Aphetic f. O.F. *escalope*, a shell. Cf. M.Du. *schelpe*, a shell, esp. a scallop-shell. Cogn. with SHELL. An edible shell-fish; its shell; an object like the shell; a utensil in which oysters, &c., are cooked and served.—*vt.* To shape in the form of the shell; to cook in a scallop.

Scalp, *n.* Northern M.E. *scalp*, app. of Scand. orig. The skin of the top of the head with its hair.—*vt.* To cut off the scalp of.

Scal'pel, *n.* L. *scalpellum*, dim. of *scalprum*, knife, f. *scalpěre*, to cut. A small surgical knife.

Scamp, *n.* From. dial. *Scamp*, v. = (and app. [cogn. with) SCAMPER. A rascal.

Scamp, *vt.* Of uncertain orig. To do (a task, &c.) negligently or hurriedly.

Scam'per, *vi.* Of uncertain orig. To run about nimbly, go hastily from place to place.—*n.* A scampering.

Scan, *vt.* L. *scanděre*, *scansum, to climb, in L.L. to 'scan' verses. (See next.) ASCEND. SCALE.[3] To measure or read (verse) by its metrical feet; to look at searchingly, examine.—**Scan'**SION, *n.*

Scan'dal, *n.* Early M.E. *scandle*—O.N.F. *escandle*—L. *scandalum*, cause of offence or stumbling—G. *skandalon*, trap (occurring, however, only *fig.*), prob. cogn. with *scanděre* (see prec.) and f. Indo-Germanic *skand-*, to spring up. Damage to reputation; something grossly discreditable; a cause of disgrace; offence to moral feeling or decency; defamatory talk.—**Scan'dal**IZE, *vt.* To shock by an action deemed disgraceful.—**Scan'dal**OUS, *a.*

Scant, *a.* O.N. *skamt*, neut. of *skammr*, short, brief = O.H.G. *scamm.* Barely sufficient; not full or copious; not wide or spacious; poorly supplied; meagre.—*vt.* To put on short allowance *of*, keep short *of*; to reduce, to be niggardly of.—**Scant'**Y,[2] *a.* Not ample or copious; deficient in size or extent.—**Scant'**LY,[2] **Scant'**ILY,[2] *advv.*

Scant'ling, *n.* Var. of obs. *Scantillon*—O.F. *escantillon*, *eschantillon* (F. *échantillon*), small piece, sample, of uncertain orig. An allotted portion; a scanty allowance; a small piece of wood; a piece of stone of a fixed size.

Scape, *n.* Aphetic var. of ESCAPE. An act of escaping.—*vi.* and *t.* In senses of ESCAPE.—**Scape'goat**, *n.* In the Mosaic ritual, a goat supposed to bear away the sins of the people; one punished for another's sins.—**Scape'grace**, *n.* Lit., 'one who escapes the grace of God'. A reckless, incorrigible fellow.

Scap'ula, *n.* L. The shoulder-blade.—**Scap'ul**AR,[1]*a.*—**Scap'ular**, **Scap'ulary**, *nn.* Med.L. *scapulāre*, *scapulārium*, f. *scapula.* A monk's short cloak covering the shoulders; a religious badge passing over the shoulders.

Scar, *n.* Prob. f. O.F. *escare*—L.L. *eschara*, a scar, esp. of a burn—G. *eschara*, a hearth, a scar of a burn. The trace of a healed wound, sore, or burn.—*vt.* To mark with a scar.—*vi.* With *over*, to heal.

Scar'ab, *n.* F. *scarabée*—L. *scarabaeus.* Cf. G. *karabos*, horned beetle. The sacred beetle of ancient Egypt; an ancient gem cut in the form of a beetle with a design on the flat under-side.

Scarce, *a.* O.N.F. *scars*, *escars*, as if f. a Pop.L. *scarsus, abb. f. *excarpsus, pa.pple. of an *excarpěre representing L. *excerpěre*, to pick out, select. EXCERPT. Existing or available in insufficient quantity; seldom seen, rare.—**Scarce**, **Scarce'**LY,[2] *advv.* Barely, only just, not quite.—**Scarce'**NESS, **Scarc'**ITY, *nn.*

Scare, *vt.* M.E. *skerren*, f. *skerre*, O.N. *skiarr*.

shy, timid. Cf. Norw. *skjerra*, to scare. To frighten, terrify; to frighten away.—*n*. A sudden fright, a panic.

Scarf, *n*.; *pl*. **Scarfs**, **Scarves**. Prob. f. O.N.F. *escarpe* (F. *écharpe*)=O.F. *escharpe*, a pilgrim's scrip hung from the neck, of Teut. orig. A band worn round the body or over the shoulders.

Scar'ify, *vt*. F. *scarifier*—L.L. *scarīficāre*—L. *scarīfāre*—G. *skaripha-esthai*, to scratch, f. *skariphos*, a pointed instrument, allied to L. *scrībere*, to write. SCRIBE. To make a number of slight cuts in (often *fig*.).

Scar'let, *n*. O.F. *escarlate*, said to be f. Per. *saqalāt*, *siqalāt*, a kind of rich cloth. A brilliant red colour.—*a*. Of the colour.—**Scar'let fe'ver**, *n*. Also **Scarlati'na**. It. *scarlattina*, f. *scarlatto* = O.F. *escarlate*. A contagious febrile disease characterized by a red rash.

Scarp, *n*. It. *scarpa*, so called f. being cut sharp, *i.e*. steep—Du. *scherp*, M.H.G. *scharf*, SHARP. ESCARP. The interior slope of a ditch.—*vt*. = ESCARP, *v*.—**Scarp'**MENT, *n*. = ESCARPMENT.

Scathe, *n*. O.N. *skathe*, harm=O.E. *sc(e)atha*. Cf. Sw. *skada*, Da. *skade*, Ger. *schade*. Hurt, harm. —*vt*. To injure, esp. by blasting or withering up (often *fig*.).—**Scathe'**LESS, *a*.

Scat'ter, *vt*. Supposed to be the northern, with SHATTER as the southern representative of an O.E. **sc(e)aterian*, f. a supposed Teut. root *skat-* cogn. with G. *skedannunai*, to scatter. To disperse; to place here and there; to sprinkle, strew.—*vi*. To disperse.

Scav'enger, *n*. The same, with intrusive *n* (as in *messenger*, *passenger*), as *Scavager* (now rare)—A.F. *scawager*, f. *scawage*, scavage (see below), f. O.F. *escauwer*, to inspect, f. Flemish *scauwen*=O.E. *scēawian*, to SHOW. Formerly, a collector of a toll called *scavage* on goods sold by strangers in London and elsewhere, on whom the care of the streets afterwards devolved. One employed to clean streets.—**Scav'enge**, *vt*. Back-formation f. *scavenger*. To clean (streets).—*vi*. To clean streets.

Scene, *n*. F. *scène*—L. *scēna*, *scaena*, stage, scene—G. *skēnē*, tent or booth, stage. The place of the action in a play, a novel, &c.: the place of any action; a subdivision of a play; stage apparatus or a part thereof; a view presented to the eye; an action, episode, situation; a stormy colloquy.—**Sce'n**ERY, *n*.

Scent, *vt*. F. *sentir*, to feel, perceive, esp. to smell—L. *sentīre*, to feel, perceive. SENSE. Of a hound, to track by smell; to find out instinctively, detect; to give an odour to.—*n*. The sense of smell; the odour by which a hound pursues; distinctive odour.

Scep'tic, **Skep'tic**, *n*. L. *Skeptici*, pl., the Sceptic Philosophers, followers of Pyrrho—G. *skeptikos*, thoughtful, inquiring, in pl. *Skeptikoi*, the Sceptic Philosophers, f. *skeptesthai*, to look out, consider, cogn. with *skope-ein*, to look, *skopos*, mark, watchman. ESPY. SCOPE. One who doubts the possibility of real knowledge; one who maintains a doubting attitude.—**Scep'tic**AL, **Skep'tic**AL, *a*.—**Scep'tic**ISM, **Skep'tic**ISM, *n*.

Scep'tre, *n*. O.F. *ceptre*, *sceptre*—L. *scēptrum*—G. *skēptron*, staff, sceptre, f. *skēptesthai*, to prop oneself. SHAFT. An ornamental rod as a symbol of regal or imperial power; royal or imperial dignity, sovereignty.

Sched'ule, *n*. O.F. *cedule*—L. *schedula*, small leaf of paper, dim. of *scheda*, *scida*, strip of papyrus-bark, f. G. *schizein*, to cleave. SCHISM. An appendix to an Act of Parliament or a deed; a tabular or classified statement.—*vt*. To enter in, or affix as a schedule.

Scheme, *n*. Med.L. *schēma*—G. *schēma*, form, figure, f. root *sch-*, whence *echein*, to have, hold, to be (in such or such a condition). EPOCH. A table, list; a plan, design; a project, enterprise; a system.—*vt*. To devise.—*vi*. To lay schemes, devise plans.—**Schem'**ER, *n*.

Schism, *n*. O.F. *scisme*—Eccles.L. *schisma*, *schismatis*—G. *schisma*, rent, cleft, schism, f. *schizein*. SCHEDULE. Division in the Church or in a party, &c.—**Schismat'**IC, *a*. and *n*.—**Schismat'**ICAL, *a*.

Schist, *n*. F. *schiste*—G. *schistos*, cleft, easily cleft, f. *schizein*. SCHEDULE. ZEST. A rock of a slaty structure.

Scho'lium, *n*.; *pl*. **Scho'lia**. G. *scholion*, f. *scholē*, school. (See next.) An explanatory note.—**Scho'liast**, *n*. G. *scholiastēs*, f. *scholion*. One who writes such notes.

School, *n*. O.E. *scól*—L. *schola*—G. *scholē*, leisure, employment of leisure, study, school. An establishment for teaching; a body of disciples or followers.—*vt*. To educate; to make wise or skilful, to discipline.—**School'man**, *n*. One of the writers of the Middle Ages who treat of logic, metaphysics, &c., as then taught in the 'schools' or universities.—**Schol'ar**, *n*. O.E. *scolere*—L.L. *scholāris*, f. *schola*. One who is taught in a school; with qualifying *a*., one who is quick (or slow) at learning; a learned person; a student receiving emoluments from school or college funds.—**Schol'ar**LY,[1] *a*.—**Schol'ar**SHIP, *n*. Learning, erudition; the status or emoluments of a scholar at a school, &c.—**Scholas'tic**, *a*. G. *scholastikos*, studious, f. *scholē*. Pertaining to the schoolmen; pedantic, needlessly subtle; pertaining to schools.

Schoo'ner, *n*. Of uncertain orig. A vessel with fore-and-aft sails on two or more masts.

Schottische', *n*. Ger. (*der*) *schottische* (*tanz*), (the) Scottish (dance). A dance resembling the polka; music written for it.

Sciat'ic, *a*. F. *sciatique*—L. *sciaticus*, a corr. of *ischiadicus*, G. *ischiadikos*, subject to pains in the hips, f. *ischion*, the hip joint. Of the hip.—**Sciat'ic**AL, *a*.—**Sciat'ica**, *n*. Med. L., fem. of *sciaticus*. Pain in the sciatic nerve.

Sci'ence, *n*. F. *science*—L. *scientia*, f. *sciens*, *scientis*, pres.pple. of *scīre*, to know. CONSCIENCE. NESCIENT. Trained skill; a branch of study concerned with a connected body of observed facts; the sciences collectively.—**Scientif'**IC, *a*. —**Scientif'ically**, *adv*. -AL. -LY.[2]—**Sci'ent**IST, *n*.

Scim'itar, *n*. Adopted in the 16th cent. in various forms f. different Romance langs. Ultimate orig. unknown. A short curved single-edged sword.

Scintil'la, *n*. L. A spark (always *fig*.).—**Scin'tillate**, *vi*. L. *scintillāre*, *scintillātum*, f. *scintilla*. To sparkle, twinkle, emit sparks. —**Scintill**A'TION, *n*.

Sci'olist, *n*. With -IST f. L.L. *sciolus*, smatterer, dim. f. *scius*, knowing, f. *scīre*. SCIENCE. A superficial pretender to knowledge.

Sci'on, *n*. O.F. *cion* (F. *scion*). of obscure orig. A slip for grafting; an heir, descendant.

Scir'rhus, *n*. G. *skirrhos*, conn. with *skiros*, hard. A hard tumour.

Scis'sors, *n.pl*. O.F. *cisoires*, pl. (in F. only of large shears, the sense 'scissors' being expressed by the cogn. *ciseaux*, pl. of *ciseau*, O.F. *cisel*. CHISEL)—L.L. **cisōria*, pl. of *cisō-*

rium, cutting instrument, f. L. *caedĕre*, *caesum* (in composition *-cīdĕre*, *-cīsum*), to cut. CÆSURA. A small double cutting instrument.

Sclerot'ic, *a.* Med. and Mod.L. *sclērōticus*—Late G. **sklērōtikos*, a. f. *sklēro-ein*, to harden, f. *sklēros*, hard. In *sclerotic coat*, &c., the hard outer coat forming the white of the eye.—*n.* The sclerotic coat.

Scoff, *n.* M.E. *scof*, *skof*, of obscure orig. A derisive jest; a mark for derision.—*vi.* To speak derisively, mock, jeer.—**Scof'f**ER, *n.*

Scold, *n.* App. f. O.N. *skáld*, poet, SCALD, with intermediate sense 'lampooner'. A railing woman.—*vi.* To rail, find fault noisily.—*vt.* To rate, rebuke.

Sconce, *n.*[1] Aphetic f. O.F. *esconse*, lantern, also, hiding-place—Monastic L. *sconsa*, abb. f. *absconsa*, fem. of L. *absconsus*, pa.pple. of *abscondĕre*, to hide. ABSCOND. A bracket-candlestick against a wall. [head.

Sconce, *n.*[2] Orig. obscure. The top of the

Sconce, *n.*[3] Du. *shans*, brushwood, earthwork made with gabions, of obscure orig. A small fort or earthwork.

Scone, *n.* Perh. a shortened adoption of M.Du. *schoonbrot*, M.L.G. *schonbrot*, a kind of loaf, lit., 'fine bread'. A round cake of wheat- or barley-meal baked on a griddle.

Scoop, *n.* Prob. f. M.L.G. *schôpe*, or M.Du. *schôpe*, *schoepe*, vessel for drawing water, corn-scoop, f. O.Teut. root *skap-*, *skōp-*, to draw water. A utensil for ladling; a kind of shovel; an implement for hollowing out; a scooping; something scooped out.—*vt.* To ladle out; to rake in or hollow out with a scoop; to form by scooping.

Scope, *n.* It. *scopo*, aim, purpose—G. *skopos*, mark, watcher. BISHOP. SCEPTIC. Intention, drift; reach of mental activity; range of application; free course or play; room, range.

Scorbu'tic, *a.* Mod.L. *scorbūticus*, f. *scorbūtus*—F. *scorbut*, scurvy, of doubtful orig. Pertaining to, affected with, scurvy.

Scorch, *vt.* Of doubtful orig. Cf. O.N. *skorpna*, to be shrivelled. To burn superficially.—*vi.* To be scorched.

Score, *n.* Late O.E. *scoru*—O.N. *skor*, notch, tally, the number of twenty, f. Teut. root *sker-*, *skar-*, *skur-*, to cut. SHEAR. A cut, notch; a line drawn, a stroke; a written or printed piece of concerted music; an account kept by marks; reason, ground, sake; points made in a game; a group or set of twenty.—*vt.* To cut, notch; to mark with a line; to cancel with a line; to record by marks, write down as a debt; to make (points) in a game, to set down in the score, to count for (so many points).—*vi.* To achieve a success.—**Scor'**ER, *n.*

Sco'ria, *n.*; *pl.* **Sco'riæ**. L. *scōria*—G. *skōria*, f. *skōr*, dung. Dross of metals; rough masses of cooled lava.

Scorn, *n.* O.F. *escarn*, *escharn*, of Teut. orig. Derision, indignant contempt.—*vt.* To despise; to disdain *to do*.—**Scorn'**ER, *n.*—**Scorn'**FUL, *a.*—**Scorn'ful**LY,[2] *adv.*

Scor'pion, *n.* O.F. *scorpion*—L. *scorpio*, *scorpiōnis*—G. *skorpiōn* or *skorpios*. An animal like a small lobster with a sting at the end of a jointed tail.

Scot, *n.*[1] Ultimately identical with O.E. *sc(e)ot*, *gesc(e)ot*, SHOT. A payment or contribution, or one's share thereof.—**Scot-free'**, *a.* Free from payment of 'scot', exempt from punishment, &c.

Scot, *n.*[2] O.E. *Scot*—L.L. *Scottus*, of obscure orig. A native of Scotland.—**Scot'tish**, *a.* *Scot* + -ISH. Var. **Scotch**. Also **Scots**, orig. *Scottis*, northern var. of *Scottish*. Of or belonging to Scotland or its people.—**Scotch'man**, **Scots'man**, *nn.*—**Scot'ticism**, *n.* L.L. *Scotticus*, a. + -ISM. A Scottish idiom.

Scotch, *vt.* Orig. obscure. To gash.—*n.* A gash.

Scoun'drel, *n.* Orig. unknown. An audacious rascal.—**Scoun'drel**ISM, *n.*—**Scoun'drel**LY,[1] *a.*

Scour, *v.*[1]*i.* Of obscure orig. To move *about* hastily; to hasten, run.—*vt.* To pass rapidly over or along, esp. in quest of something.

Scour, *v.*[2]*t.* Prob. f. M.Du. or M.L.G. *schûren*, prob. f. O.F. *escurer*, f. Pop.L. **excūrāre*, to scour, f. EX- + L. *cūrāre*, to take care of, f. *cūra*, care. CURE. To cleanse or polish by rubbing; to clear out (a channel, &c.); to clear *away* or *off*.

Scourge, *n.* A.F. *escorge*, related to O.F. *escorgiee*, f. Pop.L. *excoriāta*, a scourge, lit. 'flayed off', hence, a strip of leather, fem. pa.pple. of L.L. *excoriāre*, to strip off the hide, f. EX- + L. *corium*, hide. EXCORIATE. A whip, lash.—*vt.* To whip, lash.

Scout, *n.* O.F. *escoute*, a listening, a listener, f. *escouter* (F. *écouter*), L. *auscultāre*, to listen. AUSCULTATION. A spying or watching; one sent ahead for information.—*v.*[1]*i.* To act as a scout.

Scout, *v.*[2]*t.* Scand. Cf. O.N. *skúta*, a taunt, prob. cogn. with SHOOT. SHOUT. To treat as absurd, to reject or dismiss with scorn.

Scowl, *vi.* Prob. Scand. Cf. Da. *skule* in same sense. To frown, to look sullenly or gloomily.—*n.* A scowling aspect.

Scrag, *n.* Prob. alteration of obs. *Crag*, neck, corresp. to Du. *kraag*, Ger. *kragen*, neck, collar. A lean person or animal; the lean end of a neck of mutton, &c.—**Scrag'g**Y,[2] *a.*

Scram'ble, *vi.* Orig. obscure. To make way, struggle along or up, by crawling, clambering, &c.; to strive with others *for*.—*vt.* To collect or gather *up* hastily or in disorder; *scrambled eggs*, eggs broken into a pan and fried with milk, butter, &c.—*n.* A scrambling; a disorderly proceeding.

Scran'nel, *a.* Cf. Norw. *skran*, lean, shrivelled. Thin, meagre; harsh, unmelodious.

Scrap, *n.* O.N. *skrap*, scraps, f. *skrapa*, to SCRAPE. In *pl.*, the remains of a meal; in *sing.*, a fragment; a small picture, &c., cut from a book, &c.—**Scrap'p**Y,[2] *a.*

Scrape, *vt.* O.E. *scrapian* or O.N. *skrapa* = M.Du. *schrapen*. SCRAP. To take *off*, *away*, &c., with something sharp; to clean or smooth thus; to get *together*, gather *up*; to rub harshly on.—*vi.* To make an awkward bow.—*n.* An act or sound of scraping; an embarrassing situation.—**Scrap'**ER, *n.*

Scratch, *vt.* App. produced by a confusion of obs. *Scrat* and *Cratch* in sim. senses, of obscure orig. To wound superficially, or rub lightly, with the claws or nails or with anything pointed; to make marks on or to mark out with a pointed instrument; to remove from a list.—*vi.* To use the claws or nails.—*n.* A slight tearing of the skin; a shallow mark; a line drawn as a starting-point, &c.—*a.* Gathered together promiscuously.

Scrawl, *vt.* Perh. a use of obs. *Scrawl*, to sprawl with the limbs, shuffle, app. an alteration of CRAWL, perh. after SPRAWL. To write or draw untidily; to cover with untidy marks.—*n.* Something scrawled; a careless style of handwriting.

Scream, *vi.* Early M.E. *scræmen, screamen*, perh. f. an O.E. **scrǽman*. Cf. Mod. West Fris. *skrieme*, to weep. To utter a shrill piercing cry; to make a noise like a scream.—*n.* A shrill piercing cry.

Screech, *vi.* A modification of imitative **Scritch** in same sense. To scream.—*n.* A scream.

Screed, *n.* A var. of SHRED. A fragment; a long list; a lengthy discourse or letter.

Screen, *n.* M.E. *skrene, skreene*, of doubtful orig. App. in some way conn. with F. *écran*, screen, O.F. *escran*, also *escrin, escren*, prob. of Teut. orig. Something to ward off heat or a draught; a contrivance for displaying objects or receiving an image; a partition, esp. one between the chancel and the other parts of a church; an apparatus for sifting; a means of securing from attack, punishment, &c.—*vt.* To shelter, hide from view, shield, protect; to sift.

Screw, *n.* App. f. O.F. *escroue* (F. *écrou*), nut, of obscure orig. A cylinder with a spiral ridge running round it outside or inside; a ship's screw-propeller; a turn of the screw; a contortion; a small portion of a commodity in a twist of paper; a miserly person; an unsound horse.—*vt.* To attach with a screw; to press or stretch with or as with a screw; to extort by pressure; to oppress; to work by turning; to fix *in, into, together*, &c., by a turning movement; to twist round.

Scrib'ble, *vt.* App. f. late Med.L. *scrībillāre* (cf. the rare L. *conscrībillāre*), a dim. formation on L. *scrībere*, to write. SCRIBE. To write or draw carelessly; to cover with scribblings.—*vi.* To write or draw carelessly.—*n.* Something scribbled; careless writing.

Scribe, *n.* L. *scrība*, writer, secretary, f. *scrībĕre, scriptum*, to write. CONSCRIBE. POSTSCRIPT. An interpreter of the Law among the Jews; a copyist; a penman; an author, writer.

Scrim. Orig. obscure. A kind of thin canvas used for lining in upholstery, &c.

Scrim'mage, *n.* Altered f. obs. *Scrimish*, var. of SKIRMISH. A noisy struggle, a scuffle; at *football*, a close mass of players with the ball on the ground in the middle.

Scrimp, *a.* Orig. obscure. Cf. Sw., Da. *skrumpen*, shrivelled, M.H.G. *schrimpfen*, to contract. Scanty, meagre.—*vt.* To keep on short allowance; to be sparing of.—*vi.* To economize.

Scrip, *n.*[1] Prob. f. O.F. *escrepe*, wallet, purse, prob. of Teut. orig. A small bag or wallet.

Scrip, *n.*[2] Short for SUBSCRIPTION (*receipt*). A provisional certificate entitling the bearer to shares or stock (often in *collective sing.*); a share certificate in general.

Script, *n.* L. *scriptum*, neut. pa.pple. of *scrībĕre*. SCRIBE. A piece of writing; handwriting; written characters.—**Scrip'ture**, *n.* L. *scriptūra*, f. *scrībĕre*. The Bible; so in *pl.*; in *sing.* or *pl.*, sacred writings.—**Scrip'tur**AL, *a.*—**Scrip'tural**LY,[2] *adv.*

Scriv'ener, *n.* With superfluous -ER = obs. *Scrivein*—O.F. *escrivain*—L.L. *scrībānus*, a notary, f. *scrībĕre*. SCRIBE. A copyist, clerk, amanuensis.

Scrof'ula, *n.* Med.L. *scrōfula*, in form dim. of *scrōfa*, a breeding sow, supposed to be subject to the disease. A disease characterized by glandular tumours in the neck.—**Scrof'u**LOUS, *a.*

Scroll, *n.* Altered f. earlier form *Scrow*—A.F. *escrowe*—M.Du. *schrôde*, O.H.G. *scrôt*, SHRED. A roll of paper or parchment; a list or roll; an ornament like a scroll of paper.

Scro'tum, *n.* L. *scrōtum*. The pouch enclosing the testicles.

Scrub, *n.*[1] A var. of SHRUB.[1] A stunted tree; brushwood; an insignificant person.—**Scrub'**BY,[2] *a.* Stunted; covered with scrub; insignificant, mean.

Scrub, *vt.* Orig. obscure. Corresp. to L.G. *schrubben*, Du. *schrobben*. To clean with a hard brush and water.—*n.*[2] A scrubbing.

Scruff, *n.* A var. of SCUFF.

Scru'ple, *n.* F. *scrupule*—L. *scrūpulus*, dim. of *scrūpus*, a pebble, a cause of anxiety. A small weight; a hesitation as to duty, &c.—*vi.* To hesitate *to do.*—**Scru'pul**OUS, *a.* Troubled with scruples; strict in matters of duty, attentive to details; of actions, characterized by such strictness or attention.—**Scru'pulous**LY,[2] *adv.*

Scru'tiny, *n.* L.L. *scrūtinium*, f. L. *scrūtāri*, to search into as if among broken pieces, f. *scrūta*, pl., broken stuff. INSCRUTABLE. Investigation, an investigation; an official examination of votes; a searching gaze.—**Scru-tin**EER', *n.* An examiner of votes.—**Scru'-tin**IZE, *vt.* To examine closely.

Scud, *vi.* Orig. obscure. To run nimbly; to run before the wind.—*n.* The action of scudding; a driving shower; light driven clouds; driven spray.

Scuff, *n.* Orig. obscure. SCRUFF. The nape [of the neck.

Scuf'fle, *vi.* A frequentative, perh. f. Scand. Cf. Sw. *skuffa*, to push, f. the root of SHOVE. To struggle confusedly at close quarters.—*n.* Such a struggle.

Scull, *n.* Of obscure orig. An oar used over a boat's stern; a short oar used in pairs.—*vi.* and *t.* To proceed or propel by means of sculls or a scull.

Scul'lery, *n.* O.F. *escuelerie, esculerie*, the office of keeping the dishes, f. *escuelle* (F. *écuelle*), a dish—L. *scutella*, a dish, dim. of *scutra*, a flat tray. SCUTTLE.[1] A place for washing dishes.

Scul'lion, *n.* Perh. alteration, with assimilation to prec., of F. *souillon*, in same sense, f. *souiller*, to SOIL. A kitchen menial.

Sculp'ture, *n.* L. *sculptūra*, f. *sculpĕre, sculptum*, to carve. The art of forming figures in the round or in relief; the product or a production of the art.—*vt.* To represent in sculpture.—**Sculp'**TOR, *n.*—**Sculp'tur**AL, *a.*

Scum, *n.* Of uncertain orig. Corresponds to M.H.G. *schûm* (Ger. *schaum*), Da., Sw. *skum*. SKIM. Floating matter on a liquid; the worst part.—*vi.* To form scum.

Scup'per, *n.* Orig. uncertain. Poss. conn with SCOOP, *v.*, as if 'ladler out of water'. A hole in a ship's side level with the deck.

Scurf, *n.* Sw. *skorf*, Da. *skurv*, prob. f. O. Teut. root seen in O.E. *sceorfan*, to gnaw. Flakes detached from the skin.—**Scurf'**Y,[2] *a.* —Also **Scurv'**Y,[2] *a.* In fig. sense, sorry, contemptible.—As *n.* A disease induced by excess of salted foods.—**Scurv'**ILY,[2] *adv.* Meanly, shabbily.

Scur'rile, Scur'ril, *a.* L. *scurrīlis*, f. *scurra*, buffoon. Also, with -OUS, **Scur'ri-lous**. Coarse or indecent in language.—**Scurril'**ITY, *n.*

Scur'ry, *vi.* Perh. taken f. HURRY-SCURRY. To run hurriedly.—*n.* Haste, bustle.

Scut, *n.* Orig. obscure. A short erect tail.

Scut'cheon, *n.* An aphetic var. of ESCUTCHEON.

Scutt'le, *n.*[1] O.E. *scutel*, dish, f. L. *scutella*. SCULLERY. A large open basket; a receptacle for coal.

Scutt'le, *n.*[2] Orig. obscure. Corresp. to F. *écoutillon*, Sp. *escotillon*, formed f. *écoutille*, *escotilla*, hatchway. A hole with a lid in a ship's deck, &c.—*v.*[1]*t.* To pierce the bottom of (a ship).

Scutt'le, *v.*[2]*i.* Perh. alteration of dial. *Scuddle*, freq. of SCUD. To hurry off.—*n.*[3] Hurried flight.

Scythe, *n.* O.E. *síthe*, lit. cutter'. Root *sek-*. SAW.[1] A mowing implement.—*vt.* To cut with a scythe.

Sea, *n.* O.E. *sǽ*. Common Teut. The body of salt water covering most of the earth; in *pl.* different tracts of this; a particular tract; a heavy swell, rough weather.—**Sea'-board**, *n.* BOARD. The coast-line, a coast region.

Seal, *n.*[1] O.E. *seolh*. Cf. O.N. *selr*, O.H.G. *selah*. An aquatic carnivorous mammal.

Seal, *n.*[2] O.F. *seel* (F. *sceau*)—L. *sigillum*, dim. of *signum*, a mark. SIGN. A piece of wax impressed with a device authenticating a document or securing a letter; a stamp for making the impression.—*vt.* To put a seal upon; to set apart, destine.

Seam, *n.* O.E. *séam*, conn. with *siwan*, to SEW. A junction made by sewing; a crevice between planks or plates; a thin layer or stratum.—*vt.* To mark with lines or furrows.—**Seam'ster**, **Semp'ster**, *n.* O.E. *séamestre*, orig. fem. of *séamere*, tailor. One who sews for a living, gen. of a man.—Fem. forms **Seam'str**ESS, **Semp'str**ESS.—**Seam'**Y,[2] *a.* Having seams; the worst (side of life, &c.).

Sear, *vi.* O.E. *séarian*, f. *séar*, SERE. To dry up.—*vt.* To dry up, blight; to burn, char; to deaden, make incapable of feeling.

Search, *vt.* O.F. *cerchier* (F. *chercher*)—L. *circāre*, to go about, traverse, f. *circus*, CIRCLE. To explore or examine in quest of something; to seek *out* diligently.—*vi.* To make a search.—*n.* A searching.

Sea'son, *n.* O.F. *seson*, *seison*, *saison*—L. *satio*, *satiōnis*, a sowing (in Pop.L., seed-time), f. *serĕre*, *satum*, to SOW. A period of the year; a year; a period marked by a festival; a period with reference to agriculture, &c., or to a sport, business, &c.; a period during which something happens, prevails, &c.; an indefinite period; the right time.—*vt.* O.F. *saisonner*, to ripen, make (fruit) palatable, f. *saison*. To make palatable; to adapt *to* a particular taste; to ripen, make fit for use; to harden or fortify (a person).—**Sea'son**ABLE, *a.* Suitable to the season, opportune.

Seat, *n.* O.N. *sǽti*, cogn. with O.E. *sittan*, to SIT. Manner of sitting (on horseback); that on which one sits; a right to sit as a member of a body; the sitting part of the body; the locality of a disease, an activity, &c.; a place of habitation; a large country house.—*vt.* To make to sit; to afford seats for; in *pass.*, to be situated, to be furnished with seats.

Secede', *vi.* L. SE*cēdĕre*, *sēcessum*, to go apart. CEDE. To withdraw from an alliance, an association, &c.—**Seces'**SION, *n.*

Seclude', *vt.* L. *sēclūdĕre*, *sēclūsum*, to shut up apart, f. SE- + *claudĕre*, to shut. CLAUSE. To remove or guard from view or resort.—**Seclu'**SION, *n.*

Sec'ond, *a.* F. *second*—L. *secundus*, following (hence, favourable), next, second, f. *sequi*, *secūtus*, to follow. SECT. SEQUEL. Coming next after the first; other, another.—*n.*[1] One who or something which is second or gives aid; one who assists a principal in a duel or pugilistic fight; in *mus.*, the next part to the highest.—*n.*[2] F. *seconde* — Med.L. *secunda* for *secunda minūta*, 'second MINUTE', *i.e.* the result of a second division of an hour, that of the first being 'first minute', or 'minute' simply. The sixtieth part of a minute.—*vt.* F. *seconder*—L. *secundāre*, f. *secundus*. To support; to further; to support (a motion or the mover) in order that discussion may be in order.—**Sec'ond**LY,[2] *adv.*—**Sec'ond**ARY, *a.* Subsidiary; derivative; of education, between the primary and university stages.—**Sec'ondari**LY,[2] *adv.* — **Sec'ond**ER, *n.*—**Sec'ond-hand**, *a.* Bought after use by a previous owner; not due to original observation or research.

Se'cret, *a.* F. *secret*—L. *sēcrētus*, secret (in neut. *sēcrētum*, a secret), orig. pa.pple. of *sēcernĕre*, to set apart, f. SE- + *cernĕre*, to separate. CONCERN. Hidden; clandestine.—*n.* Something kept secret; that which accounts for, or is necessary to secure something.—**Se'cret**LY,[2] *adv.*—**Se'crecy**, *n.* Formerly *secretee*, *-tie*, app. f. *secret*, a. + -Y.[1] A keeping or being kept secret; ability or tendency to keep secret, reticence. — **Sec'retary**, *n.* Med.L. *sēcrētārius* in sim. senses f. *sēcrētum*. One who writes for another; an officer of a company, &c., who writes letters, keeps records, &c.; applied officially to certain ministers of state.—**Secreta'ri**AL, *a.*-**Secreta'ri**ATE,[1] **Sec'retary**SHIP, *nn.*—**Secrete'**, *vt.* From *sēcrētus*. To hide; of a gland, &c., to extract (certain matters) from the blood.—**Secre'**TION, *n.*—**Secre'**TORY, *a.*—**Secre'**TIVE, *a.* Reticent.—**Secre'tive**NESS, *n.*

Sect, *n.* L. *secta*, a school, sect, f. *sequi*. SECOND. A party within a religious body; a separately organized religious body; the followers of a philosopher or school of thought.—**Sect'**ARY, *n.*—**Secta'ri**AN, *a.*

Sec'tion, *n.* L. *sectio*, *sectiōnis*, f. *secāre*, *sectum*, to cut. BISECT. SAW.[1] SEGMENT. A cutting; a portion, division; a subdivision of a book, &c.; a drawing of an object as if cut through.—**Sec'tion**AL, *a.*

Sec'ular, *a.* O.F. *seculer* (F. *séculier*)—L. *saeculāris*, in Eccles.L., 'of the world', f. L. *saeculum*, generation, age, in Eccles.L., 'the world'. Of clergy, living in 'the world', not in monastic seclusion; worldly, lay, temporal.—Directly f. *saeculāris* in classical sense 'of a generation or age'. Occurring once in, lasting for, an age.—**Sec'ular**IST, *n.* One sceptical of religion or opposed to religious education.—**Sec'ular**ISM, *n.*—**Sec'ular**IZE, *vt.* To convert to non-religious purposes.—**Seculariz**A'TION, *n.*

Secure', *a.* L. *sēcūrus*, f. SE- + *cūra*, care. CURE. SURE. Free from care; out of danger; involving no danger; trustworthy; firmly fixed; having a safe prospect *of*.—*vt.* To make safe from attack; to free (a creditor) from risk of loss; to make a payment certain by a mortgage, &c., *upon*; to make firm; to get possession of.—**Secure'**LY,[2] *adv.*—**Secur'**ITY, *n.*

Sedan', *n.* Orig. obscure. Connection with *Sedan* in France unlikely. A covered vehicle borne on poles. So **Sedan' chair**.

Sedate', *a.* L. *sēdātus*, pa.pple. of *sēdāre*, to settle, make calm, causal of *sedēre*, to SIT. ASSESS. Calm, cool, collected.—**Sed'**ATIVE, *a.* Soothing.—*n.* A soothing medicine.

Sed'entary, *a.* F. *sédentaire*—L. *sedentārius*, f. *sedēre*, to SIT. Involving, addicted to, much sitting.
Sedge, *n.* O.E. *secg*, lit. 'cutter', *i.e.* 'sword-grass', from the shape. Root *sek-*. SAW.[1] A coarse grassy flag-like plant.—**Sedg'**Y,[2] *a.*
Sedi'le, *n.*; *pl.* **Sedi'lia**. L. *sedīle*, seat, f. *sedēre*, to SIT. Us. in *pl.*, a series of seats on the south side of the chancel near the altar for the use of the clergy.
Sed'iment, *n.* F. *sédiment*—L. *sedimentum*, a settling down, f. *sedēre*, to SIT. Matter which falls to the bottom of a liquid.
Sedi'tion, *n.* O.F. *sedition*—L. *sēditio, sēditiōnis*, a going apart, dissension, f. *sēd-* (= SE-) + *itio*, a going, f. *īre*, to go. A rebellion, mutiny; conduct or language inciting to rebellion or mutiny.—**Sedi'tio**US, *a.*
Seduce', *vt.* L. SE*dūcĕre, sēductum*, to lead aside. DUKE. To lead into wrong; to induce (a woman) to surrender her chastity.—**Seduc'**ER, *n.*—**Seduc'tio**N, *n.*—**Seduc'**TIVE, *a.* Alluring, winning.
Sed'ulous, *a.* L. *sēdulus*, careful + -OUS. Diligent in application.—**Sedu'li**TY, *n.*
See, *vt.* O.E. *séon*. Common Teut. To perceive with the eyes or mentally; to contemplate; to ascertain; to escort; to regard as *good*, &c.; to observe, come to know; to experience; to call upon, to give an interview to.—*vi.* To perceive, understand, consider.—**See**R, *n.* A prophet.—**See'ing**, quasi-*conj.* Inasmuch as, since.
See, *n.* O.F. *sé, sed*—L. *sēdēs*, a seat, f. *sedēre*, to SIT. The throne of a bishop; the position of being bishop of a diocese.
Seed, *n.* O.E. *sǽd*, f. *sáwan*, to SOW. Cogn. with L. *sēmen*. A plant's reproductive germ; seeds collectively; offspring.—*vi.* To produce seed.—*vt.* To sow with seed.—**Seed'ling**, *n.* -LING (1). A plant raised from seed.—**Seed'**Y,[2] *a.* Full of seed, run to seed; shabby; unwell.
Seek, *vt.* O.E. *sécan*. Common Teut. Cogn. with G. *hēge-esthai*, to lead, L. *sāgīre*, to discern acutely. BESEECH. RANSACK. SAGACIOUS. To go in quest of; to try to get, aim at; to ask for.—*vi.* To make search.
Seem, *vi.* M.E. *sēme*—O.N. *sœma*, to honour, conform to, f. *sœmr*, fitting, seemly. Formerly, to be suitable to, beseem. To appear to be (something); to appear *to be* or *to do*.—**Seem'ing**LY,[2] *adv.* Apparently.—**Seem'**LY,[1] *a.* O.N. *sœmiligr*, f. *sœmr*. Becoming, decorous.—**Seem'li**NESS, *n.*
See'-saw, *n.* Perh. reduplicated f. SAW, *v.*, and imitative of a sawyer's movements. A game in which children swing on the ends of a balanced plank; a plank so used.—*vi.* To move with a see-saw motion.
Seethe, *vt.* O.E. *séothan*. Common Teut. SODDEN. To boil; to soak or steep.—*vi.* To be boiled; to surge or foam up; to be in agitation or turmoil.
Seg'ment, *n.* L. *segmentum*, f. *secāre*, to cut. SECTION. A piece cut off; a division, section.
Seg'regate, *vt.* L. SE*gregāre, sēgregātum*, to separate from the flock, set apart, f. *grex, gregis*, flock. GREGARIOUS. To set apart, isolate.—**Segrega'**TION, *n.*
Seid'litz pow'der, *n.* From *Seidlitz* in Bohemia, with a medicinal spring, the name being given arbitrarily merely on account of aperient quality. A dose consisting of two powders dissolved separately and taken after mixture and during effervescence.
Seigneur', *n.* F.—L. *senior*, SENIOR. Also **Seig'nior**. A.F. *segnour*, O.F. *seignor*—L. *senior*. A feudal lord, the lord of a manor.—**Seig'nior**AGE, *n.* A duty levied by the sovereign on the coining of money; a duty levied on minerals. — **Seignio'**RIAL, *a.*—**Seig'niory**, *n.* O.F. *seignorie*. Feudal lordship or dominion; a feudal lordship or domain; a body of seigniors.
Seine, *n.* O.E. *segne* = O.S., O.H.G. *segina*—L. *sagēna*—G. *sagēnē*. A vertically hanging fishing net.
Seis'mic, *a.* G. *seismos*, earthquake (f. *seiein*, to shake) + -IC. Pertaining to earthquakes.
Seize, *vt.* O.F. *saisir, seisir*, to put in possession, take possession of—Frankish L. *sacīre*, to put, place, of doubtful orig. To put in legal possession (in this technical sense spelt *seise*); to take possession of under a judicial order; to lay hold of, grasp; to apprehend, perceive.—*vi.* To lay hold *upon*.—**Sei'sin**, *n.* O.F. *saisine*, f. *saisir*. In *law*, possession.—**Seiz'**ABLE, *a.*—**Seiz'**URE, *n.*
Sel'dom, *adv.* O.E. *seldan, seldum*=O.H.G. *seltan* (Ger. *selten*), conn. with Goth. *sildaleiks*, wonderful. Not often, rarely.
Select', *vt.* L. *sēligĕre, sēlectum*, to choose out, f. SE- + *legĕre*, to collect. choose. LEGEND. To choose, pick out.—*a.* Choice, picked, the best; exclusive.—**Selec'tio**N, *n.*
Self, *pron.*; *pl.* **Selves**. O.E. *self, selfa*. Common Teut. Added to a pronoun in oblique case to express emphasis, distinction, or a reflexive usage.—*a.* Of a colour, the same throughout, uniform.—*n.* One's own individuality or essence; one's personal interests.—**Self'**ISH, *a.* Devoted unduly to self.—**Self'ish**LY,[2] *adv.*—**Self'ish**NESS, *n.*—**Self-conceit'**, *n.* An exaggerated opinion of oneself.—**Self-con'scious**, *a.* Unduly preoccupied with one's own personality.—**Self-possessed'**, *ppl.a.* Composed.—**Self-posses'**SION, *n.*—**Self'same**, *a.* Two synonymous words joined for emphasis. (The) very same.—**Self-suffic'ient**, *a.* Sufficient in or for oneself; presumptuous.—**Self-suffic'**IENCY, *n.*
Sell, *vt.* O.E. *sellan*, to hand over. Common Teut. SALE. To betray; to hand over for a price; to make profit of; to disappoint, cheat.—*vi.* Of a commodity, to find purchasers.—*n.* A disappointment.—**Sell'**ER, *n.*
Sel'vage, Sel'vedge, *n.* App. SELF + EDGE, aft. the equivalent early Mod.Du. *selfegghe*. An edge of cloth so finished as to prevent ravelling out; a strip at the edge of a web of cloth.
Sem'aphore, *n.* G. *sēma*, sign + *-phoros*, bearing, f. *pherein*, to BEAR. A post with one or more movable arms used for signalling.
Sem'blance, *n.* F. *semblance*, f. *sembler*, to seem—L. *simulāre, similāre*, to make like. SIMULATE. RESEMBLE. Appearance; likeness, image.
Se'men, *n.* L. *sēmen, sēminis*, seed, f. *serĕre*, to SOW. The impregnating fluid of male animals.—**Sem'in**AL, *a.*
Sem'ibreve, *n.* SEMI- + BREVE. *Mus.*, a note having half the length of a breve.
Sem'icircle, *n.* SEMI- + CIRCLE. The half of a circle; anything in this form.—**Semicir'cul**AR, *a.*
Semico'lon, *n.* SEMI- + COLON. A punctuation mark, a dot above a comma (;).
Sem'inary, *n.* L. *sēminārium*, seed-plot, f. SEMEN. A place of education.
Sem'iquaver, *n.* SEMI- + QUAVER. *Mus.*, a note having half the length of a quaver.

Sem'itone, *n.* SEMI- + TONE. *Mus.*, an interval approximately equal to half a tone.
Semoli'na, *n.* It. *semolino*, dim. of *semola*, bran — L. *simila*, fine wheaten flour. The hard portions of wheat which escape grinding.
Sempiter'nal, *a.* L.L. *sempiternālis*, f. L. *sempiternus*, f. *semper*, always. Everlasting.
Semp'stress, *n.* See SEAMSTRESS under SEAM.
Sen'ate, *n.* O.F. *senat*—L. *senātus*, lit. 'council of old men', f. *sen-* as in *senex*, old. SENESCHAL. SENILE. SENIOR. A state-council of citizens, esp. that of ancient Rome; a similar body.—**Sen'at**OR, *n.*—**Senato'ri**AL, *a.*
Send, *vt.* O.E. *sendan*. Common Teut. To cause to go or to be conveyed; to impel; to dispatch (a message, &c.); to cause to happen, ordain; to discharge (a missile); to emit.—*vi.* To send a messenger or a message.
Sen'dal, *n.* O.F. *cendal*, prob. ultimately f. G. *sindōn*, fine linen. A thin rich silken material.
Sen'eschal, *n.* O.F. *seneschal*, f. O.Teut. **seni-*, old (cogn. with L. *senex*. SENATE) + *skalkoz*, servant. MARSHAL. A steward in a mediæval great house.
Se'nile, *a.* L. *senīlis*, f. *senex*. SENATE. Incident to old age; showing the weakness of old age.—**Senil'**ITY, *n.*
Se'nior, *a.* L. *senior*, comp. of *senex*. SENATE. SEIGNEUR. SIR. SIRE. Older, elder; superior *to* in standing.—*n.* An elder person, a superior.—**Senior'**ITY, *n.*
Sen'na, *n.* Mod.L. *senna*, *sena*—Arab. *sanā*. The shrub known as Cassia; the dried leaflets used as a medicine.
Sen'night, *n.* Orig. two words, O.E. *seofon*, SEVEN, *nihta*, pl. of *niht*, NIGHT. A week.
Sense, *n.* F. *sens*—L. *sensus*, f. *sentīre*, *sensum*, to feel, perceive. CONSENT. SCENT. SENTENCE. Each of the bodily faculties of perception; these faculties viewed as one, the exercise or function of this faculty; the faculties viewed as means of gratifying desires; soundness of judgement; feeling, consciousness, recognition; opinion; meaning; something with a satisfactory or intelligible meaning; what is wise or reasonable.—**Sensa'**TION, *n.* An operation of a sense; the operation of the senses; a mental feeling; mental apprehension; an excited feeling; a state of excited feeling; an exciting event.—**Sensa'tion**AL, *a.* Relating to sensation; aiming at producing, calculated to produce, exciting effects.—**Sensa'tional**ISM, *n.* The theory that sensation is the only source of knowledge; addiction to sensational writing, &c.—**Sense'**LESS, *a.* — **Sense'less**LY,[2] *adv.* — **Sens'**IBLE, *a.* Perceptible by the senses; appreciable, considerable; aware, not unmindful; of good sense, reasonable. — **Sens'ib**LY,[2] *adv.* — **Sensi**BIL'ITY, *n.*—**Sens'itive**, *a.* F. *sensitif*—Med. L. *sensitīvus*, f. *sentīre*. Having sensation; feeling quickly and acutely; very open to external impressions; readily altered or affected. —**Sens'itive**LY,[2] *adv.*—**Sens'itive**NESS, *n.* —**Sens'it**IZE, *vt.* To make sensitive, esp. to render (a photographic film, &c.) sensitive to light.—**Senso'rium**, *n.* L.L., f. *sentīre*. The seat of sensation; the brain.—**Sens'ual**, *a.* L.L. *sensuālis*, f. *sensus*. Relating to the gratification of the senses; lewd.—**Sens'ual**ISM, *n.* — **Sens'ual**IST, *n.* — **Sensual'**ITY, *n.*— **Sens'u**OUS, *a.* Pertaining to the senses.
Sen'tence, *n.* F. *sentence* — L. *sententia*, opinion, maxim, &c., f. *sentīre*. SENSE. The determination of punishment, the punishment; a series of words expressing a thought. —**Senten'ti**OUS, *a.* Of the nature of a maxim; abounding in maxims.
Sen'tient, *a.* L. *sentiens*, *sentientis*, pres. pple. of *sentīre*. SENSE. Feeling; capable of feeling.
Sen'timent, *n.* F. *sentiment*—Med.L. *sentimentum*, f. *sentīre*. SENSE. A tendency or view; an emotion; a tersely expressed thought; appeal to the tender emotions; emotional regard to considerations.—**Sentimen't**AL, *a.*
Sen'tinel, *n.* F. *sentinelle*—It. *sentinella*, of doubtful orig. A sentry.
Sen'try, *n.* Perh. shortened or formed f. *centrinel*, *centronel*, varr. of SENTINEL. A soldier on guard.
Sep'arate, *vt.* L. *sēparāre*, *sēparātum*, f. SE- + *parāre*, to make ready, PREPARE. PARE. SEVER. SEVERAL. To put apart; to occupy the space between.—*vi.* To withdraw; to quit company; to become disjoined *from*. — *a.* Parted, disconnected; having independent existence; belonging or peculiar to one; individual.—**Sep'arate**LY,[2] *adv.*—**Sep'ar**ABLE, *a.* — **Separ**A'TION, *n.* — **Sep'arat**IVE, *a.* — **Sep'arat**IST, *n.* An advocate of ecclesiastical or political independence.
Se'pia, *n.* L. *sēpia*—G. *sēpia*. The cuttlefish; a paint made from its inky secretion.
Se'poy, *n.* Urdu and Per. *sipāhī*, horseman, soldier, f. *sipāh*, army. A native of India in British service as a soldier.
Sept, *n.* Prob. a var. of SECT. A clan.
Septem'ber, *n.* L., f. *septem*, SEVEN. The seventh of the Roman months; our ninth.— **Septet(t)'**, **Septette'**, *n.* Ger. *septet*, f. *septem*. A composition for seven voices or instruments.—**Septuages'ima**, *n.* L. *septuāgēsima* (*dies*), seventieth (day), f. *septuāginta*, seventy, f. *septem*. The third Sunday before Lent. (It is not clear why it is so called.)—**Sep'tuagint**, *n.* From *septuāginta*. The Greek version of the Old Testament, said to have been made by 72 translators in 72 days.
Sep'tic, *a.* G. *sēptikos*, f. *sēpein*, to putrefy. Causing or caused by putrefaction.
Sep'ulchre, *n.* O.F. *sepulcre*—L. *sepulcrum* (less correctly *sepulchrum*), f. *sepelīre*, *sepultum*, to bury. A tomb. — *vt.* To bury.— **Sepul'chr**AL, *a.*—**Se'pult**URE, *n.* Burial.
Se'quel, *n.* O.F. *sequelle*—L. *sequēla*, result, f. *sequi*, to follow. CONSECUTION. ENSUE. PERSECUTE. SUIT. A consequence, after effects; a following part or continuation.— **Se'qu**ENT, *a.* Following. — **Se'qu**ENCE, *n.* Succession; a connected series.
Seques'ter, *vt.* L.L. *sequestrāre*, *sequestrātum*, to separate, put in safe keeping, f. L. *sequester*, one holding as depositary the subject of a suit, perh. lit. '(one) standing apart', conn. with *secus*, otherwise. To seclude; to take temporary possession of; to divert (income).—**Seques'tr**ATE,[3] *vt.* To divert (income); to take temporary possession of; to confiscate.—**Sequestr**A'TION, *n.* A diverting of income; temporary seizure; confiscation.
Se'quin, *n.* F. *sequin*—It. *zecchino*, f. *zecca*, mint—Arab. *sicca*, die. An Italian gold coin = about 9*s.*; a coinlike ornament on a dress, &c.
Seragl'io, *n.* It. *serraglio*, enclosure, place of confinement (used, from likeness of sound, to render Turkish *serāī*, lodging, palace)—L. *serāre*, to lock up, close, f. *sera*, bar, bolt, f. *serĕre*. SERIES. SERRIED. A harem; a Turkish palace, esp. that of the Sultan.

Ser'aph, *n.* Back-formation f. the pl. *seraphim*—Heb. *serāphīm*, only in Isa. vi, pl. of **sārāph*. Meaning not determined. In Christian use, an angel of the highest order.—**Seraph'**IC, *a.*

Sere, Sear, *a.* O.E. *séar*. Cogn. with G. *auos* (*sausos*), dry, f. *auein* (*sausein*), to dry. AUSTERE. SEAR. Dry, withered.

Serenade', *n.* F. *sérénade*, app. f. It. *serenata*, evening song, app. f. *sereno*, the open air, use as *n.* of *sereno*, L. *serēnus*. (See next.) An evening performance of music, esp. under a lady's window.—*vt.* To entertain with a serenade.

Serene', *a.* L. *serēnus*. Of the weather, &c., clear, calm; tranquil; an epithet given to certain princes, &c., esp. of Germany.—**Serene'**LY,[2] *adv.*—**Seren'**ITY, *n.*

Serf, *n.* O.F. *serf*—L. *servus*, slave. SERVE. One whose service is attached to the soil.

Serge, *n.* O.F. *serge*—L. *sērica*, fem. of *sēricus*. SILK. A durable woollen fabric. (App. orig. applied to a *silk* fabric.)

Ser'geant, Ser'jeant, *n.* O.F. *sergent*, *serjant*—L. *serviens*, *servientis*, an officer, orig. pres.pple. of *servīre*, to SERVE. One of a (now abolished) order of barristers (in this sense *Serjeant*); a non-commissioned officer ranking above a corporal (in this sense *Sergeant*); applied to officers of Parliament, the Royal Household, &c.—**Ser'gean**CY, **Ser'jean**CY, *n.*

Se'ries, *n.* L. *seriēs*, f. *serĕre*, *sertum*, to join together. ASSERT. DESERT, *a.* SERMON. A number *of* things of one kind arranged in line or following in time, &c.; a succession of books, &c.; a set.—**Se'ri**AL, *a.* Of, in, forming a series; published in instalments.—*n.* A serial publication.—**Seria'tim**, *adv.* Med.L. One after another.

Se'rious, *a.* F. *sérieux*—L.L. *sēriōsus*, f. L. *sērius*, grave, earnest. Earnest in purpose or thought; not jesting; requiring, performed with, earnestness; of grave demeanour; important, not slight.—**Se'rious**LY,[2] *adv.*

Ser'mon, *n.* A.F. *sermun* = O.F. *sermon*—L. *sermo*, *sermōnis*, connected discourse, f. *serĕre*. SERIES. A discourse in church.—*vt.* To admonish.—**Ser'mon**IZE, *vt.* and *i.*

Ser'pent, *n.* O.F. *serpent*—L. *serpens*, *serpentis*, creeping thing, serpent, orig. pres.pple. of *serpĕre* = G. *herpein*, to creep. A scaly, limbless reptile; a kind of firework; an obsolete wind instrument.—**Ser'pent**INE, *a.*—*vi.* To move like a serpent.

Serrate', *vt.* L. *serrāre*, *serrātum*, to saw, f. *serra*, saw. To make notched or jagged.—**Ser'rate, Serrat'ed**, *aa.* Notched.—**Ser**RA'TION, *n.*

Ser'ried, *ppl.a.* F. *serrer*, to press close, lock—L. *serāre*. SERAGLIO. Pressed close, in close order.

Se'rum, *n.* L. *serum*, whey. Watery animal fluid.—**Se'**ROUS, *a.*

Serve, *vi.* O.F. (and F.) *servir*—L. *servīre*, *servītum*, f. *servus*, slave, servant. DESSERT. To do work under another; to take one's part in war; to do duties; to answer a purpose; to be of use or capable of being used *as*, *for*, &c.; to be favourable or suitable; to suffice; in tennis, &c., to start the play by striking a ball.—*vt.* To work for; to attend upon; to help to food; to fulfil one's duty to; to fight for in war; to be useful to; to contribute or conduce to; to attend to (a customer); to supply *with* something; to set (meat, &c.) on the table; to deliver formally (a document. &c.) to a person concerned; to treat in a specified way.—**Ser'**VANT, *n.* A personal or domestic attendant; one who serves under another.—**Ser'vice**, *n.*[1] O.F. *servise*, *service*. The condition or occupation of being a servant; work done by a servant; public religious worship; a serving or benefiting; a useful office, benefit; a waiting at table; a set of dishes, &c.; provision (of labour, conveyance, &c.).—**Ser'vice**ABLE, *a.* Profitable, useful.—**Ser'vile**, *a.* L. *servīlis*, f. *servus*. Of, being, a slave; befitting a slave; meanly submissive. — **Ser'vile**LY,[2] *adv.*—**Servil'**ITY, *n.*—**Ser'vit**OR, *n.* A servant. —**Ser'vi**TUDE, *n.* Slavery.

Ser'vice, *n.*[2] Orig. *serves*, pl. of M.E. *serve*—O.E. *syrfe*—L. *sorbus*. A European tree bearing small pear-shaped or round fruit.

Ses'ame, *n.* F. *sésame*—G. *sēsamē*. A widely cultivated East Indian plant; the seeds.

Sesquipeda'lian, *a.* L. *sesquipedālis* (f. *sesqui-*, a half in addition + *pēs*, *pedis*, FOOT) + -AN. Of a word, 'a foot and half long', of many syllables.

Ses'sion, *n.* F. *session*—L. *sessio*, *sessiōnis*, f. *sedēre*, *sessum*, to SIT. A meeting of a court, &c.; a continuous series of such meetings.

Sestet(t)', Sestette', *n.* It. *sestetto*, f. *sesto*, L. *sextus*, sixth. A composition for six voices or instruments; the last six lines of a sonnet.

Sesti'na, *n.* It., f. *sesto*. (See prec.) A poem of six six-line stanzas (concluding with an envoy), in which the line-endings of the first stanza are repeated in a different order in the other five.

Set, *vt.* O.E. *settan*. Common Teut. Causal of Teut. type **setjan*, to SIT. To cause to sit; to put (a thing) in its place; to put, cause to be; to put (a thing) in the balance *against*; to fix (a price) *upon*; to appoint (a time); to propound (a question); to present (an example), introduce (a fashion); to fix (a gem, &c.) in metal; to put up (a sail); to make ready (a (table); to put (words) *to* music; to put (a broken bone) in position; to adjust (a cloak, &c.); of a hunting dog, to mark the position of game by stopping.—*pass.* To have one's mind fixed *upon*.—*vi.* Of the sun, &c., to go down; to become firm; to have a certain course or direction; to set game.—*ppl.a.* Deliberate, intentional; elaborately composed; pre-arranged, formal; unvarying.—*n.*[1] A setting (of the sun, &c.); tendency; fixed habit. —**Set-off**, *n.* Something that sets off or adorns; a reckoning of one thing as counterbalancing another; an item so treated.—**Set'**TER, *n.* One who or that which sets; a dog trained to set game.

Set, *n.*[2] O.F. *sette*—L. *secta*, SECT. A number of persons or things associated in intercourse or use as being essentially similar or as being complementary to each other.

Se'ton, *n.* Med.L. *sēto*, *sētōnis*, app. f. *sēta*. SATIN. A thread, &c., drawn under the skin to maintain an opening for discharges.

Settee', *n.* Perh. a fanciful var. of next. A long seat (for indoors) with a back.

Set'tle, *n.* O.E. *setl*, a seat. Cogn. with SIT. A bench with a back and arms and gen. with a locker below.—*vt.* O.E. *setlan*, f. *setl*. To place in order or position; to cause to take up residence; to establish (a colony); to consolidate, compact; to quiet, tranquillize; to fix; to establish *in*; to secure (property, &c.) *to*, *on*, *upon*; to bring into order, &c.; to decide upon; to come to a decision on (a question, &c.), to bring (a dispute, &c.) to an end; to pay.—*pass.* To have taken up abode.—*vi.* To alight *on*; to come to rest; to take up abode; to sink, subside; to become consolidated; of a liquid, to become clear; to subside; to come to an agreement *with*; to settle accounts.—**Set'tle**MENT, *n.*—**Set'tl**ER. *n.*

Sev'en, *a.* and *n.* O.E. *seofon.* Common Teut. Cogn. with G. *hepta*, L. *septem.* The cardinal number next after six.

Sev'er, *vt.* O.F. *sevrer*—L. *sēparāre*, to SEPARATE. To separate, divide, keep apart; to cut or tear off.—*vi.* To separate, divide.—**Sev'er**ABLE, *a.*—**Sev'er**ANCE, *n.*

Sev'eral, *a.* A.F. *several*—Med.L. *sēparālis*, f. L. *sēparāre.* (See prec.) Separate, distinct, individual; more than two, but not many.—*pron.* A moderate number.—**Sev'eral**LY,[2] *adv.*—**Sev'eral**TY, *n.* Unshared tenure.

Severe', *a.* F. *sévère*—L. *sevērus*, serious, strict, stern. ASSEVERATE. PERSEVERE. Rigorous, strict, austere; involving effort, trying, hard to endure.—**Severe'**LY,[2] *adv.*—**Sever'**ITY, *n.*

Sew, *vt.* O.E. *siwan, siwian.* Common Teut. and Indo-Germanic. Cogn. with G. *(kas)suein*, L. *suěre.* SUTURE. To join or attach with thread.

Sew'er, *n.* O.F. *se(u)wiere*, channel for draining a pond—L. type **exaquāria*, f. EX- + *aqua*, water. AQUATIC. EWER. An underground drain for carrying off waste water and refuse.—**Sew'**AGE, *n.* Refuse so carried off.—**Sew'er**AGE, *n.* Drainage by sewers; sewers collectively; sewage.

Sex, *n.* L. *sexus.* The condition of being male or female; males or females collectively.—**Sex'u**AL, *a.*—**Sex'ual**LY,[2] *adv.*—**Sexual'**ITY, *n.*

Sexages'ima, *n.* L. *sexāgēsima (dies)*, sixtieth (day), f. *sexāginta*, sixty. The second Sunday before Lent. (It is not clear why it is so called.)

Sexen'nial, *a.* L. *sexennis*, of six years (f. *sex*, SIX + *annus*, year) + -AL. Lasting six years; recurring every six years.

Sex'tant, *n.* L. *sextans, sextantis*, a sixth part, f. *sextus*, sixth. An instrument with a graduated arc equal to a sixth of a circle used for measuring angular distances.

Sex'ton, *n.* M.E. *segerstane, sekesteyn*, &c.—A.F. *segerstaine* = O.F. *segrestein, secrestein*, &c.—Med.L. *sacristānus*, SACRISTAN under SACRED. An official in charge of a church and its contents, and often acting as grave-digger.

Shab'by, *a.* With -Y[2] f. *shab* (now only dial.)—O.E. *sceabb*, corresp. to O.N. **skabbr*, SCAB. Cogn. with SHAVE. Dingy, faded, worn; poorly dressed; dishonourable, ungenerous.—**Shab'bi**LY,[2] *adv.*—**Shab'bi**NESS, *n.*

Shack'le, *n.* O.E. *sceacul*, fetter. Cf. L.G. *schakel*, link of a chain, hobble for a horse, Du. *schakel*, link of a chain. A fetter.—*vt.* To confine with or as with shackles.

Shad, *n.* O.E. *sceadd*, of unknown orig. A deep-bodied fish.

Shade, *n.* M.E. *schade*, representing O.E. *sceadu* and its by-form *scead.* Cogn. with G. *skotos*, darkness. Partial darkness; the darker part of a picture; degree of darkness or of depth of colour; a tinge, a hardly perceptible degree; a ghost; shelter from light, heat, &c.; a place sheltered from the sun; something sheltering from light, &c.—*vt* To shelter from light, &c.; to screen; to obscure or darken; in drawing, &c., to represent the shades on; to cause to pass (also, as *vi.*, to pass) imperceptibly *into.*—**Shad'ow**, *n.* Reps. O.E. *sceadwe* oblique case of *sceadu.* Partial darkness; a figure projected by the interception of light; a trace; a ghost; protection or shelter.—*vt.* To cast a shadow over; to symbolize, typify, gen. with *out, forth*, &c.; to follow closely.—**Shad'ow**Y,[2] *a.*—**Sha'd**Y,[2] *a.* Affording shade; shaded; disreputable.

Shaft, *n.* O.E. *sceaft.* Common Teut. App. cogn. with L. *scāpus*, shaft, stem, shank, and poss. with G. *skēptron*, staff, SCEPTRE. The rod forming the body of a spear, arrow, &c.; a stem, straight part, handle; one of the bars between which a horse is harnessed; a rotating rod for the transmission of power; a vertical or slightly inclined access to a mine, &c.

Shag, *n.* O.E. *sceacga.* Cf. O.N. *skegg*, beard. Rough matted hair, wool, &c.; cloth with a long nap on one side; tobacco cut into fine shreds.—**Shag'g**Y,[2] *a.*

Shagreen', *n.* Var. of CHAGRIN in orig. sense. A kind of untanned leather with a rough surface.

Shah, *n.* Per. *shāh*, king, shortened f. Old Per. *khshāyathiya*, prob. orig. an *a.* = 'mighty', cogn. with G. *kta-esthai*, to acquire. CHECK. A Persian title equivalent to 'king'.

Shake, *vi.* O.E. *scacan.* Cf. O.N. *skaka.* To move irregularly and quickly to and fro, up and down, &c.; to totter; to tremble; *mus.*, to execute a trill.—*vt.* To cause to shake; to impair the stability of; with *off*, &c., to get rid of by shaking.—*n.* An act of shaking; tremulous or vibratory movement; a jolt, jerk, shock; *mus.*, a trill.—**Shak'**Y,[2] *a.*

Shak'o, *n.* Magyar *csákó.* A military cap with a peak.

Shale, *n.* Perh. a use, suggested by the derived sense 'loose ore' of obs. *Shale*, dish, shell, husk—O.E. *sc(e)alu*, cogn. with O.N. *skál.* SCALE.[1] A clay rock with a slaty structure.—**Shal'**Y,[2] *a.*

Shall, *v.aux.* O.E. *sceal*, pa. *sceolde*, I should. Common Teut. Orig. sense 'to owe, be liable for'. Helps to form the future tense, in the first person expressing futurity, in the second and third gen. expressing the speaker's will.

Shalloon', *n.* F. *chalon*, app. f. *Chalons-sur-Marne*, the original place of manufacture. A woven woollen material used chiefly for linings.

Shal'lop, *n.* F. *chaloupe*, prob. the source of Du. *sloep*, SLOOP. A dinghy.

Shallot', *n.* O.F. *eschalote*, var. of *escalogne*—L. *ascalōnia*, orig. fem. of *Ascalōnius*, belonging to Ascalon, a city of the Philistines. A small onion, native in Syria.

Shal'low, *a.* M.E. *schalowe.* Prob. related in some way to SHOAL. Not deep; lacking depth of mind; superficial.—*n.* A shallow place.

Sham, *n.* Orig. obscure. Appears as slang about 1677. Originally, a trick, fraud. A counterfeit, imitation.—*a.* Counterfeit.—*vt.* To feign, pretend to be.—*vi.* To pretend.

Sham'ble, *n.*[1] O.E. *sc(e)amel*, stool—L. *scamellum*, dim. of *scamnum*, bench. In *pl.*, a butcher's stall, a slaughter-house.

Sham'ble, *vi.* Prob. f. the rare *Shamble*, a., ungainly, gen. of the legs, prob. attrib. use of prec. (*shamble legs* app. meaning orig. 'legs straddling like those of a butcher's trestles'). To go with an awkward, unsteady gait.—*n.*[2] Such a gait.

Shame, *n.* O.E. *sc(e)amu.* Common Teut. The painful emotion from being conscious of something dishonouring, ridiculous, or indecorous in one's conduct or situation; disgrace; a cause of disgrace.—*vt.* O.E. *sc(e)amian.* To cause to feel shame; to disgrace.—**Shame'fast**, *a.* O.E. *scamfæst*, f. *sc(e)amu* + *fæst*, FAST. Orig. app. 'restrained by shame'. Modest, bashful, shy. Sim. **Shame'faced**, orig. an etymological misinterpretation of *shamefast*.—**Shame'**FUL, *a.*—**Shame'ful**LY,[2] *adv.*—**Shame'**LESS, *a.*

Shampoo', *vt.* Prob. f. Hindī *chāmpo*, imp. of *chāmpnā*, to press. To rub and wash (the scalp) with a cleansing agent.—*n.* The act or operation.

Sham'rock, *n.* Ir. *seamróg*, dim. of *seamar*, clover. A trefoil plant, the Irish national emblem.

Shank, *n.* O.E. *sc(e)anca*, corresp. to L.G. *schanke*, leg, thigh, Flemish *schank*, bone. The leg from the knee to the ankle; the shinbone; the leg; a stem or straight part.

Shan'ty, *n.*[1] Prob. f. F. *chantier*, work-yard, in Canadian senses 'establishment for felling trees', 'place at which the workers assemble at night'. A cabin or hut.

Shan'ty, *n.*[2] Said to be f. F. *chantez*, imp. of *chanter*, to sing. CHANT. A sailor's song.

Shape, *vt.* O.E. *scieppan.* Common Teut. (The present word descends f. M.E. *schapen*, formed f. *scapen*, the pa.pple.) To make, fashion, mould; to devise, plan.—*n.* External form; appearance, guise; definite form; a mould for forming jelly, &c.; a portion of moulded jelly, &c.—**Shape'**LESS, *a.*—**Shape'**LY,[1] *a.* Well-formed.

Shard, *n.*[1] O.E. *sceard*, a fragment, lit., 'cut thing', from root *skar-* of SHEAR. POTSHERD. A fragment, esp. of broken earthenware.

Shard, *n.*[2] Evolved from a misunderstanding of Shakespeare's 'shard-borne beetle', Macb. III. ii. 42. Really 'dung-born', f. dial. *shard*, patch of cow-dung, app. cogn. with dial. *sharn* in sim. sense—O.E. *scearn*, f. root *skar-*, to separate, of SHEAR. The wing-case of an insect. [The blade of a plough.

Share, *n.*[1] O.E. *scear*, f. root *skar-* of SHEAR.

Share, *n.*[2] O.E. *scearu*, cutting, division, f. root *skar-* of SHEAR. A portion allotted, belonging or contributed; a part taken *in* (an action, &c.); each of the parts into which a company's capital is divided.—*vt.* To apportion; to give away part of; to get or have a share of.—*vi.* To have a share.

Shark, *n.*[1] Orig. obscure. App. introduced by Capt. (afterwards Sir John) Hawkins's sailors in 1569. A voracious fish.

Shark, *n.*[2] Orig. obscure. A parasite; a sharper.

Shark, *vi.* Orig. obscure. Prob. formed f. both the *nn.* To act the parasite or sharper.—*vt.* To steal, pilfer.

Sharp, *a.* O.E. *scearp.* Common Teut. SCARP. Having a fine edge or point; quick-witted; apt, pointed; of the sight, &c., acute, keen; brisk, energetic, business-like; taking unfair advantage; severe, harsh; cutting in rebuke; pungent; shrill, penetrating; distinct in outline, abrupt, strongly marked.—*n.* *Mus.*, a note half a tone above the natural pitch; the sign (♯) marking this.—*vi.* To swindle.—**Sharp'**LY,[2] *adv.*—**Sharp'**EN,[2] *vt.*—**Sharp'**ER, *n.* A swindler.—**Sharp'**NESS, *n.*—**Sharp'shooter**, *n.* A skilled marksman.

Shat'ter, *vt.* See SCATTER. To break in pieces, destroy.—*vi.* To fly in pieces.

Shave, *vt.* O.E. *sceafan.* Common Teut. To pare away; to cut (the hair, &c.) off close; to tonsure as a cleric; to remove the hair from (the chin, &c.); to graze.—*vi.* To shave oneself.—*n.*[1] A shaving; a narrow escape.—**Shave'ling**, *n.* -LING (1). A tonsured cleric.

Shave, *n.*[2] O.E. *sceafa*, f. root of prec. A tool adapted for removing thin slices.

Shawl, *n.* Per. *shāl.* An article of dress used chiefly as a covering for the shoulders.

She, *pron.* Of doubtful orig. Prob. altered form of the O.E. fem. demonstrative pron. *sío*, *séo*, &c. The feminine pronoun of the third person.

Sheaf, *n.*; *pl.* **Sheaves**. O.E. *scéaf.* Common Teut. (Not in Goth.) A bundle of cornstalks bound together after reaping; any similar bundle.

Shear, *vt.* O.E. *sceran.* Common Teut. O. Teut. root *sker-*, *skar*, *skur-*, to cut, divide, shear. Cogn. with G. *keirein* (*skeryein*), to cut. SCORE. SHARD. SHARE. To cut through; to cut *off*, *away*, &c.; to clip, to cut the hair or the fleece from.—*n.pl.* A double instrument for cutting; a device for raising and fixing masts, boilers, &c. (often spelt *sheers*).—**Shear'**ER, *n.*—**Shear steel**, *n.* Steel improved in quality by heating, rolling, &c. (The steel orig. so called was stamped with the figure of a pair of shears.)

Sheath, *n.* O.E. *scǽth*, *scéath*, app. f. Teut. root *skaith-*, to separate, divide. SHED, *v.* (Primary notion perh. that of a stick split to receive a blade.) A close-fitting cover, esp. for a sword, &c.—**Sheathe**, *vt.* To put into a sheath; to cover.

Sheave, *n.* Cogn. with O.S. *scîva*, O.H.G. *scîba* (Ger. *scheibe*), disk, wheel, pulley, &c. A pulley.

Shed, *n.*[1] App. a var. of SHADE. A slight structure for shelter, storage, &c.; a large strong structure with a roof on pillars.

Shed, *vt.* O.E. *sc(e)ádan.* Common Teut. (Not in Scand.) Teut. root *skeith-*, *skeid-*; *skaith-*, *skaid-*, to separate. Prob. cogn. with G. *schizein*, to split, L. *scindĕre*, to cut, cleave. Formerly, to separate. To pour forth, diffuse, spread abroad; to lose, cast off (hair, leaves, &c.)—*n.*[2] A ridge dividing two valleys.

Sheen, *a.* O.E. *sciene.* Teut. root *skau-*, to see, look. SHOW. Influenced by root of SHINE. Beautiful, bright.—*n.* Brightness; bright attire.—**Sheen'**Y,[2] *a.*

Sheep, *n.* O.E. *scǽp*, *scéap.* Cf. Du. *schaap*, Ger. *schaf.* A well-known animal.—**Sheep'cot**, **Sheep'cote**, *nn.* COT.[1] COTE. A shelter for sheep.

Sheer, *a.* M.E. *schēre*, bright, perh. from O.N. *skǽrr.* Teut. root *ski-*, to SHINE. Unmixed, mere, absolute; perpendicular.—*adv.* Completely; perpendicularly.

Sheer, *vi.* Poss. a use, difficult to explain, of SHEAR. Of a ship, to deviate from its course; to depart, go *off*.—*n.*[1] A swerve.

Sheer, *n.*[2] Perh. formed on SHEAR. The fore-and-aft upward curvature of the deck or bulwarks of a vessel.

Sheers, *n.pl.* See SHEAR.

Sheet, *n.*[1] O.E. *sciete*, f. Teut. root *skaut-*, of which one of the senses was 'to project'. Hence 'corner', 'fold of a garment', 'cloth'. SHOOT. A large oblong piece of linen, &c., for a bed; a broad piece of some thin material; a piece of paper printed and folded; a broad expanse.—*vt.* To wrap in or cover with a sheet.

Sheet, *n.*[2] O.E. *scéata*, f. root *skaut-*. (See prec.) A rope attached to a corner of a sail.

Sheet-an'chor, *n.* Orig. uncertain. A large anchor used only in an emergency.
Sheikh, *n.* Arab. *shaikh*, properly 'old man', f. *shākha*, to grow or be old. An Arab chief.
Shek'el, *n.* Heb. *sheqel*, f. *shāqal*, to weigh. A Babylonian and Jewish weight and coin.
Shelf, *n.*[1]; *pl.* **Shelves**. App. f. (M.)L.G. *schelf*, shelf, set of shelves, cogn. with M.Du. *schelve*, stack (of hay, &c.). A slab fixed horizontally to hold vessels, books, &c.—**Shelve**, *v.*[1]*t.* To fit with shelves; to put on a shelf; to put aside, to defer.
Shelf, *n.*[2] Of obscure orig. A sand-bank.
Shell, *n.* O.E. *sciell*, *scill*. Teut. root *skal-*. SCALE.[1] The hard covering of an animal, a fruit, &c.; an explosive projectile; an inner coffin; the outer part of a fabric left after removal of the interior.—*vt.* To take out of the shell; to remove the shell of; to fire at with shells.
Shellac', *n.* Translation of F. *laque en écailles*. LAC in scales or thin plates.
Shel'ter, *n.* Orig. obscure. Poss., in former form *shelture*, f. *sheld*, early spelling of SHIELD, *v.* + -URE, after *jointure*, &c. A structure affording protection; a place of safety; sheltered condition.—*vt.* To protect, screen.—*vi.* To take shelter.
Shelve, *v.*[2]*i.* Of obscure orig. Prob. not f. SHELF[1] or [2]. Of a surface, to slope gradually.
Shep'herd, *n.* O.E. *scéaphirde*, SHEEP. HERD. A man who tends sheep.—**Shep'herd**ESS, *n.*
Sher'bet, *n.* Turkish and Per. *sherbet*, f. Arab. *sharbat*, f. *shariba*, to drink. SYRUP. SHRUB.[2] A cooling drink of the East.
Sher'iff, *n.* O.E. *scírgeréfa*, f. *scír*, SHIRE + *geréfa*, REEVE. A county, city and borough officer with various duties; in Scotland, a local judge.
Sher'ry, *n.* A sing. form evolved f. archaic *Sherris* taken as a pl.—Sp. (*vino de*) *Xeres*, (wine of) Xeres. A white Spanish wine.
Shib'boleth, *n.* Heb. See Judges xii. 4-6. A test word; a distinguishing custom, mode of speech, &c.; an old-fashioned doctrine.
Shield, *n.* O.E. *sceld*. Common Teut. A piece of armour carried on the left arm (often *fig.*); an escutcheon.—*vt.* To protect, screen.
Shift, *vt.* O.E. *sciftan*, to divide, corresp. to M.L.G., Du. *schiften*, to divide, M.H.G. *schihten*, to divide, to classify, O.N. *skipta*, to share, to change. To change, move, remove.—*vi.* To make a livelihood, get along; to employ evasions; to change one's clothes; to change, move, remove.—*n.* An expedient or evasion; a forced measure; a relay of workmen, the time during which they work; a removal.—**Shift'**LESS, *a.* Lacking in resource.—**Shift'**Y,[2] *a.* Full of evasions.—**Shift'i**NESS, *n.*
Shil'ling, *n.* O.E. *scilling*. Common Teut. A silver coin of the value of 12 pence.
Shil'ly-shal'ly, *vi.* Orig. *Shill I*, *shall I* = *Shall I*, *shall I*. To vacillate.—*n.* Vacillation.
Shim'mer, *vi.* Late O.E. *scymrian* = West Fris. *skimerje*, to shimmer, (M.)L.G. *schēmeren*, to be shadowy, to glimmer. To gleam faintly. —*n.* A shimmering light.
Shin, *n.* O.E. *scinu* = West Fris. *skine*, (M.)L.G. *schēne*, O.H.G. *scina*. Orig. meaning app. 'thin or narrow piece'. The front of the lower leg.—*vi.* To climb with arms and legs.
Shin'dy, *n.* Perh. alteration of *Shinty* (used in the same sense) = *shinny*, a north-country and American game like hockey, app. f. a cry used in the game *shin ye*, of obscure orig. A row or disturbance.
Shine, *vi.* O.E. *scínan*. Common Teut. Teut. root *skī*. SHEER, *a.* To give out or reflect light.—*n.* Brightness.—**Shin'**Y,[2] *a.*
Shin'gle, *n.*[1] M.E. *scincle*, *shyngle*, app. representing L. *scindula*, a later form of *scandula*, a shingle. A thin piece of wood used as a house-tile.—*vt.* To cover with shingles.
Shin'gle, *n.*[2] Orig. obscure. Cf. Norw. *singl*, coarse sand, N.Fris. *singel*, gravel. Small rounded pebbles on the sea-shore.
Shin'gles, *n.pl.* Representing L. *cingulus* (var. of *cingulum*, girdle, f. *cingère*, to gird), used to render G. *zōnē* or *zōstēr*, girdle, shingles. CINCTURE. An eruptive disease often extending round the body like a girdle.
Ship, *n.* O.E. *scip*. Common Teut. EQUIP. SKIFF. SKIPPER. A large sea-going vessel.—*vt.* To put, take, send away on board ship.—*vi.* To embark; to engage for service in a ship.—**Ship'**MENT, *n.*—**Ship'ping**, *vbl.n.* Ships collectively.—**Ship'-shape**, *a.* As things ought to be on board ship; trim, orderly.—**Ship's hus'band**, *n.* An agent of the owners who attends to the business of a ship while she is in port.
Shire, *n.* O.E. *scír* = O.H.G. *scira*, care, official charge. Equivalent to COUNTY.
Shirk, *vt.* Belongs to obs. *Shirk*=SHARK, *n.*[2] To evade (one's duty, &c.).—*n.* One who does this.—**Shirk'**ER, *n.*
Shirt, *n.* O.E. *scyrte*, corresp. to M.Du. *schorte*, M.L.G. *schōrt*, apron, O.N. *skyrta*, shirt (whence, with unexplained difference in sense, SKIRT). Teut. type **skurto-*, SHORT. (Prob. the notion in the various senses is 'short garment'.) An undergarment for the upper part of the body.
Shiv'er, *n.*[1] Early M.E. *scifre*, cogn. with O.H.G. *scivero*, splinter. Teut. root *skīf-*, to split. A fragment, splinter.—*v.*[1]*t.* and *i.* To break in pieces.
Shiv'er, *v.*[2]*i.* Early M.E. *chiveren*, of obscure orig. To tremble, esp. with cold or fear.—*n.*[2] An act or the condition of shivering.
Shoal, *a.* O.E. *sceald*, of doubtful orig. SHALLOW is app. a parallel formation. Of water, not deep.—*n.*[1] A sand-bank or bar.—*v.*[1]*i.* To become shallow.
Shoal, *n.*[2] O.E. *scolu*, troop, division of an army = O.S. *scola*, multitude, M.Du. *schole*, multitude, shoal of fish. Teut. root *skul-*. SCALE.[1] A multitude, esp. of fish, &c., swimming together.—*v.*[2]*i.* To collect in shoals.
Shock, *vt.* App. f. F. *choquer* = Sp. *chocar*, of obscure orig. To scandalize, horrify; to outrage (feelings, &c.).—*n.*[1] A violent blow, &c.; a damaging blow (to health, &c.); a sudden disturbing emotion.
Shock, *a.* Prob. a back-formation f. obs. *Shock*, *Shock-dog*, a dog with shaggy hair, of doubtful orig. Having rough thick hair; of hair, shaggy.—*n.*[2] A thick mass (of hair).
Shod'dy, *n.* Of obscure orig. Shreds of refuse wool mixed with new wool; cloth made of shoddy.—*a.* Worthless and pretentious.
Shoe, *n.* O.E. *scóh*. Common Teut. A covering for the foot, slighter than a boot; a metal protection on a horse's hoof; various things like a shoe.—*vt.* To put shoes on.
Shoot, *vi.* O.E. *scéotan*. Common. Teut. Teut. root *skeut-*, *skaut-*, *skut-*. SHEET[1] and [2]. SHOT. SHOUT. SHUT. To go swiftly and suddenly; to sprout; to discharge a missile; to engage in killing game with a gun.—*vt.* To

pass quickly under; to descend (a rapid); to send forth suddenly; to dump; to slide (a bar or bolt); to discharge (a missile); to discharge (a gun, &c.); to kill or wound with a missile from a weapon.—*n.* An act of shooting; a game-shooting expedition; a young branch; a place where rubbish may be shot.

Shop, *n.* M.E. *schoppe*—O.E. *sceoppa*, cogn. with *scypen*, cattle-shed, O.H.G. *scopf*, porch, M.L.G. *schoppe*, *schuppe*, shed. A place where goods, &c., are sold or made.—*vi.* To visit a shop or shops in order to buy.—**Shop'lifter**, *n.* One who steals from a shop.

Shore, *n.*[1] M.E. *schore*, f. or cogn. with M.L.G. *schore*, *schare*, shore, late M.Du. *schore*, *schor*, shore, sea-marsh. Poss. f. the root of SHEAR, with notion 'division between land and sea'. The land bordering on the sea or on a large lake or river.

Shore, *n.*[2] Late M.E. *schore*, f. or cogn. with M.L.G., M.Du. *schōre*, *schāre*, prop. Cf. O.N. *skortha* in same sense. A prop, support.—*vt.* To prop, support.

Short, *a.* O.E. *sc(e)ort* = O.H.G. *scurz*. Teut. type **skurto-*, poss. an altered adoption of L. *curtus*. SHIRT. Measuring little from end to end; of sight, &c., of small range; brief; rudely curt; of the temper, hasty; inadequate; friable, easily crumbled; of a vowel, having the lesser of the two recognized measures of duration.—*n.* In *pl.*, knee-breeches; *in short*, briefly, concisely.—*adv.* Abruptly, suddenly; curtly.—**Short'**AGE, *n.* Deficiency in quantity.—**Short'**EN,[2] *vt.* and *i.*—**Short'hand**, *n.* A method of speedy writing by means of contractions or signs.—**Short'**LY,[2] *adv.* Briefly; curtly; soon.

Shot, *n.* O.E. *sc(e)ot*. Teut. type **skuto-* f. *skut-*. SHOOT. A shooting; the range of a shot; lead in small pellets; one who shoots; a reckoning at a tavern, &c.—*ppl.a.* Woven so that the fabric changes in tint when viewed from different points.

Shoul'der, *n.* O.E. *sculder*, corresp. to M.L.G. *schulder*, M.H.G. and Ger. *schulter*. The part of the body to which the arm or the fore-leg is attached; a projection or support.—*vt.* To push with the shoulder; to put on one's shoulder.—*vi.* To make one's way by shouldering.—**Shoul'der-blade**, *n.* The bone of the shoulder.

Shout, *n.* Corresponds formally to O.N. *skúta*, *skúte*. SCOUT, *v.*[2] Prob. f. the root of SHOOT. A loud cry.—*vi.* To utter a shout.—*vt.* To utter with a loud voice.

Shove, *vt.* O.E. *scúfan*. Common Teut. Teut. root *skeub-*: *skaub-*: *skub-*. SCUFFLE. SHOVEL. To push along with effort, to move by a push.—*n.* An act of shoving.

Shov'el, *n.* O.E. *scofl*, corresp. to M.L.G., L.G. *schuffel*, M.Du. *schofel*. App. f. root of SHOVE. A broad spade-like implement.—*vt.* To move with a shovel.

Show, *vt.* O.E. *scéawian*. Common W. Germanic. Teut. root *skau-*, to see, look, whence SHEEN. SCAVENGER. To expose to view; to produce for inspection; to point out; to guide; to accord (favour, &c.); to be an indication of.—*vi.* To be visible, appear.—*n.* An appearance, display; something shown, a sight, spectacle.—**Show'**Y,[2] *a.*—**Show'**ILY,[2] *adv.*

Show'er, *n.* O.E. *scúr*. Cf. O.N. *skúr*, Du. *schoer*. A short fall of rain; anything coming like a shower.—*vi.* and *t.* To rain, fall, pour in a shower.—**Show'er**Y,[2] *a.*

Shrap'nel, *n.* From the inventor, General H. *Shrapnel*. A shell containing bullets, which can be scattered at a given point.

Shred, *n.* O.E. *scréade*. Teut. root *skraud-*, *skreud-*, *skrūd-*, to cut. SCREED. SCROLL. SHROUD. A fragment, a strip.—*vt.* and *i.* To reduce, to be reduced, to shreds.

Shrew, *n.*[1] O.E. *scréawa*, *scrǽwa*. Not elsewhere in Teut. A small mouse-like mammal with a long sharp snout.—So **Shrew'mouse**.

Shrew, *n.*[2] Perh. a fig. use of prec. Formerly, a malicious person. A scolding woman.—**Shrew'**ISH, *a.*

Shrewd, *a.* M.E. *schrewed*, &c. Prob. f. SHREW[2] (or SHREW[1]) + *-ed*. Formerly, malicious, shrewish. Astute, sagacious; of a suspicion, &c., coming near the truth.—**Shrewd'**LY,[2] *adv.*—**Shrewd'**NESS, *n.*

Shriek, *vi.* Imitative. Cf. SCREECH. To utter a loud shrill cry.—*n.* Such a cry.

Shrie'valty, *n.* From *Shrieve*, obs. var. of SHERIFF + *-alty*—O.F. *-alte*—L. *-ālitas*. The office, jurisdiction, term of office, of sheriff.

Shrike, *n.* App. repg. O.E. *scríc*, *scréc*, perh. applied generally to birds with shrill cries. The name of various birds with strong toothed and hooked bills.

Shrill, *a.* M.E. *shrille*, related to L.G. *schrell*, of sharp tone, Ger. *schrill*, shrill. Sharp, piercing.—**Shril'**LY,[2] *adv.*

Shrimp, *n.* Prob. cogn. with M.H.G. *schrimpen*, to shrivel up. A small crustacean allied to the prawns.—**Shrimp'**ER, *n.*

Shrine, *n.* O.E. *scrín*, corresp. to M.L.G. *schrīn*, O.H.G. *scrīni*—L. *scrīnium*, case, chest. A case containing a saint's relics; a temple.

Shrink, *vi.* O.E. *scrincan* = M.Du. *schrinken*, Sw. *skrynka*, to wrinkle. To become smaller; to retire, recoil, flinch.—*vt.* To cause to shrink.—**Shrink'**AGE, *n.*

Shrive, *vt.* O.E. *scrífan*, to allot, decree, impose as a sentence or penance. Common Teut. (Wanting in Goth.) Cf. Old Fris. *scriva*, to write, impose penance, O.H.G. *scrīban*, M.H.G. *scrīben*, to write, draw, appoint. All prob. f. L. *scrībĕre*. SCRIBE. To hear the confession of, give absolution to.—*vi.* To confess one's sins.—**Shrift**, *n.* O.E. *scrift*. Absolution; confession.

Shriv'el, *vi.* and *t.* Orig. unknown. Cf. Sw. dial. *skryvla*, to wrinkle. To become, to cause to become, contracted or wrinkled.

Shroud, *n.*[1] O.E. *scrúd*, garment, f. Teut. root *skrūd-*. SHRED. A sheet for a corpse; a defence, covering.—*vt.* To put a shroud on; to cover, screen.

Shroud, *n.*[2] Prob. a use of the prec. with notion of clothing the mast with the shrouds. Gen. in *pl.*, a set of ropes leading from the head of the mast.

Shrove'-tide, *n.* The first element conn. with SHRIVE. Quinquagesima Sunday and the two following days.

Shrub, *n.*[1] App. repg. O.E. *scrybb*, presumed to mean 'underwood, shrubbery'. SCRUB, *n.*[1] A woody plant smaller than a tree.—**Shrub'b**Y,[2] *a.*—**Shrub'b**ERY, *n.* A plantation of shrubs; shrubs collectively.

Shrub, *n.*[2] Prob. f. Arab. *shurb*, drink, draught, f. *shariba*. SHERBET. A drink of fruit-juice and rum.

Shrug, *vt.* Of obscure orig. To raise and contract (the shoulders) to express disdain, &c.—*n.* The motion.

Shud'der, *vi.* M.E. *schoderen*, cogn. with M.L.G. *schōderen* (Ger. *schaudern*), M.Du. *schūderen*. Teut. root *skūd-*, to shake. To tremble from fear, &c.; to quiver.—*n.* An act of shuddering; a quiver.

Shuf'fle, *vi.* From or cogn. with L.G. *schüffeln*, to walk clumsily, shuffle (cards), deal dishonestly. Teut. root *skuf-* (*skub-*), to SHOVE. To move the feet withou lifting them; to act evasively.—*vt.* To mix (cards); with *off*, to evade; to put (a thing) *off*, *from*, one person *to* or *upon* another.—*n.* An evasive trick; a shuffling movement; a rude dance; the act of shuffling cards.—**Shuf'fl**ER, *n.*

Shun, *vt.* O.E. *scunian* of obscure orig. To avoid; to abstain from.

Shunt, *vt.* Of obscure orig. To move (a train) from one line of rails to another.

Shut, *vt.* O.E. *scyttan*, f. root *skut-*, SHOOT. Cf. next. Formerly, to shoot (a bar or bolt). To close; to enclose or confine *in* or *within*.—*vi.* To close, become closed.—**Shut't**ER, *n.* A movable screen for a window.

Shut'tle, *n.* O.E. *scytel*, f. root *skut-*. SHOOT. An instrument for shooting the woof between the threads of the warp.—**Shut'tlecock**, *n.* A feathered cork for use with a battledore.

Shy, *a.* O.E. *scéoh*, corresp. to M.H.G. *schiech* (Ger. *scheu*). Teut. root *skeuhw-*, to fear, to terrify. ESCHEW. Timid; uneasy in company; chary, reluctant.—*v.*[1]*i.* To start back or aside through sudden fear.—*n.*[1] A sudden start by a horse.—**Shy'**LY,[2] **Shi'**LY,[2] *adv.*—**Shy'**NESS, **Shi'**NESS, *n.*

Shy, *v.*[2]*t.* Of obscure orig. To throw, jerk.—*n.*[2] A throw, a jerk; a trial, an experiment.

Sib'ilant, *a.* L. *sibilans*, *sibilantis*, pres pple. of *sibilāre*, to hiss. Having a hissing sound.—*n.* A speech sound having a hissing effect.

Sib'yl, *n.* O.F. *Sibile*—L. *Sibylla*—G. *Sibulla*. A pagan prophetess.—**Sibyl'l**INE, *a.*

Sic'cative, *a.* L. *siccātivus*, f. *siccāre*, *siccātum*, to dry. DESICCATE. Causing to dry.

Sick, *a.* O.E. *séoc*. Common Teut. Ill; inclined to vomit; weary *of*.—**Sick'**EN,[2] *vi.* and *t.*—**Sick'**ISH, *a.*—**Sick'**LY,[1] *a.*—**Sick'**NESS, *n.*—**Sick'-bay**, *n.* BAY,[3] a recess. A place set apart for invalids, &c.

Sick'le, *n.* O.E. *sicol*, *sicel* = M.L.G. *sekele*, O.H.G. *sichila* (Ger. *sichel*). Poss. f. Campanian L. *secula*, f. *secāre*. SAW.[1] A reaping-hook.

Side, *n.* O.E. *síde*. Common Teut. (not in Gothic). One of the longer (gen. vertical) surfaces of an object; a bounding line or surface; a bank or shore; place or direction; the space on either hand *of*; a part *of* a place, &c.; a party or faction.—*vi.* To take part *with*.—**Side'-arms**, *n. pl.* Weapons worn at the side.—**Side'board**, *n.* A piece of dining-room furniture for holding dishes, &c.—**Side'ling**, *adv.* *-Ling*, expressing direction. Sideways, obliquely.—*a.* Oblique.—**Side'**LONG, *adv.* Obliquely.—*a.* Inclining to one side, oblique.—**Sides'man**, *n.* An assistant to the churchwardens of a parish.—**Side'**WAYS, **Side'**WISE, *advv.*—**Sid'ing**, *vbl.n.* A short additional line of rails.—**Sid'le**, *vi.* Prob. a back-formation f. SIDELING. To go sideways, edge along, esp. furtively or unobtrusively.

Side'real, *a.* L. *siderius*, f. *sidus*, *sideris*, star + -AL. CONSIDER. Relating to the stars.

Siege, *n.* O.F. *sege*, *seige*, *sieze*, a seat (F. *siège*), as if f. a Pop.L. *sĕdicum*, f. **sĕdes* = L. *sēdes*, seat, f. *sedēre*, to SIT. BESIEGE. The action of beleaguering a town, &c.

Sien'na, *n.* Short for It. *terra di Sienna*, earth of Sienna, or Siena in Tuscany. A reddish-brown earth used as a pigment.

Sier'ra, *n.* Sp. *sierra*—L. *serra*, saw. A mountain-range rising in peaks like the teeth of a saw.

Sies'ta, *n.* Sp., f. L. *sexta*, sixth (hour), the hottest part of the day. An afternoon rest.

Sieve, *n.* O.E. *sife* = M.L.G. *seve*, O.H.G. *sib* (Ger. *sieb*). A utensil for sifting.

Sift, *vt.* O.E. *siftan*, *syftan*, f. stem of *sife*. (See prec.) To separate the coarser particles of (a substance) from the finer (often *fig.*).

Sigh, *vi.* M.E. *sihen*, *sighen*, &c.—O.E. *sícan*. Imitative. Cf. Sw. *sucka*, Da. *sukke*. To make a long audible breath.—*n.* Such a breath.

Sight, *n.* O.E. *sihth* (us. *gesihth*, *gesiht*), f. *sih-*, stem of SEE + -TH.[1] Something seen; a seeing; the faculty or range of vision; a device for guiding the eye.—*vt.* To catch sight of.—**Sight'**LESS, *a.*—**Sight'**LY,[1] *a.* Comely.

Sigmat'ic, *a.* With -IC f. L. *sigma*, *sigmatis* = G. *sigma*, the 18th letter of the Greek alphabet = Eng. *s*. Formed with sigma, esp. of the Greek aorist.

Sign, *n.* F. *signe*—L. *signum*, mark, token. ASSIGN. INSIGNIA. SEAL.[2] A gesture to convey an order, &c.; a mark or device; a token or indication.—*vt.* To affix one's signature to; to affix (one's signature).—*vi.* To affix one's signature; to make a sign, give an order, &c., by gesture.—**Sig'nature**, *n.* Med.L. *signātūra*, f. L. *signāre*, *signātum*, to mark, seal, f. *signum*. RESIGN. One's name used in signing.—**Sig'nat**ORY, *a.* and *n.* Forming one, one, of those who sign a document. So **Sig'nat**ARY, *n.*—**Sign-man'ual**. An autograph authenticating signature.

Sig'nal, *n.* F. *signal*—Med.L. *signāle*, a Romanic formation on L. *signum*, SIGN. A sign to convey an order, &c.—*vt.* To make signals to; to communicate thus.—*vi.* To convey an order, &c., thus.—*a.* F. *signalé*, pa.pple. of *signaler*, to distinguish. Striking, remarkable.—**Sig'nal**LY,[2] *adv.*—**Sig'nal**IZE, *vt.*

Sig'net, *n.* O.F. *signet*, dim. of *signe*. SIGN. A small seal.

Sig'nify, *vt.* F. *signifier*—L. *significāre*, f. *signum*, SIGN + *facĕre*, to make. To be a sign of; to mean; to intimate.—*vi.* To be of importance.—**Signif'ic**ANT, *a.* Expressive, suggestive.—**Signif'icant**LY,[2] *adv.*—**Signif'ic**ANCE, *n.*—**Significa'**TION, *n.* Meaning.

Si'lence, *n.* O.F. *silence*—L. *silentium*, f. *silēre*, to be silent. Abstinence from speech; stillness; omission of mention or notice.—*vt.* To force into silence.—**Si'l**ENT, *a.*

Si'lex, *n.* L. *silex*, *silicis*, flint. Also **Sil'ica**. A mineral substance occurring in the form of flint, quartz, &c.

Sil'houette, *n.* From Etienne de *Silhouette* (1709-67). The word is said to have been applied in ridicule of the politician's petty economies. A portrait in outline filled in with black.

Silk, *n.* O.E. *sioloc*, *seoloc*, &c.—O.N. *silki*. Not in the other Germanic languages. Supposed to be ultimately f. L. *sēricus* or G. *sērikos*, silken, f. L. *Sēres*, G. *Sēres*, the people (perh. the Chinese) from whom silk first came. SERGE. A fibre produced by the larvæ of certain moths; the fabric made from this.—**Silk'**EN,[1] *a.*—**Silk'**Y,[2] *a.*

Sill, *n.* O.E. *syll*, *sylle*. Cf. O.N. *svill*, *syll*, Sw. *syll*, Da. *syld*. The timber or stone at the foot of a door or window.

Sil'labub, **Syl'labub**, *n.* Of obscure orig. A dish made of milk with wine or cider.

Sil'ly, *a.* M.E. *sely*—O.E. (*ge-*)*sǽlig* (f. *sǽl*, time season, happiness) = Old Fris. *sēlich*, O.S.

and O.H.G. *sâlig.* Formerly, 'timely', 'happy', 'blessed', 'innocent', 'simple'. Weak in intellect; foolish, senseless; characterized by foolishness.—**Sil'li**LY,[2] *adv.*—**Sil'li**NESS, *n.*

Si'lo, *n.* Sp. *silo*—L. *sirus*—G. *siros.* ENSILAGE. A pit for storing grain or fodder.

Silt, *n.* Of doubtful orig. Cf. Da. and Norw. *sylt*, O.L.G. *sulta*, O.H.G. *sulza*, salt-marsh. Fine matter deposited by water.—*vi.* and *t.* To become filled, to fill, with silt.

Sil'van, Syl'van, *a.* L. *silvānus*, a. f. *silva*, a wood. SAVAGE. Of a wood; wooded; rural.

Sil'ver, *n.* O.E. *siolfor*, *seolfor*, &c. Common Teut. A white malleable precious metal; silver coin; articles made of silver.—*vt.* To cover with, to make like silver; **Sil'ver**Y,[2] *a.*

Sim'ian, *a.* L. *simia*, an ape + -AN. Of, pertaining to, comprising apes; ape-like.

Sim'ilar, *a.* F. *similaire*, as if f. a L. **similāris*, f. *similis*, like, conn. with *simul.* SIMULATE. Of the like nature or kind.—**Sim'ilar**LY,[2], *adv.*—**Similar'**ITY, *n.*—**Sim'ile**, *n.* L. *simile*, neut. sing. of *similis.* A comparison of one thing with another, esp. in poetry.—**Simil'i**TUDE, *n.* Likeness, appearance; a simile.

Sim'mer, *vi.* and *t.* Later form of obs. *Simper* in sim. sense, prob. imitative. To be, to keep, just below boiling-point.

Sim'nel, *n.* O.F. *simenel*, app. in some way conn. with L. *simila* or G. *semidalis*, fine flour. A rich currant cake eaten in certain districts on Mid-Lent Sunday.

Si'mony, *n.* O.F. *simonie*—Med.L. *simōnia*, f. *Simon* Magus. See Acts, viii, 18-19. The buying or selling of ecclesiastical preferments. —**Simo'niac**, *n.* Med.L. *simōniacus.* One guilty of simony.—**Simoni'ac**AL, *a.*

Simoom', *n.* Arab. *semūm*, f. root *samm*, to poison. A dry suffocating wind.

Sim'per, *vi.* Of obscure orig. To smile in a silly, affected, or self-conscious way.

Sim'ple, *a.* O.F. *simple*—L. *simplex*, *simplicis*, lit., 'one-fold', f. *sem-*, one + *plic-*, stem of *plicāre*, to fold. SIMULATE. SINGLE. APPLY. Straightforward; humble; plain; of low rank; ordinary; lacking acuteness; mere; not complicated.—**Simp'**LY,[2] *adv.*—**Sim'pleton**, *n.* A fanciful formation. A foolish person.—**Simplic'**ITY, *n.*—**Sim'pli**FY, *vt.* —**Simpli**FICA'TION, *n.*

Sim'ulate, *vt.* L. *simulāre*, *simulātum*, to make like, counterfeit, f. *similis*, like, conn. with *simul*, together, lit., 'at once', f. Indo-Germanic root *sem-*, one. ASSEMBLE. SAME. SIMILAR. SIMPLE. To feign, to pretend to be.—**Simula'crum**, *n.*; *pl.* **Simula'cra**. L., f. *simulāre.* A material image of something; a mere image or appearance.—**Simula'**TION, *n.*—**Simulta'neous**, *a.* L. type **simultāneus*, formed on *simul* + -OUS. Happening, &c., at the same time.—**Simulta'neous**LY,[2] *adv.*—**Simultane'**ITY, *n.*

Sin, *n.* O.E. *synn.* Cf. M.Du. *sonde*, O.S. *sundea*, Ger. *sünde.* Poss. cogn. with L. *sons*, guilty. Violation of divine law; an instance of this; conduct or a state characterized by this. — *vi.* To commit sin. — **Sin'**FUL, *a.* — **Sin'**LESS, *a.*—**Sin'n**ER, *n.*

Sin'apism, *n.* L. *sinăpismus*—G. *sinapisma*, mustard plaster, *sinapismos*, the use of one, f. *sinapi*, mustard. A mustard plaster.

Since, *adv.* Shortened f. obs. *Sithence* = (with advbl. suff.) obs. *sithen* — O.E. *siththon*, for **sīth thon*, after that. Cf. Ger. *seitdem.* From that time till now; subsequently, later; ago. —*prep.* Continuously from; at some time subsequent to.—*conj.* From the time that; seeing that, inasmuch as.

Sincere', *a.* L. *sincērus*, clean, pure, &c. Not feigned, real; honest; straightforward.—**Sincere'**LY,[2] *adv.*—**Sincer'**ITY, *n.*

Sin'ciput, *n.* L. *sinciput*, *sincipitis*, earlier **senciput*, f. *sēmi*, half (SEMI-) + *caput*, head. CAPITAL.—The front part of the head.—**Sincip'it**AL, *a.*

Si'necure, *n.* L. *sine cūrā*, without CURE (of souls). A benefice without cure of souls; an office with emolument but no duties.

Sin'ew, *n.* O.E. *seon(o)we*, *sionwe*, &c., oblique forms f. the nom. *sionu*, *sinu* = M.L.G. *sene*, M.H.G. *sene*, *senne* (Ger. *sehne*). A fibrous cord uniting a muscle to a bone; strength, main strength (often in *pl.*)—**Sin'ew**Y,[2] *a.*

Sing, *vi.* O.E. *singan.* Common Teut. SONG. To utter musical sounds.—*vt.* To utter (words, &c.) with musical modulations; to celebrate in song or verse.—**Sing'**ER, *n.*

Singe, *vt.* O.E. *sencgan* = M.Du. *zengen*, M.L.G., M.H.G., Ger. *sengen.* To burn superficially.—*n.* The act or effect of singeing.

Sin'gle, *a.* O.F. *single*—L. *singulus*, one, individual, separate (in classical L. only in *pl.* *singuli*, &c., one by one). (The first syllable is *sem-* as in SIMPLE.) Alone; separate, distinct; one only; sole; unmarried; consisting of only one part, &c.; simple, sincere.—*vt.* To pick or mark *out.*—**Sin'glet**, *n.* After DOUBLET. An unlined woollen garment.—**Sin'gleton**, *n.* Cf. SIMPLETON. The only card of a suit in a hand; a single thing.—**Sin'g**LY,[2] *adv.*—**Sin'gle-stick**, *n.* Fencing with a stick requiring only one hand; the stick.

Sin'gular, *a.* L. *singulāris*, f. *singuli.* (See prec.) Unique; denoting one person or thing; remarkable, extraordinary, odd.—*n.* A word in its singular form.—**Sin'gular**LY,[2] *adv.*—**Singular'**ITY, *n.*

Sin'ister, *a.* L. *sinister*, left, left-handed, unlucky, bad. Wicked; of evil omen, ill-looking; in *heraldry*, on the left-hand side (from the point of view of the bearer of the shield).

Sink, *vi.* O.E. *sincan.* Common Teut. To become submerged in water, &c.; to drop down, give way; to degenerate or decline; to pass *into* (sleep, &c.).—*vt.* To cause to sink; to make by excavation; to invest.—*n.* A receptacle from which waste water, &c., is carried off.—**Sink'**ER, *n.* One who sinks; a weight.

Sinol'ogist, *n.* *Sino-*, combining form of G. *Sinai*, L. *Sinae*, the Chinese + LOG(Y) + -IST. One versed in things Chinese.

Sin'uous, *a.* L. *sinuōsus*, f. *sinus*, curve, bend. INSINUATE. With many turns, curving.—**Sin'uous**LY,[2] *adv.*—**Sinuos'**ITY, *n.*

Sip, *vi.* Of obscure orig. Poss. a modification of SUP to express a slighter action. To take up liquid in small quantities with the lips.—*vt.* To drink thus.—*n.* Something sipped.

Si'phon, *n.* L. *sipho*, *siphōnis*—G. *siphōn*, pipe. A bent tube for drawing off liquids.

Sir, *n.* Reduced form of SIRE. The title of a knight or baronet; a respectful or polite form of address.

Sir'dar, *n.* Urdū (Per.) *sardār*, f. Per. *sar*, head + *dār*, possessor. In India, &c., a military chief; the commander-in-chief of the Egyptian army.

Sire, *n.* O.F. *sire*—L. *senior*, SENIOR. A term of address to a sovereign; a father.

Si'ren, *n.* Through L. *Sīrēn*, f. G. *Seirēn.* One of the fabulous female monsters supposed to lure sailors to destruction by their singing (often *fig.*); a fog-signal.

Sir'loin, *n.* O.F. *surlonge*, f. *sur*, over, above + *longe*, LOIN. The upper and choicer part of a loin of beef.

Siroc'co, *n.* It. *sirocco*—Arab. *sharq*, east, f. *sharaqa*, (the sun) rose. An oppressively hot Mediterranean wind.

Sis'ter, *n.* Common Teut. Cogn. with L. *soror* (*swesor). The modern Eng. form is app. f. O.N. *systir*. COUSIN. A daughter of the same parents or having a common parent. —**Sis'ter**LY,[1] *a.*—**Sis'ter**HOOD, *n.* The relation of a sister; an order or band of females. —**Sis'ter-in-law**, *n.* The sister of one's husband or wife; the wife of one's brother.

Sit, *vi.* O.E. *sittan*. Common Teut. Cogn. with G. *hezesthai*, L. *sedēre*. ASSESS. SET. To rest on the lower part of the body; to seat oneself; to occupy a seat as judge, member of parliament, &c.; to hold a session; to place oneself in position for having one's portrait made; to incubate.—*vt* To sit upon (a horse).

Site, *n.* L. *situs*, place, position. Situation; a plot of ground built or to be built upon.

Sit'uate, *ppl.a.*; also **Sit'uated**. L.L. *situātus*, pa.pple. of *situāre*, to place, f. L. *situs*. (See prec.) Placed.—**Situ**A'TION, *n.* Place, position; a place; a post or employment; position of affairs.

Sitz' bath, *n.* G. *sitzbad*, f. *sitzen*, to sit. A bath in which one sits; a bath taken thus.

Six, *a.* and *n.* O.E. *six*. Common Teut. Cogn. with G. *hex*, L. *sex*. The cardinal number next after five.—**Six**TH,[2] *a.* The corresponding ordinal number.—*n.* A sixth part.—**Six'pence**, *n.* A sum equal to, a coin worth, six pennies.—**Six'penny**, *a.*

Size, *n.*[1] O.F. *sise*, shortened f. *assise*. ASSIZE. Magnitude; a particular magnitude.

Size, *n.*[2] Of doubtful orig. A semi-solid glutinous substance.—*vt.* To treat with size.

Skate, *n.*[1] O.N. *skata*. A flat-fish.

Skate, *n.*[2] Orig. in pl. *schates*, &c.—Du. *schaats*, sing.—O.N.F. *escache* (F. *échasse*), stilt, supposed to be f. L.G. *schake*, shank, leg. A steel blade, with means of attaching it to the boot, used for gliding over ice.—*vi.* To glide over ice upon skates.

Skein, *n.* O.F. *escaigne*, of obscure orig. A quantity of yarn, &c., put up in a loose knot.

Skel'eton, *n.* G. *skeleton* (*sōma*), dried (body), neut. of *skeletos*, a. f. *skellein*, to dry up. The bony framework of an animal.

Sketch, *n.* Du. *schets* or Ger. *skizze*—It. *schizzo*, supposed to be f. L. **schedius* representing G. *schedios*, done off-hand, extempore. A rough or slight drawing; a short account or essay.—*vt.* To make a sketch of.—*vi.* To practise sketching.—**Sketch**'Y,[2] *a.*

Skew, *vi.* O.N.F. *eskiu(w)er*, var. of O.F. *eschuer*, *eschever*, to shun. ESCHEW. To take an oblique course.—*a.* Slanting.

Skew'bald, *a.* Cf. obs. *Skewed* in same sense, perh. (in some way difficult to explain) f. O.F. *escu*, shield. PIEBALD. Irregularly marked with white and brown or red.

Skew'er, *n.* A var. of dialectal *Skiver* of unknown orig. A pin to fasten meat together. —*vt.* To pierce with a skewer.

Ski, *n.* Norw.—O.N. *skíth*, snow-shoe. A wooden runner fastened on the foot for sliding over snow.—*vi.* To slide on skis.

Skid, *n.* Of doubtful orig. A drag for a wheel.—*vt.* To apply a skid to.—*vi.* Of a wheel, to slip without revolving; to slip sideways.

Skiff, *n.* F. *esquif*—Sp. *esquife* or It. *schifo*, prob. f. O.H.G. *scif*, SHIP. A light boat.

Skill, *n.* O.N. *skil*, distinction, difference, &c., conn. with M.L.G. and M.Du. *schele*. Teut. root *skel-*. SCALE.[1] Formerly, discrimination, discretion, knowledge. Practical knowledge with ability, cleverness, expertness. —**Skil'**FUL, *a.*—**Skil'ful**LY,[2] *adv.*

Skil'let, *n.* Orig. obscure. Prob. f. A.F. or O.F. A cooking utensil usually having three or four feet and a long handle.

Skim, *vt.* Prob. f. O.F. *escumer*, f. Teut. SCUM. To clear of floating matter; to remove by skimming; to read carelessly; to move over lightly and rapidly.—*vi.* To move thus.

Skimp, *a.* and *v.* = SCRIMP.

Skin, *n.* O.N. *skinn*, conn. with O.H.G. *scindan*, M.L.G. and Du. *schinden*, to flay, peel. The stripped-off integument of an animal; the integument; an outer covering.—*vt.* To deprive of skin.—*vi.* To form skin.—**Skin'n**Y,[2] *a.* Thin.

Skip. *vi.* App. conn. with M.Sw. *skuppa*, *skoppa*, in same sense. To leap lightly; to move by skips.—*vt.* To pass over in reading; to pass over, omit.—*n.* An act of skipping.

Skip'per, *n.* M.Du. or M.L.G. *schipper*, f. *schip*, SHIP. The captain of a ship.

Skir'mish, *vi.* O.F. *eskirmir*—O.H.G. *skirman*, *scirman* (Ger. *schirmen*), to defend, f. *scirm*, *scerm*, shield, defence. (Properly, to fight behind cover.) To fight in small parties. —*n.* Such a fight.

Skirt, *n.* O.N. *skyrta* = O.E. *scyrte*, SHIRT. The lower part of a woman's dress, a coat, &c.; outlying part; edge.—*vt.* To bound or border; to go round.—*vi.* To lie or run *along* or *round*.

Skit, *n.* Perh. a back-formation f. SKITTISH. A piece of light satire or caricature.

Skit'tish, *a.* Of obscure orig. Characterized by levity or frivolity; fickle, tricky.

Skit'tles, *n.pl.* Of obscure orig. NINEPINS.

Skulk, *vi.* App. of Scand. orig. Cf. Norw. *skulka*, to lurk, Da. *skulke*, Sw. *skolka*, to shirk. To lurk; to shirk duty.

Skull. *n.* Of obscure orig. The bony case of the brain; the framework of the head.

Skunk, *n.* American Indian (Abenaki) *segankw* or *segongw*. An evil-smelling N. American animal of the weasel kind; a mean or contemptible person.

Sky, *n.* O.N. *sky*, cloud = O.S. *skio*, O.E. *sceo*. The apparent arch of heaven; the celestial regions.

Slab, *n.* Of obscure orig. A flat, broad, and comparatively thick piece of anything.

Slack, *a.* O.E. *sleac*, *slæc*. Common Teut. Cogn. with L. *laxus*. LAX. Sluggish; not busy; of the tide, having little strength; loose; soft, crumbling.—*n.* A loose part.—*vt.* To disintegrate (lime) with water.—*vi.* To be inactive.—**Slack'**LY,[2] *adv.*—**Slack'**EN,[2] *vt.* and *i.*

Slag, *n.* M.L.G. *slagge* = Ger. *schlacke*, of obscure orig. Refuse of smelted metal.

Slake, *vi.* O.E. *sleacian*, *slacian*, f. *slæc*, SLACK. To abate, moderate.—*vt.* To slack (lime); to allay; to quench.

Slam, *vt.* Poss. of Scand. orig. Cf. Sw., Norw. *slamra*. To shut noisily; to dash, throw. —*vi.* To shut noisily.—*n.* A noisy shutting.

Slan'der, *n.* A.F. *esclaundre*, O.F. *esclandre*, an alteration of O.N.F. *escandle*. SCANDAL. Calumny; a false or malicious statement concerning a person.—*vt.* To calumniate or defame.—**Slan'der**ER, *n.*—**Slan'der**OUS, *a.*

Slang, *n.* Of doubtful orig. The vocabulary

of a class; colloquial language.—*vt.* To scold violently.

Slant, *vi.* A var. of dial. *Slent*, as if f. O.N. **slenta* (Norw. *slenta*, older Da. *slente*), to slope, slant, slip. To slope; to take an oblique course.—*vt.* To cause to slope.—*n.* A slope; an oblique movement; slope, inclination.—*adv.* In a slanting manner or direction.—*a.* Sloping; oblique.—**Slant'**WISE, *adv.* and *a.*

Slap, *n.* L.G. *slapp*, of imitative orig. A smart blow, esp. with the open hand.—*vt.* To strike smartly with the open hand.

Slash, *vt.* Perh. f. O.F. *esclachier*, to break. To make gashes in; to lash.—*vi.* To make gashes.—*n.* A cutting stroke; a gash.

Slat, *n.* O.F. *esclat* (F. *éclat*). splinter, conn. with *esclater*, to burst, of doubtful orig. A long narrow strip of wood or metal.

Slate, *n.* O.F. *esclate*, fem. = *esclat*, masc. SLAT. A thin piece of certain varieties of stone used for covering roofs or set in a frame for writing on; the rock which is split into slates.—*v.*[1]*t.* To cover with slates.

Slate, *v.*[2]*t.* App. f. SLATE, *n.* To scold or criticize severely; to castigate, cut up.

Slat'tern, *n.* Conn. with the dial. v. *Slatter*, to spill or splash awkwardly. Orig. obscure. A sluttish woman.—**Slat'tern**LY,[1] *a.*

Slaugh'ter, *n.* O.N. **slahtr*, early form of *slátr*, butcher-meat, cogn. with SLAY. The killing of cattle, &c., for food; killing, a killing. —*vt.* To kill.—**Slaugh'ter**OUS, *a.*

Slave, *n.* O.F. *esclave*—L.L. *Sclavus*, Slav, many of the Slavs of Central Europe having been enslaved. One without freedom or personal rights.—*vi.* To toil like a slave.—**Slav'**ER, *n.*[1] A vessel or person engaged in slave-traffic.—**Slav'**ERY, *n.*—**Slav'**ISH, *a.*

Sla'ver, *vi.* App. of Scand. orig. Cf. Icel. *slafra* in sim. sense. To let saliva run from the mouth.—*vt.* To wet with saliva.—*n.*[2] Saliva running from the mouth; gross flattery.

Slay, *vt.* O.E. *sléan*, orig., to smite. Common Teut. SLAUGHTER. SLEDGE.[1] SLY. To kill.

Sledge, *n.*[1] O.E. *slecg* = M.Du. *slegge*. Cogn. with SLAY. A blacksmith's hammer.—Also **Sledge-ham'mer**.

Sledge, *n.*[2] M.Du. *sleedse*, *slede* = O.N. *slethi*. Stem *slid-* of SLIDE. SLEIGH. A carriage mounted upon runners.

Sleek, *a.* Var. of M.E. *slike*, prob. representing an O.E. **slice* related to *-slician*, to make smooth. Cf. O.N. *slíkr*, smooth. Smooth and glossy; plump.

Sleep, *vi.* O.E. *slápan*, *slǽpan*, *slepan*=M.Du. and Du. *slapen*, O.H.G. *slâfan* (Ger. *schlafen*). To take rest in sleep; to be inert or inactive. —*n.* The unconscious state regularly assumed by men and animals.—**Sleep'**ER, *n.* One who sleeps; on a railway, one of the beams supporting the rails.—**Sleep'**LESS, *a.*—**Sleep'less**NESS, *n.*—**Sleep'**Y,[2] *a.*

Sleet, *n.* Prob. representing an O.E. (Anglian) **slét*, conn. with M.L.G. *slôte*, M.H.G. *slôze* (Ger. *schlosse*), hail. Partially thawed snow.—*vi. It sleets*, sleet is falling.

Sleeve, *n.* O.E. *slýf*, Anglian *sléfe* = East Fris. *slêwe*, N.Fris. *slêv*, conn. with M.Du. *slove*, covering. The part of a coat, &c., which covers the arm.

Sleigh, *n.* Orig. U.S. f. Du. *slee* = *slede*. SLEDGE.[2] A sledge.

Sleight, *n.* O.N. *slǽgth*, f. *slǽgr*. SLY. Dexterity; a feat of jugglery, &c.

Slen'der, *a.* Of obscure orig. Prob. A.F. Slim; inadequate, slight; small, limited.

Sleuth'-hound, *n.* O.N. *slóth*, track, trail. SLOT.[2] A species of bloodhound.

Slew, **Slue**, *vt.* Orig. unknown. To swing round.—*vi.* To turn about, swing *round*.

Slice, *n.* O.F. *esclice*, *esclisse*, f. *esclicer*, *esclisser*, to reduce to splinters—O.H.G. *slizan*, SLIT. A thin piece cut off; a flattish implement.—*vt.* To cut into slices; to cut *out* or *off*.

Slide, *vi.* O.E. *slídan* = Older L.G. *sliden*, M.H.G. *slîten*. SLEDGE.[2] To pass smoothly and continuously.—*vt.* To cause to slide.—*n.* A sliding; a track on ice made by sliding; a sliding part of a mechanism.

Slight, *a.* M.E. *slight*, *sleght*, even, smooth, slender, trivial, &c., f. Old Scand. type **sleht-* (O.N. *sléttr*) = M.Du. and M.L.G. *slecht*, *slicht*, M.H.G. *sleht* (Ger. *schlicht*, smooth. *schlecht*, bad). Slender, slim; light, not substantial; small in amount, &c.; trifling.—*vt.* To disregard, disdain.—*n.* Indifference, disregard; an instance of this.—**Slight'**LY,[2] *adv.*

Slim, *a.* Du. or L.G. *slim* = M.H.G. *slim* (Ger. *schlimm*), crooked, bad, mean, &c. Slender, thin; small, slight; crafty.

Slime, *n.* O.E. *slím*. Common Teut. Soft glutinous mud; a viscous substance.—*vt.* To smear or cover with slime.—**Slim'**Y,[2] *a.*

Sling, *n.*[1] Of obscure orig. Corresponds to M.L.G. *slinge*, O.H.G. *slinga*. An implement for throwing stones.—*vt.* To throw with or as with a sling.

Sling, *n.*[2] Orig. obscure. Perh. ultimately the same as prec. Cf. Ger. *schlinge*, loop, Sw. *slinga*, noose, arm-sling, &c. A device for grasping articles while being hoisted or lowered; a support for an injured arm.—*vt.* To place in a sling; to hang up.

Slink, *vi.* O.E. *slincan*, to creep, crawl=L.G. *slinken*. To move stealthily.

Slip, *n.*[1] App. f. M.Du. or M.L.G. *slippe*, cut, strip, &c. A twig cut to be grafted or planted; a long and narrow piece or strip.

Slip, *n.*[2] From or related to SLIP, *v.* A landing-place; a slope on which ships are built; a leash; a woman's undergarment; an act of slipping; an error.

Slip, *vi.* Prob. f. M.L.G. *slippen* (Ger. *schlippen*) = O.H.G. *slipfan*, to slip, slide, &c. LUBRICATE. To pass lightly or quietly; to lose one's foothold; to err.—*vt.* To cause to slip; to strip *off*, to put *on*; to insert gently; to neglect; to release (a dog).—**Slip'p**ER, *n.* A light shoe easily slipped on.—**Slip'pery**, *a.* An alteration of obs. *Slipper*—O.E. *slipor*, f. the stem of the *v.* So smooth as to cause slipping; difficult to catch or hold; unstable; shifty.—**Slip'shod**, *a.* Wearing shoes down at the heel; slovenly, careless.

Slit, *vt.* Obscurely related to O.E. *slítan* = O.N. *slíta*, corresp. to M.Du. *sliten*, O.H.G. *slizan*. SLICE. To cut into, cut open; to divide, sever.—*ppl.a.* Rent, torn; cut, divided. —*n.* A straight narrow cut.

Sliv'er, *n.* From dial. *Slive*, to cleave, split —O.E. **slífan*. Not in the cogn. languages. A piece split off, a long thin piece.

Slob'ber, *vi.* Corresp. to Du. *slobbern*, to eat or work in a slovenly way. To slaver.—*vt.* To wet with saliva; to do carelessly.—*n.* Running saliva.—**Slob'ber**Y,[2] *a.*

Sloe, *n.* O.E. *slá(h)*, &c. = Fris. *slé*, M.L.G. *slee*, O.H.G. *slêha* (Ger. *schlehe*). A shrub of the plum kind; its fruit.

Sloop, *n.* Du. *sloep* = Fris. and L.G. *slûp*, Ger. *schlupe*. Prob. f. F. *chaloupe*. SHALLOP. A small vessel differing little from a cutter.

Slop, *n.*[1] In the first sense occurring in O.E. *oferslop*. OVER. Cf. M.Du. *slop*, also in the first sense. A loose outer garment; in *pl.*, wide breeches, ready-made clothing.

Slop, *n.*[2] Prob. representing an O.E. *sloppe as in *cúsloppe*, var. of *cúslyppe*, COWSLIP. Dirty liquid; in *pl.*, weak liquid or semi-liquid food; refuse liquid.—*vt.* To spill or splash.—*vi.* To flow *over* or *up*.—**Slop'**PY,[2] *a.*

Slope, *n.* Shortened f. ASLOPE, which app. = A[1] + archaic *slope*, a. (itself app. = O.E. *slopen*, 'slipped', pa.pple. of *slúpan*, to slip). A declivity; upward or downward inclination; a slant.—*vi.* To move obliquely, to incline.—*vt.* To form with or place at a slope.

Slot, *n.*[1] O.F. *esclot*, the hollow of the breast. Orig. obscure. A narrow depression or perforation.

Slot, *n.*[2] O.F. *esclot*, hoof-print, prob. f. O.N. *slóth*. SLEUTH-HOUND. The trail of an animal, esp. of a deer.

Sloth, *n.* Early M.E. *slāwth(e)*, *slōwth(e)*, f. *slāw*, *slōw*, SLOW. Sluggishness; a sluggish S. American mammal.—**Sloth'**FUL, *a.*

Slouch, *n.* Of obscure orig. Cf. Norw. *slōk*, Icel. *slókr*, lazy fellow. A stooping ungainly gait.—*vi.* To walk with a slouch.—*vt.* To pull down (one's hat).

Slough, *n.*[1] O.E. *slóh*. Orig. doubtful. A place or hole filled with mud or mire.

Slough, *n.*[2] M.E. type *sloh*, of doubtful orig., perh. conn. with L.G. *sluwe*, *slu*, husk, peel. The outer skin shed by a snake, &c.; dead tissue on a wound.—*vi.* Of such tissue, to be shed.—*vt.* To shed (the skin).

Slov'en, *n.* Perh. an A.F. formation on Flemish *sloef*, dirty, or Du. *slof*, careless. An untidy or dirty person.—**Slov'en**LY,[1] *a.*

Slow, *a.* O.E. *sláw*. Common Teut. Dull; sluggish; tedious, tardy; behind in time; moving, &c., at a low speed.—*vi.* To slacken in speed.—**Slow'**LY,[2] *adv.*—**Slow'**NESS, *n.*

Slow'-worm, *n.* O.E. *slá-wyrm*. WORM. The obscure first element appears also in Middle Sw. *slā*, Norw. *slo*, slow-worm. A small harmless lizard, the blind-worm.

Sludge, *n.* Var. of dial. *Slutch*. Orig. uncertain. Mud, mire.

Slug, *vi.* Perh. of Scand. orig. Cf. Sw. dial. *slogga*, to be slow. To be lazy.—*n.* A lazy fellow: a slow-moving land-snail; a roughly formed bullet (in this sense perh. a different word).—**Slug'**GARD, *n.*—**Slug'**GISH, *a.* Lazy; dull; moving slowly.—**Slug'gish**NESS, *n.*

Sluice, *n.* O.F. *escluse*—Med. and L.L. *exclūsa*, lit. 'shut off (water)', orig. fem. pa.pple. of *exclūdere*. EXCLUDE. A structure or device to control the flow of water.—*vt.* To pour water over.

Slum, *n.* Of cant orig. A street, &c., inhabited by the very poor.—*vi.* To visit slums.

Slum'ber, *vi.* M.E. *slūmeren*, corresp. to Fris. *slûmerje*, M.L.G. *slômeren*, late M.H.G. *slum(m)ern* (Ger. *schlummern*). To sleep, esp. lightly.—*n.* Sleep, a light sleep.—**Slum'ber**OUS, **Slum'br**OUS, *a.*

Slump, *vi.* Prob. imitative. Of values, &c., to fall heavily or suddenly.—*n.* Such a fall.

Slur, *vt.* From dial. *Slur*, thin or fluid mud, of obscure orig. To disparage, depreciate; to pass *over* lightly.—*n.* A slight; a stain, blot.

Slush, *n.* Of doubtful orig. Cf. SLUDGE. Half-melted snow; liquid mud.—**Slush'**Y,[2] *a.*

Slut, *n.* Orig. doubtful. Cf. dial. Ger. *schlutt*. A dirty, untidy woman.—**Slut'**TISH, *a.*

Sly, *a.* O.N. *slǿgr*, clever, cunning, orig., 'able to strike', f. *slóg-*, preterite stem of *slá*, to strike. SLAY. SLEIGHT. Guileful, wily; waggish.—**Sly'**LY,[2] *adv.*—**Sly'**NESS, *n.*

Smack, *n.*[1] O.E. *smæc* = M.L.G. *smak*, M.Du. and M.H.G. *smac* (Ger. *geschmack*). A taste, flavour; a mouthful.—*v.*[1]*i.* To taste *of*.

Smack, *v.*[2]*t.* Prob. imitative. Corresp. to M.Du., M.L.G. *smacken*. To open (the lips) with a sharp sound; to slap.—*n.*[2] The sound of smacking; a slap.

Smack, *n.*[3] Prob. f. Du. *smak* = L.G. *smakke*. Orig. uncertain. A small sailing-vessel.

Small, *a.* O.E. *smæl*. Common Teut. Of limited size or amount; not much; brief; of low alcoholic strength; low, soft; mean-souled.—**Small'**ISH, *a.*—**Small'**NESS, *n.*—**Small'-clothes**, *n.pl.* Breeches.—**Small'-pox**, *n.* *Pox* = *pocks*, pl. of POCK. (*Great pox* was syphilis.) A contagious disease characterized by pustules on the skin.

Smalt, *n.* F. *smalt*—It. *smalto*, of Teut. orig. and conn. with SMELT, *v.* Glass coloured blue and pulverized to serve as a pigment, &c.

Smart, *vi.* O.E. *smeortan* = M.L.G. *smerten*, O.H.G. *smerzan* (Ger. *schmerzen*). Prob. cogn. with G. *smerdnos*, terrible. L. *mordēre*, to bite. To be very painful; to suffer acutely.—*a.* O.E. *smeart*, conn. with *smeortan*. Causing sharp pain; brisk, prompt; clever; trimly dressed; fashionable.—*n.* Sharp pain.—**Smart'**EN,[2] *vt.*—**Smart'**LY,[2] *adv.*—**Smart'**NESS, *n.*

Smash, *vt.* Prob. imitative. Cf. Norw. dial. *smaska*, to crush. To shatter; to dash.—*vi.* To dash; to fly in pieces.—*n.* A heavy blow; a shattered condition.

Smat'ter, *vi.* Orig. uncertain. To have superficial knowledge.—**Smat'tering**, *vbl.n.* Such knowledge.—**Smat'ter**ER, *n.*

Smear, *vt.* O.E. *smerian*, f. *smeoru*, *smeru*, fat, grease. Common Teut. Perh. cogn. with G. *muron*, ointment. To rub with grease, &c. —*n.* A mark made by smearing.

Smell, *vt.* M.E. *smellen*, *smüllen*. Not in O.E. or the cogn. langs. To perceive by the nose; to inhale the odour of.—*vi.* To use the sense of smell; to give out an odour.—*n.* The faculty of smelling; odour.

Smelt, *n.* O.E. *smelt* = obs. Ger. *schmelt*, Da. *smelt*. A small fish of the salmon kind.

Smelt, *vt.* Prob. f. M.Du. or M.L.G. *smelten* = O.H.G. and M.H.G. *smelzen* (Ger. *schmelzen*). App. the stem is a var. of that of MELT. To melt (ore) in order to extract the metal; to extract (the metal).

Smi'lax, *n.* L. *smilax*, G. *smilax*, convolvulus, &c. A genus of climbing shrubs some of which yield sarsaparilla.

Smile, *vi.* M.E. *smilen* = Da. *smile*, Sw. *smila*. Cogn. with Skr. *smi*, G. *meida-ein*, to smile, L. *mīrāri*, to wonder. To give to the face a look expressing pleasure, amusement, disdain, &c.—*n.* An act of smiling.

Smirch, *vt.* App., with transference of sense, f. O.F. *esmorcher*, to torture (as with hot metal). To soil; to cast disgrace upon.

Smirk, *vi.* O.E. *smearcian*, *smercian*, to smile. Not in the cogn. langs. To smile in an affected way.—*n.* Such a smile.

Smite, *vt.* O.E. *smītan* = Old. Fris. *smīta*, to throw, M.Du. *smiten*, to throw, strike, M.H.G. *smīzen* (Ger. *schmeissen*), to throw, strike, smear. ('Throwing' is perh. the orig. sense.) To strike; to destroy; to attack, affect; to enamour.—*vi.* To give a blow.

Smith, *n.* O.E. *smith*. Common Teut. Orig. sense app. 'craftsman in metal, wood, &c.'

One who works in iron or other metals.—**Smith'y**, *n.* O.N. *smithja* = O.E. *smiththe.* His workshop.

Smock, *n.* O.E. *smoc.* Prob. conn. with O.E. *smúgan*, to creep, O.N. *smjúga*, to creep into, put on. A woman's undergarment.—*vt.* To gather by sewing in diagonal lines.—**Smock-frock**, *n.* A farm-labourer's loose garment with the upper part gathered.

Smoke, *n.* O.E. *smoca*, f. stem of *sméocan* (strong *v.*), to smoke. Cf. M.Du. *smōken*, Ger. *schmauchen.* The visible volatile product of burning; fume, vapour, &c.; a spell of smoking tobacco, &c.—*vi.* O.E. *smocian* (weak *v.*) To emit smoke, &c.; to inhale and expel the fumes of tobacco, &c.—*vt.* To expose to smoke; to use in smoking.—**Smok'**ER, *n.*—**Smok'**Y,[2] *a.*

Smooth, *a.* O.E. *smóth*, found only once. Us. form *sméthe.* Not clearly repd. in the cogn. langs. Even on the surface, not rough; flowing evenly; plausible, insinuating.—*vt.* To make smooth; to soothe.—**Smooth'**LY,[2] *adv.*

Smoth'er, *n.* Early M.E. *smorther*, f. stem of O.E. *smorian*, to smother = M.Du., M.L.G. *smoren.* Dense stifling smoke, &c.—*vt.* To suffocate.—*vi.* To be suffocated.

Smoul'der, *vi.* Poss. conn. with L.G. *smōlen*, Du. *smeulen.* To burn without flame.

Smudge, *vt.* Orig. obscure. Cf. SMUTCH. To soil, smear.—*n.* A stain or smear.

Smug, *a.* Of doubtful orig. Self-satisfied, conceited; complacently respectable.

Smug'gle, *vt.* App. of L.G. or Du. orig. Agrees with L.G. *smuggeln*, and the earlier form *smuckle* with L.G. *smukkeln*, Du. *smokkelen.* To convey clandestinely in evasion of the law.—**Smug'gl**ER, *n.*

Smut, *vt.* Cf. M.H.G. *smutzen* (Ger. *schmutzen*, to get dirty), to dirty. To blacken, smudge.—*n.* A disease in grain; a smudge; soot, a particle of soot; obscene language.

Smutch, *n.* Orig. obscure. Cf. SMUDGE. A smudge; a slight touch.—*vt.* To smudge.

Snack, *vi.* and *t.* Orig. doubtful. Cf. M.Du. *snacken*, to snap (of a dog), Norw. dial. *snaka*, to snatch (of animals). To bite or snap *at*, to share (now dial. or obs.); to take a snack (from the *n.*).—*n.* A share; a light repast.

Snaf'fle, *n.* Orig. doubtful. A simple form of bit.—*vt.* To put a snaffle on (a horse).

Snag, *n.* Prob. of Scand. orig. Cf. Norw. dial. *snag*, stump, spike = Icel. *snagi*, peg. A stump; a tree-trunk in a river.

Snail, *n.* O.E. *snegel*, *snægel* = M.L.G. *sneil*, O.H.G. *snegil.* A slow-moving mollusc.

Snake, *n.* O.E. *snaca* = M.L.G. *snake.* Cf. Sw. *snok*, Da. *snog.* A serpent.—**Snak'**Y,[2] *a.*

Snap, *vi.* App. f. M.Du. or M.L.G. *snappen* = M.H.G. *snappen* (Ger. *schnappen*). To make a quick bite or snatch *at*; to break suddenly.—*vt.* To snatch; to break suddenly. *n.* A quick bite; a quick sharp sound; a break. —**Snap'p**ISH, *a.* Sharp in speech.—**Snap'-dragon**, *n.* A plant bearing showy flowers (supposed to resemble a dragon's mouth); a game consisting of snatching raisins out of burning brandy.

Snare, *n.* O.N. *snara* = O.H.G. *snarahha*, conn. with O.S. *snari*, M.Du. *snare*, string. A string with a running noose used as a trap.—*vt.* To catch in a snare.

Snarl, *vi.* = obs. *Snar*, corresp. to Du., (M.)L.G., M.H.G. *snarren* (Ger. *schnarren*), to rattle, whirl, snarl, &c., prob. imitative. Of a dog, to show the teeth with an angry sound; to quarrel; to grumble.—*n.* An act of snarling.

Snatch, *vi.* Orig. obscure. Poss. conn. with SNACK. To make a quick bite or catch *at.*—*vt.* To seize, catch.—*n.* A quick catch; a short burst or spell.

Sneak, *vi.* Orig. doubtful. To go stealthily, to slink.—*n.* A mean-spirited or shifty person.

Sneer, *vi.* Prob. imitative. Orig. of a horse, to snort. To smile, also to speak or write, scornfully.—*n.* An act of sneering.

Sneeze, *vi.* App. an alteration, due to confusion between *f* and the old long *s* (ſ), of obs. *Fnese* — O.E. *fnéosan* (implied in *fnéosung*, vbl.n.), cogn. with Du. *fniezen*, O.N. *fnýsa.* To emit breath suddenly by an involuntary and convulsive action.—*n.* An act of sneezing.

Sniff, *vi.* Imitative. To draw in air through the nose sharply and audibly; to express disdain, &c., by sniffing.—*vt.* To take *up*, draw *in*, through the nostrils; to smell.—*n.* An act of sniffing.

Snig'ger, *vi.* Imitative. To laugh in a covert manner.—*n.* An act of sniggering.

Snip, *vt.* Prob. f. Du. or L.G. Cf. Du. and L.G. *snippen*, to snip, snatch, &c. To cut up or off.—*n.* A small piece cut off; a small cut. —**Snip'pet**, *n.* Dim. suff. *-et.* A shred.

Snipe, *n.* Of doubtful orig. Prob. f. Scand. A bird frequenting marshy places.—*vi.* To shoot singly at the enemy, generally at long range and from under cover or at night.—*vt.* To hit by shooting thus.—**Snip'**ER, *n.*

Sniv'el, *vi.* O.E. *snyflan* (implied in *snyflung*, vbl. n.), f. *snofl*, mucus. Cf. Da. *snövle*, to snuffle. To make a sniffing sound expressive of real or assumed emotion.

Snob, *n.* Orig. slang. Of obscure orig. One who vulgarly admires, and imitates or seeks to associate with, his superiors in rank.—**Snob'b**ERY, *n.*—**Snob'b**ISH, *a.*

Snood, *n.* O.E. *snód*, of obscure orig. A fillet or ribbon for confining the hair.

Snooze, *vi.* Of obscure orig. App. a cant word. To slumber, doze.—*n.* A nap, a doze.

Snore, *vi.* Prob. imitative. Cf. SNORT. To make harsh sounds with the breath in sleep.—*n.* An act of snoring.

Snort, *vi.* Prob. imitative. Cf. SNORE. To make a harsh sound by driving breath through the nostrils.—*n.* An act of snorting.

Snout, *n.* M.E. *snūt(e)* = M.Du. *snūte*, M.L.G. *snût(e)* (Ger. *schnauze*). The nose of an animal.

Snow, *n.* O.E. *snáw.* Common Teut. Cogn. with L. *nix*, *nivis*, snow, G. *niphein*, to snow. Frozen vapour falling in flakes.—*vi. It snows*, snow is falling.—*vt.* To let fall like snow; to cover with or as with snow.—**Snow'**Y,[2] *a.*—**Snow'drop**, *n.* Cf. Ger. *schneetropfen.* An early bulbous plant with white flowers.

Snub, *vt.* O.N. *snubba*, to rebuke. Cf. Norw. and Sw. dial. *snubba*, Da. *snubbe*, also in sense 'to cut short, make stumpy'. To treat so as to repress or mortify.—*n.* A snubbing.—**Snub nose**, *n.* Cf. Norw. dial. *snubbnos.* A short stumpy turned-up nose.

Snuff, *n.*[1] Orig. obscure. The charred part of a candle-wick.—*v.*[1]*t.* To free from this; to extinguish; to efface.—**Snuff'**ER, *n.*

Snuff, *v.*[2]*t.* Prob. f. M.Du. *snoffen*, *snuffen*, prob. of imitative orig. To draw *up* or *in* through the nostrils.—*vi.* To draw air into the nostrils.—*n.*[2] A snuffing.

Snuff, *n.*[3] Prob. f. Du. and Flemish *snuf*, *snuif*, app. an abb. of *snuiftabak*, 'snuff-tobacco'. Cf. prec. Powdered tobacco for inhalation.—*v.*[3]*i.* To take snuff.

Snuf'fle, *vi.* Prob. f. Du. and Flemish *snuffelen.* Cf. SNUFF, *v.*[2] To smell *at*; to speak through the nose; to inhale through the nostrils audibly.—*n.* A snuffling; a nasal tone.

Snug, *a.* Orig. doubtful. Of a ship, trim, prepared for bad weather; comfortable, cosy; in concealment.—**Snug'**LY,[2] *adv.*—**Snug'-ger**Y, *n.* A cosy room or house.—**Snug'gle**, *vi.* Vbl. suff. *-le.* To lie snug, nestle.

So, *adv.* O.E. *swa, swá.* Common Teut. ALSO. SUCH. In this or that manner; to that degree; thus; very; the case being such; thereby. —*conj.* Provided that, in case that; therefore.

Soak, *vi.* O.E. *socian*, f. weak grade of stem of *súcan*, to SUCK. To lie in a liquid; to percolate.—*vt.* To wet thoroughly; to steep.

Soap, *n.* O.E. *sápe* = M.L.G. *sêpe*, O.H.G. *seifa* (Ger. *seife*). Cogn. with L. *sāpo*, which is f. Teut. A compound of oil or fat with an alkali used in washing.—*vt.* To treat with soap.

Soar, *vi.* F. *essorer*, representing Pop.L. *EX*aurāre*, to expose to air, f. L. *aura*, air. To fly high.

Sob, *vi.* App. imitative. To catch the breath convulsively, esp. in weeping.—*n.* A sobbing.

So'ber, *a.* O.F. *sobre*—L. *sōbrius.* Temperate; not addicted to strong drink; not drunk; staid; subdued in tone.—*vt.* and *i.* To make, to become, sober.—**So'ber**LY,[2] *adv.*—**Sobri'ety**, *n.* F. *sobriété*—L. *sōbrietas.* The quality of being sober.

Sob'riquet, *n.* F. orig. uncertain. A nickname.

So'cial, *a.* L. *sociālis*, f. *socius*, friend, companion, f. root of *sequi*, to follow. ASSOCIATE. CONSECUTION. Sociable; living in communities; pertaining to society.—**So'cial**LY,[2] *adv.* —**So'cia**BLE, *a.* Disposed to be friendly; characterized by companionship.—**So'ciab**LY,[2] *adv.*—**Socia**BIL'ITY, *n.*—**So'cial**ISM, *n.* A policy of social organization which aims at the ownership of the means of production by the community.—**So'cial**IST, *n.*

Soci'ety, *n.* O.F. *societe*—L. *societas*, f. *socius.* (See prec.) Companionship, one's companions; a living in association with others, those living thus; the leisured or fashionable class; an association.—**Sociol**OL'OGY, *n.* Social science.

Sock, *n.* O.E. *socc*—L. *soccus.* SOCLE. A light shoe worn by Greek and Roman comic actors; a short stocking.

Sock'et, *n.* A.F. *soket*, dim. of *soc*, ploughshare, prob. of Celtic orig. A hollow for something to fit into.

Soc'le, *n.* F. *socle*—It. *zoccolo* (also a clog)—*socculus*, dim. of *soccus.* SOCK. A low plain block forming a pedestal to a statue, column, &c.

Sod, *n.* App. f. M.Du. *sode*, *soode* or M.L.G. *sode* = Old Fris. *sātha*, *sāda*, of doubtful orig. A slice of earth with the grass growing in it.

So'da, *n.* Med.L. *soda.* Orig. unknown. An alkaline substance in common use.—**So'da-wa'ter**, *n.* Water (orig. containing a compound of sodium) charged with a gas under pressure.

Sodal'ity, *n.* L. *sodālitas*, fellowship, f. *sodālis*, fellow. Fellowship; a brotherhood.

Sod'den, *ppl.a.* Pa.pple. of SEETHE. Of the features, &c., dull and expressionless; doughy; soaked.

So'dium, *n.* SODA with a L. termination. The metal forming the basis of soda.

Sod'omy, *n.* O.F. *sodomie*, f. the name of the town *Sodom.* Genesis xviii–xix. An unnatural form of sexual intercourse.

So'fa, *n.* F. *sofa*, *sopha*—Arab. *soffah.* A long stuffed seat with a back and ends or an end.

Sof'fit, *n.* After F. *soffite*, f. It. *soffitta*, f. *sof-* (= SUB-, under) + *figgere*, L. *figere*, to FIX. *Arch.*, the under surface of an architrave, cornice, arch, &c.

Soft, *a.* O.E. *sófte*, *sóft*, more us. *séfte*, corresp. to West Fris. *séft*, *seaft*, O.H.G. *semfti.* Producing agreeable sensations; involving little effort; of a sound, &c., low, subdued; not crude or glaring; mild, gentle; not harsh; impressionable; compliant; silly, simple; yielding easily to pressure; insufficiently hard.—**Soft'**LY,[2] *adv.*—**Soft'**EN,[2] *vt.* and *i.*

Soil, *n.*[1] A.F. *soil*, *soyl*, a piece of ground, app. repg. L. *solium*, seat, in sense of *solum*, the ground. The earth or ground; mould, earth; a particular kind of mould or earth.

Soil, *vt.* O.F. *suill(i)er*, *soill(i)er* (F. *souiller*) —Pop.L. type **suculāre*, f. L. *suculus* or *sucula*, dim. of *sūs*, pig. SOW, *n.* To make dirty; to sully.—*vi.* To become soiled.—*n.*[2] Soiling; a stain; filth, sewage.

Soirée, *n.* F., f. *soir*, evening—L. *sērum*, late hour, neut. of *sērus*, late. An evening party or social meeting.

So'journ, *vi.* O.F. *sojorner*, *sojourner*, repg. a Pop.L. *SUB*diurnāre*, to stay temporarily under (a roof), f. L. *diurnus*, daily, of a day, f. *dies*, day. DIURNAL. To make a temporary stay.—**So'journ**ER, *n.*

Sol'ace, *n.* O.F. *solas*—L. *sōlātium*, f. *sōlāri*, *sōlātus*, to CONSOLE. Comfort, consolation; that which gives solace.—*vt.* To cheer, comfort.—**Sola'tium**, *n.* L. as above. A money compensation.

So'lan, *n.* O.N. and Icel. *súla*, the bird + (poss.) O.N. *and-*, duck. A large sea-fowl resembling a goose.

So'lar, *a.* L. *sōlāris*, f. *sōl*, SUN. SOLSTICE. Of, determined by, proceeding from, the sun.

Sol'der, *n.* O.F. *soudure*, *soldure*, f. *souder*, *soulder*—L. *solidāre*, to make firm, f. *solidus*, SOLID. (See next.) A fusible metallic substance for joining metals.—*vt.* To join by means of solder.

Sol'dier, *n.* O.F. *soud(i)er*, *soldier*, f. *soude*, *soulde*, pay—L. *solidus*, a piece of money, orig. 'a solid piece', f. *solidus.* (See prec.) One in military service.—**Sol'dier**LY,[1] *a.*—**Sol'dier**Y,[1] *n.* Soldiers collectively.

Sole, *n.*[1] O.F. *sole*—Pop. and Med.L. *sola* for L. *solea*, sandal, sole-fish. (See next.) The under surface of the foot; the bottom of a boot, &c.—*vt.* To furnish with a sole.

Sole, *n.*[2] O.F. *sole*, of the same orig. as prec. A British and European flat-fish.

Sole, *a.* O.F. *soul*, *sol*—L. *sōlus*, alone. DESOLATE. SOLILOQUY. SOLITARY. SULLEN. Alone, solitary, one and only; unique, exclusive.—**Sole'**LY,[2] *adv.*

So'lecism, *n.* G. *soloikismos*, f. *soloikos*, speaking incorrectly, said to refer to corruption of Attic speech at *Soloi* in Cilicia. An impropriety in speech or diction.

Sol'emn, *a.* L. *sōlemnis*, established, customary, festive. Having a religious character; accompanied by due ceremony; formal, deliberate; serious, grave; impressive.—**Sol'emn**LY,[2] *adv.*—**Solem'ni**TY, *n.*—**Sol'emn**IZE, *vt.* To celebrate, hold, perform; to make solemn.—**Solemniz**A'TION, *n.*

Sol-fa, *n.* From the syllables *sol* and *fa* of the gamut. The set of syllables sung to the notes of the gamut.—*vt.* and *i.* To sing to these syllables.—**Solfeg'gio**, *n.* It., f. *sol-fa.* An exercise in which the syllables are used.

Solic'it, *vt.* L. *sollicitāre, sollicitātum*, f. *sollicitus*, lit., 'wholly agitated', f. *sollus*, whole + *citus*, pa.pple. of *ciēre*, to set in motion. CITE. To entreat, urge; to entice, allure; to request, sue for.—**Solicit**A'TION, *n.*—**Solic'it**OR, *n.* One admitted to practise as a law-agent in any court; one who solicits. —**Solic'it**OUS, *a.* Troubled, anxious.—**Solic'i**TUDE, *n.*

Sol'id, *a.* F. *solide*—L. *solidus.* CONSOLIDATE. SOLDER. Not hollow; of three dimensions; compact; substantial.—*n.* A body of three dimensions.—**Sol'id**LY,[2] *adv.*—**Solidar'ity**, *n.* F. *solidarité*, f. *solidaire*, solid, f. *solide.* A state of being united or at one.—**Solid'i**FY, *vt.* and *i.*—**Solidi**FICA'TION, *n.* —**Solid'**ITY, *n.*

Solil'oquy, *n.* L. *sōliloquium*, f. *sōlus*, alone + *loqui*, to speak. SOLE, *a.* ALLOCUTE. A talking with oneself.—**Solil'oqu**IZE, *vi.*

Sol'itary, *a.* L. *sōlitārius*, f. *sōlus*, alone. SOLE, *a.* Living alone; lonely; single.—*n.* A hermit.—**Sol'itaire**, *n.* F. *solitaire.* A precious stone set by itself; various games for one person.—**Sol'i**TUDE, *n.*—**So'lo**, *n.* It. *solo.* A song or piece of instrumental music for a single performer.—**So'lo**IST, *n.*

Sol'stice, *n.* O.F. *solstice*—L. *solstitium*, f. *sōl*, sun + *stit-*, ppl. stem of *sistĕre*, to stand still. SOLAR. ASSIST. One of the two periods in the year, midway between the equinoxes, when the sun is farthest from the celestial equator and seems to stand still.—**Solstit'**IAL, *a.*

Solve, *vt.* L. *solvĕre, solūtum*, to loose, dissolve. ABSOLVE. To explain, clear up, work out.—**Sol'uble**, *a.* O.F. *soluble*—L. *solūbilis*, that may be loosed, f. *solvĕre.* Capable of being dissolved or explained.—**Solu**BIL'ITY, *n.*—**Solu'**TION, *n.*—**Solv'**ABLE, *a.*—**Solv'**ENT, *a.* Able to pay one's debts.—*n.* A liquid having the power of dissolving.—**Solv'**ENCY, *n.*

Somat'ic, *a.* G. *sōmatikos*, a. f. *sōma, sōmatos*, body. Of or affecting the body.

Som'bre, *a.* F. *sombre*, of uncertain orig. Depressingly dark or obscure, gloomy.

Sombre'ro, *n.* Sp., f. *sombra*, shade. Cf. F. *sombre* in prec. A broad-brimmed hat.

Some, *pron.* O.E. *sum.* Common Teut. Cogn. with Skr. *sama*, any, every, G. *hamo-* (as in *hamothen*, from some place). One or other (in phrase *some of these days*); a portion; certain persons or things.—*a.* One or other, an undetermined or unspecified; a certain amount, &c., of; certain (taken individually); approximately.—**Some'body**, *n.* Some person; one of note.—**Some'how**, *adv.* In some manner.—**Some'thing**, *n.* Some unspecified thing; a certain part, amount, &c.; a thing, &c., of some value.—**Some'time**, *adv.* Formerly.—*a.* Former.—**Some'times**, *adv.* At times, now and then.—**Some'what**, *n.* Something.—*adv.* To some extent, slightly. —**Some'where**, *adv.* In, at, to some place.

Som'ersault, *n.* Also in altered form **Som'erset**. O.F. *sombresaut, -sault*, alteration of *soubresaut, -sault*, f. L. *suprā*, above + *saltus*, leap, f. *salīre*, to leap. ASSAIL. A leap in which one turns heels over head.

Somnam'bulance, *n.* L. *somnus*, sleep + *ambulāre*, to walk + -ANCE. AMBLE. Sleep-walking.—**Somnam'bul**IST, *n.*

Som'nolent, *a.* L. *somnolentus*, f. *somnus*, sleep. Causing sleepiness; sleepy.—**Som'no**LENCE, *n.*

Son, *n.* O.E. *sunu.* Common Teut. Cf. Skr. *sūnu*, G. *huios* (root *su-*). A male child.—**Son'-in-law**, *n.* A daughter's husband.

Sona'ta, *n.* It., orig. fem. pa.pple. of *sonare*, L. *sonāre*, to sound. ASSONANCE. A piece of music in several movements.—**Sonati'na**, *n.* It., dim. of *sonata.* A short simple form of sonata.

Song, *n.* O.E. *sang*, f. root of *singan*, to SING. The act or art of singing; a poem adapted for singing.—**Song'**STER, *n.*—**Song'str**ESS, *n.*

Son'net, *n.* It. *sonetto*, dim. of *suono*, L. *sonus*, sound. ASSONANCE. A rhymed poem of fourteen lines.—**Sonnet**EER', *n.*

Sono'rous, *a.* L. *sonōrus*, f. *sonor*, sound, cogn. with *sonus.* (See prec.) Giving out a deep sound, resonant.—**Sono'rous**LY,[2] *adv.*

Soon, *adv.* O.E. *sóna* = O.S. *sâna, sâno*, O.H.G. *sân.* Before long; early; willingly.

Soot, *n.* O.E. *sót* = M.Du. *soet*, N.Fris. *sött, sutt*, O.N. *sót.* A black substance formed by the combustion of coal, &c.—**Soot'**Y,[2] *a.*

Sooth, *n.* O.E. *sóth*, true, as *n.*, truth = O.N. *sannr, sathr*, conn. with Skr. *satyas*, true. Truth.—**Sooth'sayer**, *n.* One who foretells.

Soothe, *vt.* O.E. *sóthian*, f. *sóth.* (See prec.) Formerly, to prove to be true, to support in an assertion, to cajole by assent. To mollify, appease; to calm; to assuage, mitigate.

Sop, *n.* O.E. *sopp*, app. f. the weak grade of *súpan.* SUP. SOUP. A piece of bread, &c., steeped in water, &c.; a bribe.—*vt.* To steep in water, &c.; to soak.

Soph'ist, *n.* L. *sophista*—G. *sophistēs*, f. *sophizesthai* (pass.), to become skilled, f. *sophos*, skilled. PHILOSOPHY. A specious reasoner. —**Soph'ism**, *n.* G. *sophisma*, clever device, f. *sophizesthai* (middle), to devise. A specious argument.—**Sophis'**TIC, **Sophis'**TICAL, *aa.* —**Soph'ist**RY, *n.*—**Sophis'ticate**, *vt.* Med. L. *sophisticāre, sophisticātum.* To render artificial; to corrupt, spoil, pervert; to falsify.—**Sophistic**A'TION, *n.*

Soporif'ic, *a.* From L. type **sopōrificus*, f. *sopor*, sleep. -FIC. Inducing sleep.

Sopra'no, *n.* It., f. *sopra*, L. *suprā*, above. The highest voice in women and boys; the part for this voice; a singer with a voice of this pitch.

Sorb, *n.* L. *sorbum*, the fruit. Cf. *sorbus*, SERVICE.[2] The fruit of the service-tree; the tree.

Sor'cerer, *n.* With superfluous -ER f. obs *Sorcer* in same sense—O.F. *sorcier*—Pop.L. **sortiārius*, f. *sors, sortis*, lot. CONSORT. A wizard, magician.—**Sor'cer**ESS, *n.*—**Sor'cery**, *n.* O.F. *sorcerie.* Witchcraft.

Sor'did, *a.* L. *sordidus*, dirty, base, f. *sordēre*, to be dirty. SWART. Mean, squalid; ignoble.—**Sor'did**LY,[2] *adv.*—**Sor'did**NESS, *n.*

Sore, *a.* O.E. *sár.* Common Teut. SORRY. Distressing; painful; suffering pain; distressed; morbidly sensitive.—*adv.* Severely, grievously. —*n.* A sore place.—**Sore'**LY,[2] *adv.*

Sori'tes, *n.* L. *sōrītēs*—G. *sōreitēs*, f. *sōros*, heap. A series of propositions in which the predicate of each is the subject of the next.

Sor'rel, *n.*[1] O.F. *surelle, sorele*, f. *sur*, Germanic *sūr*, SOUR. A plant with a sour taste.

Sor'rel, *a.* O.F. *sorel*, f. *sor* (F. *saur*), sorrel in colour. Of a bright chestnut colour.—*n.*[2] The colour; a horse of the colour.

Sor'row, *n.* O.E. *sorh, sorg.* Common Teut. Distress of mind.—*vi.* To feel sorrow.—**Sor'row**FUL, *a.*

Sor'ry, *a.* O.E. *sárig*, f. *sár*, SORE. Distressed; mean, poor.—**Sor'ri**LY,[2] *adv.* Meanly, poorly.

Sort, *n.* O.F. *sorte*—Pop.L. **sorta*—L. *sors, sortis*, lot, share, condition. CONSORT. SORCERER. A species or class.—*vt.* To classify.

Sor'tie, *n.* F., f. *sortir*, to go out, of doubtful orig. A sally by a besieged force.

Sor'tilege, *n.* Med.L. *sortilegium*, f. L. *sortilegus*, diviner, f. *sors* (SORT) + *legĕre*, to choose. The practice of casting lots; an instance.

So so, **So-so**, *adv.* SO, *adv.* Cf. Ger. *so so*, Du. *zoo zoo* in sim. use. Not very well.—*a.* Not very good.

Sot, *n.* O.F. *sot*, of unknown orig. One who stupefies himself with drinking.—**Sot'**TISH, *a.*

Soufflé, *n.* F., orig. pa.pple. of *souffler*, to blow—L. *sufflāre*, f. *suf-* (= SUB-, under) + *flāre*, to blow. A light and frothy dish made by beating up with white of egg.

Sough, *vi.* O.E. *swógan*. Cf. O.S. *swógan*, in sim. sense, W.Fris. *swoegje*, to pant. SURF. SWOON. To make a rushing or rustling sound. —*n.* Such a sound.

Soul, *n.* O.E. *sáwol, sáwel, sáwl*, &c. Common Teut. The spiritual or emotional part of man; intellectual power; a person.

Sound, *n.*[1] A.F. *soun*, O.F. *son*—L. *sonus*. ASSONANCE. SONATA. SONNET. UNISON. The sensation of hearing: that which is heard. —*v.*[1]*i.* To make a sound.—*vt.* To cause to sound; to give a signal, &c., for by a sound.

Sound, *n.*[2] Partly f. O.E. *sund*, swimming, sea, and partly f. O.N. *sund* in sim. senses, both cogn. with SWIM.[1] The swimming-bladder of a fish; a channel or stretch of water.

Sound, *a.* M.E. *sund*, repg. O.E. *gesund*. Cf. W.Fris. *soun*, Du. *gezond*, Ger. *gesund*. Healthy; in good condition; solid, substantial; of sleep, profound; valid; based on good principles or knowledge; of good judgement.—**Sound'**LY,[2] *adv.* With reference to sleep, profoundly; thoroughly; severely.

Sound, *v.*[2]*i.* O.F. *sonder*, f. *sonde*, app. f. O.E. or O.N. *sund*. SOUND, *n.*[2] To ascertain the depth of water.—*vt.* To ascertain the depth of; to try to discover the opinions, &c., of.

Soup, *n.* F. *soupe*, in obscure relation to SOP. A liquid food made by boiling.

Sour, *a.* O.E. *súr*. Common Teut. SORREL.[1] Of an acid taste; peevish.—*vi.* and *t.* To become or to make sour.—**Sour'**LY,[2] *adv.*

Source, *n.* O.F. *sors*, masc. *surse, source*, fem., uses as n. of the pa.pple. of *sourdre*, L. *surgĕre*, to rise. SURGE. RESOURCE. The fountain-head of a river, a spring; origin.

Souse, *vt.* From dial. *Souse*, pickled pigs' feet, &c.—O.F. *sous, souce*, f. the Germanic stem seen in SALT. To pickle; to plunge *in* or *into* water; to drench, soak.—*vi.* To soak; to fall with a plunge.—*n.* An act of sousing.—*adv.* With a plunge.

South, *adv.* O.E. *súth*. Common Teut. Towards the part of the heavens which is directly opposite to the north.—*n.* The cardinal point opposite to the north; the southern part of the world, a country, &c.—*a.* That is towards the south.—*vi.* Of a star, &c., to cross the meridian of a place.—**South'er**LY,[1] *a.* Cf. EASTERLY, &c. — **South'**ERN, *a.*—**South'**WARD(S), *adv.* and *a.* — **Southwest'**ER, *n.* A large water-proof hat or cap.

Sou'venir, *n.* F. *souvenir*, memory, keepsake, use as *n.* of *souvenir*, to remember—L. *subvenire*, to come to one's assistance, to come into the mind, f. SUB-(5) + *venīre*, to come. ADVENT. A keepsake.

Sov'ereign, *n.* O.F. *soverain, suverain, souverein*, &c. (F. *souverain*)—Pop.L. **superānus*, f. L. *super*, above. SUZERAIN. A king; a gold coin = 20 shillings.—*a.* Supreme; efficacious.—**Sov'ereign**TY, *n.*

Sow, *n.* O.E. *sugu*=M.Du. *soge, seuge*, M.L.G. *soge, suge*. Cogn. with G. *hus*, L. *sūs*. SOIL, *v.* SWINE. The female of swine.

Sow, *vi.* O.E. *sáwan*. Common Teut. Cogn. with L. *serĕre* (perf. *sēvi*), and perh. with G. *hienai* (*sisenai*), to send, throw. SEASON. SEED. To scatter seed.—*vt.* To scatter seed upon; to scatter or deposit (seed); to scatter like seed; to spread abroad.—**Sow'**ER, *n.*

Spa, *n.* The name of a Belgian town with a medicinal spring. A medicinal spring; a place possessing such a spring.

Space, *n.* O.F. *espace*—L. *spatium*. EXPATIATE. Extent or period of time; interval between points; area; an expanse; the immeasurable expanse of the universe; an empty place, a blank.—*vt.* To place at intervals.—**Spa'**CIOUS, *a.* Wide, roomy, ample.

Spade, *n.*[1] O.E. *spadu* = M.Du. *spade*, Ger. *spaten*. Cogn. with G. *spathē*. SPATULA. A tool for digging.

Spade, *n.*[2] It. *spade*, pl. of *spada*, sword, used as a mark on cards—L. *spatha*, SPATULA, a kind of sword. In *pl.*, one of the suits at cards, with black (in England spade-shaped) marks; in *sing.*, a card of this suit.

Span, *n.* O.E. *span(n), spon(n)* = M.Du. *spanne*, O.H.G. *spanna* (Ger. *spanne, spann*), app. conn. with *spannan*. (See next.) The space between the thumb and the little finger (as a measure = 9 inches); a small extent or space; the stretch of an arch, &c.—*v.*[1]*t.* To measure or encircle with the outstretched hand; to form an arch across, to extend over.

Span, *v.*[2]*t.* From Flemish, Du., or L.G. *spannen* = O.H.G., O.E. *spannan* (Ger. *spannen*), to fasten, draw tight, &c. (See prec.) To harness or yoke.—*n.* A team of oxen.—**Span'ner**, *n.* Ger. *spanner*, f. *spannen*. A tool for gripping the nut of a screw, &c.

Span'drel, *n.* App. a dim. f. A.F. *spaundre*, perh. = (*e*)*spandre*, L. *expandĕre*, to EXPAND. The space between the outer curve of an arch and a surrounding rectangular framework.

Span'gle, *n.* With dim. suff. *-le* f. obs. *Spang*, prob. f. M.Du. *spange* = O.H.G. *spanga* (Ger. *spange*), clasp, brooch, &c. A small thin piece of glittering metal.

Span'iel, *n.* O.F. *espaignol, espaigneul*, 'Spanish dog'—Sp. *español*, Spanish, f. *España*, L. *Hispania*, Spain. A dog with large drooping ears and long hair.

Span'king, *ppl.a.* Orig. doubtful. Cf. Da. *spanke*, to strut. Fine, big; moving briskly; blowing briskly.—**Spank**, *vi.* Prob. a back-formation from the *ppl.a.* To move briskly.

Span'-new, *a.* O.N. *spán-nýr*, lit. 'new as a (freshly severed) chip', f. *spán(n)*, chip + *ný-r*, new. SPOON. Quite new.

Spar, *n.*[1] Cf. M.Du., M.L.G. *sparre*, O.H.G. *sparro* (Ger. *sparren*), O.N. *sparri*. A ship's mast, yard, &c.

Spar, *n.*[2] M.L.G. *spar, sper*, conn. with O.E. *spæren*, gypsum. A crystalline mineral.

Spar, *vi.* Orig. obscure. To box; to dispute.

Spare, *a.* Conn. with next. Cf. O.N. *sparr*, (that may be) spared, O.E. *spær*, O.H.G. *spar*, M.Du. *spaer*, sparing. Not in use, additional; lean; not abundant.

Spare, *vt.* O.E. *sparian.* Common Teut. To leave unhurt; to deal gently with; to preserve (life); to abstain from using, &c.; to avoid incurring; to give, lend, to do without.

Spark, *n.* O.E. *spærca, spearca* = M.Du., M.L.G. *sparke.* A small ignited particle; a trace, indication.—*vi.* To emit sparks.

Spark'le, *n.* From prec. with dim. suff. *-le.* A small spark; glittering appearance. —*vi.* Freq. suff. *-le.* To glitter.

Spar'row, *n.* O.E. *spearwa,* &c. = Goth. *sparwa,* M.H.G. *sparwe.* A small brownish-grey bird.

Sparse, *a.* L. *sparsus,* pa.pple. of *spargĕre,* to scatter. ASPERSE. Thinly scattered.

Spar'tan, *a.* L. *Spartānus,* f. *Sparta,* G. *Sparta, Spartē.* Of Sparta; characteristic of Sparta, hardy, frugal, sparing of speech.—*n.* A native of Sparta.

Spasm, *n.* L. *spasmus, spasma*—G. *spasmos, spasma,* f. *spa-ein,* to draw, tug, &c. A convulsive muscular contraction.—**Spasmod'ic**, *a.* G. *spasmōdēs* + -IC. Of the nature of a spasm; intermittent; agitated, emotional; disjointed in style.

Spat, *n.* Abb. of SPATTERDASH. A short gaiter worn over the instep.

Spate, *n.* Orig. obscure. A sudden flood in a river.

Spat'ter, *vt.* App. a freq. of the stem found in Du. and L.G. *spatten,* to burst, spout, &c. To cast in drops; to splash, stain.—*vi.* To fly in drops. —*n.* A slight splash.—**Spat'terdash**, *n.* DASH, *v.* A gaiter to keep the trousers or stockings from being spattered.

Spat'ula, *n.* L. *spatula,* var. of *spathula,* dim. of *spatha,* flat instrument for stirring, broad sword—G. *spathē,* flat blade. EPAULET. SPADE[1] and [2]. A broad blade used by painters.

Spav'in, *n.* O.F. *espavain, esparvain,* of obscure orig. A hard tumour on a horse's leg.

Spawn, *vi.* App. for **spaund,* f. A.F. *espaundre* = O.F. *espandre,* to shed, spill—L. *expandĕre.* EXPAND. Of fish, to cast eggs.—*vt.* To engender.—*n.* The eggs of fish.

Spay, *vt.* A.F. *espeier* = O.F. *espeer,* to cut with a sword, f. *espee* (F. *épée*), sword. To destroy the reproductive power of (a female).

Speak, *vi.* O.E. *sprecan,* later *specan* = M.Du. *spreken,* O.H.G. *sprehhan* (Ger. *sprechen*). SPEECH. To utter words; to converse; to deliver an address.—*vt.* To utter; to declare, make known; to communicate with (a passing vessel).—**Speak'**ABLE, *a.*—**Speak'**ER, *n.*—One who speaks; the representative and president of the House of Commons.

Spear, *n.* O.E. *spere* = Old Fris. *spiri,* M.Du. *spere,* O.H.G. *sper* (Ger. *speer*). A long pointed weapon.—*vt.* To pierce with a spear.

Spec'ial, *a.* O.F. *especial* or L. *speciālis,* not general, individual, f. *species,* SPECIES. ESPECIAL. Beyond the usual; distinct or individual in character; limited or individual in application, &c.—**Spec'ial**LY,[2] *adv.*—**Spec'ial**IST, *n.* One devoted to a particular subject or branch of a subject.—**Spec'ial**ISM, *n.* —**Special'**ITY, *n.* A particular point, matter, &c.; a peculiarity or characteristic; a special occupation, study, &c.; a special or characteristic product.—**Spec'ial**IZE, *vt.* To mention specially; to make special.—*vi.* To be a specialist.

Spe'cie, *n.* L. *speciē,* ablative sing. of *species,* SPECIES, orig. in phrase *in specie,* in the (actual) form. Coined money.

Spe'cies, *n.* L. *species,* appearance, form, kind, &c., f. *specĕre,* to look, look at. ASPECT. CONSPICUOUS. ESPY. SPECIAL. A class; a subdivision; a sort or kind.—**Specif'**IC, *a.* Belonging to and characteristic of a class or thing; specially or exclusively efficacious for a particular ailment; definite, explicit.—*n.* A specific remedy.—**Specif'ically**, *adv.* -AL. -LY.[2]—**Spec'**IFY, *vt.* To state definitely or in detail.—**Speci**FICA'TION, *n.* Esp., a detailed description of an invention or of some projected work in building, &c.

Spec'imen, *n.* L. *specimen,* f. *specĕre.* (See prec.) A part intended to typify the whole.

Spe'cious, *a.* L. *speciōsus,* fair, fair-seeming, f. *species,* SPECIES. Having a delusively fair appearance; plausible.—**Spe'cious**LY,[2] *adv.*

Speck, *n.* O.E. *specca.* Not in the cogn. languages. A small spot. —*vt.* To mark with specks.—**Speck'le**, *n.* Dim. suff. *-le.* A speck.—*vt.* To mark with speckles.

Spec'tacle, *n.* L. *spectāculum,* f. *spectāre, spectātum,* freq. of *specĕre,* to look. ASPECT. A display or show; a person or thing exhibited; in *pl.*, a device for assisting defective eyesight by means of lenses.—**Spectac'ul**AR,[1] *a.* Of the nature of a show.—**Specta't**OR, *n.* One who looks on or is present.—**Spec'tre**, *n.* L. *spectrum,* f. *specĕre.* An apparition or phantom.—**Spec'tr**AL, *a.*

Spec'trum, *n.*; *pl.* **Spec'tra**, **Spec'trums**. L. *spectrum.* (See prec.) A spectre; the coloured band into which a beam of light can be decomposed.—**Spec'troscope**, *n.* G. *skope-ein,* to look. SCEPTIC. An instrument for decomposing light and examining spectra.

Spec'ulate, *vi.* L. *speculāri, speculātus,* to spy out, observe, examine, &c., f. *specula,* a watch-tower, f. *specĕre,* to look. ASPECT. To form conjectures or theories; to engage in a risky transaction promising gain.—**Specul**A'TION, *n.*—**Spec'ul**ATIVE, *a.*—**Spec'ulat**OR, *n.*

Speech, *n.* O.E. *sprǽc, spréc,* later *spǽc, spéc,* f. *sprecan, specan,* to SPEAK. The act or faculty of speaking; words; a language; conversation; a formal discourse.—**Speech'**IFY, *vi.* To make a speech.—**Speech'**LESS, *a.*

Speed, *n.* O.E. *spéd,* success, haste, f. *spówan,* O.H.G. *spuon,* to prosper. Swiftness; rate of progress; promptness. —*vi.* To succeed; to move with speed.—*vt.* To further; to expedite; to bid farewell to.—**Speedom'eter**, *n.* G. *metre-ein,* to measure. A speed-indicator, esp. on a motor car.—**Speed'**Y,[2] *a.*—**Speed'**ILY,[2] *adv.*—**Speed'well**, *n.* App. f. the *vi.*, to succeed. A common herbaceous plant with blue flowers.

Spell, *n.*[1] O.E. *spel, spell* = O.S., O.H.G. *spel,* O.N. *spjall,* recital, tale, &c. GOSPEL. A set of words supposed to have magical power.

Spell, *v.*[1]*t.* O.F. *espeller* (F. *épeler*), f. the Germanic stem *spell-* as in prec. To read letter by letter; to give the letters of in order; to amount to, imply.—*vi.* To repeat or set down the letters of words.

Spell *v.*[2]*i.* Later form of dial. *Spele,* to represent—O.E. *spelian,* of obscure orig. To take turns at work.—*n.*[2] A turn of work; a bout; a short period of time.

Spelt, *n.* O.E. *spelt* = O.S. *spelta,* O.H.G. *spelza*—L.L. *spelta* of uncertain orig. A kind of grain.

Spel'ter, *n.* Corresponds in form to O.F. *espeautre,* PEWTER. Zinc; an alloy of zinc.

Spen'cer, *n.* Earl *Spencer* (d. 1834). A close-fitting bodice worn by women and children.

Spend, *vt.* O.E. *spendan—L. *expendĕre.* EXPEND. To lay out, disburse; to employ (labour, time, &c.); to exhaust.—**Spend'-thrift**, *n.* An improvident or wasteful person.

Sperm, *n.* L. *sperma*—G. *sperma*, f. *speirein*, to sow. SPORADIC. The seminal fluid.—**Spermace'ti**, *n.* Med.L., f. *sperma* + *cēti*, genit. of *cētus*, whale (from an erroneous notion of the nature of the substance). A fatty substance found in certain whales.

Spew, *vi.* and *t.* O.E. *spīwan*, *spéowan* = O.S., O.H.G. *spīwan*. Cogn. with G. *ptuein*, to spit, L. *spuĕre*, to spit, spew. To vomit.

Sphe'noid, *a.* G. *sphēnoeidēs*, f. *sphēn*, wedge. -OID. Wedge-shaped; *sphenoid bone*, a bone at the base of the skull wedged in between other bones.

Sphere, *n.* L.L. *sphēra*, earlier *sphaera*—G. *sphaira*. The vault of heaven; one of the concentric hollow globes formerly supposed to carry the heavenly bodies round the earth; range, domain, province; a globe or ball.—**Spher'**ICAL, *a.*—**Spher'**OID, *n.* A body approaching in shape to a sphere.—**Spher-**OID'AL, *a.*

Sphinc'ter, *n.* L. *sphincter*—G. *sphinktēr*, f. *sphiggein*, to draw tight. A contractile muscular ring closing an orifice of the body.

Sphinx, *n.* L. *sphinx*—G. *sphigx*, app. f. *sphiggein*. (See prec.) A monster, half woman, half lion, which infested Thebes till a riddle which it propounded was solved; an enigmatic person.

Spice, *n.* O.F. *espice* (F. *épice*)—L. *species*, kind, in L.L. a spice. SPECIES. A pungent or aromatic vegetable substance; spices collectively; a slight trace.—*vt.* To season with spice.—**Spic'**Y,[2] *a.*—**Spic'**ILY,[2] *adv.*

Spick and Span, *a.* Shortening of *spick and span new*, an emphatic extension of SPAN-NEW. Quite new; very neat and trim.

Spi'der, *n.* App. repg. O.E. *spīthre, *spinthre, f. *spinnan*, to SPIN. An animal which spins a web in which to catch its prey.

Spi'got, *n.* Prob. f. Early Pr. *espigot, f. *espiga*, L. *spīca*. (See next.) A peg for insertion in a hole in a cask.

Spike, *n.*[1] L. *spīca*. An ear of corn.

Spike, *n.*[2] Orig. doubtful. Cf. Sw. and Norw. *spik*, nail. A sharp-pointed piece of metal or wood.—*vt.* To secure with spikes; to furnish with spikes; to drive a spike into.

Spike'nard, *n.* L. or Med.L. *spīca nardi* = G. *nardou stachus*, spike of nard. SPIKE.[1] NARD. An aromatic substance got from an Eastern plant, known also as *nard*; the plant.

Spill, *n.*[1] App. conn. with dial. *Spile*, splinter, spigot—M.Du. or M.L.G. *spīle*, splinter, peg, &c. A thin slip of wood or twisted piece of paper for lighting a candle, &c.

Spill, *vt.* O.E. *spillan* = M.Du., M.L.G. *spillen*, to destroy, slay. To shed (blood); to allow or cause (a liquid) to pour out; to throw from a horse, &c.—*vi.* To flow over the brim.—*n.*[2] A fall from a horse, &c.

Spin, *vi.* O.E. *spinnan*. Common Teut. SPIDER. To twist fibres into a thread; to move or revolve rapidly.—*vt.* To twist (fibres) into a thread; to make by spinning; to contrive; to prolong, draw *out*; to cause to revolve rapidly.—*n.* A rapid ride or run.—**Spin'dle**, *n.* O.E. *spinel*, f. stem of *spinnan*. A slender rod used in spinning; a rod serving as an axis.—**Spin'**NER, *n.*—**Spin'**STER, *n.* A woman who spins; an unmarried woman.

Spin'ach, *n.* O.F. *espinage*, (*e*)*spinache*, of doubtful orig. A well-known vegetable.

Spin'drift, *n.* Var. of SPOONDRIFT

Spine, *n.* O.F. *espine* (F. *épine*), thorn—L. *spīna*, thorn, backbone, &c. PORCUPINE. A thorn; various things like this; the backbone.—**Spin'**AL, *a.*

Spinet', *n.* Older F. *espinette* = It. *spinetta*. Perh. after Giovanni *Spinetti*, said to have been the inventor. An instrument like the harpsichord, but smaller.

Spin'naker, *n.* Said to be formed on *Spinx*, mispronunciation of *Sphinx*, the name of the first yacht which commonly carried the sail. A large three-cornered sail boomed out at right angles to a yacht's side.

Spin'ney, *n.* O.F. *espinei*, a thorny place, f. *espine*. SPINE. A small wood.

Spiræ'a, *n.* L. *spiraea*—G. *speiraia*, app. f. *speira*. SPIRE.[2] A genus of plants with small white or pink flowers; a plant of the genus.

Spire, *n.*[1] O.E. *spīr* = M.Du. *spier*, M.H.G. *spir*, sprout, shoot, &c. A stalk or stem; something elongated or tapering; the tapering portion of a steeple.

Spire, *n.*[2] F. *spire*—L. *spīra*—G. *speira*, anything wound or coiled. A coil; a spiral.—**Spir'**AL, *n.* A continuous curve like that of a screw.—**Spir'**AL, *a.*—**Spir'al**LY,[2] *adv.*

Spir'it, *n.* A.F. *spirit* = O.F. *esperit*, *esprit*—L. *spīritus*, breathing, breath, spirit, conn. with *spīrāre*, to breathe. ASPIRE. The vital principle; a supernatural incorporeal rational being; a frame of mind; essential character, broad meaning; ardour, courage, liveliness; in *pl.*, the mind, cheerfulness, liveliness; a liquid, esp. alcoholic, obtained by distillation.—*vt.* To inspirit; to carry *away* mysteriously.—**Spir'it-**LESS, *a.*—**Spir'itu**AL, *a.* Of the spirit; ecclesiastical; not material.—**Spir'itual**LY,[2] *adv.*—**Spiritual'**ITY, *n.*—**Spir'itual**ISM, *n.* The belief that the spirits of the dead can communicate with the living.—**Spir'itual-**IST, *n.*—**Spir'itu**OUS, *a.* Alcoholic.

Spirt, Spurt, *vi.* Orig. obscure. Cf. M.H.G. *spirzen*, to spit. To issue in a jet.—*vt.* To emit in a jet.—*n.* A jet.

Spit, *n.*[1] O.E. *spitu* = M.Du. *spit*, O.H.G. *spiz* (Ger. *spiess*). A sharp rod thrust through meat which is to be roasted; a small low point of land projecting into water.—*v.*[1]*t.* To thrust through with a spit.

Spit, *v.*[2]*t.* Northern O.E. *spittan* = Ger. dial. *spitzen*, of imitative orig. To eject from the mouth.—*vi.* To eject saliva.—*n.*[2] Saliva; an act of spitting.—**Spit'tle**, *n.* Modification of obs. *Spettle*, *Spattle*—O.E. *spǽtl*, *spátl*. Saliva.—**Spittoon'**, *n.* Suff. *-oon*. Cf. *buffoon*, *dragoon*. A receptacle for spittle.

Spite, *n.* Shortened f. DESPITE. Envious malice; a malignant feeling; *in spite of*, notwithstanding.—*vt.* To annoy or thwart spitefully; to offend, irritate.—**Spite'**FUL, *a.*

Splash, *vt.* Alteration of PLASH, *v.* To spatter with liquid.—*vi.* Of liquids, to dash or fly.—*n.* The result or sound of splashing.

Splay, *vt.* Shortened f. DISPLAY. To spread out, expand, extend; to make slanting.—*n.* A slanting surface.—*a.* Slanting.

Spleen, *n.* L. *splēn*—G. *splēn*, cogn. with Skr. *plīhan*. An organ in the abdomen; irritable or peevish temper; moroseness.—**Splenet'ic**, *a.* L.L. *splēnēticus*. Of or pertaining to the spleen; irritable, peevish; morose.

Splen'did, *a.* L. *splendidus*, f. *splendĕre*, to be bright. RESPLEND. Sumptuous, gorgeous, magnificent; brilliant.—**Splen'did**LY,[2] *adv.* —**Splen'dour,** *n.* L. *splendor.* Brilliancy; magnificence.

Splice, *vt.* M.Du. *splissen,* of doubtful orig. To join (ropes, &c.) by interweaving of strands; to join (timber, &c.) by overlapping.—*n.* A union made by splicing.

Splint, *n.* M.Du. or M.L.G. *splinte,* metal plate or pin, of doubtful orig. A strip of rigid material for confining a broken bone.

Splin'ter, *n.* M.Du. *splinter* = L.G. *splinter,* conn. with prec. A chip or fragment.—*vt.* and *i.* To break into splinters.

Split, *vt.* and *i.* M.Du. *splitten,* of obscure orig. To break asunder.—*n.* A crack or fissure.

Splotch, *n.* Orig. obscure. A blot or smear.

Splut'ter, *vt.* and *i.* and *n.* = SPUTTER.

Spoil, *vt.* O.F. *espoillier*—L. *spoliāre,* f. *spolium,* booty. To strip (a defeated foe); to pillage; to damage; to injure by indulgence.—*vi.* To go bad, decay.—*n.* Booty (often in *pl.*). —**Spoli**A'TION, *n.*

Spoke, *n.* O.E. *spáca* = O.S. *spêca,* O.H.G. *speicha* (Ger. *speiche*). A bar of a wheel; a round of a ladder; a handle of a steering-wheel.—**Spoke'shave.** SHAVE, *n.*[2] A tool for shaping spokes, &c.

Spokes'man, *n.* From *spoke,* pa.pple. of SPEAK, after *craftsman,* &c. One deputed to speak for others.

Spon'dee, *n.* L. *spondēus, spondaeus*—G. *spondeios,* as a stately foot befitting a *spondē* or solemn drink-offering. A metrical foot consisting of two long syllables.—**Sponda'**IC, *a.*

Sponge, *n.* O.E. *sponge*—L. *spongia*—G. *spoggia,* later form of *spoggos.* A light porous marine substance which readily absorbs fluids. —*vt.* To wipe with a sponge.—*vi.* To live on others by mean arts.—**Spong'**Y,[2] *a.*

Spon'son, *n.* Orig. obscure. A triangular platform before and abaft the paddle-boxes of a steamer; a gun platform projecting from the side of a vessel.

Spon'sor, *n.* L. *sponsor,* agent-n. f. *spondēre,* to promise. SPOUSE. One who answers for an infant at baptism; a surety.

Sponta'neous, *a.* L. *spontāneus* (f. *sponte,* of one's own accord) + -OUS. Voluntary; without apparent external cause.—**Sponta'neous**LY,[2] *adv.*—**Spontane'**ITY, *n.*

Spook, *n.* Du. *spook,* Ger. *spuk,* app. of L.G. orig. A spectre or apparition.

Spool, *n.* M.Du. *spoele,* O.H.G. *spuōla* (Ger. *spule*). A reel to wind thread, &c., on.

Spoon, *n.* O.E. *spón,* a chip. Common Teut. A utensil for conveying soft or liquid food to the mouth.—*vt.* To transfer with a spoon.

Spoon'drift, *n.* From obs. *Spoon,* to sail before the wind, of obscure orig. + DRIFT, *n.* Spray swept by wind from the tops of waves.

Sporad'ic, *a.* Med.L. *sporadicus*—G. *sporadikos,* scattered, f. *sporas, sporados,* in sim. sense, f. *spora,* a sowing, f. *speirein,* to sow. SPERM. Scattered; occurring singly, in small numbers, or at intervals.

Sport, *n.* Shortened f. DISPORT. Pastime, esp. hunting, shooting, &c.; mirth; a particular kind of pastime; an object of mirth, &c.—*vi.* To divert oneself, take part in some game, &c.; to trifle *with* something.—**Sport'**IVE, *a.* Playful.—**Sports'man,** *n.* One who hunts, shoots, &c.

Spot, *n.* M.E. *spot* = M.Du. *spotte,* L.G. *spot.* A moral stain; a small mark; a particular place.—*vt.* To mark with spots; to detect.—**Spot'**LESS, *a.*

Spouse, *n.* O.F. *spus, spous,* masc., *spuse,* fem., varr. of *espus,* &c.—L. *sponsus.* ESPOUSE. SPONSOR. A husband or wife.

Spout, *vi.* M.E. *spouten,* corresp. to M.Du. *spouten,* Sw. dial. *spūta.* SPUTTER. To pour forth in a copious stream; to talk copiously.—*vt.* To discharge copiously; to utter volubly.—*n.* A projecting tube for the discharge of water, &c.; a copious discharge of water, &c.

Sprain, *vt.* Of doubtful orig. To wrench or twist (a part of the body).—*n.* A wrench or twist of the ligaments, &c., of a joint.

Sprat, *n.* Later form of *sprot*—O.E. *sprott.* Cf. Du. *sprot,* sprat, O.E. *sprot* (conn. with **sprútan*), SPROUT. A small sea-fish.

Sprawl, *vi.* O.E. *spreawlian* = N. Fris. *spraweli.* To toss about or spread oneself out; to lie awkwardly stretched out.

Spray, *n.*[1] Orig. obscure. Small twigs; a slender or graceful shoot or twig.

Spray, *n.*[2] App. conn. with M.Du. *sprayen* = M.L.G. *sprœjen,* to sprinkle. Water flying in small particles.—*vt.* To send in the form of spray; to sprinkle with spray.

Spread, *vt.* O.E. *sprǽdan* (in combination) = M.Du. *spre(e)den,* O.H.G. *spreitan* (Ger. *spreiten*). To stretch out; to disperse, scatter, diffuse.—*vi.* To become expanded or diffused; tc extend.—*n.* Extent, diffusion.

Sprig, *n.*[1] Orig. obscure. A small nail.

Sprig, *n.*[2] Orig. obscure. A shoot or twig.

Spright'ly, *a.* From *Spright,* var. of SPRITE + -LY.[1] Lively, brisk.—**Spright'li**NESS, *n.*

Spring, *vi.* O.E. *springan.* Cf. O.N. *springa,* to burst, split, Ger. *springen,* to jump, to crack. Orig. sense 'to split or crack'. To split, crack; to leap; to move rapidly; to arise, appear.—*vt.* To bring up or produce unexpectedly.—*n.* A flow of water from the earth; a coming into being; the first season of the year; a quick movement from a constrained position, recoil; resilience; a contrivance of bent or coiled resilient metal.—**Spring'-tide,** *n.* The high tide at the new and full moon.—**Springe,** *n.* Orig. made with a flexible or *springing* rod. Cf. O.H.G. *springa.* A snare.

Sprin'kle, *vt.* and *i.* Formerly *sprenkle.* Conn. with Du. *sprenkelen,* Ger. *sprenkeln.* To scatter, to fall, in small drops or particles.

Sprint, *vi.* Early Scand. **sprinta* (O.N. *spretta,* Sw. *spritta*). To run a short distance at full speed.—*n.* Such a run.

Sprit, *n.* O.E. *spréot* = M.Du., M.L.G. *spriet.* Conn. with SPROUT. A pole, esp. one for propelling a boat; a small spar reaching diagonally from the mast to the upper outward corner of a sail.—**Sprit'sail,** *n.* A sail extended by a sprit.

Sprite, *n.* F. *esprit*—L. *spiritus.* SPIRIT. SPRIGHTLY. A fairy or goblin.

Sprout, *vi.* O.E. **sprútan.* Cf. Du. *spruiten,* Ger. *spriessen.* SPRAT. To put forth shoots, spring up.—*n.* A shoot.

Spruce, *a.* Prob. alteration of M.E. and O.F. *Pruce,* Prussia, referring to some Prussian fashion. Neat in dress.—**Spruce'**LY,[2] *adv.*—Sim. **Spruce fir, Spruce,** *n.* 'Prussian fir.' A kind of fir.

Spud, *n.* Orig. obscure. A small spade for cutting the roots of weeds.

Spume, *n.* L. *spūma.* Foam.—*vi.* To foam.

Spunk, *n.* Orig. obscure. Courage, spirit.

Spur, *n.* O.E. *spura, spora.* Common Teut. SPURN. A pricking instrument on a horseman's heel; a hard projection on a cock's leg;

an incentive or stimulus; a projecting mountain range.—*vt.* To apply spurs to; to incite. —*vi.* To ride hard.

Spurge, *n.* O.F. *espurge*, f. *espurgier*, L. *expurgāre*, to cleanse. EXPURGATE. A plant with an acrid purgative juice.

Spu'rious, *a.* L. *spurius*+-OUS. Not genuine, not what it pretends to be.

Spurn, *vt.* O.E. *spurnan*, *spornan*, to kick against, prob. conn. with *spura*, SPUR. To thrust back with the foot; to reject with disdain.

Spurt, Spirt, *n.* Orig. obscure. A short, sudden effort, esp. in racing.—*vi.* To make such an effort.

Sput'ter, *vt.* = Du. *sputteren*, W.Fris. *sputterje*. Imitative. To emit with a spitting sound; to utter rapidly or incoherently.—*vi.* To speak thus.—*n.* Such speech.

Spu'tum, *n.* L. *spūtum*, orig. neut. pa.pple. of *spuĕre*, to spit. Spittle, saliva.

Spy, *vt.* Short for ESPY. To catch sight of.—*vi.* To play the spy.—*n.* One in hostile territory to observe and report; one keeping a secret watch.

Squab'ble, *vi.* Prob. imitative. Cf. Sw. dial. *skvabbel*, dispute. To engage in a noisy and petty quarrel.—*n.* Such a quarrel.

Squad, *n.* F. *esquade*, *escouade*, varr. of *esquadre*—It. *squadra*, square, squadron, conn. with O.F. *esquare*. SQUARE. A small party, esp. of soldiers.—**Squad'ron**, *n.* It. *squadrone*, aug. of *squadra*. A division of a cavalry regiment or of a fleet.

Squal'id, *a.* L. *squālidus*, f. *squālēre*, to be rough, parched, dirty. Dirty, mean.—**Squal'or**, *n.* L. *squālor*. The state of being squalid.

Squall, *vi.* Imitative. Cf. SQUEAL. To cry out, scream.—*n.*[1] A scream.

Squall, *n.*[2] Perh. conn. with prec. A sudden gust of wind.

Squan'der, *vt.* Orig. obscure. To spend wastefully.

Square, *n.* O.F. *esquare*—Pop.L. *EX*quadrāre*, intensive of L. *quadrāre*. QUADRATE. SQUAD. An instrument for drawing right angles; an equilateral rectangle; an area of this shape built round; the product of a number multiplied by itself.—*a.* In the form of a square; thorough; fair, honest.—*vt.* To make square or rectangular; to multiply (a number) by itself; to adjust; to pay; to bribe.—*vi.* To suit; to take the attitude of a boxer.—**Square'**LY,[2] *adv.*—**Square root**, *n.* The number of which a given number is the square.

Squash, *vt.* O.F. *esquasser* = It. *squassare*—Pop. L. *EX*quassāre*. QUASH. (A reference of the word to L. *cōgĕre* seems to be mistaken.) To crush or squeeze flat or into pulp.—*n.* A squashed mass; a crowd.

Squat, *v.refl.* and *i.* O.F. *esquatir*, *esquater*, f. *es*-(= EX-) + *quatir*, to beat or press down, f. **quait*, L. *coactus*, pressed together, pa.pple. of *cōgĕre*. COAGULATE. To sit upon the heels. —*a.* Short and thick.—**Squat'**TER, *n.* One who settles on land without a title.

Squaw, *n.* From native *squa*. An American-Indian woman or wife.

Squawk, *vi.* Imitative. To utter a harsh cry.—*n.* Such a cry.

Squeak, *vi.* Imitative. To make a short shrill sound.—*n.* Such a sound.

Squeal, *vi.* Imitative. Cf. SQUALL, *v.* To utter a shrill cry.—*n.* Such a cry.

Squea'mish, *a.* Var. of dial. *Squeamous*—A.F. *escoymous*, delicate, nice as to food, of doubtful orig. Easily nauseated; excessively scrupulous.

Squeeze, *vt.* Perh. strengthened form of obs. *Quease* in same sense, of obscure orig. To press; to thrust *into*; to subject to extortion.—*n.* An act of squeezing.

Squib, *n.* Orig. obscure. Perh. imitative. A small firework; a short satirical composition, a lampoon.

Squid, *n.* Orig. obscure. A kind of cuttle-fish.

Squill, *n.* L. *squilla*—G. *skilla*. The sea-onion; its bulb.

Squint, *vi.* Aphetically f. *Asquint*, obliquely, app. f. A-[1] + a word corresp. to Du. *schuinte*, slope, slant. To look obliquely, to have the eyes turned in different directions.—*n.* Such an affection of the eyes; a look or glance; a hagioscope.

Squire, *n.* Short for ESQUIRE. A country gentleman; a lady's escort.—*vt.* To escort (a lady).

Squirm, *vi.* App. imitative. To wriggle, writhe.—*n.* A wriggling motion.

Squir'rel, *n.* A.F. *esquirel*, O.F. *escureul*, &c.—Med.L. *scūrellus*, for **sciūrellus*, dim. of L. *sciūrus*, G. *skiouros*, squirrel, popularly explained as f. *skia*, shadow + *oura*, tail. A small arboreal quadruped with a bushy tail.

Squirt, *vt.* and *i.* Orig. obscure. Cf. L.G. *swirtjen*. To eject, to be ejected, in a jet.—*n.* An instrument for squirting.

Stab, *vt.* App. f. Sw. dial. *stabbe*, thick stick. Cf. O.N. *stabbi*, stump. To pierce with a pointed weapon.—*vi.* To aim a blow with such a weapon.—*n.* Such a blow; the wound inflicted.

Sta'ble, *n.* O.F. *estable*—L. *stabulum*, stall, stable, f. *stāre*, to STAND. STALL. A building for lodging horses.—*vt.* To put in a stable.—*vi.* To be stabled.

Sta'ble, *a.* O.F. *stable*, *estable*—L. *stabilis*, f. *stāre*. (See prec.) ESTABLISH. Firmly fixed or established; resolute, firm.—**Sta**BIL'ITY, *n.* —**Sta'**BLY,[2] *adv.*

Stacca'to, *a.* and *adv.* It. *Mus.*, in an abrupt, sharply detached, or pointed manner.

Stack, *n.* O.N. *stakkr*, haystack. Cf. Sw. *stack* in sim. sense. A pile of hay, grain, &c.; a pile or heap; a number of chimneys standing together, a tall chimney.—*vt.* To pile in a stack.

Staff, *n.*; *pl.* **Staffs**, in *mus.* **Staves**. O.E. *stæf*. Common Teut. STAVE. A stick or pole; a body of officers attached to a commander; a body of workers; the five parallel lines on which musical characters are placed.

Stag, *n.* Prob. repg. O.E. **stacga*, app. meaning properly a male animal in its prime. Cf. O.N. *steggr*, *steggi*, he-bird. The male of the deer.

Stage, *n.* A.F. *estage*, storey, loft, dwelling-house, &c.—Pop.L. **staticum*, f. L. *stāre*, *statum*, to STAND. A raised floor, platform, or surface; the platform of a theatre; dramatic art or literature; scene of action; point of progress or development; a stopping-place on a road, the distance between two stopping-places.—*vt.* To put (a play) on the stage.—**Stag'**ER, *n.* An experienced person.—**Stag'**Y,[2] *a.* Theatrical in manner, dress, &c.

Stag'ger, *vi.* Alteration of dial. *Stacker*—O.N. *stakra*, freq. of *staka*, to push, to stagger. To walk or stand unsteadily; to hesitate.—*vt.* To cause to stagger; to shock.—*n.* A tottering movement.

Stag'nate, *vi.* L. *stagnāre*, *stagnātum*, f.

stagnum, pond. STANCH. TANK. To cease to flow; to become motionless, dull or sluggish. —**Stag'n**ANCY, *n.*—**Stagn**A'TION, *n.*—**Stag'n**ANT, *a.*

Staid, *a.* Formerly *stay'd*, pa.pple. of STAY, to make steady. Of steady and sober character.—**Staid'**LY,[2] *adv.*—**Staid'**NESS. *n.*

Stain, *vt.* Shortened f. O.F. *desteindre*, to discolour, f. *des-* (= DIS- (4)) + *teindre*, L. *tingĕre*, to dye. TAINT. To discolour, soil; to impart a colour to; to blemish, sully.—*vi.* To become stained.—*n.* A spot or mark.—**Stain'**LESS, *a.*

Stair, *n.* O.E. *stǽger*, conn. with *stigan*, to climb. Cf. Du. *steiger*, stair, Ger. *steg*, path. STILE. A set of steps (us. in *pl.*).—**Stair'case**, *n.* The part of a building containing the stairs.

Stake, *n.*[1] O.E. *staca*. Cf. M.Du., M.L.G. *stake*. Teut. **stak-*, var. of **stek-*, to pierce, thrust in. STICK. STOCKADE. A sharpened stick driven in as a support, a boundary, &c.—*v.*[1]*t.* To secure with a stake or stakes, to mark *off* or *out* with stakes.

Stake, *n.*[2] Orig. uncertain. Money wagered or to be contended for.—*v.*[2]*t.* To wager.

Stalac'tite, *n.* With suff. *-ite* of scientific terms f. G. *stalaktos*, vbl.a. f. *stalassein*, to let drop, to drip. A calcareous deposit hanging like an icicle from the roof of a cave.—**Stalag'mite**, *n.* Like *stalactite* f. G. *stalagmos*, a dropping, f. *stalassein*. A similar deposit on the floor.

Stale, *a.* Orig. obscure. Prob. ultimately f. the Teut. root *sta-*, to STAND. That has been too long on view, not fresh; lacking novelty.

Stale, *n.*[1] A.F. *estale*, perh. of Eng. orig. Also **Stale'mate**. MATE.[1] In chess, a draw, one player being unable to move.

Stale, *vi.* Perh. f. O.F. *estaler* = It. *stallare*, in some way conn. with L.G., H.G. *stallen*, Sw. *stalla*. Of horses, &c., to make water.—*n.*[2] Urine of horses, &c.

Stalk, *n.* M.E. *stalke*, dim. of *stale*, *stele*, O.E. *stela*, stalk, stem. Cf. Du. *steel*, Ger. *stiel*. The stem of a plant, &c.; a factory chimney.

Stalk, *vi.* O.E. **stealcian*, to walk warily, conn. with STEAL. To steal up to game; to walk in a stately manner.—*vt.* To steal up to (game).—*n.* The act of doing this; a stately gait.

Stall, *n.* O.E. *steall*, standing-place, stall. Common Teut. Prob. f. root *sta-*, to STAND. INSTALL. STILL, *a.* A compartment in a stable, &c.; a place in or on which goods are exposed; a seat in the chancel of a church; a front seat on the floor of a theatre.—*vt.* To put in a stall.—*vi.* To stick fast in mud, &c.

Stal'lion, *n.* O.F. *estalon* (f. Teut. **stallo-*, stall (see prec.)), as kept in a stall. An uncastrated horse.

Stal'wart, *a.* Formerly *stalworth*—O.E. *stǽlwierthe*, f. *stǽl*, place + *wierthe*, *wyrthe*, WORTH. Strongly built, sturdy; resolute, courageous.

Sta'men, *n.* L. *stāmen*, the upright warp, f. *stāre*, to STAND. The male organ of a flowering plant.—**Stam'ina**, *n.* Pl. of *stāmen*, now gen. used as sing. Power of endurance.

Stam'mer, *vi.* O.E. *stamerian* = W.Fris. *stammerje*, M.Du. *stameren*. Cf. Ger. *stammeln*. STUMBLE. To speak with repetitions of a syllable.—*vt.* To utter thus.—*n.* The habit of speaking thus.

Stamp, *vi.* Early M.E. *stampen*, perh. repg. O.E. **stampian*. Cf. Du. *stampen*, Ger. *stampfen*. STEP. To bring down one's foot heavily. —*vt.* To impress a mark, &c., upon; to affix a postage stamp to; *to stamp out*, to put an end to, crush.—*n.* A stamping with the foot; an instrument for impressing marks, &c.; an official mark; a piece of paper bearing this as evidence of payment of postage, &c.; character, kind.—**Stampede'**, *n.* Sp. *estampido*, conn. with *estampar*, to stamp, of Teut. orig. A sudden rush due to fright.—*vi.* and *t.* To take part in a stampede, to cause to do so.

Stanch, **Staunch**, *vt.* O.F. *estanchier*, perh. f. Pop.L. **stagnicāre*, f. *stagnāre*. STAGNATE. STAUNCH. To check the flow of (blood, &c.); to check the flow from (a wound).

Stan'chion, *n.* O.F. *estanchon*, dim. of *estance*, situation, stanchion—Pop.L. **stantia*, vbl.n. f. *stāre*, to STAND. STANZA. A prop or support.

Stand, *vi.* O.E. *standan*. Common Teut. Cogn. with Skr. *sthā*, G. *sta-*, *stēnai*, L. *stāre*. ASSIST. STABLE. STAGE. STALE, *a.* STALL. STANCHION. STEAD. STATE. STOW. To have or assume an upright position; to be situated; to become stationary; to maintain one's position; to hold good; to be an equivalent.—*vt.* To set upright or in some position; to endure. —*n.* Stoppage; a standing and resisting; position; something on which things may be placed; a raised structure for spectators.

Stan'dard, *n.* O.F. *estandard*, perh. f. L. *extendĕre*, to EXTEND + -ARD. A distinctive flag; a weight or measure to which others are to conform; degree of excellence, &c.; average quality; an upright support; a tree or shrub that stands alone.

Stan'nary, *n.* L.L. *stannāria*, tin-mine, f. L. *stannum*, tin. A tin-mine; a tin-mining district; *stannary court*, a court dealing with matters relating to tin-mining in Cornwall and Devon.

Stan'za, *n.* It. *stanza*, chamber, stanza (as having a pause at the end)—Pop.L. **stantia*. STANCHION. A group of lines of verse.

Sta'ple, *n.*[1] O.E. *stapol*, post, pillar. Orig. sense, 'prop'. Cf. Du. *stapel*, staple, heap, Ger. *staffel*, rung, step, *stapel*, heap, emporium. (See next.) A hoop-shaped piece of wire with pointed ends.

Sta'ple, *n.*[2] O.F. *estaple*, market, f. L.G., the same word as prec. A principal commodity; chief element or material; the fibre of wool, &c.

Star, *n.* M.E. *sterre*—O.E. *steorra*. Cf. Du. *ster*, Ger. *stern*. Cogn. with G. *astēr*, *astron*, L. *stella*, *astrum*. ASTER. ASTERISK. ASTROLOGY. ASTRONOMY. DISASTER. STELLAR. A celestial body seen as a luminous point; an asterisk.—*vt.* To set or adorn with or as with stars; to put an asterisk against.—**Star-cham'ber**, *n.* Late M.E. *sterre-chambre*, also *sterred chamber*, a room in Westminster Hall in which the court met, said to be so called because the roof was originally ornamented with stars. A civil and criminal court (abolished 1640) dealing primarily with offences affecting the interests of the crown, noted for its arbitrary procedure.

Star'board, *n.* O.E. *stéorbord*, 'steering side', f. *stéor*, steering-oar, rudder (conn. with *stéoran*, to STEER) + *bord*, ship's side. BOARD. The right-hand side of a ship.—*a.* Belonging to or on this side.—*vt.* To put (the helm) to starboard.

Starch, *n.* From STARK. Cf. Ger. *stärke*, strength, starch, f. *stark*, strong. A substance used for stiffening linen.—*vt.* To stiffen with starch.

Stare, *vi.* O.E. *starian*, f. root seen in Ger. *starr*, stiff. Cf. Da. *stirre*, Du. *staren*. (See next.) To look with fixed, wide-open eyes; to be prominent, evident, imminent.—*vt.* To abash by staring.—*n.* A staring gaze.

Stark, *a.* O.E. *stearc*, stiff, strong. Cf. Du. *sterk*, Ger. *stark*. Cogn. with prec. and G. *stereos*, firm. STARCH. Stiff; downright, sheer.—*adv.* Wholly, quite.

Stark-na'ked, *a.* M.E. *start-naked*, lit., 'tail-naked', f. O.E. *steort*, tail. Cf. Du. *staart*, Ger. *sterz*, tail. Quite naked.

Star'ling, *n.* M.E. *sterling*, dim. of *stare*, O.E. *stær*, starling. Cf. O.N. *starri*, Ger. *staar*. A bird with blackish-brown speckled plumage showing metallic reflections.

Start, *vi.* M.E. *sterten*, conn. with Du. *storten*, to fall, rush, Ger. *stürzen*, to fall. To make a sudden movement; to begin a journey; to make a beginning.—*vt.* To rouse, to set going; to begin, originate.—*n.* A sudden movement; a beginning; an advantage conceded in a race. —**Start'le**, *vt.* Freq. suff. *-le*. To cause to start, to give a shock to, frighten.

Starve, *vi.* M.E. *sterven*, O.E. *steorfan*, to die. Cf. Du. *sterven*, Ger. *sterben*, to die. To die of hunger; to lack food; to suffer from cold.—*vt.* To kill or distress with hunger or cold.—**Starve'ling**, *n.* -LING (1). A starving or ill-fed person or animal.—*a.* Starving.—**Starv**A'TION, *n.* (A hybrid word.)

State, *n.* O.F. *estat*—L. *status*, position, condition, status, f. *stāre*, *statum*, to STAND. STATUE. STATUTE. Condition; mode of existence; an organized political community; civil government; rank, dignity, pomp.—*vt.* To express in speech or writing; to fix, specify.—**State'**LY,[1] *a.* Dignified, imposing.—**State'**MENT, *n.* Expression in words; a thing stated; a formal account of facts.—**State'-room**, *n.* A separate cabin in a steamer.—**States'man**, *n.* One prominent or versed in state affairs.

Stat'ic, *a.* G. *statikos*, causing to stand, f. *sta-*, root of *stēnai*, to STAND. Also **Stat'**ICAL. Dealing with forces in equilibrium.—In *pl.* as *n.*, the branch of dynamics dealing with such forces.

Sta'tion, *n.* F. *station*—L. *statio*, *stationis*, n. of action f. *stāre*. STATE. A place where a person or thing stands or is placed; a stopping-place on a railway; position in life.—*vt.* To assign a position to.—**Sta'tion**ARY, *a.* Not moving or changing; not meant to be moved.—**Sta'tion**ER, *n.* Orig. a bookseller having a *station* or stall. One who sells writing-materials, &c. — **Sta'tion**ERY, *n.* His wares.

Sta'tist, *n.* STATE + -IST. One who deals with statistics.—**Statis'**TICS, *n.pl.* Numerical facts systematically collected; the science of dealing with these.—**Statist'**IC, **Statis'**TICAL, *aa.*—**Statist**IC'IAN, *n.*

Stat'ue, *n.* O.F. *statuë*—L. *statua*, f. *stāre*. STATE. An image of a person, &c., in a solid substance.—**Stat'u**ARY, *a.* Of statues.—*n.* A maker of statues; the statuary art; statues collectively.—**Statuesque'**, *a.* Suff. *-esque* of likeness. Like a statue.—**Statuette'**, *n.* Dim. suff. *-ette*. A small statue.

Stat'ure, *n.* F. *stature*—L. *statūra*, f. *stāre*. STATE. The height of one's body.

Sta'tus, *n.* L. *status*, f. *stāre*. STATE. Position, rank; relation to others; position of affairs.

Stat'ute, *n.* F. *statut*—L. *statūtum*, neut. pa.pple. of *statuĕre*, to place, causal of *stāre*. STATE. CONSTITUTE. A written law.—**Stat'u**TORY, *a.*

Staunch, **Stanch**, *a.* O.F. *estanche*, watertight, conn. with *estanchier*. STANCH. Trustworthy, loyal.

Stave, *n.* Var. of STAFF. One of the pieces forming a cask; a stanza or verse.—*vt.* To break a hole in (a cask, ship, &c.); to ward *off*.

Stay, *vt.* O.F. *estayer*, f. *estaye*, prop, stay—M.Du. *stade*, *staeye*, prop, cogn. with STEAD. STAID. To check, stop; to support, prop —*vi.* To remain; to dwell temporarily; to pause. —*n.* A remaining, a dwelling; a check, restraint; a support; in *pl.*, a corset.

Stay, *n.* O.E. *stæg*, poss. f. O.F. *estaye*. (See prec.) A rope supporting a mast.

Stead, *n.* O.E. *stede*, a place. Cf. Du. *stede*, a place, *stad*, Ger. *stadt*, town. Cogn. with STAND and STAY, *v.* Cf. BEDSTEAD, HOMESTEAD, ROADSTEAD. *In* (one's) *stead*, in (his) place, instead (of him); *to stand* (one) *in good stead*, to be of service (to him).—**Stead'fast**, *a.* O.E. *stedefæst*. FAST, *a.* Firm, constant. —**Stead'**Y,[2] *a.* Firmly fixed; regular, equable; constant; of temperate habits.—*vt.* and *i.* To make, to become steady.—**Stead'**ILY,[2] *adv.* —**Stead'**INESS, *n.*

Steak, *n.* O.N. *steik*. Cf. *steikja*, to roast on a spit, conn. with O.E. *stician*. STICK. A slice of meat cut for broiling or broiled.

Steal, *vt.* O.E. *stelan*. Cf. Du. *stelen*, Ger. *stehlen*. To take without right or leave; to take surreptitiously or by surprise.—*vi.* To move secretly or silently.—**Steal**TH,[1] *n.* Secrecy, surreptitious procedure.—**Stealth'**Y,[2] *a.*—**Stealth'**ILY,[2] *adv.*

Steam, *n.* O.E. *stéam*, vapour, smoke, smell. Cf. Du. *stoom*. The vapour of water.—*vt.* To cook by, treat with steam.—*vi.* To give out steam; to rise in vapour; to move by the agency of steam.—**Steam'**ER, *n.* A ship propelled by steam; a vessel for steaming things.

Ste'arin, *n.* G. *stear*, stiff fat + chemical suff. *-in*. The chief component of animal fats.

Steed, *n.* O.E. *stéda*, stallion, war-horse, f. *stód*, STUD.[2] A horse, esp. a war-horse.

Steel, *n.* O.E. *stýle*. Cf. Du. *staal*, Ger. *stahl*. Cogn. with Skr. *stak*, to resist. A hard and malleable alloy of iron and carbon; a sharpening tool.—*vt.* To harden (one's heart, &c.).

Steel'yard, *n.* Named f. the *Steelyard*, the meeting-place in London of German merchants—L.G. *staal-hof*, sample-yard, *staal*, STALL, being confused with *steel*. A kind of balance with unequal arms.

Steep, *a.* O.E. *stéap*, steep, high. Cf. O.N. *steypthr*, conn. with *steypa*, causal of *stúpa*, to STOOP. STEEPLE. Having a decided slope. —*n.* A steeply sloping place.—**Steep'**EN,[2] *vt.* and *i.*—**Steep'**LY,[2] *adv.*

Steep, *vt.* O.N. *steypa* (see prec.), to overturn, pour out, steep. To soak; to impregnate.

Steep'le, *n.* O.E. *stýpel*, high tower, f. *stéap*. STEEP, *a.* A church tower surmounted with a spire.—**Steep'lechase**, *n.* A horse-race across country (perh. orig. with a steeple as goal).

Steer, *n.* O.E. *stéor*. Cf. Du. and Ger. *stier*, bull. Cogn. with G. *tauros*, L. *taurus*, bull. A young male of the ox kind.

Steer, *vt.* O.E. *stéoran*, *stýran*, conn. with *stéor*. STARBOARD. Cf. Du. *stuur*, Ger. *steuer*, rudder. STERN, *n.* To direct the course of (a ship); to direct (one's course).—*vi.* To direct one's course.—**Steer'**AGE, *n.* The effect of a ship's helm; the part of a ship (now us. in the bow) allotted to passengers paying the lowest fare.—**Steers'man**, *n.* One who steers a ship.

Stel'lar, *a.* L.L. *stellāris*, f. L. *stella*, STAR. Of or pertaining to stars.

Stem, *n.* O.E. *stefn*, *stemn*, stem of a tree or a ship. Cf. O.N. *stafn*, *stamn*, stem of a ship, Ger. *stamm*, stem of a tree. The main body of a tree or plant; the part of a word to which case-endings, &c., are added; the foremost part of a ship.

Stem, *vt.* Cf. E. Fris., Ger. *stemmen*. To check, dam up; to make way against.

Stench, *n.* O.E. *stenc*, strong (often pleasant) smell, conn. with *stincan*. STINK. An ill smell.

Sten'cil, *vt.* Perh. f. O.F. *estenceler*, to sparkle, to cover with stars, f. *estencele*, *estincelle* (F. *étincelle*), spark—Pop. L. **stincilla* for L. *scintilla*, spark. SCINTILLA. TINSEL. To paint in figures by means of a pierced plate. —*n.* The plate; the pattern produced.

Sten'ograph, *n.* G. *stenos*, narrow + *graphein*, to write. GRAPHIC. A character used in shorthand writing. — **Stenog'raphy**,[1] *n.* Shorthand writing.—**Stenog'rapher**, *n.*—**Stenograph'**IC, *a.*

Stento'rian, *a.* *Stentor*, a Greek with a loud voice (Iliad, 5, 785) + -IAN. Very loud.

Step, *vi.* O.E. *steppan*. Cf. Du. *stap*, footstep. Cogn. with STAMP. To move and set down a foot or the feet.—*vt.* To set up (a mast).—*n.* The completed movement of a leg in walking, &c., the distance covered; a mark left by the foot; a measure adopted, an act; something to support the foot in ascending or descending; a degree in a scale; a socket to hold a mast.

Step'child, *n.* O.E. *stéopcild*, f. *stéop*, orphaned + *cild*, CHILD. Cf. Du., Ger. *stiefkind*. One's wife's or husband's child by a former marriage. So of other relationships regarded as similar—**Step'brother, Step'sister**, a child of a former marriage of one's stepfather or stepmother; **Step'father, Step'mother**, one's parent's later husband or wife.

Stephano'tis, *n.* G. *stephanos*, wreath + *ous*, *ōtos*, ear, referring to the form of the flowers. A climbing plant with fragrant waxy flowers.

Steppe, *n.* Russian *stepe*. A bare level plain.

Ster'eoscope, *n.* G. *stereos*, solid + *skope-ein*, to behold. An optical instrument by which two views of an object taken at different angles are combined into one image so as to give an effect of solidity.—**Stereoscop'**IC, *a.* —**Ster'eotype**, *n.* *Stereos* + TYPE. A printing-plate cast from a mould of an assemblage of types.—*vt.* To make a stereotype from.

Ster'ile, *a.* O.F. *sterile*—L. *sterilis*. Barren, unfruitful; free from disease-germs.—**Steril'**ITY, *n.*—**Ster'il**IZE, *vt.*—**Ster'ilizer**, *n.* An apparatus for destroying disease-germs.

Ster'ling, *a.* M.E. *sterling*, a coin of true weight. Poss. = STARLING, referring to birds depicted on coins, or *starling* (-LING (3)), referring to stars thus depicted. Of standard value or purity; of solid worth.

Stern, *a.* O.E. *styrne*. Cf. Ger. *störrig*, morose, stubborn. Severe, strict, rigid.—**Stern'**LY,[2] *adv.*—**Stern'**NESS, *n.*

Stern, *n.* O.N. *stjórn*, a steering, helm. Cogn. with STEER, *v.* The hind part of a ship.

Ster'num, *n.* L., f. G. *sternon*, chest. The breastbone.

Sternuta'tion, *n.* L. *sternūtātio*, *sternūtātiōnis*, f. *sternūtāre*, freq. of *sternuĕre*, to sneeze. A sneezing, a sneeze.

Ster'torous, *a.* L. *stertĕre*, to snore + -*or*, suff. of condition + -OUS. Making snore-like sounds.

Steth'oscope, *n.* G. *stēthos*, breast + *skopeein*, to behold, examine. An instrument used in auscultation, esp. of the heart.

Ste'vedore, *n.* Sp. *estivador*, f. *estivar*, to compress wool, stow cargo—L. *stīpāre*, to compress. CONSTIPATE. STIFF. One who loads or unloads ships.

Stew, *n.* O.F. *estuve*, stew, stove, hothouse, f. Teut. Cf. O.H.G. *stupa*, bathroom, Ger. *stube*, room. Cogn. with STOVE. A brothel.

Stew, *vt.* and *i.* From prec. in sense 'hot bath'. To cook slowly in a closed vessel.—*n.* A dish thus made; a state of anxiety.

Stew'ard, *n.* O.E. *stíweard*, lit. 'styward', f. *stigu*, STY[1] + *weard*, WARD. One who manages another's property; an attendant on passengers in a ship; an official managing a race-meeting, &c.—**Stew'ard**ESS, *n.*

Stick, *vt.* Two words blended — (1) M.E. *steken*, to pierce, fix. Cf. Ger. *stechen*. Teut. type **stek*-. (STAKE.) Cogn. with L. *instigāre* (INSTIGATE): (2) M.E. *stikien*, to be infixed—O.E. *stician*, to pierce, prick. Cf. Ger. *stecken*. STEAK. STITCH. To thrust the point of *in*, &c.; to stab; to fix, fasten; to cause to project.—*vi.* To be fixed, adhere; to project; to be brought to a stop; to scruple.—*n.* O.E. *sticca*, peg, stick, conn. with *stician*. A staff or rod; a slender cylindrical piece.—**Stick'y**,[2] *a.* Tending to adhere, viscous.

Stick'leback, *n.* O.E. *sticel*, prickle, sting, f. *stician*. (See prec.) A small fish with sharp spines on its back.

Stick'ler, *n.* Obs. *Stickle*, to part combatants, be umpire (prob. f. M.E. *stightlen*, to arrange, freq. f. O.E. *stihtan*, to control, cogn. with Da. *stifte*, Ger. *stiften*, to institute) + -ER. One who insists on authority, trifles, &c.

Stiff, *a.* O.E. *stíf*. Cf. Da. *stiv*, Du. *stijf*. Cogn. with L. *stīpāre*. STEVEDORE. Rigid, not flexible; unyielding, obstinate; lacking ease or grace; hard to cope with.—**Stiff'**EN,[2] *vt.* and *i.*—**Stiff'**LY,[2] *adv.*—**Stiff'**NESS, *n.*

Sti'fle, *vt.* O.N. *stífla*, to dam up, freq. conn. with prec. To smother.

Stig'ma, *n.* G. *stigma*, *stigmatos*, prick, brand, f. *stizein*. DISTINGUISH. INSTIGATE. A branded mark; a stain on reputation; the part of the pistil which receives the pollen; in pl. *stigmata*, marks corresponding to those made on Christ's body.—**Stig'mat**IZE, *vt.* To describe opprobriously *as*.

Stile, *n.* O.E. *stigel*, f. *stígan*, to climb. STAIR. STIRRUP. Steps for climbing a fence.

Stilet'to, *n.* It., dim. of *stilo*, dagger, f. L. *stilus*. STYLE. A small dagger.

Still, *a.* O.E. *stille*, conn. with *stillan*, to be still. Cogn. with *stellan*, to place, conn. with *steall*, STALL. Without or nearly without motion or sound; not effervescing.—*vt.* To quiet, calm.—*adv.* Even to this or that time; nevertheless; with *comp.*, even, yet.—**Still'**NESS, *n.*—**Still'**Y,[2] *a.* Still, quiet.—**Still'born**, *a.* Born dead.—**Still life**, *n.* The representation in painting of inanimate things.

Still, *n.* Short for M.E. *stillatorie*, f. L. *stillāre*. DISTIL. An apparatus for distilling. —**Still'-room**, *n.* A housekeeper's storeroom.

Stilt, *n.* Sw. *stylta.* Cf. Du. *stelt*, Ger. *stelze.* One of a pair of poles with rests for the feet raising the user in walking.—**Stilt'ed**, *ppl.a.* As if on stilts, bombastic, pompous.

Stilt'on, *n.* From *Stilton* in Huntingdonshire. A rich white cheese.

Stim'ulus, *n.* L. *stimulus*, goad. Something that rouses, a rousing, to activity.—**Stim'ulate**, *vt.* L. *stimulāre, stimulātum*, to prick forward. To animate, excite, spur on.—**Stim'ul**ANT, *a.* Producing a rapid temporary increase of vital energy.—*n.* A stimulant or exciting agent or substance.—**Stim'u**LATIVE, *a.*—**Stimul**A'TION, *n.*

Sting, *vt.* O.E. *stingan.* Cf. O.N. and Sw. *stinga.* To thrust the sting into (often *fig.*).—*vi.* To be affected by acute pain.—*n.* A sharp-pointed weapon, often connected with a poison-gland, with which certain animals and plants are furnished; the thrust of a sting, the wound made, the pain caused (often *fig.*).—**Sting'**Y,[2] *a.* From the *n.*, with sense 'nipping, unkindly'. Niggardly, meanly parsimonious.

Stink, *vi.* O.E. *stincan*, to smell strongly (sweetly or evilly). Cf. Du., Ger. *stinken*, to stink. STENCH. To emit or have a strongly offensive smell.—*n.* Such a smell.

Stint, *vt.* O.E. (*for-*)*styntan*, properly, to make short of wit, f. *stunt*, short of wit, dull. Cf. O.N. *stytta*, to shorten, f. *stuttr*, short, stunted. STUNT. To keep on short allowance; to supply grudgingly.—*n.* Limitation of supply or effort.

Sti'pend, *n.* L. *stīpendium*, tax, soldier's pay, f. *stips, stĭpis*, gift, alms + *pendĕre*, to pay. EXPEND. A fixed periodical payment for services.—**Stipen'di**ARY, *a.* Receiving a stipend.—*n.* One receiving a stipend; a paid police magistrate.

Stip'ple, *vt.* Du. *stippelen*, to dot over, f. *stippel*, speckle, dim. of *stip*, point. To engrave in dots, as distinguished from lines.—*n.* Engraving by this process.

Stip'ulate, *vi.* L. *stipulāri, stipulātus*, to make an agreement, f. Old L. *stipulus*, firm, fast, conn. with *stipes*, stock, post. STUBBLE. With *for*, to mention or insist upon in making a bargain; to demand *that.*—**Stipul**A'TION, *n.*

Stir, *vt.* O.E. *styrian.* Cf. O.H.G. *stōren*, to scatter, destroy, disturb (Ger. *stören*, to disturb). Prob. cogn. with STORM. To set or keep in motion; to move a spoon, &c., round and round in; to agitate, rouse.—*vi.* To begin to be in motion; to be out of bed.—*n.* Commotion, disturbance, excitement.

Stir'rup, *n.* O.E. *stí-ráp, stig-ráp*, f. *stigan*, to climb (STILE) + *ráp*, ROPE. A metal loop, hung by a strap, for mounting a horse and for supporting the foot.—**Stir'rup-cup**, *n.* A drink given to a departing rider.

Stitch, *n.* O.E. *stice*, pricking sensation, f. *stician.* STICK. A sharp pain in the side; a complete movement of a needle in sewing, &c.; the result.—*vt.* and *i.* To sew.

Sti'ver, *n.* Du. *stuiver*, a small coin now obsolete. The smallest coin imaginable.

Stoat, *n.* M.E. *stot*, stoat, stallion, male animal. Cf. O.N. *stútr*, bull, Ger. *stossen*, to push. The ermine, esp. in its summer fur.

Stock, *n.* O.E. *stocc*, stock, stump. Cf. Du. *stok*, Ger. *stock.* STOKER. STUCCO. A stump, post, stem; a handle or holding-piece; a store for drawing upon; lineage; the animals and implements on a farm, the requisites for a trade; liquor forming a foundation for soups, &c.; various kinds of sweet-smelling flowers; money lent or contributed by various persons and united into one fund; in *pl.*, a frame, formerly in use, for confining the feet of offenders, the timbers supporting a ship which is being built.—*vt.* To fit or provide with a stock; to lay up in store.—*attrib.* Kept in stock; often repeated or brought forward.—**Stock'-broker**, *n.* One who acts for clients in the purchase or sale of interests in stocks and of shares in companies.—**Stock'-jobber**, *n.* One whose occupation it is to deal in such things on his own account.—**Stock' Exchange'**, *n.* A place where such transactions are carried out; an association of persons engaged in such transactions.—**Stock'-still**, *a.* 'Still as a stock', motionless.

Stockade', *n.* Assimilated to prec. f. Sp. *estacada*, f. *estaca*, M.Du. *stake*, STAKE. An enclosure or defence of upright stakes.

Stock'ing, *n.* With dim. suff. *-ing* f. *stock*, short for *nether-stock, i.e.* docked lower part of the 'hose' covering the lower part of the body and the legs. STOCK. A close-fitting covering for the foot and leg.

Stod'gy, *a.* Of obscure orig. Indigestible, heavy; dull and crammed with facts or details. —**Stodge**, *n.* App. a back-formation f. the *a.* Heavy food; a full meal.

Sto'ic, *n.* L. *stōicus*—G. *stōikos*, lit., 'of the colonnade', referring to the *stoa* or colonnade under which Zeno taught. One of a school of philosophers, founded at Athens (c. 300 B.C.) by Zeno, who held virtue to be the highest good and inculcated control of the passions and indifference to pleasure and pain; a person of great self-control.—**Sto'ic**AL, *a.*—**Sto'ical**LY,[2] *adv.*—**Sto'ic**ISM, *n.*

Sto'ker, *n.* Du. *stoker*, f. *stoken*, to kindle or stir a fire, prob. conn. with *stok* (STOCK) in sense 'poker'. One who tends a fire.—**Stoke**, *vt.* Back-formation f. the *n.* To feed and tend (a fire).

Stole, *n.* L. *stola*, robe—G. *stolē*, equipment, robe, f. *stellein*, to equip. APOSTLE. DIASTOLE. A long strip of silk, &c., worn by a priest, &c., round the neck.

Stol'id, *a.* L. *stolidus*, firm, stupid. Phlegmatic, hard to stir.—**Stolid'**ITY, *n.*

Stom'ach, *n.* F. *estomac*—L. *stomachus*—G. *stomachos*, gullet, stomach, conn. with *stoma*, mouth. A cavity forming the principal digestive organ; appetite; readiness, inclination. —*vt.* To put up with (an affront, &c.).—**Stom'ach**ER, *n.* A piece of female dress formerly worn on the front of the body.—**Stomach'**IC, *a.* Of the stomach; promoting digestion.

Stone, *n.* O.E. *stán.* Cf. Du. *steen*, Ger. *stein.* A piece of rock; a gem; rock or stones as a material; a shaped slab of rock; a concretion occurring in the body, esp. in the bladder; the nut or seed of a fruit; a weight of 14 lbs.—*vt.* To pelt with stones; to free (fruit) from stones.—**Stone'-blind**, *a.* Quite blind.—**Stone'-ware**, *n.* Common glazed pottery.—**Ston'**Y,[2] *a.*

Stool, *n.* O.E. *stól*, seat. Cf. Du. *stoel*, Ger. *stuhl*, chair. FALDSTOOL. A backless seat for one; a place for evacuating, the evacuation, of the bowels; the fæces evacuated.

Stoop, *vi.* O.E. *stúpian.* Cf. O.N. *stúpa*, M.Du. *stuypen.* STEEP, *a.* To lean forward; to deign *to do*, to lower oneself *to.*—*n.* A stooping carriage of the body.

Stop, *vt.* O.E. *stoppian* (in combination)—L.L. *stuppāre*, to stop up with tow, f. L. *stuppa*, tow. Cf. G. *stuppē*, tow. STUFF. To stuff up, prevent passage through; to fill up a cavity in (a tooth); to check; to cease to give or allow; to regulate the sounds of (a stringed instrument).—*vi.* To cease, pause; to remain, stay.—*n.* A stopping or being stopped; a pause; a punctuation mark; a set of organ-pipes having a special tone, the means of putting it in and out of action.—**Stop'p**AGE, *n.*—**Stop'p**ER, *n.* Also **Stop'ple**. Instrumental suff. *-le.* A plug for closing a bottle.

Store, *n.* O.F. *estor*—L.L. *staurum* = *instaurum*, f. L. *instaurāre*, to build, restore, in L.L., to provide necessaries, f. IN-[1] + **staurāre* (f. **staurus* = G. *stauros*, stake), to set up, place. RESTORE. Abundance, provision; a place for keeping goods; in *pl.*, articles laid up for use, a commercial establishment dealing in goods of different kinds.—*vt.* To stock or furnish; to deposit for keeping.—**Stor'**AGE, *n.*

Sto'rey, Sto'ry, *n.* O.F. *estorée*, a building, fem. pa.pple. of *estorer*, to build—L.L. **staurāre.* (See prec.) One of the horizontal divisions of a house.

Stork, *n.* O.E. *storc.* Cf. Du. *stork*, Ger. *storch.* A tall wading bird.

Storm, *n.* O.E. *storm.* Cf. Du. *storm*, Ger. *sturm.* STIR. A violent atmospheric disturbance; assault on a fortified place.—*vi.* To rage, be violent.—*vt.* To take by storm.—**Storm'**Y,[2] *a.*

Sto'ry, *n.* A.F. *storie*, O.F. *estoire*—L. *historia.* HISTORY. History; an account of an incident, a narrative, tale.—**Sto'ried**, *a.* Celebrated in, associated with, legends or tales.

Stout, *a.* O.F. *estout*—M.Du. *stolt.* Cf. Ger. *stolz*, proud. Perh. f. L. *stultus.* STULTIFY. Brave, sturdy, strongly built or made; corpulent.—*n.* The strongest kind of beer.—**Stout'**LY,[2] *adv.*—**Stout'**NESS, *n.*

Stove, *n.* O.E. *stofa*, heated room, bath. Cf. M.Du. *stove* in sim. sense. An apparatus for warming a room, cooking, &c.

Stow, *vt.* M.E. *stowen*, lit., 'to put in a place'—O.E. *stówigan*, f. *stów*, a place. Cogn. with STAND. To put in a convenient place or out of the road; to stow articles in.—**Stow'**AGE, *n.*—**Stow'away**, *n.* A person who conceals himself on board a ship to secure a passage.

Strad'dle, *vi.* Formerly *striddle*, f. STRIDE + freq. suff. *-le.* To spread the legs wide apart.—*vt.* To stand or sit across (something) in this attitude.

Strag'gle, *vi.* App. f. M.E. *strāken*, to wander + freq. suff. *-le.* Cf. M.Da. *strage*, to wander. To stray from the main body, get dispersed, occur at intervals.—**Strag'gl**ER, *n.*

Straight, *a.* O.E. *streht*, pa.pple. of *streccan*, to STRETCH. Without curve or bend; honest, upright; level; in proper order or place.—*n.* Straight condition; a straight part.—*adv.* In a straight line; without circumlocution.—**Straight'**EN,[2] *vt.* and *i.*—**Straightfor'ward**, *a.* Open, frank; without complications.—**Straightfor'ward**LY,[2] *adv.*—**Straight'way**, *adv.* Immediately, at once.

Strain, *vt.* O.F. *estreindre*—L. *stringĕre.* ASTRINGENT. STRICT. To stretch tightly; to exercise or use to the utmost or to excess; to wrest from the true meaning; to filter.—*vi.* To make a strong effort.—*n.*[1] Stretching force; violent effort; injury from being strained; a burst or spell of music or poetry; tone adopted in writing or speaking, tendency of discourse (this sense app. associated with next).—**Strain'**ER, *n.* A filter.

Strain, *n.*[2] O.E. *stréon*, gain, product, progeny, whence *strýnan*, to beget. A breed of animals; a human stock or race; a moral tendency; a trace or streak.

Strait, *a.* A.F. *estreit*, O.F. *estroict* (F. *étroit*)—L. *strictus*, pa.pple. of *stringĕre.* STRICT. Narrow, confined; confining; strict.—*n.* A narrow passage of water connecting two large bodies (often in *pl.*); in *pl.*, a position of difficulty, distress.—**Strait'**EN,[2] *vt.*—**Strait'-laced**, *a.* Severely virtuous.—**Strait-waist'coat**, *n.* A contrivance for confining the arms of maniacs.

Strand, *n.*[1] O.E. *strand.* Common Teut. The margin of a sea, lake, or river.—*vt.* To run (a ship) aground.—*vi.* To run aground.

Strand, *n.*[2] O.N.F. *estran*—O.H.G. *streno*, cord (Ger. *strähne*, skein, hank). One of the strings or wires composing a rope.

Strange, *a.* O.F. *estrange*—L. *extrāneus.* EXTRANEOUS. ESTRANGE. Foreign; not familiar; singular, surprising; unaccustomed *to.*—**Strange'**LY,[2] *adv.*—**Strange'**NESS, *n.*—**Strang'**ER, *n.* A foreigner; an unknown person; one unaccustomed *to.*

Strang'le, *vt.* O.F. *estrangler*—L. *strangulāre*—G. *straggalizein*, f. *straggalē*, halter, f. *straggos*, twisted. STRETCH. To kill by compressing the windpipe.—**Strangul**A'TION, *n.*

Stran'gury, *n.* L. *strangūria*—G. *straggouria*, f. *stragx*, *straggos*, drop + *ouron.* URINE. A disease in which the urine is discharged painfully and in drops.

Strap, *n.* O.E. *stropp*—L. *struppus*, cogn. with G. *strophos*, twisted band, f. *strephein*, to twist. STROP. A strip of leather or metal.—*vt.* To fasten with a strap; to beat with a strap.—**Strap'ping**, *ppl.a.* Cf. '*thumping*', big, huge. Tall and well made.

Strappa'do, *n.* It. *strappata*, f. *strappare*, to pull, wring—Swiss H.G. *strapfen*, to pull tight—Du. *straffen*, to punish, f. *straf*, severe. A military punishment consisting in raising the culprit to a height by a rope, and suddenly letting him fall half-way with a jerk.

Strat'agem. *n.* O.F. *stratageme*—L. *stratēgēma*—G. *stratēgēma*, a device of a general, a stratagem. f. *stratēge-ein*, to be general, f. *stratēgos*, general, f. *stratos*, army + *agein*, to lead. An artifice in war, a trick, device.—**Strat'egy**, *n.* G. *stratēgia*, generalship. The art of moving or disposing troops, ships, &c., to the best advantage.—**Strateg'**IC, **Strateg'**ICAL, *aa.*—**Strat'eg**IST, *n.*

Stra'tum, *n.*; *pl.* **Stra'ta**. L. *strātum*, something spread out, neut. pa.pple. of *sternĕre*, to spread, cover, pave, throw down. CONSTERNATE. PROSTRATE. STREET. A layer.—**Strat'i**FY, *vt.* To arrange in strata.—**Strati**FICA'TION, *n.*

Straw, *n.* O.E. *streaw.* Cf. Du. *stroo*, Ger. *stroh.* Cogn. with L. *sternĕre.* (See prec.) STREW. The dry cut stalks of grain.—**Straw'berry**, *n.* O.E. *streawberige*, f. *streaw* + *berige* = *berie*, BERRY (perh. from its propagation by runners). A plant producing a red fruit studded with yellow seeds; the fruit.

Stray, *vi.* O.F. *estraier*, prob. ultimately f. L. *strāta* (STREET) with notion 'to wander about the streets'. To wander, go astray.—*n.* An animal that has strayed.—*a.* Strayed; scattered, occurring or met with now and then.

Streak, *n.* O.E. *strica.* Cogn. with STRIKE. A long narrow band or line.—*vt.* To mark with streaks.—**Streak'**Y,[2] *a.*

Stream, *n.* O.E. *stréam.* Cf. Du. *stroom*,

Ger. *strom*. Cogn. with Skr. *sru*, G. *rhe-ein*, to flow. CATARRH. A flowing body of water or other liquid.—*vi*. To flow in a stream; to run with liquid; to float or wave in the air.—**Stream'**ER, *n*. A ribbon attached at one end and streaming in the air; a beam or column of light.—**Stream'let**, *n*. Dim. suff. *-let*. A small stream.

Street, *n*. O.E. *strǣt*—L. *strāta*, paved way, fem. pa.pple. of *sternĕre*. STRATUM. STRAY. Cf. Du. *straat*, Ger. *strasse*. A town or village road with houses on one side or both; the road with the houses.

Strength, *n*. O.E. *strengthu*, conn. with *strang*, STRONG. The quality of being strong, the degree in which a person or thing has this quality; that which makes strong; the proportion of a whole number present or available.—**Streng'th**EN,[2] *vt*. and *i*.

Stren'uous, *a*. L. *strēnuus* (cogn. with G. *strēnēs*, strong) + -OUS. Energetic, vigorous, earnestly persistent.—**Stren'uous**LY,[2] *adv*.

Stress, *n*. O.F. *estrecier*, to straiten, contract.—Pop. L. type **strictiāre*, L. *strictus*. STRICT. Constraint, impelling force; effort, demand upon energy; emphasis, accent.—*vt*. To emphasize; to put under mechanical stress.

Stretch, *vt*. O.E. *streccan*, f. *stræc*, rigid, strong. Cf. Du. *strekken*, Ger. *strecken*. Cogn. with L. *stringĕre*, G. *straggos*. STRAIGHT. STRANGLE. STRICT. STRONG. To draw taut, tighten; to place somewhere in a taut state; to straighten; to reach *out*; to exert to the utmost or in excess; to exaggerate.—*vi*. To reach or extend; to have elasticity.—*n*. A stretching or being stretched; a continuous expanse or spell.—**Stretch'**ER, *n*. A person or thing that stretches; a plank in a boat to take the pressure of a rower's feet; an appliance for carrying a disabled person.

Strew, *vt*. O.E. *strēowian*, conn. with *strēaw*, STRAW. Cf. Ger. *streuen*. To scatter over a surface; to cover partly by scattering.

Stri'a, *n*.; *pl*. **Stri'æ**. L. *stria*, furrow, hollow. A slight ridge or furrow; a line or streak.—**Stri'**ATE,[2] *a*.—**Stri'**ATE,[3] *vt*.

Strict, *a*. L. *strictus*, pa.pple. of *stringĕre*, to draw tight, compress, also to graze, stroke. ASTRINGENT. PRESTIGE. STRAIN. STRAIT. STRESS. STRETCH. STRINGENT. Exactly defined; without exception; not lax.—**Strict'**LY,[2] *adv*.—**Strict'**NESS, *n*.—**Strict'**URE, *n*. A morbid contraction; a critical remark.

Stride, *vi*. O.E. *strīdan*. Cf. L.G. *striden*, to strive, to stride, Ger. *streiten*, to strive, O.N. *strīth*, STRIFE. Orig. sense app. 'to strive', hence, 'to take long steps' (as if in strife). STRADDLE. To walk with long steps.—*vt*. To pass over with one step; to bestride.—*n*. A step, esp. in respect of length.

Stri'dent, *a*. L. *strīdens*, *strīdentis*, pres. pple. of *strīdĕre*, to creak. Loud and harsh in sound.

Strife, *n*. O.F. *estrif*, app. f. O.N. *strīth*. STRIDE. STRIVE. A contest; a state of conflict.

Strig'il, *n*. L. *strigilis*, f. *stringĕre*, in sense 'to graze'. STRICT. A skin-scraper used by the ancients at the bath.

Strike, *vt*. O.E. *strīcan*, to proceed swiftly and smoothly, to strike. Cf. Ger. *streichen*, to go, strike. Cogn. with L. *stringĕre*, to graze. STRICT. STREAK. STROKE. To hit; to cause to penetrate; to ignite (a match); to occur to; to impress strongly; to lower (a flag, &c.); **of a** clock, to indicate (the time) audibly.—*vi*. To deliver a blow; to cease work in order to enforce some demand.—*n*. Such a ceasing.

String, *n*. O.E. *streng*, f. *strang*, STRONG (app. as being tightly twisted). Cf. Ger. *strang*. Fine cord; something for tying up, &c.; a stretched piece of catgut, &c.; a row or series.—*vt*. To supply with a string; to tie up, &c., with a string; to make tense.—**String'**Y,[2] *a*. Fibrous; viscous.

Strin'gent, *a*. L. *stringens*, *stringentis*, pres. pple. of *stringĕre*. STRICT. Strict, rigorous.—**Strin'g**ENCY, *n*.—**Strin'gent**LY,[2] *adv*.

Strip, *vt*. O.E. *strȳpan*, to plunder, strip. Cf. Du. *stroopen*, Ger. *streifen*. To lay bare, to deprive *of*; to pull a covering, &c., off; to pull (a covering, &c.) *off*.—*vi*. To take off one's clothes.—*n*. Prob. f. the *v*., or perh. var. of next. A long narrow piece.

Stripe, *n*. M.Du. *strijpe*, a stripe in cloth. Cf. Norw. *stripa*, Da. *stribe*, stripe. A narrow marking or band; a blow with a scourge.—**Strip'ling**, *n*. -LING (3). A slender youth.

Strive, *vi*. O.F. *estriver*, f. *estrif*, STRIFE. To endeavour, make efforts; to contend, vie.

Stroke, *n*.[1] O.E. *strac*, f. *strīcan*, to STRIKE. A blow; a sudden attack (of paralysis, &c.); an effort; a complete performance of some repeated action or movement; a mark made with a pen, &c.; the sound of a striking clock; the rower sitting nearest the stern and setting the time to the rest.

Stroke, *vt*. O.E. *strācian*, f. *strac*. (See prec.) To pass the hand gently over.—*n*.[2] The action or an act of stroking.

Stroll, *vi*. Perh. = TROLL, *v*., in obs. sense 'to range', with *s-* (O.F. *es-* = EX-) prefixed. To take a leisurely walk; to go about giving performances.—*n*. A leisurely walk.

Strong, *a*. O.E. *strang*. Cogn. with STRETCH. Cf. Ger. *streng*, strict. STRENGTH. STRING. Having force or power of resistance; healthy; powerfully affecting the senses; highly flavoured; forming inflections by internal vowel-change. — **Strong'hold**, *n*. A place of strength, a fortress.—**Strong'**LY,[2] *adv*.

Strop, *n*. Var. of STRAP. A strip of leather for sharpening a razor.—*vt*. To sharpen on a strop.

Stro'phe, *n*. G. *strophē*, f. *strephein*, to turn. A turn made in dancing by the Greek tragic chorus; the lines sung during the movement. (The returning movement and the lines then sung are named the **Antis'trophe**. ANTI-.)

Struc'ture, *n*. F. *structure*—L. *structūra*, f. *struĕre*, *structum*, to build. CONSTRUCT. Manner of construction, make; something constructed, a building.—**Struc'tur**AL, *a*.

Strug'gle, *vi*. M.E. *strogelen*, *strugelen*. Orig. doubtful. Cf. O.E. *thryccan*, to force, Norw. *stru*, refractory. To throw oneself about violently; to strive, contend, proceed with difficulty.—*n*. A struggling; a contest or effort.

Strum, *vi*. and *t*. Formed f. THRUM, *v*. with *s-* (as in STROLL) prefixed. To play unskilfully on a stringed instrument.

Strum'pet, *n*. Poss. f. O.F. *strupe* = *stupre*, concubinage (L. *stuprum*, dishonour, disgrace) + dim. suff. *-et*. A prostitute.

Strut, *v*.[1]*i*. M.E. *strouten*—Da. *strutte*. Cf. Sw. dial. *strutta*, to walk with a jolting step, L.G. *strutt*, rigid. To walk with a pompous gait.—*n*.[1] Such a gait.

Strut, *n*.[2] Cogn. with prec. Something rigid set obliquely in a framework.—*v*.[2]*t*. To strengthen with a strut or struts.

Strych'nia, *n*. Also (with chemical suff.

-*ine*) **Strych'nine.** L. *strychnos*—G. *struchnos*, nightshade. A poisonous alkaloid obtained from nux vomica seeds.

Stub, *n.* O.E. *stybb.* Cf. O.N. *stubbi*, Du. *stobbe.* Cogn. with STUMP and G. *stupos*, stump. STUBBORN. A stump.—*vt.* To clear (land) of stubs.

Stub'ble, *n.* A.F. *estuble*, O.F. *estouble*—L.L. *stupula*, *stupla* = L. *stipula*, stubble, dim. of *stipes.* STIPULATE. The stumps of cut grain.

Stub'born, *a.* M.E. *stoburn*, *stiborn*, prob. f. O.E. *stybb*, STUB. Obstinate, unyielding.—**Stub'born**LY,[2] *adv.*—**Stub'born**NESS, *n.*

Stuc'co, *n.* It.—O.H.G. *stucchi*, crust (Ger. *stück*, piece). Cogn. with STOCK. A kind of plaster or cement.—*vt.* To coat with stucco.

Stud, *n.*[1] O.E. *studu*, post. Cf. Da. *stöd*, stump, Ger. *stütze*, prop. A projecting large-headed nail, a boss; a movable button.—*vt.* To set with studs.

Stud, *n.*[2] O.E. *stód.* Cf. O.N. *stóth*, M.H.G. *stuot* (Ger. *gestüt*). STEED. A number of horses kept for breeding, &c.

Studding-sail, *n.* (*stun'sl*). Of doubtful orig. A sail added to a square sail.

Stud'y, *n.* A.F. and O.F. *estudie* (F. *étude*)—L. *studium*, zeal, study. Effort expended in acquiring knowledge; a subject of study or effort; a room for study; a preliminary sketch.—*vt.* To make a study of; to try constantly *to do.*—**Stu'dent**, *n.* L. *studens*, *studentis*, pres.pple. of *studēre*, to be busy about, study, conn. with *studium.* One who studies; one given to studying.—**Stu'dio**, *n.* It., f. L. *studium.* The working-room of a painter, &c.—**Stu'di**OUS, *a.*—**Stu'dious**LY,[2] *adv.*

Stuff, *n.* O.F. *estoffe*—L. *stūpa*, *stuppa.* STOP. Material; a woollen fabric; the material forming the gown of a barrister below the rank of a King's Counsel, who wears silk; useless matter.—*vt.* To stop *up*, fill; to fill up the emptied skin of (an animal, &c.); to ram *into* something.—*vi.* To eat greedily.—**Stuf'f**Y,[2] *a.* Lacking fresh air, close.

Stul'tify, *vt.* L. *stultus*, foolish + -FY. To reduce to absurdity, to make of no effect; to cause to appear ridiculous.—**Stulti**FICA'TION, *n.*

Stum'ble, *vi.* A doublet (with inserted -*b*-) of STAMMER (with freq. suff. -*le* = -*er*), referring to hesitation of step. To have a partial fall in walking; to come accidentally *on*, &c.—*n.* A stumbling.—**Stum'bling-block**, *n.* An obstacle.

Stump, *n.* O.N. *stumpr.* Cf. Du. *stomp*, Ger. *stumpf.* Cogn. with STUB. The remnant of a tree, tooth, &c.; one of the uprights forming a wicket in cricket; a tree-stump mounted by a speaker (whence **Stump-or'ator**).—*vi.* To walk stiffly and noisily.—*vt.* To go through (the country) making speeches; to put out of play (a batsman out of his ground) by disturbing the wicket with the ball.—**Stump'**Y,[2] *a.* Short and thick.

Stun, *vt.* O.E. *stunian*, to make a din. Cf. O.N. *stynja*, Ger. *stöhnen*, to groan. To deafen; to knock senseless; to overwhelm.

Stunt, *vt.* O.E. *stunt*, dull, stupid, orig. 'short'. Cf. O.N. *stuttr.* STINT. To check the growth or development of.

Stu'pefy, *vt.* F. *stupéfier*—L. *stupefacĕre*, f. *stupēre*, to be amazed or benumbed + *facĕre*, to make. FACT. To make stupid, deprive of sensibility.—**Stupe**FAC'TION, *n.*—**Stupen'dous**, *a.* L. *stupendus*, to be wondered at, ger. of *stupēre* + -OUS. Amazing, astounding.

Stu'pid, *a.* F. *stupide*—L. *stupidus*, f. *stupēre.* STUPEFY. In a stupor; slow-witted, dull.—**Stupid'**ITY, *n.*—**Stu'pid**LY,[2] *adv.*—**Stu'por**, *n.* L. *stupor* f. *stupēre.* The state of being dazed or torpid.

Stur'dy, *a.* M.E. *sturdi*, *stordy*, rash, reckless—O.F. *estourdi*, amazed, rash, pa.pple. of *estourdir* (F. *étourdir*), to amaze, of unknown orig. Strongly built, robust.—**Stur'di**LY,[2] *adv.*—**Stur'di**NESS, *n.*

Stur'geon, *n.* O.F. *esturgeon*—Med.L. *sturio*, *sturiōnis*—O.H.G. *sturjo*, *sturo*, of doubtful orig. A large fish making good food.

Stut'ter, *vi.* Obs. *Stut* in same sense (for which cf. Ger. *stossen*, to strike, cogn. with L. *tundĕre*, to beat) + freq. suff. -*er*. Cf. Ger. *stottern*, to stutter. Orig. sense 'to strike against, trip'. To speak with difficulty, esp. with repetition of initial consonants.—*n.* An act or habit of stuttering.

Sty, *n.*[1] O.E. *stigu*, sty, cattle-pen. Cf. O.H.G. *stiga*, cattle-pen. STEWARD. An enclosure for pigs.

Sty, *n.*[2] **Stye.** Earlier *styan*, *stiony*, poss. lit. 'rising', f. O.E. *stīgan*, to climb. STILE. An inflamed swelling on the eyelid.

Styg'ian, *a.* L. *Stygius* (G. *Stugios*, a. f. *Stux*, *Stugos*, the Styx) + -AN. Pertaining to the Styx, the fabled river over which the shades of the dead passed; dark, gloomy.

Style, *n.* O.F. *stile*, *style*—L. *stilus.* STILETTO. A pointed rod for writing on waxed tablets; manner of writing, doing, &c.; a characteristic mode in any of the arts; a designation; kind, sort; superior quality or manner.—*vt.* To designate.—**Styl'**ISH, *a.* Fashionable.—**Styl'**IST, *n.* One cultivating literary style.

Styp'tic, *a.* and *n.* F. *styptique*—L. *stypticus*, G. *stuptikos*, astringent, f. *stuphein*, to draw together. Checking, something checking bleeding.

Sua'sion, *n.* F. *suasion*—L. *suāsio*, *suāsiōnis*, n. of action f. *suādēre*, *suāsum*, to urge, conn. with *suāvis*, pleasant. SWEET. ASSUAGE. DISSUADE. Persuasion.

Suave', *a.* F. *suave*—L. *suāvis.* (See prec.) Blandly polite.—**Suav'**ITY, *n.*

Sub'altern, *a.* L.L. *subalternus*, f. SUB- (4) + L. *alter*, another. Of inferior rank.—*n.* An officer below the rank of captain.

Subcommit'tee, *n.* SUB- (4). A section of a committee charged with a special function.

Subdivide', *vt.* L.L. *subdividĕre*, *subdivisum*, f. SUB- (4) + *dividĕre*, to DIVIDE. To divide again.—**Subdivi'**SION, *n.*

Subdue', *vt.* M.E. *sodewe*, *subdewe*, &c., repg. A.F. **soduer*, **su(b)duer* (= O.F. *so(u)duire*, *su(d)duire*, &c., to deceive, seduce—L. *subdūcĕre*, to draw up or away, withdraw, f. SUB (1) + *dūcĕre.* DUKE), app. in sense of L. *subdĕre*, to subdue, f. SUB- (4) + *dăre*, to put. To conquer, overcome; to soften, mitigate.—**Subdu'**AL, *n.*

Sub'ject, *a.* O.F. *suget*, *subject* (F. *sujet*)—L. *subjectus*, pa.pple. of *subjicĕre*, to subject, f. SUB- (4) + *jacĕre*, to throw, put. JET, *v.* Owing allegiance *to*; liable or prone *to*; *subject to*, conditional upon.—*n.* One owing allegiance; the member of a proposition about which something is predicated; the mind, the conscious self; a theme or topic.—**Subject'**, *vt.* To subdue; to expose, make liable.—**Subjec'tion**, *n.*—**Subjec'**TIVE, *a.* Relating to the mind or conscious self; displaying the artist's individuality.—**Subjectiv'**ITY, *n.*

Subjoin', *vt.* Obs. F. *subjoindre*—L. *subjungĕre, subjunctum*, f. SUB- (3) + *jungĕre*, to join. To add at the end, annex, append.

Sub'jugate, *vt.* L. *subjugāre, subjugātum*, f. SUB- (1) + *jugum*, YOKE. To bring into subjection, subdue.—**Subjuga'**TION, *n.*

Subjunc'tive, *a.* L. *subjunctivus*, f. *subjungĕre*, to SUBJOIN. Applied to a mood of a verb used chiefly in subjoined or subordinate clauses expressing condition, &c. — *n.* The mood; a verb in the mood.

Sublet', *vt.* SUB- (4). Of a lessee, to let the subject of the lease to another.

Sublime', *a.* L. *sublīmis*, perh. f. SUB- (1) + *līmen*, lintel, 'up to the lintel'. Inspiring awe or wonder.—*vt.* O.F. *sublimer*—L. *sublīmāre, sublīmātum*, to raise on high, in Med. L., to sublimate. To sublimate.—*vi.* To undergo sublimation.—**Sub'limate**, *vt.* From *sublīmāre*. To convert by heat into vapour and allow to solidify again; to purify, refine. —*n.* A sublimated substance.—**Sublima'**TION, *n.*—**Sublime'**LY,[2] *adv.*—**Sublim'**ITY, *n.* The quality of being sublime.

Sublu'nary, *a.* SUB- (1) + L. *lūna*, the moon + ARY. LUNAR. Of this world, earthly.

Submarine', *a.* SUB- (1) + MARINE. Lying, existing, &c., beneath the surface of the sea. —*n.* A war-vessel that can be submerged.

Submerge', *vt.* L. *submergĕre, submersum*, f. SUB- (1) + *mergĕre*, to dip. MERGE. To place under or cover with water.—**Submer'**SION, *n.*

Submit' *vt.* L. *submittĕre, submissum*, to let down, lower, f. SUB- (1) + *mittĕre*. MISSION. To surrender; to present for consideration, &c.—*vi.* To represent, urge; to yield.—**Submis'**SION, *n.*—**Submis'**SIVE, *a.*

Subor'dinate, *a.* Med.L. *subordinātus*, pa.pple. of *subordināre*, to place in a lower rank, f. SUB- (1) + L. *ordināre*, to set in order. ORDAIN. Of inferior rank or importance.—*n.* One under the orders of another.—*vt.* To treat as or make subordinate.—**Subor'dinate**LY,[2] *adv.*—**Subordina'**TION, *n.*

Suborn', *vt.* L. *subornāre*, f. SUB- (2) + *ornāre*, to equip. ORNAMENT. To bribe to do evil.—**Suborna'**TION, *n.*

Subpoe'na, *n.* L. *sub poenā*, under penalty, the first words of the writ. PENAL. A writ requiring attendance in a court of justice.—*vt.* To serve such a writ upon.

Subscribe', *vt.* L. *subscrībĕre, subscriptum*, f. SUB- (1) + *scrībere*, to write. SCRIBE. To write (one's name) at the foot of a document, &c.; to write one's name at the foot of; to make or promise (a contribution to some object). — **Subscrib'**ER, *n.* — **Subscrip'**TION, *n.*—**Sub'script**, *a.* From the pa.pple. of *subscrībĕre*. In Greek grammar applied to an iota (ι, Eng. *i*) written below another vowel.

Sub'section, *n.* SUB- (4). A division of a section.

Sub'sequent, *a.* L. *subsequens, subsequentis*, pres.pple. of *subsequi*, to follow close after, f. SUB- (3) + *sequi*, to follow. SEQUEL. Following in time; posterior in time *to*.—**Sub'sequ**ENCE, *n.*—**Sub'sequent**LY,[2] *adv.*

Subserve', *vt.* L. *subservīre*, to serve under another, f. SUB- (4) + *servīre*, to SERVE. To be a means of promoting (a purpose, &c.).—**Subser'vi**ENT, *a.* Serving as a means; obsequious, cringing.—**Subser'vi**ENCE, **Subser'vi**ENCY, *nn.*—**Subser'vient**LY,[2] *adv.*

Subside', *vi.* L. *subsīdĕre*, to settle down, to lie in wait, f. SUB- (1) + *sīdĕre*, to settle, cogn. with *sedēre*, to sit. (Cf. next.) ASSESS. To sink in level, to settle down lower; to abate.—**Sub'sid**ENCE, *n.*

Sub'sidy, *n.* A.F. *subsidie* = O.F. *subside*—L. *subsidium*, reserve troops, assistance, f. *subsidēre* (SUB- (1) + *sedēre*) = *subsīdĕre*. (See prec.) Money granted for some purpose.—**Sub'sid**IZE, *vt.* To pay a subsidy to.—**Subsid'i**ARY, *a.* Assisting or supplementing.

Subsist', *vi.* L. *subsistĕre*, to stay, abide, f. SUB- (3) + *sistĕre*, to stand. ASSIST. To exist, remain in being, support life. — **Subsist'**ENCE, *n.* Subsisting; means of subsisting.

Sub'soil, *n.* SUB- (1). The soil below the surface soil.

Sub'stance, *n.* O.F. *substance*—L. *substantia*, substance, essence, f. *substans, substantis*, pres.pple. of *substāre*, to exist, lit., 'to stand near', f. SUB- (3) + *stāre*, to stand. STATE. Essential nature; the most important part, the purport; material as distinguished from form; reality, solid worth, actual possessions; a particular kind of matter.—**Substan'ti**AL, *a.* Having substance or actual existence; of importance, considerable; solid; well-to-do; deserving the name in essentials.—**Substantial'**ITY, *n.* — **Substan'tial**LY,[2] *adv.*—**Substan'ti**ATE,[3] *vt.* To adduce grounds for. —**Substantia'**TION, *n.*—**Sub'stant**IVE, *a.* Expressing existence; having independent existence.—*n.* A noun.

Sub'stitute, *n.* L. *substitūtus*, pa.pple. of *substituĕre*, to put in the place of another, f. SUB- (6) + *statuĕre*, to place, STATUTE. A person or thing put in the place of another.—*vt.* To put in the place of another, to put in exchange *for*.—**Substitu'**TION, *n.*

Subsume', *vt.* From SUB- (1) + L. *sūmĕre, sumptum*, to take. ASSUME. To include under a rule or in a class.—**Subsump'**TION, *n.*

Subtend', *vt.* L. *subtendĕre*, to stretch beneath, f. SUB- (1) + *tendĕre*, to stretch. ATTEND. To be opposite to.

Sub'terfuge, *n.* L.L. *subterfugium*, f. L. *subterfugĕre*, to escape by stealth, f. *subter*, secretly + *fugĕre*, to flee. FUGITIVE. An evasion; an evasive statement, &c.

Subterra'nean, *a.* L. *subterrāneus* (f. SUB- (1) + *terra*, earth) + -AN. TERRESTRIAL. Underground.

Subt'le, *a.* O.F. *sutil*—L. *subtīlis*, fine, thin, accurate, subtle, perh. orig. 'finely woven', f. SUB- (3) + *tēla*, web. TOIL, *n.*[2] Tenuous and pervasive; evasive, hard to grasp; making fine distinctions, acute; ingenious, clever; crafty.—**Subt'**LY,[2] *adv.*—**Subt'le**TY, *n.*

Subtract', *vt.* L. *subtrahĕre, subtractum*, to draw away underneath, f. SUB- (1) + *trahĕre*, to draw. ABSTRACT. To take away (a number, &c.) *from* a greater.—**Subtrac'**TION, *n.*

Sub'urb, *n.* O.F. *suburbe*—L. *suburbium*, f. SUB- (3) + *urbs*, city. URBANE. An outlying district of a city.—**Subur'**BAN, *a.*

Subven'tion, *n.* L. *subventio, subventiōnis*, assistance, f. *subvenīre, subventum*, to come to assistance, f. SUB- (5) + *venīre*, to come. ADVENT. A subsidy.

Subvert', *vt.* F. *subvertir*—L. *subvertĕre, subversum*, f. SUB- (1) + *vertĕre*, to turn. ADVERSE. To overturn, to overthrow.—**Subver'**SION, *n.*—**Subver'**SIVE, *a.*

Sub'way, *n.* SUB- (1). An underground passage.

Succeda'neum, *n.* Neut. of L. *succedāneus*, substituted, f. *succēdĕre*. (See next.) Something substituted.—**Succeda'ne**OUS, *a.*

Succeed′, *vt.* F. *succéder*—L. *succēdĕre, successum*, to go under, to follow, to take the place of, to prosper, f. *suc-* (= SUB- (1)) + *cēdĕre*, to go. ACCEDE. To take the place of; to follow.—*vi.* To follow; to acquire right by inheritance, &c., *to*; to accomplish one's purpose.—**Success′**, *n.* O.F. *succes*—L. *successus*, f. *succēdĕre*. Issue; favourable issue, accomplishment, attainment; a thing or person that turns out well. — **Success′**FUL, *a.* — **Success′ful**LY,[2] *adv.*—**Succes′**SION, *n.* A following in order; a series; a succeeding, the right of succeeding, *to*. — **Succes′**SIVE, *a.* Following, consecutive. — **Succes′sive**LY,[2] *adv.*—**Succes′**SOR, *n.*

Succinct′, *a.* L. *succinctus*, pa.pple. of *succingĕre*, to gird up, f. *suc-* (= SUB- (1)) + *cingĕre*, to gird. CINCTURE. Terse, concise.—**Succinct′**LY,[2] *adv.*—**Succinct′**NESS, *n.*

Suc′cour, *vt.* O.F. *sucurre* (F. *secourir*)—L. *succurrĕre*, to run to the aid of, f. *suc-* (= SUB- (5)) + *currĕre*, to run. CONCUR. To aid in need.—*n.* O.F. *socors*—Med.L. *succursus*. Aid given in need.

Suc′culent, *a.* F. *succulent*—L. *sūculentus*, full of juice, f. *sūcus*, juice, conn. with *sūgĕre*, to SUCK. Juicy; thick and fleshy, having such leaves or stems.—**Suc′cul**ENCE, *n.*

Succumb′, *vi.* L. *succumbĕre*, to lie or sink down, to yield, f. *suc-* (= SUB- (1)) + **cumbĕre*. INCUMBENT. To yield, be overcome.

Such, *a.* M.E. *swulc, swilc, swich, such*—O.E. *swylc*, f. *swá*, SO + *-l(i)c*, -LY.[1] Cf. Du. *zulk*, Ger. *solch*. Of the same kind or degree; so great, so constituted, &c., *as to do* or *that*; of the kind or degree mentioned.

Suck, *vt.* O.E. *súcan*. Cogn. with L. *sūgĕre, suctum*. SUCCULENT. Cf. Ger. *saugen*. HONEYSUCKLE. SOAK. To draw into the mouth; to suck liquid from; to roll in the mouth.—*n.* Opportunity of sucking the breast; a sucking.—**Suck′**ER, *n.* A person or thing that sucks; an organ enabling some animals to adhere by suction; the piston of a pump; a shoot of a plant.—**Suck′le**, *vt.* Freq. suff. *-le*. To give suck to.—**Suck′ling**, *n.* Obs. *Sokel*, one who sucks + *-ing*, denoting one concerned. An unweaned child, &c.—**Suc′t**ION, *n.* The action of sucking; a drawing in of air to produce a partial vacuum.

Suda′tion, *n.* L. *sūdātio, sūdātiōnis*, f. *sūdāre, sūdātum*, conn. with *sūdor*, SWEAT. Sweating.—**Su′dat**ORY, *a.* Promoting sweating.—*n.* A hot-air bath.—**Sudorif′erous**, *a.* L. *sūdōrifer* (f. *sūdor*, + *-fer*, bringing, f. *ferre*, to bring) + -OUS. Of glands, producing sweat. — **Sudorif′**IC, *a.* Inducing sweating.—*n.* A sudorific medicine.

Sud′den, *a.* O.F. *sodain*—L. *subitāneus*, lengthened f. *subitus*, sudden, ppl. a. f. *subīre, subitum*, to go stealthily, f. SUB- (2) + *īre*, to go. Occurring, done, &c., unexpectedly; abrupt, hurried.—**Sud′den**LY,[2] *adv.*

Suds, *n.pl.* From *sud-*, weak grade of O.E. *séothan*, to SEETHE. Froth of soap and water.

Sue, *vt.* A.F. *suer* = O.F. *suir* (F. *suivre*), to follow—L.L. *sequĕre* for L. *sequi*. SEQUEL. ENSUE. PURSUE. SUIT. To seek justice from.—*vi.* To make entreaty or an application.

Suède, *n.* F., Swedish. Undressed kid.

Su′et, *n.* With dim. suff. *-et* f. O.F. *seu* (F. *suif*). L. *sēbum*. Hard animal fat.—**Su′ety**, *a.*[2].

Suf′fer, *vt.* O.F. *souffrir*—Pop.L. *sufferire* for L. *sufferre*, f. *suf-* (= SUB- (5)) + *ferre*, to BEAR. To undergo, be subjected to; to permit.—*vi.* To undergo pain, damage, &c. — **Suf′fer**ABLE, *a.* — **Suf′fer**ANCE, *n.* Tacit permission, toleration.—**Suf′fer**ER, *n.*

Suffice′, *vi.* F. *suffire* (pres.pple. *suffisant*)—L. *sufficĕre*, to supply, f. *suf-* (= SUB (5)) + *facĕre*, to make. FACT. To be enough.—*vt.* To satisfy, meet the needs of.—**Suffic′i**ENT, *a.* Enough.—**Suffic′i**ENCY, *n.*

Suffix′, *vt.* L. *suffigĕre, suffixum*, to fix beneath, fix on, f. *suf-* (= SUB (1)) + *figĕre*, to FIX. To append in forming a word.—**Suf′fix**, *n.* A suffixed letter or syllable.

Suf′focate, *vt.* L. *suffōcāre, suffōcātum*, lit., 'to squeeze the throat', f. *suf-* (= SUB- (1)) + *fauces*, throat. To kill by stopping respiration. —*vi.* To feel suffocated.—**Suffoca′**TION, *n.*

Suf′fragan, *a.* Med.L. *suffrāgāneus*, assisting, esp. of a bishop, f. L. *suffrāgāri*, to support with one's vote, f. *suffrāgium*. (See next.) Assisting (a bishop).—*n.* An assistant bishop; a bishop in relation to his archbishop.

Suf′frage, *n.* F. *suffrage*—L. *suffrāgium*. A vote; the right of voting.

Suffuse′, *vt.* L. *suffundĕre, suffūsum*, to pour over, f. *suf-* (= SUB (1)) + *fundĕre*, to pour. CONFOUND. Of colour or moisture, to well up and overspread.—**Suffu′**SION, *n.*

Su′gar, *n.* F. *sucre*—Sp. *azucar*—Arab. *sakkar* — Per. *shakar* — Skr. *çarkarā*, gravel, candied sugar. SACCHARINE. A sweet crystalline vegetable substance.—*vt.* To sweeten with sugar.—**Su′gar**Y,[2] *a.*

Suggest′, *vt.* L. *suggerĕre, suggestum*, to bring under, supply, suggest, f. *sug-* (= SUB- (1)) + *gerĕre*, to bring. CONGEST. To call up the idea of; to propose. — **Sugges′t**ION, *n.* —**Sugges′t**IVE, *a.*—**Sugges′tive**LY,[2] *adv.*

Su′icide, *n.* L. *sui*, genit. of *se*, self + -CIDE (1). One who kills himself intentionally.—-CIDE (2). Intentional self-killing.—**Suicid′**AL, *a.*—**Suicid′al**LY,[2] *adv.*

Suit, *n.* O.F. *suite*, a following—Med.L. *secūta*, f. L. *sequi*. SUE. The action of suing; an action at law; one of the four sets forming a pack of cards; a set, esp. of a man's outer clothes.—*vt.* To adapt, make fitting; to meet the demands, &c., of; to be consistent with the health of; to become, go well with.—*vi.* To be convenient.—**Suit′**ABLE, *a.* Fitting, convenient. — **Suita**BIL′ITY, *n.* — **Suit′ab**LY,[2] *adv.* —**Suite**, *n.* F. A retinue; a set of things going or used together (esp. of rooms, &c.).—**Suit′**OR, *n.* A party to a lawsuit; a petitioner; a wooer.

Sul′ky, *a.* Back-formation f. obs. *Sulkeness*, O.E. *solcenes*, sloth, f. *solcen*, slothful, of obscure orig. Sullen, morose.—**Sulk**, *n.* Back-formation f. the *a.* A sulky fit (gen. in *pl.*).—*vi* To be sulky.—**Sul′ki**LY,[2] *adv.*

Sul′len, *a.* M.E. *solain, sulain*, O.F. *solain*, solitary—L.L. **sōlānus*, f. L. *sōlus*, alone. DESOLATE. Passively resentful, obstinately ill-humoured; dismal, gloomy.—*n.pl.* A sullen frame of mind.—**Sul′len**LY,[2] *adv.*

Sul′ly, *vt.* O.E. *sylian*, f. *sol*, mire. Or perh. to be regarded as a doublet of SOIL, *v.* To soil, tarnish.

Sul′phur, *n.* L. *sulphur*. Cf. Skr. *çulvāri-*. A pale-yellow non-metallic element.—**Sulphu′r**EOUS, *a.* Of or like sulphur.—**Sulphu′r**IC, *a.* Containing sulphur in its higher combining proportion. — **Sul′phur**OUS, *a.* Sulphureous; containing sulphur in its lower combining proportion.

Sul′tan, *n.* F. *sultan*—Arab. *sultān*, victorious, a ruler. A Mohammedan sovereign.—**Sultan′a**, *n.* It., fem. of *sultano*, f. Arab.

His mother, wife or daughter; a Smyrna raisin.—**Sul'tan**ATE,[1] *n.*

Sul'try, *a.* Earlier *sweltry*, f. SWELTER + -Y.[2] Oppressively hot and close.

Sum, *n.* F. *somme*—L. *summa*, chief point, sum total, amount, orig. fem. of *summus*, highest. SUMMIT. A total amount; substance, essence; a particular amount of money; an arithmetical problem.—*vt.* To add into a total; to gather *up* and recapitulate (evidence, &c.). —**Sum'mary**, *a.* L. **summārius*, f. *summa*. Brief, done with dispatch.—*n.* L. *summārium*. An abridgment.—**Sum'mar**ILY,[2] *adv.*—**Sum'mar**IZE, *vt.* To make or be a summary of.—**Summa**'TION, *n.* An adding up.

Sum'mer, *n.* O.E. *sumer*, *sumor*. Cf. Du. *zomer*, O.H.G. *sumar* (Ger. *sommer*). The second season.—*vi.* To pass the summer.

Sum'mit, *n.* F. *sommet*, dim. of O.F. *som*, top—L. *summum*, neut. of *summus*. SUM. The highest point or degree.

Sum'mon, *vt.* A.F. *sommoner*, O.F. *somoner* —L. *summonēre*, to remind privily, f. *sum*- (= SUB- (2)) + *monēre*, to remind, warn. ADMONISH. To demand the presence of, esp. in a court of law; to call upon (a town, &c.) to surrender; to gather *up* (one's energies, &c.). —**Sum'mons**, *n.* A.F. *somons*, O.F. *semonse*, orig. fem. pa.pple. of *semondre*, alteration of *somoner*. An authoritative invitation; a citation to a court.—*vt.* To serve a summons upon.

Sump'ter, *n.* O.F. *sommetier*, pack-horse driver, L.L. **sagmatārius* — G. *sagma*, *sagmatos*, pack-saddle, f. *sattein*, to pack or load. A pack-horse driver, a pack-horse.

Sump'tuary, *a.* L. *sumptuārius*, f. *sumptus*, cost, f. *sūmere*, *sumptum*, to take up, use, spend, f. *sum*- (= SUB- (1)) + *emĕre*, to buy, acquire. Regulating expenditure.—**Sump'tuous**, *a.* L. *sumptuōsus*, costly, f. *sumptus*. Costly, expensive, magnificent.—**Sump'tuous**LY,[2] *adv.*—**Sump'tuous**NESS, *n.*

Sun, *n.* O.E. *sunne*. Cf. Du. *zon*, Ger. *sonne*. Cogn. with L. *sōl*. PARASOL. SOLAR. The self-luminous body round which the earth revolves; the rays of the sun.—*vt.* To expose to the rays.—**Sun'day**, *n.* O.E. *sunnan-dæg*, DAY of the sun. The first day of the week.—**Sun'flower**, *n.* A plant with golden-rayed flowers.—**Sun'**LESS, *a.*—**Sun'n**Y,[2] *a.*

Sun'der, *vt.* and *i.* O.E. *syndrian*, f. *sundor*, asunder, apart. Cf. O.N. *sundra*, Ger. *sondern*. To separate. — **Sun'dry**, *a.* O.E. *syndrig*, f. *sundor*. Divers, several. —*n.pl.* Items not requiring to be stated in detail.

Sup, *vt.* O.E. *sūpan*. Cf. O.N. *súpa*, Du. *zuipen*, L.G. *supen*, O.H.G. *sūfan* (Ger. *saufen*). SIP. SOP. SUPPER. To take by sips.—*vi.* To take supper.—*n.* A mouthful of liquid.

Su'perable, *a.* L. *superābilis*, f. *superāre*, to overcome, f. *super*. SUPER-. That may be overcome.

Superabound', *vi.* SUPER- (4). To be present in excess.—So **Superabun'dance**, *n.*; **Superabun'dant**, *a.*; **Superabun'dantly**, *adv.*

Superan'nuate, *vt.* App. formed f. L.L. *superannātus*, that has lived beyond a year, f. SUPER- (4) + *annus*, year. ANNUAL. To discharge or pension off as too old for service. —**Superannu**A'TION, *n.*

Superb', *a.* F. *superbe*—L. *superbus*, proud, superb. Of the most exalted kind, impressive, grand.—**Superb'**LY,[2] *adv.*

Su'percargo, *n.* Sp. *sobrecargo*, f. *sobre*- = SUPER- (2) + *cargo*, CARGO. One in charge of the commercial affairs of a trading ship.

Supercil'ious, *a.* L. *superciliōsus*, f. *supercilium*, an eyebrow, also, haughtiness (as expressed by raising the eyebrows), f. SUPER- (1) + *cilium*, eyelid. Haughtily indifferent, contemptuous.—**Supercil'ious**LY,[2] *adv.*

Superoga'tion, *n.* L.L. *superērogātio*, *superērogātiōnis*, a payment in addition, f. L. *superērogāre*, to pay out over and above, f. SUPER- (4) + *ērogāre*, to expend, f. E- + *rogāre*, to ask, propose. ABROGATE. A doing of more than duty requires.—**Supererog'a**TORY, *a.*

Superfic'ies, *n.* L., f. SUPER- (1) + *facies*, FACE. A surface.—**Superfic'i**AL, *a.* Of or on the surface; without depth of knowledge or feeling.—**Superficial'**ITY, *n.*

Su'perfine, *a.* SUPER- (4). Of extra quality; affecting great refinement.

Super'fluous, *a.* L. *superfluus* (f. SUPER- (4) + *fluĕre*, to flow) + -OUS. AFFLUENT. More than enough, needless.—**Superflu'**ITY, *n.*

Superheat', *vt.* SUPER- (4). To raise (steam) to a temperature above that of boiling water.

Superhu'man, *a.* SUPER- (4). More than human. [something else.

Superimpose', *vt.* SUPER- (1). To lay on

Superincum'bent, *a.* SUPER- (1). Lying on something.

Superinduce', *vt.* SUPER- (3). To bring in or develop as an addition.

Superintend', *vt.* Eccles. L. *superintendĕre*, f. SUPER- (2) + L. *intendĕre*. INTEND. To have the charge and management of, to arrange and look after the working of.—**Superinten'd**ENCE, *n.*—**Superinten'd**ENT, *n.*

Supe'rior, *a.* O.F. *superieur*—L. *superior*, comp. of *superus*, high, conn. with *super*. SUPER-. SUPREME. Upper; in higher position or rank; above the average in quality, ability, &c.; having or showing consciousness of being so.—*n.* One who is superior to another; a feudal lord; the head of a monastery, &c.—**Superior'**ITY, *n.*

Super'lative, *a.* F. *superlatif*—L. *superlātivus* (as a grammatical term), f. *superlātus*, excessive, lit., 'borne beyond', f. SUPER- (4) + *lātus*, pa.pple. of *ferre*, to BEAR. Of the highest degree; applied to a form of an *a.* or *adv.* expressing the highest or a very high degree of a quality or attribute.—*n.* The superlative degree of an *a.* or *adv.*

Super'nal, *a.* L. *supernus*, upper (conn. with *super*. SUPER-) + -AL. Celestial, heavenly.

Supernat'ural, *a.* SUPER- (4). Above or beyond nature, miraculous.

Supernu'merary, *a.* F. *supernumeraire*—L. *supernumerārius*, f. SUPER- (4) + *numerus*, NUMBER. In excess of the normal number. —*n.* A supernumerary person or thing.

Su'perscribe, *vt.* L. *superscrībĕre*, *superscriptum*, f. SUPER- (1) + *scrībĕre*, to write. SCRIBE. To write at the top of or outside something; to write something over or on.—**Superscrip'**TION, *n.* Something superscribed; the address on a letter.

Supersede', *vt.* O.F. *superseder*, to desist, hence, to defer—L. *supersedēre*, *supersessum*, to sit upon, to be superior to, to desist from, f. SUPER- (1) + *sedēre*, to sit. ASSESS. To set aside, to appoint another in place of; to oust, supplant.—**Superses'**SION, *n.*

Supersti'tion, *n.* O.F. *superstition* — L. *superstitio*, *superstitiōnis*, orig., a standing over or by a thing, hence, dread, religious awe, f. SUPER- (2) + *stāre, statum*, to STAND. Credulity in regard to the supernatural; a religion or opinion based on this.—**Superstit'**IOUS, *a.*

Su'perstructure, *n.* SUPER- (1). A structure resting on something else.

Supervene', *vi.* L. *supervenīre*, to come upon or over, arrive, come upon, f. SUPER- (1) + *venīre*, to come. ADVENT. To happen by way of interruption or change.—**Superven'**TION, *n.*

Supervise', *vt.* L.L. *supervidēre, supervīsum*, f. SUPER- (2)+L. *vidēre*, to see. ADVICE. SURVEY. To superintend, oversee.—**Supervi'**SION, *n.*

Su'pine, *a.* L. *supīnus*, f. stem of *super* (SUPER-) + *-īnus*, -INE. Lying face upward; indolent.—*n.* L. *supīnum* (*verbum*, WORD), poss. as falling back or resting on the verb. A verbal noun formed from Latin verbs.

Sup'per, *n.* O.F. *soper* (F. *souper*), f. *soper*, to sup or sip—L.G. *supen*. SUP. The last meal of the day when dinner is not the last. —**Sup'per**LESS, *a.*

Supplant', *vt.* O.F. *supplanter*—L. *supplantāre*, to put something under the sole of the foot, trip up, f. *sup-* (= SUB- (1)) + *planta*, sole. PLANT. To take the place of, esp. by underhand means.—**Supplant'**ER, *n.*

Sup'ple, *a.* F. *souple*—L. *supplex, supplicis*, submissive, beseeching, orig., bending the knees, f. *sup-* (= SUB- (1)) + *plicāre*, to fold. APPLY. SUPPLICATE. Pliant, flexible; artfully submissive.—**Sup'p**LY,[2] *adv.*

Sup'plement, *n.* F. *supplément*—L. *supplēmentum*, f. *supplēre*, to fill up, f. *sup-* (= SUB- (6)) + *plēre*, to fill. COMPLETE. SUPPLY. Something added to supply a deficiency.—**Supplement'**, *vt.* To add to.—**Supplement'**AL, **Supplement'**ARY, *aa.*

Sup'plicate, *vt.* L. *supplicāre, supplicātum*, f. *supplex*. SUPPLE. To entreat humbly; to beg humbly for.—*vi.* To make humble petition.—**Sup'pliant**, *a.* F. *suppliant*, pres. pple. of *supplier*, to supplicate, f. L. *supplicāre*. Supplicating, expressive of supplication.—*n.* A humble petitioner.—**Supplica'**TION, *n.* —**Sup'plicat**ORY, *a.*

Supply', *vt.* O.F. *supploier* (F. *suppléer*)—L. *supplēre*. SUPPLEMENT. To furnish; to make up for; to fill (an office, &c.) as substitute. —*n.* A supplying; a stock or store; in *pl.*, collected necessaries, money provided.

Support', *vt.* F. *supporter*—L. *supportāre*, to carry to a place, in L.L. to endure, f. *sup-* (= SUB- (1)) + *portāre*, to carry. COMPORT. To hold up; to endure; to provide with necessaries; to further, assist; to substantiate; to sustain adequately (a part, &c.).—*n.* A supporting or being supported; something that supports; means of living.—**Support'**ABLE, *a.*—**Support'**ER, *n.*

Suppose', *vt.* F. *supposer*, f. *sup-* (= SUB- (1)) + *poser*, to place. POSE.[1] To assume as a hypothesis; to imply, take for granted, accept as probable.—**Suppos'**ABLE, *a.*—**Supposi'tion**, *n.* F. *supposition*—L. *suppositio, suppositiōnis*, a putting under, f. *suppōnĕre, suppositum*, to put under, substitute, f. *sup-* (= SUB- (1)) + *pōnĕre*, to put. POSITION. In senses from the *v.*—**Supposititious**, *a.* L. *suppositicius* (f. *suppōnere*) + -OUS. Substituted for the real, spurious.

Suppress', *vt.* L. *supprimĕre, suppressum*, f. *sup-* (= SUB- (1)) + *premĕre*, to press. COMPRESS. To put down, quell; to restrain; to keep or withdraw from publication, to keep secret.—**Suppres'**SION, *n.*

Sup'purate, *vi.* L. *suppūrāre, suppūrātum*, to gather pus underneath, f. *sup-* (= SUB- (1)) + *pūs, pūris*, PUS. To form pus, fester.—**Suppura'**TION, *n.*

Supramun'dane, *a.* L. *suprā*, above, conn. with *super*. SUPER-. Above or superior to the world.

Supreme', *a.* F. *suprême*—L. *suprēmus*, highest, superl. of *superus*. SUPERIOR. Highest, greatest.—**Supreme'**LY,[2] *adv.*—**Suprem'**ACY, *n.*

Surcharge', *n.* A.F. *surcharge*, an overcharge, f. *sur-* (= SUPER- (4)) + *charge*, conn. with *charger*, to CHARGE. An excessive or additional burden or charge; a sum in an official account charged by an auditor against a person responsible.—*vt.* To overburden; to exact a surcharge from.

Surd, *a.* L. *surdus*, deaf, noiseless. (The mathematical sense seems to have come from the word being used to translate G. *alogos*, speechless, irrational.) ABSURD. Of a consonantal sound, uttered with the breath and not the voice; of a quantity, irrational.—*n.* A surd sound or quantity.

Sure, *a.* O.F. *seür*, *sur* (F. *sûr*)—L. *sēcūrus*, SECURE. Convinced; trustworthy; certain.—*adv.* Certainly.—**Sure'**LY, *adv.*—**Sure'**TY, *n.* One who makes himself responsible for an engagement of another.

Surf, *n.* Earlier *suffe*. Perhaps a var. of SOUGH, *n.* The foam and commotion of breaking waves.

Sur'face, *n.* F. *surface*, f. *sur-* (= SUPER- (1)) + *face*, FACE. The outside or outward aspect of a body; that which has length and breadth without thickness.—**Sur'faceman**, *n.* One in charge of the permanent way of a railway.

Sur'feit, *n.* O.F. *surfait, sorfait*, orig. pa.pple of *sorfaire*, to augment, exaggerate, f. *sur-*, *sor-* (= SUPER- (4)) + *faire*, L. *facĕre*. FACT. Excess, esp. in eating and drinking; the result. —*vt.* and *i.* To feed to excess.

Surge, *vi.* O.F. *surgir*, L. *surgĕre* (contracted f. *surrigĕre*), to rise, f. *sur-* (= SUB- (1)) + *regĕre*, to direct. REGENT. INSURGENT. SOURCE. To move in or as in waves.—*n.* Waves; a wave; a surging motion.

Sur'geon, *n.* Altered f. obs. *Chirurgeon* —O.F. *cirurgien*, f. *cirurgie*, L.L. *chirurgia*, surgery—G. *cheirourgia*, a working by hand, surgery, f. *cheir*, hand + *-ergia*, working, f. *ergon*, WORK. CHIROPODIST. A medical man who treats by operation.—**Sur'gery**, *n.* O.F. *cirurgerie*=*cirurgie*. Treatment of injuries or disorders by operation; a doctor's consulting room and dispensary.—**Sur'g**ICAL, *a.*

Sur'ly, *a.* Prob. = SOUR + -LY.[1] Uncivil, churlish. —**Sur'l**ILY,[2] *adv.*—**Sur'li**NESS, *n.*

Surmise', *n.* O.F. *surmise*, an accusation, orig. fem. of *surmis*, pa.pple. of *surmettre*, to put upon, lay to one's charge, f. *sur-* (= SUPER- (1)) + *mettre*, L. *mittĕre*, to send. ADMIT. A conjecture or suspicion.—*vt.* To suspect the existence of.—*vi.* To conjecture.

Surmount', *vt.* F. *surmonter*, f. *sur-* (= SUPER- (1)) + *monter*, to MOUNT. To be or get on the top of; to overcome, get over.—**Surmount'**ABLE, *a.*

Sur'name, *n.* From *name* after F. *surnom*, f. *sur-* (= SUPER- (3)) + *nom*, L. *nōmen*, NAME. Orig., an additional name attached to a person and often becoming hereditary. The common name of a family.

Surpass', *vt.* F. *surpasser*, f. *sur-*(= SUPER- (4)) + *passer*, to PASS. To outdo, excel.
Sur'plice, *n.* O.F. *surplis* (i.e. *superplis*)—Med.L. *superpelliceum*, f. SUPER- (1) + *pellicia*. PELISSE. A loose white vestment worn by the clergy and by choristers.
Sur'plus, *n.* O.F. *surplus*—Med.L. *superplūs*, f. SUPER- (3) + L. *plūs*, more. PLUS. What remains over or unexpended (often *attrib.*).—Sim. **Sur'plus**AGE, *n.*
Surprise', *n.* O.F. *surprise*, orig. fem. of *surpris*, pa.pple. of *surprendre*, to surprise, f. *sur-*(= SUPER- (1)) + *prendre*, L. *prehendĕre*, to seize. PREHENSILE. A catching unprepared; the emotion excited by anything unexpected; that which excites surprise.—*vt.* To take by surprise, to come upon unprepared; to affect with surprise.—**Surpri'**SAL, *n.*
Surren'der, *vt.* O.F. *surrendre*, f. *sur-* (= SUPER- (1)) + *rendre*, to RENDER. To hand over, give up.—*vi.* To yield, give oneself up.—*n.* A surrendering or being surrendered.
Surrepti'tious, *a.* L. *surrepticius* (f. *surripĕre, surreptum*, to pilfer, f. *sur-*(= SUB- (2)) + *rapĕre*, to seize. RAPE, *v.*) + -OUS. Clandestine.—**Surrepti'tious**LY,[2] *adv.*
Sur'rogate, *n.* L. *surrogātus*, pa.pple. of *surrogāre*, to substitute, f. *sur-*(= SUB- (6)) + *rogāre*, to ask, to propose for election. ABROGATE. A deputy, esp. of a bishop.
Surround', *vt.* O.F. *surunder* (i.e. *superunder*), L. *superundāre*, to overflow, f. SUPER- (1) + *undāre*, to flow. ABOUND. Formerly, to overflow. By confusion with *round*, to be or come all round, encompass.
Sur'tax, *n.* F. *surtaxe*, f. *surtaxer*, to surtax, f. *sur-*(= SUPER- (3)) + *taxer*, to TAX. An additional tax.—*vt.* To impose such a tax on.
Surveil'lance, *n.* F. *surveillance*, f. *surveiller*, to superintend, f. *sur-*(= SUPER- (2)) + *vigilāre*, to watch, f. *vigil*, awake. VIGIL. Close watching, supervision.
Survey', *vt.* A.F. *surveier* (i.e. *superveier*) (O.F. *surveoir*)—L.L. *supervidēre*, to SUPERVISE. To view or examine; to measure and examine (land).—**Sur'vey**, *n.* A general view; an inspection of condition, a report of the result; a surveying of land, a map, &c., showing the result.—**Survey'**OR, *n.*
Survive', *vt.* F. *survivre* (i.e. *supervivre*)—L. *supervivĕre*, f. SUPER- (4) + *vīvĕre*, to live. CONVIVIAL. To outlive; to come alive through.—*vi.* To continue to live, to be still alive.—**Survi'**VAL, *n.*—**Survi'**VOR, *n.*
Suscep'tible, *a.* F. *susceptible*—Med.L. **susceptibilis*, f. L. *suscipĕre, susceptum*, to support, to undertake, to receive, f. *sus-* (= SUB- (5)) + *capĕre*, to take. ACCEPT. Admitting *of*; open or sensitive *to*; impressionable.—**Suscepti**BIL'ITY, *n.*
Suspect', *a.* F. *suspect*—L. *suspectus*, pa.pple. of *suspicĕre*, to look up at, to look at secretly, to suspect, f. *sus-* (= SUB- (1) (2)) + *specĕre*, to look. ASPECT. SUSPICION. Of suspected character.—*n.* A suspected person.—*vt.* To have an impression of the presence or existence of; to be inclined to believe *to be*; to doubt the innocence, genuineness or truth of.
Suspend', *vt.* F. *suspendre*—L. *suspendĕre, suspensum*, f. *sus-* (= SUB- (1)) + *pendĕre*, to hang. APPEND. To hang up; to sustain in the air or a fluid; to keep undecided; to cause to cease for a time; to debar temporarily.—**Suspend'**ER, *n.* In senses from the *v.* In *pl.*, straps, &c., for holding up the trousers, &c.—**Suspense'**, *n.* F. *suspense* (now *suspens*), orig. a fem. pa.pple. of *suspendre*. A state of uncertainty or expectation.—**Suspen'**SIBLE, *a.* — **Suspen'**SION, *n.* — **Suspen'sion-bridge**, *n.* A bridge hung over a stream, &c.—**Suspen'**SIVE, *a.* Effectual only for a time.—**Suspen'**SORY, *a.*
Suspi'cion, *n.* A.F. *suspeciun*, O.F. *suspeccion* (F. *soupçon*)—L. *suspīcio, suspīciōnis*, f. *suspicĕre*, to SUSPECT. A suspecting or being suspected; a being inclined to believe; a trace or small amount.—**Suspi'cious**, *a.*—**Suspi'cious**LY,[2] *adv.*
Suspire', *vi.* O.F. *souspirer*—L. *suspīrāre*, f. *sus-*(= SUB- (1)) + *spīrāre*, to breathe. ASPIRE. To draw a deep breath, sigh.
Sustain', *vt.* O.F. *sustener*—L. *sustinēre, sustentum*, f. *sus-*(= SUB- (5)) + *tenēre*, to hold. ABSTAIN. To bear up; to inspirit; to endure; to decide in favour of; to confirm; to act adequately (a part, &c.).—**Sustain'**ABLE, *a.*—**Sus'tenance**, *n.* O.F. *sustenance*—L.L. *sustinentia*, endurance, f. *sustinēre*. Nourishing; nourishing quality; food.—**Sustenta'tion**, *n.* O.F. *sustentation*—L. *sustentātio, sustentātiōnis*, n. of action f. *sustentāre*, freq. of *sustinēre*. Maintenance (esp. of clergy).
Sut'ler, *n.* Du. *zoetelaar*, scullion, sutler. Cogn. with Ger. *sudeln*, to sully, and SUDS. A camp-follower who sells provisions, &c.
Suttee', *n.* Skr. *satī*, true wife. A Hindu widow who immolates herself on her husband's funeral pyre; the custom.
Su'ture, *n.* F. *suture*—L. *sūtūra*, f. *suĕre, sūtum*, to SEW. A seamlike joining of bones; a stitching of the edges of a wound.
Su'zerain, *n.* O.F. *suzerain*, formed (after *suverain*, SOVEREIGN) f. *sus*, above, L. *sursum*, up, on high. A feudal lord; a sovereign having certain rights over an autonomous state.—**Su'zerain**TY, *n.*
Swab'ber, *n.* Du. *zwabber*, ship-drudge. Cf. *zwabbern*, to drudge, Sw. *svabla*, to swab. One who swabs.—**Swab**, *vt.* Back-formation f. *swabber*. To clean (esp. decks) with a mop and water.—*n.* A mop so used.
Swad'dle, *vt.* M.E. *swathlen*—O.E. *swethel*, swaddling-band, conn. with SWATHE. To swathe.—**Swad'dling-bands**, *n.pl.* Bands of cloth in which infants are swathed.
Swag'ger, *vi.* Freq. of obs. *Swag*, to sway from side to side. Conn. with SWAY. To strut; to talk boastfully.—*n.* A strutting gait; boastful talk; an over-confident manner.
Swain, *n.* O.N. *sveinn*, lad. Orig doubtful. Cf. O.E. *swān*, swine-herd. A young rustic; a lover.
Swal'low, *n.* O.E. *swealwe, swalewe*. Cf. Du. *zwaluw*, Ger. *schwalbe*. A well-known migratory bird.
Swal'low, *vt.* M.E. *swelwen, swolwen*—O.E. *swelgan*. Cf. Ger. *schwelgen*, to feast. GROUNDSEL. To cause or allow to pass down the gullet (often *fig.*).—*n.* A swallowing; the gullet.
Swamp, *n.* Cf. Da., Sw. *svamp*, sponge, Ger. *sumpf*, swamp. A piece of wet spongy ground.—*vt.* To entangle in a swamp; to flood, soak, overwhelm.—**Swamp'**Y,[2] *a.*
Swan, *n.* O.E. *swan*. Cf. Du. *zwaan*, Ger. *schwan*. A well-known water-bird.
Sward, *n.* O.E. *sweard*, bacon-rind. Cf. Icel. *svörthr*, skin, sward, Du. *zwoord*, bacon-rind. Turf; a stretch of turf-covered ground.
Swarm, *n.* O.E. *swearm*, lit. 'that which hums', perh. cogn. with L. *susurrus*, hum. Cf. Du. *zwerm*, Ger. *schwarm*. SWIRL. A large

cluster of insects, &c.—*v.*[1]*i.* To move in a swarm, esp. of bees emigrating from the hive; to gather in numbers, be numerous.

Swarm, *v.*[2]*i.* Orig. uncertain. To climb *up* a pole, &c., by clasping with hands and knees.

Swart, *a.* O.E. *sweart.* Cf. Ger. *schwarz*, black. Cogn. with L. *sordēre.* SORDID. Dark-hued.—**Swarth'y**, *a.* Obs. *Swarth*, var. of *swart* + Y.[2] Dark-complexioned.

Swath, *n.* O.E. *swæth*, *swathu*, track, band. Cf. E. Fris. *swad*, Du. *zwad*, L.G. *swad*, swath, L.G. *swade*, scythe. A line of cut grass, corn, &c.; a track left clear in mowing.

Swathe, *vt.* M.E. *swathen*—O.E. *swathu.* (See prec.) SWADDLE. To bind with bandages, to cover up with wraps.

Sway, *vi.* M.E. *sweiyen.* Cf. Du. *swaaijen*, to sway, Sw. *svaja*, to jerk. SWAGGER. To have an unsteady swinging motion.—*vt.* To give such a motion to; to wield; to govern.—*n.* Swaying motion; government.

Swear, *vt.* O.E. *swerian.* Cf. Du. *zweren*, Ger. *schwören.* Orig. sense 'to speak'. ANSWER. To promise on oath; to declare emphatically; to take (an oath); to cause to take an oath.—*vi.* To use profane oaths.

Sweat, *n.* O.E. *swát.* Cf. Du. *zweet*, Ger. *schweiss.* Cogn. with Skr. *svēda-*, G. *hidrōs*, L. *sūdor.* SUDATION. Moisture oozing out from the skin.—*vi.* To exude sweat; to toil.—*vt.* To cause to sweat; to employ at unduly low wages.—**Sweat**'ER, *n.* In senses from the *v.*; a thick woollen jersey worn by athletes.

Swede, *n.* A *Swedish* turnip.

Sweep, *vi.* M.E. *swēpen*, formed f. O.E. *swápan*, to SWOOP. Cf. O.N. *sveipa*, and Ger. *schweifen*, to ramble. Conn. with SWIPE. To pass swiftly or majestically; to extend in a continuous line, curve, &c.—*vt.* To carry impetuously *off*, *away*, &c.; to sweep over; to clear of dust, &c., with a broom, &c.—*n.* Sweeping motion or extension; range, compass; an act of cleaning with a broom, &c.; a long oar; one who sweeps chimneys.—**Sweep'stake**, **Sweep'stakes**, *n.* A form of gambling in which stakes are contributed by the participators and are taken by the winners.

Sweet, *a.* O.E. *swéte.* Common Aryan. Cogn. with Skr. *svad*, to please, G. *hēdus*, sweet, L. *suāvis*, pleasant. HEDONISM. SUASION. Tasting like sugar; fragrant; melodious; fresh and in good condition; fit for drinking; attractive, agreeable.—*n.* The sweet part; a sweetmeat; in *pl.*, sweet dishes served at table, fragrance, delights.—**Sweet'bread**, *n.* The pancreas of an animal used as food.—**Sweet-bri'er**, *n.* A wild rose with fragrant leaves and flowers.—**Sweet**'EN,[2] *vt.* and *i.*—**Sweet'heart**, *n.* Either of a pair of lovers.—**Sweet**'ISH, *a.*—**Sweet**'LY,[2] *adv.*—**Sweet'meat**, *n.* A piece of confectionery.—**Sweet-pea'**, *n.* A plant of the pea kind with fragrant flowers.—**Sweet-wil'liam**, *n.* A garden plant of the pink kind.

Swell, *vi.* O.E. *swellan.* Cf. Du. *zwellen*, Ger. *schwellen.* To grow larger or louder, to expand, to bulge *out.*—*vt.* To cause to swell.—*n.* The act of swelling, the state of being swollen; a heaving of the sea after a storm; mechanism in an organ for varying the intensity of the sound; a person of distinction or fashionable appearance.

Swel'ter, *vi.* Freq. f. M.E. *swelten*, to swoon, to die—O.E. *sweltan*, to die. Cf. O.N. *svelta*, O.S. *sweltan*, to die, O.H.G. *schwelzan*, to be consumed by fire or love. SULTRY. To be faint with heat; to be oppressive with heat.—*n.* A sweltering state or atmosphere.

Swerve, *vi.* O.E. *sweorfan*, to rub, file, hence, to move to and fro, turn aside in moving. Cf. O.N. *sverfa*, to file, O.H.G. *swerban*, to whirl round. To deviate, change direction.—*n.* Deviation, swerving motion.

Swift, *a.* O.E. *swift*, f. *swífan*, to move quickly. Cf. O.N. *svífa*, to rove, turn, sweep. SWIVEL. Rapid, quick; ready, prompt.—*n.* A bird like the swallow.—**Swift**'LY,[2] *adv.*

Swill, *vt.* O.E. *swilian*, to wash. Cf. O.N. *skyla.* To rinse, pour water over or through; to drink greedily.—*vi.* To drink greedily.—*n.* A rinsing; liquid food for pigs.

Swim, *v.*[1]*i.* O.E. *swimman.* Cf. Du. *zwemmen*, Ger. *schwimmen.* SOUND, *n.*[2] To float; to propel oneself on water; to be flooded.—*vt.* To traverse by swimming; to cause to swim.—*n.* A spell of swimming.—**Swim'm**ER, *n.*

Swim, *v.*[2]*i.* O.E. *swíma*, a swoon. Cf. Du. *zwijm*, a swoon, Ger. *schwindeln*, to be dizzy, act thoughtlessly, swindle. (See next.) To have a dizzy effect or sensation.

Swin'dler, *n.* Ger. *schwindler*, f. *schwindeln.* (See prec.) One who swindles, a cheat.—**Swin'dle**, *vt.* Back-formation f. *swindler.* To cheat.—*n.* A fraudulent scheme; something counterfeit.

Swine, *n.* (*Pl.* the same.) O.E. *swín*, sing. and pl. Cf. Du. *zwijn*, Ger. *schwein.* App. orig. adjectival forms like and cogn. with L. *suīnus*, a. f. *sūs.* SOW. A pig.—**Swine'-herd**, *n.* One who tends swine.

Swing, *vi.* O.E. *swingan*, to scourge, to fly, flutter. Cf. Sw. *svinga*, Ger. *schwingen*, to swing. To move to and fro in the manner of a suspended body; to oscillate, revolve.—*vt.* To cause to swing; to fix so as to be free to swing.—*n.* An act of swinging; a suspended seat for swinging in.

Swinge, *vt.* O.E. *swengan*, causal of *swingan* (see prec.), as if 'to cause (a whip) to swing upon'. To beat soundly.

Swipe, *vi.* and *t.* O.E. *swipian*, to beat, conn. with SWEEP. To hit (esp. at cricket) hard and recklessly.—*n.* A hit of this kind.

Swipes, *n.pl.* From prec. in obs. sense 'to drink off'. Poor washy beer.

Swirl, *vi.* and *t.* Norw. *svirla*, to whirl round, freq. of *sverra*, to whirl, orig., to hum. Cf. Ger. *schwirren*, to whirl. Cogn. with SWARM, *n.* To be carried or to carry with an eddying motion.—*n.* Such a motion.

Swish, *vt.* Imitative. To lash.—*vi.* To swing a cane, &c., audibly; to move with a sound like that thus caused.—*n.* Such a sound; a stroke with a cane, &c.

Switch, *n.* M.Du. *swick*, whip. Cf. Ger. *zwecke*, tack, wooden peg. A flexible twig or rod; a mechanism for completing or interrupting an electric circuit.—*vt.* To strike with a switch; to swing round suddenly; to affect (an electric current) by means of a switch.

Swiv'el, *n.* With instrumental suff. *-el* f. *swif-*, weak grade of O.E. *swífan.* SWIFT. A mechanism so connecting two parts that one can revolve on the other.—*vt.* and *i.* To turn on a swivel.

Swoon, *vi.* M.E. *swounen*, *swoghenen*, *swowenen*, with formative *n.* f. *swowen*, *swoghen*, to sigh, to swoon—O.E. *swógan.* SOUGH. To have a fainting fit.—*n.* A fainting fit.

Swoop, *vi.* O.E. *swápan*, to rush, swoop. SWEEP. To come down like a bird of prey.—*vt.* To snatch *up* with a swoop.—*n.* An act of swooping.

Sword, *n.* M.E. *swerd*—O.E. *sweord.* Cf. Du. *zwaard*, Ger. *schwert.* A weapon for cutting and thrusting.—**Sword'-fish**, *n.* A fish with a long sharp upper jaw.

Syb'arite, *n.* L. *Sybarita*, G. *Subaritēs*, an inhabitant of the luxurious city of Sybaris in Magna Graecia. A luxurious and effeminate person.

Syc'amore, *n.* Formerly *sycomore*—L. *sycomoros*—G. *sukomoros*, perh. f. Heb. *shiqmāh* assimilated to G. *sukon*, fig, and *moron*, mulberry. A Syrian and Egyptian kind of fig-tree; a timber-tree of the plane kind.

Sy'cophant, *n.* L. *sycophanta*, informer, sycophant—G. *sukophantēs*, false accuser, lit. 'fig-shower' (but in what sense is not known), f. *sukon*, fig + *-phantēs*, shower, f. *phainein*, to show. A flatterer or parasite.—**Sy'cophancy**, *n.*—**Sycophan'tic**, *a.*

Syl'lable, *n.* With intrusive *l* f. O.F. *sillabe* —L. *syllaba*—G. *sullabē*, lit., 'that which is taken together', f. *sul*- (= SYN-) + *lab*-, root of *lambanein*, to take. A unit of pronunciation. —*vt.* To pronounce by syllables; to utter.—**Syllab'ic**, *a.*—**Syl'labus**, *n.* L.L. *syllabus*, f. G. *sullambanein*, to bring together, f. *sul*- + *lambanein.* An abstract; a programme.

Sylle'psis, *n.* L. *syllēpsis*—G. *sullēpsis*, f. *sullambanein.* (See prec.) An application of a word to two others in different senses, or to two words of which grammatically it suits only one.

Syl'logism, *n.* O.F. *silogime*—L. *syllogismus* —G. *sullogismos*, an inference, a syllogism, f. *sullogizesthai*, to reckon together, infer, f. *sul*- (= SYN-) + *logizesthai*, to reckon, infer, f. *logos*, account, reason. A form of reasoning consisting of two premisses and a resulting conclusion.—**Syllogis'tic**, *a.* -IST. -IC.—**Syl'logize**, *vi.* To use syllogisms.—*vt.* To throw into syllogistic form.

Sylph, *n.* F. *sylphe*, a word due to Paracelsus, and app. formed f. G. *silphē*, a moth or beetle. An elemental spirit of the air.

Sym'bol, *n.* F. *symbole*—L. *symbolum*—G. *sumbolon*, sign, token, f. *sumballein*, to throw together, infer, f. *sum*- (= SYN-) + *ballein*, to throw. A thing typifying or representing something; a character or mark.—**Symbol'ic**, **Symbol'ical**, *aa.*—**Sym'bolism**, *n.*—**Sym'bolize**, *vt.*

Sym'metry, *n.* O.F. *symmetrie*—L. *symmetria*—G. *summetria*, f. *summetros*, commensurate, f. *sum*- (= SYN-) + *metron*, measure. Due proportion between the parts of a whole, harmony; correspondence of arrangement.—**Symmet'ric**, **Symmet'rical**, *aa.*

Sym'pathy, *n.* L. *sympathīa*—G. *sumpatheia*, f. *sumpathēs*, sympathetic, f. *sum*- (= SYN-) + *pathos*, feeling. PATHOS. Feeling for another in trouble, compassion; a sharing of an emotion, &c., of another; agreement in opinion or desire.—**Sympathet'ic**, *a.* G. *sumpathētikos.* Of, feeling, apt to feel, displaying, due to sympathy.—**Sympathet'ically**, *adv.* -ICAL. -LY.[2]—**Sym'pathize**, *vi.*

Sym'phony, *n.* O.F. *symphonie*—L. *symphōnia*—G. *sumphōnia*, f. *sumphōnos*, agreeing in sound, f. *sum*- (= SYN-) + *phōnē*, sound. PHONETIC. Consonance of sounds; an orchestral composition consisting of several contrasted but related movements.—**Symphon'ic**, *a.*

Sympo'sium, *n.*; *pl.* **Sympo'sia.** G. *sumposion*, f. *sum*- (= SYN-) + *po*-, root seen in *pepōka*, perfect of *pinein*, to drink. A drinking-party; a friendly discussion; a set of magazine articles on a subject by various hands.

Symp'tom, *n.* O.F. *symptome*—G. *sumptōma*, *sumptōmatos*, a chance or casualty, a symptom, f. *sumpiptein*, to fall together, to fall in with, f. *sum*- (= SYN-) + *piptein*, to fall. A change in the body forming an indication of its state in reference to disease; a sign or token.—**Symptomat'ic**, *a.*

Synæ'resis, **Syne'resis**, *n.* G. *sunairesis*, f. *sun*- (SYN-) + *hairesis*, a taking, f. *haire-ein*, to take. The contraction of two vowels or syllables into one.

Syn'agogue, *n.* F. *synagogue*—L. *synagōga* —G. *sunagōgē*, a bringing together, place of assembly, f. *sun*- (SYN-) + *agōgē*, a bringing, f. *agein*, to bring. A Jewish congregation; its meeting-place.—**Synagog'ical**, *a.*

Syn'chronize, *vi.* G. *sugchronizein*, to be a contemporary of, f. *sug*- (= SYN-) + *chronos*, time. CHRONIC. To occur at the same time. —*vt.* To make to agree in time.—**Syn'chronism**, *n.*—**Syn'chronous**, *a.*

Syn'cope, *n.* L. *syncopē*—G. *sugkopē*, f. *sug*- (= SYN-) + *kop*-, root of *koptein*, to strike, cut. A syncopated spelling or pronunciation; a fainting from loss of blood.—**Syn'copate**, *vt.* L. *syncopāre*, *syncopātum*, recorded in sense 'to swoon', f. *syncopē.* To shorten (a word) by omission of interior letters.

Syn'dic, *n.* F. *syndic*—L. *syndicus*—G. *sundikos*, an advocate, f. *sun*- (SYN-) + *dikē*, justice. An official of different kinds at different times and in different places.—**Syn'dicate**, *n.* Med.L. *syndicātus*, f. *syndicus.* A body of syndics; a body of persons combined to promote some enterprise.

Synec'doche, *n.* L. *synecdochē*—G. *sunekdochē*, lit., 'a receiving together', f. *sun*- (SYN-) + *ek*, out + *dechesthai*, to receive. A figure of speech in which a part is made to stand for the whole.

Syn'od, *n.* F. *synode*—L. *synodus*—G. *sunodos*, assembly, f. *sun*- (SYN-) + *hodos*, way. METHOD. An ecclesiastical council; a meeting for debate.—**Syn'odal**, **Synod'ical**, *aa.*

Syn'onym, *n.* F. *synonyme*—L. *synōnyma*, pl. of *synōnymum*, synonym—G. *sunōnumos*, of like name or meaning, in neut. pl., synonyms, f. *sun*- (SYN-) + *onoma* (in Æolic *onuma*), NAME. A word conveying the same sense as another. —**Synonym'ity**, *n.*—**Synon'ymous**, *a.*—**Synon'ymy**,[1] *n.* The quality of being synonymous; the use of synonyms for emphasis.

Synop'sis, *n.* L. *synopsis*—G. *sunopsis*, a general view, a synopsis, f. *sun*- (SYN-) + *opsis*, sight. AUTOPSY. A summary.—**Synop'tic**, **Synop'tical**, *aa.* Affording a general survey.—**Synop'tically**,[2] *adv.*

Syn'tax, *n.* F. *syntaxe*—L. *syntaxis*—G. *suntaxis*, f. *sun*- (SYN-) + *taxis*, order, f. *tassein*, to arrange. TACTIC. The grammatical arrangement of words; the rules governing this.—**Syntac'tic**, *a.* G. *suntaktikos.* Of or according to syntax.—**Syntac'tically**, *adv.* -ICAL. -LY.[2]

Syn'thesis, *n.* G. *sunthesis*, f. *sun*- (SYN-) + *thesis.* THESIS. Putting together, combination.—**Synthet'ic**, *a.* G. *sunthetikos.* Pertaining to, consisting in synthesis.—**Synthet'ical**, *a.*—**Synthet'ically**,[2] *adv.*

Syph'ilis, *n.* F. *syphilis*, f. *Syphilus*, the title-character of a 16th c. Latin poem on the subject. An infectious and hereditary venereal disease.—**Syphilit'ic**, *a.*

Syr'inge, *n.* F. *seringue*—G. *surigx, suriggos*, pipe. A tube fitted with a piston for drawing in fluid and ejecting it in a fine stream or in spray.—*vt.* To sluice or spray with a syringe.

Syr'up, *n.* O.F. *syrop* (F. *sirop*)—Arab. *sharāb*, beverage, f. *shariba*, he drank. SHERBET. A strong solution of sugar in water, often flavoured; treacle.—**Syr'up**Y,[2] *a.*

Sys'tem, *n.* L. *systēma*—G. *sustēma, sustēmatos*, a whole compounded of parts, f. *sus-* (= SYN-) + *stē-*, root of *stēnai*, to STAND. A complex whole; the body as a functional whole; method, organization, classification.—**Systemat'**IC, *a.* Methodical, according to a plan.—**Systemat'ically**, *adv.* -ICAL. -LY.[2]—**Sys'temat**IZE, *vt.*

Sys'tole, *n.* G. *sustolē*, a drawing together, f. *sustellein*, to draw together, f. *su-* (= SYN-) + *stellein*, to put APOSTLE. STOLE. The contraction of the heart or of an artery.

Syz'ygy, *n.* G. *suzugia*, a being yoked together, f. *suzeugnunai*, to yoke together, f. *su-* (= SYN-) + *zeugnunai*, to yoke, f. *zugon*, YOKE. The conjunction or opposition of two heavenly bodies.

T

Tab, *n.* Orig. obscure. A short strap, flat loop or projecting part; a luggage label.

Tab'ard, *n.* O.F. *tabart*, a kind of coat, of unknown orig. A herald's official coat.

Tab'by, *n.* F. *tabis*, earlier *atabis*, app. f. Arab. *attābiy*, a kind of silk named from the quarter of Bagdad in which it was made. Silk taffeta, striped or watered.—*Attrib.* *Tabby cat* (also *tabby*), a brindled cat; a she-cat.

Tab'ernacle, *n.* F. *tabernacle*—L. *tabernāculum*, dim. of *taberna*, hut. booth. TAVERN. A habitation of slight construction; applied to a nonconformist place of worship.

Ta'ble, *n.* F. *table*—L. *tabula*, plank, board, tablet, list, painting, &c. ENTABLATURE. TAFFEREL. A tablet; an article of furniture consisting of a flat top supported by legs; food, fare; a statement of a set of facts, &c., arranged in columns and lines.—*vt.* To lay upon a table.—**Ta'ble-land**, *n.* An elevated tract of land with a level surface.

Tab'leau, *n.*; *pl.* **Tab'leaux**. F., dim. of *table*. (See prec.) A group of persons, &c., producing a picturesque effect.

Tab'let, *n.* O.F. *tablete*, dim. of *table*. TABLE. A small slab for writing upon or for an inscription; a small flat piece.

Taboo', **Tabu'**, *a.* Tongan *tabu*. Prohibited to a particular class, forbidden, sacred; under a prohibition from certain actions, &c.—*n.* The putting of a person or thing under a prohibition; the fact or condition of being so placed; the prohibition; the institution or practice of taboo.—*vt.* To put under a taboo.

Ta'bor, **Ta'bour**, *n.* O.F. *tabour*, *tambour* (F. *tambour*), drum. Said to be of Oriental orig., and compared with Per. *tabīrah*, drum, and Arab. *tambūr*, a kind of lute. TAMBOUR. A small drum.—*vi.* To play on a tabor.

Tab'ular, *a.* L. *tabulāris*, a. f. *tabula*. TABLE. Flat; entered in, in the form of, a table.—**Tab'ul**ATE,[3] *vt.* To draw up a table of.

Tac'it, *a.* L. *tacitus*, pa.pple. of *tacēre*, to be silent. RETICENT. Not expressed but implied.—**Tac'it**LY,[2] *adv.*—**Tac'iturn**, *a.* L. *taciturnus*. Habitually silent.

Tack, *n.* Doublet of archaic *Tache*, clasp, hook—O.F. *tache*, clasp, nail, of uncertain orig. ATTACH. A small nail; a long slight stitch; a rope, &c., for securing the corners of certain sails; the course of a ship in relation to the wind.—*vt.* To attach with tacks; to append.—*vi.* To shift sails and change a ship's course.

Tack'le, *n.* App. of L.G. orig. Cf. M.L.G. *takel*, equipment, hoisting apparatus, f. *taken*, to grasp, with instrumental suff. *-el*. Equipment, apparatus; an apparatus for moving weights.—*vt.* To grip, attack, take in hand.

Tact, *n.* L. *tactus*, touch, f. *tangĕre*, *tactum*, to touch. ATTAIN. Skill in dealing with men or circumstances.—**Tact'**LESS, *a.*—

Tact'ile, *a.* L. *tactilis*. Of, perceptible to, endowed with, touch.

Tac'tic, *n.* G. *taktikē* (*technē*), (art) of arrangement, tactic, f. *taktos*, vbl. a. f. *tassein*, to arrange. SYNTAX. TAXIDERMY. The art of drawing up troops or ships for battle and performing evolutions. Sim. (and more us.) **Tac'tics**, rendering G. *ta taktika*, tactics, lit. 'matters pertaining to arrangement'.—**Tac'tic**AL, *a.*—**Tactic**'IAN, *n.*

Tad'pole, *n.* M.E. *tadde*, TOAD + (app.) POLL, head, from the size of the head. The young of a frog, &c.

Taf'ferel, *n.*; corrupted to **Taf'frail**. Du. *tafereel*, panel, board, dim. of *tafel*, f. L. *tabula*. TABLE. The rail at a ship's stern.

Taf'feta, **Taf'fety**, *n.* O.F. *taffetas*—Per. *tāftah*, silken cloth. A thin silk or linen fabric.

Tag, *n.* Orig. obscure. A ragged end; an address label; a hard point on a lace, &c.; an appendage; a trite quotation.—*vt.* To append.—**Tag-rag**, *n.* Orig. two words = both *tag* and *rag*. The rabble.

Tail, *n.* O.E. *tægel, tægl*. Common Teut. The projecting hindmost part of an animal.

Tai'lor, *n.* A.F. *taillour* = O.F. *tailleor*, *-eur* (oblique case of *tailler(r)e*)—Med.L. *tāliātor*, cutter, f. *tāliāre*, to cut. ENTAIL. A maker of outer garments.

Taint, *n.* O.F. *teint*, *taint*—L. *tinctus*, a dyeing, f. *tingĕre*, *tinctum*. TINCTURE. ATTAINT. STAIN. A stain; an infection.—*vt.* To tinge, imbue slightly; to corrupt.—*vi.* To become corrupted.

Take, *vt.* M.E. *taken*—Late O.E. *tacan*—O.N. *taka*, to grasp, seize. To seize, catch; to transfer to or bring into relation with oneself; to captivate; to assume, adopt; to choose; to make use of; to use up; to get; to receive, accept; to exact; to understand; to leap, &c., over; to consider, reckon; to convey, conduct.—*vi.* To be effective; to apply oneself *to*.

Talc, *n.* F. *talc*—Arab. *talq*. Mica; also, a compound of magnesium having a greasy feel.

Tale, *n.* O.E. *talu* = M.L.G. *tāle*, O.H.G. *zala* (Ger. *zahl*), number, O.N. *tala*, talk. O.Teut. **talā*. TELL. A narrative: number.

Tal'ent, *n.* O.E. *talente*, *-an* = O.H.G. *talenta*—L. *talenta*, pl. of *talentum*, G. *talanton*, balance, weight, sum of money. An ancient weight and money; *fig.* (see Matt. xxv. 14-30) power or ability, a special natural ability.

Tal'isman, *n.* = 17th c. F., Sp., Pg. *talisman*, It. *talismano*—Arab. *tilsam*—Late G. *telesma*, a religious rite, a consecrated object, f. G. *tele-ein*, to complete, to initiate. An object held to possess magic virtue.

Talk, *vi.* M.E. *talkien*, *talken*, a freq. derivative f. TALE OR TELL. To converse; to speak.—*vt.* To express in speech; to use as a spoken language; to discuss.—*n.* Discourse; a conversation; mention: rumour; the subject of conversation.—**Talk'**ATIVE, *a.*—**Talk'**ER, *n.*

Tall, *a.* Prob. represents (with loss of *pref.*) O.E. *getæl*, swift, prompt = O.H.G. *gizal*, quick. Formerly, meet, proper; comely; valiant. High of stature; high, lofty.

Tal'low, *n.* M.E. *talgh*, corresp. to M.L.G. and Ger. *talg*, Du. *talk*. Animal fat melted and clarified.—*vt.* To smear with tallow.

Tal'ly, *n.* A.F. *tallie* = Anglo-L. *tālea, tallia*, in same sense—L. *tālea*. ENTAIL. A notched rod for keeping accounts; an account so kept; a duplicate or counterpart.—*vt.* To record or reckon by tally.—*vi.* To agree, correspond.

Tal'mud, *n.* Late Heb. *talmūd*, instruction. The body of Jewish civil and ceremonial law.

Tal'on, *n.* O.F. *talon*, heel—Late Pop.L. *tālo, tālōnis*, heel—L. *tālus*, ankle. A claw.

Tam'arind, *n.* = Sp., It. *tamarindo*—Arab. *tamr-hindī*, date of India. The fruit of a tropical tree; the tree.

Tam'arisk, *n.* L.L. *tamariscus*, var. of *tamarix*. Orig. unknown. An evergreen shrub or small tree of S. Europe and W. Asia.

Tam'bour, *n.* F. *tambour*. TABOR. A large drum; a frame for embroidery; a cylindrical stone in a column.—**Tambourine'**, *n.* App. f. F. *tambourin*, dim. of *tambour*. A kind of half-drum with cymbals attached.

Tame, *a.* O.E. *tam* = Old Fris. *tam*, O.H.G. *zam* (Ger. *zahm*). Cogn. with G. *dama-ein*, L. *domāre*. ADAMANT. DAUNT. Reclaimed from the wild state; docile; insipid.—*vt.* To make tame.—**Tame'**LY,[2] *adv.*—**Tame'**LESS, *a.*

Tam'per, *vi.* Formerly us. spelt *temper*. App. the same as TEMPER. Formerly, to temper (clay). To try to have clandestine dealings *with*; to interfere *with* improperly.

Tan, *n.* Prob. f. F. *tan* = Med.L. *tannum*, app. of Celtic orig. TAWNY. Crushed oak-bark for tanning; the colour.—*vt.* To convert into leather; to make brown or tawny.

Tan'dem, *n.* App. L. *tandem*, at length (of time), used punningly. A vehicle drawn by two horses harnessed one behind the other.—*adv.* One behind the other.

Tan'gent, *a.* L. *tangens, tangentis*, pres.pple. of *tangĕre*. ATTAIN. TACT. Meeting, but not (though produced) intersecting.—*n.* A straight line tangent to a curve.—**Tangen'ti**AL, *a.*—**Tan'gi**BLE, *a.* That may be touched; definite, palpable.—**Tangi**BIL'ITY, *n.*

Tan'gle, *vt.* App. a var. of obs. *Tagle* in same sense, prob. of Scand. orig. To involve; to twist together confusedly.—*n.* A tangled condition; a tangled mass.

Tank, *n.* Pg. *tanque*, L. *stagnum*, pond. STAGNATE. A receptacle for storing liquids.

Tank'ard, *n.* = M.Du. *tanckaert*, F. *tanquart*. Orig. unknown. A large drinking-vessel.

Tan'talize, *vt.* With -IZE f. L. *Tantalus*, G. *Tantalos*, who was placed in water which constantly receded as he stooped to drink (Odyssey, 11 582 foll.). To torment by presenting and withdrawing a desired thing.

Tan'tamount, *a.* Orig. as *v.*, to be equivalent—A.F. *tant amunter* (= O.F. *amonter*), to AMOUNT to as much. Equivalent *to*.

Tan'trum, *n.* Orig. unknown. An outburst of petulance.

Tap, *n.*[1] O.E. *tæppa*. Common Teut. Orig. sense 'a tapering stick'. A plug for stopping a hole in a cask; a hollow plug for drawing off liquid.—*v.*[1]*t.* To put a tap in; to draw liquid from; in *surgery*, to draw accumulated fluid from.—**Tap'-root**, *n.* A root tapering to a point and growing directly downwards.—**Tap'**STER, *n.* One who draws beer, &c.

Tap, *v.*[2]*t.* Imitative. Perh. through F. *taper* in same sense. To strike lightly but audibly.—*n.*[2] A light but audible blow or rap.

Tape, *n.*[2] O.E. *tæppe* or *tæppa*. Orig. unknown. A narrow woven strip.

Ta'per, *n.* O.E. *tapur, -or, -er*. Not in the cogn. langs. A long wick coated with wax.—*a.* Diminishing gradually towards one end.—*vi.* and *t.* To become or make taper.

Tap'estry, *n.* Corr. of some form of earlier and obs. *Tapissery* in same sense—F. *tapisserie*, f. *tapisser*, to cover with carpet, f. *tapis*, carpet, table-cloth—L.L. *tapētium*—G. *tapētion*, dim. of *tapēs, tapētos*, carpet, rug. A textile fabric decorated with designs in colours.

Tapio'ca, *n.* Pg., Sp., F. *tapioca*—Brazilian *tipiōca*, 'dregs squeezed out' (*sc.* from the root of the plant). The prepared flour of the roots of a plant known as cassava.

Tar, *n.* O.E. *teru* = M.L.G. *ter* (Ger. *teer*), O.N. *tjara*. Prob. conn. with O.E. *trēow*, TREE. A black viscid liquid obtained from coal, &c.; a nickname for a sailor (perh. an abb. of TARPAULIN).—*vt.* To smear with tar.

Tar'dy, *a.* F. *tardif*—Pop.L. **tardīvus*, f. L. *tardus*, slow. RETARD. Slow, sluggish, late, delaying, dilatory.—**Tar'di**LY,[2] *adv.*

Tare, *n.*[1] Orig. unknown. Vetch.

Tare, *n.*[2] F. *tare*—Arab. *tarhah*, what is thrown away. An allowance for the weight of a box, &c., containing goods.

Targe, *n.* Late O.E. *targe, targa* = O.F. *targe*—O.N. *targa*, shield. A light shield.—**Tar'get**, *n.* Dim. A small targe; something to be aimed at in shooting.

Tar'iff, *n.* It. *tariffa*, book of rates of duties—Arab. *ta'rīf*, notification. An official list of customs duties; the system of such duties a classified list of charges.

Tarn, *n.* O.N. **tarnu, tjorn*. A small mountain lake.

Tar'nish, *vt.* F. *terniss-*, extended stem of *ternir*, f. *terne*, dull, dark, of doubtful orig. To discolour; to sully.—*vi.* To lose lustre, become sullied.—*n.* Discoloration; stain.

Tarpau'lin, *n.* Said to be f. TAR, *n.* + PALL, *n.* + *-ing*. Canvas coated with tar.

Tar'ry, *vi.* Orig. obscure. To delay, linger.

Tart, *n.* F. *tarte*, an open tart = Med.L. *tarta*. Orig. uncertain. An open piece of pastry filled with fruit, &c.; a covered fruit pie.

Tart, *a.* O.E. *teart*, of obscure orig. Poss. f. root of *teran*, to TEAR. Sour; acrimonious.

Tar'tan, *n.* Of uncertain orig. A woollen cloth woven in coloured stripes crossing at right angles; the pattern of such cloth.

Tar'tar, *n.*[1] F. *tartre*—Med.G. *tartaron*, perh. of Arab. orig. A crust deposited by wine on casks; a deposit on the teeth.

Tar'tar, *n.*[2] Med.L. *Tartarus*, prob. orig. *Tātār*, corrupted by association with *Tartarus*, hell. A native of Tartary; a savage or intractable person.

Task, *n.* O.N.F. *tasque*=O.F. *tasche*—Med.L. *tasca*, said to be for *taxa*, f. L. *taxāre*. TAX. Formerly, a tax. A piece of work imposed or undertaken.—*vt.* To impose a task on.

Tas'sel, *n.* O.F. *tasel, tassel*, clasp, of doubtful orig. Formerly, a clasp. An ornament consisting of a knob with a bunch of threads.

Taste, *vt.* O.F. *taster*, to touch, feel, app. f. **taxtāre*, **taxitāre*, as freq. of L. *taxāre*, to touch, handle. TAX. To experience; to perceive or try the flavour of; to eat or drink.—*vi.* To have a flavour *of*; to have experience *of*.—*n.* A small quantity; the sense of tasting; flavour; liking; the sense of what is beautiful or excellent; style or manner.—**Taste'**FUL, *a.*—**Taste'**LESS, *a.*

Tat'ter, *n.* Of Scand. orig. Cf. O.N. *taturr, pl. *tötrar*, rags. A rag.—*vt.* To tear to tatters.—**Tatterdema'lion,** *n.* A factitious element added to the *n.* A ragged fellow.

Tat'tle, *vi.* = M.Flemish *tatelen.* Ultimately imitative. TWADDLE. To chatter, gossip.

Tattoo', *n.*[1] Formerly *tap-too*—Du. *taptoe*, in same sense, f. *tap*, the tap (of a cask) + (*doe*) *toe*, (put) to, shut. A beat of drum or bugle-call calling soldiers to their quarters.

Tattoo', *n.*[2] Polynesian. A mark made by tattooing.—*vt.* To form marks on (the skin) by puncturing (it) and inserting a pigment.

Taunt, *n.* Orig. obscure. An insulting gibe.—*vt.* To reproach *with* contemptuously.

Taut, *a.* Orig. obscure. Perhaps conn. with *teuh-*, &c. TIE. Tightly drawn; trim.

Tautol'ogy, *n.* G. *tautologia*, f. *tautologos*, repeating what has been said, f. *tauto* (*to auto*), the same + *-logos*, saying, f. *legein*, to say. Repetition of the same thing in different words.—**Tautolog'**ICAL, *a.*

Tav'ern, *n.* O.F. *taverne*—L. *taberna*, hut, booth, tavern. TABERNACLE. A place where liquors are sold.

Taw'dry, *n.* Orig. short for *Tawdry* (i.e., *St. Awdry* [Etheldreda]) *Lace*, lace bought at St. Awdry's fair held in the Isle of Ely and elsewhere on the saint's day, Oct. 17. Cheap finery.—*a.* Cheap and showy; cheaply adorned.

Taw'ny, *a.* A.F. *taune*, O.F. *tané*, dark-coloured like tan, f. *tan*, TAN. Of a brownish-yellow colour.—*n.* The colour.

Tax, *vt.* App. f. O.F. *taxer*—L. *taxāre*, to touch, to censure, to value, in Med.L. also to impose a tax. TASK. TASTE. To examine and adjust (an account of costs, &c.); to impose a tax upon; to burden, put a strain on; to charge *with*.—*n.* A compulsory contribution to the cost of government; a burden, strain.

Tax'idermy, *n.* G. *taxis*, an arranging (f. *tassein*, to arrange) + *derma*, skin. TACTIC. DERM. The art of preparing and stuffing the skins of animals.

Tea, *n.* = F. *thé*, It. *tè*, Du. and Ger. *thee*, adaptation (perh. through Malay *te, teh*) of Chinese (Amoy dialect) *tē* = Mandarin *ch'a.* The dried leaves of a plant cultivated in China, India, &c.; a beverage made therefrom; the plant; a meal at which tea is served.

Teach, *vt.* O.E. *tǽc*(*e*)*an*, to show, to show how to do, cogn. with *tácn*, TOKEN. To impart the knowledge of; to instruct.—*vi.* To act as a teacher.—**Teach'**ER, *n.*

Teak, *n.* Pg. *teca*—Malayālam *tēkka.* An E. Indian tree with very hard wood; the wood.

Teal, *n.* M.E. *tele*—O.E. **tǽle*, **tēle.* Cf. Du. *taling, teling.* A small fresh-water fowl.

Team, *n.* O.E. *téam*, family, offspring = Old Fris. *tám*, bridle, family, O.H.G. *zoum* (Ger. *zaum*), bridle, rein, f. *tauh-*. TIE. TEEM. A set of draught animals; a number of persons associated in an action.—**Team'**STER, *n.*

Tear, *n.*[1] O.E. *téar* = Old Fris. *târ*, O.N. *tár.* Cogn. with G. *dakru*, Old L. *dacrima* (L. *lacrima*). LACHRYMAL. A drop of fluid in the eye.—**Tear'**FUL, *a.*—**Tear'**LESS, *a.*

Tear, *vt.* O.E. *teran* = Du. *teren*, O.H.G. *zeran* (Ger. *zehren*), to destroy. Cogn. with G. *derein*, to flay. To pull asunder or away; to rend, lacerate.—*vi.* To become torn; to rush.—*n.*[2] A rent.

Tease, *vt.* O.E. *tǽsan*, to pull to pieces, tease (wool, &c.) = L.G. *tēsen*, to pull, O.H.G. *zeisan*, to tease. To pull asunder the fibres of; to worry in a petty way.

Teat, *n.* App. reps. F. *tette*, O.F. *tete*, &c., prob. of Ger. orig. Cf. O.E. *tit* (whence earlier Eng. forms), M.Du. *titte.* The nipple of the female breast.

Tech'nic, *a.* L. *technicus*—G. *technikos*, a. f. *technē*, art, craft. Technical.—*n.* Technical details or methods collectively (us. *pl.*); more us. in F. form **Technique'.**—**Tech'nic**AL, *a.* Of or used in an art or the arts generally.—**Tech'nical**LY,[2] *adv.*—**Technical'**ITY, *n.*

Te'dium, *n.* L. *taedium*, weariness, f. *taedēre*, to weary. Wearisomeness.—**Te'dious,** *a.* L. *taediōsus.* Wearisome by continuance.

Teem, *vi.* O.E. *tíeman*, f. *téam.* TEAM. To be full, to be prolific, abound, swarm.

Teethe, *vi.* From *teeth*, pl. of TOOTH. To develop or 'cut' teeth.

Teeto'tal, *a.* A kind of emphasizing reduplication of TOTAL. Of or pertaining to total abstinence from alcoholic drinks; pledged to this.—**Teeto'tall**ER, **Teeto'tal**ER, *n.*

Teeto'tum, *n.* Formerly *T totum*, i.e. L. *tōtum*, all, the whole (the earlier name of the toy) with its initial (inscribed on one of the four sides of the toy) prefixed. A top, properly one with four sides with a letter on each used in a game of chance, the turning up of the T giving right to all the stakes.

Teg'ument, *n.* L. *tegumentum*, f. L. *tegĕre*, to cover. DETECT. THATCH. A covering.

Tel'egraph, *n.* F. *télégraphe*, f. G. *tēle*, afar + *-graphos*, that writes, f. *graphein*, to write. GRAPHIC. An apparatus for transmitting messages to a distance, now gen. by electricity.—*vi.* and *t.* To communicate by telegraph.—**Tel'egram,** *n.* Formed f. G. *tēle* + *gramma*, a written character, f. *graphein.* A message sent by telegraph.—**Telegraph'**IC, *a.*—**Teleg'raph**IST, *n.* A telegraph-operator.—**Teleg'raph**Y,[1] *n.*

Teleol'ogy, *n.* G. *telos*, end + -LOGY. The doctrine or study of ends or final causes.

Telep'athy, *n.* G. *tēle*, afar + *-patheia*, f. *pathos*, feeling. Action of one mind on another at a distance.—**Telepath'**IC, *a.*

Tel'ephone, *n.* G. *tēle*, afar + *phōnē*, voice, sound. An apparatus for reproducing sound at a distance.—*vi.* and *t.* To communicate by telephone.—**Telepho'n**IC, *a.*—**Teleph'on**Y,[1] *n.*

Tel'escope, *n.* It. *telescopio*, f. G. *tēleskopos*, far-seeing, f. *tēle*, afar + *scope-ein*, to look. SCEPTIC. An instrument for making distant objects appear nearer.—**Telescop'**IC, *a.*

Tell, *vt.* O.E. *tellan*, f. *talu*, TALE. To narrate; to make known; to discern; to apprise; to order.—*vi.* To give an account; to be of account or weight.

Tellu'rian, *a.* L. *tellus, tellūris*, the earth + -IAN. Of or pertaining to the earth.

Temer'ity, *n.* L. *temeritas*, rashness, f. *temere*, blindly, rashly. Rashness, foolhardiness.—**Temera'rious,** *a.* L. *temerārius* (f. *temere*) + -OUS. Rash, foolhardy.

Tem'per, *vt.* O.E. *temprian*—L. *temperāre*, *temperātum*, to proportion or mingle duly, to qualify, to regulate. TAMPER. To modify, moderate, restrain; to bring to a proper consistence; to harden (steel).—*n.* The degree of hardness of tempered steel; mental constitution; frame of mind, humour; anger.—**Tem′perament**, *n.* L. *temperāmentum*, due mixture, f. *temperāre.* Mental constitution, esp. as connected with physical constitution.—**Tem′perate**, *a.* L. *temperātus*, pa.pple. of *temperāre.* Keeping due measure, self-restrained; of mild temperature.—**Tem′per**ANCE, *n.* Self-restraint, esp. in regard to intoxicants.—**Tem′perate**LY,[2] *adv.*—**Tem′perature**, *n.* L. *temperātūra*, due measure, temperature, f. *temperāre.* State with regard to warmth or coldness.

Tem′pest, *n.* O.F. *tempeste*—Pop.L. **tempesta* for L. *tempestas*, season, weather, storm, f. *tempus*, time, season. TEMPORAL. A violent storm.—**Tempes′tuous**, *a.* L. *tempestuōsus.* Very stormy.

Tem′ple, *n.*[1] O.E. *templ, tempel*—L. *templum.* An edifice devoted to divine worship.

Tem′ple, *n.*[2] O.F. *temple*—Pop.L. type **tempula*, **templa*, app. for. L. *tempora* (taken as fem. sing.), pl. of *tempus* (see next), 'the right place, the fatal spot' (aft. G. *to kairion*), hence, temple. The flattened region on each side of the forehead.—**Tem′por**AL, *a.*[1]

Tem′poral, *a.*[2] L. *temporālis*, f. *tempus, temporis*, time. CONTEMPORANEOUS. Of this life, secular.—**Temporal′**ITY, *n.* In *pl.*, temporal or material possessions (esp. of the clergy).—**Tem′por**ARY, *a.* Lasting for a limited time.—**Tem′porari**LY,[2] *adv.*—**Tem′por**IZE, *vi.* To conform to circumstances; to negotiate so as to gain time.

Tempt, *vt.* O.F. and A.F. *tempter*—L. *temptāre*, to handle, feel, test, tempt. To provoke, defy; to entice to evil; to allure.—**Tempt**A′TION, *n.*—**Tempt′**ER, *n.*

Ten, *a.* and *n.* O.E. *tíen*, Anglian *tén.* Common Teut. Cogn. with G. *deka*, L. *decem.* The cardinal number next after nine.

Ten′able, *a.* F. *tenable*, f. *tenir*, L. *tenēre*, to hold. TENANT. Capable of being defended.

Tena′cious, *a.* L. *tenax, tenācis*, holding fast (f. *tenēre*, to hold) + -OUS. PERTINACIOUS. (See next.) Adhesive; holding fast; retentive.—**Tenac′**ITY, *n.*

Ten′ant, *n.* F. *tenant*, orig. pres.pple. of *tenir*, L. *tenēre*, to hold. ABSTAIN. CONTAIN. ENTERTAIN. One who holds lands or tenements; one who holds them by lease.—*vt.* To hold as tenant, to occupy, inhabit.—**Ten′**ANCY, *n.*—**Ten′ant**ABLE, *a.* Fit for occupation.—**Ten′ant**RY, *n.* A body of tenants.

Tench, *n.* O.F. *tenche* (F. *tanche*)—L.L. *tinca.* A thick-bodied freshwater fish.

Tend, *v.*[1]*t.* Shortened f. ATTEND. Cf. next. To attend to, take care of.—**Ten′d**ANCE, *n.* —**Ten′d**ER, *n.*[1] A vessel attending a larger one; a carriage for fuel and water attached to a locomotive.

Tend, *v.*[2]*i.* F. *tendre*—L. *tendĕre*, to stretch, extend, to direct one's course, proceed. ATTEND. OSTENSIBLE. TENDER, *v.* TENSE, *a.* To move, hold a course; to be inclined or conduce *to* or *to do.*—**Ten′d**ENCY, *n.*

Ten′der, *a.* F. *tendre*—L. *tener*, conn. with *tenuis*, THIN. Easily injured; gentle, loving; sensitive; solicitous.—**Ten′der**LY,[2] *adv.*

Ten′der, *vt.* F. *tendre*—L. *tendĕre*, to stretch, hold forth. TEND.[2] To offer, proffer.—*n.*[2] An offer; what may be legally offered in payment.

Ten′don, *n.* Med.L. *tendo, tendōnis*, app. f. G. *tenōn*, sinew, tendon, influenced by L. *tendĕre.* (See prec.) A band of fibrous tissue attaching a muscle to a bone, &c.

Ten′dril, *n.* Orig. uncertain. Perh. f. F. *tendre.* TEND, *v.*[2] A slender organ by which a climbing plant attaches itself to something.

Ten′ement, *n.* A.F. = O.F. *tenement*—Med. L. *tenēmentum*, f. L. *tenēre*, to hold (TENANT) + *-mentum*, -MENT. A piece of land; a house; a part of a house forming a separate dwelling.

Te′net, *n.* L. *tenet*, 'he holds', 3rd sing. of *tenēre.* (See prec.) A doctrine or dogma.

Ten′nis, *n.* M.E. *tenētz, tennēs*, &c., prob. f. F. Poss. f. *tenez* (A.F. *tenetz*), imp. of *tenir*, to hold (see next), 'take, receive' (a ball sent). A game in which a ball is driven to and fro in an enclosed court.

Ten′on, *n.* F. *tenon*, f. *tenir*, to hold. TENANT. A projection fitting into a mortise.

Ten′or, *n.* O.F. *tenor, tenour*, import (of a document, &c.)—L. *tenor*, course, import, f. *tenēre*, to hold. TENANT. Import; general course; the male voice between the bass and the alto (app. so called as holding or continuing the dominant note), the part for this voice, a singer with a voice of this pitch.

Tense, *n.* O.F. *tens* (F. *temps*)—L. *tempus*, time. CONTEMPORANEOUS. A modification of a verb to indicate the time of an action, &c.

Tense, *a.* L. *tensus*, pa.pple. of *tendĕre, tensum* or *tentum*, to stretch. PORTEND. TEND.[2] Drawn or stretched tight.—**Ten′sile**, *a.* Mod. L. *tensilis.* Capable of being stretched; pertaining to stretching.—**Ten′**SION, *n.*

Tent, *n.* O.F. *tente*—L.L. *tenta*, fem. of *tentus*, pa.pple. of *tendĕre.* (See prec.) A portable shelter of canvas.—*vi.* To live in a tent.

Ten′tacle, *n.* Mod.L. *tentāculum*, f. L. *tentāre* (= *temptāre.* TEMPT) + dim. suff. *-culum.* A slender organ serving as a feeler.

Ten′tative, *a.* Med.L. *tentātivus*, f. L. *tentāre.* (See prec.) Done by way of trial.—*n.* An attempt.—**Ten′tative**LY,[2] *adv.*

Ten′ter, *vt.* App. f. an A.F. or O.F. **tentour* —L. **tentor*, agent-n. f. *tendĕre*, to stretch. TEND.[2] A frame for stretching cloth.—**Ten′ter-hook**, *n.* A hook on a tenter; fig., *on tenter-hooks*, in a state of painful suspense.

Ten′uous, *a.* From L. *tenuis*, THIN + -OUS. Thin; unsubstantial.—**Tenu′**ITY, *n.*

Ten′ure, *n.* A.F., O.F. *tenure*, in Med.L. *tenitūra*, f. *tenēre*, to hold. TENANT. Manner or period of holding land, &c.

Tep′id, *a.* L. *tepidus*, lukewarm, f. *tepēre*, to be warm. Moderately warm, lukewarm.

Ter′cel, Tier′cel, *n.* O.F. *tercel*—Pop.L. *tertiolus*, dim. f. L. *tertius*, third. A male hawk (said to be so called from being a third smaller than the female, or because a third egg was believed to produce a male).

Tercen′tenary, *a.* L. *ter*, thrice + CENTENARY. Of or belonging to three hundred years.—*n.* A three-hundredth anniversary.

Ter′giversate, *vi.* L. *tergiversāri, tergiversātus*, f. *tergum*, the back + *vertĕre, versum*, to turn. ADVERSE. To desert one's party; to shift, shuffle.—**Tergivers**A′TION, *n.*

Term, *n.* F. *terme*, L. *terminus*, limit, in Med.L., word, term. DETERMINE. A limit; end; a day fixed for payment of rent, &c.; duration; a period during which courts sit, scholastic institutions are open, &c.; in *pl.*, conditions, footing, mutual relation; a technical expression; a word.—*vt.* To name, call. —**Ter′min**AL, *a.* At or forming the end; final, ultimate.—*n.* A terminal part or structure.—**Ter′min**ATE,[3] *vt.* To bring to an end; to bound, be at the end of.—*vi.* To come to an end.—**Ter′min**ABLE, *a.*—**Termin**A′TION, *n.*—**Terminol**′OGY, *n.* The study of

terms, technical terms collectively.—**Terminolog'**ICAL, *a.*—**Ter'minus**, *n.* A station at the end of a railway.
Ter'magant, *n.* An imaginary Mohammedan deity, represented on the stage as an overbearing personage. A brawling woman.
Ter'race, *n.* F. *terrace*—L. **terrācea*, fem. of **terrāceus*, a. f. *terra*, earth. TERRESTRIAL. A raised level place; a uniform row of houses.
Ter'ra-cot'ta, *n.* It., 'baked (cooked) earth' —L. *terra* (see prec.) + *cocta*, fem. pa.pple. of *coquĕre*, to COOK. A kind of hard unglazed pottery; the colour, a brownish red.
Ter'rene, *a.* L. *terrēnus*, f. *terra*. (See next.) Of the earth or this world.
Terres'trial, *a.* L. *terrestris* (f. *terra*, earth) + -AL. INTER. TERRACE. TUREEN. UMBER. Of the earth, of this world, of the land.
Ter'rible, *a.* F. *terrible*—L. *terribilis*, f. *terrēre*, to frighten. DETER. Inspiring or fitted to inspire fear; very great, excessive.—**Ter'rib**LY,[2] *adv.*—**Terrif'**IC, *a.* Terrible. —**Terrif'ical**AL, *a.*—**Terrif'ical**LY,[2] *adv.*—**Ter'rif**Y, *vt.* To inspire with fear.—**Ter'ror**, *n.* F. *terreur*—L. *terror*. The state of being terrified; the quality of causing fear.—**Ter'ror**IZE, *vt.* To coerce or deter by terror. —*vi.* To rule by terror.—**Ter'ror**ISM, *n.*
Ter'rier, *n.* F. *terrier* (sc. *chien*, dog), Med. L. *terrārius*, a. f. *terra*, earth. TERRESTRIAL. A dog which follows its quarry into its burrow.
Ter'ritory, *n.* L. *territōrium*, land round a town, territory, us. referred to *terra*. (See prec.) The land ruled by a king, &c.; a region. —**Territo'ri**AL, *a.* *Territorial Army* or *Force*, the British Army of Home Defence.
Terse, *a.* L. *tersus*, pa.pple. of *tergēre*, to wipe. Free from redundancy, pithy.
Ter'tian, *a.* L. *tertiāna* (sc. *febris*, FEVER), fem. of *tertiānus*, of the third, tertian, f. *tertius*, third. TIERCE. Having a paroxysm every third (*i.e.* every alternate) day.
Ter'tiary, *a.* L. *tertiārius*, of the third part or rank, f. *tertius*. (See prec.) Third.—*n.* The third geological period.
Test, *n.* O.F. *test*, pot—L. *testum*, var. of *testa*, tile, pot. The pot in which gold and silver are assayed; means of trial; an oath to be taken before admission to an office, &c.—*vt.* To assay; to try, put to the proof.
Tes'tament, *n.* L. *testāmentum*, f. *testāri*, to be a witness, ATTEST, call to witness, make a will, f. *testis*, a witness. OBTEST. A will; each of the two divisions of the Bible (translating G. *diathēkē*, will, covenant).—**Testamen'**TARY, *a.*—**Tes'tate**, *a.* L. *testātus*, pa.pple. of *testāri*. That has left, disposed of by, a will.—**Tes'tacy**, *n.* From *testate* after INTESTACY. The state of being testate. —**Testa'tor**, *n.*; fem. **Testa'**TRIX. One who makes a will.
Tes'ticle, *n.* L. *testiculus*, dim. of *testis*, testicle. One of the two organs in males in which the seminal fluid is secreted.
Tes'tify, *vt.* Late or Med. L. *testificāre*, L. *testificāri*, to bear witness, proclaim, f. *testis*, a witness + *facĕre*, to make. To bear witness to.—*vi.* To bear witness.—**Tes'timony**, *n.* L. *testimōnium*. Evidence.—**Testimo'nial**, *n.* O.F. *testimonial* in phrase *lettres tes(ti)moniaulx*, f. *tesmoin*, L. *testimōnium*. A certificate of character, &c.; a gift by a number of persons in token of esteem, &c.
Tes'ty, *a.* A.F. *testif*, heady, obstinate, f. *teste* (F. *tête*), head. Short-tempered, peevish.
Tet'anus, *n.* L. *tetanus*—G. *tetanos*, muscular spasm, f. *teinein*, to stretch. Spasm and rigidity of some or all of the voluntary muscles.
Tet'chy, Tech'y, *a.* Orig. uncertain. Short-tempered, peevish.—**Tet'chi**LY,[2] *adv.*
Teth'er, *n.* App. f. O.N. *tjóthr*, corresp. to M.Du., M.L.G. *tûder*, *tudder*. A rope, &c., for tying up a horse, &c.—*vt.* To tie up.
Tet'ragon, *n.* G. *tetragōnon*, a quadrangle, f. *tetra-*, combining form of *tessares*, *tettares*, FOUR + *gōnia*, angle. A figure having four angles and four sides.—**Tetrag'on**AL, *a.*—**Tetrahe'dron**, *n.* Late G. *tetraedron*, properly neut. of *tetraedros*, four-sided, f. *tetra-* + *hedra*, base. A solid figure contained by four triangular faces.—**Tetral'ogy**, *n.* G. *tetralogia*, f. *tetra-* + *logos*, discourse. A series of four related dramas.—**Tetram'eter**, *n.* L. *tetrametrus*—G. *tetrametros*, a., f. *tetra-* + *metron*, measure. A verse of four feet.
Tet'ter, *n.* O.E. *teter*, cogn. with Skr. *dadru*, a kind of skin-disease. A general term for eruptive cutaneous diseases.
Text, *n.* F. *texte*, the Scriptures, &c.—Med.L. *textus*, the Gospel, written character, L. *textus*, style of a literary work, lit., 'that which is woven', f. *texĕre*, *textum*, to weave. CONTEXT. TISSUE. TOIL, *n.*[2] The original words of an author; the main body of a book; a short passage from the Scriptures, esp. as the subject of a sermon; subject, theme.—**Text'-book**, *n.* A manual of instruction.—**Text'ual**, *a.* App. f. A.F. *textuel*—L. type **textuālis*, f. *textus*. Of or in the text.
Tex'tile, *a.* L. *textilis*, woven, f. *texĕre*. (See prec.) Woven; that may be woven.—*n.* A woven fabric.—**Tex'**TURE, *n.* The character of a textile fabric; structure.
Than, *conj.* O.E. *thanne*, *thonne*, *thænne*. THEN. Conn. with THE. (The use as *conj.* is pre-English and has not been satisfactorily explained.) Used after a comparative and also after *other*, *else*.
Thane, *n.* O.E. *thegn*, *thegen*, *thēn* = O.S. *thegan*, O.H.G. *degan*, boy, servant, warrior. Orig. sense 'child, boy'. Cogn. with G. *teknon*, child. In Anglo-Saxon times, one holding land by military service; later, a term of rank.
Thank, *n.* O.E. *thanc*, *thonc*, a thought, a grateful thought. Cogn. with THINK. In *pl.*, the expression of gratitude.—*vt.* To give thanks to.—**Thank'**FUL, *a.*—**Thank'**LESS, *a.*
That, *dem. pron.* O.E. *thæt*, nom. and acc. sing. neut. of the dem. pron. and a. *se*, *séo*, *thæt*. THE. THEY. THIS. THITHER. Denoting a thing or person pointed out or present, or that has just been mentioned.—*a.* Indicating such a thing or person.—*relative pron.* In many cases equivalent to *who*, *which*.—*conj.* Introducing various dependent clauses.
Thatch, *vt.* O.E. *thecc(e)an*. Common Teut. Cogn. with G. *tegos*, roof, L. *tegĕre*, to cover. Cf. M.Du. *deken*, to cover. DECK. TEGUMENT. To cover a house with straw or the like.—*n.* Material used in thatching.
Thau'maturgy, *n.* G. *thaumatourgia*, f. *thauma*, *thaumatos*, marvel + *-ergos*, working, f. **ergein*, to work. Miracle-working, magic.
Thaw, *vt.* O.E. *thawian*, cogn. with O.H.G. *douwen*, O.N. *theyja*. To cause to thaw.—*vi.* Of ice, &c., to melt.—*n.* A thawing.
The. The reduced stem of the O.E. dem. *se*, *séo*, *thæt*. THAT. Common Teut. and Indo-European. = G. *ho*, *hē*, *to*. Cogn. with L. *iste* and *tunc*. The definite article.
The'atre, *n.* L. *theatrum*—G *theatron*, an open-air space for viewing spectacles, f. *thea-*

esthai, to behold. THEOREM. An edifice for dramatic representations; the drama; dramatic works collectively; a surgical operating room.—**Theat'r**ICAL, *a.* Of or suited to the theatre.—In *pl.* as *n.*, amateur performances.

Theft, *n.* O.E. *théofth*, f. *théof*, THIEF. The act of stealing.

The'ine, *n.* Mod.L. *thea*, TEA + chemical suff. *-ine*. The same as CAFFEINE.

Their, *pron.* O.N. *their(r)a*, properly genit. pl. of *sá*, *sú*, *that*. THEY. Belonging to them.

The'ism, *n.* G. *theos*, god + -ISM. Belief in one God without denial of revelation.

Theme, *n.* O.F. **teme*—L. *thema*—G. *thema*, proposition, f. *the-*. ANTITHESIS. A subject of discourse, composition, &c.; an essay.

Then, *adv.* M.E. *thenne*, *than*, *then*. Orig. the same as THAN. At that time; after that; next; in that case; that being the case.

Thence, *adv.* M.E. *thennes*, f. *thenne* (see prec.) with advbl. genit. *-s*. From that place; from that as cause, ground of inference, &c.

Theoc'racy, *n.* G. *theokratia*, f. *theos*, god + *-kratia*, rule. ARISTOCRACY. A system of government directly by God; a state thus governed.—**Theocrat'**IC, *a.*

Theod'olite, *n.* Orig. unknown. A portable surveying instrument.

Theol'ogy, *n.* F. *théologie*—L. *theologia*—G. *theologia*, f. *theos*, god + *logos*, discourse. The science which treats of God.—**Theolo'g**IAN, *n.*—**Theolog'**ICAL, *a.*

The'orem, *n.* L.L. *theōrēma*—G. *theōrēma*, spectacle, theorem, f. *theōre-ein*, to be a *theōros* or spectator, to look at, f. *thea-esthai*. THEATRE. A general proposition demonstrable by argument.—**The'ory**, *n.* L.L. *theōria*—G. *theōria*, a looking at, speculation, theory, f. *theōros*. A statement of rules or principles; a supposition to account for something; rules, &c., as distinguished from practice.—**Theo**RET'IC, **Theoret'ic**AL, *aa.*—**Theoret'ic**ALLY,[2] *adv.*—**The'or**IZE, *vi.* To form theories.—**The'or**IST, *n.*

Theos'ophy, *n.* Late G. *theosophia*, abstract n. f. *theosophos*, wise concerning God, f. G. *theos*, God + *sophos*, wise. A system of speculation basing the knowledge of nature on that of the divine nature.

Therapeu'tic, *a.* G. *therapeutikos*, f. *therapeutēs*, agent—n. f. *therapeuein*, to tend, treat medically. Of or pertaining to healing.—In *pl.* as *n.*, the healing art.

There, *adv.* O.E. *thǽr*, deriv. of the dem. stem *tha-* seen in THAT, THE, with advbl. suff. *-r* as in WHERE. In that place; at that point; thither.—**There'fore**, *adv.* O.E. and early M.E. *fore*, collateral form of FOR. In consequence of that, that being so.

Ther'mal, *a.* = F. *thermal*, f. G. *thermē*, heat + -AL. Of or pertaining to heat. Also **Ther'm**IC, *a.*—**Thermom'eter**, *n.* From *thermē* + G. *metre-ein*, to measure. An instrument for measuring temperature.—**Thermomet'r**IC, **Thermomet'r**ICAL, *aa.*

The'sis, *n.* G. *thesis*, a placing, a proposition, f. *the-*. ANTITHESIS. A proposition; a dissertation.

Thew, *n.* O.E. *théaw* = O.S. *thau*, custom, O.H.G. *thau*, discipline. Formerly, a custom; a personal quality; a good quality. Bodily powers or forces, muscular development.

They, *pron.* Early M.E. *thei*—O.N. *their*, nom. pl. masc. of dem. *sá*, *su*, *that* = O.E. *se*, *séo*, *thæt*. THAT. Plural of the pronoun of the third person.

Thick, *a.* O.E. *thicce* = O.H.G. *dicchi* (Ger. *dick*), O.N. *thykkr*. Having great extension measured through; crowded; bushy; closely arranged; viscid; dense; foggy; hoarse.—*adv.* To a great depth; densely; in quick succession.—**Thick'**LY,[2] *adv.*—**Thick'**EN,[2] *vt.* and *i.*—**Thick'et**, *n.* O.E. *thiccet*, f. *thicce*. A dense growth of small trees, &c.—**Thick'-set**, *a.* Composed of parts set close together; thickly planted.—*n.* A close-grown hedge.

Thief, *n.*; *pl.* **Thieves**. O.E. *théof*, *thíof*. Common Teut. THEFT. One who steals.—**Thieve**, *vi.* and *t.* O.E. *théofian*, f. *théof*. To steal.—**Thiev'**ISH, *a.*

Thigh, *n.* O.E. *thíoh*, *théoh* = O.N. *thjó*, O.H.G. *dioh*. The upper part of the leg.

Thim'ble, *n.* O.E. *thýmel*, thumb-cover, f. *thúma*, THUMB + *-el*, *-le*, instrumental suff. A metal sheath worn on the finger in sewing.

Thin, *a.* O.E. *thynne*. Cf. O.H.G. *dunni* (Ger. *dünn*), O.N. *thunnr*. Stem *ten-*, &c., to stretch. Cogn. with L. *tenuis*. ATTENUATE. TENDER, *a.* TENUOUS. Of little thickness; slender; of small density; not closely packed.—*vt.* and *i.* To make or become thin.—**Thin'**LY,[2] *adv.*—**Thin'**NESS, *n.*

Thine, *pron.* O.E. *thín*, used as genit. of *thú*, THOU, and as possessive a. = O.S. *thín*, O.H.G. *dín* (Ger. *dein*). Thy: belonging to thee.

Thing, *n.* O.E. *thing*. Common Teut. HUSTING. Orig. sense 'dispute, council, lawsuit, cause'. An affair; an event or circumstance; a material object.

Think, *vt.* O.E. *thenc(e)an* = Old Fris. *thinka*, O.H.G. *denchen* (Ger. *denken*). THANK. THOUGHT. To conceive; to consider.—*vi.* To form ideas; to reflect; to hold a certain opinion.

Third, *a.* O.E. *thridda*. Common Teut. and Indo-European. Cogn. with Skr. *tritīyas*, G *tritos*, L. *tertius*. The ordinal number corresponding to three.—*n.* A third part.

Thirst, *n.* O.E. *thurst* = O.S. *thurst*, O.H.G., Ger. *durst*. Cogn. with L. *torrēre*. TOAST. The sensation caused by want of drink (often *fig.*).—*vi.* To feel thirst.—**Thirst'**Y,[2] *a.*

Thirteen', *a.* and *n.* O.E. *thréotiene*, *thréoténe*, f. *thréo*, THREE + *tiene*, *téne*, inflected forms of *tíen*, *tén*, TEN. The cardinal number composed of ten and three.

Thir'ty, *a.* and *n.* O.E. *thrítig*, f. *thri*, THREE + *-tig*, conn. with TEN. The cardinal number equal to three tens.

This, *dem. pron.* Orig. the sing. neut., nom. and acc., now the sole sing. form, of the O.E. dem. *thes*, *théos*, *this*, a formation produced by adding *s(e)*, *s(i)* (prob. = Goth. *sai*, 'see, behold') to the simple dem. represented by O.E. *se*, *séo*, *thæt*, the initial in the masc. and fem. changing to *th*. THAT. THE. Denoting a thing or person present or near, or that has just been mentioned, esp. as being nearer than some other.

This'tle, *n.* O.E. *thistil*, *thistel* = O.H.G. *distil* (Ger. *distel*), O.N. *thistell*, *thistill*. A prickly herbaceous plant.

Thith'er, *adv.* O.E. *thider*, earlier *thaeder*, f. *tha-*, stem of THAT, THE + suff. denoting motion towards. To or towards that place.—*a.* Situated on that side or in that direction.

Thole, *n.* O.E. *thol(l)*, corresp. to O.N. *thollr*, M.Du. *dolle*. One of a pair of pegs between which an oar works. Also **Thole'-pin.**

Thong, *n.* O.E. *thwang*, *thwong*, corresp. to O.N. *thvengr*. Cogn. with TWINGE. A narrow strip of leather.

Tho'rax, *n.* L. *thōrax*—G. *thōrax*, breastplate, breast, chest. The part of the body between the neck and the abdomen.
Thorn, *n.* O.E. *thorn* = O.H.G., Ger. *dorn*, O.N. *thorn*. A stiff sharp-pointed process on a plant, a prickle; a plant which bears thorns.
Thor'ough, *a.* Attrib. use of archaic *thorough*, adv., a development of O.E. *thurh*, THROUGH. Complete, perfect.—**Thor'ough**LY,[2] *adv.*—**Thor'oughbred**, *a.* Of pure breed.—*n.* A thoroughbred animal.—**Thor'oughfare**, *n.* From *thurh* + O.E. *faru*, passage, way. WELFARE. Passage; a main road or street.
Thorp, *n.* M.E. and O.E. *throp*, *thorp*. Common Teut. A hamlet or village.
Thou, *pron.* O.E. *thū*. Common Teut. and Indo-European. Cogn. with G. *su*, L. *tu*. THINE. The pronoun of the second person.
Though, *adv.* O.N. *thó* (contracted f. **thauh*), corresp. to O.E. *théah*, *théh*, O.S. *thōh*. For all that, nevertheless.—*conj.* Notwithstanding that; even if; and yet, but yet, nevertheless.
Thought, *n.* O.E. *thoht*, shortened f. **thóht*, f. stem of *thencan*, to THINK + suff. *-t*. The process of thinking; the thinking faculty; what one thinks; what is or has been thought collectively; a notion; heed; meditation; intention; an opinion; a very small amount.
Thou'sand, *a.* and *n.* O.E. *thúsend* = O.H.G. *dūsunt* (Ger. *tausend*), O.N. *thúsuna*. The cardinal number equal to ten times a hundred.
Thrall, *n.* O.E. *thrǽl*—O.N. *thrǽll*, perh. f. O.Teut. root *threh-*, to run, 'one who runs on errands'. A slave; servitude (in this sense f. the *v.*).—*vt.* To enslave.—**Thral'**DOM, *n.*
Thrash, Thresh (the latter only in the first sense), *vt.* O.E. *therscan*, rarely *threscan*. Common Teut. Orig. sense prob. 'to stamp heavily with the feet'. To beat out the grains of (wheat, &c.); to beat.
Thrason'ical, *a.* From *Thrasōn*, name of a braggart soldier in Terence's *Eunuchus* (f. G. *thrasus*, bold) + -ICAL. Bragging, boastful.
Thread, *n.* O.E. *thrǽd*—O.H.G. *drāt* (Ger. *draht*), O.N. *thrathr*, f. O.Teut. root *thræ-*. THROW. A fine cord; yarn; the spiral ridge on a screw.—*vt.* To put a thread in (a needle); to string on a thread; to pick (one's way); to pick one's way through.—**Thread'bare**, *n.* Having the nap worn off, well-worn.
Threat, *n.* O.E. *thréat*. Cf. Ger. *ver-driessen*, to vex. Cogn. with L. *trūdĕre*, to thrust, push. A declaration of intention to punish or hurt.—**Threat'**EN,[2] *vt.* To use threats against; to presage; to appear likely *to do*.
Three, *a.* and *n.* O.E. *thrí*, *thrío*, *thréo*. Common. Teut. and Indo-European. Cogn. with Skr. *trayas*, G. *treis*, L. *trēs*. TRINITY. The cardinal number next after two.—**Three'**FOLD, *a.* Three times as great or numerous; triple.—*adv.* Triply.
Threne, *n.* G. *thrēnos*, funeral lament. A song of lamentation, a dirge.—**Thren'ody**, *n.* G. *thrēnōidia*, f. *thrēnos* + *ōidē*, song. ODE. The same.—**Thren'od**IST, *n.*
Thresh'old, *n.* O.E. *therscold*, *threxold*, &c. = O.N. *threskjöldr*. The first element gen. identified with *thresh* in its orig. sense. THRASH. Second doubtful. The piece of stone or wood below the bottom of a door.
Thrice, *adv.* M.E. *thriës*, *thryës*, f. earlier *thrië*, *thryë* (O.E. *thriwa*, thrice, f. *thrí*, THREE), with *s* of advbl. genit. Three times.
Thrift, *n.* THRIVE + formative suff. *-t*. Frugality.—**Thrift'**LESS, *a.*—**Thrift'**Y,[2] *a.*
Thrill, *vt.* Alteration of *Thirl* (now dial.), to pierce—O.E. *thyrlian*, f. *thýr(e)l*, for **thyrhil*, **thurh-il*, hole, f. *thurh*, THROUGH. Formerly, to pierce. To send a quiver of emotion through.—*vi.* To produce or feel a thrill.—*n.* A quiver of emotion; a throbbing.
Thrive, *vi.* M.E. *thrive*—O.N. *thrífa-sk*, to thrive, refl. of *thrífa*, recorded in sense 'to clutch, grasp' (hence perh. 'to brace oneself', 'to make a (successful) effort'). THRIFT. To grow or develop well; to prosper, be fortunate.
Throat, *n.* M.E. *throte*—O.E. *throte*, *throtu* = O.H.G. *drozza*, app. cogn. with O.E. *thrútian*, O.N. *thrútna*, to swell. (Perh. the name had reference to the external appearance of the throat.) THROTTLE. The front of the neck; the gullet or windpipe.
Throb, *vi.* App. imitative. No cognate in Teut. or Romanic. Of the heart, to beat strongly; to quiver.—*n.* A throbbing.
Throe, *n.* M.E. *throwe*. Orig. obscure. A violent spasm or pang.—*vi.* To suffer throes.
Throne, *n.* O.F. *trone*—L. *thronus*—G. *thronos*, seat, throne. A seat of state, esp. that of a king.—*vt.* To place on a throne.
Throng, *n.* M.E. *thrang*, *throng*, prob. shortened f. O.E. *gethrang*, f. *thringan* (a common Teut. verb), to press, crowd. Cf. Ger. *drang*. A crowd.—*vt.* and *i.* To crowd.
Thros'tle, *n.* O.E. *throstle*. Cf. M.H.G. *drostel*. Prob. cogn. with L. *turdus*. The song-thrush.
Throt'tle, *n.* In form a dim. of THROAT. Cf. Ger. *drossel*, dim. of O.H.G. *drozza*. The throat.—*vt.* Perh. f. THROAT + formative suff. *-le*. (App. not f. the *n.*, which appears much later.) To choke, strangle.
Through, *prep.* O.E. *thurh*. Common W. Germanic. NOSTRIL. THOROUGH. THRILL. From end to end of; all over, everywhere in; by means of; by reason of.—*adv.* From end to end; all the way; to the end.—**Throughout'**, *prep.* In O.E. two words, *thurh* and *út*, OUT. Through the whole of, in every part of.—*adv.* Through the whole, in every part.
Throw, *vt.* O.E. *thráwan*, to turn, twist, corresp. to M.Du. *draeien*, M.H.G. *dræjen* (Ger. *drehen*). O.Teut. root *thræ-*, pre-Teut. *trē-*, *ter-*, to turn. Cogn. with G. *teirein*, L. *terĕre*, to rub. THREAD. To twist (silk) into thread; to fling, project; to prostrate.—*n.* An act of throwing; distance of throwing.
Thrum, *n.* M.E. *thrum*, *throm*—O.E. *thrum* (in combination) = M.Du. *drom*, O.H.G., *drum*, end-piece, remnant. Cogn. with G. *terma*, L. *terminus*, end. The end of a warp-thread left on the loom when the web is cut off.
Thrum, *vi.* Imitative. STRUM. To pluck the strings of an instrument, to strum.
Thrush, *n.*[1] O.E. *thrýsce*, later *thryssce*. Orig. obscure. A well-known bird.
Thrush, *n.*[2] Orig. obscure. A disease, chiefly of infants; a disease of the horse.
Thrust, *vt.* Early M.E. *thrusten*, *thrysten*—O.N. *thrýsta*, poss. cogn. with L. *trūdĕre*. THREAT. To push, force; to put forth.—*vi.* To push one's way; to make a thrust.—*n.* A thrusting; a lunge or stab with a weapon.
Thud, *n.* App. imitative. A dull heavy sound.—*vi.* To produce a thud.
Thumb, *n.* O.E. *thúma* = O.Fris. *thûma*, O.H.G. *dûmo* (Ger. *daumen*). Cogn. with G. *tulos*, lump, L. *tumēre*, to swell. THIMBLE. TUMID. The short thick digit of the hand.—*vt.* To handle or soil with the thumb.

Thump, *vi.* and *i.* Imitative. To strike heavily.—*n.* A heavy dull blow; the sound.

Thun'der, *n.* M.E. *thoner*, &c.—O.E. *thunor* = O.H.G. *donnar* (Ger. *donner*), O.N. *thórr*. Cogn. with L. *tonāre*, to thunder. ASTONISH. DETONATE. THURSDAY. The loud noise accompanying lightning.—*vi. It thunders*, thunder sounds; to utter denunciation.—*vt.* To utter (violent threats).—**Thun'derbolt**, *n.* A bolt or dart formerly supposed to accompany a lightning-flash.—**Thun'der**OUS, *a.*

Thu'rible, *n.* L. *t(h)ūribulum*, f. *t(h)ūs*, *t(h)ūris*, incense. A censer.—**Thu'rifer**, *n.* L. *t(h)ūrifer*, incense-bearing, f. *t(h)ūs*+*ferre*, to BEAR. One who carries a thurible.

Thurs'day, *n.* O.E. *thunresdæg*, DAY of Thunor or Thor, god of THUNDER. The fifth day of the week.

Thus, *adv.* O.E. *thus* = O.S. *thus*, M.Du. *dus*, app. f. the dem. stem of THAT or THIS. In this way; as follows; therefore.

Thwack, *vt.* App. imitative. To beat vigorously, whack.—*n.* A vigorous stroke.

Thwart, *adv.* Early M.E. *thwert*, a.—O.N. *thvert*, adv., orig. neut. of *thverr*, transverse, cross. Cf. O.H.G. *twer* (Ger. *quer*). Cogn. with L. *torquēre*, to twist. TORMENT. Across. —*a.* Transverse, cross; obstinate; adverse.—*vt.* From the *adv.* To frustrate.—*n.* App. f. the *adv.* and *a.* A seat across a boat.

Thy, *pron.* Early M.E. *thī*, reduced form of *thīn*, THINE. Belonging to thee.

Thyme, *n.* F. *thym*—L. *thymum*—G. *thumon*, f. *thuein*, to burn sacrifice. A shrubby herb with aromatic leaves.

Thyr'sus, *n.* G. *thursos*. TORSO. A staff wreathed with ivy and vine-leaves borne by the votaries of Dionysus (Bacchus).

Tia'ra, *n.* L. *tiāra*—G. *tiara*. A kind of turban; a diadem worn by the pope; a jewelled ornament worn above the forehead.

Tib'ia, *n.* L. *tibia*. The inner bone of the lower leg, the shin-bone.

Tic, *n.* F. *tic*, of uncertain orig. A spasmodic twitching of the muscles of the face.

Tick, *n.*[1] Poss. shortened f. *teke*, corresp. to M.L.G. *tēke*, Du. *teek*. Orig. uncertain. A mite infesting the hair or fur of various animals.

Tick, *n.*[2] Earlier *tikke*, *tēke*, *tyke*, app. ultimately f. L. *thēca*, G. *thēkē*, case, sheath. The covering or case of a mattress or pillow.

Tick, *n.*[3] Perh. imitative. Cf. Du. *tik*, a pat, tick, L.G. *tikk*, a touch. A quick, light, distinct sound; a small dot or dash.—*vi.* To make a tick.—*vt.* To mark with a tick.

Tick, *n.*[4] App. abb. of TICKET in obs. sense 'promise to pay', 'score', in phrase *on (the) ticket*, on credit. Credit, trust.

Tick'et, *n.* Obs. F. *etiquet*, a little note, a notice, O.F. *estiquet*, f. *estiquer*, to stick, fix—O.L.G. *stekan* = O.H.G. *stehhan*. ETIQUETTE. A label; a slip of cardboard, &c., bearing evidence of right to a service, &c.—*vt.* To label.

Tick'le, *vi.* Of obscure orig. To tingle, to itch.—*vt.* To touch lightly so as to cause a feeling of tickling; to amuse.—**Tick'l**ISH, *a.* Easily tickled; risky.

Tide, *n.* O.E. *tíd*, time, season = O.H.G. *zit* (Ger. *zeit*), O.N. *títh*, referred by some to root *ti-*. TIME. A time or season; the recurrent rising and falling of the sea; a stream.—*vi.* To drift with the tide; *to tide over*, to get over or surmount.—*vt.* To enable (a person, &c.) to do this.—**Ti'dings**, *n.pl.* Prob. f. O.N. *títhendi*, events, news, f. *títhr*, happening, f. *títh*. News, intelligence.—**Ti'dy**, *a.* M.E., f. *tíd*+-Y.[2] Formerly, timely, opportune. Pretty good; keeping things neat and in order; neat, in order.—*vt.* To put in order.

Tie, *vt.* O.E. *tígan*, f. *téag*, *teáh* = O.N. *taug*, rope, f. stem *teuh-*, *tauh-*, *tug-* (*tog-*), to draw, cogn. with L. *dūcĕre*, to lead. TEAM. TOW, *v.* TUG. To bind, fasten; to restrict.—*n.* O.E. *teáh*, *téag*. That with which anything is tied; a cravat; a restraint; a bond of union; a drawn match; a deciding match.

Tier, *n.* Orig. *tire*—F. *tire*, in O.F. range, rank, order, f. *tirer*, to draw, of unknown orig. ATTIRE. TIRADE. A row, range, rank, course.

Tierce, *n.* O.F. *tierce*, fem. of *tierz* (F. *tiers*) —L. *tertius*, third. TERTIAN. An old measure equal to one third of a pipe.

Ti'ger, *n.* O.F. *tigre*—L. *tigris*—G. *tigris*, an Oriental word. A large carnivorous feline quadruped; a boy in livery.—**Ti'gr**ESS, *n.*

Tight, *a.* App. an altered form of dial. *Thight*, dense, app. f. early O.N. **théhtr*, later *thettr*, water-tight, solid, corresp. to M.Du., M.L.G., Ger. *dicht*. Impervious to water, &c.; firmly fixed; tense; fitting closely.—**Tight'**EN,[2] *vt.* and *i.*—**Tights**, *n.pl.* Tight-fitting breeches; tight-fitting thin elastic garments.

Tike, Tyke, *n.* M.E. *tike*—O.N. *tík*. A low-bred dog, a cur; a low or rough fellow.

Tile, *n.* O.E. *tigule*, *tigele*—W. Germanic *tegala*—L. *tēgula*, f. *tegĕre*, to cover. DETECT. A thin slab of baked clay.—*vt.* To cover with tiles; to keep secret, to bind to secrecy.

Till, *n.* Orig. obscure. A money-drawer.

Till, *vt.* O.E. *tilian*, to strive, acquire = O.S *tilian*, to acquire, O.H.G. *zilôn*, to strive (Ger *zielen*, to aim, strive). TILL, *prep.* To cultivate.—**Til'l**AGE, *n.*—**Til'l**ER, *n.*[1]—**Tilth**, *n.* O.E. *tilth*. Cultivation.

Till, *prep.* O.Northumb. *til*—O.N. *til*, prob. orig. a n. = O.E. *till*, fixed point, station, O.H.G. *zil*, Ger. *ziel*, end, limit, goal, and cogn. with O.E. *tilian*. TILL, *v.* UNTIL. Up to the time of.—*conj.* To the time that; so that at length; with negative, before.

Til'ler, *n.*[2] O.F. *telier*, *tellier*, stock of a cross-bow, orig., a weaver's beam—Med.L. *tēlārium*, f. L. *tēla*, web. TOIL, *n.*[2] The handle of a rudder.

Tilt, *n.*[1] Collateral form of M.E. *tild*—O.E. *teld*, tent = O.H.G., Ger. *zelt*, O.N. *tjald*. An awning; a cover for a cart or waggon.

Tilt, *vt.* M.E. *tylten*, to fall, to cause to fall—O.E. **tyltan* for **tieltan*, f. *tealt*, unsteady, of obscure orig. To slope, slant; to pour out by tilting a vessel.—*vi.* To slope, slant; to engage in a tilt (in this sense f. the *n.* in the first sense).—*n.*[2] From the *v.* in sense 'to cause to fall'. A combat of two mounted men with lances. From the *v.* in the first sense. Slope.

Tim'ber, *n.* O.E. *timber*, a building, house, building material = O.H.G. *zimbar* (Ger. *zimmer*), room, O.N. *timbr*, timber. Cogn. with G. *demein*, to build, L. *domus*, house. DOME. Wood for building; a beam.

Tim'bre, *n.* F. *timbre*, bell, timbre, in O.F. in sense 'timbrel'—L. *tympanum*. TYMPANUM. The quality of a musical sound.

Tim'brel, *n.* App. f. obs. *Timbre* in same sense (O.F. *timbre* (see prec.)) + dim. suff. *-el*. A kind of tambourine.

Time, *n.* O.E. *tíma* = O.N. *tími*, app. f. a root *ti-*, to stretch, extend. TIDE. A space of continued existence; a period; leisure; the rate of musical movement; a point in duration, an occasion; the due time; opportunity; each occasion of a recurring action; finite duration.—*vt.* To choose the time of; to note the time taken in (a race, &c.).—**Time′**LY,[1] *a.* Seasonable, opportune.—**Time′piece,** *n.* An instrument for measuring time.

Tim′id, *a.* L. *timidus,* f. *timēre,* to fear. INTIMIDATE. Lacking courage, easily frightened.—**Timid′**ITY, *n.*—**Tim′orous,** *a.* = O.F. *temeros, -ous,* Med.L. *timōrōsus,* f. *timor,* fear, f. *timēre.* Timid.

Tin, *n.* O.E. *tin* = O.H.G. *zin* (Ger. *zinn*), O.N. *tin.* A malleable white metal; a vessel of tin or tinned iron.—*vt.* To coat with tin; to put in a tin.

Tinc′ture, *n.* L. *tinctūra,* a dyeing, tinging, f. *tingĕre, tinctum,* to dye, colour. MEZZOTINT. TAINT. TINGE. TINT. Colour, a tint; a trace or flavour; a solution of a medicinal substance.—*vt.* To colour, tinge; to imbue.

Tin′der, *n.* O.E. *tynder,* f. *tund-,* weak grade of O.Teut. root *tind-,* to kindle. Cf. Du. *tonder,* O.N. *tundr.* A dry substance readily taking fire from a spark.

Tinge, *vt.* L. *tingĕre.* TINCTURE. To colour or flavour slightly.—*n.* A trace of colour, &c.

Ting′le, *vi.* App. a modification of TINKLE. Of the ears, to ring; to thrill, vibrate.

Tin′ker, *n.* Orig. uncertain. A mender of pots, &c.—*vi.* and *t.* To work *at* or mend clumsily.

Tink′le, *vi.* App. a freq. of obs. *Tink,* to clink, chink, tingle, of imitative orig. Cf. E. Fris. *tinken.* To give forth a series of short, light, sharp ringing sounds.—*vt.* To cause to tinkle.—*n.* An act or the action of tinkling.

Tin′sel, *n.* O.F. *estincelle.* STENCIL. Thin glittering metallic plates; anything showy.

Tint, *n.* App. altered f. earlier *Tinct* in sim. sense—L. *tinctus,* a dyeing, f. *tingĕre.* TINCTURE. A colour or hue, usually slight or delicate, a tinge.—*vt.* To impart a tint to.

Tintinnabula′tion, *n.* N. of action f. L. *tintinnābulum,* bell. The sound of bells.

Tiny, *a.* App. f. obs. *Tine* in sim. sense, of unknown orig. + -Y.[2] Very small.

Tip, *n.*[1] = M.Du., M.L.G. *tip,* M.H.G. *zipf,* point, extreme end. The slender extremity of a thing; a piece of metal protecting a tip.—*v.*[1]*t.* To protect with a tip.—**Tip′staff,** *n.* Contraction of *tipped* or *tipt staff.* An official carrying a tipped staff, a sheriff's officer, the usher of a court.—**Tip-top,** *n.* App. *tip* + TOP. The very top.—*a.* The very highest.

Tip, *v.*[2]*t.* Agrees with Du., L.G., Ger. *tippen,* Sw. *tippa,* of obscure orig. To strike smartly but lightly.—*n.*[2] Perh. f. this *v.* with the notion of tipping the arm or elbow by way of a hint. A piece of useful private information; a device or dodge.

Tip, *v.*[3]*t.* Orig. rogues' cant of obscure orig. To give, let one have; to give a small money present to.—*n.*[3] A small money present.

Tip, *v.*[4]*t.* Orig. obscure. To upset; to tilt; to empty out by tilting.—*vi.* To topple *over*; to tilt.—*n.*[4] A place where carts are tipped; tipped rubbish, &c.

Tip′pet, *n.* Orig. uncertain. A covering for the shoulders or the neck and shoulders.

Tip′ple, *vi.* Orig. uncertain. To take strong drink habitually.—*vt.* To drink (intoxicating liquor), esp. often and in small quantities.—*n.* Drink, esp. strong drink.

Tip′sy, *a.* App. f. TIP, *v.*[4] in sense 'to topple over'. Cf. *tricksy.* Partly intoxicated.

Tirade′, *n.* F. *tirade,* draught, pull, shot, declamation, passage of verse or prose—It. *tirata,* a pulling, a volley, &c., f. pa.pple. of *tirare* = F. *tirer,* to draw, to shoot. TIER. A long vehement (generally hostile) speech.

Tire, *n.*[1] Shortened f. ATTIRE. Attire; a head-dress.—*v.*[1]*t.* To dress (the hair or head).

Tire, *n.*[2], **Tyre.** Prob. the same as prec., the tire being regarded as the 'clothing' of the wheel. A rim of metal round a wheel; a cushion of rubber, &c., on a rim.

Tire, *v.*[2]*i.* O.E. *tíorian, téorian,* of unknown orig. To become fatigued; to become weary *of.*—*vt.* To fatigue.—**Tire′**SOME, *a.*

Ti′ro, Ty′ro, *n.* L. *tīro,* young soldier, recruit. A beginner, a novice.

Tis′sue, *n.* O.F. *tissu,* f. pa.pple. of *tistre,* L. *texĕre,* to weave. TEXT. Any fine woven fabric; the substance of an animal, &c., body.—**Tis′sue-pa′per,** *n.* Very thin paper.

Tit, *n.* App. imitative. Cf. Norw. dial. *titta,* little girl, Icel. *tittr,* little plug, titmouse. A small horse; in combination in the names of small birds, as TITLARK, TITMOUSE, TOMTIT.

Titan′ic, *a.* G. *titanikos,* f. *Titanes,* the Titans, a race of gods subdued by Zeus. Like a Titan, gigantic, huge.

Tit′-bit, Tid′-bit, *n.* Orig. *tyd bit, tid-bit,* f. dial. *Tyd, Tid,* nice, delicate, of unknown orig. + BIT. A nice or toothsome morsel.

Tithe, *n.* M.E. *tīthe, tythe*—O.E. *teogotha, téotha,* forms of the ordinal of TEN. A tenth part of annual agricultural produce (gen. in *pl.*); a tenth part.—*a.* App. revived f. the *n.* Tenth.—*vt.* To exact tithes from.

Tit′illate, *vt.* L. *tītillāre, tītillātum,* to tickle. To excite or stimulate as by tickling to excite agreeably.—**Titill**A′TION, *n.*

Tit′lark, *n.* TIT + LARK.[1] A bird like a lark.

Ti′tle, *n.* O.F. *title*—L. *titulus,* superscription, inscription. TITTLE. A heading; the name of a book; a name, appellation; just claim; legal right, the evidence thereof.

Tit′mouse, *n.*; *pl.* (by confusion with the unrelated *mouse*) **Tit′mice.** M.E. *titmōse,* f. TIT + obs. *Mose,* titmouse—O.E. *máse,* a name for several small birds. Cf. Du. *mees,* Ger. *meise,* titmouse. A small active bird. (Commonly shortened to *tit.*)

Tit′ter, *vi.* App. imitative. To laugh in a suppressed or covert way.—*n.* Such a laugh.

Tit′tle, *n.* M.E. *titel, titil,* orig. the same as TITLE, but with the L.L. sense of *titulus,* 'a little stroke or mark over a letter'. A whit.

Tit′tle-tattle, *n.* Reduplicated f. TATTLE. Petty gossip.—*vi.* To gossip.

Tit′ular, *a.* L. type **titulāris,* f. *titulus.* TITLE. Held in virtue of a title; existing, that is such, in name only.—**Tit′ular**LY,[2] *adv.*

To, *prep.* O.E. *tó* = O.S. *tō* (Du. *toe*), O.H.G. *zō, zuo, zua* (Ger. *zu*). INTO. UNTO. In the direction of; as far as; indicating comparison, ratio, &c.; introducing an indirect object; the sign of the infinitive mood.—*adv.* To the normal or required position or state; *to and* FRO, backwards and forwards.

Toad, *n.* O.E. *tádige.* Orig. unknown. An animal like a frog.—**Toad′-eater,** *n.* Orig. one who ate or pretended to eat toads (held poisonous) that a charlatan, his master, might show skill in expelling poison. A fawning parasite, a sycophant.—**Toad′stool,** *n.* A kind of fungus.—**Toad′**Y,[2] *a.* Toad-like; infested with toads.—*n.* Perh. a use of the *a.* A toad-eater.—*vt.* From the *n.* To fawn servilely upon.

Toast, *vt.* O.F. *toster,* to roast or grill—L. *torrēre, tostum,* to parch, scorch, burn. THIRST. TORRENT. TORRID. To brown at the fire; to warm; to drink in honour of (in this sense f.

the *n.*).—*n.* A slice of bread browned at the fire; bread so browned; a person, orig. a lady, whose health is drunk (the lady's name being supposed to flavour the drink like a spiced toast); the call or act of proposing a health.

Tobac'co, *n.* Sp. *tabaco*, taken f. the language of Hayti. (Said to have meant a pipe.) A plant the leaves of which are used for smoking; the leaves prepared for smoking.—**Tobac'co**NIST, *n.* A dealer in tobacco.

Tobog'gan, *n.* From a Canadian Indian name for a sledge. A light sledge for sliding down a slope of snow.—*vi.* To slide thus.

Toc'sin, *n.* F. *tocsin*, O.F. *toquesin*, &c.—Pr. *tocasenh*, f. *tocar* (F. *toucher*), to TOUCH, strike + *senh*, call of a bell, bell—L. *signum*, SIGN, in L.L. also bell. An alarm-signal on a bell.

To-day', *adv.* O.E. *tó daeg*, TO, *prep.* (in former sense 'at (a time)', 'on (a day)') + DAY. On this day.—*n.* This day.

Tod'dle, *vi.* Originally Scotch and N.Eng. Orig. obscure. To go with short unsteady steps; to saunter, stroll.—*n.* A toddling.

Tod'dy, *n.* Hind. *tāri*, *tādī*, f. *tār*, palm. The sap of palm-trees as a beverage; a sweetened mixture of whisky, &c., and hot water.

Toe, *n.* O.E. *tá* = O.H.G. *zêha* (Ger. *zeh*, *zehe*), O.N. *tá*. Each of the digits of the foot.—*vt.* To touch, reach, kick with the toe.

Tof'fee, **Tof'fy**, *n.* Orig. uncertain. A sweetmeat made of sugar boiled with butter.

Togeth'er, *adv.* O.E. *tógædere*, f. *tó*, TO + *geador*, together, whence *gad(e)rian*, to GATHER. Into or in company or conjunction; simultaneously; continuously.

Toil, *vi.* A.F. *toiler*, to strive, wrangle = O.F. *toeillier*, &c., to stir up, agitate, perh. f. L. *tudiculāre*, to stir, f. *tudicula*, a machine for bruising olives. To strive, labour arduously.—*n.*[1] A heavy task; labour.—**Toil'**SOME, *a.*

Toil, *n.*[2] F. *toile*, cloth, in *pl.*, toils—L. *tēla*, web, prob. conn. with *texĕre*, to weave. TEXT. SUBTLE. TILLER.[2] A net or system of nets for catching game (us. in *pl.*).

Toi'let, *n.* F. *toilette*, dim. of *toile*. (See prec.) A cover for a dressing-table; the articles used in dressing; the process of dressing; style of dressing; a dress or costume.

Tokay', *n.* A wine of *Tokay* in Hungary.

To'ken, *n.* O.E. *tácen*, *tácn* = O.S. *têcan*, O.H.G. *zeihhan* (Ger. *zeichen*). Cogn. with O.E. *tǽc(e)an*. TEACH. A sign or evidence.

Tol'erate, *vt.* F. *tolérer*—L. *tolerāre*, to bear, endure, conn. with *tollĕre*, to lift, raise. EXTOL. To allow to exist, be practised, &c.; to endure; to put up with.—**Tol'er**ABLE, *a.* Endurable; moderately good.—**Tol'erab**LY,[2] *adv.* —**Tol'er**ANCE, *n.*—**Tol'er**ANT, *a.* Disposed to tolerate.—**Tolera'**TION, *n.*

Toll, *n.*[1] O.E. *toll* = O.H.G. *zol* (Ger. *zoll*), O.N. *tollr*, gen. referred to Pop.L. *tolōneum* for L. *telōnium*, G. *telōnion*, toll-house, f. *telos*, tax. A tax or impost, esp. for permission to pass along a road, over a bridge, &c.

Toll, *vt.* Prob. orig. particular use of dial. *Toll*, to entice, to pull—M.E. *tollen*, *tullen*, of obscure orig. To cause (a bell) to sound slowly at regular intervals; to announce (a death) by tolling, to toll for (a dead person).—*vi.* To be tolled.—*n.*[2] The act or sound of tolling.

Tom'ahawk, *n.* Renâpe (N.Amer. Indian of Virginia) *tāmāhāk*. The axe of the N.Amer. Indians.—*vt.* To strike or kill with this.

Tomat'o, *n.* F. *tomate*, or Sp., Pg. *tomate*—Mexican *tomatl*. The fleshy fruit of a plant a native of tropical America; the plant.

Tomb, *n.* Early M.E. *toumbe*, *tumbe*—A.F. *tumbe*, O.F. *tombe*—L.L. *tumba*—G. *tumbos*, sepulchral mound. A grave; a sepulchral monument.—*vt.* To bury.

Tom'boy, *n.* *Tom*, familiar shortening of *Thomas* + BOY. A wild romping girl.

Tom cat, **Tom-cat**, *n.* *Tom* (see prec.) + CAT. A male cat.

Tome, *n.* F. *tome*—L. *tomus*, G. *tomos*, volume, section of a book, conn. with *temnein*, to cut. A volume, a large book.

To-mor'row, *adv.* M.E., f. *to morwen*, TO (as in TO-DAY) + *morwen*, MORN. For or on the day after to-day.—*n.* The day after to-day.

Tom-tit, **Tomtit**, *n.* *Tom* (as in TOMBOY) + TIT. A species of titmouse.

Ton, *n.* In orig. the same as TUN. A unit of a ship's carrying capacity (orig. the space occupied by a tun of wine); a measure of weight, 20 cwt.—**Ton'n**AGE, *n.* A charge per ton; carrying capacity; ships collectively.

Tone, *n.* F. *ton*—L. *tonus*—G. *tonos*, a stretching, pitch of the voice, musical mode, conn. with *teinein*, to stretch. INTONATE. TUNE. A musical sound in relation to its quality; a fixed interval between notes; quality of voice; healthy condition; prevailing character; a quality of colour.—*vt.* To impart a tone to.—**Ton'**IC, *a.* Improving bodily tone; relating to tone.—*n.* A tonic medicine.

Tongs, *n.pl.* O.E. *tang*, *tange*, sing. = O.H.G. *zanga* (Ger. *zange*), O.N. *tōng*. Prob. cogn. with G. *daknein*, to bite. A double instrument for grasping objects.

Tongue, *n.* M.E., O.E. *tunge* = O.S. *tunga*, O.H.G. *zunga* (Ger. *zunge*). Prob. cogn. with L. *lingua*. LINGUAL. The organ of taste and speech; language; a language.

To-night', *adv.* O.E. *tó niht*, TO (as in TO-DAY) + NIGHT. On this night; on the night following this day.—*n.* This night; the night following this day.

Ton'sil, *n.* L. *tonsillae*, pl. Either of the glands on each side of the throat.

Ton'sure, *n.* L. *tonsūra*, a shearing or clipping, f. *tondēre*, *tonsum*, to shear, clip. The shaving of the head or part of it as a religious rite; the part shaved.—*vt.* To give tonsure to.

Tontine', *n.* F. *tontine*, f. *Tonti*, a Neapolitan banker, the inventor. An annuity paid to subscribers or the survivors or survivor.

Too, *adv.* Stressed form of TO, *prep.* In addition; in excess, more than enough.

Tool, *n.* O.E. *tól* = O.N. *tól*, pl. O.Teut. root *tōw-*, to prepare, make. A mechanical implement.—*vt.* To work on with a tool.

Toot, *vi.* App. imitative. Cf. Du. *tuyten*, *toeten*, Ger. *tuten*, to blow a horn. To sound a horn, &c.; of a horn, &c., to sound.—*vt.* To sound (a horn, &c.).—*n.* An act of tooting.

Tooth, *n.*; *pl.* **Teeth**. O.E. *tóth*. Common Teut. and Indo-European. Cogn. with Skr. *danta*, G. *odous*, *odontos*, L. *dens*, *dentis*. MASTODON. DENTAL. One of the hard processes of the jaws; various projections like these.—**Tooth'**SOME, *a.* Pleasant to eat.

Top, *n.*[1] O.E. *top*. Common W. Germanic and Norse. The highest point, part, position, &c.; a platform on a ship's mast.—*vt.* To cut off the top of; to put a top on; to exceed in height, &c., to surpass; to reach the top of.

Top, *n.*[2] M.E. *top* (app. also in late O.E.). Orig. obscure. A toy made to spin on a point.

To'paz, *n.* O.F. *topaze*—L. *topazus*—G. *topazos*, a foreign word. A precious stone.

Tope, *vt.* and *i.* Poss. conn. with obs. *Tope*, int., an exclamation in drinking, app. = 'I pledge you', gen. derived f. F. *top, tope* (said to be for *je* (I) *tope*, f. *toper*, to accept a wager) = It. *toppa*, 'done!'. To drink copiously and habitually.—**To'per**, *n.*

Top'ic, *n.* L. *topica* = G. (*ta*) *topika* (neut. pl. of *topikos*, a. f. *topos*, place, commonplace), '(the) Topics', lit. 'matters concerning commonplaces', the title of a work of Aristotle. UTOPIAN. A subject or matter of discourse, &c.—**Top'ical**, *a.* Of the topics of the day.

Topog'raphy, *n.* L.L. *topographia* — G. *topographia*, f. *topos* (see prec.) + *-graphia*, writing, f. *graphein*, to write. A description of a place; its features collectively.—**Topog'rapher**, *n.*—**Topograph'ic**, -**ical**, *aa.*

Top'ple, *vi.* TOP[1] + freq. suff. *-le.* To totter and fall—*vt.* To cause to do so.

Top'sy-tur'vy, *adv.* App. the first element contains TOP.[1] The second may be conn. with obs. *Tirve, Terve*, to turn, turn over, app. repg. an O.E. **tierfan*. (Cf. O.E. *tearflian*, to wallow.) Upside down; in disorder.

Torch, *n.* O.F. *torche*, by some referred to Pop.L. **torca*, f. stem of *torquēre*. (See next.) A portable light of twisted hemp, &c.

Tor'ment, *n.* O.F. *torment*—L. *tormentum* (**torqu(e)mentum*), an engine for hurling missiles, an instrument of torture, torture, f. *torquēre, tortum*, to twist. TORSION. TORT. TORTUOUS. TORTURE. Great suffering, bodily or mental; a source of suffering or of worry.—**Torment'**, *vt.* To afflict, distress.

Torna'do, *n.* Orig. *ternado*, prob. adapted f. Sp. *tronado*, thunderstorm (f. *tronar*, L. *tonāre*, to THUNDER), and associated with *tornar*, to turn. A whirlwind, a hurricane.

Torpe'do, *n.* L. *torpēdo*, numbness, the fish, f. *torpēre*, to be numb. A flat fish which emits electric discharges; a self-propelled submarine explosive missile.—*vt.* To destroy with a torpedo.—**Tor'pid**, *a.* L. *torpidus*. Benumbed, dormant; sluggish.—**Torpid'ity**, *n.*—**Tor'por**, *n.* L. *torpor*. Torpid state.

Tor'rent, *n.* F. *torrent*—L. *torrens, torrentis*, burning, boiling, rushing, as *n.*, a torrent, pres.pple. of *torrēre*. TOAST. A swift and impetuous stream.—**Torren'tial**, *a.*

Tor'rid, *a.* L. *torridus*, f. *torrēre*. TOAST. Scorched, burned; scorching, hot.

Tor'sion, *n.* Through F. f. L.L. *torsio, torsiōnis*, by-form of *tortio*, n. of action f. L. *torquēre*. TORMENT. The action of twisting.

Tor'so, *n.* It., stalk, trunk of a statue—L. *thyrsus*, stalk, stem, the thyrsus—G. *thursos*, THYRSUS. The trunk of a statue.

Tort, *n.* O.F. *tort*, Med.L. *tortum*, wrong, use as *n.* of neut. pa.pple. of L. *torquēre*. TORMENT. A breach of legal duty.

Tor'toise, *n.* Late Pop.L. *tortūca*, believed to be a deriv. of L. *tortus*, twisted (pa.pple. of *torquēre*. TORMENT), referring to the crooked feet of one of the species. TURTLE.[2] A four-footed reptile covered with horny plates.

Tor'tuous, *a.* A.F. *tortuous* = F. *tortueux*—L. *tortuōsus*, f. *tortus*, a twisting, f. *torquēre*. TORMENT. Winding; not straightforward.

Tor'ture, *n.* F. *torture*—L. *tortūra*, f. *torquēre*. TORMENT. The infliction of excruciating pain.—*vt.* To subject to torture.

To'ry, *n.* Ir. **tóraidhe*, pursuer, f. *tóir*, to pursue. Orig., a dispossessed Irish outlaw living by plunder. The name of that one of the two great political parties which is now represented (more or less) by the Conservatives.

Toss, *vt.* Orig. uncertain. Cf. Norw. and Sw. dial. *tossa*, to spread, strew. To throw about; to disturb, disorder; to cast, fling; to throw into the air; to jerk up.—*vi.* To fling oneself about, be flung about.—*n.* An act of tossing.

Tot, *n.*[1] Orig. uncertain. A tiny child; a minute quantity; a very small thing.

Tot, *n.*[2] Short for TOTAL. An addition sum. —*vt.* To add *up*.—*vi.* With *up*, to amount to.

To'tal, *a.* F. *total*—Scholastic L. *tōtālis*, f. L. *tōtus*, entire. Complete, absolute.—*n.* The whole amount.—*vt.* To amount to; to add up. —**Total'ity**, *n.* Entirety; the total, a whole.

To'tem, *n.* From some N. American Indian dialect. Among these Indians, the hereditary emblem or badge of a tribe or group, consisting of the figure of an animal, plant, &c., after which the tribe, &c., is named; extended to refer to other savage races similarly divided into tribes, &c., named after animals, &c.

Tot'ter, *vi.* In form a freq. f. a stem *tot-* expressing instability. Perh. f. Norse. Cf. Norw. dial. *tutra, totra*, Sw. dial. *tuttra*, to quiver. To be about to fall; to walk unsteadily.

Touch, *vt.* O.F. *tochier, tuchier* (F. *toucher*, to touch) = Sp., Pg., *tocar*, It. *toccare*, to strike, hit, touch. Perh. imitative f. *toc* imitating a knock. To put the hand, &c., on; to come into or be in contact with; to reach; to move the feelings of.—*vi.* Of a ship, to call *at*; with *on, upon*, to refer or allude to.—*n.* A touching; the sense by which contact is perceived; a slight blow; a slight stroke with a pencil, &c.; a trace or smack; artistic manner.—**Touch'-stone**, *n.* A kind of stone used for testing gold and silver.—**Touch'wood**, *n.* Wood or a woody substance used as tinder.

Touch'y, *a.* Perh. an alteration of TETCHY. Short-tempered, irritable, tetchy.

Tough, *a.* O.E. *tóh*. Cf. Du. *taai*, Ger. *zähe*. Pliable, and not brittle; sturdy; stubborn; difficult, trying.—**Tough'en**,[2] *vt.* and *i.*

Tour, *n.* F. *tour*—L. *tornus*. TURN. A travelling round from place to place.—*vi.* To make a tour.—*vt.* To tour in.—**Tour'ist**, *n.* One who makes a pleasure-tour.

Tour'nament, *n.* O.F. *tournoiement*, f. *tournoier*, to engage in a tournament—L. *tornāre*. TURN. A meeting for knightly sports; a series of contests of skill.

Tour'niquet, *n.* F. *tourniquet*, deriv. of *tourner*, to turn—L. *tornāre*. TURN. A bandage with a tightening device for stopping the flow of blood.

Tous'le, *vt.* With freq. suff. *-le* f. obs. *Touse*, prob. repg. an O.E. **túsian*, cogn. with M.H.G. *erzûsen, erzousen* (Ger. *zausen*) in sim. sense. TUSSLE. To pull about roughly; to disorder.

Tout, *vi.* App. repg. an O.E. **tútian* = *tótian*, to stick out, hence, to peep out, of obscure orig. To solicit custom.—*n.* One who does this.

Tow, *n.* Orig. doubtful. Perh. conn. with O.N. *tó*, uncleansed wool or flax. Coarse and broken fibre of flax or hemp.

Tow, *vt.* O.E. *togian*, to pull, drag = O.H.G. *zogôn*, O.N. *toga*, f. *tog-*. TIE. To draw a vessel by a rope.—*n.* A towing, a being towed; a vessel in tow.—**Tow'age**, *n.*

Tow'ard, *a.* O.E. *tóweard*, f. TO, *prep.* + -WARD. Docile.—Sim. **Tow'ardly**,[1] *a.*

Toward', *prep.* O.E. *tóweard*. (See prec.) Orig. the uninflected form or neut. sing. of the *a.* Also **Towards'**. -WARDS. In the direction of; in relation to, as regards; shortly before; by way of contribution to; for.

Tow'el, *n.* O.F. *toaile* (F. *touaille*), f. Teut. Cf. O.H.G. *dwahilla*, f. *dwahan*, O.E. *thwéan*, to wash. A cloth for wiping dry after washing.
Tow'er, *n.* O.F. *tor, tur* (F. *tour*)—L. *turris*. TURRET. A tall square or circular structure; a fortress.—*vi.* To rise aloft, stand high.
Town, *n.* O.E. *tuun, tún*, enclosed place, homestead, hamlet = O.H.G. *zûn* (Ger. *zaun*), hedge, fence, L.G. *tuun*, hedge, fence, enclosed place. An inhabited place larger than a village; the capital.—**Town'ship**, *n.* O.E. *túnscipe*. -SHIP. Each of the divisions of a large parish, each containing a village or town.
Tox'ic, *a.* Med.L. *toxicus*, poisoned, f. L. *toxicum*, poison—G. *toxikon* (*pharmakon*), (a preparation, poison) for smearing arrows, also *toxikon* alone in sense 'poison', neut. of *toxikos*, a. f. *toxon*, bow, in pl. bow and arrows. INTOXICATE. Poisonous; due to poison.—**Toxicol'**OGY, *n.* The science of poisons.
Toy, *n.* Orig. unknown. A trifle; a plaything.—*vi.* To act idly; to dally, sport.
Trace, *n.*[1] O.F. *traiz, trais*, pl. of *trait*, action of drawing, trace—L. *tractus*, draught, a track or course, a region, f. *trahĕre*, to draw. TREAT. TRACT, *n.*[2] TRAIT. (See next.) A strap or chain by which a horse draws a vehicle.
Trace, *vt.* O.F. *tracier* (F. *tracer*), pointing to a Pop.L. **tractiāre*, f. L. *tractus*. (See prec.) To follow the traces or course of; to ascertain, find out; to make a plan of; to draw.—*n.*[2] A track left by the passage of anything; an indication; a minute quantity.—**Trac'**ERY, *n.* Interlaced work, network.
Trache'a, *n.* Med.L. *trāchēa*—G. *tracheia* (*artēria* (whence ARTERY)), the rough, *i.e.* gristly (air-passage), as distinguished from the arteries (by the ancients regarded as air-passages), fem. of *trachus*, rough. The windpipe.—**Tracheot'omy**, *n.* *-tomy* = *-tomia* as in LITHOTOMY. Incision of the windpipe.
Track, *n.* O.F. *trac*, prob. of Teut. orig. Poss. conn. with M.L.G. and Du. *treck, trek*, draught, pull, line drawn, &c., f. *trecken, trekken*, to draw, pull. TRIGGER. A mark left by the passage of anything; a path; a course.—*v.*[1]*t.* To follow up the track of.
Track, *v.*[2]*t.* App. f. Du. *trekken*. (See prec.) To tow a vessel, esp. from the bank.
Tract, *n.*[1] App. abb. f. L. *tractātus*, TRACTATE. A short pamphlet.
Tract, *n.*[2] L. *tractus*. TRACE, *n.*[1] A space or extent; a region, district.
Tract'able, *a.* L. *tractābilis*, f. *tractāre*. TREAT. Easy to manage or deal with; docile.
Trac'tate, *n.* L. *tractātus*, a handling, a tractate, f. *tractāre*. TREAT. A treatise.
Trac'tion, *n.* Med.L. *tractio, tractiōnis*, n. of action f. *trahĕre*. TREAT. The action of drawing.
Trade, *n.* M.L.G. *trade*, O.S. *trada*, track = O.H.G. *trata*, track, way, passage, f. *tred-, trad-*, to TREAD. Formerly, a track; a course; a course of life. The practice of an occupation, esp. for gain; anything practised for a livelihood; those engaged in a trade; commerce, traffic.—*vi.* To resort *to* a place for trade; to engage in trade.—*vt.* To buy and sell, to barter.—**Trade'-mark**, *n.* A distinctive mark on a manufacturer's goods.—**Trad'**ER, *n.*—**Trade-u'nion**, **Trades-u'nion**, *n.* An association of workers for the protection of their interests.—**Trade'-wind**, *n.* App. originating in obs. phrase *to blow trade*, to blow in a regular course. A wind blowing constantly towards the equator.

Tradi'tion, *n.* O.F. *tradicion*—L. *trāditio, trāditiōnis*, a delivering up, a tradition, f. *trādĕre*, to deliver, transmit, hand down, betray, f. *trā-* (= TRANS-) + *dăre*, to give. DATE.[2] BETRAY. EXTRADITION. TRAITOR. TREASON. Transmission of statements, &c., without writing; what is so transmitted.—**Tradi'tion**AL, **Tradi'tion**ARY, *aa.*
Traduce', *vt.* L. *trādūcĕre*, to lead across, to make a show of, dishonour, f. *trā-* (= TRANS-) + *dūcĕre*, to lead. DUKE. To vilify, slander.
Traf'fic, *vi.* O.F. *trafiquer*, app. f. It. *trafficare*, of unknown orig. To trade.—*n.* Trade; the passing to and fro of persons, vehicles, &c., on a road, &c.—**Traf'fick**ER, *n.* A trader.
Trag'edy, *n.* O.F. *tragedie*—L. *tragoedia*—G. *tragōidia*, f. *tragōidos*, tragic singer, app. lit. 'goat-singer', f. *tragos*, goat + *aoidos*, singer, f. *aeidein*, to sing; but the reason of the name has not been explained. The branch of the drama which deals in a serious and dignified style with sorrowful or terrible events; a drama of this kind.—**Trage'di**AN, *n.* A player in or a writer of tragedies.—**Trag'**IC, *a.* Of, in the style of tragedy; sad; disastrous.—In the last two senses also **Trag'**ICAL, *a.*—**Trag'ical**LY,[2] *adv.*—**Tragi-com'edy**, *n.* F. *tragicomédie*—L.L. *tragi-cōmoedia*, shortened f. L. *tragico-cōmoedia*, f. *tragicus* + *cōmoedia*, COMEDY. A play with tragic and comic elements.
Trail, *vt.* M.E. *traylen, traille*, app. the same word as O.N.F. *trailler*, E.Fris. *treilen, trailen*, M.L.G. *treilen*, to haul (a boat), supposed all to go back to a L.L. **trāgulāre*, to drag—L. *trāgula*, a drag-net, a small sledge, f. *trahĕre*, to drag. TREAT. To draw along behind one.—*vi.* To be drawn along behind; to hang loosely.—*n.* Something that trails; the hinder end of a gun-carriage; a trace, track.
Train, *vt.* F. *traîner*, in O.F. *traïner, trahiner*, app. a deriv. of L. *trahĕre*, to draw. TREAT. To cause (a plant, &c.) to grow in a particular way; to educate, instruct, exercise; to point (a firearm).—*vi.* To follow a course of training.—*n.* A trailing part of a robe, &c.; a body of attendants; a series; a line of gunpowder, &c., to carry fire to a mine, &c.; a coupled line of railway carriages with the locomotive.
Train'-oil, *n.* From obs. *Train* in same sense—M.L.G. *trân*, M.Du. *traen* (Ger. *tran*), oil made to exude, train-oil, app. the same word as M.L.G. *trân, trâne*, M.Du. *traen*, exuding gum, tear (Ger. *träne*, tear). Oil obtained by boiling the blubber of whales.
Trait, *n.* F. *trait*, in obs. F. *traict*, draught, touch, line—L. *tractus*. TRACE, *n.*[1] A stroke; a lineament of the face; a characteristic.
Trai'tor, *n.* O.F. *traitor*, acc. form of *traitre*—L. *trāditor*, f. *trādĕre*. TRADITION. A betrayer; one guilty of treason.—**Trai'tor**OUS, *a.*—**Trai'tr**ESS, *n.*
Trajec'tory, *n.* Through F. f. *trājectōria*, fem. of Mod.L. *trājectōrius*, pertaining to throwing across, f. L. *trājicĕre, trājectum*, to throw across, f. *trā-* (= TRANS-) + *jacĕre*, to throw. JET, *v.* The path of a projectile.
Tram, *n.* App. the same word as L.G. *traam*, handle of a barrow, E.Fris. *trame, trâm*, beam, step of a ladder. A small truck used in mines; a line of beams or metal rails; a waggon-road at a mine consisting of two such lines laid parallel; a tram-car.—**Tram'-car**, *n.* A car running on a tramway.—**Tram'-way**, *n.* A set of rails in a street on which cars are run for the conveyance of passengers.

Tram'mel, *n.* O.F. *tramail*, in the first sense below—Late Pop.L. *tramaculum* for *trimaculum*, a kind of fishing-net, explained as f. TRI- + L. *macula*, mesh. MACULATE. Various kinds of fishing-net: anything that restrains (this sense *fig.* f. obs. sense 'a hobble for a horse').—*vt.* To restrain.

Tramp, *vi.* M.E. *trampen* = L.G. *trampen*, whence Da. *trampe*, Sw., Norw. *trampa*, to stamp. To walk heavily; to travel on foot, to travel as a tramp.—*vt.* To traverse on foot.—*n.* An act or the sound of tramping; a bout of travelling on foot; a vagabond.

Tram'ple, *vi.* M.E. *trampelen*, *tramplen*, f. prec. + freq. suff. -*(e)len*. To tread heavily *on* or *upon*.—*vt.* To tread underfoot.

Trance, *n.* O.F. *transe*, passage, passage from life to death, vbl. n. f. *transir*, to pass, depart, to die—L. *transīre*. TRANSIENT. A suspension of consciousness; a state of rapture or ecstasy.—*vt.* To entrance.

Tran'quil, *a.* L. *tranquillus*. Free from agitation, calm, serene.—**Tranquil'l**ITY, *n.* —**Tran'quil**lIZE, *vt.*—**Tran'quil**LY,[2] *adv.*

Transact', *vt.* L. *transigĕre*, *transactum*, to drive through, to accomplish, f. TRANS- + *agĕre*, to drive. ACT. To carry on, carry through, conduct.—**Transac'tion**, *n.*

Transcend', *vt.* L. *transcendĕre*, to climb or step over, surpass, f. *tran-* (= TRANS-) + *scandĕre*, to climb. ASCEND. To go beyond, exceed; to surpass, excel. — **Transcen'd**ENCE, **Transcen'd**ENCY, *nn.* — **Transcen'd**ENT, *a.* Surpassing, excelling; transcending experience. — **Transcenden'tal**, *a.* Not derived from experience, concerned with the presuppositions of experience; supernatural; abstract, abstruse. — **Transcenden'tal**ISM, *n.* Transcendental philosophy. —**Transcenden'tal**IST, *n.*

Transcribe', *vt.* L. *transcrībere*, *transcriptum*, to write over from one book into another, copy, f. *tran-* (= TRANS-) + *scrībĕre*, to write. SCRIBE. To copy out.—**Tran'script**, *n.* O.F. *transcrit*—L. *transcriptum*, neut. pa.pple. of *transcrībĕre*. A copy.

Tran'sept, *n.* Med. or Mod.L. **transseptum*, f. TRANS- + L. *septum*, *saeptum*, fence, f. *saepīre*, to fence. App. 'the cross fenced piece'. The transverse part of a cruciform church; each of the two arms of this.

Transfer', *vt.* L. TRANS*ferre*, to BEAR across. To convey; to make over, esp. by deed.—**Trans'fer**, *n.* A transferring or being transferred; making over by deed; the deed. —**Trans'fer**ABLE, *a.* — **Transferee'**, *n.* — **Trans'fer**ENCE, *n.* — **Trans'fer**OR, **Transfer'r**ER, *nn.*

Transfig'ure, *vt.* L. *transfigūrāre*, to change in shape, f. TRANS- + *figūra*, shape. FIGURE. To alter the appearance of; to elevate, glorify. —**Transfigur**A'TION, *n.*

Transfix', *vt.* L. TRANS*figĕre*, *transfixum*. FIX. To pierce through.—**Transfix'**ION, *n.*

Transform', *vt.* L. *transformāre*, f. TRANS- + *formāre*, to form, f. *forma*, FORM. To change the form of; to change in character or condition.—**Transform**A'TION, *n.*

Transfuse', *vt.* L. TRANS*fundĕre*, *transfūsum*. FUSE, *v.* To cause to pass from one vessel into another.—**Transfu'**SION, *n.*

Transgress', *vt.* F. *transgresser*—L. *transgredi*, *transgressus*, to step across, f. TRANS- + *gradi*, to step. AGGRESSION. To break, violate (a law, &c.).—*vi.* To offend, sin.—**Transgres'**SION, *n.*—**Transgres'**SOR, *n.*

Tranship', *vt.* and *i.* TRANS- + SHIP, *v.* To transfer or change from one ship, railway train, &c., to another.—**Tranship'**MENT, *n.*

Tran'sient, *a.* L. *transiens*, *transientis*, pres.pple. of TRANS*īre*, *transitum*, to go or pass across. TRANCE. Passing away quickly, brief, shortlived.—**Tran'si**ENCE, -ENCY, *nn.*

Tran'sit, *n.* L. *transitus*, vbl. n. f. *transīre*. (See prec.) Passage or conveyance; the passage of one heavenly body over the disk of another.—**Transi'tion**, *n.* Change or passage from one state, &c., to another.—**Transi'tion**AL, **Transi'tion**ARY, *aa.*—**Tran'sit**IVE, *a.* Expressing action passing over to an object.—**Tran'sit**ORY, *a.* Transient.

Translate', *vt.* Prob. first used in *translat(e)* as pa.pple.—L. *translātus*, pa.pple. of *transferre*. TRANSFER. To remove (a bishop) to another see; to turn from one language *into* another.—**Transla'tion**, *n.*

Translit'erate, *vt.* TRANS- + L. *lit(t)era*, LETTER + -ATE.[3] To write in the characters of another alphabet.—**Transliter**A'TION, *n.*

Translu'cent, *a.* L. *translūcens*, *translūcentis*, pres.pple. of TRANS*lūcēre*, to shine through. LUCID. Semi-transparent.—**Translu'c**ENCE, **Translu'c**ENCY, *nn.*

Transmarine', *a.* L. *transmarīnus*, f. TRANS- + *mare*. MARINE. Beyond the sea.

Trans'migrate, *vi.* L. TRANS*migrāre*, *transmigrātum*. MIGRATE. To migrate; of the soul, to pass into another body.—**Transmigr**A'TION, *n.*

Transmit', *vt.* L. TRANS*mittĕre*, *transmissum*. MISSION. To cause to pass to another place, person, or thing; to allow (light, &c.) to pass through.—**Transmis'**SION, *n.*

Transmute', *vt.* L. TRANS*mūtāre*. MUTABLE. To change in nature, properties, or form.—**Transmut**A'TION, *n.*

Tran'som, *n.* M.E. *traunsum*, *traunsom*, app. a corr. of L. *transtrum* in same sense, f. *trans* (TRANS-)+instrumental suff. -*trum*. TRESTLE. A cross-beam or cross-piece, a lintel.

Transpa'rent, *a.* Med. L. *transpārens*, *transpārentis*, pres.pple. of TRANS*pārēre*, to shine through, f. *pārēre*, to come in sight, APPEAR. That can be seen through distinctly; frank, candid; manifest, obvious.—**Transpa'r**ENCE, *n.*—**Transpa'r**ENCY, *n.* Transparence; a picture, &c., made visible by means of a light behind it.—**Transpa'rent**LY,[2] *adv.*

Transpire', *vt.* *Tran-* (= TRANS-) + *spīrāre*, to breathe. SPIRIT. To discharge through the skin, to exhale.—*vi.* To exhale; to come to be known, 'leak out'.—**Transpir**A'TION, *n.*

Transplant', *vt.* L. TRANS*plantāre*, f. *planta*. PLANT. To plant in another place; to transport.—**Transplant**A'TION, *n.*

Transport', *vt.* L. TRANS*portāre*. PORT, *v.*[2] To convey from one place to another; to carry into banishment; to put into an ecstasy, enrapture. — **Trans'port**, *n.* Conveyance; ecstasy; a ship engaged in transporting troops or stores.—**Transport**A'TION, *n.*

Transpose', *vt.* F. *transposer*, f. TRANS- + *poser*, to place. POSE.[1] To alter the order of (a set or series), to alter the order of (a thing) in a set or series; to put (music) into a different key. — **Transpos'**AL, *n.* — **Transposi'tion**, *n.* Prob. f. F. *transposition* or Med.L. *transpositio*, *transpositiōnis*, n. of action f. L. TRANS*pōnĕre*, to place across, to transfer. POSITION. Transference; alteration of order or of key.

Transubstan'tiate, *vt.* Med.L. *tran(s)-substantiāre, tran(s)substantiātum,* f. TRANS- + L. *substantia,* SUBSTANCE. To change in substance, esp. of conversion in the Eucharist of the elements into the body and blood of Christ.—**Transubstanti**A'TION, *n.*

Transverse', *a.* L. *transversus,* pa.pple. of TRANS*vertĕre,* to turn across. ADVERSE. TRAVERSE. Lying across, at right angles.

Trap, *n.* O.E. *treppe,* snare = M.Du. *trappe,* Mod. W. Flemish *traap, trape,* also Med.L. *trappa, trapa,* O.F. *trape* (F. *trappe*). (The relations between the Teutonic and the Romanic words are uncertain.) ENTRAP. A contrivance for catching game, &c., a snare; a movable covering on an opening; a door flush with a floor, a roof, &c. (also **Trap-door**); a two-wheeled carriage on springs; a contrivance for preventing the escape of gases from a drain-pipe.—*v.*[1]*t.* To ensnare, entrap; to furnish with a trap or traps.

Trap, *v.*[2]*t.* From obs. *Trap,* caparison, altered form of F. *drap.* DRAPE. To caparison. —**Trap'pings**, *n.pl.* A caparison; ornaments.

Trape'zium, *n.* Mod.L.—G. *trapezion,* dim. of *trapeza,* table. A quadrilateral having only one pair of its opposite sides parallel.—**Trap'ez**OID, *n.* Such a figure having no two of its sides parallel.—**Trapeze'**, *n.* F. *trapèze,* A horizontal bar suspended by two ropes.

Trash, *n.* Orig. obscure. Cf. Norw. dial. *trask,* lumber, Icel. *tros,* rubbish, fallen twigs, &c. Broken-off pieces, as twigs, splinters, &c.; rubbish; nonsense.—**Trash'**Y,[2] *a.*

Trav'ail, *vi.* O.F. *travaillier,* gen. taken to represent a late Pop.L. **trepāliāre,* to torture, deriv. of *trepālium,* an instrument of torture, prob. f. L. *trēs, tria,* three + *pālus,* stake (being so named from its structure). PALE, *n.* (See next.) To toil; of a woman, to be in labour. —*n.* Toil; the pains of childbirth.

Trav'el, *vi.* Orig. the same as prec. To make a journey; to move, proceed, pass.—*vt.* To journey through, traverse.—*n.* The action of travelling: in *pl.*, an account of occurrences during a journey.—**Trav'ell**ER, *n.*

Trav'erse, *n.* Repg. (1) O.F. *travers,* masc., a traversing, an obstacle—Pop.L. *trāversum* for L. *transversum,* neut. of *transversus,* TRANSVERSE; (2) O.F. *traverse,* fem., cross-piece, barrier, app. repg. a L.L. *trāversa,* fem. n. f. *transversus.* A traversing; an obstacle, a mishap; a cross-piece or cross-beam.—*vt.* O.F. *traverser,* to cross, thwart, f. *travers.* To pass or journey over or through; to cross, intersect; to thwart, oppose.

Trav'esty, *n.* F. *travesti,* pa.pple. of (*se*) *travestir,* to disguise oneself—It. *travestire,* to disguise, f. *tra-* (= TRANS-) + *vestire,* L. *vestīre,* to clothe. DIVEST. A ludicrous imitation.—*vt.* To make ridiculous by a travesty.

Trawl, *n.* Orig. obscure. A net dragged along the bottom of the sea.—*vi.* To fish with such a net.—**Trawl'**ER, *n.* A trawling vessel.

Tray, *n.* O.E. **trieg, trīg.* O.Teut. root *trau-,* in relation with *treu-,* whence *tréow,* TREE. Primary sense perh. 'wooden (vessel)'. A flat utensil for carrying small articles.

Treach'ery, *n.* O.F. *trecherie, tricherie,* f. *trechier, trichier,* to cheat, commonly referred to a L.L. **triccāre* for L. *trīcāri,* to trifle, play tricks, f. *tricae.* EXTRICATE. TRICK. Deceit, perfidy; the perfidy of a traitor, an instance of this.—**Treach'er**OUS, *a.*

Treac'le, *n.* O.F. *triacle,* a medicinal compound—Late Pop.L. **triaca* for L. *thēriaca* = G. *thēriakē* (*antidotos*), (an antidote) against a poisonous bite, f. *thēriakos,* a. f. *thērion,* wild beast, serpent, in form dim. of *thēr,* wild beast. FIERCE. Formerly in the O.F. sense. Now applied to sugar-cane juice remaining uncrystallized in the process of refining.

Tread, *vt.* O.E. *tredan.* Common Teut. TRADE. To set foot on; to oppress.—*vi.* To walk, go; to trample *on* or *upon.*—*n.* A treading; manner of walking; the upper surface of a step in a stair.—**Tread'le**, *n.* Instrumental suff. *-le.* A lever worked by the foot.

Trea'son, *n.* A.F. *tresun, treson,* O.F. *traïson* (F. *trahison*)—L. *trāditio.* TRADITION. Treachery; violation of allegiance.—**Trea'son**ABLE, *a.* Of the nature of, involving treason.—**Trea'son**OUS, *a.*

Treas'ure, *n.* O.F. *tresor*—Pop.L. (Gaulish) *trēsaurus,* for L. *thēsaurus* = G. *thēsauros.* Stored wealth, riches.—*vt.* To store up; to prize.—**Treas'ur**ER, *n.* An official in charge of funds.—**Treasure-trove'**, *n.* Orig. two words as in A.F. *tresor trové* (TROVER) = L. *thēsaurus inventus* (*inventus* being pa.pple. of *invenīre.* INVENT). Treasure of unknown ownership found hidden.—**Treas'ury**, *n.* O.F. *tresorie,* f. *tresor.* A place for treasure or for the funds of a state, &c.; the department of state in charge of the revenue.

Treat, *vi.* O.F. *tretier, traitier, traiter*—L. *tractāre,* to drag, to transact, to discuss, freq. of *trahĕre, tractum,* to draw. ABSTRACT. TRACE. TRACTABLE. TRACTION. TRAIL. TRAIN. To negotiate *with*; with *of,* to deal with, discuss.—*vt.* To deal with, discuss; to act towards in a specified way; to entertain, regale.—*n.* An entertainment, a pleasure party.—**Treat'ise**, *n.* A.F. *tretiz,* repg. O.F. **traitëiz,* f. *traitier.* A book dealing with some particular subject.—**Treat'**MENT, *n.*—**Treat'y**, *n.* A.F. *treté,* O.F. *traité,* ppl.n. f. *traiter.* Negotiation; a contract between states, the document embodying it.

Treb'le, *a.* O.F. *treble*—L. *triplus.* TRIPLE. Threefold, triple.—*n.* A soprano voice; the part for this voice; a singer with a voice of this pitch.—*vt.* and *i.* To make, to become three times as many or great.—**Treb'**LY,[2] *adv.*

Tree, *n.* O.E. *tréow, tréo* = O.Fris. *trê,* O.N. *tré.* Cogn. with Skr. *dru,* tree, wood, G. *drus,* oak (orig. tree). TAR. TRAY. TROUGH. A perennial plant with a woody stem and branches; a beam, bar, &c., as in AXLE-TREE. —**Tree'nail, Tren'ail**, *n.* A wooden pin for binding timbers.

Tre'foil, *n.* A.F. *trifoil*—L. *trifolium,* f. TRI- + *folium,* leaf. FOIL, *n.*[1] A plant having triple leaves.

Trel'lis, *n.* O.F. *treliz, trelis* (orig. an a. and app. receiving the particular sense by contact with *treille,* bower, lattice—L. *trichila,* later *tricla,* bower)—Late Pop. L. **trilīcius,* for L. *trilix, trilīcis,* having three threads in the warp, f. TRI- + *licium,* a thread of the warp. TWILL. A lattice or grating of light cross-bars.—*vt.* To furnish with a trellis.

Trem'ble, *vi.* F. *trembler*—Pop. and Med.L. *tremulāre*—L. *tremulus,* trembling, f. *tremĕre,* to tremble, to tremble at. To shake or quiver. —*n.* A trembling.—**Tremen'dous**, *a.* From *tremendus* (ger. of *tremĕre*) + -OUS. Exciting awe; immense.—**Trem'or**, *n.* O.F. *tremor* —L. *tremor,* f. *tremĕre.* Trembling, a trembling.—**Trem'ulous**, *a.* From *tremulus* + -OUS. Timorous; vibrating easily.

Trench, *vt.* O.F. *trenchier, trencher* (F.

trancher), to cut, referred to a Pop.L. **trincāre* for L. *truncāre*. TRUNCATE. TRINKET. To cut a groove in; to make trenches in (ground) so as to bring up the lower soil (in this sense f. the *n.*).—*vi.* To infringe *on* or *upon*.—*n.* A long narrow hollow for shelter in warfare; a deep furrow.—**Tren'chant**, *a.* O.F. *trenchant*, pres.pple. of *trencher*. Incisive.—**Tren'cher**, *n.* A.F. *trenchour*=O.F. *trencheoir*, f. *trenchier*. A wooden platter.

Trend, *vi.* O.E. *trendan*, to roll, cogn. with *trinde*, round lump, M.L.G. *trent*, ring, also with TRUNDLE. To have a specified general direction.—*n.* General direction or tendency.

Trepan', *n.*[1] F. *trépan*—Med.L. *trepanum*—G. *trupanon*, borer. A cylindrical surgical saw for removing portions of the skull.—*v.*[1]*t.* To operate on with a trepan.

Trepan', *n.*[2] Prob. orig. rogues' slang. One who entraps or inveigles.—*v.*[2]*t.* To entrap.

Trephine', *n.* According to the inventor f. L. *trēs fīnes*, three ends, from the shape. An improved form of trepan.—*vt.* To operate on with a trephine.

Trepida'tion, *n.* L. *trepidātio*, *trepidātiōnis*, f. *trepidāre*, to be agitated, f. *trepidus*. INTREPID. Agitation, alarm, tremor.

Tres'pass, *n.* O.F. *trespas*, a passing across, a transgression, f. *trespasser*, to pass across, f. *tres-* (= TRANS-) + *passer*, to PASS. A transgression; a wrongful entering upon the lands of another.—*vi.* To commit a trespass.

Tress, *n.* F. *tresse*, in O.F. *tresce*. Orig. doubtful. A plait or long lock of hair.

Tres'tle, *n.* O.F. *trestel*, transom—Pop.L. **transtellum*, dim. of L. *transtrum*. TRANSOM. A supporting bar with diverging legs.

Tri'ad, *n.* L. *trias*, *triadis*—G. *trias*, *triados*, f. *treis*, three. A group of three.

Tri'angle, *n.* L. *triangulum*, neut. n. f. *triangulus*, three-cornered, f. TRI- + *angulus*, ANGLE. A figure having three angles.—**Trian'gul**AR,[1] *a.*

Tribe, *n.* L. *tribus*. TRIBUNE. A group or race of people.—**Tri'b**AL, *a.*

Tri'brach, *n.* L. *tribrachys*—G. *tribrachus*, f. TRI- + *brachus*, short. A metrical foot consisting of three short syllables.

Tribula'tion, *n.* O.F. *tribulacion*—Eccles. L. *tribulātio*, *tribulātiōnis*, f. *tribulāre*, to afflict, f. L. *tribulum*, a threshing-sledge, app. f. *trī*, a stem of *terĕre*, *tritum*, to rub + instrumental suff. *-bulum*. TRITE. A condition of affliction, oppression, or misery.

Trib'une, *n.*[1] L. *tribūnus*, lit., 'head of a tribe', f. *tribus*, TRIBE. One of the officers (the 'tribunes of the people') appointed to guard the interests of the Roman plebeians; a popular leader.—**Tribu'nal**, *n.* L. *tribūnal*, f. *tribūnus*. A judgement-seat; a law-court.

Trib'une, *n.*[2] F. *tribune*—It. and Med.L. *tribūna* = L. *tribūnal*. (See prec.) A raised platform for a speaker; the throne of a bishop.

Trib'ute, *n.* L. *tribūtum*, neut. n. f. *tribūtus*, pa.pple. of *tribuĕre*, to assign, give, pay. ATTRIBUTE. An impost paid by one state to another.—**Trib'ut**ARY, *a.* Paying tribute; auxiliary; of a stream, flowing into another.

Trice, *vt.* M.Du. *trīsen*, to hoist = M.L.G. *trissen*, *tritsen*. Orig. obscure. To haul *up* and secure with a rope.

Trice, *n.* First in obs. phrase *at a trice*, app. orig. 'at one pull', *trice* being app. vbl.n. f. prec. *In a trice*, in an instant, forthwith.

Trick, *n.* O.F. *trique* (Picard and Norman form of *triche*, deceit, cheating), prob. vbl.n. f. *trikier* = *trichier*, *trechier*. TREACHERY. An artifice or stratagem; a practical joke; a feat of dexterity or skill; a characteristic quality or habit; the cards played in one round.—*vt.* To cheat; to attire, deck.—**Trick'**ERY, *n.*—**Trick'**ISH, *a.*—**Trick'**STER, *n.*—**Trick's**Y,[2] *a.* Spruce, smart; sportive, mischievous; crafty, cheating.—**Trick'**Y,[2] *a.* Crafty, cheating; ticklish.

Trick'le, *vi.* Orig obscure. Doubtfully explained as (with loss of *s*) freq. or dim. of M.E. *striken*, to strike, to flow—O.E. *strican*. STRIKE. To fall in drops; to flow scantily.

Tri'colour, *a.* F. *tricolore*—L.L. *tricolor*, f. TRI- + L. *color*, COLOUR. Three-coloured.—*n.* A tricolour flag, esp. the French flag.

Tri'cycle, *n.* F. *tricycle*, f. TRI- + G. *kuklos*, circle, wheel. A three-wheeled vehicle propelled by the rider.—**Tri'cycl**IST, *n.*

Tri'dent, *n.* L. *tridens*, *tridentis*, f. TRI- + *dens*, *dentis*, tooth. DENTAL. An instrument or weapon with three prongs.

Trien'nial, *a.* L. *triennis*, of three years, f. TRI- + *annus*, year. Lasting three years; happening every three years.

Tri'fle, *n.* M.E. *trufle*, &c.—O.F. *trufle*, *treufle*, *truffle*, parallel forms of *trufe*, *truffe*, raillery, cheating, of uncertain orig. Formerly, a lying story, an idle tale. A thing of small moment; flavoured sponge-cake or the like with custard, &c.—*vi.* With *with*, to treat without proper consideration, to finger idly; to speak or act frivolously.—*vt.* To fritter *away*.—**Tri'fl**ER, *n.*—**Tri'fling**, *ppl.a.* Frivolous; of small moment.

Trifo'rium, *n.* Orig. unknown. A gallery over the nave and choir of a church.

Trig'ger, *n.* In form *tricker* f. Du. *trekker* f. *trekken*, to pull. TRACK, *n.* A catch which releases a spring, esp. a catch which releases the hammer of a gun.

Tri'glyph, *n.* L. *triglyphus*—G. *trigluphos* thrice grooved, f. TRI- + *gluphein*, to carve. A block with three vertical grooves used as an ornament in Doric architecture.

Trigonom'etry, *n.* G. *trigōnon*, triangle (f. TRI- + *gōnia*, angle) + *-metria*, f. *metre-ein*, to measure. The branch of mathematics dealing with the relations of the sides and angles of triangles.—**Trigonomet'r**IC, **Trigonomet'r**ICAL, *aa.*

Trill, *vi.* and *t.* It. *trillare*, us. referred to a German source. To sing with tremulous vibration.—*n.* Such singing.

Tril'ogy, *n.* G. *trilogia*, f. TRI- + *logos*, discourse. A series of three related dramas.

Trim, *a.* App. deriv. of next. In good order, sound; neat, spruce.—**Trim'**LY,[2] *adv.*

Trim, *vt.* App. represents O.E. *trymman*, *trymian*, to strengthen, set in array, &c., f. *trum*, strong, stable, &c., of unknown orig. To fit out for sea; to put into good order; to dress *up*, array; to cut off irregularities from; to adjust properly the load of (a ship, &c.).—*vi.* To suit oneself to the times.—*n.* Of a ship, the state of being trimmed; dress; state.

Trim'eter, *n.* L. *trimetrus*, a. and n.—G. *trimetros*, a., f. TRI- + *metron*, measure. A verse of three measures.

Trin'ity, *n.* O.F. *trinite*—L. *trīnitas*, the number three, later, the Trinity, f. *trīnus*, triple, f. *trēs*, THREE. The state of being threefold; the three persons of the Godhead.—**Trinit**A'RIAN, *a.* and *n.*

Trin'ket, *n.* M.E. *trenket*, *trynket*, shoemaker's knife, whence app. toy-knife, trinket, perh. f. O.N.F. *trenquer* = O.F. *trencher*. TRENCH. A small personal ornament.

Tri'o, *n.* It.,—L. *trēs, tria*, THREE. A musical composition for three parts; a set of three performers; a group of three.—**Tri'olet**, *n.* F. *triolet*, f. It. *trio*. A rhyming poem of eight lines with recurring lines.

Trip, *vi.* M.E. *trippen*, to step lightly. Cf. Du. *trippen*, to skip, Sw. *trippa*, to step lightly. To move lightly; to stumble; to commit a fault.—*vt.* To cause to stumble.—*n.* A light step; a stumble; a journey.

Tri'partite, *a.* O.F. *tripartite*—L. *tripartītus*, f. TRI- + *partītus*, pa.pple. of *partīre*, to divide. BIPARTITE. Having three parts.

Tripe, *n.* F. *tripe* = Sp., Pg. *tripa*, It. *trippa*. Orig. unknown. The stomach of a ruminating animal prepared for food.

Trip'le, *a.* F. *triple*—L. *triplus*, threefold, f. TRI- + *-plus*, f. root *ple-*, to fill. DOUBLE. TREBLE. Threefold.—*vt.* and *i.* To treble.—**Trip'**LY,[2] *adv.*—**Trip'let**, *n.* F. *triplet*, f. *triple* + dim. suff. *-et*. Three of a kind; three lines rhyming together.

Trip'licate, *vt.* L. *triplicāre, triplicātum*, f. TRI- + *plicāre*, to fold. APPLY. To make threefold.—*a.* Threefold.—*n.* Each of a set of three copies; the state of being triplicate.—**Triplica'**TION, *n.*

Tri'pod, *n.* L. *tripūs, tripodis*—G. *tripous, tripodos*, f. TRI- + *pous*, FOOT. A three-footed stool, utensil, &c.

Trip'tych, *n.* G. *triptuchos*, threefold, f. TRI- + **ptux, ptuchos*, a fold. A picture or carving in three compartments.

Tri'reme, *n.* L. *trirēmis*, having three ranks of oars, f. TRI- + *rēmus*, OAR. A galley with three ranks of oars.

Trite, *a.* L. *trītus*, pa.pple. of *terĕre* = G. *teirein*, to rub. DETRIMENT. TRIBULATION. Hackneyed, stale. — **Trit'urate**, *vt.* L.L. *trītūrāre, trītūrātum*, to thresh (corn), f. L. *trītūra*, a rubbing, f. *terĕre*. To rub to powder.—**Tritura'**TION, *n.*

Tri'umph, *n.* O.F. *triumphe* (F. *triomphe*, also the name of a card game and the trump at it)—L. *triumphus*, the solemn entrance of a victorious general into Rome, a victory. TRUMP.[2] Victory, signal success; something constituting a triumph; exultation.—*vi.* To gain victory, be successful; to exult.—**Trium'phal**, *a.*—**Trium'phant**, *a.*

Trium'vir, *n.* L. *triumviri*, pl., three men, formed f. *trium virōrum*, genit. of *trēs viri*, THREE men. VIRILE. One of three men joined in office.—**Trium'vir**ATE,[1] *n.*

Tri'une, *a.* TRI- + *ūnus*, ONE. Three in one.

Triv'et, *n.* O.E. *trefet*—L. *tripēs, tripedis*, f. TRI + *pēs*, FOOT. An iron tripod or bracket to support a pot, &c.

Triv'ial, *a.* F. *trivial*—L. *triviālis*, belonging to cross-roads, common—L. *trivium*, a place where three roads meet, f. TRI- + *via*, way. DEVIATE. Of small importance; trifling; commonplace.—**Trivial'**ITY, *n.*

Tro'chee, *n.* L. *trochaeus*—G. *trochaios*, running, also, a trochee, f. *trechein*, to run. TRUCK, *n.*[2] A metrical foot giving a tripping effect consisting of a long syllable followed by a short.—**Trocha'**IC, *a.*

Trog'lodyte, *n.* F. *troglodyte*—L. *trōglodyta*—G. *trōglodutēs*, one who creeps into holes, f. *trōglē*, (mouse's) hole (f. *trōgein*, to gnaw) + *-dutēs*, who enters, f. *duein*, to enter. TROUT. A cave-dweller.

Troll, *vt.* M.E. *trollen*, to roll, ultimately f. O.F. *trauler*, to run or draw hither and thither —Ger. *trollen*, to roll, troll, of uncertain orig. To pass (a drinking-vessel) round; to sing in a full voice.—*vi.* To be passed round; to fish in a particular manner.—*n.* A part-song.—**Trol'ley, Trol'ly**, *n.* Dim. suff. *(e)y*. A small truck; an electric tram-car's power-conductor.

Trombone, *n.* It. *trombone*, aug. of *tromba* = O.F. *trompe*, trumpet. TRUMP.[1] A large musical instrument of the trumpet kind.

Troop, *n.* F. *troupe*, earlier *trope*, of unknown orig. An assemblage of persons or animals; a unit of cavalry; in *pl.*, soldiers.—*vi.* To gather or move in a troop.—**Troop'**ER, *n.* A private cavalry-soldier.

Trope, *n.* L. *tropus*—G. *tropos*, a turn, a trope, f. *trepein*, to turn. A figurative use of a word.—**Trop'ic**, *n.* F. *tropique*—L. *tropicus*, tropical—G. *tropikos* (sc. *kuklos*, circle), tropic, f. *tropos*. Either of the two celestial circles at which the sun appears to turn at the solstices, or of the two corresponding terrestrial circles; in *pl.*, the hot region of the earth between the latter circles.—*a.* Of the tropics.—**Trop'**ICAL, *a.* Tropic; figurative.

Tro'phy, *n.* F. *trophée*—L. *tropaeum*, G. *tropaion*, f. *tropē*, a putting to flight, f. *trepein*. (See prec.) A memorial of a victory.

Trot, *vi.* F. *trotter*, O.F. *troter*, conn. with *trotier*, Med.L. *trotārius*, one who trots, messenger, said to be f. L. *tolūtārius*, going at a trot, f. *tolūtim*, at a trot, f. *tollĕre*, to lift (*sc.* the feet). EXTOL. Of a horse, to go by lifting each diagonal pair of feet alternately; to run with short strides.—*n.* The action of trotting.

Troth, *n.* Var. of TRUTH. Truth, faith.

Trou'badour, *n.* Through F. f. Pr. *trobador*, f. *trobar* = F. *trouver*. CONTRIVE. One of a class of lyric poets originating in Provence in the eleventh century.

Troub'le, *vt.* F. *troubler*, O.F. *trubler*—L.L. **turbulāre*, f. L. *turbula*, dim. of *turba* crowd. TURBID. To agitate, disturb.—*vi* To be agitated or disturbed.—*n.* Agitation, affliction; labour, inconvenience.—**Troub'le**SOME, *a.*—**Troub'l**OUS, *a.*

Trough, *n.* M.E. *trogh*—O.E. *troh, trog*. Cf. Du., Ger., *trog*, Da. *trug*. Prob. f. same root as Skr. *dru*, G. *drus* (TREE), and thus orig. 'wooden receptacle'. A long narrow open vessel; the hollow between two waves.

Trounce, *vt.* O.F. *trons, tronson*. TRUNCHEON. To beat soundly.

Trou'sers, *n.pl.* Formerly *trouses* — F. *trousses*, breeches, pl. of *trousse*, O.F. *tourse*, bundle, f. O.F. *tourser*, to pack up. TRUSS. A two-legged outer garment.—**Trousseau'**, *n.* F., dim. of *trousse*. A bride's outfit.

Trout, *n.* O.E. *trūht*—L. *tructa*, G. *trōktēs*, gnawer, a fish with sharp teeth, f. *trōgein*. TROGLODYTE. A fresh-water fish.

Tro'ver, *n.* O.F. *trover*, to find. CONTRIVE. The acquisition of goods by finding them.

Trow, *vi.* O.E. *trēowian*, conn. with *trēowe*, TRUE. To believe, to suppose.

Trow'el, *n.* F. *truelle*—L.L. *truella*, trowel, dim. of L. *trua*, ladle. A small tool for spreading mortar, &c., or for lifting plants, &c.

Troy'-weight, *n.* App. orig. a weight used at the fair of *Troyes* in France. A system of weights used for gold and silver.

Tru'ant, *n.* F. *truand*, vagabond, of Celtic orig. One absent from duty without leave.

Truce, *n.* Orig. a pl. form f. O.E. *trēow*, compact, pledge. Cf. *trēowe*, TRUE. A temporary cessation of hostilities.

Truck, *vi.* and *t.* M.E. *trukken*—F. *troquer*, to barter, of doubtful orig. To barter.—*n.*[1] Barter; a paying of workmen in goods.

Truck, *n.*[2] L. *trochus*, a hoop—G. *trochos*, a running, a wheel, f. *trechein*, to run. TROCHEE. An open vehicle for heavy goods.—**Truck'le-bed**, *n.* L. *trochlea*, a pulley, conn. with *trochus*. A low bed on wheels capable of being pushed under a superior's larger bed.—Hence **Truck'le**, *vi.* To submit servilely.

Truc'ulent, *a.* F. *truculent*—L. *truculentus*, f. *trux*, *trucis*, fierce. Fierce, ferocious.

Trudge, *vi.* Obs. F. *trucher*, to beg, app. of Teut. orig. Cf. M.Du. *truggelen* in sim. sense. To walk laboriously.—*n.* Such a walk.

True, *a.* O.E. *tréowe*, *trýwe*. Orig. 'believed'. Cf. Goth. *trauan*, to believe, O.H.G. *trūwēn* (Ger. *trauen*), to trust. TROTH. TROW. TRUCE. TRUTH. In accordance with fact; genuine; loyal, faithful; exact, correct.—**Tru'**ISM, *n.* A self-evident truth.—**Tru'**LY,[2] *adv.*

Truf'fle, *n.* F. *truffe*. Said to be orig. **tufre*, answering to L. *tūbera*, pl. of *tūber*, bump, knob, truffle, conn. with *tumēre*. TUMID. PROTUBERANT. TUBER. An edible fungus growing underground.

Trump, *n.*[1] F. *trompe*—O.H.G. *trumpa*, *trumba*, of Slavonic orig. TROMBONE. A trumpet.—**Trump**, *v.*[1]*t.* F. *tromper*, to deceive, orig., to play on a *trompe*, whence, to play (with any one), amuse oneself (at his expense). To get *up*, fabricate.—**Trump'et**, *n.* O.F. *trompette*, dim. of *trompe*. A musical wind-instrument of metal.—*vt.* To proclaim as by sound of trumpet.—*vi.* To blow a trumpet, make a sound as of a trumpet.

Trump, *n.*[2] A corr. of TRIUMPH. A card of a suit ranking conventionally above the other suits.—*v.*[2]*t.* To take with a trump.

Trump'ery, *n.* F. *tromperie*, a wile, fraud, f. *tromper*. TRUMP.[1] Worthless finery, rubbish.—*a.* Showy and worthless, delusive.

Trun'cate, *vt.* L. *truncāre*, *truncātum*, f. *truncus*. TRUNK.[1] TRENCH. To cut short.

Trun'cheon, *n.* O.N.F. *tronchon*, O.F. *tronson*, thick stick, f. *tronc*. TRUNK.[1] TROUNCE. A short club; a staff of office.

Trund'le, *vt.* and *i.* L.G. *tröndeln*, cogn. with TREND. To roll *along*, *down*, &c.

Trunk, *n.*[1] O.F. *tronc*—L. *truncus*, stem, tree-trunk, f. *truncus*, maimed. TRUNCATE. TRUNCHEON. The main body of a tree; the body of a person or animal without the head and limbs; a box for clothes, &c.

Trunk, *n.*[2] App. corr. of TRUMP.[1] An elephant's proboscis, with which it *trumpets*.

Truss, *vt.* O.F. *trousser*, *tourser*, to pack up, of doubtful orig. TROUSERS. To fasten or tighten *up*; to tie up the wings of (a fowl); to support.—*n.* A support; a bundle (of hay, &c.); a belt used in cases of rupture.

Trust, *n.* O.N. *traust*, trust, protection, firmness, conn. with TRUE. Cf. Ger. *trost*, consolation. Firm belief, confidence, reliance; the legal relationship arising from making over property to be held for another; the property.—*vt.* To believe in, rely upon.—**Trust**EE', **Trust'**ER, *nn.*—**Trust'**FUL, *a.*—**Trust'worthy**, *a.* Worthy of trust.—**Trust'**Y,[2] *a.* Trustworthy.

Truth, *n.* O.E. *tréowth*, f. *tréowe*, TRUE. The quality or state of being true; something that is true.—**Truth'**FUL, *a.*

Try, *vt.* M.E. *trien*, to pick out—F. *trier* in sim. sense—L.L. *tritāre*, to pound small, f. L. *terĕre*. TRITE. To test; to subject to suffering, &c.; to investigate judicially; to investigate the case of; to attempt.—*vi.* To attempt, endeavour.—**Tri'**AL, *n.*

Tryst, *n.* O.F. *trist(r)e*, hunting station, watching-place, prob. of Scand. orig. and cogn. with TRUST. An appointment to meet.

Tub, *n.* M.Du. *tobbe*, of doubtful orig. An open wooden vessel; a bath.

Tube, *n.* F. *tube*—L. *tubus*, conn. with *tuba*, trumpet. A long hollow cylinder.—**Tu'bu**LAR,[1] *a.* (From L. *tubulus*, dim. of *tubus*.)

Tu'ber, *n.* L. *tūber*. TRUFFLE. A short thick underground stem or root.—**Tu'bercle**, *n.* L. *tuberculum*, dim. of *tūber*. A small tumour formed within an organ tending to degeneration.—**Tuber'cul**AR,[1] *a.*—**Tuberculo'sis**, *n.* Suff. *-osis* of condition. A disease marked by the presence of tubercles.

Tuck, *vt.* M.E. *tukken*—L.G. *tukken*. Cf. O.H.G. *zucchen* (Ger. *zucken*), to twitch. To gather into folds for stitching; to draw or roll close together or into small compass.—*n.* A flat fold stitched.

Tues'day, *n.* O.E. *tíwes dæg*, the DAY of *Tíw*, O.N. *Týr*, god of war, cogn. with L. *deus*, god, G. *Zeus*. The third day of the week.

Tuft, *n.* F. *touffe*, app. of Teut. orig. Cf. Ger. *zopf*, pigtail. A bunch of threads, feathers, &c.; a titled undergraduate (who formerly wore a tufted cap).—**Tuft'-hunter**, *n.* One who seeks the society of titled persons.

Tug, *vt.* M.E. *toggen*—O.N. *tog*, rope, f. *tog-*. TIE. To pull with effort.—*vi.* To make a tug *at*.—*n.* A violent pull; a steam-vessel used for towing other vessels.

Tui'tion, *n.* F. *tuition*—L. *tuitio*, *tuitiōnis* protection, f. *tuēri*, *tuitus* or *tūtus*, to watch. INTUITION. Teaching.

Tu'lip, *n.* F. *tulipan*, *tulippe*—It. *tulipa(no)*—Turkish *tulbend*, a TURBAN (which the flower was thought to resemble). A plant with bright bell-shaped flowers.

Tum'ble, *vi.* M.E. *tumblen*, freq. of *tumben* in sim. sense—O.E. *tumbian*, to turn heels over head, dance. Cf. O.H.G. *tūmōn* (Ger. *tummeln*), to turn over and over. To fall or move suddenly; to do acrobatic feats.—*vt.* To throw or push down; to rumple.—*n.* A fall; a somersault.—**Tum'bl**ER, *n.* An acrobat; a flat-bottomed drinking-glass (formerly one rounded at the base which would not stand).

Tu'mid, *a.* L. *tumidus*, f. *tumēre*, to swell. THUMB. TRUFFLE. Swollen; bombastic.—**Tu'mi**FY, *vt.* and *i.* To cause to swell, to swell.—**Tume**FAC'TION, *n.*—**Tu'mour**, *n.* F. *tumeur*—L. *tumor*. A morbid swelling.

Tu'mult, *n.* F. *tumulte*—L. *tumultus*, f. *tumēre*. (See prec.) A commotion; uproar; confused or excited state.—**Tumul'tu**OUS, *a.*

Tu'mulus, *n.* L., f. *tumēre*. TUMID. A sepulchral mound.—**Tu'mul**AR,[1] *a.*

Tun, *n.* O.E. *tunne*, barrel. Cf. Du. *ton*, O.N. *tunna*, O.F. *tonne*. TON. A large cask.

Tune, *n.* A.F. *tun*, F. *ton*. TONE. A melody; correct adjustment of a musical instrument; concord, agreement.—*vt.* To put in tune.—**Tune'**FUL, *a.* Melodious.

Tu'nic, *n.* O.F. *tunique*—L. *tunica*, a body-garment. A short military coat.

Tun'nel, *n.* O.F. *tonnel* (dim. of *tonne* (TUN)), a tunnel-shaped trap for birds, hence, a tunnel or shaft. An artificial subterranean passage.—*vt.* To make a tunnel through.

Tun'ny, *n.* F. *thon*—L. *thunnus*—G. *thunnos*. A large edible fish.

Tur'ban, *n.* F. *turbant, turban*—It. *turbante*—Turkish *tulbend*, more properly *dulbend*—Per. *dulband.* TULIP. An Oriental head-dress.

Tur'bid, *a.* L. *turbidus*, disturbed, f. *turbāre*, to disturb, f. *turba*, a crowd. DISTURB. TROUBLE. TURBULENT. Thick, muddy; confused, disordered.—**Turbid'**ITY, *n.*

Tur'bine, *n.* F. *turbine*—L. *turbo, turbinis*, whirlwind, spinning-top, whirling motion, in L.L. turbot, f. *turbāre.* (See prec.) A kind of water-wheel; a form of steam-engine.

Tur'bot, *n.* F. *turbot*—L. *turbo.* (See prec.) A large kind of flat-fish.

Tur'bulent, *a.* F. *turbulent*—L. *turbulentus*, f. *turba.* TURBID. In commotion, riotous.

Tureen', *n.* F. *terrine*, earthen pan—L. *terra*, earth. TERRESTRIAL. A soup-dish.

Turf, *n.* O.E. *turf.* Cf. Du. *turf*, O.N. *torf.* Surface earth filled with roots of grass, &c.; a cut piece of this.

Tur'gid, *a.* L. *turgidus*, swollen, f. *turgēre*, to swell. Morbidly swollen; bombastic.

Tur'key, *n.* F. *Turquie*, Turkey, whence the bird was supposed to come. A large domestic bird, a native of America.

Tur'meric, *n.* F. *terre-mérite*, prob. a corr. of an Arab. word. An E. Indian plant; the root, used as a dye, a test for alkalis, &c.

Tur'moil, *n.* Poss. f. MOIL with pref. *tur-* (*tra-*, TRANS-) as intensive. Agitation.

Turn, *vt.* O.E. *tyrnan, turnian*—L. *tornāre*, to turn on a lathe, f. *tornus*, lathe—G. *tornos*, a tool for drawing a circle. ATTORNEY. TOUR. TOURNAMENT. To cause to move round or rotate; to shape on a lathe; to put in position; to change, to reverse.—*vi.* To move round; to change course; to have recourse; to become.—*n.* An act of turning; a bend; character, disposition; a short walk, performance, &c.; opportunity, occasion or obligation coming in succession; purpose; service, disservice. —**Turn'cock**, *n.* One in charge of public water-taps, &c.—**Turn'**ER, *n.* Esp., one who works with a lathe.—**Turn'key**, *n.* One in charge of prison keys.—**Turn'pike**, *n.* Formerly, a defensive frame set with pikes. A gate set across a road to ensure payment of tolls; the road.—**Turn'stile**, *n.* A revolving means of giving and controlling entrance.

Tur'nip, *n.* M.E. *nepe*, O.E. *nǽp*, L. *nāpus*, turnip. Orig. of *tur-* unknown. A plant of the mustard family cultivated for its root.

Tur'pentine, *n.* F. *turbentine*—L. *terebinthus*, G. *terebinthos*, the terebinth or turpentine tree. A resinous substance produced by certain trees, used for mixing paints, &c.

Tur'pitude, *n.* F. *turpitude*—L. *turpitūdo*, f. *turpis*, base. Depravity, vileness.

Tur'quoise, *n.* F., orig. fem. of *Turquois*, Turkish. A blue or greenish-blue gem.

Tur'ret, *n.* F. *tourette*, dim. of *tour*, TOWER. A small tower; a revolving tower for a gun in a ship or fort.

Turt'le, *n.*[1] O.E. *turtle*—L. *turtur*, imitative of the bird's sound. A kind of dove.

Turt'le, *n.*[2] Corr., with assimilation to prec., of Pg. *tartaruga* or Sp. *tortuga*—Late Pop.L. *tortūca*, TORTOISE. The sea-tortoise.

Tusk, *n.* O.E. *tusc, tux.* Cf. Old Fris. *tusk*, O.N. *toskr.* A long protruding tooth.

Tus'sle, *vi.* The same as TOUSLE. To struggle, scuffle.—*n.* A struggle or scuffle.

Tus'sock, *n.* Cf. TOUSE (under TOUSLE) and Sw. dial. *tuss*, wisp of hay. Dim. suff. *-ock.* A clump or hillock of grass, &c.

Tu'telage, *n.* L. *tūtēla*, protection (f. *tuēri* TUITION) + -AGE. Guardianship; period of being under guardianship.—**Tu'tel**AR,[1] **Tu'tel**ARY, *aa.*—**Tu'tor**, *n.* L. *tūtor*, guardian. A guardian; a private teacher; a college official directing studies.—**Tuto'r**IAL, *a.*

Twad'dle, *vi.* Formerly *twattle*, var. of TATTLE. To talk in a senseless or prosy way.—*n.* Such talk.—**Twad'dl**ER, *n.*

Twain, *a.* O.E. *twegen.* TWO. Two.—*n.* Two persons or things.

Twang, *vi.* and *t.* Imitative. To make, to cause to make, a ringing metallic sound.—*n.* Such a sound or a nasal sound.

Tweak, *vt.* M.E. *twikken*—O.E. *twiccian.* Cf. Ger. *zwicken*, to pinch. TWITCH. To pinch and pull sharply.—*n.* A tweaking.

Tweed, *n.* App. a corr. of TWILL by association with the *Tweed.* A twilled fabric used for men's clothes largely made in S. Scotland.

Twee'zers, *n.pl.* With -ER(*s*) f. obs. *tweezes*, small surgical instruments, f. *tweeze, twees*, surgeon's box of instruments, pl. of *twee, etwee*, F. *estuy* (now *étui*), sheath, case, of doubtful orig. Small pincers or forceps.

Twelve, *a.* and *n.* O.E. *twelf*, lit., 'two over (ten)', f. TWO + *-lif*, cogn. with LEAVE, *v.* The cardinal number next after eleven.—**Twelfth'-day**, *n.* The twelfth day after Christmas, the Epiphany. — **Twelfth'-night**, *n.* The eve of this.

Twen'ty, *a.* and *n.* O.E. *twentig*, f. *twen* = *twēn*, short for *twegen*, TWAIN + *-tig*, conn. with TEN. The cardinal number equal to two tens.

Twice, *adv.* M.E. *twiës*—O.E. *twiges*, earlier *twiwa*, f. root *twi*(*s*)-, double, conn. with *twá*, TWO. TWIST. Two times.

Twid'dle, *vt.* and *i.* Norw. *tvidla*, var. of *tvirla.* TWIRL. To twirl idly.

Twig, *n.* O.E. *twig*, orig., the fork of a branch, f. *twi-.* TWIST. A small branch.

Twi'light, *n.* *Twi-*, double, hence, between, doubtful. TWIST. The light when the sun is below the horizon; faint light.

Twill, *vt.* L.G. *twillen* = M.H.G. *zwilhen*, to double (*sc.* the warp-threads), f. *zwilch*, O.H.G. *zwilih*, two-threaded (a word app. suggested by L. BI*lix*, f. *licium*, thread. TRELLIS). To weave with certain warp-threads doubled so as to produce ribs.—*n.* The fabric thus woven.

Twin, *a.* O.E. *ge-twinnas*, twins, f. *twi-.* TWIST. Cf. O.N. *tvinnr*, in pairs. Forming one of a pair, esp. of children born together. *n.* One of a pair, esp. of such children.

Twine, *vt.* M.E. *twinen*—O.E. *twin*, a twisted thread. Cf. O.N *tvinni.* Root *twis-* as in TWIST. To form (a thread, &c.) by twisting; to coil, wind.—*vi.* To wind round.—*n.* String made of twisted strands; a coil or twist.

Twinge, *vt.* O.E. *twengan.* Cf. Ger. *zwingen*, to constrain. Cogn. with THONG. To affect with a sharp darting pain.—*n.* Such a pain.

Twink'le, *vi.* O.E. *twinclian*, freq. of *twink*, whence M.E. *twinken*, to blink, wink, conn. with *twikken.* TWEAK. To shine with a quivering light.—*n.* A gleam or sparkle.

Twirl, *vt.* and *i.* Freq. of O.E. *-thweran*, to turn. Cf. Norw. *tvirla.* To turn round rapidly; to turn round and round.

Twist, *vt.* M.E. *twisten*—O.E. *twist*, a rope. O.Teut. root *twi*(*s*)-, double, cogn. with G. *dis*, L. *bis*, TWICE. TWILIGHT. TWIN. TWINE. To wind (one thing) about another, to form (a cord, &c.) thus; to turn (a body) spirally by the operation of contrary forces acting at right angles to its axis; to wrench out of shape, distort.—*n.* Something twisted; the act of twisting; the state of being twisted.

Twit, *vt.* Shortened f. M.E. *atwiten*, O.E. *ætwītan*, to reproach, f. *æt*, AT, upon + *witan*, to blame, orig. to observe, cogn. with Goth. *witan*, to know. WIT. To reproach, taunt.

Twitch, *vt.* M.E. *twicchen*, var. of *twikken*. TWEAK. To pull *off* with a light jerk; to pluck at.—*vi.* To contract spasmodically.—*n.* Such a contraction; a pull or jerk.

Twit'ter, *vi.* Prob. imitative with freq. suff. *-er*. To utter a succession of light tremulous notes.—*n.* Such a succession of notes.

Two, *a.* and *n.* O.E. *twá*, fem., *twá*, *tú*, neut. For *twegen*, masc., see TWAIN. Cf. Du. *twee*, Ger. *zwei*. Cogn. with G. *duo*, L. *duo*. TWICE. The cardinal number next after one.—**Two'**FOLD, *a.* Double.—*adv.* Doubly.

Tym'panum, *n.* L. *tympanum*, G. *tumpanon*, TIMBREL, kettledrum. The ear-drum.

Type, *n.* F. *type*—L. *typus*—G. *tupos*, blow, mark, model or type, f. *tuptein*, to strike. ARCHETYPE. An illustration or specimen; a class; characteristic structure; a piece of metal bearing a letter, &c., for use in printing; such pieces collectively.—**Type'-writer**, *n.* A writing machine.—**Typ'**ICAL, *a.*—**Typ'i**FY, *vt.* To serve as a type of.—**Typi**FICA'TION, *n.*—**Typog'raphy**, *n.* G. *graphein*, to write. The art of printing; style of printing.—**Typograph'**IC, **Typograph'**ICAL, *aa.*

Ty'phoid, *a.* TYPHUS + -OID. Like typhus. *n.* A fever with intestinal irritation, enteric.

Typhoon', *n.* Arab. *ṭūfān*—G. *tuphōs*, cogn. with *tuphos*. (See next.) A violent hurricane.

Ty'phus, *n.* G. *tuphos*, smoke, fever-stupor. A fever with eruption of purple spots and (usually) delirium.

Ty'rant, *n.* O.F. *tiran*, *tyrant*—L. *tyrannus*—G. *turannos*, absolute ruler, tyrant. A cruel or oppressive ruler.—**Tyran'n**ICAL, *a.*—**Tyran'nicide**, *n.* L. *tyrannicīda*. -CIDE (1). A killer of a tyrant. -CIDE (2). The killing of a tyrant.—**Tyr'ann**IZE, *vi.*—**Tyr'ann**OUS, *a.*—**Tyr'ann**Y,[1] *n.*

U

Ubiq'uity, *n.* F. *ubiquité*, as if f. a L. **ubiquitas* formed f. *ubīque*, everywhere. A being everywhere.—**Ubiq'uit**OUS, *a.*

Ud'der, *n.* O.E. *úder*, corresp. to M.Du. *uder*, O.H.G. *ûter* (Ger. *euter*). Cogn. with Skr. *ūdhar*, G. *outhar*, L. *ūber*. EXUBERANT. The milk-bag of the cow, &c.

Ug'ly, *a.* M.E. *uglike*, *ugly*—O.N. *uggligr*, fearful, f. *uggr*, fear + *-ligr* = O.E. *-líc*, -LY.[1] Repulsive; ill-omened.—**Ug'li**NESS, *n.*

Ul'cer, *n.* F. *ulcère*—L. *ulcus*, *ulceris*, a sore. A sore discharging pus.—**Ul'cer**ATE,[3] *vi.* To form an ulcer.—*vt.* To affect with or as with an ulcer.—**Ulcer**A'TION, *n.*—**Ul'cer**OUS, *a.*

Ul'na, *n.* L. = G. *ōlenē*, elbow. The longer of the two bones of the forearm.

Ulte'rior, *a.* L. *ulterior*, comp. of **ulter*, beyond, on the other side. On the further side; beyond what is seen or avowed.

Ul'timate, *a.* L. *ultimātus*, pa.pple. of *ultimāre*, to come to an end, f. *ultimus*, last, superl. of **ulter*. (See prec.) Furthest; last.—**Ul'timate**LY,[2] *adv.* Finally, in the end.—**Ultima'tum**, *n.* Neut. of *ultimātus*. A final proposal or request the rejection of which involves war.—**Ul'timo**, *adv.* Ablative sing. masc. (sc. *mense*, month) of *ultimus*. Belonging to last month.

Ul'tramarine', *a.* Sp. *ultramarino*, beyond the sea, as *n.*, a blue colour—L. *ultrā*, beyond + *mare*, sea (MARINE) + *-īnus* (-INE). Beyond the sea.—*n.* A natural blue pigment.

Ultramon'tane, *a.* F. *ultramontain*—It. *ultramontano*—L. *ultrā*, beyond + *mons*, *montis*, mountain (MOUNT) + *-ānus* (-AN). South of the Alps; Italian.—*n.* One of the Italian party in the R.C. Church.—**Ultramon'tan**ISM, *n.*

Ultro'neous, *a.* L.L. *ultrōneus*, of one's own accord, f. *ultro*, spontaneously. Spontaneous.

Um'ber, *n.* F. *ombre*, short for *terre d'ombre*, It. *terra d'ombra*, 'earth of shadow'—L. *terra*, earth (TERRESTRIAL) + *dē*, of + *umbra*, shadow (UMBRAGE). A natural dark brown pigment.

Umbili'cal, *a.* O.F. *umbilical*, a. f. *umbilic*, L. *umbilicus*, navel, cogn. with G. *omphalos*. Pertaining to the navel.

Um'brage, *n.* O.F. *ombrage*, *umbrage*, f. *ombre*, L. *umbra*, shadow + -AGE. ADUMBRATE. PENUMBRA. Shade; that which affords shade; offence, resentment.—**Umbra'**GEOUS, *a.* Affording shade; shady.—**Umbrel'la**, *n.* It. *ombrella*, *umbrella*, a parasol, dim. of *ombra*, L. *umbra*. A portable collapsible shade carried for protection against rain.

Um'pire, *n.* M.E. *nompere*, *noumpere*, &c., lit., 'an odd man', hence, one called in to arbitrate—O.E. *nonper*, *nomper*, peerless, odd, f. L. *non*, not + *pār*, equal. PAR. One to whose sole decision a controversy is referred.—*vi.* To act as umpire.—*vt.* To act as umpire in.

Unabashed', *a.* UN-[2]; **Unarm'**, *vt.* UN-[1]; &c. &c.

Note.—The derivatives in UN-[1] and UN-[2] are practically unlimited in number. As almost all of them explain themselves and are of no etymological interest, they are not here recorded. A few exceptions are inserted in their places. Examples of the formations are given in the List of Prefixes.

Unan'imous, *a.* L. *ūnanimus*, f. *ūnus*, ONE + *animus*, mind. Of one mind.—**Unan'imous**LY,[2] *adv.*—**Unanim'**ITY, *n.*

Unaware', *a.* UN-[2]. Not aware, unconscious.—**Unawares'**, *adv.* With advbl. genit. *-s*. Unexpectedly; unconsciously.

Unbo'som, *v.refl.* UN-[1]. To make a disclosure *of* one's secret opinions or feelings.

Un'cial, *a.* L. *unciālis*, inch-long, f. *uncia*, INCH. The variety of majuscule writing commonly found in the earlier manuscripts, as opposed to the later minuscule or cursive.

Un'cle, *n.* A.F. *uncle* (F. *oncle*)—L. *avunculus*, a mother's brother, lit., 'little grandfather', dim. of *avus*, grandfather. The brother of one's father or mother; also, an aunt's husband.

Uncouth', *a.* O.E. *uncúth*, unknown, hence, strange, odd, f. UN-[2] + *cúth*, pa.pple. of *cunnan*, to know. CAN, *v.* KITH. Clumsy.

Unc'tion, *n.* F. *onction*—L. *unctio*, *unctiōnis*, f. *ungĕre*, *unctum*, to ANOINT. UNGUENT. The act of anointing; a quality of speech exciting fervour, devotion, &c.; emotional warmth; simulated fervour, devotion, &c.—**Unc'tu**OUS, *a.* Greasy, oily; having or characterized by unction.

Un'der, *prep.* O.E. *under*. Cf. O.N. *undir*, Du. *onder*, Ger. *unter*. Below, beneath; inferior to; subject to; in conformity with;

bound by; included in; in the time of.—*adv.* In a lower place, condition, or degree.—*a.* Lower; lower in rank or degree.
Underbred′, *a.* UNDER-. Ill-bred, vulgar.
Undercharge′, *vt.* UNDER-. To charge less than a fair sum for.—**Un′dercharge**, *n.* Too low a charge.
Undergo′, *vt.* UNDER-. To endure, sustain; to be subjected to, experience.
Undergrad′uate, *n.* UNDER-. One who has not taken a degree.
Un′dergrowth, *n.* UNDER-. Shrubs or small trees growing beneath large trees.
Underhand′, *adv.* UNDER-. By secret means; by fraud.—*a.* Secret; sly, deceitful.
Underhung′, *a.* UNDER-. Of the lower jaw, projecting beyond the upper.
Underlie′, *vt.* UNDER-. To lie beneath; to form the foundation or basis of.
Underline′, *vt.* UNDER-. To draw a line beneath.
Un′derling, *n.* UNDER, *a.* + -LING (2). A subordinate.
Undermine′, *vt.* UNDER-. To make an excavation beneath; to injure insidiously.
Underneath′, *adv.* M.E. *undernethe*, &c., f. UNDER- + *nethe*, O.E. *neothan*, below, f. *neothera*, NETHER. Below, in a lower place. —*prep.* Under, beneath.
Un′dershot, *a.* UNDER-. Moved by water passing under.
Undersized′, *a.* UNDER-. Of less than the usual size or stature.
Understand′, *vt.* O.E. *understandan*, lit. 'to stand under or among', hence, to comprehend, f. *under-* (UNDER-) + *standan*, to STAND. To perceive the meaning or significance of; to infer; to take for granted.—*vi.* To be informed, learn.—**Understand′ing**, *n.* The power of knowing or of abstract thought; agreement of minds; something agreed upon.
Undertake′, *vt.* M.E. *undertaken*, f. UNDER- + *taken*, to TAKE. To take upon oneself; to take in hand; to answer for.—*vi.* To assume responsibility; to become bound. —**Un′dertaker**, *n.* One who undertakes; one who manages funerals.—**Undertak′ing**, *vbl.n.* An act of undertaking; an enterprise; an obligation.
Un′dertone, *n.* UNDER-. A low tone.
Un′dertow, *n.* UNDER-. A current below the surface moving in a direction different from that of the surface-current; the backward flow of a breaking wave.
Un′derwood, *n.* UNDER-. Small trees or bushes growing beneath large trees.
Underwrite′, *vt.* UNDER-. To write below; to agree to pay by signing one's name, esp. in marine insurance; to agree to take up (shares, &c., of a company, &c., which the public may not take up).—**Un′derwriter**, *n.* One who underwrites; one who undertakes marine insurance.
Undo′, *vt.* UN-[1]. To annul; to ruin; to unfasten, unloose.
Un′dulate, *vi.* L. *undulātus*, wavy, f. **undula*, dim. of *unda*, wave. ABOUND. WATER. To move in or as in waves.—**Undula′tion**, *n.*—**Un′dulatory**, *a.*
Ungain′ly, *a.* With -LY[1] f. M.E. *ungein*, inconvenient, f. UN-[2] + O.N. *gegn*, ready, convenient, conn. with O.E. *gegn*. AGAIN. Uncouth, clumsy, awkward.
Un′guent, *n.* L. *unguentum*, f. L. *ungĕre* or *unguĕre*. UNCTION. An ointment.

U′nicorn, *n.* O.F. *unicorne*—L. *ūnicornis*, one-horned, f. *ūnus*, ONE + *cornū*, HORN. A fabulous animal with a single long horn.
U′niform, *a.* F. *uniforme*—L. *ūniformis*, having only one form, f. *ūnus*, ONE + *forma*, FORM. Not variable or changing; of the same form or character with others.—*n.* A distinctive dress worn by members of the same body.—**Un′iformly**,[2] *adv.*—**Unifor′mity**, *n.*—**U′nify**, *vt.* To form into one.—**Unifica′tion**, *n.*
U′nion, *n.* F. *union*—L. *ūnio*, *ūniōnis*, oneness, f. *ūnus*, ONE. ONION. The act of joining into one; the state of being so joined; the result of such joining; a combination, confederation; a trade-union.—**U′nionist**, *n.* One opposed to the dissolution of the legislative union between Great Britain and Ireland. —**Union Jack′**, *n.* JACK.[2] The national flag of the United Kingdom.
Unique′, *a.* F. *unique*—L. *ūnicus*, f. *ūnus*, ONE. Single in its kind or excellence.
U′nison, *n.* F. *unisson*—Med.L. *ūnisonus*, having one sound, f. *ūnus*, ONE + *sonus*, SOUND.[1] ASSONANCE. The state of sounding at the same pitch; agreement, harmony.
Unite′, *vt.* L. *ūnīre*, *ūnītum*, f. *ūnus*, ONE. To join into one, to connect, associate.—*vi.* To become one, to combine.—**U′nity**, *n.* O.F. *unite*—L. *ūnitas*, f. *ūnus*. The state of being one; harmony, concord; artistic symmetry.—**U′nit**, *n.* Shortened f. *unity*. A single thing or person; a group regarded as an individual; a standard quantity; the number 1.—**Unita′rian**, *n.* One who denies the doctrine of the Trinity.—**Unita′rianism**, *n.*
Univer′sal, *a.* F. *universel*—L. *ūniversālis*, belonging to the whole, f. *ūniversus*, turned into a whole, f. *ūnus*, ONE + *vertĕre*, to turn. ADVERSE. Pertaining to all things or to all men; that can be predicated of all the members of a class.—**Univer′sally**,[2] *adv.*—**Universal′ity**, *n.*—**U′niverse**, *n.* F. *universe*—L. *ūniversum*, neut. of *ūniversus*. The whole system of existing things.—**Univer′sity**, *n.* F. *université*—L. *ūniversitas*, the whole, the universe, a society, in Med.L., a university, f. *ūniversus*. An institution for the purpose of study which has power to confer degrees.
Unkempt′, *a.* For *unkemb'd*, uncombed—O.E. *cemban*, to comb, f. *camb*, COMB. UN-.[2] Uncombed, rough.
Unless′, *conj.* Formerly *on lesse that*, in less than, on a less supposition than. If not, except when.
Unrav′el, *vt.* UN-[1] (1). To disentangle.
Unru′ly, *a.* UN-[2] + RULE, *n.* + -Y[2]. Disregarding rules, ungovernable.
Until′, *prep.* Altered f. UNTO. Cf. TILL, *prep.* Up to the time of.—*conj.* To the time that; so that at length; with negative, before.
Un′to, *prep.* Not in O.E. M.E. *unto*, f. Goth., Old Fris., O.S. *und*, up to, as far as + TO. To.
Up, *adv.* O.E. *úp*, *upp* = Goth. *iup*, O.H.G. *uf* (Ger. *auf*), O.N. *upp*, Du. *op*. ABOVE. OPEN. In or to a higher position; at or to a head, source, &c.; at or to a higher point or degree; in or into activity, &c.; wholly, quite. —*prep.* To or toward the head, &c., of.—**Up′ward**, *adv.* and *a.*—**Up′wards**, *adv.*
U′pas, *n.* Malay *ūpas*, a poisonous juice, (*pūhun*) *ūpas*, poison(-tree). The poisonous sap of an Eastern tree; the tree.
Upbraid′, *vt.* M.E. *upbreiden*, orig. app. 'to attack', f. UP-, on + *bregdan* (BRAID) in sense 'to lay hold of, seize'. To reproach.

Up'bringing, *n.* UP-. The process of bringing up; training, education.
Upheave', *vt.* UP-. To lift or raise up.—**Upheav'**AL, *n.*
Uphold', *vt.* UP-. To hold up; to support, maintain.—**Uphold'**ER, *n.* A supporter.
Uphol'sterer, *n.* With -ER f. *upholster* for *upholdSTER* = UPHOLDER in obs. sense 'one who carries on a business, an upholsterer'. One who supplies and fits in carpets, curtains, &c.—**Uphol'ster**, *vt.* Back-formation f. the *n.* To furnish with carpets, &c.; to put a textile covering on.—**Uphol'st**ERY, *n.*
Up'land, *n.* M.E. *upland*, f. UP, *adv.* The higher ground of a district.
Upon', *prep.* O.E. *uppon* = *upp*, UP + *on*, ON. Up and on, on.
Up'per, *a.* M.E. *upper*, comp. of UP. Higher in place or rank.—*n.* The upper part of a boot.
Up'pish, *a.* UP + -ISH. Assuming airs of superiority, arrogant.
Up'right, *a.* O.E. *upriht*, f. UP- + *riht*, straight. RIGHT. Erect, vertical; honest, just.—*n.* Something standing upright.
Up'roar, *n.* Du. *oproer*, f. *op*, UP + *roeren*, to stir, agitate = Ger. *rühren*, O.E. *hréran*. REARMOUSE. A tumult; disturbance.—**Uproa'r**IOUS, *a.*—**Uproa'rious**LY,[2] *adv.*
Upset', *vt.* UP-. Formerly, to set up. To overturn.—*n.* An upsetting or being upset.
Up'shot, *n.* UP-. Final issue, end.
Upstart', *vi.* UP-. To start up.—**Up'start**, *n.* One suddenly raised to wealth, power, &c.
U'ranus, *n.* L. *Uranus*—G. *Ouranos*, a personification of *ouranos*, heaven. The most distant but one of the planets.
Urbane', *a.* L. *urbānus*, belonging to a city, f. *urbs*, city. SUBURB. Having manners suited to a city, courteous.—**Urban'**ITY, *n.*—**Ur'ban**, *a.* Doublet of *urbane*. Of or pertaining to a city or town.
Ur'chin, *n.* Walloon *urechon*, O.F. *ireçon*, *eriçon*, *herisson*, hedgehog—L. *ēricius*. A hedgehog; a roguish or mischievous boy.
Urge, *vt.* L. *urgēre*, to press, push, urge. To request with earnestness; to press upon attention.—**Urg'**ENT, *a.* Demanding immediate action, cogent, vehement.—**Urg'ent**LY,[2] *adv.*—**Urg'**ENCY, *n.*
U'rine, *n.* F. *urine*—L. *ūrīna*, cogn. with G. *ouron*; also with Skr. *vāri*, *vār*, water. DIURETIC. The fluid secreted by the kidneys.—**U'ric**, *a.* F. *urique*, f. G. *ouron*. Of, pertaining to, obtained from urine.—**U'rin**AL, *n.* A place for urinating.—**U'rin**ARY, *a.*—**U'rin**ATE,[3] *vi.* To discharge urine.
Urn, *n.* F. *urne*—L. *urna*. A vase with a rounded body.
Use, *n.*[1] O.F. *us*—L. *ūsus*, f. *ūti*, *ūsus*, to use. ABUSE. USUFRUCT. USURY. UTENSIL. UTILITY. The act of employing or availing oneself of anything, employment; serviceableness, help, profit; occasion to employ, necessity; custom, habit.—*vt.* F. *user*—L.L. *ūsāre*, freq. of *ūti*. To employ, avail oneself of; to behave towards, treat; to accustom.—*vi.* To be accustomed (only in *pa.t.*)—**Us'**ABLE, *a.*—**Us'**AGE, *n.* The act of using; treatment; custom; the customary mode of employing a word, &c.—**Use'**FUL, *a.*—**Use'ful**LY,[2] *adv.*—**Use'ful**NESS, *n.*—**Use'**LESS, *a.*—**Use'less**NESS, *n.*—**U'sual**, *a.* In common use, habitual.—**U'sual**LY,[2] *adv.*
Use, *n.*[2] A modern spelling of A.F. *oeps*, *oes*, *uoes*, O.F. *oes*, *ues*—L. *opus*, employment, need. The benefit or profit of property held in trust.
Ush'er, *n.* A.F. *usser*, O.F. *ussier* (F. *huissier*), door-keeper, usher—L. *ostiārius*, door-keeper, f. *ostium*, door. A door-keeper; an officer who introduces strangers, &c.; an under-teacher.—*vt.* To introduce, announce.
U'sufruct, *n.* F. *usufruit*—L. *ūsusfructus*, f. *ūsus* (USE[1]) + *fructus*, FRUIT. The use of something belonging to another.
Usurp', *vt.* F. *usurper*—L. *ūsurpāre*, to employ, acquire, usurp. To seize by force or without right.—**Usurp**A'TION, *n.*—**Usurp'**ER, *n.*
U'sury, *n.* F. *usure*—L. *ūsūra*, use, interest, usury, f. *ūti*. USE.[1] Excessive interest on money lent; the practice of exacting such interest.—**U'sur**ER, *n.*—**Usu'r**IOUS, *a.*
Uten'sil, *n.* O.F. *utensile*—L. *ūtensilia*, utensils, neut. pl. of *ūtensilis*, fit for use, for **ūtentilis*, f. *ūtens*, *ūtentis*, pres.pple. of *ūti*. USE.[1] An instrument or implement.
U'terus, *n.* L. *uterus*, cogn. with G. *hustera*. HYSTERIC. The womb.—**U'ter**INE, *a.* Of or pertaining to the womb; born of the same mother, but by a different father.
Util'ity, *n.* F. *utilité*—L. *ūtilitas*, f. *ūtilis*, useful, f. *ūti*. USE.[1] Usefulness, profitableness; a useful thing.—**Utilita'rian**ISM, *n.* The doctrine that any useful act is justifiable; the doctrine of the greatest happiness of the greatest number.—**Utilita'r**IAN, *n.*—**U'til**IZE, *vt.* To make use of, turn to account.
Ut'most, *a.* M.E. *outemest*—O.E. *úte-m-est*, double superl. f. *út*, OUT. Furthest, extreme.—*n.* The furthest, the extreme.
Uto'pian, *a.* From Sir Thomas More's *Utopia* an imaginary island situated *nowhere*, f. G. *ou*, not + *topos*, place. TOPIC. Characteristic of an ardent but unpractical reformer.
Ut'ter, *a.* O.E. *útera*, *uttera*, comp. of *út*, OUT. Complete, total.—*vt.* Cf. Ger. *äussern*, f. *äusser*, outer. To emit audibly; to give expression to; to put in circulation.—**Ut'ter**ANCE, *n.*—**Ut'ter**LY,[2] *adv.*
U'vula, *n.* Mod.L. *ūvula*, dim. of L. *ūva*, grape, cluster, uvula. The pendent fleshy part of the palate.
Uxo'rious, *a.* With -OUS f. L. *uxōrius*, in sim. sense, f. *uxor*, wife. Excessively or foolishly fond of one's wife.

V

Vacate', *vt.* L. *vacāre*, *vacātum*, to be empty or at leisure. VACUUM. To quit the possession of, leave empty; to annul.—**Va'c**ANT, *a.* Empty; not filled, unoccupied; not engaged, idle; thoughtless, inane.—**Va'cant**LY,[2] *adv.*—**Va'c**ANCY, *n.*—**Vac**A'TION, *n.* The act of vacating; holidays.
Vac'cinate, *vt.* As if f. a L. v. **vaccināre*, **vaccinātum*, f. *vaccīnus*, a. f. *vacca*, cow. To inoculate with cow-pox in order to secure immunity from small-pox.—**Vaccin**A'TION, *n.*—**Vac'c**INE, *a.* Of cows or vaccination.
Vac'illate, *vi.* L. *vacillāre*, *vacillātum*, to sway to and fro, vacillate. To waver in opinion or resolution.—**Vacill**A'TION, *n.*
Vac'uum, *n.* L. *vacuum*, an empty space, f. *vacuus*, empty, f. *vacāre*. VACATE. Space void of matter.—**Vac'u**OUS, *a.* Empty; without intelligence.—**Vacu'**ITY, *n.*
Vag'abond, *n.* F. *vagabond*—L. *vagābundus*, wandering about, f. *vagāri*, to wander. EX-

TRAVAGANT. VAGUE. A vagrant; a rascal.—*a.* Vagrant.—**Vag'abond**AGE, *n.*

Vaga'ry, *n.* Orig. used as a *v.*—L. *vagāri.* (See prec.) A freak or whim.

Vagi'na, *n.* L. *vāgina.* A sheath; the passage leading to the womb.

Va'grant, *n.* A.F. *wakerant*, a vagrant, O.F. *walcrant*, pres.pple. of *walcrer*, to wander—M.H.G. *walgern*, to walk about, cogn. with WALK. An idle wanderer, a tramp.—*a.* Wandering idly.—**Va'gr**ANCY, *n.*

Vague, *a.* F. *vague*—L. *vagus*, wandering, whence *vagāri.* VAGABOND. Indefinite, indeterminate.—**Vague'**LY,[2] *adv.*

Vain, *a.* F. *vain*—L. *vānus*, empty, vain. EVANESCE. VANITY. VAUNT. Worthless, trivial; useless, ineffectual; foolish; conceited, foolishly proud.—**Vain'**LY,[2] *adv.*

Val'ance, *n.* Prob. f. *Valence*, near Lyons, still famous for silks. A kind of damask; a short curtain on a bedstead, &c.

Vale, *n.* F. *val*—L. *vallis.* A VALLEY.

Valedic'tion, *n.* With -ION f. L. *valēdictus*, pa.pple. of *valēdicĕre*, to say farewell, f. *valē* (imp. of *valēre*, to be strong), farewell + *dicĕre*, to say. AVAIL. DICTION. A farewell.—**Valedic't**ORY, *a.*

Val'et, *n.* F. *valet*, groom, O.F. *varlet.* VARLET. A male personal attendant.

Valetu'dinary, *a.* O.F. *valetudinaire*—L. *valētūdinārius*, sickly, f. *valētūdo, valētūdinis*, health (good or bad), f. *valēre.* AVAIL. Sickly.—**Valetudina'ri**AN, *a.* In same sense.—*n.* A sickly person.

Val'iant, *a.* F. *vaillant*, O.F. *vailant*, pres. pple. of *valoir.* AVAIL. Brave, courageous.

Val'id, *a.* F. *valide*—L. *validus*, strong, f. *valēre.* AVAIL. Well grounded, sufficient in law.—**Val'id**ATE,[3] *vt.*—**Valid'**ITY, *n.*

Valise', *n.* F. *valise*—It. *valigia*, of unknown orig. A travelling-bag.

Val'ley, *n.* O.F. *valee* (F. *vallée*), lengthened from *val.* VALE. AVALANCHE. A relatively low tract of land between hills.

Val'our, *n.* O.F. *valor*, L. *valor*, value, f. *valēre*, to be strong or worth. AVAIL. Bravery, courage, intrepidity.—**Val'or**OUS, *a.*

Val'ue, *n.* O.F. *valuë*, orig. fem. of *valu*, pa.pple. of *valoir.* AVAIL. Worth, importance; price, equivalent.—*vt.* To estimate the value of; to have in high esteem; to take into account, care for.—**Val'u**ABLE, *a.* Capable of being valued; of great value or worth.—*n.* A thing of value.—**Valu**A'TION, *n.*—**Val'ue**LESS, *a.*—**Val'u**ER, *n.*

Valve, *n.* F. *valve*—L. *valva*, gen. in *pl.*, folding-door. A device controlling the flow of a liquid, &c., through a pipe or outlet.—**Val'vul**AR,[1] *a.* (With *-ul-* of *aa.*)

Vamp, *n.* M.E. *vampay*—O.F. *avant-pied*, the fore-part of the foot, f. *avant*, in front, forward (AVAUNT) + *pied*, L. *pēs, pedis*, foot. The upper front part of a boot; a piece added for the sake of appearance; an improvised accompaniment.—*vt.* To repair, furbish up.

Vam'pire, *n.* F. *vampire*—Ger. *vampir*—Servian *vampir*, blood-sucking ghost, prob. of Turkish orig. A spectre supposed to quit the grave at night and to suck human blood.

Van, *n.*[1] Short for *Van-guard*—M.E. *vantwarde*—O.F. *avant-warde, avant-garde*, f. *avant*, in front (AVAUNT) + *warde, garde*, GUARD. ADVANCE. The foremost division or front of an army or fleet.

Van, *n.*[2] Short for CARAVAN. A vehicle for goods, generally covered.

Van'dal, *n.* One of the barbarian tribe *Vandali.* A wilful or ignorant destroyer of a work of art or the like.—**Van'dal**ISM, *n.*

Vane, *n.* O.E. *fana*, a small flag. Cf. Du. *vaan*, Ger. *fahne.* A weather-cock.

Vanil'la, *n.* Sp. *vainilla*, dim. of *vaina*, scabbard, pod—L. *vāgina.* VAGINA. A tropical plant; a fragrant oil obtained from it.

Van'ish, *vi.* M.E. *evanisshen, vanissen, vanisshen*—A.F. *evaniss-*, lengthened stem of *evanir*, O.F. *esvanir*—L.L. type **exvanīre* for L. *ēvānescĕre.* EVANESCE. To disappear.

Van'ity, *n.* F. *vanité*—L. *vānitas*, f. *vānus.* VAIN. The character or state of being vain; that which is vain.

Van'quish, *vt.* M.E. *venkisen, venquishen*—A.F. *venquiss-*, lengthened stem of *venquir*, O.F. *veinquir*, var. of *veincre* (F. *vaincre*), L. *vincĕre*, to conquer. CONVICT. To conquer.

Van'tage, *n.* Shortened f. *avantage*, M.E. form of ADVANTAGE. Advantage.

Vap'id, *a.* L. *vapidus*, stale, flat. Insipid, flat; dull, spiritless.—**Vapid'**ITY, *n.*

Va'pour, *n.* F. *vapeur*—L. *vapor.* EVAPORATE. Cogn. with G. *kapnos*, smoke. An exhalation of moisture; the gaseous form assumed by a solid under heat.—*vi.* To boast or vaunt.—**Va'por**IZE, *vt.*—**Va'por**OUS, *a.*

Var'icose, *a.* L. *varicōsus*, f. *varix, varicis*, a dilated vein. Morbidly dilated.

Var'let, *n.* O.F. *vaslet, varlet*, groom, dim. of *vasal, vassal*, VASSAL. VALET. A rascal.

Var'nish, *n.* F. *vernis.* Cf. It. *vernice*, Sp. *berniz.* Orig. unknown. A clear fluid which hardens without losing transparency; a lustrous or specious appearance.—*vt.* To lay varnish on; to give a specious appearance to.

Va'ry, *vt.* F. *varier*—L. *variāre*, f. *varius*, various. To change, diversify, modify.—*vi.* To be changed or modified; to differ or be different, be unlike or diverse.—**Va'ri**ABLE, *a.*—**Vari**ABIL'ITY, *n.*—**Va'ri**ANCE, *n.* Dissension.—**Va'ri**ANT, *a.* Different, diverse.—*n.* Something substantially the same but in a different form.—**Vari**A'TION, *n.*—**Va'riegate**, *vt.* L. *variegāre, variegātum.* (*Varius* + *agĕre*, to drive, to make). To diversify by means of different colours.—**Variega**'TION, *n.*—**Vari'ety**, *n.* L. *varietas.* The state or quality of being varied or various; a varied assortment; a sort or kind.—**Va'ri**OUS, *a.* Diverse, manifold; divers, several.

Vas'culum, *n.* L. *vasculum*, dim. of *vās*, a vessel. (See next.) A botanist's specimen-case.—**Vas'cul**AR,[1] *a.* Of or pertaining to vessels in the body which convey fluids.

Vase, *n.* F. *vase*—L. *vāsum* = *vās*, a VESSEL. A vessel of various materials and forms generally used as an ornament.

Vas'sal, *n.* F. *vassal*, of Celtic orig. VARLET. One holding land by the obligation to render services to his lord; a dependent or retainer.—**Vas'sal**AGE, *n.*

Vast, *a.* F. *vaste*—L. *vastus*, desert, vast. WASTE. Very great in extent, degree or power.—**Vast'**LY[2], *adv.*—**Vast'**NESS, *n.*

Vat, *n.* O.E. *fæt.* Cf. Du. *vat*, Ger. *fass.* A large tub.—*vt.* To put or treat in a vat.

Vatic'inate, *vi.* and *t.* L. *vāticināri, vāticinātus*, f. *vāticinus*, prophetic, f. *vātes*, prophet. To foretell.—**Vaticin**A'TION, *n.*

Vault, *n.*[1] M.E. *voute, vaute*, &c.—O.F. *voute* (F. *voûte*), earlier *volte*, orig. fem. of *volt*, bent, bowed, f. **voltus* for L. *volūtus*, pa.pple. of *volvĕre*, to roll, turn round. CONVOLVE. An arched roof; an arched apartment; a continued arch; a cellar.—*v.*[1]*t.* To form with an arched roof.

Vault, *v.*[2]*i.* O.F. *volter*, f. *volte*, a round, turn, gambol—It. *volta*, a sudden turn, f. **voltus*. (See prec.) To leap or spring with the hand resting on something.—*vt.* To vault over.—*n.*[2] Such a leap or spring.

Vaunt, *vi.* F. (*se*) *vanter*, to flatter oneself, to boast—L.L. *vānitāre*, to speak vanity, flatter, f. L. *vānus*, VAIN. To boast.—*vt.* To boast of.—*n.* A boast.

Veal, *n.* O.F. *veël*, calf—L. *vitellus*, dim. of *vitulus*, calf. VELLUM. The flesh of a calf.

Vedette′, **Vidette′**, *n.* O.F. *vedette*—It. *vedetta*, horse-sentry, orig., watch-tower, f. *vedere*, L. *vidēre*, to see. ADVICE. A mounted sentinel.

Veer, *vi.* F. *virer*, of doubtful orig. ENVIRON. To turn, change direction; to change one's mind.—*vt.* To slacken, let out.

Veg′etable, *a.* O.F. *vegetable*, fit or able to live—L. *vegetābilis*, animating, f. *vegetāre*, to animate, f. *vegetus*, animated, f. *vegēre*, to quicken, arouse, conn. with *vigēre*. VIGOUR. Having life such as a plant has; of or pertaining to plants.—*n.* A plant, esp. one used for culinary purposes.—**Veget**A′RIAN, *n.* One who eats vegetables only.—**Veg′et**ATE,[3] *vi.* To live a mere inactive physical life.—**Vege-t**A′TION, *n.* The process of the growth of plants; plants collectively.

Ve′hement, *a.* O.F. *vehement*—L. *vehemens*, *vehementis*. Impetuous, violent.—**Ve′he-ment**LY,[2] *adv.*—**Ve′hem**ENCE, *n.*

Ve′hicle, *n.* L. *vehiculum*, f. *vehĕre*, to convey. CONVEX. INVEIGH. WEIGH. A carriage moving on land; a means of transmission, application, &c.—**Vehic′ul**AR,[1] *a.*

Veil, *n.* O.F. *veile* (F. *voile*)—L. *vēlum*, a cloth, a sail. An article of dress shading the face; a disguise or pretext.—*vt.* To cover with or as with a veil.

Vein, *n.* F. *veine*—L. *vēna*. A blood-vessel taking blood to the heart; an occurrence of ore; a streak or stripe; mood, cast of mind.—*vt.* To streak as with veins.—**Ve′n**OUS, *a.*

Vel′lum, *n.* M.E. *velim*—O.F. *velin*. Cf. L.L. *vitulinium*, f. L. *vitulīnus*, a. f. *vitulus*, calf. VEAL. The skin of calves (sometimes of goats) prepared for writing, printing, &c.

Veloc′ity, *n.* O.F. *velocité*—L. *vēlōcitas*, f. *vēlox*, *vēlōcis*, swift. Swiftness; rate of speed.

Vel′vet, *n.* A.F. *velwet*, *veluet*—L.L. *velluctum*—L. *villus*, shaggy hair, conn. with *vellus*. WOOL. A silk stuff with a thick, short, soft pile.—**Vel′vet**Y,[2] *a.*—**Velveteen′**, *n.* -*Een* = n. suff. -*ine*. Imitation velvet.

Ve′nal, *a.* O.F. *venal*, L. *vēnālis*, saleable, f. *vēnus* or *vēnum*, sale. Cogn. with G. *ōnos*, price. Open to receiving a bribe.—**Venal′**ITY, *n.*

Vend, *vt.* F. *vendre*—L. *vendĕre*, shortened f. *vēnundăre*, f. *vēnum*, sale (see prec.) + *dăre*, to give, offer. To sell.—**Vend′**IBLE, *a.*

Vendet′ta, *n.* It.—L. *vindicta*, vengeance, f. *vindicāre*. AVENGE. A state of private war in which the nearest of kin avenge the slaying of a relative.

Veneer′, *vt.* Formerly *fineer*—Ger. *furniren*, to furnish small pieces of wood, veneer—F. *fournir*, to FURNISH. To put a thin layer of fine wood on (inferior wood).—*n.* A thin piece of wood used for this purpose.

Ven′erate, *vt.* L. *venerāri*, *venerātus*. To reverence, revere.—**Ven′er**ABLE, *a.*—**Ven-er**A′TION, *n.*

Vene′real, *a.* Formed with -AL f. L. *Venereus*, pertaining to VENUS. Arising from or connected with sexual intercourse.

Ven′ery, *n.* O.F. *venerie*, f. *vener*, L. *vēnāri*, to hunt. VENISON. Hunting.

Ven′geance, *n.* F. *vengeance*, f. *venger*, to avenge—L. *vindicāre*. AVENGE. Punishment inflicted for wrong.—**Venge′**FUL, *a.*

Ve′nial, *a.* O.F. *venial*—L. *veniālis*, f. *venia*, pardon. That may be pardoned, excusable.

Ven′ison, *n.* M.E. *veneison*—A.F. *veneisun*, O.F. *venaison*—L. *vēnātio*, *vēnātiōnis*, the chase, game, f. *vēnāri*. VENERY. The flesh of deer.

Ven′om, *n.* A.F. and O.F. *venim* (F. *venin*)—L. *venēnum*, poison. Poison; spite, malignity.—**Ven′om**OUS, *a.*

Vent, *n.* O.F. *fente*, cleft, f. *fendre*, L. *findĕre*, to cleave (FISSURE), influenced by F. *vent*, L. *ventus*, wind. (See next.) A small hole; an outlet; utterance.—*vt.* To give vent to.

Ven′tilate, *vt.* L. *ventilāre*, *ventilātum*, to toss in the air, winnow, f. *ventulus*, dim. of *ventus*, WIND. To supply with fresh air; to bring forward, make public.—**Ventil**A′TION, *n.*—**Ven′tilat**OR, *n.*

Ven′tricle, *n.* F. *ventricule*—L. *ventriculus*, dim. of *venter*, *ventris*, belly. A small cavity in the body; a hollow part or organ.—**Ventric′ul**AR,[1] *a.*—**Ventril′oquist**, *n.* Formed with -IST f. L. *ventriloquus*, a ventriloquist, lit. 'one who speaks from his belly', f. *venter* + *loqui*, to speak. One who can so utter sounds that they appear to proceed from some source other than the speaker.—**Ventril′o-qu**ISM, *n.*

Ven′ture, *n.* Shortened f. *aventure*, M.E. form of ADVENTURE. An undertaking involving risk; a commercial speculation; something hazarded.—*vi.* To dare; to run a hazard.—*vt.* To expose to hazard; to run the hazard of.—**Ven′ture**SOME, *a.*—**Ven′tur**OUS, *a.*

Ven′ue, *n.* O.F. *venuë*, a coming, orig. fem of *venu*, pa.pple. of *venir*, L. *venīre*, to come, app. confused with O.F. *visne*, neighbourhood, venue—L. *vicīnia*, neighbourhood, f. *vīcīnus*, neighbouring. ADVENT. VICINAGE. The district in which a trial takes place.

Ve′nus, *n.* L. *Venus*, *Veneris*. The Roman goddess of Love; one of the seven planets.

Vera′cious, *a.* L. *vērax*, *vērācis*, true (f. *vērus*, true) + -OUS. VERDICT. VERY. Truthful, true.—**Verac′**ITY, *n.*

Veran′da, **Veran′dah**, *n.* Pg. *varanda*—Old Sp. *varanda*, a stair-railing, of doubtful orig. A light gallery attached to the outside of a building.

Verb, *n.* F. *verbe*—L. *verbum*, WORD. A word that asserts or declares.—**Ver′b**AL, *a.* Of, pertaining to, consisting in words; relating to or concerned with words only; spoken, not written; of or pertaining to a verb.—**Ver′-bal**LY,[2] *adv.*—**Verba′tim**, *adv.* Med.L. Word for word.—**Ver′biage**, *n.* F. *verbiage*—O.F. **verbier*, to talk. The use of too many words, prolixity.—**Verb**OSE′, *a.* Wordy, prolix.—**Verbos′**ITY, *n.*

Ver′dant, *a.* As if f. F. **verdant* for *verdissant*, pres.pple. of *verdir*, to flourish—O.F. *verd*, L. *viridis*, green. Green, fresh.—**Ver′-d**URE, *n.* The fresh green of vegetation; green vegetation.—**Ver′dur**OUS, *a.*

Ver′dict, *n.* A.F. and O.F. *verdit*—L.L. *vērēdictum*, true saying, verdict, f. L. *vērē*, truly (adv. f. *vērus* (VERACIOUS)) + *dictum*, neut. pa.pple. of *dicere*, to say. ADDICT. The decision of a jury; decision, judgement.

Ver′digris, *n.* M.E. *verdegrece*—O.F. *verd*

de gris, f. *verd*, green (VERDANT) + *de*, of + *Gris*, pl. of *Gri*, L. *Graecus*, Greek. A substance obtained by exposing copper to air in presence of acetic acid.

Verge, *n.* M.E. *verge*, F. *verge*, wand, rod—L. *virga*, rod. A rod of office, a mace; edge, brink, border; scope, room.—**Verg'**ER, *n.* A mace-bearer; an official in charge of the interior of a church.

Verge, *vi.* L. *vergĕre*, to incline. To border *upon*, approach closely.

Ver'ify, *vt.* O.F. *verifier*—L.L. *vērificāre*, to make true, f. *vērus*, true + *facĕre*, to make. VERACIOUS. To prove or confirm the truth of; to ascertain to be correct.—**Ver'ifi**ABLE, *a.*—**Veri**FICA'TION, *n.*—**Verisimil'itude**, *n.* L. *vērisimilitūdo*, f. *vēri* (genit. neut. of *vērus*) + *similis*, like. ASSIMILATE. The appearance of truth, probability, likelihood.—**Ver'itable**, *a.* O.F. *veritable*. True, real.—**Ver'ity**, *n.* O.F. *verité*—L. *vēritas*. Truth.

Ver'ily, *adv.* VERY + -LY.[2] In truth.

Ver'juice, *n.* O.F. *verjus*, lit. 'green juice', 'juice of green grapes', f. *verd* (VERDANT) + *jus*, JUICE. An acid liquid obtained from fruit; sourness of temper, manner, &c.

Vermicel'li, *n.* It. *vermicelli*, lit., 'little worms', from the shape, pl. of *vermicello*, dim. of *verme*, L. *vermis*, WORM. An Italian paste of flour, &c., manufactured in long slender threads.—**Ver'micide**, *n.* -CIDE (1). A substance which destroys intestinal worms.—**Ver'mifuge**, *n.* L. *fugāre*, to drive away. A substance which expels such worms.

Vermil'ion, *n.* O.F. *vermillon*, little worm (*i.e.* the kermes insect), vermilion—L. *vermiculus*, dim. of *vermis*. (See prec.) A bright red pigment; the colour.—*a.* Of the colour.

Ver'min, *n.* F. *vermine*—L. **verminus*, a. f. *vermis*. VERMICELLI. *Collectively*, noxious or troublesome animals.—**Ver'min**OUS, *a.*

Vernac'ular, *a.* L. *vernāculus*, native, f. *verna*, a home-born slave. Of one's country or mother-tongue.—*n.* One's mother-tongue.

Ver'nal, *a.* L. *vernālis*, f. *vēr*, spring, cogn. with G. *ear*, O.N. *vár*. Of spring.

Ver'nier, *n.* Invented by Pierre *Vernier*, 1580-1637. A small sliding scale attached to a barometer, &c., for fine measurement.

Ver'satile, *a.* L. *versātilis*, f. *versāre*, *versātum*, freq. of *vertĕre*. (See next.) Turning with ease from one thing or subject to another.—**Versatil'**ITY, *n.*

Verse, *n.* M.E. *fers*, *vers*, O.E. *fers*—L. *versus*, a line, row, verse, f. *vertĕre*, *versum*, to turn. ADVERSE. DIVERT. PROSE. A line of poetry; metrical composition, poetry; a short division of a composition.—**Versed**, *ppl.a.* Imitated f. L. *versātus*, pa.pple. of *versāre*. (See prec.) Conversant, skilled.—**Ver'sicle**, *n.* L. *versiculus*, dim. of *versus*. A short verse said or sung in a church service.—**Ver'si**FY, *vt.* To turn into verse.—*vi.* To make verses.—**Versi**FICA'TION, *n.*—**Ver'**SION, *n.* A translation; a statement, account, or description.—**Ver'so**, *n.* L., ablative neut. of *versus*, pa.pple. of *vertĕre*. The back of an object; a left-hand page.

Ver'tebra, *n.*; *pl.* **Ver'tebræ**. L. *vertebra*, f. *vertĕre*. (See prec.) Any bone of the spine.—**Ver'tebr**AL, *a.*—**Ver'tebr**ATE,[2] *a.* Having a spine.

Ver'tex, *n.*; *pl.* **Ver'tices**, **Ver'texes**. L. *vertex*, *verticis*, whirl, summit, f. *vertĕre*. VERSE. The highest point, the summit.—**Ver'tic**AL, *a.* Directly overhead; upright.

Verti'go, *n.* L. *vertigo*, *vertīginis*, f. *vertĕre*. VERSE. Giddiness.—**Vertig'in**OUS, *a.*

Ver'y, *a.* M.E. *verrai*—O.F. *verai* (F. *vrai*), true—L.L. type **vērācus*, conn. with L. *vērax*. AVER. VERACIOUS. True, real.—*adv.* In a high degree, to a great extent.

Ves'icle, *n.* L. *vēsicula*, dim. of *vēsica* bladder. A small cavity or cell in the body.—**Vesic'ul**AR,[1] *a.*

Ves'per, *n.* L. *vesper*, evening-star, evening, cogn. with G. *hesperos*. The evening-star, evening; in *pl.*, an evening service, evensong.

Ves'sel, *n.* A.F. *vessel*, O.F. *vaissel*—L. *vascellum*, dim. of *vās*. VASE. A utensil for holding liquids and other things; a ship; a canal or tube in the body in which a fluid is secreted, contained, or conveyed.

Vest, *n.* L. *vestis*, a garment, clothing, cogn. with G. *hennunai*, to clothe, Skr. *vas*, to put on clothes. DIVEST. WEAR.[1] A waistcoat.—*vt.* To clothe; to endow; with *in*, to commit to.—*vi.* To come or descend, to take effect.

Ves'tal, *a.* F. *vestale*, vestal virgin—L. *vestālis*, of or pertaining to Vesta, as *n.*, a vestal virgin, f. *Vesta*, goddess of flocks and herds and of the household. Of Vesta; of or characteristic of a vestal.—*n.* A virgin consecrated to Vesta; a virgin, a nun.

Ves'tibule, *n.* L. *vestibulum*, a fore-court. A space inside an outer door.

Ves'tige, *n.* F. *vestige*—L. *vestigium*, footprint. INVESTIGATE. A mark or trace.

Vest'ment, *n.* O.F. *vestement*—L. *vestimentum*, f. *vestire*, to clothe, f. *vestis*. VEST. A garment; a ceremonial or official garment or robe, esp. when worn by the clergy.—**Vest'ry**, *n.* O.F. *vestiarie*—L. *vestiārium*, a wardrobe, neut. of *vestiārius*, a. f. *vestis*. A room attached to a church in which vestments are kept; a board elected by the ratepayers of a parish.—**Vest'**URE, *n.* Clothing, dress.

Vetch, *n.* O.F. *veche*—L. *vicia*. A climbing plant cultivated for fodder.

Vet'eran, *a.* L. *veterānus*, tried, experienced, f. *vetus*, *veteris*, old, cogn. with G. *etos*, year. INVETERATE. Grown old in service; practised and skilful.—*n.* One long practised; a veteran soldier.

Vet'erinary, *a.* L. *veterinārius*, of or pertaining to beasts of burden (as *n.*, a cattle-doctor), f. *veterīnus* (contr. f. *vehiterinus*, f. *vehĕre* (VEHICLE)), of or pertaining to carrying burdens. Of or pertaining to domestic animals and their diseases. Hence, **Vet'erinary sur'geon**, *n.*

Ve'to, *n.* L. *veto*, I forbid. A power of prohibition or of preventing from coming into effect.—*vt.* To interpose a veto to.

Vex, *vt.* F. *vexer*—L. *vexāre*. To annoy or distress.—**Vexa'**TION, *n.*—**Vexa'tious**, *a.*

Vi'able, *a.* F. *viable*—Med.L. *vītābilis*, capable of life, f. L. *vita*, life. VITAL. Of a newly-born child, capable of living.

Vi'aduct, *n.* L. *via ducta*, a road conducted, f. *via*, road, and *dūcĕre*, to lead, conduct. CONVEY. DUKE. A long bridge over a valley.

Vi'al, **Phi'al**, *n.* M.E. *viole*, *fiole*—O.F. *viole*, *fiole*—L. *phiala*, G. *phialē*, a bowl. A small glass bottle.

Vi'and, *n.* F. *viande*, food—Med.L. *vivenda*, things to be lived upon, provisions, neut. pl. of the gerundive of L. *vīvĕre*, to live. CONVIVIAL. In *pl.*, food, victuals.

Viat'icum, *n.* F. *viatique*—L. *viāticum*, provision for a journey, neut. of *viāticus*, of a journey, f. *via*, way, journey. CONVEY. VOYAGE. Provision for a journey; the eucharist, when administered to a dying person.

Vi'brate, *vt.* L. *vibrāre, vibrātum*, to agitate, to quiver. WHIP. To cause to move to and fro.—*vi.* To swing; to quiver.—**Vibra'**TION, *n.*—**Vi'brat**ORY, *a.*

Vic'ar, *n.* F. *vicaire*, deputy—L. *vicārius*, deputy, orig. a. f. *vicis* (genit., the nom. does not occur), change, alternation. A deputy; the incumbent of a parish the tithes of which are held by another.—**Vic'ar**AGE, *n.* His benefice; his residence. — **Vica'r**IAL, *a.*—**Vica'r**IOUS, *a.* Deputed, delegated; acting, performed or suffered for another.

Vice, *n.*[1] F. *vice*—L. *vitium*, blemish, fault. VITIATE. Fault; a defect or blemish; an evil habit or practice; depravity.—**Vic'**IOUS, *a.*

Vice, *n.*[2] M.E. *vice*, F. *vis*, screw, winding stair—L. *vītis*, a vine, which twines. WITHY. An instrument for holding fast something that is being worked upon.

Vicege'rent, *n.* F. *vicegerent*, deputy, f. VICE- + *gerens, gerentis*, pres.pple. of *gerĕre*, to carry on. CONGEST. One who acts in the place of a superior.

Vice'roy, *n.* F. *viceroi*, f. VICE- + *roi*, L. *rex, rēgis*, king. One who governs as representing a king or queen.—**Vicere'g**AL, *a.*

Vic'inage, *n.* F. *voisinage*, f. *voisin*, L. *vicīnus*, near, f. *vicus*, village, street. Neighbourhood.—**Vicin'**ITY, *n.*

Vicis'situde, *n.* L. *vicissitūdo*, change, conn. with *vicissim*, by turns, f. *vicis*. VICAR. Alternation; a passing from one state or condition to another.

Vic'tim, *n.* F. *victime*—L. *victima*. A living being sacrificed; a person killed, ruined, or injured; one who is cheated.—**Vic'tim**IZE, *vt.* To cheat.

Vict'or, *n.* L. *victor*, f. *vincĕre, victum*, to conquer. CONVICT. INVINCIBLE. One who vanquishes another. — **Vic'tory**, *n.* A.F. *victorie*—L. *victōria*. The vanquishing of an enemy; advantage or superiority gained in a contest.—**Victo'rious**, *a.*

Vic'tual, *n.* O.F. *vitaille*, us. in pl. *vitailles*, provisions—L. *victuālia*, provisions, neut. pl. of *victuālis*, relating to nourishment, f. *victus*, food, conn. with *vivĕre, victum*, to live. CONVIVIAL. Food, provisions (gen. in *pl.*).—*vt.* and *i.* To supply with victuals, to obtain victuals.—**Vic'tuall**ER, *n.*

Vie, *vi.* M.E. *vien*, shortened f. *envien*—O.F. *envier*, lit. 'to invite' (*sc.* to a contest)—L. *invitāre*, to INVITE. To contend.

View, *n.* A.F. *view, vewe, vue*, O.F. *veuë*, fem. pa.pple. of *veoir* (F. *voir*), L. *vidēre*, to see. ADVICE. The act of viewing; reach of sight; that which is seen, scene, prospect; a picture or sketch; an opinion; a purpose.—*vt.* To look at, examine; to survey mentally.—**View'**LESS, *a.* Invisible.

Vig'il, *n.* F. *vigile*—L. *vigilia*, a watch, f. *vigil*, awake, f. *vigēre*. VIGOUR. SURVEILLANCE. A keeping awake; the day and night preceding a church festival.—**Vig'il**ANT, *a.* Watchful, alert.—**Vig'il**ANCE, *n.*

Vignette', *n.* F. *vignette*, a little vine, in *pl.*, branch-like flourishes, dim. of *vigne*, VINE. An illustration, esp. at the beginning of a book or of a chapter (orig. often enclosed in a border representing trailing vines).

Vig'our, *n.* O.F. *vigor*—L. *vigor*, f. *vigēre*, to be lively. INVIGORATE. VEGETABLE. VIGIL. Strength, force.—**Vig'or**OUS, *a.*

Vi'king, *n.* O.N. *víkingr*, prob. conn. with *víg*, war, Goth. *weihan*, to fight, L. *vincĕre*. VICTOR. A northern sea-robber.

Vile, *a.* F. *vil*, fem. *vile*—L. *vīlis*, cheap, mean. Mean, despicable; depraved, bad.—**Vile'**LY,[2] *adv.*—**Vile'**NESS, *n.*—**Vil'i**FY, *vt.* To slander, defame. — **Vili**FICA'TION, *n.*—**Vil'ipend**, *vt.* F. *vilipender*—L. *vilipendĕre*, to hold in slight esteem, f. *vīlis* + *pendĕre*, to weigh, weigh out. COMPEND. To vilify.

Vil'la, *n.* L. *villa*, country-house, farm. A country or suburban house.—**Vil'lage**, *n.* F. *village*—L. *villāticus*, a. f. *villa*. A small assemblage of houses.—**Vil'lag**ER, *n.*

Vil'lain, *n.* M.E. *vilein*—A.F. *vilein*, servile, as *n.*, serf—L.L. *villānus*, farm-servant, serf, f. *villa*. (See prec.) A feudal serf (in this sense also **Vil'lein**); a scoundrel.—**Vil'lain**OUS, *a.*—**Vil'lain**Y,[1] *n.*

Vinaigrette', *n.* F. f. *vinaigre*, VINEGAR. A small bottle or case containing some substance with a strong and pungent odour.

Vin'dicate, *vt.* L. *vindicāre, vindicātum*, to lay claim to, to avenge. AVENGE. VENDETTA. VENGEANCE. To maintain the cause of; to support, maintain, justify.—**Vindica'**TION, *n.*—**Vindic'tive**, *a.* F. *vindicatif*, revenging, f. *vindicāre*. Revengeful.

Vine, *n.* O.F. *vine, vigne*—L. *vīnea*, vineyard, vine, fem. of *vīneus*, a. f. *vīnum*, WINE, grapes. VIGNETTE. A climbing plant from the fruit of which (the grape) wine is made.—**Vine'yard**, *n.* O.E. *win-geard*, f. *win*, WINE + *geard*, YARD.[1] A plantation of vines.—**Vi'n**OUS, *a.* Of, like, due to wine.—**Vin'tage**, *n.* M.E. *vindage, vendage* (altered by association with *vintner*)—O.F. *vendenge*, L. *vindēmia*, f. *vīnum* + *-dēmia*, f. *dēmĕre*, to take away. The gathering of a crop of grapes; the crop; the wine made from the crop.—**Vint'ner**, *n.* M.E. *vineter, viniter, vintener*—O.F. *vinetier*—L.L. *vīnētārius*, f. *vīnētum*, vineyard, f. *vīnum*. A dealer in wine.

Vin'egar, *n.* O.F. *vin egre* (F. *vinaigre*), i.e. *vin*, L. *vīnum* (see prec.), and *egre*, L. *ācer*, sharp, conn. with *acuĕre*, to sharpen. EAGER. An acid liquid got from wine, &c.

Vi'ol, *n.* O.F. *viole, violle*, Pr. *viula*—L.L. *vīdula, vītula*, viol, whence O.H.G. *fīdula*, O.E. *fithele*, FIDDLE. A musical instrument resembling the violin.—**Vi'ola**, *n.* It. *viola* = O.F. *viole*. A large kind of violin.—**Violin'**, *n.* It. *violino*, dim. of *viola*. A fiddle.—**Violoncel'lo**, *n.* It., dim. of *violone*, bass-viol, aug. form of *viola*. A large powerful instrument of the violin kind.

Vi'olate, *vt.* L. *violāre, violātum*. To outrage; to desecrate; to infringe, transgress.—**Vi'ol**ABLE, *a.*—**Viol**A'TION, *n.*

Vi'olent, *a.* F. *violent*—L. *violentus*. Impetuous, furious; fierce, passionate; produced by force; intense; extreme.—**Vi'olent**LY,[2] *adv.*—**Vi'ol**ENCE, *n.*

Vi'olet, *n.* O.F. *violet*, dim. of *viole*—L. *viola*, violet. A plant with a bluish-purple flower; the colour of the flower.—*a.* Of the colour.

Vi'per, *n.* F. *vipère*—L. *vipera*. A venomous serpent.

Vira'go, *n.* L. *virāgo*, man-like woman, f. *vir*. VIRILE. A turbulent woman.

Vi'relay, *n.* F. *virelai*, f. *virer*, to turn (VEER) + *lai*, LAY. A short poem with a refrain and with only two rhymes throughout.

Vir'gin, *n.* O.F. *virgine*—L. *virgo, virginis*. A woman who has had no carnal knowledge of man.—**Vir'gin**AL, *a.*—**Virgin'**ITY, *n.*

Vir'ile, *a.* F. *viril*—L. *virīlis*, f. *vir*, man. Pertaining to a man or to procreation; manly, strong.—**Viril'**ITY, *n.*

Vir'tue, *n.* F. *vertu*—L. *virtus*, *virtūtis*, manly excellence, f. *vir*. (See prec.) Moral goodness; a particular moral excellence or good quality; an inherent power, efficacy.—**Vir'tu**AL, *a.* That is such in effect though not in name.—**Vir'tual**LY,[2] *adv.*—**Virtuo'so**, *n.*; *pl.* **-i**. It., f. *virtù*, shortened f. *virtute*, virtue, love of the fine arts, f. L. *virtus*. One having special knowledge of the fine arts, antiquities, &c.—**Vir'tu**OUS, *a.*

Vi'rus, *n.* L. *vīrus*, poison. Contagious poisonous matter; acrimony, bitterness.—**Vir'ulent**, *a.* F. *virulent*—L. *vīrulentus*, poisonous, f. *vīrus*. Having poisonous or deadly effects; acrimonious, bitter.—**Vir'ulent**LY,[2] *adv.*—**Vir'ul**ENCE, *n.*

Vis'age, *n.* F. *visage*, O.F. *vis*—L. *visus*, sight, a thing seen, f. *vidēre*, *visum*, to see. ADVICE. VISOR. The face.

Vis'cera, *n.pl.* L. *viscera*. EVISCERATE. The entrails.—**Vis'cer**AL, *a.*

Vis'cid, *a.* L. *viscidus*, f. *viscum*, mistletoe, birdlime. Sticky, adhesive.—**Viscid'**ITY, *n.* —**Vis'**COUS, *a.*—**Viscos'**ITY, *n.*

Vis'count, *n.* A.F. *visconte*, *viconte*, O.F. *viscomte*—L. *vice* (VICE-) + *comes*. COUNT, *n.*[2] A degree of nobility ranking next above that of baron.—**Vis'count**ESS, *n.*

Vis'ion, *n.* F. *vision*—L. *visio*, *visiōnis*, f. *vidēre*, *visum*, to see. ADVICE. Sight; the faculty of sight; an apparition; a creation of the fancy.—*vt.* To see or show in or as in a vision.—**Vis'ion**ARY, *a.* Impracticable; imaginative, apt to act on fancies.—*n.* One apt to act thus.—**Vis'**IBLE, *a.* That can be perceived by the eye.—**Vis'ib**LY,[2] *adv.*—**Visi**BIL'ITY, *n.*—**Vis'ta**, *n.* It., orig. fem. of *visto*, seen, f. *vedere*, L. *vidēre*. A view, esp. between rows of trees.—**Vis'ual**, *a.* O.F. *visual*—L. *visuālis*, attained by sight, f. *visus*, sight. VISAGE. Of or pertaining to sight.—**Vis'ual**IZE, *vt.* To make visible.

Vis'it, *vt.* F. *visiter*—L. *visitāre*, freq. f. *visĕre*, to view, freq. f. *vidēre*, to see. ADVICE. To go or come to see in the way of friendship, business, &c.; to afflict.—*n.* A visiting.—**Vis'it**ANT, *n.*—**Visit**A'TION, *n.* A formal visit of inspection, &c.; an affliction.—**Vis'it**OR, *n.*

Vi'sor, **Vi'zor**, **Viz'ard**, *n.* M.E. *visere*—O.F. *visiere*, f. *vis*, VISAGE. The movable front of a helmet.

Vi'tal, *a.* F. *vital*—L. *vitālis*, f. *vita*, life, conn. with *vivĕre*, to live. CONVIVIAL. Of, pertaining to, necessary to life; indispensable. —In *pl.* as *n.*, the organs which are essential to life.—**Vi'tal**LY,[2] *adv.*—**Vital'**ITY, *n.* Vital force; manifestation of a capacity for existing.—**Vit'al**IZE, *vt.* To give life to.

Vit'iate, *vt.* L. *vitiāre*, *vitiātum*, to injure, f. *vitium*. VICE.[1] To spoil, corrupt; to render invalid or of no effect.—**Viti**A'TION, *n.*

Viticul'ture, *n.* L. *vitis*, vine + *cultūra*. ARBORICULTURE. VICE.[2] The cultivation of the vine.

Vit'reous, *a.* L. *vitreus* (f. *vitrum*, glass) + -OUS. Of or pertaining to glass; like glass; consisting of glass.—**Vit'ri**FY, *vt.* To convert into glass.—*vi.* To become glass.—**Vitri**FAC'TION, *n.*—**Vitri**FICA'TION, *n.*

Vit'riol, *n.* F. *vitriol*, as if 'glassy substance'—L. *vitreolus*, glassy, f. *vitreus*. (See prec.) Sulphuric acid; caustic speech.—**Vitriol'**IC, *a.*

Vitu'perate, *vt.* L. *vituperāre*, *vituperātum*, to blame, lit. 'to prepare (or find) a blemish', f. *vitium* (VICE[1]) + *parāre*. PARE. To abuse in words, censure abusively.—**Vitupera'**TION, *n.*—**Vitu'per**ATIVE, *a.*

Vivac'ity, *n.* F. *vivacité*—L. *vīvācitas*, f. *vīvax*, *vīvācis*, tenacious of life, lively, f. *vīvĕre*, to live. CONVIVIAL. VICTUAL. Liveliness, animation.—**Viva'cious**, *a.*—**Viv'id**, *a.* L. *vividus*, lively, f. *vīvĕre*. Lifelike; bright, clear; producing a strong impression on the mind.—**Viv'id**LY,[2] *adv.*—**Viv'**IFY, *vt.* To endow with life; to animate, inspire.—**Vivip'arous**, *a.* L. *vīviparus* (f. *vīvus*, living, conn. with *vīvĕre* + *parĕre*, to bring forth) + -OUS. Bringing forth young in a living state.—**Vivisec'tion**, *n.* Formed f. L. *vīvus* + SECTION. Dissection of a living body.—**Vivisec'tor**, *n.*

Vix'en, *n.* M.E. *fixen*, *vixen*—O.E. *fyxen*, formed f. *fox*, FOX, with vowel-change and fem. suff. *-en*. A female fox; a quarrelsome woman.—**Vix'en**ISH, *a.*

Viz'ier, *n.* F. *vizir*—Arab. *wazīr*, state-councillor, orig., porter, hence 'one who bears the burden of state', f. *wazara*, to bear, sustain. In Mohammedan countries, a chief minister of state.

Vo'cable, *n.* F. *vocable*—L. *vocābulum*, an appellation, f. *vocāre*, *vocātum*, to call, conn. with *vox*, *vōcis*, VOICE. ADVOCATE. INVOKE. VOUCH. A word.—**Vocab'ulary**, *n.* L.L. *vocābulārium*. An alphabetical list of words with explanations; range of words employed. —**Vo'cal**, *a.* F. *vocal*—L. *vōcālis*, f. *vox*. VOWEL. Uttering sound or words; pertaining to the voice.—**Vo'cal**LY,[2] *adv.*—**Vo'cal**IST, *n.* A public singer.—**Vo'cal**IZE, *vt.* To form into, to utter with voice.—**Voca'**TION, *n.* A summons; employment, occupation, business. —**Voc'**ATIVE, *a.* and *n.* The case used in calling to or addressing a person or thing.—**Vocif'erate**, *vi.* L. *vōciferārī*, *vōciferātus*, f. *vox* + *ferre*, to BEAR, carry. To cry out noisily.—*vt.* To utter with a loud voice, shout.—**Vocifera'**TION, *n.*—**Vocif'er**OUS, *a.* Clamorous, noisy.

Vogue, *n.* F. *vogue*, in older F., sway, power, orig. 'sway of a ship', f. *voguer*, to sail—It. *vogare*, to row, *voga*, oar-stroke—M.H.G. *wâgen* (Ger. *wogen*), to fluctuate, move on the sea, *wâg* (Ger. *woge*), wave. Conn. with O.E. *wegan*, to carry, move. WAG. Mode or fashion prevalent at a particular time.

Voice, *n.* O.F. *vois* (F. *voix*)—L. *vox*, *vōcis* (conn. with *vocāre*, to call), cogn. with G. *epos*, a word. VOCABLE. The sound uttered by a person in speaking, singing, &c.; the character or quality of the sound; the faculty of speaking; the body of inflexions of a verb which shows the relation of the subject to the action.—*vt.* To give utterance to.—**Voice'**LESS, *a.*

Void, *a.* O.F. *vuit*, fem. *vuide*, *voide*, of unknown orig. AVOID. DEVOID. Empty, ineffectual.—*n.* An empty space.—*vt.* To emit (excrement, &c.); to nullify.

Vol'atile, *a.* F. *volatil*—L. *volātilis*, flying, transitory, f. *volāre*, *volātum*, to fly. VOLLEY Evaporating rapidly; fickle, apt to change.—**Volatil'**ITY, *n.*—**Volat'il**IZE, *vt.* To cause to evaporate.—*vi.* To pass off in vapour.

Volca'no, *n.* It. *volcano*—L. *Volcānus*, *Vulcānus*, Vulcan, the god of fire, fire. A mountain with an opening through which heated materials are expelled.—**Volcan'**IC, *a.*

Voli'tion, *n.* F. *volition*—L.L. **volitio*, **volitiōnis*, f. L. *velle*, to wish. VOLUNTARY. The act of willing; the power of willing.
Vol'ley, *n.* F. *volée*, a flight, a flight of shot, a volley—L. *volāre*. VOLATILE. A simultaneous discharge of missiles.—*vt.* To discharge in a volley.—*vi.* To fly in a volley; to sound together.
Vol'uble, *a.* O.F. *voluble*—L. *volūbilis*, easily turned about, voluble, f. *volvĕre*, to roll. CONVOLVE. Fluent, too fluent, in speech.—**Vol'ubly**,[2] *adv.*—**Volubil'ity**, *n.*
Vol'ume, *n.* F. *volume*—L. *volūmen*, *volūminis*, a roll, a roll of writing, f. *volvĕre*. (See prec.) Printed sheets bound together; a rounded mass, wreath, coil; bulk.—**Volu'minous**, *a.* Bulky; having written much.
Vol'untary, *a.* O.F. *voluntaire*—L. *voluntārius*, willing, f. *voluntas*, free will, conn. with *volens*, *volentis*, pres.pple. of *velle* (pres. indic. *volo*), to wish. VOLITION. WILL. Done of or due to one's own free choice.—*n.* An organ prelude to a service (app. as not being prescribed).—**Vol'untarily**,[2] *adv.*—**Volunteer'**, *n.* One who enters into a service of his own free will.
Volup'tuous, *a.* F. *voluptueux*—L. *voluptuōsus*, full of enjoyment, delightful, f. *voluptas*, pleasure, conn. with *velle*. (See prec.) Pertaining, addicted, contributing to sensual pleasure.—**Volup'tuary**, *n.* One addicted to sensual pleasure.
Volute', *n.* F. *volute*—L. *volūta*, orig. fem. of *volūtus*, pa.pple. of *volvĕre*. CONVOLVE. A spiral scroll characteristic of Corinthian and Ionic capitals.—**Volu'tion**, *n.* A rolling or winding; a spiral turn.
Vom'it, *vi.* L. *vomitāre*, freq. of *vomĕre*, *vomitum*, to vomit, cogn. with G. *eme-ein*. EMETIC. To eject the contents of the stomach through the mouth.—*vt.* To eject from the stomach through the mouth.—*n.* What is so ejected; an emetic.
Vorac'ity, *n.* F. *voracité*—L. *vorācitas*, f. *vorax*, greedy to devour, f. *vorāre*, to DEVOUR. CARNIVOROUS. Greediness in eating.—**Vora'cious**, *a.*—**Vora'ciously**,[2] *adv.*
Vor'tex, *n.*; *pl.* **Vor'tices**, **Vor'texes**. L. *vortex*, var. of *vertex*. VERTEX. A whirl of fluid; any whirling motion.
Vote, *n.* L. *vōtum*, a wish, orig., a vow, f. *vovēre*, *vōtum*, to vow. VOW. The formal expression of wish or choice; that which is allowed or bestowed by vote; the result of voting.—*vi.* To give a vote.—*vt.* To enact, choose, grant by vote.—**Vot'er**, *n.*—**Vot'ary**, *n.*; *fem.* **Vot'aress**. One devoted to a service, pursuit, &c.—**Vot'ive**, *a.* Given or consecrated in accordance with a vow.
Vouch, *vt.* O.F. *vochier*—L. *vocāre*, to call to, summon. AVOUCH. VOCABLE. To attest, warrant.—*vi.* To bear witness, give assurance.—**Vouch'er**, *n.* A writing proving the correctness of an item in an account.—**Vouchsafe'**, *vt.* Formerly two words, *i.e.* 'to warrant as safe'. To condescend to grant or *to do*.
Vow, *n.* O.F. *veu*, *vou* (F. *vœu*)—L. *vōtum*. VOTE. A solemn promise.—*vt.* To undertake solemnly to perform or give; to swear.
Vow'el, *n.* O.F. *vouel*, *voiel* (F. *voyelle*)—L. *vōcālis* (*littera*), a 'vocal' letter, a vowel. VOCABLE. One of the open and resonant sounds uttered in speaking; a letter representing such a sound.
Voy'age, *n.* M.E. *viage*, *veage*—O.F. *veiage* (F. *voyage*), journey—L. *viāticum*. VIATICUM. A journey by sea to a distance.—*vi.* To make a voyage.—**Voy'ager**, *n.*
Vul'canize, *vt.* Formed with -IZE, f. *Vulcan*. VOLCANO. To harden (caoutchouc) by heating it with sulphur.—**Vul'canite**, *n.* Coined f. the *v.* with suff. *-ite* of scientific terms. The product.
Vul'gar, *a.* F. *vulgaire*—L. *vulgāris*, a. f. *vulgus*, the common people. DIVULGE. Of the common people; common; not refined, coarse; *vulgar* (or *common*) *fraction*, one written with the numerator above and the denominator below a horizontal or diagonal line.—**Vul'garly**,[2] *adv.*—**Vulga'rian**, *n.* A vulgar person.—**Vul'garism**, *n.* Coarseness of manners; a coarse expression.—**Vulgar'ity**, *n.*—**Vul'garize**, *vt.*—**Vul'gate**, *n.* L. (*ēditio*) *vulgāta*, the common or published (edition), fem. pa.pple. of *vulgāre*, to make common, to publish. The Latin version of the Bible accepted by the Roman Catholic Church.
Vul'nerable, *a.* F. *vulnérable*—L. *vulnerābilis*, f. *vulnerāre*, to wound, f. *vulnus*, wound. VULTURE. Capable of being injured.
Vul'pine, *a.* O.F. *vulpin*—L. *vulpīnus*, a. f. *vulpes*, fox. Pertaining to or like the fox.
Vul'ture, *n.* L. *vultur*, 'the tearer', f. *vellĕre*, *vulsum*, to tear, conn. with *vulnus*. VULNERABLE. A bird which preys on carrion.

W

Wab'ble, **Wob'ble**, *vi.* Cf. L.G. *wabbeln*, to wabble, M.H.G. *wabelen*, to move hither and thither. To rotate unsteadily; to rock.
Wad, *n.* Sw. *vadd*, wadding. Cf. Ger. *watte*, wadding, wad. A soft mass of fibrous material used for stuffing; something used in a gun to hold the charge in place.—*vt.* To line with wadding; to pad, stuff; to put a wad into.—**Wad'ding**, *n.* Wads collectively, stuffing.
Wad'dle, *vi.* Freq. of WADE. To walk with a rolling gait.
Wade, *vi.* O.E. *wadan*. Cf. Du. *waden*. Cogn. with L. *vādĕre*, to go. EVADE. To walk through a substance that impedes free movement, esp. water.—**Wad'er**, *n.* One who wades; a high waterproof boot.
Wa'fer, *n.* O.F. *waufre* (F. *gaufre*)—M.Du. *waefel*, L.G. *wafel*. A thin cake of bread, &c.; a thin disk of dried paste for fastening papers.—*vt.* To fasten with a wafer.
Waft, *vt.* A var. of WAVE. To convey through water or air.—*n.* A sweep of a wing; a breath of odour.
Wag, *vt.* Early Sw. *wagga*, to wag, sway. Cogn. with O.E. *wagian*, to wag, f. *wegan*, to carry, move. VOGUE. WEIGH. To cause to shake or oscillate slightly.—*vi.* To oscillate, sway, swing.—**Wag**, *n.* Short for *wag-halter*, one who deserves hanging (jocosely). A droll fellow.—**Wag'gery**, *n.*—**Wag'gish**, *a.*—**Wag'tail**, *n.* A small bird so called from the wagging motion of its tail.
Wage, *n.* O.F. *wage*, *g(u)age* (F. *gage*), a GAGE, pledge, hence, a stipulated payment—L.L. *wadium*—Goth. *wadi*, a pledge. ENGAGE. WED. Payment for work done (gen. in *pl.*).—*vt.* To pledge oneself to, engage in, carry on (a contest).—**Wag'er**, *n.* O.F. *wageure* (F. *gageure*)—L.L. *wadiātūra*, f. *wadium*. A bet.—*vt.* and *i.* To bet, to stake.

Wag'gle, *vi.* and *t.* Dim. and freq. of WAG. Cf. DRAGGLE. To wag.

Wag'gon, Wag'on, *n.* Du. *wagen.* Cogn. with WAIN. A four-wheeled vehicle for heavy loads.—**Wag'gon**ER, **Wag'on**ER, *n.* —**Waggonette', Wagonette'**, *n.* Diminutive. A four-wheeled pleasure vehicle with seats running lengthwise.

Waif, *n.* O.F. *waif*, lost (*choses waives*, things lost and not claimed)—O.N. **weif*, Icel. *veif*, anything flapping about, allied to **weifa.* WAIVE. A stray article; a homeless wretch.

Wail, *vi.* and *t.* M.E. *weilen*—O.N. *vœla*, lit. 'to cry woe', f. *vœ, vei*, woe! WOE. To lament.—*n.* A plaintive cry or sound.

Wain, *n.* O.E. *wægn, wǽn*, f. *wegan*, to carry. WEIGH. A waggon.

Wain'scot, *n.* Du. *wagenschot*, M.Du. *waeghe-schot*, oak-wood with a waving grain, f. *waeghe*, wave + *schot*, a wainscot, partition. Formerly, a fine kind of oak. A wooden lining of the walls of a room.—*vt.* To put such a lining on.

Waist, *n.* M.E. *wast*, lit. 'growth', the part where strength is developed = M.E. *wacst*, strength, allied to O.E. *wæstm*, growth, f. *weaxan*, to grow. WAX, *v.*[1] The part of the body between the ribs and the hips; anything bearing an analogy to this.—**Waist'coat**, *n.* A sleeveless garment worn under the coat.

Wait, *n.* O.F. *waite* (F. *guet*, night-watch), a watchman—O.H.G. *wahta*, in same sense, orig., a watch, a being awake, f. Teut. root *wak-*, as in Goth. *wakan.* AWAIT. WAKE, *v.* Formerly, a watchman. A musician who sings out of doors at Christmas; the act of waiting; ambush.—*vi.* O.F. *waiter* (F. *guetter*), to watch, wait, f. *waite.* To be, or to continue, in expectation; to serve at table.—*vt.* To await.—**Wait'**ER, *n.* One who waits; one who serves at table; a salver.—**Wait'**RESS, *n.*

Waive, *vt.* A.F. *weiver*—O.F. *guesver*, to waive—O.N. **weifa*, Icel. *veifa*, to vibrate, flutter. WAIF. To relinquish, forgo.

Wake, Wa'ken, *vv.* Two O.E. intrans. verbs, *wacian*, weak verb, and *wæcnan*, with strong pa.t. *wók*, confused, as explained under AWAKE, AWAKEN. Cogn. with Goth. *wakan*, to be awake. WAIT. WATCH. *Intrans.* To cease from sleep; to bestir oneself. *Trans.* To rouse from sleep; to stir up, make active.—**Wake**, *n.*[1] An all-night watch by the body of the dead.—**Wake'**FUL, *a.*

Wake, *n.*[2] Properly 'an opening in, passage through, ice'. Icel. *vak-*, stem of *vök*, Sw. *vak*, Norw. *vok*, a hole, an opening in ice. The track left by a ship; a track in general.

Wale, Weal, *n.* M.E. *wale*—O.E. *walu.* Cogn. with E.Fris. *wale*, wale, Old Fris. *walu*, rod, wand, Icel. *völr*, a round stick. (The sense of rod or beam is preserved in GUNWALE.) A streak produced by the blow of a rod or whip.—*vt.* To mark with such streaks.

Walk, *vi.* O.E. *wealcan*, to roll, rove. Cf. M.Du. *walcken*, to full, press cloth, Sw. *valka*, to roll, full, work. To pursue a particular course of life; to move with the gait called a walk.—*vt.* To traverse; to cause to walk.—*n.* Course of life; range of action; the slowest gait of land-animals; the act of walking; gait; a place for walking.—**Walk'**ER, *n.*

Wall, *n.* O.E. *weall*—L. *vallum*, a rampart. INTERVAL. A structure of stone, &c., serving to enclose, divide, support, &c.—*vt.* To furnish with a wall; to block *up* with a wall.—**Wall'-flower**, *n.* A fragrant garden plant.

Wal'let, *n.* M.E. *walet*, of doubtful orig. A kind of bag: a pocket-book.

Wall'-eyed, *a.* Icel. *vald-eygthr*, a corr. of *vagleygr*, f. *vagl*, a beam, a 'beam' in the eye + *eygr*, eyed, f. *auga*, EYE. Having an eye with little colour in the iris.—**Wall'-eye**, *n.* Such an eye.

Wal'low, *vi.* M.E. *walwen*—O.E. *wealwian*, to roll round. Cogn. with L. *volvĕre.* VOLUBLE. To roll the body in water or mire.

Wal'nut, *n.* Old Mercian *walh-hnutu*, f. *walh*, O.E. *wealh*, a Celt (*i.e.* Welsh or Gaulish), cogn. with O.H.G. *walah*, a foreigner + *hnutu*, NUT. WELSH. Lit., 'Gaulish or foreign nut', as having been first brought from France and Italy. The fruit of a well-known nut-bearing tree; the tree.

Wal'rus, *n.* Du. *walrus*—Sw. *vallross*, Da. *hvalros*, f. Sw. *vall*, Da. *hval*, whale + Icel. *hross*, horse. The same as O.E. *hors-hwæl*, HORSE-WHALE. A large marine carnivorous mammal, said to be named from its neighing.

Waltz, *n.* Ger. *walzer*, f. *walzen*, to roll. WELTER. A revolving dance for two.—*vi.* To dance a waltz.

Wan, *a.* O.E. *wann, wonn*, dark, colourless. Orig. uncertain. Gloomy; pale, sickly of hue.

Wand, *n.* O.N. *vöndr.* Cf. Goth. *wandus*, a rod, perh. (from its pliancy) f. *-windan*, to WIND. A slender stick; a staff of office.

Wan'der, *vi.* O.E. *wandrian*, used as freq. of *wendan*, to go, WEND, but formed from *windan*, to WIND. To ramble without any certain course; to stray, deviate; to rave.

Wane, *vi.* O.E. *wanian*, f. *wan, won*, deficient. Cf. O.N. *vana*, to decrease, f. *vanr*, deficient. Cogn. with Skr. *ūna-*, wanting, G. *eunis*, bereft of. (See next.) To decrease, esp. of the moon; to decline.—*n.* Decline.

Want, *n.* M.E. *want*, orig. an *a.* f. O.N. *vant*, neut. of *vanr.* (See prec.) Lack; something lacking; poverty.—*vt.* To lack; to require, to desire.—*vi.* To be lacking; to be in need.

Wan'ton, *a.* M.E. *wantoun, wantowen*, unrestrained, uneducated, f. *wan-* (f. O.E. *wan*, see WANE) + *-towen*, f. O.E. *togen*, pa.pple. of *téon*, to draw, to educate, cogn. with *togian.* TOW, *v.* Unrestrained; playful; dissolute; motiveless, serving no purpose.—*vi.* To frolic; to sport lasciviously.—**Wan'ton**LY,[2] *adv.*

War, *n.* M.E. and late O.E. *werre*—O.F. *werre* (F. *guerre*)—O.H.G. *werra*, broil, confusion, f. *werran*, to confuse, entangle. GUERRILLA. WORSE. A contest between states or parties in a state carried on by force; a state of hostility; the art of war.—*vi.* To carry on war.—**War'fare**, *n.* O.E. *faran*, to go. FARE. Military service; hostilities.—**War'like**, *a.* Having a military appearance; pertaining to war; disposed for war.—**War'rior**, *n.* A.F. *werreiur*, f. *werreier*, to make war, f. *werre.* A distinguished or veteran soldier.

War'ble, *vt.* and *i.* M.E. *werbeln*—O.F. *werbler*—M.H.G. **werbelen*, assumed as old form of Ger. *wirbeln*, to WHIRL, to warble. To sing with trills or melodious turns.—*n.* A warbled strain.—**War'bl**ER, *n.*

Ward, *n.* O.E. *weard*, masc., a guard, also fem., a guarding, cogn. with *wær*, cautious. O.Teut. type **wardâ.* GUARD. LORD. STEWARD. WARE, *a.* A guarding; a defensive motion in fencing; guardianship; one under guardianship; a division of a town, a hospital, &c.; a piece in a lock.—*vt.* To guard; to fend *off.*—**Ward'**ER, *n.*—**Ward'**SHIP, *n.*—**Ward'robe**, *n.* Cf. F. *garderobe.* A place

where clothes are kept.—**Ward'-room**, *n.* An officers' mess-room in a warship.

War'den, *n.* M.E. *wardein*—O.F. *g(u)arden*, f. *g(u)arde*, GUARD. A guardian, governor.

Ware, *a.* M.E. *war*—O.E. *wær*, cautious. Cf. O.N. *varr*, Da., Sw. *var*, Ger. *gewahr*. Cogn. with G. *hora-ein*, to perceive, L. *verēri*, to regard, dread. WARD. On one's guard, aware.—*vt.* To beware of, take heed of.

Ware, *n.* O.E. *waru*. Cf. Du. *waar*, Ger. *waare*. In *pl.*, goods, commodities; *collectively*, articles of a certain kind. —**Ware'house**, *n.* A storehouse for goods; a large shop.—*vt.* To put in a warehouse.

Warm, *a.* O.E. *wearm*. Cf. Du., Ger. *warm*. Perh. cogn. with G. *thermos*, L. *formus*. FURNACE. Moderately hot; ardent, earnest. —*vi.* and *t.* To become, to make, warm.—**Warm'**LY,[2] *adv.*—**Warm**TH,[1] *n.*

Warn, *vt.* O.E. *wearnian*, *warenian*, to take heed, also, to warn. Cf. Ger. *warnen*, to warn. GARNISH. To put on guard, caution; to admonish; to inform previously.

Warp, *n.* O.E. *wearp*, a warp in weaving, f. *weorpan*, to throw, hence, to throw the shuttle. Cf. O.N. *varp*, a throwing, f. *varpa*, to throw. The threads extended lengthwise in a loom. From the *v.*, a twist, the state of being twisted; a rope used in moving a ship. —*vt.* From *varpa* in sense 'to twist'. To give a twist to; to move (a ship) by a rope fixed to a buoy, &c.—*vi.* To become twisted.

War'rant, *n.* O.F. *warant*, *guarant*—O.H.G. *werênt-*, stem of pres.pple. of *werên* (Ger. *gewähren*), to certify, warrant, of obscure orig. GUARANTY. Assurance, evidence; authorization; an act or instrument giving authority. —*vt.* To give an assurance in regard to; to authorize, to justify.—**War'rant**Y,[1] *n.*

War'ren, *n.* O.F. *warenne*, *varenne* (F. *garenne*)—O.H.G. *warjan*, to protect. Ground appropriated to rabbits.

Wart, *n.* O.E. *wearte*. Cf. Du. *wrat*, Ger. *warze*. A hard growth on the skin.

Wa'ry, *a.* M.E. *war* + -Y.[2] WARE, *a.* Cautious, careful, prudent.—**Wa'ri**LY,[2] *adv.*

Wash, *vt.* M.E. *waschen*—O.E. *wæscan*, *waxan*. Cf. Du. *wasschen*, Sw. *vaska*, Ger. *waschen*. To cleanse with liquid; to remove thus; to carry along by or as by a rush of water; to tint lightly.—*vi.* To cleanse oneself, to cleanse clothes, &c., with liquid; to endure washing.—*n.* The act of washing; clothes, &c., washed at once; the sweep of water; the rough water behind a moving vessel; the noise of moving water; a thin coat of colour.—**Wash'**ER, *n.* One who washes; a ring of leather, &c., put under a screwed-up nut.—**Wash'**Y,[2] *a.* Diluted, thin; weak, feeble.

Wasp, *n.* O.E. *wæps*. Cf. Ger. *wespe*. Cogn. with L. *vespa*. A stinging bee-like insect.

Was'sail, *n.* Orig., a drinking of a health. Norman *weisseil*, as if f. an O.N. **wesheill*, be WHOLE, be well. A drinking-bout; the liquor used.—*vi.* To carouse.

Waste, *a.* O.F. *wast*, in phrase *faire wast*, to lay waste—M.H.G. *waste*, a waste—L. *vastus*, waste, desolate. VAST. Desert; superfluous. —*n.* A desert; gradual diminution; superfluous material; useless expenditure.—*vt.* To devastate; to wear away, use up; to expend, &c., uselessly.—*vi.* To diminish gradually.—**Wast'**AGE, *n.*—**Waste'**FUL, *a.*

Watch, *n.* M.E. *wacche*—O.E. *wæcce*, a watch, guard. Cogn. with WAKE, WAKEN. Vigilance, close observation; the time during which one is on duty; a part of a ship's crew on duty together; a small portable timepiece. —*vi.* To be closely observant. —*vt.* To observe closely; to guard.—**Watch'**FUL, *a.*—**Watch'word**, *n.* A motto, a rallying-cry.

Wa'ter, *n.* O.E. *wæter*. Cf. Du. *water*, Ger. *wasser*. Cogn. with OTTER, and with G. *hudōr*, L. *unda*. A transparent inodorous tasteless fluid; a body of water; the transparency and brilliancy of a gem.—*vt.* To put water into or upon; to cause to drink; to produce irregular wavy markings on (a fabric).—*vi.* To gather saliva in the mouth; to get or take in water. —**Wa'terproof**, *a.* Proof against water.—*n.* A waterproof garment, &c. —**Wa'termark**, *n.* A device made in the substance of paper during manufacture.—**Wa'ter**Y,[2] *a.*

Wat'tle, *n.* M.E. *watel*—O.E. *watel*, *watul*, hurdle. Cf. O.E. *wætla*, a bandage. A wicker hurdle.—*vt.* To interlace (twigs, &c.), form into basket-work.

Wave, *vi.* M.E. *waven*—O.E. *wafian*, to wave with the hand, to waver. Cf. *wæfre*, wavering, restless, Icel. *vafra*, *vafla*, to waver. WAFT. To move to and fro; to have an undulating form; to beckon.—*vt.* To move to and fro; to shape in undulations; to express by a waving gesture.—*n.* A ridge on water, &c.; a waving gesture.—**Wa'v**Y,[2] *a.*

Wa'ver, *vi.* O.E. *wæfre*. (See prec.) To flutter; to be irresolute, vacillate.

Wax, *v.*[1]*i.* M.E. *waxen*—O.E. *weaxan*. Cf. Du. *wassen*, Ger. *wachsen*. Cogn. with G. *auxanein*, L. *augēre*. WAIST. To grow, increase; to grow, become.

Wax, *n.* O.E. *weax*. Cf. Du. *was*, Ger. *wachs*. A thick sticky substance produced by bees; various things like this; a substance used for sealing.—*v.*[2]*t.* To smear or rub with wax.—**Wax'**EN,[1] *a.*

Way, *n.* M.E. *wey*, *way*—O.E. *weg*. Cf. Icel. *vegr*, Da. *vei*, Ger. *weg*. A track; progress; length of space; distance; direction; condition, state; plan, course; method.—**Way'farer**, *n.* O.E. *faran*, to go. FARE. A traveller, esp. one on foot.—**Waylay'**, *vt.* App. f. LAY, *v.*, though the development of sense is not clear. (Prob. there has been confusion with *to lay wait*, *to lie in wait*, &c.) To lie in wait for.—**Way'ward**, *a.* M.E. *weiward*, abb. f. *aweiward*, in a direction away from a thing, f. *awei*, away + -WARD. Capricious, perverse.—**Way'ward**LY,[2] *adv.*

We, *pron.* O.E. *wé*. Cf. Da., Sw. *vi*, Du. *wij*, Ger. *wir*, Skr. *vay-am*. Plural of the pronoun of the first person.

Weak, *a.* A back-formation f. M.E. *wēken*, to make weak—O.E. *wǽcan* (for *wácian*), f. *wák*, weak. Cf. Icel. *veikr*, Ger. *weich*, weak, Sw. *vek*, Da. *veg*, pliant. Lacking firmness or strength, physical or mental; forming inflections by syllabic addition.—**Weak'**LY,[1] *a.* Sickly.—**Weak'**LY,[2] *adv.*—**Weak'**EN,[2] *vt.* and *i.*—**Weak'ling**, *n.* -LING (2). A feeble creature.—**Weak'**NESS, *n.*

Weal, *n.*[1] M.E. *wele*—O.E. *wela*, allied to *wel*, well. WELL, *adv.* Riches, well-being.—**Wealth**, *n.* M.E. *welthe*, extended f. *wele*. Riches, abundance.—**Wealth'**Y,[2] *a.*

Weal, *n.*[2] See WALE.

Wean, *vt.* M.E. *wenen*—O.E. *wenian*, to accustom. Teut. root *wenan-*, to crave. WEEN. To accustom to food other than the mother's milk (often *fig.*).—**Wean'ling**, *n.* -LING (1). A new-weaned child, &c.

Weap'on, *n.* M.E. *wepen*—O.E. *wǽpen*. Cf.

Icel. *vápn*, Du. *wapen*, Ger. *waffe*. An instrument of offence or defence.

Wear, *v.*[1]*t.* M.E. *weren*—O.E. *werian*. Cf. O.N. *verja*, O.H.G. *werian*. Cogn. with L. *vestis*. VEST. To carry on the body; to consume by use; to waste or to produce by rubbing; to bear, exhibit, show.—*vi.* To last; to become worn; of time, to move slowly *on*.—*n.* The act of wearing; impairment, diminution; *collectively*, things to wear.—**Wear'**ER, *n.*

Wear, *v.*[2] The same as VEER.

Wea'ry, *a.* M.E. *weri*—O.E. *wérig*, f. *wór-*, a moor or marsh (tedious to traverse), in *wórhana*, moor-cock. Cf. O.S. *wôrig*, weary. Tired; impatient *of*; causing fatigue.—*vt.* and *i.* To make, to become, weary.—**Wea'ri**LY,[2] *adv.*—**Wea'ri**NESS, *n.*—**Wea'ri**SOME, *a.*

Wea'sel, *n.* O.E. *wesle*, *wesulæ*. Cf. Du. *wezel*, Da. *væsel*. A small carnivorous mammal akin to the ferret.

Weath'er, *n.* M.E. *weder*—O.E. *weder*. Cf. Du. *weder*, Ger. *wetter*. WITHER. The atmospheric conditions at a particular time.—*a.* Towards the wind.—*vt.* To affect by weather; to sail to windward of; to come safely through.—**Weath'er-cock**, *n.* A device in the shape of a cock to show the wind's direction.

Weave, *vt.* O.E. *wefan*. Cf. Du. *weven*, Ger. *weben*; also G. *huph-ainein*. WEB. WEFT. WOOF. To form by interlacing threads, &c.; to form a texture from.—**Weav'**ER, *n.*

Web, *n.* O.E. *webb*, f. Teut. *wab-*, *weban-*, to WEAVE. A woven fabric; the threads spun by a spider; the membrane between the toes of water-fowl.

Wed, *vt.* O.E. *weddian*, to pledge, to betroth, f. *wedd*, pledge, cogn. with Goth. *wadi*. WAGE. Cogn. with L. *vas*, *vadis*, pledge. To marry; to unite closely.—**Wed'ding**, *n.* A marriage.—**Wed'lock**, *n.* O.E. *wedlác*, f. *wedd* + *lác*, a gift, often a mere suff. Marriage.

Wedge, *n.* O.E. *wecg*. Cf. Icel. *veggr*, O.H.G. *wecki*. A body sloping to an edge.—*vt.* To split with a wedge; to crowd, compress.

Wed'nesday, *n.* O.E. *wódnesdæg*, Woden's DAY. The fourth day of the week.

Weed, *n.*[1] O.E. *wéod*, *wíod*, corresp. to O.S. *wiod*. Orig. unknown. A plant regarded as useless or troublesome.—*vt.* To free from weeds.—**Weed'**Y,[2] *a.*

Weeds, *n.*[2] *pl.* O.E. *wǽde*, garment. Cf. Old Fris. *wēde*, O.S. *wādi*. A widow's mourning.

Week, *n.* O.E. *wice*, *wicu*. Cf. Du. *week*, O.H.G. *wecha*, *wehha* (Ger. *woche*). A period of seven days.—**Week'**LY,[1] *a.* Happening or done once a week.—**Week'**LY,[2] *adv.*

Ween, *vi.* O.E. *wénan*, to imagine, f. *wén*, expectation, orig., a striving after, f. Teut. root *wenan-*. WEAN. To think, suppose.

Weep, *vi.* O.E. *wépan*, to cry aloud. Cf. O.S. *wōpian*, Goth. *wōpjan*, to shout. To show grief by shedding tears; to give out moisture.—*vt.* To lament; to let fall as tears.

Wee'vil, *n.* O.E. *wifel*, *wibil*. Cf. M.Du. *wevel*, O.H.G. *wibil*. A kind of beetle.

Weft, *n.* O.E. *weft*, *wefta*, f. *wefan*, to WEAVE. The woof in weaving.

Weigh, *vt.* O.E. *wegan*, to carry, raise, weigh. Cf. Du. *wegen*, to move, lift. Cogn. with L. *vehĕre*. WAG. WAIN. To raise; to find the weight of; to estimate.—*vi.* To have weight; to be or amount in weight.—**Weight**, *n.* O.E. *wiht*, f. *wegan*. The downward force of a body; a heavy mass; a body of known mass as a standard for weighing; importance.—*vt.* To add a weight to; to burden.—**Weight'**Y,[2] *a.*

Weir, *n.* O.E. *wer*. Cf. L.G. *ware*, weir, M.Du. *weer*, rampart. A dam across a river.

Weird, *a.* O.E. *wyrd*, fate. Teut. root *werthan-*, to become, happen. Connected with fate; unearthly.

Wel'come, *a.* For *well come*. Gladly received; conferring gladness; gladly permitted or privileged.—*n.* A kindly greeting; kind reception.—*vt.* To receive gladly.

Weld, *vt.* Late M.E. *well*. The *d* is modern. Believed to be the same word as WELL, *v.*, re-adopted from Sweden with a technical sense given by the iron-workers there. To unite (metal) by hammering; to bring into close union.—*n.* A welded junction.

Wel'fare, *n.* M.E., f. *wel*, well + *fare*—O.E. *faru*, a faring, f. *faran*, to FARE. Well-being.

Wel'kin, *n.* O.E. *wolcnu*, clouds, pl. of *wolcen*. Cf. Du. *wolk*, L.G. *wulke*, Ger. *wolke*. The sky, the heavens.

Well, *adv.* M.E. *wel*—O.E. *wel*, orig., 'agreeably to a wish', allied to *willan*, to WILL. WEAL.[1] Rightly, suitably; favourably; satisfactorily; in reality, fully; to a good degree; to a large extent; conveniently.—*a.* Satisfactory; suitable; in a good state of health.

Well, *n.* O.E. *wylla*, *wella*. Cf. Icel. *vell*, ebullition, Du. *wel*, a spring. A spring; a shaft sunk for water; a well-like cavity.—*vi.* and *t.* To flow or pour forth.

Welsh, *a.* O.E. *wælisc*, *welisc*, Celtic, f. *wealh*, a Celt + *-isc* (= -ISH). WALNUT. Of Wales.—*n.* The Welsh language or people.

Welt, *n.* M.E. *walt*, *welte*, poss. f. O.E. *wyltan*, *wæltan*. (See next.) An applied hem or bordering; a weal on the skin.—*vt.* To put a welt on; to beat severely.

Wel'ter, *vi.* Formerly also *Walter*. Freq. f. M.E. *walten*, to roll over, tumble—O.E. *wæltan*, to roll. Cf. O.N. *velta*, to roll; Ger. *wälzen*, to welter, f. *walzen*, to roll. WALTZ. Cogn. with L. *volvĕre*. To roll or tumble about.—*n.* A turmoil.

Wen, *n.* O.E. *wenn*. Cf. L.G. *ween*, Du. *wen*. A harmless fatty tumour.

Wench, *n.* M.E. *wenche*, earlier *wenchel*, prob. f. O.E. *wencel*, child, occurring only in *pl.* Perh. conn. with O.E. *wancol*, tottery. Cf. Ger. *wanken*, to totter. A young woman.

Wend, *vt.* O.E. *wendan*, to turn oneself, to go, causal of *windan*, to WIND. WANDER. To direct (one's way).—*vi.* To proceed, go.

Wer'wolf, **Were'wolf**, *n.* O.E. *werwulf*, f. *wer*, man + *wulf*, WOLF. A man-wolf.

West, *adv.* O.E. *west*, westward. Cf. Du. and Ger. *west*. In the direction of the setting sun.—*n.* The part of the sky where the sun sets; the western part of the world, a country, &c.—*a.* That is towards the west.—**West'er**LY,[1] *a.*—**West'**ERN, *a.*—**West'**WARD, *adv.* and *a.*—**West'**WARDS, *adv.*

Wet, *a.* O.E. *wǽt*. Cf. O.N. *vátr*, Da. *vaad*. Covered or soaked with moisture; rainy.—*n.* Moisture; rain.—*vt.* To make wet.—**Wet'-nurse**, *n.* A nurse who suckles the child.

Weth'er, *n.* O.E. *wethr*. Lit., 'a yearling'. Cogn. with Skr. *vatsa-*, year. A castrated ram.

Whack, *vt.* App. imitative. Cf. East Fris. and Prov. Ger. *wackeln* in sim. sense. To give a resounding blow to.—*n.* Such a blow.

Whale, *n.* O.E. *hwæl*. WALRUS. The largest sea animal.—**Whale'bone**, *n.* An elastic horny substance got from the upper jaw of certain whales.—**Whal'**ER, *n.* A person or ship employed in capturing whales.

Wharf, *n.* O.E. *hwerf*, a dam or bank. Cf.

Du. *werf*, Da. *værft*, wharf. A quay for loading or unloading ships.—**Wharf'**AGE, *n.*—**Wharf'inger**, *n.* For *Wharfag*ER, with intrusive *n.* Cf. MESSENGER. One who owns or has charge of a wharf.
What, *pron.* O.E. *hwæt*, neut. of *hwá*, WHO. Used interrogatively, chiefly of things; also in adjectival sense with interrogative force; that which.—**Whatev'er**, *pron.* EVER. Anything which; of what kind it may be.
Wheat, *n.* O.E. *hwǽte*, cogn. with WHITE. A cereal plant; its seeds, from which a white flour is prepared.—**Wheat'**EN,[1] *a.*
Wheed'le, *vt.* Poss. f. O.E. *wǽdlian*, to beg, f. *wǽdl*, poverty. To coax, cajole.
Wheel, *n.* O.E. *hwéol*, shortened f. *hweowol*, *hweogul*. Cf. Da. *hiul*. Cogn. with G. *kuklos*. CYCLE. A circular frame turning on an axis. —*vt.* To cause to rotate; to convey by vehicle. —*vi.* To rotate; to change one's direction.
Wheeze, *vi.* O.E. *hwésan*. Cf. O.E. *hwósta*, Du. *hoest*, Ger. *husten*, a cough. To breathe with difficulty and audibly.—**Wheez'**Y,[2] *a.*
Whelk, *n.* M.E. *wilk*—O.E. *wiloc*. Cf. Du. *wulk*, *welk*. A well-known shell-fish.
Whelm, *vt.* M.E. *whelmen*, to overturn, app. (through **whelm* = **hwelfm*, n.) conn. with *whelven* in same sense. Cf. O.E. *hwealf*, convex, a vault, Ger. *wölben*, to vault. To engulf, submerge.
Whelp, *n.* O.E. *hwelp*. Cf. Icel. *hvelpr*, Du. *welp*. The young of the dog, wolf, &c.—*vi.* and *t.* To bring forth whelps.
When, *adv.* M.E. *whan*—O.E. *hwænne*, *hwonne*. Cf. M.Du. *wan*, Ger. *wann*. At what or which time?—*conj.* At the time that; at which time; at the same time that.—**Whenev'er**, *conj.* EVER. At whatever time.
Whence, *adv.* M.E. *whennes*, earlier, *whanene* —O.E. *hwanon*, conn. with WHEN. From what place, source, &c.?—*conj.* From what or which place, &c.
Where, *adv.* O.E. *hwǽr*, conn. with *hwá*, WHO. Advbl. suff. *-r*. Cf. Icel. *hvar*, Du. *waar*. At or in what place, &c.? whither?—*conj.* At or in what or which place, &c.; the place in which.—**Whereas'**, *conj.* The thing being so that; while on the contrary.—**Where'fore**, *adv.* Formed like THEREFORE. For what reason, purpose, &c.?—*conj.* For which reason, consequently.—**Wherev'er**, *conj.* EVER. At or to whatever place.
Wher'ry, *n.* Of unknown orig. A light shallow boat.
Whet, *vt.* O.E. *hwettan*, f. *hwæt*, keen, bold. Cf. Du. *wetten*, Ger. *wetzen*. To sharpen; to excite, stimulate.—*n.* An act of whetting; something that whets the appetite.—**Whet'stone**, *n.* A stone for sharpening tools, &c.
Wheth'er, *a.* and *interrog.* and *rel. pron.* O.E. *hwæther*, which of two, f. the base of WHO + comp. suff. *-ther*. EITHER. NEITHER. Which of the two.—*conj.* Introducing the first of two alternatives; introducing also an alternative with a second unexpressed.
Whey, *n.* O.E. *hwǽg*. Cf. M.Du. *wey*. The watery part of milk.
Which, *pron.* O.E. *hwilc*, short for *hwi-líc*, of what form, f. *hwi-*, conn. with *hwá*, WHO + *-líc*. -LY.[1] An interrogative pronoun, used adjectivally or substantively; a relative pronoun, the neuter of *who*.—**Whichev'er**, *pron.* EVER. No matter which; any one.
Whiff, *n.* Imitative. A puff of air, odour, &c.—*vi.* To puff.—*vt.* To puff out, exhale.
Whig, *n.* App. short for *Whiggamore*, of uncertain orig. The name of that one of the two great political parties which is now represented (more or less) by the Liberals.
While, *n.* O.E. *hwíl*, a pause, a time. Cf. Icel. *hvíla*, place of rest, Ger. *weile*, a time. A space of time; expenditure of time.—*conj.* During or in the time that; at the same time that. (Also **Whilst**, with gen. suff. -(*e*)*s* and added *t*.)—*vt.* To cause (time) to pass *away*.
Whim, *n.* Cf. O.N. *hvima*, to wander with the eyes, Norw. *kvima*, to whisk about, trifle. A caprice. Sim. **Whim'sy**, **Whim'sey**. Cf. Norw. *kvimsa*, app. in sim. relation to *kvima*.—**Whim'**SICAL, *a.*
Whim'per, *vi.* App. a freq. of WHINE. To cry and whine softly—*n.* Such a sound.
Whine, *vi.* O.E. *hwinan*. Cf. O.N. *hvína*, Da. *hvine*, to whir, whine. To utter a long-drawn complaining cry.—*n.* Such a cry.
Whin'ny, *vi.* App. a freq. of WHINE. To neigh softly or joyfully.
Whip, *vi.* M.E. *wippen*, to jump up and down. Cf. Du. *wippen*, to skip, L.G. and Ger. *wippen*, to bob up and down. Cogn. with L. *vibrāre*. VIBRATE. To move nimbly. —*vt.* To move, pull, &c., suddenly; to punish or drive by lashing; to beat into a froth.—*n.* Something for punishing or driving by lashing; a member of parliament who looks after the attendance of his party; his summons.—**Whip'per-snap'per**, *n.* Prob. *Whip-snapper* (with the first element assimilated to the second), 'one who does nothing but snap or crack his whip'. An insignificant person. Sim. **Whip'ster**. -STER.
Whir, *vi.* Imitative. To fly, dart, &c., with a buzzing sound.—*n.* Such a sound.
Whirl, *vt.* and *i.* M.E. *whirlen* for *whirflen*, freq. of *wherfen*, to turn—O.N. *hvirfla*, to whirl, freq. of *hverfa*, to turn round. Cf. Ger. *wirbeln*. WARBLE. To turn round rapidly. —*n.* A rapid turning.—**Whirl'igig**, *n.* GIG in obs. sense 'whipping-top'. A spinning toy. —**Whirl'pool**, *n.* A circular current.—**Whirl'wind**, *n.* A wind moving round a progressive axis.
Whisk, *vt.* Properly *wisk*—Da. *viske*, to wipe, rub, f. *visk*, a wisp, rubber = Icel. *visk*, in same sense. Cf. Ger. *wischen*, to wipe. To sweep, agitate, or move with a light rapid motion.—*vi.* To move nimbly.—*n.* A kind of brush; an instrument for whisking eggs, &c.; a quick movement.—**Whisk'**ER, *n.* Hair on the sides of a man's face (likened to a brush).
Whisk'y, *n.* Prob. = (in the sense of the compound) the first element of *usquebaugh*, whisky—Ir. *uisge beatha*, water of life. A spirit distilled chiefly from barley.
Whis'per, *vi.* and *t.* O.E. (Northumb.) *hwisprian*, to murmur. Imitative. Cf. M. Du. *wisperen*, Ger. *wispern*. To speak or utter with a low rustling voice.—*n.* Such a voice.
Whist, *int.* Like HUSH a sound suggesting silence. Silence! hush!—*n.* Orig. *whisk*, from the sweeping up of the tricks (WHISK); renamed from the *int.* as requiring silence. A game at cards for four.
Whist'le, *vi.* O.E. *hwistlian*, to hiss. Imitative. Cf. Da. *hvisle*, to hiss, Sw. *hvissla*, to whistle. To utter a shrill sound through an orifice in the closed lips; to warble; to sound a whistle.—*vt.* To utter or direct by whistling. —*n.* The sound of whistling; an instrument for making the sound.
Whit, *n.* The same (with misplaced *h*) as WIGHT. The smallest particle, a jot or tittle.

White, *a.* O.E. *hwít.* Cf. Du. *wit*, Ger. *weiss.* Cogn. with Skr. *çvēta-*, white, f. *çvit*, to shine. WHEAT. Of snow-colour; pallid; pure, stainless; of wine, of a golden or amber colour, as opposed to red.—*n.* The colour; a pigment of the colour; a white part.—**Whit'**EN,[2] *vt.* and *i.*—**White'**NESS, *n.*—**Whit'**ISH, *a.*—**White'bait**, *n.* App. 'white refreshment or food'. BAIT. A small edible fish.—**White'smith**, *n.* A smith who works in tin; one who finishes and polishes forged iron.—**White'wash**, *n.* A liquid composition for whitening.—*vt.* To cover with this; to restore the reputation of.—**Whit'ing**, *n.*[1] Dried chalk.—**Whit'ing**, *n.*[2] A fish with delicate white flesh.

Whith'er, *adv.* O.E. *hwider, hwæder*, conn. with WHO. To what place? to which place.

Whit'low, *n.* A corr. of *whickflaw*, i.e. *whick*, northern dial. form of QUICK, sensitive part + FLAW,[1] a crack; hence, crack near the quick, painful sore. A painful swelling on the finger.

Whit'sunday, *n.* O.E. *hwíta sunnan-dæg*, WHITE SUNDAY, said to be so named from the white garments of candidates for baptism, who presented themselves in the largest number on this day. The seventh Sunday after Easter.—**Whit-Mon'day**, *n.* The following day.—**Whit'suntide**, *n.* Short for *Whitsundaytide.* The following week.

Whit'tle, *vt.* From obs. *Whittle*, knife—M.E. *thwitel*, f. O.E. *thwítan*, to cut. To cut or pare with a knife.

Whiz, Whizz, *vi.* Imit., like WHISTLE. To make a hissing sound.—*n.* Such a sound.

Who, *pron.* O.E. *hwá*, neut. *hwæt.* Cf. Du. *wie*, Da. *hvo*, Ger. *wer*; also Skr. *kas*, L. *quis.* HOW. An interrogative and relative pronoun, always used substantively and with reference to persons.—**Whoev'er**, *pron.* EVER. Any one without exception.

Whole, *a.* M.E. *hole*, the southern and midl. dial. rep. of O.E. *hál.* Cf. Icel. *heill*, Du. *heel*, Ger. *heil.* HAIL, *int.* HALE, *a.* HOLY. WASSAIL. Healthy; healed; unimpaired, intact; entire, complete; all, every part.—*n.* An entire thing; a complete system.—**Whol'**LY,[2] *adv.*—**Whole'sale**, *n.* Sale of goods by the piece or in large quantities.—*a.* Dealing by wholesale; pertaining to the wholesale trade; extensive and indiscriminate.—**Whole'**SOME, *a.* Salubrious, salutary.

Whoop, *vi.* M.E. *houpen*—F. *houper*, f. imitative int. *houp!* Cf. East Fris. *hup!* up! To shout.—*n.* A loud call or shout.

Whore, *n.* M.E. *hore*—O.N. *hóra*, adulteress. Cf. Du. *hoer*, Ger. *hure.* A prostitute.

Whorl, *n.* Said to be the same as dial. *Wharl*, a piece of bone on a spindle for twisting it by—M.E. *wharl, whorl*, contr. f. *whorvil*—O.E. *hweorfa*, f. *hweorfan*, to turn. Cf. O.N. *hverfa.* WHIRL. A ring of leaves, &c.; a volution, turn.

Whort'leberry, *n.* The first element of uncertain orig. The bilberry, a dark-blue berry, the fruit of a small shrub; the shrub.

Why, *adv.* O.E. *hwí*, in what way, instrumental case of *hwá*, WHO. For what cause?—*conj.* For what cause.

Wick, *n.* O.E. *weoce.* Cf. Da. *væge*, M.H.G. *wieche.* The twist of threads in a lamp, &c.

Wick'ed, *a.* Orig. a ppl. form with sense 'rendered evil', f. obs. *wikke*, wicked, conn. with O.E. *wicce*, WITCH. Evil in principle or practice, sinful.—**Wick'ed**LY,[2] *adv.*

Wick'er, *n.* M.E. *wiker*, pliant twig—O.E. *wícan*, to bend, conn. with *wæcan.* WEAK. WITCH-ELM. Plaited twigs.

Wick'et, *n.* A.F. *wiket, wisket*—O.F. *guischet* (F. *guichet*), of uncertain orig. A small gate; in *cricket*, a set of three stumps at which the bowler aims.

Wide, *a.* O.E. *wíd.* Cf. Du. *wijd*, Ger. *weit.* Broad; spacious; embracing much, applicable to many cases; remote.—**Wide'**LY,[2] *adv.*—**Wid'**EN,[2] *vt.* and *i.*—**Wid**TH,[1] *n.*

Wid'geon, *n.* O.F. *vigeon*, prob. f. L. *vipio, vipiōnis*, a kind of small crane. A water-fowl.

Wid'ow, *n.* O.E. *widwe.* Cf. Du. *weduwe*, Ger. *witwe.* Cogn. with L. *vidua.* A woman whose husband is dead, and who has not married again.—*vt.* To make a widow of.—**Wid'ower**, *n.* M.E. *widewer.* -ER. A man whose wife is dead, and who has not married again.—**Wid'ow**HOOD, *n.*

Wield, *vt.* M.E. *welden*—O.E. *gewyldan*, to have power over. Cf. O.N. *valda*, Ger. *walten.* To govern, rule; to sway; to use as a weapon, &c.—**Wield'**Y,[2] *a.* Easily wielded.

Wife, *n.* O.E. *wíf*, woman, wife. Cf. Du. *wijf*, Ger. *weib.* A woman joined to a man by marriage.—**Wife'**LIKE, **Wife'**LY,[1] *aa.*—**Wive**, *vi.* O.E. *wífian*, f. *wíf.* To take a wife.—*vt.* To provide with a wife.

Wig, *n.* Short for PERIWIG. An artificial covering of hair for the head.

Wight, *n.* O.E. *wiht*, a creature, person, thing. Cf. Du. *wicht*, child, Ger. *wicht*, wight. WHIT. AUGHT. NAUGHT. A person.

Wig'wam, *n.* Corrupted f. N. American Indian. The hut of a N. American Indian.

Wild, *a.* O.E. *wilde.* Cf. O.N. *villr*, wild, also astray, bewildered, Ger. *wild*, wild. BEWILDER. Not domesticated or cultivated; furious; excited; rash.—*n.* A desert.—**Wild'**LY,[2] *adv.*—**Wil'derness**, *n.* O.E. *wilder*, wild animal + -NESS. A desert; a confused mass or collection.—**Wild'-fire**, *n.* An inflammable composition.

Wile, *n.* Late O.E. *wíl*, perh. f. O.F. *guile.* GUILE. A trick or stratagem.—*vt.* To lure, entice; to cause (time) to pass *away* (prob. by confusion with WHILE, *v.*).—**Wil'**Y,[2] *a.*

Wil'ful, *a.* M.E. *wille*, WILL, *n.* + -FUL. Intentional; stubborn, wayward.

Will, *vt.* O.E. *willan, wyllan.* Cf. Du. *willen*, Ger. *wollen.* Cogn. with L. *velle.* To wish.—*vi.* To have a wish.—*v.aux.* Helps to form the future tense, in the first person expressing the speaker's will, in the second and third futurity.—*vt.* From O.E. *willian*, secondary *v.* f. *willan.* To intend, purpose; to give as a legacy.—*n.* Wish; purpose; a formally expressed wish as to the disposal of one's property after death; the faculty of conscious and deliberate action.—**Wil'ling**, *a.* Ready, inclined; voluntary; prompt.—**Wil'ling**LY,[2] *adv.*—**Wil'ling**NESS, *n.*—**Wil'ly-nil'ly**, *adv. Will he, nill he*—O.E. *nillan*, short for *ne willan*, not to wish. Willing or unwilling.

Will'-o'-the-wisp', *n.* *Will(iam) of the handful* (of lighted tow, &c.). The *ignis fatuus.*

Wil'low, *n.* O.E. *welig.* Cf. Du. *wilg*, L.G. *wilge.* A tree or shrub furnishing material for basket-making, &c.—**Wil'low**Y,[2] *a.*

Wim'ble, *n.* Cf. Da. *vimmel*, L.G. *wemel*, in sim. sense. GIMLET. A kind of gimlet.

Win, *vt.* O.E. *winnan*, to struggle, try to get. Cf. Du. *winnen*, Ger. *gewinnen.* Root *wen-*. WISH. To get or accomplish by labour or effort; to be successful in; to reach; to attract, allure.—*vi.* To succeed.

Wince, *vi.* A.F. **wencir*, older form of *guencir*, O.F. *guenchir*, f. Teut. Cf. O.S. *wenkian*, M.H.G. *wenken*. Cogn. with WINK. To flinch, start back.—*n.* An act of wincing.

Winc'ey, *n.* Said to be an abb. and corr. of LINSEY-WOOLSEY. A durable cloth with a cotton warp and a woollen weft.

Winch, *n.* O.E. *wince*, bent handle. Cf. *wincel*, corner, lit., 'bend', f. **wincan*. WINK. A crank of a wheel, &c.; a hoisting-machine.

Wind, *n.* O.E. *wind*. Cf. O.N. *vindr*, Du. and Ger. *wind*. Cogn. with Skr. *vā*, to blow, *vātas*, wind, L. *ventus*. VENTILATE. WINNOW. Air in motion; breath; anything ineffectual or empty.—*v.*1*t.* To sound by blowing; to render scant of breath; to allow to rest to recover breath.—**Wind'fall**, *n.* Fruit blown down; an unexpected piece of good fortune.—**Wind'-pipe**, *n.* The passage for the breath.—**Wind'**WARD, *a.* On the side toward the wind—**Wind'**Y,2 *a.*

Wind, *v.*2*i.* O.E. *windan*. Cf. O.N. *vinda*, Du. and Ger. *winden*, Goth. *-windan*. WAND. WANDER. WEND. To vary from the direct line, go in a devious course; to twine.—*vt.* To bend, turn, twist round, wrap; to adjust for work by coiling a spring more tightly.—**Wind'lass**, *n.* M.E. *windelas*—O.N. *vindiláss*, f. *vindill*, a winder (f. *vinda*)+*áss*, pole, rounded beam, cogn. with Goth. *ans*, beam. A revolving cylinder on which a rope is wound used for raising weights.

Win'dow, *n.* M.E. *windoge*, *windowe*—O.N. *vindauga*, lit. 'wind-eye', f. *vindr*, WIND+*auga*, EYE. An opening in a wall for the admission of light and air.

Wine, *n.* O.E. *win*—L. *vinum*, cogn. with G. *oinos*. VINE. VINEGAR. The fermented juice of the grape.

Wing, *n.* M.E. *wenge*, *winge*—Norw. *vengja*, Cf. Da., Sw. *vinge*. One of the limbs with which birds, &c., fly; flight; a lateral extension.—*vt.* To furnish with wings; to traverse in flight; to wound in the wing.—*vi.* To fly.

Wink, *vi.* O.E. *wincian* (also strong v. **wincan*). Cf. M.Du. *wincken*, O.N. *vanka*; also Ger. *winken*, to nod. WINCE. WINCH. To open and close the eyelid quickly; to convey a hint, &c., by winking; to be wilfully blind.—*n.* An act of winking.

Win'kle, *n.* O.E. *-wincla* (in a form variously read as *pine-wincla* (whence poss. PERIWINKLE2) and *wine-wincla*). Cf. Da. dial. *vinkel*, snail-shell. A periwinkle.

Win'now, *vt.* O.E. *windwian*, to expose to wind, winnow, f. *wind*, WIND. To expose to wind to separate chaff, &c. (often *fig.*).

Win'some, *a.* O.E. *wynsum*, delightful, f. *wynn*, joy (root *wen-*. WISH) + *-sum*, -SOME. Charming, attractive, winning.

Win'ter, *n.* O.E. *winter*, winter, also, a year. Cf. Du., Ger. *winter*. The fourth or cold season.—*vi.* To pass the winter.—*vt.* To keep or tend during the winter.—**Win'try**,2 *a.*

Wipe, *vt.* O.E. *wipian*. Cf. E.Fris. *wip*, L.G. *wiep*, a WISP of straw. To rub in order to clean; to efface, remove.—*n.* A wiping.

Wire, *n.* O.E. *wir*. Cf. O.N. *vírr*, wire, Sw. *vira*, to twist. Cogn. with L. *viriae*. FERRULE. A slender bar of metal.—*vt.* To fit or provide with wire.—**Wir'**Y,2 *a.* Made of wire; tough, sinewy.

Wise, *a.* O.E. *wís*. Cf. Du. *wijs*, Ger. *weise*. Indo-Germanic root *weid-*. WIT. WIZARD. Sagacious, judicious; dictated or directed by wisdom. —**Wise'**LY,2 *adv.* —**Wis'**DOM, *n.* The property of being wise.

Wise, *n.* O.E. *wise*, way. Orig. sense, wisdom, skill, f. *wís*. (See prec.) GUISE. Manner, mode.

Wise'acre, *n.* M.Du. *wijssegger*, wise sayer —Ger. *weissager*, taken in sim. sense, a corruption of O.H.G. *wizago*, seer, f. *wizan*, to see. A pretender to wisdom.

Wish, *vi.* O.E. *wýscan*. Cf. M.Du., Ger. *wunsch*, a wish. Root *wen-*. Cogn. with Skr. *vāñch*, to wish. WIN. WINSOME. WONT. To have a desire or longing *for*.—*vt.* To desire, long for.—**Wish'**FUL, *a.*

Wisp, *n.* Cf. L.G. *wiep*, Norw. *vippa*. WIPE. A small bundle; a twisted handful.

Wist'ful, *a.* Perh. a substitution for WISHFUL by association and confusion with obs. *Wistly*—M.E. *wisly*, certainly, f. O.N. *viss*, certain, orig. pa.pple. of *vita*, to know. (See next.) Wishful, longing; musing, pensive.

Wit, *vt.* and *i.* O.E. *witan*. Cf. Goth. *witan*, O.N. *vita*, Du. *weten*, Ger. *wissen*. O.Teut. root *weid-*. Cogn. with G. *ide-ein*, L. *vidēre*, to see. GUIDE. HISTORY. IDEA. WISE. WITNESS. To know.—*n.* O.E. *witt*, knowledge. Wisdom, sagacity; understanding, intellect; the apt association of incongruous ideas. From O.E. *wita*, 'one who knows'. One possessing the faculty of this.—**Wit'ticism**, *n.* WITTY +C+-ISM. A witty phrase or remark.—**Wit'ting**LY,2 *adv.* Consciously, by design.—**Wit'**TY,2 *a.* Brilliantly original in expressing amusing notions; characterized by wit.—**Wit'**TILY,2 *adv.*

Witch, *n.* M.E. *wicche*, masc. and fem.—O.E. *wicca*, masc., *wicce*, fem., conn. with *wiccian*, to practise witchcraft. Cf. M.Du. *wicker*, soothsayer, L.G. *wikken*, to predict. WICKED. A woman supposed to have magical powers.—*vt.* To enchant.—**Witch'craft**, *n.* The practices of witches; enchantment.—**Witch'**ERY, *n.*

Witch'-elm, **Wych'-elm**, *n.* O.E. *wice*, the name of several trees with pendulous branches, f. *wicen*, pa.pple. of *wícan*, to bend. WICKER. A kind of elm.

With, *prep.* O.E. *with*, by, near, among; also, against. Cf. O.N. *vidh*, against, by, at, Da. *ved*, Sw. *vid*, near, by, at. Against; in the company of; as a property, &c., of, in the possession, &c., of; having, possessing; in relation to; by; through.—**Withal'**, *adv.* M.E. *with alle* (dat. of *al*, O.E. *al*, ALL). Moreover, likewise.—*prep.* An emphatic form of with, used after the object (gen. a relative).—**Withdraw'**, *vt.* From *with*, against, opposite, towards oneself, back. To draw back, aside, or away; to retract; to divert.—*vi.* To go away, retire.—**Withdraw'**AL, *n.*—**Withhold'**, *vt.* To refrain from giving, &c.—**Within'**, *adv.* O.E. *withinnan*. In or into the interior. —*prep.* In or into the interior of; included in; not beyond or more than; in.—**Without'**, *adv.* O.E. *withútan*. On or as to the outside. —*prep.* Beyond; lacking, destitute of.—**Withstand'**, *vt.* To stand against, oppose.

With'er, *vt.* M.E. *widren*, *wederen*, to expose to weather, f. *weder*, WEATHER. To cause to fade; to blight.—*vi.* To fade.

With'ers, *n.pl.* O.E. *wither* (conn. with WITH), against, as *n.*, resistance, hence, 'the resisting or pulling part'. The ridge between a horse's shoulder-blades.

With'y, **Withe**, *n.* M.E. *withi*—O.E. *withig*, willow. Cf. Da. *vidie*, Ger. *weide*, willow. Root *wei-*, to twine. Cogn. with G. *itea*, willow, L. *vitis*, vine. VICE.[2] A flexible twig.

Wit'ness, *n.* O.E. *witnes*, testimony, f. *witan*, to know (WIT) + *-nes* (-NESS). Testimony; one who gives testimony; one who sees, hears, &c. —*vi.* To give testimony.—*vt.* To attest; to see, &c.; to see the execution of (a deed) and sign as having done so.

Wiz'ard, *n.* M.E. *wisard*, f. O.E. *wís*, WISE + F. suff. *-ard*, 'one who affects to be wise'. A sorcerer.

Wiz'en, *a.* O.E. *wisnian*, to become dry. Cf. O.N. *visna*, to wither. Dry, shrivelled. Also **Wiz'ened**.

Woe, *int.* O.E. *wá*, int. and adv., *wéa*, n. Cf. Du. *vee*, int. and n., O.N. *vei*, Goth. *wai*, int., Ger. *weh*, int. and n. WAIL. An exclamation of pain or grief.—*n.* Grief, misery.—**Woe'begone**, *a.* 'Woe-surrounded', f. M.E. *begōn*, pa.pple. of *begōn*, O.E. *begán*, to surround, f. BE-, about + *gán*, to GO. Overwhelmed with woe, sorrowful. — **Woe'**FUL, *a.* — **Woe'ful**LY,[2] *adv.*

Wold, *n.* M.E. *wold*, *wald*—O.E. *weald*, *wald*, a wood, hence, waste ground. Cf. Du. *woud*, O.S. *wald*, O.H.G. *walt* (Ger. *wald*), a wood. An open tract of country.

Wolf, *n.*; *pl.* **Wolves**. O.E. *wulf*, pl. *wulfas*, corresp. to Du., Ger. *wolf*. Cogn. with G. *lukos*, L. *lupus*. A carnivorous quadruped akin to the dog.

Wo'man, *n.*; *pl.* **Wom'en**. O.E. *wífman*, later *wimman*, lit., woman-man (*man* being formerly applied to both sexes). WIFE. MAN. An adult human female; the female sex; a female attendant. — **Wo'man**HOOD, *n.* — **Wo'man**ISH, *a.*—**Wo'mankind**, *n.* The female sex.—**Wo'man**LY,[1] *a.*

Womb, *n.* O.E. *wamb*, *womb*, belly. Cf. Ger. *wampe*, Da. *vom*, belly. The part of a female in which the ovum is nourished.

Won'der, *n.* O.E. *wundor*. Cf. Du. *wonder*, Ger. *wunder*. A strange thing, a marvel; the feeling excited by a wonder.—*vi.* To be affected with wonder; to speculate expectantly. — **Won'der**FUL, *a.* — **Won'derful**LY,[2] *adv.*—**Won'der**MENT, *n.*—**Won'dr**OUS, *a.* —**Won'drous**LY,[2] *adv.*

Wont, *a.* M.E. *woned*, pa.pple. of *wonien*, O.E. *wunian*, to dwell, be used to, f. *gewuna*, custom, use, f. *wun-*, weak grade of *wen-*. WISH. Accustomed.—*n.* Custom.—**Wont'ed**, *ppl.a.* Formed f. the *n.* Habitual.

Woo, *vt.* O.E. *wógian*, of obscure orig. To court, seek in marriage.—**Woo'**ER, *n.*

Wood, *n.* O.E. *wudu*, orig. *widu*, a wood, a tree, wood. Cf. O.N. *vithr*, a tree, wood, O.H.G. *witu*, wood. A large collection of growing trees; the substance of trees; timber. —**Wood'bine**, **Wood'bind**, *n.* O.E. *wudubind*, 'that which binds or winds round trees', f. *bindan*, to BIND. The wild honeysuckle.—**Wood'cock**, *n.* O.E. *wuducoc*. A bird allied to the snipe.—**Wood'cut**, *n.* An engraving on wood; a print from such an engraving.—**Wood'**EN,[1] *a.*—**Wood'land**, *n.* Land covered with trees.—**Wood'pecker**, *n.* A bird with a bill adapted for boring wood.—**Wood'**Y,[2] *a.*

Woof, *n.* Altered by initial conformity with *weave*, *weft*, &c., f. M.E. *oof*—O.E. *ówef*, f. *ó-* (=A-[3]) + *wef*, f. *wefan*, to WEAVE. The threads that cross the warp in weaving.

Wool, *n.* O.E. *wull*, *wul*. Cf. Du. *wol*, Ger. *wolle*. Cogn. with L. *vellus*, fleece. VELVET. The soft hair covering the sheep and some other animals.—**Wool'l**EN,[1] *a.*—**Wool'**LY,[1] *a.*—**Wool'sack**, *n.* A cushion stuffed with wool, applied to the seat of the Lord Chancellor in the House of Lords.

Word, *n.* O.E. *word*. Cf. Du. *woord*, Ger. *wort*. Cogn. with L. *verbum*. VERB. An articulate sound used as the sign of an idea; talk (gen. in *pl.*); a saying, remark; information; an order; a promise.—*vt.* To express in words.—**Word'**Y,[2] *a.*

Work, *n.* M.E. *werk*—O.E. *weorc*, *werc*. Cf. Du., Ger. *werk*. Cogn. with G. *ergon*. ENERGY. WRIGHT. Labour; something to do; a task; something accomplished; something made or manufactured; a place for manufacturing, &c. (gen. in *pl.*).—*vi.* To put forth effort; to act, operate; to ferment; to make way; to be engaged in a trade, &c.—*vt.* To prepare by labour; to make, form; to perform; to set in motion; to achieve; to exact labour from.—**Work'**ABLE, *a.*—**Work'**ER, *n.* — **Work'house**, *n.* An institution for paupers.—**Work'man**, *n.* A man employed in manual labour.—**Work'man**SHIP, *n.* The art or skill of a workman; the finish shown in anything made.—**Work'shop**, *n.* A place where work is carried on.

World, *n.* O.E. *weoruld*, *weorold*, lit. 'age of man', 'course of man's life', hence, a lifetime, experience of life, &c., f. *wer*, a man + *eld*, an age. Cf. Du. *wereld*, O.H.G. *weralt* (Ger. *welt*). A state or sphere of existence; the system of created things; the human race; a class or section of men; the earth; secular affairs or interests, those devoted thereto; life in society; the practices of life; a domain.—**World'**LING, *n.* -LING (1). One devoted to secular affairs.—**World'**LY,[1] *a.*

Worm, *n.* O.E. *wyrm*, a worm, snake = O.S. *wurm*, Du., L.G. *worm*. Cogn. with L. *vermis*. A small creeping animal.—*vi.* and *refl.* To insinuate oneself, to crawl sinuously.—*vt* To extract (a secret, &c.) insidiously.

Worm'wood, *n.* M.E. *wormwod*, alteration of *wermode*—O.E. *wermód*. Orig. unknown. Cf. Ger. *wermut*. A bitter herb.

Wor'ry, *vt.* M.E. *wirien*, *worowen*, orig., to strangle—O.E. *wyrgen*, to strangle, harm. Cf. Du. *worgen*, Ger. *würgen*, to strangle. To seize by the throat with the teeth; to trouble, harass.—*vi.* To be unduly anxious.—*n.* Care, anxiety.

Worse, *a.* M.E. *wurse*, *werse*, a., *wurs*, *wers*, adv.—O.E. *wyrsa*, a., *wyrs*, adv. Cf. O.S. *wirsa*, a., *wirs*, adv., M.H.G. *wirser*, a., *wirs*, adv. Cf. also O.H.G. *werran* (Ger. *wirren*), to confuse, entangle. WAR. *Comp.* of BAD, EVIL, ILL.—*adv.* In a manner or to a degree more bad or evil.—**Wors'**EN,[2] *vi.* and *t.*

Wor'ship, *n.* Short for *worthship*—O.E. *weorthscipe*, *wyrthscipe*. WORTH. -SHIP. Reverence; deference; adoration; devotion, admiration; a title of honour.—*vt.* To show respect to; to adore; to love or admire.—**Wor'ship**FUL, *a.*—**Wor'shipp**ER, *n.*

Worst, *a.* O.E. *wyrsta*, a. (contracted f. **wyrsesta*), *wyrst*, adv. Cf. O.S. *wirsista*, a. *Superl.* of BAD, EVIL, ILL.—*adv.* In a manner or to a degree the extreme of bad or evil.—*vt.* To defeat, overthrow.

Wor'sted, *n.* From *Worsted* in Norfolk, as orig. made there. A variety of woollen yarn.

Wort, *n.*[1] O.E. *wyrt*, a wort, plant, herb. Cf. O.S. *wurt*. Cogn. with G. *rhiza*, L. *rādix*, root. ERADICATE. A plant, herb.

Wort, *n.*[2] O.E. *wyrt* (only in combination).

MASH. Cf. M.H.G. *wirz.* The infusion of malt which by fermentation becomes beer.

Worth, *a.* O.E. *wyrthe*, alteration of *weorth*, valuable. Cf. Ger. *wert.* Cogn. with L. *verēri.* WARE, *a.* Having value in a given degree; possessing; meriting.—*n.* O.E. *weorth, wyrth.* Excellence, merit; value, importance.—**Worth'**LESS, *a.*—**Worth'**Y,[2] *a.*—**Worth'i**LY,[2] *adv.*—**Worth'**INESS, *n.*

Wound, *n.* O.E. *wund.* Cf. Du. *wond*, Ger. *wunde.* A lesion of the body due to external violence; an injury or hurt.—*vt.* To inflict a wound upon; to cause injury to, pain.

Wrack, *n.* M.E. *wrak*, 'what is cast on shore', a wreck, f. O.E. *wræc*, 'what is driven', f. *wrecan.* WREAK. WRECK. RACK, *n.*[3] Seaweed; wreckage; destruction, ruin.

Wraith, *n.* Scotch. Orig. doubtful. An apparition of one about to die or newly dead.

Wran'gle, *vi.* M.E. *wranglen*, to wrestle, to dispute, freq. f. O.E. *wrang-*, 2nd grade of *wringan.* WRING. To dispute, argue noisily.—*n.* A noisy quarrel.

Wrap, *vt.* M.E. *wrappen.* Cf. N.Fris. *wrappe*, to stop up. To envelop, surround; to cover; to put or arrange *round* or *about.*—*n.* An outer article of dress.—**Wrap'**PER, *n.* An outer covering; a loose garment.

Wrath, *n.* O.E. *wrǽththu*, f. *wráth*, WROTH. Violent anger.—**Wrath'**FUL, *a.*

Wreak, *vt.* O.E. *wrecan*, to revenge, orig., to drive, urge. Cf. Ger. *rächen*, to revenge. WRACK. To inflict (vengeance, &c.).

Wreath, *n.* O.E. *wrǽth*, twisted band, f. *wráth-*, 2nd grade of *wrīthan.* WRITHE. WREST. Something twisted into a circular form; a garland.—**Wreathe**, *vt.* To form into a wreath; to wind *round*; to encircle.

Wreck, *n.* The same as WRACK. Destruction of a ship; a ship ruined by wreck; ruin; something in a state of ruin.—*vt.* To cause the wreck or ruin of.—**Wreck'**AGE, *n.*

Wren, *n.* O.E. *wrenna, wrænna.* Cf. O.N. *rindill.* A very small bird.

Wrench, *n.* M.E. *wrenche*, only *fig.*, 'perversion, deceit'—O.E. *wrenc*, guile, fraud, orig., crookedness. Cf. Ger. *ränke*, tricks. Formerly, a deceit, trick. A violent twist or turn; a tool for screwing.—*vt.* To twist; to distort; to take by force.

Wrest, *vt.* O.E. *wrǽstan*, to twist forcibly, f. *wrǽst*, tightly twisted (hence, firm), formed f. *wráth-.* WREATH. To twist or turn (often *fig.*); to take by force.—*n.* A tool for tuning a harp, &c.—**Wres'tle**, *vi.* O.E. *wrǽstlian*, freq. of *wrǽstan.* To contend by grappling and trying to throw down.

Wretch, *n.* O.E. *wrecca, wræcca*, an outcast, cogn. with *wrecan.* WREAK. A miserable person; a contemptible creature.—**Wretch'ed**, *a.* For the form cf. WICKED. Miserable; causing unhappiness; contemptible, worthless.

Wrig'gle, *vi.* Freq. of obs. *Wrig*, to move about, a weakened form of M.E. *wrikken*, to twist. Cf. O.E. *wrigian*, which passed into WRY; also Du. *wriggelen*, L.G. *wrickeln.* To twist to and fro; to move sinuously.—*n.* A quick twisting motion.

Wright, *n.* O.E. *wyrhta*, worker, f. *wyrht*, deed, work, f. *wyrcan*, to work, f. *weorc*, WORK. An artificer, workman, maker.

Wring, *vt.* O.E. *wringan*, to press, strain, wring. Cf. Ger. *ringen*, to wrestle, to wring. WRANGLE. To twist; to distress, pain; to extract, to extort.

Wrin'kle, *n.*[1] M.E. *wrinkel.* Cf. M.Du. *wrinckel.* A slight ridge on a surface.—*vt.* To form wrinkles in.—*vi.* To become wrinkled.

Wrin'kle, *n.*[2] Perh. a dim. of O.E. *wrenc.* WRENCH. A valuable hint.

Wrist, *n.* O.E. *wrist*, f. *writh-*, weak grade of *wrīthan.* WRITHE. The joint between the arm and the hand.—**Wrist'let**, *n.* Dim. suff. *-let.* A band, &c., worn on the wrist.

Write, *vt.* O.E. *wrītan.* Orig. sense, to score, scratch. Cf. O.S. *wrītan*, to cut, write, Ger. *reissen*, to cut, tear. To trace or form upon a surface; to set down in words; to communicate in writing; to compose.—*vi.* To form written words; to practise written composition; to conduct correspondence, send a letter.—**Writ**, *n.* O.E. *gewrit, writ.* That which is written; a legal precept, a formal writing.

Writhe, *vi.* O.E. *wrīthan.* Cf. O.N. *rītha*, Da. *vride*, to wring, twist, turn. WREATH. WRIST. WROTH. To turn and twist about.

Wrong, *a.* Late O.E. *wrang*, a wrong, orig. *a.*—Icel. *rangr* (O.N. *vrangr*), awry, wrong. Cogn. with WRING. Not right or suitable.—*n.* That which is wrong; wrong conduct; harm done; a being wrong or acting wrongly.—*adv.* In a wrong manner.—*vt.* To do wrong to.—**Wrong'**LY,[2] *adv.*—**Wrong'**FUL, *a.*

Wroth, *a.* O.E. *wráth*, f. *wráth*, 2nd grade of *wrīthan*, to WRITHE. WRATH. Angry.

Wry, *a.* M.E. *wrien*, to twist, bend aside—O.E. *wrigian*, to turn, incline towards WRIGGLE. Turned to one side, distorted.

Y

Yacht, *n.* M.Du. *jacht*, Du. *jagt*, a hunting, a swift boat, f. *jagen*, to hunt. Cf. Ger. *jagen*, to hunt. YAW. A light vessel for racing or pleasure.—*vi.* To sail in a yacht.

Yard, *n.*[1] O.E. *geard*, an enclosure, court. Cf. O.N. *garthr*, Du. *gaard.* GARDEN. GARTH. ORCHARD. A piece of enclosed ground.

Yard, *n.*[2] O.E. *gyrd, gerd*, rod. Cf. Du. *garde*, twig, rod, Ger. *gerte*, switch. GAD, *n.* A measure of 3 feet; a spar slung across a mast.

Yarn, *n.* O.E. *gearn*, thread. Cf. Du. *garen*, Ger. *garn.* Cogn. with G. *chordē.* CORD. Thread prepared for weaving, &c.; a tale.

Yaw, *vi.* O.N. *jaga*, to hunt, to move to and fro. Cf. Du. *jagen.* YACHT. To go unsteadily.—*n.* A deviation from the straight course.

Yawl, *n.* Du. *jol.* Cf. Da. *jolle*, Sw. *julle.* A small yacht of the cutter class.

Yawn, *vi.* M.E. *geonien, yonien*—O.E. *geonian.* Cf. O.H.G. *ginēn.* Cogn. with L. *hiāre*, to gape. HIATUS. To gape; to open the mouth wide through drowsiness.—*n.* A yawning.

Ye, *pron.* O.E. *gé*, genit. *eówer*, dat. and acc. *eów.* Cf. Du. *gij*, Ger. *ihr.* Cogn. with G. *hu-meis.* YOU. YOUR. Archaic plural of the second personal pronoun.

Yea, *int.* M.E. *ye*—O.E. *géa, geá.* Cf. Du., Da., Ger. *ja.* Yes.

Year, *n.* O.E. *geár, gér.* Cf. Du. *jaar*, Ger. *jahr.* Prob. cogn. with G. *hōra* (*yōra*), season. YORE. The period of the earth's revolution round the sun; twelve months.—**Year'ling**, *n.* -LING (1). A beast one year old.—**Year'**LY,[1] *a.*—**Year'**LY,[2] *adv.*

Yearn, *vi.* O.E. *giernan*, f. *georn*, desirous, conn. with O.H.G. *gerōn*, Ger. *begehren*, to long for. Cogn. with G. *chairein*, to rejoice. To feel desire or longing.

Yeast, *n.* O.E. *gist*. Cf. Du. *gest*, Ger. *gischt*; also O.H.G. *jesan*, to ferment. Cogn. with G. *ze-ein*, to boil. A substance inducing fermentation and used in making bread.

Yell, *vi.* O.E. *gellan*, *giellan*, to cry out, resound. Cf. Du. *gillen*, Ger. *gellen*, to sound loud and shrill. NIGHTINGALE. To cry out with a sharp loud noise.—*n.* Such a cry.

Yel'low, *a.* O.E. *geolo*, *geolu*. Cf. Du. *geel*, Ger. *gelb*. Cogn. with G. *chloē*, young herbage, L. *helvus*, light yellow. GALL, *n.*[1] GOLD. YOLK. Of a colour like that of a lemon or of gold.—*n.* The colour.—**Yel'lowhammer**, *n.* From (*h*)*ammer*, corresp. to O.E. *amere*, *amore*—M.L.G. *amere*, O.H.G. *amero* (Ger. *ammer*), bunting. The yellow bunting.

Yelp, *vi.* O.E. *gielpan*, to boast, talk noisily. Cf. O.N. *gjálpa*, to yelp. To give a sharp, shrill, quick cry.—*n.* Such a cry.

Yeo'man, *n.* M.E. *yoman*, app. pointing to an O.E. **géaman*. Poss. conn. with Old Fris. *gāman*, villager, f. *gā*, village + *man*, MAN. One owning (and usually himself cultivating) a small landed property.—**Yeo'man**RY, *n.* Yeomen collectively; a volunteer cavalry force.

Yes, *int.* M.E. *yis*, *yus*—O.E. *gise*, *gese*, prob. short for *géa swá*, YEA SO. Expressing affirmation or consent.

Yes'terday, *n.* O.E. *geostra*, *giestra*, yester- (cf. Du. *gistern*, Ger. *gestern*, yester(day)) + *dæg*, DAY. The day last past.

Yet, *adv.* O.E. *git*, *get*, *giet*, moreover. Cf. Old Fris. *ieta*, *ita*, M.H.G. *iezuo*, *ieze*, yet. At present, now; in addition; still; at or before some future time; hitherto, thus far; nevertheless.—*conj.* Nevertheless.

Yew, *n.* O.E. *iw*. Cf. O.H.G. *īwa* (Ger. *eibe*). An evergreen tree.

Yield, *vt.* M.E. *gelden*, *yelden*—O.E. *gieldan*, *gildan*, to pay, give up. Cf. Du. *gelden*, to pay, Ger. *gelten*, to be worth. O.Teut. root *geld-*, to pay. GUILD. To give as fruit, &c.; to grant; to give up, surrender.—*vi.* To produce; to give way.—*n.* Amount produced.

Yoke, *n.* O.E. *geoc*, *gioc*, *ioc*. Cf. Du. *juk*, Ger. *joch*. O.Teut. root *juk-*, Indo-European *yug-*. Cogn. with G. *zugon*, L. *jugum*. CONJUGAL. JOIN. A contrivance for fastening together a pair of draught animals (often *fig.*); various things resembling this; a couple.—*vt.* To put a yoke on (often *fig.*).

Yo'kel, *n.* Orig. obscure. A rustic.

Yolk, *n.* O.E. *geoleca*, *geolca*, lit., 'yellow part', f. *geolu*, YELLOW. The yellow part of an egg.

Yon, *a.* O.E. *geon*. Cf. Goth. *jains*, G. *jener*, yon, that. Cogn. with Skr. *yas*, who, orig., that, G. *hos* (*yos*), who. That or those, referring to a distant object. Sim., **Yon'der**, *a.* Cf. Goth. *jaindre*.

Yore, *n.* O.E. *geára*, formerly, lit. 'of years', genit. pl. of *geár*, YEAR. Old times.

You, *pron.* Properly dat. and acc. of YE. Plural of the pronoun of the second person, often applied to a single person.

Young, *a.* O.E. *geong*, *giung*, *iung*. Cf. Du. *jong*, Ger. *jung*. Cogn. with L. *juvenis*. JUVENILE. In the early stage of life, growth or existence; vigorous.—*n.* Offspring collectively.—**Young'**STER, *n.* An active or lively boy.

Your, *pron.* O.E. *éower*, orig. genit. of *gé*, YE. Belonging to you.

Youth, *n.* O.E. *geogoth*, *geoguth*, *iuguth*, f. *geong*, &c., YOUNG. The condition or period of being young; a young person; young persons collectively.—**Youth'**FUL, *a.*

Yule, *n.* O.E. *géol*, *geohol*. Orig. unknown. The feast or season of Christmas.

Z

Zana'na, **Zena'na**, *n.* Hindustani *zanāna*—Pers. *zanān*, pl. of *zan*, woman. The women's quarters in a Hindu house.

Za'ny, *n.* Old It. *Zane*, It. *Zanni* for *Giovanni*, John, used in derision. A clown who mimics the professional clown; a buffoon.

Zeal, *n.* O.F. *zele*—L.L. *zēlus*. JEALOUS. Passionate ardour.—**Zeal'ot**, *n.* G. *zēlōtēs*. One passionately devoted to a cause.—**Zeal'**OUS, *a.*—**Zeal'ous**LY,[2] *adv.*

Ze'bra, *n.* Pg. *zebra*, app. of W. African orig. A striped animal allied to the horse.

Zen'ith, *n.* O.F. *cenith*—Sp. *zenit*—Arab. *semt*, lit. 'way, tract, quarter', in full *semt-er-ras*, lit. 'the way of the head'. The vertical point of the heavens at any place.

Zeph'yr, *n.* O.F. *zephyre*, L. *zephyrus*, G. *zephuros*, the west wind. The west wind; a gentle breeze.

Zep'pelin, *n.* After Count *Zeppelin*, the constructor. A German military air-ship.

Ze'ro, *n.* It. *zero*, abb. f. *zefiro*—L.L. *zephyrum*—Arab. *sifr*. CIPHER. A cipher; nothing.

Zest, *n.* O.F. *zest*, slice of lemon-peel (giving a flavour)—L. *schistos*, G. *schistos*, cleft, divided. SCHIST. Piquancy, relish.

Zig'zag, *n.* F. *zigzag*—Ger. *zickzack*, reduplicated f. *zacke*, tooth (with reference to notched work). Something in the form of straight lines placed at angles.—*a.* Having such a form.—*vi.* To move as on the lines of a zigzag.

Zinc, *n.* F. *zinc*—Ger. *zink*, of uncertain orig. A bluish-white metal.—*vt.* To coat with zinc.

Zo'diac, *n.* F. *zodiaque*—L. *zōdiacus*—G. *zōdiakos* (*kuklos*), 'animal (circle)', f. *zōidion*, dim. of *zōion*, animal. A belt in the heavens divided into twelve parts or 'signs' chiefly represented by animals.—**Zodi'ac**AL, *a.*

Zone, *n.* F. *zone*—L. *zōna*—G. *zōnē*, girdle. A girdle; one of the five divisions of the earth bounded by circles parallel to the equator; a continuous tract or belt.

Zool'ogy, *n.* G. *zōion* (ZODIAC) + -LOGY. The science of animals.—**Zoolog'**ICAL, *a.*

Zo'ophyte, *n.* F. *zoophyte*—G. *zōophuton*, an animal-plant, f. *zōos*, living + *phuton*, a plant, f. *phuein*, to produce. A plant-like animal such as a sponge.

Zymot'ic, *a.* G. *zumōtikos*, causing to ferment, f. *zumo-ein*, to leaven, f. *zumē*, leaven. Pertaining to fermentation; of a disease, due to the multiplication within the body of a germ introduced from without.

PREFIXES AND SUFFIXES

PREFIXES

A-[1]. A worn-down form of O.E. *an, on.* On, into, in, at.
A-[2]. A worn-down form of O.E. *of.* Of, off.
A-[3]. An O.E. pref. of somewhat indefinite meaning, sometimes intensive.
A-[4], **An-**. G. and L. Privative. Not, without.
Ab-, **Abs-**. L. prep. and pref. Also in form *a-*. From, off, away.
Ad-. L. prep. and pref. Also in forms *a-*, *ac-*, *af- ag-*, *-al-*, *an-*, *ap-*, *ar-*, *as-*, *at-*. To, towards, upon, at.
An-. See A-[4].
Ante-. L. prep. and pref. Before in position, order, or time.
Anti-. G. prep. and pref. Cogn. with UN-[1]. Also in forms *ant-*, *anth-*. Opposite, against; in exchange; representing; rivalling, simulating.
Apo-. G. prep. and pref. Also in form *aph-*. Away, apart, off.
Arch-, **Archi-**. G. pref., f. *archē*, rule. Chief, head, ruling.
Auto-. G. pref., f. *autos*, self. Self; one's own; by oneself.

Be-. O.E. Weak form of BY. Orig. meaning 'about'. (1) Adding notion of 'all over', 'all round'; (2) intensive; indicating thoroughness or excess; (3) forming transitive *vv.* from intransitive; (4) forming from *aa.* and *nn. vv.* expressing the imparting of a quality; (5) forming from *nn. vv.* expressing treatment or the producing of a state.
Bi-. L. pref., f. *bis*, twice. Twice; having two; two-.

Cata-, **Cat-**, **Cath-**. G. prep. and pref. *kata.* Down; down upon; away, entirely; implying disparagement or abuse; subsidiary, inferior; answering to, according to, each to each; intensive.
Circum-. L. prep. and pref. Round, around, all round.
Co-, **Col-**, **Com-**, **Con-**, **Cor-**. L. pref. repg. prep. *cum* (archaic form *com*). With, together; intensive, altogether, completely. Sometimes the pref. does not appreciably alter the sense.
Contra-. L. prep. and pref. *contrā.* Against.
Counter-. F. *contre*—L. *contrā* (see prec.). Against, in return. Gives notion of (1) reciprocation; opposition, rivalry; frustration; (2) opposite position or direction; (3) correspondence; a duplicate or substitute.

De-. L. prep. and pref. *dē* (in composition *dĕ* before a vowel), indicating departure, removal, separation. (1) Down, down from, down to; (2) off, away, aside; away from one self; (3) down to the bottom, completely, thoroughly, on and on; methodically, formally; to exhaustion, to the dregs; (4) so as to put down or subject to indignity; (5) the undoing or reversing of the action of a *v.*; the depriving of a thing or character; negation; (6) forms from *nn. vv.* of this type.
Dia-, **Di-**. G. prep. and pref. *dia.* Cogn. with DIS-. Through, across, apart, asunder; thorough, thoroughly.
Dis-. L. pref. Also in forms *di-*, *dif-*. Indicates (1) in twain, apart, asunder; hence, abroad, away, aside; (2) between; so as to separate or distinguish; (3) away, completely, thoroughly; (4) the undoing or reversing of the action of a *v.*; (5) forms *vv.* from *nn.* in senses 'to strip or deprive of, free of'; 'to deprive of the character or rank of'; 'to turn out, expel'; (6) forms *vv.* from *aa.* with sense of doing away with or reversing the quality expressed by the *a.*; (7) forms from *nn.* new *nn.* expressing the opposite or denoting the absence (of the thing in question); (8) prefixed to *aa.* with negative force.

E-, **Ex-**. L. prep. and pref. Also in form *ef-*. Out of, out, from, forth; bringing into a condition; removal, expulsion; relief, deprivation, lacking; intensive. Sometimes the pref. does not appreciably alter the sense.
En-[1], **Em-**[1]. F. *en-*, *em-*—L. *in.* IN-[1]. Forms *vv.* (1) from *nn.* with sense 'to put (something) into or upon what is denoted by the *n.*', or 'to put what is denoted by the *n.* into or upon (something)'; (2) from *nn.* or *aa.* with sense 'to bring or come into a certain condition, to give a certain quality to'; (3) from other *vv.* with added notion of 'within', 'into', 'upon', 'against', or with merely intensive force.
En-[2], **Em-**[2]. G. prep. and pref. *en*, in, cogn. with prec. Also in form *eg-*. In.
Epi-. G. prep. and pref. Also in form *eph-*. Upon, on, at, close upon, among; to; on, for, during; on the ground or occasion of; in addition, besides.
Equi-. L. *aequi-*, f. *aequus*, EQUAL.
Ex-. See E-.

For-. O.E. *for-*, *fær-*. (1) Away, off, apart; (2) prohibition; warding off; (3) abstention; neglect; (4) destruction, prejudicial effect; (5) intensive.
Fore-. FORE, *adv.* Prefixed to *vv.* gives sense of 'before' in time, position, order, or rank;

prefixed to *nn.* forms designations of objects or parts of objects occupying a front position, or expresses anteriority in time.

Geo-. G. *geō-*, combining form of *gē*, earth.

Hemi-. G. *hēmi-*. = SEMI-.
Hyper-. G. prep. and pref. *huper*. Over, above, beyond; exceeding, excessive.
Hypo-, **Hyp-**. G. prep. and pref. *hupo*. Under, below; slightly.

In-[1]. L. prep. and pref. *in*. IN. Also in forms *il-*, *im-*, *ir-*. In, into, within; on, upon; towards, to, against; continuance or onward motion; intensive; transitive; sometimes with little appreciable force.
In-[2]. L. *in-*, cogn. with A-[4] and UN-[2]. Also in forms *i-*, *il-*, *im-*, *ir-*. Expressing negation or privation.
Inter-. L. prep., adv. and pref. Also in form *intel-*. Between, among, within; at intervals; mutually, reciprocally.

Mal-. F. *mal*, L. *male*, badly, f. *malus*, bad. (1) Bad, badly; (2) = IN-[2], UN-[2].
Meta-. G. prep. and pref. Also in forms *met-*, *meth-*. With; after; change of position, place, &c.
Mis-[1]. O.E. *mis-* = O.N. *mis-*, Du. *mis-*, Ger. *miss-*. MISS, *v.* Amiss, badly, wrongly, unfavourably; expressing negation.
Mis-[2]. O.F. *mes-*—L. *minus*, less, not. = prec.
Mono-, **Mon-**. G. *mono-*, *mon-*, combining form of *monos*, single, alone. Single, alone, sole.

Non-. A.F. *noun-* = O.F. *non-*—L. *nōn*, not. Prefixed (1) to *nn.* giving notion (*a*) of failure to do, abstention from doing; as *non-payment*, *non-compliance*; (*b*) of a person or thing that is not something specified; as *non-member*, *non-metal*; (*c*) of 'not connected with', 'not involving'; as *non-party* (man), *non-jury* (trial); (*d*) of simple negation; as *non-combatant*, *non-existence*; (2) to *aa.* = not, not coming under the description of; as *non-commissioned*, *non-effective*; (3) to *advv.* = not; as *non-contentiously*, *non-officially*.

Ob-. L. prep. and pref. Also in forms *o-*, *oc-*, *of-*, *op-*. (1) In the direction of, towards; facing, in front of; (2) against, in opposition; indicating injuriousness or objectionable character; (3) upon or over; down upon, down; (4) completely; sometimes merely pleonastic; (5) on account of.
Omni-. Combining form of L. *omnis*, all. All-; of all things; in all ways or places.
Out-. OUT, *adv.* Out, out of, outwards, on the outside: going beyond, surpassing.
Over-. OVER. (1) Over, above, beyond, down, by way of cover: (2) excess beyond the desirable, proper, &c.; (3) more than: (4) effectually; into submission: (5) doing something to excess and so hurting oneself; (6) of higher kind; in higher position: (7) making transitive *vv.* from intransitive or from *nn.*, with sense of exceeding.

Para-, **Par-**. G. prep. and pref. *para*. Beside, besides, aside; extra; beyond, contrary to; wrong, irregular; alteration, perversion.
Per-. L. prep. and pref. Also in form *pel-*. Through: all over, thoroughly, completely, very; to destruction, to the bad.
Peri-. G. prep. and pref. Round, around, round about, about.

Poly-. G. *polu-*, combining form of *polus*, much, in *pl.*, many. Many, several, various.
Pre-. L. adv., prep., and pref. *prae*. Before in time, place, order, degree, importance.
Pro-. L. prep. and pref. *prō*. In front of; for, on behalf of, instead of, on account of; forth, forward.
Pseudo-. G. pref., f. *pseudein*, to beguile. False, spurious.

Quadri-. L. pref., conn. with *quattuor*, FOUR. Four-.
Quasi-. L. *quasi*, as if, as it were. (A) kind of; in appearance; almost.

Re-. L. pref. *re-*, *red-*. (1) In return, back, mutual, mutually; (2) against; (3) behind, after; (4) secrecy, retirement; (5) off, away, down; (6) freq. or intensive; (7) the undoing of an action; negation; (8) again, once more, repeated; (9) back, back to the previous state.
Retro-. L. adv. and pref. *retrō*. Backwards.

Se-. Old L. prep. and adv. *sē* (also *sēd*). Without, aside, apart.
Semi-. L. *sēmi-* = G. *hēmi-*, O.E. *sam-*, Skr. *sámi-*. Half; partly, partially, to some extent, imperfectly, incompletely.
Sub-. L. prep. and pref. Also in forms *suc-*, *suf-*, *sug-*, *sum-*, *sup-*, *sur-*, *sus-*. Under. Denoting (1) lower position; change of position to or from a lower; (2) covertness, secrecy; (3) nearness, closeness; (4) inferiority, subordination; further; (5) aid, support; (6) addition; substitution; (7) rather, not quite.
Super-. L. adv., prep., and pref. Above, over. Denoting (1) above; on the top; (2) observation from above; being in charge; (3) besides, in addition; (4) to a degree beyond the normal or right; exceeding, transcending.
Syn-. G. prep. and pref. *sun*. Also in forms *sy-*, *syl-*, *sym-*, *sys-*. With, together, alike.

Trans-. L. prep. and pref. Also in forms *tra-*, *tran-*. Across, beyond, on or to the other side, through, into a different state or place.
Tri-. G. *tri-* (*treis*, *tria*), L. *tri-* (*trēs*, *tria*), THREE. Having or composed of three; three-.

Un-[1]. O.E. Cogn. with ANTI-. Pref. of *vv.* denoting the undoing or reversing of action, deprivation, release, degradation, &c. (1) Prefixed to a *v.* to denote the undoing or reversing of the action of the *v.* (occasionally (as in *unloose*) with merely intensive force): as *uncover*, *undeceive*; (2) prefixed to a *n.* with sense 'to deprive of', 'to separate from'; as *unsex*, *uncloak*; (3) prefixed similarly with sense 'to release from', 'to remove or displace from'; as *uncage*, *unhorse*; (4) prefixed to a *n.* with sense 'to cause to be no longer', 'to degrade from the rank of'; as *unman*, *unking*.
Un-[2]. O.E. Cogn. with A-[4] and IN-[2]. Giving negative sense. (1) Prefixed to *aa.* (including participles) and to *advv.*; as *uncivil*, *unmerited*; *unequally*, *unexpectedly*, *unwillingly*; (2) prefixed to *nn.*; as *unbelief*, *unceremoniousness*, *unrest*, *untruth*.
Under-. UNDER, prep., adv., and a. Below, beneath, lower than; insufficiently, incompletely, too low; low; subordinate.
Up-. UP.

Vice-. L. *vice*, in the place (of). Denoting a substitute or deputy.

SUFFIXES

-able. F.—L. *-ā-* of the 1st conjugation + *-bilis*. -BLE. Forms *aa.* with notion 'able to', 'inclined to', 'able to be', 'fit for'.

-acious. L. *-ax*, *-āci-s* + -OUS. Forms *aa.* with notion 'characterized by', 'inclined to', 'abounding in'.

-acity. L. *-ācitas*. Forms *nn.* of quality.

-acy. L. *-ācia*. Forms *nn.* of state or quality.

-age. O.F. — L.L. *-āticum*. Forms *nn.* with notion of an aggregate or collective assemblage, a total; as *assemblage, cellarage, tonnage*; a concrete result of action; as *package*; function, condition; as *tutelage, bondage*; action; as *breakage, passage, storage*; place of abode; as *parsonage, vicarage*; an institution for; as *orphanage*; fees for, cost of using; as *postage, wharfage*.

-al. L. *-ālis*. Forms (1) *aa.* with notion 'pertaining or belonging to'; (2) *nn.* of action.

-ality. -AL + -ITY. Forms *nn.* with notion of quality or of an instance of this.

-an. L. *-ānus*. Forms (1) *aa.* with notion 'of, belonging to', 'like', 'engaged in'; (2) *nn.* with similar sense.

ance. F. *-ance*—L. *-antia*. Forms *nn.* of quality or state, also of action or process.

ancy. -ANC(E)+-Y.[1] Forms *nn.*, us. denoting only quality or state.

-ant. F. *-ant*—L. *-ans*, *-antis*, the termination of pres.pples. of *vv.* of the 1st conjugation. Cf. -ENT. Forms (1) *aa.* indicating the action of a *v.*; (2) agent-*nn.* and *nn.* denoting a thing producing an effect.

-ar.[1] L. *-āris*. Forms *aa.* with notion 'of, pertaining to', 'of the kind of', 'characterized by'.

-ar.[2] Var. of -ER, -OR.

-ard. M.E. and O.F.—Ger. *-hart*, *-hard*, hardy (in proper names). Forms *nn.*, denoting a person who does something discreditable or to excess, or a person or thing characterized by something.

-arian. L. *-āri-us* + -AN. Forms *aa.* and *nn.* denoting a member of a body, sect, &c., or a person of a specified age.

-ary. L. *-ārius* and *-āris*. Forms (1) *aa.* with notion 'pertaining to', 'of the kind of', 'characterized by'; (2) *nn.* with notion 'one belonging to or engaged in', 'something connected with or employed in', 'a place for'.

-ate.[1] L. *-ātus* (genit. *-ūs*). Forms *nn.* of office, state, &c.

-ate.[2] L. *-ātus*, termination of pa.pples. of the 1st conjugation. Forms *aa.* (sometimes used as *nn.*) corresponding to pa.pples.

-ate.[3] L. *-āt-*. (See next.) Forms *vv.* to represent L. *vv.* in *-āre* or *-āri*, or F. *vv.* in *-er*.

-ation. *-āt-* of ppl. stems of L. 1st conjugation + -ION. = -ION.

-ative. L. *-āt-* (see prec.) + -IVE. Forms *aa.* like those in *-ive*.

-bility. L. *-bilitas*. Forms abstract *nn.* from *aa.* in *-ble*, *-able*, *-ible*.

-ble. L. *-bilis*. -ABLE. -IBLE. Forms *aa.* with notion 'able to', 'inclined to', 'able to be', 'fit for'.

-cide L. *caedĕre*, to kill. Forms *nn.* with sense (1) slayer of (L. *-cida*); (2) slaughter of (L. *-cidium*).

-cy. L. *-cia*. Forms abstract *nn.*

-dom. O.E. *-dom*. Forms *nn.* expressing state, condition, rank, domain, from *nn.* and *aa.*

-ean. = -AN.

-ee. A.F. *-é*—L. *-ātus*. -ATE.[2] Forms *nn.* denoting the person affected by the action of a verb.

-eer. L. *-ārius*. Denotes a person concerned.

-en.[1] L. *-inus*. Forms *aa.*, usually denoting material, from *nn.*

-en.[2] O.E. Forms from *aa.* and *nn.* *vv.* generally denoting the imparting of a quality or the bringing or coming into a condition.

-ence. F. *-ence*—L. *-entia*. Forms *nn.* of quality or state, also of action or process.

-ency. -ENC(E) + -Y.[1] Forms *nn.*, us. denoting only quality or state.

-ent. F. *-ent*—L. *-ens*, *-entis*, the termination of pres. pples. of *vv.* of the 2nd, 3rd, and 4th conjugations. Cf. -ANT. Forms (1) *aa.* indicating the action of a *v.*; (2) agent-*nn.* and *nn.* denoting a thing producing an effect.

-eous. L. *-e-us* + -OUS. Forms *aa.* with notion 'of the nature of'.

-er. Teut. Forms from *nn.* and *vv.* *nn.* denoting an agent, an instrument, a person concerned.

-ern. Teut. suff. of *aa.*, as in *northern*, &c.

-ery, -ry. Reps. F. *-ier*, *-er* (f. L. *-ārius*) + *-ie* = -Y[1]; and O.F. *-ere*, *-eor*, F. *-eur* (f. L *-ātor*) + *-ie*. Forms *nn.* denoting a class of goods, &c., wares; as *drapery, mercery*; condition; as *outlawry*; that with which one has to do, employment; as *archery, gunnery*; a place of work, for keeping something, &c.; as *brewery, piggery*; conduct, repeated action; as *foolery, trickery*; the result of repeated action; as *tracery*; that which has to do with, things like; as *popery, witchery*.

-ess. F. *-esse*—L.L. *-issa*, G. *-issa*. Forms fem. *nn.*

-eth. = -TH.[2] [*nn.* and *aa.*

-etic. G. agent-suff. *-et-* or *-ēt-* + -IC. Forms

-faction. L. *-factio*, *-factiōnis*, f. *facĕre*, to make. Forms *nn.* of action or condition from *vv.* in -FY.

-fic. L. *-ficus*, f. *facĕre*, to make. Forms *aa.* with notion 'making, causing, producing', 'performing', 'bringing into a state'.

-fication. L. *-ficātio*, *-ficātiōnis*. = -FACTION.

-fold. O.E. *-feald*, conn. with *fealdan*. FOLD.[2] Added to cardinal numbers to form *aa.* denoting 'multiplied by'.

-ful. Orig. = FULL, *a.* Forms *aa.* with sense 'full of' or 'having the qualities of'.

-fy. L. *-facĕre*, *-ficāre*, *-ficāri*, f. *facĕre*, to make. Forms *vv.* with sense 'to make so and so'; also 'to become so and so'.

-head. M.E. *-hēde*, *-hēd*. Not in O.E. **-hood**. M.E. *-hod* — O.E. *-hād*. Both corresp. to O.H.G., Ger. *-heit*. Forms *nn.* of condition or quality from *nn.* and *aa.*

-ial. L. *-i-ālis*. = -AL.
-ian. L. *-i-ānus*. = -AN.
-ible. L. *-i-bilis*. -BLE. Forms *aa*. with notion 'able to', 'inclined to', 'able to be', 'fit for'.
-ic. F. *-ique*—L. *-icus*, G. *-ikos*. Forms *aa*. with notion 'after the manner of', 'of, pertaining to', 'of the nature of'.
-ical. -IC + -AL. Forms *aa*. similar to those in -IC. Many *aa*. have a form both in *-ic* and *-ical*. In such cases the form in *-ic* often denotes only 'of, pertaining to', 'of the nature of', while the form in *-ical* denotes 'connected or dealing with', 'practising'.
-ician. F. *-icien*. Forms *nn*. denoting one skilled in or concerned with.
-ier. In earlier examples, as *collier*, *grazier*, of doubtful orig. In later, as *financier*, *gondolier*, f. F. *-ier*—L. *-ārius*. -EER. Forms personal *nn*. denoting occupation, &c.
-ine. L. *-inus*. Forms *aa*. with notion 'pertaining to', 'of the nature of'.
-ion. L. *-io*, *-iōnis*. Forms abstract *nn*. with notion of verbal action; an instance of this; a resulting state; a concrete result.
-ious. L. *-i-ōsus*. = -OUS.
-ise. = -IZE.
-ish. O.E. *-isc*. Common Teut. Forms *aa*. with notion 'pertaining to', 'of the nature of'; 'to some degree', 'somewhat'.
-ism. F. *-isme*—L. *-ismus*, G. *-ismos*, *-isma*. Forms abstract *nn*. with notion of action; as *criticism*, *exorcism*; typical conduct or condition; as *heroism*, *barbarism*; a system or principle; as *agnosticism*, *stoicism*; a peculiarity or characteristic; as *archaism*, *Hellenism*; a morbid condition induced by the abuse of something; as *alcoholism*.
-ist. F. *-iste*—L. *-ista*, G. *-istēs*. Forms personal *nn*. denoting an agent; as *bigamist*, *plagiarist*; a person practising or studying an art, science, &c.; as *economist*, *etymologist*; an adherent, a person holding certain views; as *atheist*, *hedonist*; one concerned; as *cyclist*, *tobacconist*.
-ition. *-it-* of L. ppl. stems + -ION. = -ION.
-itis. G. *-itis*, fem. of adjectival ending *-itēs* (with *nosos*, disease, understood). Denotes inflammation.
-ity. = -TY.
-ive. F. *-if*—L. *-īvus*. Forms *aa*. with notion 'tending to', 'given to', 'having the nature of'.
-ize, -ise. F. *-iser*—L.L. *-izāre*, G. *-izein*. Forms *vv*. with notion to treat in such a way; as *canonize*, *idolize*; to follow such a system or principle, to have such a feeling; as *philosophize*, *theorize*, *sympathize*; to bring or come into such a state; as *civilize*, *cicatrize*; to treat on the system of; as *macadamize*; to treat or affect with; as *oxidize*.

-less. O.E. *-léas*. LOOSE, *a*. Forms *aa*. with sense 'free from', 'devoid of'.
-like. LIKE in composition. Gives notion of likeness or resemblance.
-ling. Common Teut. (1) Added to *nn*. denotes a person or thing belonging to or concerned with (what is denoted by the *n*.); sometimes by analogy added to *v*. stems (taken in passive sense); (2) added to *aa*. denotes a person or thing having the quality denoted by the *a*.; (3) diminutive.
-logy. G. *-logia*, f. *logos*, discourse. Forms *nn*. denoting the action, character or speciality of one who writes or speaks in a certain way or deals with a certain subject.
-long. LONG, *a*. Expresses direction.
-ly.[1] O.E. *-līc* = *gelic*, LIKE. Forms *aa*. with notion 'having the qualities of', or denoting recurrence.
-ly.[2] O.E. *-lice*, f. *-līc*. (See prec.) Forms adverbs.

-ment. L. *-mentum*. Forms *nn*. denoting result or means of verbal action.

-ness. O.E. *-nes*. Forms *nn*. denoting state or condition.

-oid. G. *-oeidēs*, f. *eidos*, form. Forms *aa*. and *nn*. with notion 'resembling', 'something resembling'.—**-oidal**. -AL. Similarly forming *aa*.
-or. L. *-or*. Forms *nn*. denoting an agent or an instrument.
-ory. L. *-ōrius*. Forms (1) *aa*. with notion 'of the nature of', 'characterized by', 'tending to'; (2) *nn*. with similar sense.
-ose, -ous. L. *-ōsus*. Forms *aa*. with notion 'abounding in', 'characterized by'.
-ous. See prec.

-ry. Shortened f. -ERY.

-ship. O.E. *-scipe*. Forms from *nn*. and *aa*. *nn*. denoting the being so-and-so, status, office; tenure of office; skill in a certain capacity.
-some. O.E. *-sum*. Adjectival suff. added to *nn*. to give sense of 'adapted to', 'productive of'; to *vv*. to give sense of 'apt to'; to *aa*.
-ster. O.E. *-estre*. Forms agent-*nn*. and *nn*. denoting occupation.

-th.[1] O.E. Forms abstract *nn*. from *aa*. and *vv*.
-th.[2], **-eth**. O.E. *-thon*. Forms ordinal numbers and *nn*. denoting fractions.
-tion. *-t-* of L. ppl. stems + -ION. = -ION.
-tory. *-t-* of L. ppl. stems + -ORY. = -ORY.
-trix. L. Forms feminine *nn*.
-tude. L. *-tūdo*. Forms abstract *nn*.
-ty, -ity. L. *-tas*, *-itas*. Forms abstract *nn*.

-ulent. L. *-ulentus*. Forms *aa*. with notion 'of the nature of', 'characterized by'.—**-ulence**. -ENCE. Forms abstract *nn*.
-ure. L. *-ūra*. Forms *nn*. denoting verbal action; the result; a collective body.

-ward; also, with advbl. genit. *-s*, **-wards**. O.E. *-weard*, repg. *weard*, towards, f. *weorthan*, to become, turn to. Gives sense of direction.
-ways. WAY + advbl. genit. *-s*. Gives notion of position, way or manner.
-wise. O.E., f. *wisian*, to show the way. Gives notion of position, way or manner.

-y.[1] Reps. F. *-ie*—L. *-ia*, G. *-ia*; and F. pa. pple. termination *-é*, *-ée*—L. *-ātus*, *-āta*, *-ātum*. Forms *nn*., generally abstract *nn*.
-y.[2] O.E. *-ig*. Forms *aa*. with notion 'full of', 'made of', 'characterized by'.
-y.[3] Orig. dim. Forms *nn*. f. monosyllabic *aa*.

APPENDIX

TERMS OF SPECIAL NOTE IN MODERN WARFARE

Ac-emma. A.M. (of time). So called by signallers to prevent mistakes.
Aerial Torpedo. A torpedo-shaped missile designed to be discharged from an air-ship or a gun, and constructed with a view to its taking a course through the air which can be determined with more or less accuracy.
Aeroplane. Any flying-machine in which the carrying or supporting surfaces are roughly of the nature of planes (though with a 'camber' or under curvature) and that depend on the principle of the kite and are driven through the air by one or more screw propellers worked by a petrol engine. A *monoplane* has one main carrying surface, a *biplane* two—one over the other. There is a *chassis* or under-carriage with wheels, skids, or runners, &c., to aid in making a start from the ground and in coming to rest.
A. frame. A large wooden frame, shaped like an inverted A, used for revetting, and supporting duck-boards.
Aileron. (F., f. *aile*, wing.) Any one of certain small movable planes fixed to the main planes of an aeroplane and used as 'balancing flaps', or to give stability, being actuated by suitable leverage.
Air-boat. See *Hydroplane* below.
Air-craft. A general name for any of those structures by means of which the air is navigated or traversed, as an aeroplane, a dirigible balloon (air-ship), &c. These may be armed and armoured in a special way. Air-craft are indispensable for gaining knowledge of an enemy's doings, and may do great damage by dropping bombs. Guns firing at very high angles are specially mounted as *anti-air-craft* guns for protection against attack by hostile air-craft.
Air-pocket. Part of the atmosphere where an aeroplane drops suddenly. It is believed that this sudden drop is caused by the air being more rarefied than in the surrounding parts.
Air-ship. An apparatus for navigating the air, but more especially one on the principle of the balloon, being buoyed up by a gas (hydrogen) that is lighter than air, and driven through the air by one or more special motors and propellers, steering-gear being also provided; otherwise called 'dirigible balloon' or 'dirigible'. Such air-ships may be rigid, non-rigid, or semi-rigid, according to the nature of the gas envelope. The air-ship of Count Zeppelin is rigid, its shape being maintained by an aluminium framework. The gas is contained in a set of separate bags or *ballonets*.
Anti-air-craft gun. See *Air-craft* above.
Anzac. (Formed from the initials of the words *Australian* (and) *New Zealand Army Corps.*) A name given to a portion of the Gallipoli Peninsula which was occupied by Australian and New Zealand troops; hence applied to these troops.
Archie. An anti-air-craft gun, or its shell.
Armageddon. The last great battle-field of the nations (Revelation, xvi, 16).
Army Corps. A large section or division of an army, complete in itself, embracing all arms, such as infantry, cavalry, and artillery, and having a permanent position in several of the European armies. An army corps may number from 30,000 to 45,000 or more.
Army Council. A body consisting of five military members, with a 'Civil Member' and a 'Finance Member'. It is charged with a general superintendence of British military affairs. The Secretary of State for War is president. Established in 1904.
Army List. A British official publication containing the names of all the officers in the army, the stations of regiments, &c.
Army Medical Corps, Royal. The main body of the medical service of the army, in time of peace employed at home, in India, and in the colonies, in time of war divided among the different bodies of troops employed. The officers hold ranks corresponding with those of the combatant forces.
Army Service Corps, Royal. A corps or branch of the army employed in connection with providing food, transport, &c., for the troops.
Artillery. The artillery of the British army forms one great body, the Royal Regiment of Artillery. Special divisions of it are the Royal Horse Artillery, in which the men are all mounted so that it may act with cavalry, and the Royal Field Artillery. Two batteries of horse artillery or three of field artillery form a brigade.
Aussies. Australian soldiers.
Automatic gun. A gun that after the first shot continues firing automatically a number of other shots in rapid succession. Specially mounted guns of this kind may be used against air-craft, torpedo-boats, &c., or may be carried by dirigibles, sea-planes, &c.; calibre from that

of the rifle to that for a 2-lb. shell. See *Machine-gun* below.

Aviation. The navigation of the air by machines that are heavier than air, their buoyancy in air being thus far analogous to that of birds (hence the name—L. *avis*, a bird), though it is on the principle of the kite that they depend. Such machines or apparatus comprise monoplanes, biplanes, &c. See *Aeroplane.*

B.A.B. code. The cipher most commonly in use in the trenches.

Back-flash. The burning gas remaining in a gun after firing.

Ballonet. (Dim. of *balloon.*) See *Air-ship* and *Compensator.*

Bangalore Torpedo. A long pipe-like torpedo ignited by a fuse, used for destroying enemy wire.

Banking. The tilting up of an aeroplane at a sharp angle sideways when flying swiftly round a curve, on the same principle as that on which a cycle track is 'banked' steeply at corners which are often rounded at high speed.

Bantam. A soldier below 5 feet 3 inches in height.

Barbette. (F., dim. of *barbe,* beard.) A fixed armoured shelter on a war-ship inside which a gun revolves on a turn-table. Distinguished from TURRET.

Barrage fire, Barrier fire, Barrage. See *Curtain fire.*

Batman. An officer's servant. (Properly, a man in charge of a pack-horse.)

Battalion. A body of infantry or engineers comprising several companies and forming part of a regiment. The number of battalions in a regiment varies.

Battery. As applied to horse, field, or mountain artillery, consists of two or three 'sections', each of two guns, with the complement of men, horses, ammunition-wagons, &c. Also, a group of guns as mounted on a war-ship.

Battleship. A war-vessel of the highest grade or rank, very powerful for offence and defence alike. Guns in British battleships can send with high effect a projectile weighing nearly a ton the distance of 10 or 12 miles, the calibre being 17 inches. The next size is 15 inches.

Bertha, Big. A German long-range gun, called after Frau Krupp, especially used of the heavy guns that bombarded Paris in 1918.

Biplane. An aeroplane with two carrying surfaces or planes one over the other. See *Aeroplane.*

Black Maria. A large German shell.

Blighty. The British Isles. *Blighty one.* A wound severe enough to ensure being sent home.

Blimp. A small air-ship, often used for scouting.

Blob Formation. Artillery formation, usually into sections.

Boche. (F. Of disputed orig. By some considered as contracted from *Alboche,* slang for *Allemand,* German.) A term of opprobrium for a German.

Boloism. (From *Bolo Pasha,* a Frenchman executed in 1918.) Treason in high places.

Bolshevik. A member of the extremist revolutionary party in Russia. This party, led by Lenin, seized power in 1917.

Bond Street ribbon. A medal or decoration given for Home Service.

Box-respirator. The most effective kind of gas-helmet, issued in 1916, and several times re-issued with improvements.

Brassard. (F., f. *bras,* arm.) A badge worn round the arm to give various indications, often to denote that the person wearing it belongs to some force not forming part of the regular forces of the Crown.

Brass Hat. A staff-officer.

Bridge-head. A fortified work protecting the end of a bridge nearest to the enemy.

Bridging-train. A body of engineer troops specially instructed in the making of temporary bridges.

Brigade. A subdivision of an army varying in different countries.

Brigade-major. The principal staff-officer of a brigadier-general, usually a captain in rank.

British warm. A short warm coat worn by British officers.

Buckshee. A windfall; something obtained for nothing.

Bully beef. Corned beef in a tin.

Bus. An aeroplane, especially a large heavy machine.

Buzz. To telephone in Morse code on an instrument equipped with a special key for the purpose.

Cadre. (F.) The permanent establishment of a regiment, forming a framework or nucleus for expansion.

Camouflage. Deception of the enemy, as by artificial scenery, dummy cannon, &c.

Cashier. To discard from the army with dishonour. An officer may only be cashiered for some very grave fault, and the result is that he is thenceforth incapable of serving His Majesty in any capacity, his social position being seriously affected also. A person simply dismissed from the army may be again employed in a military capacity.

Censor. An officer appointed to see that no communication is transmitted which is likely to be of service to the enemy or prejudicial to the welfare of the country, all private communications as well as those to newspapers and journals being in time of war or under martial law subject to censorship. As *v.*, to subject to the attentions of the censor.

Chevron. A V-shaped stripe; used especially for the stripes of an N.C.O.; also for the overseas service stripes first issued in 1918.

Civies. Plain clothes, as opposed to uniform.

Click. To get what you want; especially to get home.

Coal-box. A heavy German shell.

Cold feet. An attack of cowardice.

Column. A formation consisting of bodies of troops on parallel and successive lines of frontage, with distances between varying according to circumstances. *Column of route,* a column with not more than four men abreast, the normal formation for troops on the march. *Double column,* two parallel columns.

Comb-out. To clear out men of military age from an office or other civilian work.

Company. A division of a battalion, consisting of four platoons (each of four sections), and commanded by a major or mounted captain, with a captain as second in command.

Company officers. Captains, lieutenants, and second-lieutenants.

Compensator. A small interior balloon or ballonet forming part of an air-ship, used in pairs, and inflated and deflated as desired, to give the balloon the necessary inclination or position in its flight.

Concertina. A peculiar formation of barbed wire.

Conchy. A conscientious objector; one who attributed his unwillingness to fight to his conscience.

Conning-tower. An armoured structure on a war-ship from which the officer in charge issues his orders during the time the ship is in action.

Conspicuous Gallantry Medal. A medal bestowed on warrant officers and men of the navy.

Contain. To keep in check or hold back (an enemy's troops); to keep occupied or unable to make progress.

Cordite. (So called from its cord-like appearance.) A smokeless explosive introduced in 1889.

Counter-attack. An attack made by a force with a view to recapturing a position from which it has been ousted. Such an attack is generally delivered with as little delay as possible, in order that the new occupants of the position may not have time to 'consolidate' their gain by adapting the position to defence against attack from what is now its front and was, of course, formerly its rear.

Crater. The hole made by a mine or a large shell.

Crimed. Entered on the sergeant-major's 'crime sheet' as an offender (e.g. for being dirty on parade).

Cruiser. One of a class of war-ships of high speed designed for the protection of friendly, and the destruction of enemy, commerce, for scouting, &c. *Light cruiser*, a cruiser of this class lightly armoured. *Battle-cruiser*, a powerful vessel of this class and of very high speed. The more powerful approach the battleship type in armament, and are of higher speed than vessels of that type.

Crump. The sound of the explosion of a large shell; also any shell from a 5·9 upwards.

Curtain fire. The discharge of artillery in such a manner as to keep a selected zone under continuous fire, with a view to preventing the passage of enemy troops through the zone. Also called *barrage* or *barrier fire*. The zone is called the *barrage*. See *Tir de barrage*.

Cushy. Safe and comfortable; usually applied to someone else's job.

Cuthbert. One who avoided military service on the grounds of being indispensable elsewhere.

Depot-ship. A ship forming a floating base for a number of other vessels, especially for a patrol flotilla of destroyers, and serving as a store-house and a repairing-shop, being fitted with appliances of all kinds necessary for this purpose.

Destroyer (in full, **Torpedo-boat destroyer**). A swift class of vessel of no great size, intended for the destruction of torpedo-craft — submarines or other—and itself armed with guns and torpedoes. Such boats defend battleships against submarines and torpedo-boats, and are extensively employed in patrol-work. Many destroyers are specially classed as 'ocean-going'.

Detail. An individual or a small body; a small detachment on special service.

Detonator. The device by which fulminate of mercury is made to explode the charge in a torpedo or submarine mine.

Dirigible balloon (also called simply **Dirigible**). A balloon or air-ship whose course can be directed by means of steering or guiding appliances. See *Air-ship* above.

Distance. The space between bodies of troops from front to rear; the space between units in column measured from the heels of the front rank of one unit to those of the next front rank following.

Distinguished Conduct Medal (D.C.M.). A medal that may be granted to warrant officers, non-commissioned officers and men of the army for individual acts of gallantry in the field.

Distinguished Service Cross (D.S.C.). Instituted 1914 for bestowal on account of distinguished services in war on officers of the navy below the rank of lieutenant-commander.

Distinguished Service Medal. Instituted 1914 for bestowal on account of distinguished services in war on chief petty officers, petty officers, men and boys of all branches of the navy and on other persons holding corresponding positions in His Majesty's service afloat.

Distinguished Service Order (D.S.O.). Instituted 1886. An honour bestowed upon commissioned officers in the navy and army for meritorious or distinguished services in war, and often for conspicuous gallantry under fire.

Division. A self-contained formation or body forming the basis of an army in the field, comprising all arms and services in due proportion, complete in itself, and equipped for independent action. A division comprises three infantry brigades, three field-artillery brigades, &c., the total personnel being fully 18,000. A cavalry division comprises four cavalry brigades, two horse-artillery brigades, &c.; total personnel, 9815.

Divisional Cavalry. The squadrons that form an integral portion of a division of all arms.

Dixie. A camp caldron.

Dock. A military hospital.

Dreadnought. The general term for a class of very large and powerful battleships, adopted from this having been the name of the first vessel of the type. *Superdreadnought* is one of still greater power. See *Battleship*.

Dressing-station. A place where wounded are collected and attended to by the personnel of a field-ambulance.

Drift. The deflection of a shell to the right of its proper course, due to the resistance of the air and the right-hand spin or rotation imparted by the rifling. Also, the deviation of an air-craft due to the wind.

Driving-band. The copper band round a shell near its base, which takes the grooves of the rifling when fired, rotation being thus imparted.

Duck-boards. Boards laid in the bottom of a trench, or over a muddy piece of open ground, to keep the feet from getting wet.

Dud. A shell that fails to explode; hence any inefficient person or defective thing.

Dug-out. An underground shelter in the trenches; an officer on the retired list recalled to active service.

Dumdum bullet. (From *Dumdum*, in India, with an arsenal.) A soft-nosed bullet which expands and lacerates on striking.

Elephant-gun. A large pistol for firing 1½ inch Véry lights.

Elevator. One of the small planes, attached to the main planes of an aeroplane, that can be moved or tilted up or down so as to cause the machine to rise or sink.

Emplacement. A position specially assigned to a gun or group of guns; a solid platform with accessories prepared for the support of a gun or guns.

Enfilade. (F., f. *enfiler*, to thread on a string.) Fire from artillery, &c., so directed as to sweep along and through a line of works or men. As *v.*, to subject to enfilade fire.

Engineers, Royal. A division of the army composed of men trained to engineering work, charged with the duty of designing and seeing to the construction of mines, trenches, &c., and of bridges, roads, &c., for the passage of the army.

Envelop. To outflank or turn both ends of an enemy's line so that it is partially surrounded and placed in great danger.

Envelope. The outer covering of a balloon or air-ship distended by means of the enclosed gas, usually a fabric into the construction of which rubber enters.

Eye-wash. Something done for show; humbug.

Field-gun. A cannon for use in the field, acting with infantry or cavalry. The chief gun of the British army in the field is the 18-pounder quick-firing gun, which can be fired about twenty-five times in a minute. For the leading French field-gun see *Soixante-quinze*.

Field officers. Colonels, lieutenant-colonels, and majors.

File. A front-rank man and his rear-rank man or 'coverer'.

Fire. The general direction in which ordnance makes its attack; as *frontal fire*, when it is directed perpendicularly on the front of the object; *reverse fire*, when the rear is assailed; *high-angle fire*, when the angle of elevation of the gun exceeds 25 degrees. See also *Enfilade*.

Fire-control. The system of controlling and directing the fire from the guns of a war-vessel, a highly scientific operation.

Fire-unit. Any number of men firing at the command of one, the normal fire-unit being the section. See *Battery*.

Firing-tube. A tube containing an explosive which when fired ignites the cordite with which a gun is loaded.

Flag-wagger. A signaller.

Fokker. A German fighting aeroplane, used for short flights.

Foot-slogger. An infantryman.

Franc-tireur. (F., f. *franc*, free+*tireur*, shooter, f. *tirer*, to shoot.) One of a corps of light infantry enrolled for the duration of a war, and not forming part of the regular army; sometimes applied to an irregular combatant in general.

Frog. The loop which holds a sword or bayonet.

Fuselage. (L. *fusus*, a spindle.) The long, narrow, somewhat spindle-shaped body of an aeroplane, having a midway position in the structure, and having at one end a 'rudder' for steering and a 'tail'.

Gliding angle. The angle, slope, or natural gradient which an aeroplane assumes of its own accord in the air when the engine-power is cut off, so that it will glide gradually to the earth, the angle varying for each machine.

Good Conduct Medal. A medal given to a soldier as a reward for 'long service with irreproachable character and conduct'.

Gooseberry. A small ball of barbed wire.

Greenjacket. A member of a rifle regiment; applied to all ranks.

Grenade. A small shell filled with some high explosive, usually intended to be thrown by hand and used at close quarters. The principal British hand-grenade is the 'Mills'. Rifle-grenades are also used at distances of 200 or 300 yards.

Gum-boots. Long waterproof boots made of india-rubber.

Gun-boat. A small vessel of light draught fitted for carrying one or more guns.

Gun-layer. One who 'lays' or gives the proper position to a gun before firing; an artilleryman who aims or lays a gun, particularly one with special qualifications or training.—**Gun-laying.** See *Laying*.

Gunner. A member of the Royal Regiment of Artillery; applied to all ranks.

Hangar. (F.) A shed constructed for the housing of aeroplanes.

High-angle fire. See *Fire*. *High-angle gun*, one so mounted that a very large angle of elevation may be given to it, as high as 80 degrees.

High explosives. Explosives of the extremely powerful modern class, especially such as are based on nitro-glycerine.

Howitzer. A short gun that fires a heavy shell with a low velocity, being always fired at a high angle, and so that it may reach objects that could not be reached by direct fire; it represents the old *mortar*. There are field-howitzers as well as siege-howitzers. The largest siege-howitzers are of 16-inch calibre at least.

Hun. A German. (Derived from the ex-Kaiser's advising the German troops sent to China in 1900 to act like the Huns under Attila.)

Hydroplane. An aeroplane fitted with floats (or a float) instead of wheels to enable it to rise from or alight on the surface of the water, in the former case having to 'taxi' or glide for some distance so as to gain the necessary flying speed. Called also *Water-plane*, *Sea-plane*, *Air-boat*. These craft are both armed and armoured, and of high importance in naval warfare.

Identity disc. A disc carried on a string round the neck by every officer and man, showing name, number, unit, and religion.

Indian Order of Merit. Instituted 1837, as a reward for personal bravery, to native Indian officers and men.

Internal combustion. The principle employed in the engines or motors of air-craft, motor-cars, &c., by which a mixture of petrol gas and air is exploded in the cylinder, so that the explosive force acts directly on the piston.

Interval. The lateral space between units having the same alignment or frontage.

Iron-ration. A soldier's emergency ration, not supposed to be eaten except by permission of an officer, but not uncommonly 'destroyed by shell-fire'. **Jerry's iron-ration.** A humorous expression for the shells fired at the Germans by our artillery.

Jack Johnson. A large low-velocity German shell.

Jerry. A German soldier.

Jolly. A Royal Marine.

Joy-stick. The starting-lever of an aeroplane.

Knife-rest. An iron bar equipped with several spikes and laid amongst the barbed wire. Also, a wooden framework shaped like a domestic knife-rest and surrounded by barbed wire; used for the purpose of a quickly-made obstruction.

Kultur. German education; of which the chief doctrines were that the State should be supreme in Germany and Germany supreme in the world.

Lance-jack. A lance-corporal.

Laying. The placing or aiming of a gun so that it points in the proper direction, by moving it vertically so that it has the proper 'elevation', and by 'traversing' it or moving it in the horizontal direction, special mechanical devices being provided. The large guns on board ship are worked by hydraulic power.

Lewis gun. An automatic rifle, gas-operated and air-cooled, capable of firing forty-seven rounds without reloading. During most of the war there were eighteen of these guns per battalion; during 1918, however, this establishment was doubled.

Liaison officer. An officer employed in linking up troops under different commands.

Listening post. A position in front of the lines occupied by a sentry or sentries charged with the duty of detecting enemy movements by hearing.

Looping the loop. Making a complete circle vertically in the air, the aeronaut and his machine being momentarily upside down.

Lyddite. (From *Lydd*, in Kent, as first used there.) A high explosive used in the manufacture of shells.

Machine-gun. A machine-gun in action may be said to represent the fire of a body of riflemen. It has generally a support of tripod form and is very portable. The most famous British machine-gun is the Maxim (invented by Sir H. *Maxim*), which is single-barrelled and entirely automatic. After the first cartridge is inserted by hand and fired the gun goes on firing of its own accord, the motive-power being the recoil aided by a strong spring, while the rate of fire is over 500 rounds a minute.

Maconochie. A tinned meat and vegetable ration.

Marines, Royal. Soldiers who serve in British war-ships, and also at dockyards and elsewhere on shore in certain circumstances.

Mask. To render (a fortress or other strong position) inactive or powerless by leaving sufficient troops to command it while the main body proceeds to other operations.

Maxim. See *Machine-gun* above.

Mekometer. (Gk. *mēkos*, length + *metron*, measure.) A sort of range-finder or device employed for similar purposes, consisting of a pair of sextants used together at the ends of a cord of fixed length, an observer being required for each sextant.

Military Cross (M.C.). A decoration, instituted in 1915, and awarded to captains, lieutenants, and warrant officers in the army and the Indian and Colonial forces.

Mine. An arrangement, structure, or contrivance which produces a sudden explosion, and is used against enemies whether on land or at sea. Land mines have long been known. Submarine mines have become prominent chiefly in recent times, their efficacy mostly depending on gun-cotton, which may be caused to explode when a ship comes in contact with the mine. The explosion may also be brought about by means of an electric connection with the shore and an operator there.

Mine-laying. The laying or dropping into the sea of mines intended to act against an enemy's vessels, such mines having a weight attached by way of 'anchor'. Mines are often used in territorial waters as defences for harbours and coast-lines, it being illegal to scatter them in the open sea, though the Germans have frequently done so, even to the risk of their own vessels.

Mine-sweeping. The 'sweeping' of the sea to clear an area of hostile mines carried out especially by boats of the trawler type, two of which work together, steaming slowly along at a considerable distance apart, having a 'sweeping-wire' extended between them which catches the mooring-chains of the mines, and brings them together so that they may be dealt with.

Minnie. A minnenwerfer, or large German trench-mortar.

Monoplane. A flying apparatus with its wings or carrying surfaces arranged in the same plane. See *Aeroplane.*

Moral. (F. Often wrongly written *morale*, which means 'morals'.) The condition of troops, &c., with respect to discipline, spirit, &c.

Mustard gas. A poisonous gas with a pungent smell resembling that of mustard.

Muzzle energy. The force or weight of the blow which a projectile can deliver when leaving the muzzle of the gun.

Muzzle velocity. The velocity in feet per second with which a projectile leaves the muzzle of the gun.

Napoo. There is no more (il n'y en a plus). Napooed, killed.

Naval General Service Medal. Instituted 1915 for officers and men of the navy. It is awarded in connection with minor naval warlike operations in cases in which no other medal would be appropriate.

Navy List. A British official publication containing the names of all the officers in the navy, the names of the vessels composing the fleet, with particulars of the power, armament, &c., of the vessels, and other naval information.

Newton pippin. A kind of rifle-grenade.

Nissen hut. A fairly portable wooden hut with iron roof. It was said to be warm in winter and cool in summer; actually it was the reverse.

No Man's Land. The ground between hostile trenches, as belonging to neither side.

Nose-dive. A headlong dive of an aeroplane, with the 'nose' of the machine pointing downwards.

Objective. The point to which troops are to advance.

Observation officer. An artillery officer placed so as to command a view of enemy positions, and in communication by telephone with those in charge of the guns to which he is attached. He directs the laying of the guns so as to bring selected objects under fire, the objects being commonly invisible to the gunners.

Observation post. The position occupied by an observation officer. Often called an 'O. Pip'.

Old Contemptibles. The original British Expeditionary Force, so called from the Kaiser's sneer at our 'contemptible little army'.

Over the top, or Over the lid (to go). To leave the trench and take part in an attack on the enemy.

Padre. A chaplain.

Patrol flotilla. A flotilla or fleet of vessels acting by way of patrol, that is moving about and keeping guard against the approach of hostile craft and against attempts to break a blockade. There are a number of patrol flotillas guarding the British shores, and consisting mainly of destroyers, each flotilla being accompanied by a depot-ship (which see above).

Periscope. An apparatus or structure rising above the deck of a submarine vessel, giving by means of mirrors, &c., a view of outside surroundings though the vessel itself remains submerged, and enabling the crew to see how to direct torpedoes. A device of a similar kind is used on land in trenches or elsewhere.

P.H. helmet. A primitive kind of gas-helmet, superseded by the box-respirator.

Pill-box. A small concrete block-house, used by the Germans as a machine-gun emplacement.

Pineapple. A light trench-mortar.

Pip-emma. P.M. (of time). So called by signallers to prevent mistakes.

Pip-squeak. A small high-explosive shell.

Platoon. A body consisting of four sections and about 40 men, commanded by a subaltern, with a sergeant as second in command.

Playfair. A cipher sometimes employed when on active service.

Poilu. (F., lit. 'hairy', from the custom of allowing the hair on the face to grow when on active service.) A soldier of the French army.

Post. A bugle call giving notice to soldiers to retire to their quarters for the night, sounded at tattoo, there being a first post and a last post, the latter sounded also at military funerals.

Profiteer. To make excess profits at the expense of the public during a national crisis such as the Great War; (noun) a person guilty of making excess profits.

Provost-sergeant. A sergeant detailed in charge of the work of policing a post, camp, &c.

Push. An offensive on a large scale.

Quick-firing gun. A gun or piece of ordnance that is loaded and fired with great rapidity. The projectile and powder are contained in a metallic cartridge-case; and the carriage is furnished with a steel shield to protect the gunners. Not to be confounded with a machine-gun (which see).

Railhead. A locality on a railway where ammunition and supplies are transferred to road transport; the point where a railway stops short.

Ramp. A sloping platform such as may be used in getting ordnance or horses into railway wagons.

Range-finding. The measurement of the distance in yards between a gun and the object of its aim, effected by means of instruments called a range-finder, a mekometer, &c. The noun 'range-finder' is used of the instrument, while 'range-taker' is applied to the man using it.

Ranging. The process of finding the elevation which should be given to a gun in order that the projectile may hit the object aimed at.

Red Hat. A military policeman.

Regiment. A body of troops having a permanent organization and forming the command of a colonel. A regiment of infantry consists of a varying number of battalions. See *Battalion*. A regiment of cavalry comprises three squadrons, each of four troops, a troop consisting of three or four sections (of four to eight men each).

Rookie. An unfledged recruit.

Rooty. Bread. (An old army word derived from Tamil).

R. T. O. Railway Transport Officer, an officer in charge of railways. (In the South African War called 'Railway Staff Officer').

Rudder. The small plane or planes set vertically which steer an aeroplane sideways.

S. A. A. Small-arms ammunition; ammunition for rifles, machine-guns, and revolvers.

Salvo. The simultaneous discharge of artillery for some special purpose, especially to prevent the smoke from one gun interfering with the laying of another.

Sam Browne. A belt with a shoulder-strap worn by British officers and first-class warrant officers.

Sapper. One of the Royal Engineers.

Sausage. An observation balloon.

Screw gun. A gun, designed for mountain warfare, which can be taken to pieces and conveyed in sections.

Screw-picket. An iron picket made to screw noiselessly into the ground, and used as the framework of a barbed-wire fence.

Scrounge. To pilfer; to cadge.

Sea-plane. See *Hydroplane* above.

Section. A small division of some military body, more especially the fourth part of a platoon, consisting of about ten men commanded by a non-commissioned officer, and forming the normal fire-unit: there are sixteen sections in a company. A cavalry section consists of from four to eight men. An artillery section comprises two guns, with the necessary men, horses, and ammunition-wagons.

Shell. A projectile containing an explosive or bursting charge, and now always of cylindrical form. *Common* shells contain a charge of powder only. *High-explosive* shells are charged with *lyddite* or some similar substance, and act with tremendous power. (German shells of this kind have been nicknamed by British soldiers 'Jack Johnsons' and 'Black Marias'—the latter giving out poisonous black smoke.) See also *Shrapnel* (in Dict.). *Armour-piercing* shells are used against armoured ships.

Shell-shock. Neurosis caused by shell-fire.

Side-slip. A dangerous movement sideways of an aeroplane that may occur when the propeller is allowed to stop and the forward speed of the machine is unduly diminished.

Skid. A sort of runner attached to the under part of an aeroplane to assist it in rising from the ground.

Skrimshanker. A soldier who shirks duty, especially by malingering.

Slope arms, to. To place the rifle flat on the left shoulder, magazine outwards.

Snotty. A midshipman.

Soixante-quinze. (F., seventy-five, denoting the calibre of the gun.) The leading French field-gun, the finest weapon of the kind in existence, designed by MM. Deport and Sainte-Claire Deville.

S.O.S. signal. A signal (usually some sort of rocket) sent up to start an artillery barrage. It was supposed to be sent up only when the Germans were actually seen advancing to the attack.

Spartacist. A member of the extreme Anarchist party in the German revolution of 1918.

Spin. The rotation of an elongated projectile (a shell) about its long axis, imparted to it by the rifling of the gun. See *Twist* below.

Spotter. An officer on board a ship who by watching the fall of shells helps to ascertain the range for which the guns should be set.

Squadron. A body of cavalry consisting of four troops, each of three or four sections. See *Section* above.

Stand-to. Standing to arms, which was done in the trenches at dusk and dawn, and at other times when there was an alarm.

Star-shell. A shell containing a number of 'stars' that ignite and give illumination when the shell bursts.

Stokes mortar. A light portable trench-mortar.

Strafe. (Ger. *strafen*, to punish, as in the German aspiration '*Gott strafe England*', 'God punish England'.) To inflict chastisement upon, to harass, 'pitch into'.

Strombos horn. A horn worked by compressed air, used as a warning against a German cloud-gas attack.

Stunt. A remarkable feat of skill; used especially about flying feats, but also used when speaking of some special job, e.g. a bombing-raid.

Submarine vessel, Submarine. A vessel that can sail on the surface like an ordinary vessel, and can also be submerged at will and sail through the water, being then in a watertight and air-tight condition. Submarines are chiefly intended to attack other vessels by means of torpedoes, and have many special features in regard to construction, propulsion, steering, diving, &c. The complement of crew is usually from about twenty to thirty or more, and they use oil fuel.

Subsection. Half an artillery section, that is, one gun with its complement of men, horses, and ammunition-wagons.

Sump-hole. A pit dug in a trench for drainage purposes.

Supernumeraries. In drill, the N.C.O's., &c., forming the third rank.

Swing the lead, to. Originally 'to tell a tall story', but used especially of a soldier who made the most of some trifling ailment.

Tail-dive. A dive or sudden descent in the air with an aeroplane, the 'tail' part of it being foremost.

Tank. A heavily armoured motor vehicle running on caterpillar-wheels, and armed with quick-firing and machine-guns. First used by the British, 15th September, 1916.

Taube. (Ger. *taube*, pigeon.) A common German form of monoplane somewhat birdlike in general appearance.

Tear-shell. A shell containing gases that cause the eyes to water profusely.

Ticket. A discharge from the army.

Tin hat. The British shrapnel helmet introduced in 1916.

Tir de barrage. (F., lit. 'barring fire'.) The same as *Curtain fire*.

Toc-emma. A trench-mortar. So called by signallers to prevent mistakes.

Tommy (in full **Tommy Atkins**). (From the name *Thomas Atkins* used casually in specimen forms given in Army Regulations.) A private soldier in the British army.

Torpedo-boat. A vessel specially intended to attack with torpedoes, and fitted with torpedo-tubes.

Torpedo-net. A strong steel net suspended vertically in the water by means of booms to intercept a torpedo aimed at a vessel—a device not generally regarded as of much real utility.

Torpedo-tube. A tube for the discharge of torpedoes from a torpedo-boat, submarine, &c.

Tractor. (L. *trahĕre*, *tractum*, to draw, pull.) A screw propeller that may be said to 'pull' an aeroplane, being placed in front of the pilot, the ordinary propeller being in his rear.

Trade, the. In the navy commonly used to denote the various forms of submarine activity.

Trail arms, to. To carry the rifle horizontally at the full extent of the right arm.

Trench feet. A condition of the feet resembling frost-bite, frequently terminating in gangrene, and caused by exposure to wet and cold.

Trench fever. An infectious disease with feverish symptoms, transmitted by vermin.

Tripod mast. In a war-vessel, a great mast the lower part of which forms a tripod, and in which are stations for important officers, as a range-finder, a fire-control officer, searchlight director, &c.

Troop. A body of cavalry consisting of three or four sections. See *Section* above.

Turbine. A steam engine, in common use for the propulsion of vessels, in which rotary motion is produced by the direct impact of steam upon a series of projections on the circumference of a cylinder free to revolve.

Turret. An armoured shelter on a war-ship containing, and revolving with, a gun. Distinguished from *Barbette*.

Twin-screw. Having two screw propellers on separate shafts and revolving in opposite directions so as to counteract the tendency to lateral vibration.

Twist. The spiral direction given to the grooves of the bore of a gun, which may be uniform throughout the bore or may increase towards the muzzle: the 'spin' or rotation of the shell depends on the twist.

U-boat. A German submarine (from German *unterseeboot*).

Umpteen. An indefinite number.

Unit. Any self-contained portion of a military force, comprising men, horses, vehicles, &c., ready to act or be employed together. There may be fighting units, medical units, transport units, &c.

Véry light. The commonest make of British star-shell.

Victoria Cross (V.C.). A small bronze cross bearing the words 'For Valour', bestowed in recognition of conspicuous bravery evinced in some act performed 'in the presence of the enemy', with a clasp and ribbon which since 1918 is crimson for all branches of the service. (In service-dress uniform a small bronze replica of the cross is worn in the centre of the ribbon.) It was instituted in 1856 on the close of the Crimean War, and may be held by all grades up to Field-Marshals and Admirals of the Fleet, including native officers and men of the Indian Army. Recipients under the rank of commissioned officer receive also a pension of £10, with £5 a year additional for each clasp if the cross has been gained more than once.

Vol-plane. The gliding downwards of an aeroplane when the rate of descent is about one in six. The word is used similarly as a verb. If the descent is almost vertical it is called a *vol-pique*.

Waacs. Members of the Women's Army Auxiliary Corps. (From the initials.)

Wangle. To gain one's ends by devious and unscrupulous methods.
Warping. The bending of the flexible edge of the plane of an aeroplane so as to maintain its due stability.
Wash-out. (Originally used for 'a shot that misses the target'.) A failure; a take-in.
Water-plane. See *Hydroplane* above.
Waves. Lines of men advancing to attack; each wave is separated from the next by about 100 yards.
Whippet. A light tank which can move quickly; first used 24th April, 1918.
Whizz-bang. A small high-velocity shell which bursts before the report of the gun is heard.
Wind up, to get the. To become nervous and excited.
Wing. The half of a regiment or larger body, termed 'right' and 'left' when in line, 'leading' and 'rear' when in column.
Wire-gun. A gun which is greatly strengthened by having layers of flattish steel wire of great strength wound tightly round an inner tube—120 miles of wire in some cases—there being also an outer 'jacket' over the wire.
Wooly-bear. A large German shrapnel shell which burst into a cloud of brownish-black smoke.
Wound-stripe. A small stripe of gold braid worn on the left fore-arm, denoting that the name of the wearer has appeared in the casualty list. The wound-stripe was first sanctioned in 1916.
Wrens. Members of the Women's Royal Naval Service. (From the initials.)
Zeppelin. See *Air-ship.*

ABBREVIATIONS AND CONTRACTIONS COMMONLY USED

A. or *ans.* Answer.
a. or @ (L. *ad*). To or at.
A.B. (L. *Artium Baccalaureus*). Bachelor of Arts.
A.B. Able-bodied seaman.
Abl. Ablative.
Abp. Archbishop.
A.C. (L. *Ante Christum*). Before Christ.
a/c or *Acct.* Account.
A.D. (L. *Anno Domini*). In the year of our Lord.
A.D.C. Aide-de-camp.
Adj. Adjective.
Adjt. Adjutant.
Ad lib. or *Ad libit.* (L. *ad libitum*). At pleasure.
Adm. Admiral.
Adv. Adverb.
Æ. or *æt.* (L. (*anno*) *ætatis*). Of the age of, aged.
A.H. (L. *Anno Hegiræ*). In the year of the Hegira.
A.Inst.C.E. Associate of the Institution of Civil Engineers.
A.K.C. Associate of King's College (London).
Ala. Alabama.
A.M. (L. *Anno Mundi*). In the year of the world.
A.M. (L. *Ante Meridiem*). Before noon.
A.M. (L. *Artium Magister*). Master of Arts.
A.M.Inst.C.E. Associate Member of the Institution of Civil Engineers.
Anon. Anonymous.
Ans. Answer.
Ap. or *Apr.* April.
A.R.A. Associate of the Royal Academy.
A.R.H.A. Associate of the Royal Hibernian Academy.
Ari., *Ariz.* Arizona.
Ark. Arkansas.
A.R.S.A. Associate of the Royal Scottish Academy.
A.R.S.M. Associate of the Royal School of Mines.
A.S., *A.-Sax.* Anglo-Saxon.
A.U.C. (L. *Anno Urbis Conditæ* or *Ab Urbe Condita*). In the year from the building of the city (*i.e.* Rome).
Aug. August.
A.V. Artillery Volunteers; Authorized Version (of the Bible).
Avoir. Avoirdupois.

b. Born.
B.A. Bachelor of Arts. See *A.B.*
Bart. or *Bt.* Baronet.
B.C. Before Christ.
B.C.L. Bachelor of Civil Law.
B.D. Bachelor of Divinity.
Bk. Book.
B.L. Bachelor of Law.
B.M. Bachelor of Medicine.
B.Mus. Bachelor of Music.
Bp. Bishop.
Brit. Britain, British.
B.S. Bachelor of Surgery.
B.Sc. Bachelor of Science.
B.Th. Bachelor of Theology.
B.V. Blessed Virgin.—*B.V.M.* Blessed Virgin Mary.

C. Centigrade (thermometer).
C. or *Cap.* (L. *caput*). Chapter.
C.A. Chartered Accountant.
Cal. California.
Cantab. (L. *Cantabrigiensis*). Of Cambridge.
Cantuar. (L. *Cantuariensis*). Of Canterbury.
Cap. (L. *caput*). Chapter.
Capt. Captain.
Card. Cardinal.
Cath. Catholic.
C.B. Companion of the Bath
C.C. Catholic clergyman.
C.D.V. Carte-de-visite.
C.E. Civil Engineer.
Cent (L. *centum*). A hundred.
Centig. Centigrade (thermometer).
Cf. (L. *confer*). Compare.
C.F.I. Cost, freight, and insurance.
C.G. Coast-guard.
C.G.S. (used adjectively). Centimetre, Gramme, Second (as units of length, mass, and time).
Ch. Chapter; church.
Chap. Chapter.
C.I. Order of the Crown of India.
Cicestr. (*Cicestrensis*). Of Chichester.
C.I.E. Companion of the Order of the Indian Empire.
Clk. Clerk.
C.M. (L. *Chirurgiæ Magister*). Master in Surgery.
C.M. Common Metre.
C.M.G. Companion of the Order of St. Michael and St. George.
Co. Company; County.
Col. Colonel; Colonial; Colossians; Column; Colorado.
Coll. College.
Comp. Compare; comparative
Conn. Connecticut.
Cor. Mem. Corresponding Member.
Cor. Sec. Corresponding Secretary.
Coy. Company.
C.P. Clerk of the Peace.
C.P.C. Clerk of the Privy Council.

C.P.S. (L. *Custos Privati Sigilli*). Keeper of the Privy Seal.
Cr. Credit or Creditor.
Crim. con. Criminal conversation (*i.e.* adultery).
C.S. Civil Service; Clerk to the Signet; Court of Session.
C.S.I. Companion of the Order of the Star of India.
Ct. Connecticut.
Cum div. With dividend.
Cur. or *Curt.* Current; this month.
C.V.O. Commander of the Royal Victorian Order.
Cwt. (L. *centum*, a hundred + Eng. *weight*). A hundredweight or hundredweights.
Cyc. Cyclopædia.

d. (L. *denarius*, pl. *denarii*). A penny or pence.
d. died.
Dak. Dakota.
D.C. District of Columbia.
D.C. (It. *Da Capo*). From the beginning; again.
D.C.L. Doctor of Civil Law.
D.C.M. Distinguished Conduct Medal.
D.D. Doctor of Divinity.
Dec. December.
Del. Delaware.
Del. (L. *delineavit*). He (or she) drew it.
Dep. Deputy.
D.F. Defender of the Faith; Dean of the Faculty.
D.G. (L. *Dei Gratia*). By the Grace of God.
Dict. Dictionary.
D.L. Deputy Lieutenant.
D.Litt. Doctor of Literature.
Do. (It. *ditto*). The same.
Dols. Dollars.
Doz. Dozen.
D. P. H. Diploma in Public Health.
D.Phil. Doctor of Philosophy.
Dr. Debtor; Doctor; drams.
D.Sc. Doctor of Science.
D.S.C. Distinguished Service Cross.
D.S.O. Distinguished Service Order.
Dunelm. (*Dunelmensis*). Of Durham.
D.V. (L. *Deo volente*). God willing.
Dwt. (L. *denarius*, penny + Eng. *weight*). A pennyweight or pennyweights.

E. East or Eastern.
Eblan. (*Eblanensis*). Of Dublin.
Ebor. (L. *Eboracensis*). Of York.
E.C. East Central (postal dist. London); Established Church.
Ed. Edition; editor; edited by.
E.E. Errors excepted; Electrical Engineer.
E.E.T.S. Early English Text Society.
E.G. (L. *exempli gratia*). For example.
E.I.C.S. East India Company's Service.
Ency. or *Encyc.* Encyclopædia.
E.N.E. East-north-east.
Eng. England or English.
E.S.E. East-south-east.
Esq. or *Esqr.* Esquire.
Etc. (L. *et cœteri, cœteræ*, or *cœtera*). And others; and so forth.
Et seq. (L. *et sequentes* or *sequentia*). And the following.
Ex. Example.
Ex div. Exclusive of dividend.
Exon. (L. *Exoniensis*). Of Exeter.

F., *Fahr.* Fahrenheit (thermometer).
F.A.S. Fellow of the Antiquarian Society.
F.B.A. Fellow of the British Academy.
F.C. Free Church (of Scotland).
Fcp. Foolscap.
F.C.S. Fellow of the Chemical Society.
F.D. (L. *Fidei Defensor* or *Defensatrix*). Defender of the Faith.
Feb. February.
Fec. (L. *fecit*). He (or she) did it.
F.E.I.S. Fellow of the Educational Institute of Scotland.
F.E.S. Fellow of the Entomological Society; Fellow of the Ethnological Society.
F.F.A. Fellow of the Faculty of Actuaries.
F.F.P.S. Fellow of Faculty of Physicians and Surgeons (Glas.).
F.G.S. Fellow of the Geological Society.
F.I.A. Fellow of the Institute of Actuaries.
F.I.C. Fellow of the Institute of Chemistry.
Fid. Def. = *F.D.*
Fig. Figure or figures; figurative or figuratively.
Fl., *Fla.*, or *Flor.* Florida.
F.L.S. Fellow of the Linnæan Society.
F.M. Field-marshal.
Fo. or *Fol.* Folio or folios.
F.O.B. Free on board (goods delivered).
F.P. Fire-plug.
F.P.S. Fellow of the Philological Society.
F.R.A.S. Fellow of the Royal Astronomical Society.
F.R.C.P. Fellow of the Royal College of Physicians.
F.R.C.P.E. Do., Edinburgh.
F.R.C.S. Fellow of the Royal College of Surgeons.
F.R.C.S.E. Do., Edinburgh.
F.R.C.S.I. Fellow of the Royal College of Surgeons, Ireland.
F.R.C.S.L. Fellow of the Royal College of Surgeons, London.
F.R.G.S. Fellow of the Royal Geographical Society.
F.R.I.B.A. Fellow of the Royal Institute of British Architects.
F.R.S. Fellow of the Royal Society.
F.R.S.E. Do., Edinburgh.
F.R.S.L. Fellow of the Royal Society of Literature.
F.S.A. Fellow of the Society of Antiquaries.
F.S.A.Scot. Do., Scotland.
F.S.S. Fellow of the Statistical Society.
Ft. Foot or feet.
F.T.C.D. Fellow of Trinity College, Dublin.
F.Z.S. Fellow of the Zoological Society.

Ga. Georgia.
Gal. or *Gall.* Gallon or Gallons.
G.C.B. Grand Cross of the Bath.
G.C.I.E. Grand Commander of the Indian Empire.
G.C.M.G. Grand Cross of St. Michael and St. George.
G.C.S.I. Grand Commander of the Star of India.
G.C.V.O. Grand Cross of the Royal Victorian Order.
Gen. or *Genl.* General.
gm. Grammes.
G.M. Grand Master.
Gov.-Gen. Governor-general.
G.P.O. General Post-office.
gr. Grain or Grains.
G.R. (L. *Georgius Rex*). King George.
G.R.I. (L. *Georgius Rex Imperator*). George King and Emperor.

H.B.M. His (or Her) Britannic Majesty.
H.C.M. His (or Her) Catholic Majesty.
H.E.I.C.S. Honourable East India Company's Service.
Hf.-bd. Half-bound.
H.G. Horse Guards.
H.H. His (or Her) Highness.
Hhd. Hogshead or Hogsheads.
H.I.H. His (or Her) Imperial Highness.
H.J. or *H.J.S.* (L. *Hic Jacet* or *Hic Jacet Sepultus*). Here lies, or here lies buried.
H.L. House of Lords.
H.M. His (or Her) Majesty.
H.M.P. (L. *Hoc Monumentum Posuit*). Erected this monument.
H.M.S. His (or Her) Majesty's Service; His (or Her) Majesty's Ship.
Hon. or *Honbl.* Honourable.
H.P. Horse-power.
H.R. House of Representatives.
H.R.H. His (or Her) Royal Highness.
H.R.I.P. (L. *Hic Requiescit In Pace*). Here rests in peace.

H.S. (L. *Hic Situs*). Here lies.
H.S.H. His (or Her) Serene Highness.

I. Island.
Ia. Iowa.
Ib. or *ibid.* (L. *ibidem*). In the same place.
Id. (L. *idem*). The same.
I.e. (L. *id est*). That is.
I.H.S. Usually looked upon as the initials of *Iesus* (*Jesus*) *Hominum Salvator*, Jesus the Saviour of Men, but originally ΙΗΣ the first three letters of ʼΙΗΣΟΥΣ (*Iēsous*), the Greek form of *Jesus*.
Ill. Illinois.
Imp. (L. *imperator*). Emperor; Imperial.
In. Inch or inches.
Incog. (It. *incognito, incognita*). Unknown.
Ind. Indiana.
Ind. T. Indian Territory.
In loc. (L. *in loco*). In its place.
I.N.R.I. (L. *Iesus Nazarenus Rex Iudaeorum*). Jesus of Nazareth, King of the Jews.
Inst. Instant; the present month.
I.O.G.T. Independent Order of Good Templars.
I.O.O.F. Independent Order of Oddfellows.
I O U. I owe you—an acknowledgment for money.
Ir. Irish.
Isl. Island.
I.S.O. Imperial Service Order.

Jan. January.
J.C. JESUS CHRIST.
J.H.S. See I.H.S.
J.P. Justice of the Peace.
Jr. or *Junr.* Junior.
J.U.D. (L. *Juris Utriusque Doctor*). Doctor of both Laws (that is, Civil and Canon).
Jul. July.

K.C. King's Counsel.
K.C.B. (*K.B.*). Knight Commander of the Bath.
K.C.I.E. Knight Commander of the Indian Empire.
K.C.M.G. Knight Commander of St. Michael and St. George.
K.C.S.I. Knight Commander of the Star of India.
K.C.V.O. Knight Commander of the Royal Victorian Order.
K.G. Knight of the Garter.
K.G.C.B. Knight Grand Cross of the Bath.
Kilog. Kilogramme.
Kilom. Kilometre.
K.M. Knight of Malta.
Knt. Knight.
K.P. Knight of St. Patrick.
Kt. Knight.
K.T. Knight of the Thistle.
Ky. Kentucky.

L., l., or £ (L. *libra*). Pound or pounds (sterling).
L., lb., or ℔. Pound or pounds (weight).
La. Louisiana.
L.A. Law Agent; Literate in Arts.
L.A.H. Licentiate Apothecaries' Hall (Ireland).
L.A.S. Licentiate of the Apothecaries' Society.
Lat. Latin; latitude.
Lb. or ℔. Pound or pounds (weight).
L.C. Lord Chamberlain; Lord Chancellor.
L.c. (L. *loco citato*). In the place quoted.
L.C.J. Lord Chief-justice.
L.C.P. Licentiate of the College of Preceptors.
Ld. Lord; *Ldp.* Lordship.
L.D.S. Licentiate of Dental Surgery.
L.G. Life Guards.
L.I. Light Infantry; Long Island.
Lib. (L. *liber*). Book.
Lieut. Lieutenant.
Lieut.-Col. Lieutenant-colonel.
Lieut.-Gen. Lieutenant-general.
Lieut.-Gov. Lieutenant-governor.
Linn. Linnæus or Linnæan.
Litt.D. (L. *Literarum Doctor*). Doctor of Literature.
L.L. or *L.Lat.* Late Latin.
L.L.A. Lady Literate in Arts.
LL.B. (L. *Legum Baccalaureus*). Bachelor of Laws.
LL.D. (L. *Legum Doctor*). Doctor of Laws.
L.M. Long Metre; Licentiate in Midwifery.
Lon. or *long.* Longitude.
Loq. (L. *loquitur*). Speaks.
L.R.C.P. Licentiate Royal College of Physicians.
L.R.C.S. Licentiate Royal College of Surgeons.
L.S. Linnæan Society.
L.S. (L. *locus sigilli*). Place of the seal.
L.S.A. = *L.A.S.*
L.S.D. (L. *Libræ, Solidi, Denarii*). Pounds, shillings, pence.
Lt. Lieutenant.

M. (L. *mille*). Thousands.
M. (L. *meridies*). Noon.
M. Mile or miles; Monsieur.
m. Minute or minutes.
M.A. Master of Arts. See *A.M.*
Ma. Minnesota.
Mad. or *Madm.* Madam.
Maj. Major.
Maj.-Gen. Major-general.
Mar. March.
Mass. Massachusetts.
M.B. (L. *Medicinæ Baccalaureus*). Bachelor of Medicine.
M.C. Military Cross; Master of Ceremonies; Member of Congress; Master in Surgery = *C.M.*
M.D. (L. *Medicinæ Doctor*). Doctor of Medicine.
Md. Maryland.
M.E. Military, Mining, or Mechanical Engineer.
Me. Maine.
Mem. Memorandum.
Messrs. Messieurs, Gentlemen
M.F.H. Master of Fox Hounds.
Mi. Mississippi.
Mich. Michigan.
M.I.E.E. Member of the Institution of Electrical Engineers.
M.I.Mech.E. Member of the Institution of Mechanical Engineers.
Minn. Minnesota.
M.Inst.C.E. Member of the Institution of Civil Engineers.
Miss. Mississippi.
Mlle. Mademoiselle or Miss.
mm. Millimetres.
Mme. Madame.
Mn. Michigan.
Mo. Missouri.
Mon. Montana.
Mons. Monsieur; Sir.
M.P. Member of Parliament.
M.P.S. Member of the Pharmaceutical Society.
Mr. Master (pron. *Mister*).
M.R. Master of the Rolls.
M.R.A.S. Member of the Royal Academy of Science; Member of the Royal Asiatic Society.
M.R.C.P. Member of the Royal College of Physicians.
M.R.C.S. Member of the Royal College of Surgeons.
M.R.C.V.S. Member of the Royal College of Veterinary Surgeons.
M.R.I.A. Member of the Royal Irish Academy.
Mrs. Mistress.
M.R.S.L. Member of the Royal Society of Literature.
M.S. (L. *Memoriæ Sacrum*). Sacred to the Memory.
MS. Manuscript; *MSS.* Manuscripts.
M.S.S. Member of the Statistical Society.
Mt. Mount or Mountain.
Mus.B. (L. *Musicæ Baccalaureus*). Bachelor of Music.
Mus.D. or *Mus.Doc.* (L. *Musicæ Doctor*). Doctor of Music.
M.V.O. Member of the Royal Victorian Order.

N. Noon; North; Northern.
N.A. North America or North American.
N.B. North Britain (Scotland); New Brunswick.
N.B. (L. *Nota Bene*). Note well or take notice.
N.C. North Carolina.
N.E. New England; North-east; North-eastern.
Neb. Nebraska.
Nem. con. (L. *nemine contradicente*). No one contradicting, unanimously.
Nem. dis. (L. *nemine dissentiente*). No one dissenting.
Neth. Netherlands.

Nev. Nevada.
N.H. New Hampshire.
N.J. New Jersey.
N.Lat. North Latitude.
N.M. New Mexico.
N.N.E. North-north-east.
N.N.W. North-north-west.
No. (L. *numero*). Number.
Non Con. Not-content, dissentient (House of Lords).
Non obst. (L. *non obstante*). Notwithstanding.
Non seq. (L. *non sequitur*). It does not follow.
Nov. November.
N.P. Notary-public.
N.S. New Style; Nova Scotia.
N.S.W. New South Wales.
N.T. New Testament.
N.W. North-west; North-western.
N.Y. New York.
N.Z. or *N.Zeal.* New Zealand.

O. Ohio.
Ob. (L. *obiit*). Died.
O.C. Officer in Command.
Oct. October.
O.F. Oddfellows.
O.H.M.S. On His (or Her) Majesty's Service.
O.M. Order of Merit.
Or. Oregon.
Ord. Ordinance; ordinary.
O.S. Old Style.
O.T. Old Testament.
Oxon. (L. *Oxoniensis*). Of Oxford.
Oz. Ounce. [*Note.* The *z*, as in *viz.*, represents an old symbol for a terminal contraction.]

p. Page; *pp.* Pages.
Pa. Pennsylvania.
Par. Paragraph.
Parl. Parliament or parliamentary.
P.C. Privy Council or Privy Councillor; Police Constable.
Pd. Paid.
Penn. Pennsylvania.
Per an. (L. *per annum*). By the year, yearly.
Per cent, or *per ct.* (L. *per centum*). By the hundred.
P.G.M Past Grand Master.
Ph.D. (L. *Philosophiæ Doctor*). Doctor of Philosophy.
Phil. Philosophy; philosophical.
Pinx. or *pxt.* (L. *pinxit*). He (or she) painted it.
P.L. Poet Laureate.
P.L.C. Poor Law Commissioners.
P.M. (L. *Post Meridiem*). Afternoon.
P.M. Past Master; Postmaster.
P.M.G. Postmaster-general.
P.O. Post-office.
P. & O. Co. Peninsular and Oriental Steam Navigation Company.
P.O.O. Post-office Order.
Pos. Positive.
Pp. Pages.
P.P. Parish Priest.
P.P.C. (Fr. *pour prendre congé*). To take leave.
P.R. Prize Ring.
P.R.A. President of the Royal Academy.
Pres. President.
Prof. Professor.
Pro tem. (L. *pro tempore*). For the time being.
Prox. (L. *proximo*). Next, or of the next, month.
P.R.A. President of the Royal Academy.
P.R.S. President of the Royal Society.
P.R.S.A. President of the Royal Scottish Academy.
P.S. (L. *post scriptum*). Postscript.
P.S. Privy Seal.
Pt. Part.
P.T. Post Town; Pupil Teacher.
P.T.O. Please turn over.
Pxt. See *Pinx.*

Q. or *Qu.* Query or question.
Q.B. Queen's Bench.
Q.C. Queen's College; Queen's Counsel.
Q.E.D. (L. *quod erat demonstrandum*). Which was to be demonstrated.
Q.E.F. (L. *quod erat faciendum*). Which was to be done.
Q.E I. (L. *quod erat inveniendum*). Which was to be found out.
Q.-M. Quarter-master.
Q.-M.-G. Quarter-master-general.
Qr. Quarter; quire.
Q.S. Quarter Sessions.
Q.s. (L. *quantum sufficit*). A sufficient quantity.
Qt. Quart.
Qu. Query or question.
Q.v. (L. *quod vide*). Which see.
Qy. Query.

R. (L. *Rex, Regina*). King, Queen.
R. Réaumur (thermometer).
R.A. Royal Academy; Royal Artillery.
R.A.M. Royal Academy of Music.
R.A.M.C. Royal Army Medical Corps.
R.A.S. Royal Asiatic Society; Royal Astronomical Society.
R.C. Roman Catholic.
R.C.P. Royal College of Physicians.
R.C.S. Royal College of Surgeons.
R.D. Rural Dean.
R.E. Royal Engineers.
Ref. Ch. Reformed Church.
Reg. or *Regt.* Regiment.
Reg. Prof. Regius Professor.
Regt. Regent: Regiment.
Rem. Remark or remarks.
Rev., *Revd.* Reverend.
R.F.A. Royal Field Artillery.
R.G.S. Royal Geographical Society.
R.H.A. Royal Horse Artillery.
R.H.S. Royal Horticultural or Royal Historical Society.
R.I. Rhode Island.
R.I.B.A. Royal Institute of British Architects.
R.I.P. (L. *Requiescat In Pace*). May he (or she) rest in peace!
R.M. Royal Mail; Royal Marines; Resident Magistrate (Ireland).
R.M.A. Royal Military Academy.
R.N. Royal Navy.
R.N.R. Royal Naval Reserve.
Roffen. (*Roffensis*). Of Rochester.
Rom. Cath. Roman Catholic.
R.S. Royal Society.
R.S.A. Royal Scottish Academy.
R.S.E. Royal Society of Edinburgh.
R.S.L. Royal Society of London.
R.S.N.A. Royal Society of Northern Antiquities.
R.S.V.P. (Fr. *Répondez, s'il vous plait*). Answer, if you please.
Rt. Right.
Rt. Hon. Right Honourable.
Rt. Rev. Right Reverend.
R.U.I. Royal University of Ireland.
R.W. Right Worshipful or Right Worthy.
R.W.G.M. Right Worshipful Grand Master.
R.W.G S. Right Worthy Grand Secretary.
R.W.G.T. Right Worth, Grand Treasurer; Right Worthy Grand Templar.
R.W.G.W. Right Worshipful Grand Warden.
R.W.S. Royal Society of Painters in Water-colours.
R.W.S.G.W. Right Worshipful Senior Grand Warden.
Ry. Railway.

S. Saint; Signor; south; southern; sun.
s. Second or seconds; shillings.
S.A. South Africa or South Australia.
S.C. South Carolina.
Sc. (L. *scilicet*). To wit; namely; being understood.
Sc. (L. *sculpsit*). He (or she) engraved it.
Sc.B. (L *Scientiæ Baccalaureus*). Bachelor of Science.
Sc.D. (L. *Scientiæ Doctor*). Doctor of Science.
Scil. (L. *scilicet*). To wit; namely; being understood.
Sculp. or *Sculpt.* (L. *sculpsit*). He (or she) engraved it.
S.E. South-east; south-eastern.
Sec. or *Secy.* Secretary.
Sec. Second.
Sec. or *Sect.* Section.
Sec. Leg. Secretary of Legation.

Sen. or *Senr.* Senior.
Seq. (L. *sequentes* or *sequentia*). The following or the next.
Serg. or *Sergt.* Sergeant.
Serj. or *Serjt.* Serjeant.
S.J. Society of Jesus (that is, the Jesuits).
Soc. or *Socy.* Society.
Sol.-Gen. Solicitor-general.
S.P.C.A. Society for the Prevention of Cruelty to Animals.
S.P.C.C. Society for the Prevention of Cruelty to Children.
S.P.C.K. Society for the Promotion of Christian Knowledge.
S.P.G. Society for the Propagation of the Gospel.
S.P.Q.R. (L. *Senatus Populusque Romanus*). Senate and People of Rome.
Sq. Square. Hence, *sq. ft.*, square foot or feet; *sq. in.*, square inch or inches; *sq. m.*, square mile or miles; *sq. yds.*, square yards.
SS. Saints.
S.S. Sunday (or Sabbath) School.
s.s. Steam-ship.
S.S.C. Solicitor before the Supreme Courts (of Scotland).
S.S.E. South-south-east.
S.S.W. South-south-west.
St. Saint; strait; street.
S.T.D. (L. *Sacræ Theologiæ Doctor*). Doctor of Divinity.
Ster. or *Stg.* Sterling.
S.T.P. (L. *Sacræ Theologiæ Professor*). Professor of Divinity.
Superl. Superlative.
Supp. Supplement.
Supt. Superintendent.
Surg. Surgeon or surgery.
Surv. Surveying or surveyor.
S.v. (L. *sub voce*). Under the word or title.
S.W. Senior Warden; south-west; south-western.

T. Tenor; ton or tun.
T.C.D. Trinity College, Dublin.
Tenn. Tennessee.
Tex. Texas.
T.O. Turn over.
Tom. Tome or volume.
Tr. Transpose; treasurer; trustee.
Trans. Transactions; translation; translator.
Trin. Trinity.
T.T.L. To take leave.

U.C. (L. *Urbis Conditæ*). From the building of the city (Rome).
U.F. United Free Church.
U.K. United Kingdom.
Ult. (L. *ultimo*). Last, or of the last, month.
Unit. Unitarian.
Univ. University.
U.S. United States.
U.S.A. United States of America, or United States Army.
U.S.N. United States Navy.
U.S.S. United States Senate; United States ship or steamer.
U.T. Utah.

V. (L. *versus*). Against.
V. (L. *vide*). See.
V.A. Vicar-Apostolic; Vice-Admiral; Royal Order of Victoria and Albert.
Va. Virginia.
V.A.D. Voluntary Aid Detachment.
V.C. Vice-chancellor; Victoria Cross.
V.D.M. (L. *Verbi Dei Minister*). Minister of the Word of God.
Ven. Venerable.
V.G. Vicar-general.
V.G. (L. *verbi gratia*). For example.
Vid. (L. *vide*). See.
Vigorn. (*Vigornensis*). Of Worcester.
Vis. or *Visc.* Viscount.
Viz. (L. *videlicet*). Namely; to wit. See note under *Oz.*
Vol. Volume; *Vols.* Volumes.
V.P. Vice-president.
V.R. (L. *Victoria Regina*). Queen Victoria.
V.Rev. Very Reverend.
V.R.I. (L. *Victoria Regina Imperatrix*). Victoria Queen and Empress.
Vs. (L. *versus*). Against.
V.S. Veterinary surgeon.
Vul. or *Vulg.* Vulgate.

W. West; western.
Wash. Washington (State).
W.C. Water-closet; West Central (postal district, London).
w.f. Wrong fount (in printing).
W.I. West Indies.
Winton. (*Wintoniensis*). Of Winchester.
Wis. or *Wisc.* Wisconsin.
W.Lon. West longitude.
W.M. Worshipful Master.
W.N.W. West-north-west.
Wpful. Worshipful.
W.S. Writer to the Signet.
W.S.W. West-south-west.
Wt. Weight.
W. Va. West Virginia.

X. Christ. (*Note.* The X represents the Greek X (= CH) in
X.d. Exclusive of dividend.
Xm. or *Xmas.* Christmas.
Xn. Christian.
Xnty. Christianity.
ΧΡΙΣΤΟΣ (*Christos*).
Xt. Christ.
Xtian. Christian.

Y. Year.
Yd. Yard; *Yds.* Yards.
Yͤ. The. [The *Y* in this and similar instances is a substitute for or representative of the Anglo-Saxon þ (=th).]
Y.M.C.A. Young Men's Christian Association.
Yr. Year; younger.
Yrs. Yours.

Z.S. Zoological Society.

FORMS OF ADDRESS

IN CEREMONIOUS COMMUNICATIONS WITH PERSONS OF TITLE OR OFFICIAL POSITION

Ambassador. The title 'Excellency' belongs specially to ambassadors, as well as to governors of colonies and the Lord-Lieutenant of Ireland. Address letters: 'His Excellency (with name or distinctive title following) His Britannic Majesty's Ambassador and Minister Plenipotentiary to the Court of ——'. Begin: 'Sir', 'My Lord', according as the ambassador possesses title or not. When personal reference is made say 'Your Excellency'. An envoy extraordinary or chargé d'affaires, though inferior to an ambassador strictly so called, also usually receives the title 'Excellency'; and the wives of ambassadors are generally addressed similarly during their husbands' tenure of office and while residing abroad.

Archbishop. Address: 'His Grace the Lord Archbishop of ——'. Begin: 'My Lord Archbishop'. Refer to as 'Your Grace'. In formal documents the Archbishop of Canterbury is styled 'The Most Reverend Father in God, James (or whatever the Christian name is), by Divine Providence Lord Archbishop of Canterbury, Primate of All England and Metropolitan'. The Archbishop of York is similarly styled 'The Most Reverend Father in God, ——, by Divine Permission Lord Archbishop of York, Primate of England and Metropolitan'. An Irish archbishop is now addressed as 'The Most Reverend the Archbishop of ——'. An archbishop may be addressed as 'The Right Honourable and Most Reverend the Archbishop of ——' if he have a claim to be called 'Right Hon.' apart from his ecclesiastical position. In America the common form of address is 'The Most Reverend A— B—, D.D.'. The wife of an archbishop has no special title in right of her husband's dignity.

Archdeacon. An archdeacon is styled 'Venerable': 'The Venerable the Archdeacon of ——'. Begin: 'Venerable Sir', or 'Reverend Sir', or (especially in speaking) 'Mr. Archdeacon'.

Baron. Address: 'The Right Hon. Lord ——'; less formally 'The Lord ——'. Begin: 'My Lord'. Refer to as 'Your Lordship'.

Baron's Daughter. Baron's daughters are all entitled to be called 'Honourable'. Unmarried they are addressed as 'The Hon. A— B—', with Christian name and surname. They retain the title 'Hon.' after marriage, the wife of a commoner being 'The Hon. Mrs.' with husband's surname, the wife of a knight or baronet being 'The Hon. Lady', with husband's surname. Begin: 'Madam'; refer to as 'Your Ladyship' if so entitled by marriage. If a higher rank is conferred by the husband the title of course corresponds.

Baron's Son. All the sons are 'Honourable', with Christian name and surname. In Scotland the eldest son is addressed as 'The Hon. the Master of' (peerage title), or 'The Hon. John (or whatever the Christian name is), Master of'. Begin: 'Sir'. The wife of a baron's son is 'The Hon. Mrs.', with husband's surname or both Christian name and surname. Begin: 'Madam'. If the daughter of an earl, marquis, or duke she must be addressed accordingly.

Baroness. Address: 'The Right Hon. the Baroness ——', or 'The Right Hon. Lady ——', or 'The Lady ——'. Begin: 'Madam'; refer to as 'Your Ladyship'.

Baronet. Address: 'Sir A— B—, Bart.', giving Christian name and surname. The Christian name *must* be given; it is quite wrong to speak, for instance, of 'Sir Vernon Harcourt', where 'Vernon' is merely one of the surnames. Begin: 'Sir'. A baronet's wife is addressed as 'Lady' with husband's surname (her Christian name would also be used if the daughter of a duke, marquis, or earl, and in this case she would also be 'Right Hon.'). Begin: 'Madam'; refer to as 'Your Ladyship'.

Bishop. Address: 'The Right Rev. the Lord Bishop of ——', or 'The Right Rev. A— B—, Lord Bishop of ——', or simply 'The Lord Bishop of ——'. Begin: 'My Lord Bishop'; refer to as 'Your Lordship'. In formal documents a bishop is styled 'The Right Reverend Father in God, John (or whatever the Christian name is), by Divine Permission Lord Bishop of ——'. A bishop suffragan is addressed as 'The Right Rev. the Bishop Suffragan of ——'. Begin: 'Right Rev. Sir'. Bishops' wives have no share in their husbands' titles.

In Ireland the bishops of the Protestant church are now most correctly addressed as 'The Right Reverend the Bishop of ——' (or in the case of Meath 'The Most Reverend'). Begin: 'Right Rev. Sir'. In Scotland the usage is similar—'The Right Rev. the Bishop of ——'; or 'The Right Rev. A— B—, Bishop of'; or 'The Right Rev. Bishop ——' (with surname). Begin: 'Right Rev. Sir'. The Primus of the Episcopal Church in Scotland is addressed as 'The Most Rev.'. Begin: 'Most Rev. Sir'. Neither Irish nor Scottish bishops can claim to be spoken of as 'Lord Bishop', 'Your Lordship', though the form of words is commonly used.

A retired bishop is still addressed as 'Right Reverend'; 'The Right Reverend Bishop ——', 'Right Rev. Sir'.

Roman Catholic bishops in Ireland are accorded the title 'Most Reverend'.

In America the form of address to a bishop is generally 'The Right Rev. A— B—'.

Canon. Address: 'The Rev. Canon ——'. Begin: 'Reverend Sir'.

Cardinal. The special title of a cardinal as such is 'His Eminence'. Begin: 'Your Eminence'.

Chargé d'Affaires. See *Ambassador*.

Clergy. The general form of address is 'The Reverend A— B—'. Begin: 'Rev. Sir' or simply 'Sir'. If a clergyman is the son of a duke or marquis he is to be addressed as 'The Rev. Lord A— B—'; if the son of an earl, viscount, or baron: 'The Rev. the Honourable A— B—', or 'The Hon. and Rev. A— B—'. If he is a baronet, 'The Rev. Sir A— B—, Bart.'.

Congress, Members of (U.S.). Addressed generally as 'The Honourable A— B—'.

Consul. There is no special form of address to a consul as such. 'A— B—, Esq., H. B. M.'s Consul', 'Consul-general', or as the case may be. In the U. States, however, a consul is commonly called 'Honourable'.

Countess. Address: 'The Right Honourable the Countess of ——'. Begin: 'Madam'; refer to as 'Your Ladyship'.

Dean. Address: 'The Very Reverend the Dean of ——'. Begin: 'Very Rev. Sir'; more familiarly 'Mr. Dean' (especially in speaking).

Doctor. The initials denoting the particular degree, whether D.D., LL.D., M.D., D.Sc., &c., are placed after the usual form of address: 'The Rev. A— B—, D.D.; 'A— B—, Esq., M.D.' Less formally: 'The Rev. Doctor B—'; 'Doctor A— B—'.

Dowager. When the holder of a title marries, the widow of a previous holder of the same title becomes 'dowager', this being often inserted in addressing her: 'The Right Hon. the Dowager Countess of ——'; 'The Dowager Lady ——'. Instead of 'Dowager', to which some ladies object, the Christian name may be used: 'The Right Hon. Mary Countess of ——'. Begin: 'Madam'; refer to as 'Your Ladyship'.

Duchess. Address: 'Her Grace the Duchess of ——'. Begin: 'Madam'; refer to as 'Your Grace'.

Duke. Address: 'His Grace the Duke of ——'. Begin: 'My Lord Duke'; refer to as 'Your Grace'. Royal dukes are different. See *Prince*.

Duke's Daughter. Address: 'The Right Hon. Lady', with Christian name and surname, or 'The Lady', with Christian name and surname. Begin: 'Madam'; refer to as 'Your

Ladyship'. If married to a commoner or a peer by courtesy, the surname is derived from the husband's name or title; if to a peer the wife takes a title corresponding to her husband's.

Duke's Son. A duke's eldest son takes by courtesy one of his father's secondary titles, and is thus usually a marquis or an earl, being addressed exactly as if really a peer with the corresponding rank. His wife receives the corresponding title, being thus a marchioness or countess: and their eldest son takes also a courtesy title belonging to the family, being thus usually either a viscount or a baron.

A duke's younger son is addressed similarly to his sisters: 'The Right Honourable Lord A— B—', or 'The Lord A— B—'. Begin: 'My Lord'; refer to as 'Your Lordship'. Their wives are treated in a corresponding manner: 'The Right Honourable Lady A— B—', or 'The Lady A— B—'. Begin: 'Madam'; refer to as 'Your Ladyship'.

Earl. Address: 'The Right Honourable the Earl of ——', or 'The Earl of ——'. Begin: 'My Lord'; refer to as 'Your Lordship'. The wife of an earl is a countess. (See *Countess* above.)

Earl's Children. The eldest son of an earl (like the eldest son of a duke) takes a courtesy title from his father and thus ranks usually either as a viscount or a baron, being treated as if really a peer and his wife being treated as a peeress.

The younger sons of an earl are all called Honourable' (their eldest brother is 'Right Honourable')—'The Hon. A— B—', the same as the sons of a baron. (See *Baron's Son* above.)

The daughters of an earl are all 'Right Honourable', and are addressed as the daughters of a duke. (See *Duke's Daughter* above.)

Envoy. See *Ambassador*.

Executive Council, Members of (in colonial governments). Generally addressed as 'The Honourable A— B—'.

Governor of Colony. Colonial governors have the title of 'Excellency' in virtue of their office. Address: 'His Excellency A— B—, Esq. (Sir A— B—, The Right Honourable the Earl of, &c.), Governor of ——'. Begin according to rank; refer to as 'Your Excellency'. A duke holding such a position would, however, be 'His Grace', 'Your Grace'. A governor's wife has no claim to be called 'Her Excellency'. Lieutenant-governors, as in India and the Dominion of Canada, are styled 'Honourable', 'His Honour', 'Your Honour'.

Governor of State (U.S.). Usually addressed as 'His Excellency'. 'His Excellency A— B—, Governor of ——', or 'His Excellency the Governor of ——'. A lieutenant-governor is called 'Honourable'.

Judge. This in Britain has not a very distinctive meaning. In England and Ireland the judges of the supreme courts are called Lords Justices and Justices; in Scotland the judges are the Lords of Session. (See *Justice, Lord Justice, Lords of Session.*) In England the county court judges are regularly called 'Judge'. 'His Honour Judge ——' (surname); on the bench referred to as 'Your Honour'.

In many British colonies the members of the higher courts are called judges and addressed as 'The Honourable A— B—'. In the U. States the term judge is regularly applied to all such functionaries; and all are addressed in the same way.

Justice. Judges of the High Court of Justice in England, in the Chancery and other divisions, are called justices. Address: 'The Honourable Mr. Justice ——'; or if a knight, 'The Hon. Sir A— B—'. Begin in both cases: 'Sir'. On the bench they are addressed as 'My Lord'; and referred to as 'Your Lordship'.

Justice of Peace. In England is formally addressed in documents as 'The Worshipful', and on the bench is referred to as 'Your Worship'.

King. To be addressed as 'The King's Most Excellent Majesty'. Begin: 'Sire', or 'May it please Your Majesty'; refer to as 'Your Majesty'.

Knight Bachelor. Treated as a baronet (of course with the omission of 'Bart.'). 'Kt.' is not usually appended to the name in addressing a letter. As in the case of a baronet, carefully avoid using a surname instead of a Christian name.

Knight of the Bath, St. Michael and St. George, Star of India. Address: 'Sir A— B—, G.C.B.', or K.C.B., K.C.M.G., K.C.S.I., as the case may be. Begin: 'Sir'.

Knight of the Garter, Thistle, St. Patrick. As above, with the initials K.G., K.T., K.P. respectively following the name.

Knight's Wife (of any class). As baronet's wife.

Legislative Council, Members of (in colonial governments). Generally addressed as 'The Honourable A— B—'.

Lieutenant-governor. See *Governor*.

Lord Advocate of Scotland. Address: 'The Right Honourable the Lord Advocate'. Begin: 'My Lord'; refer to as 'Your Lordship'.

Lord Chancellor. Address: 'The Right Hon. the Lord High Chancellor'; or 'The Right Hon. Earl —— (or as the case may be), Lord High Chancellor'. Begin: 'My Lord'; refer to as 'Your Lordship'.

Lord Chief Justice (England). Address: 'The Right Honourable the Lord Chief Justice', or 'The Right Honourable Sir A— B—, Lord Chief Justice'. Begin: 'My Lord' or 'Sir', as the case may be.

Lord Justice (English Court of Appeal). Address: 'The Right Honourable the Lord Justice ——', or 'The Right Honourable Sir A— B—'. Begin: 'Sir'. On the bench they are addressed as 'My Lord'; and referred to as 'Your Lordship'.

Lord Lieutenant of Ireland. Address: 'His Excellency the Lord Lieutenant', or if a duke, 'His Grace the Lord-Lieutenant'. How to begin and refer will also be determined by rank ('My Lord Duke', 'My Lord Marquis').

Lord Mayor. Only London, York, and a few other cities have a Lord Mayor. Address: 'The Right Honourable the Lord Mayor of ——', or 'The Right Hon. A— B—, Lord Mayor of ——'. Begin: 'My Lord'; refer to as 'Your Lordship'.

The Lord Mayor's wife is addressed: 'The Right Honourable the Lady Mayoress of ——'. Begin: 'My Lady'; refer to as 'Your Ladyship'.

Lord Provost. Address: 'The Right Hon. the Lord Provost of Edinburgh'; 'The Hon. the Lord Provost of Glasgow'; 'The Lord Provost of Aberdeen', 'Perth', or 'Dundee'. Begin: 'My Lord', or 'My Lord Provost'; refer to as 'Your Lordship'. The Lord Provost's wife has no share in the title.

Lords of Appeal (in Ordinary). These are

judicial members of the House of Lords, who rank as barons and are so addressed. Their wives are baronesses; their children are not specially distinguished.

Lords of Session. These are the judges of the supreme court of Scotland. Some of these lords retain their surname when elevated to the bench ('Lord Young'), others substitute the name of an estate. Address: 'The Honourable Lord ——'. Begin: 'My Lord'; refer to as 'Your Lordship'. Their wives take the title 'Lady'.

Maid of Honour. Address: 'The Honourable Miss ——'. Begin: 'Madam'.

Marchioness. Address: 'The Most Honourable the Marchioness of ——'. Begin: 'Madam'; refer to as 'Your Ladyship'.

Marquis. Address: 'The Most Hon. the Marquis of ——'. Begin: 'My Lord Marquis'; refer to as 'Your Lordship'.

Marquis's Children. All are 'Right Honourable' like those of a duke. The eldest son takes a courtesy title like the eldest son of a duke, and is similarly addressed. Younger sons and daughters are treated like those of a duke.

Mayor. Address: 'The Mayor of ——', or in formal documents 'The Right Worshipful the Mayor of ——'. Address: 'Sir'; refer to as 'Your Worship'.

In the United States mayors are usually styled 'Honourable'; 'The Hon. A— B—, Mayor of'.

Member of Parliament. Not specially recognized except by adding 'M.P.' to the ordinary address: 'A— B—, Esq., M.P.'; 'Sir A— B—, Bart., M.P.'.

Minister. See *Ambassador, Clergy*.

Moderator of General Assembly (Scotland). 'The Right Rev.'; the assembly itself is 'The Venerable'.

Officers, Military and Naval. Their professional rank is put before any title they may independently possess: 'General' or 'Admiral the Right Hon. the Earl of ——'; 'Colonel the Honourable A— B—'.

President (U.S.). Address: 'His Excellency the President of the United States'; 'His Excellency A— B—, President of the U. States'. The Vice-president and ex-presidents are 'Honourable': 'The Honourable the Vice-president'; 'The Honourable A— B—'.

Prime Minister. No special title or address as such.

Prince. Address: 'His Royal Highness the Prince of Wales'; 'His Royal Highness Prince A—' (Christian name). If a royal duke: 'His Royal Highness the Duke of ——'. Begin in any case: 'Sir'; refer to as 'Your Royal Highness'.

Princess. Address: 'Her Royal Highness the Princess of Wales'; 'Her Royal Highness the Princess A—' (Christian name). If a royal duchess: 'Her Royal Highness the Duchess of ——'. Begin: 'Madam'; refer to as 'Your Royal Highness'.

Privy Councillor. All members of the privy council are entitled to be addressed as 'Right Honourable'; 'The Right Honourable A— B—, P.C.' (omit 'Esq.'). Otherwise according to rank.

Queen. Address: 'The Queen's Most Excellent Majesty'. Begin: 'Madam', or 'May it please Your Majesty'; refer to as 'Your Majesty'.

Recorder (judge regularly acting at courts of quarter sessions in cities and boroughs). Addressed as 'The Worshipful'; in London 'The Right Worshipful'. Begin: 'Sir'; refer to as 'Your Worship'.

Senators (Canada and U. States). Addressed as 'The Honourable A— B—'.

Serjeant-at-law. Address: 'Serjeant ——', or 'Mr. Serjeant ——'.

Sheriff of London. As recorder of London.

Viscount. Address: 'The Right Hon. the Lord Viscount ——', or 'The Right Hon. Lord ——', or 'The Lord Viscount ——'. Begin: 'My Lord'; refer to as 'Your Lordship'.

Viscount's Children. Are addressed in the same way as those of a baron.

Viscountess. Address: 'The Right Honourable the Viscountess ——', or 'The Viscountess ——'; 'The Right Hon. Lady ——'. Begin: 'Madam'; refer to as 'Your Ladyship'.

PRINCIPAL MONEYS OF THE WORLD

AND THEIR EQUIVALENTS OR APPROXIMATE EQUIVALENTS IN ENGLISH CURRENCY

Abyssinia. Since 1894 the unit has been the *talaro* (value 3*s.* 11½*d.*). Silver and copper coins.

Afghanistan. As in India, with the rupee a little over a shilling.

Algeria. As in France.

Anam. Accounts are kept in dollars (= 2*s.*) and cents. Silver and bronze coins.

Argentine Republic. The dollar (peso or patacon) of 100 centavos is valued in gold at 3*s.* 11½*d.*, in paper at 1*s.* 9*d.* Gold 5-peso piece = 19*s.* 10*d.* Few gold and silver coins; currency mainly paper and nickel and bronze coins.

Australia. Coinage as in Britain. There are mints at Sydney, Melbourne, and Perth.

Austria-Hungary. The unit (since 1892) is the krone or crown of 100 heller, value 10*d.* Gold, silver, nickel, and bronze coins.

Basutoland. As in Britain; barter prevails.

Bechuanaland. As in Britain.

Belgium. As in France. Gold, silver, nickel, and bronze coins.

Bermudas. As in Britain.

Bolivia. The unit is the boliviano or dollar of 100 centavos, with a value of about 1s. 8*d.* There are silver, nickel, and bronze, but few gold coins.

Brazil. The unit is the milreis of 1000 reis, par value 2*s.* 3*d.* There are gold and silver coins. British sovereigns are current.

British East Africa. As in India.

British North Borneo. The standard coin is now the Straits Settlements silver dollar, value 2*s.* 4*d.* So with Sarawak and Labuan. See STRAITS SETTLEMENTS.

Bulgaria. As in France, francs and centimes being represented by levs and stotinki. There are gold, silver, nickel, and bronze coins. Gold was made the standard in 1897.

Canada. The chief coins of the Dominion of Canada are the half-dollar, quarter-dollar, and minor subdivisions, all in silver, as in the United States, accounts being kept in dollars, cents, and mills (10 mills = 1 cent). By law it is fixed that the sovereign is equal to 4 dollars 86⅔ cents. United States gold coins are a legal tender; but not much gold is in circulation, government notes and bank bills taking its place.

Cape Colony. The coinage is that of Britain.

Ceylon. The rupee is the standard coin as in India, but here it is divided into 100 cents. There are silver and bronze coins. See INDIA.

Chili. Gold standard since 1895. The dollar or peso of 100 centavos (value 1*s.* 6*d.*) is coined both in silver and in gold. The gold coins include British sovereigns.

China. There is no official coinage except copper cash, of which about 30 = 1 penny. Payments are made in silver by weight, and values reckoned by the tael, the Haikwan or customs tael of pure silver being at present worth about 3*s.* Mexican and American trade dollars circulate.

Colombia. The unit is the peso or dollar of 100 centavos; gold peso value 4*s.* There are gold, silver, nickel, and bronze coins.

Congo Free State. As in Belgium.

Costa Rica. Gold standard since 1896. The gold colon of 100 centimos is valued at nearly 1*s.* 11*d.* There are gold, silver, and copper coins.

Denmark. See NORWAY.

Ecuador. The unit is the sucre or dollar, a silver coin equal to about 2*s.* It is divided into 100 centavos.

Egypt. Since 1885 the unit is the Egyptian gold pound of 100 piastres or 1000 ochr'-el-guerch. The pound is equal to £1, 0*s.* 6½*d.* Under the former system the piastre of 40 paras was the unit. There are gold, silver, nickel, and bronze coins.

Finland. The unit is the markka or mark of 100 penni, equivalent to the franc (see next). There are gold, silver, and bronze coins.

France. The unit is the franc (divided into 100 centimes), the approximate value of which is 9½*d.* sterling, or 25·22 francs to £1 sterling. The smallest gold coin is the 10-franc piece; the 20-franc piece is called a Napoleon. The highest silver coin is 5 francs. There are bronze coins from 1 centime to 10 centimes. Bank notes from 50 to 1000 francs.

The coinage of France has been accepted as the model for that of Belgium, Switzerland, Italy, Greece, Spain, Servia, Roumania, Bulgaria, &c.

Germany. The unit is the mark (or Reichsmark) of 100 pfennige, which on a gold basis is nearly equivalent to 1*s.* sterling, or 20·4 marks = £1. The lowest gold coin is the half-crown of 5 marks, and the highest silver coin is a 5-mark piece. There are also bronze and nickel coins.

Gibraltar. British sterling money since 1898; previously Spanish currency.

Great Britain. The money unit is the pound sterling, represented as a coin by the sovereign and divided into twenty shillings, each shilling being divided into 12 pence. The sovereign consists of gold of 22 carats or $\frac{11}{12}$ or 916̇ fine, and it weighs 123·27 grains troy. Hence 40 lbs. of gold = 1869 sovereigns; 1 lb. = £46, 14*s.* 6*d.*; 1 oz. = £3, 17*s.* 10½*d.*

The guinea, a gold coin worth 21*s.*, has long been withdrawn from circulation, though it is still used as a money of account.

Gold Coins.—The sovereign and half-sovereign are the only gold coins that really form part of the currency, though 2-sovereign and 5-sovereign pieces have been coined.

Silver Coins.—The crown or five-shilling piece; the half-crown or two shillings and sixpence; the florin or two-shilling piece; the double florin or four-shilling piece (not coined since 1893); the shilling, the sixpence, and the threepenny piece. The fourpenny piece is now only coined, like the silver twopenny and penny pieces, for the so-called *maundy money*.

The coins of inferior denomination are the bronze penny, halfpenny, and farthing.

In many British colonies and possessions the above coins form the chief currency, though in some of the colonies and possessions special coins are also in use. In Hong-Kong and the East the dollar is the chief coin. See CANADA, INDIA, HONG-KONG.

Greece. As in France, the franc and centime being called the drachma and lepton. There are gold, silver, nickel, and bronze coins.

Guatemala. Accounts are kept in dollars or piastres (value 2*s.* 8*d.*) = 100 centavos. There are gold, silver, and bronze coins.

Guiana, British. Accounts are commonly kept in dollars and cents, 1 dollar = 100 cents. The dollar is reckoned at 4*s.* 2*d.* The ordinary British denominations of pounds, shillings, and pence are also used. British, United States, Mexican, and other gold and silver coins are in circulation.

Haiti. A gourde or dollar (gold 3*s.* 11½*d.*, silver 2*s.*) = 100 centavos. There are gold, silver, nickel, and bronze coins.

Holland. See NETHERLANDS.

Honduras. Gold standard since 1894. The dollar (value in gold 4*s.* 2·21*d.*, in silver 2*s.*) = 100 centavos. There are gold, silver, and bronze coins.

Honduras, British. United States gold has been adopted as the standard of currency. British coins circulate, and the sovereign and half-sovereign are legal tender (1 sovereign = 4 dols. 86 cents).

Hong-Kong. Accounts are kept in dollars and cents. The standard coin is the Mexican dollar, varying in actual value according to the price of silver, being now worth about 2*s.* British dollars of similar value are also current. Silver coins less than a dollar are legal tender for amounts of not more than two dollars. There is no gold coinage.

India. The unit is the rupee, a silver coin which used to be regarded as equivalent to 2*s.* sterling, but since the introduction of a gold standard (1899) has been fixed at 1*s.* 4*d.* (15 rupees = £1). The rupee is divided into 16 annas, the anna into 4 pice, the pice into 3 pies. The sum of 100,000 rupees is called a lac, of 10,000,000 a crore. There are mints at Calcutta and Bombay. British gold coins are legal tender, and there are also silver and copper coins and local notes.

Italy. As in France, the franc and centime being represented by the lira and centesimo. There are gold, silver, nickel, and bronze coins.

Jamaica. Accounts kept as in Britain, and all British gold and silver coins circulate and are legal tender. American gold coins are also current. Mexican and old Spanish doubloons are current at £3, 4*s*. each. There are nickel pennies, halfpennies, and farthings.

Japan. Gold standard since 1897. The gold yen or dollar is now the unit, value about 2*s*., divided into 100 sens. The lowest gold coin is 5 yens; the highest silver one 50 sens; and there are nickel and bronze coins.

Korea. Under the regulations of 1894 the moneys of account are the dollar (about 2*s*.) = 5 liang = 100 cents = 500 cash. The money is now assimilated to the Japanese.

Labuan. The same as in British North Borneo and Straits Settlements.

Liberia. Money chiefly British. Accounts kept also in dollars and cents.

Madagascar. As in France; the chief legal coin is the silver 5-franc piece.

Mauritius. As in Ceylon.

Mexico. The standard coin is the dollar or peso of 100 centavos; value about 2*s*. There are gold, silver, and copper coins.

Montenegro. The money of the adjacent countries.

Morocco. A mithkal (value 4*s*. 3·83*d*.) = 10 ounces = 40 blankeels = 960 flues. There are silver coins; also Spanish dollars and cents.

Natal. The money is the same as in Britain.

Netherlands. The unit is the gulden, guilder, or florin of 100 cents, a silver coin equivalent to about 1*s*. 8*d*., or twelve to the £ sterling. The lowest gold coin is the ducat (value 9*s*. 6*d*.); the highest silver coin the 2½-gulden piece (rix-dollar). There are also bronze and copper coins.

Newfoundland. As in Canada, with two-dollar gold coins in addition.

New Zealand. Coinage as in Australia.

Nicaragua. Practically the same as in Honduras.

Nigeria. As in Britain; barter prevails.

Norway and Sweden. Norway, Sweden, and Denmark have the same coinage, though the names of the pieces differ slightly. The unit is the crown, called krone (plural kroner) in Norway and Denmark, krona (plural kronor) in Sweden; value 1*s*. 1⅓*d*., or about 18 to the £1 sterling. The krone or krona is divided into 100 öre. There are gold coins from 5-kroner upwards; silver from 2-kroner downwards; also bronze coins.

Orange River Colony. English money is used as formerly.

Ottoman Empire. See TURKEY.

Paraguay. The chief coin is the peso or dollar of 100 centavos, nominally equal to 4*s*. The actual currency is paper.

Persia. The monetary unit is the krân, a silver coin which may be compared to the franc. The krân is divided into 20 shâhis or 1000 dinâs, the dinâ being an imaginary coin. There are gold coins, mostly expressed in terms of the toman of 10 krâns; also silver and copper coins.

Peru. A gold standard was introduced in 1901. The standard coin is the libra of 10 soles = a pound sterling. The sole is divided into 100 centavos.

Portugal. The chief money unit is the milreis, the value of which in gold is 4*s*. 5⅓*d*. The milreis is divided into 1000 reis (plural of real), which are only money of account. Large sums are stated in contos or millions of reis, a conto being equal to £222, 4*s*. 5⅓*d*. There are gold coins from one milreis upwards, including the corôa or crown of 10 milreis; silver coins from 500 reis downwards, including the testoon of 100 reis; also bronze coins. The British sovereign and half-sovereign are legal currency at the respective values of 4500 and 2250 reis.

Rhodesia. As in Britain.

Roumania. As in France, the franc and centime being represented by the leo (plural lei) and the bano. There are gold, silver, and bronze coins.

Russia. The monetary unit is the rouble of 100 copecks. The silver rouble is of the value of about 2*s*. 1½*d*. sterling, or £1 sterling = about 9·46 roubles. A law of 1897 established the currency upon a gold basis, fixing the relation of gold to paper money at 1 rouble in gold = 1½ rouble in paper. There are gold coins from 3 roubles upwards, including the imperial (10 roubles); silver coins from one rouble downwards; also copper coins.

St. Helena. As in Britain.

Salvador. Gold standard since 1897. The dollar (value 2*s*.) = 100 centavos. Coins as in Guatemala and Honduras.

Samoa. American money.

Santo Domingo. The gold dollar of 100 centavos is valued at 4*s*. 1·31*d*. There are gold, silver, nickel, and bronze coins.

Sarawak. As in British North Borneo.

Servia. As in France, the franc and centime being represented by the dinar and para (or cent). There are gold coins, including the milan (20 dinars); also silver, nickel, and bronze coins.

Siam. The chief coin is the tical or bat, a silver piece of the fixed value of 1*s*. 6½*d*., or 13 ticals = £1 sterling. There are silver and bronze coins.

Singapore. The Straits Settlements silver dollar is the standard coin.

Spain. As in France, the franc and centime being represented by the peseta and centesimo. There are gold coins from 5 pesetas upwards; silver coins from 5 pesetas downwards; also bronze coins.

Straits Settlements. The Straits Settlements silver dollar, value 2*s*. 4*d*., with subsidiary silver and other coins. The British sovereign is legal tender at the rate of 7 for 60 dollars.

Sweden. See NORWAY.

Switzerland. The money is the same as in France, the unit being the franc, divided into 100 centimes or rappen. Of gold coins only 20-franc pieces are coined by the republic itself.

Tasmania. As in Australia.

Transvaal. As in Britain.

Trinidad. British gold, silver, and bronze coinage, with U. States and Mexican gold.

Tripoli. A mahbub (value 4*s*. 2*d*.) = 20 piastres = 800 paras.

Tunis. As in France.

Turkey. The reckoning is by Turkish pounds of 100 piastres each, equal to about 18*s*. There are gold coins from a quarter-lira or pound upwards; silver coins from 20 piastres downwards; also bronze or copper coins.

United States. The dollar of 100 cents has been the money unit of the United States since 1786. The coinage at present is as follows:—*Gold Coins*—Double-eagle or 20-dollar piece =

£4, 2*s.* 2·33*d.*; eagle or 10 dollars; half-eagle or 5-dollar piece; quarter-eagle or 2½-dollar piece. *Silver Coins*—Dollar: 4*s.* 1½*d.*; half-dollar or 50 cents; quarter-dollar or 25 cents; dime or 10 cents (5*d.*). There are also 5-cent pieces coined in nickel and cent pieces in bronze.

Uruguay. The peso or dollar is the unit, divided into 100 centavos; theoretical value 4*s.* 3*d.*, or £1 = 4·7 pesos. United States gold coins circulate, and there are silver coins representing the dollar and certain fractions of it.

Venezuela. The chief coins are the silver venezolano or dollar of 100 centavos, and the bolivar of 20 centavos. The former is identical with the 5-franc piece, and the latter with the franc (see FRANCE). There are also gold venezolanos.

West African Colonies. As in Britain, with a few other coins in addition.

West Indies. In the British islands the currency is nearly that of the home countries, though reckoning by dollars and cents is common, and American coins are also current. See JAMAICA.

Zanzibar. Accounts are kept in dollars and cents, the standard being the Maria Theresa silver dollar. The Indian rupee is the coin now in chief currency, standard value 47 cents, or dollar = 2 rupees 2 annas. See INDIA.

WEIGHTS AND MEASURES

I.—BRITISH

Avoirdupois Weight

(for general use)

16 drams	=	1 ounce (oz.).
16 oz.	=	1 pound (lb.).
14 lb.	=	1 stone.
2 st. or 28 lb.	=	1 quarter.
4 qr. or 112 lb.	=	1 hundredweight.
20 cwt. or 2240 lb.	=	1 ton.
7000 grains	=	1 lb.

Troy Weight

(used in weighing gold and silver, &c.)

4 grains	=	1 carat.
24 grains	=	1 pennyweight.
20 dwt.	=	1 ounce (oz.).
12 oz.	=	1 pound (lb.).
5760 grains	=	1 lb.

Apothecaries' Weight

(used in compounding medicines)

20 grains	=	1 scruple (℈).
3 scr.	=	1 drachm (ʒ).
8 drachms	=	1 ounce (℥).
12 oz.	=	1 lb.

Apothecaries' Measure

1 fluid minim (♏)	=	·0045 cu. in.
60 „ minims	=	1 fl. dr. (ʒ).
8 drachms	=	1 fl. oz. (℥).
20 oz.	=	1 pint (O).

Wool Weight

7 lb.	=	1 clove.
2 cl.	=	1 stone.
2 st.	=	1 tod.
6½ tods	=	1 wey.
2 weys	=	1 sack.
12 sacks	=	1 last.
240 lb.	=	1 pack.

Long Measure

12 lines	=	1 inch.
12 in.	=	1 foot.
3 ft.	=	1 yard.
5½ yd.	=	1 rod or pole.
4 po.	=	1 chain.
10 ch.	=	1 furlong.
8 fur.	=	1 mile.
3 ml.	=	1 league.
1760 yd. or 5280 ft.	=	1 mile.

Nautical Measures

6 feet	=	1 fathom.
6080 feet	=	1 nautical mile or knot.

Square Measure

144 square inches	=	1 sq. foot.
9 „ feet	=	1 „ yard.
30¼ „ yards	=	1 „ pole.
40 „ poles	=	1 rood.
4 roods	=	1 acre.
640 acres	=	1 sq. mile.

Surveyors' Measure

7·92 inches	=	1 link.
100 links	=	1 chain.
80 chains	=	1 mile.
100,000 sq. links or 10 „ chains	=	1 acre.

Cubic Measure

1728 cu. inches	=	1 cu. foot.
27 „ feet	=	1 „ yd.
40 „ „	=	1 load of rough timber.
50 „ „	=	1 load of squared timber.

Dry Measure

4 gills	=	1 pint.
2 pt.	=	1 quart.
4 qt.	=	1 gallon.
2 gall.	=	1 peck.
4 pecks	=	1 bushel.
8 bus.	=	1 quarter.
36 bus.	=	1 chaldron.

Ale and Beer Measure

2 pints	=	1 quart.
4 qt.	=	1 gallon.
9 gall.	=	1 firkin.
2 firk.	=	1 kilderkin.
2 kil.	=	1 barrel.
1½ bar.	=	1 hogshead.
2 hog.	=	1 butt.
2 butts	=	1 tun.

Wine Measure

4 gills	=	1 pint.
2 pints	=	1 quart.
4 qt.	=	1 gallon.
10 gall.	=	1 anker.
18 ,,	=	1 runlet.
42 ,,	=	1 tierce.
84 ,,	=	1 puncheon.
63 ,,	=	1 hogshead.
2 hog.	=	1 pipe.
2 pipes	=	1 tun.

Linen Yarn

300 yards	=	1 cut.
2 cuts	=	1 heer.
6 heers	=	1 hasp.
4 hasps	=	1 spindle.

Cotton Yarn

120 yards	=	1 skein.
7 skeins	=	1 hank.
18 hanks	=	1 spindle.

Miscellaneous

56 lb.	=	1 firkin of butter.
112 ,,	=	1 quintal of fish.
280 ,,	=	1 sack of flour.
4 pecks	=	1 bushel of coal.
3 bushels	=	1 sack ,,
24 sheets	=	1 quire of paper.
20 quires	=	1 ream ,,
10 reams	=	1 bale ,,
3 inches	=	1 palm.
4 ,,	=	1 hand.
9 ,,	=	1 span.
18 ,,	=	1 cubit.
5 feet	=	1 pace.
272¼ sq. ft.	=	1 rod of brickwork.
100 ,,	=	1 square of flooring.
30 acres	=	1 yard of land.
100 ,,	=	1 hide of land.
2240 yards	=	1 Irish mile.
4840 sq. yd.	=	1 English acre.
6250 ,,	=	1 Scotch ,,
7840 ,,	=	1 Irish ,,
12 articles	=	1 dozen.
20 ,,	=	1 score.
5 score	=	1 hundred.
6 ,,	=	1 long hundred.
12 dozen	=	1 gross.
108 gallons	=	1 butt of sherry.
19½ cwt.	=	1 fodder of lead.
24 oz.	=	1 great pound of silk.

Time Measure

60 seconds	=	1 minute.
60 min.	=	1 hour.
24 hr.	=	1 day.
7 days	=	1 week.
4 weeks	=	1 month.
13 Lunar mo.	=	1 year.
12 Calendar mo.	=	1 year.
365 days	=	1 com. year.
366 ,,	=	1 leap year.
365¼ ,,	=	1 Julian year.
365 d. 5 h. 48 m. 51 sec.	=	1 Solar year.
100 years	=	1 century.

Circular Measure

60 thirds (‴)	=	1 second (″).
60 seconds	=	1 minute (′).
60 minutes	=	1 degree (°).
90 degrees	=	1 quadrant.
360 ,,	=	1 circle.

Sizes of Books

(4to = Quarto; 8vo = Octavo)

Foolscap 8vo	=	6¾ × 4¼ inches.
Crown 8vo	=	7½ × 5 ,,
Demy 8vo	=	8¾ × 5⅝ ,,
Royal 8vo	=	10 × 6¼ ,,
Imperial 8vo	=	11 × 7½ ,,
Crown 4to	=	10 × 7½ ,,
Demy 4to	=	11¼ × 8¾ ,,
Crown Folio	=	15 × 10 ,,
Royal Folio	=	20 × 12½ ,,

II.—METRIC

(The use of the metric system was made permissive in the United Kingdom in 1897.)

Units of Measurement

Length....Metre (m.)	=	about	39 in.
Area......Are (a.)	=	,,	120 sq. yd.
Solidity....Stere (s.)	=	,,	35 cu. ft.
Capacity ..Litre (l.)	=	,,	1¾ pt.
Weight ...Gram (g.)	=	,,	¼ dram.

Prefixes

LATIN (for sub-multiples)	GREEK (for multiples)
milli- = $\frac{1}{1000}$ part.	deka- = 10 times.
centi- = $\frac{1}{100}$,,	hecto- = 100 ,,
deci- = $\frac{1}{10}$,,	kilo- = 1000 ,,
	myria- = 10,000 ,,

Length

TERMS.—Millimetre, Centimetre, Decimetre, METRE, Dekametre, Hectometre, Kilometre, Myriametre.

10 millimetres (mlm.)	=	1 centimetre.
10 centimetres (cm.)	=	1 decimetre.
10 decimetres (dcm.)	=	1 METRE.
10 metres (m.)	=	1 dekametre.
10 dekametres (dkm.)	=	1 hectometre.
10 hectometres (hm.)	=	1 kilometre.
10 kilometres (km.)	=	1 myriametre (mrm.).

Area

TERMS.—Centiare, Deciare, ARE, Dekare, Hectare.

10 centiares (ca.)	=	1 deciare.
10 deciares (dca.)	=	1 ARE.
10 ares (a.)	=	1 dekare.
10 dekares (dka.)	=	1 hectare (ha.).

Solidity

TERMS.—Decistere, STERE, Dekastere.

10 decisteres (dcs.)	=	1 STERE.
10 steres (s.)	=	1 dekastere (dks.).

Capacity

TERMS. — Millilitre, Centilitre, Decilitre, LITRE, Dekalitre, Hectolitre, Kilolitre.

10 millilitres (mll.)	=	1 centilitre.
10 centilitres (cl.)	=	1 decilitre.
10 decilitres (dcl.)	=	1 LITRE.
10 litres (l.)	=	1 dekalitre.
10 dekalitres (dkl.)	=	1 hectolitre.
10 hectolitres (hl.)	=	1 kilolitre (kl.).

Weight

TERMS.—Milligram, Centigram, Decigram, GRAM, Dekagram, Hectogram, Kilogram, Myriagram.
Extra Terms.—Quintal, Millier or Ton.

10 milligrams (mlg.)	=	1 centigram.
10 centigrams (cg.)	=	1 decigram.
10 decigrams (dcg.)	=	1 GRAM.
10 grams (g.)	=	1 dekagram.
10 dekagrams (dkg.)	=	1 hectogram.
10 hectograms (hg.)	=	1 kilogram.
10 kilograms (kg.)	=	1 myriagram.
10 myriagrams (mrg.)	=	1 quintal.
10 quintals (q.)	=	1 millier or ton.

Alternative Metric Measures

Square.—Sq. Centimetre, Sq. Decimetre, SQ. METRE (= centiare), Sq. Dekametre, Sq. Hectometre, Sq. Kilometre.

100 sq. cm.	=	1 sq. dcm.
100 sq. dcm.	=	1 SQ. M.
100 sq. m.	=	1 sq. dkm.
100 sq. dkm.	=	1 sq. hm.
100 sq. hm.	=	1 sq. km.

Cubic.—Cubic Centimetre, Cubic Decimetre, CU. METRE (= stere), Cu. Dekametre, Cu. Hectometre.

1000 cu. cm.	=	1 cu. dcm.
1000 cu. dcm.	=	1 CU. M.
1000 cu. m.	=	1 cu. dkm.
1000 cu. dkm.	=	1 cu. hm.

Metric Money Table (Decimal Coinage)

10 mils	=	1 cent (c.).
10 cents	=	1 florin (fl.).
10 florins	=	1 pound (£).

£1 and florin same as at present.
Cent = about 2½*d.*; 6*d.* = 2½ cents.
Mil = about ¼*d.*; 6*d.* = 25 mils.

DECIMAL COINAGE ABROAD

United States Money

10 mils	=	1 cent.
10 cents	=	1 dime.
10 dimes	=	1 dollar (= 50*d.* English).

French Money

10 centimes	=	1 decime.
10 decimes	=	1 franc (9½*d.* English).

Metric Measures and Weights in Terms of British

Length

1 centimetre	=	0·3937 inch.
1 decimetre	=	0·3281 foot.
1 metre	=	1·0936 yard.
1 dekametre	=	1·9884 pole.
1 hectometre	=	0·4971 furlong.
1 kilometre	=	0·6214 mile.

Area

1 are	=	0·0988 rood.
1 hectare	=	2·4711 acres.
1 sq. kilometre	=	0·386 sq. mile.

Capacity

1 centilitre	=	0·0704 gill.
1 decilitre	=	0·1759 pint.
1 litre	=	0·8799 quart.
1 dekalitre	=	2·1997 gallons.
1 hectolitre	=	2·7497 bushels.

Weight

1 centigram	=	0·1543 grain.
1 decigram	=	1·5432 ,,
1 gram	=	15·4323 grains.
1 dekagram	=	5·6438 drams.
1 hectogram	=	3·5274 oz.
1 kilogram	=	2·2046 lb.
1 myriagram	=	1·5747 stone.
1 quintal	=	1·9684 cwt.
1 millier	=	0·9842 ton.

British Measures and Weights in Terms of Metric

Length

1 inch	=	25·3995 millimetres.
1 foot	=	30·479 centimetres.
1 yard	=	0·9144 metre.
1 furlong	=	201·164 metres.
1 mile	=	1·6093 kilometre.

Area

1 rood	=	10·1168 ares.
1 acre	=	0·4047 hectare.
1 sq. mile	=	2·5899 sq. kilometres.

Capacity

1 pint	=	0·5679 litre.
1 quart	=	1·1359 litre.
1 gallon	=	4·5435 litres.
1 bushel	=	36·3477 litres.

Weight

1 grain	=	0·0648 gram.
1 oz.	=	28·35 grams.
1 lb.	=	453·59 grams.
1 cwt.	=	50·802 kilograms.
1 ton	=	1016·04 kilograms.